Employment

Wolters Kluwer (UK) Limited
145 London Road
Kingston upon Thames
Surrey KT2 6SR
Tel: 020 8247 1175
www.croner.co.uk

Published by
Wolters Kluwer (UK) Limited
145 London Road
Kingston upon Thames
Surrey KT2 6SR
Tel: 020 8247 1175
www.croner.co.uk

First published September 2007

© Wolters Kluwer (UK) Limited

All rights reserved. No part of this work may be reproduced, stored in a retrieval system or transmitted in any form or by any means, electronic, mechanical, photocopying, recording or otherwise, without the prior permission of Wolters Kluwer (UK) Limited.

Crown copyright is reproduced with the permission of the Controller of Her Majesty's Stationery Office and the Queen's Printer for Scotland.

Although great care has been taken in the compilation and preparation of this book to ensure accuracy, the publishers cannot in any circumstances accept responsibility for any errors or omissions.

Readers of this book should be aware that only Acts of Parliament and Statutory Instruments have the force of law and that only the courts can authoritatively interpret the law.

British Library cataloguing in Publication Data. A catalogue record for this book is available from the British Library.

ISBN 978-1-85524-706-2

Printed and Bound in Great Britain by Latimer Trend & Company Limited, Plymouth

Contents

Chapter 1 Absence and Working Time — 1
Holidays and Extended Leave — 2
Overseas Workers — 11
Part-Time and other Atypical Workers — 18
Sabbaticals and Secondments — 25
Sickness Absence — 32
Statutory Time Off — 39
Time Off at the Employer's Discretion — 46
Time Off for Dependants — 56
Working Time — 60
Working Time for Mobile Workers — 74

Chapter 2 Contracts of Employment — 81
Appearance and Dress Codes — 82
Breach of Contract — 87
Common Clauses — 94
Contract Formation — 103
Contract Terms — 114
Data Protection — 121
Email and Internet — 132
Employer/Employee Relationship — 138
Employment Agencies and Employment Businesses Regulations — 152
Staff Handbooks — 159
Types of Contract — 166
Varying the Contract of Employment — 178

Chapter 3 Discipline and Grievance — 185
Bullying — 186
Disciplinary Offences and Penalties — 195
Disciplinary Procedures — 204
Grievance Procedures — 223
Resolving Disputes through Tribunals and other Methods — 234

Chapter 4 Discrimination and Diversity — 245
Age Discrimination — 246
Disability Discrimination — 262
Discrimination Claims — 278
Diversity and Equality in the Workplace — 290
Equal Pay — 304
Fair Employment (Northern Ireland) Act 1989 — 313
Race Discrimination — 322
Religion or Belief Discrimination — 337
Sex Discrimination — 352
Sexual Orientation Discrimination — 367

Chapter 5 Industrial and Employee Relations — 379
Collective Agreements — 380
Collective Redundancies — 391
Employee Representatives — 401

Industrial Action	410
Information and Consultation	418
Trade Union Membership and Employers	437
Trade Unions and Employers	447
Whistleblowing	456
Works Councils	465

Chapter 6 Maternity and Parental Leave — 473

Adoption Rights	474
Flexible Working	480
Maternity Rights	490
Parental Leave	499
Paternity Rights	506
Statutory Maternity, Paternity and Adoption Pay	512

Chapter 7 Pay and Benefits — 531

Attachment of Earnings	532
Benefits	540
Cars, Fuel, Vans and Related Benefits	554
Deductions from Pay	567
Employee Share and Share Option Schemes	572
National Insurance	585
National Minimum Wage	594
PAYE and Income Tax	602
Pensions	609
Statutory Sick Pay	633

Chapter 8 Recruitment and Selection — 643

Advertising and Sourcing Applicants	644
Induction	654
Interviewing	661
Job Descriptions and Person Specifications	669
Job Evaluation	678
Probationary Periods	686
Recruitment — Legal Issues	692
Recruitment and Migrant Workers	709
References and Medical Checks	722
Selection Process	728
Succession Planning	739

Chapter 9 Termination of Employment — 747

Employment Tribunal Proceedings and Remedies	748
Insolvency	760
Redundancy	770
Resignation and Constructive Dismissal	785
Retirement	791
Settlements and Compromise Agreements	801
Summary Dismissal	810
Transfer of Undertakings	818
Unfair Dismissal	833
Wrongful Dismissal	843

Appendix Key Rates and Data — 853

Chapter 1
Absence and Working Time

Holidays and Extended Leave

> This topic covers the following.
> - The Definition of a Worker
> - Policy and Procedure for Holidays and Extended Leave
> - Policy and Procedure for Sabbaticals and Long-Service Leave
> - Entitlement to Annual Leave
> - Agency Staff
> - Periods of Absence
> - The Minimum Entitlement
> - Definition of a Week's Leave
> - Definition of a Leave Year
> - Public Holidays
> - Bank Holidays
> - Religious Holidays and Festivals
> - Specifying Particulars of Holidays
> - Payment during Annual Leave
> - Accrual of Holiday in First Year of Employment
> - Timing of Holidays — Notice of Intention to Take Holidays
> - Employees' Notice of Intention
> - Employers' Right of Counter-Notice
> - Carrying over Holiday Entitlements
> - Payment in Lieu of Holiday
> - Deductions for Holiday Taken in Excess
> - Extended Leave

1.1 All workers are entitled to take a minimum of four weeks' paid leave in any leave year. Statutory holiday requirements are now largely governed by the Working Time Regulations 1998 (WTR) and the Employment Rights Act 1996 (ERA), both modified by case law. The entitlement is a minimum only and, in practice, many employers choose to give greater holiday entitlements. Workers do not need any minimum period of continuous service in order to qualify for the right to minimum holiday.

Employers' Duties

1.2 Employers must:
- allow workers to take their minimum period of leave each year
- give workers payment for annual leave
- specify holiday entitlements in all employees' statements of terms and conditions of employment
- pay in lieu of accrued but untaken holiday on termination.

Employees' Duties

1.3 Employees must:
- comply with the notice requirements when they wish to take holiday

- check for any specific contractual obligations imposed by their employer over and above those that are statutory.

In Practice

The Definition of a Worker

1.4 The definition of worker for the purpose of the Working Time Regulations 1998 includes not only employees but also:
- casual staff
- freelance workers
- agency staff
- home workers.

1.5 It also includes those who contract to perform personally any work or services for the employer.

1.6 The definition of a worker will generally not include individuals who are genuinely self-employed where the organisation is the individual's client rather than their employer. There have, however, been a number of cases where individuals, who might at first sight appear to be self-employed (eg certain sub-contractors), have been found to be workers since they contracted to perform work personally (eg *Torith Ltd v Flynn* 21 November 2003 EAT and *Byrne Brothers (Formwork) Ltd v Baird* [2002] IRLR 96).

Policy and Procedure for Holidays and Extended Leave

1.7 Details of procedures for holidays and extended leave should include:
- when the holiday year starts and finishes
- the number of working days' holiday employees are entitled to during each holiday year, which must be not less than four weeks
- for any employees without fixed hours, how their holidays and holiday pay will be calculated
- whether employees are entitled to bank and public holidays in addition to the specified number of days' holiday
- whether there are any periods when employees will be required to take holiday, eg a Christmas shutdown
- what procedure employees must follow to obtain approval for holiday requests
- how payment in lieu of any accrued but untaken holiday will be calculated on termination of employment
- whether employees will have deductions made from final salary payments in respect of any holiday taken in excess of entitlement and how these deductions will be calculated
- how much holiday can be taken at any one time and whether holidays should be taken in minimum blocks
- whether holiday can be carried over from one holiday year to the next (subject to the provision in the Working Time Regulations that statutory annual leave, ie the four weeks' minimum entitlement, cannot be carried forward) and, if so, whether there is a maximum number of days that can be carried over.

Holidays and Extended Leave

Policy and Procedure for Sabbaticals and Long-Service Leave

1.8 Details of procedures for sabbaticals and long-service leave should include:
- whether employees will be entitled to extended leave or whether it will be purely discretionary
- the length of service required to qualify for extended leave (since the implementation of age discrimination legislation, any length of service requirement that is more than five years will have to be objectively justified)
- whether such leave will be paid or unpaid and whether benefits will continue to accrue during leave
- whether employees will be required to continue in work for a certain period following return from such leave, failing which they might be required to make a specified repayment.

Entitlement to Annual Leave

Agency Staff

1.9 Agency staff are entitled to annual leave. Whether it is the responsibility of the agency or the client organisation to pay holiday pay will generally be set out in the commercial documentation. If an agency worker has no contract with either the agency or the client organisation, it is the party who pays the agency staff who is responsible for holiday pay. Normally this will be the agency.

Periods of Absence

1.10 A worker's entitlement to annual leave is generally not affected by periods of absence. Employees who are on maternity, adoption, paternity or parental leave will continue to accrue holiday entitlement under the Working Time Regulations, provided that there is still a contract governing their employment. Employees who return from such periods of leave are, therefore, entitled to take their annual paid holiday entitlement on return (subject to notification requirements).

1.11 Until recently, employees who were absent from work on long-term sick leave were able to request, while still on sick leave, to take their holiday entitlement. However, the Court of Appeal has overturned the EAT's decision in *Commissioners of Inland Revenue v Ainsworth* [2005] IRLR 465, CA, finding that the EAT was wrong in deciding that the right to statutory paid holiday continues to accrue while an employee is off on long-term sick leave and has exhausted his or her entitlement to sick pay.

1.12 The decision may now mean that employees who are on sick leave are no longer able to request that a period of sick leave be converted to holiday and to be paid holiday pay. The decision may also mean that, where an employee is off work on sick leave for an entire year, he or she has no right under the Working Time Regulations to holiday leave or pay in that year (although any contractual entitlement must still be honoured). It should be noted, however, that the *Commissioners of Inland Revenue v Ainsworth* ruling leaves open the question of what defines long-term sickness. It implies at the outset that this is where entitlement to pay, statutory or otherwise, comes to an end but then fails to provide a decision of authority on this point.

1.13 It should also be noted that the question of whether employees who return to work from long-term sick leave during a holiday year are entitled to the full four weeks' statutory holiday is unclear and, until further guidance is available, employers should continue to provide employees in these circumstances the statutory four weeks' holiday entitlement.

1.14 The case has now been referred to the European Court of Justice (ECJ) under the name of *HM Revenue and Customs v Stringer and others*.

The Minimum Entitlement

1.15 All workers are entitled to a minimum of four weeks' paid holiday in each "leave year".

1.16 For workers who start or leave employment part way through a leave year, the entitlement is to a *pro rata* proportion of four weeks' leave, based on the portion of the year worked.

1.17 Part-time employees have a right to a pro rata proportion of the annual leave entitlement. For example, a part-time worker, who works three days a week, is entitled to take four weeks' holiday but will only be paid holiday pay for 12 days.

1.18 The four weeks' entitlement is not currently in addition to public holidays but see Public Holidays below for details of a new Government proposal.

1.19 Workers do not need any minimum period of continuous service in order to qualify for the right to minimum holiday.

1.20 Employees do not have an automatic right to more holiday than the statutory minimum although the courts may be prepared to imply such a right, eg as a result of custom and practice.

1.21 In practice, many employers choose to give employees more holiday than the minimum statutory entitlement, eg 25 working days plus public and bank holidays.

Definition of a Week's Leave

1.22 A "week's leave" is the length of time that the specified worker is employed in a normal working week. So:
- an individual working six days a week is entitled to 24 days' annual leave
- a worker who works five days a week is entitled to 20 working days' annual leave
- a worker who works three days a week is entitled to 12 working days per year.

Definition of a Leave Year

1.23 A "leave year" is the holiday year as set out in the employee's contract of employment, or in a workforce or collective agreement. In the absence of any specified leave year, the year will commence either on 1 October 1998 (for any worker employed on or before that date) and on each subsequent 1 October, or (for all other workers) on the date on which a worker commences employment and each subsequent anniversary.

Public Holidays

1.24 Under the Working Time Regulations, employees do not have a right to take public and bank holidays as paid time off in addition to the four weeks' annual entitlement. An employer may, if it wishes, include public and bank holidays as part of the four weeks' entitlement. The Work and Families Act 2006, however, will prevent bank holidays from being included in the statutory annual leave entitlement, thereby giving full-time employees a statutory right to 28 days' annual leave (*pro rata* for part-time employees). The Government proposes to phase in the additional leave, with an increase to 24 days from 1 October 2007. This part of the Act is still under consultation.

1.25 At the moment, if an employee works five days a week and the employer requires him or her to take the normal bank and public holidays as part of the statutory entitlement, the individual will only be entitled to 12 additional working days' leave.

1.26 It may be possible for employees in some industries to argue that they have an implied contractual right to take bank and public holidays as leave because of past custom and practice.

Bank Holidays

1.27 The lists of bank holidays in England and Wales, Scotland and Northern Ireland are based on:
- common law holidays (public holidays)
- the schedule to the Banking and Financial Dealings Act 1971
- holidays made by royal proclamation to substitute holidays falling at the weekend or to announce additional holidays
- alternative arrangements announced by the Government.

1.28 In general, there is no statutory obligation to observe bank holidays designated under the provisions of the Banking and Financial Dealings Act 1971 and employers and employees are not precluded from making their own alternative arrangements.

1.29 In England, Wales and Northern Ireland, Good Friday and Christmas Day are public holidays, not bank holidays.

1.30 See the calendars for Bank and Public Holidays for details of the holidays in England, Ireland, Scotland, Wales and Northern Ireland in the appendix to this book.

Religious Holidays and Festivals

1.31 When staff ask for holiday for fast days, to celebrate religious festivals or attend ceremonies, employers should sympathetically consider whether:
- the request is reasonable
- it is practical for the employees concerned to be absent from work at the time requested
- whether they have enough accrued holiday entitlement.

1.32 If there will be difficulties caused by a number of staff making requests for time off at the same time, employers should:
- discuss the matter with the employees affected
- discuss it with any recognised trade union
- aim to balance the needs of the business (and remaining staff) with the affected employees
- when agreeing criteria to decide who is granted leave, be careful to avoid indirect discrimination.

1.33 See the calendars of Religious Holidays and Festivals in the appendix to this book.

Specifying Particulars of Holidays

1.34 Employers are obliged under s.1 of the Employment Rights Act 1996 to

provide each employee with a basic statement of terms and conditions of employment. The statement must set out terms:
- specifying the employee's entitlement to holiday including public holidays
- relating to holiday pay.

1.35 The statement must be clear enough to allow the employee to calculate his or her entitlement (eg to payment in lieu of accrued holiday on termination). This is often done by specifying that one day's holiday will be paid at a rate of 1/260th of annual salary.

Payment during Annual Leave

1.36 A worker is entitled to be paid at the rate of a "week's pay" for each week of holiday taken under the Working Time Regulations 1998.

1.37 For employees who have normal working hours, a week's pay is the amount payable by the employer assuming the worker works during his or her normal working hours. Normally overtime pay is not counted in calculating the holiday pay for such workers.

1.38 For employees who do not have normal working hours, a week's pay is calculated by taking average remuneration over the previous 12 working weeks.

Accrual of Holiday in First Year of Employment

1.39 Until 2001, employees needed to have been employed for a minimum of 13 weeks before they had any right to take annual leave. This is no longer the case.

1.40 Under the Working Time Regulations, the amount of holiday employees can take in the first year of their employment is restricted. Workers will only be entitled to take that amount of holiday that has accrued at the rate of 1/12th of the annual entitlement on the first day of each month.

1.41 There is no such restriction after the first year of employment. So, for example, if an employee took an agreed two weeks' leave in the first month of the leave year, the employee would be obliged to pay holiday pay for the whole two weeks.

Timing of Holidays — Notice of Intention to Take Holidays

Employees' Notice of Intention

1.42 The employee must give the employer notice of intention to take holiday. The notice must be at least equal to twice the number of days' holiday the employee wishes to take. These notice requirements can be varied or disapplied by agreement.

Employers' Right of Counter-Notice

1.43 The employer can refuse a request to take statutory holiday by serving a counter-notice on the employee.

1.44 The counter-notice must be served on the employee at least as many days before as are in the requested leave, eg to refuse a request for one week's holiday the employer must give at least one week's notice prior to the requested start date.

1.45 The employer can compel the employee to take holiday on specific dates, eg over a Christmas or summer shutdown period, by serving a notice to that effect on the employee. The employee must be given notice at least equal to twice the number of days holiday the employee is required to take.

1.46 Employers should ensure that any requirements for when employees take holiday (eg Christmas shutdowns) do not discriminate against employees unjustifiably (eg on ground of race or religion). However, a decision not to allow workers to work on Christmas and Boxing Day, for example, may be considered reasonable, if the cost of opening and heating an office would be excessive, or if there is no work to be carried out on such a day.

Carrying over Holiday Entitlements

1.47 Under the Working Time Regulations, employees have no statutory right to carry over any unused statutory holiday from one leave year to the next.

1.48 Employers can, however, allow employees to carry over contractual holiday entitlements, ie holiday entitlement in excess of the four weeks' statutory minimum, from one year to the next.

Payment in Lieu of Holiday

1.49 An employer may not pay an employee for giving up any of his or her statutory holiday entitlement.

1.50 However, an employer may pay an employee for giving up any of his or her holiday in excess of the statutory minimum entitlement.

1.51 On termination of employment, workers are entitled to payment for any accrued but untaken statutory entitlement, whatever the circumstances of termination.

1.52 The amount to be paid following termination is calculated by a formula set out in the Working Time Regulations or as agreed in the employment contract or collective agreement.

Deductions for Holiday Taken in Excess

1.53 On termination of employment, the employer is entitled to "claw back" any holiday taken in excess of what the employee has accrued that year. However, an employer may not deduct sums for holiday taken in excess of accrued entitlement from the employee's pay unless the employee's employment contract allows it or the employee has signed a document in advance consenting to the deduction.

Extended Leave

1.54 Employers should be aware that employees on any form of leave, eg maternity, adoption, paternity and parental leave, sick leave and sabbaticals, continue to accrue annual leave.

Training

1.55 Human Resources personnel should be trained to ensure a good understanding of:
- employees' basic minimum entitlements to annual leave
- additional entitlements the employer has granted
- the relevant procedures for taking leave

Holidays and Extended Leave

- how discrimination legislation affects when employees may be permitted to take leave
- the issues arising from employees who are granted extended leave, eg sabbaticals.

List of Relevant Legislation

1.56
- Work and Families Act 2006
- Working Time Regulations 1998
- Employment Rights Act 1996

List of Relevant Cases

1.57
- *Robinson-Steele v RD Retail Services Ltd, Clarke v Frank Staddon Ltd and Caulfield & ors v Hanson Clay Products Ltd (formerly Marshalls Clay Products Ltd)* C-131/04, ECJ and C-257/04, ECJ — the ECJ ruled that rolled-up holiday pay is technically unlawful. The BERR (formerly DTI) amended its guidance notes to s.7 of the Working Time Regulations 1998 on annual leave and makes it clear that rolled-up holiday pay is unlawful, although, where rolled-up holiday payments have been made in the past, they can be set off against future leave payments.
The BERR stated: "Rolled-up holiday is considered unlawful and employers should renegotiate contracts involving rolled-up holiday pay for existing employees/workers as soon as possible so that payment for statutory annual leave is made at the time when the leave is taken. Where an employer has already given rolled-up holiday pay in relation to work undertaken, and the payments have been made in a transparent and comprehensible manner, they can be set off against any future leave payments made at the proper time."
- *Commissioners of Inland Revenue v Ainsworth* [2005] IRLR 465, CA — the Court of Appeal overturned the EAT's decision, finding that the EAT was wrong in deciding that the right to statutory paid holiday continues to accrue while an employee is off on long-term sick leave and has exhausted his or her entitlement to sick pay.
- *Smith v Morrisroes (AJ) and Sons Ltd* [2005] IRLR 72, EAT — where an employer contests holiday pay claims on the basis that holiday pay was "rolled up" in the basic rate of pay, the key issue will be whether or not there was a mutual agreement for genuine payment of holidays, representing a true addition to the contractual rate of pay for the time worked.
- *Caulfield v Marshalls Clay Products* [2004] IRLR 564, CA — employers may "roll up" holiday pay under the WTR provided there is a relevant contractual term and the amount of the holiday pay element is specified.
- *Hill v Chappell* [2003] IRLR 19 — an employer cannot recover money from a departing employee for holiday taken in excess of entitlement unless the employer has express authority to do so in the employment contract or a collective agreement.
- *MPB Structures Ltd v Munro* [2003] IRLR 350, CS — Scottish Court of Session hold that employers cannot "roll up" holiday pay.

- *Torith Ltd v Flynn* 21 November 2003 EAT — an apparently self-employed joiner was a "worker" within the WTR and therefore entitled to holiday pay.
- *Byrne Brothers (Formwork) Ltd v Baird* [2002] IRLR 96 — apparently self-employed labour-only subcontractors were "workers" within the WTR and therefore entitled to holiday pay.
- *Campbell & Smith Construction Group Ltd v Greenwood* [2001] IRLR 588 — confirms that employees have no statutory right to take leave on bank or public holidays. An employee's entitlement in this respect is purely a matter of contract.
- *Witley & District Men's Club v Mackay* [2001] IRLR 595 — a collective agreement (or employment contract) which provides that no payment will be made on summary dismissal in respect of accrued holiday is void. At least some payment must be made.

Further Information

Organisations

- **Department for Business, Enterprise and Regulatory Reform (BERR)**
  Web: *www.berr.gov.uk*
  The Department for Business, Enterprise and Regulatory Reform brings together functions from the former Department of Trade and Industry (DTI), including responsibilities for productivity, business relations, energy, competition and consumers. It also drives regulatory reform.

Overseas Workers

This topic covers the following.
- Statement of Particulars
- Posted Workers Directive
- EU Member States
- Enforcement
- Working Outside Europe
- Territorial Jurisdiction and Unfair Dismissal
- Discrimination
- Other Considerations
- Statutory Employment Rights
- Health and Safety
- Policy and Procedure

1.58 It is common for employers in certain types of industry to send employees to work abroad on a temporary basis. Many employees welcome the opportunity and it can provide them with additional skills, which are then transferred back into the workplace when they return to the UK.

1.59 It is important, however, for employers to be aware of the legal considerations of posting workers abroad. The considerations to be borne in mind depend on whether employees are being sent to work in an EU Member State or outside the EU. Employees posted to another EU Member State are protected by the Posted Workers Directive.

1.60 There is no such equivalent outside the EU and it is essential that employers seek legal advice in the country in question.

1.61 Regardless of where the posting is to be, employers may not post workers abroad unless they have a contractual right to do so. Where no contractual right exists, employers must obtain the employee's agreement.

1.62 It is sometimes possible to imply that the employer has the right to post employees abroad, for example where an employer conducts much of its business abroad, and the employee was aware of this when he or she accepted the contract.

Employers' Duties

1.63 Employers must:
- ensure that they have the employee's agreement if they wish to send an employee abroad
- ensure that employees who are required to work abroad for more than one month have, in their statement of particulars:
  - the length of time they are expected to work abroad
  - the currency in which remuneration will be paid
  - any benefits or additional remuneration applicable
  - terms and conditions relating to the employee's return to the UK
- put into place the appropriate systems to ensure that employees who are required to work abroad receive a statement of particulars before they leave the UK, even if that is before the expiry of the eight-week deadline for issuing a statement

- be aware of the Posted Workers Directive if sending employees to work in the European Union
- contact a liaison officer in the relevant Member State to ensure that employment laws in that Member State are not breached
- be aware that a worker whose pay and conditions are less favourable than the statutory minimum in the Member State to which they are posted may apply to a tribunal or court, either in that Member State or the Member State in which they live
- ensure that employees working abroad are fully informed of the organisation's policy on issues such as removal costs, medical treatments and travel back home.

Employees' Duties

1.64 Employees must:
- ensure that they are fully informed of their rights in the Member State in which they are to work, if being sent to work in Europe
- be clear as to the employment laws relating to them if working outside Europe
- obtain visas and other travel documents as required
- be aware of day-to-day living conditions in the relevant country, particularly where communicable disease is rife
- understand the culture of the country they will be working in before their departure
- ensure that any vaccinations are up to date and that any medication required is obtained before departure.

In Practice

Statement of Particulars

1.65 All employees are entitled to receive a written statement of particulars within eight weeks of starting employment.

1.66 Where employees are to be posted abroad, they must receive the statement of particulars before they leave the UK. This may be before the expiry of the eight-week deadline.

1.67 Section 1 of the Employment Rights Act 1996 states that, where employees are to be sent abroad for one month or more, the statement of particulars must provide information on:
- the length of the posting
- the currency in which remuneration will be paid
- any benefits or additional remuneration applicable
- any terms and conditions relating to the employee's return to the UK.

1.68 It is also important that the statement of particulars specifies by which country the contract is governed. In the absence of a choice of law clause, the contract will normally be governed by the law of the country in which the employee habitually carries out his or her work.

1.69 This does not mean, however, that an employer may deprive an employee of mandatory rights of the country to which he or she is posted. This is particularly true of the EU, where employees are protected under the Posted Workers Directive.

Posted Workers Directive

1.70 The Posted Workers Directive came into effect in December 1999. As well as protecting workers, the directive ensures that employers sending workers on temporary assignments to other EU Member States do not have a competitive advantage by offering these workers terms and conditions that are less favourable than the statutory minimums provided by the country to which the individual is being posted.

EU Member States

Austria	Belgium	Bulgaria*	Cyprus
Czech Republic	Denmark	Estonia	Finland
France	Germany	Greece	Hungary
Ireland	Italy	Latvia	Lithuania
Luxembourg	Malta	The Netherlands	Poland
Portugal	Romania*	Slovakia	Slovenia
Spain	Sweden	United Kingdom	

*Romania and Bulgaria joined the EU on 1 January 2007. People from these countries have the right to travel freely throughout the EU, but are not automatically allowed to work in the UK, due to the Government's decision to place restrictions on them.

1.71 Skilled workers are allowed to come to the UK on work permits to take up specific jobs. Low-skilled migrants from Romania and Bulgaria are, however, restricted to a total of 20,000 workers per year and such people are only permitted to work in jobs covered by existing schemes.

1.72 The key areas covered by the Posted Workers Directive are:
- minimum annual paid holiday
- maximum working hours and rest breaks
- minimum rates of pay (including overtime rates)
- protective measures for new mothers and pregnant workers
- health and safety
- protective measures for the employment of children and young persons, and
- discrimination laws.

1.73 This means that where an employee is posted to France, for example, the employee will be entitled to France's maximum working week of 35 hours, instead of the UK's 48-hour working week. In other EU Member States, all employees who work over their contractual hours are entitled to overtime pay. It is essential, therefore, that employers obtain full employment advice in the EU Member State in which the posting is to take place to ensure that the Posted Workers Directive is not breached.

1.74 The directive states that each EU Member State must have at least one liaison officer, whose role it is to advise employers in other Member States on legislation applicable to that Member State. Employers should contact the liaison officer at the relevant embassy before sending employees to that country.

1.75 However, where terms in the Member State are less favourable, the more favourable terms under the UK contract apply.

1.76 Note that the Posted Workers Directive does not apply to rights on termination of employment.

Enforcement

1.77 Workers whose pay and/or other terms and conditions in the key areas set out above are less favourable may apply to either a court or tribunal in the Member State in which they are working or the Member State in which they normally live and work.

Working Outside Europe

1.78 There is no equivalent to the Posted Workers Directive outside the EU and employers must ensure that they obtain full information and legal advice on any employment laws that apply in the country to which they are posting employees.

1.79 The US is an example of a particularly complex area. As a confederacy of 50 states, with three different types of statutes, employers must have an understanding of the federal, state and local municipal laws relating to each particular state. In addition, employers must ensure that they are fully informed of the discrimination laws in each state — US culture is considered particularly litigious and discrimination claims are common and often highly publicised.

1.80 Employers should ensure, therefore, that employees posted to the US are aware of its discrimination laws and what is, and is not, acceptable behaviour.

Territorial Jurisdiction and Unfair Dismissal

1.81 The issue of whether employees working abroad can claim unfair dismissal is an important one for employers and employees to be aware of. Much will depend on where the employee habitually works.

1.82 The case of *Serco Ltd v Lawson; Botham v Ministry of Defence; Crofts and others v Veta* [2006] UKHL 3 has provided some much needed guidance in this area.

1.83 Lawson was employed as a security supervisor on Ascension Island in the South Atlantic by Serco, a UK registered organisation with its head office in the UK. Mr Lawson's contract referred only to English law and he was paid in sterling. In 2001, Lawson brought an unfair constructive dismissal claim for asserting a right under the Working Time Regulations 1998 but the employment tribunal dismissed his claim on the grounds that it did not have the jurisdiction to hear it.

1.84 Lawson subsequently successfully appealed to the Employment Appeal Tribunal. It held that Lawson was entitled to make a claim for unfair dismissal, even though he had never worked in the UK on the grounds that his employer had a place of business in England. The Court of Appeal overturned this decision, however. It held that Lawson was not employed in the UK for the purposes of the Employment Rights Act 1996. It was an important factor, it said, that he worked solely on Ascension Island and it was of no consequence that he and his organisation had strong links with the UK.

1.85 The case was recently revisited in the House of Lords in the joint case of *Serco Ltd v Lawson; Botham v Ministry of Defence; Crofts and others v Veta Ltd and others* [2006] IRLR 289.

1.86 The House of Lords clarified the situation by ruling that claims may be brought by employees:
- who normally work in the UK
- who are sent to work outside the UK on a temporary basis
- who normally work outside the UK but whose base of employment is the UK.

1.87 It is important that individuals are employed by a UK organisation and there is a strong connection with the UK.

Discrimination

1.88 Employees who work *wholly* outside of the UK are unable to bring a discrimination claim, unless the:
- employer has a place of business in the UK
- employee's work is for the business in the UK
- employee is ordinarily a resident of the UK at the time he or she applies or is offered the job, or at any time during the course of employment.

1.89 In the case of *Saggar v Ministry of Defence* [2005] IRLR 618, the Court of Appeal held that the whole of an employee's contract must be taken into account when determining whether an employee has worked "wholly" outside the UK for purposes of determining whether a tribunal can hear a claim for discrimination.

1.90 Lieutenant Colonel Saggar, who was of Indian origin, worked as a consultant anaesthetist in the Royal Army Medical Corps from 1982 until his retirement in 2002.

1.91 Until 1998, Saggar worked mainly in the UK, apart from a few short postings abroad. From September 1982 to December 1999, however, he undertook a tour of duty in Cyprus. He complained to an employment tribunal that while he was in Cyprus he had been the victim of race discrimination.

1.92 The Employment Tribunal and EAT dismissed the case as Saggar had been working in Cyprus and not in the UK when the alleged discrimination took place.

1.93 The Court of Appeal held that the employment tribunal had erred, as it should have considered the whole period of employment when determining whether the employee had worked "wholly or mainly" in the UK, and not just the time spent in Cyprus and the case was, therefore, sent to another tribunal for reconsideration.

Other Considerations

Statutory Employment Rights

1.94 Although an employee's service continues to accrue while he or she is working abroad, employers should ensure that they inform employees of any statutory employment rights they currently enjoy which they may not benefit from while working abroad.

1.95 For example, if a redundancy occurs, weeks spent working abroad do not count towards continuous service, unless the employee is paying UK National Insurance contributions, although continuity of employment is preserved.

1.96 Likewise, there is no entitlement to Statutory Maternity, Paternity or Adoption Pay, unless UK National Insurance contributions are paid.

Health and Safety

1.97 Employers posting workers abroad should ensure that a risk assessment is carried out for each placement. The risk assessment should include contacting the Foreign and Commonwealth Office and the World Health Organisation.

1.98 Employers should also bear in mind that employees have the right to refuse to travel overseas if they consider that their safety will be put at risk, eg if the posting is to a war zone.

1.99 In addition, employers should:
- ensure that adequate arrangements are in place for in-country medical assistance
- make clear to employees who they should contact in the event of an emergency
- ensure that employees have adequate travel insurance
- provide information to employees on any vaccinations or other medications required.

Policy and Procedure

1.100 Employers who regularly post employees abroad should consider creating a policy and procedure on overseas working. The policy and procedure should include, in addition to the above, information on the following:
- mobility and repatriation costs
- accommodation arrangements
- allowances and any additional monies awarded
- return visits home
- any partner benefits or child education costs awarded
- work permits.

Training

1.101 All managers should be made aware of the legal implications of posting workers abroad, in particular their rights and responsibilities under the Posted Workers Directive. Where employees are being posted to countries outside of the European Union, they should be trained on any laws applicable to the relevant country and provided with guidance on unacceptable social behaviour to avoid causing embarrassment or committing a criminal offence.

List of Relevant Legislation

1.102
- Employment Equality (Religion or Belief) Regulations 2003
- Employment Equality (Sexual Orientation) Regulations 2003
- Employment Rights Act 1996
- Disability Discrimination Act 1995
- Sex Discrimination Act 1975
- Race Relations Act 1976
- Posted Workers Directive 96/71/EC

List of Relevant Cases

1.103
- *Serco Ltd v Lawson; Botham v Ministry of Defence; Crofts and others v Veta Ltd and others* [2006] UKHL 3
- *Crofts v Cathay Pacific Airways Ltd* [2005] IRLR 624, CA
- *Saggar v Ministry of Defence* [2005] IRLR 618, CA

Further Information

Organisations
- **Foreign and Commonwealth Office**
  Web: *www.fco.gov.uk/knowbeforeyougo*
  The Foreign and Commonwealth Office website provides up-to-date information for people travelling overseas.
- World Health Organization (WHO)
  Web: *www.who.int*
  The WHO is the United Nations' specialised agency for health and was established in 1948.

Part-Time and Other Atypical Workers

> This topic covers the following:
> - What is a Part-Time Worker?
> - Comparable Full-Time Worker
> - Part-time Workers (Prevention of Less Favourable Treatment) Regulations 2000
> - Annual Holiday Entitlement
> - Public and Bank Holidays
> - Remedies
> - Fixed-Term Employees
> - Definition of Fixed-Term Employee
> - Comparable Permanent Employee
> - Right Not to be Treated Less Favourably
> - Termination
> - Waiver Clauses

1.104 In the UK an increasing number of people are choosing not to work full time. Many of them are working parents but others are people wishing to obtain a better balance between work and their personal lives.

1.105 Part-time work is the most common form of atypical working but other types of atypical working include:
- temporary work
- fixed-term work
- seasonal work
- term-time working
- casual working
- home working.

1.106 There are many issues that employers need to consider when employing atypical workers. These range from the legal considerations, eg the protection afforded to such workers under the Part-time Workers (Prevention of Less Favourable Treatment) Regulations 2000, to administrative and practical issues, such as how to calculate holiday entitlement for an employee who does not work full time or is on a fixed-term contract.

Employers' Duties

1.107 Employers have a duty to:
- be aware of the status of workers under different types of contract
- observe the rights of employees
- not treat part timers less favourably than full timers on the grounds of their part-time status
- not treat employees on fixed-term contracts less favourably than comparable permanent employees unless there are objective reasons for doing so.

Employees' Duties

1.108 Employees must:
- accept work provided by the employer when he or she has agreed to a contract of employment that is governed by minimum requirements of mutuality of obligation and control.

In Practice

Part-Time Workers

What is a Part-Time Worker?

1.109 A part-time worker is an employee who works fewer hours than full-time employees within an organisation.

1.110 For example, if most employees work a 40-hour week, this would be considered to be full-time work. An employee who works fewer than 40 hours a week would be considered to be part time.

Comparable Full-Time Worker

1.111 A worker who considers that they have been treated less favourably because he or she works part time has to compare him or herself to a comparable full-time worker.

1.112 A comparable full-time worker is a worker who works in the same establishment as the part-time worker or, if there is no comparable full-time worker at the same establishment as the part-time worker, at a different establishment within the same organisation, and:
- is employed under the same type of contract as the part-time worker, and
- carries out the same or broadly similar work.

Part-time Workers (Prevention of Less Favourable Treatment) Regulations 2000

1.113 The Part-time Workers (Prevention of Less Favourable Treatment) Regulations 2000 apply not only to employees but also to workers who work under a contract for services and who do not have employment status. This includes many atypical workers such as freelances, casual workers, home workers and temporary staff. The regulations do not, however, apply to the genuinely self-employed.

1.114 The main difference between an employee and a worker working under a contract for services is the lack of mutuality of obligation between the worker and the employer. The employer does not have a duty to provide work and the worker has no obligation to accept it. The employer also lacks control over the work carried out.

1.115 Under the regulations, part-time workers have the right to be treated no less favourably than a comparable full time worker with regard to all contractual terms and non-contractual policies, practices and benefits. This includes, for example, promotion, selection for redundancy, training and pay.

1.116 Other examples in which it would be considered unlawful to treat a part-time worker less favourably include access and qualifying conditions relating to:
- occupational sick pay schemes
- enhanced maternity and paternity leave provisions
- occupational pension schemes.

1.117 Full-time workers who reduce their working hours or are transferred to part-time work are also covered by the regulations.

1.118 While part-time workers have the right to be paid the same as a comparable full-time worker, it should be noted that part-time workers are not entitled to enhanced overtime pay until they have worked the same number of hours as a comparable full-time worker.

1.119 Part-time workers are also protected by the following legislation.
- Employment Equality (Religion or Belief) Regulations 2003.
- Employment Equality (Sexual Orientation) Regulations 2003.
- Working Time Regulations 1998.
- National Minimum Wage Act 1998.
- Disability Discrimination Act 1995.
- Sex Discrimination Act 1975.
- Race Relations Act 1976.

1.120 A part-time worker, therefore, not only has the right not to be discriminated against on grounds of part-time status, but also has the right not to be subjected to discrimination on grounds of sex, race, religion or belief, age, sexual orientation or disability, and to be paid the national minimum wage for all work carried out. He or she also has the right not be forced to work an average of more than 48 hours a week, to minimum daily and weekly rest breaks and to four weeks' paid holiday (*pro rata*) per annum.

1.121 Workers also have the right not to be subjected to a detriment for having made a protected disclosure.

Annual Holiday Entitlement

1.122 All employees, including part-time workers, are entitled to a minimum statutory entitlement of four weeks' paid holiday. This may be inclusive of public holidays as there is no statutory entitlement to public holidays. Where, however, an employer offers its employees more than the statutory minimum, it must be sure to offer its part-time workers the same benefit on a *pro rata* basis.

1.123 Annual holiday entitlement should be "pro-rated" for part-time workers. Where a full-time employee would get 20 days for working a five-day week, for example, a part-time worker who only works 2.5 days a week would be entitled to 10 days' holiday in a leave year.

1.124 Where a worker has no normal working hours, holiday entitlement should be calculated by taking the average number of hours worked over a 12-week period.

Public and Bank Holidays

1.125 Part-time workers must not be discriminated against on grounds of their part-time worker status, therefore, where an employer grants full-time employees public holidays, part-time employees should also be entitled to these, albeit on a *pro rata* basis. It is usual for part-time employees to be granted only those public holidays that fall on days that he or she would normally work. The issue of whether a part-time employee who does not work on Mondays should be compensated for bank holidays that fall on a Monday is often raised. The case of *McMenemy v Capita Business Services Ltd [2007] IRLR 400 CS* implies that this is not necessary where an employee who works full time would be treated in the same way (in this case the business operated seven days a week and there were full-time employees who would not work on Mondays).

1.126 The law is unclear as to how public holidays should be calculated for part-time employees and it may, therefore, be more straightforward for employers to calculate public holidays on a *pro rata* basis, depending on the number of days they actually work.

Remedies

1.127 An employer who treats a part-time worker less favourably than a full-time worker because of his or her part-time status, will be in breach of the regulations unless it can justify the treatment on wholly objective grounds.

1.128 Part-time workers who believe they have been denied their statutory rights under the Part-time Workers (Prevention of Less Favourable Treatment) Regulations may demand a written statement from their employer explaining the reasons for being treated less favourably than a comparable full-time employee. This must be provided within 21 days and any statement provided may be admissable in evidence at an employment tribunal.

1.129 A claim to tribunal must be made within three months of the less favourable treatment taking place or the date of the worker's termination if he or she has resigned or been dismissed. A worker does not, however, need to resign in order to bring a claim under the regulations. A tribunal will order the employer to put matters right and/or pay the worker compensation as it sees fit.

Fixed-Term Employees

1.130 Employees employed under fixed-term contracts are protected by the Fixed-term Employees (Prevention of Less Favourable Treatment) Regulations.

1.131 The regulations came into force on 1 October 2002 and provide that employees on fixed-term contracts have the legal right not to be treated less favourably than comparable permanent employees.

1.132 It should be noted that the regulations apply only to employees and not to workers.

1.133 The regulations also do not apply to students on work placements of one year or less, apprentices or agency temps. Employees taken on for a fixed period for work experience or training purposes (where such experience or training is funded by an EU institution) are also not covered.

Definition of Fixed-Term Employee

1.134 A fixed-term employee is an employee who is employed under a contract that is due to end:
- on the expiry of a specific term
- on completion of a particular task
- or when a specific event either happens or does not happen.

1.135 The Department for Business, Enterprise and Regulatory Reform's guide to the regulations provides some examples of fixed-term employees as follows.
- Those who are employed for a fixed term to cover for maternity, paternity, parental or sick leave.

- Those who are employed to cover for peaks in demand and whose contracts expire when demand returns to the normal level.
- Those whose contracts expire when a specific task is finished.
- Seasonal or casual workers who are taken on for a short period or task and whose contracts come to an end when that period expires or the task is finished.

1.136 Under the regulations, if an employee completes four years' continuous service under a series of consecutive fixed-term contracts, or has his or her fixed-term contract renewed after four years' continuous service on a single contract, the employee will be considered as permanent unless the fixed-term status can be justified.

Comparable Permanent Employee

1.137 An employee on a fixed-term contract who feels he or she has been treated less favourably must compare him or herself with a comparable permanent employee.

1.138 A comparable permanent employee is an employee employed by the same employer who is employed on an open-ended contract. He or she must also carry out the same or broadly similar work and work at the same establishment or, where there is no comparable permanent employee at the same establishment, at another of the employer's establishments.

Right Not to be Treated Less Favourably

1.139 Employees on fixed-term contracts have the right not to be treated less favourably than comparable permanent employees in relation to:
- terms and conditions of employment (eg pay and bonus schemes) unless there are objective reasons for the less favourable treatment
- training, promotions or transfers
- permanent positions within the company — employees on fixed-term contracts must be informed of any permanent vacancies that arise.

1.140 If the fixed-term employee is treated less favourably than a comparable permanent employee, then the employer must be able to justify this treatment on objective grounds.

1.141 Examples might include the employer's need to achieve a genuine business objective, or a situation where the cost of providing a benefit to someone on a fixed-term contract would be disproportionately high compared with the value of the benefit they would receive.

1.142 Fixed-term employees who believe that their employer has treated them less favourably without proper justification may complain to an employment tribunal.

1.143 When comparing terms and conditions the regulations make it clear that there is no absolute right for every item to be identical, provided the overall package is no less favourable. Also, there may be circumstances where it is appropriate to give only a proportion of a benefit to reflect the short duration of a fixed-term contract.

Termination

1.144 When a fixed-term contract comes to an end and is not renewed, the law regards this as a dismissal and the employee will be able to claim unfair dismissal and/or a redundancy payment, subject to the requisite periods of qualifying service, and the circumstances of the termination.

Waiver Clauses

1.145 In the past it was common for employers to insert waiver clauses for unfair dismissal and redundancy pay into fixed-term contracts. It is now no longer possible to agree these terms with employees.

1.146 Unfair dismissal waiver clauses are now only still valid if they were entered into prior to 25 October 1999 for the remainder of that fixed-term contract. Similarly, a waiver clause in respect of statutory redundancy pay can no longer be inserted into a fixed-term contract, although any valid waiver clause in a fixed-term contract entered into before 1 October 2002 will remain valid and enforceable until the expiry of the contract.

List of Relevant Legislation

1.147
- Employment Equality (Religion or Belief) Regulations 2003
- Employment Equality (Sexual Orientation) Regulations 2003
- Fixed-term Employees (Prevention of Less Favourable Treatment) Regulations 2002
- Part-time Workers (Prevention of Less Favourable Treatment) Regulations 2000
- Working Time Regulations 1998
- Employment Act 2002
- Public Interest Disclosure Act 1999
- National Minimum Wage Act 1998
- Employment Rights Act 1996
- Disability Discrimination Act 1995
- Race Relations Act 1976
- Sex Discrimination Act 1975

List of Relevant Cases

1.148
- *McMenemy v Capita Business Services Ltd* [2007] IRLR 400, CS
- *Matthews v Kent & Medway Towns Fire Authority* [2003] IRLR 732
- *Whiffen v Milham Ford Girls' School* [2001] IRLR 468, CA

Further Information

Publications
- PL520 *Flexible Working — The Right to Request and the Duty to Consider: Guidance for Employers and Employees*, Department for Business, Enterprise and Regulatory Reform (BERR)
- *Flexible Working — The Right to Request and the Duty to Consider*, Department for Business, Enterprise and Regulatory Reform (BERR) URN 06/2158/A1

Organisations
- **Employers and Work-life Balance**
  Web: *www.employersforwork-lifebalance.org.uk*
  Employers and Work-life Balance aims to help all UK organisations implement and continuously improve sustainable work-life strategies that meet customer needs, corporate goals and enhance the quality of life for individuals.

Sabbaticals and Secondments

> This topic covers the following.
> - Who Initiates Sabbaticals or Career Breaks and Why?
> - A Valued Benefit
> - The Scope and Benefits of Secondments
> - Duration
> - Disadvantages and Dangers
> - A Policy on Sabbaticals
> - Setting up Secondments
> - During the Period of Absence
> - When Employees Return

1.149 A "secondment" is the fixed-term transfer of a senior manager to an external organisation. Mid-level managers can be seconded to external organisations; all staff can be seconded within a given organisation. A "sabbatical" is a period of paid or unpaid leave granted to an employee, normally for the purpose of study or travel. A "career break" is a similar suspension of work, often unpaid.

1.150 Both sabbaticals and secondments involve employees taking a period of time away from their existing job, then either returning to this job or taking up a different position within the organisation. In each case, there are important matters to be considered before, during and at the end of the period of absence. There are however several differences between sabbaticals and secondments, relating to factors such as:

- why and by whom they are initiated
- who benefits from them and in what ways.

1.151 There is also an overlap between sabbaticals and career breaks. Furthermore, the management of career breaks presents some of the same problems as the management of secondments.

Employers' Duties

1.152 Employers have a duty to ensure that:

- no applicant is treated less favourably in the sabbatical and secondment process on the grounds of sex, race, age, disability, sexual orientation, gender reassignment, religion or belief, or trade union membership or non-membership
- consideration is given to any provision, criterion or practice, eg any condition attached to the secondment or sabbatical, which, although apparently neutral in effect, might be indirectly discriminatory against particular groups of applicants
- contractual obligations are fully understood by both parties
- terms and conditions of employment are consistent with statutory requirements and minimum standards
- data relating to sabbaticals and secondments is processed in accordance with data protection legislation and guidance from the Information Commissioner.

Employees' Duties

1.153 Employees have a duty to ensure that:
- they abide by any agreement they reach relating to a secondment or sabbatical.

In Practice

Who Initiates Sabbaticals or Career Breaks and Why?

1.154 Until recently, the initiative for taking sabbaticals tended to come from employees. The most common reasons were:
- to undertake an extended period of travel
- to study full time, either for a career-related qualification or for personal development
- to reassess priorities because of a desired career change.

1.155 Career breaks are also usually requested by employees. Two major reasons for career breaks are:
- parents want to take time out to be with young children
- employees with a terminally ill spouse or close relative want to provide care or support.

A Valued Benefit

1.156 It is becoming common, however, for employers, eg Microsoft, to offer sabbaticals as part of a standard benefits package. Advantages to the employer include:
- the goodwill such schemes generate
- reductions in staff turnover
- improving the employer's ability to attract new staff
- better performance from the individuals who take sabbaticals on their return
- development opportunities for the covering staff — who are able to take on new responsibilities.

1.157 Even more widespread is the practice of offering career breaks as part of the benefits package. Career breaks can help to attract and retain female employees and employees with caring responsibilities in particular.

The Scope and Benefits of Secondments

1.158 Secondments are usually initiated by the donor organisation, but employees seeking development opportunities may also request them — as do recipient organisations such as charities looking for staff on "free loan".

Scope

1.159 The term "secondment" commonly refers to the fixed-term transfer of a senior manager to an external organisation. There is also scope for:

- seconding mid-level managers to external organisations
- arranging secondments for staff at all levels to other operating sites or departments within a given organisation.

1.160 Secondments can also be made, for example:
- to a one-off project team
- for an employee to work with external consultants for the duration of an assignment
- to a trial or pilot operation
- in multinational organisations, from one country to another.

1.161 Secondments are normally one way but it is possible to arrange a swap between two employees from different parts of the same organisation or from two completely separate organisations.

1.162 These external secondments usually require an existing link between the two organisations, ie one may be a customer of, or supplier to, the other. Secondments can also take place between public and private sector organisations or when organisations second employees to a charity.

Benefits

1.163 Secondments offer benefits for the parent or donor organisation, the recipient organisation, and the individual employee.

1.164 The parent organisation benefits from:
- the forging of closer links with the recipient organisation
- the opportunity to contribute to the community (when seconding to charities)
- "new blood" ideas and procedures brought back by the secondee
- the improved performance of the secondee.

1.165 Benefits to recipient organisations include:
- in secondments to charities — a free resource, assuming that the parent organisation continues to pay the individual's salary
- in secondments to suppliers or customers — the creation of greater understanding between the organisations and a cementing of their working relationship
- in internal secondments — overcoming the "us and them" feeling that often exists, eg between head office and operating units
- in international secondments within an organisation — opportunities to train and develop local staff and to understand and overcome cultural differences.

1.166 Benefits to the seconded individual include:
- the opportunity to obtain training or experience that may not be available in the parent organisation
- exposure to a different culture and to different methods of working, which may creatively challenge the individual's ideas.

Duration

1.167 Sabbaticals, secondments and career breaks can last from a few weeks to several years.

Disadvantages and Dangers

Sabbaticals and Career Breaks

1.168 The disadvantages of sabbaticals from the employer's point of view are:

- disruption to work
- additional stress on other members of the department who may have to provide cover
- the cost of a temp or interim to cover
- the risk that employees may not want to return.

1.169 From the viewpoint of employees there are the risks that they may:
- be perceived as less committed to their careers than those who do not take breaks
- not be able to return to their old job, eg due to restructuring, after long breaks
- not want to return to their old jobs.

1.170 These risks are greater with career breaks, which tend to be longer than sabbaticals.

Secondments

1.171 With regard to secondments, there are potential disadvantages to both the employer and the employee.

1.172 From the parent organisation's angle:
- secondments are an expensive form of development, since the parent organisation usually pays the secondee's salary and other employment costs
- the organisation loses the secondee's output and expertise, at least for a time
- there is a risk that the secondee will be poached by the other party, or revalue his or her career aims and not return.

1.173 In the case of international secondments, the costs and risks are significantly greater.
- when an employee is seconded overseas his or her living and travel costs increase — especially if he or she is accompanied by a spouse or partner and children.
- there is a greater risk of the secondment being prematurely terminated due to the employee's family failing to settle in.

1.174 From the point of view of the secondee the potential disadvantages are:
- the desired learning may not take place, particularly if the recipient organisation uses the secondee at a low level
- secondments may be used by employers as a way of off-loading under-performing or surplus individuals rather than taking positive steps to deal with under-performance
- individuals may not be able to return to their role due to restructuring or other changes in the parent organisation.

A Policy on Sabbaticals

1.175 Before adding sabbaticals and career breaks to the range of flexible benefits they offer, employers should consider the implications and lay down a clear policy. This will ensure consistency and avoid situations in which individual line managers set precedents by their responses to specific requests.

Key Issues

1.176 Equal opportunities legislation favours allowing all staff to request sabbaticals, although it is possible to set a period of employment that is necessary before an employee becomes eligible to request a secondment. To avoid claims of age discrimination, this should be no more than five years, unless a longer period of time can be objectively justified.

1.177 Other key issues to define include the following.
- The purpose of sabbaticals — are they to be granted only if they directly add value to the organisation, eg a research project or MBA, or is their value in allowing employees to achieve a personal ambition?
- Length of service qualifying periods, especially where sabbaticals are used as a reward or as an opportunity for rest.
- Pay and benefits — whether during unpaid sabbaticals, employees will continue to enjoy benefits, eg insurance cover and company car, and be eligible for salary reviews.
- Continuity of employment and the applicability of the terms of an employee's contract of employment during the sabbatical.
- Undertakings regarding an employee's return, including:
  - the employer's provision of a same-level post if it cannot guarantee return to the same job
  - making the sabbatical conditional on an employee's agreement to return for a defined period
  - stating what will happen if the employee resigns during the sabbatical or decides not to return.
- Timing — the employer needs to control the number of staff on sabbatical at any one time, by considering:
  (a) how the policy links to policy on absences such as maternity or parental leave
  (b) length of break — should a time limit be imposed?

Setting up Secondments

1.178 Since secondments arise on an *ad hoc* basis and are not part of a benefits package, a specific policy may not be appropriate. It is vital to set each secondment up properly by:
- agreeing both its objectives and the responsibilities of all three parties
- formalising its terms in a written contract
- guaranteeing a same-level post on the employee's return from secondment.

1.179 The written contract should define the duration of the secondment, who pays the secondee and what expenses he or she may claim and from whom. A clause preventing the recipient organisation from poaching the secondee can be inserted.

During the Period of Absence

1.180 Where the purpose of a sabbatical is for the employee to have a complete break, contact may be inappropriate until shortly before the individual's return. In other cases, eg career breaks lasting for several years, it is important to maintain contact. Ways of doing this include:
- inviting the employee to attend training courses, meetings or social events
- posting or emailing appropriate material about the organisation
- encouraging the individual's line manager and colleagues to keep in touch socially.

1.181 Secondments must be properly managed throughout their duration as follows:
- specify named individuals as contacts in both the parent and recipient organisations
- provide an induction programme in the recipient organisation
- maintain contact between the parent organisation and the individual
- ensure that the secondee receives appropriate training and is included in performance management programmes, eg annual appraisals.

Sabbaticals and Secondments

1.182 The management of secondments is particularly important in multinational organisations where employees undertake overseas assignments. The expatriate has to adjust not only to a new organisation but also to an unfamiliar country — and the same may be true of his or her partner and family.

1.183 The home-country organisation should stay in contact with the expatriate as well as offering local help. This contact:
- increases the chances of defining and resolving problems which might jeopardise the assignment
- makes expatriates feel cared for and responsible to the organisation.

When Employees Return

1.184 When employees are returning to their old job, it is important to:
- make them feel welcome
- bring them up to date with changes
- introduce them to new members of staff
- ensure that they are clear about their objectives
- ensure they have an appropriate workload.

1.185 In the case of secondments there should be a formal review of how the individual's development can be used for the benefit of the organisation.

1.186 Where longer breaks are involved, other factors must be considered, eg the employee's old job may no longer be available and it may be necessary to identify a suitable alternative. Employees may not want the same job or not on the same terms. This can happen when returning employees:
- have increased ambitions due to gaining a qualification such as an MBA
- find that their work-life balance priorities have changed
- want to work part time or on a job-sharing basis.

1.187 Those who have been on extended career breaks at home will need most help re-assimilating into the workplace. Employers should therefore treat the return of a member of staff from a career break in much the same way as the induction of a new employee by:
- providing an orientation programme
- providing specific support from the line manager
- monitoring the individual's re-integration into the organisation.

Training

1.188 Prior to the commencement of secondments, training or briefing prepares employees for the lifestyle and cultural differences they will encounter, especially when the secondee is moving abroad.

1.189 Although some large companies run their own briefing sessions for international assignments, many use the courses developed by external specialist organisations. These cover everything from cultural differences to taxation and children's education. There is a strong case for giving training to employees' spouses or partners as well.

1.190 At the beginning of a secondment, it is important for the recipient organisation to provide an induction programme.

1.191 During sabbaticals and secondments it is important to enable employees to

Sabbaticals and Secondments

keep up with their CPD (continuing professional development) where appropriate. Providing relevant training is also a useful means of keeping in touch.

1.192 When employees return, an induction programme should be provided, together with any necessary training on new systems.

Sickness Absence

Sickness Absence

This topic covers the following.
- Identifying Reasons for Absence
- Sickness Absence Policy and Procedure
- Management Commitment
- Managing Short Term Absence
- Managing Long Term Absence
- Dismissal on Capability Grounds
- Keeping in Touch with Absent Employees
- Improving Levels of Absence

1.193 For many organisations, sickness absence is a considerable concern. The UK as a whole has a poor absence record. The CBI reported that, in 2006, the number of working days lost in the UK was 175 million, an increase of 6% over the previous year, resulting in a total cost in lost productivity of around £13.4 billion. While employees will, on occasions, be sick, organisations should try to ensure that effective absence management procedures are in place to minimise the impact of sickness within the organisation.

1.194 There is no doubt that effective absence management can have a substantial impact on an organisation's bottom line. The cost of occupational sick pay can be high, but the indirect costs should not be underestimated. Some of these indirect costs can be high yet difficult to price, for example the impact on customer service, the quality of the service provided and the training of temporary staff.

1.195 Many organisations are aware that they have an absence "problem" but find it difficult to quantify this as they do not monitor the type of absences and do not have an understanding of the issues relating to absence within their workplace. Different organisations, by the very nature of their workforce, will experience absence in different ways. An employee who is stressed, for example, and has a negative opinion towards his or her employer, may find it easier to call in sick for a day or two with a minor ailment rather than face a day at work. An organisation that does not provide flexible working may find employees calling in sick when in fact it is their children who are unwell and off school.

Employers' Duties

1.196 Employers have a duty to:
- communicate rules and procedures on sickness absence
- pay employees, subject to qualifying conditions, statutory sick pay and any contractual sick pay specified in the contract of employment
- assist employees who are off sick to return to work by making reasonable adjustments as specified by a GP or other doctor
- keep in touch with employees who are off sick.

Employees' Duties

1.197 Employees have a duty to:

- attend work and only take time off due to sickness absence where the absence is genuine and justified
- comply with organisational absence reporting procedures
- co-operate and attend medical appointments as stated in their contract of employment.

In Practice

1.198 There are several hands-on ways to reduce levels of sickness absence.

Identifying Reasons for Absence

1.199 In order to determine effectively the level of absence within an organisation, data on individual absence must be collated and the causes of absence identified.

1.200 Employees who are absent for one day or more should be required to complete a self-certification sickness form, which should be handed to the employee's immediate line manager at a return-to-work interview which should take place on the employee's first day back at work. The self-certification sickness form should require employees to give their reason for their absence against meaningful categories. Where employees are absent from work for seven or more days, a medical certificate should be provided. The certificate should clearly state the reason for absence.

1.201 Such information, although basic, once collated and analysed is essential to gaining an understanding of absence issues at an organisational level. However this data is collated, the process should include the ability to analyse the following.
- The reasons for absence:
  - categorisation should not be overly complex or too generic so that the data is easy to analyse as well as meaningful.
- The levels of absence within specific departments, job levels and job roles:
  - it is essential to be able to analyse data relating to a specific grouping. Is absence particularly high in a specific role, for example?
- The pattern of absence:
  - are employees frequently off sick on a Monday or a Friday? Is there a certain shift where sickness is particularly prevalent?

1.202 The data may be gathered through a comprehensive HR system or even manually in smaller organisations. It does not matter which method is used, as long as the reasons for absence are clear and that any patterns in absence can be identified.

1.203 The data should be reviewed by the organisation as a whole, but also by individual managers who may be able to identify potential problems and provide guidance as to why an individual is taking time off. It is worth bearing in mind, however, that not all employees will complete self-certification forms honestly. In addition, even where an employee does complete the form to the best of his or her ability, it may not provide the organisation with the full picture. An employee, for example, who is highly stressed may not cite stress as being the reason for his or her absence — he or she may genuinely have a minor ailment which he or she feels is bad enough to take a day off work. An employee who is not suffering from stress in the same circumstances would not have taken the time off. The underlying reason for the employee's absence in such circumstances would be stress and not the cause given for the absence.

Sickness Absence Policy and Procedure

1.204 In order to manage sickness effectively within an organisation, it is essential to have a clearly defined policy and procedure. The policy and procedure should be clear and communicated to managers and employees regularly.

1.205 The following areas should be covered in a policy and procedure.
1. A clear statement on the organisation's attitude to sickness absence. It should be made clear that employees should attend work unless they have a genuine and legitimate reason for absence. The policy should also recognise, however, that employees will, from time to time, be unwell and unable to attend work and that the organisation will support such employees with the aim of assisting them in their return to work as soon as possible.
2. Procedures to be followed in the event of sickness absence. Employees should be made aware of how sickness absences should be reported. Ideally, employees should, where physically possible, report their absence personally to their line manager within a defined time scale, eg by their normal start time.
It should be made clear to employees that text messaging, leaving voicemail messages and asking partners/relatives to contact the organisation are not acceptable. The process to be followed when employees return to work should also be set out, eg the requirement for self-certification forms to be completed at a meeting with the line manager on the first day back at work or, for longer absences, the submission of medical certificates.
Employees should be made aware that failure to comply with the organisation's absence reporting procedures may result in disciplinary action and/or occupational sick pay being withheld.
3. Procedures for dealing with persistent short-term absence. Employees who are regularly absent for short periods should be aware that these absences will be identified by the company and that formal disciplinary action may be taken where an employee exceeds a certain number of absences or a specified number of days within a defined time frame. Managers should, however, be aware that it may not always be appropriate to take formal disciplinary action as the circumstances surrounding each individual case should be determined. An employee with MS, for example, who takes genuine time off for reasons relating to his or her disability, should not be disciplined, however, an employee who takes Mondays off, for no apparent reason, may well be subject to the organisation's disciplinary procedure.
4. Procedures for dealing with long-term absence. The procedures for dealing with extended timescales should be clearly set out, for example at what point employees are expected to submit medical certificates, when occupational health will be contacted and for how long company sick pay, if relevant, will run.
5. Details on occupational sick pay if relevant and details of qualifying conditions.

Management Commitment

1.206 In order to ensure that a sickness absence policy and procedure operates effectively, it is essential to have management buy-in. While senior management commitment is essential, more often than not it will be line managers who will be dealing with day-to-day absence issues and it is important that these managers understand the rationale behind the policy and procedure and how it operates. The policy and procedure should be robust and credible and take into account organisational needs as well as best practice.

Managing Short-Term Absence

1.207 Short-term absences are very often the most problematic for an organisation. Such absences are usually without notice leaving organisations very often struggling to provide an effective service. It can sometimes be difficult to determine whether short-term absences are legitimate, since the employee will usually self-certify rather than provide a medical certificate.

1.208 Where an employee is persistently off sick for short periods of time, or has reached the organisational "trigger" for days off work, a full investigation should be carried out.

1.209 The investigation should determine whether the absences are due to an underlying medical condition. An employee who is always off sick with a bad back, for example, may be suffering from a condition which requires medical intervention. In determining whether there is a genuine medical underlying cause, the employer will, in most cases, obtain specialist advice either from the employee's GP or the organisation's occupational health service (having obtained the necessary consents under the Access to Medical Records Act). This specialist advice should assist the employer in identifying steps that should be taken to improve the individual's attendance record.

1.210 Where, following investigation, it is determined that there is no underlying medical problem that has led to the absences and that the employee has taken time off for minor ailments, it may be appropriate to instigate the organisation's disciplinary procedures on grounds of misconduct. Alternatively, it may be the case that the individual has been suffering from genuine, non-serious medical conditions that have made him or her too ill to attend work. In such cases, it is would be reasonable to simply reiterate the required level of absence. Where disciplinary action is taken, it is usual to start with the lowest sanction so that the employee has the opportunity to realise how seriously the organisation takes excessive sickness absence and has the opportunity to improve his or her absence record. Where persistent absence does eventually lead to dismissal, a tribunal will consider a variety of factors to determine whether the dismissal was fair, including the employee's past attendance record, the likelihood of the employee's attendance improving and any other mitigating factors. The statutory dismissal procedure should always be followed.

Managing Long-Term Absence

1.211 Where an employee is likely to be absent for a prolonged length of time, appropriate medical investigations should take place.

1.212 Medical investigations should include contacting the employee's GP and requesting the employee attend an appointment with the organisation's occupational health department or an independent doctor.

1.213 In order to do any of the above, employers must adhere to the Access to Medical Reports Act 1988. Written consent from the employee must be obtained and this consent should be forwarded to the GP. Employees also have the right to:
- withhold consent to an application being made
- withhold consent to the report being supplied to the organisation
- see the report before it is sent to the organisation
- request amendments to the report, or add their own comments to the report.

1.214 When contacting the GP, it is helpful to provide as much information as possible about the nature of the employee's role. This will help the GP to provide detailed guidance as to the prognosis relating to the employee's return to work given the employee's job.

1.215 It is usual for a doctor's report to make recommendations as to adjustments that will enable an employee to return to work, eg a phased return, reduced hours for a period of time, etc. Where an employee has a disability that falls under the Disability Discrimination Act 1995, it is essential that the organisation takes heed of such recommendations.

1.216 The Act expects employers to make reasonable adjustments to their employment arrangements and/or their premises. The definition of "reasonable" will depend on the employer's individual circumstances. Examples of adjustments can include:
- allowing the employee to work reduced hours
- changing start or end times so that the employee can travel to work on public transport
- providing specialist equipment to facilitate the employee's work.

1.217 A blanket refusal to make reasonable adjustments would be likely to lead to a finding of discrimination on the grounds of disability.

1.218 Where reasonable adjustments have been made but have failed to improve an employee's attendance record or where an employee is not disabled, it may be necessary to terminate an employee's employment on the grounds of capability.

Dismissal on Capability Grounds

1.219 A decision to terminate employment on capability grounds should never be made without a thorough medical investigation. Suitable alternative employment should also be considered. An employer may not be required to create a new role to accommodate an employee's needs, but it should consider other roles within an organisation. In doing so, the employer should exercise flexibility. A vacant position may be full time (9am to 5pm) but could this role be carried out at different times or part time, or can certain elements of the role be reduced or removed where such factors may adversely affect the ability of the individual to carry it out? How much flexibility is required will depend on the size of the organisation, its capacity to be flexible, the nature of the employee's illness and his or her skills and abilities.

1.220 Where, despite all of the above, a dismissal is the only available option, it is important that the statutory dismissal procedure is carried out and that the employer is satisfied that all other options have been explored.

Keeping in Touch with Absent Employees

1.221 Employees who are off work for an extended period often feel out of touch with the working environment. Such detachment may result in the employee becoming fearful of returning to work, thereby resulting in the sickness becoming more prolonged. In some cases, valuable employees may even choose not to return to work.

1.222 It is important for managers to keep in touch with employees who are off sick. The mechanisms for doing so will depend on the circumstances of each individual case. Contact by telephone at intervals agreed between the manager and the employee is usual, but home visits (as long as the employee agrees to these) can also be of benefit. Home visits as well as telephone calls can be used to identify how the employee is feeling and when he or she will feel well enough to return to work. The manager can also use these meetings to communicate company news and consult on company changes if necessary.

Improving Levels of Absence

1.223 Once an organisation has collated data relating to reasons for absence, it is

possible to identify ways of improving absence levels by modifying existing policies or creating new ones that take account of the needs of the workforce. The following examples will depend on the size of the organisation and available resources.
- Health programmes — providing discounted rates to health clubs or sporting facilities, vaccination programmes (eg free influenza injections), health education and advice, stress counselling.
- Flexible working — where it is identified that sickness is taken as an excuse for time off to deal with domestic incidents, a flexible working policy where an individual can take time off, eg first thing in the morning and make up the time at a later stage may encourage employees not to take time off sick for domestic emergencies. Employers should note that employees have a right to emergency time off under Time off for Dependants legislation, although the right is to unpaid time off.
- Employee Assistance Programmes.
- Training for managers on absence management and company absence procedures.

Training

1.224 There are three levels of training required.

1.225 Line managers and supervisors should:
- understand the regulations relating to sickness absence and related topics such as statutory sick pay
- understand the importance of accurate record-keeping
- have the ability to conduct interviews and to support staff as appropriate during and after sickness absence.

1.226 Senior managers should:
- appreciate their responsibilities and influence in the field of sickness absence management
- have the ability to conduct sensitive and high impact meetings with employees.

1.227 HR support personnel should:
- set up and continually update reporting and monitoring systems
- have the ability to assist and support in sensitive and high impact meetings with employees
- understand the process that must be followed if contemplating dismissing or taking relevant disciplinary action against an employee.

List of Relevant Legislation

1.228
- Data Protection Act 1998
- Employment Rights Act 1996
- Disability Discrimination Act 1995
- Access to Medical Reports Act 1988

Further Information

Publications
- IR CA30 *Statutory Sick Pay — A Manual for Employers*, available from HM Revenue & Customs.

Organisations
- **Advisory Conciliation and Arbitration Service (Acas)**
  Web: *www.acas.org.uk*
  Acas aims to improve organisations and working life through better employment relations. It provides up-to-date information, advice, high-quality training, and works with employers and employees to solve problems and improve performance.
- **HM Revenue & Customs**
  Web: *www.hmrc.gov.uk/home.htm*
  HM Revenue & Customs (HMRC) is the department responsible for the business of the former Inland Revenue and HM Customs and Excise. HMRC is responsible for lecting the bulk of tax revenue as well as paying tax credits and child benefit.
- **Disability Rights Commission**
  Web: *www.drc-gb.org*
  An independent body established by Act of Parliament to eliminate discrimination against disabled people and promote quality of opportunity. It provides information and advice to disabled people and employers about their rights and duties. From October 2007 this organisation will be replaced by the Commission for Equality and Human Rights (**Web:** *www.cehr.org.uk*).
- **NHS Plus**
  Web: *www.nhsplus.nhs.uk*
  NHS Plus is a network of occupational health services based in NHS hospitals providing occupational health services to NHS Staff and the private sector.
- **Managing Absence**
  Web: *www.managingabsence.co.uk*
  This site provides employers with comprehensive information on cost-effective approaches to managing short-term sickness absenteeism.

Statutory Time Off

> This topic covers the following.
> - Unpaid Time Off to Perform Public Duties
> - Reasonable Time Off
> - Jury Service
> - Paid Time Off to Perform Duties
> - Trade Union Activities
> - The Right of Accompaniment
> - Employee Representatives
> - European Works Council Representatives
> - Pension Fund Trustees
> - Ante-natal Care
> - Young Employees
> - Redundancy

1.229 Employees have a number of different statutory rights to ask for time off work. Employees have the right to seek unpaid time off work to carry out functions connected with certain public duties. Some categories of employees have the right to request paid time off work. The right is to request time off work, not an absolute right to take time off when the individual sees fit. An employee whose request for time off has been unreasonably refused can bring an action in an employment tribunal. Such a claim must be brought within three months of the date of the employer's failure to allow the employee to take time off. In exceptional circumstances, the tribunal may extend this period. Most of the statutory rights to time off work are set out in the Employment Rights Act 1996 and the Trade Union and Labour Relations (Consolidation) Act 1992.

Employers' Duties

1.230 Employers must permit employees to take unpaid time off:
- to perform public duties
- for jury service (not for statutory reasons, but to avoid contempt of court).

1.231 Employers must permit employees to take paid time off to:
- carry out duties as an official of a recognised trade union
- accompany a fellow employee to a formal grievance or disciplinary interview
- carry out duties as an employee representative on collective redundancies/ transfers of undertakings consultations
- undertake duties as a European Works Council representative
- undertake duties as a pension fund trustee
- receive ante-natal care, if pregnant
- undertake study or training, if aged between 16 and 18
- look for alternative employment during a redundancy notice period.

Employees' Duties

1.232 Employees have a duty to:
- agree any time off work with their employer
- follow the company policy and procedure on time off.

In Practice

Unpaid Time Off to Perform Public Duties

1.233 Under s.50 of the Employment Rights Act 1996 (ERA) employees must be permitted to take time off work to carry out certain public duties. There is no minimum qualifying period. The relevant public duties are where the employee is acting as a Justice of the Peace or as a member of:
- a local authority, the Common Council of the City of London or a National Parks Authority
- a statutory tribunal
- a police authority
- the Service Authority for the National Criminal Intelligence Service or the Service Authority for the National Crime Squad
- a board of prison visitors or a prison visiting committee
- a health authority, special health authority, primary care trust or health board
- certain education bodies (eg school council, school board or the managing body of a school or college maintained by a local education authority)
- the General Teaching Councils for England and Wales
- the Environment Agency or the Scottish Environment Protection Agency
- a water and sewerage agency in Scotland.

1.234 The above employees can request time off to:
- attend meetings of the body
- perform duties relating to the function of that body.

1.235 Individuals who are members of a recognised independent union have the right to seek time off work to participate in the activities of the union or consult with a union learning representative. However, there is no statutory right to be paid during such time off. This right does not include the right to participate in industrial action, but does cover voting in workplace and union ballots and consulting union officials.

Reasonable Time Off

1.236 Employees may request a reasonable amount of time off. What is reasonable will depend on:
- how much time is required to perform the particular duties
- how much time the employee has already been permitted
- the effect of the individual's absence on the employer's business.

Statutory Time Off

1.237 Employers must actually permit the individual to take time off. Simply rearranging an employee's work so that the individual makes up the time taken off is not sufficient.

1.238 Employees do not have any right to be paid whilst taking time off to perform the above public duties.

1.239 The employee should give the employer "reasonable" notice and details of required time off.

Jury Service

1.240 On 6 April 2004, the Employment Relations Act 2004 came into effect, providing employees who are summoned for jury service, or have had time off for jury service, with greater protection.

1.241 The regulations provide that employees have the right not to be subjected to any detriment for being summoned for jury service or having time off for jury service.

1.242 There is no right to be paid by an employer while absent on jury service. A detriment, therefore, excludes not paying employees' their normal remuneration for the period that they are on jury service, unless the contract of employment specifies otherwise. If an employer chooses not to pay, jurors may claim compensation for loss of earnings. The loss of earnings allowances for 2007–2008 are as follows.

Jury Service — Loss of Earnings Allowances

Time spent on jury service		Loss of earnings allowance
Up to and including 4 hours	In the first 10 days of jury service	£29.19
	On day 11 up to 200th day of jury service	£58.38
	On the 201st and all subsequent days	£102.50
More than four hours	In the first 10 days of jury service	£58.38
	On day 11 up to 200th day of jury service	£116.78
	On the 201st and all subsequent days	£205.00

1.243 Jurors may also claim a subsistence allowance for their time away. The current rates for 2007–2008 are as follows.

Jury Service — Subsistence Allowances

Period of absence	Maximum daily allowance
Up to and including 10 hours	£5.13
10 hours or more	£10.94
Overnight stay	Accommodation will be arranged by the court

1.244 Travel allowance may also be claimed by jurors at the 2007–2008 rates shown below.

Jury Service — Travel Allowances

Mode of Transport	Allowance
Train, underground or bus	The cost of the ticket (2nd class, if applicable)
Motorcycle	28p per mile
Motorcycle if no alternative public transport available	29.8 per mile
Bicycle	7p per mile
Car	28p per mile
Car if no alternative public transport available	42.5 p per mile
Car supplement if other jurors are passengers	For the first passenger, 2p per mile. For each additional passenger, 1p per mile

Note also that parking fees will be paid only where permission to claim for them has been given before travel. Taxi fares will be paid only where permission to use a taxi has been given.

1.245 Employees also have the right not to be unfairly dismissed for being absent from work on jury service. However, where an employer can show that its circumstances are such that the employee's absence would cause substantial injury to its business and communicates this to the employee, and where the employee unreasonably fails or refuses to apply for excusal or deferral, this subsection does not apply.

Paid Time Off to Perform Duties

1.246 The categories of employees with the right to paid time off work — and the relevant functions — are:
- officials of recognised trade unions, to perform union duties
- employee representatives in consultation about collective redundancies or transfers of undertakings
- members of European Works Councils
- employees who are trustees of occupational pension funds
- pregnant employees, for ante-natal care
- employees aged 16 to 18, to undertake study or training
- employees with over two years' service under notice of redundancy, to look for other employment.

Trade Union Activities

1.247 Employees who are officials of a trade union recognised by the employer for collective bargaining purposes have the right to seek paid time off for certain duties. The relevant duties are:
- negotiations with the employer as part of collective bargaining
- consultations on collective redundancies and transfer of undertakings
- training in these areas.

1.248 Union learning representatives (ULRs) also have the right to request paid time off from work.

1.249 Union-appointed safety representatives have the right to time off work to perform safety functions or undergo relevant training.

1.250 Acas has produced a Code of Practice on Time Off that sets out practical guidance on taking time off for trade union related matters.

The Right of Accompaniment

1.251 Employees now have a statutory right to be accompanied to grievance and disciplinary hearings by a trade union officer or official or a fellow employee. The Employment Relations Act 1999 gives those individuals a statutory right to take paid time off to accompany employees to such hearings if the employees concerned work for the same employer.

Employee Representatives

1.252 Employee representatives and candidates standing in elections are entitled to take a reasonable amount of time off from work to perform their functions. Employee representatives are entitled to be paid for time taken off. This right to pay does not extend to hours that an employee is not contractually required to work (eg voluntary overtime).

European Works Council Representatives

1.253 The Transnational Information and Consultation of Employees Regulations 1999 gives rights to employees associated with European Works Councils (EWCs). Representatives of or candidates for an EWC have the right to seek paid time off work to perform their functions. Members of any Special Negotiating Body established to negotiate the terms of an EWC are also allowed paid time off.

Pension Fund Trustees

1.254 Employees who are trustees of an occupational pension scheme have the right to take paid time off for their duties or relevant training.

Ante-natal Care

1.255 Pregnant employees have the right to seek paid time off during work to attend appointments for ante-natal care. The appointment must have been made on the advice of a registered medical practitioner, registered midwife or registered health visitor.

1.256 The employer may require the employee to produce:
- a certificate showing she is pregnant
- some evidence of the appointment.

1.257 The employer cannot require this for the employee's first appointment during pregnancy.

1.258 The individual has a right to be paid at the appropriate hourly rate. For employees with fixed hours this is simply a week's pay divided by the number of normal working hours.

Young Employees

1.259 Certain young employees have the right to seek paid time off for study or training. The right is available to employees aged 16 or 17 who are not in full-time secondary or further education and who have not attained a certain standard of academic achievement specified by the Government. Eighteen-year olds have the same right if they began current study or training prior to their 18th birthday. This right promotes the undertaking of study or training that leads to a relevant qualification. It should also enhance the individual's employment prospects.

1.260 The amount of time off will depend on a number of factors, including what the employee is studying, the employer's business and the effect the individual taking the time off will have on the business. Employers have the right to request evidence as to the amount of time off that the employee would reasonably require for study, eg a letter from a college tutor.

Redundancy

1.261 Eligible employees who are given notice of redundancy are entitled to seek reasonable paid time off at any point in the notice period to train or look for new employment.

1.262 The right is only available to employees with at least two years' continuous service who are under actual notice of redundancy.

1.263 The employer is only liable to pay up to 40% of one week's pay for the time taken during the whole of the notice period. This provision does not mean that further time off should not be granted beyond two days, but rather that when the time is granted, it need not be paid for.

1.264 The rights to seek paid time off while under notice of redundancy are minimums only. The employer is free to choose to give employees greater entitlements.

Training

1.265 Human Resources and line managers should be made aware of:
- the categories of employees who have rights to seek time off work
- the categories of employees who have a right to be paid during time off
- whether the company grants additional rights not required by law
- who needs to be consulted on the granting and refusing of requests
- what records need to be kept of the decision making process relating to such requests.

List of Relevant Legislation

1.266
- Collective Redundancies and Transfer of Undertakings (Protection of Employment) (Amendment) Regulations 1999
- Right to Time Off for Study or Training Regulations 1999
- Transnational Information and Consultation of Employees Regulations 1999
- Employment Relations Act 2004
- Employment Relations Act 1999
- Employment Rights Act 1996
- Trade Union and Labour Relations (Consolidation) Act 1992

List of Relevant Cases

1.267

- *Ryford Ltd v Drinkwater* [1996] IRLR 16, EAT — an employer cannot fail to permit time off and therefore be in breach of regulations unless he or she knows of the employee's request for time off.
- *Hairsine v Kingston upon Hull City Council* [1992] IRLR 211, EAT — employers are only obliged to pay for time off during those hours the employee would have been working, plus practical guidance on the difficult position of shift workers.
- *London Ambulance Service v Charlton* [1992] IRLR 510, EAT — employees may be entitled to paid time off to attend union-only meetings to prepare for negotiations if the meeting has sufficient nexus with collective bargaining.
- *Luce v London Borough of Bexley* [1990] IRLR 422, EAT — to qualify for time off, union activity must be related to the employment relationship.
- *Wignall v British Gas Corporation* [1984] IRLR 493, EAT — an employer, when assessing a request from a member of an independent trade union for time off to take part in union activities, may take into consideration any time off already granted and may refuse.
- *Ministry of Defence v (1) Crook and (2) Irving* [1982] IRLR 488 and [1982] IRLR 43, EAT — an employer is entitled to decide whether a course is relevant to a union official's duties on the basis of information supplied.
- *Davies v Head Wrightson Teesdale Ltd* [1979] IRLR 170, IT — employers are only obliged to pay for time off to undertake trade union duties for those hours where the employee is contractually obliged to work.
- *Sood v GEC Elliott Process Automation Ltd* [1979] IRLR 416, EAT — exchange of information among trade union representatives does not qualify under the time off provisions.
- *Dutton v Hawker Siddeley Aviation Ltd* [1978] IRLR 390, EAT — redundant employees have the right to paid time off to look for another job or to arrange retraining; an employer cannot insist as a precondition that the employee give details of appointments.

Further Information

Publications

- PL702 *Time Off for Public Duties*, Department for Business, Enterprise and Regulatory Reform (BERR)
- *Acas/CP03 Code of Practice on Time Off for Trade Union Duties and Activities* (2003)

Time Off at the Employer's Discretion

This topic covers the following.
- Bereavement and Compassionate Leave
- Religion and Belief
- Time Off Work for Fertility Treatment
- Time Off Work for Medical and Dental Appointments
- Time Off Work for Retiring Employees
- Time Off Work for Territorial Duties
- The Reserve Forces

1.268 Employees have a statutory right under the Employment Rights Act 1996 to take time off when a dependant is ill or dies.

1.269 When a close friend or non-dependant family member becomes ill or dies; however, there is no statutory entitlement to take time off work.

1.270 In practice most employers allow employees who are dealing with the death or illness of someone close to them, or who wish to attend a funeral or cremation to take leave, albeit unpaid.

1.271 There is no statutory right to take time off work for fertility treatment. As fertility treatment can be a long and painful process, employers may, at their discretion, allow an employee who is undergoing fertility treatment or his or her partner, a certain number of paid or unpaid days off work in any given year.

1.272 There is no statutory entitlement to take time off work to attend medical or dental appointments and an employer may request that an employee use annual leave in such circumstances. Care must be taken; however, where an employee is disabled under the Disability Discrimination Act 1995.

1.273 In practice, many employers allow employees paid or unpaid time off in order to attend medical or dental appointments, as long as appointments are made at a time convenient to the organisation.

1.274 An employer may also allow employees who are close to retirement age to take time off work in the period before they retire in order to help them to make the adjustment gradually.

Employers' Duties

1.275 Employers should make sure that employees are aware of the following with regard to discretionary time off.
- The organisation's policy on bereavement and compassionate leave, time off for fertility treatment and time off for medical/dental appointments.
- The organisation's policy on retirement and the opportunity to reduce working hours.
- The types of situations that would qualify for bereavement or compassionate leave.
- Any qualifying length of service required.
- The number of days that may be taken under each policy.

- Whether the leave is paid or unpaid.
- Where leave is paid, that it will be paid at the employee's basic rate of pay.

Employees' Duties

1.276 Employees have a duty to:
- inform the employer as soon as possible if they wish to take time off work, and follow the organisation's procedure
- inform the employer of when they intend to return to work
- in the case of time off for fertility treatment or medical/dental appointments, produce appointment cards or statements from a qualified medical practitioner when required
- in the case of time off for fertility treatment or medical/dental appointments, try to make appointments at times convenient to the organisation.

In Practice

Bereavement and Compassionate Leave

1.277 Compassionate leave is generally defined as time off when someone the employee is close to is seriously ill or dies. Some organisations have a broader approach to compassionate leave and allow employees time off work, eg where a marriage breaks down.

1.278 Bereavement leave is defined as time off in order to mourn the death of someone close to the employee, or time off to attend a funeral or cremation.

1.279 It is beneficial, therefore, to have a policy in place to ensure that a consistent approach is taken when employees require leave at a difficult time. It is particularly important that employers define the maximum number of days that may be taken and whether the leave is paid or unpaid.

1.280 As both bereavement leave and compassionate leave are at the discretion of the employer, there is no right to be paid for any leave taken.

1.281 In practice, some employers allow employees to take paid leave where a member of their immediate family is ill or dies. In order to ensure that a consistent approach is taken, it is useful to define what the employer considers "immediate family" to be, eg parent, child, sibling, grandparent.

1.282 When defining who qualifies as "immediate family" it is important to ensure that discrimination on the grounds of sexual orientation does not take place. Where paid time off is allowed; eg where an employee's husband or wife dies, paid time off should also be allowed where an employee's civil partner dies.

1.283 Where no policy on bereavement and compassionate leave is in place employers may request that employees take annual leave, if possible, in such circumstances. However, this is not always practical as an employee may have exhausted his or her holiday entitlement and would still require time off.

Religion and Belief

1.284 Employers should note that, while there is no statutory right to bereavement leave, failure to allow an employee time off work when an employee suffers a loss, may lead to a claim of unlawful discrimination on the grounds of religion or belief.

1.285 The Acas guide *Religion or Belief and the Workplace: Putting the Employment Equality (Religion or Belief) Regulations 2003 into Practice* considers the implications of failing to accommodate a request for bereavement leave. It lists the main religions in the UK and gives examples of the requirements that must be observed following bereavement. For example, in the Hindu religion, following a cremation close relatives will observe a 13-day mourning period, during which time they are required to remain at home.

Time Off Work for Fertility Treatment

1.286 With the improvements in medical science, employers may be faced with an employee who requires time off to undergo fertility treatment or to support his or her partner.

1.287 Employees undergoing fertility treatment may be required to take annual leave. However, an employer may wish to provide paid or unpaid leave where an employee has the requisite service.

1.288 It is important to ensure that a procedure is in place, setting out notice requirements and providing for the right to see appointment cards and/or a statement from a qualified medical practitioner that fertility treatment has been approved.

Time Off Work for Medical and Dental Appointments

1.289 While there is no statutory right to time off work for medical or dental appointments (except for ante-natal care) most employers allow employees to make appointments during working time, as long as the appointments are made at a time convenient to the organisation and, where appropriate, time lost is made up.

1.290 It is advisable to request that employees produce appointment cards where possible.

1.291 Where an employee is disabled under the Disability Discrimination Act 1995, care must be taken as unreasonably refusing time off could lead to a claim for disability discrimination.

Time Off Work for Retiring Employees

1.292 Retirement may provide employees with the opportunity to enjoy their leisure activities to the full, or it may be an extremely traumatic event. Much depends on whether the employees have prepared themselves for the adjustment.

1.293 Employers can help by allowing employees who are close to retirement to reduce their working hours in the period before they retire in order to help them to make the adjustment gradually.

1.294 Time off in these circumstances may be paid or unpaid. If the time off is unpaid, it is important that the employee is made fully aware of the impact on his or her occupational pension. Such implications should be discussed in detail with the employee before any decision on time off is made.

Time Off Work for Territorial Duties

1.295 There is no statutory right for employees to have time off to undertake territorial duties. However, an employer is free to come to an agreement with the employee concerned on arrangements for time off.

The Reserve Forces

1.296 The UK's volunteer reserve forces are made up of civilians prepared to accept an annual training commitment and a liability to be called out for service. They may belong to the Royal Naval Reserve, the Royal Marines Reserve, the Territorial Army or the Royal Auxiliary Air Force. Many ex-regular service personnel also retain a liability to call-out, and are members of the Royal Fleet Reserve, the Army Reserve or the Air Force Reserve.

Training and Duties

1.297 Members of the reserve forces are required to undertake one or more periods of training each year, up to a maximum of 16 days. This figure was increased from 15 days by the Reserve Forces Act 1996. Reservists may also enter into a commitment to undertake additional duties, either on a part-time or full-time basis, if their circumstances allow. Such arrangements, however, are purely voluntary, and do not provide reservists with the special employment protection which is extended to them in the event of call-out.

1.298 There is no statutory obligation on employers to release reservists either for training or for voluntary service. In many cases, though, employers are happy to be flexible with annual leave or to grant additional leave of absence. When reservists are served with a call-out notice, employers must release them (subject to certain exemption and deferral provisions — see below) — and they will be entitled to reinstatement when they return (subject to certain conditions — see Reinstatement of Reservists in Civil Employment).

1.299 From 1 April 2004, it became a condition of joining the reserve forces that a reservist must give the Ministry of Defence (MoD) consent to notify his or her employer that he or she is a reservist. The MoD now automatically gives such notification to the employers of new entrants to the Volunteer Reserve Forces and for all current reservists as they re-engage. Should the reservist change jobs, the MoD will also notify his or her new employer. Since 1 April 2005, the MoD also notifies the employers of reservists who do not routinely re-engage, such as commissioned officers.

Call-out

1.300 All reservists may be called out in the following circumstances:
- the Queen may call out members of the reserve forces in the event of a great emergency or an actual or apprehended attack on the UK
- the Secretary of State may make an order authorising call-out if it appears to him or her that:
  - warlike operations are in preparation or progress, or
  - it is necessary or desirable to use armed forces on operations outside the UK for the protection of life or property, or for the alleviation of distress or preservation of life or property in time of disaster or apprehended disaster.

1.301 This power to call out reservists for peacekeeping, humanitarian and disaster relief operations was first introduced by the Reserve Forces Act 1996, giving volunteers a greater opportunity to serve. Once the Queen or the Secretary of State has made a call-out order, then individual reservists may be served notices requiring them to present themselves for service at a specified time and place, and to remain there until they are either accepted into service or told they are not required. A call-out notice may be served either by personal delivery, or by sending it to the person's last known address. Failure to comply with a call-out notice may result in the reservist being charged with desertion or absence without leave.

Duration of Call-out

1.302 The maximum obligatory periods of service for different categories of call-out are as follows:
- when national danger is imminent or a great emergency has arisen: three years in any six, extendable to five years in any six
- for warlike operations: 12 months in any three years, extendable to two years in any three
- for peacekeeping, humanitarian or disaster relief operations: nine months in any 27 months, with no provision for extension.

1.303 Although reservists will normally be entitled to be released from service at the end of the above periods, this entitlement may be postponed for up to 12 months in the case of call-out for national danger, great emergency or warlike operations or nine months in the case of peacekeeping or humanitarian operations. Also, reservists may voluntarily agree to extend their service beyond the obligatory periods, for up to 12 months at a time.

Exemption or Deferral

1.304 When a reservist is served with a call-out notice, then he or she has the right to apply for exemption or deferral of the obligation to present themselves for service. The grounds on which application may be made are where the reservist:
- needs to care for someone with a severe physical or mental disability
- has sole parental responsibility for a child
- is engaged in education or training which is intended to prepare or qualify them for a vocation or a job, and which would be seriously disrupted by absence on service
- has entered into a contract of employment but has not yet started work, and the employer refuses to postpone the commencement date
- is making the request on other compassionate grounds.

1.305 Employers also have a right to apply for the exemption of an employee from call-out or for deferral. Application must be made to the person specified on the call-out notice or to an adjudication officer not more than seven days after the notice has been served. Late applications may be considered, however, where the employer has not found out about the notice until after that time. The grounds on which an employer may make application are that the absence of the reservist would cause serious harm to the business. Such harm may include:
- loss of sales, markets, reputation, goodwill or other financial harm
- impairment of ability to produce goods or provide services
- harm to research into or development of new products, services or processes.

1.306 Exemption or deferral is more likely to be granted when call-out is for peacekeeping or humanitarian purposes rather than in the event of war. Once an adjudication officer has received an application, it must be considered promptly, and the employer must be sent written notification of the outcome within two days of a decision being made.

1.307 If the employer is dissatisfied with the decision, he or she can appeal to a Reserve Forces Appeal Tribunal. Where an employer's application is granted, the reservist cannot have that decision altered.

1.308 The rules governing applications for exemption and deferral either by reservists or their employers are contained in the Reserve Forces (Call-out and Recall) (Exemptions Etc) Regulations 1997.

Financial Assistance

1.309 Financial assistance is available for reservists and employers who suffer loss as a result of call-out for service in the armed forces.

1.310 New financial assistance regulations for reservists and their employers came into force in April 2005. They streamline the claims process and improve the level of financial assistance payable to both reservists and their employers (under the Reserve Forces (Call-out and Recall) (Financial Assistance) Regulations 2005). These regulations will be reviewed each year from April 2006 by the Ministry of Defence (MoD).

1.311 Employers of reservists who are mobilised do not have to continue to pay them. They are able to claim the additional costs associated with employing a temporary replacement, or with overtime payments to other employees covering the reservist's work, subject to a cap of £110 per day (equivalent to about £40,000 a year). In addition, they will be able to reclaim in full any one-off or non-recurring costs of replacing a reservist, such as agency fees and advertising costs. A re-training payment can also be claimed. There is no payment cap on these payments.

1.312 The forms that the reservist and his or her employer need to complete have been revised and simplified. Reservists whose civilian pay is higher than their service pay will now receive an additional payment to make up the difference between the two. This will be subject to an overall cap of £548 per day (equivalent to around £200,000 a year). For medical consultants serving with the Defence Medical Services the cap is £822 per day (equivalent to around £300,000 a year).

1.313 Reservists will also be able to claim the cost of replacing certain benefits in kind that they lose on mobilisation, such as health insurance and company cars. Any payments to a reservist for these purposes will count towards the payment cap.

1.314 Reservists can also claim for certain additional expenses incurred when they are mobilised. These include, for example, costs associated with childcare and the care of dependant relatives. These costs are not included in the payment cap. A reservist who is called out is entitled to remain a member of his or her occupational pension scheme. Provided that the reservist continues to pay contributions to the scheme, the MoD will pay the employer contributions that it would have made.

Time Limits

1.315 Reservists or employers who wish to claim financial assistance, other than for training, can do so at any time up to within four weeks of the reservist being demobilised.

1.316 Claims for retraining awards must be made within eight weeks of the training being undertaken. Normally training must be undertaken within six months of the reservist's return to work. However, if this is not possible, it can be undertaken within 12 months, provided notice is given by the employer to the Adjudication Officer of its intention to do this within the initial six months.

Reserve Forces Appeal Tribunals

1.317 Reserve Forces Appeal Tribunals were set up under the Reserve Forces Act 1996 to hear appeals against decisions affecting reservists or their employers in relation to:
- a request for exemption or deferral of liability for call-out or recall, or
- an application for financial assistance for those who suffer loss as a result of call-out.

1.318 Appeal Tribunals are independent of the Ministry of Defence (MoD), and are made up of a legally qualified chairman and two lay members. In order to appeal against an adjudication officer's decision, the reservist or the employer must send a notice of appeal to the Tribunal Secretary. This must arrive not later than five days after the date on which written notification of the adjudication officer's decision was received by the appellant. In certain circumstances, however, a request may be made for an extension of time.

1.319 At the hearing, there is no requirement for appellants to have legal representation, but this is not excluded. The Appeal Tribunal makes its decision either unanimously, or by a majority. Once it has done so, the outcome is made known to the parties either at the end of the hearing or in writing. The regulations governing appeals are set out in the Reserve Forces Appeal Tribunals Rules 1997.

Reinstatement of Reservists in Civil Employment

1.320 The Reserve Forces (Safeguard of Employment) Act 1985 provides members of the Reserve and Auxiliary Forces, who are called up for whole-time service with a statutory right, subject to certain conditions (see Obligation of Employers to Reinstate Former Employees), to reinstatement in their previous employment. The statutory right to reinstatement is, in most cases, only applicable where the whole-time service is a consequence of an Order authorising call-out.

1.321 However, there is no statutory requirement on an employer to maintain an employee's contract of employment during their absence for whole-time service and so an employer is not obliged to pay salary or provide for the accrual of holiday entitlement or other benefits during this time.

Dismissal of Employees Called Out for Whole-Time Service

1.322 The employer is prohibited from dismissing an employee, before the date on which he or she is required to attend for whole-time service, for a reason arising from the employee's call out. An employer found guilty of such an offence is liable on summary conviction to heavy penalties.

Application for Reinstatement

1.323 The applicant must make an application for reinstatement to the former employer in writing by the third Monday after the end of whole-time service. If this is not possible because of sickness or some other reason, the application must be made as soon as possible after that time.

Notification of Availability for Work

1.324 Not later than the sixth Monday after the end of whole-time service, the applicant must write to the former employer stating the date of availability for work. This date must be within the six-week period, or as soon as possible afterwards if sickness or some other reason makes this impossible.

Whole-Time Service

1.325 Whole-time service begins on the date specified in the call-out notice as the date on which applicants are required to present themselves to the service authority in order to take up duty. The end of whole-time service is treated as being either the day the:
- applicant goes on final leave, pending release on discharge, or
- applicant's full pay ends, when final leave is not granted.

Renewal of Application

1.326 An application for reinstatement ceases to have effect 13 weeks after the day it was made. However if the applicant wishes to preserve the right to be reinstated

Time Off at the Employer's Discretion

the application must be renewed in writing before the 13 weeks have elapsed. The application then remains in force for 13 more weeks from the date of renewal, and may be further renewed providing it is still in force.

Obligation of Employers to Reinstate Former Employees

1.327 As long as a valid application remains in force the former employer is under an obligation to take the applicant into employment at the first opportunity on or after the notified date of availability. The applicant should be taken into employment:

- in the occupation in which he or she was last employed before whole-time service began, and on terms and conditions not less favourable than those which would have applied had there been no call-out, or
- if that is not reasonable and practicable, in the most favourable occupation and the most favourable terms and conditions which are reasonable and practicable.

1.328 A reinstated employee has the right to remain in employment for a specified minimum period, which is dependent on the length of his or her continuous employment prior to the beginning of whole-time service.

Reserve Forces: Minimum Periods of Reinstatement

Length of Service	Minimum Period of Reinstatement
Less than 13 weeks	13 weeks
More than 13 but less than 52 weeks	26 weeks
More than 52 weeks	52 weeks

1.329 The obligation on the former employer to reinstate ceases six months from the end of the applicant's whole-time service, unless reinstatement has been ordered by the reinstatement committee or the umpire.

Reinstatement: Reasonable and Practicable

1.330 In order to decide what is or is not reasonable or practicable regarding reinstatement, an employer may have to take into account a variety of circumstances, and there is little guidance on the matter in the Act. However, what the Act does say is that a former employer is not required to reinstate an applicant if this can only be done by dismissing some other person who:

- was employed by the former employer before the beginning of the applicant's whole-time service
- had been employed before that date for a longer period than the applicant
- was employed in employment of a kind not less permanent than the applicant's employment.

1.331 If these conditions are not satisfied by the other person, then the applicant must be reinstated regardless of the fact that the other person must be dismissed.

Continuous Employment

1.332 For the purpose of computing a period of continuous employment, providing the applicant enters the employment of the former employer within the six-month period after the end of whole-time service, the previous employment with that employer and the renewed employment shall be treated as continuous within the provisions of the Employment Rights Act 1996.

1.333 However, the period of absence from employment due to call-out does not count under part XIV Chapter 1 of the Employment Rights Act 1996. To determine length of service, the start date of the contract of employment is deemed to have been postponed by the number of days the employee was absent.

Settlement of Disputes — Reinstatement Committees

1.334 A person who claims that he or she has been denied his or her rights under the Act may apply to a reinstatement committee. Each committee will consist of a chairman, an employer's representative and a representative of employed persons.

1.335 This committee will decide the matters in dispute between the applicant and the employer concerned and, if it decides that the employer is in breach of the provisions of the Act, it may make an order requiring the employer to make employment available to the applicant, specifying the occupation, terms and conditions. It may also order compensation to be paid for any loss suffered by the applicant.

1.336 Appeals can be made against any decision or order of the reinstatement committee to the umpire appointed for the purpose. An employer who fails to obey an order for reinstatement will be liable to heavy penalties.

Training

1.337 It is important that managers are aware of the organisation's policies on time off at the employer's discretion and the consequences of not granting leave. It is essential that managers adopt a fair approach throughout.

List of Relevant Legislation

1.338
- Reserve Forces (Call out and Recall) (Financial Assistance) Regulations 2005
- Employment Equality (Religion or Belief) Regulations 2003
- Employment Relations Act 1999
- Employment Rights Act 1996
- Disability Discrimination Act 1995

List of Relevant Cases

1.339
- *R v Randles Garages* (2006), Kidderminster Magistrates Court — the employer was fined £750 and ordered to pay £986 compensation to one of its former employees, a reserve forces worker who was dismissed when he was called up to fight in Iraq. Under the Reserve Forces (Safeguard of Employment) Act 1985 employers are required to reinstate their former staff once they have completed their tour of duty. This was the first case of its kind under the 1985 Act.

Further Information

Publications
- EEL01 *Acas Religion or Belief and the Workplace — A Guide for Employers and Employees (November 2003)*

- PL506 *Family Emergency: Your Right to Time Off*, Department for Business, Enterprise and Regulatory Reform (BERR)
- URN 99/1186 *Time Off for Dependants — Detailed Guidance for Employers and Employees*, Department for Business, Enterprise and Regulatory Reform (BERR)

Organisations

- **Advisory Conciliation and Arbitration Service (Acas)**
  Web: *www.acas.org.uk*
  Acas aims to improve organisations and working life through better employment relations. It provides up-to-date information, advice, high-quality training, and works with employers and employees to solve problems and improve performance.
- **Department for Business, Enterprise and Regulatory Reform (BERR)**
  Web: *www.berr.gov.uk*
  The Department for Business, Enterprise and Regulatory Reform brings together functions from the former Department of Trade and Industry (DTI), including responsibilities for productivity, business relations, energy, competition and consumers. It also drives regulatory reform.
- **Employers and Work-life Balance**
  Web: *www.employersforwork-lifebalance.org.uk*
  Employers and Work-life Balance aims to help all UK organisations implement and continuously improve sustainable work-life strategies that meet customer needs, corporate goals and enhance the quality of life for individuals.

Time Off for Dependants

> This topic covers the following.
> - General Qualifying Conditions
> - What is a Dependant?
> - Reasons for Time Off
> - Notification Requirements
> - Reasonable Time Off

1.340 The right to time off for dependants came into force on 15 December 1999. The provisions have been implemented into the Employment Rights Act 1996 and set out an employee's right to take a reasonable amount of unpaid time off work for urgent family reasons.

1.341 The right to time off for dependants is available to every employee, regardless of length of service.

Employers' Duties

1.342 Employers should make sure that employees are aware of the following.
- What time off for dependants means.
- The definition of a dependant.
- The kinds of situations that would qualify as a family emergency.
- The notification requirements.

Employees' Duties

1.343 Employees have a duty to:
- notify the employer of his or her absence as soon as is reasonably practicable
- inform the employer of how long he or she expects to be off work.

In Practice

General Qualifying Conditions

1.344 The right to time off for dependants applies to all employees, regardless of gender or length of service. There are only three classes of employees that are excluded from the right to time off, ie those employed in:
- the armed forces
- share fishing
- the police service.

What is a Dependant?

1.345 The legislation makes it clear that employees may take time off work to provide assistance or take appropriate action to care for a dependant.

1.346 A dependant is a:
- spouse
- partner
- parent
- child
- person who lives in the same household as the employee but who is not his or her lodger, employee or boarder.

1.347 A dependant, therefore, does not have to be related to the employee.

1.348 A dependant may also be a person who reasonably relies on the employee for assistance when that person falls ill or is assaulted or injured. This extended definition of a dependant may apply, eg where an employee cares for a neighbour outside of work and where this person unexpectedly falls ill.

Reasons for Time Off

1.349 An employee may take time off work to provide assistance or to take appropriate action when:
- a dependant is suddenly taken ill, or has been assaulted or injured
- a dependant gives birth
- a dependant dies
- existing arrangements for the care of a dependant are unexpectedly disrupted or come to an end, eg an employee's childminder calls in sick
- his or her child is involved in an incident at school.

Notification Requirements

1.350 In order to take time off to deal with a family emergency, employees must, as soon as is reasonably practicable, inform the employer of:
- the reason for his or her absence
- how long he or she expects to be away from work.

1.351 Notice does not have to be given in writing. If an employee does not comply with the notification requirements, the employer may treat the absence as unauthorised leave.

Reasonable Time Off

1.352 The legislation does not make clear how much time off work should be granted to deal with a family emergency. When deciding what is reasonable, a tribunal will consider what is reasonable to the employee, given his or her circumstances and discount any inconvenience to the employer.

1.353 The Department for Business, Enterprise and Regulatory Reform (BERR) suggests that one or two days would normally be sufficient for an employee to deal with a family emergency and, if necessary, to make alternative arrangements for the continuing care of the dependant. The actual circumstances of each case should, however, be considered on its own merits.

Time Off for Dependants

Statutory Rights During Time Off for Dependants

1.354 Employees have the right not to be victimised, dismissed or subjected to any detriment for exercising their statutory right to take time off for dependants.

Training

1.355 It is important that all line managers are familiar with the employee's statutory right to take time off for dependants as it is likely that notification for time off will come to them. All managers should:

- understand the law surrounding time off for dependants
- be aware of the notification requirements.

List of Relevant Legislation

1.356
- Employment Relations Act 1999
- Employment Rights Act 1996

Further Information

Publications
- E15 *Pay and Time Off Work for Parents*, available from HM Revenue & Customs.
- PL520 *Flexible Working — The Right to Request and the Duty to Consider: Guidance for Employers and Employees*, Department for Business, Enterprise and Regulatory Reform (BERR)
- *Flexible Working — The Right to Request and the Duty to Consider*, Department for Business, Enterprise and Regulatory Reform (BERR) URN 06/2158/A1
- URN 99/1186 *Time Off for Dependants — Detailed Guidance for Employers and Employees*, Department for Business, Enterprise and Regulatory Reform (BERR)
- PL506 *Family Emergency: Your Right to Time Off*, Department for Business, Enterprise and Regulatory Reform (BERR)

Organisations
- **Advisory Conciliation and Arbitration Service (Acas)**
  Web: *www.acas.org.uk*
  Acas aims to improve organisations and working life through better employment relations. It provides up-to-date information, advice, high-quality training, and works with employers and employees to solve problems and improve performance.
- **Employers and Work-life Balance**
  Web: *www.employersforwork-lifebalance.org.uk*
  Employers and Work-life Balance aims to help all UK organisations implement and continuously improve sustainable work-life strategies that meet customer needs, corporate goals and enhance the quality of life for individuals.
- **Tommy's**
  Web: *www.tommys.org*
  Tommy's aims to end the heartache caused by premature birth, miscarriage and

stillbirth. It funds a national programme of research, education and information aimed at understanding and preventing these tragedies.

Working Time

This topic covers the following.
- To Whom do the Working Time Regulations Apply?
- Exemptions — Excluded Sectors
- Exemptions — Other Cases
- Unmeasured Working Time
- Workers Employed Outside Great Britain
- The 48-Hour Weekly Maximum
- The Working Time (Road Transport) Regulations 2005
- Calculating the Weekly Average
- Opt-Out Agreements
- Opt-Out Restrictions
- Record Keeping
- Daily Rest Breaks
- Rest Breaks and Monotonous Work
- Daily Rest Periods
- Weekly Rest Periods
- Night Work
- Calculating Average Night Work Hours
- Annual Leave
- Workforce and Collective Agreements
- Drivers' Hours and Records
- Shift Workers

1.357 Under the Working Time Regulations 1998 employers may not require workers to work more than 48 hours per week on average. However, workers may opt out and work more by agreeing to do so in writing.

1.358 Young workers (ie aged 15 or over but under 18 and over school leaving age) may not work more than 8 hours per day or 40 hours per week.

1.359 Night workers cannot be required to work more than an average of 8 hours in each 24 hours. Night workers whose work involves special hazards or strenuous physical work or mental strain must not work more than 8 hours in each 24 hours (rather than an average limit over 17 weeks).

1.360 All workers are entitled to the following rest breaks and rest periods under the regulations.
- Daily rest breaks of at least 20 minutes if working time is more than 6 hours.
- A daily rest period of at least 11 consecutive hours in each 24-hour period.
- A weekly rest period of at least 24 hours in each 7-day period. All workers are entitled to a minimum of four weeks' paid holiday in any leave year. This currently includes bank holidays. Following a consultation, the Government has confirmed its intention to add eight extra days to the statutory annual entitlement, although its original plan to complete their introduction by October next year has been amended. While the first four will come in October 2007 as expected, the second instalment has been deferred until 1 April 2009.

Employers' Duties

1.361 Employers must:

- permit all workers to take a minimum of four weeks' paid holiday each leave year
- ensure that the working hours of their workers do not exceed the set limits — an average of 48 working hours per week, including overtime (calculated over any rolling 17-week period), unless opt-outs have been signed, and no more than 60 hours in a single week for mobile workers
- enforce the maximum average working hours for young workers at 40 hours per week, including overtime (calculated over any rolling 17-week period) and a further limit of 8 hours of work a day
- ensure that night workers do not work more than an average of 8 hours in each 24-hour period (or 10 hours for mobile workers)
- limit the hours of night workers whose work involves special hazards or strenuous physical work or mental strain to at most 8 hours in each 24-hour period (as opposed to an average of 8 hours in each 24-hour period)
- allow workers to have a daily rest period of at least 11 consecutive hours in each 24-hour period (12 hours in each 24-hour period for young workers)
- allow workers to have a weekly rest period of at least 24 hours in each 7-day period, which can be taken as two 24-hour rest periods in a 14-day period or one 48-hour rest period in a 14-day period
- allow young persons to have a 48-hour rest period in each 7-day period
- permit workers to take a minimum 20 minute rest break after 6 hours of work
- permit young persons to take a minimum 30 minute break if their working day is longer than 4.5 hours
- ensure that young persons do not work between 10pm and 6am, except after assessment
- ensure that mobile workers take the appropriate and necessary rest breaks
- keep adequate records.

Employees' Duties

1.362   Employees are required to:
- give written notice to the employer in order to opt back in to the 48-hour limit
- understand the record keeping system they must complete if required to do so by their employer.

In Practice

To Whom do the Working Time Regulations Apply?

1.363   The Working Time Regulations 1998 apply to all workers. Workers include not only employees but also individuals who contract to perform personally any work for an employer.

1.364   The definition does not include genuinely self-employed individuals. It does however include casual and freelance workers. Most agency staff will also be classed as workers.

1.365   In many areas the regulations have stricter protections for young workers. A young person is someone who is at least 15 but under 18 and who is over the compulsory school age.

Exemptions — Excluded Sectors

1.366 There are certain sectors of employment to which particular provisions of the regulations do not apply.

1.367 The working hour element of the Working Time Regulations do not apply to the following categories of adult worker.
- Workers employed as domestic servants in private households.
- Seafarers to whom Council Directive 1999/63/EC applies.
- Workers on board a sea-going fishing vessel.
- Workers on board a ship or hovercraft that operates services for passengers or goods via inland waterway or lake transport.
- Where characteristics peculiar to certain specific services, such as the armed forces or police, conflict with the provisions of the regulations.
- Workers in the civil aviation industry to whom Council Directive 2000/79/EC applies.
- Mobile road transport workers to whom Council Directive 2002/15/EC applies.

1.368 With effect from 1 August 2004 doctors in training are now covered by the regulations, although the limits on average weekly working time will be phased in, as follows.
- 58 hours from 1 August 2004 to 31 July 2007.
- 56 hours from 1 August 2007 to 31 July 2009.
- 48 hours from 1 August 2009.

Exemptions — Other Cases

1.369 Employers of certain types of workers may derogate from the rest break and night working provisions contained in the Working Time Regulations. Where these derogations apply, it is also open to the employer to extend the reference period for averaging working hours from 17 to 26 weeks.

1.370 Furthermore, where there are objective, technical or organisational reasons for doing so, the reference period may, by agreement, be extended to 52 weeks in relation to that particular group of workers. The workers to whom these derogations apply are those:
- who work far away from where they live or constantly have to work in different places making it difficult to work to a set pattern
- who are involved in security or surveillance work that requires a permanent presence (eg to protect property or individuals)
- who work in jobs in which round-the-clock staffing is required, eg hospitals, residential institutions, prisons, media production companies, public utilities, or in industries where work cannot be interrupted on technical grounds
- whose work involves a foreseeable surge of activity (eg postal services, tourism)
- whose work is affected by unforeseeable events beyond the employer's control.

1.371 Whenever a worker in one of the derogated categories is not granted a rest break or rest period at the time it is due, equivalent compensatory rest will have to be offered unless exceptional circumstances apply.

1.372 Compensatory rest is normally a period of rest the same length as the period of rest, or part of a period of rest, that a worker has missed. The total entitlement under daily and weekly rest periods amounts to 90 hours of rest per week. The exceptions allow this rest to be taken in a different pattern to that set out in the regulations. The principle is that everyone gets his or her entitlement of 90 hours rest a week on average, although some rest may come slightly later than normal.

Working Time

1.373 The following provisions do not apply to domestic servants in private households.
- Maximum working hours.
- Length of night work.
- Health assessments.

1.374 However, domestic workers do have the right to daily rest, weekly rest, rest breaks and annual leave under the regulations.

Unmeasured Working Time

1.375 The provisions relating to maximum weekly working time, night work, daily and weekly rest periods and rest breaks do not apply to workers:
- who can decide their own working hours
- whose working time is not measured or predetermined due to the nature of their work.

1.376 Employees who fall within this exemption include managing executives or other people with autonomous decision-making powers and family workers and workers officiating at religious ceremonies in churches and religious communities. The right to annual leave still applies to such workers.

Workers Employed Outside Great Britain

1.377 The regulations state that they "extend to Great Britain" only. Guidance from the Department of Business, Enterprise and Regulatory Reform (BERR) states that time spent abroad by a worker whose employer carries on business in Great Britain would be working time. However recent case law has cast some doubt on whether the regulations will apply to workers working outside Great Britain, although the issue is still uncertain.

The 48-Hour Weekly Maximum

1.378 Under the Working Time Regulations 1998 a worker's working time must not exceed 48 hours per week on average, unless the worker has voluntarily signed an opt-out.

1.379 A young person's working time must not exceed 8 hours a day or 40 hours per week.

1.380 Mobile workers' working time must not exceed an average of 48 hours per week, averaged out over a typical 17-week period, and no more than 60 hours in any single week.

1.381 An individual's working time means any:
- period during which he or she is working, at the employer's disposal and carrying out duties (this will include overtime)
- period during which he or she is receiving in-house training or work experience
- other period agreed as working time under a workforce or collective agreement.

Road Transport (Working Time) Regulations 2005

1.382 Working time is not the same as shift time or attendance, a key point especially important for mobile workers. The Road Transport (Working Time)

Regulations 2005 define working time as the time an employee spends at the disposal of the employer carrying out his or her duties. This includes, for example, not only driving but:

- cleaning and maintaining the vehicle
- loading and unloading goods
- training that is part of normal work
- waiting periods where the foreseeable duration is not known in advance.

1.383 Working time does not include:

- rest breaks and breaks where no work is carried out
- periods of availability (waiting time where the mobile worker knows before the start of the relevant period about that period of availability and can foresee how long it is likely to last)
- travel between home and the normal place of work.

1.384 Time spent "on call" is likely to be working time if the individual is at the employer's disposal, even if he or she is not actually working (eg a doctor on call at a hospital). Business travel that is part of the job will count as working time but travel that is outside normal hours is unlikely to count.

1.385 The Road Transport (Working Time) Regulations 2005 affect mobile workers (mainly drivers and crew) travelling in vehicles subject to EU drivers' hours rules. Mobile workers need to comply with these regulations as well as existing EU drivers' hours rules. Self-employed drivers are excluded from all the requirements until March 2009.

1.386 The definition of "self-employed driver" under the regulations has been tightly drawn, so only a limited number of drivers are likely to be excluded from their scope. The amount of control that the drivers have over their work is crucial, as is their reliance on profits as their main source of income. For example, if the worker is restricted (either implicitly or explicitly) from working for another client or customer, then he or she would be covered by all the requirements of these regulations.

1.387 In addition, most agency workers would not count as self-employed because they are normally paid at a fixed rate. Once they accept a job, an agency worker is not free to organise his or her working activities.

1.388 Drivers who do not satisfy the criteria for being self-employed under these regulations are (along with employees) subject to them. The regulations introduce:

- limits on weekly working time (excluding breaks and periods of availability) and
- a limit on the amount of work that can be done at night.

1.389 They also specify how much continuous work can be done before taking a break.

Calculating the Weekly Average

1.390 The limit of 48 hours is an average calculated over a 17-week reference period (or less if the worker has been working for fewer than 17 weeks). The reference period can be longer than 17 weeks (up to a maximum of 52 weeks) if agreed in a workforce or collective agreement.

1.391 For mobile workers, employers and employees must agree what reference period is to be used. The regulations provide for a default calendar option which includes some 18-week periods. It is also possible to agree a fixed reference period or a rolling reference period through workforce or collective agreement, but the reference period should not result in an average working week of more than 48 hours.

1.392 Working time is calculated by dividing the individual's total number of hours worked by the number of weeks in the reference period (usually 17). Using an example from the BERR, if an employee works a standard 40 hours a week and does 12 hours a week overtime for 10 weeks, his or her total hours will be 800 hours (ie (17 x 40) + (12 x 10) = 800). His or her average working time is therefore 47.1 hours a week (ie 800/17 = 47.1).

1.393 If a worker is off work during the reference period because of annual leave, maternity, paternity, adoption, parental or sick leave, an allowance must be made for this. The calculation should include the hours worked in the equivalent number of days following the end of the reference period. Using another BERR example, assume an individual works 40 hours a week (8 hours a day) and does overtime of 8 hours a week for the first 12 weeks. The individual is off on leave for 4 days during the 17 week reference period. The calculation would be:

1.394 (16 weeks x 40 hours) + (1 day x 8 hours) + (10 weeks x 8 hours' overtime) = 744 hours.

1.395 It would then be necessary to add time in respect of the 4 days' leave, using the working time in the 4 days following the end of the reference period. Assuming the worker does no overtime on those 4 days and works 8 hours per day, he or she will work 32 hours. The worker's average is therefore 45.6 hours per week (ie (744 + 32)/17 = 45.6).

Opt-Out Agreements

1.396 Under UK law, workers are free to agree to work more than the average 48-hour limit. For such an agreement to be valid, the worker must sign an opt-out agreement.

1.397 An opt-out agreement should state clearly that a worker has the right to "opt back in" to the working time element of the Regulations on giving a specified period of notice. This period of notice must be no fewer than seven days but no more than three months.

1.398 An opt-out agreement should be quite separate to an employee's contract of employment and is a matter for each individual. Employees cannot be bound by collective agreements in this regard. Workers must not be subjected to any detriment for refusing to sign an opt-out agreement.

1.399 Young workers cannot sign opt-outs.

Opt-Out Restrictions

1.400 The European Commission and the UK Government have been reviewing whether the future use of the opt-out should be restricted in any way or prohibited altogether. The European Commission has recently decided to allow the UK to retain its opt-out from the 48 hour working week but has imposed "stricter conditions to prevent abuse".

1.401 Where collective bargaining agreements exist between unions and employers, opt-outs will be undertaken through collective agreements, although individuals will still be able to opt-out if no collective agreement is reached.

1.402 All opt-out agreements will have to be renewed annually. The proposals will be voted on by the European Parliament before they come into force.

Record Keeping

1.403 Employers need to keep records to show:
- that weekly and night working time limits are being complied with
- who has opted out of the 48-hour working time limit
- health assessments offered and carried out for night workers.

1.404 For the first time, employers are required to keep records of the number of hours worked by their mobile workers. The regulations do not specify what kinds of records should be kept but it is important that the system used demonstrates that limits on working time and night work are complied with. These records must be kept for a minimum of two years.

Daily Rest Breaks

1.405 If an adult worker is required to work for more than six hours, a rest break of at least 20 minutes (or longer, if agreed by a workforce or collective agreement) must be permitted. The break should be taken during those six hours, not at the start or end of the six hours.

1.406 Workers must be permitted to spend the rest break away from their work station, if they have one.

1.407 Employers do not have to ensure that workers actually take their rest breaks — instead, workers must be permitted to take rest breaks if they wish and not prevented from doing so.

1.408 Young workers are entitled to rest breaks of at least 30 minutes where daily working time is more than 4.5 hours. The 30 minutes must be consecutive if possible.

1.409 Mobile workers must receive a break of at least 30 minutes during their period of work time if the working day is between six and nine hours long. If the working day is longer than nine hours mobile workers are entitled to a minimum break of 45 minutes.

Rest Breaks and Monotonous Work

1.410 If the pattern of an individual's work puts his or her health and safety at risk (eg because the work is monotonous or the work rate is predetermined) the employer must provide adequate work breaks. This might apply to assembly line workers doing repetitive jobs, or call centre staff.

1.411 The regulations do not state that this must be in addition to the daily 20 minute rest break, although it is probably best to assume that this is the case.

Daily Rest Periods

1.412 Adult workers are entitled to a daily rest period of 11 hours in each 24-hour period during which they work. The 11 hours' rest period does not have to fall in the same calendar day — if a worker leaves work at 8pm and starts again at 7am the next day, he or she will have been given his or her full entitlement.

1.413 Young workers are entitled to an uninterrupted 12 hours of daily rest in each 24-hour period during which they work. This may be interrupted in situations where the work activities are split up over the day or are of short duration. In these circumstances, compensatory rest must be offered within three weeks.

1.414 Mobile workers may reduce their daily rest period to nine hours up to three times a week as long as compensatory rest is taken.

1.415 Recent case law has confirmed that being on call counts as working time. Employees are entitled to compensatory rest if the on-call hours lead to a reduction in the minimum daily rest period of 11 consecutive hours. This is regardless of whether they are on the employer's premises during the on-call duty.

1.416 In *Landeshauptstadt Kiel v Jaegar* (2003) ECJ, the court held that a doctor who was required to be physically present in the hospital during working hours could not be regarded as being at rest during the periods of on-call duty, even if no work was actually carried out.

1.417 In the more recent case of *MacCartney v Oversley House Management* [2006] IRLR 514, the EAT ruled that a break should be uninterrupted and the worker must not be at the employer's disposal.

Weekly Rest Periods

1.418 Adult workers are entitled to a rest period of 24 hours in each 7-day period. This requirement can be fulfilled by giving one rest break of 48 hours or two rest breaks of 24 hours each in each 14-day period.

1.419 Young workers are entitled to weekly rest periods of at least 48 hours in each 7-day period. It is not possible to average this out over a 2-week period as with adult workers. The weekly rest entitlement for young workers may be interrupted in situations where the work activities are split up over the day, or are of short duration, or for technical or organisational reasons, but may not be reduced to fewer than 36 hours. In these circumstances, compensatory rest must be offered.

1.420 Mobile workers may reduce their daily rest period to nine hours up to three times a week as long as compensatory rest is taken.

1.421 In principle, a worker's weekly rest must not include any of his or her 11-hour daily rest periods unless there are "objective, technical or organisational reasons" justifying it.

Night Work

1.422 The regulations provide special protection for night workers. A worker will be a night worker if:
- he or she works at least three hours of his or her daily working time between 11pm and 6am ("night hours") as a normal course
- he or she is likely, during night-time, to work at least such proportion of his or her annual working time as is agreed in a workforce or collective agreement.

1.423 The definition of night hours can be changed by a workforce or collective agreement, but it must include a period of at least 7 hours and must include midnight to 5am.

1.424 Night workers must not work more than an average of 8 hours in each 24-hour period. This average is calculated over a 17-week reference period, unless otherwise agreed in a workforce or collective agreement.

1.425 However, night workers who undertake work involving special hazards or heavy physical or mental strain are subject to greater restrictions. Their actual hours (rather than average hours) must not exceed eight hours in any 24-hour period during which they are performing night work. A night worker's work will be regarded as involving special hazards or heavy physical and mental strain if a workforce or collective agreement identifies the work as such or if a risk assessment carried out under the Management of Health and Safety at Work Regulations 1999 identifies this.

Working Time

1.426 Night workers are entitled to free health assessments from their employer before taking up night work. Health assessments must also be carried out at regular intervals thereafter.

1.427 Young workers may not ordinarily work at night between 10pm and 6am, or between 11pm and 7am if the contract of employment provides for work after 10pm. However, there are some exceptional cases where young people can work at night (eg where they are required to ensure continuity of production). A health assessment must be carried out to ensure suitability before a young worker is assigned to night work.

1.428 Mobile workers are limited to 10 hours' night work in any 24 hour period unless a relevant agreement is in place. The 10-hour limit does not include rest breaks, breaks where the worker is not required to work or periods of availability.

Calculating Average Night Work Hours

1.429 In order to calculate average night work hours, the number of actual hours worked in the reference period should be divided by the number of days in the period, after deducting that number of rest days taken by the worker.

1.430 Using an example given by BERR, a night worker works 4 x 12 hour shifts each week. Over the 17 week reference period his or her total hours are 816: 17 x (4 x 12) = 816.

1.431 There are 119 days in the 17 weeks and the worker takes 17 weekly rest periods — as he or she is entitled under the regulations. Therefore the number of days the worker could be asked to work is 102: 119 − 17 = 102.

1.432 To calculate the daily average working time, the total of hours is divided by the number of days a worker could be required to work: 816/102 = 8.

1.433 This equals an average of 8 hours per day.

Annual Leave

1.434 All workers (including young workers) are entitled to a minimum of four weeks' paid annual leave. At present, employees have no statutory right to take bank holidays as leave in addition to this minimum entitlement and so employers may, if they wish, nominate any bank holidays that are granted as paid leave as part of the four week statutory entitlement. Following a consultation, however, the Government has confirmed its intention to add eight extra days to the statutory annual entitlement, although its original plan to complete their introduction by October 2008 has been amended. While the first four will come in October 2007 as expected, the second instalment has been deferred until 1 April 2009.

1.435 A week's leave should correspond to the amount of time worked by the worker during a week. For someone working six days a week, a week's leave should be six days' leave (thereby giving him or her 24 working days of annual leave).

1.436 The regulations contain further provisions on statutory holiday entitlements, payment during annual leave and notice required to take annual leave.

Workforce and Collective Agreements

1.437 Many of the features of the regulations can be altered for specific circumstances by using a collective agreement (with a trade union) or a "workforce agreement". A workforce agreement is an agreement reached with (non-union) elected employee representatives (or with a majority of the workforce if the employer employs 20 or fewer workers).

1.438 Collective/workforce agreements can be used to:
- identify persons who will be night workers
- identify work that involves special hazards or heavy physical or mental strain for the purpose of night work
- agree the length of rest breaks for adult workers
- modify various aspects of night work, including the reference period for measuring the average
- change the entitlement to daily rest, weekly rest and rest breaks for adult workers
- change the start and end of the holiday year in terms of annual leave
- alter the reference period (normally 17 weeks) for measuring average working time for the 48-hour limit.

Drivers' Hours and Records

1.439 EC Regulations 561/2006 (the drivers' hours rules) and 3821/85 (Recording equipment in road transport) govern the driving time and record keeping requirements for drivers of goods vehicles exceeding 3.5 tonnes permissible maximum weight (including the weight of any trailer drawn), engaged on journeys within the UK and/or other Member States.

1.440 The main requirements of the regulations are as follows.
- *Total daily driving* — the maximum is 9 hours (extended to 10 hours' maximum not more than twice a week).
- *Weekly driving* — this will be governed by the requirement that a driver must, after no more than six daily driving periods, take a weekly rest period. This weekly rest period can be postponed until the end of the sixth day if the total driving time over the six days does not exceed the maximum corresponding to six daily driving periods.
- *Total driving time in a fortnight* — the maximum is 90 hours.
- *Driving time* — this must total not more than 4.5 hours after which a break must be taken. Breaks from driving — after a total of 4.5 hours driving a minimum break of at least 45 minutes must be taken unless the driver begins a rest period. This break can be split into shorter periods that must be of at least 15 minutes' duration to qualify as a break so that when spread over the driving period or immediately following it the aggregate is at least 45 minutes. If a driver has taken a break of 45 minutes, either as a single break of 45 minutes, or as several breaks of at least 15 minutes during or at the end of the 4.5 hour period, the calculation should begin afresh — without taking into account the driving time and breaks previously completed.
- *Daily rest period* — in each period of 24 hours a driver must have a daily rest of at least 11 consecutive hours which may be reduced to no fewer than 9 consecutive hours on 3 days a week. Any reduction in the daily rest must be made up before the end of the following week. However, on days when the daily rest period is not reduced a driver is allowed to split this 11 hours into 2 or 3 separate periods (minimum 1 hour) during the 24 hours, one period of which must be of at least 8 consecutive hours' duration. When the daily rest period is split in this manner the minimum length of the daily rest must be increased to 12 hours. Where a vehicle is double manned each driver must have a rest period of no fewer than 8 consecutive hours during each period of 30 hours. Daily rest periods may be taken in the vehicle provided it is fitted with a bunk and the vehicle is stationary.

- *Weekly rest period* — the definition of a week is the period between 0000 Monday to 2400 Sunday, ie a fixed period. During each week a daily rest period must be extended into a weekly rest period totalling 45 consecutive hours; however, this may be reduced to 36 consecutive hours if taken where the vehicle or driver is normally based, or to a minimum of 24 consecutive hours if taken elsewhere. Each reduced rest period must be made good by the driver taking an equivalent rest period, *en bloc*, before the end of the third week following the week in question. A weekly rest period beginning in one week and continuing into the next can be attached to either week. Any compensatory rest period taken for the reduced daily and/or weekly rest periods must be attached to another rest period of at least eight hours and be granted at the request of the driver, at the vehicle's parking place or driver's base.
- *Work records* — drivers of goods vehicles exceeding 3.5 tonnes permissible maximum weight (including the weight of any trailer drawn) used for carrying goods and who are subject to EC Regulations, must record their hours of work by using a tachograph fitted in the vehicle. A chart fitted in the instrument automatically records the distance travelled and the speed of the vehicle, driving time, periods of other work of the driver, breaks in the working day, daily rest periods, etc.
- *Domestic hours laws* — certain vehicle operations are exempt from EC requirements but are nonetheless covered by the Transport Act 1968, as modified. For drivers operating under domestic legislation the permanent hours limits are:
  – 10 hours' maximum daily driving
  – 11 hours' maximum daily duty.

A driver is exempt from the duty limit on non-driving days. This also applies when a driver does not drive for more than four hours on each day of the week. Where a driver is required to keep records of his or her working day a simplified weekly record sheet must be used.

Shift Workers

1.441 Employers should take particular care when creating rosters or shift patterns for workers to ensure that the Working Time Regulations 1998 are not breached. The key areas to consider are:
- maximum weekly hours
- night working
- rest breaks.

1.442 One of the advantages of working to shift patterns is that employers have flexibility in matching staffing levels to service production requirements.

1.443 It is common for shift workers not to be contracted to work regular hours each week, but for their hours to vary with demand. Logistically, it can be difficult for employers to keep tab of how many hours are being worked by individuals, particularly where time sheets are not completed on a daily or weekly basis or, in the case of 24-hour production, where the roster is being created by a number of managers. In addition, where workers are paid an hourly rate, workers often try to work as many hours as they can to increase their income.

1.444 Where it is likely that workers will work over 48 hours a week, it is essential that they are made aware of their right not to work more than 48 hours on average. If they wish to work more than this, then they should sign an opt-out agreement.

1.445 Employers should ensure that workers take adequate rest breaks during their shifts and have enough of a break between one shift and the next. Particular care must be taken to ensure that night workers also have adequate rest.

Training

1.446 Training in relation to hours of work is mostly covered during worker induction, backed up by on-the-job training if working time appears to be an issue. Induction training could include:

- the organisation's policy on hours of work
- the legal limits on working time and workers' rights to rest breaks and rest periods
- the adverse health effects that are associated with excessive hours of work
- what workers should do to avoid suffering from fatigue when driving long distances on company business
- the increased accident risks associated with fatigue and how to reduce these risks
- the importance of taking regular breaks.

1.447 Managers should be trained on the record keeping systems to be used and how to monitor and maintain records.

List of Relevant Legislation

1.448

- Road Transport (Working Time) Regulations 2005
- Working Time (Amendment) Regulations 2003
- Management of Health and Safety at Work Regulations 1999
- Working Time Regulations 1998
- Health and Safety at Work, etc Act 1974
- Working Time Directive (2003/88/EC)
- Road Transport Directive (2002/15/EC)
- EC Regulation on Drivers' Hours of Work (561/2006/EC)
- EC Regulation on Recording Equipment in Road Transport (3821/85/EC)

List of Relevant Cases

1.449

- *MacCartney v Oversley House Management* [2006] IRLR 514 — the EAT ruled that a daily break should be uninterrupted and the worker must not be at the employer's disposal.
- *Clamp v Aerial Systems* (2004) UKEAT/0266/04 — if, as a result of the Working Time Regulations 1998 applying, an employee worked fewer hours so that his or her salary was reduced, this amounted to a consequence and not a detriment. There was no victimisation in this case.
- *Redrow Homes (Yorkshire) Ltd v Wright* [2004] IRLR 720 — bricklayers who were ostensibly engaged as subcontractors were "workers" under the regulations as they were intended to carry out the work personally.
- *Barber v RJB Mining (UK) Ltd* [1999] IRLR 308 — the 48-average weekly working time limit will be an implied term of each contract of employment, potentially allowing employees to bring claims for constructive dismissal/breach of contract if required to work in excess of that limit without an opt-out having been signed.

- *Addison t/a Brayton News v Ashby* [2003] IRLR 211 — a child who was not above compulsory school age was not a "worker" and therefore not entitled to annual leave under the regulations.
- *Landeshauptstadt Kiel v Jaeger* ECJ, 9.9.03 (C-151/02) — time spent by a doctor on call was "working time", even though it included periods of inactivity when the doctor was sleeping, provided that the doctor was required to remain at the hospital.
- *Cavil v Barratt Homes Ltd* EAT (1 July 2003) — a joiner working as a labour-only subcontractor was obliged to render personal service and was therefore a "worker" under the regulations.
- *Torith Ltd v Flynn* EAT (21 November 2003) — an apparently self-employed joiner was a "worker" under the regulations.
- *Hill v Chappell* [2003] IRLR 19 — an employer cannot recover money from a departing employee for holiday taken in excess of entitlement unless the employer has express authority to do so in the employment contract or a collective agreement.
- *Marshalls Clay Products v Caulfield* [2003] IRLR 552 — employers may "roll up" holiday pay under the WTR provided there is a relevant contractual term and the amount of the holiday pay element is specified.
- *MPB Structures Ltd v Munro* [2003] IRLR 350, CS — the Scottish Court of Session held that employers cannot "roll up" holiday pay.
- *Torith Ltd v Flynn* EAT(21 November 2003) — an apparently self-employed joiner was a "worker" within the WTR and therefore entitled to holiday pay.
- *Byrne Brothers (Formwork) Ltd v Baird* [2002] IRLR 96 — self-employed labour-only subcontractors were "workers" within the Working Time Regulations and therefore entitled to holiday pay.
- *Kigass Aero Components Ltd v Brown* [2002] IRLR 312 — employees on sick leave will continue to accrue rights to annual leave under the Working Time Regulations.
- *List Design Group Ltd v Douglas; LDG Ltd v Catley* [2003] IRLR 14 — employees can bring claims for unlawful deductions from wages in respect of unpaid holiday pay.
- *Campbell & Smith Construction Group Ltd v Greenwood* [2001] IRLR 588 — employees have no statutory right to take leave on bank or public holidays; an employee's entitlement in this respect is purely a matter of contract.
- *Witley & District Men's Club v Mackay* [2001] IRLR 595 — a collective agreement (or employment contract) which provides that no payment will be made on summary dismissal in respect of accrued holiday is void. At least some payment must be made.

Further Information

Publications
- *A Guide to Working Time Regulations*, Joint BERR/HSE Guidance
- HSC 2000/025 *Legislation: Human Rights Act, Working Time Regulations, Parental and Maternity Leave Regulations and Part-time Workers Regulations*
- HSG122 (rev 2002) *New and Expectant Mothers at Work: A Guide for Employers*
- HSG165 (rev 2000) *Young People at Work: A Guide for Employers*

Organisations
- **Department of Health**
  Web: *www.dh.gov.uk*
  The Department of Health provides health and social care policy, guidance and publications.
- **Department for Business, Enterprise and Regulatory Reform (BERR)**
  Web: *www.berr.gov.uk*
  The Department for Business, Enterprise and Regulatory Reform brings together functions from the former Department of Trade and Industry (DTI), including responsibilities for productivity, business relations, energy, competition and consumers. It also drives regulatory reform.

Working Time for Mobile Workers

> This topic covers the following.
> - Who is Affected by the Road Transport (Working Time) Regulations?
> - What is Working Time?
> - What Does Not Count as Working Time?
> - The Working Week
> - Night Working
> - Rest Breaks
> - Record Keeping
> - Enforcement

1.450 On 4 April 2005, the Road Transport (Working Time) Regulations 2005 came into effect. The new regulations affect mobile workers who are subject to the EU drivers' hours rules (561/2006). This is the first time that mobile workers will be subject to restrictions on the number of hours they may work on average each week and at night.

1.451 It is important to note that the Road Transport (Working Time) Regulations do not supersede the EU drivers' hours rules. Instead, mobile workers will have to abide by both sets of regulations.

1.452 Under the new regulations, working times for mobile workers must not exceed:

- an average of 48 hours per week, calculated over a reference period of 4 months
- 60 hours in any one week
- 10 hours in any 24-hour period if working at night.

1.453 It is not possible to opt out of the 48-hour working week. The reference period for the average 48-hour working week, however, may be extended from 4 to 6 months by a collective or workforce agreement.

1.454 Likewise, the limit on night work may be increased through a collective or workforce agreement, although employers should ensure that they do not breach the EU drivers' hours rules on daily and weekly rest breaks.

1.455 Employers will be responsible for ensuring that the new working time limits are not breached by monitoring working time and keeping records.

Employers' Duties

1.456 Employers must:

- ensure that workers do not exceed the 48-hour average working limit or work more than 60 hours in any single week
- ensure that if a relevant agreement is in place, that agreement is reached on the reference period to be used
- be aware that where agreement on the reference period is not reached, the default arrangement is automatically applicable
- identify those activities that count as working time and those that do not

- request that where employees work for another employer they provide written information on the amount of time they work elsewhere
- identify those workers who are likely to work at night and ensure that they do not breach the night-time limit of 10 hours during any 24-hour period
- ensure that all mobile workers take the appropriate and necessary rest breaks
- put into place adequate record keeping systems and keep records of hours worked for at least two years.

Employees' Duties

1.457 Employees have a responsibility to:
- ensure that they do not breach the limits on working time and night-time work
- understand the record keeping system they must complete if required to do so by their employer
- provide their employer with information on work carried out for another employer on request
- understand that they, along with the employer, may be potentially liable for prosecution if the working time limits are breached.

In Practice

Who is Affected by the Road Transport (Working Time) Regulations?

1.458 The regulations affect drivers and other mobile workers who are subject to the EU drivers' hours rules (561/2006/EC). It is important to note that workers, not only employees, are covered by the regulations.

1.459 All workers who drive or form part of the vehicle crew or travelling staff of vehicles with tachographs are covered by the regulations, unless the vehicle has an exemption from 561/2006/EC. This means that the kind of worker covered by the regulations is very broad and can include, for example, bus conductors, porters in household removals, etc.

1.460 The regulations do not apply to:
- self-employed drivers as defined by the regulations
- mobile workers who are not covered by the EU drivers' hours rules, eg van drivers
- workers who only occasionally carry out work within the scope of the EU drivers' hours rules
- any worker who does not fall under the definition of a mobile worker in the Road Transport Directive.

Self-Employed Drivers

1.461 The definition of "self-employed drivers" has been tightly defined by the new regulations and differs to the definition of self-employed in the Employment Rights Act 1996. The HM Revenue and Customs test also does not apply. Drivers who fall under the definition provided by the Road Transport (Working Time) Regulations are exempt from the regulations until 2009.

1.462 The regulations define "self employment" as follows.

1.463 *"Self employment shall mean anyone whose main occupation is to transport passengers or goods by road for hire or reward within the meaning of Community legislation under cover of a Community licence or any other professional authorisation to carry out such transport, who is entitled to work for himself and who is not tied to an employer by an employment contract or any other type of working hierarchical relationship, who is free to organise the relevant working activities, whose income depends directly on the profits made and who has the freedom to, individually or through a co-operation between self-employed drivers, have commercial relationships with several customers."*

1.464 A key point, therefore, is the driver's reliance on profits, as well as the amount of control that the driver has over the work.

Occasional Mobile Workers

1.465 Occasional mobile workers are workers who only occasionally work within the scope of the EU drivers' hours rules in that they work fewer than:
- 11 days within scope of the EU drivers' hours in a 26-week reference period
- 16 days within scope of these rules in a 26-week or more reference period.

1.466 These workers are subject to the Working Time Regulations 1998, instead of the Road Transport (Working Time) Regulations 2005.

What is Working Time?

1.467 A key point to note is that working time is not the same as shift time or attendance. The Working Time (Road Transport) Regulations define working time as the time an employee spends at the disposal of the employer carrying out his or her duties. This includes, for example, not only driving but:
- cleaning and maintaining the vehicle
- loading and unloading goods
- training that is part of normal work
- waiting periods where the foreseeable duration is not known in advance.

1.468 In fact, any time where workers cannot freely dispose of their time and are required to be at their workstations with certain tasks associated with being at work, is classified as working time.

What Does Not Count as Working Time?

1.469 Working time does not include:
- rest breaks and breaks where no work is carried out
- periods of availability
- travel between home and the normal place of work.

Periods of Availability

1.470 A period of availability is waiting time where the mobile worker knows before the start of the relevant period about that period of availability and can foresee how long it is likely to last. In order for waiting time to fall under the category of a period of availability, the worker must be free to leave his or her workstation (although the worker can choose to remain at the workstation if he or she wishes), as long as he or she is available to start work on request.

1.471 A typical example of a period of availability could be accompanying a vehicle being transported by sea or time spent waiting in a queue for the vehicle in question to be unloaded. In addition, time spent by a mobile worker who is travelling in the vehicle, but not driving it, will be classed as a period of availability for that person.

1.472 It is important that the worker has a reasonable amount of freedom to do as he or she wishes, ie eat or read.

1.473 Time spent sitting in traffic, however, is unlikely to count as a period of availability as a driver would be required to concentrate and stop and start the vehicle.

The Working Week

1.474 Under the regulations, workers cannot work more than an average of 48 hours per week, averaged out over a typical 17-week period, and no more than 60 hours in any single week.

1.475 For calculation purposes, the working week must start and finish at 0000 hours on a Monday morning.

The Reference Period

1.476 Employers and employees must agree what reference period is to be used. The regulations provide for a default calendar option which includes some 18-week periods. It is also possible to agree a fixed reference period or a rolling reference period through a collective or workforce agreement.

1.477 The default calendar option, as provided by the regulations, is the option that must be used where agreement over what reference period to use is not achieved. The default reference period begins at 0000 hours on the nearest Monday morning or on 1 April, 1 August and 1 December each year. The start and finishing times dates for the reference period for 2007/2008 are, therefore:
- 2 April 2007 to 5 August 2007 (18 weeks)
- 6 August 2007 to 2 December 2007 (17 weeks)
- 3 December 2008 to 7 April 2008 (18 weeks).

1.478 If there are objective or technical reasons or reasons concerning the organisation of the work, employers and employees may, via a collective or workforce agreement, agree different start and finish times for the reference period and extend the reference period to a period of up to 26 weeks.

1.479 The rolling reference period is the normal method of calculating working time under the Working Time Regulations 1998. Again, it is possible for employers and employees to agree to use this method via a relevant agreement. The key point is that the reference period should not result in an average working week of more than 48 hours.

1.480 A collective or workforce agreement must be a genuine agreement between the employer and the workers, and not a unilateral change imposed by the employer.

Calculating the Average Weekly Working Time

1.481 A worker's average weekly working time is calculated by dividing the number of hours worked by the number of weeks in the reference period.

1.482 It is not possible to use sickness absence or statutory annual leave to reduce the average working week. Where annual leave is taken, 48 hours for each week should be added to the worker's total working time for the current reference period, with an additional 8 hours for each additional day's leave that is taken. However, contractual holiday over the statutory entitlement of four weeks may be used to reduce the average working week.

Night Working

1.483 Unless a relevant agreement is in place, workers are limited to 10 hours' night work in any 24-hour period. The 10-hour limit does not include rest breaks, breaks where the worker is not required to work, and periods of availability.

1.484 Although more than 10 hours work a night may be carried out if there are objective or technical reasons or reasons concerning the organisation of work and if a relevant agreement is in place, employers must still ensure that the minimum rest break requirements under the EU drivers' hours rules are adhered to.

Definition of Night-Time

1.485 Night-time must include the period between midnight and 4am for drivers and other mobile worker on goods vehicles and the period between 1am and 5am for workers on passenger services.

Rest Breaks

1.486 The EU drivers' hours rules 561/2006/EC apply minimum daily and weekly rest breaks. The Road Transport (Working Time) Regulations give non-driver workers the right to these same minimum daily and weekly rest breaks, as well as imposing additional rest break requirements.

1.487 Under the EU drivers' hours rules, workers are entitled to:
- 11 consecutive hours rest in each period of 24 hours — this can be reduced to 9 hours up to 3 times a week as long as compensatory rest is taken
- a weekly rest period of 45 hours' consecutive rest — again this can be reduced to 36 or 24 hours, as long as compensatory rest is taken.

1.488 The new regulations provide that, in addition, workers must not work more than six hours without a break. If the working day is between six and nine hours long, workers are entitled to a rest break of at least 30 minutes during their period of working time. If the working day is longer than nine hours workers are entitled to a minimum break of 45 minutes.

Record Keeping

1.489 For the first time, employers are required to keep records of the number of hours worked by their mobile workers. The regulations do not specify what kinds of records should be kept but it is important that the system used demonstrates that limits on working time and night work are complied with.

1.490 Existing records such as tachograph sheets may be used, although where this is not practicable, eg for non-driving staff and workers who do not use a tachograph each day, the employer will have to adopt another method of recording working time.

1.491 Where a relevant agreement is in place, this must be kept and made available for inspection.

1.492 Records must be kept for a minimum of two years.

1.493 Where workers work for more than one employer, it is important that the employer ask the worker in writing for an account of the time worked for the other employer. The worker must respond to this in writing and the employer should keep this information and monitor it regularly to ensure that the working time limits are not breached.

Enforcement

1.494 The regulations are enforced by the Vehicle and Operator Services Agency (VOSA) in Great Britain and the Driver and Vehicle Testing Agency (DVTA) in Northern Ireland.

Training

1.495 Managers should be trained on the record keeping systems to be used and how to monitor and maintain records.

List of Relevant Legislation

1.496
- Road Transport (Working Time) Regulations 2005
- Working Time Regulations 1998
- Road Transport Directive (2002/15/EC)
- EC Regulation on Drivers' Hours of Work (561/2006/EC)

Further Information

Publications
- *Draft Format Guidance for Industry*, Department for Transport (DfT)

Organisations
- **Department for Transport (DfT)**
  Web: *www.dft.gov.uk/roadsafety*
  The DfT oversees the delivery of a reliable, safe and secure transport system that responds efficiently to the needs of individuals and business while safeguarding the environment.

Chapter 2
Contracts of Employment

Appearance and Dress Codes

> This topic covers the following.
> - Dress Codes
> - Sex Discrimination
> - Discrimination on the Grounds of Race, or Religion or Belief
> - Human Rights
> - Gender Reassignment

2.1 Social norms and legal requirements regarding dress and general appearance at work are constantly evolving.

2.2 Public opinion regarding religious dress and the fashions carried by either sex are the most obvious areas that are continually subject to changing social views. Various legislation and court decisions have affected the legal rules on appearance and dress. These include the Sex Discrimination Act 1975, Race Relations Act 1976, Employment Equality (Religion or Belief) Regulations 2003 and the cases such as *Thompson v Department of Work and Pensions*, *Mohmed v West Coast Trains Ltd* and *Azmi v Kirklees Metropolitan Borough Council*.

Employers' Duties

2.3 An employer must ensure the following.
- Dress codes for men and women are equivalent and do not place an onerous burden on one sex rather than another.
- If an employee or worker dresses in a manner particular to his or her religion or belief, this should be respected so long as it does not impact on the safety practices of the workplace or the effective performance of the work that he or she is required to undertake.
- An employee's dress or appearance should be respected unless it creates a hostile or offensive atmosphere for others.
- There should be a legitimate reason or aim for the requirements of a dress code and the requirements should be proportionate to achieving that aim.
- It is the responsibility of an employer to ensure that employees are actively made aware of any code on dress or appearance at work.
- An individual who is undergoing gender reassignment should be allowed to dress appropriately for the relevant sex.

Employees' Duties

2.4 Employees must ensure that:
- they comply with their employer's dress code
- they do not wear or display insignia that could cause offence or create an intimidating environment for others.

In Practice

Dress Codes

2.5 Employers should ensure that any policy they design places equivalent requirements on all employees regardless of the sex or race of the employee.

2.6 Once in place there is a duty on an employee to comply with the code, but he or she may have a claim against the employer if the code places him or her at a disadvantage compared to other employees, on the grounds of his or her sex or race or the individual's religion or belief.

Sex Discrimination

2.7 Setting different dress code standards for men and women can lead to claims of sex discrimination under the Sex Discrimination Act 1975.

2.8 Requiring either men or women as a class of people to uphold more onerous standards of appearance can amount to sex discrimination. Policies within an organisation should be fair to both sexes.

Proving Sex Discrimination

2.9 Proving discrimination has been difficult in the past because, historically, men and women have tended to dress differently. This has meant that the courts have found it inappropriate to compare the dress of men and women on a garment-by-garment approach. Proving, therefore, that one sex has been discriminated against has often been problematic.

2.10 The general guidance for employers is that they should ensure that the dress requirements for one sex are not any more demanding overall than the requirements for the other sex.

Skirt Wearing

2.11 In the past, employers sometimes drafted dress codes specifically forbidding female employees from wearing trousers. A court decision in 1978 (*Schmidt*) found that women did not look suitably professional if wearing trousers.

2.12 A requirement now for women to wear a skirt at work would probably be seen as discriminatory. Tribunals would now view a smart trouser suit on a woman as smart and professional business wear.

2.13 The question a tribunal would ask is whether one sex is being asked to adhere to a higher level of smartness than the other. Sexes can be treated differently so long as neither is treated less favourably.

Men with Long Hair

2.14 In the past, men wearing their hair long have been found to contravene dress code standards. For example, a male employee working at a delicatessen counter was dismissed from work because his hair was too long.

2.15 Nowadays, it is likely that such a decision would be found to be unreasonable. The question that the courts would ask is whether a requirement for men to wear their hair short would be fair if women in similar circumstances could wear their hair long.

2.16 If long hair results from a religious requirement, an employer's code forbidding long hair could be found to be indirectly discriminatory under the Employment Equality (Religion or Belief) Regulations 2003. The employer would need to reasonably justify its decision. An individual's beard length (or wearing of a beard) may also lead to allegations of discrimination if the beard is worn long for reasons related to the individual's religion.

Wearing a Shirt and Tie

2.17 Employment handbooks frequently require employees to dress "in a professional and business-like manner". This phrasing can be interpreted in a variety of ways.

2.18 In the recent case of *Thompson v Department of Work and Pensions*, Mr Thompson claimed that, while he had to wear a shirt and tie with a suit, women in similar work were allowed to wear a T-shirt with their suit.

2.19 The Employment Appeal Tribunal stated that employers should consider whether the requirement that all staff dress "in a professional and business-like manner" could be achieved without imposing the requirement that all male employees wear a shirt and tie. If a more flexible approach could in practice be taken, then failure to be more flexible could amount to discrimination against men.

Discrimination on the Grounds of Race, or Religion or Belief

2.20 If an employee feels that an organisation's dress code restricts his or her rights to religious freedom, the employee could bring a claim under the Employment Equality (Religion or Belief) Regulations 2003.

2.21 Protection was previously only available to individuals who could demonstrate that their religion demonstrated an ethnic origin. In such cases, the Race Relations Act 1976 could be used.

2.22 The practicalities of specific religious appearance have generally been dealt with in legislation. For example, the rules on the use of hard hats in the building industry were specifically amended to allow for the wearing of turbans.

2.23 A claim against Virgin Trains pursued by a customer service assistant, Mr Mohmed, who had been dismissed for a failure to comply with a requirement to wear his beard shorter than a fist length as this was against his Islamic faith, was pursued as religious discrimination and race discrimination. He was, however, unsuccessful with both arguments at tribunal. Similarly, a claim of direct and indirect discrimination under the 2003 regulations brought by a female Muslim teacher, who said she must wear a full face veil as a requirement of her faith, also failed in an employment tribunal although she was given an award on grounds that she had suffered victimisation at the hands of her employer, Kirklees Metropolitan Borough Council.

Justification

2.24 Employers are advised to exercise flexibility whenever possible to allow for religious requirements.

Appearance and Dress Codes

2.25 An employer that wishes to defend a claim of discrimination on the basis of religion or belief would need to show that the refusal to allow the individual to wear what he or she wished was justified.

2.26 Any justification must not be based on a reason connected with the religion or belief of the individual. The employer must be able to justify the dress code requirements, which must be a proportionate means of achieving a legitimate aim. An employer must have a very good reason for the particular dress code requirement or restriction and the requirement must not be more than is absolutely necessary to achieve a stated business or organisational need.

2.27 Health and safety tends to be the most common justification used by employers. An employer may need special rules for food handling. The wearing of a beard for religious reasons has previously been found to pose a food hygiene risk (although there is now specially designed equipment available to deal with this risk).

Human Rights

2.28 Claims could be brought directly against a public authority employer on the grounds that appearance restrictions infringe the employee's human right to freedom of expression.

2.29 For individuals employed by private sector employers, the Human Rights Act 1998 can only be relied on indirectly, ie if dismissed for reasons relating to appearance, by arguing that the reasonableness of the dismissal must take into account human rights issues.

2.30 There is no current case law to suggest whether such a claim would succeed, but it is likely that the courts would find that freedom of expression should be allowed so long as it does not impact on the rights of others.

2.31 For example, an individual might wear an insignia that might be viewed as hostile or intimidating to others (eg a swastika). In such circumstances, it is likely that the need to protect those being made to feel uncomfortable would outweigh the right of the individual concerned to freedom of expression.

2.32 Behaviour such as wearing a swastika might also be seen as harassment on the grounds of religion or belief: protection from such behaviour is specifically included in the regulations.

Gender Reassignment

2.33 An individual who intends to undergo gender reassignment is likely to start wearing the clothing of the sex he or she intends to take on. If this happens, an employer can still insist on smart dress if this is what is normally required of all employees.

2.34 However, the employer must accept the change of gender or it may face claims under the Sex Discrimination (Gender Reassignment) Regulations 1999.

Training

2.35 Any induction to an organisation should cover the expected dress codes. An employer must bring any code to the attention of its employees and if any breaches occur the employer should ensure that the relevant employees are fully aware of the organisation's expectations.

2.36 HR professionals should, at the very least, read the guidance on religion and belief in the workplace issued by the Advisory, Conciliation and Arbitration Service (Acas). In particular, Appendix 2 provides very useful information on specific religious practices.

2.37 Training of managers on the subjects of equal opportunities and diversity should also include information about the rules governing appearance and dress.

List of Relevant Legislation

2.38
- Employment Equality (Religion or Belief) Regulations 2003
- Sex Discrimination (Gender Reassignment) Regulations 1999
- Human Rights Act 1998
- Race Relations Act 1976
- Sex Discrimination Act 1975

List of Relevant Cases

2.39
- *Mohmed v West Coast Trains* EAT/0682/06
- *Azmi v Kirklees Metropolitan Borough Council* EAT/0009/07
- *Thompson v Department of Work and Pensions* [2004] IRLR 348
- *Smith v Safeway plc* [1996] IRLR 456, CA
- *Schmidt v Austicks Bookshops Ltd* [1977] IRLR 360, EAT

Further Information

Publications
- EEL01 *Acas Religion or Belief and the Workplace — A Guide for Employers and Employees (November 2003)*

Organisations
- **Advisory Conciliation and Arbitration Service (Acas)**
  Web: *www.acas.org.uk*
  Acas aims to improve organisations and working life through better employment relations. It provides up-to-date information, advice, high-quality training, and works with employers and employees to solve problems and improve performance.
- **Commission for Racial Equality**
  Web: *www.cre.gov.uk*
  The Commission for Racial Equality is a publicly funded, non-governmental body set up under the Race Relations Act 1976 to tackle racial discrimination and promote racial equality. From October 2007 this organisation will be replaced by the Commission for Equality and Human Rights.

Breach of Contract

This topic covers the following.
- Contractual Terms
- Employer's Rights
- Withholding or Making Deduction from Wages
- Employees' Remedies
- Fundamental Breach
- Unilateral Variation
- Variation Clauses
- Employer Discretions
- Types of Breach of Contract
- Claims Prior to Employment
- Breach of Trust and Confidence
- Injury to Feelings
- Injunctions by Employees
- Jurisdiction of Employment Tribunals

2.40 Breach of contract can be pursued in employment tribunals, county courts and the High Court. An employer or employee can seek payment of sums outstanding under the contract and also damages for losses suffered. Employees also have statutory protection if the breach of contract is for unpaid wages. Employers and employees may pursue injunctions against the other as well as damages, although this is very unusual.

2.41 The employer has various remedies for breaches of contract by the employee. These include:
- withholding or deducting wages (if the contract allows and agreed in writing)
- pursuing the case through the courts for damages or injunctions.

Employers' Duties

2.42 Employers should take steps to ensure:
- employees are aware of contractual terms
- any changes to terms are clearly notified to the employee
- compliance with the terms of the contract
- they do not alter terms without the consent of the employees unless flexibility is drafted into the contract
- they include, somewhere in the contractual documentation, disciplinary rules and information regarding to whom a grievance can be made and how to pursue that complaint.

Employees' Duties

2.43 Employees have a duty to:
- comply with the terms of their contract of employment
- not to unilaterally change the contract

- comply with implied terms of the contract including their duty of trust and confidence.

In Practice

Contractual Terms

2.44 Contractual terms should be recorded in a written contract or other document, eg a staff handbook or offer letter. If an employer or employee wishes to prove that the contract of employment has been breached they have to convince a court or tribunal that the term was part of the contract. The strongest evidence of this is when the terms are in a written document signed by both parties. Employers who can give evidence of employee agreement to a contractual term are in a much stronger position.

2.45 Some contractual terms remain unwritten. These can be considered express or implied terms by the courts. Implied terms are points that are not expressly agreed by the parties but that are implied into the contract, eg by custom and practice, or because such a term is necessary to make the contract comply with statute.

2.46 The most important of these implied terms is the implied duty of trust and confidence, which is binding on both employer and employee.

2.47 It is up to an employment tribunal to decide whether an implied term is incorporated into a contract of employment. The tribunal's decision will be partly based on whether the terms were understood and familiar to both parties, despite not being written down. It will also depend on whether the contract contains any express terms that would be inconsistent with any such implied term.

2.48 Contracts can also contain discretionary terms, eg terms that relate to employee benefits (such as the supply of a mobile phone). Discretionary terms and benefits may be altered by the employer, whereas any breach of contractual terms by the employer can be contested by the employee, or vice versa.

Employer's Rights

2.49 It may be possible to restrain an employee from working for a competitor if the employee has not given proper notice or is in breach of a contractual term prohibiting such employment.

2.50 An injunction may also be granted if an employee is in breach of a "garden leave" contractual term, ie when he or she does not do any work for the employer during a period of notice, but must not work for anyone else either.

2.51 Where an employer is pursuing damages for the breach of a restrictive covenant, employees can be asked to account for profits they have made as a result of the breach of the term.

2.52 If an employee is in breach of implied duties to the employer, eg duties of trust and confidence, the employer can seek damages for any losses (although claims of this sort are rare).

2.53 If the employee's breach is a fundamental breach of a contractual obligation, eg gross misconduct or extreme incompetence, the employer can bring the contract to an immediate end without any further payments due under the contract.

Withholding or Making Deduction from Wages

2.54 If an employee refuses to perform a substantial part of his or her contractual duties, eg when on strike, the employer can withhold salaries and wages.

2.55 The daily rate of salary deduction is generally calculated as 1/365th of the annual salary, subject to contrary provision in the contract. For hourly paid employees, the deduction is based on the hourly rate of pay.

Employees' Remedies

2.56 If an employer is in breach of contract, an employee may bring proceedings in the High Court or county court for sums due under the contract of employment and damages. Damages are unlimited. The employee can pursue the claim while still employed.

2.57 An employee may also bring a claim for breach of contract to an employment tribunal, but the claimant must have left employment in order to so. This is because the jurisdiction of the tribunal depends on the claim arising from or being outstanding at termination of employment. There is also a limit on the amount that can be claimed in the tribunal of £25,000.

2.58 An employee cannot pursue the same claim through both the courts and a tribunal.

2.59 Where the employer's breach relates to the non-payment of wages, the employee may have a separate claim in an employment tribunal for unlawful deductions from wages under the Employment Rights Act 1996.

Fundamental Breach

2.60 If the breach of contract by the employer is sufficiently serious the employee can resign in response to that breach but will still be treated as if he or she has been dismissed (this is known as constructive dismissal). The employee can resign with or without giving contractual notice so long as the breach is sufficiently serious to have fundamentally breached the implied term of trust and confidence. He or she can bring proceedings for loss of the contract as well as for sums outstanding at the date of dismissal. If the employee has a one-year qualifying period, he or she can also pursue a claim of unfair dismissal.

Unilateral Variation

2.61 Contractual terms cannot be unilaterally varied by either party. If an employer attempts to change the terms of the contract unilaterally, this could be seen as a fundamental breach of contract.

2.62 An employer can seek consent from an employee for changes to the contract of employment. If changes are agreed this should be recorded in writing.

Variation Clauses

2.63 Certain contractual clauses are often drafted to allow the employer the right to change certain aspects of the employment at the employer's discretion, ie a location clause may permit the employer to change the employee's workplace without his or her consent. Such flexibility clauses will however be subject to the implied term of trust and confidence. In practice this will mean that the employer would need to give the employee reasonable notice of the required change, ie change of work location. If this was not done it could entitle the employee to claim constructive dismissal if he or she resigned.

2.64 A clause purportedly giving the employer the right to change any term of the contract it wishes without the employee's consent is likely to be interpreted as applying only to changes of a less fundamental nature.

Employer Discretions

2.65 Contracts of employment are often drafted so that certain contractual benefits may be payable "at the absolute discretion of" the employer, ie bonuses are often stated to be wholly discretionary. Even where the contractual benefit is stated to be wholly discretionary, the courts are now more willing to imply a term that such discretions will not be exercised irrationally or capriciously. So, for example, if all employees are generally paid bonuses by reference to their performance but one high-performing employee is paid nothing because his or her manager simply does not like him or her, this might be open to challenge as a breach of contract, even though if the bonus was expressed to be at the "absolute discretion" of the employer in the contract.

Types of Breach of Contract

Summary Dismissal

2.66 If an employer summarily dismisses an employee, the employee can — if there has been no gross misconduct — pursue a claim for the wages and benefits he or she would have received during the contractual or statutory notice period.

2.67 The applicable notice period will be outlined in the contract or, if greater, one week's notice for each year worked up to a maximum of 12 weeks (eg over one month but less than two years would require one week's notice, over two years but less than three would require two weeks' notice, etc under the statutory notice provisions in the Employment Rights Act 1996). If no notice period has been agreed, the employee will be entitled to a "reasonable" notice period. What is reasonable will depend on what is reasonable in the particular industry and the seniority of the employee, but in any case statutory notice would always apply.

2.68 An employee may also argue that the employer should have followed a contractual disciplinary procedure. In this case an amount may be awarded to recompense the employee for wages he or she would have been paid during the procedure. See *Focsa Services (UK) Limited v Birkett*.

2.69 If an employer dismisses an employee without giving him or her the notice required by the employment contract, and at the date of termination the employee has less than one year's service (but would have had one year's service if notice had been served), the employee will not be able to bring a breach of contract action for loss of the chance to bring an unfair dismissal claim. However, in these circumstances statutory notice provisions will still apply so that if an employee has reached 51 weeks' service at the date of termination, the courts will add one week's statutory notice which will bring the employee up to the required one year's service to be able to bring a claim of unfair dismissal before an employment tribunal.

2.70 An employee can claim damages for any loss of pension rights and other contractual benefits caused by the employee's summary dismissal.

2.71 An employee can pursue claims for unlawful deductions from wages under their statutory rights.

Claims Prior to Employment

2.72 There is a valid contract of employment as soon as an offer of employment is made and accepted. If an employer wishes to withdraw the offer and terminates the contract before the start date then the employee will have a claim for wrongful dismissal.

2.73 However, employers can make offers of employment conditional on certain requirements which have to be met in order for the contract to be valid. If these conditions are not met, the employer can withdraw the offer of employment without being in breach. For example, if an employer wishes to take up references before employment, he or she must make clear that any employment contract is subject to satisfactory references.

Breach of Trust and Confidence

2.74 An employee may be able to recover damages for loss of reputation if an employer has behaved in such a way that it has affected the employee's reputation, eg the employer can be held to have breached the implied trust and confidence clause if it has been operating a dishonest business. See *Malik v BCCI SA (in compulsory liquidation) [1997] IRLR 462, HL*. In practice, however, the circumstances in which such claims will be successful will be extremely rare.

Injury to Feelings

2.75 It now is clear that an employee cannot claim for damages for non-financial losses. It had been argued in the past that, if the manner of dismissal has caused injury to feelings (eg distress and humiliation), an ex-employee might be able to claim damages because of the manner of his or her dismissal. The most recent decision on this point however emphasises that only financial loss can be claimed and that the emotional impact does not give rise to a claim for financial recompense (see *Dunnachie v Kingston upon Hull City Council*).

2.76 If an individual is suspended from work unfairly and suffers psychological injury there may be a claim that a person can pursue regarding breach of the implied term of an organisation to support and assist its employees (see *Gogay v Hertfordshire County Council*).

Injunctions by Employees

2.77 An employee may seek an injunction to restrain an employer from taking action to breach the contract, eg failing to follow contractual disciplinary procedures. In practice, courts only grant an employee's application for an injunction against an employer in very limited circumstances.

Jurisdiction of Employment Tribunals

2.78 Employment tribunals have jurisdiction to hear claims for breach of contracts of employment or contracts connected with employment. Employment tribunals are not able to consider general personal injury claims and the claim must be one which arises, or is outstanding, on the termination of the employee's employment.

2.79 There are specific exclusions for claims relating to:
- living accommodation
- intellectual property
- imposing an obligation of confidence

- any term which is in restraint of trade.

2.80 As with many other tribunal claims, the claim must be brought within three months of the effective date of termination.

2.81 Employers are entitled to counter-claim. The time limit for presenting a counter-claim is six weeks from the date when the employer received a copy of the originating application.

2.82 The maximum award a tribunal can make for breach of contract is £25,000.

Training

2.83 A potential employee should be made aware of all the terms of a provisional contract when offered a job. Contractual terms should be explained to the potential employee and he or she should be asked to sign and return his or her contract.

2.84 Managers should be educated on the effects of agreeing to requests by employees to change contracts.

2.85 It is important to train managers and HR staff to record changes to contractual terms in writing.

2.86 Managers should also be trained in the risks of offering jobs without stating that the offer is subject to satisfactory references or other conditions, such as clearance by the criminal records bureau, security clearance, medical checks, etc.

List of Relevant Legislation

2.87
- Employment Rights Act 1996
- Employment Tribunals Extension of Jurisdiction (England and Wales) Order 1994

List of Relevant Cases

2.88
- *Dunnachie v Kingston upon Hull City Council* [2004] IRLR 727, HL
- *Eastwood v Magnox Electric plc; McCabe v Cornwall County Council* [2004] IRLR 733, HL
- *Harper v Virgin Net Ltd* [2004] IRLR 390, CA — employee not entitled to bring contractual claim for loss of the chance to bring an unfair dismissal claim when dismissed prior to one year's qualifying service.
- *Clark v Nomura International plc* [2000] IRLR 766, HC — court indicates that a discretionary bonus clause will be subject to the implied term that discretion should not to be exercised capriciously or irrationally.
- *Gogay v Hertfordshire County Council* [2000] IRLR 703 — an employee placed on suspension was held to have the right to pursue such a claim where there was an implication that by suspending an employee an employer had made public allegations of abuse.

- *Malik v BCCI SA (in compulsory liquidation)* [1997] IRLR 462, HL — BCCI's behaviour was held to have been corrupt and dishonest, which tainted the employee in the jobs market because of his or her connection with the former employer.
- *Focsa Services (UK) v Birkett* [1996] IRLR 325 — an employee's damages were limited to the losses suffered for the notice period and once that was discharged it was irrelevant for a tribunal to consider what might have happened had the disciplinary procedure been followed.

Further Information

Publications
- FSA's *Factsheet: Challenging Unfair Contract Terms*

Common Clauses

This topic covers the following.
- Garden Leave
- Right to Search
- Fidelity
- Restrictive Covenants
- Relocation and Mobility Clauses
- Intellectual Property
- Confidential Information
- Flexibility Agreements
- Medical Examinations
- Reimbursement of Training Costs Clauses

2.89 This topic looks at some of the common clauses that may be used in a contract of employment. The list is not exhaustive, but shows some common examples of how an employer might protect its own interests within the employer-employee relationship, particularly in relation to competitors.

2.90 This topic does not cover how to create a contract of employment or the legal obligations relating to the employer/employee relationship. See the Contract Formation or Employer/Employee Relationship topic.

Employers' Duties

2.91 Employers have a duty to:
- comply with the terms of the contract
- notify employees of any changes to their contract terms
- not alter the contract terms without the agreement of the employee, unless there is a flexibility clause
- where there is a flexibility clause, to be reasonable in the way in which they implement changes
- inform employees of their contractual rights
- comply with the implied duty of trust and confidence.

Employees' Duties

2.92 Employees have a duty to:
- render faithful service, eg not work for a competitor
- obey lawful and reasonable orders
- comply with the implied duty of trust and confidence
- act honestly in dealings with the employer.

In Practice

Garden Leave

2.93 Garden leave is a term in a contract of employment under which the employee is not required to attend work during the notice period but in all other respects remains an employee bound by the contract and receives pay and all other contractual benefits. The employee is requested by the employer to stay at home, hence the term "garden leave".

2.94 A garden leave clause is useful in protecting an employer when the employee is serving his or her notice period before leaving to join a competitor, and has the following benefits.
- It prevents the employee from working against his or her organisation's interest by doing work for a competitor.
- It stops the employee from passing on sensitive information to a competitor during the notice period.
- It gives the employer time to re-establish the client contact by preventing the employee from moving to the competitor until after the expiry of the notice period.
- It binds the employee to the other terms of his or her contract, such as the duty of fidelity.

2.95 The case of *Symbian Ltd v Christensen* has cast doubt on the proposition that the duty of good faith continues during a period of garden leave (although the case in this respect may be of doubtful authority now). To overcome this problem it is sensible for employers to provide expressly that the duty of good faith continues during garden leave in the contract of employment.

2.96 It is best practice for employers to use garden leave clauses in a reasonable way, eg by not enforcing a long notice period through garden leave as an employee may need to keep skills up to date. A court may refuse to enforce an excessively long garden leave period if it is thought that it will cause the former employee's skills to atrophy.

Right to Search

2.97 An employer may wish to carry out a search, eg in the following circumstances:
- to screen for drugs or alcohol abuse
- to search for theft of the organisation's property
- as part of a routine security operation.

2.98 However, employers should be aware that there is no automatic right to search employees. A clause in the contract giving the employer the right to search will be essential.

2.99 Employers should be aware that searches might:
- cause offence to employees
- cause an assault charge to be brought against the employer
- be a breach of mutual trust and confidence
- be a breach of human rights.

Common Clauses

2.100 Employers should consider the following points when considering inserting a clause on the right to search into a contract of employment.
- An employer must obtain consent from the individual employee on each occasion.
- Additional protection could be provided to the employer by having a search authorisation form signed by the employee on each occasion. The employee should be told the reason for each search and a written record of the search should be kept.
- There may be circumstances where an employer wishes to carry out a search routinely as part of security operations or as part of an investigatory process when items of value may have gone missing.
- If the contract gives the employer the right to search and the employee subsequently refuses permission, the employer should treat this as a disciplinary matter rather than attempting the search without consent.
- The mutual obligation of confidence and trust is implied into every contract of employment and both parties should not act in a way so as to destroy that relationship.
- Care should be taken to respect the dignity of employees — therefore a search should be carried out by a person of the same sex as the person searched and be carried out in a private room.
- It is recommended that a witness be present during any search in case of any dispute as to what took place.
- It is advisable to have a clause in the contract of employment allowing the employer to carry out periodic locker searches at work. The employer should not search through the contents of personal belongings. A witness should be present during a locker search and a written record kept.

Fidelity

2.101 A fidelity clause helps to prevent employees from working simultaneously for a rival organisation or in a role which would present a conflict of interests. It is implied into every contract of employment that the employee will faithfully serve the employer and will not act in a way that is contrary or damaging to the employer's interests. The duty of fidelity may be contained in either an express (explicitly stated) or an implied term of the contract of employment.

2.102 Working for a rival organisation at the same time as the existing employer would breach this term, as would personally tendering for the business of the employer's customers.

2.103 The following points should be kept in mind when deciding whether to include a fidelity clause in a contract of employment.
- The duty of fidelity exists during employment and the employee is released from the duty after employment subject to any restrictive covenants that may have been agreed and subject to the rules on confidential information.
- A contract may contain a clause that prohibits the taking up of any secondary employment without the consent of the employer. Such consent should not be unreasonably withheld. It would normally be considered reasonable to prevent the employee from working concurrently with a competitor.
- An employer may also be reasonable in refusing consent where the second job would place a strain on the employee, eg the standard of work would suffer or the duty of fidelity owed to the two employers is likely to lead to a conflict.
- In relation to more senior employees, it is more common to impose an absolute prohibition on any outside employment, whether competing or not.
- There should be no problem with an employee working for a non-competing organisation in the absence of an express clause.

Restrictive Covenants

2.104 A restrictive covenant is an express (explicitly stated) term in a contract of employment restraining the employee from certain activities following employment. The object of the covenant is to protect the employer from competition brought about by the employee's departure, which may be in the form of restraining the former employee's ability to deal with clients or customers or from making use of clearly defined categories of confidential information or trade secrets.

2.105 It should be noted that restrictive covenants:
- are often considered unenforceable
- are held to be in restraint of trade and contrary to public policy and so must be justified if an employer wishes to rely on them
- restrict an individual's right to work freely for whomsoever he or she chooses.

2.106 For a restrictive covenant to be upheld, two conditions must be met.
- The covenant must be reasonable as between the parties.
- It must be reasonable in the interests of the public.

2.107 The employer seeking to enforce the covenant must also show that there is a protectable interest. The two well established categories of protectable interest are:
- customer connection
- trade secrets.

2.108 There has recently emerged a third category of protecting the stability of the workforce by restraining the employee's ability to "poach" other members of staff.

2.109 To be enforceable a restrictive covenant must be no wider than is reasonably necessary for the protection of the interest. Careful drafting of the covenant is required — if it is too wide it will be unenforceable. Consider the duration of the covenant and the geographical extent of the restriction.

2.110 There can be no standard format for an enforceable restrictive covenant. The facts of each individual case will have to be considered. The nature of the work, the extent to which the work brings the employee into contact with customers or trade secrets and the seniority of the employee will all be relevant.

Removal of Invalid Sub-Clauses

2.111 If a covenant is badly or too widely drafted a court will refuse to enforce it.

2.112 A court will not rewrite the covenant and it will be invalid unless the "blue pencil test" can be applied. This tests whether a badly drafted clause (or part of a clause) can be struck out without the remaining words losing their meaning. If so, the remaining words will be allowed to stand.

2.113 Often restrictive covenants are drafted with a number of sub-clauses, so that if one part is invalid, it can be "blue pencilled" or crossed out leaving the other sub-clauses intact. Due to the complexity of the law surrounding restrictive covenants, it is often worth seeking professional advice on this matter.

Preventing Poaching of Customers

2.114 There are two types of covenant used to protect customer connection.
- A non-solicitation clause.
- A non-dealing clause.

2.115 It is important to identify the pool of customers who are to be covered by the restriction. The covenant is most likely to be enforced if it clearly specifies the customers with whom the employee had dealings within a set period of time prior to termination of employment. The covenant should not generally cover customers who have used the employer's services for the first time since the employee left or those with whom the employee had no dealings.

2.116 A non-solicitation clause prevents the employee from actively seeking business from his or her ex-employer's customers. A non-dealing clause is more stringent as it restrains the employee from dealing with the customers whether or not he or she actively sought their business. It is often hard to establish how a customer came to the employee and therefore a non-dealing clause is more likely to be enforceable if carefully and narrowly drafted.

Scope of Restrictive Covenants

2.117 Both the geographical area covered by the covenant and its duration are key to the enforceability of restrictive covenants.

2.118 The reasonableness of a covenant may vary from region to region and a one-mile radius in a country area may be enforceable whereas the same radius in the City of London may not.

2.119 The duration of the covenant should be defined and will be dependent on individual circumstances. A covenant in excess of 12 months would require special circumstances in order to be enforceable.

Stability of the Workforce

2.120 Recently courts have upheld covenants that allow an employer to prevent the poaching of its employees by a former employee. The basis is that the employer's interest in maintaining a stable and trained workforce is one that can be properly protected within the limits of reasonableness. To be enforceable the covenant requires narrow drafting to clarify exactly which staff are protected. For example, it could be applied to those with particular seniority or who are of particular importance to the business whose departure may cause loss or damage to the organisation.

2.121 A covenant is likely to be unenforceable if it prevents the former employee soliciting employees even if their employment commenced after the former employee left. A wide clause restricting the poaching of any staff over a long period of time is unlikely to be enforced.

Transfer of Undertakings

2.122 When a transfer of an undertaking (business) takes place the existing terms and conditions of employment are protected. When the contract contains a restrictive covenant it may be enforced by the transferee (the buyer) but only to the extent to which it protects the customers of the transferor (the seller). The scope of the restrictive covenant is not widened on the transfer to cover customers of the transferee.

2.123 The details of dealing with an employee's terms and conditions of employment relating to the transfer of an undertaking is covered elsewhere. See Transfer of Undertakings topic.

Trade Secrets and Confidential Information

2.124 The obligations placed upon employees are stricter during employment than afterwards. To be capable of restriction, the trade secret or confidential information must genuinely fall within the category of information which can be protected or must be a trade secret, eg secret processes of manufacture or detailed product information

Relocation and Mobility Clauses

2.125 As with flexibility clauses, where an employer wishes to have the discretion to relocate its employees, there should be a good reason for exercising this power, the employer must act reasonably and must also consult.

2.126 Distance and the seniority of the employee in question can be key factors. An employer could not, for example, rely on a standard relocation clause to move all its employees, including administrative and manual workers, a long distance. However, it could be considered reasonable to require a managing director to relocate in such circumstances.

2.127 Requiring employees to be widely mobile may also be indirectly discriminatory. While it may be reasonable to expect a male sales representative to travel around the country, requiring all employees at a certain level or grade to be mobile could lead to claims of sex or disability discrimination.

Intellectual Property

2.128 Intellectual property rights give protection to:
- copyright works
- designs
- patents.

2.129 Copyright works include:
- original literary, dramatic or artistic works
- sound recordings
- films
- broadcasts or cable programmes
- typographic arrangements of published editions
- computer programmes
- graphic works
- photographs.

2.130 The employer has certain rights relating to the following.
- Literary, dramatic, musical or artistic works created in the course of employment — the employer is the first owner of any copyright in the work, subject to any agreement to the contrary.
- Copyright works of value created in the course of employment — it is common to find an express clause in the contract of employment stating that ownership of the copyright work shall belong to the employer.
- Original designs created by an employee in the course of his or her employment — the employer is the first owner of any design right.
- Patents — the employee may be entitled to compensation where the patent is of outstanding benefit to the organisation.

Confidential Information

2.131 Confidential information may be protected during employment either by express or implied terms. During employment the employee is under a greater restriction because of the greater duty of fidelity owed to the employer. After employment the employee has more freedom to divulge information, especially where this information forms part of his or her general skills and knowledge.

2.132 Confidential information can only be protected after employment to the extent to which the courts regard the information as properly confidential. All the facts must be considered but the following will be of special importance.
- The nature of the employment and whether the employee is expected to realise the sensitive nature of the information handled.
- The nature of the information itself, eg a secret process of manufacture.
- Whether the employer has impressed upon the employee the confidentiality of the information.
- Whether the confidential information is readily isolated from information that the employee is entitled to disclose.

2.133 An express covenant may help to identify information as being confidential but it may not protect the employer if the information is not properly regarded as confidential.

2.134 Without an express clause in the contract prohibiting unauthorised use or disclosure, an employee will only be prevented after termination of employment from using or disclosing "trade secrets" or equivalent categories of information, rather than merely confidential information.

Flexibility Agreements

2.135 A flexibility agreement will assist the employer in making changes without the difficulties normally associated with variations of the contract.

2.136 A flexible agreement may cover:
- a flexible duties clause
- flexible hours
- moving employees from one department to another or between associated companies by giving the employer the contractual right to do so.

2.137 Flexibility terms in contracts of employment should be drafted with care. If terms are too vague, eg invoking the right to vary all or any of the terms of the contract, a court may refuse to enforce them. The types of flexible arrangements available, eg hours or duties, should be set out. Ambiguity in the flexibility agreement may be construed against the employer.

2.138 Good practice in operating flexible terms would include:
- reasonable and sufficient grounds for exercise of the agreement — arbitrary reasons may run the risk of a constructive dismissal claim
- consideration of the implied obligation of mutual trust and confidence — reasonable notice should be given and the employees should not be asked to do anything which is wholly impractical
- an obligation to consult with the employees concerned, giving them the opportunity to state the implications for them as individuals.

Medical Examinations

2.139 The employer may wish employees to undergo a medical examination in a number of circumstances including:
- long-term ill health situations
- drug and alcohol screening
- health and safety reasons.

2.140 As the requirement to undergo a medical examination may only be implied into a contract of employment in limited circumstances, it is advisable to state the right to ask an employee to undergo a medical examination expressly. An implied term may only exist where it is directly relevant to the work, eg those working in the medical profession or those working in close contact with food for hygiene reasons.

2.141 The following points should be kept in mind.

- There is an implied term in every contract of employment that the parties will not act in a manner likely to destroy the mutual relationship of confidence and trust.
- The respect and dignity of the employee must be preserved as any treatment of a humiliating or degrading nature may be in breach of this implied term.
- Even where the contractual right to require a medical examination exists, the employee cannot be compelled to undergo an examination without consent.
- If the employee refuses to be examined despite the term in the contract, this should be treated as a disciplinary matter and the employee's reasons for refusal considered.
- The employee may have the right under the Access to Medical Reports Act 1988 to view any medical reports produced as a result of such examination, if carried out by a medical practitioner who was responsible for the clinical care of the individual.
- Medical reports obtained by the employer should not be disclosed to third parties without the employee's consent.

Reimbursement of Training Costs Clauses

2.142 The costs involved in training employees can be considerable and employers may wish to protect the investment they have made in training.

2.143 It is possible to provide for the reimbursement of training costs upon termination of employment. Such clauses should be drafted with care and a balance should be struck between the interests of the employer and employee. The obligation to refund costs should last for a certain period of time only, the costs to be refunded should be direct costs only and the reimbursement to be reduced on a sliding scale to reflect the benefit the employer has obtained from the employee's service during the period of employment.

Training

2.144 It is advisable for employers to explain contractual terms to new employees at their induction.

2.145 Employees should be asked to sign and return contracts, confirming that they understand and agree to abide by the terms.

2.146 Managers should be educated on the effects of agreeing requests by employees to change contracts.

2.147 Managers and HR staff need to be trained to record changes to contractual terms in writing.

List of Relevant Legislation

2.148
- Transfer of Undertakings (Protection of Employment) Regulations 2006
- Employment Act 2002 (Dispute Resolution) Regulations 2004

- Working Time Regulations 1998
- Contracts (Rights of Third Parties) Act 1999
- Employment Relations Act 1999
- Employment Rights Act 1996
- Disability Discrimination Act 1995
- Trade Union and Labour Relations (Consolidation) Act 1992
- Access to Medical Reports Act 1988
- Copyright Designs and Patents Act 1988
- Patents Act 1977
- Unfair Contract Terms Act 1977
- Sex Discrimination Act 1975
- Health and Safety at Work, etc Act 1974
- Rehabilitation of Offenders Act 1974
- Equal Pay Act 1970
- Employment Tribunals Extension of Jurisdiction (England and Wales) Order 1994
- Treaty of Rome (1960)

List of Relevant Cases

2.149
- *Department for Work and Pensions v Thompson* [2004] IRLR 298
- *Symbian Ltd v Christensen* [2001] IRLR 77, CA
- *William Hill Organisation Ltd v Tucker* [1998] IRLR 313
- *Meade-Hill v British Council* [1995] IRLR 478, CA

Contract Formation

> This topic covers the following.
> - Formation
> - Offers
> - Acceptance, Counter Offers and Withdrawal of Offer
> - Conditional Offers
> - Misrepresentation
> - Written Statement of Particulars of the Contract
> - Excluded Employees
> - Identifying the Contract Terms
> - Custom and Practice
> - Mutual Obligations
> - Employee Handbooks
> - Reference Documents
> - Variation of the Contract
> - Transfer of Undertakings
> - Breach of Contract

2.150 A contract is an agreement between two or more parties. It may be oral, written or both. In common law, the employer/employee relationship is governed by the contract of employment. Legislation since the Contracts of Employment Act 1963 has developed the rights and obligations of both parties.

2.151 An understanding of the employment contract and its formation is fundamental to an understanding of employment law, especially when many claims to employment tribunals concern disputes over contract terms.

Employers' Duties

2.152 Employers should ensure that they:
- present the terms and conditions of employment on offer openly and in good faith
- pay agreed wages
- provide work if not doing so affects earnings or would cause loss of skills
- take reasonable care to ensure employees' health and safety
- handle grievances promptly and in good faith
- inform employees of contractual rights and benefits
- comply with the implied duty of trust and confidence.

Employees' Duties

2.153 Employees should ensure that they:
- present themselves honestly and fully in the contract formation process
- render faithful service, eg not work for a competitor
- obey lawful and reasonable orders
- exercise reasonable care and skill, ie possess skills as claimed, and not act negligently

Contract Formation

- comply with the implied duty of trust and confidence.

In Practice

Formation

2.154 A contract of employment can only be deemed "formed" if a number of conditions have been satisfied, including:
- agreement between the parties following the acceptance of an offer
- the intention to create a legal relationship
- consideration, ie that the contract should benefit all parties
- certainty of terms, ie the terms of the contract must be clear in their meaning.

Offers

2.155 After interviews, tests and other selection methods, as the parties approach agreement, employers can make an oral offer which is only open for a defined period. Any subsequent written offer should outline the main terms and conditions of employment.

Oral Offers

2.156 Making an offer means the employer is willing to be bound by a contract. The offer must be:
- capable of immediate acceptance
- sufficiently clear for the person receiving it to understand it
- communicated to the intended recipient
- made by an authorised person.

2.157 Oral offers can be used for:
- checking an applicant's freedom to take up a post
- agreeing start dates
- ensuring that the recipient is aware of conditions attached to the offer, eg satisfactory references.

2.158 Oral offers should always be confirmed in writing.

Written Offers

2.159 Follow up an oral offer in writing or by email. Before making a written offer, employers should:
- define who has authority to offer employment
- check any constraints, eg funding and pay rate.

2.160 When making an offer in writing, employers should give sufficient information to enable the recipient to decide whether to accept the job, including details of:
- the job title and description
- the name and title of the line manager
- salary
- annual holiday

- hours of work
- any additional considerations, eg assistance with relocation
- any trial or probationary period
- a contact person for further discussion
- the timescale and method for acceptance, eg in writing
- whether the offer is subject to receipt of satisfactory references or any other conditions, eg pre-employment medical checks.

Acceptance, Counter Offers and Withdrawal of Offer

2.161 If no time period for acceptance is specified, the person receiving the offer will be deemed to have refused it after a "reasonable period". Unless the means of acceptance is defined in the written offer, acceptance may be in writing (including email), oral or implied by the employee's conduct, eg by simply starting work.

2.162 After unconditional acceptance, an offer may not be withdrawn without risking a breach of contract claim. This would make the employer liable for damages equivalent to pay and benefits for the notice period and/or discrimination claims.

2.163 A conditional acceptance may contest a proposed term of the contract, eg pay, overtime or hours worked. Employers should not permit new employees to start work unless these counter-offer issues have been resolved.

2.164 Conditional acceptance is statutorily provided for when an employee tries out a new job for four weeks following redundancy.

Conditional Offers

2.165 Any conditions must be made absolutely clear. Candidates should not give notice to their current employer until the following have been supplied to the new employer's satisfaction:
- references
- qualifications
- medical or health check
- rehabilitation of offenders records
- criminal records bureau records
- asylum and immigration records.

References

2.166 At the very least, an employer should verify the information on a candidate's CV or application form. A written offer that is conditional on receipt of satisfactory references should include the statement that the offer is "subject to the receipt of references satisfactory to the company/organisation".

Qualifications

2.167 If required, qualifications must be verified by seeing original certificates or confirmation from the awarding body.

Medical or Health Check

2.168 The employment offer should state the purpose of any health check, eg fitness for proposed work, and employers should be aware of potential disability discrimination if the offer is withdrawn on health grounds.

2.169 Subject to this, a candidate should give details of the number of days' sickness in the previous two years. A comprehensive questionnaire is possible, so long as it is confidential and competently assessed. Questionnaires may be followed up with enquiries to the candidate's doctor or an examination by an appropriately qualified person.

2.170 This subject is dealt with in more detail in References and Medical Checks.

Rehabilitation of Offenders

2.171 Candidates should declare any convictions not spent under the Rehabilitation of Offenders Act 1974. Employers should assess the convictions' relevance to the job.

Criminal Records Bureau Checks

2.172 Checks are desirable for certain jobs, whereas for others they are mandatory. If checks are only desirable, assess the information carefully before deciding whether any conditional offer should stand.

Asylum and Immigration Act 1996

2.173 Employers must check candidates' eligibility to work in the EU. In order to avoid potential race discrimination claims, all candidates should be asked for evidence of their right to work in the UK prior to appointment (eg a passport or a P45, P60 and a full birth certificate).

Other Conditions

2.174 Candidates may be asked to warrant that they are not subject to any agreement, arrangement, contract or court order restricting or prohibiting them from taking up employment or carrying out duties under specified terms and conditions. This often covers restrictive covenants which might be enforced by previous employers.

Misrepresentation

2.175 Prospective employers should not make erroneous or misleading statements about the job or terms and conditions at any stage during contract formation.

2.176 Candidates should be asked to warrant on an application form that they have made no false claims. The form should also state that a job offer will be withdrawn if any falsehoods emerge.

Written Statement of Particulars of the Contract

2.177 Section 1 of the Employment Rights Act 1996 (ERA) stipulates that new employees must receive a statement of written particular terms of the contract of employment within two months of starting work. Employers should note that this document is not a contract of employment in itself although it is often mistakenly referred to as such. The statement can be a standalone document or the information can be included in an offer letter or written contract of employment but must include the following particulars.
1. Names of employer and employee.
2. Date employment began.

Contract Formation

3. Date on which any continuous employment began (including employment that counts with a previous employer).
4. Scale or rate of pay or how it is calculated.
5. How often employees are paid.
6. Terms and conditions concerning hours of work.
7. Terms and conditions concerning holidays, holiday pay and entitlement on termination.
8. Terms and conditions concerning sickness or incapacity, sick pay, pensions and pension schemes.
9. Notice period required to terminate the employment on each side.
10. Job title or brief description of work.
11. Expected length of employment if not permanent.
12. Place of work and employer's address.
13. Details of collective agreements affecting terms and conditions.
14. Details of the duration, currency of payment, benefits and terms and conditions on return if the employee is required to work outside the UK for over one month.
15. Disciplinary rules and procedure (or where these can be found).
16. Grievance process and to whom a grievance can be raised and to whom an appeal against a disciplinary decision can be raised.
17. Whether or not the employment is contracted out of the state second pension.

2.178 Numbers 1 to 7, 10 and 12 must be in one document. Numbers 8 and 15 may refer to another document, and number 9 may refer to a relevant collective agreement or applicable law, so long as all are reasonably accessible to the employee.

Excluded Employees

2.179 The following employees are not entitled to receive a s.1 (ERA) statement:
- members of the armed forces
- employees of under one month
- merchant sailors.

Identifying the Contract Terms

2.180 A contract may include express, implied and statutory terms and terms incorporated from other sources, eg works' rules or collective agreements.

2.181 Under the Contracts (Rights of Third Parties) Act 1999, third parties may become involved, eg a survivor may claim pension rights, or an employee permanently unable to work may claim permanent health benefits as an insured right.

Express Terms

2.182 Express terms:
- may be oral or written
- should be written to minimise areas of dispute
- must be as or more favourable than statute, eg as regards notice periods or the National Minimum Wage.

2.183 Terms setting out the right to dismiss an employee immediately and withhold a contractual or statutory right to notice, or notice pay, would be potentially unfair under the unfair dismissal provisions of the Employment Rights Act 1996. The right to dismiss an employee immediately without any notice or payment in lieu of notice is only available if the employee has breached the contract and been guilty of gross misconduct.

2.184 If a contract is ambiguous, tribunals may consider the circumstances of recruitment and selection, including the job advertisement and subsequent exchanges between parties.

Implied Terms

2.185 Implied terms may supplement but must not override express terms. Courts only infer that a term is implied if they consider parties originally intended it, and they must be satisfied it was:
- intended; or
- necessary to give the contract business efficacy; or
- normal custom and practice; or
- so obvious it must have been intended.

2.186 However, there are also implied terms binding on both employers and employees, eg the mutual duty of trust and confidence.

Incorporated Terms

2.187 Incorporated terms are usually collective agreements, works rules and disciplinary rules.

2.188 Incorporated terms are binding on individual employees even if they are unaware of them.

2.189 Employers may choose to incorporate contractual disciplinary and grievance procedures, in which case they become binding. If not incorporated these procedures are easier to change without requiring the agreement of employees and/or trade unions.

2.190 A collective agreement may include terms taken to be inserted into a contract. This occurs when the term can be shown to be collective custom and practice or it is so obvious that it must be taken to be included. It may cover matters of an advisory or good practice nature that are unsuitable for incorporation into individuals' contracts.

Statutory Terms

2.191 Statutory terms include:
- minimum notice period for employee (see Employment Rights Act 1996)
- equality clause relating to equal pay between men and women (see Equal Pay Act 1970)
- working time regulations — including minimum holiday entitlement (see Working Time Regulations 1998)
- the provision of a working environment that is safe, without risks to health and adequate as regards facilities and arrangements for welfare at work (see Health and Safety at Work, etc Act 1974).

2.192 Employers need not act to include clauses, but should consider how they relate to existing and possibly more generous contractual terms, particularly working time regulations.

Void Terms and Illegality

2.193 Terms withholding employees' statutory rights, eg concerning unfair dismissal, maternity leave, the National Minimum Wage or discrimination are illegal. Such terms may be excluded leaving the remainder of the contract intact. If the term is criminal, immoral or fraudulent, it may make the whole contract unenforceable.

Custom and Practice

2.194 Terms may also be implied if regularly adopted in a particular industry or employer. The tests here are normally whether the practice is:
- reasonable, ie fair
- notorious, ie well-known and established
- certain, ie clear-cut.

2.195 In *Scott v Blagden*, pay rises determined by industry-wide national agreement over many years and the fair dismissal of a worker who refused to do essential maintenance which was always carried out at weekends were cited as examples of customary practices.

Mutual Obligations

2.196 After agreement, each party has obligations to the other. Employees must work and employers must pay for that work. However, the implied term of mutual trust and confidence underpins the whole employment relationship. This implied term applies to every aspect of the employment relationship, except dismissal. See *Johnson v Unisys Ltd*.

2.197 The implied duty of mutual trust and confidence is relied on in:
- providing references in a fair manner
- implementing procedures, eg discipline, in a non-oppressive way
- operating discretionary clauses fairly and in good faith
- not humiliating or undermining employees
- not conducting business in a corrupt or dishonest manner
- protecting whistleblowers.

2.198 No action is needed to include implied terms into a contract.

Employee Handbooks

2.199 The s.1 statement may refer to the employee handbook.

2.200 It is important to state whether employment terms are contractual, ie incorporated into the contract, or non-contractual. Contractual terms must be clear and may only be changed by agreement. Non-contractual terms are easier to vary.

Reference Documents

2.201 The s.1 statement may also refer to another document, eg a collective agreement, relating to:
- sickness absence
- pension schemes
- notice, statutory and contractual
- disciplinary procedures.

2.202 Reference documents must be reasonably accessible, so employers should:
- say where they are held
- avoid extensive cross-referencing, and
- state details in full.

Variation of the Contract

2.203 Any party may wish to change terms over time. Most are changed by mutual consent. It is difficult to change a contract unilaterally without it amounting to a breach of contract. There are several change strategies open to employers and employees. More detail can be found in Varying the Contract of Employment.

Variation by Agreement

2.204 Employers should consider the necessity of any agreement. Changes may already be within the scope of the contract:
- where managerial prerogative is permitted, eg in relation to work organisation
- where handbooks state that policies and procedures constitute guidance and can be "amended from time to time".

2.205 Any agreement to change terms must be communicated to the employee(s). A formal notification should follow within one month of the agreement to changes. Acceptance of the changes may be implied when an employee continues to work, without making any protest clear to the employer, although courts will be reluctant to infer such acceptance by "silence" where the change has no immediate impact on the employee, eg the imposition of restrictive covenants.

2.206 Employers should be alert to the possibility of constructive unfair dismissal following an alleged fundamental breach of contract.

2.207 Employers should also not apply duress with regards to any changes.

Incorporating the Right to Vary within the Contract

2.208 Employers should define contracts sufficiently for a section 1 statement, but with enough flexibility for their anticipated needs. Clauses must not be so widely drawn as to be meaningless. For example, a clause permitting unfettered changes to duties would be difficult to rely upon.

2.209 Employers are advised to write clauses incorporating the right to vary with care and clarity.

Variation through Collective Agreement

2.210 Collective agreements may be incorporated into an individual's contract, either expressly or implicitly, regardless of whether the employee is a trade union member. They may be implied into individual contracts by custom and practice and they bind both sides. Employers may not vary them without further agreement.

Unilateral Variation

2.211 Employers may wish to change the terms of a contract without the agreement of the employee. They have two options:
- introduce new terms as a *fait accompli*
- terminate contracts and include variations in new contracts.

2.212 Employers should be aware that unilateral change will constitute breach of contract.

2.213 In response, employees may:
- acquiesce and carry on working, resulting in no claims
- resign and claim constructive unfair dismissal, forcing the employer to justify the changes

Contract Formation

- refuse to work under the new conditions
- "stand and sue", ie work under protest and bring a claim for breach of contract or wages to the court or tribunal for unlawful deductions from pay
- if the change to the contract is particularly fundamental, claim constructive dismissal as it it may be regarded as a termination of the old contract although compensation will probably be limited.

2.214 Changes to contracts linked with the Transfer of Undertakings (Protection of Employment) Regulations 2006 (TUPE) are described in more detail in Transfer of Undertakings.

2.215 Employers wishing to change the terms and conditions in a contract of employment should also consider the implications of health and safety legislation, discrimination, the National Minimum Wage, Sunday working provisions and working time regulations.

Transfer of Undertakings

2.216 The Transfer of Undertakings (Protection of Employment) Regulations 2006 (TUPE) protect the contracts of employees and affect the ability to agree new terms and conditions after a business is transferred to a new owner.

2.217 An employee cannot validly agree to a variation of his or her terms and conditions if the change is by reason of the transfer, although it is sometimes difficult to determine if the variation is in fact due to the transfer or to another reason. As a rule of thumb, however, the closer the variation is introduced to the date of transfer, the more likely it will be interpreted as being reason of the transfer.

2.218 In a situation where the new employer terminates the contract of employment and offers re-engagement under a new contract on different terms and conditions, the dismissal will be for a reason connected with the transfer. This means that the employee could bring a claim for automatically unfair dismissal if he or she has one year's service or more.

2.219 The new regulations incorporate much of the case law developed since the first TUPE regulations came into force in 1981.

2.220 Employers should take expert advice on this complex area of employment law.

2.221 If an organisation is acquired through share transfer, TUPE does not apply and contractual changes may be negotiated.

Breach of Contract

2.222 A breach of contract generally entitles the other party to sue for damages, but not necessarily to terminate the contract.

2.223 Breaches are most likely when an employer varies a contract unilaterally. Employees may:
- accept the breach and work on without protest
- work on but protest and seek damages
- accept the breach and resign, suing for damages and/or for constructive unfair dismissal.

2.224 Note that industrial action may constitute a breach of contract. More detail on this area can be found in Breach of Contract.

Training

2.225 Writing contracts of employment is specialist work. Employers should determine who has the authority to make job offers and who follows them up. All the relevant managers and staff need a basic understanding of contract law, provided by:
- tailored short courses on that subject
- contract-writing courses
- visits to employment tribunals to highlight the pitfalls of loose drafting.

List of Relevant Legislation

2.226
- Transfer of Undertakings (Protection of Employment) Regulations 2006
- Conduct of Employment Agencies and Employment Businesses Regulations 2003
- Working Time Regulations 1998
- Contracts (Rights of Third Parties) Act 1999
- National Minimum Wage Act 1998
- Asylum and Immigration Act 1996
- Employment Rights Act 1996 (ERA)
- Access to Medical Reports Act 1988
- Unfair Contract Terms Act 1977
- Health and Safety at Work, etc Act 1974
- Rehabilitation of Offenders Act 1974
- Equal Pay Act 1970
- Proof of Employment Relationship Directive (91/533/EEC) 14 October 1991
- Article 39 of Treaty of Rome (1960) on Freedom of Movement

List of Relevant Cases

2.227
- *Cable & Wireless plc v Muscat* EAT 25/02/05 (0661/04)
- *Dacas v Brook Street Bureau (UK) Ltd* [2004] IRLR 358, CA
- *Scott v Blagden (Barking) Ltd* EAT 367/82
- *Wilson v St Helens Borough Council* [1998] IRLR 706, HL
- *Brookes v Borough Care Services* [1998] IRLR 636
- *Johnson v Unisys Ltd* [2001] IRLR 279, HL

Further Information

Publications
- *Acas Contracts of Employment*

Contract Formation

- *G01 Acas Producing a Written Statement* (written statements of particulars of employment only)

Organisations

- **Advisory Conciliation and Arbitration Service (Acas)**
  Web: *www.acas.org.uk*
  Acas aims to improve organisations and working life through better employment relations. It provides up-to-date information, advice, high-quality training, and works with employers and employees to solve problems and improve performance.

- **Chartered Institute of Personnel and Development (CIPD)**
  Web: *www.cipd.org.uk*
  The CIPD is a professional body for those involved in the management and development of people.

- **Commission for Racial Equality**
  Web: *www.cre.gov.uk*
  The Commission for Racial Equality is a publicly funded, non-governmental body set up under the Race Relations Act 1976 to tackle racial discrimination and promote racial equality. From October 2007 this organisation will be replaced by the Commission for Equality and Human Rights.

- **Criminal Records Bureau (CRB)**
  Web: *www.crb.gov.uk*
  The CRB — an executive agency of the Home Office — is set up to help organisations make safer recruitment decisions.

- **Disability Rights Commission**
  Web: *www.drc-gb.org*
  An independent body established by Act of Parliament to eliminate discrimination against disabled people and promote quality of opportunity. It provides information and advice to disabled people and employers about their rights and duties. From October 2007 this organisation will be replaced by the Commission for Equality and Human Rights (**Web:** *www.cehr.org.uk*).

- **Disclosure Bureau**
  Web: *www.disclosurescotland.co.uk*
  Disclosure Scotland is part of the Scottish Criminal Record Office providing security and clearance checks especially for employers. The disclosure service is aimed at public safety and protecting vulnerable people form those who may harm them.

- **Equal Opportunities Commission**
  Web: *www.eoc.org.uk*
  An agency working to eliminate sex discrimination and put equality into practice in the workplace. From October 2007 this organisation will be replaced by the Commission for Equality and Human Rights (**Web:** *www.cehr.org.uk*).

- **Health and Safety Executive (HSE)**
  Web: *www.hse.gov.uk*
  The HSE and the Health and Safety Commission (HSC) are responsible for the regulation of almost all the risks to health and safety arising from work activity in the UK.

- **Office of Public Sector Information (OPSI)**
  Web: *www.opsi.gov.uk*
  The Office of Public Sector Information (OPSI) — formerly known as Her Majesty's Stationery Office (HMSO) — provides online access to UK legislation, licenses the re-use of Crown copyright material, manages the Information Fair Trader Scheme, maintains the Government's Information Asset Register and provides advice and guidance on official publishing and Crown copyright.

Contract Terms

> This topic covers the following.
> - Express Terms
> - Implied Terms
> - Employer's Common Law Duties
> - Employee's Duties
> - Mutual Duties
> - Discretionary Terms
> - Written Particulars of Terms of Employment
> - Complaint to Tribunal
> - Procedures on Dispute Resolution
> - Other Common Contract Terms

2.228 Contract terms can be implied, express or discretionary.
- Express terms are those that are specifically agreed between the employer and employee. Express terms are the key terms of the contract and will prevail, unless the terms are void because they limit or restrict a statutory right or they are contrary to public policy.
- Implied terms are terms that are not mentioned or written down, but are implied into the contract; eg by custom and practice, conduct, statute or common law.
- Discretionary terms are binding but allow the employer a certain amount of discretion to change them. However unless they are drafted with great care, discretionary terms can lead to disputes that only a tribunal or court can resolve.

2.229 All new employees whose employment continues for one month or more, are entitled to receive a written statement of particulars of employment. The employer must provide the statement no later than two months after the employee's start date.

2.230 Any employee who has not been given a statement, or who thinks a statement given is incorrect or incomplete, may complain to an employment tribunal within three months of the employer's failure to provide the statement.

2.231 A complaint may be made at any time while the employment continues, and up to three months after it ends. The three-month period may be extended if the tribunal is satisfied that it was not reasonably practicable to present the application within the period.

Employers' Duties

2.232 Employers have a duty to:
- provide eligible employees with a written statement of particulars within two months of commencing employment
- provide reasonable notice
- pay wages
- indemnify employees against expenses and liabilities incurred in the course of employment
- take reasonable care for the safety of employees
- maintain a relationship of mutual trust and confidence.

Employees' Duties

2.233 Employees have a duty to:
- be ready and willing for work
- use reasonable skill and care in the performance of duties
- take reasonable care of property entrusted to them in the course of employment
- obey reasonable orders, ie those that are not unlawful or dangerous
- act in good faith, eg not divulge confidential information to third parties and not compete with the employer
- maintain a relationship of mutual trust and confidence.

In Practice

2.234 Contract terms can be:
- implied
- express, or
- discretionary.

Express Terms

2.235 Express terms are those that are specifically agreed between the employer and employee.

2.236 These may be:
- oral terms, eg agreed at the time of making the job offer over the telephone, or
- written terms, eg those set out in various documents, such as an offer letter or the contract of employment.

2.237 Express terms are the key terms of the contract. They will prevail, unless they are:
- void because they limit or restrict a statutory right
- contrary to public policy.

2.238 Oral express terms are difficult to prove and can lead to problems when written documents differ from what was agreed orally. In such a situation, the precedence is dependent on whether the job was offered and accepted (and the contract formed) before the documents were issued. Employers should, therefore, always put oral express terms into writing as soon as possible, in order to avoid any problems later in an employment relationship.

2.239 An express term can be used to prevent oral representations acquiring contractual status — and are best professionally drafted.

2.240 It is possible that express terms are not written in the statement of particulars or contract of employment itself, but are instead incorporated into the statement or contract from another document, eg an employee handbook, policy or collective agreement.

2.241 If an employer does not intend to incorporate an entire document into the contract, it should make clear which parts of the document should be considered

Contract Terms

contractual and which parts should not. For example, a statement of particulars that mentions an employee handbook should specify the parts of the employee handbook that are relevant to the contract if the whole book is not to be considered contractual.

2.242 Employers should ensure that the terms of the incorporated document do not differ from the terms in the statement of particulars, and that all employees are aware of any incorporated terms (see *Scally UK Ltd v Lee*).

Implied Terms

2.243 Implied terms are terms that are not mentioned or written down, but are implied by the contract. This could be by:
- custom and practice
- conduct
- statute
- common law.

2.244 For example, if no written term on breaks exists, the custom of taking a one-hour stoppage at lunchtime may imply entitlement to a paid lunch break.

2.245 Terms can also be incorporated by statute. For example, the Equal Pay Act 1970 has the effect of implying an equality clause into every contract of employment. This ensures that men and women receive pay for equal work in circumstances prescribed by the Act.

2.246 An employer cannot override statutory rights with a term in an employee's contract of employment. So, for example, an employer cannot include a term allowing for payment below the National Minimum Wage or employment without the minimum required breaks. Any such contractual terms will generally be deemed void and illegal.

2.247 There are also a number of common law rights and duties that are implied into every contract of employment. Some common law duties apply to both parties, others only apply to one party.

Employer's Common Law Duties

Duty to Pay Wages

2.248 Wages are part of the "consideration" necessary for an employment contract to be formed and an employer has a duty to pay them. Failure to do so will be a breach of contract. Generally the amount and the method of payment is expressly agreed between the employer and the employee. Failure to pay wages will amount to an unlawful deduction of wages.

Duty to Provide Work

2.249 There is no general duty on an employer to provide work to an employee, provided the employer pays the employee. An obligation may arise in certain cases, however, such as where:
- pay is dependent on work done (eg piece work)
- a failure to be working has an adverse effect on an employee's reputation (eg actors and musicians).

Duty of Care

2.250 An employer has an implied duty to take reasonable care of an employee's safety. Although this common law duty has now been largely overtaken by a substantial body of health and safety legislation, it nevertheless remains in place.

Duty to Pay Costs and Expenses

2.251 There is a duty on the employer to indemnify employees against costs incurred in carrying out their duties (eg travel expenses and cost of equipment). The extent of this duty depends on the seniority and type of employee concerned.

Duty to Provide a Reasonable Period of Notice

2.252 If an employment contract does not contain any provisions setting out what notice must be given to terminate the employment, common law will imply a term that the employee is entitled to reasonable notice. For senior employees what is "reasonable" may substantially exceed the statutory minimum.

Employee's Duties

Duty to Obey the Employer's Orders

2.253 The employee must obey the employer's instructions provided these are reasonable, lawful and are not beyond the scope of the contract.

Duty to Work with Reasonable Care and Skill

2.254 The employee must take reasonable care to ensure the work performed for the employer is carried out safely and efficiently.

Duty to be Loyal

2.255 The employee must not behave dishonestly or compete with the employer.

Mutual Duties

2.256 Employers and employees have a duty to act reasonably towards one another, with mutual trust and confidence. A contract can be breached if either party acts in a way that makes the employment relationship impossible to continue. If the employer's conduct seriously damages or destroys the relationship of trust and confidence, employees may be entitled to resign and consider themselves constructively dismissed (see *Malik v BCCI SA (in compulsory liquidation)*).

Discretionary Terms

2.257 Discretionary terms are binding but allow the employer a certain amount of freedom to change them. However, even if certain terms are stated to be wholly discretionary, eg a bonus clause in which the amount is decided at the employer's absolute discretion, a term may still be implied that the discretion will not be exercised irrationally or capriciously.

Written Particulars of Terms of Employment

General Obligations

2.258 All new employees whose employment continues for one month or more are

Contract Terms

entitled to receive a written statement of particulars of employment. The employer must provide the statement no later than two months after the employee's start date.

2.259 The statement must include the following key information.
- The names of the employer and employee.
- The date when employment began.
- The date on which the employee's period of continuous employment began (taking into account any employment with a previous employer that counts).
- The scale or rate of pay, or the way pay is calculated.
- The pay intervals (ie whether the employee will be paid hourly, weekly, monthly, etc).
- Terms and conditions relating to hours of work (including normal working hours, if applicable).
- Terms and conditions relating to holiday entitlement including public holidays and holiday pay (enough information must be given to enable entitlement to be calculated precisely).
- Job title or a brief job description.
- Place of work or, if the employee is required or permitted to work at various places, an indication of that fact and the employer's address.

2.260 The employer must also provide the following written particulars within the two-month period (either in further instalments or with the principal statement).
- Any terms and conditions relating to sickness/injury, including sick pay.
- Details relating to pensions and pension schemes, including whether or not employment is contracted out of the state pension scheme.
- Length of notice to be given to terminate the employment contract by both employer and employee.
- If the contract is temporary, an indication of the expected duration of the contract, or, if the contract is for a fixed term, the date when it is to end.
- Particulars of any collective agreements that directly affect the terms and conditions of the employment including, where the employer is not a party, the persons by whom they were made.
- Where the employee is required to work outside the UK for a period of more than one month details of the length of the posting, the currency in which payment will be made, details of any additional benefits arising from the posting and any terms and conditions relating to the employee's return to the UK.
- A note on disciplinary and grievance procedures, including:
  - any disciplinary rules applicable (it is usual to refer to a separate document or an employee handbook)
  - the name (or description) of the person to whom an employee can apply if dissatisfied with a disciplinary decision and the manner in which such applications can be made
  - the name or description of the person with whom the employee can raise a grievance and the manner in which such applications should be made
  - an explanation of any additional steps in the disciplinary or grievance procedures.

2.261 The written statement can refer employees to another document for particulars on:
- sickness
- pensions
- disciplinary rules and the various steps in the disciplinary and grievance procedures.

2.262 However, it is important that employees have a reasonable opportunity to read the reference document. For example, while it may not be necessary for all employees to have a copy of an employee handbook, it is essential that the handbook be easily accessible and readily available.

Complaint to Tribunal

2.263 Any employee who has not been given a statement, or who thinks a statement given is incorrect or incomplete, may complain to an employment tribunal within three months of the employer's failure to provide the statement.

2.264 A complaint may be made at any time while the employment continues and up to three months after it ends. The three-month period may be extended if the tribunal is satisfied that it was not reasonably practicable to present the application within the period.

2.265 A tribunal may:
- confirm the particulars as they stand, amend them or substitute others as it thinks appropriate (the original statement given by the employer is then deemed automatically to include the tribunal's alterations)
- determine the particulars that ought to have been given (it can only declare those terms and conditions it believes the parties agreed to; it is not entitled to set any for itself)
- make an increased financial award of between two and four weeks' pay if the employee is also bringing a claim of unfair dismissal or discrimination.

Procedures on Dispute Resolution

2.266 Under Part 3 of the Employment Act 2002, statutory dismissal and disciplinary procedures came into effect from 1 October 2004. These procedures affect all employers.

2.267 The procedures must be followed in all cases when a dismissal could be the result. Therefore they must be followed not only when managing a disciplinary process but also when dealing with redundancies, performance management issues and the expiry of fixed term contracts.

Other Common Contract Terms

2.268 Most contracts of employment will make reference to a number of terms other than those that must be included in the written particulars. Some of the more common terms are discussed in the topic Common Clauses.

List of Relevant Legislation

2.269
- Employment Act 2002
- National Minimum Wage Act 1998
- Working Time Regulations 1998
- Employment Rights Act 1996
- Trade Union and Labour Relations (Consolidation) Act 1992

List of Relevant Cases

2.270
- *Kerry Foods Ltd v Lynch* [2005] IRLR 680 EAT
- *Royal National Lifeboat Institution v Bushaway* [2005] IRLR 674, EAT
- *Scully UK Ltd v Lee* [1998] IRLR 259, CA
- *Malik v BCCI SA (in compulsory liquidation)* [1997] IRLR 462, HL
- *Meade-Hill v British Council* [1995] IRLR 478
- *Scally v Southern Health and Social Services Board* [1991] IRLR 522, HL
- *United Bank Ltd v Akhtar* [1989] IRLR 507
- *Faccenda Chicken Ltd v Fowler and Others* [1986] IRLR 69, CA
- *Western Excavating (ECC) Ltd v Sharp* [1978] IRLR 27, CA

Further Information

Publications
- FSA's *Factsheet: Challenging Unfair Contract Terms*

Organisations
- **Department for Business, Enterprise and Regulatory Reform (BERR)**
  Web: *www.berr.gov.uk*
  The Department for Business, Enterprise and Regulatory Reform brings together functions from the former Department of Trade and Industry (DTI), including responsibilities for productivity, business relations, energy, competition and consumers. It also drives regulatory reform.
- **Employment Lawyers Association**
  Web: *www.elaweb.org.uk*
  The Employment Lawyers Association's members are qualified barristers and solicitors who practice employment law in the UK, and organisations engaged in the practice of employment law.

Data Protection

This topic covers the following.
- Conditions for Processing Personal Data
- Processing of Sensitive Personal Data
- Data Controller
- Penalties
- Applications
- Verifying Applicants' Claims
- Shortlisting
- Pre-employment Vetting
- Retention of Recruitment Records
- Collecting and Storing Records
- Sickness and Accident Records
- Pension and Insurance Schemes
- Equal Opportunities Monitoring
- Fraud Detection
- Workers' Access to Own Information
- Employment References
- Disclosure Requests
- Mergers and Acquisitions
- Discipline, Grievance and Dismissal
- Outsourcing Data Processing
- Retention of Records
- Employee Monitoring
- Medical Records

2.271 The Data Protection Act 1998 came into force on 1 March 2000 and aims to balance the entitlement of organisations to collect, store and manage various types of personal data, with the privacy rights of the individual about whom the data is held. It introduced the principles of good practice, a registration system, an independent supervisory authority and the data subject's right to access personal data held about him or her and have inaccuracies corrected or removed.

2.272 The Act covers manual and computerised records and processing data related to identifiable living individuals. It gives individuals certain rights, and requires decision-makers to be open about processing and to comply with the data protection principles.

2.273 The Information Commissioner's Office is charged with oversight of the Act and has published codes of practice on:
- recruitment and selection
- employment records
- monitoring at work
- information about workers' health.

2.274 All four sections are now available under the Employment Practices Code. The Information Commissioner also supplies a guide to the code entitled "A Quick Guide to the Employment Practices Code".

Employers' Duties

2.275 Employers have a duty to:
- give accurate information if they decide to supply a reference for an employee/ex-employee
- only request personal data from employees that is relevant and not excessive in relation to the purpose it was requested for
- not retain personal data for longer than is necessary
- update personal data where necessary to ensure the information is accurate
- put in place technical and organisational measures against unauthorised access
- arrange safeguards to prevent the accidental loss, destruction or damage of data
- not process data without the employees' explicit consent, except where there is a legal obligation on the employer to do so or a number of other exceptions apply
- not process sensitive personal data without first satisfying the legal requirements
- request permission from the employees when obtaining third party records, eg medical records
- supply personal data to an employee on request.

Employees' Duties

2.276 Employees have a duty to:
- not provide information that is misleading or inaccurate
- only request to see information that is personal data.

In Practice

Conditions for Processing Personal Data

2.277 Personal data is information which relates to a living person. It covers all computerised and automated data and data held on paper or microfiche in any relevant filing system. (See *Durant v Financial Services Authority,* Court of Appeal, 2003.)

2.278 Processing of personal data includes obtaining, keeping, using, accessing, disclosing and destroying data andmay only be carried out when one of the following conditions has been satisfied.
- The individual has given consent.
- It is necessary for the performance of a contract with the individual, such as to make payments.
- There is a legal obligation on the employer, such as to comply with Statutory Sick Pay (SSP) or PAYE.
- It is necessary to protect the vital interests of the individual.
- It is necessary to carry out public functions.
- It is necessary to pursue the legitimate interests of the data controller.

- It is necessary for the administration of justice.
- It is necessary for the exercise of any functions conferred by or under any enactment.

Processing of Sensitive Personal Data

2.279 Sensitive personal data relates to:
- ethnic or racial origin
- political opinions
- religious or other similar beliefs
- trade union membership
- physical or mental health
- sexual life
- the commission or alleged commission of any offence and any related proceedings or sentence.

2.280 Processing of sensitive data is only permitted where:
- the individual has given his or her explicit consent to the processing
- it is necessary to protect the vital interests of the individual or another person, in cases where consent either cannot be given, has been unreasonably refused or where the employer cannot reasonably be expected to get consent
- it may be carried out by a non-profit-making body which exists for philosophical, political or trade union purposes
- the data has already been made public by the subject
- it is necessary in connection with actual or prospective legal proceedings
- it is necessary for the administration of justice
- it is necessary for medical purposes and is carried out by someone with a duty of confidentiality
- it is necessary for equal opportunity monitoring and the data relates to racial or ethnic origin.

Data Controller

2.281 In a limited company the Data Controller is the organisation, but in partnerships or sole traders it is the owners. Large employers should allocate responsibility for compliance with the Data Protection Act to a specific person or department.

2.282 Data Controllers must notify the Commissioner they are processing personal data.

Penalties

2.283 Failure to process any personal data in a fair and proper way can lead to a criminal offence or a claim for compensation.

2.284 The Data Protection Codes state what employers need to check and what action they need to take. They cover how workers should be treated relating to:
- recruitment and selection
- employment records
- employee monitoring
- medical records.

Data Protection

2.285 Workers includes job applicants and employees, both current and former, agency, casual and contract workers. It may also include volunteers and work experience personnel. Most information about workers is likely to fall under the Act.

Applications

2.286 There are certain data protection considerations that should be observed in the recruitment and selection process. When advertising a vacancy, the advertisement or the agency should state the employer's name and how the information provided by job applicants will be used.

2.287 When dealing with job applications, including curriculum vitae and unsolicited applications, employers should:
- state who will receive information and how it will be used
- only obtain relevant/necessary personal data
- only seek information about criminal convictions if justified by the role
- tell candidates what checks will be undertaken, eg references, qualifications and health checks
- in the case of sensitive data, ensure that at least one sensitive data condition is satisfied
- provide confidential means of sending/receiving applications.

Verifying Applicants' Claims

2.288 When verifying candidates' claims through references, verifying qualifications and financial information, employers should:
- explain what checks they intend to make
- obtain consent before obtaining third party records
- seek candidate's comments if discrepancies show up
- only seek verification on a need-to-know basis.

Shortlisting

2.289 When shortlisting applicants, employers should:
- use personal data consistently
- tell candidates if only automated shortlisting is used and allow them to comment on results
- ensure psychological testers are fully trained.

2.290 Following interviews of candidates, the employer should ensure that any personal data retained afterwards are necessary for justifying the selection decision.

Pre-employment Vetting

2.291 Employers should take care when carrying out pre-employment checks as it may seem intrusive. It is advisable to carry out checks only where:
- employer, clients or customers may be at significant risk and there is no alternative
- a candidate has been offered the position
- candidates have been informed that the checks will be carried out
- information sought has been specified
- reliable sources have been used
- exceptionally, the family needs to be approached

Data Protection

- the person's consent to approaching third parties has been obtained
- medical checks are required.

Retention of Recruitment Records

2.292 Employers should consider the following guidance when retaining records relating to recruitment.
- Formulate criteria on clear business basis.
- Destroy vetting information within six months, retaining only the result.
- Keep only necessary information on a successful candidate's record.
- Delete information about criminal convictions once verified by Criminal Records Bureau, unless strictly necessary for ongoing relationship.
- Securely store or delete personal data.

2.293 Consideration should be given to whether the data is classed as sensitive personal data. This could include:
- candidates' competencies with respect to safe systems of working
- the reliability of recruits who will have access to personal data
- avoiding discrimination on the grounds of race, sex, sexual orientation, disability or religion/belief or age
- immigration status.

Collecting and Storing Records

2.294 When collecting and keeping employment records:
- inform new workers what is held, its source and how it will be used and/or disclosed
- inform all workers about access rights to their own data and whether a fee will be charged
- collect and hold only necessary and relevant information
- allow workers to verify and amend their own data
- take measures to ensure accuracy of all personal data held
- prevent unauthorised access, accidental loss, damage and destruction
- use audit trails for tracking
- train staff in understanding confidentiality
- put clauses in the contracts of employees involved in accessing personal data, requiring them to comply with the provisions of the Data Protection Acts
- write rules for records which leave site, eg on laptops
- assess the risks of using faxes and emails and use encryption for security.

Sickness and Accident Records

2.295 When keeping sickness and accident records on employees, the following should be observed.
- Separate sickness and accident records from absence records and only use sickness or accident records if essential.
- Protect accident logs from unauthorised viewing.
- Satisfy conditions for use of sensitive data.
- Only disclose data when legally obliged or explicit consent is given.
- Only make data available on a need-to-know basis.

Pension and Insurance Schemes

2.296 When handling data relating to pensions or insurance schemes, the following best practice should be observed.
- Do not use third party data (eg a pension provider's), information from trustees, or medical insurance information for general employment purposes.
- Limit information exchange with the scheme provider to that needed to satisfy funding obligations.
- Advise workers joining health or insurance schemes on what information will be passed to scheme administrators.

Equal Opportunities Monitoring

2.297 When performing equal opportunities monitoring, employers should be aware that:
- the information is likely to be sensitive personal data, so conditions apply
- the monitoring should be anonymous where practicable
- personal information ought to be accurate and not excessive in relation to its purpose.

Fraud Detection

2.298 Where electronic data matching is involved, consult trade unions and inform workers that payroll information might be used.

2.299 Only disclose data if:
- it is legally required
- failure to disclose might prejudice the prevention or detection of crime
- employment contracts permit it.

Workers' Access to Own Information

2.300 All workers, ex-workers and job applicants have the right to request the employer for access to any specified personal data held about them. Personal data includes details of:
- sickness
- discipline
- training
- appraisal
- emails
- word-processed documents
- email logs
- audit trails
- information on personnel files
- interview notes.

2.301 In order to prepare for this, employers should:
- install manual and computerised systems to enable location and supply of all information about a worker within 40 days
- tell workers what automatic decision-making is used.

2.302 Employers may charge up to £10 each time for access. Responding to employee requests for data should involve:

- checking who is seeking information
- telling the worker if personal information is kept about him or her
- describing it, how it is used and who it may be passed to
- providing the information in an appropriate form
- disclosing the information source.

2.303 Employees have the right to obtain access to personal data except where the information is:
- for management forecasting including succession planning or redundancy
- about intentions in negotiations or bargaining
- given in confidence in a reference
- held for the prevention or detection of crime or for assessment or collection of tax.

Employment References

2.304 Employment references usually involve disclosing personal data to prospective employers, landlords or financial institutions. Employers should:
- devise a policy on the giving and receiving of references
- define who may give references and policy on access
- obtain consent from the individual concerned before requesting or providing references
- determine when workers may see received references.

2.305 Workers have no right to see references from the provider, but may access them via the recipient, who should either obtain the author's consent to disclosure or conceal the author's identity before disclosure.

Disclosure Requests

2.306 If disclosure is not legally necessary, employers' primary duty of care is to workers. Employers should establish:
- a clear policy about who may respond to requests
- what to do about those falling outside the policy, eg in an emergency
- a method to detect deception that might be used to obtain unauthorised disclosure.

Mergers and Acquisitions

2.307 When handling personal data relating to mergers and acquisitions, employers should:
- supply anonymous information about the employees to the potential purchaser
- before final agreement, supply personal information only for evaluation purposes in confidence
- advise workers about extent of disclosure, certainly if the merger/acquisition proceeds
- ensure compliance with sensitive personal data conditions
- ensure proper basis to transfer any information outside of the EEA.

Discipline, Grievance and Dismissal

2.308 Workers may access information about themselves on discipline, grievance and dismissal, unless a crime is being investigated. However, employers should:

- not use obtained information about an employee for any purpose other than the one for which it was obtained
- be proportionate about the seriousness of the matter being investigated
- adopt clear procedures about disposing of "spent" warnings
- keep accurate records of reasons for leaving, especially if dismissed.

Outsourcing Data Processing

2.309 When outsourcing data processing, usually from the payroll department, employers should:
- ensure data processors have sound security
- obtain written agreement for compliance with the Data Protection Act
- ensure proper basis for any data transfer outside the EEA
- comply with sensitive personal data conditions.

Retention of Records

2.310 Records should only be kept for the minimum period necessary for particular purposes. Statutory requirement for wages records is seven years; statutory maternity pay (SMP) and statutory sick pay (SSP) is three years and health and safety (eg accident logs) must be kept for three years. In addition, employers should:
- establish policies for the retention of different types of information based on business needs
- make information anonymous wherever possible
- delete any information about "spent" convictions at the appropriate time
- dispose of information securely and effectively.

Employee Monitoring

2.311 Workers may be monitored:
- for quality control
- to ensure safe working
- to identify training needs
- to ensure proper use of the employer's computer system
- for financial or security reasons.

2.312 Any adverse impact of monitoring involving manual recording or automated processing must be justified. Employers should carry out impact assessments to evaluate whether the potential infringement of the individual's privacy is justified by a benefit to the business.

2.313 The purpose of monitoring should be clear and all workers informed about the purpose, extent and types of monitoring the employer carries out. Employees have a reasonable expectation that private calls and emails will not be monitored.

2.314 Electronic, video and audio monitoring may be systematic (eg of emails or the organisation's drivers), or occasional (eg by covert CCTV). Employers should:
- devise policies on the use of telephones (including mobiles), voicemail, email, Internet and the organisation's vehicles
- define disciplinary penalties
- assess the impact of proposed monitoring, balancing employee privacy with the employer's need to know
- publicise purposes of monitoring and ensure minimal intrusion

- authorise covert monitoring at very senior level only if crime or fraud is suspected
- not use information about workers obtained from other sources, unless justified by risk to the business
- train the people carrying out the monitoring.

Medical Records

2.315 Processing of medical records is governed by sensitive personal data requirements.

2.316 Information from health questionnaires about disabilities, eye tests, blood type, tests to check for substance abuse or genetic tests may be held electronically or in a filing system. Employers should observe the following best practice.
- Identify policies and procedures considering use, relevance and extent of information obtained.
- Publicise the policies and procedures in the staff handbook and link with disciplinary rules.
- Ensure that only necessary information is requested.
- Separate health information from other records.
- Do not hold information obtained for pensions or insurance purposes.
- Receive employees' consent for testing, recording, use and disclosure of results.
- Inform workers how occupational health information will be used.
- Ensure that all information is confidentially treated by health professionals.
- Set out purpose of examination and testing, eg
  - for assessing fitness for work
  - to meet legal requirements
  - to detect alcohol or drug use
  - to prevent a significant risk to health and safety
  - to determine entitlement to sick pay
  - to prevent discrimination on grounds of disability.
- Ensure that any testing is carried out competently.

Training

2.317 Employers should understand both corporate responsibilities and the rationale behind data protection legislation. Although the legal responsibilities of the Data Controller cannot be delegated, a senior person or department should have devolved responsibility. He or she should ensure that line managers become familiar with policy and procedures, including responsibilities of third parties such as contractors and agencies. An in-house training session will ensure that managers:
- understand the law surrounding data protection and legal obligations, including the principles and the overriding need for proportionality
- understand the employer's policy and procedure on data protection
- develop awareness of HR policies on recruitment and selection, equal opportunities and record retention, monitoring, etc.

2.318 Data handlers also need to be trained in the principles and practice of data protection. This can also be done in-house on a structured basis. "Barry's Bad Data Day" is an introductory video available free of charge from the Information Commissioner.

List of Relevant Legislation

2.319
- Telecommunications (Lawful Business Practice) Regulations 2000
- Freedom of Information Act 2000
- Regulation of Investigatory Powers Act 2000
- Data Protection Act 1998
- Human Rights Act 1998
- Public Interest Disclosure Act 1998
- Asylum and Immigration Act 1996
- Employment Rights Act 1996
- Access to Medical Reports Act 1988
- Rehabilitation of Offenders Act 1974
- Data Protection Directive 95/46/EC
- EC Convention on Human Rights and Fundamental Freedoms 1950

List of Relevant Cases

2.320
- *Durant v Financial Services Authority* [2003] EWCA Civ 1746 December 2003, Court of Appeal narrowly interpreted the meanings of "personal data" and a "relevant filing system". This case is currently on appeal to the House of Lords.
- *Halford v United Kingdom* [1997] IRLR 471, ECHR concerned covert interception of private telephone conversations to obtain information about the sex discrimination claim the individual was bringing. Brought under the European Convention on Human Rights, it reinforced an employee's expectation of reasonable privacy at work.

Further Information

Publications
- *B03 Acas Personnel Data and Record Keeping*
- *Conducting an Equal Pay Review in Accordance with Data Protection Act Principles*, Equal Opportunities Commission (EOC)
- *Employment Practices Data Protection Code — Part 1: Recruitment and Selection*, from the Information Commissioner's Office
- *Employment Practices Data Protection Code — Part 2: Employment Records*, from the Information Commissioner's Office
- *Employment Practices Data Protection Code — Part 3: Monitoring at Work*, from the Information Commissioner's Office
- *Employment Practices Data Protection Code — Part 4: Information about Workers' Health*, from the Information Commissioner's Office

- *Responding to an Equal Pay Questionnaire and Requests for Information During Tribunal Procedures in Accordance with Data Protection Act Principles*, Equal Opportunities Commission (EOC)
- *The Employment Practices Code*, from the Information Commissioner's Office, 2005

Organisations

- **Advisory Conciliation and Arbitration Service (Acas)**
  Web: *www.acas.org.uk*
  Acas aims to improve organisations and working life through better employment relations. It provides up-to-date information, advice, high-quality training, and works with employers and employees to solve problems and improve performance.
- **Commission for Racial Equality**
  Web: *www.cre.gov.uk*
  The Commission for Racial Equality is a publicly funded, non-governmental body set up under the Race Relations Act 1976 to tackle racial discrimination and promote racial equality. From October 2007 this organisation will be replaced by the Commission for Equality and Human Rights.
- **Criminal Records Bureau (CRB)**
  Web: *www.crb.gov.uk*
  The CRB — an executive agency of the Home Office — is set up to help organisations make safer recruitment decisions.
- **Disability Rights Commission**
  Web: *www.drc-gb.org*
  An independent body established by Act of Parliament to eliminate discrimination against disabled people and promote quality of opportunity. It provides information and advice to disabled people and employers about their rights and duties. From October 2007 this organisation will be replaced by the Commission for Equality and Human Rights (**Web:** *www.cehr.org.uk*).
- **Equal Opportunities Commission**
  Web: *www.eoc.org.uk*
  An agency working to eliminate sex discrimination and put equality into practice in the workplace. From October 2007 this organisation will be replaced by the Commission for Equality and Human Rights (**Web:** *www.cehr.org.uk*).
- **Health and Safety Executive (HSE)**
  Web: *www.hse.gov.uk*
  The HSE and the Health and Safety Commission (HSC) are responsible for the regulation of almost all the risks to health and safety arising from work activity in the UK.
- **Information Commissioner's Office**
  Web: *www.ico.gov.uk*
  The Information Commissioner enforces and oversees the Data Protection Act 1998 and the Freedom of Information Act 2000. It is an independent UK supervisory authority, reporting directly to the UK Parliament. It has an international role as well as a national one.
- **Office of Public Sector Information (OPSI)**
  Web: *www.opsi.gov.uk*
  The Office of Public Sector Information (OPSI) — formerly known as Her Majesty's Stationery Office (HMSO) — provides online access to UK legislation, licenses the re-use of Crown copyright material, manages the Information Fair Trader Scheme, maintains the Government's Information Asset Register and provides advice and guidance on official publishing and Crown copyright.

Email and Internet

> This topic covers the following.
> - Monitoring Communications
> - The Regulation of Investigatory Powers Act 2000 (RIPA)
> - The Data Protection Act 1998
> - The Human Rights Act 1998
> - Contract Law
> - Copyright
> - Criminal and Other Offences
> - Other Disciplinary Matters
> - Policy on Email and Internet Use

2.321 Email and Internet misuse by employees concerns most organisations. A balance between employee privacy and the risks of computer misuse needs to be found and then employers need to tell employees how and when they can use computers in the workplace. A clear, well-communicated and well-understood policy on the use of email and the Internet is essential to achieve this end.

2.322 The Office of the Information Commissioner has published codes of practice including guidance on monitoring employees in the workplace, based on the Data Protection Act 1998.

Employers' Duties

2.323 Employers should designate a person in the organisation to be responsible for ensuring compliance with the data protection principles. Employers should also ensure that systems provide for an assessment of who has access to data and that this is not excessive. See Data Protection topic for more details.

2.324 Employers should make sure that employees are aware:
- whether there is monitoring of their email and Internet systems
- how this monitoring will be carried out
- that misuse of email or the Internet is a misconduct offence and can also be a criminal offence
- that if email is used to harass others this could lead to dismissal
- that email communications can lead to legally binding agreements
- that if they process information about workers they understand their data protection responsibilities — especially with regard to ensuring the security of the data
- that statements made in emails or posted on Internet sites can give rise to actions for defamation
- that the risks involved in the misuse of the Internet and email are clearly set out in the organisation's policy
- how their particular organisation will ensure the rules on email and Internet use are complied with.

Employees' Duties

2.325 Employees have a duty to do the following.
- Not to forward material which could cause offence.
- Avoid accessing sites which contain obscene images.
- Avoid language in emails that might make or change contracts without the consent of their employer.
- Not to publish defamatory statements on the Internet or by email.
- Not to download copyright material or software without a licence.
- Not to select offensive images as screen savers.
- Not to download computer games or other material from outside sources without prior permission.
- Not to negligently disclose personal information.
- If working at home to ensure that the rules relating to computer systems are followed on home-based systems.

In Practice

Monitoring Communications

2.326 A legal framework now governs the interception of communications. Even where they have legitimate reasons for monitoring employee communications, employers must ensure that their policies and practices do not conflict with the law.

2.327 The relevant legislation is contained in the Regulation of Investigatory Powers Act 2000 (RIPA), especially the Telecommunications (Lawful Business Practice) (Interception of Communications) Regulations 2000. These regulations came into effect on 24 October 2000.

2.328 In general, employers should consider whether monitoring can be done in the least intrusive manner, eg by the use of a record of email traffic rather than by reading email contents. If emails are read, discretion should be exercised, especially where they are marked private and confidential.

2.329 Under this legislation, spot checks are more likely to be justifiable than continuous monitoring. It is not always necessary to open and read emails to establish a breach of policy.

The Regulation of Investigatory Powers Act 2000 (RIPA)

2.330 RIPA makes it illegal to intercept communications unlawfully on a public or private telecommunications system.

2.331 The Telecommunications (Lawful Business Practice) (Interception of Communications) Regulations set out the circumstances where it is lawful for an employer to monitor and record communications without the consent of those involved.

2.332 The regulations state that interceptions are authorised where there are "reasonable grounds to believe that both the sender and the intended recipient have

Email and Internet

consented to that interception". It is usually sufficient for an employer to make reasonable efforts to inform those affected, eg by mentioning monitoring in the organisation's automated signature. Interception can then be allowed in order to:
- establish business related information
- ensure compliance with regulatory or self-regulatory practices
- monitor standards and training
- prevent or detect crime or unauthorised use
- ensure effective operation of the system.

The Data Protection Act 1998

2.333 The employer must also comply with the Data Protection Act 1998 (DPA) when monitoring or recording use of email or the Internet. The DPA sets out the principles by which such information must be processed.

2.334 A relevant Code of Practice was published in 2003.

The Human Rights Act 1998

2.335 Article 8 of the Human Rights Act 1998 (HRA) gives employees a "right to respect for private and family life, home and correspondence". Employers need to consider whether this will be breached by their actions (see *Halford v United Kingdom*).

Contract Law

2.336 It is possible to make a legally binding contract by email in the same way as it is in writing or orally. Employees need to be aware of this as they can inadvertently create contracts with which their employer must comply. Employees can similarly vary the terms of existing contracts unless the contract is drafted in such a way as to prevent this.

Copyright

2.337 Employees must be aware that under the Copyright Designs and Patents Act 1988, digital and electronic publications are protected by copyright, as are websites and software. None of these should be downloaded without the agreement of the copyright holder — unless the employer is licensed to do so.

Criminal and Other Offences

2.338 The Computer Misuse Act 1990 aims to prevent hacking, ie unlawful access to computer programs and data.

2.339 Accessing or downloading certain types of obscene material on the Internet can be seen as criminal behaviour under the Obscene Publications Act 1959, the Protection of Children Act 1988 and the Criminal Justice Act 1988.

2.340 The employer may be liable for defamation if an employee emails or posts a defamatory remark on the Internet. In fact, employers are vicariously liable for all email abuse that takes place on work computers, even where there is no work related reason for the email being sent. See *Moonsar v Fiveways Express Transport Ltd*, *Jones v Tower Boot Co Ltd* and *Chief Constable of the Lincolnshire Police v Stubbs*.

2.341 Offensive email and Internet images may create a hostile work environment and be discriminatory – both the employer and the employee could be liable.

Employees should not make screensavers out of offensive images; nor should they send offensive emails or forward offensive images.

Other Disciplinary Matters

2.342 In order to prevent the transfer of viruses into an employer's computer system, importing information from an outside source without authorisation should probably be stated to be a potential disciplinary offence in the organisation's disciplinary policy.

Policy on Email and Internet Use

2.343 It is difficult to discipline employees who misuse communications systems unless an employer can show that employees knew that their behaviour was unacceptable.

2.344 Employers should ensure that employees are aware of the possible consequences of their action through the publication of a clear policy stating:
- what is required of the employee
- that monitoring and/or recording may take place
- the consequences of breaching policy.

2.345 The policy should:
- make it clear that communications systems are provided to promote effective business communication
- set out the restrictions governing personal use
- make it clear that policies on sexual harassment and discrimination will apply to communications
- inform users that interceptions, monitoring and recording may take place
- give examples of reasons for interceptions, such as ensuring compliance, monitoring standards and preventing or detecting unauthorised use
- make it clear that interceptions will be used to counter legal action against the employer
- make it clear that passwords and terminals are not to be made available to unauthorised persons
- set out the disciplinary consequences of breaching policy
- emphasise that it also applies to home workers.

2.346 It is also a good idea to emphasise email best practice as follows.
- Employees should review the content of all emails they send because emails can easily be misinterpreted.
- Confidential or sensitive matters are best dealt with in person or on the telephone.

Training

2.347 Formal training is recommended so that staff and managers who use email and the Internet are aware of relevant policies. There should be frequent reminders of the rules, especially when compliance proves to be a problem. In disciplinary matters, employers will need to show that they have consistently made individual employees aware of policy.

List of Relevant Legislation

2.348
- Telecommunications (Lawful Business Practice) (Interception of Communications) Regulations 2000
- The Regulation of Investigatory Powers Act 2000
- Data Protection Act 1998
- Human Rights Act 1998
- Computer Misuse Act 1990
- Copyright Designs and Patents Act 1988
- Criminal Justice Act 1988
- Protection of Children Act 1988
- Obscene Publications Act 1959

List of Relevant Cases

2.349
- *Moonsar v Fiveways Express Transport Ltd* [2005]IRLR 9, EAT
- *Chief Constable of the Lincolnshire Police v Stubbs* [1999] IRLR 81
- *Halford v United Kingdom* [1997] IRLR 471, ECHR This case suggests that employees should have reasonable levels of privacy in the workplace and that employers should provide them with access to unmonitored personal communications. It was also suggested that a private staff telephone line be provided.
- *Jones v Tower Boot Co Ltd* [1997] IRLR 168, CA

Further Information

Publications
- *Acas Guide to Internet and Email Policies (2004)*
- *CCTV Data Protection Code of Practice*, from the Information Commissioner's Office www.informationcommissioner.gov.uk/eventual.aspx
- *The Employment Practices Code*, from the Information Commissioner's Office, 2005
- *Employment Practices Data Protection Code — Part 1: Recruitment and Selection*, from the Information Commissioner's Office
- *Employment Practices Data Protection Code — Part 2: Employment Records*, from the Information Commissioner's Office
- *Employment Practices Data Protection Code — Part 3: Monitoring at Work*, from the Information Commissioner's Office
- *Employment Practices Data Protection Code — Part 4: Information about Workers' Health*, from the Information Commissioner's Office

Organisations
- **Advisory Conciliation and Arbitration Service (Acas)**
  Web: *ww.acas.org.uk*
  Acas aims to improve organisations and working life through better employment relations. It provides up-to-date information, advice, high-quality training, and works with employers and employees to solve problems and improve performance.
- **Information Commissioner's Office**
  Web: *www.ico.gov.uk*
  The Information Commissioner enforces and oversees the Data Protection Act 1998 and the Freedom of Information Act 2000. It is an independent UK supervisory authority, reporting directly to the UK Parliament. It has an international role as well as a national one.

Employer/Employee Relationship

> This topic covers the following.
> - Employee, Worker or Self-employed?
> - Who is an Employee?
> - Who is a Worker?
> - What is Self-employment?
> - Employees and Office Holders
> - The Employment Relationship
> - Express and Implied Terms
> - Written Statement of Terms
> - Common Law
> - Statutory Terms
> - Statutory Protection
> - Collective Agreements
> - Permanent Full-Time Contracts
> - Permanent Part-Time Contracts
> - Fixed-Term Contracts
> - Job-share Contracts
> - Temporary Contracts
> - Casual Contracts
> - Agency Workers
> - Overseas Workers
> - Government-sponsored Apprenticeships
> - Young Workers
> - Home Workers
> - Income Tax
> - National Insurance Contributions
> - Part-Time Worker Regulations
> - Fixed-Term Employee Regulations
> - General Protection
> - Wrongful Dismissal
> - Unfair Dismissal Awards
> - Discrimination

2.350 The employer/employee relationship is based on a combination of contract (whether written or oral), common law and statute.

2.351 The existence of an employment contract is a major factor in determining whether or not an individual is an employee or self-employed.

2.352 The Employment Rights Act 1996 sets out the requirement for a written statement of terms and conditions of employment and is the main statute on which the employment relationship is based.

2.353 The Employment Act 2002 has inserted various amendments into the ERA 1996.

2.354 Understanding the employer/employee relationship is vital for the understanding of the duties and obligations owed by employers and is vital for the maintenance of a stable workforce.

Employers' Duties

2.355   Employers have a duty to
- comply with the obligation to pay an employee
- indemnify the employee in respect of expenses and liabilities incurred by the employee in the course of his or her duties
- take reasonable care of the employee's health and safety and working conditions
- ensure that the relationship of trust and confidence between the employer and employee is not destroyed
- take reasonable care in giving references.

Employees' Duties

2.356   Employees have a duty to:
- give personal service — an employee is not allowed to delegate the performance of his or her duties
- obey lawful and reasonable orders from the employer
- exercise reasonable skill and care in the performance of his or her duties
- treat the employer with fidelity and act in good faith.

In Practice

2.357   The growth of flexible working practices and of regulations governing them makes defining the categories of individuals in paid work vitally important.

Employee, Worker or Self-employed?

2.358   Most individuals in paid work are either:
- employees
- workers, or
- self-employed individuals.

2.359   There is often a fine line between the statuses of such individuals. That status can have a huge impact on the obligations owed by individuals in the working relationship.

Who is an Employee?

2.360   An employee is someone who has entered into or works under a contract of employment. To determine in common law whether there is a contract of employment it is necessary to ask three questions.
- Does the person engaging the individual tell him or her what, where, when and how to carry out his or her duties?

Employer/Employee Relationship

- Does the organisation pay the individual in exchange for the individual providing services to the organisation?
- Is there a degree of personal responsibility on the part of the individual for the work carried out?

2.361 "Yes" answers to these questions — while indicative of an employment relationship — are not sufficient for determining the existence of a contract of employment. It is also necessary to determine the exact nature of the relationship between the two parties. Questions providing further clarification include the following.

- Does the individual provide his or her own equipment?
- Does the individual take any degree of financial risk?
- Is the individual allowed to take paid holidays?
- Is the individual subject to disciplinary proceedings?

2.362 If the answers to the first two questions are in the negative and the second two answered positively, there is likely to be an employment relationship in existence. If not, the individual may be self-employed.

Who is a Worker?

2.363 A worker is defined as an individual who:
- has entered into or works under a contract of employment or some other contract, and
- undertakes to do or perform personally any work or services for another party to the contract, but is not self-employed.

2.364 The three definitive factors to look for are whether the individual:
- has a contract (whether written or oral, express or implied)
- is obliged to personally provide services
- is not in business on his or her own account.

2.365 The classic example of a worker is someone who is employed through an agency. There are risks, however, that the traditional agency worker temp might be protected by an employment tribunal as an employee if he or she has been with an organisation for a long period of time. This is because over a period of years the tribunal is prepared to accept that an implied employment contract can build up between the agency worker and the end user *(Dacas v Brook Street Bureau (UK) Ltd [2004])*. Some organisations also use workers on casual or "bank" contracts.

What is Self-employment?

2.366 If an individual does not fall within either of the above categories, he or she is likely to be self-employed. A self-employed individual is:
- somebody who is neither employed nor a worker
- engaged under an agreement traditionally referred to as a "contract for services".

Employees and Office Holders

2.367 There is a further distinction between employees employed under a contract of employment and office holders. Office holders (eg an organisation's directors) are not necessarily employees. The factual details of the relationship should be examined on a case-by-case basis to determine if the individual is also an employee. The greater the control that a director has over an organisation, and the more shares he or she holds the less likely it is that he or she will be found to be an employee by a tribunal.

Why is the Distinction Important?

2.368 The distinction between employees, workers and the self-employed is important because employees have a greater range of rights than the others. Conversely, the employer has more duties to comply with in relation to employees.

2.369 Even when an organisation and individual agree that an individual is a contract worker, that individual may be treated as an employee for tax and/or legal purposes that override any specific contractual arrangements.

2.370 Please see the table below which sets out the statutory rights applicable to employees, workers and the self-employed.

The Employment Relationship

2.371 The main basis of an employment relationship is the terms and conditions of employment between the parties. There is no legal requirement for a contract of employment to be in writing; it can be oral or written or a mixture of both.

2.372 For more information on the employment relationship, refer to the topic on Contracts of Employment.

Express and Implied Terms

2.373 A full written contract of employment contains express (ie written and agreed) terms and conditions. The employment relationship can be subject to terms that are implied by the courts, custom, practice and law. These are called implied terms.

Written Statement of Terms

2.374 In the absence of a written contract of employment, an employer must provide the employee with a written statement of the terms of his or her contract within two months of employment commencing. The statement must contain details of the:
- identity of the parties
- date employment began
- date continuous employment began (taking into account any relevant employment with a previous employer)
- scale or rate of remuneration and intervals of pay
- hours of work
- holidays and holiday pay, sickness and sick pay, pensions and pension schemes
- length of notice required to determine the contract
- period for which non-permanent employment is expected to continue or the date employment is to end if it is fixed term
- job title or a brief description of the work
- place or places of work
- collective agreements which directly affect the terms and conditions of employment
- period of work, currency of payment, benefits and terms relating to return to the UK, applicable where employees are required to work outside the UK for a period of more than one month

- disciplinary rules or reference to where these can be easily found
- person to whom a complaint about the disciplinary procedure or grievance can be made and details of the procedure, or where the procedure can be easily located.

2.375 The written statement must specify if any of these terms do not apply.

2.376 The statement must be given to the employee. The statement may refer the employee to another document, eg a staff handbook, which contains full details of some of the terms that may be too lengthy for the statement.

Common Law

2.377 A duty of trust and confidence is implied in the employment contract. This duty applies to both employer and employee. It is widely applicable and means that rights must be exercised reasonably. For example, even where the employer has an express right to change terms and conditions, this must only be done for a fair reason.

2.378 The main terms implied by common law can be separated into obligations on the employer and those on the employee.

2.379 Terms may be implied into the employment contract where the employer has consistently provided certain benefits or applied certain procedures, eg where an employer has always calculated bonus payments or contractual redundancy payments according to a certain formula (commonly referred to as Custom and Practice).

Statutory Terms

2.380 Statutory minimum requirements override express terms that fall short of the statutory requirements. The statutory entitlements implied in the employment contract are stated in the table of statutory rights below.

Statutory Protection

Statutory Rights	Employees	Workers	Self-employed
Written statement of employment particulars	*		
Itemised pay statement	*		
Protection against unlawful deductions from wages	*	*	
Guarantee payments	*		
Protection in relation to Sunday trading and Sunday betting	*		
Protection for making a protected disclosure	*	*	

Statutory Rights	Employees	Workers	Self-employed
Protection against detriment for exercising rights in respect of: • health and safety cases • Sunday working • trustees of occupational pensions schemes • employee representatives • time off work for study and training • leave for family and domestic reasons • trade union membership • European works council	*		
Protection against detriment for exercising rights in respect of: • working time cases • protected disclosures • National Minimum Wage • part-time work • right to be accompanied	*	*	
Time off work for public duties	*		
Time off work to look for work or arrange training in the event of redundancy	*		
Time off work for ante-natal care	*		
Time off for dependants	*		
Time off for pension trustees	*		
Time off for employee representatives	*		
Time off for young person for study or training	*		
Time off for members of a European Works Council	*		
Remuneration on suspension on medical grounds	*		
Suspension on maternity grounds	*		
Ordinary maternity leave	*		
Additional maternity leave	*		
Parental leave	*		
Right to a minimum period of notice	*		
Written statement for reasons for dismissal	*		
Right not to be unfairly dismissed (or selected for redundancy)	*		
Right to a redundancy payment	*		
Right for an insolvency payment	*		
Protection of acquired rights on the transfer of an undertaking	*		

Statutory Rights	Employees	Workers	Self-employed
Right to be accompanied	*	*	
Right to be informed and consulted through representatives about collective redundancies	*		
Right to holidays under Working Time Regulations	*	*	
Right to the National Minimum Wage	*	*	
Right to rest breaks and to maximum weekly working time	*	*	
Right for part-time workers not to be treated less favourably than comparable full time workers	*	*	
Right to belong or not to belong to a trade union	*		
Time off for carrying out trade union duties	*		
Time off for union activities	*		
Right not to suffer deductions for unauthorised union subscriptions	*		
Right not to be discriminated against on grounds of sex, race, disability, religious belief and sexual orientation and age	*	*	*
Right to paternity leave	*		
Right to adoption leave	*		
Right to dispute resolution procedures	*		
Time off for union learning representatives	*		
Right for fixed term employees not to be treated less favourably than comparable employees in permanent employment	*		
Right to request flexible working for parents of young disabled children	*		

For more information regarding employee's various rights, refer to the topic on.
- Working Time.

Collective Agreements

2.381 Collective agreements between unions and employers are reasonably common in manufacturing industries and in public services. The main issues covered by collective agreements are pay, hours of work, health and safety and disciplinary issues.

Permanent Full-Time Contracts

2.382 Employees under permanent contract are not exempt from dismissal but such contracts do provide a certain amount of job security. Permanent, full-time employees have the benefit of the full range of protective employment legislation. So do temporary part-time employees, provided that they have at least one year's continuous service.

Permanent Part-Time Contracts

2.383 A permanent part-time employee will be entitled to the same benefits as a full-time employee (potentially on a *pro rata* basis) and will have the benefit of protective employment legislation.

Fixed-Term Contracts

2.384 Fixed-term contracts end when a specific period of time expires or a specific task ends. An example of a fixed-term contract is a seasonal worker who will only be working on a farm at harvest time.

2.385 If an employee completes four years' continuous service under a series of consecutive fixed-term contracts, or has his or her fixed-term contract renewed after four years' continuous service on a single contract, the employee will be considered as permanent unless the fixed-term status can be justified.

Job-share Contracts

2.386 Job-share contracts occur where two part timers share one job. Benefits and pay are pro-rated to the number of hours worked. Variations to standard contracts will be necessary and clarification on the following areas is required:
- procedures for work handover
- procedures for covering the absence of one employee
- procedure if one of the employees leaves the organisation or moves to another role
- requirements to attend meetings, courses, etc outside of normal working hours.

Temporary Contracts

2.387 Temporary contracts are no different from open-ended contracts other than that the nature of their work is short term.

2.388 Temporary employees are therefore entitled to the same rights and benefits as permanent employees and may be protected by the Fixed-Term Employees (Prevention of Less Favourable Treatment) Regulations 2002.

Casual Contracts

2.389 Casual contracts are generally used where an employer requires workers to work on an "as and when" basis and are particularly common in the hospitality and catering industries. The workers are not required to be available for work or accept work. As a result there is no mutuality of obligation or continuing contract.

2.390 However, if workers undertake to work on a regular basis, continuity could result or mutuality of obligation could be implied, leading to an employment relationship.

Agency Workers

2.391 The issue of whether agency workers are employed by their agency, their hirer, or indeed by anyone, has been the subject of much case law. Agency workers are not entitled to the benefits enjoyed by employees, other than rights under the Working Time Regulations 1998 and the right to the National Minimum Wage. They are also protected by discrimination legislation.

2.392 Where a worker is taken on from an agency for a short period of time, in general, there are no foreseeable problems. However, where a worker is taken on for a longer length of time (coming up to or over one year) and is treated by management as an employee, the question of employment rights may arise, including the right to claim unfair dismissal.

Overseas Workers

2.393 All overseas workers are entitled to receive a written statement of particulars before they leave the UK. Section 1 of the Employment Rights Act 1996 states that where employees are to be sent abroad for one month or more, the statement of particulars must provide information on:
- the length of the posting
- the currency in which remuneration will be paid
- any benefits or additional remuneration applicable, and
- any terms and conditions relating to the employee's return to the UK.

2.394 Although an employee's service continues to accrue while he or she is working abroad, employers should ensure that they inform employees of any statutory employment rights they currently enjoy which they may not benefit from while working abroad.

Government-sponsored Apprenticeships

2.395 The Government's Apprenticeships are now more common than traditional apprenticeships and involve employees combining on-the-job training with college courses to achieve NVQs or (in Scotland) SVQs. They are available across a wide range of industries and lead to NVQ/SVQ Level 2 qualifications. Advanced Apprenticeships lead to NVQ/SVQ Level 3 qualifications. Apprenticeships were previously only available to people aged 16 to 24, but, following the implementation of the Employment Equality (Age) Regulations 2006 (on 1 October 2006), the Government abolished the upper age limit. In Wales, Scotland and Northern Ireland they are known as Modern Apprenticeships. Each industry has its own apprenticeship route, details of which can be obtained from Learning and Skills Councils (LSCs) and Local Enterprise Companies (LECs) in Scotland. The website *www.apprenticeships.org.uk* provides useful information.

2.396 Note that where an employer is unable to allow the apprentice to complete the training, the apprentice may claim for breach of contract and compensation for the remainder of a period of training, or compensation until the date another training provider is found to enable him or her to continue training. Traditional apprenticeships were protected in this manner, but the Court of Appeal decided in the case of *Flett v Matheson* [2006] IRLR 277, CA that Mr Flett, who was employed under a Modern Apprenticeship in order to qualify as an electrician and who was dismissed by his employer because of a downturn in business during the apprenticeship period, should enjoy similar contractual protection.

2.397 There is no obligation for an employer to provide work for the apprentice at the end of the apprenticeship period, but it is important that the employer is reasonable in this respect. Where, quite clearly, there is a suitable vacancy, the apprentice should be offered a position. It should be remembered that apprentices with over one year's service have the right to claim unfair dismissal.

Young Workers

2.398 Employers must ensure that the law relating to children and young people is complied with when recruiting young persons. Young workers are those who are over the compulsory minimum school leaving age but have not yet reached the age of 18. A child is defined as someone who is under the compulsory minimum school leaving age. The date on which a child is eligible to leave full-time education varies in England and Wales, Scotland and Northern Ireland.

2.399 No child may be employed in any industrial undertaking, in any mine or quarry, or in construction or demolition work, or in any premises, such as a factory or workshop, in which articles are manufactured, altered, cleaned, repaired, ornamented, finished, broken up or demolished, or in which materials are transformed.

2.400 Within seven days of having employed a child, an employer must apply to the relevant local education authority for an Employment Certificate. The authority will forward an application form and a copy of its bylaws on the employment of children.

2.401 It devolves on the employer to inform the parents or guardians of any health and safety risks associated with the type of work in which the child is employed and the steps taken to minimise those risks.

2.402 For more information on employment law regarding young workers, refer to the topic on Working Time.

Home Workers

2.403 Home workers may be on any of the above contracts. It is advisable to establish a policy setting out the employer's expectations and the employee's obligations when working from home. The home worker should be made aware of and comply with standards and rules regarding:

- segregating work from domestic duties
- working only the hours which might be expected of an office worker
- adhering to the employer's guidelines when working on display screen equipment
- reporting all accidents, hazards and near misses to Health and Safety immediately
- maintaining high standards of housekeeping.

Income Tax

2.404 Employees will be taxed on the income earned from their employment. This includes salary and any other payments which have financial value for the employee. The rate of tax deducted is dependent on the level of the employee's salary.

National Insurance Contributions

2.405 Employers have to pay National Insurance contributions in relation to earnings paid to employees. Employees must also pay contributions.

Part-Time Workers Regulations

2.406 The Part-time Workers (Prevention of Less Favourable Treatment) Regulations 2000 apply to workers as well as employees and require that part-time workers are not treated less favourably in their contractual terms and conditions than comparable full-timers, unless the employer can justify the less favourable treatment on grounds of a genuine business objective.

2.407 The contractual benefits covered by the regulations include access to occupational pension schemes. Employers should therefore consider whether the rules of their occupational pension schemes restrict part-timers from becoming members. Employers also need to consider whether employers' contributions to part-timers' pensions are disproportionately less than contributions to full-timers' pensions.

Fixed-Term Employee Regulations

2.408 The Fixed-term Employee (Prevention of Less Favourable Treatment) Regulations 2002 require that fixed term employees (not workers) are not treated less favourably (on a *pro rata* basis) in respect of their contractual terms and conditions (including pension benefits) than comparable permanent employees, unless the employer can objectively justify the treatment.

General Protection

2.409 Employees are entitled to a statutory minimum period of notice. After one month's employment, an employee is entitled to a minimum of one week's notice per complete year of service. This entitlement rises to a maximum of 12 weeks after 12 years' service.

2.410 Employees are eligible for statutory redundancy pay after two years of continuous employment.

2.411 If an individual is transferred to a new business entity, he or she retains continuous employment if the new entity is an associated employer. Associated employers are created when an employer is an organisation controlled by another employer, or where both employers are companies controlled by a third person. The employee also retains continuous employment after the transfer of a business if the TUPE regulations apply.

Wrongful Dismissal

2.412 An employee has the right to bring a claim of wrongful dismissal if an employer acts in breach of either contractual obligations or statutory obligations in respect of notice. An employer will be liable for a claim of damages unless it can establish that it was acting in response to a serious breach of contract by the employee. There is no qualifying period for bringing a claim for wrongful dismissal.

2.413 Employees who have at least one year's continuous employment can claim unfair dismissal. Employers should note that an employment tribunal will add statutory notice to the effective date of a summary dismissal at 51 weeks' continuous service, thereby enabling employees to make an unfair dismissal claim. Such a claim must be brought within three months of the effective date of termination of employment. It is then for the employer to show that the:
- dismissal was for a potentially fair reason
- dismissal was fair in all the circumstances, including the procedure followed leading to the dismissal.

2.414 Potentially fair reasons are set out in the relevant legislation and consist of reasons relating to:
- the capability or qualifications of the employee
- the conduct of the employee
- statutory bar (ie when it would be illegal to continue to employ the individual)
- redundancy

- retirement
- some other substantial reason.

Unfair Dismissal Awards

2.415 If an employee succeeds in a claim for unfair dismissal, the employee is entitled to a basic and a compensatory award. The basic award is calculated by reference to age and length of service (capped at 20 years) and consists of:
- half a week's pay for each complete year of service up to and including the age of 21
- one week's pay per complete year of service between the ages of 22 and 40 inclusive
- one-and-a-half week's pay per complete year of service from age 41.

2.416 A week's pay for these purposes is, for 2007/08, capped at £310 per week.

2.417 The compensatory award is based on losses arising from the dismissal and is subject to a maximum of £60,600 for 2007/08. The maximum compensatory award and the statutory amount of a week's pay are reviewed annually.

2.418 Employees do not need one year's service to claim unfair dismissal if the reason for dismissal is for:
- being a health and safety representative or raising such issues
- being an employee representative
- making a protected disclosure
- asserting a statutory right
- pregnancy
- maternity leave, adoption leave or parental leave, or
- time off for dependants.

Discrimination

2.419 Employees, workers, the self-employed and job candidates are protected against discrimination on the grounds of sex, race, disability, sexual orientation, age and religion or belief. Discrimination legislation also covers protection from harassment and victimisation. Compensation for discrimination is based on financial losses and emotional impact (injury to feelings) and is unlimited.

2.420 For more information, refer to the topic on Discrimination and Equality.

Training

2.421 Employers are advised to ensure that human resources staff are fully trained in the necessity of providing the correct contract of employment to employees.

2.422 To ensure the employer/employee relationship is not breached, managers should be made aware of employees' protection from unfair or wrongful dismissal.

2.423 All employees should receive awareness training regarding discrimination in the workplace and the consequences of such behaviour.

List of Relevant Legislation

2.424

- Employment Equality (Age) Regulations 2006
- Employment Equality (Religion or Belief) Regulations 2003
- Employment Equality (Sexual Orientation) Regulations 2003
- Fixed-term Employees (Prevention of Less Favourable Treatment) Regulations 2002
- Part-time Workers (Prevention of Less Favourable Treatment) Regulations 2000
- Working Time Regulations 1998
- Employment Relations Act 2004
- Employment Act 2002
- Employment Rights Act 1996
- Disability Discrimination Act 1995
- Race Relations Act 1976
- Sex Discrimination Act 1975

List of Relevant Cases

2.425

- *Flett v Matheson* [2006] IRLR 277, CA
- *Dacas v Brook Street Bureau (UK) Ltd* [2004] IRLR 358, CA
- *Franks v Reuters Ltd* [2003] IRLR 423, CA
- *Scally v Southern Health and Social Services Board* [1991] IRLR 522, HL
- *Robertson and Jackson v British Gas Corporation* [1983] IRLR 302, CA
- *Liverpool City Council v Irwin* [1977] AC 239

Further Information

Organisations

- **Advisory Conciliation and Arbitration Service (Acas)**
  Web: *www.acas.org.uk*
  Acas aims to improve organisations and working life through better employment relations. It provides up-to-date information, advice, high-quality training, and works with employers and employees to solve problems and improve performance.
- **Department for Business, Enterprise and Regulatory Reform (BERR)**
  Web: *www.berr.gov.uk*
  The Department for Business, Enterprise and Regulatory Reform brings together functions from the former Department of Trade and Industry (DTI), including responsibilities for productivity, business relations, energy, competition and consumers. It also drives regulatory reform.

- **Employment Tribunals**
  Web: *www.employmenttribunals.gov.uk*
  Contains useful information about employment tribunals, which resolve disputes between employers and employees over employment rights.

Employment Agencies and Employment Businesses Regulations

> This topic covers the following.
> - Introduction
> - Industrial Disputes
> - Payment of Workers
> - Restrictions on Fees Charged to Work-Seekers
> - Restrictions on Charges to Employers
> - Terms and Conditions between Employment Business or Agency and Hirer
> - Information to be Provided by the Hirer to an Employment Agency or Business
> - Information to be Provided by the Employment Agency or Business to the Hirer
> - Implied Contracts of Employment — Employment Agencies
> - Prohibition Orders

2.426 The Conduct of Employment Agencies and Employment Businesses Regulations 2003 came into effect on 6 April 2004. As the purpose of the regulations is to govern the conduct of the private recruitment industry, employers do not need to be familiar with the regulations in their entirety. However, as more and more employers seek to recruit temporary or permanent staff through employment agencies or businesses it is important that they are aware of the minimum standards that they can expect under the regulations, as well as what their obligations to the recruitment agency or business and the work-seeker are.

2.427 In addition to these regulations, employment agencies and businesses are expected, as are employers, to follow equality of opportunity legislation and treat work-seekers and workers in a fair manner.

Employers' Duties

2.428 Employers have a duty to:
- recognise the differences between employment agencies and employment businesses
- provide the employment agency or business with the information it requires on the position or positions available
- understand that where permanent workers are taken on that they are responsible for paying workers' remuneration and any applicable statutory benefits
- ensure that they do not directly or indirectly pay temporary workers' pay or benefits
- be aware of any charges that may be applicable to them under their agreement with the agency or business.

In Practice

Introduction

2.429 When seeking temporary or permanent staff through the private recruitment industry, employers will either use an employment business or an employment agency.

2.430 An employment business will normally supply an employer (the hirer) with temporary workers. The employment business engages work-seekers under either contracts for services or contracts of employment. While the work-seekers are working for the hirer, however, they are under the hirer's supervision or control.

2.431 An employment agency, on the other hand, will introduce work-seekers to employers for direct employment by that employer in permanent (or fixed-term) positions.

2.432 Some recruitment organisations will be involved in the supply of both temporary workers and permanent recruitment and will therefore fall under the definition of both an employment agency and an employment business. The Conduct of Employment Agencies and Employment Businesses Regulations 2003 require agencies and employment businesses to provide employers with clear terms setting out under which capacity they are operating in relation to the service being provided at the time.

Industrial Disputes

2.433 Employers sometimes seek temporary staff to replace employees taking part in an official strike. Employment businesses may not provide employers with workers in these circumstances, nor may they provide an employer with workers to cover the work of someone who has been transferred by the employer to perform the duties of an employee who is on strike or taking industrial action. There are, however, no restrictions on employment businesses supplying staff to replace employees involved in unofficial strike action.

Payment of Workers

2.434 As only employment businesses, as opposed to employment agencies, may provide an employer with temporary workers, the employment business is responsible for the worker's pay and any statutory benefits such as holiday pay.

2.435 An employer that takes on temporary workers via an employment business is not obliged to pay the worker in question or to provide the worker with any statutory benefits. This is the sole responsibility of the employment business.

2.436 With regard to permanent workers, however, the regulations specify that where an employment agency provides an employer with a work-seeker it has no responsibility to pay the work-seeker either his or her salary or other statutory benefits. Nor may it directly or indirectly pay workers on behalf of the hirer. In such circumstances, remuneration and benefits are the sole responsibility of the hirer.

Restrictions on Fees Charged to Work-Seekers

2.437 The Employment Agencies Act 1973 prohibits employment agencies and employment businesses from charging fees to individuals seeking work through them. Breach of this prohibition is a criminal offence. The only exceptions to this, where fees may be charged to work-seekers, is in the areas of the entertainment industry, modelling and in relation to au pairs.

2.438 Nevertheless, neither the Employment Agencies Act 1973 nor the Conduct of Employment Agencies and Employment Businesses Regulations 2003 prevent an employment agency or business from charging a work-seeker for ancillary services provided to the individual (eg CV writing, photographic services or training). The regulations do however make it illegal for the employment agency or business to make provision of its work-finding services conditional on the individual using any such ancillary services.

Restrictions on Charges to Employers

2.439 Many employers, after a while, choose to take on temporary workers on a permanent basis. The regulations ensure that employment businesses do not use transfer fees unreasonably as a means of discouraging employers from offering temporary workers permanent employment. The regulations do, however, allow employment businesses to protect their business interests.

Introduction of a Temporary Worker by Employment Business to Hirer — No Supply

2.440 Where there has been an introduction of a temporary worker by an employment business to a hirer but where there has been no supply (ie no actual work has been carried out) any term in a contract between an employment business and a hirer in which it is seeking to charge a transfer fee in a temp-to-perm situation (where a temporary worker is taken on directly by the hirer) or temp-to-temp situations (where a worker is supplied to the same employer by a different employment business), will be unenforceable. The only circumstances where such a term would be enforceable would be where the contract also contains a term giving the employer the option, instead of paying a fee, to choose to have that worker supplied by the employment business for a specified extended period of time, at the end of which he or she will transfer without charge.

Introduction of a Temporary Worker by Employment Business to Hirer — Supply

2.441 Where there has been a supply, ie the temporary worker has carried out work for the hirer, the situation is very similar, although additional restrictions apply.

2.442 Where there has been a supply, an employment business can set out in its agreement with the hirer, transfer fees that would apply in "temp-to-perm" and "temp-to-temp" situations provided that the:
- hirer is given the option to have the worker supplied by the employment business for a specified extended period of hire, at the end of which the worker will transfer without charge instead of paying the transfer fee, and
- transfer takes place within either 14 weeks of the start of the first assignment or within 8 weeks of the end of any assignment, whichever period ends later.

Engagement of a Temporary Worker by a Third Party — Supply

2.443 Where an employment business has supplied a temporary worker to a client and there is a "temp-to-third party" situation (ie the temporary worker is taken on directly by a third party to whom the client introduced him or her), the employment business can charge a transfer fee. However, in order to do so, the employment business must set out in its agreement, the method of calculating the transfer fee in such temp-to-third party situations and ensure that the transfer takes place within either 14 weeks of the start of the first assignment or within 8 weeks of the end of any assignment, whichever period ends sooner.

Terms and Conditions between Employment Business or Agency and Hirer

2.444 The regulations provide that an employment business or agency must, prior to providing the services, agree with the hirer the terms and conditions which will apply between them, including the following.

- Whether the services provided will be that of an employment agency (introduction of permanent workers) or employment business (the supply of temporary workers).
- The details of the fees which may be payable to the employment agency or employment business by the hirer, setting out in particular how such fees are calculated and what refunds or rebates, if any, are payable to the hirer under what circumstances.
- The procedure to be followed if an employment business provides the hirer with an unsatisfactory work-seeker. This should include a timescale by which the hirer must inform the employment business of the work-seeker's unsuitability and what the employment business will do to rectify the situation.

2.445 All the terms between the hirer and the employment agency or employment business must be recorded in a single document and the hirer provided with a copy of the document as soon as is practicable.

2.446 If there are any changes to the agreed terms the agency or employment business must provide the hirer with a document setting out details of the changes and stating the date that the varied terms take effect.

Information to be Provided by the Hirer to an Employment Agency or Business

2.447 In order to select a suitable worker for a hirer, the regulations state that an employment agency or employment business may not introduce or supply a work-seeker until it has obtained the following information from the hirer.

- The identity of the hirer and the nature of the hirer's business (which may include identifying which particular organisation in a group of organisations is the actual hirer).
- The likely start date of the placement and the anticipated duration of the placement.
- The position and the type of work the work-seeker is required to do.
- The work-seeker's place of work.
- The hours the work-seeker would be required to work.
- Any health and safety risks known to the hirer and the steps that the hirer has taken to prevent or minimise the risks.
- What qualifications, experience or training the hirer considers the work-seeker needs to have, or is required to have by law or by the requirements of a professional body in order to successfully carry out the work.
- Any expenses payable by or to the work-seeker, including any expenses incurred in attending interviews prior to the commencement of the placement.

2.448 In the case of employment agencies, the following information must also be obtained from the hirer.

- The minimum rate of pay and benefits offered by the hirer.

- The intervals at which the work-seeker would be paid.
- Where applicable, the length of notice the work-seeker would be required to give (and be entitled to receive) to end his or her employment with the hirer.

Information to be Provided by the Employment Agency or Business to the Hirer

2.449 An employment agency or employment business may not introduce or supply a work-seeker to a hirer without first having obtained confirmation of the following.
- The identity of the work-seeker (in order to do so the agency or business must obtain evidence of identity such as thorough sight of a passport, driving licence or birth certificate).
- That the work-seeker has the experience, qualifications or training that the hirer considers necessary for the work-seeker to successfully perform the job in question, or which the work-seeker is required to have by law or by the requirements of a professional body.
- That the work-seeker is willing to work in the position offered.

2.450 In order to protect both the hirer and the work-seeker the regulations provide that an employment business or agency must carry out all checks to ensure that the work-seeker and the hirer are both aware of any legal or professional body requirements which the work-seeker is required to have in order for the work-seeker to work for the hirer. This of course means that the employment agency or business must have a good knowledge of the sector in which it is operating. The agency or business must keep a record of the fact that these checks were carried out.

2.451 The employment agency or employment business also has an obligation under the regulations to make enquiries to ensure that the placement would not be detrimental to the interests of either the hirer or the work-seeker (eg checking that the hirer is not in financial difficulties or engaged in illegal or immoral activities).

2.452 Where an employment business or agency is introducing or providing the hirer with work-seekers who are to work with vulnerable persons, additional checks must be carried out, namely that the employment business or agency must:
- obtain copies of any relevant qualifications or authorisations that the work-seeker needs in order to work in the position in question
- offer the hirer copies of these
- obtain two references from persons not related to the work-seeker
- confirm that the work-seeker is not unsuitable to work with vulnerable persons.

2.453 Where the employment business or agency, having already taken all reasonable steps, is unable to comply fully with these checks, it must inform the hirer of this.

2.454 The regulations also provide that if an employment business, once having supplied a work-seeker, obtains information to suggest that the work-seeker is unsuitable for the position in which he or she has been placed, it must inform the hirer without delay and end the work placement. An example could be that of a youth worker where it later comes to light that the worker is unsuitable to work with children. "Without delay" is defined in the regulations as the same day or where that is not reasonably practicable on the next business day.

2.455 Where, on the other hand, the employment business receives information that suggests that the work-seeker may be unsuitable, it must inform the hirer and investigate the matter further. Where its investigations find that the work-seeker is, in fact, unsuitable, it must inform the hirer immediately and terminate the placement without delay.

2.456 In relation to an employment agency (as opposed to an employment business) if it receives information within three months of the introduction which suggests that the individual is or may be unsuitable, it must pass that information to the hirer. However, where such information comes to light three months after the date the worker is introduced, the employment agency has no obligation to inform the hirer. There is no definition of what date the "introduction" should be, but the Department for Business, Enterprise and Regulatory Reform (BERR) Guidance suggest interpreting "introduction" as the date the worker is actually employed or engaged by the hirer.

Implied Contracts of Employment — Employment Agencies

2.457 It is important for organisations to bear in mind that, due to a number of recent court decisions, it is now increasingly possible for an individual supplied through an employment business in some circumstances to establish that there is an implied contract of employment between him or her and the end-user. This may particularly be the case if:
- the end user has practical day-to-day control over the individual
- the individual has effectively been treated in a similar manner to permanent employees of the end-user and integrated into the workforce generally; and/or
- the individual is obliged to provide the services personally and no replacement or substitute personnel can be provided.

Prohibition Orders

2.458 The Employment Agencies Act 1973 gives the Secretary of State power to apply to an employment tribunal for an order prohibiting an individual from carrying on an employment agency or business. A tribunal may only make such an order if it is satisfied that the person is unsuitable because of misconduct or any other sufficient reason. Such an order cannot exceed ten years.

Training

2.459 All managers involved in the recruitment of temporary or permanent staff should be made aware of their obligations to employment businesses or agencies; in particular the need to provide employment businesses and agencies with detailed information on the role and the work-seeker required. They should also ensure that they are familiar with the terms and conditions agreed with the agency or business.

List of Relevant Legislation

2.460
- Employment Equality (Age) Regulations 2006
- Conduct of Employment Agencies and Employment Businesses Regulations 2003
- Employment Equality (Religion or Belief) Regulations 2003
- Employment Equality (Sexual Orientation) Regulations 2003
- National Minimum Wage Act 1998

- Disability Discrimination Act 1995
- Race Relations Act 1976
- Sex Discrimination Act 1975
- Employment Agencies Act 1973

List of Relevant Cases

2.461
- *Cable & Wireless plc v Muscat* [2006] IRLR 354, CA
- *Astbury v Gist* (2005) UKEAT/0446/04/LA
- *Bunce v Postworth Ltd t/a Skyblue* [2005] IRLR 557, CA
- *Dacas v Brook Street Bureau (UK) Ltd* [2004] IRLR 358, CA
- *Franks v Reuters Ltd* [2003] IRLR 423, CA

Further Information

Organisations

- **Department for Business, Enterprise and Regulatory Reform (BERR)**
  Web: *www.berr.gov.uk*
  The Department for Business, Enterprise and Regulatory Reform brings together functions from the former Department of Trade and Industry (DTI), including responsibilities for productivity, business relations, energy, competition and consumers. It also drives regulatory reform.
- **Recruitment and Employment Confederation**
  Web: *www.rec.uk.com*
  The Recruitment and Employment Confederation is a body representing the private recruitment industry in the UK.
- **Recruitment Society**
  Web: *www.recruitmentsociety.org.uk*
  The Recruitment Society aims to help everyone with a stake in recruitment by encouraging the exchange of ideas.

Staff Handbooks

This topic covers the following.
- Purpose of the Staff Handbook
- Information and Consultation of Employees Regulations 2004
- Key Terms of Employees' Employment
- Structure of the Handbook
- Format
- Style
- Consultation During Development
- Updating the Handbook
- Content of the Handbook
- Possible Topics
- Equal Opportunities Statement
- Introduction
- About the Organisation
- Terms and Conditions of Employment
- Policies and Procedures

2.462 A staff handbook may be used:
- as a basic point of reference for the benefit of employees on all employment issues
- to act as an aid to communication between employer and employee
- to act as an aid to induction training
- to fulfil statutory requirements.

2.463 A good staff handbook will reflect the ethos and style of a particular organisation and consolidate its organisational values.

2.464 There is no specific legislation on the topic of staff handbooks, although the content is the expression of a combination of good employment practice and statutory obligations.

2.465 Since there are no specific employers' duties in respect of a staff handbook, there is scope for choice and judgment in the purpose, style and content of the final document.

Employers' Duties

2.466 Employers have a duty to:
- give all employees (including part-time employees) who are engaged for more than one month a written statement setting out the main particulars of their employment within two months of starting work
- provide a written health and safety policy when they have five or more employees
- implement a procedure of information and consultation if they have 100 or more employees (50 or more from 6 April 2008) and it is required by their employees.

Employees' Duties

2.467 Employees have a duty to abide by the terms and conditions set out in their contracts of employment, some of which may be contained in the staff handbook.

In Practice

Purpose of the Staff Handbook

2.468 By creating a staff handbook that is a comprehensive resource and then distributing it to employees, the employer will be providing:
- readily available, relevant and accurate information on terms and conditions of employment
- a resource that addresses all employment policies and procedures, and is available to employees individually for their use at any time.

2.469 A staff handbook may be used:
- as a point of reference for employees on all employment issues, including general terms and conditions of employment
- to fulfil statutory requirements
- to clarify the duties and responsibilities of both employer and employee
- to set out the policies and procedures that relate to employment
- to act as a resource for trainers as an aid to induction training
- to act as an aid to communication between employer and employee
- to increase employees' understanding of how the business operates.

2.470 As an aid to communication, a staff handbook should give the following information about a business.
- Market-place and environment.
- Products and services.
- Performance and future prospects.

Information and Consultation of Employees Regulations 2004

2.471 Use of a staff handbook for communication may become more widespread since implementation of the Information and Consultation of Employees Regulations 2004.

2.472 The Information and Consultation of Employees Regulations 2004 give employees in larger UK businesses a right to request the establishment of information and consultation procedures which must cover such matters as:
- recent and probable developments in the business, including its economic situation
- planned structural changes which might affect employment prospects
- decisions likely to lead to substantial changes in work organisation
- prospective changes to the terms and conditions of employees' employment.

2.473 The regulations came into force on 6 April 2005 for organisations with 150 or more employees and from 6 April 2007 have applied to organisations with 100 or more employees. The implementation date for those with 50 or more employees is April 2008. Employers with fewer than 50 employees will not be affected.

Key Terms of Employees' Employment

2.474 All employees (including part-time employees) who are engaged for more than one month are entitled to a written statement setting out the particulars of their employment. The statement must be issued within two months of the employee starting work. Some of the particulars that employers are required to put in writing may be included in a separate document to which employees have reasonable access, such as a staff handbook. These particulars include:
- terms related to sickness absence and sick pay
- pensions and pension schemes
- disciplinary rules and procedures
- grievance procedures.

Structure of the Handbook

2.475 It is advisable to structure the staff handbook in separate sections so that it is made clear to employees which items form part of their contracts of employment and which are intended to be for information and/or guidance only.

2.476 Organisations have choices as to the level of detail to be included in the handbook. Options include making the handbook:
- comprehensive and complete with all details of all policies and procedures
- complete as to issues, but with more detailed documents elsewhere
- directional (eg web-based — with signposts to topics in detail).

Format

2.477 The options for format are also a matter of organisational choice and include:
- hard-copy document
- loose-leaf folder
- full access on the Internet or the organisation's intranet.

2.478 The choice of format will depend on:
- the type and size of the organisation
- other documents and guides available within the organisation
- the degree to which employees have access to computers.

Style

2.479 Making the document user-friendly is important. Options include:
- the use of graphics, tables and attractive textual styling
- signposting the document to highlight important examples (eg of best practice and disciplinary issues)
- cross-references from one topic to another.

2.480 The staff handbook should be written in a user-friendly style avoiding legalese, technical jargon and abbreviations. It should be capable of being understood readily at a first reading by any employee, whatever his or her background or discipline.

Consultation During Development

2.481   During development of a staff handbook, it is advisable to consult with:
- managers within the organisation with relevant responsibilities
- recognised trade unions or workforce representatives where appropriate
- legal advisors to check that the content of the handbook is compliant with legislation
- IT staff.

Updating the Handbook

2.482   Information should be updated at appropriate intervals to ensure that the handbook remains accurate and useful. It is also advisable to appoint a nominated individual to be responsible for keeping the handbook up to date.

2.483   It is important to bear in mind that employees' contractual terms cannot be varied unilaterally. In other words, if any changes are to be made to any elements in the staff handbook that form part of employees' contracts, then the agreement of the relevant employees (or their representatives) will first have to be obtained through a process of consultation.

Content of the Handbook

2.484   The guiding principle in developing the content of a staff handbook is to take into account what employees will need and want to know during the course of their employment.

2.485   The handbook should therefore include:
- information about the structure of the organisation
- information about the organisation's aims and values
- details about the organisation's activities, including their products and/or services
- general terms and conditions of employment
- all current policies and procedures
- the standards expected of employees in performance and behaviour.

Possible Topics

2.486   Handbook content may be arranged around the following, non-comprehensive list of topics — with as much detailed information as is deemed appropriate to each organisation.

Equal Opportunities Statement

2.487   The equal opportunities statement should reflect current legislation, organisational values and good practice.

Introduction

2.488   The introduction should:
- offer a welcome to the organisation
- outline the organisation's aims and values
- clarify the employer's responsibility to offer employment and other relevant information

Staff Handbooks

- clarify the employee's responsibility to become familiar with the information and to use it to best effect.

About the Organisation

2.489 This section should detail the organisation's:
- products and services
- objectives and performance in its market
- people and their roles
- facilities
- physical environment.

Terms and Conditions of Employment

2.490 This section should include such details as:
- pay policy and when/how pay is reviewed
- job evaluation and any grading system in place
- expenses paid
- hours of work, any shift systems and overtime requirements
- policies on sickness absence and attendance and on sick pay
- general information about holiday entitlements and any rules about scheduling of holidays
- pension schemes and entitlements
- disciplinary rules and procedures
- grievance procedures.

Policies and Procedures

2.491 This section will include some or all of the employer's policies and procedures on:
- health and safety at work (a written health and safety policy is a legal requirement for organisations with five or more employees)
- the environment
- business ethics
- security and confidentiality issues
- equal opportunities and diversity
- bullying and harassment
- performance management and appraisal schemes
- recruitment, selection and promotion
- training and development
- relocation and temporary assignment policies
- information and consultation
- communication
- data protection and disclosure of information
- employee conduct (including at work-related events)
- maternity, paternity, adoption and parental leave schemes
- flexible working policy
- rules on use of email and the Internet
- use of office telephones and mobile phones

Staff Handbooks

- whistleblowing policy
- access to and use of any sport/social premises or facilities provided by the employer.

Training

2.492 Those responsible for induction training will need training on the use of the staff handbook as it will normally be used as part of the induction process.

2.493 Areas covered in the training should include:
- familiarity with the content of the staff handbook
- familiarity with the priorities and relevance for each employee
- understanding of how the individual employee might use the handbook
- how to navigate online documents.

2.494 Induction training should always be held over a period of time, as the new employee will understand the significance of certain policies only with a growing understanding of the organisation and his or her role.

List of Relevant Legislation

2.495
- Employment Equality (Age) Regulations 2006
- Employment Equality (Sex Discrimination) Regulations 2005
- Information and Consultation of Employees Regulations 2004
- Employment Equality (Religion or Belief) Regulations 2003
- Employment Equality (Sexual Orientation) Regulations 2003
- Employment Relations Act 2004
- Employment Act 2002
- Employment Relations Act 1999
- Data Protection Act 1998
- Public Interest Disclosure Act 1998
- Employment Rights Act 1996
- Disability Discrimination Act 1995
- Race Relations Act 1976
- Sex Discrimination Act 1975
- Health and Safety at Work, etc Act 1974
- Equal Pay Act 1970

Further Information

Organisations
- **Advisory Conciliation and Arbitration Service (Acas)**
  Web: *www.acas.org.uk*
  Acas aims to improve organisations and working life through better employment

relations. It provides up-to-date information, advice, high-quality training, and works with employers and employees to solve problems and improve performance.

- **Criminal Records Bureau (CRB)**
  Web: *www.crb.gov.uk*
  The CRB — an executive agency of the Home Office — is set up to help organisations make safer recruitment decisions.

- **Department for Business, Enterprise and Regulatory Reform (BERR)**
  Web: *www.berr.gov.uk*
  The Department for Business, Enterprise and Regulatory Reform brings together functions from the former Department of Trade and Industry (DTI), including responsibilities for productivity, business relations, energy, competition and consumers. It also drives regulatory reform.

- **Information Commissioner's Office**
  Web: *www.ico.gov.uk*
  The Information Commissioner enforces and oversees the Data Protection Act 1998 and the Freedom of Information Act 2000. It is an independent UK supervisory authority, reporting directly to the UK Parliament. It has an international role as well as a national one.

Types of Contract

This topic covers the following.
- Employed or Self-employed
- Employee or Worker
- Part-Time Contracts
- Fixed-Term Contracts
- Job Share Contracts
- Temporary Contracts
- Annualised Contracts
- Home Working Contracts
- Nil Hours Contracts
- Casual Contracts
- Agency Workers
- Draft Directive on Agency Workers
- Apprenticeship Agreements

Open-ended contracts are not the only option open to employers when employing workers. Employers need to be able to react to changes in the market, be competitiveand have flexibility in staffing. arrangements available, including:

2.496 Employers need to be aware of the status of workers employed or engaged under different types of contracts. Home workers, for example, may or may not be employees (see *Airfix Footwear Ltd v Cope*) and casuals may be classified as workers, and therefore not entitled to full employment protection. Much depends on the circumstances of each individual case. The first issue to be determined is whether mutuality of obligation exists and whether the employer can exercise control over the work carried out.

2.497 In such cases, the key consideration is whether the agency worker is employed by the hirer. The absence of a contract of employment does not necessarily mean that the worker is not an employee of the end-user organisation. Tribunals will look at a range of factors, including control, mutuality of obligation and how the worker was treated.

Employers' Duties

2.498 Employers must:
- be aware of the status of workers employed or engaged under different types of contracts
- observe the rights of employees
- respect the mutual implied duty of trust and confidence between employers and employees
- not treat part-time staff less favourably than full-time staff
- not treat employees on fixed-term contracts less favourably than comparable permanent employees unless there are objective reasons for doing so
- take care of employees' health and safety.

Employees' Duties

2.499 Employees must:
- accept work provided by the employer when he or she has agreed to a contract of employment governed by minimum requirements of mutuality of obligation and control
- follow the reasonable instructions of the employer
- work with due diligence and care
- not use or disclose trade secrets or confidential information
- respect the mutual implied duty of maintaining trust and confidence between employers and employees.

In Practice

Employed or Self-employed

2.500 There is a difference in law between a contract:
- "for service", ie one that is used for appointing an independent contractor on a freelance basis
- "of service", ie one that establishes the relationship of employer and employee between the parties.

2.501 There are a number of differences indicating that a contract is one "of service" rather than "for service".

Differences between Contracts "Of Service" and Contracts "For Service"

	Contract "of service"	Contract "for service"
Degree of Control	The employee is told what to do, how and when to do it.	The contractor is taken on to do a particular job and decides how it should be done.
Integration	The employee forms part of the organisation.	The contractor is in business on his or her own account — he or she can work for other people and employ others.
Obligations	The organisation is obliged to provide work, and the employee is obliged to do it.	There is no obligation on either side.

Types of Contract

	Contract "of service"	Contract "for service"
Payments	The employee receives pay or salary with PAYE deductions, a payslip, etc.	The contractor issues an invoice when the job is finished and receives a fee with no deductions. The worker may also have the ability to make a profit or loss.
Benefits	The employee has the right to paid holiday and sick leave.	The organisation has no involvement when the contractor is unavailable for work.
Ownership of Equipment	Equipment and materials are provided by the organisation.	The contractor may use his or her own premises, tools and materials.

2.502 The minimum requirements for the existence of a contract of employment are:

- mutuality of obligation, and
- control.

2.503 It is likely that if these exist a tribunal will conclude that an employment relationship exists.

Employee or Worker

2.504 The term "worker" is relatively new and was first introduced with the arrival of the Working Time Regulations 1998. These regulations apply not only to employees but also to "workers". A "worker" is any person who personally performs or undertakes work or services for an employer, whatever the nature of the relationship.

2.505 The regulations, therefore, apply to freelancers, casuals and seasonal workers. The term "worker" does not include those individuals who are genuinely self-employed on their own account. Both workers and employees have the right to make use of the provisions set out in the Working Time Regulations, including the right to four weeks' paid annual leave per year.

2.506 Other legislation also applies to "workers", such as the Part-time Workers (Prevention of Less Favourable Treatment) Regulations 2002, the Sex Discrimination Act 1975 and the National Minimum Wage Act 1998.

2.507 However, workers do not enjoy the entire raft of employment rights available to employees, such as the right to redundancy pay, remedies for unfair dismissal or to a written statement of particulars.

2.508 It can sometimes be difficult to determine whether someone is a worker or an employee. An employee is someone who is employed under a contract of employment and the minimum requirements of mutuality of obligation and control exist. The employee agrees to carry out work for the employer in return for an agreed wage or salary. The employer, in turn, controls how the work is carried out.

2.509 A worker will include employees but will also extend to someone who performs personally work or services for another. It would therefore include an individual providing services on a freelance basis.

Part-Time Contracts

2.510 With the coming into force of the Part-time Workers (Prevention of Less Favourable Treatment) Regulations 2000, part-time employees have the same rights to benefits as comparable full-time employees. There is no real difference, therefore, between a contract of employment for a part-time employee and a full-time employee other than that certain benefits may be prorated, eg holiday, public holiday and bonus scheme entitlements. Training however cannot be prorated.

2.511 Employers must not treat part-timers less favourably than other workers employed on the same type of contract. A full-time worker, for example, who changes his or her contract to a part-time one, has the right to enjoy the same terms and conditions as those he or she enjoyed when he or she worked full time. An employer's only defences are if the treatment is unconnected to the fact that the employee is a part-timer or if the treatment is justified, eg if there is a genuine business reason for the different treatment.

2.512 A part-time worker must compare himself or herself with other workers employed by the employer at the same establishment and who carry out broadly similar work and who have similar relevant qualifications, skills and experience. Where there are no suitable comparators at the establishment where the part-timer works, he or she may use a comparator at another establishment of the same employer.

2.513 A part-time employee who feels that he or she has been subject to unfavourable treatment may ask the employer for a written reason for the unfavourable treatment. The employer must provide the employee with a response within 21 days of the request being made.

2.514 In the case of *Pipe v Hendrickson Europe Ltd* [2003] IDS Brief 738, it was held that selecting an employee for redundancy because she could not work full time was in breach of the Part-time Workers (Prevention of Less Favourable Treatment) Regulations 2000. The employee was also successful in her claim for sex discrimination.

Fixed-Term Contracts

2.515 A fixed-term contract is one that specifies a start date and expiry date. Fixed-term contracts can give employers control over the shape of the workforce and allow for changes to be made if required. It is usual to put employees on fixed-term contracts where the completion of a particular task will end the relationship within a certain timeframe, ie a language teacher employed solely to teach at a summer school.

2.516 Under the Fixed-term Employees (Prevention of Less Favourable Treatment) Regulations 2002, if an employee completes four years' continuous service under one or more fixed-term contracts, the employee will be considered as permanent unless the fixed-term status can be justified. As the regulations specifically discount service prior to 10 July 2002, fixed-term employees, employed under one or more successive fixed-term contracts lasting four years, have been able to claim that they are permanent from 10 July 2006. Service prior to that 2002 date, whether permanent or for a fixed-term, is irrelevant for these purposes.

2.517 A fixed-term employee who considers himself or herself to be a permanent employee on this four-year basis will be entitled to ask his or her employer to confirm in writing that his or her contract is no longer fixed-term in nature. The employer must respond within 21 days of the request. If it does not agree, then it must give reasons as to why it believes the contract remains fixed-term. A tribunal may take any statement of this kind (or a failure to provide one) into account in the event that the

Types of Contract

employee later presents a complaint under the regulations. An employee will also be able to ask a tribunal for a declaration that he or she has become a permanent employee, without any parallel claim for compensation being necessary.

Notice

2.518 While there is no requirement to have a notice clause in a fixed-term contract, it may in some circumstances be advisable to have one as it allows an employer to end the relationship before the expiry date should it be genuinely necessary to do so.

2.519 A project may, for example, come to an early end. If there is no notice period in the contract allowing the employer to give notice and end the contract early, the employee may be able to claim damages to cover his or her losses for the outstanding period of the contract.

Less Favourable Treatment

2.520 Employees on fixed-term contracts have the right not to be treated less favourably than comparable permanent employees in relation to:
- terms and conditions of employment (eg pay and bonus schemes) unless there are objective reasons for the less favourable treatment
- training, promotions or transfers
- permanent positions within the organisation — employees on fixed-term contracts must be informed of any permanent vacancies that arise.

2.521 In *Coutts & Co plc (2) Royal Bank of Scotland v (1) Mr Cure (2) Mr Fraser* EAT/0395/04, the employer refused to pay fixed-term employees a non-contractual bonus. The EAT held that the employment tribunal was correct in determining that the reason for the less favourable treatment was on grounds of the employees' status as fixed-term workers.

Termination

2.522 When a fixed-term contract comes to an end and it is not renewed, the law regards this as a dismissal and the employee will be able to claim unfair dismissal if there is still work for him or her to do or a redundancy payment where the need for the work has ended, subject to the requisite qualifying service. Waiver clauses in contracts, where employees agree to waive their rights to claim unfair dismissal and/or a redundancy payment, are no longer lawful.

2.523 The very nature of fixed-term contracts, however, is that they end after a certain period and an employee on a fixed-term contract cannot claim that he or she has been treated less favourably than a permanent employee simply because his or her contract has been terminated (*Department for Work and Pensions v Webley* [2005] IRLR 288).

2.524 In light of the points outlined above, employers should consider taking the following practical steps.
- Identify any individuals on fixed-term contracts who have been continuously employed on such an arrangement since 10 July 2002. Ensure that managers are aware of this.
- Check whether there is any collective or workforce agreement in place that varies the four-year limit on successive fixed-term contracts, or sets out good and applicable reasons for renewing an employee's fixed-term contract after this period.

- Consider, even where there is no collective or workforce agreement, whether there are any good reasons to require employees to remain on a fixed-term contract after this four-year period.
- Ensure that managers are aware of the need:
  - to deal with any requests from employees who think they are no longer fixed-term employees within 21 days of receiving a request
  - thereafter to treat such employees as part of the permanent complement and not as a disposable resource.

Temporary Cessation of Work

2.525 Gaps between periods of employment may count as continuity of employment in some circumstances.

2.526 The gap between the periods of employment must be due to a temporary cessation of work and the length of the gap must be reasonable. Tribunals will determine whether continuity of employment is broken or not on a case by case basis. In the case of *Ford v Warwickshire County Council* [1983] IRLR 126 the House of Lords held that school teachers who had a three-month gap (ie no contract, during the summer holidays) had continuity of employment during the gap.

2.527 However, in *Berwick Salmon Fisheries Co Ltd v Rutherford* [1991] IRLR 203, the EAT held that the fishermen concerned spent too much time out of work between seasonal contracts for the gap to be considered temporary and that therefore continuity of employment was, in this case, broken.

Job Share Contracts

2.528 Job share contracts occur where two part-timers share one job. Benefits and pay are *pro rata* the number of hours worked. Variations to standard contracts will be necessary and clarification on the following areas is required:
- allocation of bank/public holidays (must be shared on a *pro rata* basis)
- procedures for work handover
- procedures for covering the absence of one employee
- requirements to attend meetings, courses, etc outside of normal working hours.

2.529 Consideration should also be given to what would happen if one partner left. For example can the job be offered on a full-time basis to the remaining partner, or can a new job share partner be sought?

Temporary Contracts

2.530 Temporary contracts are no different from open-ended contracts other than that the nature of their work is short term.

2.531 Temporary employees are therefore entitled to the same rights and benefits as permanent employees and may be protected by the Fixed-Term Employees (Prevention of Less Favourable Treatment) Regulations 2002.

Annualised Hours Contracts

2.532 The basic principle of annualised hours is that, instead of defining working time in terms of a standard working week, the number of hours is averaged over the year. In its simplest form, the calculation of annual working hours is based on the number of weeks in a year multiplied by the number of hours in a working week less the number of holidays and public holidays.

2.533 Further variable elements such as shift arrangements and overtime will add complexity to the calculation. Whichever the formula chosen, it is essential that this should be reflected in the contract of employment.

2.534 As with traditional contracts based on normal working hours, annualised hours contracts should specify whether employees will receive overtime pay for working additional hours. This will normally depend on how the annualised hours contract compares with existing contractual provisions.

2.535 In addition, an annualised hours contract should make clear:
- the number of hours an employee will be expected to work in any given period
- the procedure by which employees are to be notified of this
- any "protected" periods, ie periods when employees will not be required to work
- any "rest" periods and periods when the employee is "on call"
- procedures to enable employees to notify their employers if their particular shift is inconvenient, eg if the employee has booked holiday which falls within one of the rostered periods
- provision which allows the employer to vary the arrangements upon notice.

2.536 Annualised hours contracts may also have an impact on other contractual terms and benefits such as holiday arrangements and payment structures and these should also be specified.

Home Working Contracts

2.537 In general the particulars of employment for homeworkers follow the standard form for all employees but take account of the particular position of home working.

2.538 A degree of flexibility will not necessarily prevent an employment relationship from arising. However, there must be minimum obligation on both sides. For example, although the hours of work may not be specified (eg where payment is by piece-work alone), there must be some minimum obligation on the employee to complete the tasks allocated within a certain timeframe. A deductions clause allowing the employer to make deductions from wages if work is not of the required standard will enable the employer to impose certain standards of quality on the home worker.

2.539 It is also prudent to set out the system of work and arrangements relating to the provision of equipment and insurance in some detail and ensure that home workers are aware of the main provisions of the Health and Safety at Work, etc Act 1974 and that a risk assessment is undertaken.

Nil Hours Contracts

2.540 Under a nil hours contract the employee agrees to be available for work but the employer does not agree to provide work. Payment is only made for work that is carried out.

2.541 Employers should note that employees on nil hours contracts have continuity of employment from the date the contract started, despite the fact that the employee may not actually work for some time.

Casual Contracts

2.542 Casual contracts are generally used where an employer requires workers to work on an "as and when" basis and are particularly common in the hospitality and catering industries. The workers are not required to be available for work or accept work and are free to turn work down. As a result there is no mutuality of obligation or continuing contract and the individuals may not be categorised as "employees" (see *Carmichael v National Power PLC*).

2.543 If workers undertake to work on a regular basis, however, continuity could result or mutuality of obligation could be implied, leading to an employment relationship.

2.544 The key factors relating to casual contracts are as follows.
- Where work is of a truly casual nature workers are free to turn down work if they choose to do so.
- The absence of mutual obligation, on the part of the organisation to provide work and on the worker to accept work, means that normally the contract of a casual worker will be a contract for services rather than a contract of employment.
- Casual workers will therefore be excluded from many employment protection rights.
- Whether a "casual worker" is an employee or not depends upon all the circumstances of the particular case.
- Even where there is no mutuality of obligation it is open to a tribunal to find that over the course of several years an "umbrella" contract may be inferred.
- Where it is the recognised custom and practice for casual workers to be engaged under contracts for services, even a long period of casual working may not result in an employment relationship.
- If organisations have a regular need for casual labour, it is advisable to:
  – maintain a list of individuals who are prepared to take on casual work
  – offer jobs on a rotating basis
  – avoid approaching the same workers repeatedly.
- Casual workers who are not employees are still protected against unlawful disability, sex and race discrimination. They are entitled to bring equal pay claims. They are also covered by the unlawful deduction provisions in the Employment Rights Act 1996.

Agency Workers

2.545 The issue of whether agency workers are employed by their agency, their hirer or indeed by anyone, has been the subject of much case law.

2.546 Agency workers are not entitled to the benefits enjoyed by employees, other than rights under the Working Time Regulations 1998 and the right to a national minimum wage. They are also protected by discrimination legislation.

2.547 Many organisations use agency workers when there is a surge in work that requires a temporary role to help manage it. Where a worker is taken on from an agency for a short period of time, in general, there are no foreseeable problems. However, where a worker is taken on for a longer length of time (coming up to or over a year) and is treated by management as an employee, the question of employment rights may arise, including the right to claim unfair dismissal.

2.548 In *Motorola Ltd v Davidson* [2001] IRLR 4, EAT, it was held that Davidson was an employee of the end-user organisation. Davidson's contract with the agency meant that Motorola could specifically ask for Davidson's services. Davidson also wore the Motorola uniform. The tribunal held that Motorola had control over Davidson and his work and therefore Davidson had employment rights and could claim unfair dismissal.

2.549 In the case of *Esso Petroleum Company v (1) Jarvis and ors (2) Brentvine*

Types of Contract

Ltd EAT/0831/00, the tribunal held that as the employees did not have a contract with the hirer, there was no employment, despite the workers having worked for Esso for a number of years.

2.550 However, in *Franks v Reuters Ltd* [2003] IRLR 423, CA, it was held that a contract does not have to be express and can be implied from the way in which the worker has been treated. In the *Reuters* case, Franks had been with the end-user organisation for five years, had been promoted within Reuters and was subject to the organisation's rules on appearance and hours. As a result, it was held that he was, in fact, an employee of the organisation.

2.551 The important case of *Dacas v Brook Street Bureau (UK) Ltd* [2004] IRLR 358, CA, increases the likelihood of a tribunal finding that a "worker" is employed by the hirer, and not an agency.

2.552 Mrs Dacas was supplied by Brook Street Bureau to Wandsworth Council to work in one of its hostels. She provided this service for a number of years, until Wandsworth Council decided it no longer required her services. Mrs Dacas brought unfair dismissal claims against both Brook Street Bureau and the council. The appeal concerned Brook Street Bureau but the Court of Appeal took the opportunity to give guidance on Ms Dacas' relationship with Wandsworth Council also. It held that there was an implied contract between Ms Dacas and Brook Street Bureau but that there was also an express one between Ms Dacas and Wandsworth Council. The council had control over her work, controlled her hours, paid her wages direct to the agency and ultimately, had decided to end her employment. Crucially, Brook Street had little control over Ms Dacas' work and therefore her relationship with Brook Street Bureau was not one of employment.

2.553 The recent case of *Cable & Wireless plc v Muscat* [2006] IRLR 354, CA mirrored the findings in *Dacas* and concentrated on which party exercised control over the worker. Again, it was found that the middle party, the agency, had no control and that the worker was employed by Cable & Wireless.

2.554 These cases illustrate the importance of employers exercising caution when using agency workers for a year or more. Employers should avoid taking responsibility for the payment of holidays and sickness and should not subject agency workers to the organisation's disciplinary or grievance procedures.

2.555 Where an agency worker is taken on a temporary basis and then made permanent, it should be noted that his or her continuous employment will date back to the date that he or she first started as an agency worker.

2.556 Agency workers can also be found to be employed by the agency. Once again, a tribunal would consider a range of factors, including the terms offered to the worker during the course of assignment, control and whether mutuality of obligation exists (*Bunce v Postworth Ltd t/a Skyblue* [2005] IRLR 557, CA).

Draft Directive on Agency Workers

2.557 The draft Agency Workers Directive has been under consideration for some time now and is still being negotiated. The main aim of the directive is to improve the quality of temporary work and provides, among other things, that temporary workers will be entitled to pay and basic working and employment conditions which are at least as good as those they would benefit from if employed directly by the hiring organisation. The working and employment conditions include pay, work and rest periods, paid holidays, overtime pay and health and safety.

2.558 Temporary workers will also have the right to be informed of any permanent positions within the organisation and not be prevented from applying for permanent work. Where a temporary worker is successful in his or her application for permanent work, no fee will be payable to the agency.

Apprenticeship Agreements

2.559 Apprenticeship agreements can either be traditional or common law apprenticeships, or a government-sponsored Apprenticeship.

Traditional Apprenticeships

2.560 These are far less common now than government-sponsored Apprenticeships but still exist in some types of industry.

2.561 In a traditional apprenticeship, the employer (the master) undertakes to train the apprentice in a particular industry or skill. The apprentice agrees to learn his or her trade and obey the master.

2.562 Apprenticeships are a very special type of employment contract. To start, it is difficult to dismiss an apprentice during the course of his or her apprenticeship. Although an apprentice who continually does not carry out his or her duties may be dismissed at lesser risk, occasional neglect of duties will not normally suffice for a dismissal to be fair, regardless of length of service.

2.563 If circumstances mean that an employer cannot complete an apprentice's training, the apprentice will be entitled to pay and benefits up to the end of the apprenticeship period, as well as damages for the employer's failure to complete the apprenticeship.

2.564 It is also not normally possible to make an apprentice redundant. An apprentice will not be automatically redundant at the end of his or her apprenticeship period as once the training is complete he or she will be entitled to a position in the organisation in the trade that he or she has trained in. However, it could be possible for an apprentice to be made redundant in certain circumstances, eg a fundamental reorganisation of the organisation or if the organisation ceases trading.

2.565 Regardless of their training status, apprentices are employees of the organisation and should be treated as such.

Government-sponsored Apprenticeships

2.566 Under the government-sponsored Apprenticeship Scheme, the employer does not have the same training responsibility as the "master" in the traditional scheme. The employer provides on-the-job training and experience, while local learning providers provide off-the-job training (normally at college, on a day-release basis). The employer may therefore have to allow the apprentice to attend college or training during normal working hours.

2.567 Each apprentice should have an apprenticeship plan drawn up between him or her and the employer, detailing the training activities and the qualifications to be gained. Both parties are expected to be committed to this and the relevant Learning and Skills Council (LSC) (or equivalent body) will monitor progress against this plan. Funding is available from the LSC; wages and travel expenses are a matter between the employer and the individual apprentice.

2.568 The employer will agree to train the apprentice in the specified trade and to ensure that the apprentice has time off to attend the off-the-job training provided by the local learning provider. The apprentice in turn will agree to attend the course provided and endeavour to progress to a satisfactory standard through the training

Types of Contract

programme. Finally, the training provider will agree to provide appropriate off-the-job training and to counsel the apprentice should he or she find the course difficult.

2.569 In most cases the parties will also agree that, where the employer is unable to allow the apprentice to complete his or her training, the provider will do all it can to find the apprentice another employer. Note that where an employer is unable to allow the apprentice to complete the training, the apprentice may claim for breach of contract and compensation for the remainder of a period of training required to complete his or her training, or compensation until the date another training provider is found to enable him or her to continue training (*Flett v Matheson* [2006] IRLR 277, CA). Where an employer ceases training, an apprentice with over two years' service will be entitled to redundancy pay, even though an alternative employer may be found to allow the apprentice to complete his or her training. However, an apprentice is not redundant when his or her apprenticeship comes to an end.

2.570 By the very nature of apprenticeships, apprentices under the Government's Apprenticeship scheme will be on a fixed-term contract. However, despite this, the expiry of a contract of apprenticeship does not constitute a dismissal. This is because a contract of apprenticeship is a one-off contract which cannot be renewed as the training will be complete. There is no obligation, therefore, for an employer to provide work for the apprentice at the end of the apprenticeship period but it is important that the employer is reasonable. Where, quite clearly, there is a suitable vacancy, the apprentice should be offered a position. It should be remembered that apprentices with over one year's service have the right to claim unfair dismissal.

Employment Status of Apprentices

2.571 Apprentices — whether traditional or modern — are employees, much in the same way as other employees, but are further protected by their apprentice status.

2.572 Apprentices should be provided with a Statement of Particulars within two months of the apprenticeship commencing and are subject to the same rules regarding disciplinary and grievances (although dismissal, regardless of length of service is more difficult).

National Minimum Wage and Apprentices

2.573 Apprentices are entitled to be paid the national minimum wage if they are 19 and have completed the first year of their apprenticeship. Apprentices who start their apprenticeship aged 26 or over, are entitled to be paid the national minimum wage. An apprentice who turns 26 during the first year of his or her apprenticeship is entitled to receive the national minimum wage from his or her birthday. In practice, therefore, an apprentice who is under 26 and has not yet completed the first year of his or her apprenticeship is not entitled to be paid the national minimum wage.

List of Relevant Legislation

2.574
- Working Time Regulations 1998
- Employment Act 2002
- National Minimum Wage Act 1998
- Employment Rights Act 1996
- Trade Union and Labour Relations (Consolidation) Act 1992

List of Relevant Cases

2.575
- *Bunce v Postworth Ltd t/a Skyblue* [2006] IRLR 557 CA
- *Cable & Wireless plc v Muscat* EAT 25/02/05 (0661/04)
- *Flett v Matheson* [2006] IRLR 277, CA
- *Department for Work and Pensions v Webley* [2005] IRLR 288
- *Giles v Cornelia Care Homes* 3100720/2005 (unreported)
- *Coutts & Co plc (2) Royal Bank of Scotland v (1) Mr Cure (2) Mr Fraser* EAT/0395/04
- *Dacas v Brook Street Bureau (UK) Ltd* [2004] IRLR 358, CA
- *Franks v Reuters Ltd* [2003] IRLR 423, CA
- *Pipe v Hendrickson Europe Ltd* [2003] IDS Brief 738
- *Motorola Ltd v Davidson* [2001] IRLR 4, EAT
- *Carmichael v National Power plc* [2000] IRLR 43, HL
- *Esso Petroleum Company v (1) Jarvis and ors (2) Brentvine Ltd* EAT/0831/00
- *Berwick Salmon Fisheries Co Ltd v Rutherford* [1991] IRLR 203
- *Nethermere (St Neots) Ltd v Taverna and Gardiner* [1984] IRLR 240, CA
- *Ford v Warwickshire County Council* [1983] IRLR 126, HL
- *Airfix Footwear Ltd v Cope* [1978] IRLR 396, EAT
- *Ready Mixed Concrete v Ministry of Pensions and National Insurance* [1968] 2 QB 497

Further Information

Organisations

- **Department for Business, Enterprise and Regulatory Reform (BERR)**
  Web: *www.berr.gov.uk*
  The Department for Business, Enterprise and Regulatory Reform brings together functions from the former Department of Trade and Industry (DTI), including responsibilities for productivity, business relations, energy, competition and consumers. It also drives regulatory reform.
- **Employment Lawyers Association**
  Web: *www.elaweb.org.uk*
  The Employment Lawyers Association's members are qualified barristers and solicitors who practice employment law in the UK, and organisations engaged in the practice of employment law.

Varying the Contract of Employment

This topic covers the following.
- The Principal Reasons for Contract Variation
- When a Contract can be Altered
- Management of Contract Changes
- Breach of Contract
- Statutory Restrictions to Change
- Justify Changes
- Consultation
- Grievance Procedure
- An Employer Cannot Impose Changes
- Employee's Response to Imposed Changes

2.576 A contract of employment is an agreement between an employee and an employer that sets out terms and conditions of employment and is enforceable in the courts.

2.577 Some terms are express (ie explicitly agreed in written or oral form). Such terms normally relate to pay and other remuneration, working hours, holidays etc.

2.578 Others terms are implied into employment contracts. These include, for example, the duty to obey lawful and reasonable instructions, and the duty of an employee to promote the employer's business.

2.579 A variety of legislation also implies terms into employment contracts, such as the prohibition of pay inequality based on gender incorporated by the Equal Pay Act 1970.

Employers' Duties

2.580 Employers should:
- provide all new employees within two months of starting employment with information about certain key contractual terms in their initial statement of employment particulars. The matters which must be addressed are set out in s.1 of the Employment Rights Act 1996 (as amended by the Employment Rights Act 2002). If any changes are subsequently made, these should be recorded within one month of the change being agreed
- ensure discussion and agreement with the relevant employee before making any changes to the contract of employment
- must respect the mutual implied duty of trust and confidence between employers and employees
- negotiate in good faith with any relevant trade union
- make sure that any changes do not breach implied terms of mutual trust and confidence
- provide appropriate training and support if it is necessary to introduce new working practices
- if it is necessary to terminate an existing contract and offer a new one, consider the provisions of the law on unfair dismissal and redundancy

- should take care of employees' health and safety.

Employees' Duties

2.581 Employees should:
- be aware of the contractual duty to co-operate with their employer and to obey lawful and reasonable instructions
- make full use of the grievance procedure if they have a complaint about an unacceptable contractual change
- not complain to an employment tribunal without having first pursued the matter through an internal grievance and appeal procedure
- consider being accompanied at any formal grievance hearing by a fellow worker or a union representative.

In Practice

The Principal Reasons for Contract Variation

2.582 The main reasons for an employer wanting to vary an existing employment contract are:
- pay and other forms of remuneration
- hours of work
- holiday entitlements
- working practices
- promotion
- location of work.

When a Contract can be Altered

- There may be express provision within a contract for change to the existing terms. For example, there may be a mobility clause that allows the employer to relocate staff in certain circumstances.
- An implied duty within the contract for an employee to obey lawful and reasonable instructions may enable the employer to change working practices.

Management of Contract Changes

2.583 There are four options for contract change.

Consensual Variation

2.584 The employer might agree a change to a particular term of the contract with the employee or with a recognised trade union. If a change is agreed with the employee, as a matter of best practice, this should be clearly recorded in writing with the employee signing an acknowledgment to indicate agreement. If a change is agreed with a recognised trade union, a collective agreement can be made and provisions of that agreement need to be incorporated into the employee's contract of employment.

Express Provision Within a Contract for Flexibility

2.585 An example of such express provision might be a clause allowing the employer to change the employee's place of work. Any exercise of such express provision must be reasonable and must not breach the implied term of mutual trust and confidence.

Implied Terms

2.586 The duty to obey lawful and reasonable instructions is an example of an implied term, ie a term that is not explicitly set out in a contract of employment but may be inferred as in the contract.

Termination

2.587 If a business need exists or if there is some other substantial reason, an employer can terminate an existing contract and offer a new contract incorporating changed terms and conditions. The employer must give the employee contractual notice of such a termination and must follow the statutory dismissal procedure under the Employment Act 2002 (Dispute Resolution) Regulations 2004 before effecting the dismissal.

2.588 If the employee chooses not to accept the new contract and has one year's service, he or she may be able to claim unfair dismissal and redundancy. An employment tribunal would decide on the facts of the case whether the dismissal was fair.

Breach of Contract

2.589 The courts will tend to regard any attempt by an employer to impose change without using one of the above methods as breach of contract. In such circumstances, the employee may be able to resign and claim constructive unfair dismissal.

Statutory Restrictions to Change

2.590 A variety of legislation affects potential changes to contracts. For example, proposed changes must be consistent with the Working Time Regulations 1998 and the National Minimum Wage Act 1998.

Justify Changes

2.591 The employer should be able to justify the changes in light of, as appropriate, the organisation's operational needs, financial circumstances and business requirements.

Consultation

2.592 A consultation process is nearly always necessary before changing contract terms. It is good practice to allow the employee to be accompanied by another employee or a union representative to consultation meetings.

2.593 If there are 20 or more employees affected by the proposed changes, collective consultation must also take place with a recognised trade union's representatives or elected representatives from the group of workers affected. Collective consultation is necessary in case any decision is made to terminate existing contracts of employment and offer re-engagement under a new contract incorporating the changes. Collective consultation should commence 30 days before notice of dismissal is effected in the case of 20 to 99 employees and 90 days before when 100 or more employees are affected. Failure to do so may give rise to a claim for protective award.

2.594 Employers should consider offering a concession in an attempt to obtain agreement from employees to any proposed changes.

Grievance Procedure

2.595 Employers should be prepared to deal with any queries and grievances that may arise. They should use the appropriate internal grievance procedure, and ensure compliance with the statutory standard grievance procedure and advice in the Acas *Code of Practice on Grievance Procedures*. Employers should try, as far as practicable, to take account of the interests and concerns of employees.

An Employer Cannot Impose Changes

2.596 An employer cannot impose changes without being in breach of contract and should be careful even if a degree of flexibility is written into the contract. The following two examples illustrate this.

A Mobility Clause

2.597 An employer may write into an employee's contract an option to change the employee's work location. Even if such an explicit provision exists, the employer could be found to have breached an implied duty of mutual trust and confidence if the employer fails to consider the interests of the employee when implementing such a change. See *United Bank v Akhtar*.

2.598 When trying to implement such a change, an employer should consider factors such as whether the express clause is discriminatory, whether the employee has been given reasonable notice of the change or whether any special arrangements can be made to assist the employee.

Lawful and Reasonable Instructions

2.599 Any change on this implied basis needs to be consistent with an employee's position and status within the organisation. The change must be something that the employee can reasonably be expected to do. Furthermore no employee can expect his or her job to remain unchanged throughout its tenure (eg the introduction of new technology may change established working practices). See *Cresswell and others v Board of Inland Revenue*.

Information and Training

2.600 The employer should give information in writing about the changes and the reasons for making them to any affected employees. Appropriate training and support should be provided if the change is substantial.

Employee's Response to Imposed Changes

2.601 The employee can take one of three courses of action if an employer imposes a change on him or her.

Accept the Change

2.602 The employee could accept the change. Express acceptance by the employee will usually constitute agreement to vary the contract. Acceptance may also be implied by performance; so an employee, who continues to work without objection after the variation has been imposed, may be deemed to have consented to the change. Employers should be wary, however, of assuming consent by performance, unless the change has an immediate practical impact on the employee. See *Aparau v Iceland Frozen Foods plc*.

Sue the Employer

2.603 The employee could argue that there has been a breach of contract and that the employer should comply with the existing contract. So if, for example, an employer imposes a pay cut, an employee could sue for unpaid wages due under the existing contract. Any claim for breach of contract other than unlawful deductions of pay would have to be claimed through the civil courts if the employee remained in employment.

2.604 In such circumstances, an employee should make clear to the employer that he or she does not accept the imposed terms. The employee should initially use any grievance procedure available within the organisation.

Resign

2.605 If an employee resigns, he or she might be able to claim constructive unfair dismissal at employment tribunal. Success would depend on whether or not the tribunal considered that there had been a fundamental breach of contract and that the employer had not acted reasonably in all the circumstances. When an employer terminates an old contract and attempts to impose a new one, the employee could let the employer terminate the old contract but not accept the new one — this would count as dismissal rather than resignation.

2.606 Should there be an employment tribunal claim, an employer should be able to demonstrate that:
- there was some substantial reason for dismissal (eg a genuine business need)
- it was reasonable in the circumstances to dismiss the employee
- the procedure used to dismiss the employee was fair.

Training

2.607 Employers have a responsibility to manage change. Failure by an employer to deal effectively with contractual changes could result in an employment tribunal complaint.

2.608 Employers are advised to train human resources staff sufficiently in the issues involved in change management. Managers play a key role in effective change management.

2.609 Manager's training needs depend on the scale of the change being proposed and implemented. Employers should:
- inform managers about the nature of any changes and the reasons for them
- tell managers where they can obtain advice in dealing with specific human resource problems and issues — about terms and conditions of employment and/or employment law
- explain the processes of consultation and discussion that should be used
- clarify how managers should deal with any queries or grievances

- ensure that managers have appropriate communication skills.

2.610 Employees should be kept informed of any changes and the reasons for them. There should always be a clear and accessible system for dealing with queries or grievances.

List of Relevant Legislation

2.611
- Employment Act 2002 (Dispute Resolution) Regulations 2004
- Employment Relations Act 1999
- National Minimum Wage Act 1998
- Working Time Regulations 1998
- Employment Act 2002
- Employment Rights Act 1996
- Trade Union and Labour Relations (Consolidation Act) 1992
- Sex Discrimination Act 1975
- Equal Pay Act 1970

List of Relevant Cases

2.612
- *GMB v Man Truck & Bus UK Ltd* [2000] IRLR 636
- *Aparau v Iceland Frozen Foods plc* [1996] IRLR 119, EAT
- *United Bank v Akhtar* [1989] IRLR 507
- *Rigby v Ferodo* [1987] IRLR 516, HL
- *Burdett-Coutts v Herefordshire County Council* [1984] IRLR 91, HC
- *Cresswell v Board of Inland Revenue* [1984] IRLR 190, HC
- *Aparau v Iceland Frozen Foods plc* [1996] IRLR 119, EAT

Further Information

Publications
- *Acas/CP01 Code of Practice on Disciplinary and Grievance Procedures (2004)*
- *Acas/AL02 Varying a Contract of Employment*

Organisations
- **Advisory Conciliation and Arbitration Service (Acas)**
  Web: *www.acas.org.uk*
  Acas aims to improve organisations and working life through better employment relations. It provides up-to-date information, advice, high-quality training, and works with employers and employees to solve problems and improve performance.

- **Department for Business, Enterprise and Regulatory Reform (BERR)**
  Web: *www.berr.gov.uk*
  The Department for Business, Enterprise and Regulatory Reform brings together functions from the former Department of Trade and Industry (DTI), including responsibilities for productivity, business relations, energy, competition and consumers. It also drives regulatory reform.
- **Equal Opportunities Commission**
  Web: *www.eoc.org.uk*
  An agency working to eliminate sex discrimination and put equality into practice in the workplace. From October 2007 this organisation will be replaced by the Commission for Equality and Human Rights (**Web:** *www.cehr.org.uk*).
- **Low Pay Commission (LPC)**
  Web: *www.lowpay.gov.uk*
  The LPC was established as a result of the National Minimum Wage Act 1998 to advise the Government about the National Minimum Wage and assists employees and employers alike with advice.

Chapter 3
Discipline and Grievance

Bullying

This topic covers the following.
- Examples of Bullying
- Why Employers Need to Take Action
- Effects of Stress on Individuals
- Effects of Stress on Employers
- Personal Injury Claims
- Health and Safety at Work Claims
- Breach of Contract or Unfair Dismissal Claims
- Discrimination Claims
- Intentional Harassment Claims
- Protection from Harassment Claims
- Developing a Formal Policy
- Investigating Bullying
- Counselling
- Formal Disciplinary Measures
- Suspension
- Unfounded Allegations

Employers' Duties

3.1 Employers have a duty to:
- ensure that the working environment is safe and without risk to health
- ensure the workplace is free of discrimination and harassment.

Employees' Duties

3.2 Employees have a duty to:
- co-operate with their employers to enable the employers to comply with their legal duties
- take reasonable care for the health and safety of themselves and others.

In Practice

3.3 Bullying at work causes a considerable amount of stress-related absenteeism.

3.4 Bullying may be characterised as targeted and persistent offensive, intimidating, malicious or insulting behaviour; and can include the abuse or misuse of power intended to undermine, humiliate, denigrate or injure the recipient.

3.5 Bullying can give rise to complaints of unfair dismissal, discrimination and harassment as well as claims for personal injury if the bullying causes psychological harm. Employers will be vicariously liable for the acts of its employees during the course of their employment, even if it has no knowledge of employees' acts and has not approved them.

3.6 Bullying can give rise to allegations of breach of health and safety legislation if an individual feels in danger of physical harm. Bullying can increase staff turnover, thereby increasing costs for the organisation.

3.7 Employers should consider the development of a policy on preventing bullying and consult with those who will be affected by its introduction, including employees and relevant trade union representatives.

Examples of Bullying

3.8 Examples of what may be considered bullying are provided below for guidance purposes. For practical purposes, complainants often define bullying as something that is unwelcome, unwarranted, targeted, persistent and causes a detrimental effect.

3.9 Bullying may include repeated occurrences of the following behaviour or actions targeted at individuals or groups.
- Constant criticism, fault finding or undermining.
- Being excluded, marginalised or isolated.
- Being treated differently from everyone else.
- Being threatened, shouted at or humiliated.
- Being either over-burdened with work or denied work.
- Being set unreasonable targets and deadlines.
- Having authority removed but responsibility increased.
- Denial of annual leave, sickness or compassionate leave.
- Unjustified disciplinary action.
- Being forced into early or ill-health retirement.
- Distorting or misrepresenting actions.

3.10 Bullying can give rise to complaints of breach of contract leading to claims of constructive dismissal and harassment claims.

3.11 Harassment is generally described as unwanted conduct affecting the dignity of employees in the workplace. It may be connected to sex, disability, race, age, religion or any personal characteristic of the individual. However, bullying differs from harassment and discrimination in that the focus of the unfair treatment is not the gender, race, age, disability, sexual orientation or religion of the individual. The treatment is more often focused on the competence or alleged lack of competence of the bullied person.

3.12 Extreme cases of bullying are usually quite easy to spot and it is often "grey" areas that cause problems, eg one person's "bullying" can be another's "firm management".

3.13 Bullying and harassment sometimes do not take place in face-to-face situations. They may also occur in written communications, email, phone calls and by unfair supervision of the individual — this can include the use of automatic supervision such as computer recording of downtime from work or the number of calls handled, if these are not applied to all workers.

3.14 Many people who claim to have been bullied say it has affected their health, causing stress and depression. It is this connection between bullying and stress which also gives rise to potentially costly claims for personal injury.

Bullying

Why Employers Need to Take Action

3.15 Bullying and harassment are not only unacceptable on moral grounds but may, if unchecked or badly handled, create serious problems for an organisation including:
- poor morale
- loss of respect for managers and supervisors
- poor performance
- loss of productivity
- high staff turnover
- poor retention of staff.

3.16 Employers must make it clear that on no account will bullying be tolerated within their organisation.

Effects of Stress on Individuals

3.17 Effects can be:
- mental
- physical
- behavioural or psychological.

3.18 Symptoms can include:
- anxiety
- sleeplessness
- tearfulness
- anger
- irritability
- headaches
- skin problems
- depression
- poor concentration and memory
- sweating
- panic attacks
- obsessiveness
- isolation
- low self-confidence
- suicidal thoughts
- indecision
- alcoholism
- mental breakdown
- heart disease.

Effects of Stress on Employers

3.19 Effects for employers can include:
- an increase in absence levels
- an increase in sick pay costs
- an increase in staff turnover
- a decrease in efficiency

- a decrease in quality
- employee relations problems
- resignations
- damage to the organisation's reputation
- tribunal and other court cases.

Personal Injury Claims

3.20 The case establishing stress as a potential personal injury issue was *Walker v Northumberland County Council*. This case established that the risk of mental damage could not be excluded from the scope of an employer's duty.

3.21 For a personal injury claim to succeed, the employee has to overcome a number of hurdles:
- the employer must owe the employee a duty of care
- the employer must be in breach of that duty
- the employee must suffer an injury
- the employer's breach must have caused the injury
- it must have been reasonably foreseeable on the part of the employer that injury to the employee would result from the breach of duty.

3.22 The House of Lords, in *Barber v Somerset County Council*, confirmed that the overall test for determining whether the employer has breached the duty of care to employees was:
- the conduct of the "reasonable and prudent" employer
- taking positive thought for an employee's safety in the light of what the employer knows or ought to know.

Health and Safety at Work Claims

3.23 The Health and Safety at Work, etc Act 1974 (HSWA) requires an employer to take reasonably practicable measures to ensure the health, safety and welfare of its employees and others sharing the workplace.

3.24 The Management of Health and Safety at Work Regulations 1999 (MHSWR) impose an obligation on employers to carry out a risk analysis of the workplace and put in place appropriate preventive and protective measures to keep employees safe from harm.

3.25 Breaches of the HSWA and/or MHSW regulations can result in criminal prosecution.

Breach of Contract or Unfair Dismissal Claims

3.26 Failure by employers to deal with stress and bullying-related issues may result in a fundamental breach of an implied term of an employee's contract. Such implied terms include the following duties, to:
- keep employees safe from harm
- maintain reasonable working hours
- provide support and assistance
- maintain trust and confidence between the employer and the employee.

3.27 Where an employee has unfair dismissal rights, if the employee can establish that the employer has fundamentally breached his or her contract, he or she may resign and claim constructive dismissal. Since 1 October 2004 the employee must have raised a grievance with the employer and allowed 28 days for a resolution before starting tribunal proceedings.

Discrimination Claims

3.28 Where bullying is based on gender, sexual orientation, ethnic origin, race, age, disability, colour, nationality or religion or belief, such bullying may amount to discrimination under the Race Relations Act, Sex Discrimination Act, Employment Equality (Sexual Orientation) Regulations, Disability Discrimination Act, Employment Equality (Age) Regulations 2006 or Employment Equality (Religion or Belief) Regulations. Employers will be vicariously liable for the acts of their employees during the course of their employment, even if they have no knowledge of the employees' acts and have not approved them. For further information see the Discrimination and Diversity chapter.

Intentional Harassment Claims

3.29 The Public Order Act 1986 (as amended) created an offence of intentional harassment. Intentional harassment in these circumstances is a criminal offence and it is the individual perpetrator who is prosecuted. A person is guilty of an offence if, with an intent to cause a person harassment, alarm or distress, he or she:
- uses threatening or insulting words or behaviour, or disorderly behaviour
- displays any writing, sign or other visible representation which is threatening or insulting.

Protection from Harassment Claims

3.30 The Protection from Harassment Act 1997 (PHA) makes it an offence for an individual to pursue a course of conduct which:
- amounts to harassment of another
- he or she knows or ought to know amounts to harassment of the other.

3.31 The person whose conduct is in question ought to know that it amounts to harassment of another if a reasonable person in possession of the same information would think the same.

3.32 The House of Lords has ruled in the case of *Majrowski v Guys and St Thomas' NHS Trust*, that an employer can be held vicariously liable for breaches of statutory duties, as well as for breaches of common law duties. The facts of this case are that Majrowski was bullied and harassed by a female manager partly on grounds of his sexuality. He had raised an internal grievance, which the employer upheld, and his manager subsequently resigned from the organisation. By this time, however, Majrowski had already suffered psychiatric ill health as a result of his treatment but his personal injury claim could not succeed because it was unlikely that he could show that his injury had been reasonably foreseeable by his employer.

3.33 Majrowski's lawyers instead argued that his manager had breached the PHA during the performance of her employment and that his employer was consequently vicariously liable for her actions. The House of Lords said that there was nothing in the wording of the PHA that prevented employers from being vicariously liable under the Act, so long as there was a sufficiently close connection between the act of harassment and the employment. In this case, there was a sufficiently close connection and Majrowski was awarded significant damages for the suffering he had experienced and the consequential detrimental impact on his state of health.

3.34 In another case, the High Court has also found in favour of an employee who was bullied by her line reports and a peer (*Green v DB Servces Ltd*). The employer failed to take what was considered to be appropriate action to remedy the situation at work, despite the fact that Green suffered two mental breakdowns during her employment as a result of daily bullying, which should have alerted the employer to the magnitude of the problem. The judge said that the employer had closed its eyes to the problem, hoping that it would go away and had dismissed the bullying as office banter. The employer was held to be vicariously liable for its employees' actions and was ordered to pay Green substantial damages.

3.35 The PHA provides an alternative route for employees, who have suffered bullying and harassment at work, to pursue a claim for damages against their employers and the time limit to bring a claim is six years from the date the last act of bullying or harassment took place.

Developing a Formal Policy

3.36 Employers should develop a formal policy in consultation with those who will be affected by its introduction, including any relevant trade union representatives. The policy could include:
- a definition and explanation of bullying
- a statement of commitment from senior management
- acknowledgement that bullying and harassment may be problems in any organisation
- a clear statement that bullying and harassment will not be tolerated
- examples of unacceptable behaviour
- a statement that bullying and harassment may be treated as disciplinary offences under the organisation's disciplinary procedure.

3.37 The policy could then give details of the:
- procedures to be taken if bullying is experienced
- person to contact if bullying is experienced
- steps the organisation will take to prevent bullying and harassment
- responsibilities of supervisors and managers
- confidentiality and protection provided to the complainant
- investigation procedures, including timescales for action
- disciplinary procedures, including timescales for action
- counselling and support available
- training available to managers
- protection provided from unfounded allegations
- implementation, review and monitoring of the policy.

Investigating Bullying

3.38 An employer should investigate the complaint promptly, objectively and to relevant timescales within the bullying procedure.

3.39 The complainant must be assured of confidentiality.

3.40 In some cases matters may be rectified informally. The individual may:
- choose to do this alone
- need support from a colleague, the HR department, a manager, an employee representative, or a counsellor.

Counselling

3.41 Counselling can play a vital role in complaints about bullying and harassment by providing:
- a confidential avenue for an informal approach
- the opportunity to resolve the complaint without need for any formal action.

3.42 Counselling can be particularly useful where investigation shows no cause for disciplinary action, or where doubt is cast on the validity of the complaint. Counselling helps support the person accused as well as the complainant.

Formal Disciplinary Measures

3.43 Where an informal resolution is not possible, the employer may decide that the matter is a disciplinary issue that needs to be dealt with formally by the organisation's disciplinary procedure. As with any disciplinary problem it is important to follow a fair procedure. In the case of a complaint of bullying or harassment there must be fairness to both the complainant and the person accused.

Suspension

3.44 In cases which appear to involve serious misconduct, it may be necessary to suspend the alleged bully/harasser for a short period while the case is being investigated.

3.45 This suspension should be with pay, failure to make payment would be seen as a breach of contract and would give the suspended individual the right to claim unfair dismissal.

3.46 A long suspension, even with pay, should be exceptional as these in themselves may amount to disciplinary penalties. Employers should not transfer the person making the complaint unless he or she asks for such a move.

Unfounded Allegations

3.47 There may be cases where somebody makes an unfounded allegation of bullying and/or harassment for malicious reasons. These cases should also be investigated and dealt with fairly and objectively under the disciplinary procedure. In reality it is difficult in most cases to prove malice as the perception of bullying is subjective.

Training

3.48 Employers should ensure that all employees receive training and information in the policy and procedures of the bullying policy, including what will happen to those employees who do not adhere to it.

3.49 Employers may also want to consider training for all employees in diversity issues.

List of Relevant Legislation

3.50
- Employment Equality (Age) Regulations 2006

- Employment Equality (Religion or Belief) Regulations 2003
- Employment Equality (Sexual Orientation) Regulations 2003
- Management of Health and Safety at Work Regulations 1999
- Protection from Harassment Act 1997
- Disability Discrimination Act 1995
- Public Order Act 1986
- Race Relations Act 1976
- Sex Discrimination Act 1975
- Health and Safety at Work, etc Act 1974

List of Relevant Cases

3.51
- *Majrowski v Guy's and St. Thomas' NHS Trust* [2006] IRLR 695, HL
- *Green v DB Services Ltd* [2006] IRLR 764, HC
- *Hartman v South Essex Mental Health and Community Care NHS Trust* [2005] EWCA Civ 06
- *Barber v Somerset County Council* [2004] IRLR 475, HL
- *Sutherland v Hatton* [2002] IRLR 263
- *Walker v Northumberland County Council* [1995] IRLR 35

Further Information

Publications
- Acas/AL04 Advice Leaflet: *Bullying and Harassment at Work: A Guide for Managers and Employers* (2004)
- Acas/AL05 Advice Leaflet: *Bullying and Harassment at Work: Guidance for Employees*
- *Bullying at Work: How to Confront and Overcome It*, Andrea Adams and Neil Crawford, Virago Press, 1992

Organisations
- **Advisory Conciliation and Arbitration Service (Acas)**
  Web: *www.acas.org.uk*
  Acas aims to improve organisations and working life through better employment relations. It provides up-to-date information, advice, high-quality training, and works with employers and employees to solve problems and improve performance.
- **Andrea Adams Trust**
  Web: *www.andreaadamstrust.org*
  The UK's only charity dedicated to tackling workplace bullying, through advice-lines, publications, services and specialist consultancy services and training programmes.
- **Commission for Racial Equality**
  Web: *www.cre.gov.uk*
  The Commission for Racial Equality is a publicly funded, non-governmental body

set up under the Race Relations Act 1976 to tackle racial discrimination and promote racial equality. From October 2007 this organisation will be replaced by the Commission for Equality and Human Rights.

- **Disability Rights Commission**
  Web: *www.drc-gb.org*
  An independent body established by Act of Parliament to eliminate discrimination against disabled people and promote quality of opportunity. It provides information and advice to disabled people and employers about their rights and duties. From October 2007 this organisation will be replaced by the Commission for Equality and Human Rights (**Web:** *www.cehr.org.uk*).

- **Equal Opportunities Commission**
  Web: *www.eoc.org.uk*
  An agency working to eliminate sex discrimination and put equality into practice in the workplace. From October 2007 this organisation will be replaced by the Commission for Equality and Human Rights (**Web:** *www.cehr.org.uk*).

Disciplinary Offences and Penalties

This topic covers the following.
- The Need for Disciplinary Rules
- Drawing up Disciplinary Rules
- Examples of Disciplinary Rules
- Examples of Misconduct
- Examples of Gross Misconduct
- Dealing with Poor Performance
- Criminal Offences Outside Employment
- Disciplinary Sanctions
- Warnings
- Other Sanctions
- Dismissal on Notice
- Dismissal Without Notice
- Remedies for Inappropriate Disciplinary Action

Employers' Duties

3.52 Employers:
- must provide details of their disciplinary rules, procedures and disciplinary sanctions in the statement of written particulars of employment
- should have a separate procedure for dealing with poor performance issues
- should ensure line managers are trained on the type of behaviour that is subject to disciplinary action and the availability of disciplinary sanctions
- should identify the misconduct or lack of capability which may result in a warning to the employee and the required improvement
- should provide the employee with a written statement of the reasons for any decision to take disciplinary action against or dismiss the employee
- should refer to the Acas Code of Practice on Discipline and Grievance for guidance on the standards and principles that need to be applied in dealing with disciplinary matters, including drawing up disciplinary rules.

Employees' Duties

3.53 Employees must:
- follow any code of conduct and/or any disciplinary rules in their terms and conditions of employment and be aware that non-compliance is likely to result in a disciplinary procedure being followed
- co-operate with the employer in any disciplinary proceedings.

> # In Practice

The Need for Disciplinary Rules

3.54 An employer's statement of written particulars must specify any disciplinary rules applicable to the employee or refer the employee to a document which is reasonably accessible, such as the company intranet or a staff handbook. This means that if disciplinary rules are in place (which is strongly recommended), they should be brought to the attention of all staff.

3.55 Employment tribunals can award four weeks' compensation for the lack, incompleteness or inaccuracy of any written statement of particulars where such a claim is linked with a separate tribunal claim.

Drawing up Disciplinary Rules

3.56 When making disciplinary rules, the aim should be to specify those that are necessary for maintaining good employment relations and for ensuring a safe and efficient workplace.

3.57 Rules should be specific, clear and recorded in writing. Management should do all that it can to ensure that every employee knows and understands the rules, including those whose first language is not English and those who have difficulty reading.

3.58 Rules and procedures should be kept under review to ensure that they are always relevant and effective. Best practice is for new or additional rules to be introduced only after reasonable notice has been given to employees or (where applicable) employee representatives have been consulted.

Examples of Disciplinary Rules

3.59 Employers may choose to devise and implement rules covering some or all of the following matters.
- Timekeeping.
- Requests for holiday and/or absence from work for personal reasons.
- Sickness absence — including notification requirements, the provision of medical certificates and a requirement to attend a medical examination with an occupational doctor on request.
- Hours of work and overtime working.
- Health and safety.
- Accident reporting.
- Dress and appearance requirements, including any banned items of clothing or jewellery.
- Smoking on the organisation's premises.
- Use of the organisation's vehicles.
- Use of the organisation's resources, including stationery, office equipment and materials.
- Care in handling money, materials, tools and equipment, and safekeeping of the organisation's property.
- Removal of the organisation's property from the premises.

Disciplinary Offences and Penalties

- Access to and use of confidential, personal and/or sensitive information.
- Use of email, the Internet and the organisation's telephones, including whether reasonable personal use is permitted.
- General behaviour towards colleagues and a requirement of co-operation.
- Raising grievances.

Examples of Misconduct

3.60 Rules commonly cover the following areas of misconduct.
- Poor timekeeping.
- Minor breaches of health and safety requirements.
- Unauthorised absence.
- Breach of dress code
- Failing to obey a lawful and reasonable instruction.
- Breach of employer's smoking policy.
- Misuse of the organisation's computer facilities, including misuse of email and Internet access.
- Using company time for personal purposes.
- Rudeness or offensive behaviour, including the use of swear words.
- Bullying and harassment.
- Negligence or carelessness in carrying out the work.
- Failure to take proper care of company property.
- (possibly) Unsatisfactory job performance.

3.61 Employers often have rules of behaviour particular to their own organisation or even department.

Examples of Gross Misconduct

3.62 Employees should be given a clear indication of the types of conduct that may be treated as gross misconduct and warrant dismissal without notice. Types of gross misconduct would include:
- theft
- fraud or deliberate falsification of records
- fighting or physical violence
- serious bullying or harassment, including threatening behaviour
- misuse of an organisation's property
- deliberate, wilful or malicious damage to property
- serious insubordination
- deliberate or flagrant failure to follow the organisation's procedures and regulations
- bringing the employer into serious disrepute
- being under the influence of alcohol or illegal drugs at work
- serious negligence which causes or might cause unacceptable loss, damage or injury
- serious infringement of health and safety rules
- disclosure without authority of confidential information to an outside person or organisation
- serious breach of confidence subject to statutory whistleblowing protection
- raising a grievance or making an allegation maliciously

Disciplinary Offences and Penalties

- serious misuse of the organisation's computer facilities, including misuse of email and Internet access
- driving a vehicle belonging to the organisation without permission
- disqualification from driving in circumstances where the possession of a driving licence is essential for the performance of the job
- criminal conduct outside of work that is relevant to the employment, or that might cause damage to the organisation's reputation
- refusal to attend a medical examination with an occupational doctor if reasonably asked to do so
- refusal to agree to undergo a test for alcohol or substance abuse.

Dealing with Poor Performance

3.63 Some employers use disciplinary rules and procedures to deal with instances of poor performance as well as conduct. Best practice is to have a separate procedure for dealing with poor performance. This avoids the stigma attached to the disciplinary process and can be viewed as a positive way of improving performance by both employer and employee.

3.64 "Warnings" can be given to the effect that unless required standards of performance are met by the end of a stipulated review period, further action will be taken, ie a further review or a further warning and ultimately dismissal will result.

3.65 If the same procedure is to be used for both poor performance and misconduct matters, it should be ensured that the disciplinary rules include poor performance as a disciplinary matter.

Criminal Offences Outside Employment

3.66 It may be appropriate to discipline an employee for conduct outside work where it affects, or could be thought to affect, the employee's employment.

3.67 As the Acas Code of Practice states, a criminal conviction in itself is not a reason for disciplinary action. The main consideration should be whether the offence impacts on the employee's suitability to do the job in question or if it brings the organisation into serious disrepute. Much will depend on the nature of the job. While it could be appropriate to dismiss a shop worker convicted of shoplifting, even if the offence was committed in a different store, it may not be appropriate to dismiss an office typist for the same offence, unless there is a real security risk, for example if the typist has access to cash at work.

Disciplinary Sanctions

3.68 There are a number of disciplinary sanctions at the disposal of the employer. The possible sanctions should be clearly identified in the employer's disciplinary procedure.

Warnings

3.69 The most widely used form of disciplinary action is a warning.

3.70 The Acas Code of Practice, while recognising that cases of minor instances of misconduct or unsatisfactory performance are usually best dealt with informally, no longer recommends verbal warnings as the first stage of formal action.

3.71 Acas recommends the following system of warnings.

- Written warning recorded in an informal letter to the employee — kept on file but disregarded after six months.
- Written warning putting the employee on notice that any further misconduct will result in dismissal — disregarded after 12 months.

3.72 Many employers still use verbal warnings to deal with minor misdemeanours. However, best practice is for such a warning to be confirmed in writing to the employee as well as making a record on the employee's personnel file.

Warning Levels

3.73 The level of warning given will depend on the seriousness of the employee's misconduct. An employer is not required to start the procedure with a first written warning. However, it may be problematic to miss out either of the warning levels unless an offence is sufficiently serious on its own to justify dismissal (eg the offence constitutes gross misconduct).

3.74 Employers should ensure that there is clear evidence of a warning being brought to the attention of the employee. The employee should ideally acknowledge receipt of a warning in writing.

Warning Content

3.75 A warning may be of little use at future disciplinary hearings or employment tribunals if it does not detail the:
- conduct which has prompted the warning
- consequences of a repetition of any such conduct (or further misconduct of any other kind)
- length of time the warning will remain "live" on the employee's file
- required improvement within a defined timescale
- consequences of a failure to achieve such improvement
- right for the employee to appeal against the warning.

Previous Warnings

3.76 The fact that previous warnings were issued for conduct of a different kind does not render them irrelevant when an employer is considering whether or not to take disciplinary action for a particular offence. The employer is entitled to take into account:
- the existence of previous warnings
- how many there have been
- the substance of the complaint on each occasion
- the dates and time periods between them.

3.77 The employer must not, however, seek to extend a previous warning that has expired.

Extending the Length of Warnings

3.78 There may be occasions when an employer may not wish to dismiss the employee but a more powerful penalty than a 12-month final written warning is desirable. Some of the sanctions mentioned below could be considered. Alternatively, an extended final written warning or even one which would last forever could be given.

3.79 An extended final written warning issued for an indefinite period would usually be issued on the basis that the employee could have been dismissed for the offence but, for a particular reason, the employer has chosen to exercise leniency and grant the employee a second chance. The reasons and implications of an indefinite final written warning must be clearly spelled out to the employee in writing.

Other Sanctions

3.80 Short of dismissal, other possible sanctions are:
- demotion or downgrading
- transfer to another department
- loss of privileges, such as a responsibility allowance, seniority or bonus payment
- suspension without pay for a limited period.

3.81 Such sanctions will have a serious impact on the employment relationship and should only be used after the most careful consideration. In particular, demotion and downgrading should only be used in cases where the employer is considering an alternative to dismissal when all warning levels have been exhausted. Furthermore, these sanctions should not be imposed unless specifically listed as possible disciplinary penalties within the contract of employment. To impose such a sanction without the agreement of the employee is likely to breach the implied term of trust and confidence and could lead to a claim for constructive dismissal. If such sanctions are not listed as disciplinary penalties, they should only be implemented with the agreement of the employee as an alternative to some other disciplinary penalty, eg a final written warning or dismissal. Once agreed with the employee, demotion, downgrading or transfer to another department will constitute a permanent change to the contract of employment. Loss of privileges may be a permanent or temporary change to the contract, whilst suspension without pay will, by nature, be temporary.

3.82 Suspension without pay is a rare disciplinary sanction and should not be confused with suspension on full pay during a disciplinary investigation, which is not a disciplinary penalty.

3.83 The standard dismissal and disciplinary procedures (DDP) must be followed, as a minimum, if any of the sanctions above are likely to be imposed, except where the employer's own disciplinary procedure has already commenced in relation to the misconduct in question. Employers must always give the employee clear written notice of the allegations against him or her prior to any disciplinary meeting, in order to give the employee a full and fair opportunity to explain any unsatisfactory conduct at the meeting. The employee must also be given the right to appeal, as is required under the statutory DDP, if any of the above sanctions are being contemplated.

Dismissal on Notice

3.84 If the employee's conduct or performance still fails to improve, or no other disciplinary sanction is appropriate, the final stage in the disciplinary process is dismissal on notice.

3.85 The statutory dismissal and disciplinary procedures must be followed, as a minimum, to avoid a finding of automatic unfair dismissal.

3.86 Dismissal, as the ultimate disciplinary sanction, should only normally be imposed as a last resort and where no lesser action is appropriate.

Disciplinary Offences and Penalties

Dismissal Without Notice

3.87 An employer may summarily dismiss an employee only where the employee has committed a repudiatory breach of contract. Most usually this would be for gross misconduct.

3.88 Summary dismissal means dismissal without notice or pay in lieu of notice. Thus the employee's contract and all the benefits under it come to an end on the same day as notice is given.

3.89 Some contracts of employment include a list of circumstances in which employees may be summarily dismissed. However, the danger of including such a clause is that a tribunal may find that the list is a complete and exhaustive list of situations in which summary dismissal may be justified. Any clause of this nature should always be carefully drafted so as to ensure it is clear that the list is illustrative and not exhaustive.

Remedies for Inappropriate Disciplinary Action

3.90 The disciplinary penalty imposed must be proportionate to the seriousness of the alleged misconduct.

3.91 In *Stanley Cole (Wainfleet) Ltd v Sheridan* [2003] IRLR 885, CA, an employee with a previously exemplary record was issued with a final written warning for leaving the workplace for 90 minutes without permission, following an argument with another employee. The tribunal held that she was entitled to resign and claim constructive dismissal. The issuing of a final written warning in this case amounted to a repudiatory breach of contract.

3.92 Demoting, transferring or suspending an employee without pay and without the contractual right to do so could amount to a repudiatory breach of contact entitling the employee to resign and claim constructive dismissal.

3.93 In order to defend a claim for unfair dismissal on the grounds of misconduct, the employer needs to show that at the time of dismissal and after a thorough investigation of the facts, a reasonable and genuine belief was formed on the balance of probabilities that the employee committed the offence. The employer does not need to prove that the employee actually committed the offence.

3.94 It is, however, for the employer to show that the reason for dismissal was a fair reason. If the employer fails to do so, the employee will win the case.

3.95 An employee, dismissed summarily without justification, will be entitled to claim wrongful dismissal on grounds that contractual notice was not given as well as, or instead of, unfair dismissal.

Training

3.96 It is important that managers are familiar with the organisation's dismissal and disciplinary procedures, and that they understand both the employer's and employees' responsibilities.

3.97 Training on disciplinary procedures should include the following.
- The type of behaviour which should be subject to disciplinary action.
- The availability of disciplinary sanctions.
- Who can administer disciplinary sanctions.

List of Relevant Legislation

3.98
- Employment Act 2002 (Dispute Resolution) Regulations 2004
- Employment Act 2002
- Employment Rights Act 1996

List of Relevant Cases

3.99
- *Silman v ICTS Ltd* (2006), EAT
- *Draper v Mears Ltd* [2006] IRLR 869, EAT
- *Diosynth Ltd v Thomson* [2006] IRLR 277, CA
- *Stanley Cole (Wainfleet) Ltd v Sheridan* [2003] IRLR 885, CA
- *August Noel Ltd v Curtis* [1990] IRLR 326
- *Dairy Produce Packers Ltd v Beverstock* [1981] IRLR 265, EAT
- *British Home Stores Ltd v Burchell* [1978] IRLR 379, EAT
- *Singh v London County Bus Services Ltd* [1976] IRLR 176, EAT

Further Information

Publications
- *Acas Advisory Handbook: Discipline and Grievances at Work (2005)*
- *Acas/CP01 Code of Practice on Disciplinary and Grievance Procedures (2004)*
- *Acas/S03 Dealing with Grievances*
- *Acas/S04 Discipline at Work (2004)*
- *Acas/RW01 Rights at Work Leaflets: Discipline, Grievances and Dismissal*
- *Croner's A-Z Guide to Employment*
- *Croner's Personnel in Practice*
- *Croner's Reference Book for Employers*

Organisations
- **Advisory Conciliation and Arbitration Service (Acas)**
  Web: *www.acas.org.uk*
  Acas aims to improve organisations and working life through better employment relations. It provides up-to-date information, advice, high-quality training, and works with employers and employees to solve problems and improve performance.
- **Department for Business, Enterprise and Regulatory Reform (BERR)**
  Web: *www.berr.gov.uk*
  The Department for Business, Enterprise and Regulatory Reform brings together functions from the former Department of Trade and Industry (DTI), including

responsibilities for productivity, business relations, energy, competition and consumers. It also drives regulatory reform.

Disciplinary Procedures

This topic covers the following.
- The Need for Disciplinary Rules and Procedures
- Written Statement of Particulars
- Drawing up Disciplinary Rules and Procedures
- Key Features of a Disciplinary Procedure
- The Acas Code of Practice
- Investigating a Disciplinary Offence
- Suspension from Work
- Arranging a Disciplinary Hearing
- The Purpose of a Disciplinary Hearing
- Conducting a Disciplinary Hearing
- Mitigating Factors
- Deciding the Outcome
- Written Statement of Reason(s) for Dismissal
- Statement of Reason for Any Decision
- Informal Warnings
- Formal Warnings
- The Lifespan of a Warning
- Dismissal with Notice
- Gross Misconduct and Summary Dismissal
- Sanctions Short of Dismissal
- Proof of Misconduct
- Right of Appeal
- Right to be Accompanied
- Statutory Dismissal and Disciplinary Procedures
- Criminal Offences outside Employment
- When the Handling of Disciplinary Matters can Lead to a Grievance
- Constructive Dismissal Claims
- Keeping Records

3.100 All employers are required by law to devise and implement a written disciplinary procedure and it is advisable to apply clear and comprehensive disciplinary rules to all staff covering a range of issues.

3.101 Disciplinary procedures must be carried out fairly and objectively and any penalty imposed must similarly be fair. Where the penalty is dismissal, the employee has a right not to be unfairly dismissed and the employer will need to be able to show that it acted reasonably in treating the matter as one justifying dismissal. An otherwise fair dismissal may be found to be unfair if there is procedural unfairness. There are also minimum procedural steps that employers are under a duty to take if the outcome of disciplinary proceedings is dismissal or certain forms of disciplinary action, known as "relevant disciplinary action".

Employers' Duties

3.102 Employers must ensure that they:
- provide details of their disciplinary procedure in, or along with, each employee's written statement of particulars of employment
- comply with the Acas Code of Practice

- carry out as much investigation as is reasonable into all the circumstances of the case before taking any disciplinary decision
- inform an employee in writing of any allegation of misconduct or unsatisfactory performance prior to holding a disciplinary hearing
- give full consideration to the employee's explanations and any mitigating factors put forward by the employee
- comply with an employee's request for a written statement of the reason(s) for his or her dismissal
- make sure that formal written warnings clearly identify the nature of the employee's misconduct or lack of capability, the improvement that is required and what the outcome will be if the employee fails to improve within a defined timescale
- accommodate the employee's right to be accompanied by an appropriate companion at a disciplinary hearing
- comply with the statutory dismissal and disciplinary procedure in every case.

Employees' Duties

3.103 Employees must:
- follow any code of conduct and/or any disciplinary rules contained in their written statement of particulars or within a staff handbook
- be aware that non-compliance with their employer's disciplinary rules is likely to result in disciplinary action being taken against them
- co-operate with the employer in any investigation being carried out into their own or others' alleged misconduct
- attend and take part in any disciplinary hearing set up by the employer and be prepared to put forward their version of events and/or explain their conduct fully
- use their right of appeal where there are grounds to believe that the disciplinary process was conducted unfairly or that the outcome of the proceedings was unfair or excessive
- consider whether they wish to exercise their right to be accompanied by a fellow worker or trade union official at any formal disciplinary hearing.

In Practice

The Need for Disciplinary Rules and Procedures

3.104 Disciplinary rules and procedures are helpful for employers and their employees because they set clear and consistent standards of behaviour for everyone, help employees to understand what types of conduct or behaviour are unacceptable in the workplace and give employers a framework for dealing fairly with employees who breach the rules.

Written Statement of Particulars

3.105 An employee's statement of written particulars must include any disciplinary rules applicable to the employee, or refer the employee to a reasonably accessible document that contains the rules, such as the organisation's intranet or a staff handbook. It is also a statutory requirement for every employer to devise and implement a written disciplinary procedure and provide all staff with ready access to the procedure. The procedure must contain the mandatory steps of the statutory dismissal and disciplinary procedure.

Drawing up Disciplinary Rules and Procedures

3.106 When devising disciplinary rules, the aim should be to specify the rationale behind the rules, eg whether they are in place:
- in order to ensure health and safety
- for reasons of efficiency (eg timekeeping, use of the organisation's equipment)
- in order to promote a comfortable working environment for all staff (eg rules prohibiting bullying or banning the downloading of inappropriate material from the Internet).

3.107 Rules should be specific, clear and recorded in writing. Management should do all it can to ensure that every employee knows and understands the rules, including employees whose first language is not English and those who may have difficulty with reading.

3.108 Rules and procedures should be kept under review to ensure they are always relevant, up-to-date and effective. Best practice is for new or additional rules to be introduced only after reasonable notice has been given to employees and (where applicable) after employees or their representatives have been consulted.

Key Features of a Disciplinary Procedure

3.109 The key features of a sound disciplinary procedure are as follows.
- The procedure should provide a clear and fair means of dealing with all types of misconduct.
- There should always be a proper investigation into the employee's alleged misconduct before disciplinary action is decided upon.
- The employee must be fully informed in writing of the allegations against him or her, including the content of any witnesses' statements.
- An employee should be expressly informed of his or her right to be accompanied at any forthcoming disciplinary hearing.
- An employee accused of misconduct must be afforded a full and fair opportunity to explain his or her conduct or put forward a defence before any decision is taken on whether or not to impose a disciplinary sanction, and if so what level of sanction to impose.
- Warnings that have expired should not normally be taken into account in deciding to dismiss, unless there are unusual circumstances.
- A first offence should not normally lead to dismissal unless it amounts to gross misconduct justifying summary dismissal.
- The employee must be granted the right of appeal against any decision to dismiss him or her.
- The employer must in a general sense act reasonably when dealing with employee misconduct.
- The employer should keep records of all disciplinary action taken, subject to the provisions of the Data Protection Act 1998.

The Acas Code of Practice

3.110 Guidance for employers on the design and operation of appropriate disciplinary procedures is provided in the Advisory, Conciliation and Arbitration

Service (Acas) Code of Practice on Disciplinary and Grievance Procedures. While it is not mandatory for employers to implement the provisions contained in the Code of Practice, non-compliance can be taken into account by an employment tribunal and will act to the employer's detriment.

3.111 The Acas Code of Practice suggests that good disciplinary procedures should:

- be in writing
- specify to whom they apply
- be non-discriminatory
- provide for matters to be dealt with without undue delay
- provide for proceedings, witness statements and records to be kept confidential
- indicate the disciplinary actions that may be taken by the employer
- specify the levels of management that have the authority to take the various forms of disciplinary action
- provide for workers to be informed of the complaints against them and, if possible, to be given all relevant evidence before any hearing
- ensure that, except for gross misconduct, no employee is dismissed for a first breach of discipline
- ensure that disciplinary action is not taken until the case has been carefully investigated
- ensure that employees are given an explanation for any penalty imposed
- provide a right of appeal to a more senior level of management and specify the procedure to be followed.

Investigating a Disciplinary Offence

3.112 Before any disciplinary action is instigated, the employer should carry out as much investigation into the employee's alleged misconduct as is reasonable. The requirement for reasonable investigation will be present at all stages of the disciplinary procedure, irrespective of the seriousness of the employee's misconduct. Investigation may include:

- checking the employee's personnel record to establish whether he or she has had any previous warnings, and if so whether they are unexpired
- talking in confidence to any employee who may have knowledge of the alleged misconduct
- taking statements from any witnesses
- checking telephone records
- talking to the employer's customers to seek feedback about the employee
- holding an investigatory meeting with the employee suspected of misconduct with a view to establishing the facts.

3.113 Following investigations, the investigating manager should then decide whether to:

- drop the matter (if there is no evidence of misconduct)
- deal with the issue informally in consultation with the employee
- arrange for the matter to be dealt with under the formal disciplinary procedure.

3.114 It is very important to distinguish between an investigatory hearing (the purpose of which is to establish facts, and not to make any decisions based on these facts) and a disciplinary hearing (the purpose of which is to determine whether there are grounds to impose a disciplinary sanction on the employee). Managers dealing with investigations should take care:

- not to jump to conclusions prematurely
- to restrict their activities to investigating the facts, rather than making decisions based on the facts
- not to say or do anything that implies judgment of the employee's actions or behaviour.

3.115 There is no statutory requirement to operate separate investigatory and disciplinary processes, although larger employers often do so. If the procedures are split, then the manager dealing with the disciplinary process should be a different person from the one who carried out the investigations. In this way, the employee is able to make representations at the disciplinary hearing to a person who has had no prior involvement in the matter and who is therefore likely to be more impartial.

Suspension from Work

3.116 When it is known or suspected that an employee has committed an act of misconduct, the employer may, at its discretion, suspend the employee from work in order to investigate the circumstances. Such suspension from work must be on normal pay; otherwise the employer would be acting in breach of contract and could be accused of pre-judging the employee's guilt.

3.117 Suspension is likely to be appropriate:
- in cases of known, or suspected, gross misconduct, in which case it is usually prudent to ask the employee to leave the premises at once and to stay away until called back to the workplace for a hearing
- if the relationship between the employer and employee has broken down
- if it is thought that the employee's continued presence in the workplace could create risks to the employer's property or in respect of the employer's responsibilities to other parties
- if the integrity of an investigation may be undermined by the accused employee continuing to work with witnesses.

3.118 Any suspension from work should be for as short a period as possible.

Arranging a Disciplinary Hearing

3.119 The invitation to an employee to attend a disciplinary hearing should be in writing, and should set out a summary of the complaint, but without giving the employee the impression that the employer has made up its mind already as to what the outcome will be. The allegations should be as clear and unambiguous as possible, so that the employee fully understands the reason(s) why he or she is to be disciplined. All available evidence about the employee's alleged misconduct should be provided to the employee at this stage, including the content of any witness statements (anonymised if appropriate).

3.120 It is important to strike a reasonable balance between dealing with an instance of misconduct as soon as possible in order to get it over and done with, and dealing with it in haste, ie so quickly that the employee has insufficient time to gather his or her thoughts and prepare an adequate defence. The latter would, of course, be unacceptable and unfair. The employee has the right to a reasonable time period to prepare his or her thoughts before the hearing takes place.

The Purpose of a Disciplinary Hearing

3.121 The purpose of a disciplinary hearing will normally be three-fold. To:

Disciplinary Procedures

- allow the employer to explain his or her case (ie explain in what way the employee is thought to have breached the employer's rules, behaved inappropriately, etc)
- allow the employee to respond to the accusations of misconduct or inappropriate behaviour (ie present his or her version of events)
- determine, on conclusion of the hearing, whether there are proper grounds to impose a disciplinary sanction against the employee.

Conducting a Disciplinary Hearing

3.122 There are no rigid criteria laid down for disciplinary hearings, but it is good practice for employers to comply with the following requirements.

- Disciplinary hearings must be objective, and the person conducting them must have the ability to remain open-minded.
- A disciplinary hearing should be reasonably formal, although it would not be expected to have the formality or rigour of a court of law.
- The onus on the employer is to reach a reasoned and reasonable conclusion on the balance of probability, rather than "beyond all reasonable doubt".
- Fairness must be evident.
- The complaint must be properly put to the employee, ie all the facts surrounding the employee's alleged or suspected misconduct must be fully and clearly communicated, with specific examples of relevant incidents being given.
- The employee must be granted a full and fair opportunity to offer his or her version of events or explanation.
- If the employee raises facts of which the employer was previously unaware, it may be necessary to adjourn the hearing to allow management to instigate further investigations.
- The employee should be permitted to ask questions and challenge any evidence put forward by the employer.
- Any mitigating factors put forward by the employee must be taken on board and subsequently considered when making a decision about whether or not to impose a disciplinary penalty, and the level of any such penalty.
- The employee must be given a full and fair opportunity to question or challenge anything reported in a witness statement, ie any matters raised by the employee regarding the accuracy of a witness statement must be followed up or checked out as appropriate.
- There is no legal requirement to call witnesses to a disciplinary hearing, but if a witness is called to attend the hearing, he or she should be present only for so long as is necessary to allow him or her to be questioned.
- If witnesses are called to the hearing by either party, both parties must be given the opportunity to question them.
- Notes should be taken of all the key points put forward at the hearing.
- The hearing should be adjourned to allow an informed and considered decision to be made.

Mitigating Factors

3.123 Representations made by an employee at a disciplinary hearing, or mitigating factors put forward, must be fully and fairly considered by the employer. These may be relevant in respect of the level of disciplinary sanction to be imposed. Mitigating factors could include:

- the employee's length of service
- previous good conduct

- the employee's personal circumstances, eg if he or she has recently experienced a bereavement or other family or personal upset
- the employee's general health, including mental health
- whether the employee was in any way provoked or whether another employee's conduct contributed towards his or her conduct.

Deciding the Outcome

3.124 Once the hearing is complete, the employer should carefully consider all the circumstances of the case before reaching any decision. While no decision should be made in haste, it is equally important to avoid any unnecessary delay in concluding the matter. The disciplinary procedure itself should specify within what period of time a decision will be provided.

3.125 The employee would normally be informed of the employer's decision verbally initially, with written confirmation following within a day or two. The written communication should specify the reasons for any disciplinary sanction imposed by the employer.

Written Statement of Reason(s) for Dismissal

3.126 Where the penalty is dismissal, the employee has a right to request a written statement of the reason(s) for his or her dismissal. Technically this right is dependent on the employee having gained a minimum of one year's continuous employment with the employer. It is nevertheless good practice to provide such a statement in all cases, and to ensure that it provides the true reason (or reasons) for the dismissal.

Statement of Reason for Any Decision

3.127 The Acas Code of Practice suggests that the employee should be provided with a written explanation as to the reasons for any imposed disciplinary penalty. Where the penalty is dismissal, the employee has a right to request a written statement of the reasons. This right is dependent on the employee having gained a minimum of one year's continuous employment with the employer.

Informal Warnings

3.128 Informal warnings fall outside the formal disciplinary procedure and amount to nothing more than the employee's manager or supervisor having a private word with the employee, eg to correct a problem or deliver an informal reprimand. Often informal warnings are sufficient to resolve a problem. There is no right for the employee to be accompanied at a meeting which amounts to an informal discussion, provided it is clear that it will not lead to any formal action.

3.129 An employer should also use informal meetings with staff to offer support, guidance and advice as to the steps that are necessary to change or improve conduct or behaviour, rather than only viewing such meetings as opportunities to issue warnings.

3.130 Even though a meeting may be informal, the manager should keep a record of it. The record should show:
- the date and time the meeting took place
- the key points discussed
- that there was no formal outcome.

3.131 The employee should be given a copy of the note and a copy placed on his or her personnel file.

Formal Warnings

3.132 A formal warning may be appropriate where the employee has not responded to earlier informal warnings and the misconduct in question is continuing or has been repeated. In addition, a formal warning may be appropriate if a first instance of misconduct is too serious to be dealt with through an informal warning.

3.133 Formal warnings, which should always be confirmed in writing, should state:
- that the warning is part of the employer's formal disciplinary procedure
- the nature of the employee's misconduct
- if it applies to any other similar or all future misconduct in the case of a final written warning
- the improvement required (ie a clear indication of how the employee is expected to behave in the future)
- any timescale for improvement
- the period of time the warning will remain active on the employee's file
- the outcome if there is no improvement (ie further disciplinary action at the next stage of the disciplinary procedure)
- the right to appeal against the warning and how any appeal should be raised.

The Lifespan of a Warning

3.134 Warnings are normally designed to have a limited lifespan, depending on their gravity and on the individual employer's policies. There are no time limits imposed by legislation. Typical time limits are as follows.
- A first or formal verbal warning may remain active for six months.
- A first written warning will often be regarded as active for between 6 and 12 months.
- A final written warning will often be regarded as active for between 12 and 24 months.

3.135 It is good practice for an employer to define in its disciplinary procedure the length of time that the various stages of disciplinary warning will normally remain active for disciplinary purposes. It is also advisable to state in the disciplinary procedure that the employer reserves the right to impose longer lifespan periods than the normal periods at its discretion. Any warning issued to the employee should specify the period of time that it will remain active on the employee's file.

3.136 After the defined lifespan has run its course, the warning must not be taken into account in any subsequent disciplinary action. The Scottish Court of Session ruled in 2006 that it is inherently unreasonable for an employer to rely on an expired warning when taking a decision whether or not to dismiss an employee.

3.137 There is no need, however, for the warning to be physically removed from the employee's file, so long as it is clearly marked as "expired" and not used against the employee in future disciplinary proceedings.

3.138 In very exceptional circumstances an employer may impose a warning that has an indefinite lifespan. This will usually be for very serious misconduct that might otherwise have resulted in summary dismissal but for mitigating circumstances. If such a warning is given, the employer should be very specific about the misconduct it relates to (eg sexual harassment) and it can only be used in future disciplinary action when the employee is guilty of similar misconduct.

Dismissal with Notice

3.139 If, after an appropriate number of warnings (typically one or more informal warnings followed by at least two formal warnings), the employee's conduct fails to improve to the required standard or misconduct is repeated, the final stage in the disciplinary process will be dismissal with notice. The notice due to the employee will be in accordance with the employee's contract.

3.140 The minimum steps of the statutory dismissal and disciplinary procedure must be followed to avoid a finding of automatically unfair dismissal.

3.141 Dismissal, as the ultimate disciplinary sanction, should only normally be imposed as a last resort where no other course of action is appropriate or reasonable.

Gross Misconduct and Summary Dismissal

3.142 Gross misconduct is a single act of misconduct which is of such a fundamentally serious nature that it justifies immediate dismissal. This is known as "summary dismissal". Summary dismissal means the termination of an employee's employment without notice or pay in lieu of notice on the grounds of the employee's gross misconduct.

3.143 For summary dismissal to be justified, the actions of the employee must have fundamentally undermined the duty of trust and confidence between employee and employer to the extent that the employer is no longer required to retain the employee in employment or be bound by any of the terms of the contract (including the requirement to give notice).

3.144 Care should be exercised as a summary dismissal can be an unfair dismissal if the correct procedures are not followed. Although the employer can dismiss the employee without notice following an incident of gross misconduct, the employer must nevertheless first follow through the normal procedures before taking the decision to dismiss. This means that the employer must still investigate the circumstances and give the employee an opportunity to explain his or her conduct at a disciplinary hearing, before concluding that summary dismissal is the appropriate sanction.

3.145 Some examples of gross misconduct include (but are not limited to):
- theft
- fraud or deliberate falsification of records
- fighting or physical violence
- serious bullying or harassment, including threatening behaviour
- serious misuse of the employer's resources
- deliberate, wilful or malicious damage to property
- serious misuse of the organisation's computer facilities, including misuse of e-mail and Internet access
- serious insubordination
- deliberate or flagrant failure to follow the organisation's procedures and regulations
- being under the influence of alcohol or illegal drugs at work
- serious negligence which causes or might cause unacceptable loss, damage or injury
- serious infringement of health and safety rules
- raising a grievance or making an allegation maliciously
- driving a vehicle belonging to the organisation without permission
- criminal conduct outside of work that is relevant to the employment, or that might cause damage to the organisation's reputation

- disclosure without authority of confidential information to an outside person or organisation
- refusal to attend a medical examination with an occupational doctor if reasonably asked to do so
- acting in any way that might reasonably bring the employer's name into serious disrepute.

3.146 There is no "legal list" of what constitutes gross misconduct and it is up to each employer to devise its own rules and ensure that these are properly communicated to all employees. The list should state that it is not all-inclusive, but that other offences of similar gravity may be considered to be gross misconduct, depending on the circumstances.

Sanctions Short of Dismissal

3.147 Rather than impose dismissal as the final sanction for misconduct, some employers include within their disciplinary procedures other sanctions which fall short of dismissal. Examples of possible sanctions are:
- demotion or downgrading
- removal of responsibilities or status
- transfer to another department
- loss of privileges, such as a responsibility allowance or discretionary bonus payment
- suspension without pay for a limited period.

3.148 Such sanctions will have a serious impact on the employment relationship and should only be used after very careful consideration. Furthermore, these sanctions should not be imposed unless specifically listed as authorised disciplinary penalties within the employee's contract of employment. To impose such a sanction without the authority of the contract would be a fundamental breach of contract and could lead to a claim for constructive dismissal. They can, of course, be applied as an alternative to dismissal with the employee's agreement.

3.149 Suspension without pay is a rare disciplinary sanction and should not be confused with suspension on full pay during a disciplinary investigation, which is not a disciplinary penalty.

3.150 The statutory dismissal and disciplinary procedure must be followed if any of the sanctions listed above are likely to be imposed.

Proof of Misconduct

3.151 Proof of misconduct is not required for a dismissal to be fair. Instead, the courts have ruled that a dismissal may be fair provided:
- the employer genuinely believed that the employee was guilty of a serious offence
- there were reasonable grounds on which to form such a belief (ie some evidence was available)
- the employer conducted a thorough investigation.

Right of Appeal

3.152 Where the outcome of a disciplinary hearing is an oral or written warning, there is no statutory right for the employee to be granted an appeal, although it is nevertheless best practice to give the employee the right of appeal against the imposition of a warning.

Disciplinary Procedures

3.153 Where, however, the outcome is dismissal or certain forms of disciplinary sanction short of dismissal, the right of appeal must, by law, be granted.

3.154 By law, only one level of appeal is required, but some employers may choose to have a further level of appeal (or even two further levels) so that the employee can appeal again if he or she still believes that the disciplinary process was not fairly conducted or that the outcome was unfair.

3.155 Employees should be informed of their right to appeal where appropriate and should also be told:
- the time limit for raising an appeal (which should be reasonable)
- to whom any appeal should be made
- how the appeal should be lodged (ie in writing)
- that the employee should make clear his or her grounds for appealing.

3.156 In some cases, it may be in the employer's interests to treat an appeal as a complete rehearing. In the case of *Taylor v OCS Group Ltd*, however, the Court of Appeal decided that there is no rule of law which says that only a complete rehearing of a case at a disciplinary appeal meeting can rectify earlier flaws in the exercise of an organisation's disciplinary procedure. An appeal hearing, which is a review of the case and is conducted fairly and with an open mind so that a reasonable decision can be concluded, can also rectify any earlier procedural flaws. In arriving at its decision, the Court of Appeal stated that an employment tribunal should consider the fairness of procedural issues together in order to decide if an employer has acted reasonably. In conclusion, in the event of an employee bringing a claim for unfair dismissal, it will be open to an employment tribunal to find that procedural unfairness occurring during the disciplinary process has been rectified by an appeal.

3.157 The exception to this ruling would be if there had been a flaw in the application of the statutory minimum disciplinary and dismissal procedure itself as there is no provision in the Employment Act 2002, which allows a breach of that procedure to be cured by an appeal. In this situation, however, the employer may still be able to claim under s.98A(2) of the Employment Rights Act 1996 that the breach would have made no difference to the outcome, and that the dismissal is, therefore, not automatically unfair under the Employment Act 2002 (Dispute Resolution) Regulations 2004.

3.158 Appeals and re-hearings should always be heard by an individual who was not involved in the original investigation or the disciplinary process. Wherever practicable, the appeal should be considered by an individual at a higher level in the organisation.

Right to be Accompanied

3.159 Employees have a statutory right to be accompanied at disciplinary hearings by a fellow worker or trade union official of their choice. A trade union official means a full-time official of a union or a lay official who is certified by the union as having had training in, or experience of, acting as a companion at disciplinary hearings. The trade union official does not have to belong to a union recognised by the employer. The right applies to formal disciplinary hearings that might give rise to the imposition of a formal disciplinary sanction. There is no requirement to allow an employee to be accompanied at an informal meeting or an investigatory interview, provided such meetings are not allowed to develop into disciplinary hearings.

3.160 The chosen companion is entitled to paid time off work for fulfilling the function of companion.

3.161 If the employee's chosen companion is unavailable at the time the employer has scheduled for the hearing, the employee may propose an alternative time for the hearing, provided the alternative time is reasonable and within five working days of the time suggested by the employer.

3.162 Denial of the right to be accompanied can give rise to a complaint to an employment tribunal. The tribunal can award up to two weeks' pay as compensation.

Statutory Dismissal and Disciplinary Procedures

3.163 The Employment Act 2002 (Dispute Resolution) Regulations 2004, which were implemented on 1 October 2004, require all employers (irrespective of their size) to introduce and operate a dismissal and disciplinary procedure (DDP) when contemplating dismissing an employee or taking "relevant disciplinary action".

3.164 The regulations introduced a standard three-step procedure and a modified two-step procedure.

The Scope of the Statutory Procedure

3.165 The statutory dismissal and disciplinary procedure (DDP) must be followed where:
- the employer contemplates dismissing an employee on grounds of misconduct
- the employer contemplates dismissing an employee on grounds of lack of capability, which includes unsatisfactory job performance or ill-health
- redundancies are proposed and the number of people likely to be made redundant is fewer than 20
- an employee's fixed-term contract is about to expire
- a dismissal is contemplated for "some other substantial reason"
- relevant disciplinary action is being contemplated.

3.166 Relevant disciplinary action would include sanctions short of dismissal such as:
- demotion or downgrading
- removal of responsibilities or status
- transfer to another department
- loss of privileges, such as a responsibility allowance or discretionary bonus payment
- suspension without pay for a limited period.

3.167 The DDP need not, however, be followed if the outcome of disciplinary proceedings is a verbal or written warning, although it is best practice to always follow the key procedural steps included in the DDP in all cases.

Exemptions from the Statutory Procedure

3.168 The statutory dismissal and disciplinary procedure need not be applied in any of the following circumstances:
- where the employer is proposing to make 20 or more employees redundant (because there is a duty to consult collectively instead)
- where the employer dismisses employees on the grounds that they are on strike or are taking other industrial action
- if the employer's business ceases to function because of an unforeseen event and it is impracticable to employ any employees

- where the employer is dismissing employees but at the same time offering them re-engagement on different terms, provided all employees of the same category are dismissed and offered re-engagement
- if the reason for dismissal is that the employer could not continue to employ the individual without contravening a legal duty or restriction
- where the same matter has been raised by representatives and is being dealt with collectively.

Standard Three-Step Procedure

3.169 Employers are obliged under the standard DDP to carry out three steps. The three steps are as follows.

3.170 Step One
- The employer must set out the employee's alleged "conduct or characteristics, or other circumstances" in writing and give or send a copy to the employee.
- The employer should inform the employee of the basis of the complaint against him or her.
- At the same time, the employer must invite the employee to attend a meeting/hearing.
- The written notice must give adequate information to the employee without giving the appearance that the manager has already made up his or her mind what the outcome will be.

3.171 Step Two
- Arrangements are made for the disciplinary hearing/meeting.
- The meeting must take place before any action is taken, although the employee may be suspended on full pay pending the meeting.
- The employee must take all reasonable steps to attend the meeting.
- The employee has the right to be accompanied at the meeting by a colleague or trade union official of his or her choice.
- At the meeting, both parties must have the opportunity to explain their cases prior to any decision being taken.
- After the meeting a decision is taken about whether to dismiss the employee or take relevant disciplinary action.
- The decision should be communicated to the employee in writing.
- The employer must also notify the employee of the right to appeal against the decision.

3.172 Step Three
- The employee must inform the employer of his or her right to appeal.
- If the employee does appeal, the employer must invite the employee to attend an appeal meeting.
- The employee must take all reasonable steps to attend the appeal meeting.
- The employee has the right to be accompanied at the appeal meeting by a colleague or trade union official of his or her choice.
- The appeal meeting should, where possible, be conducted by a more senior manager than the manager who led the disciplinary hearing.
- After the appeal meeting, the employer must inform the employee of the final decision in writing.

3.173 By law, only one level of appeal is required, but some employers may choose to have a further level of appeal (or even two further levels) so that the employee can appeal again if he or she still believes that the disciplinary process or the decision to dismiss was unfair.

Modified Two-Step Procedure

3.174 A modified two-step DDP is, in theory, possible where the employee has committed a very serious act of misconduct which makes it reasonable for the employer to dismiss the employee immediately on discovering the offence, without first conducting an investigation or holding a hearing. The modified procedure is unlikely to be appropriate except in the most extreme circumstances such as violent criminal activity or seriously threatening behaviour in the workplace and if it is to be relied upon, the dismissal must take place immediately without any delay whatsoever.

3.175 The two steps are as follows.

3.176 Step One

- The employer must write to the employee post-dismissal, stating the grounds for the dismissal, ie setting out the employee's alleged gross misconduct.
- The employer must set out in writing what the basis was for thinking at the time of the dismissal that the employee was guilty of the misconduct in question.
- The employer must inform the employee of the right to appeal against the dismissal.

3.177 Step Two

- If the employee wishes to appeal, he or she must inform the employer.
- If the employee informs the employer of his or her wish to appeal, the employer must invite the employee to attend an appeal meeting.
- The employee must take all reasonable steps to attend the appeal meeting.
- The employee has the right to be accompanied at the appeal meeting by a colleague or trade union official of his or her choice.
- The appeal meeting should, where possible, be conducted by a more senior manager than the manager who took the decision to dismiss.
- After the appeal meeting, the employer must inform the employee in writing of the final decision.

3.178 Using the modified procedure rather than the standard three-step procedure is likely to be risky, as it could be challenged as inherently unfair at an employment tribunal. Dismissal without a prior investigation and a hearing to establish the employee's version of events goes against the principle of natural justice. It is recommended, therefore, that employers should always apply the three-step standard DDP in all cases where dismissal is being contemplated, including cases of gross misconduct.

General Requirements of the Statutory Procedures

3.179 It is important to note that any dismissal implemented without the full and correct application of the DDP will be automatically unfair (provided non-application is the employer's fault).

3.180 The procedure, however, represents a minimum level of fairness. There is still a duty to treat employees reasonably in an overall sense; otherwise a dismissal may be unfair even if the DDP has been followed.

3.181 The following requirements apply to both the standard and the modified procedure.

- Each step and action under the procedure must be taken without unreasonable delay, although there are no prescribed timescales.
- The timing and location of meetings must be reasonable.
- If either party does not attend the meeting for a reason that was unforeseeable at the time the meeting was arranged, the employer must reschedule the meeting (but this requirement only applies once).

Disciplinary Procedures

- Meetings must be conducted in a manner that enables both the employer and the employee to explain their cases.
- Employees have a right to be accompanied at the meetings by a colleague or trade union official of their choice.
- If an employee appeals against a disciplinary decision, the appeal should be dealt with by a more senior manager than the person who dealt with the matter initially.

Financial Sanctions for Failure to Comply with the Statutory Procedure

3.182 Financial sanctions may be imposed on the employer or the employee for failing to comply with the statutory procedure. This takes the form of an increase or reduction to any compensation payable to the employee, following a successful claim to an employment tribunal. If the tribunal finds that either party failed to comply with the statutory procedure, it will:

- increase the award to the employee by 10%, if the failure is by the employer
- reduce the award to the employee by 10%, if the failure is by the employee.

3.183 In both cases, the tribunal may, at its discretion, adjust the award upwards or downwards to a maximum of 50% of the employee's compensation. In exceptional circumstances, the tribunal may apply a percentage adjustment of less than 10%.

3.184 Awards for unfair dismissal continue, however, to be subject to the statutory cap imposed on the compensatory award.

3.185 Where an employment tribunal finds that a dismissal was automatically unfair as a result of the employer's failure to adhere to the statutory dismissal and disciplinary procedure, it will be bound to award the employee a minimum of four weeks' pay in compensation.

3.186 In addition, employment tribunals can award two or four weeks' pay as compensation for the lack, incompleteness or inaccuracy of any written statement of key terms of employment where such a claim is linked with a separate tribunal claim.

Dismissal of Employees with Under a Year's Service

3.187 Generally, employees are required to have gained a minimum of one year's continuous service in order to qualify for the right to claim unfair dismissal. Nevertheless, it is best practice for employers to use the statutory dismissal and disciplinary procedure when dismissing employees with under a year's service. This helps to achieve consistency and fairness.

Inter-Relationship Between the Statutory Procedure and the Employer's Own Procedure

3.188 Over and above the duty to comply with the statutory dismissal and disciplinary procedure, employers are under a duty to act reasonably towards employees in respect of the application of disciplinary procedures leading to dismissal. Procedural fairness will generally be assessed in the light of the Acas Code of Practice.

3.189 An employer's disciplinary procedure must be at least as substantial and fair as the statutory procedure, but need not mirror it so long as it contains the key features of the statutory procedure. Any failure on the employer's part to follow one or more elements of its own disciplinary procedure will not of itself make a dismissal unfair (unless part of the statutory procedure has not been complied with). In this case, however, the employer must be able to show that the employee would have been dismissed even if the full procedure had been followed, and also that the employer acted reasonably in an overall sense. If the tribunal accepts this, there will be no finding of unfair dismissal. It is of course much safer and more appropriate to ensure that all aspects of the employer's own disciplinary procedure are complied with at all times.

Criminal Offences outside Employment

3.190 If it is established that an employee has committed a criminal offence outside of work (ie in the employee's own time and away from the workplace), this may or may not justify disciplinary action or dismissal, depending on whether the offence has any connection with the employee's employment.

3.191 The Acas Code of Practice points out that a criminal conviction unrelated to work is not in itself a reason for disciplinary action.

3.192 The main consideration should be whether the offence impacts on the employee's suitability to do his or her job. Much will depend on the nature of the job in relation to the type of offence that the employee has committed. While it could well be appropriate to dismiss a shop worker who has been convicted of shoplifting in another store, it would probably not be appropriate to dismiss a clerical worker for the same offence, unless there was a real security risk, for example if the clerical worker had access to cash at work.

3.193 In general, there may be a sufficient connection with employment if, as a result of the offence outside of work:

- the employee is judged as unsuitable to perform the job that he or she is employed to do
- there is a genuine loss of trust and confidence in the employee, eg if the employee is a manager and the offence casts doubt on his or her integrity
- the offence is likely to damage the employer's reputation
- colleagues refuse, with good reason, to continue to work alongside the individual. This is likely to be a valid reason to dismiss only in very limited circumstances, eg where the offence was one of a very serious nature such as violence or sexual assault.

3.194 There is no obligation on the employer to wait until the employee goes to trial before deciding whether or not to instigate disciplinary proceedings, particularly if the trial may not take place for some considerable time. If the offence affects the employee's work, it may be legitimate for the employer to take disciplinary action, and potentially dismiss the employee, before the case comes to trial. The burden of proof in a criminal trial is completely different from that in a claim for unfair dismissal. In the former case, the court will require proof beyond reasonable doubt to convict, while the test for employment tribunals to make a decision in an unfair dismissal case is based on the "balance of probabilities" principle. Proof of misconduct, whether at work or outside of work is not required for a dismissal to be fair.

When the Handling of Disciplinary Matters can Lead to a Grievance

3.195 In the course of a disciplinary investigation, an employee may sometimes raise a grievance about the behaviour of the manager dealing with the matter. Where this happens, it may be necessary to put the disciplinary procedure on hold while the grievance is dealt with.

3.196 In this case, the grievance should be dealt with by someone who has not been involved in either the investigation of the employee's alleged misconduct or the disciplinary process.

3.197 Once the grievance has been dealt with, the disciplinary process can be resumed. If the employee's grievance was well-founded and/or upheld, it may be appropriate to nominate a different manager to resume the disciplinary process rather than have the matter continued by the same manager.

Constructive Dismissal Claims

3.198 As stated above, any procedure involving the imposition of disciplinary penalties will need to meet the requirements of fairness. Employers need to be aware of the risk that an employee who is disciplined unfairly could have grounds to resign and claim constructive dismissal.

3.199 For example, if an employer imposed a final written warning on account of a first breach of discipline that was relatively minor or where there were genuine mitigating circumstances, an employee with a minimum of one year's continuous service could resign and claim constructive dismissal on the grounds that the employer's actions were disproportionate and amounted to a breach of the implied duty of trust and confidence.

Keeping Records

3.200 Written records should be made and kept of all disciplinary interventions, whether formal or informal. Although initial discussions may well be informal, it is important to keep notes of them, both as a record of what was discussed (to avoid any future doubt or denial) and as evidence of any support given to the employee (where appropriate). This is particularly important should a claim for unfair dismissal ultimately be brought before an employment tribunal.

3.201 At the very least, the record should show:
- the time and date the discussion took place
- the key matters that were discussed
- the key responses put forward by the employee
- any relevant mitigating factors put forward by the employee
- any agreed action points
- whether or not there was a formal outcome, eg a written warning.

Training

3.202 It is important that all line managers are familiar with the organisation's disciplinary rules and procedures, and the statutory procedures, and that they understand both the employer's and the employee's responsibilities under those rules and procedures.

3.203 Training on disciplinary matters should include the following:
- the organisation's rules and the type of behaviour which would give rise to disciplinary action
- the disciplinary sanctions listed in the disciplinary procedure and the circumstances in which each level of sanction is appropriate
- who has authority to administer disciplinary sanctions
- who has the authority to dismiss
- the steps of the disciplinary procedure and how to follow them correctly
- awareness of the law on unfair dismissal and of the statutory dismissal and disciplinary procedure.

3.204 Induction training for all new employees should inform them about:

- the details of the organisation's disciplinary procedures
- the employer's disciplinary rules and the reasons for them
- any related policies and procedures, eg those on harassment, bullying and whistleblowing.

List of Relevant Legislation

3.205
- Employment Act 2002 (Dispute Resolution) Regulations 2004
- Working Time Regulations 1998
- Employee Relations Act 2004
- Employment Act 2002
- Data Protection Act 1998
- Employment Rights Act 1996
- Trade Union and Labour Relations (Consolidation) Act 1992
- Employment Code of Practice (Disciplinary and Grievance Procedures) Order 2004

List of Relevant Cases

3.206
- *Diosynth Ltd v Thomson* [2006] IRLR 277, CA
- *Taylor v OCS Group Ltd* [2006] IRLR 613, CA
- *Silman v ICTS Ltd* (2006), EAT
- *Draper v Mears Ltd* [2006] IRLR 869, EAT
- *Skiggs v South West Trains Ltd* [2005] IRLR 459, EAT
- *Strouthos v London Underground* [2004] IRLR 636, CA
- *Billington v Michael Hunter & Sons Ltd* (2003) EAT
- *Stanley Cole (Wainfleet) Ltd v Sheridan* [2003] IRLR 885 Court of Appeal
- *A v Company B Ltd* [1997] IRLR 405, HC
- *British Home Stores Ltd v Burchell* [1978] IRLR 379, EAT

Further Information

Publications
- *Acas/B15 Advisory Booklet: Representation at Work*
- *Acas Advisory Handbook: Discipline and Grievances at Work (2005)*
- *Acas/S04 Discipline at Work (2004)*
- *Acas/RW01 Rights at Work Leaflets: Discipline, Grievances and Dismissal*
- *Croner's A-Z Guide to Employment*
- *Croner's Reference Book for Employers*
- *Croner's Personnel in Practice*

- *Guidance on the Employment Act 2002 (Dispute Resolution) Regulations 2004*, Department for Business, Enterprise and Regulatory Reform (BERR)

Organisations

- **Advisory Conciliation and Arbitration Service (Acas)**
  Web: *www.acas.org.uk*
  Acas aims to improve organisations and working life through better employment relations. It provides up-to-date information, advice, high-quality training, and works with employers and employees to solve problems and improve performance.
- **Department for Business, Enterprise and Regulatory Reform (BERR)**
  Web: *www.berr.gov.uk*
  The Department for Business, Enterprise and Regulatory Reform brings together functions from the former Department of Trade and Industry (DTI), including responsibilities for productivity, business relations, energy, competition and consumers. It also drives regulatory reform.
- **Employment Appeal Tribunal (EAT)**
  Web: *www.employmentappeals.gov.uk*
  The EAT was created by the Employment Protection Act 1975. It is a Superior Court of Record dealing with appeals from the decisions of the Employment Tribunals, the Certification Officer and the Central Arbitration Committee.
- **Employment Tribunals**
  Web: *www.employmenttribunals.gov.uk*
  Contains useful information about employment tribunals, which resolve disputes between employers and employees over employment rights.

Grievance Procedures

> This topic covers the following.
> - Issues that Can Give Rise to Grievances
> - Gravity of the Issue
> - The Role of Human Resource Practitioners
> - Requirements of Good Grievance Procedures
> - Statutory Grievance Procedure
> - Standard Grievance Procedure
> - Modified Grievance Procedure
> - General Requirements of the Statutory Grievance Procedures
> - Sanctions for Failure to Comply with the Grievance Procedure
> - Exceptions
> - Financial Sanctions for Failing to Comply with the Statutory Grievance
> - Procedures for Dealing with Particular Grievances
> - Appropriate Management Skills
> - Failure to Deal Effectively with Grievances
> - Records

3.207 Employee grievances may concern any one of a wide range of issues, including the employee's terms and conditions of employment, statutory rights or problems with work relationships. Following the implementation of the Employment Act 2002 (Dispute Resolution) Regulations 2004 in October 2004, employers must by law have a written grievance procedure and provide a copy to each employee within two months of the start of his or her employment.

3.208 The Advisory, Conciliation and Arbitration Service (Acas) provides guidance on the handling of grievances in a statutory Code of Practice.

Employers' Duties

3.209 Employers should:
- inform new employees about the arrangements and procedure for raising a grievance within two months of the start of their employment
- ensure that any internal grievance procedure conforms to the standard grievance procedure imposed by statute
- make the grievance procedure readily available to all staff in a staff handbook or on an intranet site or inform staff where they can easily locate a copy
- ensure that managers deal with grievances promptly and fairly
- encourage employees to try to resolve any grievance they may have informally in the first instance
- conduct all grievance hearings in private
- inform employees of their statutory right to be accompanied at a formal grievance hearing
- inform employees of the right of appeal to a higher level of management if they are not satisfied with the outcome of a grievance meeting
- provide managers with appropriate training on how to handle grievances effectively.

Employees' Duties

3.210 Employees should:
- make full and proper use of the employer's grievance procedure in the event of a genuine workplace grievance
- give the employer a chance to sort out any issue before making a complaint to an employment tribunal
- seek to resolve any minor grievances informally rather than invoking the formal grievance procedure
- consider being accompanied at a formal grievance hearing.

In Practice

Issues that Can Give Rise to Grievances

3.211 Workplace grievances may relate to action already taken by an employer or to action the employer proposes to take. Grievances can be about a range of issues, such as:
- pay
- hours of work or holidays
- application of the organisation's policies, eg provision of sick pay
- new working practices
- implications of organisational change
- health, safety and welfare
- equal opportunities and discrimination
- workplace relationships (including harassment and bullying).

3.212 Disciplinary or dismissal procedures may give rise to certain issues that might be raised by an employee as a grievance. Examples include suspension from work, warnings issued, allegations of discriminatory treatment during the disciplinary process or a belief that disciplinary action has been taken for a reason that is unrelated to the grounds on which the employer claimed to be taking the action.

Gravity of the Issue

3.213 The appropriate way to deal with a grievance will depend on the seriousness of the matter raised.

Minor Issues

3.214 An employee may raise a grievance which, when viewed objectively, is in reality a minor complaint or a query about his or her treatment. In such cases, an informal discussion with the manager in question may be sufficient to resolve the issue. Managers should, however, take care not to assume that an employee's grievance is minor, when it may in fact be very serious when viewed from the employee's point of view. Also minor issues, if allowed to aggregate, can become a much more serious consolidated grievance over time.

Serious Issues

3.215 An issue raised by an employee as a grievance will be serious (or potentially serious) in the following circumstances.

- It concerns terms and conditions of employment, and may have implications for other members of staff.
- There is a possibility that discrimination law (including equal pay legislation) might have been breached.
- The grievance involves an alleged breach of the employee's rights under employment legislation.
- The grievance potentially involves a breach of the employee's contract of employment.
- It is a complaint about harassment or bullying, and other members of staff are potentially involved as perpetrators or victims.
- The issue could be classed as a disclosure of malpractice under the Public Interest Disclosure Act 1998.

The Role of Human Resource Practitioners

3.216 HR managers should have the following role in dealing with grievances.

- Provide advice to managers on the organisation's policy and relevant employment law.
- Ensure consistency in the application of the organisation's policies and procedures.
- Give support for managers to help them deal with grievances.
- Provide advice to employees on the procedures available to them to deal with any grievances they may have.
- Give advice on training initiatives.

Requirements of Good Grievance Procedures

3.217 Good grievance procedures should:

- be drafted by management and representatives of the staff in consultation with each other
- clearly reflect the organisation's management structure
- embody the standard grievance procedure imposed by statute
- provide time limits for arranging hearings and for responses to be given by the employer
- be structured so as to require managers to deal with grievances promptly
- allow for grievances to be dealt with by the employee's immediate supervisor whenever possible, unless the grievance concerns the supervisor
- allow for an employee to be represented or accompanied at grievance and appeal meetings
- require all grievance meetings to be conducted in private.

Statutory Grievance Procedure

3.218 All employers, irrespective of their size, are obliged in law to devise and operate a written grievance procedure. As a minimum, the employee's written statement of particulars must state the name or job title of the person to whom he or she should apply to seek redress and the manner in which the complaint should be made. It should also make clear what further steps are consequent on making the application or where the document explaining the procedure can be found, eg in the staff handbook.

3.219 A grievance is defined as a complaint by an employee about action which his or her employer has taken, or is contemplating taking, in relation to him or her. "Action" in this context includes omission.

3.220 There are two versions of the statutory grievance procedure (GP): the standard (three-step) grievance procedure and a modified (two-step) procedure, which can be applied in certain defined circumstances (see below).

3.221 The statutory grievance procedure is intended to be viewed as a minimum standard. Employers are free to operate more comprehensive grievance procedures, provided that these include all the elements of the standard statutory procedure.

Standard Grievance Procedure

3.222 The standard grievance procedure applies to all employees who raise a grievance. The three steps are as follows.

3.223 Step One
- The employee must set out his or her grievance in writing and give or send a copy to the employer.

3.224 Step Two
- The employer must invite the employee to attend a meeting to discuss the grievance and how it might be resolved.
- The employee must take all reasonable steps to attend the meeting.
- The employee has the right to be accompanied at the meeting by a colleague or trade union official of his or her choice. A trade union official means a full-time official or a lay official certified by the union as having experience of, or training in, acting as a companion at disciplinary and grievance hearings.
- At the meeting, both parties must have the opportunity to state their cases.
- After the meeting, the employer must inform the employee of the decision in response to the grievance, preferably in writing, and notify the employee of the right to appeal against that decision.

3.225 Step Three
- The employee must inform the employer if he or she wishes to appeal.
- If the employee does appeal, the employer must invite the employee to attend an appeal meeting.
- The employee must take all reasonable steps to attend the appeal meeting.
- The employee has the right to be accompanied at the meeting by a colleague or trade union official of his or her choice.
- After the appeal meeting, the employer must inform the employee of the final decision.

Modified Grievance Procedure

3.226 The modified grievance procedure applies to employees who have left the organisation where:
- the employer was unaware of the grievance before the employee left, or
- the procedure had not been instigated or completed before the employment ended, and

Grievance Procedures

- both the employer and the employee have agreed in writing to use the modified procedure rather than the standard procedure.

3.227 If the above conditions are not all satisfied, the standard three-step procedure will apply.

3.228 The two steps of the modified procedure are as follows.

3.229 Step One
- The employee must set out his or her grievance in writing and give or send a copy to the employer.
- The employee must also state the basis for the grievance.

3.230 Step Two
- The employer must set out his or her response to the grievance in writing and send a copy of it to the employee.

3.231 There is no right of appeal when the modified procedure is operated. Best practice would dictate that this fact should be made clear to the employee before he or she agrees to the procedure.

General Requirements of the Statutory Grievance Procedures

3.232 The following requirements apply to both the standard and the modified procedures.
- Each step and action under the procedure must be taken without unreasonable delay, although there are no prescribed timescales.
- The timing and location of meetings must be reasonable.
- If either party does not attend a meeting for a reason that was unforeseeable when the meeting was arranged, the employer must reschedule the meeting (but this requirement only applies once).
- Meetings must be conducted in a manner that enables both the employer and the employee to explain their cases.
- Employees have a right to be accompanied at the meetings by a colleague or trade union official of their choice.
- If an employee appeals against the decision following a grievance meeting, the appeal should be dealt with by a more senior manager than the person who dealt with the grievance initially.

Sanctions for Failure to Comply with the Grievance Procedure

3.233 Employees are barred from bringing a range of claims to an employment tribunal if they have not:
- complied with step one of the grievance procedure (ie submitted the grievance to the employer in writing)
- waited at least 28 days since complying with step one of the grievance procedure.

3.234 In either of these cases, the tribunal will not accept the employee's claim.

3.235 Since the Employment Act 2002 (Dispute Resolution) Regulations 2004 were introduced, tribunals have taken a lenient approach to what constitutes a grievance letter. Some general principles upheld by the EAT are that:
- the employee is not required to indicate that the complaint is a "grievance" or even mention the word "grievance"

- the employee's written communication need not comply with the employer's contractual grievance procedure in order to constitute a grievance under the statutory grievance procedure
- a grievance can be contained in a letter of resignation
- a letter written by an employee's representative or agent (eg a solicitor) can constitute a grievance for the purpose of the statutory grievance procedure
- notes taken by a manager at a meeting with an employee setting down the details of a complaint can constitute a grievance for the purpose of the statutory grievance procedure
- the letter outlining the employee's complaint need not provide every detail of the complaint; it will be sufficient that the general nature of the complaint is made clear.

3.236 In essence, all the employee has to do to fulfil step one of the statutory grievance procedure is to set out his or her complaint in writing and give the employer a copy of it.

3.237 The debarment on an employee taking a case to tribunal does not apply to claims of unfair dismissal where the employee will have the opportunity to appeal against his or her dismissal under the appeal stage of the statutory dismissal and disciplinary procedure. There is no need for the employee to instigate the statutory grievance procedure as well.

3.238 If an employee's claim to tribunal is rejected on account of his or her failure to submit a written grievance and wait 28 days, the tribunal will notify the individual accordingly. The individual will then have another opportunity to raise the grievance with the employer, wait 28 days and then re-submit the claim to the tribunal (for example if the grievance has not been resolved by this time). In these circumstances, the employee must submit the written grievance to the employer within one month after the end of the time limit for bringing the claim to tribunal. The time limit for bringing most claims to tribunal is three months, but this time limit is automatically extended to six months when the employee:
- instigates step one of the grievance procedure
- is notified by the tribunal that his or her claim has been rejected because of non-compliance with step one of the grievance procedure.

Exceptions

3.239 There are some exceptions to the provision that requires employees to raise a grievance with the employer and wait 28 days before bringing a case to tribunal. Exceptions apply where:
- the person is or was not employed by the employer on a contract of employment
- the tribunal claim was brought under a law not covered by the statutory grievance procedure
- it was not practicable for the employee to put the grievance in writing to the employer, eg due to serious long-term illness
- the employee has reasonable grounds to believe that putting the grievance in writing or attending a meeting would result in a significant threat, or (if he or she has been harassed in the past) to further harassment
- the grievance has been raised collectively by an appropriate representative, or under an industry-level grievance procedure (although in these circumstances, the employee must still wait 28 days before bringing his or her claim to tribunal)
- the employee has raised the matter as a "protected disclosure" under the Public Interest Disclosure Act 1998.

Financial Sanctions for Failing to Comply with the Statutory Grievance Procedure

3.240   In addition to the above, an employment tribunal may impose financial sanctions on the employer or the employee for failing to comply with the statutory grievance procedure. This takes the form of an increase or reduction to any compensation payable to the employee, following a successful claim to an employment tribunal. If the tribunal finds that either party failed to comply with the statutory procedure, it will:
- increase the award to the employee by 10%, if the failure is by the employer
- reduce the award to the employee by 10%, if the failure is by the employee.

3.241   In both cases, the tribunal may, at its discretion, adjust the award upwards or downwards to a maximum of 50% of the employee's compensation. In exceptional circumstances, the tribunal may apply a percentage adjustment of less than 10%.

Procedures for Dealing with Particular Grievances

3.242   Some employment issues are so important or sensitive that it may be advisable to apply a separate procedure for dealing with them and also provide additional support for employees.

Harassment and Bullying

3.243   A harassment and bullying procedure could give the employee an opportunity to discuss a complaint or concern informally and confidentially with a trained harassment advisor or other impartial person (eg, an HR manager), before deciding whether or not to raise the issue through the formal grievance procedure. As an alternative to the formal grievance procedure, some employers offer mediation. The employer should consider whether or not this is appropriate in each individual case.

Whistleblowing

3.244   Public interest disclosure legislation is designed to protect employees who blow the whistle on malpractice and criminal wrongdoing within their employer's organisation. Employers are encouraged to provide a special procedure through which such complaints and allegations can be made. Where a protected disclosure has been made to a nominated senior manager, the employer should take all reasonable steps to ensure that no manager, work colleague or other person under its control victimises the whistleblower.

Health, Safety and Welfare

3.245   Many health, safety and welfare issues can be dealt with through the normal grievance procedure. However, in emergency situations where there is a serious risk, employees are entitled (or forced) to stop work. Any legal issues or concerns over hazards that arise as a result of this would normally be dealt with through discussions with safety representatives or through a safety committee.

Appropriate Management Skills

3.246   Managers and supervisors will need a range of skills if they are to deal effectively with employee grievances, including:
- the ability to listen and discern any underlying issues
- the ability to be calm, fair and sensitive in grievance handling

- the ability to investigate the issue fully and impartially
- a willingness to take appropriate advice and to obtain relevant information from, for example, other managers, the human resource department, a recognised trade union and any appropriate external agencies (eg Acas, the Health and Safety Executive, the Commission for Equality and Human Rights, etc)
- a preparedness to adjourn if necessary
- a willingness to consider whether there might be common ground for resolving the grievance
- the ability to analyse and sum up information
- the ability to deliberate on the information provided and consider the implications of any decision for other staff and for the organisation's policy and practice
- the ability to come to a practical, fair and lawful decision
- the ability to communicate the outcome of any procedure clearly.

Failure to Deal Effectively with Grievances

3.247 The possible consequences of failing to deal effectively with grievances are as follows.
- The nature of the grievance may involve a fundamental breach of the employee's contract of employment which could result in the employee's resignation and a claim for constructive dismissal being brought to an employment tribunal.
- A failure to deal with a genuine grievance may constitute a breach of trust and confidence which would also be a fundamental breach of the contract and the basis for a constructive dismissal claim.
- Under discrimination law, the employer is liable for acts of discrimination and harassment in the course of employment. The "course of employment" is defined widely and can cover work-related behaviour away from the employer's premises, including conduct at organised work-related social events. The employer can defend itself if it can show that it took all reasonably practicable steps to prevent discrimination and harassment from occurring.

Records

3.248 Confidential records should be kept and should set out:
- the details of any grievance raised
- any investigations carried out by the employer
- dates and times of grievance meetings
- the main issues discussed at grievance meetings
- the response of the employer
- any action taken and the reasons for it
- whether there was an appeal and, if so, the outcome.

3.249 The employer should comply with the guidance provided by the Information Commissioner on the retention of employment records and on the disclosure of sensitive personal data.

3.250 Copies of the records of meetings should be given to the employee although certain information may be withheld (eg to protect the identity of a witness).

Training

3.251 The effective handling of grievances is a continuing employment relations responsibility for employers. In drawing up a training programme, it is advisable to involve senior human resources staff at every stage.

3.252 Training should cover both employees and managers.

Employees

3.253 Employees (who are not managers) should receive awareness training which covers the organisation's grievance procedures and how grievances are raised and dealt with. Training should encourage employees to seek informal resolution of any grievances they may have if at all possible.

3.254 The employer should also ensure that induction training for all new employees covers the details of the grievance procedure and any related policies and procedures, eg those on harassment, bullying and whistleblowing.

Managers

3.255 Managers should be provided with detailed training covering the organisation's grievance procedures and the handling of grievances. This can often most effectively be provided through interactive workshops in which participants are encouraged to share ideas and practical experiences. Effective training in such workshops would involve the following two elements.
- Information about the relevant law, the organisation's procedures and good employment relations' practice.
- The opportunity to consider and practise particular skills. Role-play coupled with feedback and discussions are particularly useful.

Union Representatives

3.256 Employers with unionised workplaces should ensure that those workers representing or accompanying their staff are appropriately trained in both the:
- knowledge of grievance procedures and of the relevant law; and
- skills of effective grievance handling and representation.

3.257 If there is a recognised trade union, it might be useful to consider some joint training with managers to share experiences and encourage discussion and reflection on how the existing procedures are working.

List of Relevant Legislation

3.258
- Employment Act 2002 (Dispute Resolution) Regulations 2004
- Health and Safety (Consultation with Employees) Regulations 1996
- Safety Representatives and Safety Committees Regulations 1977
- Employment Act 2002
- Employment Relations Act 1999
- Data Protection Act 1998
- Public Interest Disclosure Act 1998
- Employment Rights Act 1996
- Trade Union and Labour Relations Consolidation Act 1992

- Health and Safety at Work, etc Act 1974

List of Relevant Cases

3.259

- *Kennedy Scott Ltd v Francis* EAT/0204/07 — a complaint presented by an employee to a manager who wrote it down meant that the employee had complied with step one of the statutory grievance procedure and the EAT allowed the case to proceed. The EAT said that there is no necessity for an employee personally to put a grievance in writing.
- *Commotion Ltd v Rutty* [2006] IRLR 171, EAT — a request to work part time under the Flexible Working Regulations could amount a grievance under step one of the statutory grievance procedure. "The Flexible Working Regulations" comprise the Flexible Working (Eligibility, Complaints and Remedies) Regulations 2002 and the Flexible Working (Procedural Requirements) Regulations 2002.
- *Galaxy Showers Ltd v Wilson* [2006] IRLR 83, EAT — a letter of resignation can be construed as a statement of grievance for the purposes of the statutory grievance procedure requirements, provided it sets out a statement of the employee's complaint about the actions (or omissions) of the employer.
- *Mark Warner Ltd v Aspland* [2006] IRLR 87, EAT — in determining whether a claimant has raised a statutory grievance, the question is whether there is a complaint in writing that has been made by the employee about action which the employer has taken or is contemplating taking. There does not need to have been an express intention to raise a grievance. Correspondence from a claimant's solicitor to the employer's solicitor may be capable of fulfilling these requirements and amounting to a grievance.
- *Shergold v Fieldway Medical Centre* [2006] IRLR 76, EAT — a letter of resignation could amount to a grievance for the purposes of the statutory grievance procedure. What was important was that a grievance was set out in writing. Exact particulars of each complaint did not need to be given. So long as the substance of the grievance and the subsequent claim are the same, an employment tribunal claim is admissible.
- *Skiggs v South West Trains Ltd* [2005] IRLR 459, EAT — this case is helpful in clarifying that investigative meetings — which can eventually lead to disciplinary action — are not necessarily disciplinary hearings and therefore the right to be accompanied is not triggered. Employers should be aware that if it becomes apparent during the course of an investigative meeting that it will be necessary to commence disciplinary proceedings the interview should be terminated and a formal hearing arranged at which the employee should have the right to be accompanied.
- *Thorpe and Soleil Investments Ltd v Poat and Lake* (2005) UKEAT/0503/05 — a letter bringing the employment relationship to an end without notice could constitute a grievance for the purposes of the statutory grievance procedure. The intention of the employee was irrelevant.
- *Jones v Tower Boot Company Ltd* [1997] IRLR 168, CA — employers are liable for acts committed by employees "in the course of their employment" unless they can establish the appropriate statutory defence.
- *WA Goold (Pearmak) Ltd v McConnell* [1995] IRLR 516, EAT — there is an implied term that an employer will reasonably and promptly give opportunity to its employees to seek redress of any grievance.

Further Information

Publications
- *Acas Advisory Handbook: Discipline and Grievances at Work (2005)*
- *Acas/B15 Advisory Booklet: Representation at Work*
- *Acas/CP01 Code of Practice on Disciplinary and Grievance Procedures (2004)*
- *Acas/S03 Dealing with Grievances*
- *Acas/RW01 Rights at Work Leaflets: Discipline, Grievances and Dismissal*
- *Employment Practices Data Protection Code — Part 2: Employment Records*, from the Information Commissioner's Office

Organisations
- **Advisory Conciliation and Arbitration Service (Acas)**
  Web: *www.acas.org.uk*
  Acas aims to improve organisations and working life through better employment relations. It provides up-to-date information, advice, high-quality training, and works with employers and employees to solve problems and improve performance.
- **Commission for Racial Equality**
  Web: *www.cre.gov.uk*
  The Commission for Racial Equality is a publicly funded, non-governmental body set up under the Race Relations Act 1976 to tackle racial discrimination and promote racial equality. From October 2007 this organisation will be replaced by the Commission for Equality and Human Rights.
- **Department for Business, Enterprise and Regulatory Reform (BERR)**
  Web: *www.berr.gov.uk*
  The Department for Business, Enterprise and Regulatory Reform brings together functions from the former Department of Trade and Industry (DTI), including responsibilities for productivity, business relations, energy, competition and consumers. It also drives regulatory reform.
- **Disability Rights Commission**
  Web: *www.drc-gb.org*
  An independent body established by Act of Parliament to eliminate discrimination against disabled people and promote quality of opportunity. It provides information and advice to disabled people and employers about their rights and duties. From October 2007 this organisation will be replaced by the Commission for Equality and Human Rights (**Web:** *www.cehr.org.uk*).
- **Equal Opportunities Commission**
  Web: *www.eoc.org.uk*
  An agency working to eliminate sex discrimination and put equality into practice in the workplace. From October 2007 this organisation will be replaced by the Commission for Equality and Human Rights (**Web:** *www.cehr.org.uk*).
- **Information Commissioner's Office**
  Web: *www.ico.gov.uk*
  The Information Commissioner enforces and oversees the Data Protection Act 1998 and the Freedom of Information Act 2000. It is an independent UK supervisory authority, reporting directly to the UK Parliament. It has an international role as well as a national one.

Resolving Disputes through Tribunals and other Methods

This topic covers the following.
- Employment Tribunal Practice and Procedure
- Overriding Objective
- The Claim
- Time Limits
- The Response
- Further Particulars and Disclosure of Documents
- Hearings
- Deposits
- Striking-out Claims
- Questionnaires in Discrimination and Equal Pay Cases
- Witness Orders
- The Hearing Panel
- Procedure at the Hearing
- Appeals
- Settlements and Acas Conciliation
- Costs
- Compromise Agreements
- Exempt Claims
- Qualifying Conditions
- Risk of Constructive Dismissal Claims
- Confidentiality
- The Acas Arbitration Scheme
- Procedure for Arbitration
- Practical Points on Arbitration
- Mediation
- Procedure for Mediation
- Practical Points on Mediation

3.260 There are a number of options available to employers and employees for resolving employment disputes and avoiding the public hearings that often cause adverse publicity. The options include:
- using the services of an Acas conciliation officer
- setting up a compromise agreement
- the use of professional mediators
- the use of Acas arbitration services for unfair dismissal and flexible working claims.

Employers' Duties

3.261 Employers should:
- recognise that employment legislation provides employees with a wide range of statutory employment rights
- assist the tribunal to achieve its overriding objective of dealing with the case justly and seeking to achieve a resolution of the dispute
- file a response form within 28 days if they wish to contest employment tribunal proceedings

Resolving Disputes through Tribunals and other Methods

- comply with any order from the tribunal to provide "further or better particulars" or to disclose documents
- respond within eight weeks to any questionnaire served by an employee in respect of an allegation of discrimination or unequal pay (although there is no legal duty to provide a response)
- work with the Acas conciliator to see if an agreed settlement can be reached
- act reasonably in bringing and conducting tribunal proceedings and ensure that the defence of the claim is not misconceived
- if considering setting up a compromise agreement to settle a dispute with an employee, ensure that all the qualifying conditions for a compromise agreement to be valid are met.

Employees' Duties

3.262 Employees should:
- assist the tribunal to achieve its overriding objective of dealing with the case justly and seeking to achieve a resolution of the dispute
- use form ET1 to bring the claim to tribunal
- ensure than any claim to an employment tribunal is brought within the relevant time limit
- comply with any order from the tribunal to provide "further or better particulars" or to disclose documents
- consider using the questionnaire procedure in the event of an allegation of discrimination or unequal pay
- work with the Acas conciliator to see if an agreed settlement can be reached
- act reasonably in bringing and conducting tribunal proceedings and ensure that the claim is not misconceived
- understand that if they enter into a conciliation agreement (arrived at through Acas) or a compromise agreement to settle a dispute with the employer, they will no longer have the right to pursue their complaint through the tribunal system.

In Practice

Employment Tribunal Practice and Procedure

3.263 Most employment disputes concerning the statutory rights of employees can be dealt with through employment tribunal proceedings. New legislation regulating employment tribunal procedures came into force on 1 October 2004.

Overriding Objective

3.264 The overriding objective of the tribunal rules is to enable tribunals to deal with cases justly. This includes:
- ensuring that the parties are on an equal footing and that the claim is dealt with expeditiously and fairly
- dealing with the case in a way that is proportionate to the complexity of the issues
- saving costs.

3.265 The parties involved are under a duty to assist the tribunal to further the overriding objective.

The Claim

3.266 To commence tribunal proceedings, the claimant must present a claim form (Form ET1) to the tribunal within the time limit. This can be filed by post or online.

Time Limits

3.267 For most claims, the time limit is three months from the date in respect of which the complaint is made. This time limit is, however, extended to six months where the:
- complaint is one of unfair dismissal and, at the expiry of the three-month time limit, the employee has reasonable grounds to believe that the employer is still following through an internal appeal procedure
- employee has raised a written grievance about the same subject matter under the statutory grievance procedure specified in the Employment Act 2002
- tribunal notifies the claimant that his or her claim cannot be accepted because he or she has not previously complied with the statutory grievance procedure, provided the claimant then complies with the procedure no later than one month after the expiry of the three-month time limit.

3.268 For claims of equal pay and statutory redundancy pay, the normal time limit is six months.

3.269 The tribunal will allow extensions to the relevant time limits only in very limited circumstances.

The Response

3.270 Following the receipt of a valid claim form, the tribunal will notify the employer of the claim. As well as a copy of the employee's claim form (ET1), the employer will be sent a "response form" (ET3) by the tribunal. The ET3 must be completed and returned to the tribunal within 28 days of the date on which the forms were sent. This is the date when the claim form is stamped by the tribunal. The ET3 can be filed by post, by fax or online. The employer can apply within the 28-day period for an extension of time, but the tribunal will only grant such an extension where it considers that it is just and equitable to do so.

3.271 If the employer fails to enter an ET3, he or she will not be heard or represented at the hearing, other than as a witness. Also, the tribunal has the power to enter a default judgment where no response has been lodged or accepted within the prescribed time limit.

3.272 The employer may make an application to review within 14 days of the default judgment being sent out by the tribunal. This time may be extended by the tribunal if it considers it just and equitable to do so.

Further Particulars and Disclosure of Documents

3.273 The parties are required to give particulars of the grounds on which the claim is brought and contested. Particulars should be sought voluntarily but a tribunal can order "further or better particulars" if one party does not have sufficient details of the opponent's case to enable it to prepare properly for the hearing.

3.274 In many cases, the tribunal will order the parties to disclose certain documents. Parties may also apply to the tribunal for disclosure of any documents which the other party has and which may help them prove their case. When considering an application for disclosure of documents, the tribunal must balance the importance of the disclosure for the fairness of the proceedings against the expense and inconvenience for the parties of compliance.

Hearings

3.275 There are three types of hearing that may take place.
1. Case management discussion — this deals with the procedure and management of the case. It is held in private and is conducted by the chairperson. Alternatively, it can be conducted by electronic communication, most commonly a conference telephone call. It takes place before a full hearing.
2. Pre-hearing review — this will generally be a public hearing. The hearing is designed to hear any interim or preliminary matters relating to the proceedings, any case management decisions, applications for deposits and oral and written evidence. As the name suggests, it takes place before the full hearing.
3. Full hearing — a case will normally be listed on the basis that all of the issues raised in the claim form will be dealt with at that single hearing. Simple cases will usually be listed for a full hearing without any earlier hearing taking place.

Deposits

3.276 One of the purposes of a pre-hearing review will be to consider an application for a deposit by either party. This is a procedure for weeding out hopeless cases, and is intended to save time and expense. If the tribunal decides that a case has no reasonable prospect of success, it can order the party concerned to pay a deposit of up to £500 to be allowed to continue with the proceedings.

Striking-out Claims

3.277 The tribunal has the power to strike out a claim form (ET1) or a response form (ET3) where:
- the claim or defence is scandalous, misconceived or vexatious
- a party has conducted the case in a scandalous, vexatious, abusive, disruptive or unreasonable manner
- there has been excessive delay
- a party fails to comply with an order or direction
- a party has failed to pay the deposit ordered by the tribunal.

Questionnaires in Discrimination and Equal Pay Cases

3.278 In cases of alleged discrimination, the complainant may ask certain questions of the employer, for which there are standard questionnaire forms. The questionnaires may be served on the employer either before a claim has been lodged with the tribunal, or within 21 days of claim form ET1 being presented to the tribunal.

3.279 Employers have a timescale of eight weeks to respond to a questionnaire served on them. They are not, however, under a legal duty to provide a response, but if they do not respond in time or if the replies given are evasive or equivocal, the tribunal may draw "just and equitable" inferences. Furthermore, the employer's replies will be admissible in evidence at any hearing.

Witness Orders

3.280 Tribunals may make an order requiring a person with relevant evidence to attend a hearing as a witness — this is called a witness order. If a witness order is made and the person fails to attend without a reasonable excuse, he or she will be liable to prosecution for contempt of court and, if convicted, will be fined.

The Hearing Panel

3.281 The case will usually be heard by a tribunal chairperson (who will be a qualified lawyer) and two lay members. One of the lay members will usually be a person with a background in HR management, while the other will typically be a trade union official or someone with extensive experience of industrial relations.

Procedure at the Hearing

3.282 The hearing will generally proceed as follows.
- The parties will make opening statements, outlining their cases.
- The witnesses will give evidence, be cross-examined by the other party and questioned by the tribunal panel members.
- The parties will make closing statements, summarising their case and drawing on the evidence.

3.283 The tribunal usually gives its decision at the end of the hearing, unless the case is complex, in which case it may reserve its decision. The parties subsequently receive the tribunal's written judgment. The tribunal must give either oral or written reasons for the judgment, but if the judgment is given orally at the end of the hearing, written reasons will not be produced unless requested. If the claimant's claim succeeds, compensation will either be dealt with at the end of the hearing or at a separate remedies hearing.

Appeals

3.284 The scope for appealing a tribunal's decision is limited. Appeals are made to the Employment Appeal Tribunal (EAT), which normally only deals with legal questions arising out of the tribunal's decision. The EAT may only interfere with a tribunal's findings on a point of law or if the tribunal's decision was perverse.

3.285 The time limit for appealing is 42 days from the date that extended reasons were sent to the parties. Although the EAT has the power to extend the time for appealing, the time limit is very strictly applied and rarely extended.

Settlements and Acas Conciliation

3.286 A claim may be settled before it reaches a hearing either by the parties themselves or through Acas conciliation. The Acas conciliator is an independent third party, who assists both parties to reach a settlement without the need for a tribunal hearing. Once a claim has been lodged with the tribunal, the Acas conciliator will contact the parties to see if he or she can help them to reach a binding agreed settlement. The settlement will be recorded in a COT3 agreement, drawn up by the Acas conciliator.

3.287 There are now fixed conciliation periods for most tribunal claims. Hearings may not be held during the conciliation period except for case management

Resolving Disputes through Tribunals and other Methods

discussions and pre-hearing reviews. Straightforward claims such as unauthorised deductions from wages have a period of seven weeks as the conciliation period. Other claims have a period of 13 weeks.

3.288 There is no fixed conciliation period for claims of discrimination, equal pay or under the Public Interest Disclosure Act (PIDA) provisions in the Employment Rights Act 1996.

Costs

3.289 In most tribunal cases, it is normal for each party to pay its own costs. Although costs will often be incurred for legal advice or representation, no fee is charged for making a claim to an employment tribunal or for the hearing itself.

3.290 The tribunal does, however, have the power to make a standard costs order against either party for any costs incurred by the other party in certain circumstances. The tribunal also has the power to order a party to make payment to the Secretary of State for any witness, expert, assessor expenses or fees paid out in association with the proceedings.

3.291 A costs order may be made where:
- there is a postponement or adjournment of the hearing or pre-hearing review for no good reason
- the party has in bringing the proceedings or in conducting the proceedings acted vexatiously, abusively, disruptively or otherwise unreasonably
- the bringing or conducting of the proceedings by a party has been misconceived
- the party has not complied with an order or practice direction.

3.292 The tribunal may take into consideration the party's ability to pay when considering whether it should make a costs order and how much the order should be for. The maximum a tribunal may award as costs is £10,000.

3.293 As an alternative to a costs order, a preparation time order may be made in favour of a party who has not been legally represented at a hearing. "Preparation time" is defined as time spent by the party or his or her employees carrying out preparatory work that is directly relating to the proceedings and/or time spent by the party's advisors relating to the conduct of the proceedings. It does not, however, include the time spent at the hearing itself. An hourly rate of £25 per hour is applied.

3.294 A tribunal may not make both a preparation time order and a costs order in favour of the same party in the same proceedings. Where a party continues with a case after being ordered to pay a deposit at a pre-hearing review and subsequently loses the case, there may similarly be strong grounds for making an order for costs.

3.295 The tribunal can also make a wasted costs order directly against a party's representative if it considers that the representative has caused another party to incur costs as a result of any improper, unreasonable or negligent act or omission. A wasted costs award is, however, only permissible where the representative in question is one who has been paid for his or her services.

Compromise Agreements

3.296 Compromise agreements allow parties to settle an employment dispute independently, without going through Acas.

Exempt Claims

3.297 Claims regarding a failure to inform and consult trade unions about a transfer under the Transfer of Undertakings (Protection of Employment) Regulations 1981 or proposed redundancies may not be compromised in a compromise agreement.

Qualifying Conditions

3.298 To be legally binding and to bar the employee from bringing or continuing with a claim against the employer at tribunal, the compromise agreement must:
- be in writing
- relate to particular proceedings
- state that the conditions regulating compromise agreements have been satisfied
- be subject to the employee having received legal advice from an independent advisor as to the terms of the agreement and its effect on the employee's ability to pursue claims
- identify the employee's advisor.

3.299 The relevant independent advisor must be:
- a qualified lawyer or an authorised advocate, barrister or litigator, or
- certified and authorised to give advice on behalf of a trade union, or
- certified and authorised by an advice centre to give free advice.

3.300 The relevant independent advisor must not be:
- acting in the matter for the employer or an associated employer or
- a trade union or advice centre advisor where the trade union or advice centre is the employer or associated employer.

Risk of Constructive Dismissal Claims

3.301 Including an exit package in the compromise agreement offered to an employee creates a risk that he or she will reject the package, resign and bring a claim for constructive dismissal.

3.302 To reduce this risk, employers should ensure that all compromise agreements are offered without prejudice and subject to contract. Employers should also ensure that they do not say anything during negotiations with the employee which could be detrimental to their case in an employment tribunal.

Confidentiality

3.303 A confidentiality clause should be included in the compromise agreement to prevent employees from disclosing the terms of the settlement or the circumstances surrounding the termination of their employment.

The Acas Arbitration Scheme

3.304 The Acas Arbitration Scheme is intended to provide a voluntary alternative to employment tribunals for the resolution of unfair dismissal claims and disputes over a request for flexible working. This results in a binding decision on the matter by an arbitrator appointed by Acas.

3.305 Disputes will be eligible for the Acas Arbitration Scheme only where the case is straightforward and where both parties have agreed to submit to Acas arbitration.

Procedure for Arbitration

3.306 The employee and employer must sign a binding Arbitration Agreement before a dispute can be accepted for arbitration. This has the effect of preventing the claimant from pursuing the claim through the employment tribunal system. Acas will appoint an arbitrator who will fix a date and place for the hearing. Before the hearing, the parties will provide the arbitrator with a statement outlining their cases.

Practical Points on Arbitration

3.307 A short, informal hearing is held in private. The arbitrator questions witnesses but there is no cross-examination.

3.308 If the arbitrator decides that the dismissal was unfair, he or she may award reinstatement, re-engagement and/or compensation. If the arbitrator upholds the claim in a flexible working case, he or she may order consideration of the request and/or compensation.

3.309 There are limited grounds for appeal.

Mediation

3.310 Mediation is not adjudication between the parties but an attempt to negotiate a settlement through an independent third party, ie the mediator. Mediation may be particularly useful in achieving a settlement when formal negotiations between the parties have broken down. Mediation takes place in private, so the risk of adverse publicity is avoided.

Procedure for Mediation

3.311 Mediation does not have strict procedural requirements but in most cases the parties:
- enter into a mediation agreement (agreeing to mediate, to share the costs equally and to keep the process confidential)
- agree the time, place and duration of the mediation
- agree who the mediator will be
- provide the mediator with copies of the key documentation and a mediation statement setting out its claims.

3.312 At the mediation, there will be an opening joint session where each party presents a summary of its case. The mediator will then meet with each party privately to:
- discuss the claim in more detail
- put forward propositions
- try to reach a settlement.

Practical Points on Mediation

3.313 The following are some key points on mediation.
- Parties can approach mediation organisations to assist with the appointment of a mediator.
- The costs of preparing for and attending mediation can be substantial.
- Parties should evaluate their strengths and weaknesses and calculate their respective bottom lines before the mediation.

Training

3.314 Line managers should be made aware of employees' rights, the procedures used by tribunals to hear claims and the alternative ways in which employment disputes may be resolved.

3.315 Managers or human resources professionals directly involved in negotiating and agreeing settlements with employees will need to be trained in the main principles relevant to conciliated and compromise agreements. Awareness training in the mediation process would also be useful.

List of Relevant Legislation

3.316
- Employment Appeal Tribunal (Amendment) Rules 2005
- Employment Tribunals (Constitution and Rules of Procedure) (Amendment) Regulations 2005
- Employment Tribunals (Constitution and Rules of Procedure) (Amendment) (No. 2) Regulations 2005
- Employment Act 2002 (Dispute Resolution) Regulations 2004
- Employment Tribunals (Constitution and Rules of Procedure) Regulations 2004
- Employment Tribunals (Constitution and Rules of Procedure) Regulations 2001
- Employment Act 2002
- Employment Rights Act 1996

List of Relevant Cases

3.317
- *Diosynth Ltd v Thomson* [2006] CSIH 5 XA25/05
- *Drapers v Mears Ltd* [2006] IRLR 869, EAT
- *Silman v ICTS Ltd* [2006] UKEAT/0630/05
- *Taylor v OCS Group Ltd* [2006] IRLR 613, CA
- *Skiggs v South West Trains Ltd* [2005] IRLR 459, EAT
- *Strouthos v London Underground* [2004] IRLR 636, CA
- *Billington v Michael Hunter & Sons Ltd* 16 October 2003 EAT
- *Stanley Cole (Wainfleet) Ltd v Sheridan* [2003] IRLR 885 Court of Appeal
- *A v Company B Ltd* [1997] IRLR 405, HC
- *British Home Stores Ltd v Burchell* [1978] IRLR 379, EAT

Further Information

Publications
- *Acas How We Can Help* (summary of services from information to advice on settling disputes)
- *Croner's A-Z Guide to Employment*
- *Croner's Reference Book for Employers*
- *Croner's Personnel in Practice*

Organisations
- **Advisory Conciliation and Arbitration Service (Acas)**
  Web: *www.acas.org.uk*
  Acas aims to improve organisations and working life through better employment relations. It provides up-to-date information, advice, high-quality training, and works with employers and employees to solve problems and improve performance.
- **Department for Business, Enterprise and Regulatory Reform (BERR)**
  Web: *www.berr.gov.uk*
  The Department for Business, Enterprise and Regulatory Reform brings together functions from the former Department of Trade and Industry (DTI), including responsibilities for productivity, business relations, energy, competition and consumers. It also drives regulatory reform.
- **Employment Appeal Tribunal (EAT)**
  Web: *www.employmentappeals.gov.uk*
  The EAT was created by the Employment Protection Act 1975. It is a Superior Court of Record dealing with appeals from the decisions of the Employment Tribunals, the Certification Officer and the Central Arbitration Committee.
- **Employment Tribunals**
  Web: *www.employmenttribunals.gov.uk*
  Contains useful information about employment tribunals, which resolve disputes between employers and employees over employment rights.

Chapter 4
Discrimination and Diversity

Age Discrimination

This topic covers the following.
- Defining Age Discrimination
- What Does the Law Cover?
- Employees and Other Types of Workers
- Qualifiying Conditions
- Exceptions
- Four Forms of Discrimination
- Age Discrimination in Recruitment
- Age Discrimination during Employment
- Terms and Conditions of Employment
- Setting a Retirement Age
- Right to Request to Continue Working beyond Retirement
- Notification of Retirement
- Pensions
- Claims for Age Discrimination
- Unfair Dismissal Rights
- The Questionnaire Procedure
- The Burden of Proof
- Vicarious Liability
- Case Law from Ireland
- Monitoring

4.1 Under the European Union Framework Directive 2000/78/EC, legislation to combat age discrimination was introduced on 1 October 2006.

4.2 The new regulations make all forms of age discrimination in recruitment and employment unlawful, ie direct discrimination, indirect discrimination, harassment and victimisation.

4.3 There is no qualifying period of service necessary to make a complaint to an employment tribunal and no limit on the amount of compensation that can be awarded to a successful claimant.

Employers' Duties

4.4 Under the new age discrimination legislation, employers have a duty:
- not to adopt policies, procedures, rules or practices that could put younger or older people at a disadvantage, unless the policy, procedure, rule or practice is appropriate and necessary in the circumstances
- not to victimise staff who have complained that they have suffered age discrimination nor victimise staff who assist others in making such complaints
- to take steps to outlaw harassment on the grounds of age
- not to discriminate against employees on the grounds of age during recruitment
- to avoid age discrimination when selecting candidates for promotion
- to offer equal training opportunities, regardless of age
- to ensure that employees are not discriminated against regarding redundancy selection on the grounds of their age
- not to require employees to retire before age 65, unless a younger retirement age can be justified

- to take seriously any request from an employee to work on beyond age 65 and comply with the "duty to consider" procedure
- to give employees approaching retirement between six and 12 months' written notice of their operative retirement date and at the same time inform them of their right to request to continue working longer
- to take all reasonable steps to prevent age discrimination in the workplace, eg by communicating their equal opportunities and anti-harassment policies to all staff on a regular basis, training staff on equal opportunities issues and the avoidance of all forms of discrimination, and monitoring compliance.

Employees' Duties

4.5 Employees have a duty:
- not to discriminate against any of their colleagues on the grounds of age
- not to victimise any member of staff who has complained that he or she has suffered age discrimination or helped a colleague to make a complaint of discrimination or harassment
- not to engage in any behaviour that could be interpreted as harassment on the grounds of age
- to adhere to their employer's equal opportunities and anti-harassment policies and to ensure that they treat their colleagues with respect and dignity at all times.

In Practice

Defining Age Discrimination

4.6 Age discrimination can affect old or young people. Some of the misconceptions that employers have about older job applicants compared to younger, include:
- older employees are more likely to take time off work for health reasons
- younger candidates have more energy, drive and ambition
- older candidates are not up to date technically
- younger people are more willing to work late
- older people tend to be set in their ways and be less adaptable
- younger candidates do not have to be paid such high salaries
- older employees cost more in terms of pension contributions.

4.7 Definition of the terms "older" and "younger" is open to debate, although "older" is usually taken to mean 50+. The term "younger" usually denotes people under 25 or under 30, and there is considerable evidence that this age group also faces discrimination on the grounds of age.

4.8 The above prejudices are, in general, totally without foundation. There is reliable evidence to show both that differences in levels of absenteeism between age groups is slight and that younger and older employees are equally effective in their work.

What Does the Law Cover?

4.9 The legislation on age discrimination is designed to ensure that decisions on selection, recruitment, promotion and training are made on the basis of an individual's merit and competence and not because that person has reached an arbitrary age. It takes the same approach as other equality legislation to the issues of direct discrimination, indirect discrimination, harassment, victimisation, genuine occupational requirements and positive action.

4.10 Job applicants are protected throughout the process of recruitment and limited protection against discrimination is also available to former employees.

4.11 The new legislation removed the age limits that were previously applicable to statutory sick pay, statutory maternity pay, statutory paternity pay and statutory adoption pay.

4.12 If discrimination occurs, the individual can bring a complaint to an employment tribunal irrespective of his or her length of service at the time.

Employees and Other Types of Workers

4.13 The new age discrimination regulations apply not only to employees, but also to:
- contract workers
- agency temps
- casual workers
- freelancers who provide their services personally
- directors
- company secretaries
- non-elected office holders
- partners in firms.

4.14 The only exemption is armed forces personnel.

4.15 The new pre-retirement procedures, apply only to employees, and not to other workers.

Qualifying Conditions

4.16 There is no minimum length of service required for an employee or worker to bring a claim for unlawful age discrimination to an employment tribunal.

4.17 Employees (but not other workers) must first raise a written grievance with their employer and wait 28 days. This is to allow the employer time and opportunity to deal with the complaint before it can proceed to tribunal. If a claim is lodged with the tribunal before the employee has raised a grievance and waited 28 days, the tribunal will in most cases not admit it. Where, however, the claim relates to a dismissal on the grounds of age, the potential claimant need not raise a grievance first.

Exceptions

4.18 Employers are, under the new age regulations, permitted to discriminate on the grounds of age in limited circumstances where the discriminatory treatment of an individual (whether direct or indirect) can be shown to be a proportionate means of achieving a legitimate aim. This means that discrimination will be justified only if the action taken is "appropriate and necessary" with a view to pursuing a specific,

Age Discrimination

legitimate business aim. There is no prescribed list of "legitimate aims" and so it will be up to the employer, if challenged, to provide a sound business reason for any discriminatory treatment of an individual and show that the treatment really was relevant and necessary in relation to that reason. Acas, in its guide titled "Age and the Workplace — Putting the Employment Equality (Age) Regulations 2006 into Practice", suggests that legitimate aims might include:

- economic factors such as business needs and efficiency
- the health, welfare or safety of an individual
- the particular training requirements of a job.

4.19 It is unlikely that the aim of reducing costs will, on its own, be considered legitimate if the means used to achieve the aim result in age discrimination against an employee or group of employees.

4.20 In contrast to the other anti-discrimination laws, the Employment Equality (Age) Regulations 2006 permit direct age discrimination (as well as indirect discrimination) if it can be justified in the circumstances. Employers must, however, provide concrete evidence to support any claim of justification, rather than relying on management opinion or custom and practice in the organisation.

Four Forms of Discrimination

4.21 In line with the other anti-discrimination laws, the age discrimination regulations define four different forms of discrimination.
1. Direct discrimination.
2. Indirect discrimination.
3. Victimisation.
4. Harassment.

Direct Age Discrimination

4.22 Direct discrimination means treating an individual less favourably than another person on the grounds of that person's age. Acts of direct age discrimination may include:

- deciding not to employ a particular job applicant on grounds that he or she is thought to be "too old" or "too young"
- denying someone access to training, transfer or promotion for the same reason
- giving someone less favourable terms and conditions of employment than another employee who is older (or younger) just because of the difference in age
- denying an individual access to benefits or perks for reasons related to his or her age
- selecting an employee for redundancy because he or she is close to retirement age.

Indirect Age Discrimination

4.23 The standard approach to indirect discrimination is used in the age discrimination regulations, ie that discrimination occurs when an employer applies any general policy, procedure, rule or practice which:

- puts (or would put) persons of a particular age group at a particular disadvantage when compared with others
- actually puts an individual to that disadvantage
- cannot be justified as being a proportionate means of achieving a legitimate aim.

4.24 This means that indirect age discrimination will be capable of justification

Age Discrimination

only if the employer's treatment of the individual in question was appropriate and necessary with a view to pursuing an identifiable, legitimate business aim.

Victimisation

4.25 The standard provisions on victimisation are included in the new age discrimination legislation. Thus, employers and employees are barred from discriminating against a member of staff because that person has raised a genuine complaint of age discrimination or harassment, whether under the employer's grievance procedure or before an employment tribunal. Any employee who supports or assists another employee with a complaint is also protected against victimisation.

Age Harassment

4.26 The standard definition of harassment is used in the new age discrimination legislation. Thus harassment occurs when an individual behaves in a way which:
- is related to age
- is unwanted from the perspective of the person on the receiving end; and
- has either the purpose or effect of violating a person's dignity; or
- creates an intimidating, hostile, degrading, humiliating or offensive environment for the person on the receiving end.

4.27 The most important criterion in establishing whether particular behaviour amounts to harassment is the perception of the person on the receiving end of the particular behaviour.

4.28 Examples of age harassment could include:
- jokes that make fun of older people and that cause offence
- referring to someone in a derogatory age-related way, such as "stupid old codger", "daft old bat" or "foolish young girl"
- making demeaning comments to or about someone suggesting that he or she is "past it" or "over the hill"
- refusing to co-operate with someone on grounds that he or she is "too young" to bother about
- excluding someone from team social events because he or she is much older/younger than the others in the team
- treating someone's ideas as inferior or worthless on account of his or her youth
- making demeaning remarks (whether in fun or not) alleging that someone's physical or mental abilities have declined on account of age
- teasing someone because his or her partner is much older or younger than him or her.

Age Discrimination in Recruitment

4.29 Job applicants are protected throughout the entire process of recruitment against any form of discrimination related to their age, unless specifically justified.

4.30 In recruiting workers, employers should make sure that recruitment decisions are based solely on objective criteria that are relevant to the job in question, such as competencies, experience, qualifications and skills. A staged process should be used to:
- analyse the job
- produce an accurate and up-to-date job description
- use this to develop a person specification.

4.31 Advertisements should:
- avoid the use of age limits or age ranges, even if only implicit in the use of words such as "energetic" and "dynamic"
- avoid language that implies age restrictions
- be placed in suitable media to encourage applicants of all ages.

4.32 It is not open to employers to seek to recruit an older or a younger person on the grounds of customer preference, eg the belief (whether valid or not) that customers would prefer to deal with someone of around their own age, or that employing people of a particular age group would improve the organisation's sales.

4.33 There is, however, a general exception which allows employers to reject job applicants on grounds of age if they are 65 or over at the time they apply for employment or if they would reach age 65 within six months of their application. In the case of an employer that operates a retirement age that is above or below age 65, the exception would operate in respect of any job applicant who was older than that age or who would reach that age within six months of the job application. A job applicant rejected on age grounds in these circumstances is not eligible to bring a claim for age discrimination to an employment tribunal.

4.34 It is important to note that this exception applies only to external recruitment, and not to decisions concerning the promotion or transfer of existing employees.

Positive Action

4.35 Although positive discrimination, ie discrimination in favour of a person from a minority group, is generally not permitted under UK employment law, the Employment Equality (Age) Regulations 2006 permit certain forms of positive action in recruitment and training. Positive action is not required in law, but is permitted if the reason for it is to increase the number of people from a particular age group or age range that has historically been disadvantaged within employment for reasons linked to age.

4.36 It is thus lawful for employers to apply measures specifically to encourage candidates from a disadvantaged age group to apply for employment or promotion. Examples could include placing job advertisements in a particular publication that is read predominantly by people of a particular age range. However, it is only encouragement that is permitted — at the point of selection for employment or promotion, the principles of equality must be applied and an individual candidate's age must play no part in the decision-making process.

4.37 An example of positive action in relation to training could be to offer training to employees over the age of 50 specifically to assist them to become more computer literate.

Recruitment Best Practice Checklist

4.38 Employers should take note of the following best practice guidelines to avoid age discrimination in the recruitment process.
- Do not use age limits or age ranges in job advertisements.
- Remove any questions relating to age or date of birth from application forms.
- Recognise that a requirement for a minimum and/or a maximum number of years of experience will be indirectly discriminatory (against younger and older job applicants respectively), and that such requirements will have to be justified.
- Do not require candidates to have a university degree unless this is necessary for legal reasons or for effective performance of the job in question. Since a much larger number of people attend university nowadays than, say, 30 years ago,

Age Discrimination

- insisting that job applicants possess a university degree would discriminate indirectly against older people, as they would be less likely than younger people to hold a degree.
- Avoid recruiting only by word of mouth as this practice may tend to reinforce an age imbalance in the workforce and may be indirectly discriminatory.
- Incorporate clear, objective and specific criteria against which applicants can be assessed. This should help to eliminate age bias, whether deliberate or subconscious.
- Be open-minded when assessing the skills and aptitudes of older (and younger) job applicants.
- Ensure that all staff involved in recruitment or selection have received effective equal opportunities training.
- Give guidance to recruiters on the effects which generalised assumptions and prejudices about "young" and "old" people can have on selection decisions.
- Use more than one person to carry out shortlisting and interviewing as this may help to prevent any one individual's prejudices affecting the selection decision.
- Keep notes on recruitment decisions in order to be able to demonstrate that the reason for the rejection of one candidate and the appointment of another was free from age bias.

Age Discrimination during Employment

4.39 Employees and other workers are protected against all forms of age discrimination in every aspect of their employment. This includes the terms and conditions of their contract, access to promotion, transfer and training and general treatment at work.

Terms and Conditions of Employment

4.40 It is unlawful to treat an employee less favourably than another as regards the terms and conditions of their contracts if the reason for the different treatment is related to their ages. It is however permissible to offer pay enhancements and/or additional contractual benefits based on length of service, as opposed to age.

4.41 The equality principle applies irrespective of cost. It would therefore be unlawful to deny an older worker an insurance benefit afforded to younger staff (eg health insurance) on the grounds that the cost of providing the benefit is much greater once a particular age has been reached.

4.42 Where it is agreed that an employee may work on beyond the employer's normal retirement age, the employee will continue to be entitled to equality of treatment, ie he or she must not be treated less favourably on grounds of age with respect to terms and conditions of employment.

Service-related Benefits

4.43 Many employers offer increased pay and enhanced contractual benefits to employees subject to their having worked for the organisation continuously for a defined number of years. A common example is holiday entitlement where employees may be granted an extra day's holiday after a stated number of years' service up to a maximum of, eg five extra days.

4.44 Under the age discrimination regulations, basing entitlement to pay increases or enhanced benefits on length of service is indirectly discriminatory. The regulations state, however, that length of service requirements related to increased pay and/or enhanced benefits are automatically permitted where the service requirement is five years or less. There is also a general provision that allows employers to grant employees higher pay or increased benefits if it "reasonably appears" to them that the length of service provision "fulfils a business need" such as encouraging loyalty, increasing or maintaining motivation or reflecting higher levels of relevant experience.

4.45 Pay policies that award pay increments solely on the basis that an employee has reached a particular birthday are, however, unlawful.

Sickness and Health Schemes

4.46 Some employers offer their employees benefits under life insurance schemes, permanent health insurance schemes and/or private medical insurance schemes. Typically, the insurance providers that underwrite these schemes take into account the age profile of the employer's workforce when determining the costs of providing the necessary insurance cover.

4.47 The new age regulations do not apply to the provision of goods, facilities and services and so insurance providers can continue to make such distinctions.

4.48 Employers, on the other hand, are prohibited from offering different employees different levels of benefit under such schemes if the differences are based on age (unless they can objectively justify such differences in treatment).

4.49 This could be significant for employers who encourage the employment of older workers as they may find that the cost of providing insurance cover could increase substantially where employees continue to work beyond age 65. As stated above, the aim of reducing costs is unlikely, on its own, to amount to a "legitimate aim" justifying age discriminatory treatment.

4.50 At the other end of the age scale, some insurance organisations may apply a large excess on their insurance premiums in respect of cover for certain employees who drive the organisation's vehicles, eg drivers under age 25. The employer is nevertheless prohibited from discriminating against young people, eg by refusing to employ an otherwise suitable 23-year old job applicant into a driving job because of his or her age. The employer would have to show that the refusal to employ the 23-year old was either unrelated to age or was necessary in relation to the achievement of a legitimate aim. An outright refusal on the part of the insurance organisation to provide the necessary insurance cover might provide justification for a refusal to recruit the individual, while the imposition of an excess on the insurance premium would probably not.

Promotion, Transfer and Training

4.51 It is unlawful to use age as a criterion in promotion decisions unless there is a specific reason that justifies the employer's decision to exclude a particular employee from promotion, transfer or training on grounds of age. The same sort of considerations would apply as described above in recruitment. The exception that allows employers to reject external job applicants on grounds of age if they are over the employer's retirement age at the time they apply for employment does not, however, apply to internal promotions or transfers.

4.52 The following good practice is recommended regarding promotions.
- Avoid the use of age limits or age ranges.
- Ensure that promotion opportunities are advertised so that all employees can see them.
- Ensure that opportunities are available to all staff who have demonstrated the ability or potential to do the job, irrespective of their age.

Age Discrimination

- Focus on the skills, abilities and potential of the candidates when reviewing applications for promotion.

Selection for Redundancy

4.53 It is unlawful to select older workers for redundancy first, in preference to younger people. Criteria for selection must be free from age bias.

Redundancy Pay

4.54 The system of calculating statutory redundancy pay was changed when the age regulations were introduced. Service below the age of 18 (which was previously excluded) is now taken into account and the previous system of tapering down entitlement during the 12 months prior to age 65 was removed. The upper age limit of 65 was also removed. The Government decided, however, to retain the system of using three different multipliers for three defined age brackets.

Contractual Redundancy Pay Schemes

4.55 Where an employer wishes to adopt a contractual redundancy pay scheme that is more generous than the statutory scheme, it must ensure that it is not discriminatory under the age regulations. A contractual redundancy pay scheme that bases redundancy pay on employees' length of service alone (ie one that does not use the age bands applied in the statutory scheme) would be indirectly discriminatory against younger staff (who on the whole would tend to have shorter service). Such a scheme would therefore have to be objectively justified. The exception for enhanced and increased benefits based on length of service (see above) does not apply to redundancy payments.

4.56 A contractual redundancy pay scheme that uses age bands must mirror the statutory scheme. The age bands used in the statutory scheme are 21 and under; 22–40 inclusive; and 41 and over.

4.57 Employers are permitted to make enhancements to the statutory scheme in any of the following ways, by:
- raising (or removing) the maximum amount of a week's pay so that a higher rate than that used in the statutory scheme (£310 for 2007/08) is used in the calculation
- multiplying the multipliers used for each age band in the statutory scheme by a number, eg two or three (the multipliers used in the statutory scheme are: half a week's pay (21 and under), one week's pay (age 22–40) and one and a half week's pay (age 41 and over)
- working out what each employee would receive under the statutory scheme and then multiplying the resultant figures by a number, eg two or three.

4.58 A combination of the above methods may be used.

4.59 Employers may also, if they wish, make contractual redundancy payments to employees who have less than two years continuous service (where no statutory redundancy payment is required) provided they follow the general rules above.

4.60 Because any enhanced scheme that an employer applies has to mirror the statutory scheme, the same adjustment would have to be made to all three age bands.

Setting a Retirement Age

4.61 The age discrimination legislation introduces a default retirement age of 65.

4.62 It is not, however, obligatory for employers to require employees to retire at age 65. They may choose to operate a higher retirement age, no retirement age at all or a lower retirement age, provided they can demonstrate that retiring employees at this lower age is appropriate and necessary in respect of the achievement of a legitimate business aim.

4.63 Where a retirement age below age 65 cannot be objectively justified, an employer that wishes to terminate an employee's employment before he or she reaches age 65 must ensure that they have another fair reason for dismissing the employee and that they follow the statutory dismissal procedure.

4.64 In conjunction with the introduction of the default retirement age of 65, retirement has become a potentially fair reason for dismissal. Thus an employee who is genuinely retired at age 65 will normally have no grounds on which to bring claims of either age discrimination or unfair dismissal (unless new pre-retirement procedures have not properly been followed).

4.65 If, however, a retirement does not take place at (or after) age 65 (or at a lower retirement age that the employer can objectively justify), or if proper notification of retirement has not been given, then the burden will be on the employer to convince a tribunal that the reason for the employee's dismissal was in fact retirement and not a pretext for some other reason, eg redundancy or declining job performance.

Right to Request to Continue Working beyond Retirement

4.66 Employees have the right to lodge a formal request to continue working beyond their operative retirement date, and the employer is obliged to consider all such requests through a formal "duty-to-consider" procedure. This procedure applies each time an employer wishes to retire an employee (unless the retirement is by mutual consent). The procedure obliges the employer to hold a meeting with the employee "within a reasonable period" to discuss the possibility of continued working, provide a decision as soon as is reasonably practicable after the meeting and allow a right of appeal against any refusal.

4.67 An employee making such a request is under a duty to submit the request in writing no later than three months before the operative date of retirement. The employee must also specify exactly what he or she wants, ie whether the request is to continue working indefinitely or for a defined limited period. The employee is not, however, obliged to provide any reason for his or her request. An employer who has properly complied with the statutory pre-retirement procedures is not obliged to consider a late request.

4.68 At the meeting, the employee should be allowed to put forward his or her case and the employer should remain open-minded about the possibility of agreeing to the request. It is also acceptable for the employer to propose alternatives, eg a different retirement date or a variation to the employee's working pattern.

4.69 The employee has the right to be accompanied by a fellow worker of his or her choice at any meeting or appeal meeting set up to consider continued working beyond retirement.

4.70 After the meeting, the employer should provide its decision in writing. There is no need for an employer to justify a refusal to permit an employee to work on beyond retirement age, or even to give the employee a reason for refusing his or her request. The duty on employers is only that they must follow through the statutory procedure correctly if a request is made. A failure to comply with the "duty-to-consider procedure" will, however, render the employee's termination an automatically unfair dismissal.

4.71 Despite the absence of a statutory duty on the employer to provide a reason for its decision, Acas recommends in its guide titled "Age and the Workplace —

Putting the Employment Equality (Age) Regulations 2006 into Practice" that employers should give a reason and a more detailed explanation of their retirement policy.

4.72 If an employee appeals against his or her employer's refusal to agree to continued working beyond retirement, the employer must ensure the appeal is heard by a different person from the person who made the decision not to agree to the employee's request. The appeal meeting can, if necessary, be heard after the retirement has taken effect.

Notification of Retirement

4.73 Employers are obliged to give employees approaching retirement age between six and 12 months' written notice of their retirement date and at the same time advise them of their right to lodge a request to continue working longer. The regulations state that employers cannot rely on the terms of an employee's contract or notification of retirement age contained in an organisation's policy or handbook for this purpose.

4.74 Where an employer fails completely to provide written notification to the employee of his or her retirement date, the retirement on that date will constitute an automatically unfair dismissal.

4.75 There is no duty on employers to follow the statutory dismissal and disciplinary procedure (DDP) where the reason for dismissal is retirement.

4.76 None of the provisions restrict employees from electing to take early retirement, if this is an option available to them under their contract of employment or their employer's pension scheme.

4.77 Where an employer fails to properly inform an employee of his or her proposed retirement date and the right to request to continue working, the employee may bring a complaint to an employment tribunal. If the case succeeds, the employee may be awarded up to eight weeks' pay as compensation.

4.78 The following good practice is recommended.
- Base retirement policy on business needs while also giving individuals as much choice as possible.
- Ensure that the loss to the organisation of skills and abilities is fully evaluated when operating early-retirement schemes.
- Do not see age as the sole criterion when operating an early-retirement scheme (subject to pension rules).
- Avoid making stereotypical assumptions about the capabilities of older employees.
- Use flexible retirement schemes where possible.
- Use phased retirement where possible to allow employees to alter the balance of their working and personal lives gradually and prepare for full-time retirement.

Pensions

4.79 The implementation of a default retirement age of 65 does not impact on the age at which an individual becomes entitled to a state or occupational pension.

4.80 It is unlawful for occupational pension schemes to discriminate against members or prospective members on the basis of age and trustees of such schemes are obliged to disapply or change any age-discriminatory rules. There are, however, exemptions applicable to most age-related criteria within occupational pension schemes.

4.81 The Government has committed itself to maintaining the state pension age at 65, which will be equalised for men and women by April 2010.

Claims for Age Discrimination

4.82 In the event of a claim for age discrimination, the employer will have to show a non-discriminatory reason for their actions (or inactions), otherwise an employment tribunal may draw adverse inferences and rule in favour of the claimant.

Unfair Dismissal Rights

4.83 The bar on employees aged 65 or over from bringing claims of unfair dismissal (or statutory redundancy pay) to an employment tribunal has been abolished. Correspondingly, retirement has become a potentially fair reason for dismissal.

The Questionnaire Procedure

4.84 An employee or job applicant who believes that he or she may have experienced any form of age discrimination (including discrimination after employment has ended) may serve a special questionnaire on the employer, asking for an explanation for the conduct that he or she thinks was discriminatory. The individual may instigate the procedure either before or after he or she has commenced tribunal proceedings. A pre-printed questionnaire is available, but the employee may add his or her own questions.

4.85 The employer is not under any statutory duty to respond to a questionnaire served upon them. The questions and replies are, however, admissible as evidence in tribunal cases. If the employer fails to respond to the questionnaire within eight weeks, or if the answers given are evasive or equivocal, the tribunal or court may infer that the employer did discriminate and that they are trying to avoid admitting it. It is, therefore, advisable for employers to answer the employee's questions as fully as possible.

4.86 In order to be used in tribunal cases, the questionnaire must, in cases where an application to tribunal has not yet been presented, be given or sent to the employer within three months of the act that is being complained about, or, where a complaint has already been presented to the tribunal, within 21 days of the date on which the complaint was lodged.

The Burden of Proof

4.87 Once an employee has established facts before an employment tribunal that indicate that he or she may have been the victim of unlawful age discrimination, the burden of proof shifts to the employer who must (if they are to succeed in defending the claim) persuade the tribunal that there was some other non-discriminatory reason for their actions, or that their actions were justified as being a proportionate means of achieving a legitimate aim.

Vicarious Liability

4.88 Employers are liable in law for any act of discrimination or harassment carried out by any of their employees in the course of their employment. This principle applies to age discrimination legislation in the same way as it applies to other forms of unlawful discrimination.

Age Discrimination

4.89 Employers can defend themselves against claims of age discrimination only if they show that they took all reasonably practicable steps to prevent their staff from behaving in a discriminatory way. To protect themselves from liability therefore, employers should:
- ensure age discrimination is incorporated into equal opportunities policies, anti-harassment policies and associated complaints procedures
- provide training to all employees on equality, and discrimination and harassment, with additional training to managers and supervisors who hold responsibility for recruitment and employment decisions
- communicate the policies on a regular basis to all staff and take steps to ensure they are fully understood
- effectively monitor compliance.

Case Law from Ireland

4.90 Ireland has had age discrimination legislation in force since 1999 and a number of interesting cases have been brought before the Irish courts since then, most of which have resulted from alleged age discrimination during the recruitment process. Some examples are as follows.
- In *O'Connor v Lidl Ireland GmbH* DEC-E/2005/012, the employer placed an advertisement in a newspaper for the post of district manager which stated that applicants should be graduates "ideally with not more than two to three years' experience in a commercial environment". When Mr O'Connor applied for the job, he was neither shortlisted nor invited to interview and he subsequently asserted in court that the requirement to have between two and three years' experience was indirectly discriminatory on grounds of age. The Equality Officer upheld this argument based partly on the evidence that out of 85 applicants for the job who were over the age of 40, only three had been called for interview.
- In *Hughes v Aer Lingus* DEC-E/2002/49, a 53-year old woman applied for a cabin crew job and was invited to interview. At the interview, she was asked the question, "How would you feel about working and being directed by younger employees?". Ms Hughes was subsequently not offered the job on the grounds of the employer's opinion that she was over-qualified. She complained, arguing that the employer had attached undue significance to her age, and that the term "over-qualified" was a euphemism to conceal the real reason for her rejection, namely that she was too old for the employer's liking. The employer refuted this allegation and claimed that the reason for the rejection of Ms Hughes was that the interviewers had formed the view that she had a very strong personality, was accustomed to working in a managerial role and would have difficulty in taking instructions.
- On balance, the Equality Officer held that Ms Hughes' rejection for the job was not on the grounds of age, largely because:
  - there were clear interview notes supporting the "strong personality" argument
  - the company could show that the success rate for job applicants over 50 was, in general, in line with the success rate for younger candidates.
- The Equality Officer did, however, rule that the question about how she would feel about working and being directed by younger employees was discriminatory, and might have affected her performance at the interview. A direction was therefore issued that Ms Hughes should be offered another interview with a differently constituted interview panel, or offered a job, within the next 12 weeks.
- In *Noonan v Accountancy Connections* DEC-E/2004/042, the claimant was a man in his 50s who had some 20 years' experience as a qualified accountant. He was nevertheless rejected for two accountancy posts described as "senior" because the employer (apparently) thought he was "too senior". The organisation asserted that they wanted someone who had been qualified for "about two to three years". In the case of one of the posts, Mr Noonan would have been older than the person he

would have reported to, which the employer felt would cause problems. He brought a claim for age discrimination, arguing that because accountants generally qualified by their mid-twenties, the condition that applicants should have between two to three years' experience in effect excluded most people over the age of 30. He asserted that the organisation should have addressed any concerns they might have about an applicant's motivation by discussing the issues directly with them. The Equality Officer accepted Mr Noonan's arguments and concluded that the employer's defence amounted to a series of generalisations which were unsupported by any objective evidence.

- In the case of *A Named Female Complainant v A Company* DEC-E/2002/013, a young, female manager newly recruited to a small organisation complained that she had been systematically belittled in front of colleagues by a male manager in his 60s who could not accept her position as a manager. This was the first decision in Ireland on age-based harassment in employment. The older male manager was frequently hostile, aggressive and unco-operative towards the young woman and often intervened in her responsibilities. One day he said to her face in front of others that she was "only a young fooling girl". Having eventually resigned, she succeeded in claims both for age-based harassment and gender-based harassment.

Monitoring

4.91 Application forms should make it clear that any requests for details of age or date of birth are to be used solely for monitoring purposes. Furthermore, like information on gender and ethnicity, the information should be requested on a detachable section of the form. The information would normally be treated confidentially and not disclosed to anyone responsible for making recruitment decisions.

Training

4.92 Employers should ensure that there is equal treatment and equal access to training for all staff irrespective of their ages. The criteria used to determine eligibility for training must be based on objective factors such as individuals' abilities and job duties.

4.93 Line managers, supervisors and recruiters frequently have preconceived notions or hold stereotypes regarding age. It is important that all employees with management and/or recruitment responsibilities are familiar with the organisation's policy and procedure on age equality — usually contained within the organisation's equal opportunities policy.

4.94 The following training should be carried out by all employers.

- Training in equality and the avoidance of bias for all line managers, supervisors and others responsible for recruitment and employment decisions.
- Awareness training for all staff in the organisation's equal opportunities policy, also covering the need to avoid all forms of harassment and the types of behaviour that could be viewed as age harassment.
- Induction training for all new staff to make them aware of the organisation's policies on age equality and harassment, and the importance of following them.

List of Relevant Legislation

4.95
- Employment Equality (Age) Regulations 2006
- Sex Discrimination (Indirect Discrimination and Burden of Proof) Regulations 2001
- Part-time Workers (Prevention of Less Favourable Treatment) Regulations 2000
- Employment Act 2002
- Employment Relations Act 1996
- Employment Rights Act 1996
- Pensions Act 1995
- Disability Discrimination Act 1995
- Race Relations Act 1976
- Sex Discrimination Act 1975

List of Relevant Cases

4.96
- *Rutherford and another v Secretary of State for Trade and Industry (No.2)* [2006] IRLR 551, HL
- *Taylor v Secretary of State for Scotland* [2000] IRLR 502, HL
- *Nash v Mash/Roe Group Ltd* [1998] IRLR 168
- *Simpson v British Tinken Ltd* [1998] 37 DCLD9
- *Bullock v Alice Ottley School* [1992] IRLR 564, CA
- *Barber v Guardian Royal Exchange Assurance Group Ltd* [1990] IRLR 240, ECJ
- *Perera v Civil Service Commission and Department of Customs and Excise* [1983] IRLR 166, CA
- *Price v Civil Service Commission and the Society of Civil and Public Servants* [1977] IRLR 291, EAT

Further Information

Publications
- *Acas: Age and the Workplace — Putting the Employment Equality (Age) Regulations 2006 into Practice (2006)*
- *Acas Employing Older Workers (2005)*
- *Voluntary Code of Practice: Age Diversity in Employment (Age Positive, 1999)*, Department for Work and Pensions (DWP)

Organisations
- **Age Concern**
  Web: *www.ageconcern.org.uk*

Age Concern is the UK's largest organisation working with and for older people. It provides vital local services as well as influencing public opinion and Government.

- **Chartered Institute of Personnel and Development (CIPD)**
  Web: *www.cipd.org.uk*
  The CIPD is a professional body for those involved in the management and development of people.
  Department for Children, Schools and Families (DCSF)
  Web: *www.dfes.gov.uk*
  The Department for Children, Schools and Families (DCSF) aims to give children an excellent start in education, enable young people to equip themselves with life and work skills.
- **Employers' Forum on Age (EFA)**
  Web: *www.efa.org.uk*
  The EFA is an independent network of leading employers who recognise the business value of attracting and retaining experienced employees — regardless of their age
- **Third Age Challenge**
  Web: *www.thirdagers.net*
  Third Age Challenge is a not-for-profit organisation, set up in 1993, whose primary mission is to support older people who are unemployed or at risk of unemployment.

Disability Discrimination

This topic covers the following:
- Scope of the Disability Discrimination Act
- Qualifying Conditions
- Definition of Disability
- Conditions Not to Be Treated as Impairments
- Forms of Disability Discrimination
- Direct Disability Discrimination
- Disability-related Discrimination
- Victimisation
- Disability Harassment
- Duty to Make Reasonable Adjustments
- Disability Discrimination in Recruitment
- Requirements in Job Specifications
- Disability Discrimination in the Course of Employment
- Claims of Disability Discrimination

4.97 The Disability Discrimination Act 1995 prohibits discrimination on grounds related to an individual's disability and places a duty on employers to make reasonable adjustments to working practices and premises in order to accommodate the needs of individual employees and job applicants who have a disability.

4.98 The Act prohibits various types of discrimination: direct discrimination, discrimination on disability-related grounds, victimisation, harassment and a failure to make reasonable adjustments. It also provides for limited post-employment protection and a questionnaire procedure to help claimants explore whether disability discrimination has occurred.

4.99 There is no qualifying period of service necessary to make a complaint to an employment tribunal and no limit on the amount of compensation that can be awarded to a successful claimant.

4.100 The Disability Rights Commission has published a Code of Practice on Employment and Occupation for employers.

Employers' Duties

- Employers must not treat any individual member of staff unfavourably on grounds that the employee has a disability, or on grounds related to a disability.
- Employers must not victimise staff who have complained that they have suffered disability discrimination, nor victimise staff who assist others in making such complaints.
- Employers must not allow any form of disability harassment.
- Employers are under a duty to take all reasonable steps to make changes to any provisions, criteria, practices or physical features of their premises that place a disabled employee or job applicant at a substantial disadvantage.
- Employers must take care not to commit any type of disability discrimination after a person's employment ends, eg by withholding a reference or harassing an ex-employee on grounds related to disability.
- Employers should take all reasonable steps to prevent discrimination in the workplace, eg by communicating their equal opportunities and anti-harassment

policies to all staff on a regular basis, training staff on equal opportunities issues and the avoidance of all forms of discrimination, and monitoring compliance.

Employees' Duties

- Employees have a duty not to discriminate against any colleague on any grounds related to the colleague's disability.
- Employees must not victimise any member of staff who has complained that he or she has experienced disability discrimination or helped a colleague to make a complaint of discrimination or harassment.
- Employees must not engage in any behaviour that could be interpreted as disability harassment.
- Employees should co-operate with their employer in order to facilitate the implementation of reasonable adjustments for themselves or any disabled colleagues.
- Employees are under a duty to adhere to their employer's equal opportunities and anti-harassment policies and to ensure that they treat their colleagues with respect and dignity at all times.

In Practice

Scope of the Disability Discrimination Act

4.101 The Disability Discrimination Act 1995 applies to all employers since the previous small employer exemption was abolished in October 2004.

4.102 The Act prohibits discrimination on grounds of or related to an individual's disability. Job applicants are protected throughout the process of recruitment and limited protection against disability discrimination is also available to former employees.

4.103 If disability discrimination occurs, the victim may bring a complaint to an employment tribunal.

Employees and Other Types of Workers

4.104 All workers are covered by the Disability Discrimination Act, ie not only those employed directly by the organisation, but also other workers such as:
- contract workers
- agency temps
- casual workers
- freelancers who provide their services personally
- directors
- company secretaries
- non-elected office holders
- partners in firms.

Qualifying Conditions

4.105 There is no length of service required for an employee or worker to bring a claim for unlawful disability discrimination to an employment tribunal. Equally, there is no lower or upper age limit for a claimant to bring a complaint.

4.106 Employees (but not other workers), must first raise a written grievance with their employer and wait 28 days. This is to allow the employer time and opportunity to deal with the complaint before it can proceed to tribunal. If a claim is lodged with the tribunal before the employee has raised a grievance and waited 28 days, the tribunal will in most cases not admit it. Where, however, the claim relates to a dismissal on the grounds of disability, the potential claimant need not raise a grievance first.

Definition of Disability

4.107 The Act defines disability as a physical or mental impairment that has a substantial and long-term adverse effect on a person's ability to carry out normal day-to-day activities. Many conditions with substantial, ie non-trivial, effects are considered disabilities.

4.108 The Scottish Court of Session has ruled (in *Millar v Board of the Inland Revenue* [2005] CSIH71 XA145/04) that the term "impairment" should be given its ordinary and natural meaning and that an impairment may either result from an illness or consist of an illness. It is therefore not necessary, in order for an individual to be classed as disabled under the Act, to identify the cause of the impairment or prove that some kind of illness underlies it. Instead, the question of whether someone is disabled will be judged according to the effects the impairment has on that person's everyday life.

4.109 A physical or mental impairment will be taken to affect a person's ability to carry out normal day-to-day activities if it affects:

- mobility
- manual dexterity
- physical co-ordination
- continence
- ability to lift, carry or move everyday objects
- speech, hearing or eyesight
- memory or ability to concentrate, learn or understand
- perception of the risk of physical danger.

4.110 A severe disfigurement may also qualify as a disability.

4.111 A condition that is fully controlled by medication may still amount to a disability. Thus, for example, an employee who is substantially deaf but who can hear reasonably well while using a hearing aid would still be regarded as disabled in law.

Physical Impairment

4.112 The Act does not define "physical impairment", but many conditions and illnesses may fall under the definition of disability depending always on the effects of the condition on the individual.

Mental Impairment

4.113 Mental impairment means an impairment resulting from or consisting of a mental illness. The criteria for a mental illness to amount to a disability are the same as for a physical illness, ie the illness must be one that has a substantial adverse effect on the person's ability to carry out normal day-to-day activities and must have lasted, or be expected to last, at least 12 months. This means that some stress-related illnesses may amount to disabilities, depending on whether their effects on the person are substantial and long term.

4.114 Learning difficulties and other conditions such as dyslexia may amount to disabilities. The level of adverse effect on an individual is the most relevant factor in determining whether or not the particular condition constitutes a disability.

Definition of "Substantial"

4.115 "Substantial" has been defined as "not minor or trivial" with the result that an impairment does not have to have extreme or major adverse effects on an individual in order for the condition to amount to a disability in law.

Long-Term Effects

4.116 The effect of an impairment is "long term" if it lasts, or is expected to last, at least 12 months or for the rest of the disabled person's life. If an impairment is intermittent with the result that it sometimes affects the person and sometimes does not, it can still be considered as a disability, provided it is likely to recur. In these circumstances the person with the condition will be deemed to be disabled at all times irrespective of whether the condition is affecting them at a particular time.

4.117 Similarly, conditions whose effects fluctuate between minor and substantial can amount to a disability. The person with the condition is considered to be disabled at all times including times when the condition is in remission.

Progressive Conditions

4.118 Certain serious progressive conditions are considered to be disabilities from the point at which the individual has been diagnosed and begins to experience some effects. This holds even if the effects are not yet substantial — provided that it is likely that they will become substantial in the future.

4.119 Progressive conditions include muscular dystrophy, Alzheimer's disease and Parkinson's disease.

Cancer, HIV and Multiple Sclerosis

4.120 Since the Disability Discrimination Act was amended on 5 December 2005, anyone diagnosed with cancer, HIV or multiple sclerosis is automatically protected against discriminatory treatment, irrespective of how the condition is affecting them at that time, and irrespective of the future prognosis.

Blind and Partial Sight

4.121 Under the Disability Discrimination (Blind and Partially Sighted Persons) Regulations 2003, a person is deemed to be disabled if he or she produces either a certificate:
- signed by a registered consultant ophthalmologist saying that he or she is blind or partially sighted; or
- from a local authority stated that he or she is registered by the authority as blind or partially sighted.

Conditions Not to be Treated as Impairments

4.122 The following conditions are not classed as a disability.
- Addiction to alcohol, nicotine or other substances does not amount to a disability unless it is the result of the administration of prescribed drugs or other medical treatment (but liver failure caused by alcoholism is likely to be a disability).
- Seasonal allergic rhinitis or hay fever does not amount to a disability unless the condition aggravates the effect of another condition, in which case the other condition may amount to a disability.
- Certain personality disorders do not amount to a disability. These include:
  – a tendency to set fires
  – a tendency to steal
  – a tendency to physical or sexual abuse of other persons
  – exhibitionism
  – voyeurism.

4.123 Severe disfigurements are disabilities, but unremoved tattoos or decorative, non-medical body piercings and adornments are not.

Forms of Disability Discrimination

4.124 There are five different forms of disability discrimination.
- Direct disability discrimination.
- Disability-related discrimination.
- Victimisation.
- Harassment.
- A failure to make reasonable adjustments.

Direct Disability Discrimination

4.125 Direct discrimination occurs where an employer treats a disabled person unfavourably on the grounds of the disabled person's disability. This type of discrimination can never be justified. Acts of direct disability discrimination may include:
- deciding not to employ a particular job applicant on the grounds that he or she has a particular disability
- denying someone access to training, transfer or promotion just because he or she has a disability
- giving someone less favourable terms and conditions of employment or denying him/her access to benefits or perks because of a disability
- dismissing an employee because he or she has become disabled.

Disability-Related Discrimination

4.126 Disability-related discrimination means treating a disabled employee or job applicant less favourably than others would be treated for a reason related to the fact that the person has a disability. This type of discriminatory treatment is subject to the possibility of justification, ie the employer may put forward a legitimate reason for the discriminatory treatment of the individual. Examples could include:
- deciding not to employ a particular job applicant on the grounds that he or she would be unable to perform the key functions of the job because of the effects of a disability
- denying someone access to training, transfer or promotion for the same reason

- dismissing an employee because he or she has been absent from work for a lengthy period of time following an accident that caused a disability.

Victimisation

4.127 Employers and employees should not discriminate against any member of staff because that person has raised a genuine complaint of disability discrimination or harassment, whether under the employer's grievance procedure or before an employment tribunal. Any employee who supports or assists another employee to raise a complaint is also protected against victimisation.

4.128 Claimants lose their protection if their allegations or the evidence or information they have given were false and not made or given in good faith.

Examples of Victimisation

4.129 As common examples of victimisation, Acas cites an employee being isolated by their colleagues, labelled a "trouble maker" or denied access to promotion or training because he or she has raised a complaint of discrimination or helped another employee to bring a complaint. Employers are under a duty to take reasonable steps to prevent this happening.

Disability Harassment

4.130 The Disability Discrimination Act 1995 contains a statutory definition of harassment on grounds of disability. An employer subjects someone to harassment when, for a reason that relates to the disabled person's disability, he or she engages in unwanted conduct that has the purpose or effect of:
- violating the disabled person's dignity
- creating an intimidating, hostile, degrading, humiliating or offensive environment for him or her.

4.131 The question as to whether behaviour amounts to harassment depends primarily on the perception of the person on the receiving end.

4.132 A further clause provides that behaviour will constitute harassment if, with regard to all of the circumstances — including the victim's perception — it should reasonably be seen as violating the victim's dignity or as creating an atmosphere which is intimidating, hostile, degrading, humiliating or offensive to him or her.

4.133 In practice this means that a spurious claim that someone's behaviour amounted to harassment in circumstances where no reasonable person could possibly have viewed it as harassment in the context in which it occurred, would not succeed.

4.134 Any employer who receives a complaint of harassment should take it very seriously, investigate the circumstances thoroughly and, if the complaint is well founded, take steps to put a stop to the behaviour that is causing offence. It will also be appropriate in most circumstances to take disciplinary action against the harasser.

Examples of Disability Harassment

4.135 Examples of disability harassment could include:
- behaviour connected in some way to a person's disability that is offensive, frightening or in any way distressing
- intentional bullying on grounds related to an employee's disability

- behaviour that has no malicious intent but which is upsetting to someone for reasons related to the fact he or she has a disability
- telling jokes or using nicknames that might be demeaning for a person with a disability
- mimicking a disabled person's movements or mannerisms
- persistent staring at someone who has a disability.

Duty to Make Reasonable Adjustments

4.136 Where it is reasonable to do so, employers must make suitable adjustments to any provision, criterion or practice that they apply, in order to accommodate the needs of an employee or job applicant with a disability. This means that policies, working practices, working arrangements, rules, procedures and guidelines would all stand to be reviewed and, if appropriate, adjusted to support the disabled person.

4.137 This would include policies and procedures on:
- recruitment
- terms and conditions of employment
- opportunities for promotion, transfer or training
- termination of employment, including redundancy arrangements.

4.138 Employers must also make reasonable adjustments to any physical feature of their premises that puts a disabled employee or job applicant at a disadvantage.

4.139 The case *Mid-Staffordshire General Hospitals NHS Trust v Cambridge* demonstrated that the employer is duty-bound to obtain and act on a full and proper assessment of the employee's condition and its effects in order to try to eliminate any discriminatory effect in the workplace. The EAT ruled that the making of a proper assessment was a necessary part of the duty to make reasonable adjustments. It follows that the employer must be proactive in assessing an employee's condition and in identifying and implementing reasonable adjustments. It is not up to the employee to take the initiative in making suggestions although the employer should, of course, be willing to consult the disabled employee in order to establish his or her views on what adjustments might be helpful and listen to what he or she has to say on the matter.

Examples of Reasonable Adjustments

4.140 Reasonable adjustments might include:
- allocating some of the disabled person's duties to a colleague
- transferring the employee to another job
- changing the place of work
- changing the hours of work
- allowing the employee time off work during working hours for medical treatment
- allowing homeworking
- providing special equipment
- modifying instructions, procedures or reference manuals
- providing a reader or interpreter
- providing training, mentoring, extra supervision or other form of support
- moving furniture and relocating shelves.

4.141 Some examples of specific reasonable adjustments could be to:

- remove the requirement for an employee to hold a driving licence when the job could be fulfilled by other modes of travelling. To insist on a driving licence where the requirement to drive could reasonably be modified or deleted from the job description would be discriminatory
- allow a disabled employee to take more time off work than would normally be acceptable
- provide additional rest breaks where the employee's condition means that they tire easily
- adjust sickness absence procedures so that disability-related absences are discounted
- allow an employee to return to work after a period of absence on a part-time basis, or allow him or her to work partly at home for a temporary period in order to ease him or her back into full-time employment.

4.142 In *O'Hanlon v Commissioners of HM Revenue and Customs* [2007] 404 CA, the Court of Appeal upheld an EAT decision that it would not have been reasonable for the employer to adjust its sick pay scheme so as to allow a disabled employee to receive full pay indefinitely when absent for a disability-related reason. It followed that the disability-related discrimination suffered by the claimant (ie the limits on the sick pay scheme that meant she could receive a maximum of six months on full pay and a further six months on half pay) was justified.

4.143 When considering making reasonable adjustments for a disabled person, employers should use the following best practice guidelines.
- Employers should be pro-active in their approach to reasonable adjustments for disabled employees and job applicants.
- Where an employee or job applicant has a disability, the employer should enquire as to the effect a particular disability might have on his or her ability to carry out relevant job duties.
- In making such enquiries, the employer should adopt a positive approach.
- Employers should give positive consideration to any request from a member of staff for an adjustment to be made.
- Any change to an employee's hours or duties must only be implemented with the employee's express agreement, eg a transfer to an alternative job would have to be implemented only if the employee had expressly agreed to the move, otherwise the employer would be acting in breach of contract.
- Employers should adopt a sympathetic and considerate approach to the needs of disabled people.
- It is advisable not to make assumptions about the abilities of someone with a particular disability.

4.144 If an employer wishes to write to a disabled employee's doctor in order to obtain advice on the employee's condition, the employer must obtain the employee's written consent, as per the Access to Medical Reports Act 1988.

4.145 It may be lawful for an employer not to make an adjustment for a disabled employee or job applicant where the adjustment would:
- incur excessive cost in relation to the available resources of the organisation
- be impracticable or cause major disruption to the business
- not help the employee
- be unacceptable to the employee
- breach safety, fire or other regulations, or
- where the employer does not know, or could not reasonably be expected to know, that the employee is disabled.

4.146 It is important for employers to note that any discrimination against a disabled employee will be unlawful if the employer has not first made whatever adjustments are reasonable in the circumstances.

Disability Discrimination in Recruitment

4.147 Job applicants are protected throughout the entire process of recruitment against disability discrimination. For example, if an applicant who was otherwise suitable for the job under review was refused employment because he or she had a history of mental illness, this would constitute direct disability discrimination and would be unlawful. Refusing employment because there is evidence that the applicant could not, even with reasonable adjustments, perform the job under review to a satisfactory standard could, however, be justified.

Requirements in Job Specifications

4.148 Including unnecessary or marginal requirements in a job specification can, in certain circumstances, lead to disability discrimination.

4.149 Requiring qualifications, specific experience, a high level of health or fitness, mobility or dexterity that have little relevance to the vacancy under consideration may discriminate against a person with a disability.

4.150 It is possible to stipulate essential health requirements, but only if they can be justified in relation to the needs of the particular job.

Advertisements

4.151 The Disability Discrimination Act 1995 makes it unlawful to publish an advertisement that indicates, or might reasonably be understood to indicate, that a job application may be determined by reference to:
- a requirement for applicants not to have a disability, or a particular type of disability, or
- the employer not wishing to make reasonable adjustments for the applicant.

4.152 Employers should therefore make sure that any advertisements they place neither state nor imply that the work is unsuitable for a disabled person. Similarly, the employer should make sure that any job-related requirements included in the advertisement are necessary for the performance of the job, and not excessive or overstated, eg the employer should:
- not make unjustified claims that a job requires physical fitness or energy
- avoid the use of words and phrases such as "dynamic", "articulate", "pleasing appearance and personality" in job advertisements.

4.153 Such requirements will place people with certain types of disability at a disadvantage. Unless the particular requirement is necessary in relation to the job in question, it will be discriminatory and unlawful.

4.154 Media publishers and advertisers who knowingly publish discriminatory advertisements are guilty of an offence unless they can show that:
- they acted in reliance on a statement made by the responsible employers that the advertisements or instructions were not in breach of the 1995 Act
- it was reasonable for them to rely on any such statement.

4.155 The penalty on conviction is a fine of £5000.

Applicant Information

4.156 Employers should make it clear that they can provide information to job applicants in formats such as audio tape, large print, Braille or email, and that they are happy to receive applications in such formats.

Interviews

4.157 Employers should be prepared to take reasonable steps to discover whether a job applicant is disabled, and whether there might be a need to make adjustments for the interview. Possible reasonable adjustments could include rearranging the venue or the time for the interview, allowing more time than usual to conduct it, or allowing the interviewee to be accompanied by an interpreter or lip reader.

4.158 It is unlawful for an employer to refuse to interview or shortlist any disabled job applicant, just because they have a disability.

4.159 It is permissible to ask about a person's disability at an interview, if it is relevant to his or her ability to do the job. If it is relevant it is also permissible to ask an applicant to indicate any relevant effects of his or her disability – and to involve him or her in suggesting adjustments that could be made should he or she be employed. However, if any of the answers to such questions are subsequently used to discriminate against the disabled job applicant, this will be unlawful. Interviewers should therefore seek to phrase questions in a positive rather than a negative way, and similarly view the answers given in a constructive manner.

Testing

4.160 Routine testing of applicants may inadvertently discriminate against or disadvantage people with disabilities. Best practice suggests a combination of asking the individual what would be a reasonable adjustment and consulting the test producer about proposed adjustments.

Medicals

4.161 Pre-employment health screening is permissible, as long as all job applicants are treated in the same way. Singling out a disabled person for a pre-employment medical examination when it is not the employer's normal practice may be viewed as discriminatory. An employer will need to have a material and substantial reason to justify doing so.

4.162 In contrast asking the person to undergo a medical examination after the appointment has been confirmed may be permissible, eg if the purpose of doing so is to assess the implications of the person's disability in light of safety requirements or establish what reasonable adjustments would be recommended. Questions about previous periods off work are justified to assist employers in assessing what adjustments might be made to the job to aid the disabled worker.

4.163 Medical evidence can justify a decision not to employ a disabled applicant if the person's condition is likely to have a substantial adverse effect on their ability to do the job concerned. This only holds when no adjustment is reasonable and no alternative vacant job which the person could do.

Disability Discrimination in the Course of Employment

4.164 Employees are protected against all forms of disability discrimination in every aspect of their employment. This will include the terms and conditions of their contract, access to promotion, transfer and training and general treatment at work.

4.165 There is no requirement to treat a disabled worker more favourably than others, although the employer may choose to do so if they wish. Where a disabled worker is afforded favourable treatment, this cannot be viewed as discrimination against others who are not disabled.

Terms and Conditions

4.166 It is discriminatory to employ a disabled person on terms less favourable than those available to able-bodied employees employed on the same job — if the reason for the less favourable terms relates to the person's disability.

4.167 If there is a material and substantial reason to offer a disabled person a less favourable contract, and there is no reasonable adjustment that could remove that reason, then such a contract may be justified. The employer should, however, explore all reasonable adjustments before offering less favourable terms or conditions.

4.168 It may be lawful to pay a disabled employee a lower rate of pay under the terms of a performance-related pay scheme so long as the scheme applies equally to all employees in a particular class. The duty of reasonable adjustments applies, however, and so employers must seek to make all possible reasonable adjustments to their working practices or arrangements that will enable the disabled employee to perform to the same standard as employees who do not have a disability.

Promotion, Transfer and Training

4.169 If an employee's access to opportunities for promotion, transfer or training is restricted for any reason related to disability, this would amount to unlawful disability discrimination unless the employer could justify their decision not to promote, transfer or train the disabled employee. The same sort of considerations would apply as shown in recruitment.

Selection for Redundancy

4.170 The criteria used to make selections for redundancy should be checked carefully to guard against the possibility of adverse impact on disabled employees. Taking disability-related absences into account when applying selection criteria could, for example, be unlawful.

Post-employment Discrimination

4.171 A claim for disability discrimination can be made against a former employer irrespective of how much time has passed since the employee's employment ended. Such a claim can only succeed, however, where the individual can show that the discrimination or harassment arose out of, or was closely connected with, the previous employment relationship.

Claims of Disability Discrimination

4.172 To bring a complaint of disability discrimination to an employment tribunal, an employee or job applicant has to show that he or she was treated unfavourably either directly on grounds of a disability or on grounds related to a disability. In the former case, a comparison has to be drawn with the treatment of someone who does not have a disability. In the latter case, the comparator will be someone "to whom that reason does not apply", for example someone whose performance is not affected by disability, or who is not off sick. Thus the comparator in this case can be either a disabled person or a non-disabled person so long as their circumstances are the same or similar to those of the disabled employee. In cases of harassment, and in claims for a failure to make reasonable adjustments, no comparator is required. The

Disability Discrimination

tribunal will determine whether or not the employer had done all they reasonably could to accommodate the needs of a particular disabled person.

Public Sector Disability Duty

4.173 From 4 December 2006, there is a general duty on all public authorities when carrying out their public functions to:
- eliminate all forms of disability discrimination
- be pro-active in promoting equality of opportunity for people with disabilities
- encourage participation by disabled persons in public life
- take account of disabled persons' disabilities, and, where appropriate, treat them more favourably than people who do not have disabilities.

4.174 This means in effect that public authorities are required to promote disability equality in relation to all their policies and practices, which includes the need to influence attitudes and educate the public about disability.

4.175 Over and above this "general duty", there are specific duties on public authority employers imposed by regulations as regards their employment practices.

4.176 Specifically, public authorities must produce and publish a Disability Equality Scheme, ie a scheme showing how they intend to fulfil the general duty under the Act and the specific duties imposed by regulations. The scheme must be devised with the involvement of relevant disabled people. The duty is similar to the "race duty" imposed on public authorities under the Race Relations (Amendment) Act 2000.

Employer's Defence

4.177 An employer has a defence against a charge of disability-related discrimination if it can be shown that the treatment in question is justified on grounds that are material and substantial, or that it was not reasonable for them to make a particular adjustment, or any adjustment. The burden of proof is on the employer who seeks to rely on the justification defence.

The Questionnaire Procedure

4.178 An employee or job applicant who believes that he or she may have experienced any form of disability discrimination (including discrimination after his or her employment ended) may serve a special questionnaire on the employer, asking for an explanation for the conduct that they think was discriminatory. The individual may instigate the procedure either before or after he or she has commenced tribunal proceedings.

4.179 A pre-printed questionnaire is available, but the employee may add his or her own questions.

4.180 The employer is not under any statutory duty to respond to a questionnaire served upon them. The questions and replies are, however, admissible as evidence in tribunal cases. If the employer fails to respond to the questionnaire within eight weeks, or if the answers given are evasive or equivocal, the tribunal or court may infer that the employer did discriminate and the employer is trying to avoid admitting it. It is therefore advisable for employers to answer the employee's questions as fully as possible.

4.181 In order to be used in tribunal cases, the questionnaire must (in cases where an application to tribunal has not yet been presented) be given or sent to the employer within three months of the act that is being complained about, or (where a complaint has already been presented to the tribunal) within 21 days of the date on which the complaint was lodged.

The Burden of Proof

4.182 Once an employee has established facts before an employment tribunal that indicate that he or she may have been the victim of unlawful disability discrimination, the burden of proof shifts to the employer who must (if they are to succeed in defending the claim) persuade the tribunal that there was some other non-discriminatory reason for their actions.

Vicarious Liability

4.183 Employers are liable in law for any act of discrimination or harassment carried out by any of their employees in the course of their employment.

4.184 Employers can only defend themselves against claims of disability discrimination if they can show that they took all reasonably practicable steps to prevent their staff from behaving in a discriminatory way. To protect themselves from liability therefore, employers should:
- devise and implement an equal opportunities policy and an anti-harassment policy, both of which incorporate disability discrimination and the employer's duty to make reasonable adjustments for disabled workers
- implement a complaints procedure
- provide training to all employees on equality, discrimination and harassment, with additional training for managers and supervisors who hold responsibility for recruitment and employment decisions
- communicate the policies on a regular basis to all staff and take steps to ensure they are fully understood
- effectively monitor compliance.

4.185 Whether or not an employer can defend itself from liability for the discriminatory behaviour of an individual employee, that employee may be held liable for their own actions by an employment tribunal. This tends to happen most often in claims for harassment. This can result in an individual employee being ordered by the tribunal personally to pay compensation to the person whom they harassed.

Compensation

4.186 If an employee, job applicant or former employee succeeds in a claim for unlawful disability discrimination at tribunal, the most common outcome is that the employer will be ordered to pay compensation to the claimant. There is no ceiling on the amount of money that may be awarded. During the year 2005, the average total award in successful disability discrimination cases was £18,427, while the median figure was £8373 (Source: Equal Opportunities Review, No.155).

4.187 Compensation in most cases is made up of loss of earnings (eg where the employee has left their job on account of the discriminatory treatment) and an amount for injury to feelings.

Monitoring

4.188 There is no requirement in law for employers to keep information on how the workforce is made up, other than in the public sector where racial, gender and disability monitoring are required by statute. As from 4 December 2006, public authorities are under a duty to positively promote equality of opportunity for disabled people both within employment and in the exercise of their public functions. This is similar to the duty to promote racial equality under the Race Relations (Amendment) Act 2000.

4.189 Where an employer elects to gather information about employees' physical

Disability Discrimination

or mental health or condition, it must bear in mind that such information is classed as "sensitive data" under the Data Protection Act 1998. This means that the data cannot be collected or used unless either the employee has given his or her free consent, or one of a list of other conditions is satisfied.

4.190 If employers want to gather data on employees' health and/or disability, in order to monitor whether any discrimination is occurring, they must ensure that employees:

- are told why the information is being gathered, ie for monitoring purposes or to allow the employer to ascertain what reasonable adjustments might be required for disabled job applicants and employees
- are told how the organisation intends to use the data
- are assured of the confidentiality of the data and that it will be kept securely
- freely give their written consent to the data being collected and used.

4.191 There should be a clear policy on how the gathering of information on health and disability is handled which should also comply with the provisions of the Data Protection Act 1998.

Training

4.192 It is important that all staff are given awareness training on the organisation's policy and procedure on equal opportunities and the avoidance of disability discrimination, so that they fully understand both the employer's and the employee's responsibilities.

4.193 Employers need to ensure that there is equal treatment and equal access to training for all staff, including those with disabilities (unless the exclusion of a disabled employee can be justified on grounds that are material and substantial). The following training should be carried out by all employers:

- training in equality and the avoidance of bias for all line managers or supervisors and any others responsible for recruitment and employment decisions
- awareness training for all staff in the organisation's equal opportunities policy, also covering the need to avoid all forms of harassment and the types of behaviour that could be viewed as disability harassment
- individually tailored induction programmes to suit an employee who has a particular disability

4.194 The duty to make reasonable adjustments applies to training. A person might need individual training, training over a longer period, or retraining, for example, if a person has acquired a disability and is being offered a change of role. Coaching or mentoring may also be appropriate.

4.195 If an employer buys in training from an outside provider, it is necessary to check that the training provider has sufficient awareness of the requirements of the Disability Discrimination Act.

List of Relevant Legislation

4.196
- Disability Discrimination (Blind and Partially Sighted Persons) Regulations 2003
- Disability Discrimination Act 1995 (Amendment) Regulations 2003
- Disability Discrimination Act 2005

Disability Discrimination

- Data Protection Act 1998
- Disability Discrimination Act 1995
- Access to Medical Reports Act 1988

List of Relevant Cases

4.197
- *O'Hanlon v The Commissioners for HM Revenue & Customs* EAT/0109/06
- *Dunham v Ashford Windows* [2005] IRLR 608
- *Department for Work and Pensions v Hall* EAT/0012/05
- *Home Office v Collins* [2005] EWCA Civ 598 (CA) (unreported)
- *HM Prison Service v Beart (No. 2)* [2005] IRLR 568, CA
- *Igen Ltd v Wong* [2005] IRLR 258, CA
- *Millar v Board of the Inland Revenue* [2005] CSIH71 XA145/04
- *Archibald v Fife Council* [2004] IRLR 651, HL
- *Hewett v Motorola Ltd* [2004] IRLR 545, EAT
- *Lane Group plc and anor v Farmiloe* EAT 22.01.04 (0352/03 and 0357/03)
- *Nottinghamshire County Council v Meikle* [2004] IRLR 703, CA
- *Paul v National Probation Service* [2004] IRLR 190, EAT
- *Kirton v Tetrosyl Ltd* [2003] IRLR 353, CA
- *Mid Staffordshire General Hospitals NHS Trust v Cambridge* [2003] IRLR 566
- *Murray v Newham Citizens Advice Bureau Ltd* [2003] IRLR 340
- *Power v Panasonic UK Ltd* [2003] IRLR 151
- *Purves v Joydisc Ltd* [2003] IRLR 420, Sheriff Principal
- *Relaxion Group plc v Rhys-Harper; D'Souza v London Borough of Lambeth; Jones v 3M Healthcare Ltd* [2003] IRLR 484, HL
- *Coca-Cola Enterprises Ltd v Shergill* [2002] All ER (D) 02
- *College of Ripon & York St John v Hobbs* [2002] IRLR 185
- *McNicol v Balfour Beatty Rail Maintenance Ltd* [2002] IRLR 711, CA
- *Morgan v Staffordshire University* [2002] IRLR 190
- *Mowat-Brown v University of Surrey* [2002] IRLR 235
- *Rowden v Dutton Gregory* [2002] ICR 971, EAT
- *Cosgrove v Caesar and Howie* [2001] IRLR 653
- *Ekpe v Commissioner of Police of the Metropolis* [2001] IRLR 605
- *Rugamer v Sony Music Entertainment UK Ltd* [2001] IRLR 644
- *Kapadia v London Borough of Lambeth* [2000] IRLR 699, CA
- *Kent County Council v Mingo* [2000] IRLR 90
- *London Borough of Hammersmith & Fulham v Farnsworth* [2000] IRLR 691
- *Arboshe v East London Bus and Coach Co Ltd* 17 December 1999, EAT
- *Clark v TDG Ltd t/a Novacold* [1999] IRLR 318, CA
- *Coote v Granada Hospitality Ltd (No. 2)* [1999] IRLR 452, EAT
- *Goodwin v The Patent Office* [1999] IRLR 4, EAT
- *Kenny v Hampshire Constabulary* [1999] IRLR 76
- *British Sugar plc v Kirker* [1998] IRLR 624
- *Morse v Wiltshire County Council* [1998] IRLR 352
- *Rideout v TC Group* [1998] IRLR 628

- *British Sugar plc v Kirker* [1998] IRLR 624
- *Murphy v Sheffield Hallam University* (11 November 1998)
- *Post Office v Adekeye* [1997] ICR 110
- *Kirker v British Sugar plc* (5 December 1997)
- *King v The Great Britain-China Centre* [1991] IRLR 513, CA
- *Bush v Rolls Royce* (ET 1401054/98 and 1401495/98)
- *Cox v Rentokil Initial Services Ltd* (ET 2405154/00)
- *Hardy v Gower Furniture Ltd* (Case No. 1802093/97)
- *HSBC Bank plc v Clarkson* EAT/205/01
- *Mulligan v Commissioners of Inland Revenue* (EAT 691/99)
- *Newsome v The Council and the City of Sunderland*
- *Ree v Redrow Homes (Yorkshire) Ltd* EAT 0035/03
- *Sandy v Hampshire Constabulary* (Case No. 3101118/97)
- *Wearing v John Millar & Sons* (Case No. 401464/2000)
- *Williams v Channel 5* (Case No. 2302136/97)
- *Yacoubi (now Lyons) v Tesco Ltd* (EAT 1454/00)

Further Information

Organisations

- **British Educational Communications and Technology Agency (Becta)**
  Web: *www.becta.org.uk*
  Becta aims to further the use of information communication technology (ICT) to raise educational standards and to improve the effectiveness of education professionals and institutions.
- **Disability Alliance**
  Web: *www.disabilityalliance.org*
  An advice line for disabled people and their advisors.
- **Employers' Forum on Disability**
  Web: *www.employers-forum.co.uk*
  The Employers' Forum on Disability works closely with Government and other stakeholders, sharing best practice to make it easier to employ disabled people and serve disabled customers. It is the employers' organisation focused on the issue of disability in the workplace. It is funded and managed by employers and represents organisations who employ over 20 per cent of the UK workforce.
- **Equal Opportunities Commission**
  Web: *www.eoc.org.uk*
  An agency working to eliminate sex discrimination and put equality into practice in the workplace. From October 2007 this organisation will be replaced by the Commission for Equality and Human Rights (**Web:** *www.cehr.org.uk*).

Discrimination Claims

This topic covers the following.
- Grounds for Discrimination Claims
- Time Limits on Claims
- Avoiding a Tribunal Case: the "Questions Procedure"
- Tribunal Proceedings
- The Decision
- Appeals
- Remedies
- Costs

4.198 A worker, job applicant or (in some cases) an ex-employee can bring a claim to an employment tribunal for unlawful discrimination if he or she thinks this has occurred.

4.199 However, in order to be eligible to bring a claim of discrimination to tribunal, the employee must, in most cases, first raise a grievance in writing with his or her employer and wait 28 days to allow the employer an opportunity to deal with the grievance. After 28 days, the tribunal will admit the claim, irrespective of whether the grievance is still being dealt with. An extension to the applicable time limit of three or six months can be granted only in limited circumstances. The Employment Appeals Tribunal (EAT) has held, however, that where a claim is one for discriminatory dismissal, ie where the claimant can show that he or she was dismissed for reasons associated with one of the prohibited grounds, there is no need for him or her to have first raised a grievance.

4.200 The burden of proof in cases of alleged unlawful discrimination is initially on the claimant. He or she must show facts based on which a tribunal could conclude that discrimination has occurred on the specified ground. Once such basic facts have been established, the burden of proof generally shifts to the employer who must refute the allegation by showing that there was a non-discriminatory reason for their actions or omissions.

Employers' Duties

4.201 Employers should:
- Recognise that the answers given on a questionnaire served by an employee — or the employer's failure to provide answers to the employee's questions — may be used in evidence at a tribunal hearing.
- Submit Form ET3 (Response Form) to the tribunal office within 28 days of the date on which a copy of the employee's Claim Form (Form ET1) was sent.
- Respond fully and factually to any directions communicated by the employment tribunal, eg a request for further information or disclosure of documents.
- Ensure that there are factual grounds on which to defend the claim of discrimination, eg that a non-discriminatory reason can be shown for any actions or treatment about which the employee has complained.
- Recognise that an appeal must be made within 42 days against a tribunal's decision, and can only be made on the grounds that there has been an error in law.
- Take care to ensure that the defence of the case is not misconceived, meaning that there is no reasonable prospect of the defence succeeding.

Employees' Duties

4.202 Employees should:
- Ensure that any claim for unlawful discrimination is lodged with the tribunal service within three calendar months of the alleged incident or action or within six months if an internal grievance has been raised with the employer.
- Consider using the questions procedure to seek information from the employer about its actions and the reasons for them.
- Respond fully and factually to any directions communicated by the employment tribunal, eg for further information or disclosure of documents.
- Ensure that sufficient evidence can be provided to indicate that discrimination may in fact have occurred.
- Recognise that an appeal against the tribunal's decision can be made only if there are grounds to believe that the tribunal has made an error of law.
- Prepare (for the tribunal hearing) a schedule setting out any financial losses that have occurred as a result of the discriminatory treatment and any claim for injury to feelings or injury to health.
- Take care to ensure that the case is not misconceived, meaning that there is no reasonable prospect of the complaint succeeding.

In Practice

Grounds for Discrimination Claims

4.203 Employment law in the UK provides that it is unlawful to discriminate on the following grounds.
- Sex, marital status, civil partnership status, trans-gender status, pregnancy and maternity — Sex Discrimination Act 1975.
- Colour, race, nationality, ethnic origin and national origin — Race Relations Act 1976.
- "Any religion, religious belief or philosophical belief" — Employment Equality (Religion or Belief) Regulations 2003
- Sexual orientation — Employment Equality (Sexual Orientation) Regulations 2003.
- Disability — Disability Discrimination Act 1995.
- Age — Employment Equality (Age) Regulations 2006.

Who Can Bring a Claim?

4.204 Claims under the laws listed above can be brought by:
- current employees and others who provide their services personally to an organisation
- job applicants
- workers who have left the organisation.

4.205 Legislation provides protection from discrimination to a wide range of people who provide their services personally to organisations. These types of people include:
- agency temps

- casual workers
- part-timers
- contractors' staff working on another employer's premises
- apprentices
- self-employed people (provided the person concerned is under a duty to provide his or her services personally).

4.206 Protection against discrimination in an employment area is in no way dependant on the individual's:
- length of service
- number of hours worked
- age (except in the circumstances outlined in the next two paragraphs).

4.207 An exception in the Employment Equality (Age) Regulations 2006 provides that employees aged 65 or over who are dismissed by reason of retirement are not eligible to bring claims of age discrimination to an employment tribunal. This is provided that the employer has complied with certain mandatory pre-retirement procedures. It is important to note that this exclusion applies only in respect of the retirement of employees, and not to the retirement of other workers such as agency temps or contract staff. Furthermore, there is no age barrier for employees aged 65 or over in respect of claims of discrimination on any of the other grounds listed above.

4.208 A further exemption in the age regulations provides that external job applicants who have reached, exceeded or are within six months of the employer's retirement age cannot claim age discrimination if they are refused employment on age grounds.

Time Limits on Claims

4.209 A claim for unlawful discrimination must be lodged within three calendar months of the discriminatory act although an extension to six months is granted where the employee has raised an internal grievance under the statutory grievance procedure specified in the Employment Act 2002.

4.210 If the claim relates to a series of discriminatory acts, the claim must be brought within three (or six) months of the most recent act. The tribunal will consider the series of acts as one continuing act of discrimination.

4.211 In *Virdi v Commissioner of Police of the Metropolis* [2007] IRLR 24, the EAT concluded that, where a claim concerns an alleged discriminatory decision made by the employer, the time limit in respect of bringing the claim runs from the date the decision was made, and not from the date on which the decision was communicated to the employee.

4.212 An employee who is considering bringing a complaint of discrimination to tribunal must, in most cases, first raise a grievance in writing with his or her employer and wait 28 days to allow the employer an opportunity to deal with the grievance. After 28 days, however, the tribunal will admit the claim, irrespective of whether the grievance is still being dealt with. The requirement to raise an internal written grievance does not, however, apply where the complaint is about an alleged discriminatory dismissal, as the appeal stage of the DDP would apply instead. It is important also to note that the requirement to raise an internal grievance applies only to employees, and not to other workers, nor to job applicants.

4.213 The following three representative organisations have six months within which to bring claims for unlawful discrimination.
- Equal Opportunities Commission.

- Commission for Racial Equality.
- Disability Rights Commission.

4.214 These three organisations are to be replaced by the Commission for Equality and Human Rights (CEHR) from October 2007.

4.215 An individual claiming his or her pay was not equal must present a claim to a tribunal within six months of termination of employment. This time limit cannot be extended.

Extension of Time Limit

4.216 Employment tribunals tend to strictly enforce the applicable time limit of three or six months on unlawful discrimination claims.

4.217 However, a tribunal may admit a claim beyond the time limit if it feels that on the facts of the case to do so would be just and equitable. This might occur if, for example, the claimant can show that:
- he or she did not know, and could not reasonably have known, certain key factors about the treatment received, or
- he or she has been ill and medical evidence supports the contention that he or she could not realistically have brought the claim in time.

Avoiding a Tribunal Case: the "Questions Procedure"

4.218 A procedure has been devised to help individuals deal with unlawful discrimination without having to resort to bringing a claim to an employment tribunal.

4.219 The "questions procedure" involves presenting a questionnaire to the relevant employer. The objective of the questionnaire is so that the potential claimant can obtain information from the employer as to the reasons for his or her treatment.

4.220 Prescribed questionnaire forms are available, though it is not compulsory to use them. The purpose of the forms is to help the parties identify information that is relevant to the employee's complaint. The forms consist of two parts.
- One part is for the employee to complete and submit to the employer.
- The other part is for the employer to complete in response to the employee's questions and return to the employee.

4.221 Applicants may add their own supplementary questions to the form and can use the responses to the questionnaire to:
- understand and resolve any outstanding issues
- decide whether or not to start proceedings in a tribunal
- formulate and present his or her case in the most effective way.

Use of the "Questions Procedure" in a Tribunal

4.222 A completed questionnaire could be admissible as evidence in tribunal proceedings, but for this to be the case the questionnaire must be served on the employer within three months of the alleged discrimination.

4.223 If tribunal proceedings have already been started, a questionnaire would only be admissible to the proceedings if it is presented to the employer within 21 days of the original complaint being made to the tribunal. The tribunal has discretion to extend this period.

4.224 Employers are not under any statutory duty to respond to a questionnaire.

Discrimination Claims

However, both the questionnaire and the replies given, or the fact that an employer has declined to answer the employee's questions, may be taken into consideration by the employment tribunal.

4.225 If:
- an employer fails to reply to a questionnaire without good reason, or
- the replies in the opinion of the employment tribunal are incomplete, ambiguous or evasive,

then the tribunal may draw an inference that the employer has in fact discriminated unlawfully.

Employers are therefore advised to:
- complete with care any questionnaire received
- be factual and specific in answering all the questions that the employee has asked.

Time Limits for Responding to the "Questions Procedure"

4.226 The time limits for replying to a questionnaire differ depending on the type of complaint.
- For complaints on grounds of colour or nationality, the requirement is to reply within a "reasonable" period.
- For all other types of complaint, there is a time limit of eight weeks for the employer to respond.

Tribunal Proceedings

4.227 The procedure involved in employment tribunal proceedings and the potential remedies are dealt with in more detail by a separate topic.

Beginning Tribunal Proceedings

4.228 A claimant beginning proceedings in an employment tribunal starts the procedure by filling out a claim form called Form ET1. This should be sent to the tribunal, which will then send a copy on to the employer against whom the complaint has been made. A copy will also be sent to the Advisory, Conciliation and Arbitration Service (Acas) and to the CEHR (from October 2007).

4.229 An employer that receives a Form ET1 should respond to the tribunal within 28 days by sending in a Response Form, known as Form ET3. This should explain the grounds on which the organisation intends to resist the employee's complaint. The tribunal will forward a copy of both forms to Acas and to the CEHR (from October 2007).

4.230 If the tribunal does not receive the employer's Response Form within 28 days, the employer will normally be barred from taking part in the proceedings. The tribunal also has the power to enter a default judgment where no response has been lodged by the employer within the time limit. This means in effect that the employer automatically "loses" the case.

Case Management

4.231 The tribunal has discretion to manage any case as it wishes, but will accept applications from the parties involved. Requests a tribunal may make include:
- requiring further particulars from either party on any aspect of the complaint or the defence
- asking one or both of the parties for written answers to specific questions

- ordering the disclosure or inspection of documents, including (if appropriate) confidential documents
- ordering the provision and exchange of witness statements
- issuing an order for one or more persons to attend the hearing as witnesses, although it is more common for witnesses to be asked to attend the hearing on a voluntary basis (failure to comply with a witness order without reasonable excuse is a criminal offence rendering the individual liable to a fine of up to £1000).

4.232 Where a party fails to comply with any requirement in a direction or order given by the tribunal, the tribunal may make an order of costs against that party or strike out the whole or part of the application or defence.

Striking Out

4.233 An employment tribunal may, at any stage of the proceedings, "strike out" either the application to the tribunal or the employer's defence. This means that the complaint or the defence will be cancelled and the other party will "win" the case.

4.234 Striking out may be ordered on the grounds that the complaint or the defence is vexatious, unreasonable or misconceived, or in circumstances where one of the parties has conducted the proceedings in a manner that is vexatious, abusive, disruptive or otherwise unreasonable. Tribunals' power to strike out is, however, exercised sparingly.

4.235 The grounds for striking out are similar to the grounds on which an award of costs may be made.

Burden of Proof

4.236 The principles governing the burden of proof in cases of alleged discrimination are different depending on the ground on which the complaint is brought.
- Discrimination on grounds of colour or nationality — the burden of proof is technically on the complainant to prove discriminatory treatment, although a tribunal may draw inferences of discrimination from the facts if it feels that would be just and equitable.
- All other types of discrimination — the burden of proof sits with the employer once the claimant has shown facts based on which a tribunal could conclude that discrimination has occurred on the alleged ground.

4.237 In *Oyarce v Cheshire County Council* EAT [2007] 0557/06, however, the EAT held that the reversal of the burden of proof does not apply to claims of victimisation under the Race Relations Act. This is due to the construction of the wording in the Race Relations Act itself. This decision does not apply to victimisation claims under the other discrimination statutes.

4.238 Tribunals work to the "balance of probabilities test" and will make a decision either way depending on the relative weight of the evidence before them. There is, therefore, no requirement for proof to meet the "beyond reasonable doubt" standard.

The Hearing

4.239 Tribunal hearings are informal and legal representation is not required. Parties to proceedings will, however, often have representation.

4.240 Hearings are normally presided over by a panel of three people:
- a legally qualified Chair

Discrimination Claims

- an employer representative — a lay-person from industry, typically someone with experience of human resource management
- an employee representative — usually someone with a background in industrial relations and trade unions.

4.241 In claims for discrimination, the claimant normally presents his or her evidence first. The procedure followed is then that of any other employment tribunal.

4.242 If one party fails to attend the tribunal hearing, it is likely (but not always the case) that the case will go against that party since he or she will not be in a position to refute any allegations.

4.243 Tribunal hearings are normally open to the public and the media. However in certain circumstances the tribunal may agree to a private hearing. In cases of disability discrimination or alleged sexual misconduct a tribunal may issue a restricted reporting order. This could prohibit the publication of any details that could lead to the identification of an individual involved in the case.

4.244 The tribunal's overall objective in a case of unlawful discrimination is to establish whether the employer would have treated someone from a different group (for example, someone of the opposite sex or from a different racial group) more favourably than the complainant.

The Decision

4.245 The tribunal may reach and announce a decision at the end of the hearing, or reserve judgment and announce the decision later in writing.

4.246 The decision does not need to be unanimous: a majority verdict is sufficient. This is the case even if it is the Chair who is in the minority.

4.247 Copies of the decision are entered into a register. In a case involving sexual offence allegations, any details that might identify the person affected by or making the allegations will be omitted or deleted.

Appeals

4.248 Appeals against the decision of a tribunal can be made to the Employment Appeal Tribunal, but only on a question of law.

4.249 An alternative course — useful if the disputed point is a matter of fact — is to ask the tribunal to review its own decision. This can only be done in limited circumstances, such as if:
- the tribunal staff made an error
- the decision was made in the absence of a party who was entitled to give evidence, or
- new evidence becomes available following the decision which could not reasonably have been known at an earlier time.

4.250 Appeals to the Employment Appeal Tribunal and requests for review cannot be made solely on the grounds that the decision is not to the liking of one of the parties.

4.251 The time limit for making an appeal or requesting review is 42 days from the date on which the full decision was sent to the parties.

Remedies

4.252 The remedies that can be prescribed by a tribunal are compensation,

Discrimination Claims

declaration and recommendation. Reinstatement or re-engagement of an employee cannot be ordered unless the claimant has also brought a claim for unfair dismissal under the Employment Rights Act 1996.

4.253 In cases of unlawful discrimination, if the complaint is upheld the tribunal may make a declaration to clarify the existing and future relationship between the two parties. It may also order the employer to pay compensation. A compensation award will in most cases include:

- damages for any loss of earnings — for example, if an employee has resigned because of the discrimination
- an award for injury to feelings
- an award for injury to health, if the claimant has produced concrete medical evidence that the discriminatory treatment caused him or her to become ill
- aggravated damages (not available in Scotland).

4.254 In claims for equal pay, however, no injury to feelings, injury to health or aggravated damages compensation is available. However, back-pay for up to six years (five years in Scotland) may be awarded in respect of any difference between the claimant's pay and that of his or her comparator which was found to be unlawful.

4.255 In *Bainbridge v Redcar & Cleveland Borough Council (No 3)* EAT 0424/06, however, the EAT ruled that compensation for claims argued on the basis of jobs rated as equivalent under a job evaluation scheme cannot necessarily be backdated for six years, but instead can only be backdated to the date the relevant job evaluation study was implemented. This would be the case even in circumstances where the claimant performed the same job prior to that date.

4.256 There is no maximum limit on the compensation that a tribunal may award in discrimination cases.

4.257 Any award for injury to feelings will depend on the:
- nature of the discrimination
- extent of the insult to the individual
- personal circumstances and the degree of hurt or distress suffered.

4.258 It is also open to tribunals to award a sum of money equivalent to damages for personal injury if the claimant can show (normally by producing medical evidence) that the discriminatory treatment he or she suffered caused damage to his or her health. This type of claim is most common in cases of harassment. Damages under this heading can be over and above any sum awarded for injury to feelings.

4.259 It is advisable for the claimant to come to the hearing with a schedule setting out any financial losses and claims for injury to feelings or injury to health.

4.260 Tribunals may (in addition or alternatively) make a recommendation that the employer should take specified action within a time limit to stop the complaint of discrimination. If the recommendation is ignored, the tribunal may:
- make an award of compensation if one was not previously made
- increase the employee's award of compensation.

Costs

4.261 As with most tribunal cases, it is normal for both sides to pay their own costs in cases of alleged discrimination.

4.262 Costs will normally be incurred for legal advice or representation. No fee is charged for making a claim to an employment tribunal or for the hearing itself.

Discrimination Claims

4.263 The tribunal will only order one party to pay the costs of the other party if, in the tribunal's view the party:
- acted vexatiously, scandalously or otherwise unreasonably in bringing the proceedings, or
- brought or conducted the proceedings on a misconceived basis, ie the proceedings had no reasonable prospect of success, or
- the party's representatives acted vexatiously, abusively, disruptively or otherwise unreasonably in conducting the proceedings, or
- paid a deposit to the tribunal so that it could continue with its case even though the tribunal believed the party had little prospect of success, and then the party lost its case for substantially the same reasons. If this is the case the deposit will be set off against any costs awarded.

4.264 If any of these circumstances apply, the tribunal may:
- order the offending party to pay the costs of the other party, where the latter has had legal representation, or
- make a "wasted costs award" directly against the representative, or
- where a party has been unrepresented, make a "preparation time order" in respect of the time the party spent preparing for the hearing.

4.265 A tribunal may make a wasted costs award directly against a paid representative to cover the whole or part of the wasted costs of either party in circumstances where:
- there has been an improper, unreasonable or negligent act or omission on the part of the representative, or
- in the light of such an act or omission, the tribunal considers it unreasonable for a party to have to pay the costs in question.

4.266 A "wasted costs award" is, however, only permissible where the representative in question is one who has been paid for his or her services.

4.267 A preparation time order may be made in favour of a party who has not been legally represented at a hearing. "Preparation time" is defined as time spent by the party or his or her employees carrying out preparatory work that is directly related to the proceedings and/or time spent by the party's advisors relating to the conduct of the proceedings. It does not, however, include the time spent at the hearing itself. An hourly rate of £25 per hour is applied.

4.268 A tribunal may not make both a preparation time order and a costs order in favour of the same party in the same proceedings.

4.269 In all cases, the maximum amount of costs that can be awarded by a tribunal is £10,000.

4.270 Alternatively, the tribunal may refer the matter to the county court for assessment of costs. The county court may award more than £10,000.

4.271 In making an award of costs, tribunals may take into account the party's ability to pay.

Training

4.272 Employers should provide training on equality issues to all senior staff who have responsibility for decisions concerning recruitment, selection and promotion. Such training should include the following.
- The fundamental principles of UK discrimination legislation, including information about direct and indirect discrimination, victimisation and harassment.

- Information about the forms of behaviour that may be viewed as unlawful harassment.
- The grounds on which individuals can bring complaints of discrimination to an employment tribunal.
- Encouragement to adopt a positive attitude towards the concepts of equality and diversity.
- Raising awareness about prejudice and stereotypical views.
- The need to assess job applicants and applicants for promotion on their individual merits and abilities to perform a particular job, rather than on personal attributes.

4.273 Staff who do not have a senior or supervisory role should be trained in the following.

- Understanding the effects that differences in gender, race, religion, age, etc can have on people's attitudes and behaviour.
- Awareness of the types of behaviour that can constitute unlawful harassment.
- Adopting a positive attitude towards the concepts of equality and diversity.
- Avoiding assumptions about people based on gender, marital status, sexual orientation, race, religion, disability or age.

List of Relevant Legislation

4.274
- Employment Equality (Age) Regulations 2006
- Employment Tribunals (Constitution and Rules of Procedure) (Amendment) Regulations 2005
- Employment Tribunals (Constitution and Rules of Procedure) (Amendment) (No. 2) Regulations 2005
- Employment Equality (Religion or Belief) Regulations 2003
- Employment Equality (Sexual Orientation) Regulations 2003
- Disability Discrimination Act 1995
- Race Relations Act 1976
- Sex Discrimination Act 1975

List of Relevant Cases

4.275
- *Virdi v Commissioner of Police of the Metropolis* [2007] IRLR 24
- *Council of City of Newcastle-upon-Tyne v Allan and ors; Degnan and ors v Redcar and Cleveland Borough Council* EAT [2005] 0845/04
- *Essa v Laing Ltd* [2004] IRLR 313, CA
  Where an employee suffers a psychiatric injury as a result of discrimination in the workplace, there is no need to show that the injury to health was reasonably foreseeable in order to be eligible to recover compensation for the injury.
- *Hendricks v Commissioner of Police for the Metropolis* [2003] IRLR 96, CA
  The interpretation of a discriminatory act extending over a period can include any "ongoing situation" or "continuing state of affairs" in which workers are subjected to linked incidents of discrimination.

- *Kopel v Safeway Stores plc* [2003] IRLR 753
  An employee may be ordered to pay the employer's costs where there is no basis for the complaint and the employee has refused an offer to settle.
- *Vento v Chief Constable of West Yorkshire Police* [2003] IRLR 102, CA
  The Court of Appeal laid down guidance on awards for injury to feelings by setting out three recommended bands of compensation.
- *Lewisham Guys Mental Health NHS Trust v Andrews* [1999] IRLR 407
  The personal representative of the complainant can continue a complaint of discrimination even after the complainant has died.
- *Ministry of Defence v Cannock* [1994] IRLR 509
  Damages for unlawful discrimination should be based on the concept that the claimant should be put back into the same position that he or she would have been in had the unlawful discrimination not occurred.
- *Deane v London Borough of Ealing* [1993] IRLR 209
  Awards of compensation for discrimination cannot include exemplary or punitive damages.
- *British Gas plc v Sharma* [1991] IRLR 101
  An employment tribunal is not authorised to recommend that the complainant should be promoted as such action could itself amount to unlawful discrimination.
- *King v The Great Britain-China Centre* [1991] IRLR 513, CA
  The court laid down principles governing the burden of proof in discrimination cases.

Further Information

Publications
- URN 03/595 Employment Tribunals Service booklet *How to Apply to an Employment Tribunal England and Wales*, available from Employment Tribunal offices and from the ETS enquiry line.

Organisations
- **Advisory Conciliation and Arbitration Service (Acas)**
  Web: *www.acas.org.uk*
  Acas aims to improve organisations and working life through better employment relations. It provides up-to-date information, advice, high-quality training, and works with employers and employees to solve problems and improve performance.
- **Commission for Racial Equality**
  Web: *www.cre.gov.uk*
  The Commission for Racial Equality is a publicly funded, non-governmental body set up under the Race Relations Act 1976 to tackle racial discrimination and promote racial equality. From October 2007 this organisation will be replaced by the Commission for Equality and Human Rights.
- **Department for Business, Enterprise and Regulatory Reform (BERR)**
  Web: *www.berr.gov.uk*
  The Department for Business, Enterprise and Regulatory Reform brings together functions from the former Department of Trade and Industry (DTI), including responsibilities for productivity, business relations, energy, competition and consumers. It also drives regulatory reform.

- **Disability Rights Commission**
  Web: *www.drc-gb.org*
  An independent body established by Act of Parliament to eliminate discrimination against disabled people and promote equality of opportunity. It provides information and advice to disabled people and employers about their rights and duties. From October 2007 this organisation will be replaced by the Commission for Equality and Human Rights (**Web:** *www.cehr.org.uk*).
- **Employment Appeal Tribunal (EAT)**
  Web: *www.employmentappeals.gov.uk*
  The EAT was created by the Employment Protection Act 1975. It is a Superior Court of Record dealing with appeals from the decisions of the Employment Tribunals, the Certification Officer and the Central Arbitration Committee.
- **Employment Tribunals**
  Web: *www.employmenttribunals.gov.uk*
  Contains useful information about employment tribunals, which resolve disputes between employers and employees over employment rights.
- **Equal Opportunities Commission**
  Web: *www.eoc.org.uk*
  An agency working to eliminate sex discrimination and put equality into practice in the workplace. From October 2007 this organisation will be replaced by the Commission for Equality and Human Rights (**Web:** *www.cehr.org.uk*).

Diversity and Equality in the Workplace

> This topic covers the following.
> - Equal Opportunities Policy
> - Dealing with Complaints of Discrimination or Harassment
> - Victimisation
> - Recruitment
> - Positive Action
> - Equality and Diversity During Employment
> - Harassment and Bullying
> - Employees with a Disability
> - Equal Opportunities Monitoring

4.276 Over the years, the Government has introduced different laws prohibiting discrimination in the workplace on a variety of grounds.

4.277 First came the Sex Discrimination Act 1975, followed the next year by the Race Relations Act 1976. Some 20 years later, the Disability Discrimination Act 1995 was implemented. More recently, in December 2003, the Employment Equality (Religion or Belief) Regulations 2003 and the Employment Equality (Sexual Orientation) Regulations 2003 were introduced. Finally, the Government implemented the Employment Equality (Age) Regulations on 1 October 2006.

4.278 All the laws require employers to apply the principle of equality in the workplace.

4.279 The Disability Discrimination Act goes one step further by requiring employers to make reasonable adjustments to working practices and premises to support any employee or job applicant who has a disability. None of the laws deal specifically with diversity, although the promotion of diversity is nowadays deemed to be "best practice".

4.280 Over and above the legislation, there are Codes of Practice that provide best practice guidance for employers. The Codes of Practice do not have statutory force (which means that an employer who fails to follow their recommendations will not be in breach of the law). However, employers should also take account of Codes of Practice as any failure to comply with the recommendations they contain will act against the employers' interests in the event of a claim of discrimination being brought against them in an employment tribunal.

Employers' Duties

- Employers have a duty to ensure that employees and potential employees are not subject to discrimination on any of the prohibited grounds.
- Employers are under no general legal obligation to respond to requests for references. In specific circumstances, however, employers may be victimising ex-employees by refusing to give a reference.
- An equal opportunities policy is not a legal requirement for UK organisations but it is seen as good practice to promote equality and diversity in the workplace.

Diversity and Equality in the Workplace

- It is advisable for employers to set out a positive duty on their managers and supervisors to implement an equal opportunities policy and take action to ensure compliance with it.
- Employers should place a positive duty on all their employees to comply with the employer's equal opportunities policy and to ensure that their colleagues are treated with respect and dignity.
- It is important to both communicate and promote the equal opportunities policy to employees on a regular basis.

Employees' Duties

- Employees have a duty not to discriminate against any of their colleagues on any of the prohibited grounds. Employees who nevertheless perpetrate acts of discrimination may be ordered personally to pay compensation to their victims.
- Diversity and equal opportunities policies place a positive duty on all employees to comply with the policy and to ensure that colleagues are treated with respect and dignity.
- All employees are under a duty not to engage in any behaviour that could be interpreted as harassment on any of the prohibited grounds, irrespective of motive.

In Practice

4.281 Employers have a duty to ensure that employees and potential employees are not subject to discrimination on designated grounds of sex, marital status, civil partnership status, trans-gender status, pregnancy/maternity, sexual orientation, race, religion or belief, disability, age and, in Northern Ireland, religion or political opinion.

4.282 The employer is usually responsible for paying compensation awarded by tribunals. Individual employees who are named in discrimination claims may also be ordered by a tribunal to pay compensation. There is no ceiling on the amount of compensation that can be awarded following a successful claim of discrimination.

Equal Opportunities Policy

4.283 Although it is not a legal requirement to do so, it is advisable for all employers to devise and implement an equal opportunities policy. An equal opportunities policy will take account of the relevant anti-discrimination legislation and associated Codes of Practice. It will increase awareness of the need for equality in the workplace and make it clear to all employees what behaviour is expected and the forms of conduct that are unacceptable. It should also state the benefits of promoting equality and diversity in the workplace.

4.284 Public authorities are, however, under a statutory duty to carry out certain monitoring activities in respect of their employees and job applicants, as well as being subject to a general duty to promote equality of opportunity in the exercise of their public functions. Currently, this public duty covers equality on grounds of gender, race and disability.

4.285 A statement of equal opportunities is usually drawn up as an advisory document, ie a non-contractual statement of good practice, which lays down general principles and assists employees and managers to understand what is expected of them.

4.286 Alternatively, the statement may be made contractual. In this case, any failure on the employer's part to adhere to the statement will give an employee grounds for a breach of contract claim and (subject to the employee having a minimum of one year's service) possibly a claim for constructive dismissal.

4.287 The statement should indicate the responsibilities of managers and supervisors for the implementation of the policy and any corrective action necessary to ensure compliance. The statement should also state the positive duty of all employees to comply with the policy and ensure that their colleagues are treated with respect and dignity.

4.288 Merely having an equal opportunities policy will not be enough to protect an employer from claims of discrimination. An employer should implement the policy by:
- communicating the policy and procedures to all staff on a regular basis
- training managers and staff
- monitoring the effectiveness of the policy
- dealing with complaints effectively
- seeking the commitment of senior managers.

4.289 Policies and employment practices should be reviewed periodically.

4.290 Aspects of a diversity policy may deal with:
- recruitment, interviewing and selection
- the laws on discrimination
- harassment and bullying
- training and development
- time-off for dependants
- maternity, paternity, parental and adoption leave
- flexible and part-time working
- casual, seasonal and occasional workers
- discipline and grievance
- termination of employment, including redundancy
- disability policy
- Guaranteed Interview Scheme run by the Employment Service
- positive action.

Dealing with Complaints of Discrimination or Harassment

4.291 If valid grievances, especially those relating to discrimination, harassment and victimisation are to be tackled, the complaints process must be made accessible to all workers.

4.292 For all but small employers, this will mean introducing a complaints procedure designed specifically to deal with complaints of discrimination and harassment/bullying. Using the organisation's standard grievance procedure for such complaints is often inappropriate because the:
- "discriminator" is very often the employee's immediate supervisor/line manager who is usually the person with whom grievances must also be raised in the first instance

- employee may feel uncomfortable raising complaints of harassment or bullying directly with his or her line manager, but more at ease with the prospect of approaching someone perceived to be neutral, eg an HR manager.

4.293 The main stages in the complaints procedure are:
- investigating the complaint objectively and thoroughly
- discussing the complaint with the complainant and with the alleged perpetrator separately at properly convened formal interviews
- giving the complainant and the alleged perpetrator the opportunity each to be accompanied at their interviews by a colleague or trade union official
- reaching a decision
- restoring normal working relationships
- monitoring the situation afterwards to make sure that no further acts of discrimination or harassment are taking place
- taking appropriate disciplinary action against the perpetrator of the discrimination or harassment.

4.294 Investigations should be concluded as soon as possible. If the person decides to take the complaint to a tribunal, they normally have three calendar months from the date of the incident to lodge the complaint with the tribunal service, although this is extended to six months where the complainant has raised an internal grievance under the statutory grievance procedure specified in the Employment Act 2002. So if a complaint is not dealt with speedily, it may go to a tribunal unnecessarily.

4.295 Managers and supervisors must be prepared to act in a firm but fair way against any person displaying bullying or harassing behaviour.

Victimisation

4.296 All the anti-discrimination laws include victimisation within their remit.

4.297 Victimisation occurs where an employer penalises an employee in some way for having raised a genuine complaint of discrimination, whether internally under the employer's complaints procedure, or at tribunal. The victimisation provisions also protect employees who give evidence in support of another employee who has experienced discrimination or harassment or who otherwise support such an employee.

4.298 Victimisation can take many forms and would include unfavourable treatment of any kind meted out against the employee who had complained of discriminatory treatment or supported another employee in his/her complaint. Examples could include labelling someone as a "trouble-maker", subjecting him or her to harassment or denying him or her access to training or promotion opportunities.

4.299 Claimants lose their protection if their allegations or the evidence or information given were false and not made or given in good faith.

Recruitment

4.300 Discrimination can creep in right at the start of the recruitment process, eg when it is assumed that the replacement employee needs to fit into a particular "mould". It is essential to challenge preconceived ideas at all stages in the recruitment process in:
- writing the job description
- preparing the person specification
- advertising

- designing application forms
- shortlisting
- interviewing
- selection
- writing and assessing references.

Job Descriptions

4.301 Any existing job description should be analysed and reviewed by discussing the content and any necessary changes with both the incumbent and that person's line manager.

4.302 Part-time, job-sharing and home-working options should be considered. Any refusal to consider employing a female job applicant who has children on a part-time or job-share basis may amount to indirect sex discrimination against her if she is otherwise the most suitable candidate for the job and the refusal to consider part-time working cannot be justified on objective job-based grounds. In any event, the promotion of flexible working patterns supports the concept of diversity and allows the employer to take advantage of a wider pool of candidates.

Person Specification

4.303 The task of drawing up a person specification must be approached in an objective fashion, taking care to ensure that all the criteria specified by the employer are appropriate and relevant to the performance of the job in question, and not based on the personal opinions of a particular manager.

4.304 Direct discrimination is increasingly rare in recruitment, but indirect discrimination can occur easily, and often unintentionally. It arises when a requirement applied to all job applicants has a disproportionate adverse effect on members of one group compared with another. For example, applying a minimum height requirement would indirectly discriminate against women and a requirement for fluency in English would indirectly discriminate against some candidates of foreign nationality. Unless the particular criterion is justifiable — ie appropriate and necessary for the effective performance of the job — it will be unlawful.

4.305 Since the implementation of the Employment Equality (Age) Regulations 2006 on 1 October 2006, any criterion for a minimum or maximum number of years of experience in a person specification will be indirectly discriminatory on the grounds of age.

4.306 For example, insisting that job applicants must have at least five years' post-graduate experience will discriminate against people under age 25 (because people under this age would, in effect, be ruled out), while requiring applicants to have "up to five years' experience" would disadvantage most people over that same age. Such requirements must be objectively justified, otherwise they will be unlawful. To be justified, they must be shown to be appropriate and necessary with a view to achieving a legitimate business aim, eg the length of experience requirement would have to be shown to be necessary for effective job performance.

Application Process

4.307 During the application process, the following best practice guidelines should be applied by employers.
- Design application forms so that they ask only questions that are relevant and necessary in respect of the job in question.
- If necessary, use more than one version of the application form.

- Review application form questions to ensure that they are not harder to answer for any particular group of applicants.
- Review questions to identify if any could be misinterpreted by people from any particular group or create suspicion as to the employer's reason for asking them.
- Ensure that candidates' personal details and questions designed for monitoring purposes are asked on a detachable part of the application form and are not used as part of the recruitment and selection process.
- Do not disqualify candidates for not being able to complete application forms unless the ability to write fluently or complete forms is directly relevant to the job.
- Make clear to candidates that any personal information they provide will be used only for monitoring purposes and, where appropriate, to allow appropriate adjustments to working arrangements to be considered for disabled candidates.

Advertising

4.308 It is important that all job adverts promote the employer as an equal opportunities employer and preferably also as one that promotes diversity.

4.309 Common forms of discrimination in recruitment advertising have been identified as follows.
- Disability — using terms such as "energetic" that could put off applicants who are disabled and could therefore be unlawful.
- Physical attributes — imposing requirements relating to appearance, physical strength or accent (for example) may discriminate on grounds of gender, race, disability and/or age.
- Driving licence — asking for a clean licence when this is not a necessary requirement of the job would discriminate against candidates who, due to a disability, were unable to drive.
- Gender — some advertisements continue to use jargon that is gender-specific, eg "salesman".
- Status bias — indicating a preference for people who have no children with terms like "unencumbered", which would discriminate against women in particular.
- Age — advertisers specifying or suggesting age ranges, or upper or lower limits, eg asking for "young" or "mature" candidates.

4.310 Publishers are liable to be prosecuted if they carry advertising containing discriminatory material.

4.311 Employers should consider broadening the advertising media used so as not to exclude or limit applications from some sections of the community.

Interviewing

4.312 During the interview process, employers should consider the following best practice guidelines in order to avoid discrimination.
- Where interviewing is conducted by a panel, take reasonable steps to ensure panel members are selected from a diverse pool.
- Make reasonable adjustments for the interview for any candidate with a disability. Examples could include changing the interview location for an applicant who uses a wheelchair, ensuring there is no background noise for a candidate with a hearing impairment or providing large-print handouts for a candidate with a visual impairment. What is reasonable will be a matter of judgment.
- Avoid personal questions which may discriminate against female candidates in particular, eg questions about childcare arrangements.

- Avoid asking questions that would require the applicant to disclose his or her age, eg a question about the date he or she left school.
- Ask only questions that are relevant to the job under review.
- Be aware of the risk of subjective biases and stereotyping affecting the interviewer's judgments.

4.313 All employees who will interview on behalf of the employer should receive training in interviewing techniques and the avoidance of discrimination in recruitment.

Selection

4.314 Selection systems should be designed so that people are appointed on merit and only relevant skills, experience, qualifications and competencies are measured. Using more than one interviewer can help to cut down on the potential for bias.

4.315 Provided the criteria for the job have been clearly and objectively defined at the outset of the recruitment exercise, and provided they have been applied objectively to all the candidates, the selection process should be straightforward. It will be a question of selecting the candidate whose background most closely matches the defined criteria, ideally measured by using a points system.

4.316 It is advisable to carry out checks on the recruitment process, ie monitor the numbers of people from both genders, different racial groups, people in different age groups and people with disabilities who apply for employment, who are interviewed, and who are successful in their applications. Any disproportionate outcomes should then be investigated thoroughly and appropriate measures adopted to avoid discrimination in the future.

References

4.317 Employers should take account of the following points when providing references for employees or ex-employees.
- Employers are under no general legal obligation to respond to requests for references. Some industries, however, eg financial services, are required by their regulatory bodies to obtain and provide references for employees.
- The employer can make an express contractual commitment to provide a reference for an employee. This commitment is sometimes given as part of a compromise agreement on an employee's termination of employment.
- Employers risk victimising ex-employees by refusing to give a reference — if the reason for the refusal was that the employee has brought a claim of discrimination against the employer or any other person.
- The employer is under a duty to ensure that the information given in a reference is factually accurate and is not misleading.

Positive Action

4.318 Although positive (or reverse) discrimination is not permitted under UK employment law, the laws do permit certain forms of positive action, specifically in recruitment and in training. Positive action is not required in law, but is permitted if the reason for it is to increase the number of people from under-represented or disadvantaged groups within employment.

4.319 In recruitment, it is lawful for employers to apply measures specifically in order to encourage candidates from an under-represented or disadvantaged group to apply for employment or promotion. Examples could include placing job advertisements in a particular publication that is read predominantly by people from a minority racial group or setting up a jobs-fair targeted only at women. However, it is only encouragement that is permitted — at the point of selection for employment, the principles of equality must be applied and gender, race, etc must play no part in the decision-making process.

4.320 Positive action is also similarly permitted in certain circumstances in relation to the provision of training, if the purpose of the training is to attempt to redress an existing imbalance, or if the training is specifically designed to help fit employees from an under-represented or disadvantaged group for particular work, eg to encourage or enable more women to gain promotion into management. Another example could be the provision of computer skills training targeted specifically at employees aged 55 or over.

Equality and Diversity During Employment

4.321 Employers are obliged to apply the principles of equality inherent in the various anti-discrimination laws to all aspects of employees' employment, both contractual and non-contractual. This will include:
- the terms and conditions of employees' contracts
- access to promotion, transfer and training
- the application of all policies, procedures and rules
- any perks and benefits applied on a discretionary basis.

4.322 Over and above ensuring no unlawful discrimination occurs in these areas, employers should be willing to promote diversity. This means considering the needs of individuals, eg in relation to family responsibilities or religious beliefs where these impact on issues such as working hours or shift patterns. It means not applying policies and procedures rigidly and inflexibly irrespective of individuals' needs, but being willing to consider:
- exempting a particular employee from night-shift working if she has young children and cannot work at nights for that reason
- permitting an employee who upholds a particular religion to swap shifts with others so that he/she is not obliged to work on Sunday (or Saturday, if this is the person's Sabbath)
- adjusting dress codes to accommodate a particular individual's racial or religious beliefs or customs
- being flexible as regards holiday dates to allow employees who uphold certain religious festivals to have time off on the relevant dates if at all possible
- discussing with any disabled employee what adjustments might reasonably be made to working practices to make it easier for him or her to perform the jobs to an effective standard.

Harassment and Bullying

4.323 It is advisable for all employers to introduce a policy designed to prevent all forms of bullying and harassment in the workplace.

4.324 If harassment is on any of the prohibited grounds, ie sex, race, religion or belief, sexual orientation, age or disability, it will be unlawful under the relevant statute. An employee who is the victim of unlawful harassment will have grounds to complain to an employment tribunal, irrespective of the motive of the harasser. The employee only needs to show that the particular behaviour that caused offence violated his or her dignity or created a working environment that he or she found offensive or otherwise unacceptable.

4.325 Harassment may be physical, verbal or non-verbal. Examples include:
- physical conduct such as unnecessary touching and unwelcome sexual advances

- banter that contains an element of sexual, racial, ageist, homophobic or religious content, nicknames linked to skin colour or nationality, sexist, racist or ageist jokes, derogatory or demeaning remarks made about people with a particular disability and comments or jokes that denigrate a particular person or group on any of the prohibited grounds
- insulting or abusive gestures, staring or leering, the display of pornographic or suggestive pictures, eg on computer screens or on pin-up calendars.

4.326 The question of whether a specific type of behaviour constitutes harassment depends principally on the perception of the person on the receiving end.

4.327 A claimant does not need to have any minimum period of service in order to bring a complaint of unlawful harassment to a tribunal.

4.328 Bullying at work, whether or not it is related to any of the grounds prohibited by the laws on discrimination, will often lead to stress. Its occurrence can therefore place the employer in breach of the employment contract, in terms of the implied duty of care. Bullying will also represent a breach of the implied duty of trust and confidence. Bullying at work can therefore give the bullied employee solid grounds to resign and claim constructive dismissal, subject to him or her having a minimum of one year's continuous service. A further route for a bullied employee may be to sue the employer under the Protection from Harassment Act 1997, arguing that the employer is vicariously liable under that Act for any type of employment-related harassment that caused the employee alarm or distress. Such claims may be in addition to a claim for unlawful harassment under the relevant discrimination statute, although the person will not be awarded double compensation for any loss of earnings.

4.329 Bullying can take many forms, eg:
- aggressive behaviour directed at an individual, eg shouting and swearing
- deliberately withholding important work-related information from someone in order to cause him or her a problem
- demanding that an employee takes on a grossly unreasonable workload with unachievable deadlines, coupled with threats if the work is not completed on time
- imposing unjustified disciplinary action on an employee on account of a personal dislike
- ostracising an employee
- repeated unfair or excessive criticism of an employee's work
- threatening an employee with dismissal in an aggressive manner.

4.330 In *Green v DB Group Services (UK) Ltd* [2006] IRLR 764 the High Court held that an employee who had two breakdowns as a result of a "concerted campaign of bullying" perpetrated by her peers was entitled to succeed in her claim for harassment under the Protection from Harassment Act (and in her claim for injury to health). The court held that the employer was liable under the Act and ordered them to pay compensation of over £800,000.

Employees with a Disability

4.331 The Disability Discrimination Act 1995 now applies to all employers, following the removal in October 2004 of the threshold of 15 staff that previously applied. The only remaining exemption from the Act is the armed forces.

4.332 Employers have a duty under the Disability Discrimination Act 1995 to take all reasonable and practicable steps to prevent any provisions, criteria or practices

Diversity and Equality in the Workplace

that they apply or physical features of their premises from placing a disabled person at a substantial disadvantage. This is termed the "duty to make reasonable adjustments".

4.333 In order to fulfil the duty to make reasonable adjustments, employers should:
- be pro-active, rather than waiting to see whether the disabled employee asks for any adjustments
- initiate discussions with the disabled employee to review what adjustments might be helpful for them
- where appropriate (eg if a disabled employee has been absent from work for a reason related to his/her disability) obtain and act on an up-to-date medical report
- be open-minded and flexible as regards matters such as job duties, working hours, the possibility of home working, time off work for medical treatment, the provision of aids, special equipment or support and extra training or coaching
- only refuse to make an adjustment if there are clear reasons to support the contention that it would not be reasonable for the employer to make the particular adjustment.

Equal Opportunities Monitoring

4.334 Although there is normally no need for an employer to know the ethnicity, gender, age, marital status or parental status of job applicants for the purposes of deciding whom to recruit, employers may legitimately wish to gather such information for monitoring purposes. Such information should normally be asked for on a separate equal opportunities monitoring sheet.

4.335 Employers in the public sector are under a statutory duty to carry out racial, gender and disability monitoring in respect of their workforces. There is, however, no such duty on private sector employers, nor in the voluntary sector.

Fair Employment Monitoring (Northern Ireland)

4.336 Special rules apply in Northern Ireland to promote equality in the workplace as between people of the Protestant and Catholic faiths. Under the Fair Employment and Treatment Order (Northern Ireland) 1998, employers that employ more than 10 people must:
- apply to the Equality Commission for registration
- submit an annual monitoring return about the religious composition of all job applicants and employees
- review the religious composition of their workforces at least once every three years and submit the information to the Equality Commission.

4.337 Failures to submit a proper monitoring return or to retain the monitoring information for three years are criminal offences.

4.338 The Order also covers discrimination on the grounds of political opinion.

Training

4.339 It is important that staff are familiar with the company's policy and procedure on equal opportunities and the avoidance of discrimination and understand both the employer's and the employee's responsibilities.

4.340 Employers need to ensure that there is equal treatment and equal access to training for all staff irrespective of gender, family status, race, religion, sexual orientation, age, disability and part-time status. The criteria used to determine eligibility for training must be based on objective factors such as individuals' abilities and job duties.

4.341 The following training should be carried out by all employers:
- training for all line managers and others responsible for recruitment and employment decisions in equality and the avoidance of bias
- awareness training for all staff covering the need to avoid all forms of harassment and the types of behaviour that can be viewed as harassment
- induction training for all new staff to make them aware of the organisation's policies on equality and harassment/bullying, and the importance of following them
- special training or additional training (where appropriate) for any employee who has a disability, to enable him or her to perform the job to the best of his or her ability.

4.342 Training should be flexible as regards:
- timing — so as not to disadvantage, eg female employees with children, part-time staff or those who for religious reasons cannot work on a particular day of the week
- location and venue — which should be suitable for any employee who has limited mobility or who uses a wheelchair
- duration of individual sessions and regular breaks, for example to accommodate the needs of an employee who adheres to a particular religion to pray at regular intervals, or for an employee whose disability makes it difficult for him or her to concentrate for lengthy periods
- materials — for example the provision of handouts in extra large print for an employee with a visual impairment.

4.343 If an employer buys in training from an outside provider, it is necessary to check that the provider has sufficient awareness of the requirements of discrimination legislation.

List of Relevant Legislation

4.344
- Employment Equality (Age) Regulations 2006
- Employment Equality (Religion or Belief) Regulations 2003
- Employment Equality (Sexual Orientation) Regulations 2003
- Part-time Workers (Prevention of Less Favourable Treatment) Regulations 2000
- Employment Act 2002
- Employment Rights Act 1996
- Disability Discrimination Act 1995
- Race Relations Act 1976
- Sex Discrimination Act 1975
- Equal Pay Act 1970
- Fair Employment and Treatment Order (Northern Ireland) 1998

List of Relevant Cases

4.345
- *Majrowski v Guy's and St Thomas's NHS Trust* [2006] IRLR 695
- *Bartholomew v London Borough of Hackney* [1999] IRLR 246, CA
- *Coote v Granada Hospitality (No. 2)* [1999] IRLR 452, EAT
- *Sykes v JP Morgan* (1999)
- *London Underground Ltd v Edwards (No. 2)* [1998] IRLR 364, CA
- *Ridout v TC Group* [1998] IRLR 628
- *Falkirk Council v Whyte* [1997] IRLR 560
- *HM Prison Service v Johnson* [1997] IRLR 162
- *Spring v Guardian Assurance plc* [1994] IRLR 460, HL
- *Deane v London Borough of Ealing* [1993] IRLR 209
- *Woods v WM Car Services (Peterborough) Ltd* [1982] IRLR 413, CA
- *Massey v Crown Life Insurance Company* [1978] IRLR 31, CA
- *Robinson v Crompton Parkinson Ltd* [1978] IRLR 61

Further Information

Publications
- *Croner's Workplace Diversity and Discrimination*
- Guides for small businesses: *Equal Opportunities in England: It's Your Business Too*, Equal Opportunities Commission (EOC)
- *Race Relations Code of Practice for the Elimination of Racial Discrimination and the Promotion of Equality of Opportunity in Employment ("Employment Code of Practice") (1984)*, Commission for Racial Equality
- *Code of Practice: Rights of Access — Goods, Facilities, Services and Premises (1996, rev 1999)* (available online from the Disability Rights Commission, from the Stationery Office (TSO))
- *Code of Practice for the Elimination of Discrimination in the Field of Employment against Disabled Persons or Persons Who Have Had a Disability (1996)*, Disability Rights Commission
- *Fairness for All: A New Commission for Equality and Human Rights (May 2004)*, White Paper
- Consultation documents: *Equality and Diversity: Age Matters (Age Consultation 2003)*
- *Voluntary Code of Practice: Age Diversity in Employment (Age Positive, 1999)*, Department for Work and Pensions (DWP)
- *Fair Employment Code of Practice, Department of Higher and Further Education*, Department for Work and Pensions (DWP)

Organisations
- **Advisory Conciliation and Arbitration Service (Acas)**
  Web: *www.acas.org.uk*

Acas aims to improve organisations and working life through better employment relations. It provides up-to-date information, advice, high-quality training, and works with employers and employees to solve problems and improve performance.

- **Age Concern**
  Web: *www.ageconcern.org.uk*
  Age Concern is the UK's largest organisation working with and for older people. It provides vital local services as well as influencing public opinion and Government.

- **British Chambers of Commerce**
  Web: *www.britishchambers.org.uk*
  The British Chambers of Commerce comprise nationally a network of quality-accredited Chambers of Commerce, all uniquely positioned at the heart of every business community in the UK.

- **Chartered Institute of Personnel and Development (CIPD)**
  Web: *www.cipd.org.uk*
  The CIPD is a professional body for those involved in the management and development of people.

- **Commission for Racial Equality**
  Web: *www.cre.gov.uk*
  The Commission for Racial Equality is a publicly funded, non-governmental body set up under the Race Relations Act 1976 to tackle racial discrimination and promote racial equality. From October 2007 this organisation will be replaced by the Commission for Equality and Human Rights.

- **Department for Business, Enterprise and Regulatory Reform (BERR)**
  Web: *www.berr.gov.uk*
  The Department for Business, Enterprise and Regulatory Reform brings together functions from the former Department of Trade and Industry (DTI), including responsibilities for productivity, business relations, energy, competition and consumers. It also drives regulatory reform.

- **Department for Children, Schools and Families (DCSF)**
  Web: *www.dfes.gov.uk*
  The Department for Children, Schools and Families (DCSF) aims to give children an excellent start in education, enable young people to equip themselves with life and work skills.

- **Disability Alliance**
  Web: *www.disabilityalliance.org*
  An advice line for disabled people and their advisors.

- **Employers' Forum on Age (EFA)**
  Web: *www.efa.org.uk*
  The EFA is an independent network of leading employers who recognise the business value of attracting and retaining experienced employees — regardless of their age

- **Employers' Forum on Disability**
  Web: *www.employers-forum.co.uk*
  The Employers' Forum on Disability works closely with Government and other stakeholders, sharing best practice to make it easier to employ disabled people and serve disabled customers. It is the employers' organisation focused on the issue of disability in the workplace. It is funded and managed by employers and represents organisations who employ over 20 per cent of the UK workforce.

- **Local Government Employers (LGE)**
  Web: *www.lge.gov.uk*
  The role of Local Government Employers is to work with local authorities, regional employers and other bodies to create solutions on pay, pensions and the employment contract.

- **Employers and Work-life Balance**
  Web: *www.employersforwork-lifebalance.org.uk*

Diversity and Equality in the Workplace

Employers and Work-life Balance aims to help all UK organisations implement and continuously improve sustainable work-life strategies that meet customer needs, corporate goals and enhance the quality of life for individuals.

- **Equality Commission for Northern Ireland**
  Web: *www.equalityni.org*
  An independent public body established under the Northern Ireland Act 1998. The Commission is working towards the elimination of discrimination through the promotion of equality of opportunity and the encouraging of good practice; the promotion of affirmative or positive action, reviewing relevant legislation and overseeing the implementation and effectiveness of the statutory duty on public authorities.

- **Equal Opportunities Commission**
  Web: *www.eoc.org.uk*
  An agency working to eliminate sex discrimination and put equality into practice in the workplace. From October 2007 this organisation will be replaced by the Commission for Equality and Human Rights (**Web:** *www.cehr.org.uk*).

- **Federation of Small Businesses**
  Web: *www.fsb.org.uk*
  The UK's leading lobbying benefits group for small businesses.

- **Northern Ireland Human Rights Commission**
  Web: *www.nihrc.org*
  Its role is to promote awareness of the importance of human rights, to review existing law and practice and to advise the Secretary of State and the Executive Committee of the Northern Ireland Assembly on what steps need to be taken to fully protect human rights in Northern Ireland.

- **Opportunity Now**
  Web: *www.opportunitynow.org.uk*
  Opportunity Now is a business-led campaign that works with employers to realise the economic potential and business benefits that women at all levels contribute to the workforce.

- **Race for Opportunity (RfO)**
  Web: *www.raceforopportunity.org.uk*
  The RfO works on an individual one-to-one basis, with organisations providing specialist advice and support to meet their objectives on race and diversity.

- **RADAR**
  Web: *www.radar.org.uk*
  The UK's campaigning and advisory disability body, run by and for, disabled people.

- **Redundancy Help**
  Web: *www.redundancyhelp.co.uk*
  Redundancy Help offers advice and help on all aspects of redundancy.

- **Royal National Institute of the Blind (RNIB)**
  Web: *www.rnib.org.uk*
  The RNIB offers information, support and advice to over two million people with sight problems. Their pioneering work helps anyone with a sight problem — not just with braille, talking books and computer training, but with imaginative and practical solutions to everyday challenges.

- **Royal National Institute of Deaf People (RNID)**
  Web: *www.rnid.org.uk*
  The RNID is the largest charity representing the nine million deaf and hard of hearing people in the UK.

- **Third Age Challenge**
  Web: *www.thirdagers.net*
  Third Age Challenge is a not-for-profit organisation, set up in 1993, whose primary mission is to support older people who are unemployed or at risk of unemployment.

Equal Pay

This topic covers the following.
- Agenda for Change
- Pay Disparity
- Equal Pay Policy
- Right to Equal Pay
- Material Differences Other Than Sex
- Equal Pay Questionnaire
- Equal Pay Audits
- Job Evaluation
- Part Timers and Job Sharers
- Pensions
- Indirect Discrimination in Pay Arrangements

4.346 The main legislation is the Equal Pay Act 1970 and the Sex Discrimination Act 1975. Also relevant is the Equal Opportunity Commission (EOC) Code of Practice on equal pay, revised in 2003.

4.347 Statutory Codes of Practice published in connection with the Race Relations Act and the Disability Discrimination Act also contain recommendations in relation to pay and benefits. Adherence to Codes of Practice can be taken into account by tribunals, who may draw adverse inferences about the employer in the event of evidence of non-compliance.

4.348 Note that from October 2007, the Commission for Equality and Human Rights (CEHR) will take on the work of the three current commissions, the Commission for Racial Equality (CRE), Disability Rights Commission (DRC) and Equal Opportunities Commission (EOC).

Employers' Duties

- Employers should provide equal terms and conditions of employment for men and women where fellow employees do the same sort of work, are rated in a job evaluation scheme as carrying out equivalent jobs, or are performing different jobs that have equal value.
- Under EOC recommendations, employers should implement an equal pay policy.
- The burden of proving, on the balance of probabilities, a genuine material factor defence is on the employer.

Employees' Duties

- It is up to an employee to prove to an employment tribunal that he or she is being paid less than someone of the opposite sex doing similar or equal work.
- Employees may seek information about pay levels from an employer using an equal pay questionnaire.
- Employees are entitled to seek gender parity in relation to each element of a pay package.

- Employees can rely on statistics to show that, on average, there is a disparity between men and women with the result that the employer may have to justify the pay system.
- The legislation covers part-time workers and those who share jobs.
- Employees should abide by their employer's policies and procedures on pay.

In Practice

Pay Disparity

4.349 Equal Opportunities Commission (EOC) research shows women's earnings remain stubbornly below men's. On average, women are paid about 80% of men's hourly earnings.

4.350 Some of the reasons for the continuing disparity in earnings, include:
- occupational segregation with women predominating in the lowest paid jobs
- jobs done predominantly by women being undervalued
- discrimination within payment systems, including more limited access to enhancements to pay (such as bonuses and shift premiums)
- the working patterns of women, given that they are more likely to take breaks to care for children and, when they are working, to do so part time.

4.351 In research, line managers show persistent stereotypical attitudes about:
- women's reasons for working
- the value of their skills and worth in the workplace
- women's performance, ambition and commitment.

4.352 Discriminatory attitudes can lead to women being affected by disparity in pay between men and women by:
- being appointed (either on recruitment or promotion) at lower points on a pay scale
- progressing more slowly through incremental pay scales and salary ranges
- receiving lower performance ratings on average than men.

4.353 To avoid disparity of pay, employers should consider the following relating to pay criteria.
- Are the criteria clear or do they, in practice, permit managers a good deal of discretion?
- Do managers understand the criteria relating to pay and are they applied consistently?
- Are the criteria (eg qualifications, experience, etc) in fact relevant to the demands of the particular job or could they indirectly discriminate against women?

4.354 Even where an employer has pay structures that are well established and generally appear to operate in a non-discriminatory manner, there is no guarantee that the employer is not vulnerable to equal pay claims.

Equal Pay Policy

4.355 Under EOC recommendations, employers should implement an equal pay policy that includes:
- a commitment to examine pay practices for bias and keeping pay practices under review

- carrying out regular monitoring to assess the effect of pay practices
- keeping employees informed of how pay practices work
- providing training and guidance to managers, supervisory staff and others involved in determining pay and benefits to enable them to identify and avoid sex bias
- conducting a pay review in consultation with trade unions and staff representatives.

Right to Equal Pay

4.356 Employees have a right to equal pay and terms of conditions of employment if it can be proved that an employee of the opposite sex does:
- "like work" compared with a fellow employee of the opposite sex
- work rated as "equivalent" under a job evaluation study
- work of "equal value".

4.357 A claimant for equal pay must be able to compare his or her treatment with that of someone of the opposite sex — claims comparing pay and benefits with someone who is of the same sex cannot be brought. The comparator must be an actual person as hypothetical comparisons are not permitted under the Equal Pay Act (unlike the Sex Discrimination Act where hypothetical comparisons are possible). In relation to claims for work rated as equivalent, although these are normally brought citing a comparator in the same job grade, a claimant may also nominate a worker on a lower grade as the comparator.

4.358 In *Alabaster v Barclays Bank plc* [2005] ICR 695, ECJ, the Court of Appeal decided that it was appropriate to disapply the need to cite a comparator in the case of a woman who was seeking to enforce her rights in relation to statutory maternity pay, specifically the right to benefit from a pay rise that takes place at any time during maternity leave.

4.359 As a result of another Court of Appeal decision (*Home Office v Bailey and ors* [2005] IRLR 757), female employees may be entitled to pursue a claim of equal pay even where the numbers of men and women in the group in which they work are roughly equal in numbers, so long as their comparators work in a group that is predominantly male.

4.360 An applicant and comparator will be regarded as doing "like work" if the work they do is of the same or a broadly similar nature and if there is no difference or important difference in the tasks that they actually perform.

4.361 Work can be rated as "equivalent" if a valid job evaluation study has been carried out by the employer and if, under such a study, the job has been rated equivalent with the comparators. The job evaluation must be objective in the way that it assesses the value being placed on particular tasks and the system of evaluation must not of itself be discriminatory.

4.362 Work can be regarded as being of "equal value" to another job if it involves broadly equivalent levels of demand, eg skill, effort and decision making. This can be the case even where the types of skills required in the two jobs are completely different.

4.363 Complainants are entitled to seek parity in relation to each element of a pay package and employees can rely on statistics to show that, on average, there is a disparity between men and women with the result that the employer may have to justify the pay system.

4.364 However, in *Degnan v Redcar and Cleveland Borough Council* [2005] IRLR 615, CA (an equal pay claim brought by a group of female domestic workers), the Court of Appeal ruled that neither a fixed bonus paid to male gardeners, refuse drivers and road workers nor an attendance allowance paid to the refuse drivers and the road workers was a separate or distinct part of the employees' contracts, but that these payments were instead part of the employees' basic hourly rate of pay. This was because both these payments related to the same subject matter, namely payment for performance of the contract.

Material Differences Other Than Sex

4.365 Employers may succeed in defending a claim for equal pay only if it can be shown that any difference in pay or contractual terms is attributable to a genuine and material factor other than any difference in sex. The burden of proving a genuine material factor defence is on the employer who must also, in certain circumstances, show that the application of the genuine material factor is objectively justified.

4.366 Common examples of valid defences put forward for differences in pay or benefits include:
- seniority that affects job performance
- greater skills, experience or training provided they are relevant to job performance
- the terms of a collective agreement, provided these are gender neutral
- "London weighting"
- unsociable hours
- better performance, as measured in an objective appraisal scheme.

4.367 The ECJ, in *Cadman v Health and Safety Executive* [2006] IRLR 969, ruled that employers do not, in general, need to provide specific justification for using length of service as a criterion to award higher pay. Rewarding experience that enables workers to perform their duties better represents a legitimate aim, and service-based pay increments designed to reward experience in this way do not therefore require further specific justification.

Equal Pay Questionnaire

4.368 Under the Employment Act 2002, employees who believe they are not receiving equal pay can serve a questionnaire on their employer to establish relevant facts relating to their pay and terms and conditions.

4.369 The questionnaire contains a small number of standard questions. These ask the employer to state whether complainants have received less than their comparator(s) and, if so, why; and whether they agree that the people being compared are doing equal work or work of equal value. The questionnaire then allows the complainant to ask questions of his or her own.

4.370 There is an eight-week time limit for an employer to respond to such a questionnaire. An employer is under no statutory obligation to provide answers to the questions, but if it appears that the employer is being evasive or equivocal in its response, a tribunal will be able to draw an adverse inference against the employer.

4.371 Employers may refuse to answer questions where to do so would breach confidentiality or data protection rules. However, the employer should still try to answer the question in terms that are not employee specific.

4.372 Should a complaint become the subject of employment tribunal proceedings, the tribunal can order the disclosure of relevant information, including specific pay details.

Equal Pay Audits

4.373 The EOC encourages employers to undertake "pay audits" of their existing practices and policies, both in terms of what is actually paid and in terms of how decisions about pay are reached.

4.374 The EOC's Code of Practice contains detailed recommendations for a review of pay structures and guidance for dealing with issues that may emerge.

4.375 Employers need to review their pay system and grading structures to identify any areas of vulnerability both within structures and between them where there is more than one structure, for example, where an organisation has different branches. It is important to include this in the review as equal pay claims may involve comparisons between different establishments of the same employer (where common terms and conditions apply), and between associated employers in the same group.

4.376 An effective review will analyse the distribution of employees by:
- sex between job titles
- grade
- whether part time or full time
- for each element of the pay system.

4.377 The depth of the review will depend on the complexity of the employer's pay arrangements.

4.378 Differences in pay should relate to a real difference in the jobs or the conditions in which they are performed, especially in jobs in which women predominate.

4.379 Employers should take steps to ensure that any differential in pay between jobs is phased out and is not the means whereby a previous discriminatory practice is perpetuated.

Job Evaluation

4.380 Non-analytical methods used in grading jobs, such as paired comparisons and job ranking, are more likely to incorporate sex discrimination since they are of a more subjective nature than analytical schemes.

4.381 A job evaluation scheme carried out using analytical methods is the most likely means of ensuring that a job grading scheme is free from sex bias, as long as there are no reasonable grounds for determining that the job evaluation system itself is discriminatory on the grounds of sex.

4.382 There are problems in designing a job evaluation scheme applicable to a whole work force with a diverse range of skills and duties and the implementation of such a scheme is a costly and time consuming project. However, it is the safest way to meet the requirements of the legislation.

Part Timers and Job Sharers

4.383 Employers need to ensure that part timers and job sharers are receiving their legal entitlement to equal pay. Part-time or job-share employees have the following rights.

Equal Pay

- Under the Working Time Regulations 1998, all workers, including part-time workers, must be granted a minimum paid holiday entitlement of four weeks a year, pro rated in accordance with the number of hours or days that the part timer actually works.
- Under the Part-time Workers (Prevention of Less Favourable Treatment) Regulations 2000, where employers grant paid bank or public holidays in addition to the four weeks under the Working Time Regulations 1998 (see above), then:
- part-time employees are entitled to be paid for those bank or public holidays that fall on days they are contracted to work.
- or employers may wish to grant a *pro rata* equivalent number of paid bank or public holidays in comparison to equivalent full-time workers.
- Eligibility for statutory sick pay does not depend on the number of hours per week a person works. However, it is only available to those whose earnings are not less than the lower earnings limit for National Insurance contributions purposes.
- With occupational sick pay, there must be *pro rata* entitlement for part-time workers.
- All employees, regardless of hours worked or length of service, are entitled to make a claim under the Employment Rights Act 1996 if they believe that amounts have been unlawfully deducted from their pay.
- All employees, including part timers, are entitled to receive an itemised pay statement.
- Part timers, irrespective of hours worked, are protected in pay matters if the employer becomes insolvent, and also have the right to remuneration under a protective award.
- An employer is not obliged to make overtime payments available to part-time workers until they have worked the normal weekly hours of a comparable full-time worker.
- Employers should bear in mind that, under the Sex Discrimination Act 1975, paying part timers less (*pro rata*) than equivalent full timers is likely to be viewed as indirect sex discrimination in circumstances where more women than men work part time. Further, this would not be allowed under the Part-time Workers (Prevention of Less Favourable Treatment) Regulations 2000.

Pensions

4.384 There are certain considerations for employers regarding the rights of employees to equal access to and benefits under occupational pensions schemes. Employers should consider the following to avoid sex discrimination.

- In the context of pensions, indirect sex discrimination occurs when an employer imposes a term or condition on membership of an occupational pension scheme with which members of one gender are less likely than members of the other to be able to comply.
- It will be indirect sex discrimination to refuse access to the pension scheme to part-time workers, if (as is common) the majority of part-timers in the organisation are women.
- Claims can be made to recover any lost pension benefits for up to six years prior to making a claim (five years in Scotland).
- It is possible for an employer who is found to have indirectly discriminated against employees by offering less favourable terms in the pension scheme to attempt to justify its actions. There will, however, need to be exceptional commercial needs to justify this. Employers should be aware that:
    - currently, survivors' benefits in pension schemes may only be paid to someone who is not the spouse or civil partner of the employee if he or she is a "dependant" of the deceased

- civil partners (ie the same-sex partner of a gay or lesbian employee with whom he or she has formed a legal civil partnership) are entitled (under the Civil Partnership Act 2004) to be treated for all purposes in the same way as married partners
- if a dependant's pension, under an occupational pension scheme, is payable to an employee's unmarried partner as a matter of right, or at the discretion of the trustees, a pension will have to be paid to the employee's same-sex partner in the same circumstances. This is because the Employment Equality (Sexual Orientation) Regulations 2003 prohibit discrimination on the grounds of sexual orientation.

4.385 Under the Pensions Act 1995, the state pension age will be equalised for men and women by April 2010.

4.386 As from April 2006, employers with 150 or more employees are obliged in law to consult employee representatives if they are proposing any material changes to any occupational pension scheme that they operate. Such consultation must take place no less than 60 days before the changes are intended to come into effect. As from April 2007, this requirement was extended to employers with 100 or more employees.

Indirect Discrimination in Pay Arrangements

4.387 To prepare a defence for a case of indirect sex discrimination, the employer should be aware of the following.
- The burden of proving unequal pay in comparison to someone of the opposite sex performing similar or equal work is on the complainant.
- The burden of proving a genuine material factor defence for the reason for inequality in pay is on the employer.
- Indirect sex discrimination occurs when an employer imposes a policy, criterion, rule or practice that places or would be likely to place women at a disadvantage compared to men (or vice versa).
- If a tribunal finds evidence of indirect discrimination, then the employer must show the action complained about did not occur, or that sex played no part in the reason for the action, or must justify the provision on the basis that it is appropriate and necessary for the achievement of a legitimate business aim.
- It is likely that to be successful at a tribunal an employer will have to have a properly documented, implemented and monitored equal opportunities policy, have complied with the Equal Pay Code of Practice and have good documented evidence of the reasons for any differences in pay.

Training

4.388 It is important that all line managers are familiar with the organisation's policy and procedure on pay and understand both the employer's and the employee's responsibilities. Where a number of managers need to be trained a short, in-house training session will ensure that managers understand the organisation's policy and procedures on equal pay.

4.389 When providing training to ensure that there is no discrimination relating to the provision of pay, employers should consider the following best practice.
- Those involved in implementing training policy or delivering programmes must be trained to avoid gender bias.
- Employers need to ensure that there is equal treatment for men and women by providing training and guidance to managers, supervisory staff and others involved in determining pay and benefits to enable them to identify and avoid sex bias.

Equal Pay

- In relation to pay enhancements for skills/training, the criteria used must genuinely reflect an enhanced ability to carry out a particular job.
- Employers need to ensure that certain grades or occupations in which women predominate have equal access to pay enhancements or increases based on additional skills or training.

List of Relevant Legislation

4.390
- Employment Equality (Religion or Belief) Regulations 2003
- Employment Equality (Sexual Orientation) Regulations 2003
- Part-time Workers (Prevention of Less Favourable Treatment) Regulations 2000 (Amendment) Regulations 2002
- Sex Discrimination (Indirect Discrimination and Burden of Proof) Regulations 2001
- Part-time Workers (Prevention of Less Favourable Treatment) Regulations 2000
- Maternity and Parental Leave Regulations 1999
- Working Time Regulations 1998
- Sex Discrimination and Equal Pay (Miscellaneous Amendments) Regulations 1996
- Employment Act 2002
- Employment Relations Act 1996
- Employment Rights Act 1996
- Disability Discrimination Act 1995
- Pensions Act 1995
- Social Security Act 1989
- Limitations Act 1980
- Race Relations Act 1976
- Equal Pay Act 1970

List of Relevant Cases

4.391
- *Cadman v Health and Safety Executive* ECJ 03.10.06 (Case C-17/05)
- *Alabaster v Barclays Bank plc and Secretary of State for Social Security (No. 2)* [2005] IRLR 576, CA
- *Degnan v Redcar and Cleveland Borough Council* [2005] IRLR 615, CA
- *Degnan v Redcar and Cleaveland Borough Council* [2005] IRLR 504, EAT
- *Sharp v Caledonia Group Services Ltd* 01.11.05 (0041/05)
- *Allonby v Accrington & Rossendale College* [2004] IRLR 224, ECJ
- *Preston v Wolverhampton Healthcare NHS Trust (No. 3)* [2004] IRLR 96
- *Rutherford v Secretary of State for Trade and Industry (No. 2)* [2006] IRLR 551, HL
- *Barton v Investec Henderson Crosthwaite Securities Ltd* [2003] IRLR 332, EAT
- *Julie Bower v Schroder Securities* ET 2002 (unreported)
- *Kells v Pilkington plc* [2002] IRLR 693
- *Lawrence v Regent Office Care Ltd* C-320/00 [2002] IRLR 822, ECJ
- *South Ayrshire Council v Morton* [2002] IRLR 256, CS

- *Preston v Wolverhampton Healthcare NHS Trust (No. 2)* [2001] IRLR 237, HL
- *Fletcher v Midland Bank plc* C-78/98 [2000] IRLR 506, ECJ
- *Barry v Midland Bank plc* [1999] IRLR 581, HL
- *Strathclyde Regional Council v Wallace* [1998] IRLR 146, HL
- *Magorrian v Eastern Health and Social Services Board* C-246/96 [1998] IRLR 86, ECJ
- *North Yorkshire County Council v Ratcliffe* [1995] IRLR 439, HL
- *Roberts v Birds Eye Walls Ltd* C-132/92 [1994] IRLR 23, CA
- *Barber v Guardian Royal Exchange Assurance Group Ltd* 262/88 [1990] IRLR 240, ECJ
- *Bilka-Kaufhaus GmbH v Weber Von Hartz* 170/84 [1986] IRLR 317, ECJ
- *Defrenne v Sabena (No. 2)* [1976] ECR 455
- *Boyle v Equal Opportunities Commission* C-411/96 [1998] IRLR 717, ECJ

Further Information

Publications

- *Code of Practice: Equal Pay (1997, rev 2003)*, Equal Opportunities Commission (EOC)
- *Conducting an Equal Pay Review in Accordance with Data Protection Act Principles*, Equal Opportunities Commission (EOC)
- *Equal Pay, Fair Pay*

Organisations

- **Advisory Conciliation and Arbitration Service (Acas)**
  Web: *www.acas.org.uk*
  Acas aims to improve organisations and working life through better employment relations. It provides up-to-date information, advice, high-quality training, and works with employers and employees to solve problems and improve performance.
- **Department for Business, Enterprise and Regulatory Reform (BERR)**
  Web: *www.berr.gov.uk*
  The Department for Business, Enterprise and Regulatory Reform brings together functions from the former Department of Trade and Industry (DTI), including responsibilities for productivity, business relations, energy, competition and consumers. It also drives regulatory reform.
- **Equal Opportunities Commission**
  Web: *www.eoc.org.uk*
  An agency working to eliminate sex discrimination and put equality into practice in the workplace. From October 2007 this organisation will be replaced by the Commission for Equality and Human Rights (**Web:** *www.cehr.org.uk*).
- **Institute for Employment Studies**
  Web: *www.employment-studies.co.uk*
  The Institute for Employment Studies is an independent, apolitical, international centre of research and consultancy in human resource issues.

Fair Employment (Northern Ireland) Act 1989

> This topic covers the following.
> - Religious Discrimination
> - Protected Workers
> - Forms of Discrimination
> - Liability
> - Registration and Monitoring
> - Affirmative Action
> - Complaints and Remedies
> - The Equality Commission

4.392 The Fair Employment and Treatment (Northern Ireland) Order 1998 consolidates and amends the Fair Employment Act 1976 and the Fair Employment Act 1989. The legislation covers discrimination on the grounds of both religion and political opinion. The framework of the Order mirrors that of Britain's sex and race discrimination law. It covers:

- direct discrimination
- indirect discrimination
- justification
- victimisation.

Employers' Duties

- Employers must not discriminate against employees or potential employees on the grounds of religion or political opinion in any aspect of employment.
- Employers in Northern Ireland with more than 10 employees must register with the Equality Commission.
- Registered companies must submit an annual monitoring return giving information about the religious composition of their workforce.
- Employers must review employment practices once every three years.
- Employers may consider taking affirmative action such as targeted training and targeted encouragement.

Employees' Duties

- Employees have a duty to co-operate with their employers to enable them to comply with their legal duties as regards fair employment.
- Complainants may use a questionnaire to seek information from an employer if they believe they have suffered discrimination on the grounds of religion or political opinion.
- A person claiming unlawful discrimination in employment can complain to the Fair Employment Tribunal.
- Employees must register any claim between three and six months after the employee's first knowledge of the discriminatory act.

- The burden of proof rests with the employee as the maker of the claim.

In Practice

Religious Discrimination

4.393 The Fair Employment and Treatment (Northern Ireland) Order 1998 covers discrimination on the grounds of actual, supposed or absent religion and political opinion. The legislation extends beyond employment: it is unlawful to discriminate in supplying goods, facilities or services, in providing university or further education and in the disposal or management of premises or land.

4.394 This Order updates the Northern Ireland Act 1998 which states that public authorities in Northern Ireland should promote equality of opportunity involving:
- religious belief
- political opinion
- racial groups
- age
- marital status or sexual orientation
- men and women generally
- persons with and without a disability
- persons with and without dependants.

4.395 Organisations prohibited from discriminating include:
- employment agencies
- vocational organisations
- trade unions
- training services
- those with power to confer qualifications.

Protected Workers

4.396 In employment, those protected include:
- job applicants
- employees, both full time and part time
- people who are applying for or working under a personal contract, eg many self-employed people
- contract workers
- agency workers
- casual workers
- those working for in-store concessions.

4.397 People who are not protected include:
- ministers of religion
- people working in a private household
- those in "any employment or occupation where the essential nature of the job requires it to be done by a person holding, or not holding, a particular religious belief or political opinion".

4.398 Discrimination by employers is outlawed:

- in any aspect of their recruitment process
- in terms and conditions of employment including access to benefits
- in dismissal, redundancy or other detriment.

Forms of Discrimination

4.399 A complainant may bring action on direct and indirect grounds as well as in circumstances of victimisation.

Direct Discrimination

4.400 Direct discrimination occurs where an employer treats one individual less favourably than others because of religious belief or political opinion. A comparison has to be made in order to decide what constitutes less favourable treatment.

4.401 Discrimination is prohibited:
- in respect of someone's supposed religious belief or political opinion
- in respect of the absence or supposed absence of any religious belief or political opinion.

4.402 The following have been ruled as constituting unlawful discrimination:
- to instruct a person to undertake a discriminatory act at the Northern Ireland Court of Appeal
- to discriminate against a person on the grounds of the religion of his or her spouse or child.

Indirect Discrimination

4.403 It is unlawful for an employer to have a requirement or condition that disproportionately and adversely affects those of a particular religious belief or political opinion, unless it can justify doing so.

4.404 To bring a case before a Fair Employment Tribunal (FET), an individual must be able to show:
- the nature of the requirement or condition
- that the requirement or condition has a disproportionate and adverse impact on people who belong to a particular religion or political opinion
- that he or she belongs to the disadvantaged group
- that he or she is unable to comply with the requirement or condition
- that he or she has suffered some detriment as a result.

4.405 There are several steps that the tribunal must undertake before making a decision. These include:
- undertaking a comparative statistical exercise to identify a pool of people who are in the same or similar circumstances as the complainant
- ensuring that the proportion of people in that pool who are of the same religious belief or political opinion as the complainant and who can comply with the requirement or condition is smaller than the proportion of people in the pool who are not of the same religious belief or political opinion
- hearing an employer's arguments justifying the requirement or condition if a disproportionate effect has been shown.

4.406 A balancing exercise is then undertaken involving the test of justification.

Justification

4.407 The test of justification requires the reasonable needs of the employer to be balanced against the discriminatory effect of the requirement on the complainant.

4.408 The employer must be able to show that the requirement or condition is necessary for the effective performance of the job.

Victimisation

4.409 This provision is designed to protect two categories of people:
- those bringing a complaint for discrimination
- those supporting someone else's complaint.

Sectarian Harassment

4.410 Fair employment legislation makes it unlawful for an employer to subject an employee to "any other detriment". This covers sectarian harassment. There are two issues that are relevant:
- the nature of the conduct
- the question of liability.

4.411 The Fair Employment Code of Practice states that employers should "promote a good and harmonious working environment and atmosphere in which no worker feels under threat or intimidated because of his or her religious belief or political opinion". Possible prohibitions include:
- displaying flags
- circulating particular literature, emblems, posters and graffiti
- singing and voicing slogans that "are likely to give offence or cause apprehension among particular groups of employees".

4.412 Any harassment that takes place in the course of employment makes the employer liable, whether or not the employer knows or approves of it happening.

Liability

4.413 The issue of liability is similar to that under Britain's anti-discrimination laws. An employer is liable for all acts of discrimination perpetrated by its employees in the course of employment, whether or not the acts were done with the employer's knowledge or approval. An employer can defend itself by saying that it "took such steps as were reasonably practicable to prevent" the discrimination. Employers are also liable for discriminatory acts done by their agents.

4.414 Anyone who knowingly "aids or incites ... directs, procures or induces" another person to discriminate unlawfully has done the same unlawful act. It follows that both the employer and the employee who committed an act of discrimination may be held liable.

Registration and Monitoring

4.415 There are three aspects to registration and monitoring:
- the registration of employers
- the duty to monitor
- the requirement to review workforce composition, employment policies and practices

Registration

4.416 Any organisation — except public authorities — that employs over 10 people in Northern Ireland is required to register with the Equality Commission. Only employees under contracts of employment or apprenticeship working 16 hours or more a week are recognised in this instance.

4.417 Failure to register is a criminal offence. The register is available for free public inspection. Public authorities must still file monitoring returns.

Monitoring Returns

4.418 All registered employers must submit an annual monitoring return about the religious composition – ie membership of the Protestant or Catholic religions — of their workforce.

4.419 Failures to submit a proper monitoring return or to retain the monitoring information for three years are criminal offences. Employers are required to maintain the confidentiality of the monitoring information and it is a criminal offence to disclose monitoring information other than in specified circumstances, eg to the Equality Commission in connection with a tribunal or other court proceedings.

Reviews

4.420 At least once every three years, registered employers must review both the religious composition of their workforces and certain of their employment practices to establish whether they are providing "fair participation in employment".

4.421 The employment practices relate to:
- recruitment
- pre- and post-recruitment training and promotion
- redundancy practices.

4.422 The Code of Practice states that:
- it is not possible to prescribe a rigid and predetermined level of participation
- what is fair will depend on the circumstances of each case
- employers must ask themselves whether the composition of the workforce is "broadly in line" with what might "reasonably be expected".

Affirmative Action

4.423 Where it is established by review that "fair participation" is not being achieved, the employer may voluntarily undertake action designed to improve participation – this is called affirmative action. The Equality Commission may also instruct an employer to take affirmative action.

4.424 Affirmative action does not mean positive discrimination — the fixing of recruitment quotas for under-represented groups is unlawful. Employers must still consider job applicants on their merits.

4.425 The types of affirmative action include:
- redundancy selection
- targeted encouragement
- recruiting from unemployed workers.

Redundancy Selection

4.426 Provided it is clear that redundancy is an affirmative action measure, it will be possible to target redundancy primarily at members of either the Protestant or Roman Catholic communities, depending on which group is "over-represented". It is, however, unlawful to adopt redundancy selection criteria that are framed by reference to religious belief or political opinion, even in circumstances where Catholics or Protestants are under-represented.

Targeted Encouragement

4.427 Employers can encourage members of either the Protestant or Roman Catholic communities to consider or apply for a particular job or occupation or for particular training. It is important to note that although targeted encouragement is lawful, actual decisions on recruitment and on promotion must be made on merit, with religion playing no part in the decision-making process.

Recruiting from Unemployed Workers

4.428 Employers can make it a requirement or condition in a recruitment exercise that applicants should have been unemployed for a specified period of time. This is lawful even if it has the effect of excluding a larger proportion of potential applicants from one religious community than the other.

Complaints and Remedies

4.429 A person claiming unlawful discrimination in employment can complain to the Fair Employment Tribunal (FET).

4.430 A claim must be brought by the earlier of these dates:
- the end of a three-month period that began with the day on which the complainant first had knowledge of the discriminatory act
- the end of a six-month period that began with the day of the act.

4.431 The FET can hear a complaint made out of time if it is just and equitable to do so.

4.432 There are several important aspects to the complaints and remedies process, relating to:
- the burden of proof
- the questionnaire procedure
- remedies available
- arrangements for compromise agreements.

Burden of Proof

4.433 The burden of proof rests on the applicant but is based on the balance of probabilities rather than proof beyond reasonable doubt. An employer can be required to explain the treatment of an individual.

4.434 A tribunal or court may draw adverse inferences from an employer's evasive, equivocal or incomplete answers to questions. This approach is used generally in discrimination complaints.

Questionnaire Procedure

4.435 Before tribunal proceedings, an employee who believes he or she has been the victim of discrimination may serve a questionnaire on the employer in order to obtain specified information. There is a standard form for this but an applicant can add further questions. Although the employer is not required by law to respond to a questionnaire, any failure to do so is likely to lead the tribunal to draw an adverse inference against the employer. Similarly, a complainant's questions and the employer's replies are admissible in proceedings before the tribunal.

Remedies

4.436 The remedies a tribunal can make for unfair discrimination are:
- an order declaring the rights of the parties
- a compensation order in respect of the applicant
- an order forcing the employer to remove or reduce the discrimination.

4.437 There is no limit on the amount of compensation. The award can include financial loss and a sum for injury to feelings.

The Equality Commission

4.438 The Equality Commission deals with fair employment, sex (including marital status), race, age, sexual orientation, religious belief and politcal opinion and disability discrimination. Its responsibilities include:
- working for the elimination of unlawful religious and political discrimination
- investigating employers' practices
- promoting equal opportunities and affirmative action
- securing undertakings from or serving directions on employers after an investigation into equal opportunity
- enforcing the prohibition of discriminatory advertising at the Fair Employment Tribunal (FET)
- enforcing employers' obligations to register with the Commission
- maintaining a register of employers and ensuring they file monitoring returns
- enforcing the equal opportunities duties placed on public authorities
- providing advice to complainants in FET applications
- providing further help at the FET including representation and other assistance
- reviewing the Fair Employment and Treatment Order (Northern Ireland) 1998 and putting amendment proposals to the Government
- keeping informed about proceedings in the FET
- issuing and maintaining codes of practice in respect of both employment and access to goods, facilities and services
- conducting research into equality issues.

Training

4.439 Employers can offer general or specific occupational training at either a particular place or to a particular group of people. It is lawful in these circumstances to encourage members of either the Protestant or Catholic community to apply for the training.

4.440 Employers can lawfully offer training to non-employees that is restricted to people of a particular religious belief. This is permissible in certain clearly defined circumstances.
- The training must help fit the trainees for employment at a particular establishment in Northern Ireland.
- The Equality Commission must be satisfied that people of the particular religious belief were under-represented over the previous 12 months.
- The Equality Commission has given the training its approval.

List of Relevant Legislation

4.441
- Northern Ireland Act 1998
- Fair Employment (Northern Ireland) Act 1989
- Employment Act 1976
- Fair Employment and Treatment (Northern Ireland) Order 1998
- Fair Employment and Treatment Order (Amendment) Regulations (Northern Ireland) 2003

List of Relevant Cases

4.442
- *AM v (1) WC and (2) SPV* [1999] IRLR 410
- *Baird v Cookstown District Council* (1 April 1998) 161/91
- *Jones v Tower Boot Co Ltd* [1997] IRLR 168, CA
- *Smyth v Croft Inns Ltd* [1996] IRLR 84, NICA
- *Belfast Port Employers' Association v Fair Employment Commission for Northern Ireland* (29 June 1994)
- *Grimes v Unipork Ltd* (17 February 1992) 167/90
- *Meek v Fire Authority for Northern Ireland and another* (22 July 1992) 50/90
- *King v The Great Britain-China Centre* [1991] IRLR 513, CA
- *James v Eastleigh Borough Council* [1990] IRLR 288, HL
- *Magill v Fair Employment Agency* (10 July 1987)
- *Bilka-Kaufhaus GmbH v Weber von Hartz* 170/84 [1986] IRLR 317, ECJ

Further Information

Publications
- *Fair Employment Code of Practice, Department of Higher and Further Education*, Department for Work and Pensions (DWP)

Organisations
- **Equality Commission for Northern Ireland**
  Web: *www.equalityni.org*
  An independent public body established under the Northern Ireland Act 1998. The Commission is working towards the elimination of discrimination through the promotion of equality of opportunity and the encouraging of good practice; the promotion of affirmative or positive action, reviewing relevant legislation and overseeing the implementation and effectiveness of the statutory duty on public authorities.

- **Northern Ireland Human Rights Commission**
  Web: *www.nihrc.org*
  Its role is to promote awareness of the importance of human rights, to review existing law and practice and to advise the Secretary of State and the Executive Committee of the Northern Ireland Assembly on what steps need to be taken to fully protect human rights in Northern Ireland.

Race Discrimination

This topic covers the following.
- Scope of the Race Relations Act
- Qualifying Conditions
- Comparable Person
- Four Forms of Discrimination
- Racial Discrimination in Recruitment
- Race Discrimination During Employment
- Race Equality Schemes for Public Bodies
- Claims of Race Discrimination
- Monitoring

4.443 The Race Relations Act 1976 and the Race Relations Act 1976 (Amendment) Regulations 2003 prohibit discrimination on grounds of colour, nationality, race and ethnic and national origins.

4.444 The Act prohibits four different types of discrimination in recruitment and employment: direct discrimination, indirect discrimination, harassment and victimisation. It also provides for limited post-employment protection and a questionnaire procedure to help claimants explore whether racial discrimination has occurred.

4.445 There is no qualifying period of service necessary to make a complaint to an employment tribunal and no limit on the amount of compensation that can be awarded to a successful claimant.

Employers' Duties

- Employers must not treat any individual member of staff less favourably than another on racial grounds.
- Employers may only use race as a criterion in recruitment in very limited circumstances where it is a genuine occupational qualification for the job in question.
- Employers must not commit any act of specific racial discrimination against an individual as there is no defence that justifies direct race discrimination.
- Employers must not adopt policies, procedures, rules or practices that could put people from a particular racial group at a disadvantage (known as indirect race discrimination), unless the policy, procedure, rule or practice is appropriate and necessary in the circumstances. Indirect race discrimination is unlawful whether it is intentional or unintentional.
- Employers must not victimise staff who have complained that they have suffered race discrimination, nor victimise staff who assist others in making such complaints.
- Employers must not allow any form of racial harassment.
- Public sector employers have an additional duty (in relation to the exercise of their public functions) to eliminate race discrimination and promote equality of opportunity and good relations as between people of different racial groups.
- Employers must take care not to commit any type of race discrimination after a person's employment ends, eg by withholding a reference or harassing an ex-employee on racial grounds.

- Employers should take all reasonable steps to prevent discrimination in the workplace, eg by communicating their equal opportunities and anti-harassment policies to all staff on a regular basis, training staff on equal opportunities issues and the avoidance of all forms of discrimination, and monitoring compliance.

Employees' Duties

- Employees have a duty not to discriminate against any colleague on any grounds involving colour, race, nationality or ethnic or national origins.
- Employees must not victimise any member of staff who has complained that he or she has experienced race discrimination or helped a colleague to make a complaint of discrimination or harassment.
- Employees must not engage in any behaviour that could be interpreted as racial harassment.
- Employees are under a duty to adhere to their employer's equal opportunities and anti-harassment policies and to ensure that they treat their colleagues with respect and dignity at all times.

In Practice

Scope of the Race Relations Act

4.446 The Race Relations Act 1976 (RRA) prohibits discrimination on racial grounds. "Racial grounds" is defined as covering colour, race, nationality, ethnic origins and national origins. If race discrimination occurs, the victim may bring a complaint to an employment tribunal.

4.447 The phrase "on racial grounds" can refer to not only the racial group of the claimant, but also to the race of the perpetrator and any third party, eg a close relative of an employee.

4.448 The Race Relations Act 1976 applies equally to people of all racial groups. A person may fall into more than one racial group, eg he or she may be:
- black and Jamaican
- white and Canadian
- black, Ugandan and of Indian Origin.

4.449 Nationality includes citizenship. It would, therefore, be discrimination to treat a British national who is a Belgian citizen less favourably on the grounds of citizenship, for example.

4.450 The English and the Scots are separate racial groups by reference to their national origins.

4.451 Job applicants are also protected throughout the process of recruitment and limited protection against discrimination is also available to former employees.

4.452 If discrimination occurs, the individual may bring a complaint to an employment tribunal.

Employees and Other Types of Workers

4.453 All workers are covered by the Race Relations Act, ie not only those employed directly by the organisation, but also other workers such as:
- contract workers
- agency temps
- casual workers
- freelancers who provide their services personally
- directors
- company secretaries
- non-elected office holders
- partners in firms.

Qualifying Conditions

4.454 There is no length of service required for an employee or worker to bring a claim for unlawful race discrimination to an employment tribunal. Equally, there is no lower or upper age limit for a claimant to bring a complaint.

4.455 Employees (but not other workers), must first raise a written grievance with their employer and wait 28 days. This is to allow the employer time and opportunity to deal with the complaint before it can proceed to tribunal. If a claim is lodged with the tribunal before the employee has raised a grievance and waited 28 days, the tribunal will in most cases not admit it.

Comparable Person

4.456 In order to found a claim of race discrimination, an employee will usually have to draw a comparison with someone of a different racial group in similar circumstances.

4.457 If, however, there is no actual comparator, but there is evidence to support an inference of race discrimination, an employment tribunal will construct a "hypothetical comparator" to assess how someone of a different race would have been treated in the same or similar circumstances. Thus the law allows employment tribunals to make assumptions about how an employer would have treated a comparable person who belongs to a different racial group from that of the complainant.

Four Forms of Discrimination

4.458 There are four different forms of discrimination:
- direct discrimination
- indirect discrimination
- victimisation
- harassment.

Direct Race Discrimination

4.459 For direct discrimination to occur it must be shown that the employer treated or would have treated someone from another racial group more favourably in the particular circumstances.

4.460 Direct discrimination means treating an individual less favourably on racial grounds than someone of a different racial group. Acts of direct race discrimination may include:
- deciding not to employ a particular job applicant on grounds related to his or her colour, race, nationality, ethnic origins or national origins
- denying someone access to training, transfer or promotion on racial grounds
- giving someone less favourable terms and conditions of employment than a comparable employee of a different racial group
- denying an individual access to benefits or perks for reasons related to race
- making separate arrangements for persons of different racial groups, eg segregation
- dismissing an employee for reasons related to race
- harassing an employee on racial grounds.

Indirect Race Discrimination

4.461 Indirect discrimination on grounds of colour or nationality occurs where a requirement or condition is applied in such a way that the proportion of persons of the same racial group who can comply with the condition is considerably smaller than the proportion of persons not of that racial group who can comply.

4.462 If a condition is justifiable irrespective of racial group, then there is no discrimination even though application of the condition may have a disproportionate adverse effect. However, it is for the employer against whom discrimination is alleged to prove that the condition is justifiable irrespective of racial group.

4.463 The requirement must be to the detriment of the person alleging discrimination because he or she cannot comply with it. If the condition is one with which the person can comply, then there is no discrimination.

4.464 The revised definition of indirect race discrimination introduced in July 2003 applies in cases where the discrimination alleged is on grounds of race or ethnic or national origin (but not colour or nationality). There are three aspects to the definition:
- the broader concept of a "provision, criterion or practice" replaces the phrase "requirement or condition"
- a stipulation that the provision, criterion or practice must be one that puts, or would put people of a particular racial group "at a disadvantage"
- the defence that the provision, criterion or practice is a proportionate means of achieving a "legitimate aim".

Provision, Criterion or Practice

4.465 The concept of a "provision, criterion or practice", is thought to be broader than a "requirement or condition". It captures informal practices as well as specific and identifiable rules, such as:
- selection criteria
- policies and procedures
- guidelines
- benefits
- employment rules
- informal practices

that are applied to all employees (or job applicants), but that could have a disproportionate adverse effect on people from a particular racial group.

"Put at a Disadvantage"

4.466 In order to prove that indirect discrimination has occurred, it must be shown not only that someone has personally been put at a disadvantage by the application of the provision, criterion or practice, but that the provision, criterion or practice in general *puts*, or *would put*, persons of the same race or ethnic or national origins at a particular disadvantage when compared with other persons.

4.467 It is thought that employment tribunals are unlikely to make any significant distinction between the concept of "disadvantage" and "detriment".

Identifying "a Legitimate Aim"

4.468 To establish a defence against a claim of discrimination, it is necessary for the employer applying the provision, criterion or practice to show that it is a proportionate means of achieving a legitimate aim. The aim must be related to the needs of the business or the specific job the employee is employed to do and must be unrelated to race, ethnic origins or national origins.

The Test of Proportionality

4.469 "Proportionate" in this context means that the provision, criterion or practice, when viewed in relation to the aim in question, must be:
- appropriate
- necessary
- not excessive

in relation to the defined aim.

Dress Codes

4.470 Rules on dress and appearance, eg a policy that prohibits certain forms of clothing, head coverings, hair styles or jewellery, may conflict with the customs and requirements of certain racial groups and hence be indirectly discriminatory unless justified, eg on the grounds of health or safety. Sikh men are, for example, required to wear a turban, and have their hair and beards uncut.

4.471 Whether or not an employer applies a set dress code, staff should, within reason, be able to wear clothing consistent with their racial origins and/or customs, provided it is practical and safe for them to do so.

4.472 The EAT has ruled (in *Azmi v Kirklees Metropolitan Council* [2007] IRLR 484 that an instruction to an assistant teacher (a devout Muslim) to remove her full-face veil whilst teaching children in class amounted to indirect religious discrimination against her. The employment tribunal concluded, however, that the instruction to remove the veil was justified (and therefore lawful) as it was underpinned by a legitimate aim — namely to ensure the children received effective, unhindered language instruction — and that it was proportionate in light of that aim. There was evidence that when the teacher wore the veil, this reduced the children's ability to learn language skills from her as her diction was not as clear as it would otherwise have been, and the children's learning was impeded because they could not see her facial expressions. These principles were upheld by the EAT.

4.473 Whenever an employer applies a policy regarding dress, appearance and even rules regarding hair styles, jewellery or tattoos, they should consider adjusting the policy to accommodate the needs of any employee for whom such customs are relevant or important in respect of their racial origins.

4.474 The Employment Act 1989 exempts Sikhs from any requirement to wear safety helmets on construction sites when they are wearing turbans.

Victimisation

4.475 Employers and employees should not discriminate against any member of staff because that person has raised a genuine complaint of racial discrimination or harassment, whether under the employer's grievance procedure or before an employment tribunal. Any employee who supports or assists another employee to raise a complaint is also protected against victimisation.

4.476 Claimants lose their protection if their allegations or the evidence or information they have given were false and not made or given in good faith.

Examples of Victimisation

4.477 As common examples of victimisation, Acas cites an employee being isolated by their colleagues, labelled a "trouble maker" or denied access to promotion or training because he or she has raised a complaint of discrimination or helped another employee to bring a complaint. Employers are under a duty to take reasonable steps to prevent this happening.

Racial Harassment

4.478 The Race Relations Act 1976 provides a statutory definition of harassment on grounds of race, ethnic origins or national origins. An employer subjects someone to harassment when, on grounds of race or ethnic or national origins, he or she engages in unwanted conduct that has the purpose or effect of:
- violating the other person's dignity
- creating an intimidating, hostile, degrading, humiliating or offensive environment for that person.

4.479 The question as to whether behaviour amounts to harassment depends primarily on the perception of the person on the receiving end.

4.480 A further clause provides that behaviour will constitute harassment if, with regard to all of the circumstances — including the victim's perception — it should reasonably be seen as violating the victim's dignity or as creating an atmosphere which is intimidating, hostile, degrading, humiliating or offensive to him or her.

4.481 In practice this means that a spurious claim that someone's behaviour amounted to harassment in circumstances where no reasonable person could possibly have viewed it as harassment in the context in which it occurred, would not succeed.

4.482 The Act does not contain a definition of harassment on grounds of colour or nationality. Courts and tribunals have, however, consistently held that harassment on these grounds in the workplace will be a form of direct racial discrimination and hence be unlawful.

4.483 Any employer who receives a complaint of harassment should take it very seriously, investigate the circumstances thoroughly and, if the complaint is well founded, take steps to put a stop to the behaviour that is causing offence. It will also be appropriate in most circumstances to take disciplinary action against the harasser.

Examples of Racial Harassment

4.484 Examples of racial harassment could include:
- behaviour connected in some way to race that is offensive, demeaning, frightening or in anyway distressing
- intentional bullying on racial grounds
- behaviour that has no malicious intent but which is upsetting to someone on racial grounds

- subtle and insidious behaviour that may involve nicknames, teasing or name-calling linked to colour, race, nationality, ethnic origins or national origins.

4.485 This behaviour does not need to be specifically targeted at the individual. A general culture that permits banter and teasing may create an uncomfortable working environment for some employees on account of their racial or ethnic background and thus potentially give rise to claims of racial harassment.

Racial Discrimination in Recruitment

4.486 Job applicants are protected throughout the entire process of recruitment against any form of racial discrimination. For example, if an applicant who was otherwise suitable for the job under review was refused employment because he or she could not read or write fluent English, this would constitute indirect race discrimination and would be unlawful unless the employer could show that the requirement for the person to read or write English to a standard of fluency was relevant and necessary for the effective performance of the job.

Genuine Occupational Qualifications and Requirements

4.487 The Race Relations Act 1976 (RRA) allows limited exceptions to the general principle that race must never be taken into account when determining who should be recruited, promoted or transferred. The Act contains a general provision that if it is genuinely necessary for the holder of a particular job to be of a particular race, ethnic origin or national origin, then it is lawful to discriminate in his or her favour, provided also that the race requirement is proportionate in the particular case.

4.488 Over and above this general provision, the RRA provides that it is lawful for an employer to insist on recruiting someone from a specified racial group in circumstances where race is a genuine occupational qualification (GOQ) for the job in question. There are four situations in which this may be justified.
- Where for reasons of authenticity, someone of a particular racial group is required to take part in a dramatic performance or other entertainment
- Where for reasons of authenticity, someone of a particular racial group is required for modelling. This exception applies both to artists' and photographic models. The job must involve participation in the production of a work of art, visual image or series of visual images (eg a film)
- Where for reasons of authenticity, someone of a specified racial group is required to work in an "ethnic" restaurant. This covers any place where food or drink is provided for and consumed by members of the public or a section of the public. An example could be a requirement that a waiter in a Chinese restaurant must be Chinese
- Where a job involves the provision of personal services and the employer can show that the services to be provided can most effectively be provided by persons of the particular racial group.

4.489 A genuine occupational qualification will not apply if:
- the employer already has enough staff of the racial group in question who can carry out the duties required by the job, and
- it is reasonable to allocate the duties to these other staff without undue inconvenience.

4.490 On each occasion, before an employer applies a genuine occupational qualification or requirement, he or she should review whether the requirement is still valid.

Positive Action

4.491 Although positive discrimination, eg discrimination in favour of people from minority racial or ethnic groups is not permitted under UK employment law, the Race Relations Act 1976 does permit certain forms of positive action in recruitment and training. Positive action is not required in law, but is permitted if the reason for it is to increase the number of people from a minority racial group in employment where people from that group are under-represented. Under-representation occurs where in the 12 months prior to the action being taken, there were no, or a comparatively small number of, people of the particular racial group doing the work in question.

4.492 It may thus be lawful for employers to apply measures specifically to encourage candidates from minority racial groups to apply for employment or promotion, or to offer them special training to help fit them for particular work. An example could be placing job advertisements in a particular publication that is read predominantly by Asian people. However, it is only encouragement that is permitted — at the point of selection for employment or promotion, the principles of equality must be applied and race must play no part in the decision making process (unless a genuine occupational qualification or requirement applies). An example of positive action in relation to training could be to offer English language training specifically to employees who are overseas nationals.

4.493 It is also permitted (but not obligatory) to provide education or training to individuals who are not ordinarily resident in Britain provided the individuals in question do not intend to remain in Britain after their period of education or training is complete.

Advertisements

4.494 Unless a job falls within the category of a genuine occupational qualification or requirement, it is unlawful to advertise for a person of a particular racial group.

4.495 The word "advertisement" includes any notices posted on notice boards or sent to staff, such as internal memos about a vacancy. The publisher of the advertisement is liable as well as the author.

4.496 If an advertisement indicates an intention to discriminate, the Commission for Racial Equality may initiate a tribunal case against the person responsible.

4.497 Employment agencies are also subject to the prohibition on advertising jobs that require a person of a particular racial group. Individuals working in employment agencies could also fall foul of the law if they accept instructions given to them by an employer to recruit someone who belongs or does not belong to a specific racial group for a job vacancy.

Asylum and Immigration

4.498 It is a criminal offence (under the Asylum and Immigration Act 1996) to employ people whose immigration status prevents them from working in the UK.

4.499 An employer should check that a job applicant has leave to enter and to work in the UK. From 1 May 2004, employers can accept a single "secure" document as proof of entitlement to work. Secure documents include a UK or EEA passport, an EEA national identity card or a UK residence permit. Otherwise, the employer must check two documents from a list of less secure documents, eg documents bearing a national insurance number, a birth certificate or a work permit. The employer must then either retain the document(s) or keep copies of them.

4.500 Employers need to make the same check of every recruit at the same stage of the recruitment process to avoid allegations of racially discriminatory treatment.

Recruitment Best Practice Checklist

4.501 Employers should consider the following best practice to avoid discrimination in recruitment.

- Do not advertise for a person of a particular racial group, unless a job is one in which a genuine occupational qualification or requirement applies.
- Avoid recruiting by word of mouth only as this practice may tend to reinforce a racial imbalance in the workforce and may be indirectly discriminatory.
- Incorporate clear, objective and specific criteria against which applicants (for jobs, transfers and promotions) can be assessed. This should help to eliminate racial bias, whether deliberate or subconscious.
- Avoid imposing a geographical limitation on the recruitment area as this may be found to be indirectly discriminatory.
- Avoid specifying experience or qualifications that may be considered discriminatory, eg the ability to read or write fluent English, unless this is necessary for the effective performance of the job.
- Ensure that reception and personnel staff are instructed not to treat applicants from minority racial groups less favourably than others.
- Ensure that staff responsible for shortlisting, interviewing and selecting candidates are clearly informed of selection criteria and of the need for their objective and consistent application.
- Be aware of the possible misunderstandings that can occur in interviews between persons of different racial and cultural backgrounds.
- Ensure that all staff involved in recruitment or selection have received effective equal opportunities training.
- Give guidance to recruiters on the effects which generalised assumptions and prejudices about race can have on selection decisions.
- Use more than one person to carry out shortlisting and interviewing — this may help to prevent any one individual's prejudices affecting the selection decision.
- Keep notes on recruitment decisions in order to be able to demonstrate that the reason for the rejection of one candidate and the appointment of another was free from racial bias.

Race Discrimination During Employment

4.502 Employees are protected against all forms of race discrimination in every aspect of their employment. This will include the terms and conditions of their contract, access to promotion, transfer and training and general treatment at work.

Terms and Conditions

4.503 Offering discriminatory terms and conditions of employment at the outset of employment is prohibited. Terms and conditions of employment must not in any way be linked to an employee's race.

Promotion, Transfer and Training

4.504 If an employee's access to opportunities for promotion, transfer or training is restricted for any reason related to race, this would amount to direct race discrimination. The same sort of considerations would apply as shown in recruitment.

Selection for Redundancy

4.505 The criteria used to make selections for redundancy should be checked carefully to guard against the possibility of indirect race discrimination. In addition, if a group of employees under threat of redundancy is predominantly of one racial group, the employer would be advised to review the selection criteria in order to guard against any effect which could be disproportionate.

Post-employment Discrimination

4.506 A claim for race discrimination can be made against a former employer irrespective of how much time has passed since the employee's employment ended. Such a claim can only succeed, however, where the individual can show that the discrimination or harassment arose out of, or was closely connected with, the previous employment relationship.

Race Equality Schemes for Public Bodies

4.507 Public bodies have a positive duty to promote:
- the elimination of race discrimination
- equality of opportunity as between people of different racial groups
- good race relations as between people of different racial groups.

4.508 Designated public authorities have had to submit a "race equality scheme" to the Commission for Racial Equality. As part of this, they were required to:
- audit and assess all functions and procedures for their relevance to racial equality
- from this analysis, develop an action plan to improve the authority's performance.

4.509 Such schemes are expected to evolve and overhaul public services to ensure fair and equal treatment of all sections of the community in respect of race.

Institutional Racism

4.510 Institutional racism was brought to light by the MacPherson Report in the context of the attitudes of the police to members of the public. An accusation of institutional racism might be relevant in some cases but only if it provided concrete evidence that a particular act of race discrimination had taken place. Such a charge might therefore lead to a conclusion that the employer was guilty of discrimination within the Race Relations Act 1976.

Claims of Race Discrimination

4.511 In the event of a claim for race discrimination, the employer must be able to show a non-discriminatory reason for their actions, otherwise the employment tribunal may draw adverse inferences. A tribunal is bound to uphold the complaint if the employer cannot come up with an adequate or credible explanation for its conduct.

The Questionnaire Procedure

4.512 An employee or job applicant who believes that he or she may have experienced any form of race discrimination (including discrimination after his or her employment ended) may serve a special questionnaire on the employer, asking for an explanation for the conduct that they think was discriminatory. The individual may instigate the procedure either before or after he or she has commenced tribunal proceedings.

4.513 A pre-printed questionnaire is available, but the employee may add his or her own questions.

4.514 The employer is not under any statutory duty to respond to a questionnaire served upon them. The questions and replies are, however, admissible as evidence in tribunal cases. If the employer fails to respond to the questionnaire within eight weeks, or if the answers given are evasive or equivocal, the tribunal or court may infer that the employer did discriminate and the employer is trying to avoid admitting it. It is therefore advisable for employers to answer the employee's questions as fully as possible.

4.515 In order to be used in tribunal cases, the questionnaire must (in cases where an application to tribunal has not yet been presented) be given or sent to the employer within three months of the act that is being complained about, or (where a complaint has already been presented to the tribunal) within 21 days of the date on which the complaint was lodged.

The Burden of Proof

4.516 Once an employee has established facts before an employment tribunal that indicate that he or she may have been the victim of unlawful race discrimination, the burden of proof shifts to the employer who must (if they are to succeed in defending the claim) persuade the tribunal that there was some other non-discriminatory reason for their actions.

4.517 In *Oyarce v Cheshire County Council* EAT (2007) 0557/06, however, the EAT held that the reversal of the burden of proof does not apply to claims of victimisation under the Race Relations Act. This is due to the construction of the wording in the Act itself. This decision does not, however, apply to victimisation claims under the other discrimination statutes.

Vicarious Liability

4.518 Employers are liable in law for any act of discrimination or harassment carried out by any of their employees in the course of their employment.

4.519 Employers can only defend themselves against claims of racial discrimination if they can show that they took all reasonably practicable steps to prevent their staff from behaving in a discriminatory way. To protect themselves from liability therefore, employers should:
- devise and implement an equal opportunities policy and an anti-harassment policy, both of which incorporate racial discrimination
- implement a complaints procedure
- provide training to all employees on equality, discrimination and harassment, with additional training for managers and supervisors who hold responsibility for recruitment and employment decisions
- communicate the policies on a regular basis to all staff and take steps to ensure they are fully understood
- effectively monitor compliance.

4.520 Whether or not an employer can defend itself from liability for the discriminatory behaviour of an individual employee, that employee may be held liable for their own actions by an employment tribunal. This tends to happen most often in claims for harassment. This can result in an individual employee being ordered by the tribunal personally to pay compensation to the person whom they harassed.

Harassment by Customers, Suppliers and Other Third Parties

4.521 In *Burton v De Vere Hotels* [1996] IRLR 596, the EAT held that an employer could potentially be held liable for harassment perpetrated on one of its employees by a third party, eg a member of the public. The House of Lords subsequently suggested (in *Pearce v Governing Body of Mayfield Secondary School* [2003] IRLR 512) that this decision may not have been legally correct.

4.522 More recently, in *Gravell v London Borough of Bexley* (2007) EAT 0587/06, the EAT ruled that, given the new freestanding provisions on harassment contained in s.3A of the Race Relations Act, a claimant may well be able to argue successfully that his or her employer should be held liable for harassment perpetrated by a third party. The claimant, Ms Gravell, had complained that her employer applied a policy that staff should ignore racist comments made by members of the public and that having to listen to such comments without being permitted to challenge them created an offensive working environment for her. The EAT overruled the employment tribunal's decision to strike out the case, stating that "there is considerable scope for argument" as to whether the observations of the House of Lords (in *Pearce*) on the *Burton* case hold good in a claim for harassment under the revised statutory provisions. An employer could, the EAT thought, potentially be held liable for the harassment of one of its employees by a third party, as such treatment could, as per the amended wording of the Race Relations Act, create an offensive working environment for that employee.

4.523 Employers should, in any event, never refuse to shield staff from race discrimination (particularly racial harassment) carried out by an outsider. An employer who is indifferent to discriminatory treatment meted out by third parties may, in addition to being liable for such discrimination under the Race Relations Act, also be in breach of the implied duty of trust and confidence, and hence in breach of contract.

4.524 In addition, Acas recommends as best practice that employers should protect their workers from harassment by third parties such as customers and service users.

Compensation

4.525 If an employee, job applicant or former employee succeeds in a claim for unlawful race discrimination at tribunal, the most common outcome is that the employer will be ordered to pay compensation to the claimant. There is no ceiling on the amount of money that may be awarded. During the year 2005, the average total award in successful race discrimination cases was £19,366, while the median figure was £8270 (Source: Equal Opportunities Review No.155).

4.526 Compensation in most cases is made up of loss of earnings (eg where the employee has left their job on account of the discriminatory treatment) and an amount for injury to feelings.

Monitoring

4.527 There is no requirement in law for employers to keep information on how the workforce is made up, other than in the public sector where racial, gender and disability monitoring are statutory requirements.

4.528 It is, nevertheless, good practice for all employers to gather data on the racial backgrounds of their workforce and of job applicants in order to monitor whether any discrimination (particularly indirect discrimination) is occurring.

4.529 Where an employer elects to gather information about employees' ethnic or racial origins, it must bear in mind that such information is classed as "sensitive data" under the Data Protection Act 1998. This means that the data cannot be collected or used unless either the employee has given their free consent, or one of a list of other conditions is satisfied.

4.530 If employers want to gather data on the racial and ethnic backgrounds of

their staff (and job applicants), in order to monitor whether any discrimination (particularly indirect discrimination) is occurring, they must ensure that staff:
- are told why the information is being gathered
- are told how the organisation intends to use the data
- are assured of the confidentiality of the data and that it will be kept securely
- are told that they have no obligation to give the information
- freely give their written consent to the data being collected and used.

Training

4.531 It is important that all staff are given awareness training on the organisation's policy and procedure on equal opportunities and the avoidance of discrimination, so that they fully understand both the employer's and the employee's responsibilities.

4.532 Employers need to ensure that there is equal treatment and equal access to training for all staff irrespective of their ethnic or racial background. The criteria used to determine eligibility for training must be based on objective factors such as individuals' abilities and job duties. The following training should be carried out by all employers:
- training in equality and the avoidance of bias for all line managers or supervisors and any others responsible for recruitment and employment decisions
- awareness training for all staff in the organisation's equal opportunities policy, also covering the need to avoid all forms of harassment and the types of behaviour that could be viewed as racial harassment
- induction training for all new staff to make them aware of the organisation's policies on equality and harassment, and the importance of following them.

4.533 In relation to pay enhancements for skills or training, the criteria used must genuinely reflect an enhanced ability to carry out a particular job.

4.534 If an employer buys in training from an outside provider, it will be necessary to check that the provider has sufficient awareness of the requirements of discrimination legislation.

List of Relevant Legislation

4.535
- Race Relations Act 1976 (Amendment) Regulations 2003
- Data Protection Act 1998
- Asylum and Immigration Act 1996
- Employment Rights Act 1996
- Employment Act 1989
- Race Relations Act 1976
- Fair Employment and Treatment Order (Northern Ireland) 1998

List of Relevant Cases

4.536
- *Azmi v Kirklees Metropolitan Council* [2007] IRLR 484

- *Igen Ltd v Wong* [2005] IRLR 258, CA
- *Madden v Preferred Technical Group Cha Ltd* [2005] IRLR 46, CA
- *Saggar v Ministry of Defence* [2005] IRLR 618, CA
- *Essa v Laing Ltd* [2004] IRLR 313
- *Khan v Trident* [2004] EWCA Civ 624, IRLR 961, TLR 297, CA
- *Rihal v Ealing London Borough Council* [2004] IRLR 642
- *Law Society and others v Bahl* [2003] IRLR 640
- *MacDonald v Advocate General for Scotland and Pearce v Governing Body of Mayfield Secondary School* [2003] IRLR 512
- *Relaxion Group plc v Rhys-Harper; D'Souza v London Borough of Lambeth; Jones v 3M Healthcare Ltd* [2003] IRLR 484, HL
- *Balamoody v UK Central Council for Nursing, Midwifery and Health Visiting* [2002] IRLR 288, CA
- *Commissioners of Inland Revenue v Morgan* [2002] IRLR 776
- *Jaffrey v Department of Environment Transport and Regions* [2002] IRLR 688
- *Yeboah v Crofton* [2002] IRLR 634, CA
- *Anya v University of Oxford* [2001] IRLR 377, CA
- *BBC Scotland v Souster* [2001] IRLR 150, CS
- *Derby Specialist Fabrication Ltd v Burton* [2001] IRLR 69
- *Chief Constable of West Yorkshire Police v Khan* [2001] IRLR 830, HL
- *Weathersfield Ltd v Sargent* [1999] IRLR 94, CA
- *Glasgow City Council v Zafar* [1998] IRLR 36, HL
- *West Midlands Passenger Transport Executive v Singh* [1998] IRLR 186, CA
- *Adekeye v The Post Office (No. 2)* [1997] IRLR 105, CA
- *Sheiky v Argos Distributions Ltd* 12/5/97 (1129/95), EAT
- *Burton v De Vere Hotels* [1996] IRLR 596, EAT
- *Dawkins v Dept of the Environment sub nom Crown Supplies PSA* [1993] IRLR 284, CA
- *Mecca Leisure Group plc v Chatprachong* [1993] IRLR 531
- *King v The Great Britain-China Centre* [1992] IRLR 513, CA
- *British Gas plc v Sharma* [1991] IRLR 101
- *Dhatt v McDonalds Hamburgers Ltd* [1991] IRLR 130, CA
- *Qureshi v London Borough of Newham* [1991] IRLR 264, CA
- *James v Eastleigh Borough Council* [1990] IRLR 288, HL
- *London Borough of Lambeth v Commission for Racial Equality* [1990] IRLR 231, CA
- *Aziz v Trinity Street Taxis Ltd* [1988] IRLR 204, CA
- *Commissioners of Inland Revenue v Morgan* [2002] IRLR 776
- *Mandla v Lee* [1983] IRLR 209, HL
- *Hussein v Saints Complete House Furnishers* [1979] IRLR 337
- *Ahmad v Morse Chain Division of Borg-Warner Ltd* (ET Case No. 25005/78)
- *Atrari v P K Stationery Ltd* (COET 2165/91)
- *Coles and Sodah v Bookwise Ltd* (ET Case No. 4782/89)
- *Deson v BL Cars Ltd* EAT/173/80
- *Isa and Rashid v BL Cars Ltd* COIT 1103/125
- *Nagarajan v London Regional Transport and Swiggs* [1999] IRLR 572, HL
- *R v Birmingham City Council ex parte Equal Opportunities Commission* [1989] IRLR 173, HL

- *Shasta and others v Shareporter Ltd* (Case Nos. 38528-30/H2)
- *Tottenham Green Under Fives' Centre v Marshall (No. 2)* [1991] IRLR 162

Further Information

Publications
- *Code of Practice for All Employers on the Avoidance of Race Discrimination in Recruitment Practice*, available from the Home Office
- *The Stephen Lawrence Inquiry, Macpherson Report (February 1999)*

Organisations
- **Commission for Racial Equality**
  Web: *www.cre.gov.uk*
  The Commission for Racial Equality is a publicly funded, non-governmental body set up under the Race Relations Act 1976 to tackle racial discrimination and promote racial equality. From October 2007 this organisation will be replaced by the Commission for Equality and Human Rights.
- **Equal Opportunities Commission**
  Web: *www.eoc.org.uk*
  An agency working to eliminate sex discrimination and put equality into practice in the workplace. From October 2007 this organisation will be replaced by the Commission for Equality and Human Rights (**Web:** *www.cehr.org.uk*).

Religion or Belief Discrimination

This topic covers the following.
- Religion or Belief — Scope of the Regulations
- Four Forms of Discrimination
- Direct Religious Discrimination
- Indirect Religious Discrimination
- Victimisation
- Religious Harassment
- Religious Discrimination in Recruitment
- Religious Discrimination During Employment
- Selection for Redundancy
- Post-Employment Discrimination
- Claims for Religious Discrimination
- Monitoring

4.537 The Employment Equality (Religion or Belief) Regulations 2003 came into force on 2 December 2003, as part of a package of anti-discrimination measures required by the EU. They prohibit discrimination at work against anyone on the grounds of religion or belief.

4.538 The regulations prohibit four different types of discrimination in recruitment and employment: direct discrimination, indirect discrimination, harassment and victimisation. They also provide for limited post-employment protection and a questionnaire procedure to help claimants explore whether discrimination on the grounds of religion or belief has occurred.

4.539 There is no qualifying period of service necessary to make a complaint to an employment tribunal and no limit on the amount of compensation that can be awarded to a successful claimant.

4.540 Acas has published a guidance paper that gives useful examples of situations in which discrimination may arise.

Employers' Duties

- Employers must not treat any individual member of staff less favourably than another on the basis of religion or belief.
- Employers may only use religion or belief as a criterion in recruitment in very limited circumstances where it is a genuine occupational requirement of the job that it be carried out by someone who subscribes to a specific religion or belief.
- Employers must not commit any act of specific religious discrimination against an individual as there is no defence that justifies direct religious discrimination.
- Employers must not adopt policies, procedures, rules or practices that could put people who subscribe to a particular religion at a disadvantage (known as indirect religious discrimination), unless the policy, procedure, rule or practice is appropriate and necessary in the circumstances. Indirect religious discrimination is unlawful whether it is intentional or unintentional.

- Employers must not victimise staff who have complained that they have suffered religious discrimination nor victimise staff who assist others in making such complaints.
- Employers must not allow harassment on the basis of a worker's religion or belief.
- Employers should take all reasonable steps to prevent discrimination in the workplace, eg by communicating their equal opportunities and anti-harassment policies to all staff on a regular basis, training staff on equal opportunities issues and the avoidance of all forms of discrimination, and monitoring compliance.
- Employers must take care not to commit any of the above forms of discrimination after a person's employment ends, eg by withholding a reference or harassing an ex-employee on grounds related to religion or belief.

Employees' Duties

- Employees have a duty not to discriminate against any of their colleagues on the basis of religion or belief.
- Employees must not victimise any member of staff who has complained that he or she has suffered religious discrimination or helped a colleague to make a complaint of discrimination or harassment.
- Employees must not engage in any behaviour that could be interpreted as harassment on the basis of religion or belief. Neither must they behave in a way that could amount to harassment on the basis of the actual or perceived religion or belief of a colleague or anyone with whom they associate.
- Employees are under a duty to adhere to their employer's equal opportunities and anti-harassment policies and to ensure that they treat their colleagues with respect and dignity at all times.

In Practice

Religion or Belief — Scope of the Regulations

4.541 The Employment Equality (Religion or Belief) Regulations 2003 prohibit discrimination at work on the grounds of "any religion, religious belief or philosophical belief". If discrimination occurs, the individual may bring a complaint to an employment tribunal.

4.542 This is not defined further in the legislation, although it is clear from the wording that the definition is very wide in its scope. In most cases it is likely that it will be clear what is or is not a religion or a belief system.

4.543 Where there is a dispute as to whether a religion or belief is covered by the regulations, the tribunals or courts will have to decide.

4.544 Factors likely to be taken into account are whether there is:
- collective worship
- a clear belief system
- a profound belief system affecting the person's way of life or view of the world.

4.545 Discrimination against people of less well-known faiths or beliefs, eg Paganism and Humanism, are likely, therefore, to be covered.

Religion or Belief Discrimination

4.546 The regulations also specifically cover discrimination on the grounds of an absence of religion or belief.

4.547 Job applicants are also protected throughout the process of recruitment and limited protection against discrimination is also available to former employees.

4.548 If discrimination occurs, the individual may bring a complaint to an employment tribunal.

Employees and Other Types of Workers

4.549 All workers are covered by the Employment Equality (Religion or Belief) Regulations, ie not only those employed directly by the organisation, but also other workers such as:
- contract workers
- agency temps
- casual workers
- freelancers who provide their services personally
- directors
- company secretaries
- non-elected office holders
- partners in firms.

Qualifying Conditions

4.550 There is no length of service required for an employee or worker to bring a claim for unlawful religious discrimination to an employment tribunal. Equally, there is no lower or upper age limit for a claimant to bring a complaint.

4.551 Employees, however, (but not other workers) must first raise a written grievance with their employer and wait 28 days. This is to allow the employer time and opportunity to deal with the complaint before it can proceed to tribunal. If a claim is lodged with the tribunal before the employee has raised a grievance and waited 28 days, the tribunal will in most cases not admit it.

Comparable Person

4.552 In order to found a claim of religious discrimination, an employee will usually have to draw a comparison with someone who adheres to a different religion in similar circumstances.

4.553 If, however, there is no actual comparator, but there is evidence to support an inference of religious discrimination, an employment tribunal will construct a "hypothetical comparator" to assess how someone of another religion would have been treated in the same or similar circumstances.

4.554 Thus the law allows employment tribunals to make assumptions about how an employer would have treated a comparable person who does not have the same religion or belief as the complainant.

Discrimination Outside the Employment Field

4.555 Discrimination can be perpetrated not only by employers but also by:
- trade organisations
- bodies conferring professional and trade qualifications
- training providers
- employment agencies

- further and higher educational institutions.

4.556 The regulations also apply to Crown servants and parliamentary staff.

4.557 As from 30 April 2007, the prohibition on religious discrimination was extended to the provision of goods, facilities and services, premises, and education and the exercise of public functions. This was as a result of the implementation of parts of the Equality Act 2006.

Four Forms of Discrimination

4.558 There are four different forms of discrimination:
- direct discrimination
- indirect discrimination
- victimisation
- harassment.

Direct Religious Discrimination

4.559 Direct discrimination means treating an individual less favourably than someone of a different religion on grounds related to the victim's religion or belief. Acts of direct religious discrimination may include:
- deciding not to employ a particular job applicant on grounds related to his or her religion or belief
- denying someone access to training, transfer or promotion on grounds related to religion or belief
- giving someone less favourable terms and conditions of employment than a comparable employee of a different religion
- denying an individual access to benefits or perks for reasons related to religion or belief
- dismissing an employee because of their religious beliefs or practices.

Indirect Religious Discrimination

4.560 Indirect discrimination occurs when an employer applies any general policy, procedure, rule or practice which:
- puts (or would put) persons of a particular religion or belief at a disadvantage when compared with others
- actually puts an individual to that disadvantage
- cannot be justified as being a proportionate means of achieving a legitimate aim.

Provision, Criterion or Practice

4.561 "Provision, criterion or practice" can be interpreted to mean that indirect discrimination can occur when an organisation has any of the following:
- selection criteria
- policies and procedures
- guidelines
- benefits
- employment rules
- informal practices

Put at a Disadvantage

4.562 In order to prove that indirect discrimination has occurred, it must be shown not only that someone has personally been put at a disadvantage by the application of the provision, criterion or practice, but that the provision, criterion or practice in general puts, or would put, persons of the same religion or belief at a particular disadvantage when compared with other persons.

Identifying a Legitimate Aim

4.563 Indirect religious discrimination can be justified when the employer's policy or practice is a proportionate way of achieving a legitimate business aim. The aim must be related to the needs of the business or the specific job the employee is employed to do and must be unrelated to religion or belief.

The Test of Proportionality

4.564 "Proportionate" in this context means appropriate, necessary and not excessive in relation to the defined aim.

4.565 Examples of how indirect discrimination can occur in a workplace follow.

Dress Codes

4.566 Rules on dress and appearance, eg a policy that prohibits certain forms of clothing, head coverings, hair styles or jewellery, may conflict with the religious customs or requirements of certain religious groups and hence be indirectly discriminatory unless justified, eg on the grounds of health or safety.

4.567 Whether or not an employer applies a set dress code, staff should, within reason, be able to wear clothing consistent with their religion, provided it is practical and safe for them to do so.

4.568 Whenever an employer applies a policy regarding dress, appearance and even rules regarding hair styles, jewellery or tattoos, they should consider adjusting the policy to accommodate the religious beliefs of any employee for whom such customs are relevant or important in respect of his or her religion or belief.

4.569 The EAT has ruled (in *Azmi v Kirklees Metropolitan Council* [2007] IRLR 484 that an instruction to an assistant teacher (a devout Muslim) to remove her full-face veil whilst teaching children in class amounted to indirect religious discrimination against her. The employment tribunal concluded, however, that the instruction to remove the veil was justified (and therefore lawful) as it was underpinned by a legitimate aim — namely to ensure the children received effective, unhindered language instruction — and that it was proportionate in light of that aim. There was evidence that when the teacher wore the veil, this reduced the children's ability to learn language skills from her as her diction was not as clear as it would otherwise have been, and the children's learning was impeded because they could not see her facial expressions. These principles were upheld by the EAT.

Showering and Changing Facilities

4.570 If showering facilities are necessary in the workplace, eg due to health, safety or hygiene, staff should be able to preserve their modesty when undressing or washing, as their religion or belief requires. Insistence upon same-sex communal shower or changing facilities could be indirect religious discrimination or could even be viewed as harassment if an employee felt uncomfortable as a consequence of a requirement to undress and/or wash in front of other people, even those of the same sex.

Prayer Facilities

4.571 There is no requirement for employers to provide either extra time off work or facilities for religious observance in the workplace. Employers should, however, consider whether their policies, rules and procedures indirectly discriminate against staff of particular religions or beliefs and, if so, whether reasonable changes are appropriate.

4.572 If staff ask to be allowed to hold prayer services, the request should be agreed if a quiet place is available and there will be no problems in allowing its use for prayer.

4.573 Staff generally may appreciate a specific area being designated for contemplation or prayer, rather than just a general rest room.

4.574 Acas suggests that employers might also consider providing separate storage facilities for ceremonial objects.

4.575 Employers are not, however, required to incur significant expenditure or make any building alterations to meet their employees' religious needs.

4.576 Where an employer does decide to provide facilities for religious observance, such facilities would have to be provided equally to employees of all faiths. The provision of facilities for employees of only one faith would discriminate directly against employees of other faiths who were not granted the same benefit. The best way forward for an employer who is considering providing such a facility, or who receives a request from staff for a facility, is to consult all staff or their representatives with a view to reaching agreement on provisions that will be satisfactory to all.

Time Off for Religious Festivals, etc

4.577 When staff ask for holiday leave for fast days, to celebrate religious festivals or attend ceremonies, employers should sympathetically consider whether:

- the request is reasonable
- it is practical for the employees concerned to be absent from work at the time requested
- whether they have enough accrued holiday entitlement.

4.578 If there will be difficulties caused by a number of staff making requests for time off at the same time employers should:

- discuss the matter with the employees affected
- discuss it with any recognised trade union
- aim to balance the needs of the business (and remaining staff) with the affected employees
- when agreeing criteria to decide who is granted leave, be careful to avoid indirect discrimination.

4.579 A refusal to grant holiday leave on a day or date that has important religious significance for a particular employee could amount to indirect religious discrimination against that employee, unless the employer could show that it was not possible or practicable for them to grant that employee time off on the particular day or date.

Dietary Issues

4.580 Some religions require extended periods of fasting, so employers should consider how they can support staff during these periods. It will be important, however, not to place unreasonable extra burdens on workers who are not fasting, as that may create either conflict between staff or claims of discrimination by them.

4.581 If staff bring food to work, they may need to store and heat it separately from other food. It is good practice to consult employees on these issues and find a mutually acceptable solution in order to avoid any possible problems.

4.582 Similarly, where an employer provides food in a staff restaurant or canteen, every reasonable effort should be made to offer a variety of different types of food to suit employees with different beliefs.

Sunday Working

4.583 Where religious belief is the reason for an employee wishing to be exempted from Sunday working (or from working on another day of the week, eg Saturdays in the case of Jews), the employer should consider whether:

- Sunday working is necessary in the particular circumstances of the case
- it is proportionate to apply the requirement to work on Sundays to the particular individual.

4.584 Refusal to adjust an employee's working pattern in light of religious needs may amount to indirect religious discrimination if the employer cannot show adequate justification.

4.585 As a separate measure, a provision in the Employment Rights Act 1996 allows those working in retail establishments or betting shops to opt out of Sunday working, by giving three months' notice that they intend to stop Sunday working. This right does not apply to those who are engaged specifically to work only on Sundays.

4.586 These provisions have nothing to do with employees' religious beliefs, but rather give all staff who work in shops or betting shops the right to opt out of Sunday working without the need to provide a reason.

Victimisation

4.587 Employers and employees should not discriminate against any member of staff because that person has raised a genuine complaint of religious discrimination or harassment, whether under the employer's grievance procedure or before an employment tribunal. Any employee who supports or assists another employee to raise a complaint is also protected against victimisation.

4.588 Claimants lose their protection if their allegations or the evidence or information they have given were false and not made or given in good faith.

Examples of Victimisation

4.589 As common examples of victimisation, Acas cites an employee being isolated by their colleagues, labelled a "trouble maker" or denied access to promotion or training because he or she has raised a complaint of discrimination or helped another employee to bring a complaint. Employers are under a duty to take reasonable steps to prevent this happening.

Religious Harassment

4.590 Harassment on the grounds of religion or belief occurs when an individual behaves in a way which:
- is related to the actual or perceived religion or belief of any person
- is unwanted from the perspective of the person on the receiving end, and
- has either the purpose or effect of violating a person's dignity, or
- creates an intimidating, hostile, degrading, humiliating or offensive environment for the person on the receiving end.

4.591 The most important criterion in establishing whether particular behaviour amounts to harassment is the perception of the person on the receiving end of the particular behaviour.

4.592 A further clause in the regulations provides that behaviour will constitute harassment if, with regard to all of the circumstances — including the victim's perception — it should reasonably be seen as violating the victim's dignity or as creating an atmosphere which is intimidating, hostile, degrading, humiliating or offensive to him or her.

4.593 In practice this means that a spurious claim that someone's behaviour amounted to harassment in circumstances where no reasonable person could possibly have viewed it as harassment in the context in which it occurred, would not succeed.

4.594 Any employer who receives a complaint of harassment should take it very seriously, investigate the circumstances thoroughly and, if the complaint is well founded, take steps to put a stop to the behaviour that is causing offence. It will also be appropriate in most circumstances to take disciplinary action against the harasser.

Examples of Religious Harassment

4.595 Examples of harassment include:
- behaviour linked to religion that is offensive, demeaning, frightening or in any way distressing
- intentional bullying on grounds of religion or belief
- behaviour that has no malicious intent but which is upsetting to someone on grounds of his or her religion or belief
- subtle and insidious behaviour that may involve nicknames, teasing or name-calling linked to religion or belief.

4.596 This behaviour does not need to be specifically targeted at the individual. A general culture that permits banter and teasing may create an uncomfortable working environment for some employees on account of their religious beliefs, and thus give rise to claims of harassment.

Religious Discrimination in Recruitment

4.597 Job applicants are protected throughout the entire process of recruitment against any form of discrimination related to their religion or belief. For example, if an applicant who was otherwise suitable for the job under review was refused employment because his or her religion required him/her not to work on a particular day of the week, this would constitute indirect religious discrimination and would be unlawful unless the employer could show that the requirement for the person to work on the particular day or shift was relevant and necessary for the effective performance of the job.

Genuine Occupational Requirements (GORs)

4.598 In a limited number of cases, it may be possible for an employer to recruit or promote someone on the basis that it is a requirement of the particular job that they subscribe to a specific religion or belief. For this to be lawful, it must be necessary (and not just a preference) for the effective performance of the job in question that the person recruited adheres to the religion in question.

4.599 To be a genuine requirement of a job, the individual's religion or belief must be specifically necessary and not just one of many relevant factors related to the job.

4.600 Additionally, where an organisation is one that has an ethos based on religion or belief, it may be able to specify that it is an absolute requirement of the job that the successful applicant adheres to the organisation's ethos. In this case, the employer need only show that the requirement is genuine, and not that is necessary for the performance of the particular job.

4.601 In all cases, however, the employer must show that it is proportionate to apply the requirement in the particular case.

4.602 Any employee or job applicant can challenge the requirement and the burden of proving that the requirement is genuine and necessary falls on the employer.

4.603 In *Glasgow City Council v McNab* EATS/0037/06, the EAT held that the religious GOR did not apply in respect of the post of acting principal teacher of pastoral care in a Roman Catholic school maintained by the council. The responsibilities of the post were such that the teachings and doctrines of the RC Church would only be relevant occasionally. Furthermore, the specific GOR did not apply either as an education authority does not have a religious ethos.

4.604 It is unlikely that there will be many situations in which tribunals and courts accept that there is a genuine occupational requirement. The rule operates as an exception to the principle of equal treatment.

4.605 For example, a faith-based care home may be able to show that belonging to a particular religion is a genuine requirement for its carers, because they are required to carry out their duties in a way that fulfils both the physical and spiritual needs of its residents. Applying the same requirement to other staff, such as receptionists, who are not needed to give spiritual support to patients, would not be likely to be accepted as necessary by an employment tribunal.

4.606 Furthermore, a genuine occupational requirement will not apply if:
- the employer already has enough staff who adhere to the specified religion and can carry out the duties required by the job, and
- it is reasonable to allocate the duties to these other staff without undue inconvenience.

4.607 On each occasion, before an employer uses a genuine occupational requirement, he or she should review whether the requirement is still valid.

Positive Action

4.608 Although positive discrimination, ie discrimination in favour of a person from a minority religious group, is not permitted under UK employment law, the regulations do permit certain forms of positive action in recruitment and training. Positive action is not required in law, but is permitted if the reason for it is to increase the number of people from a particular religious group that has historically been disadvantaged within employment for reasons linked to religion or belief.

4.609 It is thus lawful for employers to apply measures specifically to encourage candidates from a disadvantaged group to apply for employment or promotion, or to offer training that would help fit them for particular work. Examples could include placing job advertisements in a particular publication that is read predominantly by people of a particular religion. However, it is only encouragement that is permitted — at the point of selection for employment or promotion, the principles of equality must be applied and an individual candidate's religion or belief must play no part in the decision-making process (unless a genuine occupational requirement applies). An example of positive action in relation to training could be to offer training to Muslim employees specifically in order to enable more Muslims to gain promotion into management.

Recruitment Best Practice Checklist

4.610 Employers should take note of the following best practice guidelines to prevent religious discrimination in the recruitment process.

- Do not advertise for a person of a particular religion, unless a job is one in which a genuine occupational requirement applies.
- Avoid recruiting only by word of mouth only as this practice may tend to reinforce a religious imbalance in the workforce and may be indirectly discriminatory.
- Be aware that insisting that someone works on Sundays (or another day of the week which represents their Sabbath) is potentially indirectly discriminatory on grounds of religion and, if challenged, would have to be justified.
- Incorporate clear, objective and specific criteria against which applicants (for jobs, transfers and promotions) can be assessed. This should help to eliminate religious bias, whether deliberate or subconscious.
- Ensure that reception and personnel staff are instructed not to treat applicants who wear clothes or other items associated with religion less favourably than others.
- Be aware of the possible misunderstandings that can occur in interviews between persons of different religious and cultural backgrounds.
- Ensure that all staff involved in recruitment or selection have received effective equal opportunities training.
- Give guidance to recruiters on the effects which generalised assumptions and prejudices about religion and belief can have on selection decisions.
- Use more than one person to carry out shortlisting and interviewing — this may help to prevent any one individual's prejudices affecting the selection decision.
- Keep notes on recruitment decisions in order to be able to demonstrate that the reason for the rejection of one candidate and the appointment of another was free from religious bias.

Religious Discrimination During Employment

4.611 Employees are protected against all forms of religious discrimination in every aspect of their employment. This will include the terms and conditions of their contract, access to promotion, transfer and training and general treatment at work.

Terms and Conditions of Employment

4.612 It is unlawful to treat an employee less favourably than another as regards the terms and conditions of their contracts if the reason for the different treatment is related to religion or belief.

Promotion, Transfer and Training

4.613 If an employee's access to opportunities for promotion, transfer or training is restricted for any reason related to his or her religion or belief, this would amount to direct religious discrimination unless a genuine occupational requirement applied. The same sort of considerations would apply as shown in recruitment.

Selection for Redundancy

4.614 The criteria used to make selections for redundancy should be checked carefully to guard against the possibility of indirect religious discrimination. In addition, if a group of employees under threat of redundancy is predominantly of one religion, the employer would be advised to review the selection criteria in order to guard against any effect which could be disproportionate.

Post-Employment Discrimination

4.615 A claim for religious discrimination can be made against a former employer irrespective of how much time has passed since the employee's employment ended. Such a claim can only succeed, however, where the individual can show that the discrimination or harassment arose out of, or was closely connected with, the previous employment relationship.

4.616 This principle also applies to employment and other working relationships that ended before the regulations came into force on 2 December 2003.

Claims for Religious Discrimination

4.617 In the event of a claim for religious discrimination, the employer must be able to show a non-discriminatory reason for their actions, otherwise the employment tribunal may draw adverse inferences. A tribunal is bound to uphold the complaint if the employer cannot come up with an adequate or credible explanation for their conduct.

The Questionnaire Procedure

4.618 An employee or job applicant who believes that he or she may have experienced any form of religious discrimination (including discrimination after their employment ended) may serve a special questionnaire on the employer, asking for an explanation for the conduct that they think was discriminatory. The individual may instigate the procedure either before or after he or she has commenced tribunal proceedings.

4.619 A pre-printed questionnaire is available, but the employee may add his or her own questions.

4.620 The employer is not under any statutory duty to respond to a questionnaire served upon them. The questions and replies are, however, admissible as evidence in tribunal cases. If the employer fails to respond to the questionnaire within eight weeks, or if the answers given are evasive or equivocal, the tribunal or court may infer that the employer did discriminate and the employer is trying to avoid admitting it. It is therefore advisable for employers to answer the employee's questions as fully as possible.

4.621 In order to be used in tribunal cases, the questionnaire must (in cases where an application to tribunal has not yet been presented) be given or sent to the employer within three months of the act that is being complained about, or (where a complaint has already been presented to the tribunal) within 21 days of the date on which the complaint was lodged.

The Burden of Proof

4.622 Once an employee has established facts before an employment tribunal that indicate that he or she may have been the victim of unlawful religious discrimination, the burden of proof shifts to the employer who must (if they are to succeed in defending the claim) persuade the tribunal that there was some other non-discriminatory reason for their actions.

Vicarious Liability

4.623 Employers are liable in law for any act of discrimination or harassment carried out by any of their employees in the course of their employment.

4.624 Employers can only defend themselves against claims of religious discrimination if they can show that they took all reasonably practicable steps to prevent their staff from behaving in a discriminatory way. To protect themselves from liability therefore, employers should:
- devise and implement an equal opportunities and anti-harassment policy both of which incorporate religious discrimination
- implement a complaints procedure
- provide training to all employees on equality, discrimination and harassment, with additional training to managers and supervisors who hold responsibility for recruitment and employment decisions
- communicate the policies on a regular basis to all staff and take steps to ensure they are fully understood
- effectively monitor compliance.

4.625 Whether or not an employer can defend itself from liability for the discriminatory behaviour of an individual employee, that employee may be held liable for their own actions by an employment tribunal. This tends to happen most often in claims for harassment. This can result in an individual employee being ordered by the tribunal personally to pay compensation to the person whom they harassed.

Harassment by Customers, Suppliers and Other Third Parties

4.626 In *Burton v De Vere Hotels* [1996] IRLR 596, the EAT held that an employer could potentially be held liable for harassment perpetrated on one of its employees by a third party, eg a member of the public. The House of Lords subsequently suggested (in *Pearce v Governing Body of Mayfield Secondary School* [2003] IRLR 512) that this decision may not have been legally correct.

4.627 More recently, in *Gravell v London Borough of Bexley* [2007] EAT 0587/0 (a race case), the EAT ruled that, given the new freestanding provisions on harassment contained in the legislation, a claimant may well be able successfully to argue that his or her employer should be held liable for harassment perpetrated by a third party. The claimant, Ms Gravell, had complained that her employer applied a policy that staff should ignore racist comments made by members of the public and that having to listen to such comments without being permitted to challenge them created an offensive working environment for her. The EAT overruled the employment tribunal's decision to strike out the case, stating that "there is considerable scope for argument" as to whether the observations of the House of Lords (in *Pearce*) on the *Burton* case hold good in a claim for harassment under the revised statutory provisions. An employer could, the EAT thought, potentially be held liable for the harassment of one of its employees by a third party, as such treatment could, as per the amended wording of the statutes, create an offensive working environment for that employee. Although this was a race case, the Employment Equality (Religion or Belief)

Regulations 2003 contain parallel wording on harassment and so the decision would apply in the same way to a claim for harassment on grounds of religion or belief.

4.628 Employers should, in any event, never refuse to shield staff from discrimination (particularly harassment) carried out by an outsider because they disapprove of the individual's religion or belief. An employer who is indifferent to discriminatory treatment meted out by third parties may, in addition to being liable for such discrimination under the Employment Equality (Religion or Belief) Regulations 2003, also be in breach of the implied duty of trust and confidence, and hence in breach of contract.

4.629 In addition, Acas recommends as best practice that employers should protect their workers from harassment by third parties such as customers and service users.

Compensation

4.630 If an employee, job applicant or former employee succeeds in a claim for unlawful religious discrimination at tribunal, the most common outcome is that the employer will be ordered to pay compensation to the claimant. There is no ceiling on the amount of money that may be awarded. During the year 2005, the average total award in successful religious discrimination cases was £5186, while the median figure was £6010 (Source: Equal Opportunities Review No.155).

4.631 Compensation in most cases is made up of loss of earnings (eg where the employee has left their job on account of the discriminatory treatment) and an amount for injury to feelings.

Monitoring

4.632 There is no requirement in law for employers to keep information on how the workforce is made up, other than in the public sector where racial, gender and disability (but not religious) monitoring are statutory requirements.

4.633 Where an employer elects to gather information about employees' religious beliefs, it must bear in mind that such information is classed as "sensitive data" under the Data Protection Act 1998. This means that the data cannot be collected or used unless either the employee has given their free consent, or one of a list of other conditions is satisfied.

4.634 If employers want to gather data on religion or belief, in order to monitor whether any discrimination (particularly indirect discrimination) is occurring, they must ensure that staff:
- are told why the information is being gathered
- are told how the organisation intends to use the data
- are assured of the confidentiality of the data and that it will be kept securely
- are told that they have no obligation to give the information
- freely give their written consent to the data being collected and used.

Training

4.635 It is important that all staff are given awareness training on the organisation's policy and procedure on equal opportunities and the avoidance of discrimination, so that they fully understand both the employer's and the employee's responsibilities.

4.636 Employers need to ensure that there is equal treatment and equal access to training for all staff irrespective of their religion, belief or religious practices. The criteria used to determine eligibility for training must be based on objective factors such as individuals' abilities and job duties. The following training should be carried out by all employers.

- Training in equality and the avoidance of bias for all line managers or supervisors and any others responsible for recruitment and employment decisions.
- Awareness training for all staff in the organisation's equal opportunities policy, also covering the need to avoid all forms of harassment and the types of behaviour that could be viewed as religious harassment.
- Induction training for all new staff to make them aware of the organisation's policies on equality and harassment, and the importance of following them.

4.637 Training should be flexible as regards:
- timing — so as not to disadvantage employees who, for religious reasons, cannot work on a particular day of the week
- duration of individual sessions and regular breaks, eg to accommodate the needs of an employee who adheres to a particular religion to pray at regular intervals.

4.638 In relation to pay enhancements for skills or training, the criteria used must genuinely reflect an enhanced ability to carry out a particular job.

4.639 If an employer buys in training from an outside provider, it will be necessary to check that the provider has sufficient awareness of the requirements of discrimination legislation.

List of Relevant Legislation

4.640
- Employment Equality (Religion or Belief) Regulations 2003
- Data Protection Act 1998
- EC Council Directive 2000/78/EC

List of Relevant Cases

4.641
- *Azmi v Kirklees Metropolitan Council* [2007] IRLR 484
- *Glasgow City Council v McNab* EATS/0037/06
- *Copsey v WWB Devon Clays Ltd* [2005] IRLR 811, CA
- *Williams-Drabble v Pathway Care Solutions Ltd* [2005] Case No 2601718/04

Further Information

Publications
- EEL01 *Acas Religion or Belief and the Workplace — A Guide for Employers and Employees* (November 2003)

Organisations

- **Advisory Conciliation and Arbitration Service (Acas)**
  Web: *www.acas.org.uk*
  Acas aims to improve organisations and working life through better employment relations. It provides up-to-date information, advice, high-quality training, and works with employers and employees to solve problems and improve performance.

Sex Discrimination

This topic covers the following.
- Scope of the Sex Discrimination Act
- The Four Forms of Discrimination
- Sex Discrimination in Recruitment
- Sex Discrimination During Employment
- Marital Status Discrimination
- Civil Partnership Status
- Gender Reassignment Discrimination
- Retirement Ages
- Selection for Redundancy
- Post-Employment Discrimination
- Claims of Sex Discrimination
- Monitoring

4.642 The Sex Discrimination Act 1975 (SDA) contains provisions to prevent discrimination against men, women, trans-gender people, married persons and civil partners in recruitment and employment as well as in education, housing and the provision of goods, facilities and services. The Act prohibits four different types of discrimination: direct discrimination, indirect discrimination, harassment and victimisation. It also provides for limited post-employment protection and a questionnaire procedure to help claimants explore whether sex discrimination has occurred.

4.643 There is no qualifying period of service necessary to make a complaint to an employment tribunal and no limit on the amount of compensation that can be awarded to a successful claimant.

Employers' Duties

- Employers must not treat a woman less favourably than a man on the basis of gender.
- Employers may only use gender as a criterion in recruitment in very limited circumstances where it is a genuine occupational qualification for the job.
- Employers must not commit any act of specific sex discrimination against an individual as there is no defence that justifies direct sex discrimination.
- Employers must not adopt policies, procedures, rules or practices that could put either women or men at a disadvantage (known as indirect sex discrimination), unless the policy, procedure, rule or practice is justifiable in the circumstances.
- Employers must not victimise staff who have complained that they have suffered sex discrimination nor victimise staff who assist others in making such complaints.
- Employers must not allow sexual harassment.
- Employers should take all reasonable steps to prevent discrimination in the workplace, eg by communicating their equal opportunities and anti-harassment policies to all staff on a regular basis, training staff on equal opportunities issues and the avoidance of all forms of discrimination, and monitoring compliance.
- Employers must take care not to commit any type of sex discrimination after a person's employment ends, eg by withholding a reference.

Employees' Duties

4.644 All employees have a duty to:
- make sure they do not discriminate (whether deliberately or inadvertently) against colleagues on grounds of gender
- ensure they do not victimise a member of staff because he or she has complained of sex discrimination or helped a colleague to make a complaint of discrimination or harassment
- make sure they do not engage in any behaviour that could be interpreted as sexual harassment
- adhere to their employer's equal opportunities and anti-harassment policies and ensure that they treat their colleagues with respect and dignity at all times.

In Practice

Scope of the Sex Discrimination Act

4.645 The Sex Discrimination Act 1975 prohibits discrimination on the grounds of gender, trans-gender status, marital status, civil partnership status, pregnancy and maternity leave. If discrimination occurs on any of these grounds, the individual may bring a complaint to an employment tribunal.

4.646 The Sex Discrimination Act 1975 (SDA) applies equally to men and women, whether full time or part time.

4.647 Job applicants are also protected throughout the process of recruitment and limited protection against discrimination is also available to former employees.

Employees and Other Types of Workers

4.648 All workers are covered by the legislation, ie not only those employed directly by the organisation, but also other workers such as:
- contract workers
- agency temps
- casual workers
- freelancers who provide their services personally
- directors
- company secretaries
- non-elected office holders
- partners in firms.

Qualifying Conditions

4.649 There is no length of service required for an employee or worker to bring a claim for unlawful sex discrimination to an employment tribunal. Equally, there is no lower or upper age limit for a claimant to bring a complaint.

4.650 Employees, however (but not other workers) must first raise a written grievance with their employer and wait 28 days. This is to allow the employer time and

Sex Discrimination

opportunity to deal with the complaint before it can proceed to tribunal. If a claim is lodged with the tribunal before the employee has raised a grievance and waited 28 days, the tribunal will in most cases not admit it.

Comparable Person

4.651 In order to found a claim of sex discrimination, an employee will usually have to draw a comparison with someone of the opposite sex in similar circumstances.

4.652 If, however, there is no actual comparator, but there is evidence to support an inference of sex discrimination, an employment tribunal will construct a "hypothetical comparator" to assess how someone of the opposite sex would have been treated in the same or similar circumstances.

4.653 Thus, the law allows tribunals to make assumptions about how an employer would have treated a comparable person of the opposite sex.

4.654 In cases of pregnancy or maternity leave discrimination, since there cannot logically be a male comparator, the tribunal will simply review whether the claimant was treated unfavourably on the grounds of her pregnancy or because she exercised, or sought to exercise, her right to take maternity leave. If this is found to be the case, the tribunal will rule that the treatment amounted to unlawful sex discrimination.

The Four Forms of Discrimination

4.655 There are four different forms of discrimination:
- direct discrimination
- indirect discrimination
- victimisation
- harassment.

Direct Sex Discrimination

4.656 Direct sex discrimination is where an employer treats a woman less favourably on grounds of sex than it treats a man, or vice versa.

4.657 Acts of direct sex discrimination could include:
- deciding not to employ a suitable job applicant on grounds that someone of the opposite sex would be preferred
- deciding not to employ a suitable job applicant on grounds that she is pregnant or on grounds that her impending maternity leave will cause inconvenience for the employer
- denying a woman (or a man) access to training, transfer or promotion on grounds of gender
- giving a woman or a man less favourable terms and conditions of employment than would be granted to someone of the opposite sex
- dismissing an employee for reasons related to sex, gender or pregnancy.

Indirect Sex Discrimination

4.658 Indirect sex discrimination occurs where a provision, criterion or practice puts, or would put, women at a disadvantage when compared to men (or vice versa) and where the employer cannot show that the provision, criterion or practice was "proportionate to the achievement of a legitimate aim".

Sex Discrimination

Provision, Criterion or Practice

4.659 "Provision, criterion or practice" can be interpreted to mean that indirect sex discrimination can occur when an organisation has:
- selection criteria
- policies and procedures
- guidelines
- benefits
- employment rules
- informal practices

that are applied to all employees (or job applicants), but that could have a disproportionate adverse impact on either men or women. Informal practices will be covered as well as contractual policies and rules. In order to make out a claim for indirect sex discrimination, the employee must also show that he or she personally suffered a disadvantage as a result of the application of the particular provision, criterion or practice.

Justification

4.660 Where an employer applies a provision, criterion or practice that is indirectly discriminatory against women (or men), it may nevertheless seek to justify the application of the provision in question by showing that it was designed to achieve a genuine business aim. This means that if the employer can demonstrate that the particular provision, criterion or practice is appropriate and necessary for the effective performance of the job, then it will not be unlawful.

Dress Codes

4.661 Rules on dress and appearance, eg a policy that prohibits certain forms of clothing, hair styles or jewellery, may be discriminatory against either women or men, unless justified. For example it would be discriminatory to refuse to permit women to wear smart trousers to work.

4.662 The law does not, however, require rules on dress or appearance to be identical for men and women as this would in any event be likely to create bizarre results. Employers should, however, ensure that any rules on dress or appearance are applied only for proper business reasons, eg:
- health or safety
- hygiene, eg in jobs that involve food handling
- smartness, in the case of staff meeting the employer's customers or members of the public.

4.663 The employer should also ensure that any dress code:
- applies equal standards to both men and women, ie is not more restrictive for one gender than the other
- is enforced to the same degree for both men and women.

Victimisation

4.664 Employers and employees should not discriminate against any member of staff because that person has raised a genuine complaint of sex discrimination or harassment, whether under the employer's grievance procedure or before an employment tribunal. Any employee who supports or assists another employee to raise a complaint is also protected against victimisation.

4.665 Claimants lose their protection if their allegations or the evidence or information they have given were false and not made or given in good faith.

Examples of Victimisation

4.666   As common examples of victimisation, Acas cites an employee being isolated by their colleagues, labelled a "trouble maker" or denied access to promotion or training because he or she has raised a complaint of discrimination or helped another employee to bring a complaint. Employers are under a duty to take reasonable steps to prevent this happening.

4.667   In *St Helens Borough Council v Derbyshire and ors* [2007] IRLR 540, the House of Lords held that the content of letters sent to employees involved in equal pay claims amounted to victimisation under the Sex Discrimination Act 1975. The Council had written two letters — one to the 39 claimants who had not settled their claims saying that the council would be unable to afford any immediate pay increases; and a second letter, sent to all the catering staff, informing them of the likely consequences if the outstanding claims were successful, ie possible cut backs and redundancies. The House of Lords upheld the employment tribunal's decision that the letters went further than just stating the facts, ie the possible financial and employment consequences of the outstanding claims succeeding; they put undue pressure on the claimants to settle and had an intimidating effect on them. In writing the second letter to all the catering staff (and not just to the claimants or their representatives), the council had gone further than was reasonable to defend its interests and in so doing had caused the claimants a detriment.

Harassment

4.668   Harassment is defined in the Sex Discrimination Act as a discrete form of unlawful discrimination. The most important criterion in establishing whether particular behaviour amounts to harassment is the perception of the person on the receiving end of the particular behaviour, and whether he or she finds it offensive. The principles inherent in harassment apply equally to men and women.

4.669   Employers should include information on sex-based and sexual harassment in an equal opportunities policy or a dignity at work policy.

4.670   The amendments to the Sex Discrimination Act 1975, which came into force on 1 October 2005 under the Employment Equality (Sex Discrimination) Regulations 2005, introduced two definitions of harassment that incorporate both sex-based harassment and sexual harassment.

4.671   "Sex-based harassment" occurs where, on the grounds of gender, a woman is subjected to "unwanted conduct that has the purpose or effect of violating her dignity, or of creating an intimidating, hostile, degrading, humiliating or offensive environment for her". Sex-based harassment is thus gender-based, ie it is unwanted and offensive conduct that occurs for reasons related to the fact that the employee is a woman (or a man, as the case may be).

4.672   "Sexual harassment" occurs where someone "engages in any form of unwanted verbal, non-verbal or physical conduct of a sexual nature that has the purpose or effect of violating her dignity or of creating an intimidating, hostile, degrading, humiliating or offensive environment for her". This type of harassment has for many years been consistently ruled by courts and tribunals to constitute a form of direct sex discrimination.

4.673   A further clause in the legislation provides that behaviour will constitute sex-based or sexual harassment if, with regard to all of the circumstances (including the victim's perception), it should reasonably be seen as violating the victim's dignity or as creating an atmosphere which is intimidating, hostile, degrading, humiliating or offensive to that person.

4.674   In practice this is likely to mean that a spurious claim that someone's

Sex Discrimination

behaviour amounted to harassment in circumstances where no reasonable person could possibly have viewed it as harassment in the context in which it occurred, would not succeed.

Examples of Sexual Harassment and Sex-Based Harassment

4.675 Sexual harassment may include:
- unwelcome advances
- requests for sexual favours
- physical conduct of a sexual nature
- jokes, banter and remarks that are sexual in nature
- displaying inappropriate material, eg calendars containing naked or partially naked women or men
- inappropriate use of a computer, eg sending sexually explicit emails or attachments or displaying sexually explicit material on computer screens
- leering at someone in a sexual way.

4.676 Sex-based harassment may include:
- demeaning jokes or remarks about women (or men)
- playing pranks on a woman where she is the only female in a predominantly male environment (similarly, unwelcome pranks played on a man working in a predominantly female environment)
- deliberately placing items on high shelves out of the reach of a woman.

4.677 The behaviour does not need to be specifically targeted at an individual in order for him or her to be offended, or raise a complaint. A general culture that permits the telling of sexist jokes or sexual banter or teasing may create an uncomfortable working environment for women in particular and thus give rise to claims for sexual or sex-based harassment.

4.678 Any employer that receives a complaint of harassment should take it very seriously, investigate the circumstances thoroughly and, if the complaint is well founded, take steps to put a stop to the behaviour that is causing offence. It will also be appropriate in most circumstances to take disciplinary action against the harasser.

Sex Discrimination in Recruitment

4.679 Job applicants are protected throughout the entire process of recruitment against any form of sex discrimination.

4.680 For example, if a female applicant who was otherwise suitable for the job under review was refused employment because she was unable to work long or unsocial hours, this would constitute indirect sex discrimination and would be unlawful unless the employer could show that the requirement for the person to work the particular hours of shift pattern was necessary for the effective performance of the job. This is because courts and tribunals have consistently held over the years that fewer women than men are able to work long or unsocial hours due to the fact that more women than men have the primary responsibility for childcare. Any requirement for a woman with children to work such hours is therefore likely to place the woman at a disadvantage and be discriminatory, unless it can be justified on objective business grounds.

Genuine Occupational Qualifications

4.681 The SDA provides that it is not unlawful for an employer to insist on recruiting either a man or a woman in circumstances where gender is a genuine occupational qualification (GOQ) for the job in question, ie if the:

- essential nature of a job calls for a man or a woman for reasons of physiology, excluding physical strength or stamina
- job calls for a man or a woman for reasons of authenticity, such as in dramatic performances or other entertainment
- job needs to be held by a man or woman to preserve decency or privacy
- job is one of two to be held by a married couple
- job needs to be held by a man because it involves the performance of duties in a country whose laws or customs are such that the duties could not be performed by a woman
- holder of the job must live in premises normally lived in by men (or women) un-equipped with separate sleeping or sanitary facilities for members of the opposite sex
- job is in a single-sex establishment such as a care home, prison or hospital where the residents require special care, supervision or attention
- job involves the provision of personal services promoting the welfare or education of men or women and those services can most effectively be provided by either a man or a woman
- job involves working in a private home and objection might reasonably be taken to either a woman or a man because there is likely to be a degree of physical or social contact with the person living in the home, or exposure to intimate details of his or her life.

4.682 A genuine occupational qualification will not, however, apply if:
- the employer already has enough men or women (as the case may be) who can carry out the duties required by the job, and
- it is reasonable to allocate the duties to these other staff without undue inconvenience.

4.683 On each occasion, before an employer applies a genuine occupational qualification, it should review whether the requirement is still valid.

Positive Action

4.684 Although positive discrimination, eg discrimination in favour of women is not permitted under UK employment law, the Sex Discrimination Act 1975 does permit certain forms of positive action in recruitment and training. Positive action is not required in law, but is permitted if the reason for it is to increase the number of women (or men, as the case may be) in employment where women (or men) are under-represented. Under-representation occurs where in the 12 months prior to the action being taken, there were no, or a comparatively small number of, people of the particular gender doing the work in question.

4.685 It may thus be lawful for employers to apply measures specifically to encourage candidates from the minority gender to apply for employment or promotion, or to offer training only to women to help fit them for particular work. An example could be placing job advertisements in a particular publication that is read predominantly by women. However, it is only encouragement that is permitted — at the point of selection for employment or promotion, the principles of equality must be applied and gender must play no part in the decision-making process (unless a genuine occupational qualification applies). An example of positive action in relation to training could be to offer training to female employees specifically in order to enable more women to gain promotion into management.

Sex Discrimination

Advertisements

4.686 Unless a job falls within the category of a genuine occupational qualification, it is unlawful to advertise for either a man or a woman, or to indicate a preference for a man or woman.

4.687 The word "advertisement" includes any notices posted on notice boards or sent to staff, such as internal memos about a vacancy.

4.688 The publisher of the advertisement is potentially liable as well as the author.

4.689 If an advertisement indicates an intention to discriminate, the Equal Opportunities Commission (or Commission for Equality and Human Rights after 1 October 2007) may initiate a tribunal case against the person responsible. Employment agencies are also subject to the prohibition on advertising jobs that require either a man or a woman.

Recruitment Best Practice Checklist

4.690 Employers should take note of the following best practice guidelines to prevent sex discrimination in the recruitment process.
- Do not advertise for a person of a particular sex, unless a job is one in which a genuine occupational qualification applies.
- Avoid recruiting by word of mouth only as this practice may tend to reinforce a gender imbalance in the workforce and may be indirectly discriminatory.
- Incorporate clear, objective and specific criteria against which applicants (for jobs, transfers and promotions) can be assessed. This should help to eliminate gender bias, whether deliberate or subconscious.
- Do not refuse to employ a woman because she is pregnant or because she will require a period of maternity leave.
- Be aware that insisting that someone works full time is potentially indirectly discriminatory against women since more women than men have the responsibility for looking after children and are unable to take on full-time employment.
- Do not ask female job applicants questions at interview about their family commitments, as such questions are likely to be viewed as discriminatory.
- Ensure that all staff involved in recruitment or selection have received effective equal opportunities training.
- Give guidance to recruiters on the effects that generalised assumptions and prejudices about gender and employment can have on selection decisions.
- Use more than one person to carry out shortlisting and interviewing — this may help to prevent any one individual's prejudices affecting the selection decision.
- Keep notes on recruitment decisions in order to be able to demonstrate that the reason for the rejection of one candidate and the appointment of another was free from gender bias.

Sex Discrimination During Employment

4.691 Employees are protected against all forms of sex discrimination in every aspect of their employment. This will include the terms and conditions of their contract, access to promotion, transfer and training and general treatment at work.

Terms and Conditions of Employment

4.692 It is unlawful to treat a man more favourably than a woman, or a woman more favourably than a man, as regards the terms and conditions of their contracts.

4.693 In relation to pay, the employer must not pay a lower rate of pay to a woman

Sex Discrimination

where she is performing the same or similar work, or work of equal value to that of man for reasons related directly or indirectly to gender. If a woman is paid less than a man who is performing equal work and there is no "genuine material factor" justifying the difference, there will be a breach of the Equal Pay Act 1970. This does not preclude an employer from paying different employees different rates of pay in a general sense, but rather means that any differences must not be related to gender.

Promotion, Transfer and Training

4.694 If access to opportunities for promotion, transfer or training is restricted in any way that disadvantages women, this would amount to direct sex discrimination. The same sort of considerations would apply as shown in recruitment above.

4.695 Direct sex discrimination can occur if employers make presumptions about the mobility of a female applicant or employee based on her family commitments; and as a result subject the woman to a detriment, eg a failure to consider her for promotion.

Part-time Work

4.696 Although there is no positive duty on employers to agree to permit an employee or job applicant to work part time (as opposed to full time), any failure to agree to part-time or job-share work may be unlawful indirect sex discrimination against a female applicant unless the employer can justify the need for the job to be done full time by one person. This is because courts and tribunals have held that fewer women than men are able to work full time due to the fact that more women than men have the primary responsibility for childcare.

Pregnancy Rights and Discrimination

4.697 Pregnant employees enjoy special statutory rights from the beginning of their pregnancy through to the end of their maternity leave.

4.698 If a woman is treated unfavourably because she is pregnant or because she has indicated an intention to take, is taking, or has taken maternity leave, or for any reason linked to pregnancy or maternity leave, this will be unlawful under the Employment Equality (Sex Discrimination) Regulations 2005. There is no defence for this type of discrimination, no matter how much inconvenience may be caused to the employer as a result of the employee's pregnancy or absence on maternity leave.

Marital Status Discrimination

4.699 The Sex Discrimination Act 1975 prohibits discrimination on grounds of married status, although, curiously, does not offer the same protection to single people. Any unfavourable treatment of an employee or job applicant on the grounds that he or she is married will therefore be unlawful.

Civil Partnership Status

4.700 The Sex Discrimination Act also protects civil partners from unlawful discrimination on the grounds of their civil partnership status. This is because the Civil Partnership Act 2004, effective from 5 December 2005, allows same-sex couples to form a formal, legal commitment to each other by entering into a civil partnership. Those who have done so are entitled to be treated for all employment purposes in the same way as married people.

Gender Reassignment Discrimination

4.701 Employers must not discriminate against a person on the grounds of gender reassignment under the Sex Discrimination (Gender Reassignment) Regulations 1999. Gender reassignment — commonly referred to as "sex change" — refers to an individual:

- planning to undergo changes to their physiological or other characteristics of sex
- being in the process of changing their physiological or other characteristics of sex
- having changed their physiological or other characteristics of sex.

4.702 The following best practice applies to an employer's treatment of employees planning to undergo or in the process of undergoing a sex change.

- Do not treat an employee who requires time off work for gender reassignment treatment less favourably than an employee who is off sick would be treated.
- Take specific steps to prevent any conduct towards a trans-gender employee that could be regarded as harassment or abuse.
- Agree with an employee who is in the early stages of a sex change an appropriate statement to inform his or her colleagues of the fact he or she is undergoing a sex change.
- Include gender reassignment in the organisation's equal opportunities policy.
- Have gender neutral toilet facilities available, eg a disabled toilet (see *Croft v Consignia*) for an employee to use during the period they are undergoing gender reassignment.
- Do not select an employee for dismissal or redundancy on the grounds of gender reassignment.
- Agree when the employee will begin wearing the opposite sex's version of any staff uniform and when they may use the toilets of their new acquired gender.

4.703 Once an employee has completed the process of sex change, he or she must be regarded for all employment purposes as a member of his or her new acquired gender.

4.704 The Gender Recognition Act 2004 (which was implemented in April 2005), gave individuals who have completed a sex change the legal right to be recognised as a member of their acquired gender for all purposes. Individuals can obtain a full gender recognition certificate, after which they are entitled to a new birth certificate reflecting their acquired gender. Such individuals may also marry someone of the opposite gender to their acquired gender.

Retirement Ages

4.705 Employers that operate a compulsory retirement age must ensure that they apply the same retirement age to both men and women.

Selection for Redundancy

4.706 The criteria used to make selections for redundancy should be checked carefully for possible indirect sex discrimination. In addition, if a group of employees under threat of redundancy is predominantly of one gender, the employer would be advised to review the selection criteria in order to guard against any effect that could be disproportionate.

4.707 Any conditions for access to voluntary redundancy benefits should be made available on equal terms to male and female employees who are in the same, or not materially different, circumstances.

4.708 The selection of part-time workers before full-time workers could be indirectly discriminatory against women in certain circumstances — as well as being in breach of the Part-time Workers (Prevention of Less Favourable Treatment) Regulations 2000 which expressly require employers not to discriminate against part-time workers on grounds of their part-time status.

Post-Employment Discrimination

4.709 A claim for sex discrimination can be made against a former employer irrespective of how much time has passed since the employee's employment ended. Such a claim can only succeed, however, where the individual can show that the discrimination or harassment arose out of, or was closely connected with, the previous employment relationship.

Claims of Sex Discrimination

4.710 In the event of a claim for sex discrimination, the employer must be able to show a non-discriminatory reason for its actions, otherwise the employment tribunal may draw adverse inferences. A tribunal is bound to uphold the complaint if the employer cannot come up with an adequate or credible explanation for its conduct.

The Questionnaire Procedure

4.711 An employee or job applicant who believes that he or she may have experienced any form of sex discrimination may serve a special questionnaire on the employer, asking for an explanation for the conduct that he or she thinks was discriminatory. The individual may instigate the procedure either before or after he or she has commenced tribunal proceedings.

4.712 A pre-printed questionnaire is available, but the employee may add his or her own questions.

4.713 The employer is not under any statutory duty to respond to a questionnaire served upon it. The questions and replies are, however, admissible as evidence in tribunal cases. If the employer fails to respond to the questionnaire within eight weeks, or if the answers given are evasive or equivocal, the tribunal or court may infer that the employer did discriminate and the employer is trying to avoid admitting it. It is therefore advisable for employers to answer the employee's questions as fully as possible.

4.714 In order to be used in tribunal cases, the questionnaire must (in cases where an application to tribunal has not yet been presented) be given or sent to the employer within three months of the act that is being complained about, or (where a complaint has already been presented to the tribunal) within 21 days of the date on which the complaint was lodged.

The Burden of Proof

4.715 Under the Sex Discrimination (Indirect Discrimination and Burden of Proof) Regulations 2001, once an employee has established facts before an employment tribunal that indicate that he or she may have been the victim of unlawful sex discrimination, the burden of proof shifts to the employer that must (if it is to succeed in defending the case) persuade the tribunal that there was some other non-discriminatory reason for the actions.

Vicarious Liability

4.716 Employers are liable in law for any act of discrimination or harassment carried out by any of their employees in the course of their employment.

4.717 Employers can only defend themselves against claims of sex discrimination if they can show that they took all reasonably practicable steps to prevent their staff from behaving in a discriminatory way. To protect themselves from liability therefore, employers should:
- devise and implement an equal opportunities policy and an anti-harassment policy both of which incorporate discrimination on grounds of sex, trans-gender status, marital status, civil partnership status and pregnancy
- implement a complaints procedure
- provide training to all employees on equality and discrimination/harassment, with additional training for managers and supervisors who hold responsibility for recruitment and employment decisions
- communicate the policies on a regular basis to all staff and take steps to ensure they are fully understood
- effectively monitor compliance.

4.718 Whether or not an employer can defend itself from liability for the discriminatory behaviour of an individual employee, that employee may be held liable for his or her own actions by an employment tribunal. This tends to happen most often in claims for harassment. This can result in an individual employee being ordered by the tribunal personally to pay compensation to the person whom he or she harassed.

Harassment by Customers, Suppliers and Other Third Parties

4.719 In *Burton v De Vere Hotels* [1996] IRLR 596, the EAT held that an employer could potentially be held liable for harassment perpetrated on one of its employees by a third party, eg a member of the public. The House of Lords subsequently suggested (in *Pearce v Governing Body of Mayfield Secondary School* [2003] IRLR 512) that this decision may not have been legally correct.

4.720 More recently, in *Gravell v London Borough of Bexley* [2007] EAT 0587/0 (a race case), the EAT ruled that, given the new freestanding provisions on harassment contained in the legislation, a claimant may well be able to successfully argue that his or her employer should be held liable for harassment perpetrated by a third party. The claimant, Ms Gravell, had complained that her employer applied a policy that staff should ignore racist comments made by members of the public and that having to listen to such comments without being permitted to challenge them created an offensive working environment for her. The EAT overruled the employment tribunal's decision to strike out the case, stating that "there is considerable scope for argument" as to whether the observations of the House of Lords (in *Pearce*) on the *Burton* case hold good in a claim for harassment under the revised statutory provisions. An employer could, the EAT thought, potentially be held liable for the harassment of one of its employees by a third party, as such treatment could, as per the amended wording of the statutes, create an offensive working environment for that employee. Although this was a race case, the Sex Discrimination Act 1975 (as amended) contains parallel wording on harassment and so the decision would apply in the same way to claims for sex-based or sexual harassment.

4.721 Employers should, in any event, never refuse to shield staff from sex discrimination (particularly sexual harassment) carried out by an outsider. An employer who is indifferent to discriminatory treatment meted out by third parties may, in addition to being liable for such discrimination under the Sex Discrimination Act 1975, also be in breach of the implied duty of trust and confidence, and hence in breach of contract.

4.722 In addition, Acas recommends as best practice that employers should protect their workers from harassment by third parties such as customers and service users.

Compensation

4.723 If an employee, job applicant or former employee succeeds in a claim for unlawful sex discrimination at tribunal, the most common outcome is that the employer will be ordered to pay compensation to the claimant. There is no ceiling on the amount of money that may be awarded. During the year 2005, the average total award in successful sex discrimination cases was £10,902, while the median figure was £7497 (Source: Equal Opportunities Review No.155).

4.724 Compensation in most cases is made up of loss of earnings (eg where the employee has left their job on account of the discriminatory treatment) and an amount for injury to feelings.

Monitoring

4.725 There is currently no requirement in law for employers to keep information on how the workforce is made up, other than in the public sector where racial, gender and disability monitoring are statutory requirements.

4.726 It is nevertheless good practice for all employers to gather data on the gender make-up of their workforce and of job applicants in order to monitor whether any discrimination (particularly indirect discrimination) is occurring.

Training

4.727 It is important that all staff are given awareness training on the organisation's policy and procedure on equal opportunities and the avoidance of discrimination so that they fully understand both the employer's and the employee's responsibilities.

4.728 Training policies should be regularly reviewed to ensure they are free from sex bias. Employers need to ensure that there is equal treatment and equal access to training for all staff irrespective of gender, marital status and part-time status. The criteria used to determine eligibility for training must be based on objective factors such as individuals' abilities and job duties.

4.729 The following training should be carried out by all employers:
- training in equality and the avoidance of bias for all line managers or supervisors and any others responsible for recruitment and employment decisions
- awareness training for all staff in the organisation's equal opportunities policy, also covering the need to avoid all forms of harassment and the types of behaviour that can be viewed as sexual harassment
- induction training for all new staff to make them aware of the organisation's policies on equality and sexual harassment, and the importance of following them.

4.730 Training should be flexible as regards timing — so as not to disadvantage part-time staff or female employees with children who may not be able to work on a particular day of the week or during evenings or weekends.

4.731 In relation to pay enhancements for skills or training, the criteria used must genuinely reflect an enhanced ability to carry out a particular job.

4.732 If an employer buys-in training from an outside provider, it will be necessary to check that the provider has sufficient awareness of the requirements of discrimination legislation.

List of Relevant Legislation

4.733
- Employment Equality (Sex Discrimination) Regulations 2005
- Sex Discrimination (Indirect Discrimination and Burden of Proof) Regulations 2001
- Part-Time Workers (Prevention of Less Favourable Treatment) Regulations 2000
- Gender Recognition Act 2004
- Employment Act 2002
- Employment Rights Act 1996
- Sex Discrimination Act 1975

List of Relevant Cases

4.734
- *Alabaster v Barclays Bank plc and Secretary of State for Social Security (No. 2)* [2005] IRLR 576, CA
- *Brumfitt v Ministry of Defence* [2005] IRLR 4, EAT
- *Cross v British Airways plc* [2005] IRLR 423, EAT
- *Fletcher v Blackpool Fylde & Wyre Hospitals NHS Trust* [2005] IRLR 689
- *Hardys & Hansons plc v Lax* [2005] IRLR 726, CA
- *Igen Ltd v Wong* [2005] IRLR 258, CA
- *Moonsar v Fiveways Express Transport Ltd* [2005] IRLR 9, EAT
- *St Helens Metropolitan Borough Council v Derbyshire* [2005] IRLR 801, CA
- *Way & Intro-Cate Chemicals v Crouch* [2005] UKEAT/0614/04/CK
- *BNP Paribas v Mezzotero* [2004] IRLR 509, EAT
- *Scott v Commissioners of Inland Revenue* [2004] IRLR 713, CA
- *Visa International Service Association v Paul* [2004] IRLR 42
- *West Yorkshire Police Chief v A* [2004] IRLR 573, HL
- *Croft v Royal Mail Group plc* [2003] IRLR 592, CA
- *Coote v Granada Hospitality Ltd (No. 2)* [1999] IRLR 452, EAT
- *Reed and Bull Information Systems v Stedman* [1999] IRLR 299, EAT
- *Brown v Rentokil Ltd* C-394/96 [1998] IRLR 445, ECJ
- *Caledonia Bureau Investment & Property v Caffrey* [1998] IRLR 110
- *Hammersmith and Fulham London Borough Council v Jesuthasan* [1998] ICR 640
- *Falkirk Council v Whyte* [1997] IRLR 560
- *Meade-Hill v British Council* [1995] IRLR 478, CA
- *Webb v EMO Air Cargo (UK) Ltd* C-32/93 [1994] IRLR 482, ECJ
- *Hampson v Department of Education and Science* [1990] IRLR 302, HL
- *Rainey v Greater Glasgow Health Board Eastern District* [1987] IRLR 26, HL
- *Bilka-Kaufhaus GmbH v Weber von Hartz* 170/84 [1986] IRLR 317, ECJ
- *Community Task Force v Rimmer* [1986] IRLR 283
- *Home Office v Holmes* [1984] IRLR 299
- *Clarke v Eley (IMI) Kynoch Ltd* [1983] ICR 165

- *Horsey v Dyfed County Council* [1982] IRLR 395
- *Coleman v Skyrail Oceanic Ltd* [1981] IRLR 398, CA
- *EOC v Robertson and others* [1980] IRLR 44
- *Gubala v Crompton Parkinson Ltd* [1977] IRLR 10
- *Price v Civil Service Commission and the Society of Civil and Public Servants* [1977] IRLR 291, EAT
- *Healy v William B Morrison & Son Ltd* B648/5 EAT

Further Information

Organisations
- **Equal Opportunities Commission**
  Web: *www.eoc.org.uk*
  An agency working to eliminate sex discrimination and put equality into practice in the workplace. From October 2007 this organisation will be replaced by the Commission for Equality and Human Rights (**Web:** *www.cehr.org.uk*).

Sexual Orientation Discrimination

This topic covers the following.
- Scope of the Regulations
- Employees and Other Types of Workers
- Qualifying Conditions
- Comparable Person
- Discrimination Outside the Employment Field
- The Four Forms of Discrimination
- Sexual Orientation Discrimination in Recruitment
- Sexual Orientation Discrimination During Employment
- Post-employment Discrimination
- Claims of Sexual Orientation Discrimination
- Questionnaire Procedure
- The Burden of Proof
- Vicarious Liability
- Harassment by Customers, Suppliers and Other Third Parties
- Compensation
- Monitoring

4.735 The Employment Equality (Sexual Orientation) Regulations came into force on 1 December 2003, as part of a package of anti-discrimination measures required by the EU. They prohibit discrimination at work against gay, lesbian, heterosexual and bisexual individuals on the basis of their sexual orientation or perceived sexual orientation.

4.736 The regulations prohibit four different types of discrimination in recruitment and employment: direct discrimination, indirect discrimination, harassment and victimisation. They also provide for limited post-employment protection and a questionnaire procedure, to help claimants explore whether discrimination on the grounds of sexual orientation has occurred.

4.737 There is no qualifying period of service necessary to make a complaint to an employment tribunal and no limit on the amount of compensation that can be awarded to a successful claimant.

4.738 Acas has published a guidance paper that gives useful examples of situations where discrimination may arise.

Employers' Duties

- Employers must not treat any individual member of staff less favourably than another on the basis of his or her sexual orientation.
- Employers may only use sexual orientation as a criterion in recruitment in very limited circumstances where it is a genuine occupational requirement of the job that it be carried out by someone who is of a particular orientation.
- Employers must not commit any act of specific sexual orientation discrimination against an individual as there is no defence that justifies direct sexual orientation discrimination.

- Employers must not adopt policies, procedures, rules or practices that could put people of a particular sexual orientation at a disadvantage (known as indirect discrimination) unless the policy, procedure, rule or practice is appropriate and necessary in the circumstances. Indirect discrimination is unlawful whether it is intentional or unintentional.
- Employers must not victimise staff who have complained that they have suffered sexual orientation discrimination, nor victimise staff who assist others in making such complaints.
- Employers must not allow harassment on the basis of a worker's sexual orientation.
- Employers should take all reasonable steps to prevent discrimination in the workplace, eg by communicating their equal opportunities and anti-harassment policies to all staff on a regular basis, training staff on equal opportunities issues and the avoidance of all forms of discrimination, and monitoring compliance.
- Employers must take care not to commit any of the above forms of discrimination after a person's period of employment ends, eg by withholding a reference or harassing an ex-employee on grounds related to sexual orientation.

Employees' Duties

- Employees must not treat any individual member of staff less favourably than another on the basis of his or her sexual orientation.
- Employees must not victimise staff who have complained that they have suffered sexual orientation discrimination or helped a colleague to make a complaint of discrimination or harassment.
- Employees must not engage in any behaviour that could be interpreted as harassment on the basis of the actual or perceived sexual orientation of a colleague or anyone with whom a colleague associates.
- Employees are under a duty to adhere to their employer's equal opportunities and anti-harassment policies and to ensure that they treat their colleagues with respect and dignity at all times.

In Practice

Scope of the Regulations

4.739 The Employment Equality (Sexual Orientation) Regulations 2003 prohibit discrimination at work on the grounds of actual or perceived sexual orientation. The regulations protect people who have a sexual orientation towards those of the:
- same sex (gay and lesbian people)
- opposite sex (heterosexuals)
- same sex and of the opposite sex (bisexual people).

4.740 Job applicants are also protected throughout the process of recruitment and limited protection against discrimination is also available to former employees.

4.741 If discrimination occurs, the individual may bring a complaint to an employment tribunal.

Employees and Other Types of Workers

4.742 All workers are covered by the Employment Equality (Sexual Orientation) Regulations, ie not only those employed directly by the organisation, but also other workers such as:
- contract workers
- agency temps
- casual workers
- freelancers who provide their services personally
- directors
- company secretaries
- non-elected office holders
- partners in firms.

Qualifying Conditions

4.743 There is no length of service required for an employee or worker to bring a claim for unlawful sexual orientation discrimination to an employment tribunal. Equally, there is no lower or upper age limit for a claimant to bring a complaint.

4.744 Employees, however (but not other workers), must first raise a written grievance with their employer and wait 28 days. This is to allow the employer time and opportunity to deal with the complaint before it can proceed to tribunal. If a claim is lodged with the tribunal before the employee has raised a grievance and waited 28 days, the tribunal will in most cases not admit it.

Comparable Person

4.745 In order to found a claim of sexual orientation discrimination, an employee will usually have to draw a comparison with someone else who is of a different sexual orientation in similar circumstances.

4.746 If, however, there is no actual comparator, but there is evidence to support an inference of sexual orientation discrimination, an employment tribunal will construct a "hypothetical comparator" to assess how someone of another orientation would have been treated in the same or similar circumstances. Thus the law allows employment tribunals to make assumptions about how an employer would have treated a comparable person who does not have the same sexual orientation as the complainant.

Discrimination Outside the Employment Field

4.747 Discrimination can be perpetrated not only by employers but also by:
- trade organisations
- bodies conferring professional and trade qualifications
- training providers
- employment agencies
- further and higher educational institutions.

4.748 The regulations also apply to Crown servants and parliamentary staff.

4.749 As from April 2007, the prohibition on sexual orientation discrimination was extended to the provision of goods, facilities and services, premises, and education and the exercise of public functions. This was as a result of the implementation of regulations made under the Equality Act 2006.

The Four Forms of Discrimination

4.750 There are four different forms of discrimination:
- direct discrimination
- indirect discrimination
- victimisation
- harassment.

Direct Sexual Orientation Discrimination

4.751 Direct discrimination means treating someone less favourably because they are, or are thought to be, lesbian, gay, bisexual or heterosexual. Direct discrimination can take the form of:
- deciding not to employ a particular job applicant on grounds related to his or her actual or perceived sexual orientation
- denying someone access to training, transfer or promotion on grounds related to sexual orientation
- giving someone less favourable terms and conditions of employment than a comparable employee of a different sexual orientation
- denying an individual access to benefits or perks for reasons related to sexual orientation (although it is permitted to restrict any benefits offered to employees' partners to those who are married or have civil partnership status)
- dismissing an employee because of his or her sexual orientation.

Indirect Sexual Orientation Discrimination

4.752 Indirect discrimination occurs when an employer applies any general policy, rule or practice which:
- puts (or would put) persons of a particular sexual orientation at a particular disadvantage when compared with others
- actually puts an individual to that disadvantage
- cannot be justified as being a proportionate way of achieving a legitimate business aim.

Provision, Criterion or Practice

4.753 "Provision, criterion or practice" can be interpreted to mean that indirect discrimination can occur when an organisation has:
- selection criteria
- policies and procedures
- guidelines
- benefits
- employment rules
- informal practices

that are applied to all employees (or job applicants) but have or could have the effect of disadvantaging people of a particular sexual orientation (even though the policies, etc apply equally to all employees). Informal practices will be covered as well as contractual policies and rules.

Put at a Disadvantage

4.754 In order to prove that indirect discrimination has occurred, it must be shown not only that someone has personally been put at a disadvantage by the application of the provision, criterion or practice, but that the provision, criterion or practice in general puts, or would put, persons of the same sexual orientation at a particular disadvantage when compared with other persons.

Identifying a Legitimate Aim

4.755 Indirect sexual orientation discrimination can be justified when the employer's policy or practice is a proportionate way of achieving a legitimate business aim. The aim must be related to the needs of the business or the specific job the employee is employed to do and must be unrelated to sexual orientation.

The Test of Proportionality

4.756 "Proportionate" in this context means appropriate, necessary and not excessive in relation to the defined aim.

Victimisation

4.757 Employers and employees should not discriminate against any member of staff because that person has raised a genuine complaint of sexual orientation discrimination or harassment, whether under the employer's grievance procedure or to an employment tribunal. An employee who supports or assists another employee to raise a complaint is also protected against victimisation.

4.758 Claimants lose their protection if their allegations, or the evidence or information given, were false and not made or given in good faith.

Examples of Victimisation

4.759 As a common example of victimisation, Acas cites an employee being labelled a "trouble maker", isolated by colleagues and denied promotion or training because he or she has raised a complaint of discrimination or helped another employee to bring a complaint. Employers are under a duty to take reasonable steps to prevent this happening.

Sexual Orientation Harassment

4.760 Harassment on the grounds of sexual orientation occurs when an individual behaves in a way that:
- is related to the actual or perceived sexual orientation of any person
- is unwanted from the perspective of the person on the receiving end, and
- has either the purpose or effect of violating a person's dignity, or
- creates an intimidating, humiliating or offensive environment for that person.

4.761 A further clause in the regulations provides that behaviour will be seen as harassment if, with regard to all of the circumstances (including the victim's perception), it should reasonably be seen as violating the victim's dignity or as creating an atmosphere that is intimidating, hostile, degrading, humiliating or offensive to him or her.

4.762 In practice this means that a spurious claim that someone's behaviour amounted to harassment in circumstances where no reasonable person could possibly have viewed it as harassment in the context in which it occurred, would not succeed.

4.763 Any employer who receives a complaint of harassment should take it very seriously, investigate the circumstances thoroughly and, if the complaint is well founded, take steps to put a stop to the behaviour that is causing offence. It will also be appropriate in most circumstances to take disciplinary action against the harasser.

Examples of Sexual Orientation Harassment

4.764 Examples of harassment could include:

- behaviour linked to sexual orientation that is offensive, demeaning, frightening or in any way distressing
- intentional bullying on grounds of sexual orientation, whether violent or not
- behaviour that has no malicious intent but is upsetting to someone on grounds of their own or another person's sexual orientation
- subtle and insidious behaviour involving nicknames, teasing and name-calling linked to sexual orientation.

4.765 This behaviour does not need to be specifically targeted at the individual. A general culture that permits banter and teasing and includes the telling of homophobic jokes may create an uncomfortable working environment for some employees on account of sexual orientation and thus give rise to harassment claims.

Sexual Orientation Discrimination in Recruitment

4.766 Job applicants are protected throughout the entire process of recruitment against any form of discrimination linked to sexual orientation. For example, if an applicant who was otherwise suitable for the job under review was refused employment because the interviewer had formed the view that he was gay, this would constitute direct sexual orientation discrimination and would be unlawful.

Genuine Occupational Requirements (GORs)

4.767 In a limited number of cases, it may be possible for an employer to specifically recruit or promote someone on the basis that it is a requirement of a particular job that he or she is gay, lesbian, bisexual or heterosexual. For example, a post as a counsellor for same-sex couples may require someone with experience of such relationships.

4.768 To be a genuine requirement of a job, the individual's sexual orientation must be specifically necessary and not just a preference.

4.769 Additionally, where an organisation exists for the purposes of an organised religion (eg a church) and where the GOR is applied so as to comply with the doctrines of the religion or avoid offending a significant number of the religion's followers, the employer may be able to specify that it is an absolute requirement of the job that the successful applicant is not gay or lesbian. In this case, the employer need only show that the requirement is genuine, and not that is necessary for the performance of the particular job.

4.770 In all cases, the requirement must also be proportionate in the particular case.

4.771 Any employee or job applicant can challenge the requirement and the burden of proving that the requirement is genuine and necessary falls on the employer.

4.772 It is unlikely that there will be many situations in which tribunals and courts accept that there is a genuine occupational requirement. The rule operates as an exception to the principle of equal treatment.

4.773 Furthermore, a genuine occupational requirement will not apply if:

- the employer already has enough staff of the required sexual orientation who can carry out the duties required by the job, and
- it is reasonable to allocate the duties to these other staff without undue inconvenience.

4.774 On each occasion, before an employer uses a genuine occupational requirement, he or she should review whether the requirement is still valid.

Positive Action

4.775 Although positive discrimination, ie discrimination in favour of a person from a minority sexual orientation, is not permitted under UK employment law, the regulations do permit certain forms of positive action in recruitment and training. Positive action is not required in law, but is permitted if the reason for it is to increase the number of people from a particular group that has historically been disadvantaged within employment for reasons linked to sexual orientation.

4.776 It is thus lawful for employers to apply measures specifically to encourage candidates from a disadvantaged group to apply for employment or promotion, or to offer training that would help fit them for particular work. Examples could include placing job advertisements in a particular publication that is read predominantly by gay and lesbian people. However, it is only encouragement that is permitted — at the point of selection for employment or promotion, the principles of equality must be applied and an individual candidate's sexual orientation must play no part in the decision-making process (unless a genuine occupational requirement applies).

Recruitment Best Practice Checklist

4.777 Employers should take note of the following best practice guidelines to prevent sexual orientation discrimination in the recruitment process.
- Do not advertise for a person of a particular sexual orientation, unless a job is one in which a genuine occupational requirement applies.
- Avoid recruiting by word of mouth only as this practice may tend to reinforce an imbalance in the workforce and may be indirectly discriminatory against gay or lesbian people.
- Incorporate clear, objective and specific criteria against which applicants (for jobs, transfers and promotions) can be assessed. This should help to eliminate all forms of bias, whether deliberate or subconscious.
- Ensure that all staff involved in recruitment or selection have received effective equal opportunities training.
- Give guidance to recruiters on the effects which generalised assumptions and prejudices about gay and lesbian people can have on selection decisions.
- Use more than one person to carry out shortlisting and interviewing — this may help to prevent any one individual's prejudices affecting the selection decision.
- Keep notes on recruitment decisions in order to be able to demonstrate that the reason for the rejection of one candidate and the appointment of another was free from bias linked to actual or perceived sexual orientation.

Sexual Orientation Discrimination During Employment

4.778 Employees are protected against all forms of sexual orientation discrimination in every aspect of their employment. This will include the terms and conditions of their contract, access to promotion, transfer and training and general treatment at work.

4.779 Employers should be aware that paternity leave, adoption leave, parental leave and the right to request flexible working can apply to gay and lesbian employees, irrespective of whether they have entered into a formal civil partnership. Checks should be made to policies to ensure that gay and lesbian employees are not excluded from these rights. Likewise, if the benefit of healthcare and insurance policies are available to the unmarried partners of staff, then the same rules should be applied to employees' same-sex partners who have not entered into a civil partnership. Furthermore, those who have entered into a civil partnership with their same-sex partner are entitled to be treated for all purposes in the same way as someone who is married.

Terms and Conditions of Employment

4.780 It is unlawful to treat an employee less favourably than another as regards the terms and conditions of their contracts if the reason for the different treatment is related to sexual orientation.

Promotion, Transfer and Training

4.781 If an employee's access to opportunities for promotion, transfer or training is restricted for any reason related to his or her sexual orientation, this would amount to direct discrimination, unless a genuine occupational requirement applied. The same sort of considerations would apply as shown in recruitment.

Selection for Redundancy

4.782 The criteria used to make selections for redundancy should be checked carefully to guard against the possibility of indirect sexual orientation discrimination.

Post-employment Discrimination

4.783 A claim for sexual orientation discrimination can be made against a former employer irrespective of how much time has passed since the employee's employment ended. Such a claim can only succeed, however, where the individual can show that the discrimination or harassment arose out of or was closely connected with the previous employment relationship.

4.784 This principle also applies to employment and other working relationships that ended before the regulations came into force on 1 December 2003.

Claims of Sexual Orientation Discrimination

4.785 In the event of a claim for sexual orientation discrimination, the employer must be able to show a non-discriminatory reason for their actions, otherwise the employment tribunal may draw adverse inferences. A tribunal is bound to uphold the complaint if the employer cannot come up with an adequate or credible explanation for their conduct.

Questionnaire Procedure

4.786 An employee or job applicant who believes that he or she may have experienced any form of discrimination (including discrimination after their employment ended) may serve a special questionnaire on the employer, asking for an explanation for the conduct that they think was discriminatory. The individual may instigate the procedure either before or after he or she has commenced tribunal proceedings.

4.787 A pre-printed questionnaire is available, but the employee may add his or her own questions.

4.788 The employer is not under any statutory duty to respond to a questionnaire served upon them. The questions and replies are, however, admissible as evidence in tribunal cases. If the employer fails to respond to the questionnaire within eight

Sexual Orientation Discrimination

weeks, or if the answers given are evasive or equivocal, the tribunal or court may infer that the employer did discriminate and the employer is trying to avoid admitting it. It is therefore advisable for employers to answer the employee's questions as fully as possible.

4.789 In order to be used in tribunal cases, the questionnaire must (in cases where an application to tribunal has not yet been presented) be served on the employer within three months of the act that gave rise to the complaint or (where a complaint has already been presented to the tribunal) within 21 days of the date on which the complaint was lodged.

The Burden of Proof

4.790 Once an employee has established facts before an employment tribunal that indicate that he or she may have been the victim of unlawful sexual orientation discrimination, the burden of proof shifts to the employer who must (if they are to succeed in defending the claim) persuade the tribunal that there was some other non-discriminatory reason for their actions.

Vicarious Liability

4.791 Employers are liable in law for any act of discrimination or harassment carried out by any of their employees in the course of their employment.

4.792 Employers can only defend themselves against claims of discrimination if they can show they took all reasonably practicable steps to prevent staff from behaving in a discriminatory way.

4.793 To protect themselves from liability therefore, employers should:
- devise and implement an equal opportunities policy and an anti-harassment policy, both of which incorporate sexual orientation discrimination
- implement a complaints procedure
- communicate with staff to promote equality and the avoidance of sexual orientation discrimination
- provide training to all employees on equality, discrimination and harassment, with additional training to managers and supervisors who hold responsibility for recruitment and employment decisions
- communicate the policies on a regular basis to all staff and take steps to ensure they are fully understood
- effectively monitor compliance.

4.794 Whether or not an employer can defend itself from liability for the discriminatory behaviour of an individual employee, that employee may be held liable for their own actions by an employment tribunal. This tends to happen most often in claims for harassment. This can result in an individual employee being ordered by the tribunal personally to pay compensation to the person whom they harassed.

Harassment by Customers, Suppliers and Other Third Parties

4.795 In *Burton v De Vere Hotels* [1996] IRLR 596, the EAT held that an employer could potentially be held liable for harassment perpetrated on one of its employees by a third party, eg a member of the public. The House of Lords subsequently suggested (in *Pearce v Governing Body of Mayfield Secondary School* [2003] IRLR 512) that this decision may not have been legally correct.

4.796 More recently, in *Gravell v London Borough of Bexley* [2007] EAT 0587/0 (a race case), the EAT ruled that, given the new freestanding provisions on harassment contained in the legislation, a claimant may well be able successfully to argue that his or her employer should be held liable for harassment perpetrated by a third party. The claimant, Ms Gravell, had complained that her employer applied a policy that staff should ignore racist comments made by members of the public and that having to listen to such comments without being permitted to challenge them created an offensive working environment for her. The EAT overruled the employment tribunal's decision to strike out the case, stating that "there is considerable scope for argument" as to whether the observations of the House of Lords (in *Pearce*) on the *Burton* case hold good in a claim for harassment under the revised statutory provisions. An employer could, the EAT thought, potentially be held liable for the harassment of one of its employees by a third party, as such treatment could, as per the amended wording of the statutes, create an offensive working environment for that employee. Although this was a race case, the Employment Equality (Sexual Orientation) Regulations 2003 contain parallel wording on harassment and so the decision would apply in the same way to a claim for harassment perpetrated on grounds of sexual orientation.

4.797 Employers should, in any event, never refuse to shield staff from discrimination (particularly harassment) carried out by an outsider because they disapprove of the individual's sexual orientation. An employer who is indifferent to discriminatory treatment meted out by third parties may, in addition to being liable for such discrimination under the Employment Equality (Sexual Orientation) Regulations 2003, also be acting in breach of the implied duty of trust and confidence and hence in breach of contract.

4.798 In addition, Acas recommends as best practice that employers should protect their workers from harassment by third parties such as customers and service users.

Compensation

4.799 If an employee, job applicant or former employee succeeds in a claim for unlawful sexual orientation discrimination at tribunal, the most common outcome is that the employer will be ordered to pay compensation to the claimant. There is no ceiling on the amount of money that may be awarded. During the year 2005, the average total award in successful sexual orientation discrimination cases was £9894, while the median figure was £3500 (Source: Equal Opportunities Review No.155).

4.800 In a case decided in early 2007 (*Ditton v CP Publishing Ltd* ET (S/101638/06 and S/107918/05)), an employment tribunal ordered an employer to pay over £118,000 compensation to a gay employee who had been subjected to offensive comments about his sexual orientation by his manager, and then dismissed for no proper reason after only eight days in the job.

4.801 Compensation in most cases is made up of loss of earnings (eg where the employee has left their job on account of the discriminatory treatment) and an amount for injury to feelings.

Monitoring

4.802 There is currently no requirement in law for employers to keep information on how the workforce is made up, other than in the public sector where racial, gender and disability monitoring are statutory requirements.

4.803 Where an employer elects to gather information about employees' sexual orientation, it must bear in mind that such information is classed as "sensitive data" under the Data Protection Act 1998. This means that it cannot be collected or used unless either the employee has freely consented to the data being collected or one of a list of other conditions is satisfied. If the organisation does want to gather data on sexual orientation, in order to monitor whether any discrimination (particularly indirect discrimination) is occurring, it must ensure that staff:

- are told why the information is being gathered
- are told how the organisation intends to use the data
- are assured of the confidentiality of the data and that it will be kept securely
- are told that they have no obligation to give the information
- freely give their consent to the data being collected and used.

4.804　It would usually be appropriate for any data on sexual orientation to be gathered anonymously.

Training

4.805　It is important that all staff are given awareness training on the organisation's policy and procedure on equal opportunities and the avoidance of discrimination, so that they fully understand both the employer's and the employee's responsibilities.

4.806　Employers need to ensure that there is equal treatment and equal access to training for all staff irrespective of their sexual orientation. The criteria used to determine eligibility for training must be based on objective factors such as individuals' abilities and job duties. The following training should be carried out by all employers.

- Training in equality and the avoidance of bias for all line managers or supervisors and any others responsible for recruitment and employment decisions.
- Awareness training for all staff in the organisation's equal opportunities policy, also covering the need to avoid all forms of harassment and the types of behaviour that could be viewed as sexual orientation harassment.
- Induction training for all new staff to make them aware of the organisation's policies on equality and harassment, and the importance of following them.

4.807　In relation to pay enhancements for skills or training, the criteria used must genuinely reflect an enhanced ability to carry out a particular job.

4.808　If an employer buys in training from an outside provider, it will be necessary to check that the provider has sufficient awareness of the requirements of discrimination legislation.

List of Relevant Legislation

4.809
- Employment Equality (Sexual Orientation) Regulations 2003
- Civil Partnership Act 2004
- Data Protection Act 1998
- EC Council Directive 2000/78/EC

List of Relevant Cases

4.810
- *Macdonald v Advocate General for Scotland* [2003] IRLR 512, HL — direct discrimination and comparative situations, harassment and sexual orientation, liability of employers and principals for the acts of others.
- *Weathersfield Ltd v Sargent* [1999] IRLR 94, CA — discrimination can occur even where it is not aimed at the person who complains.
- *Insitu Cleaning Co Ltd v Heads* [1995] IRLR 4, EAT — the meaning of "detriment" in discrimination cases, constructive dismissal following harassment.
- *University of Huddersfield v Woolf* (EAT/596/02) Unreported — application of the burden of proof in proving discrimination.

Further Information

Publications
- EEL02 *Acas Sexual Orientation and the Workplace — A Guide for Employers and Employees* (November 2003)

Organisations
- **Advisory Conciliation and Arbitration Service (Acas)**
  Web: *www.acas.org.uk*
  Acas aims to improve organisations and working life through better employment relations. It provides up-to-date information, advice, high-quality training, and works with employers and employees to solve problems and improve performance.

Chapter 5
Industrial and Employee Relations

Collective Agreements

> This topic covers the following.
> - What is Collective Bargaining?
> - The Usefulness of Collective Bargaining
> - The Parties in Collective Bargaining
> - Recognition of Unions for Bargaining
> - The Law and Collective Bargaining
> - Scope of Collective Agreements
> - Working Time Legislation and Collective Bargaining
> - Workforce Agreements
> - Non-Unionised Employees
> - The Process of Bargaining
> - The Failure of the Bargaining Process
> - Information and Consultation of Employees Regulations 2004

5.1 This section on collective agreements defines collective bargaining, which is required to make an agreement. Alternative views on the legitimacy of collective bargaining are considered. The parties who make or influence a collective agreement are listed. The process of recognising unions and the law relating to recognition, bargaining and industrial action is described. The content of collective agreements is explained and the legal relationship with individual contracts of employment. There is an analysis of the process of bargaining and how to handle the failure of the process, including the role of Acas. In conclusion, the future of collective agreements is considered.

5.2 The Information and Consultation of Employees Regulations 2004 came into force in phases from April 2005 (depending on the size of the employer) and require employers to consult their employees if requested to do so on the economic position of the organisation and any changes they propose to make. This will affect relationships with employees, whether they are unionised or not, except for those in small organisations.

Employers' Duties

5.3 Employers should be aware that:
- they may be required to recognise a union for bargaining if a majority of the relevant employees are in favour of recognition
- they should not offer an inducement to a union member to discourage them from having terms and conditions negotiated through collective bargaining
- they should not threaten that there could be detrimental treatment or dismissal if the inducement is refused
- collective agreements are not normally legally enforceable, but their terms can form part of the individual contract of employment
- if industrial action is threatened by a union, it must ballot first to make the action lawful
- the Information and Consultation of Employees Regulations 2004 bring into force (depending on the size of the employer) rights relating to the disclosure of information by employers and the employer's duty to consult — in both unionised and non-union organisations.

Employees' Duties

5.4 Employees should be aware that:
- statutory recognition ballots require not just a simple majority in favour but at least 40% of employees eligible to vote in the bargaining unit to be in favour
- the employer has no right to offer them an inducement not to have their terms and conditions of employment negotiated through collective bargaining
- the employer must not threaten detrimental treatment (eg overlooking for promotion) or dismissal if the inducement is refused
- changes negotiated in a collective agreement may change the terms of the individual contract of employment
- industrial action taken without a postal ballot leaves them with no protection against dismissal and their union may also suffer punitive damages unless it repudiates their unlawful action
- the Information and Consultation of Employees Regulations 2004 may from April 2005, depending on the size of their organisation, affect their relationship with their employer and the position of their union.

In Practice

What is Collective Bargaining?

5.5 The relationship between an employer and employees over pay and conditions of employment can be an individual one. It can also be wholly or partially collective with a trade union representing employees. Collective bargaining is the process through which unions and employers negotiate terms and conditions of employment.

5.6 An employer's relationship with unions in practice is not necessarily confined to negotiating pay and conditions of employment. It can also cover the process of consultation with unions, eg on health and safety, and the handling of discipline and grievances.

5.7 A union thus becomes closely involved with a range of issues within an organisation and/or an industry and enters into collective agreements with employers.

5.8 There are two important aspects of this relationship between an employer and a union: inequality of power and joint regulation.

Inequality of Power

5.9 There is an imbalance of power in the employment relationship between the individual employee and the employer. It is arguable that individuals are relatively weak (in terms of power) to influence the terms and conditions affecting their working lives. Collective action by individual employees is one way of attempting to equalise the imbalance of power.

5.10 A group of organised workers can:
- exert more pressure on the employer
- use the expertise of a union to make and present their case.

Joint Regulation

5.11 Entering into joint regulation by employer and union of the terms and conditions of employment suits the interests of both sides.

5.12 The employer finds it easier to deal collectively with terms and conditions of employment with a representative of his or her employees. This may be an elected employee representative (ie a shopsteward or staff representatives) or an outside union official.

5.13 It saves time if agreement can be reached collectively. This agreement is then supported by the union which commits its members. The larger the organisation, or unit of an organisation, the more convenient it is to have collective agreements.

The Usefulness of Collective Bargaining

5.14 There are generally two views on the usefulness of collective bargaining, the:
- unitarist perspective
- pluralist perspective.

The Unitarist Perspective

5.15 Some employers and managers do not accept that there is any need to deal with unions. Collective bargaining is not only unnecessary but also quite wrong. They feel that there is no essential conflict of interest between employer and employee. Any difference is put down to individual interest and to poor communication of the employer's message.

5.16 If you accept this view of a natural harmony of interest then it is clear that union representation and collective agreements are neither necessary nor desirable. Collective bargaining is seen as an illegitimate intrusion into the employment relationship.

The Pluralist Perspective

5.17 Other employers take a different view on employment relations. They accept that there is a legitimate difference of interest between employer and employees. While the two sides will want the organisation to be successful and ensure job security, there will be differences over the rate of pay, hours of work and other conditions of employment. These differences of view are natural, but have to be settled. A way of doing so, particularly if there are large numbers of employees, is by collective agreement.

The Parties in Collective Bargaining

5.18 Several organisations affect collective agreements:
- trade unions
- the Trades Union Congress
- employers
- employers' associations.

Trade Unions

5.19 To bargain collectively an employer needs to recognise one or more unions. Some unions are large general unons recruiting across private and public sectors (eg the Transport and General Workers Union); some are largely public sector based (eg UNISON); and others tend to be sectorally based (eg the National Union of Teachers).

5.20 Unions could also include an independent staff association without outside union involvement. An example is the Abbey National Group Union covering the Abbey group of companies.

5.21 Under law, an independent trade union is one that is clearly not under domination or control of an employer.

The Trades Union Congress (TUC)

5.22 The Trades Union Congress (TUC) is a national organisation for British trade unions. It does not engage in collective bargaining for its members. It may however influence the conduct of bargaining of member unions, but would do so indirectly. The TUC does represent the views of the trade union movement to government and to employers' organisations.

Employers

5.23 An "employer" can be a:
- business/partnership/organisation/sole trader, etc
- government department
- voluntary organisation.

5.24 Once people are engaged on a contract of employment there exists a legal contractual relationship that may be derived from statute law, common law, a collective agreement, implied terms and custom and practice.

Employers' Associations

5.25 Employers may choose to bargain partly through the employers' association covering an industry, although it is increasingly rare for this to happen. Examples are local government and electrical contracting.

5.26 Employers' associations can provide organisations with a common voice and position to negotiate with unions. Associations may also provide advice and services to their members. A smaller organisation may find this helpful, and may not be able to access or provide such advice on its own economically. An example is the Engineering Employers' Federation, which is a grouping of regionally-based associations.

Recognition of Unions for Bargaining

5.27 Before collective bargaining takes place there needs to be an acceptance by an employer that a union is recognised for the purpose of negotiating and agreeing on terms and conditions of employment. This recognition can cover as extensive and wide a list of terms and conditions as the parties agree. It may alternatively be confined to basic terms and conditions.

5.28 The employees covered by the agreement may be widely or narrowly defined. Strictly speaking bargaining or negotiation only relates to the items agreed by the parties for that purpose.

5.29 There may be consultation on other items and on the general position of the organisation. Some consultation is merely information giving. However some consultation is, in practice, an extension of bargaining.

5.30 The bargaining unit, the level of bargaining and the scope of bargaining are covered below, after considering the role of the law.

The Law and Collective Bargaining

Recognition

5.31 The following points apply regarding the law and recognition of trades unions.

- Employers could choose to recognise a union when it has a relatively small membership among their employees, say 20%. However there is no legal compulsion to do so in Britain unless there is much stronger evidence of support for the union.
- The law (Trade Union and Labour Relations (Consolidation) Act 1992 (as amended), requires a majority voting in favour in a ballot for recognition in the bargaining unit concerned. In addition there must be at least 40% support of those eligible to vote.
- Those who do not vote are counted effectively against the bid for recognition.
- If there is a dispute over recognition, this may be settled with the help of the Advisory Conciliation and Arbitration Service (Acas).
- If a dispute cannot be settled by negotiation or through Acas, the parties can ask the Central Arbitration Committee (CAC) to adjudicate. This only applies to organisations with 21 or more employees, where there is initial evidence of at least 10% union membership.
- The CAC will try to get a voluntary settlement, but may require a ballot.
- If the union is successful in the ballot, the employer will be legally required to recognise the union for bargaining purposes. This will cover key conditions of employment for workers in a defined area of work, the bargaining unit.
- If the parties can agree on collective bargaining arrangements and the scope of the items to be negotiated they would then be expected to develop that relationship.
- If the employer and the union cannot reach a voluntary agreement, the CAC will impose prescribed items such as pay and hours. This settlement, unlike a usual collective agreement, would be legally enforceable.
- Members of an independent trade union are protected against being offered inducements by their employer to discourage them having their terms and conditions negotiated through a trade union or to give up the use of collective bargaining.

Disclosure of Information

5.32 Employers are under a general statutory duty to disclose information to an independent recognised union for collective bargaining. Acas has published a statutory Code of Practice as guidance in this area.

5.33 If an employer is unwilling to disclose information for collective bargaining purposes a union can ask the CAC to adjudicate. The CAC can require information to be disclosed. This legal process is not used often and its use would be a sign of very poor relations between management and a union.

Effect on Individual Employment Contracts

5.34 If pay or any condition of employment is agreed by collective bargaining in Britain this is not normally expressed as a legal contract and thus cannot be enforced by law. It could be legally binding, but this would be very unusual and both the employer and the trade union would have to agree.

5.35 However collective terms and conditions of employment are incorporated as appropriate into individual employment contracts by referring to the collective agreement. They are then enforceable in law by an employee.

Scope of Collective Agreements

5.36 The scope of a collective agreement includes the:
- bargaining unit (ie those covered by a recognition agreement)
- level of bargaining (eg workplace or national)
- bargaining scope (ie the range of items included in the agreement).

The Bargaining Unit

5.37 The definition of those to be covered by a recognition agreement and thus by the agreements on terms and conditions of employment is a key area for both voluntary recognition and that imposed by the CAC.

5.38 Those outside the defined bargaining unit are not covered by a recognition agreement and the union is therefore unable to fully represent the interests of these employees.

5.39 It is usually in the union's interest to cover more workers except when it wishes to represent a small clearly defined group, where its membership is concentrated. The union's goal may not be advantageous to the management. An employer may wish to confine bargaining to a specific group of employees. Alternatively, it may want common terms of employment throughout the organisation irrespective of grade or location.

The Level of Bargaining

5.40 Bargaining can take place at several levels:
- within the organisation at workplace level
- at plant level in a multi-plant or multi-site organisation
- at the level of the organisation as a whole
- at industry level
- at the national/country level.

5.41 The last item listed is more likely outside Britain, eg in Germany, although the TUC and the CBI have agreed a Framework Agreement to facilitate the implementation of the Information and Consultation Directive 2002.

5.42 There has been a trend toward the decentralisation of bargaining from organisation level down to its constituent parts. This may be for economic reasons to reflect differences in local labour markets.

5.43 However this is far more likely for pay than for an item such as leave entitlement or pensions. It suits an employer to standardise on hours, leave and pensions. Pay is a different matter and employers may seek to pay as little as they need to attract and retain labour in different areas.

Bargaining Scope

5.44 The range of items that can be covered by collective bargaining depends on the agreement of the union and management. The range can be as wide as the parties wish it to be and may extend beyond the areas laid down in law if compulsory recognition is awarded by the CAC.

5.45 Agreements could cover many items in the employment contract and consultation on the financial prospects and position of the organisation.

5.46 Under statutory recognition law, the scope of bargaining is pay, hours and holidays (known as the "core topics"). "Pay" for collective bargaining purposes excludes employer contributions to an occupational or personal pension scheme.

Working Time Legislation and Collective Bargaining

5.47 Under the Working Time Regulations 1998 (WTR), an employer can negotiate a collective agreement with a union to modify or exclude the application of certain regulations for particular groups of workers. Principally, these regulations cover the averaging of working time, the length of night work, and rest periods.

5.48 In non-union workplaces, the WTR provide for the negotiation of workforce agreements to cover such modifications and exclusions.

Workforce Agreements

5.49 Workforce agreements can be negotiated in organisations where collective bargaining does not exist for the relevant workgroup. Initially, they were introduced in working time legislation to facilitate the implementation of certain regulations. Similar provisions also exist under the Maternity and Parental Leave, etc Regulations 1999 and the Fixed-Term Employees (Less Favourable Treatment) Regulations 2002.

5.50 The requirements for a workforce agreement are:
- it must be in writing
- it must specify the date of application to the workers concerned
- all workers covered must be provided with a copy before signature
- it must be signed by a majority of the relevant workforce or a majority of the representatives of the workforce
- it must have an expiry date not later than five years from the agreement's commencement (when it can be renewed or replaced).

Non-Unionised Employees

5.51 A collective agreement within an organisation, or for an industry covering member firms of an employers' association, will cover all those employed whether union members or non-members. All will have their individual contracts affected by the outcome of collective bargaining, if the collective agreement is incorporated into their contracts of employment.

5.52 It would be neither convenient nor sensible for an employer to differentiate between employees on the basis of their union membership.

5.53 Organisations that are not unionised take account of rates agreed in collective bargaining as this affects their labour market. They may decide to pay above these negotiated rates to avoid the possibility of union recognition.

5.54 Thus, while union membership in Britain covers only a third of the labour force, the effect of collective agreements is very much wider and is said to cover about half of the working population.

The Process of Bargaining

5.55 The procedure for collective bargaining is as follows.

- To arrive at a collective agreement the employer and the union have to reach a settlement about the items concerned (eg pay, hours of work or compensation for redundancy).
- The difference between bargaining for commercial reasons and collective bargaining is that the commercial bargaining relationship is often a single bargain based on market power.
- A collective bargain relates to a continuing relationship between the employer and the union. It is not advisable to push a temporary superior power position too far, as the two sides have to live and work together.
- Union members within an organisation have an interest in the continuing health of their organisation as it provides them and their families with a living.
- An employer has to consider the labour market and the effect on motivation and morale and thus on productivity. Short-term gain is not always advisable, unlike with buying and selling a car.
- Items on the bargaining agenda have to be offset one against another. The priority is to ensure the most vital point is most strongly advanced or defended.

The Failure of the Bargaining Process

5.56 In most cases employers and unions are able to come to an agreement, which the union is satisfied will be agreed with its members. This agreement is not always possible between the negotiators, however. It is not unknown for union members to reject a proposed collective agreement. What happens next?

5.57 The alternatives are for:
- the employer to impose a settlement
- the union to threaten or take industrial action
- both sides to seek assistance to settle the dispute through conciliation, mediation or arbitration.

Imposing a Settlement

5.58 Imposing a settlement does happen. If the union realises its members are not prepared to take action, it would be foolish to threaten industrial action. It may be that the union is weak, or that the negotiators cannot sell the deal but feel it is the best they can get.

5.59 Imposition without agreement may suit them, but this cannot be admitted. Employees then receive a pay increase without delay and the union can try to return to the argument and improve the position over time.

Industrial Action

5.60 Industrial action may mean a strike, a ban on overtime, or some form of restriction on normal working.

5.61 If industrial action, particularly a strike, is taken employees will be breaching their contracts of employment. There is no legal right to strike in the United Kingdom. This contrasts with other countries in the EU, such as France. The law gives some protection (for both the union and the individual members), if the strike is authorised by the union, after a postal ballot is held and notice given to the employer of what may happen.

5.62 If there is no ballot, and if the union repudiates the actions of its members, industrial action is unofficial and those involved have no protection in law. If the union does not disassociate itself from unlawful action it is liable to punitive damages. Ballots are used to put further pressure on an employer to come to an agreement as a threat.

Conciliation, Mediation and Arbitration

5.63 Acas assists the two sides in an industrial dispute to reach an agreement if possible. Conciliation is the process where an Acas official who has the trust of the parties finds out what they would like to achieve and persuades them to come to an agreement.

5.64 Mediation is a process where a mediator is asked by the two sides to propose a solution that they can consider and may accept if they wish to do so. It will succeed if the mediator is able to bridge the gap between the two sides. The parties may want an answer to their dispute and therefore agree to an arbitrator hearing their case and making an award that is binding in honour not law.

5.65 Under arbitration, the two disputing parties agree in advance to accept the decision of the arbitrator as final and binding.

5.66 Some arbitration is conducted as "pendulum arbitration." This means that the arbitrator has to choose between the last demand of the union and the last offer of the employer. The parties have to be careful therefore not to seem unreasonable or the other side may gain the award. More usually, the arbitrator will construct and award that aims to provide a realistic outcome that is acceptable to both parties.

5.67 Arbitration awards may be about pay, or job grading or a disciplinary appeal. An award is invariably accepted by employers and unions. This may be because the issue is a technical one, the alternative such as industrial action is less acceptable, or that both parties are able to lay the blame for the outcome on an outsider.

5.68 Management can justify itself to the board or a union to its members by using arbitration as a mutually acceptable way out of an impasse.

Information and Consultation of Employees Regulations 2004

5.69 The Information and Consultation Directive 2002 is implemented in the UK under the Information and Consultation of Employees Regulations 2004. These regulations are phased in from 6 April 2005. Initially, they covered organisations employing 150 or more employees. From April 2007, they cover organisations employing 100 or more; and from April 2008, those with 50 or more. They do not apply to organisations with fewer than 50 employees.

5.70 The provisions of the regulations are not automatically implemented at workplace level. They require negotiations and balloting to approve a workplace Information and Consultation Agreement.

5.71 The duties on employers relating to information disclosure and consultation are as follows.
- Information on the recent and probable development of the organisation's activities and economic situation. It is said that the purpose of this information is to help union or employee representatives understand the context in which decisions are made affecting employment, work organisation and the employee's terms and conditions.
- Information and consultation about the employment within the organisation and about any likely expansion, contraction or reorganisation.

- Information and consultation with a view to reaching agreement on management decisions likely to lead to substantial changes in work organisation or in contractual relations with employees (in respect of terms and conditions of employment).

5.72 Unions may be able to benefit from the regulations by ensuring their members are elected; thus using another channel of communication with the employer to widen their influence to matters and areas not now covered by collective agreements.

5.73 However, the existence of a consultative council may undermine a union which is weakly represented. Employees may fail to see the value of membership and become even less likely to join or maintain union membership.

List of Relevant Legislation

5.74
- Information and Consultation of Employees Regulations 2004
- Working Time Regulations 1998
- Employment Relations Act 2004
- Trade Union and Labour Relations (Consolidation) Act 1992 (as amended)

Further Information

Publications
- *Acas/RP05 Resolving Collective Disputes at Work (Research paper, January 2001)*
- *Acas/RW07 Trade Unions and Representation (November 2003)*
- *Acas Code of Practice: Disclosure of Information for Collective Bargaining Purposes (2001)*

Organisations
- **Advisory Conciliation and Arbitration Service (Acas)**
  Web: *www.acas.org.uk*
  Acas aims to improve organisations and working life through better employment relations. It provides up-to-date information, advice, high-quality training, and works with employers and employees to solve problems and improve performance.
- **Central Arbitration Committee**
  Web: *www.cac.gov.uk*
  The Central Arbitration Committee is a permanent independent body with statutory powers, whose main function is to adjudicate on applications relating to the statutory recognition and derecognition of trade unions for lective bargaining purposes, where such recognition or derecognition cannot be agreed voluntarily.
- **Chartered Institute of Personnel and Development (CIPD)**
  Web: *www.cipd.org.uk*
  The CIPD is a professional body for those involved in the management and development of people.
- **Confederation of British Industry (CBI)**
  Web: *www.cbi.org.uk*

The CBI is a vital source of expert advice and information and a forum for the generation of ideas, best practice exchange and high-powered networking.

- **Department for Business, Enterprise and Regulatory Reform (BERR)**
  Web: *www.berr.gov.uk*
  The Department for Business, Enterprise and Regulatory Reform brings together functions from the former Department of Trade and Industry (DTI), including responsibilities for productivity, business relations, energy, competition and consumers. It also drives regulatory reform.

- **Trades Union Congress (TUC)**
  Web: *www.tuc.org.uk*
  The TUC describes itself as "the voice of Britain at work". With 71 affiliated unions representing nearly seven million working people from all walks of life, it campaigns for a fair deal at work and for social justice at home and abroad.

Collective Redundancies

> This topic covers the following.
> - Collective Redundancies Defined
> - Period of Consultation
> - Calculating the Number of Employees to be Dismissed
> - "Redundancy Selection"
> - "Dismiss as Redundant"
> - "One Establishment"
> - Notification to the Department for Business, Enterprise and Regulatory Reform
> - When An Employer Should Consult
> - Meaningful Consultation
> - Who Should Be Consulted
> - Employers' Duties on Election of Representatives
> - Election Process
> - If Employees Fail to Elect Representatives
> - Information to Appropriate Representatives/Employees
> - Subjects for Consultation
> - Consequences of a Failure to Consult
> - When Employers Are Allowed to Not Consult - Special Circumstances
> - Protective Awards
> - Unfair Dismissal
> - Other Rights and Claims
> - Assistance for Employees Selected for Redundancy
> - European Dimension

5.75 The obligation to comply with collective redundancy requirements arises when an employer is proposing to dismiss 20 or more employees as redundant at one establishment within a period of 90 days. An employer is obliged to consult the appropriate representatives of affected employees if collective redundancies are proposed.

5.76 The obligation to consult must include certain information and include ways to avoid or reduce the redundancies or mitigate the consequences.

Employers' Duties

5.77 Employers have the following duties.
- Identify the number of employees for whom dismissal is being considered.
- Identify the basis on which employees are selected for redundancy.
- Consider whether these employees are employed at "one establishment".
- Identify whether the employees have union or other appropriate representatives. If not, arrange for elections.
- Lodge Form HR1 with the BERR.
- Arrange a consultation meeting with the appropriate representatives.
- Provide appropriate representatives with a copy of Form HR1 and any other information in writing that the employer is obliged to provide.
- Agree the selection criteria with the appropriate representatives.

- Ensure consultation takes place for the minimum period and is extended beyond the minimum period if the appropriate representatives raise issues which remain unresolved.
- Arrange individual meetings with those employees identified as "at risk" of becoming redundant.

Employees' Duties

5.78 Employees have the following duties.
- Ensure the collective redundancy proposal made by the employer satisfies the statutory criteria.
- Employees should choose representatives to consult with their employer, or they should consult with the employer themselves.
- Employees should make use of any help provided by the employer to employees selected for redundancy.
- Employees at risk of redundancy should consider applying for suitable alternative positions at the employer's organisation.

In Practice

Collective Redundancies Defined

5.79 Collective redundancies occur when an employer dismisses 20 or more employees as redundant:
- at one establishment
- within a period of 90 days.

5.80 In such circumstances, the employer is obliged to consult with the appropriate representatives of affected employees.

Period of Consultation

5.81 If an employer proposes to dismiss:
- 100 or more employees from one establishment within a 90-day period, consultation must begin not less than 90 days before the first dismissal is effected
- between 20 and 99 employees from one establishment within a 90-day period, consultation must begin not less than 30 days before the first dismissal is effected.

5.82 These are minimum periods only. Employers may in fact require that for it to be "meaningful", consultation should cover a longer period of time. In practice, if the appropriate representatives raise issues that have not been sufficiently dealt with in the statutory minimum timetable, the employer must engage in further consultation until such issues have been dealt with.

5.83 The requirement on the employer is to consult "with a view to reaching an agreement" with the appropriate representatives. This duty does not, however, require the employer to actually reach an agreement. The employer must demonstrate a willingness to consider and respond to all of the points raised by the appropriate representatives.

Calculating the Number of Employees to be Dismissed

5.84 When calculating the number of redundancies for collective consultation purposes, the definition of employees should include:
- temporary employees
- those with less than one year's service
- those over normal retirement age.

5.85 Since collective consultations are intended to consider an employer's proposed redundancies, consultations must still take place even if the proposed number of redundancies is over 20 but the actual number of redundancies turns out to be less than 20. Therefore, if the employer is also considering redeployment of some of the employees, but such redeployed employees will be required to agree substantially or to wholly varied contractual terms, these employees are to be counted as "proposed redundancies".

5.86 Similarly, if an employer is proposing to vary substantially, or wholly, employees' terms of employment, the employees are deemed to be dismissed for these purposes.

"Redundancy Selection"

5.87 In selecting employees for redundancy, the employer must use fair and objective criteria against which an individual's selection could be defended. Employers should use criteria which do not just depend on the view of the person making the selection but can be objectively checked against, eg:
- attendance record
- efficiency at the job
- experience
- disciplinary record.

5.88 There is no statutory obligation to follow any particular customary arrangements such as LIFO ("last in, first out"). Employers need to be careful that any selection criteria do not infringe discrimination law (eg to select people on the basis of length of service may be indirect sex discrimination and is likely to constitute age discrimination).

5.89 Employers should agree the selection criteria with the appropriate representatives.

"Dismiss as Redundant"

5.90 "Dismiss as redundant" means — for the purposes of collective redundancy legislation — "dismissal for a reason not related to the individual concerned or for a number of reasons all of which are not so related".

5.91 The definition therefore includes normal redundancy dismissals, but can also extend to:
- the expiry of a fixed term contract
- termination of an existing employment contract and re-engagement on new terms
- a substantial variation of contractual terms.

"One Establishment"

5.92 "Establishment" does not necessarily just mean an employee's normal place

Collective Redundancies

of work. Employees can be defined as engaged at "one establishment" even when they do not work at the same premises, eg a nationwide sales team.

5.93 Factors to consider when establishing whether a number of employees work at "one establishment" include the following.
- Does the establishment have a degree of permanence?
- Is there an organisation of people working at the establishment or from the establishment?
- Even if normally working from different locations, are employees managed from and reporting to the establishment?

5.94 The courts will generally see through any attempts by an employer to avoid the "one establishment" definition by artificially dividing a workforce.

Notification to the Department for Business, Enterprise and Regulatory Reform

5.95 Employers who propose to make collective redundancies must notify the BERR of the proposed redundancies using Form HR1. Form HR1 can be obtained from the BERR on 0845 145 0004 or from www.insolvency.gov.uk/pdfs/rpforms/hr1.pdf.

5.96 Notification must be:
- 90 days before the first notice of dismissal takes effect, if 100 or more employees are to be dismissed
- 30 days before the first dismissal notice of dismissal takes effect, if 20–99 employees are to be dismissed.

5.97 Failure to notify the BERR is a criminal offence and may result in a fine of up to £5000. An employer who fails to give the required notification to the BERR may be prosecuted in a Magistrates Court.

5.98 A copy of Form HR1 must be given to the appropriate representatives at the beginning of the redundancy consultation period.

When An Employer Should Consult

5.99 Consultation must begin in good time. Effectively this means while the collective redundancy proposals are at a formative stage. The appropriate representatives must be informed that no decisions have been made about effective collective redundancies. The employer should also inform the appropriate representatives that it will undertake meaningful consultation about the proposed collective redundancies.

5.100 A tribunal has found that consultation does not need to cover "the economic background or context in which the proposal for redundancies arises" (see *Securicor Omega Express v GMB*). But it is still unclear at what stage of the collective redundancies' decision-making process consultation should begin: it is safest for an employer to consult as early on in the process as possible.

"Meaningful" Consultation

5.101 Consultation should be "meaningful", which means that the employer should be open-minded and consider the views of the appropriate representatives. The aim should be to reach agreement with the representatives. The consultation should begin early enough so that the views of the appropriate representatives can be properly considered.

5.102 The employer is not required in fact to reach an agreement with the appropriate representatives. Therefore, if the employer has considered and responded to all of the issues raised by the appropriate representatives, the employer can end the consultation process notwithstanding that it has not reached an agreement with the appropriate representatives.

Who Should Be Consulted

5.103 An employer must consult with the representatives of a trade union recognised by the organisation or in the absence of a recognised union, with whichever of the following representatives the employer chooses.

- Representatives who have been appointed or elected by employees, and who have general authority to be consulted on behalf of the employees about any proposed dismissals.
- Representatives elected by employees specifically to consult about the proposed collective redundancies in question.

5.104 Every category of worker must be represented during the consultation process. Therefore if the recognised trade union does not represent all of the affected employees, additional appropriate representatives should be elected to represent the remaining non-union employees. If no representatives can be elected or chosen, the employer should consult directly with the employees concerned.

Employers' Duties on Election of Representatives

5.105 If there are not already any appropriate representatives, the employer should arrange elections. The employer should ensure these guidelines are followed.

- Arrangements should be reasonably practical to ensure that the election is fair.
- Enough representatives should be elected so that all affected employees' interests are represented.
- It should be determined whether the elected representatives are of all the affected employees or of particular classes of those employees.
- The term of office of the elected representatives should be decided.

Election Process

5.106 The following guidelines should be adhered to for a fair election.

- Candidates for election must themselves be affected employees on the date of election.
- No affected employee must be unreasonably excluded from standing for election.
- All affected employees on the date of election must be entitled to vote.
- There must be a candidate for each representative position.
- The voting should be secret and the votes accurately counted.
- Where an elected representative ceases to act, causing any employee no longer to be represented, a new representative must be elected.

5.107 It is advisable to write to each affected employee, explaining the essentials of the representation and consultation process, and inviting nominations for each work group.

5.108 Those nominations should be returned to a specific person; generally someone in the HR department. It must be pointed out to the employees that they must first obtain the consent of the person whom they are nominating. The nominations are then counted and the person obtaining most nominations is duly appointed.

Collective Redundancies

5.109 It would be sensible for an employer to keep a record of, and any paperwork relating to employee representative elections, together with the results and the guidelines used for the election process.

5.110 Alternatively, there are independent bodies that can arrange elections in the workplace (eg Electoral Reform Ballot Services Ltd).

If Employees Fail to Elect Representatives

5.111 Where an employer has invited affected employees to elect representatives but they have failed to do so within a reasonable time, the employer should provide each affected employee with the information that would have been provided to their representatives.

Information to Appropriate Representatives/Employees

5.112 The appropriate representatives or the employees if no representatives are elected must be informed of the:
- reasons for the proposed redundancies
- numbers and descriptions of those employees it is proposed to dismiss as redundant
- total number of employees employed at each establishment from which redundancies will be declared
- proposed method of selection for redundancy
- proposed method of dismissal, including procedure and timing, having regard to any agreed procedures
- proposed method of calculating redundancy payments.

5.113 All this information must be given in writing. The information contained in the first four bullet points is contained in Form HR1.

5.114 An employer must consider and reply to any representations. Reasons should be given if suggestions from representatives or employees are rejected.

Subjects for Consultation

5.115 The employer must consult appropriate representatives about each of the following subjects:
- avoiding dismissals
- reducing the number of dismissals
- mitigating the effects of dismissals.

5.116 The requirement to consult about all three subjects is mandatory and employers cannot escape this obligation on the grounds that consultation about any one of these subjects would be futile.

5.117 If insufficient weight is given to any of these subjects, the consultation process will be considered defective. It is particularly important to consider ways of avoiding the dismissals and care should be taken not to start the procedure so late that this cannot be done.

5.118 Ways to avoid redundancies will include redeployment, training for vacant positions and considering suitable alternative positions. In addition to consulting with their representatives, employers should allow employees themselves to propose ideas about these matters.

5.119 However, it is ultimately for the employer to determine whether the redundancies should proceed or not. Notices of dismissal should not be sent out before the expiry of any statutory consultation period. The only circumstance where it may be acceptable to send out notices of dismissal is where the substance of the consultation process is completed before the end of the statutory consultation period. The employer should obtain written confirmation from the appropriate representatives that they agree that the consultation process has been completed if this is before the expiry of the minimum statutory period.

5.120 A fully completed consultation process will benefit the employer by reducing both the likelihood of successful unfair dismissal claims and the risk of a protective award claim.

Consequences of a Failure to Consult

5.121 Where the employer has failed to comply with certain requirements relating to consultation or the election of representatives, the relevant trade union, employee representative or affected employee may present a claim for a protective award to an employment tribunal. The maximum award is 90 days' pay per affected employee. The tribunals have held that the purpose of the protective award is to provide a sanction for the employer's breach rather than to compensate the employee for any loss as a result of the breach. Where there has been a complete failure to consult, the starting point will be the maximum penalty, reduced only if there are relevant mitigating circumstances.

5.122 Any claim must be presented within three months of the last dismissals taking effect. If the employees are bringing claims themselves (where there are no appropriate representatives) the employees must do so within three months from the date of their own dismissal.

5.123 The onus is on the employer to show that the requirements relating to the election of representatives have been satisfied.

When Employers Are Allowed to Not Consult — The "Special Circumstances" Defence

5.124 An employer may be excused compliance with the obligation to consult only where "special circumstances" exist, although the employer will still need to take all reasonably practicable steps to comply. All employers should bear in mind that this defence is extremely limited in scope and will only rarely apply.

5.125 The test for "special circumstances" will only be satisfied if the employer has a genuine and very serious crisis. Even insolvency has in the past been found not to constitute "special circumstances".

5.126 Should circumstances be found to be "special", an employer will still need to show it has done its best to consult in all the circumstances.

Protective Awards

5.127 Where an employer has not complied with its legal duty to consult, an employee may present a complaint to an employment tribunal. If the tribunal finds the complaint well-founded, it will make a declaration to that effect and may also make a protective award.

5.128 A protective award is an award to one or more employees:
- who have been dismissed as redundant, or whom it is proposed to dismiss as redundant, and

- in respect of whose dismissal or proposed dismissal the employer failed to comply with its legal duty to consult.

5.129 Any award will span the protected period, which:
- begins with the date on which the first of the redundancies take effect or the date of the award, whichever is the earlier
- will be a period that the tribunal thinks is just and equitable in all the circumstances taking into account the seriousness of the employer's failure to consult
- cannot exceed 90 days' pay per affected employee.

5.130 A protective award is a payment awarded to an employee to cover the protected period. The protective award is not considered remuneration for the protected period and the fact that there is no loss on the part of the employee will not necessarily prevent an award.

5.131 There are five factors that an employment tribunal will consider when deciding whether to make a protective award and for what period.
(1) The purpose of the award is not to compensate the employee but to provide a sanction for breach by the employer of its obligation to consult.
(2) What is just and equitable in all the circumstances focusing on the seriousness of the employer's default. The tribunal can exercise wide discretion in this matter.
(3) The nature and seriousness of the employer's default. This may vary in seriousness from a technical one to complete failure to consult.
(4) The deliberateness of the failure may be relevant, as may be the availability of legal advice to the employer.
(5) In assessing the length of the protective period, courts or tribunals should start with the maximum period (if there has been no consultation at all) and reduce that period only if there have been mitigating factors.

Unfair Dismissal

5.132 In addition to claiming a protective award, employees may also bring claims of unfair dismissal. They can argue that they may not have been dismissed if they had been properly consulted. The maximum compensation available following a successful unfair dismissal claim is now £60,600 (from February 2007).

Other Rights and Claims

5.133 An employee may also bring a claim in an employment tribunal if the employee feels that he or she has suffered a detriment or been unfairly dismissed because he or she was:
- an employee representative
- a candidate in an election to be an employee representative, or
- involved in the election of appropriate representatives.

5.134 An employee is entitled to paid time-off for training in connection with being an employee representative.

Assistance for Employees Selected for Redundancy

5.135 Employers should consider as a matter of good practice whether it is possible to provide assistance and advice to employees selected for redundancy. This could include advice about:
- the tax and social security implications of any termination payments
- preparing CVs
- making job applications

- interview technique
- counselling.

5.136 An employer could ask local colleges and/or recruitment agencies to visit the employer's premises to offer assistance.

European Dimension

5.137 Treatment of collective redundancy can be vastly different in other EU countries. Sanctions tend to be more severe than in the UK, so multinational companies seeking to make redundancies in other countries should take specialist advice.

5.138 In particular, works councils in Europe tend to have much greater powers to force employers to consult with them (eg applying for injunctions preventing the dismissals going ahead until the consultation process has been completed).

Training

5.139 When appropriate representatives are specially elected, for the collective consultation process, the employer should ensure that they have had an opportunity for appropriate training in time to allow for the minimum period for consultation to be met. Any time off to undertake training should be paid.

List of Relevant Legislation

5.140
- Employment Act 2002 (Dispute Resolution) Regulations 2004
- Information and Consultation Regulations 2004
- Trade Union and Labour Relations (Consolidation) Act 1992, as amended. In particular, s.188 implements the Collective Redundancies Directive (75/129/EEC) as amended in the UK. The Act has been further amended by the Collective Redundancies and Transfer of Undertakings (Protection of Employment) (Amendment) Regulations 1999.
- Collective Redundancies Directive (Consolidation) 1998 (98/59/EC)

List of Relevant Cases

5.141
- *Amicus v GBS Tooling Ltd (in administration)* UK EAT/0100/05/SM
- *GMB v Lambeth Service Team Ltd* EAT/0127/05
- *Howard v Millrise Ltd* [2005] IRLR 84, EAT
- *Junk v Kühnel* [2005] IRLR 310, ECJ
- *Leicestershire County Council v Unison* UK EAT/0066/05
- *TGWU v Lambeth Service Team Ltd* EAT/0129/05
- *Vauxhall Motors Ltd v Transport and General Workers Union* EAT/0657/05
- *GMB v Beloit Walmsley Ltd* [2004] IRLR 18
- *Hardy v Tourism South East* [2004] UKEAT/0631/04

Collective Redundancies

- *Securicor Omega Express Ltd v GMB* [2004] IRLR 9
- *Susie Radin Ltd v GMB* [2004] EWCA Civ 180
- *GMB and Others v Amicus and Others* [2003] IRLR 721
- *Middlesbrough Borough Council v TGWU & Unison* [2002] LRLR 332
- *MSF Refuge Assurance plc* [2002] IRLR 324
- *TGWU v Morgan Platts Ltd (in administration)* [2002] EAT/0646/02
- *GMB v Man Truck and Bus UK Ltd* [2000] IRLR 636
- *Mills & Allen Ltd v Bulwich* EAT/154/99 [8 June 2000]
- *Scotch Premier Meat Ltd v Burns and Others* [2000] IRLR 639
- *GMB and AEEU v Campbells UK Ltd* Industrial Tribunal, [1 May 1998]
- *Williams v Compair Maxam Ltd* [1982] IRLR 83

Further Information

Publications
- *BERR Redundancy Forms*, Department for Business, Enterprise and Regulatory Reform (BERR)

Organisations
- **Advisory Conciliation and Arbitration Service (Acas)**
  Web: *www.acas.org.uk*
  Acas aims to improve organisations and working life through better employment relations. It provides up-to-date information, advice, high-quality training, and works with employers and employees to solve problems and improve performance.
- **Chartered Institute of Personnel and Development (CIPD)**
  Web: *www.cipd.org.uk*
  The CIPD is a professional body for those involved in the management and development of people.
- **Department for Business, Enterprise and Regulatory Reform (BERR)**
  Web: *www.berr.gov.uk*
  The Department for Business, Enterprise and Regulatory Reform brings together functions from the former Department of Trade and Industry (DTI), including responsibilities for productivity, business relations, energy, competition and consumers. It also drives regulatory reform.
- **Electoral Reform Services**
  Web: *www.erbs.co.uk*
  The role of the Electoral Reform Services (ERS) is to see the fair and impartial conduct of ballots and elections. They have over a century's experience in conducting ballots for a huge range of clients in all areas of society.
- **Trades Union Congress (TUC)**
  Web: *www.tuc.org.uk*
  The TUC describes itself as "the voice of Britain at work". With 71 affiliated unions representing nearly seven million working people from all walks of life, it campaigns for a fair deal at work and for social justice at home and abroad.

Employee Representatives

This topic covers the following.
- Right to be Accompanied
- Right to Consultation
- Elections of Employee Representatives
- The Rights of Employee Representatives
- Consultation Mechanism
- Works Councils and Collective Bargaining
- The Benefits of Employee Representation

5.142 An employee representative is a worker within an organisation who is chosen by other workers within the organisation to represent a category of workers in negotiations or consultations with the employer.

5.143 The employee representative could act in group negotiations — both formal and informal — or accompany one individual in a meeting with the employer.

5.144 The role of employee representative is one that has developed with the decline in union influence. Unlike a union representative, an employee representative need not have any affiliation to an external organisation. An employee representative may not have any other experience of being a representative.

Employers' Duties

5.145 Employers should do the following.
- Make all employees aware of their statutory right to be accompanied by a trade union official or co-worker in certain meetings concerned with discipline or grievance.
- Ensure that employees or their representatives are consulted over planned collective redundancies, a transfer of undertakings, or health and safety issues.
- Facilitate elections of employee representatives if all employees and categories of employees are not already properly represented.
- Circulate certain information if an election is to take place.
- Make sure that all relevant employees should be able to vote on the date of the election — this may require facilities for postal, telephone or e-mail voting.
- Ensure that voting in any election is secret, so far as is reasonably practicable.
- Recognise the rights of employee representatives.

Employees' Duties

5.146 Employees should do the following.
- A worker facing a disciplinary, dismissal or grievance hearing should decide whether or not he or she wishes to be accompanied by a co-worker or trade union official.
- They should make every effort to vote in an election for employee representatives.

Employee Representatives

- Employees who are employee representatives should understand their rights and ensure they are properly prepared to fulfil their role.

In Practice

5.147 Legislation has developed in recent times to ensure that workers are properly consulted. Many of these rights were originally only available to trade union members where the employer recognised the trade union in the workplace.

5.148 The areas where employee representation needs to be established or considered are as follows.

Right to be Accompanied

5.149 Workers have a statutory right to be accompanied by a fellow worker or trade union official (lay or full-time) if they are asked by their employer to attend a disciplinary, dismissal or grievance hearing. The worker's request to be accompanied must be reasonable.

5.150 It is for the worker to decide whether he or she wishes to be accompanied by a co-worker or a trade union official.

5.151 The right to be accompanied applies only to:
- disciplinary, dismissal and grievance hearings that may result in a formal warning or other action being taken against a worker by his or her employer
- where the grievance is about the employer's contractual or statutory duty to the worker.

5.152 The right applies to all workers, including:
- employees
- those who perform work personally for someone else but are not genuinely self-employed
- agency workers
- home workers.

5.153 Workers also have a right to reasonable postponement of any hearing organised if the worker's chosen companion is unavailable at the time the employer proposes. The worker must suggest an alternative date which is reasonable and which falls within five working days from the first working day after the day proposed by the employer.

5.154 The person accompanying the worker can address the hearing and confer with the worker, but cannot answer questions on behalf of the worker unless the employer accepts this.

5.155 If an employer refuses to allow a worker to be accompanied at a disciplinary hearing and subsequently dismisses the worker, the dismissed worker can make a claim for "automatically unfair" dismissal at an employment tribunal.

Time Off to Accompany

5.156 A worker who is asked by a fellow worker to accompany him or her to a disciplinary, dismissal or grievance hearing is entitled to paid time off work to do so.

Accompanying a Person Requesting Flexible Working

5.157 Parents of children under the age of six or disabled children under the age of 18, and carers of specified categories of adults, have the right to apply to their employer to request flexible working. If the employer and employee need to meet to discuss a request for flexible working at a hearing, the employee can ask to be accompanied by a colleague who has the right to paid time off during working hours to attend.

Extra Rights to Accompaniment

5.158 Many employers will wish to provide employees with contractual rights over and above the statutory provisions. For example, allowing:
- workers to be accompanied on a broader range of occasions by a person of their choice (eg interviews, meetings or hearings on a range of disciplinary issues)
- workers to be accompanied by a broader range of people (eg a spouse, partner, friend, legal practitioner, or, in the case of young workers, a parent or guardian)
- the accompanying individual to take a full representational role, rather than merely acting as a companion.

Employment Act 2002 (Dispute Resolution) Regulations 2004

5.159 The Employment Act 2002 (Dispute Resolution) Regulations 2004, which came into force on 1 October 2004, set out statutory dismissal, disciplinary and grievance procedures which apply to all employers and employees.

5.160 The aim of the procedures is to encourage organisations to sort out any disagreements internally without having to resort to costly and time-consuming external procedures.

5.161 The legislation provides for a standard dismissal and disciplinary procedure, and a modified dismissal procedure. In both cases, the emphasis is on consultation with the relevant employee.

Right to Consultation

5.162 Employees have rights to be consulted over:
- planned collective and individual redundancies
- transfers of undertakings
- health and safety issues.

Consultation over Collective Redundancies

5.163 An employer must consult with a trade union or employee representative if he or she plans to dismiss as redundant 20 or more employees at one establishment within 90 days or less.

5.164 Employers should provide in writing, to employee representatives, the following information:
- reasons for the proposed redundancies
- numbers and descriptions of the employees affected
- total number of employees of this description employed at the establishment
- proposed method of selecting employees who may be dismissed
- how the dismissals are proposed to be carried out
- how redundancy payments over the legal minimum will be calculated.

5.165 If an employer decides to make 20 or more employees redundant and does not recognise a trade union, then he or she must ensure that employees:
- already have employee representatives
- are invited to hold an election to appoint employee representatives.

5.166 If employees already have employee representatives, the employer must ensure that such representatives are suitable for consultation over redundancies. So, for example, a health and safety committee might not be an appropriate representative group.

5.167 An employer who fails to consult with employee representatives over proposed redundancies could face a claim in an employment tribunal.

Consultation over Transfer of Undertakings

5.168 If a business or undertaking is to be transferred from one owner to another, the employers concerned must consult with the employees affected or their representatives. The information provided should include:
- when and why the transfer is going to take place
- the broad implications of the transfer for all employees who will be affected
- whether the employer envisages taking any action in connection with the transfer that will affect employees.

5.169 If the employer does plan to reorganise the undertaking as a result of the transfer, it must consult with employee representatives before doing so.

5.170 This consultation must take place in good time before the transfer so that the employees or their representatives can respond. The consultation should be conducted with a view to reaching agreement on contentious issues.

Health and Safety Representation

5.171 There are four routes to health and safety representation and consultation:
- through recognised trade union representatives (1977 Regulations)
- through non-union employee representatives (1996 Regulations)
- directly with the relevant workforce (1996 Regulations)
- through representatives in offshore industry (1989 Regulations).

Information and Consultation of Employees Regulations 2004

5.172 The Information and Consultation of Employees Regulations 2004 are implemented in stages, depending on the number of employees at a business, as follows.
- 150 employees or more — 6 April 2005
- 100–149 employees — 6 April 2007
- 50–99 employees — 6 April 2008.

5.173 The regulations will not apply to employers with fewer than 50 employees. They will require employers to:
- inform employees or their representatives about the economic situation of the business
- consult with employees or their representatives on employment prospects
- consult with a view to reaching agreement on any potential changes to work organisation or contractual relations (including redundancies or the transfer of the business to another owner).

5.174 If an employer does not have existing arrangements in place, the employer must initiate negotiations to reach such an agreement if requested to do so by 10% or more of its employees.

5.175 If an employer does have an information and consultation agreement in place, the employer can hold a ballot and the existing agreement will be allowed to stay in place unless at least 40% of the workforce votes in favour of change.

Consultation for European Companies

5.176 Companies with at least 1000 employees in EU Member States and with at least 150 employees in two or more Member States can request a European Works Council or equivalent procedure. This obligation stems from the Transnational Information and Consultation of Employees Regulations 1999, which implement the European Works Council Directive 1994.

5.177 The purpose of a European Works Council is to provide "transnational information and consultation" to the workforce. The regulations provide that employees should be allowed reasonable paid time off if they are a:
- member of a special negotiating body or a European Works Council
- representative for information or consultation purposes
- candidate in an election to be a member or representative.

5.178 The Working Time Regulations 1998 provide for the negotiation of workforce agreements (in organisations where collective agreements are not agreed with recognised trade unions). Such agreements — concluded with the workforce as a whole or through representatives — can modify provisions of the regulations.

Elections of Employee Representatives

5.179 If employee representatives are required, an employer should ensure that elections are held so that all employees have an opportunity to be represented. An employer must take reasonable steps to ensure that any election is conducted fairly.

5.180 The responsibility for conducting elections lies with the employer. There is no guidance on the number of representatives required or what a reasonable timescale for elections would be.

5.181 If an employer recognises an independent trade union, it may be that the union only represents certain categories of employee (eg those in particular occupational groups within the organisation). The employer then still has a duty to ensure other employees affected are offered the opportunity to consult through employee representatives.

Preparation for the Election Process

5.182 The following information should be circulated to all those involved in the election:
- the number of representatives needed to sufficiently represent the interests of the workers
- the term of office of the representatives (eg every two years)
- time frame for the election process
- instructions to potential candidates (eg suggest circulating brief information about themselves prior to the elections)
- candidate nomination forms
- an explanation of how votes will be counted.

Prior to an Election

5.183 Employers should, prior to any election, ensure that:
- all candidates legitimately represent the employees for whom they claim to stand (it is not good practice for the employer to nominate candidates)
- no relevant employee is unreasonably excluded from standing for election
- all relevant employees are able to vote on the date of the election; this may require postal, telephone or e-mail voting to allow those absent or on leave to vote
- voting papers are prepared.

The Election Process

5.184 To ensure that an election runs smoothly, an employer should ensure that:
- those voting do so in secret, so far as is reasonably practicable
- the votes cast at the election are accurately counted (NB, it is not necessary to hire an independent vote counter)
- the voting figures are made available to employees.

After the Elections

5.185 The elected employee representatives and other employees should be informed of the result after the election. The date of the first meeting that the employer intends to hold with the employees or their elected representatives should be arranged and circulated.

The Rights of Employee Representatives

5.186 Employee representatives have essentially the same rights as trade union representatives. These rights include:
- access to employees
- facilities, such as meeting rooms and telephones
- reasonable paid time off work during working hours, in order to allow them to carry out or be trained for their duties. If an employer unreasonably refuses a request for time off work, the employer can be taken to an employment tribunal.

The Right Not to be Dismissed or Victimised

5.187 Employees are protected against unfair dismissal and detrimental treatment for taking part in an election, whether as candidates or as voters. It is automatically unfair to dismiss or select for redundancy an employee representative on grounds relating to them carrying out their duties.

Consultation Mechanism

5.188 Most employers will have some form of consultation mechanism in place at their workplace. Employee representatives might meet an employer in regular meetings, variously called:
- joint consultative committees
- staff councils
- company councils
- works committees
- office committees
- participation groups

- joint panels.

5.189 Consultation undertaken by an employer should be genuine (ie it should be undertaken with the active aim of dealing with employee concerns and of reaching agreement on issues). This means that consultation should take place early, either at or before the proposal stage, and certainly before any decision is taken.

5.190 Those being consulted should be provided with the information necessary and time to consider any proposals. If employee representations are not accepted, it can bolster the employer's credibility if it gives reasons for refusal.

5.191 Regular newsletters and staff satisfaction surveys can help to facilitate communication within an organisation, but are no substitute for active consultation.

Works Councils and Collective Bargaining

5.192 If an employer does not recognise a trade union, the employer may still consult with employee representatives on works councils. This subject is dealt with in more detail in a separate topic.

5.193 A works council is a permanent body within an organisation through which representatives of the employer can consult with representatives of the employees. Validation of a business decision by a works council helps to smooth the passage of a change with employees.

5.194 The people sitting on a works council as representatives of the employees should between them cover all categories and interests of the organisation's employees. Any employee involved in a works council should be given reasonable paid time-off to carry out his or her duties on the council.

5.195 Employees should elect the individuals who represent them on works councils. If an organisation has an established trade union structure, it is often the case that the union representatives will sit on the works council along with elected employee representatives sitting for non-union employees.

5.196 If an employer does recognise a trade union, the employer needs to be aware that consulting with any other employee representatives may cause conflict with the union. A reasonable line to take with a union is that employees who are not union members also need to have their views heard through representation.

5.197 Legislation requires multi-sited EU undertakings to have, if requested, a European Works Council that spans the different sites of the organisation and consults at a European level.

The Benefits of Employee Representation

5.198 Although employers are required by law to consult employee representatives, consultation can bring considerable benefits to an employer. The benefits can include:
- harmonious working relations and positive employees building the competitiveness and performance of an organisation
- enhancing the spirit of co-operation within a business
- improving the prospects of attracting and retaining the best talent in business sectors where skilled workers are in short supply
- encouraging the commitment, energy and ideas of employees
- helping the employees to identify more closely with the policies and aims of the organisation

- improve employees' skills in negotiation and consultation, which may be of benefit to the organisation more widely.

Training

5.199 All employees should be made aware of their various rights and duties in relation to employee representatives.

5.200 Any employee chosen as a representative should be trained in the different skills and technical requirements of the role.

5.201 Works council members — and other representatives involved regularly in formal consultation — should be encouraged to learn about:
- interacting with a group
- dealing constructively with conflict and criticism
- valuing the contributions of others
- any legislation relevant to their role.

List of Relevant Legislation

5.202
- Employment Act 2002 (Dispute Resolution) Regulations 2004
- Information and Consultation of Employees Regulations 2004
- Transnational Information and Consultation of Employees Regulations 1999
- Working Time Regulations 1998
- Health and Safety (Consultation with Employees) Regulations 1996
- Offshore Safety (Safety Representatives and Committees) Regulations 1989
- Transfer of Undertakings (Protection of Employment) Regulations 1981
- Safety Representatives and Safety Committees Regulations 1977
- Trade Union and Labour Relations (Consolidation) Act 1992
- Companies Act 1985
- Business Transfers Directive 2001
- Collective Redundancies Directive 1998
- European Works Council Directive 1994
- Working Time Directive 1993
- Safety and Health of Workers Directive 1989

Further Information

Organisations
- **Advisory Conciliation and Arbitration Service (Acas)**
  Web: *www.acas.org.uk*
  Acas aims to improve organisations and working life through better employment relations. It provides up-to-date information, advice, high-quality training, and works with employers and employees to solve problems and improve performance.

Employee Representatives

- **Department for Business, Enterprise and Regulatory Reform (BERR)**
  Web: *www.berr.gov.uk*
  The Department for Business, Enterprise and Regulatory Reform brings together functions from the former Department of Trade and Industry (DTI), including responsibilities for productivity, business relations, energy, competition and consumers. It also drives regulatory reform.

- **Trades Union Congress (TUC)**
  Web: *www.tuc.org.uk*
  The TUC describes itself as "the voice of Britain at work". With 71 affiliated unions representing nearly seven million working people from all walks of life, it campaigns for a fair deal at work and for social justice at home and abroad.

Industrial Action

> This topic covers the following.
> - Subjects for Dispute
> - Categories of Dispute
> - Forms of Industrial Action
> - Legality of Industrial Action
> - Employees' Protection from Dismissal
> - Seriousness of Disputes
> - Employer's Response
> - Resolving Disputes
> - Obligation to Resolve Industrial Action
> - Illegal Union Action
> - Management Skills
> - Workplace Disputes' Procedures
> - Alternative Dispute Resolution (ADR) Defined
> - The Role of HR Practitioners
> - Trade Unions' Immunity from Legal Proceedings
> - Employees' Protection from Union

5.203 Industrial action is a sanction used by a group of employees against its employer. It usually arises when there is a failure to settle a dispute about terms and conditions of employment.

Employers' Duties

- Employers should not dismiss employees unlawfully.
- Pay should not be unlawfully deducted from employees.
- Employers should comply with all contracts (employment and commercial) to which the employer is party.
- Ensure that any response to industrial action complies with the relevant areas of law.

Employees' Duties

- Employees should ensure that any industrial action in which they take part has been approved in the required individual secret ballot.
- The union's principal executive committee should endorse any industrial action in which an employee takes part.
- Employees should be aware that, in taking strike action, they will be breaching their contracts of employment.
- "Industrial action short of a strike" is also very likely to be categorised as a breach of a contract of employment.

In Practice

Subjects for Dispute

5.204 Collective disputes in the workplace may relate to some decision already taken by an employer or to a decision the employer proposes to take. Disputes can be about a range of issues, including:
- pay, hours and holidays
- new working practices
- implications of organisational change
- technical change
- health, safety and welfare
- equal opportunities and discrimination
- whether the employer is complying with legal requirements.

5.205 For example, a union might complain that an employer is not implementing a collective agreement correctly or put in a claim for improvements to existing terms and conditions of employment.

Categories of Dispute

5.206 Disputes fall into two broad, sometimes overlapping categories.
- Disputes of "right" concern the interpretation and implementation of an existing collective agreement, contractual term or statutory entitlement.
- Disputes of "interest" relate to new claims on topics such as levels of pay, hours of work, holidays and work organisation.

Forms of Industrial Action

5.207 Industrial action can take many forms. Strikes tend to be the most highly publicised. Other forms of industrial action (sometimes called "industrial action short of a strike") include a go-slow, an overtime ban, a work-to-rule and a refusal to carry out certain tasks.

Legality of Industrial Action

5.208 An employee is breaching his or her contract of employment by taking part in a strike. The legal situation is likely to be the same for other forms of industrial action, but workers who take part in lawful industrial action have some protection against dismissal.

5.209 The overwhelming majority of industrial action involves trade union members. A union that organises industrial action has some protection against legal action if it complies with a complex range of legal obligations, both before and during the industrial action.

Employees' Protection from Dismissal

5.210 Employees involved in industrial action are "protected" for at least 12 weeks from dismissal. An employer cannot selectively dismiss an employee for taking part in official industrial action and, if an employee is dismissed, he or she cannot be selectively refused re-engagement if other workers in similar circumstances are re-engaged.

5.211 An employee may be able to make a complaint to, or bring a claim for, unfair dismissal at an employment tribunal. A successful claim could result in a basic award, a compensatory award and an additional award.

Seriousness of Disputes

5.212 Managers should treat all disputes seriously, as trivial complaints can often trigger major industrial action. This is particularly true of organisations where employment relations are generally poor, and there is little trust between the management and the workforce.

Employer's Response

5.213 An employer's response to any industrial action should consist of three interlocking strategies:
- business
- employee relations
- legal.

5.214 It is particularly important in long-running and intractable disputes that the employer's different strategies are clearly set out. The employer should communicate its case clearly to the staff.

5.215 Pursuit of one strategy will have inevitable short- and long-term consequences for other strategies. For example, an injunction against a trade union may provide short-term business benefits, but could also damage long-term employment relations.

Resolving Disputes

5.216 Resolution of industrial action normally occurs in one of the three following ways.

The Employer Sits it Out

5.217 The employer may choose to sit out the industrial action, awaiting employees to return to work under the existing or new terms of employment.

Resolution Within the Workplace

5.218 Resolution within the workplace could be achieved if the employer:
- re-opens formal negotiations with the relevant trade union, or
- agrees with the union to use one of the alternative dispute resolution (ADR) procedures.

5.219 Formal negotiations are often restarted after some form of informal contact has taken place between the parties.

Legal Action

5.220 Where appropriate, the employer could apply to the courts for the industrial action to be declared unlawful if it believed the union and/or members of the workforce had behaved (or intended to behave) unlawfully. Although a declaration would end the action itself, it is unlikely to resolve the original dispute and, therefore, ADR is a more comprehensive solution.

Obligation to Resolve Industrial Action

5.221 An employer has no direct obligation to attempt to resolve any industrial action. However, making no attempt to resolve industrial action may affect the judgment of an employment tribunal.

5.222 For example, employees are protected from unlawful dismissal for the first 12 weeks of any industrial action. Should an employment tribunal find that an employer did not take reasonable procedural steps to resolve the dispute during this period, the tribunal may extend the period of protection from unlawful dismissal.

5.223 The tribunal will consider whether, after the protected industrial action had begun, either the employer or the trade union unreasonably:
- rejected a proposal to start or re-start negotiations
- refused a request to make use of conciliation
- refused a request to use mediation.

Payment of Wages

5.224 An employer may lawfully deduct wages if an employee takes part in industrial action. If the action is a strike, the employer will normally pay no wages for the duration of the strike.

5.225 If the action is "industrial action short of a strike", employees will normally do some work. The employer must decide whether to accept or reject such partial performance of the contract of employment.

5.226 If the employer accepts the employee's partial performance of the contract, it is possible that the employer will be able to deduct a reasonable sum from the employee's wage. If the employer declines to accept part performance of the contract, then it is possible that the employer may be able to refuse to pay any wages.

Factors to Consider in Payment of Wages

5.227 The courts have found that the following factors should be considered when deciding whether or not wages should be paid.
- Employees are not entitled to pick and choose the work they do under the contract of employment.
- An employee cannot refuse to comply with the contract and then demand pay.
- An employer cannot, having told an employee not to attend work because he or she was not performing the contract, give directions to the employee if he or she turned up to work on a voluntary basis.
- An employer cannot be expected physically to prevent employees from entering work premises.
- In deciding whether to reject partial performance of a contract, the employer should take into account the nature and scale of the work not undertaken and the subsequent impact on the employer's business operations.

Illegal Union Action

5.228 An employer can, if it considers such action desirable, apply to the courts for an injunction if a trade union takes illegal industrial action.

Industrial Action

Management Skills

5.229 The key management skill for dealing with industrial action is negotiation. This could include the ability to:
- listen and discern any underlying issues in a dispute
- consider whether there might be common ground for resolving the dispute
- sift information
- be willing to adjourn negotiations as appropriate
- draw on appropriate advice within the organisation and from external agencies (such as Acas or an employers' association)
- be prepared to consider possible concessions
- sum up
- deliberate on the information provided and consider the implications of any decision for other staff and for the organisation's policy and practice
- communicate the outcome clearly.

Workplace Disputes Procedures

5.230 There is usually an agreed procedure for dealing with disputes in workplaces where trade unions are recognised. If managers and union representatives fail to resolve a dispute through the various stages of an agreed procedure, there are normally two alternative outcomes:
- the union calls some form of industrial action, or
- the parties agree to use ADR.

Alternative Dispute Resolution (ADR) Defined

5.231 ADR occurs when a third party is brought in to help resolve a dispute. The Advisory, Conciliation and Arbitration Service (Acas) is often involved in ADR. There are three possible ADR processes.

Conciliation

5.232 A third party (usually an Acas conciliation officer) assists the two parties in dispute to reach a settlement.

Mediation

5.233 This is sometimes described as a halfway house between conciliation and arbitration. A third party helps to clarify the nature of the dispute by making proposals about which the disputing parties can agree to negotiate further.

Arbitration

5.234 A third party (normally drawn from an Acas panel of trained and approved arbitrators) makes an award that resolves the dispute. Success of the arbitration depends on the parties agreeing in advance that the award will be final and binding. Since the parties pass over resolution of the dispute to a third party, arbitration is often seen as a last resort.

The Role of HR Practitioners

5.235 Human resources professionals can assist in a variety of ways when industrial action occurs. They can offer advice to the organisation on:

- standard organisation policy
- the possible uses of ADR
- the relevant law relating to industrial action
- a strategic approach to industrial action and dispute resolution
- assessing the lessons to be learned from industrial action once a dispute has been resolved.

Trade Unions' Immunity from Legal Proceedings

5.236 Trade unions will be immune from legal proceedings if industrial action is:
- mainly concerned with a dispute about terms and conditions of employment between a specific employer and its employees
- not called to support the employees of another employer (ie secondary or "sympathetic" industrial action)
- approved by a majority of the workforce concerned in an individual secret ballot (using a statutorily approved ballot paper) that has been supervised by an independent scrutineer
- not called to prevent an employer using non-union workers or to pressurise an employer or contractor into recognising a trade union
- endorsed by the union's principal executive committee
- started only after compliance with the statutory requirements on giving notice of industrial action to the employer
- not called to support an employee who has been dismissed for taking part in unlawful industrial action
- supported by peaceful picketing at the workplace which is (apart from limited exceptions in law) only conducted by employees from that workplace.

5.237 If unions break the law on industrial action, an employer can seek an injunction and claim limited damages.

Employees' Protection from Union

5.238 If an employee is a trade union member but refuses to take part in or support official industrial action by his or her union, the employee is protected from disciplinary action imposed by his or her union. Such disciplinary action might include imposing a fine, depriving the employee of union services or excluding the employee from standing in a union election.

Training

5.239 It is rare for organisations to provide special training for dealing with industrial action. It might form part of management's general training in the handling of employment relations. There are three key issues.

Employment Relations Skills

5.240 These would comprise conventional grievance handling and discipline handling skills. Some managers will require negotiating skills.

Knowledge of Legal Framework

5.241 Managers should have some basic understanding of the law on industrial

Industrial Action

action so that any context for an employer's approach to tackling industrial action is understood. Areas of law that are of particular relevance to employers include:

- breach of contracts of employment by individual employees
- the consequences of commercial contracts being breached due to industrial action
- legal requirements in relation to industrial action ballots
- when it is lawful to dismiss or deduct pay from an employee who takes part in industrial action
- trade union obligations in respect of industrial action
- when it is lawful for an employer to apply for an injunction and claim limited damages against a union.

Debrief

5.242 Once a bout of industrial action is over, managers could benefit from a facilitated workshop to explore the lessons to be learned from the employer's conduct during the dispute.

List of Relevant Legislation

5.243
- Employment Act 2002 (Dispute Resolution) Regulations 2004
- Employment Relations Act 2004
- Employment Act 2002
- Employment Relations Act 1999
- Employment Rights Act 1996
- Trade Union and Labour Relations (Consolidation) Act 1992

List of Relevant Cases

5.244
- *Gate Gourmet London Ltd v TGWU* [2005] IRLR 881, HC
- *P v National Association of Schoolmasters/Union of Women Teachers* [2001] IRLR 532, CA
- *Westminster City Council v UNISON* [2001] IRLR 524, CA
- *Intercity West Coast Ltd v RMT* [1996] IRLR 583, CA
- *London Underground Ltd v RMT* [1996] IRLR 636, CA
- *NALGO v Killorn and Simm* [1990] IRLR 464, EAT
- *London Underground v NUR* [1989] IRLR 341, HC
- *Rayware Ltd and another v Transport and General Workers Union* [1989] IRLR 134
- *Wiluszynski v London Borough of Tower Hamlets* [1989] ICR 493, CA
- *Boxfoldia v National Graphical Association* [1988] IRLR 383, HC

Further Information

Publications
- PL928 *Picketing: Code of Practice*, Department for Business, Enterprise and Regulatory Reform (BERR)
- *Acas/CP02 Code of Practice on Disclosure of Information to Trade Unions (2001)*
- *Acas/CP03 Code of Practice on Time Off for Trade Union Duties and Activities (2003)*
- *Acas/CP01 Code of Practice on Disciplinary and Grievance Procedures (2004)*

Organisations
- **Advisory Conciliation and Arbitration Service (Acas)**
  Web: *www.acas.org.uk*
  Acas aims to improve organisations and working life through better employment relations. It provides up-to-date information, advice, high-quality training, and works with employers and employees to solve problems and improve performance.
- **Commission for Racial Equality**
  Web: *www.cre.gov.uk*
  The Commission for Racial Equality is a publicly funded, non-governmental body set up under the Race Relations Act 1976 to tackle racial discrimination and promote racial equality. From October 2007 this organisation will be replaced by the Commission for Equality and Human Rights.
- **Department for Business, Enterprise and Regulatory Reform (BERR)**
  Web: *www.berr.gov.uk*
  The Department for Business, Enterprise and Regulatory Reform brings together functions from the former Department of Trade and Industry (DTI), including responsibilities for productivity, business relations, energy, competition and consumers. It also drives regulatory reform.
- **Disability Rights Commission**
  Web: *www.drc-gb.org*
  An independent body established by Act of Parliament to eliminate discrimination against disabled people and promote quality of opportunity. It provides information and advice to disabled people and employers about their rights and duties. From October 2007 this organisation will be replaced by the Commission for Equality and Human Rights (**Web:** *www.cehr.org.uk*).
- **Equal Opportunities Commission**
  Web: *www.eoc.org.uk*
  An agency working to eliminate sex discrimination and put equality into practice in the workplace. From October 2007 this organisation will be replaced by the Commission for Equality and Human Rights (**Web:** *www.cehr.org.uk*).
- **Trades Union Congress (TUC)**
  Web: *www.tuc.org.uk*
  The TUC describes itself as "the voice of Britain at work". With 71 affiliated unions representing nearly seven million working people from all walks of life, it campaigns for a fair deal at work and for social justice at home and abroad.

Information and Consultation

This topic covers the following.
- Benefits of Good Information and Consultation
- Rights to Information and Consultation
- Health and Safety
- Collective Redundancies
- Information and Consultation about a Transfer of Business
- Occupational and Personal Pensions
- European Works Councils and Consultation in Transnational Organisations
- Information and Consultation of Employees Regulations 2004
- Consultation and Collective Bargaining
- Achieving Effective Consultation
- Failure by an Employer to Consult
- Disputes
- Disclosure of Information

5.245 Employers have a duty to inform and consult their employees in certain prescribed circumstances in respect of collective redundancies, business transfers and health and safety matters.

5.246 The Information and Consultation of Employees Regulations 2004 give employees and their representatives the right to be informed and consulted about specified issues. The regulations implement the Informing and Consulting Employees Directive 2002.

5.247 Implementation of the regulations is in three stages:
- businesses with 150 employees or more (6 April 2005)
- businesses with 100–149 employees (6 April 2007)
- businesses with 50–99 employees (6 April 2008).

5.248 Employers and employees may meet their obligations by means of existing agreements on information and consultation.

5.249 Employers are also required to consult with individual employees in relation to dismissals.

5.250 Case studies detailing how four organisations have dealt with the Information and Consultation of Employees Regulations 2004 are included at the end of this topic.
- Information and Consultation - AstraZeneca
- Information and Consultation - Badenoch & Clark
- Information and Consultation - Royal London Group
- Information and Consultation - United Welsh Housing Association.

Employers' Duties

5.251 Employers have a duty to:
- consult with the union or appropriate employee representatives, or the employees directly, on changes to health and safety requirements and procedures within the organisation and other health and safety matters
- hold elections for representatives where applicable

Information and Consultation

- ensure that elected representatives receive adequate training and paid time off to undertake such training
- inform and consult with the union or appropriate employee representatives where 20 or more redundancies are proposed
- consult individual employees about prospective redundancies and suitable alternative employment
- inform and consult on transfers of employees
- consult about changes to occupational and personal pensions (depending on the size of the employer)
- inform on the organisation's economic situation, if there is a relevant Information and Consultation Agreement (ICA)
- inform and consult about employment prospects, if there is a relevant ICA
- inform and consult on any other issues likely to lead to substantial changes in work organisation or contractual relations, if there is a relevant ICA
- ensure that the timing, method and content of the consultation are appropriate
- ensure that the information supplied by the management will allow employee representatives to form opinions and undertake research to enable a proper response
- respond to requests for relevant information
- enter the consultation with a view to reaching agreement on decisions within the scope of the management's powers
- allow union or employee representatives reasonable time off with pay to perform their functions as members of a special negotiating body or a European Works Council (EWC)
- allow union or employee representatives reasonable time off with pay to perform their functions as information and consultation representatives
- allow union or employee representatives reasonable time off with pay to perform their functions as candidates in an election to be members or representatives
- disclose information to the union for collective bargaining purposes to independent recognised trade unions
- ensure that there is appropriate consultation about dismissals under the statutory dismissal and disciplinary procedure.

Employees' Duties

5.252 Under the Information and Consultation of Employees Regulations 2004, if employees wish to establish an information and consultation agreement, they:
- must request the setting-up of information and consultation procedures in writing — either to the employer or, in a dispute with the employer, to the Central Arbitration Committee
- may not make further requests or notifications for three years after a ballot, unless there are material changes to the business
- must reach a negotiated and written agreement with employers regarding information and consultation procedures within a fixed period.

5.253 Alternatively, their representatives must have approved any pre-existing agreement and there must be written proof of this.

5.254 In other circumstances, employees:
- must elect representatives if applicable

Information and Consultation

- should agree any redundancy selection criteria with the employer if applicable
- must raise questions about the substance of the consultation procedure with their appropriate representatives or management directly
- should ensure that management complies with its obligations to inform and/or consult
- should consider suitable alternative vacancies or other positions in a redundancy situation.

In Practice

Benefits of Good Information and Consultation

5.255 The benefits to organisations of good information and consultation systems include:
- raised levels of morale
- performance increases
- reduced risk of claims.

Rights to Information and Consultation

5.256 Under a range of employment law, employees or their representatives have the right to be informed and consulted by their employers in the following circumstances where:
- changes to health and safety standards and procedures are taking place
- collective bargaining is taking place
- 20 or more redundancies at one workplace within 90 days of each other are proposed within a 90-day period (collective consultation)
- any dismissal on grounds of redundancy is to be effected (individual consultation)
- there is a proposed business transfer between two employers
- where there are changes to an occupational or other pension scheme to which the employer contributes
- the employer is a specified transnational organisation and there is a European Works Council (EWC) in existence
- employees have negotiated an information and consultation agreement or a default agreement applies to discuss the following (or other matters specified in the agreement):
  – the organisation's economic situation
  – employment prospects
  – any other issues likely to lead to substantial changes in work organisation or contractual relations.
- an employee is about to be dismissed.

Health and Safety

5.257 Employers are obliged to consult on matters to do with health and safety at work, including:
- any change which may substantially affect the employees' health and safety at work

Information and Consultation

- the information employees must be given on the likely risks and dangers arising from their work, measures to reduce or get rid of these risks and what they should do if they have to deal with a risk or danger
- the planning of health and safety training
- the health and safety consequences of introducing new technology.

5.258 In unionised workplaces, two union safety representatives can request the establishment of a safety committee (under the Safety Representatives and Safety Committee Regulations 1977). In non-unionised workplaces, the establishment of a safety committee is at the management's discretion. However, the employer does have a duty to consult representatives or the relevant workforce as a whole (under the Health and Safety (Consultation with Employees) Regulations 1996).

5.259 If a union is recognised, the employer must consult those representatives on health and safety matters. If no union is recognised or does not represent all employees, the employer can choose to consult with the non-unionised employees directly or through their elected non-union representatives.

5.260 Whether or not a safety committee exists, representatives have the following key functions.

Union Representatives

- To represent employees in consultation with the employer.
- To investigate potential hazards, dangerous occurrences and the causes of accidents.
- To investigate complaints by employees relating to health, safety and welfare.
- To carry out inspections in specified circumstances.
- To represent employees in consultations with health and safety inspectors.

Non-union Representatives

- To make representations to the employer on potential hazards and dangerous occurrences.
- To make general representations to the employer.
- To represent employees in consultations with health and safety inspectors.

5.261 Employers must ensure that elected representatives receive adequate training and paid time off to undertake such training.

Collective Redundancies

Information About Proposed Redundancies

5.262 To ensure employee representatives play a useful part in consultations on proposed redundancies, the employer must disclose the following information in writing.
- The reasons for the proposed redundancies.
- The numbers and descriptions of those affected.
- The total number of employees of any such description employed at the establishment.
- The proposed method of selecting the employees who may be dismissed.
- The proposed method of carrying out the dismissals, taking account of any agreed procedure.
- How redundancy payments will be calculated (this would cover any enhancements proposed by the employer).

Consultation About Proposed Redundancies

5.263 An employer must consult with representatives of an independent recognised trade union or appropriate employee representatives when it is proposed to dismiss as redundant 20 or more employees at one place of work over a period of 90 days or less.

5.264 The consultation must take place at least 30 days before the first dismissal takes effect if between 20–99 employees are proposed to be dismissed or at least 90 days before the first dismissal takes effect if 100 or more employees are proposed to be dismissed.

5.265 This consultation must take place with a view to reaching agreement and must include discussion of:
- ways of avoiding redundancies (eg by freezing recruitment of new staff)
- reducing the numbers to be dismissed (eg by early voluntary retirements)
- mitigating the consequences of redundancies.

5.266 Employers also have a duty to act fairly and reasonably in handling redundancies and informing and consulting affected employees individually, regardless of the number of dismissals.

5.267 A redundancy is a dismissal and is covered by the statutory dismissal and disciplinary procedure (except collective redundancies).

5.268 Failure to consult with an individual (whether within the context of a collective redundancy or not) may make the dismissal unfair. Individuals have the statutory right to be accompanied by a union representative or by a fellow worker in any individual meetings.

5.269 Employers should also consult individual employees in all redundancy situations including discussions on suitable alternative employment.

Information and Consultation About a Transfer of Business

5.270 The old employer's employees affected by a business transfer have the right to be informed in advance when a business or undertaking is transferred to a new employer. The new employer's employees should also be informed of the transfer but this does not have to be in advance.

5.271 The old employer must tell representatives of an independent recognised trade union or appropriate employee representatives:
- that the transfer is going to take place
- approximately when and why it is to take place
- the legal, economic and social implications of the transfer for the affected employees
- what measures the new or old employer may take in connection with the transfer which may affect the employees (eg reorganisation; or redundancies that arise for economic, technical or organisational reasons that involve some change in the workforce).

5.272 The information and consultation (if any) must take place "in good time" before the transfer.

5.273 If any measures are proposed which will affect the old or new employees by the relevant employer, that employer must consult employee representatives.

5.274 Both the old and the new employer should give the representatives relevant information long enough before the transfer to enable effective consultation to take place. The information must be in writing.

Occupational and Personal Pensions

5.275 From 6 April 2006, employers are under a duty to consult about changes to occupational and personal pensions. The duty is phased in as follows:
- from 6 April 2006 for employers with 150 or more staff
- from 6 April 2007 for employers with 100 or more staff
- from 6 April 2008 for employers with 50 or more staff.

5.276 (The 2007 and 2008 dates coincide with those for implementing the Information and Consultation of Employees Regulations 2004).

5.277 In occupational schemes, consultation will be in relation to existing or prospective scheme members in respect of the following issues:
- proposals to increase the retirement age
- closing the scheme to new recruits or existing members
- making the scheme non-contributory or removing the employer's liability to contribute
- reducing the employer's contribution to a defined amount
- increasing member contributions
- changing from a final salary to a money purchase scheme
- reducing future accrual of benefits.

5.278 In respect of personal pensions and money purchase schemes, employers must consult if they propose any of the following, to:
- stop making pension contributions
- reduce the level of employer contributions or stopping them altogether
- increase member contributions.

5.279 Consultation should take place, as appropriate, with the following:
- representatives of a trade union recognised for collective bargaining
- information and consultation representatives (elected or appointed under the Information and Consultation of Employees Regulations 2004)
- representatives specifically elected under the proposed Occupational and Personal Pension Schemes (Consultation by Employers) Regulations 2006.

5.280 Where there are no representatives consultation can then take place directly with the pension scheme members.

European Works Councils and Consultation in Transnational Organisations

5.281 Employees in multinational organisations also have the rights to information and consultation and to employee representation under the Transnational Information and Consultation Regulations 1999.

Organisations Covered

5.282 Organisations with at least 1000 employees in EU Member States — and with at least 150 employees in two or more Member States — are liable to a request for a European Works Council (EWC).

5.283 Organisations have the following options:
- await a formal request to establish a special negotiating body (SNB)
- proactively initiate the SNB process
- operate the statutory EWC model structure.

Issues Discussed

5.284 Transnational matters covering the economic position of the organisation, investment plans, product market and sales information, technological change, restructuring and research and development.

Employee Representatives

5.285 Employees are allowed reasonable time off with pay to perform functions as:
- a member of a special negotiating body or an EWC
- an information and consultation representative
- a candidate in an election to be a member or representative.

Information and Consultation of Employees Regulations 2004

5.286 These regulations implement the EU's Information and Consultation Directive 2002. In Britain, they are implemented from April 2005 in a phased way, depending on the size of the organisation:
- 6 April 2005: organisations employing 150 or more employees
- 6 April 2007: organisations employing 100 or more employees
- 6 April 2008: organisations employing 50 or more employees.

5.287 The regulations do not apply to smaller organisations employing less than 50 employees.

5.288 The organisations covered are private and public undertakings in Great Britain that carry out an economic activity whether or not it is for gain.

5.289 Whether a specific organisation is covered may have to be decided by the courts. However, the Department for Business, Enterprise and Regulatory Reform (BERR) states in its guidance that the following are covered: companies, partnerships, co-operatives, mutuals, building societies, friendly societies, associations, trade unions, charities. It states that the following may be covered if they are carrying out an economic activity: schools, colleges, universities, NHS trusts and central and local government bodies.

5.290 Whether or not an employer is technically covered by the regulations, it is important to remember that it is good practice to inform and consult with employees to promote constructive employment relations.

Information Disclosure and Consultation

5.291 Under the regulations, employers will have to provide information to employee representatives to enable consultation to take place in procedural arrangements negotiated under an Information and Consultation Agreement or under the default procedure.

5.292 The regulations provide for:
- information on recent and probable developments in the undertaking's activities and its economic situation

- information and consultation on the structure and possible changes in employment in the organisation (this duty relates to the existing duties to consult in relation to collective redundancies and business transfers (note: it might be possible in one set of consultations to meet all the relevant statutory duties))
- information and consultation (with a view to reaching agreement) on decisions likely to lead to substantial changes in work organisation or in contractual relations with employees. This is a potentially very wide-ranging duty. It would cover variations of terms and conditions in the contract of employment. Under existing contract law, employers are expected to discuss and agree contractual changes.

5.293 Employers may restrict information disclosed on the grounds of confidentiality but it will be expected that the representatives will agree to sign confidentiality agreements before being given the information. Employers should raise this before resisting disclosure.

Proposing an Information and Consultation Agreement (ICA)

5.294 Under the regulations, negotiations to achieve an agreement must be triggered in one of two ways:
- a formal written request from employees: this must be made by at least 10% of the employees in the undertaking (subject to a minimum of 15 and a maximum of 2500)
- an initiative by the employer.

5.295 It is possible that an already-established consultation arrangement (a pre-existing agreement) might form the basis of an ICA. To do this a ballot of the workforce would have to be held to determine its acceptability. To be approved the pre-existing agreement must be supported by 40% or more of the employees and a majority of those voting and there must be written proof of this.

5.296 If there is no pre-existing agreement, then negotiations will take place between the employer and employee representatives to agree an ICA. If an employer fails to start negotiations (following a valid employee request), then the "standard information and consultation provisions" (set out in the legislation) will apply.

5.297 ICAs may cover more than one organisation. Different arrangements may be established in different parts of an organisation, ie divisions, business units, etc.

ICA Negotiations

5.298 Negotiations to agree an ICA must be started by the employer no later than three months after a valid request is made. During this period the employer must arrange for the appointment or election of employee negotiating representatives. The negotiations can last for up to six months. The employer and employee representatives can extend this period to reach an agreement.

5.299 If agreement cannot be reached, then the "standard information and consultation provisions" will apply (ie the default procedure).

Provisions of a Negotiated ICA

5.300 A negotiated ICA must:
- set out the circumstances in which the employer will inform and consult its employees
- provide for either:
  - employee information and consultation representatives; or
  - direct information and consultation arrangements with the workforce
- be in writing and dated
- cover all the employees of the undertaking
- be signed by the employer

Information and Consultation

- be approved by employees in a ballot.

5.301 Detailed issues such as topics to be discussed, frequency and timing of information and consultation will be for the parties to agree.

Developing Information and Consultation Arrangements

5.302 Employers encountering requests for ICAs may have a number of issues to consider.

Strategic Thinking

5.303 Employers should be encouraged to take an overview of employment relations and think about structures and arrangements that best suit the needs of both the organisation and its employment relations.

5.304 It is best to establish information and consultation arrangements in ways that fit with communication or business needs. The most obvious models are:
- strategic business units — often geographically based, eg by site or trade union constituency
- functional groups — emerging out of the way the organisation is constructed, eg production, sales, support and facilitating consultation on business decisions affecting specific functions.

Existing Arrangements

5.305 There may already be procedures for information and consultation, eg concerning health and safety, redundancy or transfer of undertakings. The employer may want to consider streamlining all these procedures into one information and consultation process. If this is to be so, then negotiations must take place and agreement reached to comply with the Information and Consultation of Employees Regulations 2004.

Trade Union Presence

5.306 Unions may be recognised for representation in all or part of the organisation. Most usually, they will be recognised for collective bargaining purposes but they may be recognised for other purposes excluding collective bargaining. They may also have representatives on some consultative committees. The employer should consider how all employees (whether union members or not) are provided with information and what involvement they have in consultation exercises.

5.307 There can be advantages and disadvantages to trade union involvement in developing information and consultation arrangements.

Advantages
- Access is provided to professional trade unionists.
- Gives confidence to employees that they are being fairly treated.
- Reduces the need for elections of employee representatives.
- Trade unions provide training for representatives which may lead to higher quality consultation.

Disadvantages
- It may create an adversarial relationship leading to industrial action.
- Consultation tends to become negotiation.
- Issues may become formal and legalistic.
- Even where trade unions have recognition it is not inevitable that consultation takes place.

Consultation and Collective Bargaining

5.308 Ideally, an employer will seek to separate consultation and collective bargaining when working in a unionised environment. In practice, the collective bargaining machinery will probably run in parallel to consultation. This may give trade unions a second attempt at consultation. Non-union employee representatives may also want to become involved in collective bargaining.

5.309 Managers and employee representatives, in the ICA, should do the following to keep consultation and collective bargaining as separate as possible.
- Establish a list of agreed topics for consultation.
- Negotiate and agree an agenda in advance of the consultation process.
- Establish a frequency for meetings — quarterly is probably sufficient.
- Establish the situations where representatives are entitled to time off work.
- Clarify that employee representatives are expected to treat as confidential any information identified as such by management.

Achieving Effective Consultation

5.310 In order to ensure effective and genuine consultation, the employer should work towards establishing mutual respect, trust, transparency and co-operation in their dealings with trade unions or employee representatives.

5.311 Top management needs to commit to taking information and consultation seriously, eg by chairing meetings. Middle and first-line managers need to become involved too.

5.312 Senior union representatives and full-time union officials may find it hard to embrace the information and consultation process — especially where they are used to the traditional culture of collectivism.

Failure by an Employer to Consult

5.313 Employers may be penalised under various legislation for failure to consult with appropriate employee representatives, as follows.
- Collective redundancies — an award to each affected employee of up to 90 days' pay for the period determined by the employment tribunal.
- Transfers of undertakings — an award to each affected employee of up to 13 weeks' pay.
- European Works Councils — a financial penalty of up to £75,000 against the employer.
- Informing and Consulting Employees Directive 2002 — a financial penalty of up to £75,000 imposed by the Employment Appeal Tribunal against the employer.
- Dismissal or redundancy — an employer's failure to inform properly, warn or consult an employee is likely to be grounds for a successful unfair dismissal case before an employment tribunal.
- Pension scheme changes — the Pensions Regulator can issue an improvement notice specifying steps that an employer must take and could fine a corporate employer up to £50,000 if the employer fails to comply with the improvement notice.

Disputes

5.314 Disputes, under the Information and Consultation of Employees Regulations 2004, may be brought to the Central Arbitration Committee (CAC). This body may order steps to be taken, but these steps cannot suspend or alter the effect of any act done, or any agreement made, by the employer. Where a complaint is upheld, an employer may be fined by the Employment Appeals Tribunal up to £75,000.

5.315 The employer may dispute, before the CAC, the validity of an employee request or whether the obligation to establish information and consultation procedures applies.

Disclosure of Information

5.316 Disclosure of information is the key to both effective bargaining and the establishment of trust.

5.317 Duties on employers to disclose information relate to consultation on health and safety, collective redundancies and business transfers. In addition, where an independent union is recognised for collective bargaining purposes, employers must disclose certain relevant information (under the Trade Union and Labour Relations Consolidation Act 1992). Furthermore, the Information and Consultation of Employees Regulations 2004 require information disclosure in relation to a workplace information and consultation agreement.

5.318 The employer is not required to compile or assemble information that would entail an unreasonable amount of work or expenditure.

5.319 If the trade union considers that an employer has failed to disclose relevant information it may make a complaint to the CAC.

When Not to Disclose Information

5.320 An employer is not required to disclose any information which:
- would be against the interests of national security
- would contravene a prohibition imposed by statute
- was given to an employer in confidence and relates to an individual
- would cause substantial injury to the business, eg detailed analysis of proposed investment, marketing or pricing policies
- was obtained for the purpose of legal proceedings and is privileged.

Types of Information

5.321 The following information is often requested for disclosure:
- pay and benefits — including the principles and structure of payment systems, job evaluation systems and grading criteria
- conditions of service — including policies on recruitment, redeployment, redundancy, training and equal opportunities
- manpower — including analyses of numbers employed and labour turnover
- performance — including productivity and efficiency data
- financial — including gross and net profits, assets and loans to parent or subsidiary organisations.

Training

5.322 Employees and their representatives may need technical training, eg training in reading balance sheets and profit-and-loss accounts; and also training in the appreciation of the processes of effective consultation and communication.

5.323 Managers may need skill development in communication and consultation.

Case Study — Information and Consultation — AstraZeneca

5.324 AstraZeneca, a pharmaceuticals business, is the result of a merger in 1999 between Astra AB of Sweden and Zeneca plc of the UK. The organisation's workforce spans 45 countries and numbers more than 64,000, including around 10,500 in the UK.

5.325 Zeneca was an offshoot of ICI and therefore had a long history of employee consultation. By contrast, Astra had little consultative tradition. Since the merger of the two organisations in 1999, extensive joint consultation machinery has been established throughout the UK. The organisation also uses a range of communications media, such as newsletters and intranet, as well as face-to-face meetings, to ensure that employees are kept up-to-date with business developments and are clear about their individual and team roles and targets. Two-yearly global employee surveys are conducted to identify areas of employee satisfaction and concern.

5.326 To comply with the Information and Consultation of Employees Regulations, AstraZeneca in the UK is revising its current arrangements to ensure they cover the whole workforce and are effective means of consultation as well as disseminators of information.

Joint Consultation

5.327 Each one of the organisation's nine main UK locations has its own site committee, its membership dependent on the size of the site. The largest committee has approximately 30 members, including five managers, and the smallest has around 10 members. A number of employee representatives from each site committee sit on the UK Joint Consultative Committee (UKJCC). This has around 60 attendees, of which 50 are employee representatives. Trade unions — Amicus, the GMB and the T&G — are represented at local and national meetings and for collective bargaining purposes.

5.328 A steering group, comprising around 12 senior representatives from around the UK, a senior business manager and the UK employee relations manager, shapes the agenda for UKJCC events and sets the strategic direction for consultation in the UK. AstraZeneca also operates a European consultation committee, which has four UK representatives and is chaired by the chief executive.

5.329 Site committees generally meet every 4–12 weeks (the frequency of meetings is agreed by each site). The focus is on important issues that specifically affect the location. "We have found other ways to deal with 'tea, toilets and trivia'," says Anita Roche, employee relations manager. The types of issues typically discussed at the local level include:

- business news
- updates from each area/function
- safety, health and environment/performance reporting
- policy updates
- open debates about the site challenges
- health and well-being
- security.

Information and Consultation

5.330 Local committees can invite guest speakers to broaden participants' knowledge of a particular issue.

5.331 The UKJCC is the main consultative forum for all employees in the UK. It meets twice a year and focuses on the following topics.
- Overall business updates.
- Challenges facing the business in the UK.
- Analysis of employee opinion survey.
- Pensions.
- Future of consultation.
- New products.
- Introduction of new methods and technology.
- Performance bonus plan and other employee benefits.
- Health and well-being.
- Policy development.

Consultation Proves Effective

5.332 According to Ms Roche, the consultative arrangements at AstraZeneca are highly effective. "There are many occasions where consensus decision-making has delivered a better solution for employees, managers and the business," she says. Some of its successes include the introduction of:
- individual health screening for every member of staff
- green commuting schemes
- changes to the way employee healthcare is provided
- long-service awards
- improved employee security
- flexible working in many areas
- disability access
- education workshops on pensions
- recognition for retirees
- breakfast in site restaurants.

5.333 The organisation also has collective bargaining arrangements with its blue-collar employees.

Problem Solving

5.334 The organisation is keen to develop other ways of involving staff. An example is the creation of teams comprising employee representatives and managers to identify solutions to business problems and needs. One issue that is currently the subject of such a group is the delivery by the blue-collar workforce of greater efficiency and improved effectiveness. This project is at an early stage but shows great promise, according to Ms Roche.

Partnership

5.335 The introduction of joint problem-solving and its wide-ranging consultative structure reflects the organisation's aim to work in partnership with its employees. "Partnership working is about assuming joint accountability for solving business issues and for agreeing how best to implement solutions for the benefit of the business, its customers and its employees," explains Ms Roche.

5.336   For more information visit: www.astrazeneca.com.

Case Study — Information and Consultation — Badenoch & Clark

5.337   *"We found the organisation was already operating in the spirit of the Directive, so we have decided to carry on in the same way, just doing more of what already works."* — Keith Nash, human resources director.

5.338   Badenoch & Clark, a professional services recruitment consultancy, has 530 employees operating from 18 offices in the UK and one in Luxembourg. The organisation has audited its existing information and consultation arrangements and decided to continue with what is already in place.

Roadshows

5.339   The managing director and another board member spend a month each spring, following the publication of the organisation's financial results, touring its UK offices and updating employees on corporate performance. The roadshows focus on how employees are contributing to the organisation's performance and what else they can do to improve it. Together with the senior management presentation, the half-day events involve a question and answer session, enabling staff to raise concerns and seek clarification on any issues.

5.340   As well as the annual roadshow, each business unit holds six-monthly business progress reviews, hosted by the responsible director and following the same format as the corporate-wide event. To ensure that there is ample time for employees to express their views and ask questions and that there is not too much disruption to the business, half the workforce attends in the morning and half in the afternoon.

Intranet

5.341   Badenoch & Clark operates a highly interactive corporate intranet, containing a wealth of information, including employment policies and the organisation's news and plans. User feedback is encouraged and employees are able to comment or post questions on issues featured on the site.

Employee Surveys

5.342   The organisation prefers to conduct frequent employee surveys that focus on one or two issues rather than an all-encompassing annual poll. In November 2004, for example, it conducted a survey on employee benefits, asking staff what they like and dislike about current provisions and what changes they would like to see made. A report of findings is posted on the intranet as soon as practicable, with subsequent updates showing how the organisation plans to respond. "The idea is to focus on areas, like benefits, that we feel need reviewing. Focusing on one to two issues also allows us to demonstrate better how we are responding to issues," explains Mr Nash. There are usually four such surveys a year.

Project Groups

5.343   Managers and recruitment consultants are encouraged to take part in project groups, the purpose of which is to put together proposals for improving

Information and Consultation

different aspects of the business and how it operates. For example, the recommendations on improving employee benefits that followed the staff survey were put together by a project team. Other issues that have recently been the focus of a project group include training and development, defining the values and the organisation's recruitment process. Mr Nash says that Badenoch & Clark's high standing in the training and development category (for which it won a special award) in the 2005 *Sunday Times*' "100 Best Companies to Work For" list is partly attributable to the improvement ideas contributed by employees.

Open Plan Working

5.344 As a way of encouraging informal discussion between employees and managers, there is no physical separation between directors, management and staff at Badenoch & Clark. Most managers and directors work at desks within their teams and are encouraged to move desks regularly. Senior managers also spend one or two days each month in one of the UK offices.

Information and Consultation Forum

5.345 "We are very relaxed about the ICE Regulations," says Mr Nash. "If we get an employee request to establish a formal process, it wouldn't be difficult to get one up and running." Nonetheless, he feels that the culture at the organisation and the type of people it employs make this unlikely. "We employ people who will speak up for themselves and operate an environment that assists them to do so," he says.

5.346 For more information visit: www.badenochandclark.com.

Case Study — Information and Consultation — Royal London Group

5.347 The Royal London Group is the UK's second largest mutual insurer, operating brands such as Scottish Life and Bright Grey. It employs more than 3000 staff at four sites in the UK. In response to the Information and Consultation of Employees Regulations, as well as to improve internal communications, the group has established staff committees in each of its main business units and set up an organisation-wide general council. It has also established a separate managers' committee to ensure that managers are kept regularly informed and consulted. The committees supplement the full range of communications media used by the organisation, including intranet and face-to-face communication.

Joint Consultative Groups

5.348 Each of the organisation's five main business units – Royal London Asset Management, Intermediary businesses, Servicing, Premium operations and Group functions – has a joint consultative group that provides a conduit for dialogue between the organisation and employees. As well as discussing business issues affecting staff, employee representatives (who are elected), are encouraged to contribute suggestions to improve corporate performance. Meetings take place at least every three months and are chaired by the most senior manager in the business unit. The number of staff representatives depends on the size of the business unit. The committee representing the Servicing (RLS) division, which is the largest business unit, has 20 staff representatives, with 10 each from the organisation's Edinburgh and Wilmslow offices.

5.349 The group-wide forum, called the employee central committee, is chaired by the CEO and involves the human resources director and members of his team as well as lead employee representatives from each of the business unit committees (there are two from the RLS committee). It meets at least twice a year and focuses on matters of general interest. To prepare staff representatives for their committee role, the organisation has provided extensive training, including courses in developing communication and influencing skills and knowledge of aspects of employment law. Staff representatives, whose role can include accompanying colleagues at disciplinary and grievance hearings, also have access to third-party legal support.

5.350 All managers must support the committees, and senior managers are required to demonstrate their commitment to the structures by regularly attending committee meetings.

5.351 For more information visit: www.royal-london.co.uk.

Case Study — Information and Consultation — United Welsh Housing Association

5.352 The United Welsh Housing Association (United Welsh), established in 1989, works with 12 local authorities in South Wales, providing over 3500 homes. The non-profit-making organisation is based in Caerphilly and Cardiff and employs around 125 staff. Over the past four years, United Welsh and the trade union Unison have worked together under a partnership agreement that includes a commitment to "option-based" consultation developed with the Involvement and Participation Association (IPA). As part of the agreement, a consultative forum has replaced the previous joint negotiating committee.

5.353 In terms of the Information and Consultation of Employees Regulations, the partnership agreement with Unison qualifies as a pre-existing agreement as it covers all employees, including managers, and trade union membership is currently well above 50% of the workforce.

Partnership Group

5.354 According to its principles and values, the partnership agreement between United Welsh and Unison is "based on transparency, open access to and sharing of business information and full and early participation in the decision-making process in areas of shared interest". A code of conduct governs the relationship between the two parties, committing them to the "encouragement and facilitation of two-way consultation and communication".

5.355 A consultation body called the Partnership Group (PG), set up in 2003, is central to the agreement. The main purpose of the PG is to provide a "formal mechanism" for informing and consulting with the union on matters of mutual interest. These include United Welsh's:

- business strategy and performance
- economic and financial position
- structure and changes
- terms and conditions of employment
- health and safety
- equality and diversity
- employment policies

- working environment
- staff development and training
- pay and benefits.

5.356 PG meetings are usually held every other month. There are three union and four management members of the PG and each side can, with the agreement of the other, bring one advisor to a meeting. The chair of the PG alternates between management and Unison. Any member of staff, with the exception of the chief executive and head of HR, is eligible to become an elected union representative. The workforce can access the minutes of PG meetings via the organisation's intranet, and important issues are given coverage in the United Welsh staff magazine.

5.357 One issue that was initially perceived as a potential problem was the disclosure of confidential information but this has not proved to be the case. "Union representatives see the careful management of confidential information as a key part of their role and realise that without such information they would be unable to properly influence decisions," comments Gareth Hexter, director of finance and corporate services. Any confidential information is removed from the minutes of PG meetings before they are posted on the intranet.

Direct Communication

5.358 As well as the PG, United Welsh uses a range of direct communication methods. There are regular two-way team meetings between managers and their staff and quarterly meetings of the whole workforce. The intranet enables employees to access information and a staff magazine is published every three months.

5.359 United Welsh also conducts staff surveys every two years to gauge staff opinions. Feedback from the 2002 and 2004 surveys has helped refine the partnership approach. The most recent results reveal that employees are more positive about the level of consultation in the organisation than they were in the past. More than half (56%) said in 2004 that they felt adequately consulted about matters that affected them, compared with a third in 2002. A similar proportion (57%) in 2004 also believed that consultation was used constructively to make better business decisions, compared with less than a quarter (24%) in 2002.

5.360 For more information visit: www.uwha.co.uk.

List of Relevant Legislation

5.361
- Occupational and Personal Pension Schemes (Consultation by Employers and Miscellaneous Amendment) Regulation 2006
- Transfer of Undertakings (Protection of Employment) Regulations 2006
- Employment Act 2002 (Dispute Resolution) Regulations 2004
- Information and Consultation of Employees Regulations 2004
- Transnational Information and Consultation of Employees Regulations 1999
- Health and Safety (Consultation with Employees) Regulations 1996
- Transfer of Undertakings (Protection of Employment) Regulations 1981
- Safety Representatives and Safety Committee Regulations 1977
- Employment Rights Act 1996
- Trade Union and Labour Relations Consolidation Act 1992
- Health and Safety at Work, etc Act 1974

- Informing and Consulting Employees Directive 2002
- Business Transfers Directive 2001
- Collective Redundancies Directive 1998
- European Works Council Directive 1994

List of Relevant Cases

5.362
- *Stewart v Moray Council* [2006] IRLR 168, CAC
- *Tarbuck v Sainsbury Supermarkets Ltd* [2006] IRLR 664
- *Amicus v Macmillan Publishers*IC/4/2005
- *Sweetin v Coral Racing*EAT/0039/05
- *Susie Radin Ltd v GMB* [2004] IRLR 400

Further Information

Publications
- *Acas/CP01 Code of Practice on Disciplinary and Grievance Procedures (2004)*
- *Acas/CP02 Code of Practice on Disclosure of Information to Trade Unions (2001)*
- *Acas/CP03 Code of Practice on Time Off for Trade Union Duties and Activities (2003)*
- *Acas Communicating with your Employees*
- *Acas Employee Communications and Consultation*
- *Acas/RW07 Trade Unions and Representation (November 2003)*
- *Assessing the Information and Consultation Regulations*, Mark Hall. Industrial Law Journal, Vol. 34 No. 2, June, Oxford University Press, 2005
- *Employee Consultation: Managing Best Practice.* Geldman, A and Suff, P. The Work Foundation, London, 2003
- *Making Consultation Work: The Importance of Process.* Research report. Beaumont, P and Hunter, LC. Chartered Institute of Personnel and Development, London, 2005
- *Sharing the Challenge Ahead: Informing and Consulting with Your Workforce*, Involvement and Participation Association
- *The Partnership Company: Benchmarks for the Future*, Involvement and Participation Association

Organisations
- **Advisory Conciliation and Arbitration Service (Acas)**
  Web: *www.acas.org.uk*
  Acas aims to improve organisations and working life through better employment relations. It provides up-to-date information, advice, high-quality training, and works with employers and employees to solve problems and improve performance.
- **Central Arbitration Committee**
  Web: *www.cac.gov.uk*
  The Central Arbitration Committee is a permanent independent body with statutory

powers, whose main function is to adjudicate on applications relating to the statutory recognition and derecognition of trade unions for lective bargaining purposes, where such recognition or derecognition cannot be agreed voluntarily.
- **Chartered Institute of Personnel and Development (CIPD)**
  Web: *www.cipd.org.uk*
  The CIPD is a professional body for those involved in the management and development of people.
- **Confederation of British Industry (CBI)**
  Web: *www.cbi.org.uk*
  The CBI is a vital source of expert advice and information and a forum for the generation of ideas, best practice exchange and high-powered networking.
- **Department for Business, Enterprise and Regulatory Reform (BERR)**
  Web: *www.berr.gov.uk*
  The Department for Business, Enterprise and Regulatory Reform brings together functions from the former Department of Trade and Industry (DTI), including responsibilities for productivity, business relations, energy, competition and consumers. It also drives regulatory reform.
- **Involvement and Participation Association (IPA)**
  Web: *www.partnership-at-work.com*
  An independent organisation that assists both unionised and non-union organisations to develop effective information and consultation and workplace partnership arrangements.
- **Trades Union Congress (TUC)**
  Web: *www.tuc.org.uk*
  The TUC describes itself as "the voice of Britain at work". With 71 affiliated unions representing nearly seven million working people from all walks of life, it campaigns for a fair deal at work and for social justice at home and abroad.

Trade Union Membership and Employers

> This topic covers the following.
> - Trade Union Representatives
> - Rights of Employees Relating to Trade Union Membership
> - Statutory Right to be Accompanied
> - Rights of Trade Union Members
> - Recruitment and Trade Union Membership
> - Redundancy on Trade Union Grounds
> - Dismissal on Trade Union Grounds
> - Dismissal for Safety Complaints and Representation
> - Right to Time Off
> - Right to Information
> - Right to Consultation
> - Collective Bargaining Rights
> - Expelling Members from Trade Unions
> - Right Not to be Unjustifiably Disciplined
> - Political Activity and Funds
> - Provision of Financial Information
> - Right to be Balloted Before Industrial Action
> - Requirements for a Ballot

5.363 Employees who are trade union members have certain rights in respect of their union membership. For example an employee has the right not to be dismissed for refusing to become or for choosing to join or remain a member of a trade union. Where these rights are held to have been breached, an employer may face claims of automatic unfair dismissal.

5.364 Under the Employment Rights Act 1996, all employees, regardless of length of service or number of hours worked per week, are protected from dismissal if the employer has failed to enforce or has infringed a relevant statutory right.

5.365 Members of recognised independent trade unions also have rights to reasonable amounts of unpaid time off work for union activities.

Employers' Duties

5.366 Employers have a duty:
- to recognise an independent trade union, whether they wish to or not, if that union has sufficient support in the workplace and has followed the necessary statutory procedure
- to take account of the interests of trade union members (and other employers) by complying with the duty to disclose information and consult about health and safety matters, collective redundancies, business transfers and pension scheme changes
- not to offer a worker an inducement in order to discourage his or her membership of an independent trade union, taking part in the activities of the union, or using the services of the union

Trade Union Membership and Employers

- not to offer an inducement to a worker (who is a member of an independent trade union which is recognised or seeking recognition) to deter his or her terms and conditions of employment from being negotiated through collective bargaining with the union
- not to subject a worker to detrimental treatment or dismissal if the inducement is refused
- not make an employee redundant because of his or her trade union membership or refusal to become a trade union member
- to not dismiss an employee because of his or her membership of a trade union or refusal to become a member
- to not dismiss an employee because the employee has brought proceedings against the employer for an alleged breach of a statutory right relating to trade union membership
- to not prevent or deter an employee from being or seeking to become members of an independent trade union
- not to impose penalties on an employee for his or her membership of a trade union or refusal to become a member
- not to prevent or deter an employee from taking part in the activities of an independent trade union at an appropriate time, or penalise him or her for doing so
- not to compel employees to become members of a trade union
- to give certain information to recognised trade union representatives in the course of collective bargaining
- not to reject a potential employee during the recruitment process for reasons relating to trade union membership
- to ensure compliance with the statutory right to be accompanied by either a union official or a fellow worker
- not to take disciplinary action against a workplace union representative without discussion with a senior union official or full-time union official.

Employees' Duties

5.367 Employees who are trade union members should:
- gain their employer's permission before attending workplace meetings
- if they are also trade union officials, give their line managers as much advance notice as possible when they need time off to pursue their industrial relations duties
- if they are also trade union officials, give management at least a few weeks' notice when seeking time off to attend a trade union-approved training course.

In Practice

Trade Union Representatives

5.368 Under consultation law, two broad types of workplace representatives might arise.
- *Ad hoc* non-union employee representatives elected for the specific purpose of consultation about collective redundancies, business transfers and pension scheme changes.

- More permanent representatives (whether union members of non-union) who are elected to joint consultative committees, safety committees or to committees created under an Information and Consultation Agreement (ICA).

5.369 In general, workers may elect other employees to act as their trade union representatives to represent them or their interests on:
- disciplinary and grievance matters
- works councils or other consultative bodies or joint working groups
- improving terms and conditions of employment through collective bargaining
- employee forums for making workforce agreements.

5.370 Trade union representatives represent groups of people — the bargaining unit — which may include people who are not members of the trade union.

5.371 Whether a trade union representative will represent a non-union employee is a matter for that union's policy.

Rights of Employees Relating to Trade Union Membership

5.372 Employees or potential employees should not be:
- treated differently
- dismissed
- refused employment
- made redundant

because of their membership or non-membership of a trade union. Nor should they be offered inducements not to be union members or participate in union activities. They should also not be dismissed for refusing to pay for union membership.

Trade union members have the right to a reasonable amount of paid time off work to carry out certain industrial relations duties and training.

Statutory Right to be Accompanied

5.373 Individual workers have a statutory right to be accompanied by a fellow worker, a full-time trade union official or (if a union is recognised) a workplace union representative (Employment Relations Act 1999; Employment Relations Act 2004). This right can be invoked in respect of a:
- grievance about a worker's contract or statutory entitlements
- disciplinary hearing where a worker might be subject to a formal warning, suspension, demotion or dismissal.

5.374 The companion has a statutory right to address the hearing or meeting, but he or she has no statutory right to answer questions on the worker's behalf. However, the companion should be allowed to ask questions and participate as fully as possible in the hearing; and have reasonable time to confer privately with the worker.

Rights of Trade Union Members

5.375 Trade union members have the right:
- not to be excluded or expelled from membership of a union (unless permitted by statute — this includes the ability of unions to exclude or expel an individual wholly or mainly for taking part in the activities of a political party)
- to terminate their union membership by giving reasonable notice and complying with reasonable conditions

- to be balloted prior to any industrial action.

Recruitment and Trade Union Membership

5.376 The Trade Union and Labour Relations (Consolidation) Act 1992 (TULR(C)A) makes it unlawful for an employer to reject a potential employee because he or she:
- is a member of a trade union
- is not a member of a trade union
- refuses a requirement to become a trade union member
- refuses to resign as a trade union member
- refuses to accept an inducement to discourage trade union membership or participation in union activities.

5.377 An employer that only employs people put forward by trade unions will be acting unlawfully if a non-union member is refused employment as a result of this practice.

5.378 A person refused employment may complain to an employment tribunal within three months of the conduct to which the complaint relates unless it was not reasonably practicable to do so within that time. If the tribunal considers the claim to be well founded it may award compensation and may recommend steps that the employer must take to reduce the effect on the applicant.

Redundancy on Trade Union Grounds

5.379 It is also unlawful for an employee to be selected for redundancy on trade union grounds. In such cases, the dismissal will be automatically unfair. Again, no qualifying period is needed to bring such a claim and there is no upper age limit.

Dismissal on Trade Union Grounds

5.380 If an employee is dismissed because of membership of a trade union, non-membership or participation in valid union activities, the dismissal will be automatically unfair. No qualifying service is needed to bring a claim. Where employees are selectively dismissed while taking part in official industrial action, they may assert that this was due to their union membership.

5.381 Where a dismissal is unfair on trade union grounds a minimum basic award which the tribunal deems to be just and equitable will be made. The employee will also receive a compensatory award, subject to a limit of £60,600.

5.382 Such employees may also apply to the employment tribunal for "interim relief". This comprises either an interim order for reinstatement or re-engagement, or for the contract of employment to be revived, until the complaint is settled or determined by the tribunal.

5.383 A tribunal may make an additional award if an employer refuses to comply with an order to reinstate or re-engage the employee. The additional award will not be less than 26 or more than 52 weeks' pay (set at £310 for 2007/08), so giving a maximum additional award of £16,120.

Dismissal for Safety Complaints and Representation

5.384 Under the Employment Rights Act, all employees have the right not to be dismissed or subjected to a detriment because they have:

- raised a health and safety concern with their employer
- performed certain health and safety functions.

5.385 This protection includes trade union safety representatives.

Right to Time Off

5.386 Employees who are officials of an independent recognised trade union have the right to a reasonable amount of paid time off work to perform their duties and carry out relevant training. Duties include negotiations with the employer regarding collective bargaining and dealing with workforce grievances.

5.387 The Advisory, Conciliation and Arbitration Service (Acas) has issued a Code of Practice giving examples of matters for which it may be appropriate to grant time off, ie:
- attending workplace meetings to discuss and vote on the outcome of negotiations with the employer
- discussing workplace issues with full-time officials
- voting in properly conducted ballots on industrial action and union elections.

5.388 Industrial action does not count as a union activity.

5.389 Where an employer has refused to give time off (or failed to pay a trade union official for time off), the employee may claim to an employment tribunal within three months of the employer's failure. No qualifying service is needed.

Right to Information

5.390 An employer must give certain information to trade union representatives in the course of collective bargaining, such as:
- information without which the trade union representatives would be impeded in carrying out the collective bargaining
- information which, in accordance with good industrial relations practice, should be disclosed for the purposes of collective bargaining.

5.391 Acas has issued a Code of Practice on the disclosure of information.

5.392 In addition, information must be given to representatives of a recognised union for consultation purposes on health and safety matters, collective redundancies, business transfers and where there is an Information and Consultation Agreement (ICA) in force.

Right to Consultation

5.393 A recognised independent trade union has a right to appoint safety representatives from the employer's workforce. If so requested by the representatives, the employer must set up a safety committee. The employer must consult with the representative and any safety committee.

5.394 Employers making redundancies of 20 or more people within a 90-day period at one establishment, or where there is a business transfer, are under a duty to consult with representatives of a trade union which is recognised in respect of affected employees; or alternatively with representatives elected by employees.

5.395 Under the Occupational and Personal Pension Schemes (Consultation by Employers and Miscellaneous Amendment) Regulations 2006, employers are required to consult with recognised unions regarding occupational pension schemes.

5.396 An employer may be under a duty to consult if the organisation is multinational and qualifies under the Transnational Information and Consultation Regulations 1999.

5.397 Furthermore, union members and union representatives may have triggered the relevant provisions of the Information and Consultation of Employees Regulations 2004 to negotiate an ICA.

Collective Bargaining Rights

5.398 Union members may claim recognition for collective bargaining from their employer. This can be through a voluntary agreement with the employer (possibly using the assistance of Acas). If necessary, through the union, members could activate the statutory recognition procedure (under the auspices of the Central Arbitration Committee) with a view to obtaining an approval ballot and compulsory recognition. In the course of the statutory procedure, individuals are protected from unfair practices initiated by either the employer or the union.

Expelling Members from Trade Unions

5.399 Every trade union member has a right to terminate his or her membership on giving reasonable notice and complying with any reasonable conditions.

5.400 Individuals have a statutory right not to be excluded or expelled from a trade union unless this is permitted by statute. This right gives employees considerable freedom to join the union of their choice when more than one union represents employees of a similar class.

5.401 A union may only exclude or expel members for the following reasons.
- Union rules restrict membership to workers employed in a specified trade or industry, or to workers of a particular occupational description or who hold specified qualifications or experience.
- An individual does not qualify for membership as the union only operates in certain parts of the UK.
- The union only operates in relation to one employer or group of employers and the individual is not employed by that employer.
- The individual's conduct is unacceptable.

5.402 An individual may apply to an employment tribunal for a declaration that this right has been breached. Where such a declaration is made, an individual may make an application for compensation. This must be made not before four weeks from the date of the declaration, but before the end of the six-month period following the declaration. If, when this application is made, the employee has been admitted or readmitted to the union, this application shall be made to the employment tribunal. Otherwise, it is made to the Employment Appeal Tribunal (EAT).

5.403 A tribunal may make such award as it considers just and equitable, subject to a maximum of £65,200. Awards made by the EAT are subject to a minimum of £6100.

Right Not to be Unjustifiably Disciplined

5.404 Trade union members have the right not to be unjustifiably disciplined by their unions for certain specified actions. This includes:
- failing to participate in or support industrial action
- alleging that one of the union representatives has acted unlawfully.

5.405 "Discipline" includes:
- fines
- expulsion from the union
- the withholding of union benefits.

5.406 Union members who believe they have been unjustifiably disciplined may bring a complaint to an employment tribunal within three months. If this complaint is upheld the tribunal must make a declaration to this effect. The member may then seek compensation either from a tribunal (where the union has reversed its measures) or from the EAT.

5.407 A tribunal (or the EAT) may make such award as it considers just and equitable subject to a maximum of £65,200. Awards made by the EAT are subject to a minimum of £6100.

Political Activity and Funds

5.408 A trade union is required to ballot members on the adoption of political objectives. Ballots must be held both to introduce funds for political objects and to retain them. A political fund must be administered separately from other funds and only money in the political fund may be used for political purposes.

5.409 Members of a trade union that has a political fund have the right to "contract out" of the political levy.

Provision of Financial Information

5.410 Trade union members have a right to an annual written statement of specified financial matters, including details of the auditor's report. The statement must also explain the steps a union member can take if concerned about irregularities.

Right to be Balloted Before Industrial Action

5.411 A union member who claims that members of that union (including that member) have been, or are likely to be, induced by the union to take part in, or to continue to take part in, industrial action that does not have the support of a properly conducted ballot may complain to the High Court. The High Court may then grant an injunction restraining the union from any further "inducement" (unless and until a proper ballot is held).

Requirements for a Ballot

5.412 Trade union members must comply with the following when balloting for industrial action.
- All members of the union who it is reasonable to believe will be called upon to take industrial action must be accorded entitlement to vote.
- There must be a separate ballot for each place of work.
- Before action is taken, a majority at that workplace must vote in favour.
- Voters must be asked whether they are prepared to take part in a strike or action short of a strike, whichever of the two is relevant. The majority of those voting must answer "yes" to the appropriate question.
- Ballot papers must contain the warning: "If you take part in a strike or other industrial action, you may be in breach of your contract of employment. However, if you are dismissed for taking part in a strike etc..."

- The ballot paper must also specify who, in the event of a "yes" vote, is authorised to call industrial action.

Training

5.413 It is important that all line managers understand the nature of the relationship between an employer and recognised trade union members. Where a number of managers need to be trained, a short, in-house training session will ensure that managers understand the:
- rights of trade union officials to conduct union business
- right of union members to attend meetings
- nature of trade union disputes
- organisation's dispute procedures and the roles of union representatives in these
- rights of union officials to take time off work to attend training on union activities
- skills involved in grievance handling and discipline handling
- skills involved in consultation.

List of Relevant Legislation

5.414
- Occupational and Personal Pension Schemes (Consultation by Employers and Miscellaneous Amendment) Regulations 2006
- Transfer of Undertakings (Protection of Employment) Regulations 2005 (draft)
- Information and Consultation of Employees Regulations 2004
- Management of Health and Safety at Work Regulations 1999
- Transnational Information and Consultation Regulations 1999
- Transfer of Undertakings (Protection of Employment) Regulations 1981
- Safety Representatives and the Safety Committees Regulations 1977
- Employment Relations Act 2004
- Employment Relations Act 1999
- Employment Rights Act 1996 (as amended)
- Trade Union and Labour Relations (Consolidation) Act 1992 (as amended)
- Social Security Act 1975
- Health and Safety at Work, etc Act 1974
- Informing and Consulting Employees Directive 2002
- Business Transfers Directive 2001
- European Works Council Directive 1994
- Collective Redundancies Directive 1992
- Safety and Health Directive 1989
- Acquired Rights Directive 1977

List of Relevant Cases

5.415
- *Associated Newspapers Ltd v Wilson; Associated British Ports v Palmer* [1995] IRLR 258, HL
- *O'Dea v ISC Chemicals Ltd* [1995] IRLR 599, CA

Further Information

Publications
- *Acas/CP01 Code of Practice on Disciplinary and Grievance Procedures (2004)*
- *Acas/CP02 Code of Practice on Disclosure of Information to Trade Unions (2001)*
- *Acas/CP03 Code of Practice on Time Off for Trade Union Duties and Activities (2003)*
- PL500 *Code of Practice: Access to Workers During Recognition and Derecognition Ballots (2000)*, Department for Business, Enterprise and Regulatory Reform (BERR)
- *Acas/RW07 Trade Unions and Representation (November 2003)*
- *Acas/RP05 Resolving Collective Disputes at Work (Research paper, January 2001)*
- PL869 *Industrial Action and the Law: A Guide for Employees*, Department for Business, Enterprise and Regulatory Reform (BERR)
- PL870 *Industrial Action and the Law: A Guide for Employers*, Department for Business, Enterprise and Regulatory Reform (BERR)
- PL962 *Industrial Action Ballots and Notice to Employers (Code, 2000)*, Department for Business, Enterprise and Regulatory Reform (BERR)
- PL928 *Picketing: Code of Practice*, Department for Business, Enterprise and Regulatory Reform (BERR)
- PL868 *Trade Union Political Funds*, Department for Business, Enterprise and Regulatory Reform (BERR)
- PL871 *Union Membership: Rights of Members and Non-members*, Department for Business, Enterprise and Regulatory Reform (BERR)
- PL865 *Unjustifiable Discipline by a Trade Union*, Department for Business, Enterprise and Regulatory Reform (BERR)

Organisations
- **Advisory Conciliation and Arbitration Service (Acas)**
  Web: *www.acas.org.uk*
  Acas aims to improve organisations and working life through better employment relations. It provides up-to-date information, advice, high-quality training, and works with employers and employees to solve problems and improve performance.

- **Business Link**
  Web: *www.businesslink.gov.uk*
  Business Link is managed by the BERR and offers practical advice to businesses. Its services are available online and through a network of local operators throughout England.
- **Central Arbitration Committee**
  Web: *www.cac.gov.uk*
  The Central Arbitration Committee is a permanent independent body with statutory powers, whose main function is to adjudicate on applications relating to the statutory recognition and derecognition of trade unions for lective bargaining purposes, where such recognition or derecognition cannot be agreed voluntarily.
- **Department for Business, Enterprise and Regulatory Reform (BERR)**
  Web: *www.berr.gov.uk*
  The Department for Business, Enterprise and Regulatory Reform brings together functions from the former Department of Trade and Industry (DTI), including responsibilities for productivity, business relations, energy, competition and consumers. It also drives regulatory reform.

Trade Unions and Employers

> This topic covers the following.
> - Rights of Trade Unions
> - Purpose of Trade Unions
> - Independent Trade Unions
> - Trade Union Recognition
> - Gaining Union Recognition
> - Recognition and Rights of Union Representatives

5.416 This topic covers the role of trade unions and the process by which trade unions can gain recognition. It does not cover the rights of trade union members or employee representatives.

Employers' Duties

5.417 Employers have a duty:
- to recognise independent trade unions that have sufficient support in the workplace (providing 21 or more workers)
- not to refuse employment on grounds of trade union membership or non-membership
- not to engage in unfair practices during a CAC-initiated ballot on union recognition
- to allow union officials and members time off work for union activities
- not to dismiss employees for not belonging to a trade union or for refusing to join one
- not to take action against employees to compel them to become members of a trade union
- not to select employees for redundancy because they are or are not members of a trade union
- to disclose information for collective bargaining purposes where an independent union is recognised
- to disclose information to independent recognised unions relating to health and safety matters, collective redundancies and business transfers
- to negotiate, as appropriate, with a trade union for the establishment of an information and consultation agreement
- to comply (if a designated multinational company) with transnational information and consultation requirements
- to comply with the statutory right for an employee to be accompanied, in grievance and disciplinary hearings, by either a full-time union official or a workplace union representative (or, if requested a fellow worker).

Employees' Duties

5.418 Employees who are trade union members should:
- gain their employer's permission before attending union workplace meetings.

Trade Unions and Employers

5.419 Employees who are union officials should:
- give their line managers as much advance notice as possible when they need time off to pursue their industrial relations duties
- give management at least a few weeks' notice when seeking time off to attend a trade union-approved training course.

In Practice

Rights of Trade Unions

5.420 Recognised independent trade unions have rights to:
- information for collective bargaining purposes, without which the union would be disadvantaged
- information on occupational pensions
- information and consultation on health and safety at work
- appoint safety representatives
- information and consultation of collective redundancies (involving 20 or more employees)
- information and consultation relating to business transfers
- trigger a request for negotiations on a workplace Information and Consultation Agreement (ICA)
- a reasonable amount of paid time off work to carry out industrial relations duties.

5.421 Furthermore, a recognised union may be involved in implementing transnational information and consultation requirements in a specified multinational organisation.

Purpose of Trade Unions

5.422 Trade unions are organisations formed by workers in order to:
- maintain and improve the terms and conditions of work of their members
- campaign for changes in employment legislation
- train members, usually employee representatives, in issues such as health and safety
- provide personal and professional support for individual members in grievance and disciplinary hearings
- provide expertise in negotiations
- provide advice in employment law-related issues
- provide financial assistance
- offer sickness benefits
- offer training facilities.

Independent Trade Unions

5.423 A trade union which is not under the domination or control of an employer and is independent from the employer financially is said to be an independent trade union. The Certification Officer maintains a list of trade unions and is responsible for determining whether a trade union or staff association is "independent". Unions which prove that they are "independent" will be granted a certificate of independence by the Certification Office. The Certification Officer has the power to strike out weak and vexatious claims.

Trade Union Recognition

5.424 When employers and employees agree arrangements for collective bargaining, it is said that the employer recognises a trade union. These are agreements voluntarily entered into and documented in a Procedural Agreement. Such recognition may be preceded by a campaign by the trade union and resistance by the employer. Typically the employer will agree to recognition if the majority of employees — in part or whole of the organisation — asks for it. This type of agreement is reached without any legal process and provides the opportunity for the employer to shape future relationships.

5.425 In the recognition agreement the employer and trade union will agree on a bargaining unit — this may be the whole organisation or part of it, eg the bargaining unit often excludes senior managers and personnel departments. Individuals not in bargaining units can still join trade unions but they will not be covered by the collective agreements negotiated by the trade union on behalf of the members in the bargaining unit.

5.426 There may be different unions recognised for different bargaining units, eg there may be different unions for shop floor workers and administrative staff.

5.427 Most recognition agreements are voluntary but, if a voluntary agreement cannot be reached, then an independent trade union in an organisation employing more than 20 workers has a statutory right to claim recognition.

5.428 To operate effectively, Acas strongly advises employers to take account of the interests of employees when making decisions and to give the reasons for decisions once they are made, especially when a decision is likely to be unpopular with workers.

Recognised Trade Unions

5.429 Legally, "recognition" means the recognition of the union by an employer for the purposes of collective bargaining. This covers negotiations concerning any of the following:
- terms and conditions of employment, or the physical conditions of work
- engagement or non-engagement, or termination of workers
- allocation of work and duties
- disciplinary matters
- a worker's membership of a trade union
- facilities for trade union officials
- negotiations and consultation procedures relating to the above.

5.430 This is clearest where there is a recognition agreement between the employer and a trade union. In some cases, recognition by an employer may be implied. Where unions have sufficient support within a workplace, employers may be under a statutory obligation to recognise such union for collective bargaining purposes.

5.431 Where an employer chooses to recognise a trade union, it will usually enter into an agreement setting out how such matters shall be conducted. A collective agreement will only be legally enforceable if the agreement:
- is in writing, and

- states that the parties intend that it be legally binding (which would be very unusual).

5.432 Such agreements will usually be binding in honour only, meaning that any breach would not give rise to legal proceedings between the parties themselves. An employer will therefore generally be free to end such an agreement at will without giving any stipulated notice.

Costs of Trade Union Recognition

5.433 The costs for the employer include:
- facilities for trade union representatives
- accreditation for union representatives
- payment of union contributions from wages (check-off)
- time off for trade union duties and activities
- disclosure of information.

Benefits of Trade Union Recognition

5.434 The benefits to the employer are:
- greater commitment to change because worker representatives have been involved in consultation or the decision making process, especially where an agreement is reached between employer and trade union
- emphasis on dialogue as a means of developing practices which are acceptable to both sides
- utilisation of the skills and knowledge of employees
- improved relationships and attitudes between managers and workers by effective systems of communication and consultation between employer and trade union representatives.

Gaining Union Recognition

5.435 The process of gaining recognition for an independent trade union has six stages.
1. The initial application.
2. Attempting a voluntary agreement.
3. Application to the Central Arbitration Committee.
4. Creating a bargaining unit.
5. Determining whether to award union recognition.
6. Holding a ballot and making an award of recognition.

5.436 The statutory process for recognition applies only to an independent trade union, or two or more independent trade unions acting together. An application must be made to the Central Arbitration Committee (CAC) which is required to promote voluntary settlements. The statutory process encourages the trade union (and employer) at a number of stages to withdraw its application if the parties can reach voluntary agreement. Such a voluntary agreement, at whichever stage in the process it is agreed, cannot then be terminated by the employer for a period of three years.

Approaching the Employer for Recognition

5.437 To start the statutory process, the trade union must put into writing a formal request to the employer for recognition. In order for this initial application to be valid:
- it must state that it is made under Schedule 1 to the Trade Union and Labour Relations (Consolidation) Act 1992 (as amended)

Trade Unions and Employers

- it must be received by the employer
- it must identify the union (or unions) making the request and the "bargaining unit" (the group of workers) to which it relates
- the employer (together with associated employers) must employ 21 or more workers.

Attempting a Voluntary Agreement

5.438 The employer has 10 working days (two full weeks) in which to respond. If the employer agrees voluntarily to recognise the union (or unions), the statutory recognition procedure is regarded as closed. However, in order to give confidence to the voluntary process the parties can ask the CAC to give a declaration that it is an agreement for recognition. In such instances, the parties can approach the CAC for assistance and determination if there are subsequent difficulties.

5.439 Alternatively, the employer may wish to negotiate a voluntary agreement or to negotiate about what the bargaining unit should be and whether the union should be recognised in which case the parties have 20 days to conclude negotiations — or longer by mutual agreement.

5.440 The employer and the union (or unions) may ask Acas to assist in conducting the negotiations. If the parties cannot agree, an application can be made to the CAC.

Application to the Central Arbitration Committee

5.441 If the parties cannot agree, the union may apply to the CAC to decide the appropriate bargaining unit, if necessary, and whether the union should be recognised. The CAC has 10 working days to apply a number of tests. In particular, the application should:

- not cover any workers for whom a union (whether independent or non-independent) is already recognised (with limited exceptions)
- show that at least 10% of workers in the proposed bargaining unit are members of the union
- show that a majority in the bargaining unit would be likely to favour recognition
- not include any workers for whom the CAC has already accepted an application
- not be made within three years of a union failing to achieve recognition following a ballot or of the CAC declaring that the union be de-recognised in respect of the same (or substantially the same) bargaining unit.

5.442 If the CAC rejects the application then the recognition process ends.

Creating a Bargaining Unit

5.443 If the union and the employer have already agreed on a bargaining unit, the application proceeds to the next stage. Otherwise they have 20 working days in which the CAC will either try to help them agree a bargaining unit or determine it. In doing so, the CAC must take a number of matters into account, in particular:

- the need for the unit to be compatible with effective management
- whether there is an existing recognition agreement covering any workers
- whether at least 10% of the workers in the bargaining unit are members of the union making the application
- whether a majority of the workers in the bargaining unit are likely to favour recognition
- if there are any competing applications from other trade unions, covering any workers in the bargaining unit.

5.444 The CAC can extend this period if necessary and will decide the appropriate bargaining unit if the union and the employer cannot agree.

Determining Whether to Award Recognition

5.445 Once the bargaining unit is established, the CAC must decide whether to:
- declare the union to be automatically recognised, or
- hold a ballot.

5.446 If over 50% of the bargaining unit are members of the union, the CAC will normally declare the union recognised and if membership is below 50%, will declare its intention to hold a recognition ballot. If the majority of the bargaining unit are members of the union the CAC may still hold a ballot:
- in the interests of good industrial relations, or
- if a significant number of members inform it that they do not want the union to conduct collective bargaining on their behalf.

Holding a Ballot and Making an Award of Recognition

5.447 The CAC must give notice that it intends to hold a ballot and the union has 10 working days to decide whether to withdraw. If the union withdraws, the ballot will not be held and recognition will not be granted. Otherwise the CAC will both appoint an independent scrutineer to run the ballot and determine the form of the ballot: workplace, postal, or a combination of these methods. During the ballot the employer has a general duty to co-operate with the ballot and specifically the employer must:
- give the union access to the workers in the bargaining unit during the balloting period
- supply to the CAC the names and addresses of the workers in the bargaining unit. This information is used for the ballot itself, and also, to distribute union literature to the workers.

5.448 If the result of the ballot is that the union's application is supported by a majority of all those voting and at least 40% of those entitled to vote, the CAC must issue a declaration that the union is recognised for the purposes of collective bargaining.

5.449 Recognition is for collective bargaining on pay, hours and holidays (and any other matters agreed by the parties). The definition of "pay" will exclude employer contributions to an occupational or personal pension scheme. Recognised unions also have the right to be consulted on training.

5.450 Where the CAC requires a ballot is to be held, then both the employer and the trade union must not engage in any unfair practices to influence the outcome of the ballot in that bargaining unit. Unfair practices include:
- offering money to a worker to vote in a particular way or to abstain from voting
- make an outcome-specific offer, ie paying money for a specific result
- coerce a worker to reveal his or her vote or intention to vote
- dismiss or threaten to dismiss a worker
- take or threaten to take disciplinary action against a worker
- subject or threaten to subject a worker to any other detriment, eg overlooking for promotion or some discretionary benefit
- using or attempting to use undue influence on a worker.

5.451 Complaints about unfair practice should be made to the CAC.

Method of Collective Bargaining

5.452 Once a union is recognised, a method for conducting collective bargaining on pay, hours and holidays needs to be agreed. The period for helping the parties reach agreement is 20 working days.

5.453 If the parties cannot reach agreement, either party can ask the CAC to intervene and specify a method of collective bargaining. In drawing up a method, the CAC panel will take account of the views of the parties, and also of the Trade Union Recognition (Method of Collective Bargaining) Order 2000 (the "model method").

5.454 Where the CAC specifies the method of collective bargaining, the method is legally enforceable.

Recognition and Rights of Union Representatives

5.455 Where a union is recognised, union officials and members acquire certain rights. These include a right to:
- time off work to carry out trade union duties and activities
- have information disclosed to them for the purposes of collective bargaining.

De-recognition

5.456 An employer may attempt to de-recognise a trade union. This will involve giving notice to terminate an existing recognition agreement. This may arise because the level of union membership has fallen significantly; and/or because the employer wishes to reconstitute its employment relations.

5.457 There are several factors that an employer needs to consider if de-recognition is contemplated.
- If the established recognition arrangements result from a CAC award under the statutory procedure, then these arrangements will last for three years.
- The employer may be required to undergo the statutory de-recognition procedure which, in broad terms, is similar to the recognition procedure. If certain conditions are met, the CAC will order a de-recognition ballot. If the result is that a majority of the workers voting and at least 40% of the workers constituting the bargaining unit support de-recognition of the union, the CAC will issue a declaration to that effect.
- Neither party should engage in specified unfair practices where a ballot is held.

Business Transfers and Recognition

5.458 If an undertaking is transferred but retains its identity alongside any existing undertaking of the new owner, a recognition deal with one or more unions also transfers. The union(s) will be deemed to be recognised by the new employer to the same extent. However, after the transfer, any recognition agreement may be varied or rescinded.

Training

5.459 It is important that all line managers understand the role of trade unions in the workplace. Where a number of managers need to be trained, a short, in-house training session will ensure that managers understand the:
- purposes and functions of trade unions
- rights of recognised trade unions to information and consultation
- right of trade union officials for time off to conduct union business
- right of union members to time off to attend meetings

- organisation's policy and procedures for dealing with requests for time off for trade union activities.

List of Relevant Legislation

5.460
- Transfer of Undertakings (Protection of Employment) Regulations 2005 (draft)
- Information and Consultation of Employees Regulations 2004
- Transnational Information and Consultation of Employees Regulations 1999
- Occupational Pensions Schemes (Disclosure of Information) Regulations 1996
- Transfer of Undertakings (Protection of Employment) Regulations 1981
- Safety Representatives and Safety Committees Regulations 1977
- Employment Relations Act 2004
- Employment Relations Act 1999
- Trade Union and Labour Relations (Consolidation) Act 1992
- Informing and Consulting Employees Directive 2002
- Business Transfers Directive 2001
- European Works Council Directive 1994
- Collective Redundancies Directive 1992
- Safety and Health Directive 1989
- Acquired Rights Directive 1977

Further Information

Publications
- *Acas/CP02 Code of Practice on Disclosure of Information to Trade Unions (2001)*
- *Acas/CP03 Code of Practice on Time Off for Trade Union Duties and Activities (2003)*
- PL500 *Code of Practice: Access to Workers During Recognition and Derecognition Ballots (2000)*, Department for Business, Enterprise and Regulatory Reform (BERR)

Organisations
- **Advisory Conciliation and Arbitration Service (Acas)**
  Web: *www.acas.org.uk*
  Acas aims to improve organisations and working life through better employment relations. It provides up-to-date information, advice, high-quality training, and works with employers and employees to solve problems and improve performance.
- **Department for Business, Enterprise and Regulatory Reform (BERR)**
  Web: *www.berr.gov.uk*
  The Department for Business, Enterprise and Regulatory Reform brings together functions from the former Department of Trade and Industry (DTI), including responsibilities for productivity, business relations, energy, competition and consumers. It also drives regulatory reform.

- **Trades Union Congress (TUC)**
  Web: *www.tuc.org.uk*
  The TUC describes itself as "the voice of Britain at work". With 71 affiliated unions representing nearly seven million working people from all walks of life, it campaigns for a fair deal at work and for social justice at home and abroad.

Whistleblowing

> This topic covers the following.
> - Who is Covered by Whistleblowing Legislation?
> - Qualifying Disclosures
> - Protected Disclosures
> - Whistleblowing Cases
> - Enforcement
> - Confidentiality Clauses

5.461 Whistleblowing, or public interest disclosure, occurs when a worker in good faith reports the actual or prospective improper actions of his or her organisation or colleagues. The worker could disclose the improper action:
- internally within his or her organisation using a set procedure
- to one of a number of external regulators
- more widely if neither of the other options is appropriate.

5.462 Employers should cultivate an environment within their organisation that allows workers to feel able to share their concerns internally in confidence.

5.463 Reporting concerns outside normal channels may be necessary where attempts to report them in the past have not been successful.

5.464 The Employment Rights Act 1996 as amended by the Public Interest Disclosure Act 1998 (often referred to as the Whistleblowing Act) is the primary legislation dealing with whistleblowing.

Employers' Duties

5.465 Employers should:
- develop an environment within their organisation that encourages workers to share their concerns about actual or potential breaches of duty or a particular failure internally and in confidence
- ensure that workers do not suffer any detriment or victimisation that occurs as a result of making a protected disclosure
- ensure that any action taken against workers who make a disclosure is not related to that disclosure
- under no circumstances attempt to suppress evidence of any breaches or failures
- ensure that appropriate staff are trained to deal with whistleblowing and the related procedures.

Employees' Duties

5.466 Employees should:
- always, where possible, follow the internal procedures set down for whistleblowing
- in most circumstances, raise concerns internally to an appropriate person before making a disclosure to any external body
- comply with any whistleblowing policy of the organisation

- consider making a disclosure to a prescribed regulator before disclosing it more widely
- if a case is exceptionally serious, and there are good reasons for doing so, bypass the disclosure procedures
- ensure that any disclosure of information is "reasonable in all the circumstances".

In Practice

Who is Covered by Whistleblowing Legislation?

5.467 Most employers are covered by whistleblowing legislation, including offices, shops, factories, hospitals, charities and the Government.

5.468 In addition to employees, the legislation covers trainees, agency staff, contractors and homeworkers. The usual employment law restrictions on minimum length of service do not apply so all workers are protected by the legislation.

5.469 However, the genuinely self-employed, volunteers, the intelligence services and the armed forces are currently not covered.

Qualifying Disclosures

5.470 Workers who "blow the whistle" are protected if they reasonably believe the disclosure will reveal that any of the following has occurred or is likely to occur.
- A criminal offence.
- A failure to comply with a legal obligation.
- A miscarriage of justice.
- The endangering of an individual's health and safety.
- Environmental damage or risks.
- Any concealment of the above.

5.471 In any such case the disclosure will be a "qualifying disclosure" unless:
- the person commits an offence by making it, eg a breach of the Official Secrets Acts, or
- it is a disclosure to which legal professional privilege would apply (ie it cannot be disclosed without breaching legal professional privilege).

5.472 A disclosure is covered by the whistleblowing legislation whether or not the information is confidential or the breach or failure occurred abroad.

Protected Disclosures

5.473 For a whistleblower to be protected under the Public Interest Disclosure Act 1998, the disclosure needs to be both a qualifying disclosure and a protected disclosure. Protected disclosures are made in good faith:
- to an employer (this includes the organisation which has engaged the worker)
- to the person responsible for the breach or failure
- to a legal advisor (this does not need to be in good faith)
- to a Government minister if the worker is employed by a public body, eg an NHS worker could make a disclosure to a health minister
- to prescribed persons

- as an external disclosure
- as an exceptionally serious case to a third party such as the police or a newspaper.

Internal Disclosure

5.474 A worker should, if possible, first try and deal with any concern about a breach or failure internally. A disclosure will be a qualifying disclosure and therefore protected if it is made in good faith to:
- the worker's employer, or
- another person whom the worker reasonably believes to be responsible for the relevant failure.

5.475 No other requirements are necessary and most problems should be dealt with quickly and easily.

Good Faith

5.476 Apart from disclosures made to legal advisers, all qualifying disclosures should be made in good faith. The worker's motivation for making the disclosure should be an honest one.

5.477 If the worker's disclosure is motivated by the desire to cause harm or by, eg a personal grudge or other ulterior motive, he or she will not have satisfied the good faith requirement. The employer must prove the disclosure was not made in good faith.

Internal Policy to Deal with Whistleblowing

5.478 It is best practice for an employer to introduce a whistleblowing policy, for the following reasons.
- It is better for an employer to enable workers to voice concerns within the organisation, rather than forcing a whistleblower to go public and so expose the employer to damaging media coverage.
- A whistleblower may lose the protection of the Public Interest Disclosure Act 1998 if he or she ignores any internal policy.
- An internal policy can help an employer to detect problems before they seriously damage the employer's business.
- Any attempt to suppress evidence of malpractice is likely to constitute a "cover-up", and in itself provide both a basis for protected disclosure and a potential touch paper for damaging media coverage.
- The policy should identify a specific person within the organisation to whom disclosures should be made to avoid any disputes later on as to whether the policy was followed.

5.479 Any internal policy should:
- confirm the employer's commitment to tackling allegations of failures
- identify examples of failures and state that they will be dealt with seriously
- explain the protection offered to whistleblowers who report malpractice within the workplace
- make it clear that making false accusations is unacceptable and could result in disciplinary action
- set out the procedures to be followed in reporting the failure

Whistleblowing

- set out a designated person and alternative to whom such failures should be reported since workers often prefer not to make a disclosure to their immediate line manager and the employer should make clear who is authorised to receive the disclosures
- indicate the proper way to raise concerns outside the organisation in exceptional circumstances (eg to a regulatory body)
- give an assurance that allegations will be taken seriously and investigated promptly and confidentially if requested
- make it clear that victimisation or harassment of a whistleblower will be considered a disciplinary offence
- be kept distinct from the organisation's grievance procedure
- be accessible to all employees.

5.480 The policy must be implemented and actively supported at the highest levels if it is to be effective.

5.481 An employer may wish, in addition, to designate an external organisation or individual as a contact for employees to raise concerns in confidence about failures. However, best practice is for such concerns to be raised internally if possible.

5.482 If a concern about a breach or failure cannot be dealt with internally, there are two further options for a whistleblower: they can make a discloure to a "prescribed person" or more widely.

Prescribed Regulators

5.483 First, whistleblowing legislation protects those who make disclosures in good faith to "prescribed persons". There is a full list of the approximately 50 prescribed persons in the Public Interest Disclosure (Prescribed Persons) (Amendment) Order 2003. The list includes:

- HM Revenue & Customs (HMRC)
- the Health and Safety Executive
- the Financial Services Authority
- the Food Standards Agency
- the Information Commissioner
- the Environmental Agency
- the Charity Commissioners
- the Director of the Serious Fraud Office
- the Secretary of State for Business, Enterprise and Regulatory Reform
- the Secretary of State for Transport.

5.484 The whistleblower is protected if he or she reasonably believes that the subject matter properly falls within the prescribed person's remit, the disclosure is made in good faith, and that the information and any allegation in the information are substantially true.

Wider Disclosure

5.485 Whistleblowers may disclose information more widely, eg, to the police, media, MPs and non-prescribed regulators. Such a disclosure is protected if:

- it is made in good faith and not for personal gain (including any payment by the media)
- it is reasonable in all the circumstances
- the whistleblower reasonably believes that the information and any allegations in it are substantially true.

5.486 And in addition, the disclosure fits any one of the following three criteria.
- The disclosure had already been raised internally or with a prescribed person.
- The whistleblower reasonably believed he or she would have been victimised had he or she raised the matter internally or with a prescribed regulator.
- The whistleblower reasonably believed a complaint would lead to the evidence being concealed or destroyed and there was no prescribed person.

"Reasonable in All the Circumstances"

5.487 Whether or not a disclosure will be considered "reasonable in all the circumstances" will depend on the following factors:
- the identity of the person to whom the disclosure is made
- the seriousness of the concern
- whether the matter is continuing or is likely to occur in the future
- whether the disclosure is made in breach of a duty of confidentiality owed by the employer to another person, eg to protect patient confidentiality
- any action which the employer or prescribed person has taken, or might reasonably be expected to have taken, as a result of a previous disclosure
- whether the worker complied with an authorised procedure when raising the issue with the employer.

Exceptionally Serious Cases

5.488 In certain circumstances, the subject of a disclosure made by a whistleblower may be exceptionally serious. The whistleblower will then be justified in bypassing disclosure procedures.

5.489 The whistleblower will need to show that:
- the qualifying disclosure was made in good faith
- he or she reasonably believed that the allegations were substantially true
- the disclosure was not made for personal gain
- it was reasonable in all the circumstances for the disclosure to have been made, with particular reference to the identity of the person to whom it was made.

Whistleblowing Cases

5.490 Two thirds of claims alleging victimisation under the Public Interest Disclosure Act are either settled or withdrawn without a public hearing.

5.491 Court decisions under current legislation have included the following cases.
- The EAT found that the dismissal of an employee who leaked a confidential report to a local newspaper about the potential dangers to the public of a contaminated landfill site was automatically unfair under whistleblowing legislation. In this case the employee became concerned over the National Trust's delay to close the landfill site which was dangerous to the public. He finally released a report into the dangers and gave interviews to a local newspaper which published the information. The trust disciplined the employee and dismissed him for breaching the trust's press protocol as he was already on a final written warning (for an unrelated matter). He successfully claimed that he was dismissed for making a protected disclosure about the environment being damaged, that he had a reasonable belief that members of the public might be injured and that he made the disclosure in good faith. (*Collins v The National Trust*(EAT) 250 7 255/05)
- The Court of Appeal upheld a claim made by a former employee who suffered a detriment under the Public Interest Disclosure Act 1998 after her employment was

terminated. In this case the employee claimed she made a protected disclosure while employed. Her former employer failed to provide her with a reference and she claimed this was a detriment under the Act. The Court of Appeal for the first time decided that whistleblowers did benefit from protection under the Act after their employment has ended. This is consistent with discrimination legislation. (*Woodward v Abbey National plc [2006] IRLR 677, CA*)

- A nursing home dismissed a nurse after he raised concerns about patient care first to his employer (unsuccessfully) and then to the Social Services Inspectorate (SSI). The SSI is not a prescribed person. An employment tribunal awarded the nurse £13,000 for unfair dismissal and £10,000 by way of compensation for "injury to feelings". Awards for "injury to feelings" are common in discrimination claims but the average award is usually significantly less. (*ALM v Bladon* [2002] IRLR 807, CA)

- A parking attendant successfully took a claim to an employment tribunal after raising concerns about false penalty notices being issued. (*Azzaoui v Apcoa Parking* [2001])

- A slaughterhouse worker contacted HM Revenue & Customs (HMRC) with concerns about the affairs of the slaughterhouse. He was summarily dismissed. HMRC is a prescribed person. An employment tribunal found in the worker's favour and awarded £11,000. (*Bailey v Arrow Consultants* [2001])

- The manager of a hospital ward for elderly patients raised concerns about bed shortage, but was told there were no resources. The problem worsened and some elderly patients were to be moved to a gynaecological ward. The manager wrote a satirical open letter to the Prime Minister for his local paper and with the NHS Trust's agreement was photographed for local press. When the letter was published, the trust gave the manager a final written warning for unprofessional and unacceptable conduct. The disclosure was protected because:
  – the manager did not know of the trust's whistleblowing policy
  – there was no reasonable expectation of action following earlier concerns
  – it was a serious public concern. (*Kay v Northumberland Healthcare NHS Trust* [2001])

- An employee of a national tyre firm overheard colleagues suggesting that losses at another branch should be written down against a break-in at their branch. The employee sent a tape of such conversations to his regional manager, who simply returned the tape to the employee's manager. An employment tribunal found that subsequent cold-shouldering of the employee amounted to victimisation and his disclosure was protected. (*Boughton v National Tyres* [2000])

- A senior lecturer who made factually incorrect allegations lost a claim to an employment tribunal. The Employment Appeal Tribunal ruled that the lecturer's mistake was "reasonable". (*Darnton v University of Surrey* [2002] EAT/882/01)

- An employee dismissed on grounds of redundancy countered in a heated exchange with allegations about the theft of golf clubs and breaches of safety rules at the organisation. An employment tribunal dismissed his claim under the Public Interest Disclosure Act, saying that the Act should not be used to protect when an employee "in the heat of the moment accused his employer of some nefarious activity". (*Durrant v Norfolk Sheet Metal*(2001))

- A floor-buffer was dismissed after only four months' employment. The employee said he was dismissed because he informed his manager about lack of supervision. He claimed that non-supervision constituted a breach of a "legal obligation" by the organisation under his employment contract. The employment tribunal did not consider that the Public Interest Disclosure Act applied in the circumstances, but the Employment Appeals Tribunal disagreed. The Act can apply to a disclosure of a breach of an employment contract, under the category of non-compliance with a legal obligation. (*Parkins v Sodexho* [2002] IRLR 109)

Enforcement

5.492 The following facts apply.

- If an employee is dismissed for making a protected disclosure, that dismissal will be automatically unfair. An employee can make a claim to an employment tribunal regardless of his or her age or length of service.
- Only employees can complain of unfair dismissal, but workers who are not employees can complain that they have been subjected to a detriment if their contracts are terminated because they have made a protected disclosure.
- All workers who have suffered detrimental treatment short of dismissal, eg such as loss of pay rise or promotion, may also complain to a tribunal.
- If a tribunal considers it likely that at the full hearing it will uphold a complaint for unfair dismissal, it can either order reinstatement or re-engagement or make an order for the temporary continuation of the contract of employment. This is called interim relief.
- Interim relief is available for unfair dismissal claims provided the claim is made within seven days of termination of employment.
- There is no upper limit to the level of compensation that can be awarded to a worker who is dismissed or subject to detriment for whistleblowing. A tribunal can also order re-instatement or re-engagement.
- Employees who are dismissed or suffer a detriment for whistleblowing may also be awarded compensation for injury to feelings. The minimum award on the "Vento" scale is £500 and the maximum is £25,000.

Confidentiality Clauses

5.493 Confidentiality clauses in employment contracts or severance agreements preventing disclosures of a relevant failure or breach are void to the extent that they conflict with whistleblowing legislation.

Training

5.494 All employees, including temporary workers and any other workers who are not genuinely self-employed, should be made familiar with an organisation's whistleblowing policy.

5.495 An employer should be able to demonstrate that all employees have access to its policy. Employers may wish to ask workers to sign an acknowledgement that they have read and understood the policy.

5.496 Senior employees to whom workers can address their concerns about malpractice should be trained in the organisation's whistleblowing procedures and how to deal with staff disclosures. Senior staff might mean line managers or departmental managers. In addition, HR managers should be trained on whistleblowing procedures.

5.497 All senior staff and HR managers who may have to deal with disclosures should be trained to:

- comprehend clearly the organisation's policy and procedure on whistleblowing
- treat workers (including non-employees') disclosures seriously, sensitively and in the strictest confidence
- consider the message rather than the messenger; the whistleblower should be viewed as a witness, not a complainant
- understand organisational procedures for investigating allegations and when such procedures should be followed

- keep the whistleblower informed confidentially of the progress or outcome of any investigation
- understand the hierarchy of authorities to whom whistleblowers can make disclosures
- understand the protections from detriment and unfair dismissal to which whistleblowers are entitled.

5.498 Employers sometimes appoint an external organisation to deal with staff disclosures: clearly such an external organisation should be made fully aware of any internal policies.

List of Relevant Legislation

5.499
- Public Interest Disclosure Act 1998
- Employment Rights Act 1996
- Public Interest Disclosure (Prescribed Persons) (Amendment) Order 2003
- Public Interest Disclosure Act 1998 (Commencement) Order 1999
- The Public Interest Disclosure (Compensation) Order 1999
- Public Interest Disclosure (Prescribed Persons) Order 1999

List of Relevant Cases

5.500
- *Babula v Waltham Forest College* [2007] IRLR 346, CA
- *Bolton School v Evans* [2007] IRLR 140, CA
- *Woodward v Abbey National plc* [2006] IRLR 677, CA
- *Collins v The National Trust* (EAT) 250 7 255/05
- *Bachnak v Emerging Markets Partnership (Europe) Ltd* [2003] EWCA Civ 1876
- *Darnton v University of Surrey* [2003] IRLR 133
- *ALM Medical Services Ltd v Bladon* [2002] IRLR 807, CA
- *Parkins v Sodexho* [2002] IRLR 109
- *Azzaoui v Apcoa Parking* (2001)
- *Bailey v Arrow Consultants* (2001)
- *Durrant v Norfolk Sheet Metal* (2001)
- *Kay v Northumberland Healthcare NHS Trust* (2001)
- *Boughton v National Tyres* (2000)
- *Llewelyn v Carmarthenshire NHS Trust* (2000)

Further Information

Organisations
- **Department for Business, Enterprise and Regulatory Reform (BERR)**
  Web: *www.berr.gov.uk*

The Department for Business, Enterprise and Regulatory Reform brings together functions from the former Department of Trade and Industry (DTI), including responsibilities for productivity, business relations, energy, competition and consumers. It also drives regulatory reform.

- **Freedom to Care**
  Web: *www.freedomtocare.org*
  The website includes some useful information on whistleblowing.
- **Public Concern at Work**
  Web: *www.pcaw.co.uk*
  Since 1993, Public Concern at Work has been influencing the law and practice on whistleblowing at home and abroad. Recognised as a leading authority by governments, employers, unions and international bodies, Public Concern at Work makes whistleblowing work for individuals, organisations and communities.

Works Councils

> This topic covers the following.
> - Organisations Covered by the Rules
> - Valid Request
> - Special Negotiating Body
> - European Works Council Agreement
> - Information to be Provided and Consulted on
> - Statutory European Works Council
> - European Works Council Members' Protection
> - Enforcement

5.501 The purpose of works councils is to provide a framework for information and consultation with employees or representatives. From 6 April 2005 all organisations with 150 or more employees (domestic or international) have had to set up some form of works council either voluntarily or if requested by its employees in order to comply with the Information and Consultation of Employees Regulations 2004. From 6 April 2007 this was extended to all organisations with 100 or more employees and will be extended to those with 50 or more employees from 6 April 2008. (see Information and Consultation).

5.502 The rules on information and consultation for UK-based multinationals are set out in the Transnational Information and Consultation of Employees Regulations 1999 (TICER) and came into force on 15 January 2000. These regulations implement the European Directive on the establishment of a European Works Council 94/45/EC. They set out procedures for negotiating an EWC agreement, enforcement, the processing of confidential information, provisions and exemptions and protection for employees.

Employers' Duties

5.503 Employers should:
- negotiate within six months following a valid request for an EWC
- facilitate the fair election of the employees' Special Negotiating Body (SNB) for negotiating purposes by providing time and independent ballot supervisors
- negotiate with the SNB to reach a European Works Council Agreement or equivalent procedure
- allow SNB and EWC members paid time off work to perform their functions
- pay legitimate SNB or EWC expenses (travel, accommodation, etc)
- agree the information to be provided and consulted on with the SNB
- conduct negotiations in compliance with the Transnational Information and Consultation of Employees Regulations 1999.

Employees' Duties

5.504 To establish a European Works Council (EWC) employees should:

- make a valid request from 100 or more employees or their representatives in at least two Member States
- elect a Special Negotiating Body (SNB) to negotiate an EWC
- ballot the UK workforce to elect members to the SNB
- where there already exists an elected consultative committee, appoint within its members UK representatives to the SNB
- not disclose confidential information where so required by central management or by a ruling of the Central Arbitration Committee.

In Practice

Organisations Covered by the Rules

5.505 Organisations that are covered by European Works Council rules are known as "Community-scale undertakings" and "Community-scale group of undertakings" referred to here as "undertakings".

5.506 An undertaking is an organisation that employs at least 1000 people in the European Economic Area (EEA), 150 or more of whom work in each of at least two EEA Member States.

5.507 An organisation whose central management is located outside the EEA will be an undertaking if it satisfies the above conditions. For foreign-owned undertakings, compliance will be the responsibility of either:
- a designated EEA representative or
- the undertaking's largest establishment in the EEA.

5.508 To work out how many people are employed by a UK-based undertaking:
- add together the number of people employed at each UK establishment during each of the 24 months immediately preceding receipt of a request for a European Works Council
- divide the total by 24.

5.509 Part-timers who work fewer than 75 hours a month may be treated as half employees if management so wish.

Valid Request

5.510 To be "valid", a request to negotiate agreement for a European Works Council must consist of:
- a single request by 100 or more employees in at least two establishments in at least two different Member States, or
- one or more separate requests made by employees which, taken together, are equivalent to the single request.

5.511 In addition the request must be:
- submitted in writing
- dated
- sent to the undertaking's central or local management.

5.512 Following receipt of a valid request, employers should set up a Special Negotiating Body (SNB).

Special Negotiating Body

5.513 The role of the Special Negotiating Body (SNB) is to reach agreement with central management concerning the scope, composition, functions and terms of office of the proposed European Works Council (EWC).

5.514 The SNB must comprise at least one, but no more than four, representatives from each of the EEA Member States in which the undertaking has operations or subsidiary companies.

5.515 If a high proportion of the undertaking's employees works in a particular Member State, that state must elect additional representatives to the SNB. The rules for additional representatives are:
- 25% to 50% of employees in one state — one additional member
- 50% to 75% of employees in one state — two additional members
- 75% or more of employees in one state — three additional members.

5.516 The UK members of an SNB must be elected by a secret ballot of the entire UK workforce.

5.517 Central management must negotiate with the SNB with a view to reaching a written agreement to either:
- set up an EWC, or
- set up an information and consultation procedure, or
- adopt the statutory EWC.

European Works Council Agreement

5.518 A written agreement between central management and a Special Negotiating Body (SNB) to set up a European Works Council (EWC) must:
- identify the undertaking's operations and establishments covered by the agreement
- specify the number of members to be elected to the EWC, their terms of office and the allocation of seats
- explain the EWC's functions and procedures
- specify the venues, frequency and duration of EWC meetings
- indicate financial and material resources that have been allocated to the EWC
- state the duration of the agreement and the procedure for its renegotiation.

5.519 If the parties decide to establish an information and consultation procedure instead of an EWC, the agreement must say how employee representatives are to meet to discuss information conveyed to them by central management.

Information to be Provided and Consulted on

5.520 It is up to the Special Negotiating Body (SNB) and central management to agree what information should be a matter for consultation. However, in the case of a Statutory European Works Council the information that must be provided and consulted on is prescribed.

5.521 Central management has the right to withhold any information that would "seriously harm the function of the undertaking or be prejudicial to it". It also has the right to insist that members of a European Works Council (EWC) do not disclose certain information entrusted to them.

5.522 Where members of an EWC think management is unfairly withholding information or insisting it remains confidential, they may apply to the Central

Arbitration Committee (CAC). The CAC may order the disclosure of the information. It may also rule that information must be held in confidence by members of the EWC.

5.523 Management must comply with the CAC's order, although it can appeal to the Employment Appeal Tribunal on any question of law arising from that order.

5.524 Any member of an EWC who rejects a CAC ruling by disclosing confidential information may face civil action for damages and forfeits his or her right to protection against unfair dismissal. The only exception is if the member reasonably believes he or she is making a "protected disclosure".

Statutory European Works Council

5.525 An undertaking may be ordered to set up a statutory European Works Council if:
- it does not negotiate to set up a European Works Council (EWC) or equivalent process within six months of receiving a valid request, or
- the parties fail to reach agreement on the size, establishment and operation of a EWC or equivalent process within three years.

5.526 The statutory EWC is set down in the Schedule to the Transnational Information and Consultation of Employees Regulations 1999.

5.527 A minimum of three and a maximum of 30 employees may be elected to serve on the statutory EWC. It must include at least one representative from each of the EEA Member States in which the undertaking has operations or subsidiary companies.

5.528 If a high proportion of the undertaking's employees work in a particular Member State, that State must elect additional members to the statutory EWC. The rules for additional members are:
- 25% to 50% of employees in one state — one additional member
- 50% to 75% of employees in one state — two additional members
- 75% or more of employees in one state — three additional members.

5.529 Four years after it has been established, a statutory EWC may open negotiations with central management for its dissolution or continuance.

Information and Consultation Meetings

5.530 The statutory European Works Council (EWC) has the right to meet with central management at least once a year. Prior to the meeting central management must draw up a report on the progress of the business and its prospects. During the meeting statutory EWC members must be informed and consulted regarding the information in the report. The report should also be sent to and discussed with local managements.

5.531 The statutory European Works Council has the right to be informed and consulted on:
- the structure of the undertaking
- the undertaking's economic and financial status
- new product development
- trends in production and sales
- likely new investments
- any proposed reorganisation or restructuring of the business
- the introduction of new working methods or processes
- transfers of production

- mergers
- cut-backs
- closures of existing establishments
- the possibility or likelihood of collective redundancies.

Exceptional Information and Consultation Meetings

5.532 Where there are exceptional circumstances affecting employees' interests, central management must notify the statutory European Works Council (EWC) and agree to meet with it. For example, where establishments are to be relocated or closed or where there are to be collective redundancies, a meeting must be held. Such meetings may be attended by the EWC or a select committee of the EWC that may be enlarged to include members affected by the proposals.

European Works Council Members' Protection

5.533 Employees have the right to paid time off to perform their functions as:
- a member of a Special Negotiating Body
- a member of a European Works Council
- an information and consultation representative
- a candidate in an election to be a member or representative.

5.534 If an employer fails to allow such time off, the issue may be referred to an employment tribunal. If a complaint is upheld the employer will have to pay compensation.

5.535 Employees who perform the above functions may not lawfully be:
- dismissed
- selected for redundancy
- victimised
- subjected to any detriment

for exercising their rights.

Employees are also protected if they challenge their employer's actions in relation to the Transnational Information and Consultation of Employees Regulations 1999 (TICER). An employee who suffers detriment does not need to resign to complain to an employment tribunal. No qualifying service is required to bring a claim.

Enforcement

5.536 European Works Council (EWC) rules are enforced through the Central Arbitration Committee (CAC) and the Employment Appeals Tribunal (EAT) in Great Britain and the Industrial Court in Northern Ireland.

5.537 An undertaking that contests the validity of an employee request to set up an EWC may apply to the CAC within three months of the date on which the request was made. The CAC will decide whether the undertaking is subject to the regulations.

5.538 Where an employer fails to respond to a valid request to establish an EWC, employees or their representatives may complain to the EAT. If agreement to set up an EWC has been reached, but not implemented, the EAT may order the central management to establish the EWC or an information and consultation procedure. If no agreement has been reached the EAT may order central management to set up a Statutory European Works Council.

5.539 Employees may also approach the EAT with complaints about the operation of an EWC or failure to comply with information and consultation agreements.

5.540 Where employees' complaints are upheld, an employer may be liable to a penalty notice of up to £75,000 payable to the Secretary of State with an additional £1000 per day of continued failure to comply.

5.541 Both the CAC and EAT may refer cases to Acas if conciliation is considered useful.

Training

5.542 Senior managers in undertakings covered by European Works Council (EWC) law should be made aware of the rules and their responsibilities. Senior managers should also know how to deal with works council requests if the undertaking is nearly large enough to be covered by the rules. Staff will require different types of training depending on their role.

5.543 Central management will be responsible for negotiating an agreement with the works council, or equivalent. It needs to understand the procedures for:
- electing a Special Negotiating Body
- negotiating an EWC agreement
- communicating relevant information to works council members
- conducting EWC meetings.

5.544 Both central and local management need to know:
- whether the organisation is covered by EWC rules
- how to deal with valid and invalid requests from employees.

5.545 Line managers need to understand the rights of staff involved in information and consultation procedures to:
- paid time off to perform their functions
- payment of expenses incurred in carrying out their functions
- protection from dismissal or other detriment.

5.546 Where a European Works Council Agreement is reached, the organisation could also provide training to EWC members and other staff involved in information and consultation processes to:
- clarify their role
- improve communications
- support the negotiation process.

5.547 Training is particularly important where a EWC is comprised of members from many different Member States with different attitudes and working methods. Trade unions may provide or support such training.

List of Relevant Legislation

5.548
- Transnational Information and Consultation of Employees Regulations 1999
- National Information and Consultation Directive 2002/14/EC
- Council Directive 97/74/EC (extends the provisions of the above to the UK)
- Works Councils Directive 94/45/EC, OJ L254/64

Further Information

Organisations

- **Advisory Conciliation and Arbitration Service (Acas)**
  Web: *www.acas.org.uk*
  Acas aims to improve organisations and working life through better employment relations. It provides up-to-date information, advice, high-quality training, and works with employers and employees to solve problems and improve performance.

- **Department for Business, Enterprise and Regulatory Reform (BERR)**
  Web: *www.berr.gov.uk*
  The Department for Business, Enterprise and Regulatory Reform brings together functions from the former Department of Trade and Industry (DTI), including responsibilities for productivity, business relations, energy, competition and consumers. It also drives regulatory reform.

Chapter 6
Maternity and Parental Leave

Adoption Rights

Adoption Rights

This topic covers the following.
- General Qualifying Conditions for Adoption Leave
- Statutory Rights During and After Statutory Adoption Leave
- Early Return from Adoption Leave
- Disrupted Placement
- Reasonable Contact
- Complaints and Remedies

6.1 This topic also provides guidance on employees' rights when adopting. It sets out the employer's and employee's duties and the employee's entitlements.

6.2 The Employment Act 2002 introduced a new statutory right for employees to take time off work to care for a child who has been newly placed with them for adoption. An eligible employee who has individually or jointly, as part of a couple, adopted a child may take up to 26 weeks' ordinary adoption leave, immediately followed by up to 26 weeks' additional adoption leave. Qualifying employees who earn equal to or over the average earnings limit are also entitled to be paid up to 39 weeks' statutory adoption pay (SAP) during their adoption leave period.

Employers' Duties

6.3 Employers should make sure that employees are aware of the following.
- What adoption leave is and what the qualifying conditions are.
- The period of adoption leave.
- The notification requirements.
- Their rights and responsibilities during adoption leave.
- What employees need to do if the placement is terminated.
- What employees need to do if they wish to return to work.

Employees' Duties

6.4 Employees have a duty to:
- meet the notification requirements
- provide documentary evidence if requested by the employer
- not breach their terms and conditions of employment, eg implied obligation of good faith, while on adoption leave.

In Practice

General Qualifying Conditions for Adoption Leave

6.5 Adoption leave can only be taken by employees. It does not apply to any other type of worker or the self-employed.

Adoption Rights

6.6 Men and women are both eligible, but where a couple adopt jointly, only one of them is entitled to take statutory adoption leave (the couple can choose which).

6.7 The right to take statutory adoption leave is not available to foster parents who adopt a child that they have been fostering, nor to step-parents who adopt their partner's child.

6.8 Members of the armed forces, share fishermen and the police are excluded from the statutory right to take adoption leave.

Qualifying Conditions — Adoption Within the UK

6.9 To qualify to take up to 52 weeks' adoption leave, an employee must:
- have been matched with a child for adoption by an approved adoption agency, or be one of a couple who have been jointly matched with a child
- have been continuously employed for at least 26 weeks by the end of the week in which he or she (or his or her spouse or partner) was formally notified by an approved adoption agency of being matched with a child for adoption
- have notified the agency that he or she agrees with the placement
- have complied with the notification procedures.

Qualifying Conditions — Adoption from Overseas

6.10 To qualify for adoption leave where a child is being adopted from overseas the employee must:
- be the child's adopter
- have been continuously employed for 26 weeks or more by the end of the week in which he or she received official notification of the placement
- have complied with the notification procedures.

Notification Procedures — Adoption Within the UK

6.11 To exercise the right to adoption leave, eligible employees must do the following.
- Inform their employers of their intention to take statutory adoption leave within seven days of having been notified by the adoption agency that they have been matched with a child for adoption.
- Provide documentary evidence in the form of a certificate provided by the adoption agency if requested by the employer.
- Advise their employer of the date on which the child is expected to be placed with them for adoption and when they want the adoption leave to start.

6.12 Employees can choose to start their leave from the date of the child's placement or from a fixed date, which can be up to 14 days before the expected date of placement.

6.13 Employees who have notified their employers of the date on which they intend to start their leave may change their mind, so long as they inform their employers of the revised date at least 28 days before the new start date.

Notification Procedures — Adoption from Overseas

6.14 Eligible employees adopting a child from overseas must do the following.
- Inform their employers of their intention to take adoption leave within 28 days of receiving an official notification from the relevant domestic authority.
- Notify their employers of the date on which the official notification was received.

Adoption Rights

- Produce a copy of that notification if asked to do so by the employer.
- Inform their employers of the date the child is expected to enter Great Britain.

6.15 Once the child enters Great Britain, the employee must give the employer at least 28 days' advance notice of the date on which adoption leave is to start, as well as evidence (eg a plane ticket) confirming the child's arrival.

6.16 The period of adoption may begin on the date the child enters Great Britain or on a predetermined date that is no later than 28 days after the child entered Great Britain.

6.17 Employees may change their mind about when they intend their leave to start, but must give at least 28 days' notice of the amended start date or, where this is not reasonably practicable, as soon as is reasonably practicable.

Notification — Employer's Response

6.18 Once the employer has been correctly notified of the date on which an eligible employee intends to start his or her adoption leave, it must write to the employee within 28 days setting out the date the employee would be expected to return to work if his or her full entitlement to adoption leave is taken.

6.19 An employer who does not write to the employee within the 28-day period loses the right to prevent the employee returning to work before the end of his or her ordinary or additional leave period, or to dismiss or discipline the employee for returning to work after the due return date.

Statutory Rights During and After Statutory Adoption Leave

6.20 Adoptive parents have the right:
- to be offered suitable alternative employment if made redundant during statutory adoption leave (the entire period of adoption leave)
- to the continuation of their contractual rights and duties while absent from work on ordinary adoption leave, apart from the right to be paid normal remuneration
- to return to work to their original (or substantially equivalent) jobs
- not to be dismissed, selected for redundancy or subjected to any other detriment for exercising or asserting their rights under the Paternity and Adoption Leave Regulations 2002.

6.21 During additional adoption leave, the contract of employment continues, but only with regard to:
- the employer's implied obligation of trust and confidence
- any terms and conditions relating to notice of termination of the contract by the employer; statutory or contractual redundancy pay in the event of redundancy and disciplinary and grievance procedures.

6.22 Likewise, the employee is bound by:
- any terms and conditions relating to notice of termination of the contract by the employee
- the implied obligation of good faith.

6.23 All other terms and conditions of employment are suspended during additional adoption leave.

6.24 Eligible employees have the right not to be victimised or subjected to any detriment (including selection for redundancy) for asserting their statutory right to adoption leave.

Early Return from Adoption Leave

6.25 Employees on adoption leave who wish to return to work earlier than the date on which they are due to return, must notify their employer of the proposed earlier return date at least 28 days before the date in question. Parents whose adoption placement is due to start on or after 1 April 2007 must give a minimum of eight weeks' notice. Should they fail to do so an employer is within its rights to delay their return until those 28 days (or eight weeks) have elapsed or until the date on which they are otherwise due to return, whichever is the sooner. An employer is under no obligation to pay an employee who returns to work without prior notice.

Disrupted Placement

6.26 If, after an employee has begun his or her adoption leave:
- the expected placement does not occur
- the newly-adopted child dies
- the child is returned to the adoption agency

the employee's adoption leave period ends eight weeks after the start of the ordinary adoption leave period (if the placement did not occur), or eight weeks from the end of the week in which death occurred or the child was returned to the agency (if the placement did take place and the disruption occurred later).

The same applies if a child adopted from overseas dies or ceases to live with the adoptive parents. For these purposes a "week" is the period of seven consecutive days beginning with Sunday.

Reasonable Contact

6.27 New regulations, under the Work and Families Act 2006, that came into effect on 1 October 2006 introduce "keeping in touch" days.

6.28 The regulations apply to employees who adopt on or after 1 April 2007 and allow an employee, if it is acceptable to the employer, to work or attend training for up to 10 days during his or her adoption leave without the risk of losing his or her entitlement to adoption leave or pay.

6.29 Employers and employees are free to determine how the 10 days are to be worked but for the purposes of the regulations any work or training carried out on any one day will count as a day's work.

6.30 Employers cannot, however, insist that an employee carry out this work — it is entirely up to employees whether they wish to do so. Employees who are dismissed or suffer a detriment in respect of undertaking, considering undertaking or not undertaking such work will have been unfairly dismissed.

Complaints and Remedies

6.31 Eligible employees who, on the grounds that they have requested or taken statutory adoption leave, are:
- denied their right to adoption leave
- dismissed
- selected for redundancy
- victimised
- subjected to any other detriment for asserting a statutory right

may complain to an employment tribunal and will be awarded appropriate compensation if their complaints are upheld.

Training

6.32 It is important that all line managers are familiar with the organisation's policy and procedure on adoption leave and understand both the employer's and employee's responsibilities.

6.33 Where a number of managers need to be trained, a short, in-house training session will ensure that managers:
- understand the law surrounding adoption leave
- understand the legal obligations of both the employee and the employer
- understand the organisation's policy and procedure on adoption leave.

List of Relevant Legislation

6.34
- Maternity and Parental Leave (Amendment) Regulations 2006
- Paternity and Adoption Leave (Amendment) Regulations 2006
- Paternity and Adoption Leave (Amendment) Regulations 2004
- Paternity and Adoption Leave Regulations 2002
- Statutory Paternity Pay and Statutory Adoption Pay (General) Regulations 2002
- Work and Families Act 2006
- Employment Act 2002
- Employment Rights Act 1996

Further Information

Publications
- PL515 *Adoptive Parents — Rights to Leave and Pay*, Department for Business, Enterprise and Regulatory Reform (BERR)
- PL520 *Flexible Working — The Right to Request and the Duty to Consider: Guidance for Employers and Employees*, Department for Business, Enterprise and Regulatory Reform (BERR)
- E15 *Pay and Time Off Work for Parents*, available from HM Revenue & Customs.
- URN 99/1186 *Time Off for Dependants — Detailed Guidance for Employers and Employees*, Department for Business, Enterprise and Regulatory Reform (BERR)

Organisations
- **Basic Skills Agency**
  Web: *www.basic-skills.co.uk*
  The Basic Skills Agency is an independent organisation and a registered charity supported by the Government, which is committed to working with others to make sure that opportunities exist to help children, young people and adults strengthen their basic skills to a level necessary to function at work and in society.

- **Child Support Agency**
  Web: *www.csa.gov.uk*
  The Child Support Agency offers information on the various child support schemes — part of the Department for Work and Pensions.
- **Employers and Work-life Balance**
  Web: *www.employersforwork-lifebalance.org.uk*
  Employers and Work-life Balance aims to help all UK organisations implement and continuously improve sustainable work-life strategies that meet customer needs, corporate goals and enhance the quality of life for individuals.
- **Tommy's**
  Web: *www.tommys.org*
  Tommy's aims to end the heartache caused by premature birth, miscarriage and stillbirth. It funds a national programme of research, education and information aimed at understanding and preventing these tragedies.

Flexible Working

> This topic covers the following.
> - Right to Request
> - Employee's Application
> - Employer's Response
> - Appeal
> - Time Limits
> - Unresolved Applications
> - Detriment or Dismissal

6.35 Employees with young children are entitled to make a formal request to change their working arrangements in order to enable them to work more flexibly. In order to do so they must have responsibility for a child under the age of six (or 18 if the child is disabled) and must be either the mother, father, adopter, guardian or foster parent of that child, or the partner or spouse of any of these. It is important to note, however, that working parents do not have an automatic right to work flexibly. Instead, those who qualify are entitled to request flexible working and the employer is then obliged to give that request serious consideration.

6.36 From 6 April 2007, the right to request flexible working also extends to carers of adults. The definition of carer will cover any employee who is or expects to be caring for an adult who:

- is married to, or the partner or civil partner of the employee; or
- is a "near relative" (ie parents, adoptive or step parents, parent-in-law, adult child, adopted adult child, siblings and in-law siblings, uncles, aunts or grandparents and step relatives) of the employee; or
- falls into neither category but lives at the same address as the employee.

6.37 Not all working parents or carers have the right to request flexible working; there are certain qualifying conditions. Those who wish to apply must have at least 26 weeks' continuous service with their employer and must be employees working under a contract of employment. Finally, requests cannot be made more than once a year.

Employers' Duties

6.38 Employers should make sure that their employees are aware of:
- their right to request flexible working and the qualifying conditions
- the type of flexible working arrangements that can be applied for
- how to submit an application and what needs to be included
- the procedure that the employer will follow when considering the request
- the fact that a change in their terms and conditions once agreed, will, unless agreed otherwise, be permanent, and they have no statutory right to revert to their previous working arrangement.

6.39 Employers must also:
- arrange a meeting with the employee within 28 days of receiving a request for flexible working
- provide a written decision within 14 days of that meeting

- hold a further meeting within 14 days of receiving notice if the employee decides to appeal
- provide a written decision within 14 days of the appeal hearing.

Employees' Duties

6.40 Employees have a duty to:
- comply with the requirements for making an application
- confirm that they have responsibility for a child's upbringing and that their relationship with that child meets the qualifying conditions
- confirm that they have a responsibility for caring for an adult and that their relationship with that adult meets the qualifying conditions
- provide details of the change applied for and the potential effects to the employer's organisation and suggest ways in which those effects might be dealt with.

In Practice

Right to Request

6.41 Working parents or carers who qualify are entitled to ask for a change in their terms and conditions of employment, including:
- the number of hours they work
- the times at which they are required to work
- their work location.

6.42 This could include requests for flexitime, job-sharing, part-time working, home working, shift working, term-time working, annualised hours, etc.

6.43 The change will be a permanent change to the employee's contract of employment, unless expressly agreed otherwise. The employee has no statutory right to revert to the original working arrangement (although a further change may, of course, be agreed between the employer and employee). The employer, similarly, has no statutory right to require the employee to revert to his or her previous pattern of working once the child reaches six years of age or the caring responsibilities cease.

Employee's Application

6.44 An employee who wishes to request flexible working must apply to the employer in writing (an email or fax is acceptable). The application must:
- be dated
- specify that it is an application under the statutory right to request flexible working
- explain how the employee's relationship with the child meets the qualifying conditions
- set out details of the proposed change and when this would ideally come into effect
- explain what effects the proposal is likely to have on the employer and suggest how these effects might be dealt with
- state whether a previous application has been made and, if so, when.

6.45 There is no legal requirement to provide evidence of a caring relationship or childcare responsibility and therefore no legal entitlement to request proof. However, employees are expected to provide their employer with as much information as possible, which may include evidence of a caring responsibility if there is any reasonable doubt on the employer's part.

Employer's Response

6.46 An employer who receives a request for flexible working has a duty to give it serious consideration and follow a set procedure in doing so.

6.47 Within 28 days of receiving an application, the employer must hold a meeting with the employee to discuss it. (NB if the employer agrees to the proposal in writing within 28 days, then there is no need to have a meeting.) If the person who would ordinarily consider the application is absent on sick leave or annual leave, the 28-day period may be extended.

6.48 The 28-day time limit will start either on the day that person returns or will start 28 days after the employee has submitted the application (whichever comes first).

6.49 The timing of the meeting must be convenient to both parties. The employee has the right to be accompanied by a fellow worker. This person may address the meeting and confer with the employee during the proceedings, but is not allowed to answer questions on the employee's behalf. If the employee's chosen fellow worker cannot be present on the day proposed, then the employer must rearrange the meeting for a date within seven days of the original date that is agreeable to everyone.

6.50 Within 14 days of the meeting, the employer must write to the employee with a decision and this letter must be dated. If the employee's proposal is accepted, then the employer must set out the new work pattern and when it will take effect. If the employer refuses the request, then the letter must give one of the following reasons.
- A burden of additional costs.
- A detrimental effect on ability to meet customer demand.
- An inability to reorganise work among existing staff.
- An inability to recruit additional staff.
- A detrimental impact on quality.
- A detrimental impact on performance.
- Insufficient work during the hours the employee proposes to work.
- Planned structural changes.

6.51 The letter to the employee must also explain the appeal procedure.

Appeal

6.52 An employee who decides to appeal must write to the employer within 14 days of receiving the decision. The letter must be dated and set out the grounds of appeal. Within 14 days of that date, the employer must hold another meeting with the employee to discuss the appeal. The time and place of the meeting must be convenient to both parties and the employee has the right to be accompanied by a fellow worker.

6.53 The employer must then give the employee a written decision within 14 days of the appeal hearing. If the appeal is upheld, then the letter should set out the change agreed to and state when this will come into effect. If the appeal is dismissed, then the letter must set out the grounds for refusal and explain why those grounds apply.

Flexible Working

Time Limits

6.54 Any of the time limits that are laid down for different parts of the procedure may be extended by agreement between the employer and employee. These are the time limits that apply to:
- holding a meeting to discuss the employee's proposal
- providing notice of the employer's decision
- providing notice of the employee's appeal
- holding an appeal hearing
- providing notice of the employer's decision following the appeal.

6.55 If both parties agree to extend any of these time limits, then the employer must ensure that the agreement:
- is recorded in writing
- specifies the time limit the extension relates to
- specifies the date on which the extension is to end
- is signed and dated
- is sent to the employee.

Unresolved Applications

6.56 When following the above procedure does not resolve a disagreement, the next step for the employee would be to use the organisation's internal grievance procedure. An employee may be entitled to refer the matter to an employment tribunal if the employer:
- failed to follow the statutory procedure for dealing with the employee's application (eg failed to arrange a meeting within the set timescale)
- rejected the application on grounds other than the permitted reasons
- based its decision on incorrect facts.

6.57 Employees are not entitled to apply to a tribunal simply because they disagree with the employer's decision. Provided the employee's request has been given proper consideration and the procedures have been followed, a tribunal is not allowed to question the validity of the employer's decision or substitute its own opinion.

6.58 If a tribunal finds in favour of an employee, it may order the employer to reconsider the application and/or make an award of compensation. The maximum amount of compensation is eight weeks' pay (subject to the statutory limit on a "week's pay", which is £310 from 1 February 2007).

6.59 As an alternative to a tribunal hearing, an employer and employee with a dispute over a request for flexible working may agree to refer the matter to the Advisory, Conciliation and Arbitration Service (Acas) for arbitration.

Detriment or Dismissal

6.60 If an employee is dismissed or disadvantaged at work because he or she has made, or intends to make, a request for flexible working, he or she may make a complaint to an employment tribunal. Dismissal on such grounds will be automatically unfair. No qualifying service is needed to make a claim.

Sex Discrimination

6.61 *British Airways plc v Starmer*

Flexible Working

6.62 A female pilot, who had brought a claim against her employer on the grounds that it would not allow her to work part time, recently won her sex discrimination case. Mrs Starmer had requested to work part time, following her return from maternity leave. British Airways turned down her request on health and safety grounds, stating that pilots with less than 2000 hours' flying time must work at least 75% of a normal rota. The safety rule, it said, applied to both male and female pilots. It also claimed that it would be too expensive to have another pilot cover the remainder of Mrs Starmer's duties. The tribunal found in Mrs Starmer's favour and the Employment Appeal Tribunal (EAT) rejected British Airways' appeal. This case illustrates the need for organisations to give serious consideration to flexible working requests.

Training

6.63 All line managers should be made familiar with the organisation's policy and procedure on requests for flexible working and should understand both the employer's and the employee's responsibilities. Training sessions should ensure that managers understand:

- the statutory right to request flexible working and its implications
- the qualifying conditions and the procedure to be followed (and any standardised forms for dealing with requests for flexible working)
- what constitutes a formal request for flexible working under the statutory provisions
- the importance of responding to an employee's request within the set time limits and the penalties for not doing so
- that employers are obliged to give such requests serious consideration and may only refuse them on permitted business grounds
- the importance of a constructive and open-minded attitude towards flexible working
- that they need to be well prepared for flexible working request meetings
- that the time and place of the meeting must be convenient to both parties, and that the employee has the right to be accompanied by a fellow worker
- the importance of giving a written decision within 14 days of the meeting and be familiar with the information this letter must contain
- that the employee has a right of appeal
- the effects of any change in the employee's terms and conditions on other members of staff or departments
- that employees can complain to an employment tribunal if those dealing with their flexible working applications fail to follow the correct procedure
- that it is unlawful to treat an employee badly or to dismiss them because they have made, or intend to make, a request for flexible working
- that an unreasonable or ill-prepared refusal to grant a flexible working request could lead to a successful sex discrimination claim.

Case Study — Flexible Working — Addenbrooke's NHS Trust

6.64 Addenbrooke's competes with well-paying large private sector employers in an area of low unemployment and high-cost housing, and has to work hard to attract and retain staff. Its investment in a flexible working policy supports its objective of being an employer of choice in the area. Addenbrooke's is a three-star NHS

Foundation Trust, employing some 6300 people in Cambridge. The hospital's workforce consists predominantly of women in the 23 to 35 age group, and flexible working is a real business driver.

Business Drivers

6.65 When Addenbrooke's set up its first workplace nursery in 1989, it did so in a desperate but successful attempt to recruit and retain staff, and its policies on flexible working soon followed. It now provides 406 nursery places for 600 parents, around one in six of who work full time, and the appetite for flexible working continues unabated. The Trust also believes that staff who are happy with their work-life balance will be more motivated and more productive.

Available Options

6.66 Although the Trust has had flexible working in place for over a decade, its formal policy was put in place only in 2001. This was introduced partly to ensure consistency between departments and managers. The policy states that the Trust is committed to helping all staff, including medical staff, achieve work-life balance, regardless of personal circumstances, so flexible working is not restricted to parents of young children or carers. The full range of flexible working options is available; including compressed hours, self-rostering, annualised hours, job sharing and term-time working. Home working is also possible. "Time out" schemes are available for up to 12 months. These can be for childcare, elder care, travel, voluntary work or study, and are taken as unpaid leave. The Trust also has a flexible retirement policy. Retirees are offered three options.
1. "Wind down" — where staff may reduce their hours but have their pension calculated on a whole time equivalent basis.
2. "Step down" — where staff can change to a less pressured job. Their pension is frozen at the higher rate and a new rate commenced.
3. "Retire and return" — where staff are encouraged to work on an *ad hoc* basis through a bank scheme at times of particular need.

6.67 Working life can also be extended after the age of 65, subject to six-monthly health checks and satisfactory attendance and performance.

The Process

6.68 There is a formal process for requesting flexible working at the Trust. Staff must complete a request form, which asks the following questions.
- How will you be able to continue to perform all current duties within the proposed working pattern?
- If you are not able to perform all duties, what duties will be affected and how do you propose to reallocate them?
- How does your request affect direct patient care; customer/client service; colleagues who may have to cover for you; contact with your line manager or any mentoring responsibilities?
- If you have management responsibilities, how will your proposal affect supervision; performance appraisal; training; communication and staff support?

6.69 Although there have to be good reasons for requests to work flexibly to be refused, these are not hard to find. For example, the number of staff already working part time or flexibly could mean that allowing a further request could create operational difficulties, and the effect on the working lives of other staff could also be problematic. Also some jobs require cover at specific times or full-time hours, where job sharing could be appropriate.

Flexible Working

Problems

6.70 There was some initial resistance from a few managers who did not see the business benefits of flexible working, and who were not enthusiastic about the extra work involved. There was also cynicism from full-time colleagues, and some areas where the fact that so many people were working part-time caused difficulties in maintaining a service. Other difficulties arose because staff always expected to have their request granted, and managers were worried that they could not say no, even where there were good reasons why they should. Employees can appeal if their requests are turned down, and may be offered flexible working in another department or at a later date.

Costs and Benefits

6.71 Investment in flexible working has involved the time of the HR department in researching best practice and writing policies and in training managers. The return on this investment has been a reduction in sickness absence from 5.3% to 4.1% and a fall in staff turnover from 20% to 14.9% between 1997 and 2004. The Trust includes references to its flexible working policy in its recruitment literature and believes that flexible working has made a real difference to its ability to continue to recruit and retain staff.

Case Study — Flexible Working — Yorkshire Building Society

6.72 While the demutualisation of building societies that took place in the 1990s confirmed the commitment of Yorkshire Building Society (YBS) to mutual status, it required the organisation to demonstrate that it offered better long term value than privately owned financial institutions. This resulted in a culture change whereby staff were empowered to uncover and deliver what customers need. Allowing and encouraging staff to work the hours that suit them best was part of this approach, as was setting up an employee assistance programme to support further their work-life balance. YBS has 2200 employees, located in a head office and a member contact centre in Bradford and in branches nationwide.

Business Drivers

6.73 In 2001 the Society already operated flexitime, but it wanted to improve work-life balance and give employees more choice, while tackling three other issues: retention; the need to extend the operating hours of its call centre; and the overtime culture within certain functions.

Available Options

6.74 YBS offers the full range of flexible working options to all staff, although culturally few managers operate in this way. Staff in the call centre can volunteer for a 10-week rolling period of different shift patterns, or can continue to work from 9 to 5, if that suits them better.

6.75 Around 600 staff work either part-time or compressed hours: a few are job sharers and around 40% are on flexitime. This is where staff work core hours of 10 to 4 and can take a maximum of one normal contractual working day as either a full day or two half-days off within any one accounting period (usually one month). There are a number of home workers and career breaks are available for periods of between three months and a year; there must be a two-year gap between breaks, with a maximum of two in 10 years.

The Process

6.76 When staff apply for flexible working they have to fill in a questionnaire explaining how the business can continue to operate when they are absent; this has been helpful in ironing out potential problems. This procedure is the same as that followed for applications under the statutory right to request flexible working, which is being used by everyone who returns from maternity leave. In both cases the procedure has worked extremely well the YBS says.

Problems

6.77 Term-time working is the most complicated flexible working option to administer as contractual terms have to be reviewed each year because of changing school holiday dates. The provision of suitable office equipment such as desks and chairs for homeworkers, as well as ensuring risk assessments are carried out, are ongoing requirements for people working this flexible option. In some areas of the business compressed hours are less popular with managers, especially in smaller teams where all staff in the team request this option. This becomes difficult to manage and is dealt with on a first-come first-served basis.

Managers and Work-Life Balance

6.78 All managers received training when flexible working was first implemented in 2001, and they are now coached on a one-to-one basis by their HR adviser when someone puts in a request for flexible working, with the approach being that there has to be a sound business reason why such a request should be refused. Although senior management fully supports flexible working for business reasons, none feel able to work this way themselves. There are also differences in the way different managers implement flexible working. Inevitably, some are more enthusiastic than others, which could be because of the nature of the work being done in their function. This can lead to individuals changing departments in order to have a job in which they can work flexibly. Unfortunately, perhaps, flexible working is seen by some managers more as a benefit to staff than as a way of improving business effectiveness, and this can colour their approach.

Costs and Benefits

6.79 Retention improved when flexible working was first introduced in 2001. Although it has risen over the years there are other organisational factors that have contributed to this. Absence is below the national average, at 3%. When the call centre introduced shift working, called Life-Style shifts, for which staff can volunteer, overtime was reduced, resulting in significant savings. Flexible working has resulted in a more flexible attitude from staff, which has helped in the branch network as well as in the call centre, with cover for busy periods such as lunchtime now cheaper and easier to obtain. Many customer support activities are better staffed at peak times which has led to improved customer satisfaction with the Society. From the employee perspective the changes mean that the majority of staff are happy with their work-life balance and are satisfied with the Society as an employer.

List of Relevant Legislation

6.80
- Flexible Working (Eligibility, Complaints and Remedies) (Amendment) Regulations 2006
- Flexible Working (Eligibility, Complaints and Remedies) Regulations 2002
- Flexible Working (Procedural Requirements) Regulations 2002
- Work and Families Act 2006
- Employment Act 2002

List of Relevant Cases

6.81
- *Commotion Ltd v Rutty* [2006] IRLR 171
- *British Airways plc v Starmer* [2005] IRLR 862, EAT
- *Clarke v Telewest Communications plc* ET No. 1301034/2004 (unreported)

Further Information

Publications
- PL520 *Flexible Working — The Right to Request and the Duty to Consider: Guidance for Employers and Employees*, Department for Business, Enterprise and Regulatory Reform (BERR)
- *Flexible Working — The Right to Request and the Duty to Consider*, Department for Business, Enterprise and Regulatory Reform (BERR) URN 06/2158/A1

Organisations
- **Carers UK**
  Web: *http://www.carersuk.org/Employersforcarers*
  Carers UK campaigns for equality for carers, provides information, advice and support for carers across the UK.
- **Department for Business, Enterprise and Regulatory Reform (BERR) — Employment Relations Working Parents**
  Web: *www.dti.gov.uk/er/workingparents.htm*
  This section of the Department for Business, Enterprise and Regulatory Reform (prior to July 2007, the Department of Trade and Industry) provides information and publications on parental leave and pay.
- **Department for Work and Pensions (DWP)**
  Web: *www.dwp.gov.uk*
  The DWP is responsible for the Government's welfare reform agenda. Its aim is to promote opportunity and independence for all.

- **Employers and Work-life Balance**
  Web: *www.employersforwork-lifebalance.org.uk*
  Employers and Work-life Balance aims to help all UK organisations implement and continuously improve sustainable work-life strategies that meet customer needs, corporate goals and enhance the quality of life for individuals.

Maternity Rights

> This topic covers the following.
> - Qualifying Conditions
> - Employee Notification
> - Notification of Change of Start Date
> - Responding to an Employee Notification
> - Going on Leave
> - Pregnancy-related Absences
> - Rights and Duties During Maternity Leave
> - Rights During Ordinary Maternity Leave
> - Rights During Additional Maternity Leave
> - Returning to Work Notification
> - Compulsory Maternity Leave
> - Returning from Ordinary Maternity Leave
> - Returning from Additional Maternity Leave
> - Contact During Maternity Leave
> - Small Employer Exemption
> - Stillbirth and Miscarriage
> - Redundancy
> - Detrimental Treatment
> - Maternity and Dismissal

6.82 This section provides information and guidance to employers on maternity rights and pay. It covers an employee's rights and obligations as they stand currently, as well as providing information on amendments to the legislation for employees with an expected week of childbirth on or after 1 April 2007.

6.83 At the moment, every pregnant employee is entitled to 26 weeks of ordinary maternity leave. The woman's normal wages or salary are not payable, but she must continue to benefit from all her other terms and conditions of employment while she is on ordinary maternity leave. She may be entitled to Statutory Maternity Pay (SMP).

6.84 Women are entitled to a further 26 weeks of additional maternity leave, giving them one year's leave in total if they have been working for their employer for at least 26 continuous weeks by the time they reach the beginning of the 14th week before their baby is due.

6.85 However, all women who have an expected week of childbirth (EWC) of 1 April 2007 or later are entitled to additional maternity leave, regardless of length of service.

6.86 Note that, while the period of SMP (for eligible employees) has been extended for EWCs on or after 1 April 2007, the length of ordinary and additional leave periods has **not** changed.

Employers' Duties

6.87 Employers must:
- advise pregnant employees of the two types of maternity leave and which they qualify for
- be clear as to the new maternity rights for women whose expected week of childbirth (EWC) is on or after 1 April 2007

Maternity Rights

- explain the notification requirements for maternity leave
- clarify the date when employees are due to return to work
- explain what the employee should do if she wants to come back early but cannot return because of illness, or if she decides not to come back at all
- advise employees of their rights and responsibilities during maternity leave
- respond within 28 days when an employee gives notice of her intention to go on maternity leave
- provide the employee with a revised return date if she gives notice that she has changed her mind about when to start maternity leave
- maintain the employee's terms and conditions of employment (except for wages or salary) during ordinary maternity leave and allow her to return to the job she was in before she went on leave
- be clear about which contractual benefits continue to apply during additional maternity leave
- allow the employee to return to her previous job following additional maternity leave, unless this is not reasonably practicable (for women whose EWC is before 1 April 2007)
- allow the employee to return to a similar job if her EWC is on or after 1 April 2007.

Employees' Duties

6.88 Employees must:

- comply with the notification requirements by the end of the 15th week before the baby is due
- follow the rules for notifying the employer if the employee changes her mind about when she wants to go on leave, or if she gives birth before maternity leave starts
- give the employer at least 28 days' notice if the employee decides to return early from either ordinary or additional maternity leave if the expected week of childbirth (EWC) is before 1 April 2007
- give the employer at least eight weeks' notice if the employee decides to return to work early or if the EWC is on or after 1 April 2007
- if not able to return on the due date because of illness, notify the employer in accordance with normal organisation sickness procedures
- if decides not to return at all, give the employer notice of her resignation in accordance with the terms of her employment
- not breach any terms or conditions of her contract of employment while she is on leave.

In Practice

Maternity Leave: Qualifying Conditions

6.89 The right to take 26 weeks of ordinary maternity leave applies to all pregnant employees, regardless of length of service or hours worked.

6.90 For employees who have an expected week of childbirth (EWC) before 1 April 2007, additional maternity leave is available to those who have 26 weeks' continuous service with the employer by the 15th week before the EWC.

6.91 All employees who have an EWC on or after 1 April 2007 are entitled to additional maternity leave, regardless of length of service.

6.92 Additional maternity leave starts at the end of ordinary maternity leave and lasts for a further 26 weeks, making 52 weeks in total. To qualify for maternity leave, a woman must be an employee working under a contract of employment. Other categories of worker are not eligible.

Employee Notification

6.93 By the end of the 15th week before the baby is due (unless this is not reasonably practicable) the pregnant employee must notify the employer of the following.
- The fact that she is pregnant.
- Her expected week of childbirth (the employer may ask to see a certificate from a doctor or midwife to confirm this).
- The date she intends to start her leave (this part must be in writing if the employer requests it).

Notification of Change of Start Date

6.94 The pregnant employee is entitled to change the date when she intends to start her maternity leave, providing she:
- gives her employer at least 28 days' notice (ie 28 days before the original date or 28 days before the new date, whichever comes first)
- puts the request in writing, if the employer requests it.

6.95 If it is not reasonably practicable for the woman to give 28 days' notice of the change, then she must notify the employer as soon as she can.

Responding to an Employee Notification

6.96 When an employer receives notice from a woman that she intends to go on maternity leave, then it must respond within 28 days. This reply must inform the woman of the date on which her maternity leave will end, calculated in accordance with her chosen start date. Where the woman subsequently changes her mind about when to start her maternity leave, then the deadline for writing to her to tell her when she is due to return will be within 28 days from the date she notified the new date.

Going on Leave

6.97 An employee may not start her leave before the 11th week before the expected week of childbirth (EWC) unless the baby is born before then. If the baby is born before the woman intended to start her maternity leave, then she must inform her employer as soon as possible, giving the date of birth and, if she has not already done so, a certificate showing when it was originally expected.

6.98 A pregnant woman may start her maternity leave as close to the birth as she likes. If, however, she is absent from work for a pregnancy-related reason after the beginning of the fourth week before her EWC, then her maternity leave will start automatically.

Pregnancy-Related Absences

6.99 The European Court of Justice (ECJ) has ruled that a sick pay scheme

Maternity Rights

which treats employees off work with a pregnancy-related illness in the same way as any other sickness absence is lawful and does not breach European equal pay rules.

6.100 Ms McKenna was a public sector employee in Ireland. She was off sick for most of her pregnancy, with a pregnancy-related illness. Her employer's sick pay scheme entitled employees to full pay for six months, followed by a further six months at half pay. The sick pay scheme did not distinguish between pregnancy-related absences and non-pregnancy related absences. When Ms McKenna's maternity leave ended, she was unable to return to work on medical grounds and received half pay for this period of absence. Ms McKenna claimed that she had been discriminated against contrary to the Equal Treatment Directive, the Equal Pay Directive and Article 141 of the EC Treaty and that her illness, being pregnancy related, should not have been treated in the same way as any other illness.

6.101 The ECJ found, however, that the employer had not discriminated against Ms McKenna and that pregnancy-related illnesses can, for sick pay purposes, be treated almost in the same way as non pregnancy-related illnesses. The ECJ's view was that while an employee's pay may be reduced while she is off sick with a pregnancy-related illness, it cannot, however, be stopped altogether.

6.102 The ECJ stated that women off sick with a pregnancy-related absence or who are off sick following a period of maternity leave, are entitled to receive a minimum level of income. While no specific guidance is given as to what this minimum level of income should be, it is likely that tribunals will interpret this as being statutory sick pay or the equivalent.

Rights and Duties During Maternity Leave

6.103 A woman's contract of employment continues throughout both ordinary and additional maternity leave. Her weeks of absence count as continuous service.

Rights During Ordinary Maternity Leave

6.104 During ordinary maternity leave, the employer has to maintain all contractual benefits except for wages or salary. Most women do, however, receive some payment in the form of Statutory Maternity Pay and some organisations give their female staff contractual maternity pay as well, ie continue full or part salary/wages. While absent on ordinary maternity leave, employees continue to be bound by any obligations arising from their terms and conditions of employment.

Pay Rises Awarded During Maternity Leave

6.105 In *Alabaster v Barclays Bank plc and the Secretary of State for Social Security*, Mrs Alabaster went on maternity leave. At the time of going on maternity leave, she was awarded a pay increase. However, the pay increase was not reflected in her maternity pay as it fell outside of the reference period for calculating her average weekly earnings.

6.106 In 2004 the European Court of Justice (ECJ) held that any pay rise that is awarded to a pregnant woman between the pay reference period and the end of the maternity leave period should be taken into account when calculating maternity pay. The Secretary of State had argued that Mrs Alabaster's claim under s.13 of the Employment Rights Act 1996 had been brought out of time and that s.1 of the Equal Pay Act was not appropriate in such a claim.

6.107 The Court of Appeal allowed Mrs Alabaster's appeal; however, stating that a pregnant woman does not require a male comparator if it can be shown that the only reason for not paying the pay increase is because of pregnancy. Employers should therefore ensure that any pay increases that are awarded to pregnant women be taken into account when calculating maternity pay, regardless of whether the increase falls outside of the reference period.

Rights During Additional Maternity Leave

6.108 During additional maternity leave, the situation is slightly different. The law requires that the terms relating to notice of termination, redundancy pay and disciplinary and grievance procedures must apply, and the right to accrue paid holiday under the Working Time Regulations must also continue. Mutual trust and confidence continues to apply during all maternity leave. If the employer intends to withdraw other benefits during additional maternity leave, this must be made clear at the outset. When deciding this matter, it is advisable to consider whether those benefits would be withdrawn during other sorts of extended leave. If not, then the employer could be vulnerable to a sex discrimination claim.

6.109 A woman on additional maternity leave is entitled to the benefit of her employer's implied obligation of trust and confidence, and she remains bound by the implied obligation of good faith to her employer and any terms relating to notice, disclosure of confidential information, acceptance of gifts or other benefits and participation in any other business.

Returning to Work Notification

Employees with an EWC before 1 April 2007

6.110 If an employee decides to take her full maternity leave entitlement and return either at the end of 26 weeks (ordinary maternity leave) or 52 weeks (ordinary and additional maternity leave) depending upon her service, she need not give her employer any prior notice of her return. She may simply return on the first working day after her full entitlement to leave has ended, in accordance with the date notified to her by the employer. Other circumstances, which may arise, are as follows.
1. If the woman wishes to return to work before the end of her 26 weeks or 52 weeks of leave, she must give her employer at least 28 days' notice of her intended return date. If she attempts to come back to work without having done this, then the employer may postpone her return to a date that will provide it with 28 days' notice. The employer may not, however, use this provision to postpone the woman's return beyond the date when her maternity leave was due to end anyway. It is also the case that if the employer has not given the woman proper notice of when she was due to return in the first place, it cannot prevent her from coming back early, even if she has not given it the correct notice.
2. If the woman cannot return to work at the end of her maternity leave because she is ill, she should notify the employer in accordance with the normal organisation's rules relating to sickness absence. If she qualifies, she should be paid SSP and/or the organisation's sick pay in the normal way.
3. If a woman decides not to return from maternity leave at all, then she must give her employer notice of her resignation in accordance with the terms of her contract.

Employees with an EWC on or after 1 April 2007

6.111 An employee with an EWC on or after 1 April 2007 who wishes to return to work early from her maternity leave must give her employer at least eight weeks' notice of her early return to work.

6.112 An employee who attempts to return to work early without giving the required notice can be prevented from returning to work by her employer until the eight weeks' notice has been given.

Maternity Rights

6.113 Similarly, if an employee changes her mind about her return date to work, she must give her employer eight weeks' notice of the new return to work date.

6.114 An employee who gives her employer early notice of the fact that she will not be returning to work at the end of her maternity leave period may not have her employment terminated early and she should not be deprived of any benefits to which she is entitled.

Compulsory Maternity Leave

6.115 No woman is allowed to return to work during the first two weeks after giving birth. This is the "compulsory maternity leave period". Any employer who allows a woman to return to work during this period could be fined. For factory work, the rules are stricter — women must not return within four weeks of giving birth.

Returning from Ordinary Maternity Leave

6.116 When a woman returns from ordinary maternity leave, she is entitled to return to the same job she was in before she went on leave, on terms and conditions which are no less favourable than those which would have applied if she had not been absent.

Returning from Additional Maternity Leave

6.117 A women whose EWC is before 1 April 2007, is entitled to return to her old job unless the employer can show that it is not reasonably practicable for her to do so. In these circumstances, she must be offered another job that is suitable and appropriate for her to do. Her terms and conditions must be no less favourable than those that would have applied if she had not been on leave. Where employment rights depend on seniority, the woman's employment before going on leave should be treated as continuous with her employment after coming back to work. Special rules apply to the treatment of pension rights during maternity leave.

6.118 A woman whose EWC is on or after 1 April 2007 is entitled to return to a similar job.

6.119 If there has been a general pay rise during the employee's maternity leave, her wages/salary should be increased accordingly on her return.

Contact During Maternity Leave

6.120 New regulations, under the Work and Families Act 2006, introduce "keeping in touch" days for women whose EWC is on or after 1 April 2007.

6.121 Contact with an employee during maternity leave has, in the past, been at the discretion of the employee and employees who returned to work during their period of maternity leave lost the right to both continue their maternity leave and pay.

6.122 The new regulations allow an employee, if it is acceptable to her employer, to work for up to 10 days during her maternity leave without the risk of losing her entitlement to maternity leave or pay.

6.123 Employers and employees are free to determine how the 10 days are to be worked, but for the purposes of the regulations any work or training carried out on any one day will count as a day's work.

6.124 Employers cannot, however, insist that an employee carry out this work — it is entirely up to the employee whether she wishes to do so. An employee who is dismissed or suffers a detriment in respect of undertaking, considering undertaking and not undertaking such work will have been unfairly dismissed.

Small Employer Exemption

6.125 The Maternity and Parental Leave (Amendment) Regulations 2006 abolish the small employer exemption. The exemption allowed employers with no more than five employees to dismiss an employee returning from maternity leave if it was not reasonably practicable for her to be given her old job back or be offered suitable alternative employment. However, in practice, many small employers were open to claims of sex discrimination.

Stillbirth and Miscarriage

6.126 Childbirth is defined to include the birth of a living child (however premature) or of a child living or dead, after 24 weeks' pregnancy. In these circumstances, the employee is entitled to the same leave and SMP (subject to the qualifying conditions) as other employees.

6.127 If an employee loses her child before reaching the 25th week of her pregnancy then she is not entitled to SMP or to maternity leave. However, her absence should be treated as sickness absence and she may be entitled to statutory sick pay (SSP), incapacity benefit or contractual sick pay.

Redundancy

6.128 If a woman becomes redundant during her ordinary or additional maternity leave, she is entitled to be offered a suitable alternative vacancy if there is one available. If there is a suitable job and the woman is made redundant without being offered it, her dismissal will be unfair. A claim for sex discrimination would also be likely to succeed.

Detrimental Treatment

6.129 If a woman is badly treated at work because she is pregnant or because she has had a baby and taken maternity leave, she may complain to an employment tribunal. The law protects her from detrimental treatment on such grounds.

Maternity and Dismissal

6.130 If a woman is dismissed for any reason connected with pregnancy or childbirth, or for taking maternity leave, the dismissal will be automatically unfair. No qualifying service is needed to claim unfair dismissal in such circumstances.

Training

6.131 It is important that all line managers are familiar with the company's policy and procedure on maternity leave and understand both the employer's and the employee's responsibilities. Where a number of managers need to be trained, in-house training sessions will ensure that managers are familiar with the following.
- The law surrounding maternity leave.
- Any company standardised forms for dealing with maternity leave.
- What notification they are entitled to receive from pregnant employees, including certificates showing the expected week of childbirth.

Maternity Rights

- Appreciate the importance of working out the correct date for the woman's return in accordance with her notified start date and maternity leave entitlement, and informing her of this within 28 days of receiving her notification.
- Understand that an employee is entitled to change her mind about when she will start her maternity leave, provided she gives proper notice. The manager must then work out the new return date and notify the woman of this.
- Plan for the fact that women who take their full maternity leave are entitled to return on the appropriate date without giving prior notice.
- Know that a woman must give notice if she wishes to return early and be familiar with the rules on postponement if she fails to do so.
- Understand that, in most cases, women are entitled to return to their own jobs on the same terms and conditions (and understand the limited exceptions to this rule).
- Follow up any cases where a woman does not return to work as expected.
- Understand that it is unlawful to subject a woman to detrimental treatment or to dismiss her on grounds of pregnancy or maternity leave.

List of Relevant Legislation

6.132
- Maternity and Parental Leave etc. and the Paternity and Adoption Leave (Amendment) Regulations 2006
- Statutory Maternity Pay and Maternity Allowance (Amendment) Regulations 2006
- Maternity and Parental Leave (Amendment) Regulations 2002
- Maternity and Parental Leave, etc Regulations 1999
- Work and Families Act 2006
- Employment Act 2002
- Employment Relations Act 1999
- Employment Rights Act 1996

List of Relevant Cases

6.133
- *Alabaster v Barclays Bank plc and Secretary of State for Social Security (No. 2)* [2005] IRLR 576, CA — the ECJ and Court of Appeal ruled that women who receive a pay rise that is not reflected in their Statutory Maternity Pay (SMP) may bring an equal pay claim against their employers without the need for a male comparator.
- *Hoyland v Asda Stores Ltd* [2005] IRLR 438, EAT — the EAT ruled that under the Maternity and Parental Leave Regulations 1999 Regulation 9, an employee on ordinary maternity leave is not entitled to the benefit of terms and conditions relating to remuneration. There is no legal obligation to continue payment of wages during ordinary maternity leave. Bonuses come within the definition of pay and so can lawfully take into effect work done and not done.
- *North Western Health Board v McKenna (C-191/03)* [2005] WLR (D) 120, ECJ — the ECJ ruled that a sick pay scheme which treats employees off work with a pregnancy-related illness in the same way as any other sickness absence is lawful and does not breach European equal pay rules.

Further Information

Publications

- E15 *Pay and Time Off Work for Parents*, available from HM Revenue & Customs.
- PL507 *Maternity Leave — Changes*, Department for Business, Enterprise and Regulatory Reform (BERR)
- PL958 (Rev 7) *Maternity Rights — A Guide for Employers and Employees: Guidance Giving Information on the Rights for Women whose Babies are Due before 6 April 2003*, Department for Business, Enterprise and Regulatory Reform (BERR)
- PL958 (Rev 9) *Maternity Rights — A Guide for Employers and Employees: Guidance Giving Information on the Rights for Women whose Babies are Due On or After 6 April 2003*, Department for Business, Enterprise and Regulatory Reform (BERR)
- PL705 *Suspension from Work on Medical or Maternity Grounds*, Department for Business, Enterprise and Regulatory Reform (BERR)

Organisations

- **Child Support Agency**
  The Child Support Agency offers information on the various child support schemes — part of the Department for Work and Pensions.
- **Employers and Work-life Balance**
  Web: *www.employersforwork-lifebalance.org.uk*
  Employers and Work-life Balance aims to help all UK organisations implement and continuously improve sustainable work-life strategies that meet customer needs, corporate goals and enhance the quality of life for individuals.
- **Tommy's**
  Web: *www.tommys.org*
  Tommy's aims to end the heartache caused by premature birth, miscarriage and stillbirth. It funds a national programme of research, education and information aimed at understanding and preventing these tragedies.

Parental Leave

This topic covers the following.
- Qualifying Conditions
- Entitlement
- Meaning of a Week's Leave
- Caring for a Child
- Parental Leave Schemes
- Statutory Fall-Back Scheme
- Documentary Evidence
- Notice of Intention to take Parental Leave
- How Parental Leave Can be Taken
- Postponement of Parental Leave
- Record Keeping
- Contractual Entitlement
- Returning to Work After Parental Leave
- Failure to Return to Work After Parental Leave
- Rights and Obligations During Parental Leave
- Refusing Leave
- Detriment, Victimisation or Dismissal
- Redundancy

6.134 The Maternity and Parental Leave (Amendment) Regulations 2001 give:
- parents with children under the age of five, and
- parents with adoptive children under the age of 18 (before the fifth anniversary of adoption or the child's 18th birthday, whichever is the sooner)

6.135 The legal right to take up to 13 weeks' unpaid parental leave.

6.136 Employers and employees are free to agree enhanced parental leave schemes through a collective or workforce agreement, provided the agreement is no less favourable than the statutory entitlement and it is incorporated into the employees' contracts of employment.

Employers' Duties

6.137 Employers should make sure that employees are aware of the following.
- What parental leave is and what the qualifying conditions are.
- The period of leave and how it may be taken.
- The notification requirements.
- The rights and responsibilities of the employee during parental leave.
- The fact that any parental leave taken with a previous employer counts towards the 13-week limit for each child (or 18-week limit in the case of parents of a disabled child).

Employees' Duties

6.138 Employees have a duty to do the following.

- Meet the notification requirements.
- Provide documentary evidence where this is requested.

In Practice

Qualifying Conditions

6.139 To qualify for parental leave, an employee must generally have at least one year's continuous service with his or her employer and:
- be the parent (named on the birth certificate) of a child who is under five years of age, or
- have acquired formal parental responsibility under the Children Act 1989 for a child under five, or
- have adopted a child under the age of 18.

6.140 If an employee has at least one year's service with his or her current employer and:
- adopted a child between 15 December 1994 and 15 December 1999, or
- has a child aged who qualifies for disability living allowance,

then he or she will qualify for parental leave.

Entitlement

6.141 An employee who qualifies for parental leave is entitled to 13 weeks' leave for each individual child. Both parents are potentially eligible. In most cases leave must be taken by the child's fifth birthday.

Disabled Children

6.142 Parents of disabled children may take parental leave up until the child's 18th birthday, and the amount of parental leave that may be taken is increased to 18 weeks.

Adopted Children

6.143 Parents of adopted children may take leave up until the fifth anniversary of the date on which the child was placed for adoption or the child's 18th birthday, whichever is sooner.

Change of Employer

6.144 Any leave taken with past employers will count towards the 13-week limit (18 for disabled children) for each child.

Meaning of a Week's Leave

Fixed Working Hours

6.145 For those who work the same hours each week, a week's parental leave is equal to the hours he or she normally works.

Varied Working Hours

6.146 Where the employee's hours of work vary, a week's parental leave is calculated by dividing the total number of hours he or she works in a year by 52.

Caring for a Child

6.147 The aim of parental leave is to enable employees to take time off work to care for a child. The Department for Business, Enterprise and Regulatory Reform (BERR) *Guide to Parental Leave* provides some examples of why an employee may elect to take parental leave. Such examples include:
- spending more time with young children
- settling a child into new childcare arrangements
- accompanying a child during a stay in hospital.

6.148 An employer has no right to seek evidence from the employee as to the reason for the leave. An employer would be entitled to take disciplinary action should the employee be found to have dishonestly taken the leave for purposes other than childcare.

Parental Leave Schemes

6.149 Parental leave schemes that offer more favourable terms than those laid out in the Maternity and Parental Leave (Amendment) Regulations 2001 can be put in place by collective or workforce agreements.

6.150 Employers and employees can also agree to amend the statutory fall back scheme through an individual agreement, eg the contract of employment.

6.151 If a provision relating to parental leave agreed within an individual, collective or workforce agreement is less favourable to the employee than the regulations, then the employee may elect to rely on the more generous corresponding provision in the statutory fall back scheme.

Statutory Fall-Back Scheme

6.152 The fall-back scheme applies to all employees unless a more favourable scheme has been agreed. The provisions of the statutory fall back scheme are as follows.

Documentary Evidence

6.153 Employees must comply with any reasonable request for documentary evidence relating to their responsibility for the child, eg birth certificates, adoption papers.

Notice of Intention to Take Parental Leave

6.154 Employees must give 21 days' notice of their intention to take parental leave and specify when they intend the leave to start and end. An expectant father who wants to take parental leave to attend the birth of his baby should let the employer know the expected week of childbirth.

How Parental Leave Can be Taken

6.155 Parents can take leave in one week blocks or multiples of one week blocks. If the child has been awarded a disability living allowance, leave may be taken one day at a time. Employees may take a maximum of four weeks' leave in any year, subject to the overall maximum of 13 weeks (18, if disabled).

Postponement of Parental Leave

6.156 The employer may postpone an employee's period of parental leave for up to six months, if the employee's absence from work would cause substantial disruption or harm to the employer's business.

6.157 The employer cannot postpone parental leave where the employee is the father and has given notice that he intends to start leave as soon as the child is born. The employer also cannot postpone parental leave where an employee has given notice of wishing to start parental leave on the date his or her child is placed for adoption.

6.158 To postpone a period of parental leave the employer must give the employee written notice of the postponement, stating the reason and specifying the dates between which leave may instead be taken. The notice must be given to the employee within seven days of the employee's original notice to the employer.

6.159 An employee taking a postponed period of leave may take that leave in full, even if by doing so the period of leave falls outside the statutory time limits for taking parental leave.

Record Keeping

6.160 There are no record keeping requirements in law. In practice it is likely that employers will want to keep records for management purposes, so that they can:

- demonstrate that they have given employees their full statutory entitlement, and
- co-operate with other employers in providing information (on request) about how much parental leave an employee has already taken.

6.161 There is no obligation, however, for employers to provide new or prospective employers with information on how much, if any, parental leave an employee has taken. Where such information is not available, new employers will have to accept what a new recruit says about how much parental leave he or she has taken.

Contractual Entitlement

6.162 Where an employee has both statutory and contractual rights to parental leave, then he or she can take advantage of whichever is the most favourable.

Returning to Work After Parental Leave

6.163 Employees who take parental leave of four weeks or less are entitled to return to their old jobs. Employees who take more than four weeks' leave are entitled either to return to their old jobs or, where this is not reasonably practicable, to another job that is both suitable and appropriate.

6.164 Where a woman takes parental leave for four weeks or less immediately after taking additional maternity leave then, if practicable, she is entitled to return to her old job. If it is not reasonably practicable for her to return to her old job, she is entitled to return to a job that is suitable and appropriate for her in the circumstances.

Failure to Return to Work After Parental Leave

6.165 If the employee does not wish to return to work after parental leave, he or she must give notice of termination in accordance with the contract of employment.

6.166 An employee who returns to work late after parental leave should be dealt with through the organisation's standard disciplinary procedure. However, an employee should be treated in the same way as any other employee who is absent from work.

Rights and Obligations During Parental Leave

6.167 The following requirements apply.

- Employees remain employed during periods of parental leave. They do not need to be paid and most terms of the contract may be suspended.
- Employers must, however, continue to honour any terms and conditions relating to notice of termination, statutory and contractual redundancy pay (in the event of redundancy), and disciplinary and grievance procedures.
- An employee's right to accrue statutory holiday entitlement also continues during a period of parental leave.
- The accrual of additional contractual holiday leave (over and above the four-week statutory holiday entitlement) is dependant on agreement between the employer and employee.
- Continuity of employment is not broken by parental leave.

Refusing Leave

6.168 Where an employer prevents or obstructs an employee from exercising his or her statutory right to parental leave, or unreasonably postpones it, the employee may complain to an employment tribunal within three months. The employee does not need to resign in order to do so.

6.169 If the employee's complaint is upheld, the tribunal will order the employer to pay the employee an appropriate amount of compensation. The amount of compensation will depend on the circumstances of the case. In considering the amount of compensation to be awarded, the tribunal will take into account the employer's behaviour and any loss suffered by the employee.

Detriment, Victimisation or Dismissal

6.170 Employees must not be subjected to any detriment for taking or seeking to take parental leave. Where an employee is dismissed for taking parental leave, the dismissal will be automatically unfair.

Redundancy

6.171 If employees are selected for redundancy because they are going to take or have taken parental leave, then dismissal will be automatically unfair.

6.172 Where an employee who is on parental leave is genuinely dismissed for redundancy, redundancy pay cannot be reduced if the employee is on unpaid leave on the calculation date.

Training

6.173 It is important that all line managers are familiar with the organisation's policy and procedure on parental leave and understand both employers' and employees' rights and responsibilities.

6.174 If a number of managers need to be trained, a short in-house training session will ensure that managers understand the:
- law surrounding parental leave
- legal obligations of both employers and employees, and
- organisation's policy and procedure on parental leave.

6.175 As the law surrounding parental leave and other family-friendly leave evolves, it is important that managers are kept up to date with key changes.

List of Relevant Legislation

6.176
- Maternity and Parental Leave (Amendment) Regulations 2001
- Maternity and Parental Leave, etc Regulations 1999
- Employment Rights Act 1996
- EC Parental Leave Directive (No.96/34)

List of Relevant Cases

6.177
- *Rodway v South Central Trains Ltd* [2005] IRLR 583, CA
- *Truelove v Safeway Stores plc* [2005] ICR 589, EAT

Further Information

Publications
- E15 *Pay and Time Off Work for Parents*, available from HM Revenue & Customs.
- PL515 *Adoptive Parents — Rights to Leave and Pay*, Department for Business, Enterprise and Regulatory Reform (BERR)
- PL514 *Paternity — Leave and Pay*, Department for Business, Enterprise and Regulatory Reform (BERR)
- PL515 *Adoptive Parents: Rights to Leave and Pay — A Basic Summary*, Department for Business, Enterprise and Regulatory Reform (BERR)
- PL509 (Rev 1) *Parental Leave — Detailed Guidance for Employers and Employees*, Department for Business, Enterprise and Regulatory Reform (BERR)
- PL517 *Working Fathers: Rights to Paternity Leave and Pay*, Department for Business, Enterprise and Regulatory Reform (BERR)

Organisations
- **Basic Skills Agency**
  Web: *www.basic-skills.co.uk*
  The Basic Skills Agency is an independent organisation and a registered charity supported by the Government, which is committed to working with others to make sure that opportunities exist to help children, young people and adults strengthen their basic skills to a level necessary to function at work and in society.
- **Child Support Agency**
  Web: *www.csa.gov.uk*
  The Child Support Agency offers information on the various child support schemes — part of the Department for Work and Pensions.
- **Tommy's**
  Web: *www.tommys.org*
  Tommy's aims to end the heartache caused by premature birth, miscarriage and stillbirth. It funds a national programme of research, education and information aimed at understanding and preventing these tragedies.

Paternity Rights

Paternity Rights

> This topic covers the following.
> - Qualifying Conditions
> - Statutory Paternity Leave After Birth
> - Statutory Paternity Leave After Adoption
> - Period of Leave
> - Notification Requirements
> - Rights and Responsibilities during Statutory Paternity Leave
> - Right to Return after Statutory Paternity Leave
> - Unfair Dismissal Rights

6.178 From 6 April 2003, fathers became entitled to take paid leave of either one or two weeks to care for their new baby, under the Paternity and Adoption Leave Regulations 2002.

6.179 Statutory paternity leave is also available to adoptive fathers and people in a same sex relationship, providing the qualifying criteria are met.

Employers' Duties

6.180 Employers have a duty to:
- inform employees of the qualifying conditions for statutory paternity leave
- explain the period of leave
- inform employees of the notification requirements
- make employees aware of their rights and responsibilities during leave.

Employees' Duties

6.181 Employees have a duty to:
- meet the notification requirements
- inform the employer as to the date on which he or she wishes to start paternity leave and the length of leave (one or two weeks) that he or she wishes to take
- declare his or her right to take statutory paternity leave, if requested by the employer
- provide further notice once the baby has been born or the child has been placed for adoption
- not breach any terms and conditions under the contract of employment while on paternity leave.

In Practice

Qualifying Conditions

6.182 The right to statutory paternity leave applies only to employees and not other workers or the self-employed. In addition, certain groups are excluded from the right to take statutory paternity leave, including members of the armed forces, share fishermen and the police.

6.183 Statutory paternity leave may be taken after the birth of a baby or the adoption of a child under the age of 18.

6.184 Where an employee's child is stillborn he or she will only be entitled to take statutory paternity leave if the stillbirth occurs after the 24th week of pregnancy.

Statutory Paternity Leave After Birth

6.185 In order to take statutory paternity leave after the birth of a child, an employee must:

- have at least 26 weeks' continuous service by the end of the 15th week before the expected week of childbirth (EWC)
- be the child's biological father, and must have, or expect to have, responsibility for the child's upbringing, or
- be the spouse or partner of the mother, and must have, or expect to have, the main responsibility for the child's upbringing, apart from the responsibility of the mother (same sex partners are eligible)
- have formally notified the employer of his or her intention to take statutory paternity leave
- provide documentary evidence supporting his or her right to take statutory paternity leave if requested.

Statutory Paternity Leave After Adoption

6.186 In order for an adoptive parent (who is not taking statutory adoption leave, or the partner of an adoptive parent) to be entitled to take statutory paternity leave to care for an adopted child (adopted in the UK), he or she must:

- have at least 26 weeks' continuous service by the end of the week in which he or she is formally informed by an approved adoption agency that he or she (or his or her partner) has been matched with a child for adoption
- be the joint adopter of the child or be married to, or the partner of, the adopter, and have, or expect to have, the main responsibility for the child's upbringing, apart from the responsibility of the adopter
- have formally informed the employer of his or her intention to take statutory paternity leave and provided documentary evidence supporting his or her right to take statutory paternity leave, if requested. See *Notification Requirements*.

6.187 Slightly different rules apply if the child is being adopted from overseas. In this case, the adoptive parent must have at least 26 weeks' continuous service and this must:

- end with the week in which the adoptive parent receives notification from the relevant domestic authority, or
- commence with the week in which the adoptive parent's employment began.

6.188 The latter criteria takes into account the fact that notification of the placement may have been obtained some time before the child enters the UK and the employee may have changed employers during that time.

Period of Leave

6.189 The following rules apply for the period of statutory paternity leave.

Paternity Rights

- Statutory paternity leave is for a maximum of two weeks.
- Employees can choose to take either one week or two consecutive weeks.
- The legislation does not make provision for the employee to take the leave over a number of non-consecutive days or weeks.
- If the employee elects to take only one week's leave, he or she may not take a further week's leave at a later stage.
- The leave may begin on any day of the week, which may include the day on which an employee's child is born or adopted.
- The length of statutory paternity leave is unaffected by multiple births or if more than one child is adopted as part of the same placement.
- Statutory paternity leave must be taken within 56 days of the birth of a child or, in the case of adoption, within eight weeks of the child's placement.
- In the case of birth, if the baby is born prematurely the employee may take statutory paternity leave at any time from the actual date of birth up to the end of a period of eight weeks after the week the birth was expected.
- Where the baby is born late, the employee must delay the start of the leave until the baby is actually born.

Notification Requirements

Birth

6.190 In order to take statutory paternity leave after the birth of a child, an employee must notify the employer of his or her intention to take statutory paternity leave by the end of the 15th week before the mother's EWC, or as soon as is practicable thereafter.

Adoption

6.191 In order to take statutory paternity leave after the adoption of a child in the UK, the employee must notify the employer of his or her intention to take statutory paternity leave no later than seven days after the date on which notification was received from the adoption agency of the match with the child.

6.192 If the adopted child is being placed from abroad, the employee must notify the employer of:
- the date the adoptive parent received official notification of the placement
- the date on which the child is expected to enter the UK.

6.193 This notification must be done within 28 days of the adoptive parent receiving the official notification of the placement, or within 28 days of the employee completing 26 weeks' continuous service (whichever is later).

Declaration of Right to Take Statutory Paternity Leave

6.194 Notice does not need to be given in writing. However, if the employer requests it the employee must provide a signed declaration that he or she satisfies the conditions of entitlement to statutory paternity leave, and that his or her absence from work will be for the purpose of caring for the child or supporting the child's mother or adopter.

6.195 HM Revenue & Customs (HMRC) provides a model self-certificate of entitlement to statutory paternity leave and pay (*Becoming a Parent* (SC3) or *Becoming an Adoptive Parent* (SC4)) which employees may use for this purpose. Completion of this form or the provision of equivalent information in writing is mandatory, if an employee is to be paid statutory paternity pay.

Commencement of Statutory Paternity Leave

6.196 As long as the employee takes his or her entitlement to one or two weeks of statutory paternity leave within 56 days of the birth or adoption of the child, he or she can choose when to start the leave. In general, statutory paternity leave starts on the date specified in the employee's notice.

6.197 In the case of birth, an exception to this is when the employee chooses to start his or her statutory paternity leave on the day the baby is born and he or she is at work on that date. In such a case, the leave would start the next day.

6.198 It is not possible for prospective fathers to take statutory paternity leave before the birth of a baby, eg for antenatal care.

Variation of Start Date

6.199 If, having provided notification of his or her intention to take statutory paternity leave on a specified date, the employee wishes to change the start date, he or she must give the employer at least 28 days' notice as to the revised start date. Notice of the variation should be given as soon as possible, and must be in writing if the employer requests it.

Further Notice

6.200 In all cases, once the baby has been born or the child has been placed for adoption, the employee must inform the employer of the date of birth or placement. This must be in writing, if the employer requests it.

Rights and Responsibilities During Statutory Paternity Leave

Terms and Conditions During Statutory Paternity Leave

6.201 During statutory paternity leave an employee's contract of employment continues and, apart from remuneration, he or she is entitled to the continuation of all his or her terms and conditions of employment.

6.202 This means that the employee should be treated as if he or she were not absent from work and all benefits, etc should continue. In the same way, the employee is bound by any obligations that arise under the contract of employment, eg confidentiality. He or she will obviously not be bound by any obligations that are inconsistent with taking statutory paternity leave, eg the duty to turn up for work.

Right to Return After Statutory Paternity Leave

6.203 Employees returning to work after one or two weeks' statutory paternity leave have the right to return to the job that they held immediately before their leave began, on the same terms and conditions of employment.

6.204 The same right applies to an employee returning to work after a period of statutory paternity leave that was the last of two or more consecutive periods of statutory leave (which includes additional maternity leave, adoption or parental leave) of more than four weeks. In these circumstances, if it is not reasonably practicable for the employee to return to the same job, he or she must be offered another position which is both suitable for the employee and appropriate for him or her to do in the circumstances.

6.205 After a period of one or two weeks of statutory paternity leave, there is no requirement for the employee to give the employer notice of his or her return date.

Unfair Dismissal Rights

6.206 An employee has the right not to be subjected to a detriment for a reason relating to his or her intention to take statutory paternity leave or for actually taking statutory paternity leave.

6.207 In addition, an employee who is dismissed for asserting his or her right to take statutory paternity leave will be considered to have been automatically unfairly dismissed. Unlike unfair dismissal, there is no qualifying service required to bring a claim of automatic unfair dismissal.

6.208 Furthermore, an employee denied contractual benefits during statutory paternity leave could bring a breach of contract claim.

Training

6.209 It is important that all line managers are familiar with the organisation's policy and procedure on paternity leave and understand both the employer's and the employee's responsibilities.

6.210 Where a number of managers need to be trained, a short, in-house training session will ensure that managers:
- understand the law surrounding paternity leave
- obtain proof of the right to take paternity leave if necessary
- provide appropriate written responses to employees where required
- understand the legal obligations of both the employee and the employer
- understand the organisation's policy and procedure on paternity leave.

List of Relevant Legislation

6.211
- Paternity and Adoption Leave (Adoption from Overseas) Regulations 2003
- Paternity and Adoption Leave Regulations 2002
- Adoption and Children Act 2002
- Employment Act 2002
- Employment Rights Act 1996

Further Information

Publications
- SC3 *Becoming a Parent*, available from HM Revenue & Customs
- SC4 *Becoming an Adoptive Parent*, available from HM Revenue & Customs
- PL514 *Paternity — Leave and Pay*, Department for Business, Enterprise and Regulatory Reform (BERR)
- E15 *Pay and Time Off Work for Parents*, available from HM Revenue & Customs.

- PL517 *Working Fathers: Rights to Paternity Leave and Pay*, Department for Business, Enterprise and Regulatory Reform (BERR)

Organisations

- **Child Support Agency**
  Web: *www.csa.gov.uk*
  The Child Support Agency offers information on the various child support schemes — part of the Department for Work and Pensions.
- **Employers and Work-life Balance**
  Web: *www.employersforwork-lifebalance.org.uk*
  Employers and Work-life Balance aims to help all UK organisations implement and continuously improve sustainable work-life strategies that meet customer needs, corporate goals and enhance the quality of life for individuals.
- **Equal Opportunities Commission**
  Web: *www.eoc.org.uk*
  An agency working to eliminate sex discrimination and put equality into practice in the workplace. From October 2007 this organisation will be replaced by the Commission for Equality and Human Rights (**Web:** *www.cehr.org.uk*).
- **HM Revenue & Customs**
  Web: *www.hmrc.gov.uk/home.htm*
  HM Revenue & Customs (HMRC) is the department responsible for the business of the former Inland Revenue and HM Customs and Excise. HMRC is responsible for collecting the bulk of tax revenue as well as paying tax credits and child benefit.
- **Tommy's**
  Web: *www.tommys.org*
  Tommy's aims to end the heartache caused by premature birth, miscarriage and stillbirth. It funds a national programme of research, education and information aimed at understanding and preventing these tragedies.

Statutory Maternity, Paternity and Adoption Pay

> This topic covers the following.
> - Statutory Pay
> - Statutory Maternity Pay
> - Statutory Paternity Pay
> - Statutory Adoption Pay
> - Legislative Changes
> - Practical Implications of the Legislative Changes

6.212 All eligible employees have a statutory right to receive a minimum payment during a period of leave following the birth or adoption of a child. In addition, the father, or the spouse or partner of a person adopting a child, has a statutory right to receive a minimum payment while on paternity leave, provided he or she meets the set criteria.

6.213 These payments are known as Statutory Maternity Pay (SMP), Statutory Adoption Pay (SAP) and Statutory Paternity Pay (SPP). Employers may choose to pay occupational maternity, adoption or paternity pay in addition to the statutory payments, thereby enhancing the payments.

6.214 Self-employed individuals have no right to be paid while away from work in such circumstances. However, they may be eligible for maternity allowance, payable by the Department for Work and Pensions (DWP).

6.215 The responsibility for administering these statutory payments rests with the HM Revenue & Customs National Insurance Contributions Office. The Department for Work and Pensions (DWP) is responsible for policy and the HM Revenue & Customs is the authority that deals with appeals regarding an employee's entitlement to receive statutory maternity, adoption or paternity pay.

6.216 The rates for the statutory payments are set at the beginning of each tax year.

6.217 The Work and Families Act 2006 and associated regulations (the Maternity and Parental Leave etc and the Paternity and Adoption Leave (Amendment) Regulations 2006):

- extend the payment period for SMP and SAP from 26 weeks to 39 weeks
- remove the additional qualifying conditions for additional maternity leave so that all employees who qualify for ordinary maternity leave will also qualify for additional maternity leave
- allow employees to work for up to 10 "keeping in touch" days during maternity or adoption leave without loss of entitlement to SMP or SAP
- allow the maternity pay period to start on any day of the week
- increase the notice that an employee is required to give if intending to return to work before the end of the additional maternity leave from 28 days to eight weeks
- propose to give fathers and partners a right to additional paternity leave, that may be paid if certain criteria are met. This will not be introduced before 2008 at the earliest.

6.218 The changes applied in respect of babies due or children expected to be placed for adoption on or after 1 April 2007, regardless of actual birth or placement date. The previous rules continue to apply in relation to babies who were due prior to

1 April 2007 and children who were placed for adoption prior to this date, irrespective of whether the actual birth or placement date fell on or after 1 April 2007. This means that some employers may have to administer the old and new rules concurrently.

Employers' Duties

6.219 All employers, regardless of size, are responsible for paying eligible employees a minimum payment for periods of leave relating to the birth or adoption of a child. Employers have a duty to ensure the following.
- They understand the regulations regarding the statutory payments.
- They keep abreast of changes to the law and understand the practical implications of the changes.
- Employees know the terms and conditions required to retain their right to be paid during periods of maternity, paternity and adoption leave.
- Employees know the evidence required to retain their right to be paid during periods of maternity, paternity and adoption leave.
- Employees are paid the correct statutory payments during periods of absence relating to the birth or adoption of a child.
- Employees are allowed to return to work at the end of the payment period.

Employees' Duties

6.220 Employees have a duty to do the following.
- Notify the employer that they intend to take leave as the result of the birth or adoption of a child.
- Provide evidence of the pregnancy or adoption of a child in the required format.
- Provide evidence of the due date or expected placement date.
- Provide the dates of the birth and adoption of a child.
- Comply with notification requirements regarding their return to work.
- Not to breach any terms and conditions under their contracts of employment while in receipt of the statutory payments.

In Practice

Statutory Pay

6.221 Statutory maternity pay (SMP) is paid at two rates. The higher rate, being 90% of average weekly earnings paid, is payable for the first six weeks of the maternity pay period. This is followed by a maximum 33 weeks for babies due on or after 1 April 2007 and a maximum of 20 weeks for babies due before 1 April 2007 at the lower of £112.75 or 90% of average weekly earnings.

6.222 Statutory paternity pay (SPP) is payable for the two weeks of paternity leave at the lower of £112.75 or 90% of average weekly earnings.

6.223 Statutory adoption pay (SAP) is payable for a maximum of the first 39 weeks of adoption leave for children placed on or after 1 April 2007 and for a maximum of the first 26 weeks of the adoption leave where the placement date was before 1 April 2007 at the rate of the lower of £112.75 or 90% of average weekly earnings.

6.224 These rates apply in relation to payment weeks starting on or after 1 April 2007.

Statutory Maternity Pay

6.225 Statutory maternity pay is payable to women employees who are pregnant and:
- have been employed continuously for at least 26 weeks in the qualifying week
- have average weekly earnings in the qualifying period above the lower earnings limit for National Insurance purposes
- are still pregnant at the 11th week before the baby is due, or have had the baby by then, due to early birth or have stopped working for the employer.

6.226 Statutory maternity pay is part of gross pay and is subject to deductions for PAYE tax and National Insurance contributions in the usual way. All lawful deductions can be taken from SMP, eg pension contributions and Give-As-You-Earn (GAYE), except attachment of earnings orders and deductions from earnings orders (DEOs) from the Child Support Agency.

6.227 All employers can recover SMP paid to employees. Most employers can recover 92% of the sums paid to their employees. Small employers can recover 100% of the SMP, plus 4.5% National Insurance compensation.

6.228 The recovery is made by deducting the relevant amount from the gross National Insurance element of the monthly payroll payment due to the Collector of Taxes. If there is insufficient National Insurance to cover the recovery, a deduction can be made from the PAYE element of the remittance.

6.229 To be classified as a small employer, the gross National Insurance contributions of the business (employees and employers) in the last qualifying tax year must be less than £45,000.

6.230 The qualifying tax year is the last completed tax year before the pregnant employee's qualifying week.

Useful Terminology
- Qualifying Week — the qualifying week is the 15th week before the expected week of childbirth, previously known as the expected week of confinement.
- Expected Week of Childbirth — this is the week in which the baby is due to be born.
- Maternity Pay Period — this is the period for which SMP may be paid. This a maximum of 26 weeks in respect of babies due before 1 April 2007 and 39 weeks in respect of babies due after 1 April 2007.
- MAT B1 form — this form is the written medical evidence of the pregnancy required by the employer under the regulations. It gives the date on which the baby is expected to be born and is signed by the doctor or midwife.

Who is Entitled to Receive Statutory Maternity Pay?

6.231 Statutory Maternity Pay is payable to a female employee who has been continuously employed by the organisation for at least 26 weeks in the qualifying

Statutory Maternity, Paternity and Adoption Pay

week — the 15th week before the baby is due. Agency workers, part-time workers and married women paying reduced rate National Insurance contributions can be paid SMP if they meet all the conditions.

6.232 The employee's average weekly earnings in the *qualifying week* must equal or exceed the lower earnings limit (LEL) for National Insurance purposes. An employee will qualify for SMP if she earned at least £84 per week if the baby was due between 16 July 2006 and 14 July 2007 and at least £87 per week if the baby was due between 15 July 2007 and 19 July 2008. Average weekly earnings are calculated over the eight weeks prior to the end of the qualifying week. However, pay rises that take effect at any time before the end of the maternity leave period must be taken into account. This may mean that average weekly earnings need to be recalculated to take account of pay awards.

6.233 The employee must also still be pregnant in the 11th week before the expected week of childbirth or have had the baby by then. She must also have actually stopped working for the employer.

6.234 The HM Revenue & Customs Booklet E15 *Pay and time off work for parents* gives a table of weeks, starting on a Sunday, which correspond to the expected week of childbirth throughout the tax year. This table helps the employer check whether the employee qualifies for SMP. Having established the expected week of childbirth for the relevant employee, the employer can use the table to ascertain the latest start date for the 26 weeks' employment rule to have been met.

6.235 *Example: The baby is due 25 August 2007, the expected week of childbirth begins 19 August 2007, the qualifying week begins Sunday 6 May 2007, the latest start date for the 26 weeks' continuous employment rule is 18 November 2006.*

6.236 Refer to the HM Revenue & Customs Booklet E15 *Pay and time off work for parents* for further information.

Continuous Employment Rule

6.237 There are certain interruptions of work where the breaks are treated as part of a continuing contract of employment. These include previous pregnancy, temporary cessation of work, reinstatement after unfair dismissal, trade dispute, agency workers, transfer of business where TUPE applies, holidays both statutory and public, adoption and parental leave, sickness or injury and change of employer.

6.238 If the employee's baby is born early, before or during the qualifying week and the employee would have completed 26 weeks of employment into the qualifying week but for the early birth, then the continuous employment rule is met.

Who is Not Eligible for SMP

6.239 A pregnant employee will not be eligible to receive SMP in the following circumstances.
- If she is not employed during the qualifying week.
- If average weekly earnings are less than the lower earnings limit.
- If she does not satisfy the 26 weeks' continuous employment rule.
- If she gives late notice of maternity absence.
- If she does not give medical evidence of pregnancy.
- If she is in legal custody at any time in the first week of the maternity pay period.

6.240 When the employee is not entitled to SMP at the start of the maternity pay period, she continues not to be entitled during the maternity pay period. The exception to this rule is if she fails to qualify because her average weekly earnings are too low but a subsequent pay rise takes the average weekly earnings (as recalculated) above the lower earnings limit.

6.241 If an employee does not meet the criteria to receive SMP, the employer must give her a form called the SMP1 Change Over Form. This form can be used by the employee to make a claim for maternity allowance.

6.242 Being ineligible to receive SMP does not affect the employee's right to take maternity leave — which will be unpaid — or her right to return to work after the birth of her child. All employees have a statutory right to take the maternity leave, regardless of length of service or the payment of SMP. Where the baby was due before 1 April 2007, the mother has a statutory right to ordinary maternity leave of 26 weeks, regardless of whether she is entitled to SMP. Mothers of babies due before April 2007 are also entitled to a further 26 weeks of additional maternity leave, provided that certain qualifying conditions are met.

6.243 For babies due on or after 1 April 2007, the additional conditions for entitlement to additional maternity leave have been removed so that all women qualify for a total of 52 weeks' maternity leave regardless of the length of their service.

Evidence and Notification for Statutory Maternity Pay

6.244 The employee must provide the employer with medical evidence of the pregnancy, usually on a form MAT B1. This form cannot be accepted if it is issued more than 20 weeks before the expected week of childbirth. The date of issue is the date it was signed by the doctor or midwife. An employer can refuse to pay SMP if the medical evidence is not produced by the third week of the maternity pay period.

6.245 The employee also needs to notify the employer that she wants to take maternity leave. If the employee is late in notifying the employer of her maternity absence, the employer can withhold SMP. The employee must notify the employer during the qualifying week that she is pregnant, the expected week of childbirth and the intended start date of the leave. Within 28 days of receipt, the employer must, in writing:

- acknowledge the intended leave start date
- make clear the employee is expected to return to work at the end of her ordinary maternity leave (or, if she is entitled to additional maternity leave, that she is expected to return at the end of her additional maternity leave period)
- specify her return to work date.

6.246 Should the employee wish to return to work early, she must give her employer the required notice. This is 28 days if the baby was due before 1 April 2007 and eight weeks in respect of babies due on or after 1 April 2007.

Payment of Statutory Maternity Pay

6.247 The rule governing the payment of SMP changed in respect of babies due on or after 1 April 2007. The new rules apply to babies due on or after 1 April 2007, regardless of the actual birth date.

6.248 The old rules continue to apply in relation to babies due before 1 April 2007, regardless of whether the baby was actually born after 1 April 2007.

6.249 This means that an employer may have to operate both sets of rules concurrently. This is illustrated by the following example.

Employee	Due date	Actual birth date	Old or new rules?
Anna	25 March 2007	19 March 2007	Old rules

Employee	Due date	Actual birth date	Old or new rules?
Beth	30 March 2007	4 April 2007	Old rules
Claire	2 April 2007	28 March 2007	New rules
Dawn	14 April 2007	11 April 2007	New rules

6.250 The old rules apply to Anna and Beth as their babies were due before 1 April 2007. It does not matter than Beth's baby was actually born after 1 April 2007 as it is the due date rather than the actual date which determines which rules apply.

6.251 The new rules apply in relation to Claire and Dawn as their babies were due after 1 April 2007. Again, it does not matter that Claire's baby was actually born before 1 April 2007 as it is the due date that is the deciding date.

6.252 Although Claire's baby was born earlier than Beth's baby, Claire benefits from the new rules, including payment of SMP for 39 weeks. Beth is not entitled to 39 weeks' SMP as her baby was actually due before 1 April 2007.

6.253 To avoid misunderstanding, employers should ensure that employees understand how the changes affect them.

6.254 Statutory Maternity Pay is paid for the maternity pay period. The maternity pay period is 26 weeks in respect of babies due before 1 April 2007 and 39 weeks in respect of babies due on or after 1 April 2007. It is the due date that determines the length of the maternity pay period rather than the date that the baby is actually born.

6.255 SMP is payable by the employer, provided the employee is eligible, whether or not the employee intends to return to work. The employer may make the payment for less than 26 or 39 weeks, as appropriate, if the employee:
- returns to work before the end of the leave period
- starts work after the birth with a new employer who is not liable to pay the SMP
- dies
- is taken into legal custody.

6.256 Once on maternity leave, mothers of babies due before 1 April 2007 lost the right to one week of lower rate SMP for every week or part week worked during the maternity pay period. This rule is relaxed for employees whose babies were due on or after 1 April 2007, who may work a maximum of 10 "keeping in touch" days during their maternity leave without losing entitlement to SMP.

6.257 The payment of SMP cannot begin until the employee starts maternity leave. The maternity pay period cannot start earlier than the 11th week before the expected week of childbirth, unless the baby is born prematurely. Generally the employee decides when her maternity leave period will start — for example three weeks before the birth or the day of the birth. The maternity pay period and the payment of SMP normally begin from the Sunday of the week following the week in which the woman ceased work. For babies due on or after 1 April 2007, the maternity pay period can start on any day of the week.

6.258 *Example: The baby is due on 25 August 2007, the maternity pay period can start at any time on or after 3 June 2007, or if the employee works up to the birth, as late as the Sunday following the day the baby is born.*

6.259 In the case of babies being born more than 15 weeks before the expected date of the birth, the maternity pay period will run for 26 weeks from the day after the actual date of the birth. The same would apply where the baby is born early, ie before the start of the planned maternity leave: the pay period starts the day after the actual date of birth. If the child is stillborn after the beginning of the 16th week before the expected week of childbirth, SMP is paid in the normal way. However if the baby is stillborn before the start of the 16th week SMP is not due for payment.

Statutory Maternity, Paternity and Adoption Pay

6.260 If the employee leaves employment after the qualifying week SMP is still payable providing the employee qualifies and does not start work for a new employer after the birth of the baby. The payment of SMP would begin at either the start of the 11th week before the expected birth if she left before that date, or the Sunday after the last day she worked if she left after the 11th week.

6.261 For babies due prior to 1 April 2007, SMP is payable at a weekly rate. Payment can only be made in multiples of whole weeks. This meant a monthly paid employee could receive four weeks' SMP one month and five weeks the next month.

6.262 For babies due on or after 1 April 2007, a daily rate was introduced to enable payments of SMP to correspond to the employer's normal pay interval. The daily rate is 1/7th of the weekly rate. This means that if an employee is paid each calendar month and the month has 31 days, she can be paid 31 days' SMP for that month.

6.263 All employees meeting the qualifying conditions will qualify for SMP regardless of age. Prior to 1 October 2006, a lower age limit of 16 applied. This was removed by the Employment Equality (Age) Regulations 2006.

Keeping in Touch Days

6.264 Under the rules that apply in relation to babies due before 1 April 2007, a woman on maternity leave loses a week's SMP at the lower rate for each week in which she undertakes some paid work for her employer. This rule applies even if the woman only does one hour's work.

6.265 Keeping in touch (KIT) days have been introduced in relation to mothers of babies due on or after 1 April 2007. The aim of KIT days is to help ease a woman's eventual return to work and make it easier for her to keep in touch with her employer during her leave from work.

6.266 Keeping in touch days enable a woman to do some work for the employer paying her SMP during her maternity pay period without losing SMP for that week. The woman can work for up to 10 days, whether consecutive or not, without losing SMP. Once the 10 days have been worked, SMP will be lost should the woman undertake any further work for the employer.

6.267 Any day on which the woman does some work for her employer will count as a KIT day, even if she only works for one hour.

6.268 The employee and employer must agree keeping in touch days between themselves. The employee has no right to work the days nor can the employer require that the employee undertake the work.

6.269 Keeping in touch days only apply to mothers of babies due on or after 1 April 2007.

Relationship Between Statutory Sick Pay and Statutory Maternity Pay

6.270 A pregnant employee who is sick before the start of her maternity pay period can be paid statutory sick pay up to the start of the maternity pay period if the sickness is not due to pregnancy. However, once she starts her maternity pay period, statutory sick pay cannot be paid. Where the employee's sickness is due to pregnancy and she is off sick on or after the start of the fourth week before the expected week of childbirth, her maternity pay period automatically begins on the day after the first complete day of absence due to sickness.

6.271 If the employee is already sick with a pregnancy-related illness — say in the fifth week before the expected week of childbirth — and the illness carries on into the fourth week, the maternity pay period must start on first day of absence after the start of the fourth week before the expected week of childbirth.

Statutory Maternity, Paternity and Adoption Pay

Rates of Statutory Maternity Pay

6.272 For payment weeks starting on or after 1 April 2007, SMP is paid at two weekly rates, the:
- higher rate — 90% of the employee's average weekly earnings — is payable for the first six weeks
- lower rate is set each year and currently stands at the lower of £112.75 or 90% of average weekly earnings and is payable for the remainder of the maternity pay period (20 weeks for babies due before 1 April 2007 and 33 weeks for babies due on or after 1 April 2007).

Calculating Average Weekly Earnings

6.273 Average weekly earnings are calculated by taking the average of the earnings paid in the "relevant period". This is the period between the last normal pay day before the end of the qualifying week and the payday falling at least eight weeks before that. Earnings include all gross earnings that are treated as earnings for National Insurance purposes. In the case of the employee with average earnings below the National Insurance threshold of £87 a week (£84 per week if the baby was due on or before 14 July 2007), SMP is not payable and she may be able to claim maternity allowance.

Change of Circumstances

6.274 An employer's liability to pay SMP ends if the employee:
- returns to work
- starts work after the birth with a new employer who is not liable to pay her SMP, ie she did not work for them at the qualifying week
- dies
- goes into legal custody.

Returning to Work

6.275 An employee who wishes to return to work before the end of her maternity leave entitlement must give her employer notice of her intention to return to work. The notice requirement is 28 days where the baby was due before 1 April 2007 and eight weeks in respect of employees whose babies are due on or after 1 April 2007.

Forms for Statutory Maternity Pay

6.276 *SMP1 — Change Over Form.* An employer must complete this if the employee is not entitled to SMP or her entitlement stops. She may be entitled to claim Maternity Allowance. The form tells the employee and the DWP why SMP is not payable and how to claim Maternity Allowance. The form must be issued within seven days of the employer deciding SMP is not payable. Failure to issue this form can result in a fine of £1000, with a further £40 per day that the failure continues.

6.277 *SMP2 — Record Sheet.* This is a sheet to assist in the operation of SMP. Employers do not have to use this form and there are similar commercial systems available for use with computerised payroll systems.

6.278 *SMP3 — Checklist.* This shows employers how to pay, record and recover SMP.

Statutory Maternity, Paternity and Adoption Pay

Records for Statutory Maternity Pay

6.279 All employers must, by law, keep the following records for at least three years following the end of the tax year to which they relate:
- all medical evidence, eg MAT B1 form
- copies of the medical evidence if the original has been returned to the employee
- dates of the maternity absence notified by the employee
- details of weeks within the maternity pay period for which SMP paid and the amounts
- details of weeks within the maternity pay period when SMP was not paid and the reasons.

6.280 HM Revenue & Customs may inspect the records during an audit visit, so the records must be accessible and clear. Other useful documents are copies of the organisation's rules on notifying maternity absence, records of average weekly earnings calculations, records of the start date of employments and the number of hours worked.

Statutory Paternity Pay

6.281 Under the Employment Act 2002, most fathers of babies due on or after 6 April 2003 are entitled to two weeks' paternity leave. An adoptive parent who is not taking statutory adoption leave is also eligible to take paternity leave. This legislation applies to all employers, regardless of the size of the workforce. During the two weeks' leave, most employees will be paid a minimum statutory sum, known as SPP. However some employees will only be eligible to take the unpaid leave.

Who is Entitled to Receive Statutory Paternity Pay

6.282 To be eligible to receive SPP the employee must have:
- average weekly earnings that equal or exceed the lower earnings limit for National Insurance contributions at the *qualifying week* — £87 if the baby is due between 15 July 2007 and 19 July 2008 and £84 if the baby was due between 16 July 2006 and 14 July 2007.
- a relationship with the child and mother, but cannot be an immediate family member
- 26 weeks' continuous employment by the qualifying or matching week
- remained in employment up to the date of the birth
- the intention of caring for the child and mother at the start of the leave period
- given the employer, if practicable, at least 28 days' notice of the start of the leave
- stopped working for the employer for those two weeks.

6.283 Prior to 1 October 2006, SPP was only payable to employees aged 16 and above. This age limit was removed from 1 October 2006. From that date SPP is payable to all employees meeting the qualifying conditions regardless of age.

Continuous Employment

6.284 To qualify for SPP, the employee must have at least 26 weeks' continuous service in the qualifying week, or matching week for adoptions. There are certain interruptions of work that are not seen as breaking the continuity of employment. These may include:
- temporary cessation of work
- reinstatement after unfair dismissal
- trade dispute

Statutory Maternity, Paternity and Adoption Pay

- agency workers
- transfer of business where TUPE applies
- holidays, both statutory and public
- adoption and parental leave
- sickness or injury
- change of employer.

6.285 The HM Revenue & Customs booklets E15 *Pay and time off work for parents* and E16 *Pay and time off work for adoptive parents* give the latest start date for the 26 weeks' employment rule for each notification week during the current tax year to help the employer check whether the employee qualifies for SPP.

Calculation of Average Weekly Earnings

6.286 The average weekly earnings are calculated over the eight weeks that end with the payday in or immediately prior to the qualifying week, or for adoptive parents the week in which the matching certificate was issued. If the employee's average weekly earnings are less than the lower earnings limit for National Insurance purposes or the employee does not meet the other criteria, the employer must complete and give the employee the Change Over Form — SPP1.

Evidence for Statutory Paternity Pay

6.287 Before employers can pay SPP, they must see the self-certificate form, either SC3 (birth) or SC4 (adoption). These forms are the employee's confirmation that they are responsible for the mother and child. The relevant form should be retained for record purposes.

Payment of Statutory Paternity Pay

6.288 Statutory Paternity Pay is payable for the maximum two weeks at the lower of 90% of average weekly earnings or £112.75 each week (rates applying for payment weeks starting on or after 1 April 2007). The payment of SPP is made through the payroll. It is treated as gross pay and is subject to deduction of PAYE tax and National Insurance contributions.

6.289 All employers are able to recover SPP from the Collector of Taxes, in the same way as with SMP. Large employers can recover 92% of SPP and small employers can recover 100% plus the National Insurance compensation of 4.5%. A small employer is one whose gross National Insurance contributions in the last completed tax year before the qualifying week — or matching week for adoptive parents — are £45,000 or less.

6.290 The recovery is made by deducting the sum to be recovered from the gross National Insurance element of the monthly payroll remittance due to the Collector of Taxes. If there is insufficient National Insurance to cover the SPP, then a deduction can be made from the PAYE tax element of the remittance.

Relationship Between Statutory Sick Pay and Statutory Paternity Pay

6.291 Statutory Paternity Pay cannot be paid for any week in which the employee is entitled to be paid statutory sick pay. An employee who becomes sick during the paternity pay period will be paid statutory sick pay only.

Form for Statutory Paternity Pay

6.292 *SPP1 — Change Over Form.* If the employee's average weekly earnings are less than the lower earnings limit for National Insurance contributions, or the employee does not meet the other criteria for SPP, the employer must complete and give the employee Form SPP1. The form tells the employee and the DWP why SPP is not payable and how the employee can claim income support and other benefits. The form must be issued within seven days of the employer deciding SMP is not payable. Failure to issue this form can result in a fine of £1000, with a further £40 per day that the failure continues.

When Statutory Paternity Pay Is Not Payable

6.293 Statutory Paternity Pay is not payable, or the payment must be stopped, if the employee:
- dies
- is taken into legal custody
- becomes eligible for statutory sick pay, or
- works for the employer during the SPP period.

6.294 However entitlement to SPP does not end if the mother or baby dies. Nor, once the employer has established the employee's right to SPP, is it lost if the employee is made redundant after the baby is born but before the start date of his leave.

Statutory Adoption Pay

6.295 If an employee adopts a child on or after 6 April 2003, he or she is entitled to take statutory adoption leave. This entitlement applies to any employee newly adopting a child up to the age of 18, but excludes step-family adoptions.

6.296 The rules governing the payment of statutory adoption pay changed in relation to children expected to be placed for adoption on or after April 2007. The new rules largely mirror the changes for SMP purposes applying in relation to babies due on or after 1 April 2007.

6.297 The old rules continue to apply where the expected placement date was before 1 April 2007.

6.298 In determining whether the new or old rules apply, the crucial date is the expected placement date, rather than the actual placement date if different. If the expected placement date fell before 1 April 2007, the old rules apply, even if the actual placement took place after 1 April 2007. If the expected placement takes place after 1 April 2007, the new rules apply, even if the placement actually occurred before that date.

6.299 Under the new rules, statutory adoption pay is increased from 26 weeks to 39 weeks, keeping in touch days are introduced, as is a daily rate of SAP. Adoption leave is increased to 52 weeks for all employees.

6.300 Adoption leave mirrors maternity leave. Where the expected placement date was before 1 April 2007, one adoptive parent is entitled to 26 weeks' ordinary adoption leave, regardless of whether the employee is entitled to SAP. Employees meeting certain qualifying conditions are entitled to a further period of additional leave of 26 weeks. Where the expected placement date is on or after 1 April 2007, one adoptive parent is entitled to adoption leave of up to weeks. The qualifying conditions for additional leave are removed where the expected placement date is after 1 April 2007.

6.301 The adoptive parents can decide which of them takes the adoption leave, the other parent being entitled to statutory paternity leave.

Statutory Maternity, Paternity and Adoption Pay

6.302 Statutory Adoption Pay is the minimum payment an eligible employee can receive while on adoption leave. Payment is made for 26 weeks where the expected placement date was before 1 April 2007 and for 39 weeks where the expected placement date is on or after 1 April 2007. It is the expected placement date rather than the actual placement date that determines whether the employee qualifies for 26 weeks or 39 weeks of SMP.

Who is Entitled to Receive Statutory Adoption Pay?

6.303 Statutory Adoption Pay is payable to employees who adopt a child and have:
- average weekly earnings which equal or exceed the lower earnings limit for National Insurance purposes: £87 per week if the adoption agency told the adopter that they had been matched with a child between 1 April 2007 and 5 April 2008 and £84 per week if the adoption agency told the adopter that they had been matched with a child between 2 April 2006 and 31 March 2007.
- been continuously employed for at least 26 weeks prior to the matching week
- stopped working for or have taken leave from the employer
- given the employer notice of their intended leave start date.

6.304 Prior to 1 October 2006, SAP was payable only to employees aged 16 or over. From 1 October 2006, this age limit was removed, meaning SAP is payable from that date to all employees meeting the qualifying conditions, regardless of age.

The Matching Week

6.305 The matching week is the week in which an employee is notified by an approved UK adoption agency of being matched with a child. If an employee is adopting a child from abroad, it is the week in which he or she receives official notification of adoption, usually from the Department of Health.

Continuous Employment

6.306 To qualify for SAP, employees must have at least 26 weeks' continuous service with their employer by the matching week. For adoptions from abroad, the employee must have at least 26 weeks' continuous service at the date of receiving their official notification.

6.307 There are certain interruptions of work where the breaks are treated as part of a continuing contract of employment. These include:
- previous pregnancy
- temporary cessation of work
- reinstatement after unfair dismissal
- trade disputes
- transfer of a business where TUPE applies
- holidays, both statutory and public
- paternity leave
- change of employer
- sickness or injury.

6.308 The HM Revenue & Customs Booklet E16 *Pay and time off work for adoptive parents* gives the latest start date for the 26 weeks' employment rule for each notification week during the current tax year to help the employer check whether the employee qualifies for SAP.

Calculation of Average Weekly Earnings

6.309 The average weekly earnings are calculated over the eight weeks that end with the payday in, or immediately prior to, the week in which the matching certificate was issued. Where the employee's average weekly earnings are less than the lower earnings limit for National Insurance purposes, or the employee does not meet the other criteria, the employer must complete and give the employee the Change Over Form — SAP1.

Notification and Evidence for Statutory Adoption Pay

6.310 Within one week of being told they have been matched with a child, employees taking adoption leave must tell their employer the date:
- of the placement, and
- on which they wish the adoption leave to begin.

6.311 Employees who are adopting children from abroad must notify their employer within 28 days of receiving official notification of a placement. In both cases the employee must give the employer 28 days' notice of the leave date. Having received notice of the leave date the employer is required to confirm, within 28 days, the employee's expected return to work date following the leave.

6.312 As evidence of their entitlement to SAP, the employee must provide the employer with the "matching certificate" issued by the adoption agency or — in the case of an overseas adoption — the official notification from the Department of Health. The matching certificate must be given to the employer no later than 28 days before the start of the pay period.

6.313 The certificate gives the date the employee is matched with a child and the date of the placement of the child.

Start Date for Adoption Pay

6.314 The earliest date adoption leave can start is:
- the day on which the child is placed for adoption, or
- no more than 14 days before the expected date of placement.

6.315 The latest date the leave can start is the day the child is placed with the family.

6.316 For adoptions from abroad, the adoption leave cannot start before the child enters the UK and the latest date the leave can start is 28 days after the date of entry.

Payment of Statutory Adoption Pay

6.317 For adoption weeks commencing on or after 1 April 2007, SAP is payable at the lower of £112.75 or 90% of average weekly earnings for the adoption pay period. This is 26 weeks for children who were expected to be placed before 1 April 2007 and 39 weeks where the expected placement date is on or after 1 April 2007. The SAP period can start on any day of the week.

6.318 Statutory Adoption Pay is paid by the employer through the payroll and is subject to deductions for tax and National Insurance contributions. Large employers can recover 92% of SAP paid. Small employers can recover 100% of the SAP, plus the National Insurance compensation amount of 4.5%. A small employer is one whose annual gross National Insurance contributions are £45,000 or less.

6.319 The recovery is made by deducting the total sum to be recovered from the gross National Insurance element of the monthly payroll remittance due to the

Statutory Maternity, Paternity and Adoption Pay

Collector of Taxes. If there is insufficient National Insurance to cover the SMP recovery, then a deduction can be made from the PAYE tax element of the remittance.

6.320 SAP is a weekly rate and where the expected placement date is before 1 April 2007 is paid in weekly block. However, a daily rate is introduced in respect of employees with an expected placement date on or after 1 April 2007. This is 1/7th of the weekly rate. The daily rate enables employers to align payment of SAP to the employee's pay period.

Keeping in Touch Days

6.321 Where the expected placement date fell before 1 April 2007, an employee on adoption leave lost one week's SAP for any week in which work was undertaken for the employer paying the SAP.

6.322 However, keeping in touch (KIT) days are introduced where the expected placement date falls on or after 1 April 2007. The keeping in touch days rules for SAP purposes mirror those applying for SMP purposes.

6.323 Keeping in touch days allow an employee on adoption leave to work up to 10 days during the adoption pay period without loss of SAP. Any day that the employee does work for the employer, even if only for an hour, counts as a KIT day. Any further days worked once the 10-day KIT limit has been reached will trigger a loss of SAP.

6.324 Keeping in touch days must be agreed between the employee and the employer. The employee has no right to work keeping in touch days and the employer cannot require that an employee on adoption works them.

When to Stop Paying SAP

6.325 The payment of SAP stops if the employee dies, is taken into legal custody or works during the adoption leave period.

6.326 If the child's placement ends during the adoption leave period — for example, because the baby dies or the child returns to the adoption agency — the adopter can continue with the leave for up to eight weeks after the end of the placement.

Relationship Between Statutory Sick Pay and Statutory Adoption Pay

6.327 An employee cannot be paid SAP for any week in which they are entitled to statutory sick pay. They will be paid statutory sick pay only.

Returning to Work

6.328 If the employee does not take the full leave to which he or she is entitled, the employee must give the employer notice of when he or she intends to return to work. The notice requirement is 28 days where the expected placement date was before 1 April 2007 and increases to eight weeks for employees who are expected to be placed with a child for adoption on or after 1 April 2007.

Form for Statutory Adoption Pay

6.329 *SAP1 — Change Over Form.* If the employee's average weekly earnings do not reach the lower earnings limit for National Insurance purposes, he or she will not receive SAP. The employer will instead complete Change Over Form SAP1 for the employee to take to their local benefits office.

Legislative Changes

6.330 The lower age limits on payments of SMP, SSP and SAP were removed by the Employment Equality (Age) Regulations 2006, with effect from 1 October 2006. These changes are unlikely to affect many employees as to qualify for SMP, SAP and SPP the employee must satisfy the other qualifying conditions, including conditions on average weekly earnings. This means that Saturday staff, for example, are unlikely to meet the necessary conditions.

6.331 The Work and Families Act 2006 and associated regulations:
- extend the payment period for SMP and SAP from 26 weeks to 39 weeks
- allow employees to work for up to 10 "keeping in touch" days during maternity or adoption leave without loss of entitlement to SAP or SMP
- allow the maternity pay period to start on any day of the week (currently starts on a Sunday)
- provide for SMP and SPP to be calculated by reference to a daily rate
- increase the notice period that employees returning before the end of the leave period are required to give from 28 days to eight weeks
- remove the qualifying condition for additional leave so that all employees are entitled to 52 weeks' maternity or adoption leave, regardless of whether they qualify for SMP or SAP.

6.332 The changes apply to babies due on or after 1 April 2007 and, in cases of adoption, to children expected to be placed on or after 1 April 2007.

Practical Implications of the Legislative Changes

6.333 The changes introduced by the Work and Families Act 2006, and associated regulations, have a number of practical implications. These changes are illustrated by the following examples.

Example 1 — SMP

6.334 An employee's baby is due on 6 April 2007. The baby is born on 25 March 2007. Is the employee entitled to 39 weeks' paid statutory maternity pay (SMP)?

6.335 Provided all the necessary conditions are met, the employee is entitled to 39 weeks' paid SMP as the baby was due on or after 1 April 2007. It does not matter that the baby was actually born before that date.

Example 2 — SMP

6.336 An employee's baby is due on 1 April 2007 and born on 3 April 2007. Is she entitled to 39 weeks' paid SMP?

6.337 Provided that all the necessary conditions are met, the employee is entitled to 39 weeks' paid SMP as the baby was due on or after 1 April 2007.

Example 3 — SMP

6.338 An employee's baby is due on 27 March 2007 and is actually born on 4 April 2007. Is the employee entitled to 39 weeks' paid SMP? As the baby is due before 1 April 2007 the employee is only entitled to 26 weeks' paid SMP. It does not matter that the baby is actually born after 1 April 2007.

6.339 It is important to note that it is the date that the baby is due — rather than the date that the baby is actually born — that determines whether the employee will benefit from the new rules. This means that if a baby is due on or after 1 April 2007,

Statutory Maternity, Paternity and Adoption Pay

the employee will be entitled to 39 weeks' SMP (provided that the other qualifying conditions are met), even if the baby is born before that date. By contrast, if the baby is due before 1 April 2007, the employee will only be entitled to 26 weeks' SMP, even if the baby is actually born on or after 1 April 2007.

6.340 Similar rules apply for statutory adoption pay (SAP) purposes. In this case, the critical date is the expected date of placement, rather than the actual date of placement. The employee is entitled to 39 weeks' SAP if the expected date of placement is on or after 1 April 2007, irrespective of the actual date of placement, and to 26 weeks' SAP if the expected date of placement is before 1 April 2007. The following examples illustrate the operation of the SAP rules.

Example 4 — SAP

6.341 A child is expected to be placed with an employee for adoption on 1 April 2007. The child is actually placed for adoption on 21 March 2007. Is the employee entitled to 29 weeks' paid statutory adoption pay (SAP)?

6.342 Provided that the necessary conditions are met, the employee is entitled to 39 weeks' paid SAP as the expected date of the placement was on or after 1 April 2007. It does not matter that the child was actually placed before this date.

Example 5 — SAP

6.343 A child is expected to be placed with an employee for adoption on 25 March 2007. The child is actually placed with the employee on 3 April 2007. Is the employee entitled to 39 weeks' paid SAP?

6.344 As the expected date of placement falls before 1 April 2007, the employee is only entitled to 26 weeks' paid SAP. It does not matter that the actual placement takes place after 1 April 2007.

Training

6.345 It is important that managers know the organisation's policy and procedures on employees' statutory leave entitlement and the payment of statutory maternity, paternity and adoption pay.

6.346 Payroll staff and managers need to know the circumstances in which employees may not be eligible to receive the statutory payments. The payroll staff and managers need to know what actions to take, and what forms to complete and hand to the employee.

6.347 Payroll staff and managers must be kept abreast of changes in the legislation and understand the practical implications of those changes.

List of Relevant Legislation

6.348
- Employment Equality (Age) Regulations 2006
- Statutory Paternity Pay (Adoption) and Statutory Adoption Pay (Adoption from Overseas) (Administration) Regulations 2003
- Statutory Adoption Pay (Adoption) and Statutory Adoption Pay (Adoption from Overseas) Regulations 2003

- Statutory Adoption Pay (Adoption) and Statutory Adoption Pay (Adoption from Overseas) (No. 2) Regulations 2003
- Paternity and Adoption Leave Regulations 2002
- Statutory Paternity Pay and Stautory Adoption Pay (General) Regulations 2002
- Maternity and Parental Leave etc Regulations 1999
- Maternity Allowance and Statutory Maternity Pay Regulations 1994
- Statutory Maternity Pay (Compensation of Employers) Regulations 1994
- Statutory Maternity Pay (General) Regulations 1986
- Work and Families Act 2006
- Social Security (Contributions and Benefits) Act 1991

List of Relevant Cases

6.349

- *Alabaster v Barclays Bank plc (No. 2)* [2005] IRLR 576, CA — the Court of Appeal ruled that women who receive a pay rise that is not reflected in their Statutory Maternity Pay (SMP) may bring an equal pay claim against their employers without the need for a male comparator. As a result, average weekly earnings must be recalculated to take into account pay rises effective before the end of the maternity leave period.

Further Information

Publications

- E15 *Pay and Time Off Work for Parents*, available from HM Revenue & Customs.
- E15 (Supplement) *Pay and Time Off work for Parents — Special Cases*, available from HM Revenue & Customs
- E16 *Pay and Time Off Work for Adoptive Parents*, available from HM Revenue & Customs.
- E16 (Supplement) *Pay and Time Off Work for Adoptive Parents — Special cases*, available from HM Revenue & Customs
- SC3 *Becoming a Parent*, available from HM Revenue & Customs.
- SC4 *Becoming an Adoptive Parent*, available from HM Revenue & Customs.

Organisations

- **Child Support Agency**
  Web: *www.csa.gov.uk*
  The Child Support Agency offers information on the various child support schemes — part of the Department for Work and Pensions.
- **Department for Work and Pensions (DWP)**
  Web: *www.dwp.gov.uk*
  The DWP is responsible for the Government's welfare reform agenda. Its aim is to promote opportunity and independence for all.

- **Department of Health**
  Web: *www.dh.gov.uk*
  The Department of Health provides health and social care policy, guidance and publications.
- **HM Revenue & Customs**
  Web: *www.hmrc.gov.uk/home.htm*
  HM Revenue & Customs (HMRC) is the department responsible for the business of the former Inland Revenue and HM Customs and Excise. HMRC is responsible for lecting the bulk of tax revenue as well as paying tax credits and child benefit.

Chapter 7
Pay and Benefits

Attachment of Earnings

> This topic covers the following:
> - Attachment of Earnings Act 1971
> - Schedule 5 Attachment of Earnings Orders
> - Debtors (Scotland) Act 1987
> - Northern Ireland Orders
> - Council Tax Attachment Orders
> - Orders Under the Child Support Act
> - Income Support Deduction Notices
> - Priority of Orders
> - Sanction for Non-compliance

7.1 "Attachment of earnings" is the legal phrase used to describe when a court orders an individual who defaults on a debt to have a set amount deducted from his or her wages in order to pay off the debt. For example, the courts may make an attachment order if someone fails to keep up maintenance payments to his or her family.

Employers' Duties

7.2 Employers should ensure that they:
- assess the type of order and make payments accordingly
- always pay the employee concerned his or her protected earnings if he or she earns that amount or more
- follow the procedure laid down on receipt of an attachment of earnings order
- inform any employee in writing of any amount that is deducted from the employee's earnings
- ensure that any variation required by the court is implemented correctly
- write to the court within seven days should it be found that a new employee has an existing Attachment of Earnings Act 1971 order against him or her
- deduct an administration charge in accordance with the relevant legislation controlling the order, eg 50p under the Debtors (Scotland) Act 1987
- prioritise multiple orders correctly. Often this will mean starting with the oldest.

Employees' Duties

7.3 Employees should ensure that they:
- make due payment on any debts to avoid the necessity for an attachment of earnings' order
- provide any evidence required to assess the level of protected earnings
- comply with any order and provide accurate information if requested.

In Practice

7.4 Attachment of earnings orders in slightly different forms can be granted under a variety of legislation. The legal position in England and Wales, Scotland and Northern Ireland is not entirely similar.

7.5 The most important legislation dealing with attachment orders is, in England and Wales, the Attachment of Earnings Act 1971 and, in Scotland, the Debtors (Scotland) Act 1987.

Attachment of Earnings Act 1971

7.6 The most widely used attachment of earnings orders are those used under the Attachment of Earnings Act 1971. These apply only to England and Wales: the Scotland and Northern Ireland variations are dealt with elsewhere.

When an Attachment of Earnings Order Can be Made

7.7 If a debtor with a court order against him or her does not make due payment, the creditor has four options under the Act for enforcing the debt.
- A warrant of execution — a bailiff is sent to collect money from the debtor.
- An attachment of earnings order — money is collected directly from the debtor's wages.
- A third party debt order — the debtor's financial assets are frozen.
- A charging order — money is secured and ultimately taken from the sale of an asset of the debtor.

7.8 A court can make an attachment of earnings order against an individual if the:
- individual is in arrears, or has not made at least one due payment
- amount he or she owes is at least £50.

Against Whom Orders Cannot be Made

7.9 Attachment of earnings orders under the Act cannot be made against:
- people who are self-employed or unemployed
- a firm or limited company
- a member of the army, navy or air force
- a merchant seaman.

7.10 There are other ways of obtaining a lapsed debt in these cases.

Two Types of Attachment Order

7.11 There are two types of attachment of earnings order that can be made under the Act.

7.12 Priority orders take precedence over other attachment of earnings orders. They are made to secure payment of debts such as maintenance, fines or legal aid contributions.

7.13 Non-priority orders are made to secure payment of a judgment debt or payments under an administration order.

Attachment of Earnings

Consolidated Attachment of Earnings Order

7.14 If two or more judgment debts are outstanding from the same debtor, one of the creditors can under the Act apply for a consolidated attachment of earnings. This is a single non-priority order that will cover all the outstanding debts.

Assessment of Attachable Earnings

7.15 In deciding how much the debtor should have deducted from his or her wages on a regular basis, a court will:
- hear evidence of the debtor's liabilities
- assess the level of "protected earnings"
- take into account the size of the debt to assess the deduction from the debtor's earnings.

7.16 "Earnings" in such circumstances will include:
- wages and salary, including bonuses, fees, overtime and commission
- pension
- statutory sick pay.

7.17 "Earnings" will exclude:
- disability pension
- statutory maternity pay
- guaranteed minimum pension (as provided by an occupational pension scheme).

7.18 Deductions from earnings should only be made after payment of:
- income tax (PAYE)
- National Insurance
- superannuation (regular payments towards a pension scheme).

7.19 Any earnings that fulfil these conditions are known as "attachable earnings".

Protected Earnings

7.20 The court will decide the amount that it believes the debtor needs to retain from his or her earnings for immediate resources and needs. This is called the "protected earnings". The protected earnings should be set aside from the attachable earnings before any deduction is made.

Contents of an Attachment of Earnings Order

7.21 An attachment of earnings order will specify to the employer:
- the total debt owed by the employee (unless the order is for ongoing maintenance)
- how often the employer is required to make a deduction
- the amount to be deducted on each occasion
- the protected earnings rate.

Employer's Procedure on Receipt of Attachment Order

7.22 An employer who receives an attachment of earnings order must do the following.
- Make the first deduction in accordance with the order on the first subsequent pay-day (unless it is within seven days of receipt of the order).
- Give written notification to the debtor/s concerned of the amount of every deduction made — and include notice of this in the employee's pay statement.

Attachment of Earnings

- Notify the court within 10 days if the debtor is not in the service of the employer — for a county court or maintenance order, the employer should contact the Centralised Attachment of Earnings System (CAPS) in Northampton.
- Inform the court within 10 days if the debtor subsequently leaves the employer's business.
- Give the debtor a transfer notice along with his or her P45.

7.23 In addition, an employer can take £1 to cover administration costs from the debtor's earnings each time a deduction is made. This fee can be taken from the protected earnings.

Employers' Procedure to Make Deductions

7.24 The procedure that an employer should follow to make deductions varies depending on whether the deduction is in accordance with a priority order or a non-priority order.

7.25 In both cases, the protected earnings are set aside and the required deduction should be made from the attachable earnings.

7.26 Sometimes the attachable earnings may not be enough to cover the attachment order amount. If this is the case, if the order is:
- a priority order, the remainder should be made up and paid to the court as soon as possible on successive pay-days
- a non-priority order, the shortfall should be disregarded and not carried forward to the next pay-day. The debt will simply take longer to pay off.

7.27 In other words, the normal deduction rate should never be exceeded with a non-priority order.

If the Attachable Earnings are Less Than the Protected Earnings

7.28 If the attachable earnings on any one pay-day are less than the protected earnings level, the employer should simply pay as much as possible of the protected earnings.

7.29 Under a priority order, the deficit in protected earnings should be made up on the next pay-day before the normal attachment order deduction is made up. In the case of a non-priority order, neither the protected earnings deficit nor the attachment order deduction deficit are carried forward.

Variation of an Order

7.30 The court will write to the employer if the attachment of earnings order is varied. A magistrates' court may vary the protected earnings rate for a period of up to four weeks.

7.31 The court will also inform the employer if the order is cancelled or paid in full. An employer should then stop deductions as soon as possible and at any rate within seven days of receiving notice.

Notification of Earnings and New Employee with Existing Order

7.32 An employer may be asked by a court to provide a signed statement of an employee's earnings.

7.33 Employers are also required to write to the court that made the order within

Attachment of Earnings

seven days should it be found that a new employee had an existing order against him or her. The notification should give details of the employee's earnings and anticipated earnings.

Attachment of Earnings Specifies Weekly Payment of Monthly Wage

7.34 It is possible that an attachment of earnings order may specify weekly deductions while the employee's pay may normally be paid monthly, or vice versa.

7.35 In such circumstances, the employer can ask the court to recalculate and amend it if the order comes from a county court. If the order comes from a magistrates' court, only the employee concerned can ask for the order to be amended.

Schedule 5 Attachment of Earnings Orders

7.36 Magistrates' courts in England and Wales can, under the Courts Act 2003, raise attachment of earnings orders for the collection of fines. Schedule 5 attachment of earnings orders are priority orders and are similar to orders under the Attachment of Earnings Act 1971.

Debtors (Scotland) Act 1987

7.37 The practice in Scotland is different from that in England and Wales. There are three basic types of order.
- An earnings arrestment.
- A current maintenance arrestment.
- A conjoined arrestment order.

Earnings Arrestment

7.38 An earnings arrestment is applicable to enforce ordinary debts such as:
- fuel bills
- monies due for goods and services.

7.39 If an employer receives such an order, he or she should:
- deduct the amount from the debtor's net salary
- pay such an amount to the creditor within a reasonable period
- if possible, notify the employee.

7.40 The arrestment remains in force until:
- the debt has been paid or otherwise ended
- the debtor ceases to be employed by the employer
- the arrestment has been recalled or abandoned by the creditor, or has ceased to have effect.

7.41 The employer is entitled to charge the employee 50p on each occasion he or she makes a payment to the creditor.

Current Maintenance Arrestment

7.42 A current maintenance order is used to protect the making of maintenance payments. The rules of payment are the same as for an earnings arrestment.

Conjoined Arrestment Order

7.43 An employer can act on only one order at any one time. If an order is already in operation from another creditor, a further creditor would have to apply to the courts to obtain a portion of any repayment available.

7.44 If the application is successful, the resulting "conjoined arrestment order" should be served on the employer. The employer must then:
- deduct the amount ordered from the debtor's net earnings
- pay such amount to the court that has made the order.

7.45 The deductions from the debtor's earnings will then be split and distributed to the creditors on a *pro rata* basis.

Failure to Comply with Order

7.46 If an employer fails to comply with an order, he or she must then pay the amount that the employee ought to have paid. These costs can later be recovered from the debtor.

7.47 Payments by an employer to replace money due under earnings arrestment and current maintenance arrestment are made directly to the debtor.

7.48 Payments by an employer to replace money due under a conjoined arrestment order should be made to the relevant court. The court has the right to obtain an enforcement order to secure payment should this be necessary.

Northern Ireland Orders

7.49 The High Court, Enforcement of Judgements Office and the Magistrates' Courts in Northern Ireland can raise attachment of earnings orders that are similar to those used in England and Wales.

7.50 The legislation governing such orders is the Judgement Enforcement (Northern Ireland) Order 1981 and the Magistrates' Courts (Northern Ireland) Order 1981, both of which apply only in Northern Ireland.

Council Tax Attachment Orders

7.51 Local authorities in England and Wales can in certain circumstances issue attachment orders in connection with non-payment of council tax. Many of the conditions are similar to those of orders under the Attachment of Earnings Act 1971.

7.52 This power derives from the Local Government Finance Act 1992 and the subsequent secondary legislation, the Council Tax (Administration and Enforcement) Regulations 1992.

7.53 The authority will send an order to the employer with instructions to make deductions from the debtor's earnings on each pay-day and transfer the deduction to the authority.

7.54 Many of the principles that apply for standard attachment of earnings orders apply also in the case of council tax attachment orders.

Orders Under the Child Support Act

7.55 Regulations issued under the Child Support Act 1991 provide for deductions in a manner similar to that of priority orders issued under the Attachment of Earnings Act 1971.

Attachment of Earnings

7.56 If an absent parent does not make a voluntary payment, a deduction of earnings' order may be issued under the provisions of the Child Support (Collection and Enforcement) Regulations 1992.

7.57 The two differences between this type of deduction of earnings' order and priority orders under the Attachment of Earnings Act are that the:
- deduction of earnings' order is issued to the employer by the Child Support Agency, not by the courts
- wages of seamen are not excluded from the definition of earnings.

Income Support Deduction Notices

7.58 Under the Social Security Contributions and Benefits Act 1992, the Department for Work and Pensions may issue an income support deduction notice to recover income support paid to an employee for up to fifteen days on returning to work after a trade dispute.

Priority of Orders

7.59 Where an employee is facing a number of different orders, an employer should ensure that the various orders are prioritised and dealt with in the correct order. While some attachment of earnings orders do take precedence over others, often they are processed in date order (starting with the oldest).

Sanction for Non-compliance

7.60 Failure by an employer or an employee to comply with a court order, or the deliberate distribution of false information, can lead to fines, diligence (in Scotland) or even imprisonment.

7.61 In the case of orders under the Debtors (Scotland) Act 1987, it is possible that an employer could be held liable for an employee's non-payment if this is due to the employer's failure to deduct wages as required.

Training

7.62 Senior payroll staff should be aware of how to deal with the different orders that can be made. Employees who face an order for repayment of debt should be given full explanation of their rights.

List of Relevant Legislation

7.63
- Child Support (Collection and Enforcement) Regulations 1992
- Council Tax (Administration and Enforcement) Regulations 1992
- Local Government Finance Act 1992
- Child Support Act 1991
- Social Security Contributions and Benefits Act 1992
- Debtors (Scotland) Act 1987
- Judgement Enforcement (Northern Ireland) Order 1981
- Magistrates' Courts (Northern Ireland) Order 1981

- Attachment of Earnings Act 1971

Further Information

Organisations
- **Court Service**
  Web: *www.courtservice.gov.uk*
  Contains useful information and sources about the Court Service.
- **Data Protection Registrar**
  Web: *www.dca.gov.uk*
  The Data Protection Registrar is responsible in Government for upholding justice, rights and democracy.
- **HM Revenue & Customs**
  Web: *www.hmrc.gov.uk/home.htm*
  HM Revenue & Customs (HMRC) is the department responsible for the business of the former Inland Revenue and HM Customs and Excise. HMRC is responsible for collecting the bulk of tax revenue as well as paying tax credits and child benefit.

Benefits

This topic covers the following.
- Flexible Benefits
- Introducing a Flexible Benefits Package
- Initial Considerations
- Cost Base of Employee Benefits
- Employee Attitudes to Benefits
- Categories of Benefits
- Taking a Lateral View of Employee Benefits
- Communication Programme
- Non-cash Benefits
- Service-Related Benefits and Age Discrimination Legislation
- Benefits during Maternity Leave
- Manual Workers' Allowance and Benefits
- Salary Sacrifice Arrangement
- Benefits in Kind and Taxation
- Benefits in Kind and National Insurance
- Saving work
- Compliance Obligations

7.64 Employee benefits are an important part of the employee package for recruiting and retaining employees. When it is difficult to recruit suitable skilled people, having a benefits package can often give an organisation the competitive edge. The non-cash and fringe benefit elements of a pay package can be extremely valuable to the employee and are often tax effective.

7.65 This topic discusses the different ways of providing benefits to staff and the advantages and disadvantages to the employer and employee. It does not go into detail regarding tax and National Insurance.

7.66 For information on the provision of company cars, fuel, vans and related benefits, please see the topic Cars, Fuel, Vans and Related Benefits.

Employers' Duties

7.67 Employers should make sure that employees are aware of:
- the benefits available to them
- the right to benefits of employees on maternity leave
- the right of part-time workers to the same benefits as full-time workers, but on a *pro rata* basis
- benefits that are liable for tax and National Insurance to the employee (usually by giving the employee a copy of his or her P9D or P11D).

7.68 Employers also have a duty to:
- comply with obligations in relation to benefits and expenses, eg completion of forms P9D, P11D and P11D(b)
- pay any Class 1A National Insurance to HM Revenue & Customs (HMRC) by 19 July
- pay any tax and Class 1B National Insurance on items included within a PAYE settlement agreement to HMRC by 19 October.

Employees' Duties

7.69 Employees have a duty to:
- return details of taxable expenses and benefits on the self-assessment return
- claim deductions expenses incurred as a necessary part of their employment where such deductions are permitted by HM Revenue & Customs (HMRC).

In Practice

Flexible Benefits

7.70 A flexible benefits package is where the employee is given some choice over the benefits that they receive. Often there will be a level of core benefits that they cannot go below, eg pensions and medical cover. This flexibility is usually attractive to employees who can choose the benefits most useful to them, eg a parent will value childcare benefits more than a childless employee will. In addition, employee needs change over time and a flexible benefits package shows that an employer is listening to the needs of the workforce.

7.71 A flexible benefits policy may also save tax and National Insurance if the employee chooses tax and NIC-exempt benefits in place of taxable salary or wages.

7.72 Flexible benefits may also secure cost savings because the employer does not have to pay for benefits that aren't being used.

7.73 Disadvantages of flexible benefits include the:
- danger of increasing costs
- problem of valuing benefits
- complex administration
- tax and VAT implications.

Introducing a Flexible Benefits Package

7.74 The following questions should be considered before introducing a flexible benefits system.
- What do you want to achieve?
- Which employees will be included?
- Which benefits do they have at the moment?
- Which benefits do employees value most?
- Which benefits will be included?
- Which benefits will the employee select if they are offered a choice?
- How flexible should the organisation be?
- What will be the core benefits?
- Will the organisation give cash options, or only options between benefits and options on the level of benefits?
- How will you decide each employee's budget?
- How will you value the benefits?

- How often will employees be able to choose?
- How will the scheme be administered?
- How will you communicate the scheme?
- Will you provide financial counselling?
- Do you need outside help in setting up the scheme?

Initial Considerations

7.75 Before implementing the flexible benefits scheme, the employer should consider the following.
- The cost base of the existing employee benefits.
- Attitudes of employees toward employee benefits.
- The tax implications for employee and employer.
- Organising employee benefits into categories.
- Including a lateral view to benefits in the flexible benefits package.

Cost Base of Employee Benefits

7.76 The cost base of employee benefits includes both the actual and administrative costs to the organisation of providing the benefits.

7.77 In costing the benefits, it is important to explore the market in order to ensure that the best purchasing arrangements have been negotiated. In costing the administration, it is important to identify opportunities for outsourcing, eg a benefit provider might be able to provide an administrative service at a lower cost than the in-house administrative service.

Employee Attitudes to Benefits

7.78 Consultation with employees is essential to understanding the benefits that they value. An employer can gauge the value of benefits for employees — and even further motivate employees — by using an attitude survey. The questions should make a point of relating employee benefits to the wider activities of the business. This will help employees link the benefits they value to corporate aims and objectives.

Categories of Benefits

7.79 Employee benefits can be categorised in various ways. They may be split into core benefits, such as health insurance and pensions, in respect of which employees are required to take a minimum level, and non-core benefits, which are optional within the scope of a flexible benefits package.

7.80 Alternatively, employee benefits may be split into categories, such as:
- health
- travel
- lifestyle
- leisure
- shares.

7.81 Employee choice of benefits is facilitated by the use of a points system. A number of points are ascribed to each benefit — and each employee has a number of points to "spend" on the benefits on offer.

Taking a Lateral View of Employee Benefits

7.82 Creating employee awareness of the organisational context of benefits allows the employer to present a range of other activities as employee benefits, eg annual staff appraisals, training and development, health and safety procedures.

7.83 These "lateral benefits" cannot be incorporated into the points system, but they can be included in a benefits statement. This will give them a higher profile among employees.

Communication Programme

7.84 The initial communication of the benefits on offer, eg at interview, needs to be followed up using an ongoing communication programme. The same channel used to cascade business communications down from the directors can be used to effectively communicate and promote employee benefits.

Non-cash Benefits

7.85 The non-cash benefit elements of the pay package can be extremely valuable to the employee and non-cash benefits are often tax and NIC-efficient.

7.86 The number and value of non-cash benefits usually decreases down the corporate hierarchy. On the shop floor, basic salary, bonuses, overtime and shift-work pay are not usually boosted by perks.

7.87 However, the tax advantages associated with many tax-efficient benefits are conditional on the benefit being made available to all employees. This is to encourage employers to provide non-cash benefits to all employees, not just to senior employees and directors.

7.88 The list of possible non-cash benefits is long and includes:
- accommodation
- business expenses
- cheap loans
- childcare provision
- clothing/dry-cleaning allowance
- company car
- company discounts
- company housing
- free petrol
- life assurance
- mileage allowances
- medical checks
- medical insurance
- mobile phone
- mortgage subsidy
- paid leave
- pension
- permanent health insurance
- personal financial planning
- pre-retirement planning
- professional membership subscriptions

- relocation assistance
- sabbaticals
- share schemes
- sports club membership
- subsidised meals
- subsistence allowances
- training/study leave
- work clothing.

Service-Related Benefits and Age Discrimination Legislation

7.89 The benefits that may be made available to employees are often related to the length of the employee's service.

7.90 Potential problems could arise in light of the age discrimination regulations, which came into force from 1 October 2006, as such arrangements could be construed as favouring older employees. However, the concept of offering benefits recognising length of service is widely supported and the Government appreciates their role in rewarding loyalty, providing incentives and helping motivation.

7.91 The age discrimination regulations (the Employment Equality (Age) Regulations 2006) are drafted in such a way as to avoid jeopardising service-related benefits and employers will not be required to justify every benefit on an individual basis. However, while it is justified to provide exemptions in relation to length of service, it should be noted that not all age-related aspects of benefits will always be justified.

7.92 The regulations allow benefits entitlement to be related to length of service, provided that the period that is taken into account does not exceed five years. This means that an employer could not provide a higher level of service-related benefits to an employee with 10 years' service as compared to an employee with six years' service.

7.93 Where benefit entitlement is related to age or length of service, employers should ensure compliance with the age discrimination regulations.

Benefits During Maternity Leave

7.94 While an employee is on ordinary maternity leave her employer must continue to provide her with all her contractual benefits — except those that relate directly to the pay elements of her remuneration package. If the employee is on additional maternity leave, only certain contractual benefits will apply. Employers and employees may agree for other terms to continue, but this is not required by law.

Ordinary Maternity Leave

7.95 Some examples of the benefits that must be continued include:
- accrual of holiday entitlement
- continuous service
- private health insurance
- company car
- car allowance
- use of mobile phone for personal as well as business use
- private petrol allowance

- use of personal computer
- profit-share schemes
- share-option schemes
- employer pension contributions
- professional subscriptions
- mortgage assistance/subsidy
- mortgage allowance
- lunch vouchers
- gift vouchers
- staff discounts.

7.96 Benefits that need not be continued include:
- salary
- overtime payments
- shift bonus
- attendance allowance
- London weighting
- contractual bonus (unless the payment relates to work carried out when the employee was not on maternity leave)
- commission.

Additional Maternity Leave

7.97 Subject to any additional agreement between employer and employee, the following rights apply to employees during additional maternity leave.
- The employee is entitled to benefit from her employer's implied obligation to her of trust and confidence.
- The employee is bound by her implied obligation to her employer of good faith.
- The employee is bound by any terms in her contract relating to:
  (a) disclosure of confidential information
  (b) acceptance of gifts or other benefits
  (c) participation in any other business.
- The employee is entitled to receive whatever period of notice her contract provides for if her employment is terminated (an employee who is pregnant or on maternity leave is protected from dismissal which is wholly or partly related to her pregnancy or maternity leave).
- The employee must give her employer the notice provided for by her contract of employment if she is terminating her contract.
- The employee is entitled to any contractual rights to compensation and statutory redundancy pay if she is made redundant.
- Any terms and conditions in the contract of employment relating to disciplinary or grievance procedures will continue to apply.

Manual Workers' Allowance and Benefits

7.98 Many manual workers may receive additional allowances from their employers to cover expenses associated with their employment. These include:
- the provision of protective clothing and footwear
- the provision and laundering of working clothes
- extra money for working in dirty, unsafe or unpleasant conditions
- travel away from the normal place of work as part of their job

- reimbursement for providing tools for their trade.

7.99 The sort of benefits that manual workers commonly receive include:
- subsidised meal/canteens
- subsidised housing
- subsistence allowances
- meal allowances
- overnight lodgings
- mileage and other travel allowances
- travelling time
- protective clothing and footwear
- tool allowances
- payment for working in abnormal conditions
- concessions and discounts.

7.100 In addition to these, there may be some tax benefits. HM Revenue & Customs (HMRC) may recognise that the employee has incurred costs as a legitimate part of his or her employment.

Salary Sacrifice Arrangements

7.101 Salary sacrifice arrangements often form part of a flexible benefits policy.

7.102 Under a salary sacrifice arrangement, the employee gives up some of his or her cash salary in return for a non-cash benefit. If the benefit is exempt from tax and/or National Insurance, the employee will be better off by giving up salary in return for the benefit than if he or she had received the salary and paid for the benefit out of his or her net pay.

7.103 For example, if an employee chooses to give up salary of £2860 in exchange for childcare vouchers of £2860 (£55 per week), the employee will save tax of £629.20 if he or she is a basic rate employee (£2860 x 22%) and £1144 if he or she is a higher rate employee (£2860 x 40%), as compared to taking the cash salary and paying for childcare costs out of net pay.

7.104 In addition, the employee will save a National Insurance contribution of £314.60 if earnings are below the upper earnings threshold and £286.00 if the upper earnings threshold has been reached. The employer will also save secondary Class 1 National Insurance contributions of £366.08.

7.105 Care must be taken that any salary sacrifice arrangement is regarded as effective by HM Revenue & Customs (HMRC). It is important that the change is a permanent change and recorded as such in the employee's contract of employment. The employee cannot simply choose to revert to the higher salary at will, or HMRC will deem the arrangement to be ineffective.

Benefits in Kind and Taxation

Overview of Tax Rules

7.106 Providing an employee with a benefit in kind may generate a tax charge. The tax rules governing benefits in kind are complex and professional advice should be sought.

7.107 Broadly, employees and directors are split into two categories as far as the taxability of benefits is concerned:

- employees earning at a rate of less than £8500 a year (P9D employees)
- directors, regardless of the level of their earnings, and employees earning at a rate of at least £8500 a year (P11D employees).

7.108 P9D employees are only taxed on living accommodation and other benefits and expenses provided in money or money's worth. This effectively covers items that can be turned into money by selling them (eg a painting), which would be valued at its second-hand value, and items such as vouchers, credit tokens and credit cards.

7.109 P11D employees and directors are taxable on a much wider range of benefits and expenses and where a benefit is provided to a P11D employee or director a tax charge will arise unless the benefit is exempt.

7.110 Benefits may be:
- taxable on all employees, eg living accommodation, vouchers
- taxable only on directors and P11D employees, eg company cars
- exempt from tax, eg employer-provided childcare, bus services, mobile phones
- taxable but offset by a corresponding deduction, eg professional fees and subscriptions.

7.111 Exempt benefits are outside the charge to tax and their provision need not be reported to HM Revenue & Customs (HMRC). However, in most cases, the exemption is only available if certain conditions are met. Increasingly, this includes making the benefit available to all employees. Some benefits, such as professional fees and subscriptions paid by the employer are taxable, but the employee may be able to claim a deduction to offset the tax charge that would otherwise arise. To save work, the employer is advised to seek a dispensation in respect of benefits falling within this category.

£8500 Threshold

7.112 Many benefits, including company cars, employment-related loans, vans and private medical insurance, are only taxable when provided to directors and employees earning at the rate of at least £8500 a year. The level of a director's earnings are irrelevant and the rules apply to directors, regardless of earnings, as they apply to employees earning at a rate of at least £8500.

7.113 In deciding whether an employee is a P9D employee or a P11D employee, the following points need to be remembered in relation to the £8500 threshold.
- The value of benefits in kind is taken into account in determining if the threshold is exceeded. Thus an employee with a cash salary of £5000 and a company car with a cash equivalent value of £4000 would have earnings of £9000, making the employee a P11D employee, with the result that the company car is taxable.
- Earnings for periods of less than one year must be grossed up to find the annual equivalent, so an employee who works for three months and earns £4500 would be earning at a rate of £18,000 a year, so would be a P11D employee.
- However, part-time earnings do not need to be grossed up to a fulll-time equivalent, so an employee who works 10 hours a week earning £4000 a year would be a P9D employee.

Valuing Benefits for Tax Purposes

7.114 The value of a benefit on which tax is charged is known as the cash equivalent of the benefit. It is this value which is reported on the P9D or P11D.

7.115 Some benefits, such as company cars and vans, living accommodation, employment-related loans and assets provided for the employee's personal use have special rules for determining their cash equivalent value.

Benefits

7.116 Where there is no special rule, the cash equivalent of a benefit is determined in accordance with the general rule. This provides that the cash equivalent value of a benefit is the cost to the employer of providing that benefit, less any amount made good by the employee.

Benefits Taxable on P11D — Employees and Directors Only

7.117 The list of benefits that are taxable on P11D employees and directors only includes:
- company cars
- fuel for private motoring in a company car
- private use of a company van
- employment-related loans
- private medical insurance
- relocation expenses and benefits in excess of £8000
- services supplied to an employee, eg hairdressing, accountancy services, cleaning services, gardening services, etc
- professional fees and subscriptions (but may be offset by a deduction).

7.118 Also taxable are benefits where an exemption is available, such that the benefit is provided in circumstances where the conditions for exemption are not met. No tax charge arises if these benefits are provided to a P9D employee (ie one who earns at a rate of less than £8500 a year including benefits).

Tax-exempt Benefits

7.119 Some benefits are exempt from tax and/or National Insurance. These can form a valuable part of a benefits package and enable employees to be remunerated in a cash efficient manner. However, it should be noted that the exemption is usually dependent on certain conditions being met.

7.120 In certain cases (such as that applying in respect of computer equipment loaned to an employee before 6 April 2006 and relocation expenses and benefits), the exemption is limited to a specified amount. To enable employees to benefit from the tax savings and NIC savings without increasing the employer's costs or the overall value of the employee's remuneration package, these benefits may be made available under salary sacrifice arrangements.

7.121 The list of tax-exempt benefits and expenses includes:
- approved mileage allowance payments and passenger payments
- incidental overnight expenses (£5 per night in UK, £10 per night abroad)
- works transport services
- subsidised public bus services
- employer provided cycles and cylists' safety equipment
- work-related training
- sports and recreation facilities
- Christmas parties and other annual functions (to a maximum of £150 per head)
- employer-provided childcare
- employer-contracted childcare and childcare (to maximum of £55 per week from 6 April 2006)
- removal expenses and benefits (to maximum of £8000)
- contributions to a registered pension scheme
- mobile phones (since 6 April 2006 only one phone per employee may be provided tax-free)

- computer equipment made available prior to 6 April 2006 to a limit of £2500
- suggestion scheme awards
- long service awards
- eye tests and corrective appliances.

Benefits in Kind and National Insurance

7.122 The provision of a benefit in kind may attract a National Insurance liability. In most cases, if a liability arises it will be to Class 1A contributions, which are payable only by the employer.

7.123 Where the benefit is included within a PAYE settlement agreement, a Class 1B liability arises in place of the Class 1A or Class 1 liability that would normally arise.

Class 1A National Insurance Contributions

7.124 Class 1A National Insurance contributions were introduced on taxable company car and fuel benefits from 6 April 1991. The charge was extended from 6 April 2000 to include most other taxable benefits.

When Does a Class 1A Liability Arise?

7.125 A number of conditions need to be satisfied before Class 1A contributions are due. They are:
- the employee must be within the scope of the NIC system
- there has to be a secondary contributor
- the employee must be a company director or earning at a rate of at least £8500 per annum
- the benefit received by the director or employee is chargeable to tax as employment income.

Who is Liable to Pay a Class 1A Contribution?

7.126 The liability to pay Class 1A contributions rests with the employer. There is no corresponding charge on the employee. Where a third party provides benefits and the employer has not arranged or facilitated the provision of the benefits the Class 1A liability remains with the third party.

Exceptions from the Class 1A Charge

7.127 Certain benefits are excluded from the Class 1A charge. The list includes:
- any benefit where Class 1 NIC has already been paid
- benefits covered by a PAYE Settlement Agreement where Class 1B contributions are payable
- benefits exempt from tax
- benefits covered by an HM Revenue & Customs (HMRC) extra-statutory concession
- eligible removal expenses
- childcare costs for children under 16 (subject to a limit of £55 (from 6 April 2006) for employer-contracted care and childcare vouchers)
- contributions to registered pension schemes
- shares and share options (Class 1 liabilities need to be considered).

Benefits

What is Payable and When?

7.128 Class 1A contributions are calculated on the basis of the values that are returned on form P11D for income tax purposes (ie the cash equivalent value).

7.129 To assist in identifying those benefits in respect of which a Class 1A liability arises, the P11D is colour coded. Items attracting a Class 1A charge are those that appear in the brown boxes of the P11D with a "1A indicator". The Class 1A calculation is performed on a global basis at employee level, rather than separately in respect of each employee. A pro forma calculation appears on form P11D(b), which is the employer's declaration that all required P11Ds have been submitted and also the statutory Class 1A returns. The starting point of the calculation is the sum of all the values in the brown Class 1A boxes that appear on all the employee's P11Ds for the tax year in question. This number is entered in Box A in section 1 of the P11D(b). There may be circumstances when adjustments are needed, in which case the employer must complete section 4 of the P11D(b). Any amounts liable to Class 1A NICs not included on the P11Ds must be added to the P11D total, and any amounts included in this total on which Class 1As are not due must be deducted.

7.130 The Class 1A liability is found simply by multiplying the total value of the benefits by the Class 1A rate, currently 12.8%.

7.131 The payment due needs to be with HM Revenue & Customs (HMRC) no later than 19 July following the end of the tax year in question.

Class 1B Contributions

7.132 Where the employee has entered into a PAYE Settlement Agreement (PSA) with HM Revenue & Customs (HMRC), Class 1B contributions are payable in place of the Class 1 or Class 1A liability that would otherwise arise.

7.133 Tax is due on the grossed up payments made to employees and the Class 1B contribution is payable on the amount of tax payable to HM Revenue & Customs (HMRC) and also on the payment or benefit to the employee if they would have attracted a Class 1 or Class 1A contribution but for the PSA.

7.134 The Class 1B liability is generally agreed at the same time as the income tax position. The rate of contributions is the higher standard rate contribution in force in the tax year covered by the PSA. The payment due needs to be with HM Revenue & Customs no later than 19 October following the end of the tax year. As with Class 1A contributions there is no employee liability and no benefit rights flow from the Class 1B contributions.

Saving work

Dispensations

7.135 A dispensation, or a notice of nil liability, removes the need for the employer to return a benefit or expense on the P9D or P11D and for the employee to claim a corresponding deduction.

7.136 A dispensation can be granted on items where HM Revenue & Customs (HMRC) is satisfied that no tax is due. For an item to be included within a dispensation, the following conditions must be met.
- The expense or benefit must be deductible.
- Expense claims must be independently checked and authorised.
- Where possible, expense claims must be vouched.

- Where expenses are advanced, the employer must have adequate procedures in place to ensure that they are properly accounted for and that any excess is repaid.

7.137 Dispensations can be used for any benefit or expense that meets the above conditions. Examples of items commonly included within a dispensation include:
- professional fees and subscriptions
- reasonable entertaining expenses
- certain international travelling expenses.

7.138 Mileage payments for drivers using their own cars for work can no longer be included within a dispensation. Instead, these are dealt with by the Approved Mileage Allowance Payments scheme. However, mileage payments made to company cars may be included, provided that the payments made are in line with the advisory rates published by HMRC. The employer must apply for a dispensation. A form, P11DX, exists for this purpose and is available from the HMRC website. Once in place, a dispensation remains in force until it is revoked. However, the employer must tell HMRC if any of the circumstances on which the dispensation was granted change.

PAYE Settlement Agreements

7.139 A PAYE settlement agreement (PSA) is an arrangement that enables the employer to settle, in a single payment, the tax and National Insurance on minor benefits that are provided to employees. The employer pays the tax on the employee's behalf. This is useful for preserving the "gift" nature of some benefits, eg Christmas parties in excess of the exemption limit.

7.140 The employer does not need to record items included within the PSA on the employer's P9D or P11D. Likewise, employees do not need to return items included on their personal tax returns.

7.141 Not all items can be included within a PSA. To be included, the benefit and expenses must be provided by reason of the employee's employment and must fall within one of the following categories.
- The benefit or expense is minor as regards the sums paid or the type of benefit provided or made available.
- The benefit or expense is irregular as regards the frequency in which, or the times at which, it is made available.
- The benefit or expense is paid in circumstances where deduction of tax is impracticable.
- In the case of a benefit made available to or shared between a number of employees, apportionment of that benefit between the employees is impracticable.

7.142 As the employer pays the tax on the item included within the PSA and that tax itself constitutes a benefit, the tax due is calculated on the grossed up value of the benefits. As far as National Insurance contributions are concerned, Class 1B contributions, payable on the value of the benefits that would otherwise attract a Class 1 or Class 1A liability, plus the value of the tax are payable.

7.143 Class 1B contributions replace the Class 1 or Class 1A liability that would otherwise arise. Where a PSA is required, it must be agreed with the tax inspector by 6 July following the end of the tax year to which it is to relate.

7.144 However, it is not advisable to leave it until the last minute. The tax and Class 1B National Insurance contributions on items included within the PSA are payable no later than 19 October after the end of the tax year to which they relate.

Compliance Obligations

7.145 Where taxable benefits and expenses are provided to employees, the

Benefits

employer must report details of them to HM Revenue & Customs (HMRC). Two forms exist for this purpose. Form P9D is used for benefits provided to employees earning at a rate of less than £8500 a year. Form P11D is used for directors, regardless of their earnings level, and for employees earning at a rate of at least £8500 a year.

7.146 In addition, the employer must also complete form P11D(b), which is the employer's declaration that all required P11Ds and P9Ds have been submitted and also the statutory Class 1A return. All three forms must reach HMRC no later than 6 July following the end of the tax year to which they relate. They can be filed manually or using HMRC's PAYE online service. It is important that the forms are correct and that the deadlines are met as penalties may be charged for late and incorrect returns. The penalty regime is harsh, with maximum penalties of £300 per late form and £3000 per incorrect form.

7.147 However, the maximum penalty for incorrect forms is usually only levied in cases of fraud. Employers must also supply employees with details of the benefits and expenses returned on their P9D or P11D by the same date. The easiest way to do this is to give the employee a copy of his or her P9D or P11D. Where company cars are provided, the employer must notify changes quarterly to HMRC on form P46(car).

7.148 Employers must also give employees a copy of their P11D or P9D or details of the information contained on the form no later than 6 July following the end of the tax year to which the form relates. This is to enable the employee to complete his or her self-assessment return.

Training

7.149 Managers and HR personnel may need ongoing training on the potential development of benefits packages and ongoing training on the compliance and administrative requirements once they are in place.

List of Relevant Legislation

7.150
- Employment Equality (Age) Regulations 2006
- Maternity and Parental Leave (Amendment) Regulations 2002
- Social Security (Contributions) Regulations 2001
- Part-time Workers (Prevention of Less Favourable Treatment) Regulations 2000
- Maternity and Parental Leave, etc Regulations 1999
- Income Tax (Earnings and Pensions) Act 2003
- Social Security Contributions and Benefits Act 1992

Further Information

Publications
- 490 *Employee Travel. A Tax and NICs Guide for Employers*, available from HM Revenue & Customs.

- CWG2 *Employer's Further Guide to PAYE and NICs*, available from HM Revenue & Customs.
- CWG5 *Class 1A NICs on Benefits in Kind*, available from HM Revenue & Customs.

Organisations

- **Department for Work and Pensions (DWP)**
  Web: *www.dwp.gov.uk*
  The DWP is responsible for the Government's welfare reform agenda. Its aim is to promote opportunity and independence for all.
- **Department for Business, Enterprise and Regulatory Reform (BERR)**
  Web: *www.berr.gov.uk*
  The Department for Business, Enterprise and Regulatory Reform brings together functions from the former Department of Trade and Industry (DTI), including responsibilities for productivity, business relations, energy, competition and consumers. It also drives regulatory reform.
- **Federation of Small Businesses**
  Web: *www.fsb.org.uk*
  The UK's leading lobbying benefits group for small businesses.
- **HM Revenue & Customs**
  Web: *www.hmrc.gov.uk*
  HM Revenue & Customs (HMRC) is the department responsible for the business of the former Inland Revenue and HM Customs and Excise. HMRC is responsible for collecting the bulk of tax revenue as well as paying tax credits and child benefit.
- **Opportunity Now**
  Web: *www.opportunitynow.org.uk*
  Opportunity Now is a business-led campaign that works with employers to realise the economic potential and business benefits that women at all levels contribute to the workforce.

Cars, Fuel, Vans and Related Benefits

> This topic covers the following.
> - Company Cars
> - Vans
> - Van Fuel Benefit
> - Pooled Vans
> - Cash Alternatives
> - Employee Car Ownership Schemes
> - National Insurance Contributions

7.151 Company cars are one of the most popular benefits provided to employees. An employee may be given a company car simply because it is essential to his or her job. A company car may also be provided to employees as a perk. Traditionally, company cars were seen as something of a status symbol, with more senior employees and directors qualifying for more expensive cars.

7.152 However, changes in the company car tax regime that have led to drivers of high emissions cars being heavily taxed, combined with increased environmental awareness, have led many employees to choose either smaller company cars or a cash alternative to a company car. To assist employees in purchasing a car of their own, employers may operate employee car ownership schemes.

7.153 Traditionally, company vans have been a low-tax alternative to a company car, enjoying significantly lower tax charges. However, the tax charge for vans increased significantly since 6 April 2007, putting vans on a par with company cars.

7.154 This topic discusses the provision of cars, fuel, vans and related benefits to employees.

Employers' Duties

7.155 Employers have a duty to:
- consider the policy in relation to cars, fuel and related benefits in the context of the wider goals of the organisation
- ensure the organisation's policy in relation to business travel is communicated to employees
- where company cars are offered, ensure that employees are aware of the organisation's policy and the tax and National Insurance implications of a company car
- where employees are paid mileage allowances, ensure that employees are aware of the rates and any associated tax implications
- ensure employees are kept informed of changes in policy and legislation that affect them
- comply with reporting requirements in relation to car, van and fuel benefits, eg P11Ds, P46(Car), etc
- keep abreast of changes in the legislation.

Employees' Duties

7.156 Employees have a duty to:
- adhere to the organisation's policy on company cars
- adhere to the organisation's rules in respect of the use of the employee's own vehicle for business mileage
- return details on any taxable benefits on his or her self-assessment return, and
- where appropriate, claim deductions for business expenses.

In Practice

Company Cars

7.157 The company car is now fully integrated into the UK way of life. Cars of all types are provided to about two million employees, for a range of reasons including:
- reliable basic transport
- uniformity of perception
- status symbol
- part of remuneration.

7.158 Most company cars perform several of these functions, and this flexibility makes the company car a desirable part of the employment package for employers and employees.

Allocation Policy

7.159 Control over the allocation system is important. Most company car policies use a hierarchical system with senior management allowed larger or more expensive models. There are several approaches to model selection based on different criteria.

7.160 Range of choice for drivers:
- totally free selection (usually subject to some form of cost control)
- selection from a limited range of manufacturers
- no selection, single badge.

7.161 Entitlement on cost:
- list price of car
- invoice price of car
- monthly rental cost
- full whole-life cost to include fuel, insurance, etc.

7.162 Vehicle and model types within the allocation policy may be open to choice, or may be restricted (eg no 4x4, sports or convertible vehicles). In setting this element of policy, managers must always consider fitness for purpose. This is a key starting aspect of "duty of care" and may be expressed in a number of ways. Where large and heavy loads form part of the expected job profile of drivers, mandating cars with little luggage space or high rear sills in the boot area could expose drivers to risks of back injury.

7.163 Permitting young drivers to select high-performance cars without consideration of their ability to control the vehicles safely, is inappropriate.

7.164 Similar processes are required for vans. These may have less driver input choice, but a correspondingly higher level of regulation. Vans must be selected to carry their common load types and this must balance the overall weight of the payload, the unit weight of each package forming part of the load and the volume occupied.

7.165 All vans have a plated weight, which is the maximum permitted mass of the full vehicle on the road. If there is any chance that a full load might take the van near or beyond that weight, detailed tests should be carried out at a public weighbridge to identify the safe and legal load.

7.166 If a standard van design will not fit the bill, there are various other, more specialist forms of bodywork which can be fitted to a base vehicle. This is a specialist area and expert advice should be obtained from suppliers — ideally two or three should be consulted to ensure all aspects have been considered.

7.167 The key issue is the need to include the model choice as one aspect of the overall risk assessment/risk management programme which should be applied to the fleet operation.

Overview of Company Car Taxation

7.168 The provision of company cars to employees provides an undoubted benefit of employment as it saves the employees having to buy and run cars themselves. Over time, a number of systems of charging employees tax on their benefits have evolved to try to provide a simple, fair and reasonable basis for assessing the right tax burden. This is called "benefit in kind".

7.169 What the tax systems have in common is an attempt to identify the salary equivalent or proxy for cash that the private use represents. Once this salary equivalent has been identified as a tax charge, HM Revenue & Customs (HMRC) can tax it more easily under the normal PAYE systems.

7.170 A taxable benefit arises where a company car is available for the employee's private use.

7.171 Since 6 April 2003, the cash equivalent of the benefit is determined by reference to the car's price and the level of its CO_2 emissions. The cash equivalent is the appropriate percentage of the list price. The appropriate percentage depends on the level of carbon dioxide emissions.

7.172 A separate fuel benefit arises if fuel is provided for private motoring in a company car.

Price of the Car

7.173 The cash equivalent of the benefit of a company car is the appropriate percentage of its price.

7.174 The starting point is the list price of the car. This is defined at the price published by the manufacturer, importer or distributor, as appropriate, as the inclusive price appropriate for a car of that kind if sold in the UK, singly in a retail sale on the open market on the day immediately before the date of first registration.

7.175 It is important to note that this is unlikely to be the price actually paid for the car. The employer must use the list price in the benefit calculation, not the actual price paid.

Cars, Fuel, Vans and Related Benefits

7.176 List price information is available from a variety of sources.

7.177 If the car does not have a list price, the notional price is used. This is the price that would have reasonably been expected to have been the car's list price.

Accessories

7.178 The list price of the car is adjusted to take account of accessories. Standard accessories are ignored. However, the list price of optional accessories must be taken into account. Where an accessory replaces an existing accessory, the replacement is ignored unless the replacement accessory is superior, in which case the cost of the replacement is substituted for the cost of the original accessory.

Capital Contributions

7.179 The price of the car is adjusted to reflect capital contributions made by the employee. The maximum deduction permitted in respect of capital contributions is £5000.

Price Cap

7.180 The maximum price for a car for the purposes of the cash equivalent calculation is £80,000. Where the price exceeds £80,000, a figure of £80,000 is used instead in the calculation.

Classic Cars

7.181 Special rules apply to classic cars. Classic cars are at least 15 years old and have a market value of at least £15,000 — and the market value is more than the list price of the car plus accessories, and less capital contributions. Where these circumstances apply, the market value is used in place of the cost of the car and accessories less capital contributions.

7.182 The price cap of £80,000 applies to classic cars as to other cars.

Appropriate Percentage

7.183 The second determinant of the cash equivalent of the benefit is the appropriate percentage.

7.184 The appropriate percentage depends on the level of the car's carbon dioxide emissions and ranges from 15–35%. Discounts are given for certain environmentally-friendly cars and from 6 April 2008 a new lower 10% charge is to be introduced for cars with CO_2 emissions of 120g/km or less. Diesel cars attract a supplement.

7.185 The CO_2 emissions figure (in grams per kilometre (g/km)) for cars registered on or after 1 March 2001 is recorded on the vehicle registration document. For cars registered between 1 January 1998 and 28 February 2001 the emissions figure can be ascertained from a database maintained by the Society of Motor Manufacturers and Traders or may be found on an EU certificate of conformity. Where more than one figure is given, the relevant figure is the combined figure, but where a car is a dual-fuel car, the lower emissions figure is taken.

7.186 The percentage rate of charge for these cars is calculated as follows, if:
- the CO_2 emissions figure does not exceed the lower threshold, the relevant percentage is 15% (the basic percentage), or
- it does, the basic percentage is increased by 1% for every complete 5g/km by which the lower threshold is exceeded.

7.187 The CO_2 figure is rounded down to the nearest 5g/km.

Appropriate Percentages

CO₂ emissions in g/km				Appropriate Percentage %
2003/04	2004/05	2005/06, 2006/07, 2007/08	2008/09 and subsequent tax years	
155	145	140	135	15
160	150	145	140	16
165	155	150	145	17
170	160	155	150	18
175	165	160	155	19
180	170	165	160	20
185	175	170	165	21
190	180	175	170	22
195	185	180	175	23
200	190	185	180	24
205	195	190	185	25
210	200	195	190	26
215	205	200	195	27
220	210	205	200	28
225	215	210	205	29
230	220	215	210	30
235	225	220	215	31
240	230	225	220	32
245	235	230	225	33
250	240	235	230	34
255	245	240	235	35

(Source: SMMT)

7.188 Diesel cars are subject to a 3% supplement, subject to the maximum charge of 35%. However, for 2005/06 and earlier years, the supplement is waived in respect of cars that were registered before 1 January 2006 and which meet the Euro IV emission standard. From 6 April 2006, the supplement also applies to diesel cars registered on or after 1 January 2006 and that meet the Euro IV emissions standard.

7.189 Discounts are given in respect of certain environmentally-friendly cars.

Emissions Discounts for Environmentally-friendly Cars: 2006/07

Type of fuel	Adjustment
Electric only	Discount of 6%
Hybrid electric	Discount of 3%
Gas only	Discount of 2%
Bi-fuel with CO_2 emissions figure for gas	Discount of 2% (lowest CO_2 figure used)

Cars, Fuel, Vans and Related Benefits

Type of fuel	Adjustment
Bi-fuel conversion, other bi-fuel not within above	None

7.190 For 2005/06 and earlier years, the discounts were as follows.
- For electric cars, the discount was 6%.
- For electric and petrol cars, the reduction was 2% plus 1% for each 20 g/km by which the CO_2 emissions figure was less than the lower threshold.
- For cars propelled by road fuel gas, and bi-fuel cars with a specified emissions figure, the reduction was 1% plus 1% for each 20 g/km by which the CO_2 emissions figure was less than the lower threshold.
- For other bi-fuel cars, the reduction was 1%.

7.191 From 2008/09, a lower charge of 10% of the list price applies to low emissions cars. A low emissions car is one with CO_2 emissions not exceeding 120g/km.

Cars with No CO_2 Emissions Figure

7.192 If the car was registered before 1 January 1998, or between 1 January 1998 and 30 September 1999 but has no CO_2 emissions figure, then the percentage rate of charge is given by the following table.

Percentage Rate of Charge for Cars with No Carbon Dioxide Emissions Figure

Engine Size	Registration: Pre-1 January 1998	Registration: 1 January 1998 — 30 September 1999
1400cc or less	15%	15%*
1401–2000cc	22%	25%*
2001cc or more	32%	35%
No cylinder capacity	15% if electric; 32% otherwise	15% if electric; 35% otherwise

* These figures are increased by 3% for diesel cars.

Periods of Unavailability Charge

7.193 The tax charge for a company car is reduced *pro rata* if the car is unavailable for part of the year. Periods of less than 30 consecutive days during which the car is unavailable (eg for repairs) are disregarded.

7.194 The taxable value of a company car is reduced by any amount which the employee pays to the employer for the private use of the car.

Calculating the Taxable Benefit

7.195 The value charged to tax in respect of the benefit of a company car is calculated as follows.
- Find the price of the car.
- Add the price of any optional accessories and adjust for any superior replacement accessories.
- Deduct any capital contributions made by the employee (maximum deduction £5000).

- If the result is greater than £80,000, limit to £80,000. This is the price of the car.
- Find the appropriate percentage of the tax year in question by reference to the car's CO_2 emissions from the table above, adjusting for any discounts or supplements.
- Multiply the price by the appropriate percentage.
- Reduce proportionately to take account of periods of unavailability of at least 30 days.
- Make any deduction for private use payments made by the employee.
- The result is the cash equivalent of the benefit.

Example

7.196 An employee has a company car with a list price of £20,000 when new. The car is fitted with optional accessories with a list price of £5000.

7.197 The car has CO_2 emissions of 198g/km.

7.198 For 2006/07, the cash equivalent of the benefit is 26% of (£20,000 + £5000) = £6500.

Pooled Cars

7.199 No taxable benefit arises in respect of the employee's private use of a pool car.

7.200 A car is a pool car if:
- it is made available to, and actually used by, more than one employee
- the car was made available to each employee by reason of his or her employment
- the car was not ordinarily used by one employee to the exclusion of others
- in the case of each employee, the private use of the car was incidental to other use of the car (eg the employee takes the car home to make an early start on a business journey the following morning)
- the car is not normally kept overnight at or in the vicinity of any of the employees' homes.

Fuel Benefit

7.201 If an employee is provided with fuel by the employer for private motoring in a company car, the employee is liable to a further tax charge on the value of the fuel.

7.202 For 2003/04 onwards the charge is linked to the carbon dioxide emissions of the car.

7.203 It is calculated by multiplying a statutory figure by the percentage used to calculate the car benefit. The statutory figure is set at £14,400 for 2003/04 and future tax years.

Example

7.204 The fuel scale charge in respect of a car with CO_2 emissions of 196g/km for 2007/08 is 26% of £14,400 = £3744.

7.205 Consideration should be given to whether the provision of private fuel does represent a benefit. This will involve comparing the tax charge with the amount spent on fuel for private motoring by the employee.

7.206 The fuel benefit is proportionately reduced if the car in respect of which it is provided is unavailable (such that the car benefit is reduced) or if for part of the tax year:

Cars, Fuel, Vans and Related Benefits

- fuel was not provided
- fuel was only made available for business travel, or
- the employee was required to make good the cost of any fuel for private travel.

7.207 However, the reduction does not apply if the provision of fuel for private use is withdrawn and later reinstated before the end of the tax year.

Advisory Fuel Rates

7.208 HM Revenue & Customs (HMRC) publishes advisory fuel rates for business mileage in company cars. The rates are fuel-only rates and are intended to reflect the actual average fuel costs at the time they are set.

7.209 They are relevant only where employers reimburse employees for business travel in a company car or where employees are required to repay the cost of fuel used for private purposes. They should not be used by employees to claim a deduction for business mileage. Any claim for deduction should be based on the actual costs incurred.

7.210 The rates may be used in negotiating dispensations for mileage payments for business travel in company cars.

7.211 The rates that currently apply and the new rates applicable from 1 August 2007 can be found in the National Insurance topic of the Key Rates and Data section.

Mileage Allowance Payments

7.212 The mileage allowance payments system was introduced with effect from 6 April 2002. The system allows employers to make mileage allowance payments free of tax and without the need to report those payments, provided that the payments do not exceed the approve amount. However, amounts paid in excess of the approved amounts are taxable and need to be reported to HMRC on the P11D/P9D.

7.213 The approved amount is found by applying the formula:

$$M \times R$$

Where:
- M is the number of business miles travelled by the employee in the tax year in question, and
- R is the rate applicable to that kind or vehicle.

7.214 Different rates apply to different types of vehicle. For cars only, a higher rate applies for the first 10,000 business miles in the tax year than for subsequent business miles.

Mileage Allowance Payments

Type of Vehicle	Rate per Mile
Cars	First 10,000 miles: 40p
	Subsequent miles: 25p
Motorcycles	24p
Bicycles	20p

Example

7.215 An employee drives 15,000 business miles in his own car during the tax year in question. The approved amount is (10,000 x 40p) + (5000 x 25p) = £5250.

7.216 The employer can pay up to the approved amount without needing to report the amount paid to HMRC.

7.217 If the employer does not pay a mileage allowance, the employee can claim a deduction up to the approved amount. Likewise, if the employer pays a mileage allowance but it is less than the approved amount, the employee can claim a deduction for the shortfall.

Passenger Payments

7.218 Employers can also pay tax free passenger payments to employees who carry a passenger, who is also an employee, on a business journey. Passenger payments are free to the extent that they do not exceed the approved amount, which is the number of business miles travelled by the employee carrying at least one passenger who is also an employee on a business journey multiplied by the passenger rate of 5p per mile. The approved amount is calculated separately for each passenger.

7.219 However, the employee cannot claim a deduction if the employer does not make passenger payments or makes them at a rate that is less than the approved rate.

7.220 Passenger payments made in excess of the approved amount are taxable and must be returned on the P9D or P11D as appropriate.

Vans

7.221 Employees who use company vans for their work may be able to use those vans for private journeys. A taxable benefit arises where a van is available for private use.

7.222 Historically, vans have been an attractive benefit from a tax perspective benefiting from a low tax charge as compared to cars. However, the cash equivalent values have increased dramatically from 6 April 2007, bringing the charge on vans more in line with that on company cars.

7.223 From 6 April 2005, the cash equivalent of the van depends on various factors.
- If there is no private use of the van, no taxable benefit arises.
- If the private use of the van meets the restricted private use condition, the cash equivalent of the benefit is nil. The restricted private use condition requires that the commuter use requirement and the business travel requirement are met. The commuter use requirement is broadly that the van is made available to the employee on terms that prohibit private use other than for the journey to and from work. The business travel requirement is simply that the van is available to the employee mainly for business travel.
- The restricted private use condition is regarded as being met if any private use other than that relating to the journey to work is insignificant.
- Where the employee uses the van for private journeys and the restricted private use condition is not met, a tax charge arises.

7.224 For 2005/06 and 2006/07, the amount charged to tax is £350 if the van is at least four years old at the end of the tax year and £500 if the van is less than four years old at the end of the tax year.

7.225 For 2007/08 onwards, the amount charged to tax increases to £3000, irrespective of the age of the van.

7.226 The cash equivalent is reduced proportionately for periods of at least 30 consecutive days when the van is unavailable.

7.227 The cash equivalent is also reduced by any payments made by the employee for private use of the van.

7.228 Where vans are shared, the cash equivalent is calculated separately for each employee and reduced on a just and reasonable basis. From 2005/06 there is no cap on the charge. This may mean it is better for an employee's private use to be restricted to one van.

Van Fuel Benefit

7.229 Prior to 6 April 2005, the van charge included any benefit for fuel provided for private use of the van. However, from 6 April 2005, the rules provide for a separate van fuel charge. The charge is set at nil for 2005/06 and 2006/07 so in practical terms it does not have any effect until 2007/08.

7.230 The van fuel benefit is set at £500 for 2007/08 onwards.

7.231 The charge does not apply if the employee is required to make good the cost of fuel for private motoring and actually does so.

7.232 The charge is proportionately reduced for any part of the year that:
- the van in respect of which the fuel was provided was unavailable and the van benefit proportionately reduced
- the provision of fuel was not available
- fuel was only provided for business purposes, or
- the employee was required to make good the cost of fuel for private purposes and actually did so.

7.233 However, no reduction is given if provision of fuel is withdrawn but reinstated before the end of the tax year.

Pooled Vans

7.234 Employees may not be allocated their own van, but instead drive one from a pool.

7.235 No tax charge arises in respect of a van that is included in a van pool, provided that the:
- van was made available and actually used by more than one employee
- vans were made available to those employees as result of their jobs
- van was not ordinarily used by one employee to the exclusion of other employees, and
- van was not normally kept overnight at an employee's home.

Cash Alternatives

7.236 An employee may be offered a cash alternative to a company car. This is increasingly popular and may be built into a flexible benefits package.

7.237 Where the choice is between cash and a company car, the employee is taxed on what he or she actually chooses.

Employee Car Ownership Schemes

7.238 Increases in company car and fuel tax have led many employers to introduce schemes that allow employees to buy their own cars, often within a specified financial framework. Although the exact nature of the schemes vary, they are generally referred to as employee car ownership schemes.

7.239 The Government has recently announced a review of employee car ownership schemes. The review aims to determine the format of such schemes and consideration will be given to taking any advantage gained by the employee as a benefit in kind.

National Insurance Contributions

Class 1A Contributions

7.240 The Class 1A charge was introduced in April 1991 and originally applied only to company car and fuel benefits. The charge was widened from 6 April 2000 to most taxable benefits provided to P11D employees and directors.

7.241 A Class 1A liability is an employer-only liability. The charge is calculated at the Class 1A rate (12.8%) on the cash equivalent of benefits as reported on the P11D.

7.242 A Class 1A liability arises in respect of company and fuel benefits and van benefits. The amounts recorded on employees' P11Ds in respect of these amounts are taken into account in the employer's Class 1A National Insurance computation.

7.243 Class 1A contributions are payable by 19 July following the tax year to which they relate.

National Insurance Contributions and Approved Mileage Allowance Payments

7.244 The tax exemption for approved mileage allowance payment also applies for National Insurance purposes. However, the calculation of the approved amount for National Insurance purposes differs slightly to that for tax purposes. The difference is necessitated by the non-cumulative nature of National Insurance contributions.

7.245 As for tax purposes, the exempt amount is found by multiplying the business mileage by the mileage rate. However, the calculation is performed for each earnings period rather than for the tax year as a whole. Where there is more than one rate for a vehicle, as in the case of cars, the highest rate is used. This means that for cars the rate up to 10,000 miles is used for NIC purposes, regardless of the number of business miles undertaken in the year.

7.246 Amounts paid in excess of the exempt amount are liable for Class 1 National Insurance contributions.

Compliance

7.247 Company car, van and fuel benefits need to be reported on the P11D form. Such benefits only arise when provided to directors and P11D employees, so in the unlikely event that a company car is provided to an employee earning at a rate of less than £8500 a year, the provision will be tax-free. However, as the value of the benefit is taken into account in determining whether the employee earns at a rate of £8500 a year, this is likely to be a very rare occurrence.

7.248 In addition to reporting benefits on the P11D, the employer must supply

Cars, Fuel, Vans and Related Benefits

details on the P11D information to the employee. This obligation is usually fulfilled by giving the employee a copy of his or her P11D.

7.249 The employer must also report company car changes to HMRC on a quarterly basis on form P46(Car). Care should be taken than the information supplied on the P46(Car) matches that reported on the P11D.

7.250 The employer must also complete form P11d(b), which is the employer's declaration and statutory Class 1A return.

7.251 Forms P11D and P11d(b) must reach HMRC by 6 July following the tax year to which they relate. Employees must be given a copy of their P11D by the same date.

Training

7.252 Those responsible for company cars must ensure that they understand the rules and keep abreast of any changes in the law. This applies equally in relation to other car-related benefits, such as fuel and company vans.

7.253 The key reports to be kept regarding company vehicles are as follows.
- Inventory — list summarising the data on all vehicles controlled by the organisation. This should be periodically reviewed.
- Driver details — list summarising details of licences, entitlement groups, motoring convictions, etc.
- Suppliers — important where multiple suppliers of services are in place.
- Accident history — by vehicle, cross-referenced to the driver.

7.254 Cost control reports will typically contain information about:
- fuel costs
- business mileage levels
- traffic violations — parking, congestion charge, speeding notices — by driver
- current/in progress insurance claims
- rental vehicle arrangements which are open and live
- vehicles off the road.

List of Relevant Legislation

7.255
- Road Vehicles (Construction and Use) (Amendment) (No. 4) Regulations 2003
- Income Tax (Pay As You Earn) Regulations 2003
- Social Security (Contributions) Regulations 2001
- Management of Health and Safety at Work Regulations 1999
- Provision and Use of Work Equipment Regulations 1998
- Income Tax (Earnings and Pensions) Act 2003
- Road Traffic Act 1991
- Health and Safety at Work, etc 1974

Further Information

Publications
- CWG5 *Class 1A NICs on Benefits in Kind*, available from HM Revenue & Customs.
- CA33 *Class 1A National Insurance Contributions on Car and Fuel Benefits*, available from HM Revenue & Customs.
- 490 *Employee Travel. A Tax and NICs Guide for Employers*, available from HM Revenue & Customs.
- *The Highway Code*, The Stationery Office.

Organisations
- **Association of Car Fleet Operators (ACFO)**
  Web: *www.acfo.org*
  The association aims to be the principal organisation which represents the professional interests of vehicle fleet operators, developing expertise in fleet management through meetings, informed debate, and training.
- **British Vehicle Rental & Leasing Association (BVRLA)**
  Web: *www.bvrla.co.uk*
  BVRLA is a member's organisation for all companies involved in the rental, contract hire and fleet management industry. They provide a wide range of trading assistance, information, training and networking opportunities.
- **Department for Transport (DfT)**
  The DfT oversees the delivery of a reliable, safe and secure transport system that responds efficiently to the needs of individuals and business while safeguarding the environment.
- **HM Revenue & Customs**
  Web: *www.hmrc.gov.uk/home.htm*
  HM Revenue & Customs (HMRC) is the department responsible for the business of the former Inland Revenue and HM Customs and Excise. HMRC is responsible for lecting the bulk of tax revenue as well as paying tax credits and child benefit.
- **Society of Motor Manufacturers and Traders (SMMT)**
  Web: *www.smmt.co.uk*
  The SMMT is the trade association for the motor industry in the UK. It is a key partner in the Automotive Consortium on Recycling and Disposal (ACORD).

Deductions from Pay

This topic contains the following:
- Whose Pay Can be Deducted
- When Pay Can be Deducted
- Categories of Deduction
- Enforcement

7.256 There are limited circumstances — laid out in the Employment Rights Act 1996 (ERA) — when an employer can make deductions from a worker's pay. There must be a requirement in law for a deduction to be made or the relevant worker must have given prior written permission.

Employers' Duties

7.257 Employers should ensure the following.
- No unlawful deduction from a worker's wages should occur.
- Employers must understand the regulations regarding statutory deductions.
- Employers must obtain the necessary written permission from workers before making any non-statutory wage deductions.
- Employers in the retail trade with cash shortages or stock shortfalls can normally only deduct up to 10% of gross wages due to a worker in any pay period.
- Ensure that all affected workers are provided with the training required to deal with deductions from pay and the possible pitfalls.

Employees' Duties

7.258 Workers should ensure the following.
- A worker should notify his or her employer in writing if he or she wishes the employer to make a non-statutory deduction from his or her pay.
- A worker should avoid any action that breaches a term or condition in his or her contract that allows for deductions to be made.
- It is important that workers realise that overpaid wages can be automatically deducted by the employer from a future pay packet unless such deduction would be unreasonable.
- An employee should normally lodge any complaint about unauthorised deductions with a tribunal within three months of the deduction.
- Any worker involved in the deduction of wages from other workers within an organisation (eg human resources and payroll staff) should ensure he or she is properly trained.

In Practice

Whose Pay Can be Deducted

7.259 Sums can be deducted under the ERA from the pay of workers who are:
- under a contract of employment
- in apprenticeship
- agency workers (but not self-employed people).

7.260 Armed forces personnel and certain categories of merchant shipping worker are excluded from the provisions, but Crown employees (eg those in the National Health Service) are within the scope of the Act.

When Pay Can be Deducted

7.261 The circumstances under which an employer can make deductions from a worker's pay are laid out in the Employment Rights Act 1996 (ERA).

7.262 The Act specifies that an employer can only make deductions if:
- there is a requirement by law for a deduction to be made, or
- a worker specifically gives prior written permission.

7.263 Deductions that might be required by law include:
- PAYE tax
- national insurance contributions
- student loan deductions
- payments imposed by county court judgments.

7.264 Deductions that might be specifically authorised by a worker include:
- loan repayments
- pension contributions
- other deductions agreed within the terms of a contract of employment.

7.265 If an employer makes a deduction:
- that is not provided for by statute, and
- without the authority of the worker concerned

the deduction will be automatically unlawful. The worker could take the employer to a tribunal and receive recompense for unlawful deductions.

Provision for Deduction in an Employment Contract

7.266 Authority to make deductions from pay might be included by an employer in an employment contract. Provision might be made, for example, to cover:
- loss of a uniform
- failure to return the organisation's property
- holiday taken in an excess of the worker's entitlement.

One-off Authorisation by a Worker

7.267 It might be that an employer seeks one-off authorisation from a worker to make a deduction from pay. Occasions when such a deduction might be made include:
- the repayment of a season ticket loan
- contributions to the organisation's pension scheme
- payments to an organisation's social club.

7.268 In such circumstances, the employer must be certain to receive written permission from the worker before proceeding.

Categories of Deduction

7.269 Legislation prevents employers from making unlawful deductions from the wages of workers (the ERA, previously the Wages Act 1986). There are four categories of acceptable deductions.
- Voluntary deductions.
- Contractual deductions.
- Retail trade.
- Underpayment of wages.

Voluntary Deduction

7.270 An employer may deduct from a worker any amount for which the worker has given prior written authority. Examples include:
- repayments of a loan made to a worker by an employer
- the repayment of an advance on salary
- the payment of trade union dues
- a subscription to a social club
- contributions towards the additional cost of family cover under a private medical scheme.

7.271 A deduction will be illegal if a written agreement is not in place prior to the deduction being made. If deductions are made without a written agreement, a worker could take his or her employer to an employment tribunal to recover the amounts deducted.

Contractual Deductions

7.272 If:
- a worker's contract provides for deductions to be made from his or her pay, and
- the worker has signed the contract, then

the employer has authority to deduct the relevant sums.

Such deductions might include:
- a worker's contribution to the organisation's pension scheme
- the payment of rent where a worker occupies property owned by an employer
- a payment to compensate for the loss of the organisation's property
- the recovery of holiday pay taken in excess of entitlement.

Retail Trade

7.273 The ERA contains additional sections applicable to workers in the retail trade. These allow employers to make deductions from a worker's wages because of:
- cash shortages
- stock shortfalls.

7.274 Prior to making a deduction on this basis, an employer must:
- notify the worker in writing of the total liability, and
- ask the worker to make the payment.

7.275 An employer cannot deduct more than 10% of the gross wages due to the worker in that one pay period. Any remaining shortfall should be recovered from future pay periods. The only exception to this is if the worker is leaving employment and there are outstanding deductions to be recovered. In such a situation, the 10% limit does not apply.

Underpayment of Wages

7.276 If a worker receives less wages or pay than he or she is entitled to under his or her contract of employment, due to a deduction that his or her employer has made from the worker's pay without authority, this will be considered an unauthorised deduction.

7.277 An example would be if a worker had taken holiday in excess of entitlement and the employer reduced the worker's pay to cover the extra days' holiday taken. If the worker's contract of employment did not provide for such deduction, it would be seen as unauthorised and therefore illegal. The worker could take the matter to an employment tribunal and have the underpayment repaid.

Correction of Wages Paid in Error

7.278 The rules governing the right to recover payments made in error in an employment context are the same as those applicable under the ordinary law of contract. The Employment Rights Act 1996 s.14 does allow the employer to make deductions from wages for reimbursement of an overpayment of a worker's wages or expenses made for any reason by the employer to the worker.

7.279 The employer does not need to obtain the worker's consent to make such a deduction and the worker cannot take legal action to prevent the deduction from being made.

7.280 Employers should, however, ensure that the deduction is carried out fairly and within the law. An employer's first consideration in such circumstances is whether or not it is reasonable to recover the overpayment from the worker. Factors to be considered when deciding on reasonableness could include that the worker:
- has made financial commitments on the basis of the overpayment, or
- would be unjustly enriched by the overpayment.

Enforcement

7.281 If an unauthorised deduction is made, a worker may complain to an employment tribunal.

7.282 The complaint must be lodged within three months of the date on which the deduction was made. This time limit may be extended if the tribunal considers it was not reasonably practicable for the worker to complain within three months.

7.283 If the tribunal upholds the complaint, it can order the employer to reimburse the worker.

Training

7.284 It is important that all human resources and payroll staff understand an employer's responsibilities under ERA legislation. Training should ensure that staff involved with HR and payroll matters:
- understand the regulations and law relating to non-statutory deductions from pay
- obtain signed written instructions from workers before making any non-statutory deductions from pay
- know the procedure to ensure unauthorised deductions are not made
- know the procedures on how to deal with underpayments of wages and salary if they do occur.

List of Relevant Legislation

7.285
- Employment Rights Act 1996

Further Information

Organisations
- **Advisory Conciliation and Arbitration Service (Acas)**
  Web: *www.acas.org.uk*
  Acas aims to improve organisations and working life through better employment relations. It provides up-to-date information, advice, high-quality training, and works with employers and employees to solve problems and improve performance.
- **Department for Business, Enterprise and Regulatory Reform (BERR)**
  Web: *www.berr.gov.uk*
  The Department for Business, Enterprise and Regulatory Reform brings together functions from the former Department of Trade and Industry (DTI), including responsibilities for productivity, business relations, energy, competition and consumers. It also drives regulatory reform.
- **HM Revenue & Customs**
  Web: *www.hmrc.gov.uk/home.htm*
  HM Revenue & Customs (HMRC) is the department responsible for the business of the former Inland Revenue and HM Customs and Excise. HMRC is responsible for lecting the bulk of tax revenue as well as paying tax credits and child benefit.

Employee Share and Share Option Schemes

> This topic covers the following.
> - Types of Schemes
> - Savings-Related Share Option Schemes
> - Company Share Option Plans (CSOPs)
> - Enterprise Management Incentive (EMI) Schemes
> - Unapproved Share Option Schemes
> - Share Incentive Plans
> - Age Discrimination

7.286 Employee share ownership is seen as a good thing as employees are more motivated and work harder if they own a stake in the organisation in which they work. There are various ways of passing shares to employees, either directly or by granting options to purchase shares.

7.287 A share option scheme is set up when an employer grants to an employee an option to buy a specified number of shares at some future time at a price fixed on the date on which the option is granted.

7.288 Share options are a highly attractive part of the benefits package offered to employees by corporate employers.

7.289 The benefit of a share option scheme is that it provides a risk-free way of holding an interest in shares.
- If the share price rises, the employee exercises his or her option at the lower option price and can then sell his or her shares at the higher market value.
- If the share price falls, the employee can decline to exercise his or her option and is thereby protected from loss.
- All share option schemes must come to an end when an employee stops working for the organisation running the scheme.
- There are often legislative restrictions on individuals who already have an equity interest in an organisation taking part in a share option scheme.
- Employers can also award shares directly to employees. This can be done in a tax-efficient manner as part of an approved employee share scheme. Share incentive plans (SIPs) (formerly know as all-employee share ownership plans) were introduced to promote wider share ownership among employees. They replace approved profit-sharing schemes, which were phased out after the introduction of SIPs.

Employers' Duties

7.290 Employers should ensure the following.
- Make sure that the scheme selected is suitable for the purposes of the organisation and satisfies the requirements of the organisation.
- Ensure that they advise employees of the existence and nature of any share option schemes.
- Ensure schemes comply with age discrimination legislation — the Employment Equality (Age) Regulations 2006 — from 1 October 2006.

Employee Share and Share Option Schemes

- Obtain HM Revenue & Customs approval if required.
- Include reports on the cost of share options in the organisation's annual report and accounts.
- Ensure that savings-related schemes meet the conditions laid down.
- The price at which employees can be granted share options in a Company Share Option Plan (CSOP) must not be "manifestly less" than the market value of shares at the date of grant.
- If an Enterprise Management Incentive (EMI) scheme seems most appropriate, check that the organisation meets the six conditions necessary for a scheme to be valid.
- Ensure that they comply with compliance obligations, such as annual returns.
- Ensure that non-HM Revenue & Customs criteria — such as listing and shareholder requirements — are satisfied if using a plan that is an Unapproved Share Option Scheme.
- Ensure that relevant staff are properly trained and that all employees are aware of their share scheme options.

Employees' Duties

7.291 Employees should do the following.
- Decide whether or not to take employee share options if a scheme is available.
- For all types of share option schemes, employees must remain in the employment of the organisation.
- Any employee who wishes to participate in a savings-related share option scheme must be prepared to enter into a savings contract and to permit regular payroll deductions.
- Understand when share options can be exercised, and the tax and National Insurance implications of exercise, if any.
- For an EMI share option scheme only, an employee must complete an HM Revenue & Customs form declaring that he or she is an "eligible employee".
- Fully understand any scheme offered by an employer. Make use of all available training and information about the scheme.

In Practice

Types of Schemes

7.292 There are currently three statutory share option schemes governed by legislative criteria that must be met if the schemes are to qualify for tax advantages. The schemes are:
- Savings-related schemes (sometimes called Sharesave or Save As You Earn (SAYE) schemes) — which must be open to all directors and employees of the organisation with at least five years' service.
- Company Share Option Plans (CSOPs — sometimes called Discretionary schemes) which are schemes through which an organisation can select appropriate employees considered suitable for options.

- Enterprise Management Incentive (EMI) schemes under which independent organisations in the UK, with gross assets of less than £30 million, can grant employees shares worth up to £100,000 at the time of the grant.

7.293 There is currently one type of approved employee share scheme — known as Share Incentive Plans (SIPs). SIPs are all-employee schemes under which employees can be awarded shares in the organisation for which they work.

7.294 In addition an employer may make use of Unapproved Share Option schemes, which are more flexible schemes that are not sanctioned by HM Revenue & Customs (HMRC).

7.295 All schemes — even those that are not approved by HMRC — will generally need to satisfy a range of criteria, including formal shareholder approval for listed organisation schemes, institutional investor guidelines, stock exchange listing obligations, Articles of Association requirements, etc.

HM Revenue & Customs — Tax Rates Approval

7.296 Employers should obtain HMRC approval where required. For EMI schemes a simpler notification procedure exists.

7.297 Tax and National Insurance advantages are available in respect of approved schemes. Unapproved schemes do not benefit from tax advantages.

Accounting for Share Options

7.298 Accounting rules now provide that the cost of share options must be reflected in an organisation's annual report and accounts.

Savings-Related Share Option Schemes

7.299 These schemes are aimed at the broad range of employees. They require those who wish to participate in them to enter into an SAYE contract with a bank or building society and permit regular payroll deductions.

7.300 Under the scheme, an employee is granted an option to buy the organisation's shares at a price fixed when the option is granted. The employee can then exercise this option when his or her savings contract matures. The number of shares that the employee ultimately buys on exercising the option is linked to the maturity value of the savings contract.

7.301 Generally, the burden of administration for a savings-related scheme will largely fall on the banks or building societies that will operate the savings contracts.

Conditions for Savings-Related Shares

7.302 Savings-related share options can only be granted over ordinary shares that meet the following conditions.
- The shares must be shares in the organisation that sets up the scheme (or in an organisation that controls the scheme).
- They must be fully paid non-redeemable shares.
- The shares must not be subject to any restrictions other than the restrictions that apply to all ordinary shares and the direction that the shares must be sold on termination of employment at the organisation.
- The shares must either be shares listed on a recognised stock exchange (or shares in a non-close subsidiary organisation of such listed organisation) or shares in an organisation that is not under the control of another organisation.

Employee Share and Share Option Schemes

- The shares must either be in an organisation whose ordinary share capital consists of shares of one class only or (unless the organisation is controlled by its employees) the majority of the ordinary shares must be held by people who did not also acquire them through an employee share scheme.

Option Price: Savings-Related Share Option Schemes

7.303 The price at which employees can be granted share options must be determined by the market value of the shares. The market value is usually agreed with HM Revenue & Customs (HMRC) before sending out invitations to employees to participate in the scheme.

7.304 The employer can, at its discretion, offer a discount of up to 20% on the market value. Therefore, if the market value of shares is £1, employees can be offered share options at a price of between 80p and £1.

SAYE Contract Agreement

7.305 Key features of the savings-related SAYE contract agreement are:
- monthly savings must be between £5 and £250
- savings contracts can be for three, five or seven years
- savings are made through payroll deductions
- tax-free interest is paid at current rates, varying according to the length of the contract.

Grant of Options: Savings-Related Share Option Schemes

7.306 Legislation limits the maximum value of the shares over which an option can be granted to the projected maturity value of the associated savings contract.

7.307 So, suppose an employee has entered into a three-year savings contract with monthly savings of £100. The projected maturity value is £3720, the organisation's share price is £1 and the employer is prepared to offer a 20% discount on the option.

7.308 The maximum size of the option this employee can be granted is £3720 worth of shares at 80p a share, ie 4650 shares.

7.309 If employees within an organisation apply in total for more shares than are available at the organisation, the employer can scale back applications provided this is done fairly.

7.310 Employers must offer participation to all employees, including part-time employees, who have five years' continuous service and who pay income tax on UK employment income. Other employees — such as overseas employees — may participate at the discretion of the employer.

7.311 Participation must be offered "on similar terms" to all participants, but this test can take account of factors such as seniority, salary levels, length of service and hours worked.

7.312 If the organisation's share price falls, employees can cease payments under their existing savings contracts, collect the cash redemption value and enter into a new savings contract. This enables employees to then participate in options granted at the new lower share price.

Exercise of Options: Savings-Related Share Option Schemes

7.313 Employees can normally exercise their options only within the period of six

months following the maturity date of their savings contract. Options are normally lost if employment at the organisation concerned comes to an end, but early exercise of options is usually permitted in the following circumstances:
- retirement
- ill health or injury
- death
- redundancy
- If the employee had held the option for three years, the sale out of the group of the subsidiary organisation that employs the holder of the option
- takeover.

7.314 The option can only be worth the redemption value of the associated savings contract. So if the option is exercised early, then the value of the option will be lower because the value of the associated savings contract will be lower.

7.315 Employees have the choice of keeping the cash received upon maturity of their savings contract rather than exercising their option and buying shares. This means that the scheme is risk free for the employees.

Tax Liability: Savings-Related Share Option Schemes

7.316 Provided that the conditions are met, employees will pay no UK income or capital gains tax on:
- the grant of their options
- the exercise of their options
- any repayment they receive under their savings contracts.

7.317 An exception is that income tax will be payable upon exercise of an option following a takeover which occurs earlier than three years from the date of grant of the option.

7.318 When the shares, bought through exercise of the option, are then ultimately sold by the employee, capital gains tax may ultimately be payable on any gains. However, because of annual capital gains tax exemption and taper relief, many employees may escape this charge.

7.319 A further tax benefit is that shares acquired under an approved savings-related share option scheme can be transferred into an Individual Savings Account (ISA), which is a tax-free savings vehicle. The transfer must be made within 90 days of the exercise date and the value of the shares transferred must not exceed £7000.

Compliance: Savings-Related Share Option Schemes

7.320 Employers must complete an annual return form (Form 34) and return it to HM Revenue & Customs (HMRC) by 6 July following the tax year to which it relates or, if later, within three months of the issue date.

Company Share Option Plans (CSOPs)

7.321 CSOPs, or discretionary schemes, allow an organisation to choose to which employees options are granted, when, how often and the size of the option grants. The discretionary nature means that it is often used to reward more senior employees.

7.322 CSOPs must however meet stringent criteria to qualify for HM Revenue & Customs (HMRC) approval.

Employee Share and Share Option Schemes

Conditions Relating to Shares: CSOPs

7.323 CSOP options can be granted only over ordinary shares which meet the same conditions as apply to savings-related share options.

Option Price: CSOPs

7.324 The price at which employees can be granted share options must not be "manifestly less" than the market value of shares at the date of grant.

7.325 As a matter of practice, HMRC will usually allow the market value of listed shares to be averaged over a number of trading days immediately preceding the date of grant.

7.326 In the case of AIM-traded and non-quoted shares, the market value should be agreed with HMRC prior to the grant of options.

Grant of Options: CSOPs

7.327 A CSOP option cannot be worth more than £30,000 at the date the option is granted.

Exercise of Options: CSOPs

7.328 An employee can normally exercise his or her option from three to 10 years after the date of grant. Options are normally lost upon termination of employment and lapse after 10 years. But, as with savings-related schemes, early exercise of options can be permitted in the case of:
- retirement
- ill health or injury
- death
- redundancy
- sale of the subsidiary organisation which employs the option-holder out of the group
- takeover.

7.329 Employees can simply allow their options to lapse, if the price at the time of exercise is such that exercise would not be worthwhile.

Performance Targets: CSOPs

7.330 A CSOP may contain performance targets that are set out when the option is granted and which must be met before an option can be exercised.

Tax Liability: CSOPs

7.331 Employees will pay no UK income or capital gains tax on:
- the grant of their options
- the exercise of their options after they have been held for at least three years
- if they allow their options to lapse.

7.332 In addition, if an option-holder dies less than three years after the grant of the option, no income tax will be payable upon exercise of the option.

7.333 Any gain in value of the shares following the exercise of the option may — on sale of the shares — be liable to capital gains tax.

Compliance: CSOPs

7.334 Employers must complete an annual return form (Form 35) and return it to HMRC by 6 July following the end of the tax year to which it relates, or, if later, within three months of the date of issue.

Enterprise Management Incentive (EMI) Schemes

7.335 Enterprise Management Incentive (EMI) schemes are designed to help smaller fast-growing "new economy" organisations recruit and retain high quality managers.

7.336 The considerable tax advantages conferred on EMI share options are intended to reward individuals who are prepared to leave their secure jobs with larger employers for new careers with smaller organisations.

7.337 There are no approvals processes for EMI schemes. Instead, a simpler notification process applies.

Basic Criteria for an EMI Scheme

7.338 The following six conditions must be met before a scheme will qualify as a valid EMI scheme.
- The employer must be a "qualifying company".
- The option must be granted to an "eligible employee".
- The option must be granted "by reason of employment" with a "qualifying company".
- The maximum value of an option grant to any employee must not exceed £100,000.
- The aggregate value of shares over which EMI options are granted must not exceed £3 million.
- The shares over which options are granted must meet certain conditions.

Qualifying Company: EMI Schemes

7.339 The four main criteria for determining whether an employer is a "qualifying company" are as follows.
- The organisation must be independent.
- Any subsidiaries must be "qualifying subsidiaries".
- Gross assets must not exceed £30 million.
- The organisation must be trading but certain trading activities are excluded.

7.340 These are detailed and relatively complex tests and an organisation can ask HMRC's Small Company Enterprise Centre to clarify whether or not it is a "qualifying company" for the purposes of the legislation.

An Eligible Employee: EMI Schemes

7.341 The three principal tests for determining whether an individual is an "eligible employee" are as follows.
- The employee must be working for either the organisation setting up the EMI scheme or a group organisation.
- He or she must work at least 25 hours a week for the organisation or, if less, devote 75% of his or her working time to the organisation (allowance is made for reasonable absences).

- An employee must pay income tax on earnings from the employment (self-employed workers can be included if they pay Schedule D income tax on their earnings from the organisation).

7.342 No director or employee can participate in the scheme if he or she owns or controls more than 30% of the issued ordinary share capital of the organisation.

7.343 Employees must complete an HMRC form declaring that she or he is an "eligible employee".

An Option Must Be Granted "By Reason of Employment": EMI Schemes

7.344 An EMI option must be granted for commercial reasons to recruit or retain the services of an employee.

Maximum Value of an Option: EMI Schemes

7.345 The maximum value of an employee's EMI option must not, at the date of grant, exceed a market value of £100,000. The value of any other option granted under a company share option scheme (CSOP) must be taken into account, but an option held under a savings-related scheme can be ignored.

7.346 The valuation of shares can be checked and cleared through HM Revenue & Customs's Share Valuation Division.

Conditions Relating to Shares: EMI Schemes

7.347 The shares over which an EMI option is granted must satisfy only the following three tests. They must be:
- ordinary shares
- fully paid up
- not redeemable.

Option Price: EMI Schemes

7.348 The employer is not restricted in the price he or she can set for options, provided the value does not lead any employee to exceed the £100,000 limit. However, any discount to market value will be taxed at income tax rates.

Exercise Period: EMI Schemes

7.349 The only legislative restriction is that an option must be exercised within 10 years of the date of grant.

7.350 Employees can simply allow their options to lapse, if the price at the time of exercise is such that exercise would not be worthwhile.

Disqualification of Options: EMI Schemes

7.351 An EMI option will lose its "qualifying" status if it no longer meets the qualification tests. Where a disqualifying event occurs, option-holders who wish to retain the tax advantages of their EMI option must exercise it within 40 days of the disqualifying event.

Employee Share and Share Option Schemes

Performance Targets: EMI Schemes

7.352 An EMI scheme may contain performance targets that are set out when the option is granted and which must be met before an option can be exercised.

Tax Liability: EMI Schemes

7.353 There will be no income tax payable on the grant of a qualifying EMI option. Provided the option is exercised with 10 years and is "qualifying" when exercised, there will be no income tax to pay if the shares are bought at the market value they had on the day the option was granted.

7.354 There is a legal mechanism for collecting income tax on the difference between:
- any discount to the shares' market value given at the time an option is granted
- the actual exercise price.

7.355 Capital gains tax may be due if you make a gain on the disposal of your shares. The principles of taper relief will apply: the shares are regarded as having been acquired on the date at which the option was granted; and the capital gains tax will decline according to the number of years after the grant at which the option is exercised.

7.356 EMI options do not have to go through a formal HM Revenue & Customs approval process. Under a "qualifying" EMI option, notice must merely be given in due form to HM Revenue & Customs (HMRC) within 92 days of the grant of the option. The organisation must also make an annual return of EMI options to HMRC by 6 July each year.

HM Revenue & Customs Notifications: EMI Schemes

7.357 EMI options do not have to go through a formal HM Revenue & Customs (HMRC) approval process. Under a "qualifying" EMI option, notice must merely be given in due form to HM Revenue & Customs within 92 days of the grant of the option. The organisation must also make an annual return of EMI options to HMRC by 6 July in each year.

Annual Return: EMI Schemes

7.358 An annual return, Form 40, must be completed each year and returned to HMRC by 6 July following the end of the tax year to which it relates.

Unapproved Share Option Schemes

7.359 In addition to the three types of scheme mentioned above, there are share option schemes that are not approved by HM Revenue & Customs (HMRC). Such schemes are considerably more flexible than the approved schemes, but do not benefit from tax breaks.

7.360 Organisations would tend to use unapproved share option schemes when the organisation:
- is too big to qualify for EMI share options and the £30,000 CSOP limit is too low
- wishes to use shares that would not qualify for approved share option schemes
- would like to attach performance targets that would not be acceptable under a CSOP
- wants to have more flexibility in the rules relating to share options than would be permitted under an approved share option scheme.

Employee Share and Share Option Schemes

7.361 There are no tax advantages to unapproved share options. An income tax charge arises upon the exercise of an option if there has been any increase above the option price in the value of the shares.

7.362 While the formal restrictions on unapproved share option schemes are minimal, organisations have to take a number of external factors into consideration. Listed companies, in particular, will have to consider institutional investor guidelines and stock exchange listing agreement obligations that impact on the:
- shares that can be used for such schemes
- option price
- number or value of shares over which options can be granted
- exercise of options.

Performance Targets: Unapproved Share Option Schemes

7.363 Unapproved share option schemes often contain employee performance targets that are set out when the option is granted and which must be met before an option can be exercised by the option-holder.

Tax Liability: Unapproved Share Option Schemes

7.364 Employees will pay income tax on the:
- grant of their options — if the option price is at a discount to the market value of the shares on the date of the grant and the option does not have to be exercised within 10 years
- exercise of their options — the sum assessed will be the increase in value of the shares over the option price.

7.365 Normally, the employee will enter into an arrangement allowing shares to be sold to meet the tax liability.

7.366 Any eventual gain on the sale of shares obtained on exercise of an unapproved share option may be liable to capital gains tax. The amount of tax will vary according to the difference between the actual sale price and the market value of the shares at the time of sale.

National Insurance Liability

7.367 No income tax will normally be payable if options lapse.

7.368 Employees and employers will also pay National Insurance contributions (NIC) on any share option gain.

7.369 To minimise the impact of an unpredictable secondary NIC liability, however, the employer and employee may jointly agree or elect that some or all of the secondary (employer's) NIC liability will be suffered by or transferred to the employee.

Compliance Obligations

7.370 Details of "reportable events" in relation to unapproved share options must be reported to HM Revenue & Customs on Form 42. The form must be returned to HM Revenue & Customs by 6 July following the end of the tax year to which it relates, or 30 days after issue if later.

Share Incentive Plans

7.371 A Share Incentive Plan (SIP) is an HMRC approved plan that offers tax and National Insurance advantages. The plans were introduced by the Finance Act 2000

Employee Share and Share Option Schemes

in a bid to encourage wider share ownership among employees. SIPs are all-employee plans. This means that they are not suitable for rewarding small groups of employees, eg directors.

7.372 SIPs, formerly known as all-employee share ownership plans, replace approved profit sharing plans, which were phased out following the introduction of SIPs.

7.373 SIPs can operate without HMRC approval. However, approval is required in order to benefit from the associated tax advantages.

Features of a Share Incentive Plan

7.374 A share incentive plan can provide for three main types of plan shares.
- Free shares — employers can provide employees with free shares worth up to £3000.
- Partnership shares — employees can spend up to £1500 a year out of pre-tax and NIC salary on additional shares, known as partnership shares.
- Matching shares — employers can give additional free shares to employees at a ratio of up to two matching shares for each partnership share bought by the employee.

7.375 The organisation can determine the mix on share incentive plan shares to suit its business needs, as it is not necessary to offer all types of plan shares.

7.376 Employees can also invest up to £1500 of dividends from incentive plan shares each year to buy further shares within the plan. Shares purchased from reinvested dividends are known as dividend shares.

7.377 The plan can also include a number of optional features, such as performance-related awards of free shares, the forfeiture of free or matching shares should the employee leave within three years of the award, or a holding period requiring that shares are held in trust for up to five years.

Tax and NIC Advantages: Share Incentive Plans

7.378 Where shares are awarded to an employee outside the scope of an approved plan, the employee is taxed on the shares as the shares are treated as forming part of the employee's remuneration.

7.379 Tax and NIC advantages apply in respect of shares awarded within a SIP. The extent to which a tax or NIC liability arises, if any, will depend on the type of shares purchased and the length of time that they have been held within the plan. No tax or NIC charge arises on the award or acquisition of plan shares.

7.380 Partnership shares are purchased out of pre-tax and pre-NIC pay.

7.381 No tax or NIC charge arises on dividends reinvested in plan shares, provided that they remain in the plan for at least three years. This is beneficial to higher rate taxpayers. Provided that certain conditions are met, no tax or NIC charge arises when the shares cease to be subject to the plan.

Approval Conditions: Share Incentive Plans

7.382 The tax and NIC advantages are only available while the SIP is approved. To gain HMRC approval, conditions must be met as to:
- the purpose of the plan
- the all-employee nature of the plan
- participation on same terms

- no preferential treatment for directors and senior employees
- no further conditions
- no loan arrangements.

Annual Return: Share Incentive Plans

7.383 An annual return is required each year for each approved scheme. The return form, Form 39, is available from the HMRC website. The form must reach HMRC by 6 July following the end of the tax year to which it relates, or, if later, within three months of the date of issue.

7.384 Details of shares awarded under an unapproved plan must be returned on Form 42.

Age Discrimination

7.385 The Employment Equality (Age) Regulations 2006 came into force on 1 October 2006. They prohibit discrimination on the basis of age in employment and vocational training.

7.386 Employers will need to familiarise themselves with the rules and ensure that any awards of shares or share options made to employees do not fall foul of the legislation. This is particularly important in the context of share schemes, as shares or share options are often awarded by reference to age or length of service. Where necessary, changes should be made to the scheme rules to ensure compliance.

7.387 Under the regulations, employee share and share option schemes cannot discriminate on grounds of age after 1 October 2006 unless the discrimination is required to comply with specific legislation, such as that governing the availability of tax and National Insurance advantages, or if that discrimination can be justified objectively.

7.388 Although awards of shares or share options made prior to 1 October 2006 are outside the ambit of the regulations, any discriminatory aspects in relation to the exercise of options after that date will need to be reviewed.

7.389 The regulations contain a number of exemptions of relevance to share and share option schemes. Age-related criteria imposed as a necessary condition of tax approval in order to comply with tax legislation is permitted. Similarly, service-related benefits are allowed, provided that the maximum qualifying service period is not more than five years.

7.390 Although the regulations allow age-related criteria where this can be justified objectively, this may be difficult to sustain in practice and employers are advised to err on the side of caution.

Training

7.391 The company secretary's department would normally be responsible for the internal administration of an employee share scheme or share option scheme. Computer software packages exist that can assist in managing schemes. Some training would be required to enable staff to undertake this administration.

7.392 A good quality explanatory booklet in simple English and possibly some training sessions might be necessary to clarify the share scheme option to employees.

List of Relevant Legislation

7.393
- Employment Equality (Age) Regulations 2006
- Income Tax Earnings and Pensions Act 2003

List of Relevant Cases

7.394
- *IRC v Eurocopy* [1991] STC 707 — limits on permitted amendments to CSOP schemes
- *Inland Revenue v Burton Group* [1990] STC 242 — acceptable performance targets

Further Information

Publications

The HM Revenue & Customs website contains a wealth of information on share schemes, located on the share schemes pages.

Organisations

- **HM Revenue & Customs**
  Web: *www.hmrc.gov.uk/home.htm*
  HM Revenue & Customs (HMRC) is the department responsible for the business of the former Inland Revenue and HM Customs and Excise. HMRC is responsible for collecting the bulk of tax revenue as well as paying tax credits and child benefit.
- **ProShare**
  Web: *www.ifsproshare.org*
  ifsProShare is a main point of contact with private investors and contains factsheets on different aspects of investing in shares as well as guides to information sources and professional advisers and gives access to free annual reports.

National Insurance

This topic covers the following:
- Earnings
- Earnings Period
- Calculating Class 1 National Insurance Contributions
- Class 1A Contributions
- Class 1B Contributions
- Record Keeping
- Returns
- Payment of National Insurance Contributions to HM Revenue & Customs
- Interest and Penalties
- Disclosure Rules

7.395 A liability to Class 1 National Insurance Contributions (NICs) arises on an employee's earnings, provided that the employee is aged over 16 and under the state retirement pension age, and has earnings equal to or above the lower earnings limit for Class 1 National Insurance purposes. For 2007/08 the lower earnings limit is £87 a week.

7.396 All employees should have a National Insurance number. This is a unique reference number that is used to identify each individual's National Insurance records. If an employee does not know his or her National Insurance number, the employer can find this using the HMRC's National Insurance number tracing service, form CA6855.

7.397 Class 1 contributions are payable by both the employee and the employer. Contributions payable by the employer are called primary Class 1 contributions and contributions payable by the employee are called secondary Class 1 contributions.

7.398 The liability to National Insurance arises once the lower earnings limit is reached. However, contributions are not payable until earnings reach the primary threshold of £100 week for 2007/08. On earnings between the lower earnings limit and the primary threshold, contributions are payable at a rate of 0%, thereby retaining entitlement to certain contributory benefits and Statutory Maternity Pay (SMP), Statutory Paternity Pay (SPP), Statutory Adoption Pay (SAP) and Statutory Sick Pay (SSP).

7.399 Primary contributions are payable at the main rate on earnings between the primary threshold and the upper earnings limit of £670 a week for 2007/08. Primary contributions on earnings above the upper earnings limit are payable at the additional rate of 1%.

7.400 Secondary contributions are payable on earnings once the secondary threshold (equal to the primary threshold at £100 per week for 2007/08) is reached. There is no upper limit for secondary Class 1 purposes.

7.401 The calculation of Class 1 NICs is non-cumulative. The calculation is performed separately for each earnings period on the earnings for that period. No account is taken of earnings in previous periods or in subsequent periods. This can be contrasted to the cumulative nature of income tax for PAYE purposes.

7.402 To prevent manipulation of the earnings period rule, special rules apply for directors. Directors have an annual earnings period. During the year, they can make payments on account of earnings at each pay day, the calculation being performed as for other employees. However, the liability must be recomputed on an annual basis at the end of the tax year.

585

7.403 Employees can choose whether to contract-out of the state earnings-related pension if their employer operates a pension scheme that satisfies certain conditions. Employees who contract-out pay National Insurance at a lower rate on earnings between the earnings threshold and the upper earnings limit.

7.404 Employers have to deduct primary contributions from the employee's earnings. The primary contributions, together with the employer's secondary contributions, must be paid over to HM Revenue & Customs each month with PAYE tax, student loan deductions, etc. Small employers can make their payments quarterly.

7.405 Class 1 contributions are payable on earnings. The definition of earnings for National Insurance purposes is not identical to that for tax purposes. In particular, it excludes most benefits in kind. However, since 6 April 2001, most taxable benefits payable to employees earning at the rate of at least £8500 a year (P11D employees), and directors, have attracted Class 1A contributions.

7.406 Class 1A contributions are employer-only contributions. They are payable on the value of benefits paid to P11D employees and directors at the Class 1A rate (12.8% for 2007/08).

7.407 Where the employer meets the liability to tax on certain benefits and expenses by way of a PAYE settlement agreement (PSA), the items covered by the agreement attract Class 1B NICs in place of the Class 1 or Class 1A liability that would otherwise arise. Like Class 1A contributions, Class 1B contributions are employer contributions. They are payable at the Class 1B rate (12.8% for 2007/08).

7.408 The rates and limits for 2007/08 are as follows.

National Insurance Rates and Limits 2007/08

Limits	£
Lower earnings limit (LEL): primary Class 1 contributions	£87 per week
Upper earnings limit (UEL): primary Class 1 contributions	£670 per week
Primary threshold	£100 per week
Secondary threshold	£100 per week
Employee's primary rate (payable on earnings of £100.01 to £670 per week)	11%
Employee's additional rate (payable on earnings over £670 per week)	1%
Employee's contracted-out rate (on earnings between £100.01 and £670 per week)	9.4%
Married women's reduced rate	4.85% on earnings between £100.01 and £670 per week and 1% on earnings over £670 per week
Employee's secondary Class 1 rate (on earnings over £100 per week)	12.8%
Employer's contracted-out rebate (salary-related schemes)	3.7%

National Insurance

Limits	£
Employer's contracted-out rebate (money purchase schemes)	1.4%
Class 1A rate (employer's only)	12.8%
Class 1B rate (employer's only)	12.8%

Employers' Duties

7.409 Employers have a duty to:
- deduct primary Class 1 contributions from employees' earnings
- pay primary Class 1 contributions deducted, together with secondary contributions payable on employees' earnings, over to HM Revenue & Customs
- keep records of National Insurance Contributions (NICs) deducted from each employee
- complete the employer's year-end returns showing NICs deducted during the year
- return details of Class 1A contributions due on benefits and expenses on form P11d(b)
- pay Class 1A contributions over to HM Revenue & Customs by 19 July following the end of the tax year to which they relate
- calculate Class 1B contributions on items included within PAYE settlement agreements (PSAs)
- pay Class 1B contributions over to HM Revenue & Customs by 19 October following the end of the tax year to which they relate.

Employees' Duties

7.410 Employees have a duty to:
- pay Class 1 NICs on earnings (deducted from pay by the employer)
- supply the employer with a P45 on joining, or if there is no P45 available, details of the National Insurance number.

In Practice

Earnings

7.411 Class 1 contributions are payable on earnings in the earnings period. The term "earnings" includes any remuneration or profit derived from employment. This means that Class 1 National Insurance is operated on gross pay for National Insurance purposes, which may not be the same as for tax purposes. Further guidance as to what is included within earnings from Class 1 National Insurance purposes is found in the HM Revenue & Customs (HMRC) guidance booklet CWG2 *Employer's Further Guide to PAYE and NICs*.

National Insurance

Earnings Period

7.412 The calculation of Class 1 National Insurance Contributions (NICs) is performed separately for each earnings period. Unlike PAYE income tax, the calculation of Class 1 NICs is non-cumulative.

7.413 The earnings period normally corresponds to the regular interval between which payments are made. Thus for weekly-paid employees, the earnings period is a week, for monthly-paid employees, the earnings period is a month, for employees paid four-weekly, the earnings period is four weeks, and so on.

7.414 Where employees are not paid at regular intervals, special rules apply to determine the earnings period. These are covered in detail in the HMRC guidance booklet, CWG2, *Employer's Further Guide to PAYE and NICs*.

Calculating Class 1 National Insurance Contributions

Tables Method

7.415 The tables method uses the National Insurance Contributions (NIC) tables published by HMRC. It is important that the correct table letter is used. For 2006/07 they are as follows.

NIC Tables Published by HM Revenue & Customs 2006/07

A	Not contracted-out standard rate contributions (weekly and monthly tables)
B	Married women with valid reduced rate election
C	Employees over state pension age
D	Contracted-out salary-related scheme
E	Contracted-out salary-related scheme — married women with reduced rate election
F	Contracted-out money purchase scheme
G	Contracted-out money purchase scheme — married women with reduced rate election
J	Not contracted-out where employee has deferment (weekly and monthly tables)
L	Contracted-out salary-related scheme where employee has another job in which they already pay NICs at or above the upper earnings limit (UEL).
S	Contracted-out money purchase scheme where employee has another job in which they already pay NICs at or above the upper earnings limit (UEL).

7.416 The most commonly used table is Table A. To determine the correct table to use and to fill out the correct columns in the deductions working sheet (P11) form, follow the steps below.
- Step 1: find the employee's gross pay for the earnings period.
- Step 2: look up the employee's gross pay in the relevant tables.
- Step 3: copy the figures into the relevant columns in the P11 form.

7.417 If the employee earns more than the upper earnings limit (£670 per week for 2007–08) per week, the calculation is slightly more complicated.

7.418 The additional contributions are calculated as follows.

National Insurance

- ubtract the upper earnings limit (UEL) from the total gross pay.
- Round the answer down to the nearest whole pound.
- Look this figure up in the additional pay table, available in the HM Revenue & Customs National Insurance Tables CA38, Tables A & J.
- If the figure is not shown, build it up by adding together as few entries as possible.
- Add the further total of the employee's NICs worked out on earnings above the UEL (columns 1d and 1e of the additional gross pay table) to the totals for the employee's and employer's NICs and employee's NICs due for earnings at the UEL (columns 1d and 1e of the main table) of the guidance booklet, CWG2.
- Record the figures resulting from above columns 1d and 1e on the deductions working sheet (P11).

Example

7.419 A weekly paid employee earns £1456 in one week in 2007/08. He has no contracted-out contributions and pays standard rate contributions.

7.420 The appropriate table to use is Table A.

7.421 From the main table of the HMRC guidance booklet, CWG2, *Employer's Further Guide to PAYE and NICs*, the entries for earnings at £670 per week are as follows.

Entries for Earnings at £645 per week

Earnings up to and including UEL	Earnings at Lower Earnings Limit (LEL)	Earnings above LEL, up to and including Earnings Threshold (ET)	Earnings above ET, up to and including UEL	Total of employee's and employer's contributions	Employee's contributions on earnings above ET	Employer's contributions
	1a	1b	1c	1d	1e	
£670	£87	£13	£570	£135.66	£62.70	£72.96

As the employee earned more than £670, it is necessary to calculate the additional contributions.

7.422 Earnings less UEL (to nearest whole pound) is £1456 − £670 = £786.

7.423 The additional gross pay table for £700 and £86 must now be used.

Additional Gross Pay Table for £86 and £700

	Employee's and employer's contributions 1d	Employee's contributions 1e	Employer's contributions
£86	£11.87	£0.86	£11.01
£700	£96.60	£7.00	£89.60
Additional contributions	£108.47	£7.86	£100.61

Therefore, the total contributions payable, to record on the P11 form, are as follows.

Example — Total Contributions Payable

Earnings up to and including UEL	Earnings at LEL	Earnings above LEL up to and including ET	Earnings above ET up to and including UEL	Total of employee's and employer's contributions	Employee's contributions on earnings above ET	Employer's contributions
	1a	1b	1c	1d	1e	
£670	£87	£13	£570	£135.66	£62.70	£72.96
£786	–	–	–	£108.47	£7.86	£100.61
£1456	£87	£13	£570	£244.13	£70.56	£173.57

Exact Percentage Method

7.424 This method simply means calculating the National Insurance due from the thresholds, as adjusted for the length of the earnings period.

7.425 In the previous example of a weekly paid employee earning £1456, contributions would be calculated as follows.

Primary Contributions

11% x (£670 – £100) = £62.70 PLUS.

1% x (£1456 – £670) = £7.86.

Total NICs = £70.56.

Secondary Contributions

12.8% x (£1456 – £100) = £173.57.

Class 1A Contributions

7.426 Class 1A contributions are payable annually by the employer. The starting point for the calculation is the entries returned on the P11D that appear in the brown boxes with a Class 1A indicator. The calculation is performed on the Class 1A return and employer's declaration, form P11d(b).

7.427 The calculation is performed on a global basis, rather than in respect of each employee. The total of all the entries in the brown boxes on all P11Ds is found and any necessary adjustments made, eg for items not in the P11D that attract Class 1A. The adjusted figure is simply multiplied by the Class 1A percentage for the year (12.8% for 2006/07 and 2007/08).

Class 1B Contributions

7.428 Class 1B contributions are payable on items included within a PAYE settlement agreement (PSA). The liability is on the value of the items attracting a National Insurance liability plus the value of the income tax payable on items within the PSA. The total is multiplied by the Class 1A percentage for the year.

Record Keeping

7.429 Employers must record National Insurance details in columns 1a to 1e of the employee's deductions working sheet (P11 or equivalent). Details must be kept for the current tax year and for the three previous tax years.

7.430 Details must be kept of benefits and expenses attracting Class 1A contributions.

National Insurance

7.431 Where a PAYE settlement agreement (PSA) is in force, details must be kept of the items included within the PSA and whether they would otherwise attract a liability to Class 1 or Class 1A.

Returns

7.432 The employer must record the National Insurance details on the PAYE end of year returns, P35 and P14s. Details of National Insurance Contributions (NICs) paid by each employee are recorded on the individual's P60. The P35 and P14s must reach HM Revenue & Customs by 19 May following the end of the tax year. The P60s must be given to the employee by 31 May following the end of the tax year.

7.433 Class 1A contributions are returned on form P11D(b), which must reach HM Revenue & Customs by 19 July following the end of the tax year to which they relate.

Payment of National Insurance Contributions to HM Revenue & Customs

7.434 Class 1 contributions are paid monthly to the collector, unless the employer is a small employer. Unless made electronically, payment must be made by the 19th of the month. Where payment is made electronically, payment must be made by the 22nd of the month. For large employers (more than 250 employees) electronic payment of PAYE and NICs is compulsory from April 2004. Class 1 NICs are paid with PAYE tax, student loan deductions, etc.

7.435 Class 1A contributions are payable by 19 July following the tax year to which they relate.

7.436 Class 1B contributions are payable by 19 October following the tax year to which they relate.

Interest and Penalties

7.437 Class 1 contributions not paid by 19 April following the end of the tax year to which they relate attract interest.

7.438 Interest may also be levied on Class 1A contributions paid late.

7.439 Penalties may be charged on late year-end returns.

Disclosure Rules

7.440 A separate disclosure scheme for National Insurance came into effect on 1 May 2007. The scheme works in a similar way to the tax disclosure scheme and aims to provide HMRC with an early warning of schemes that seek to avoid National Insurance.

7.441 The disclosure rules only require disclosure of a National Insurance scheme that:
- will, or might be expected to, enable any person to obtain a NIC advantage
- advantage is, or might be expected to be, the main benefit or one of the main benefits of the arrangements,
- the scheme is an NIC arrangement that falls within one of the hallmarks set out in the rules.

7.442 The obligation to disclose normally falls on the promoter. This is the person who makes the scheme available for implementation. However, employers and payroll professionals should be aware of the rules as it is possible that in certain situations the disclosure burden will fall on them.

7.443 HM Revenue & Customs had indicated that they would expect salary sacrifice schemes to be notifiable, despite the fact that they provide tangible benefits, because they will fall within the disclosure hallmarks. However, the decision as to whether to disclose a scheme must be made by the promoter, employer or payroll manager as appropriate in line with the disclosure rules. Employers should therefore be familiar with the rules.

Training

7.444 It is important that all payroll staff understand the National Insurance system. In particular, they should be familiar with:
- the different classes of National Insurance Contributions (NICs)
- when National Insurance is payable
- how to calculate NICs
- how to record NICs
- how to pay NICs over to the HM Revenue & Customs
- what year-end returns are required and when they should be submitted by
- the National Insurance disclosure scheme rules.

7.445 In addition, training should be given to ensure that all staff keep abreast of changes in both the law and in the rates of National Insurance.

List of Relevant Legislation

7.446
- Social Security (Contributions) Regulations 2001 (as amended)
- Social Security (Categorisation of Earners) Regulations 1978 (as amended)
- National Insurance Contributions Act 2006
- Social Security (Contributions and Benefits) Act 1992 (as amended)
- Social Security (Administration) Act 1992 (as amended)

Further Information

Publications
- *CCH's British NIC Guide*
- CWG2 *Employer's Further Guide to PAYE and NICs*, available from HM Revenue & Customs.
- IR LIST *Catalogue of Leaflets and Booklets*, available from HM Revenue & Customs.
- 480 *Expenses and Benefits, A Tax Guide*, available from HM Revenue & Customs.
- CA02 *NI Contributions for Self-employed People with Small Earnings*, available from HM Revenue & Customs.
- NIC2 *NI Contributions Holiday Scheme*, available from HM Revenue & Customs.

Organisations

- **HM Revenue & Customs**
  HM Revenue & Customs — National Insurance Contributions Office (NICO)
  Web: *www.hmrc.gov.uk/nic*
  The National Insurance Contributions Office of HM Revenue & Customs publishes all relevant information regarding National Insurance contributions (NICs).

National Minimum Wage

This topic covers the following.
- Current Rates
- Determining the NMW
- What is a Worker?
- What Hours are Counted as Having Been Worked?
- What Type is the Particular Worker's Job Arrangement?
- How Many Hours Have Been Worked?
- What is the Pay for the Work?
- Reductions and Deductions
- What is the Hourly Rate of Pay?
- Does this Rate Comply with the NMW?
- Enforcement Provisions

7.447 The National Minimum Wage (NMW) requires that employers pay workers a minimum hourly rate of pay. From October 2004, this covers most workers over the age of 16. The self-employed, specified vocations and certain other circumstances are excluded. Employers cannot opt out of the legislation.

7.448 Employers must comply with the NMW or face heavy sanction. Employees can complain about offences through a Government-sponsored confidential helpline (0845 600 0678).

7.449 Enforcement of the NMW is by HM Revenue & Customs through the employment tribunal system, with penalties related to non-compliance and criminal offences.

7.450 The minimum wage rate is set by the Government and is subject to periodical variation. Three different types of working arrangements are recognised, each with different implications for the assessment of working hours, the calculations of applicable pay and the resultant "National Minimum Wage pay" for an hourly rate.

7.451 Determining the effective wage for any given employee can be complex as it involves both a calculation of working time and the monies making up the wage. The NMW pay is calculated for a defined pay reference period and there are restrictions on averaging pay over several periods or offsetting time flexibility with wage payments.

7.452 From 1 October 2006, the NMW increased to £5.35 for adult workers, £4.45 for workers aged 18 to 21 and £3.30 for 16 and 17 year olds. The accommodation offset rate (where the employer provides accommodation with the job) rose from £3.90 to £4.15 per day.

7.453 A further increase for all rates is scheduled for 1 October 2007 with the adult rate increasing to £5.52, development rate £4.60 and youth rate £3.40.

7.454 Accredited training has been abolished as a result of the coming into force of the age discrimination regulations in October 2006.

Employers' Duties

7.455 Employers have a duty to:

- keep records that are sufficient for NMW purposes — the closer the wage level is to the NMW level, the better the records required
- keep records for three years plus one pay period
- respond within 14 days to a written request from an employee wishing to see his or her NMW record
- bear the burden of proof to show compliance with the NMW
- inform employees of current NMW rates and advertise the NMW helpline number (0845 600 0678)
- not use the NMW as a reason to dismiss or victimise employees
- remain liable to the requirements of the NMW even after the contract between employer and employee has ended.

Employees' Duties

7.456 Employees have a duty to:
- keep an accurate record of hours worked and provide the record to the employer as soon as possible, if home-based or travelling.

In Practice

Current Rates

7.457 The National Minimum Wage (NMW) is set by the Government and uplifted based on inflation and other economic conditions.

NMW Payment Tiers

Category	1 October 2006	From 1 October 2007
Main rate (22 years old plus) per hour	£5.35	£5.52
Development rate (18–21 years) per hour	£4.45	£4.60
Youth rate (16–17) per hour	£3.30	£3.40
Accommodation offset rate (where the employer provides accommodation with the job)	£4.15 per day	£4.30 per day

7.458 Apprentices under the age of 19 are not entitled to the NMW. Apprentices who are 19 or over and in the first 12 months of their apprenticeship are not entitled to the NMW.

7.459 An employer cannot use the fact that an employee has, due to age, entered a higher pay band under the NMW as a reason for dismissing the employee.

Determining the NMW

7.460 The seven questions that employers need to consider to ensure compliance are as follows.
- What is a worker?
- What hours are counted as having been worked?
- What type is the particular worker's job arrangement?
- How many hours have been worked?
- What is the pay for the work?
- What is the hourly rate of pay?
- Does this rate comply with the NMW?

What is a Worker?

7.461 The term "worker" is broader than a person with an employment contract and includes casual workers where their work is dictated by a single organisation. The NMW positively includes:
- agency workers
- agricultural workers (pay rates are determined by the Agricultural Wages Boards)
- commission workers
- home workers
- pieceworkers
- offshore workers in UK territorial waters
- workers usually employed in the UK but temporarily working overseas
- legally employed workers imported from outside the UK
- seafarers.

7.462 The NMW positively excludes:
- the genuinely self-employed
- workers under 16 years old, where permits are required from the Local Education Authority
- apprentices under 19
- apprentices under 26 in their first year
- students on vocational experience
- trainee teachers on work experience
- trainees on government-funded accredited training courses lasting at least 26 days over a six-month period
- members of the armed forces (regulars and reservists on duty)
- fisherman on a profit-share basis
- the unemployed
- prisoners
- homeless people working to receive shelter
- family, friends, neighbours or others working at home (eg au pairs, nannies or formal companions)
- residential members of religious communities.

7.463 Voluntary workers do not normally fall under the NMW.

7.464 For more information on employment types, refer to the topic on Contracts of Employment.

National Minimum Wage

What Hours are Counted as Having Been Worked?

7.465 It is important for an employer and his or her employee to agree on what hours will be counted as having been worked in any pay period. In general, all the hours worked in a pay reference period, usually of one month, should be counted. Some hours might be considered unproductive by employers who may wish to stipulate the arrangements for travelling sales representatives and employees who do a lot of informal evening work or business entertaining.

7.466 Times that are counted include the following.
- Time at work "at the disposal of the employer", including waiting and stoppage time.
- Travelling time, during working hours, to a place of work — including waiting time for the transport to arrive and spare time after the journey before actually starting work.
- Training time at the normal place of work or away from the normal place of work and the time taken to travel to the location.
- Standby time when the worker has actually been called out.

7.467 Times that are not counted include:
- rest periods during working hours
- breaks and lunch time
- holidays
- sickness absence
- industrial action
- contractual arrangements about lay-off or short-time working.

7.468 Recent case law has shown that sleeping time on the employer's premises may not count as time worked. See *Simap* and *Jaeger* rulings.

What Type is the Particular Worker's Job Arrangement?

7.469 The four types of work arrangement are:
- time work
- output work
- salaried work
- unmeasured work.

Time Work

7.470 Time work is when the presence of the worker is required ("at the employer's disposal") at specific times. The time counted will include non-productive time.

Output Work

7.471 Output work is work paid for by actual tangible results, eg production or sales and will include "payment by results" (PBR) schemes. Travelling time for commission-only sales staff will also be counted.

7.472 The employer will need to design any PBR scheme so that the NMW is realistically achievable and, in any event, the employer will have to pay for any shortfalls.

7.473 Home workers need a written agreement which provides a "fair estimate of hours" to achieve the anticipated output. From October 2004, this has been set at 80% of an average rated output work. The fair piece rate was initially set at 100% of the minimum wage and increased to 120% from April 2005, at which most homeworkers will receive the minimum wage.

Salaried Work and Annual Hours' Contracts

7.474 Salaried work applies to workers who are paid:
- evenly throughout the year
- for a contracted annual salary
- for a specified number of annual working hours.

7.475 The number of hours counted is potentially higher than for a "time worker" in the same time period, since it will include holidays, rest breaks, sickness, etc.

7.476 Hours worked in excess of the contracted basic hours must be included in any calculation. This can have significant impact on annual hours' contracts where the effective hourly rate is close to the NMW. For example, a worker on an annual hours' contract of 2040 hours per year and pay of £10,914 per year would be a marginal NMW case (£10,914 divided by 2040 is £5.35), but a worker on £15,000 is unlikely to fall below the NMW.

Unmeasured Work Time

7.477 Unmeasured work is where a worker is generally available all or much of the time, but not necessarily actually carrying out duties. Examples include wardens, pub managers and care workers. The rule is that if work does not fit the other three categories, this one applies. The employee's time actually working is difficult to measure, but there are two options.
1. Record the actual total hours worked.
2. Make a written agreement before the pay period starts that sets out the daily average number of hours.

How Many Hours Have Been Worked?

7.478 The regulations permit a maximum reference period of one calendar month, but employers can use four-weekly, fortnightly or weekly periods.

What is the Pay for the Work?

7.479 The regulations are specific about what can be included or deducted from pay counting towards the total in a pay reference period. The principles are as follows.
- Pay must be related to the specific pay reference period. Special provisions apply to irregular pay earned in one pay reference period, but not actually paid until a later pay reference period, eg bonuses, overtime, commissions, etc.
- Pay cannot be deferred by more than one pay reference period. This means, for example, that annual bonuses cannot be spread over the whole year for NMW purposes. If the pay reference period is monthly, $1/11$th of an annual bonus can be allocated for NMW purposes to the month before the bonus is actually given. The remaining $11/12$ths should then be incorporated into the actual bonus month.
- Pay relates to formal pay corresponding to a timesheet. Gratuities, such as directly-paid tips, are not counted.
- Employer-provided accommodation can be offset against pay counting towards the NMW. From 1 October 2006, this rose to £29.05 per week and will be raised again to £30.10 per week from 1 October 2007.

7.480 Payments excluded from gross pay include:
- the premium part of overtime or shift rates

National Minimum Wage

- a loan
- advance of wages
- pension payment
- lump sum on retirement
- redundancy payment
- rewards under staff suggestion scheme.

7.481 Payments that are not excluded include:
- incentive pay
- bonuses
- tips paid through the payroll
- income tax and employee's National Insurance contributions
- deduction or payment:
  - of a penalty
  - to repay a loan
  - to repay an advance of wages
  - to pay for purchase of shares or securities
  - to refund accidental overpayment of wages
- union subscriptions
- worker's pension contribution
- any deduction made by the employer but not for his or her use or benefit
- unforced payments by the worker for goods and services from the employer
- accommodation up to the permitted limit.

7.482 The employer is not expected to subsidise the employee for voluntary actions or honest mistakes.

Reductions and Deductions

7.483 Further basic rules protect both employer and employee.

7.484 Reductions make the pay counting towards the NMW calculation smaller, thereby helping the employee. They are largely to prevent cross-subsidy, so excluded from pay are overtime premiums, non-consolidated compensation allowances (eg shift allowances) and expenses for getting to the location.

7.485 Deductions enable the employer to claw back some of the pay. Essentially, whenever a non-voluntary deduction or direct payment is made it will not count towards the NMW calculation. This includes a variety of items such as:
- meals
- tools
- uniforms
- laundry
- materials
- fuel.

7.486 It also excludes deductions for accommodation charged above the stated limits. Fines for which the employee is contractually liable may be deducted.

What is the Hourly Rate of Pay?

7.487 The hourly rate of NMW pay for the pay reference period is the employee's gross pay divided by the eligible working hours.

Does this Rate Comply with the NMW?

7.488 A comparison of the NMW pay is made to the appropriate NMW category for the individual concerned.

Enforcement Provisions

7.489 Following are several enforcement provisions.
- HM Revenue & Customs has the responsibility for audit compliance to the NMW requirements.
- Employees can make a written request to see their own records. Employers must respond with 14 days or be fined, the payment going to the employee.
- Inspectors can require access to records and interviews with employees.
- Disputes are settled through an employment tribunal or through the civil courts. The burden of proof is on the employer.
- Employees are protected from unfair dismissal or victimisation as a result of NMW enquiries.
- Organisations may be fined through penalty notices that are set at twice the NMW rate for each employee for each day of non-compliance.
- There are six criminal offences each with a potential fine of £5000 for each offence.
  – Refusal or wilful neglect to pay NMW.
  – Failure to keep records.
  – Keeping false records.
  – Producing false records or information.
  – Intentional obstruction of enforcement officer.
  – Refusing or neglecting to give information to an enforcement officer.

Training

7.490 Training in NMW matters is required for payroll administrators and those in charge of employment matters. General awareness would be useful for managers controlling the hours of staff. Managers in charge of high-risk jobs close to the NMW should read the Department for Business, Enterprise and Regulatory Reform Employer guidance notes.

List of Relevant Legislation

7.491
- Employment Equality (Age) Regulations 2006
- National Minimum Wage Regulations 1999 (Amendment) Regulations 2005
- National Minimum Wage Regulations 1999
- Working Time Regulations 1998
- National Minimum Wage (Enforcement Notices) Act 2003
- National Minimum Wage Act 1998

List of Relevant Cases

7.492

- *Landeshauptstadt Kiel v Jaeger*C151/02 [2003] IRLR 804, ECJ — On call duty, including periods of sleep and rest, where doctors were required to be present in the hospital at which they worked constituted "working time" under Council Directive 93/104 on Working Time.
- *Davis v MJ Wyatt (Decorators) Ltd* [2000] IRLR 759 — Determines that an employer cannot make deductions from basic pay to fund holiday pay.
- *Laird v AK Stoddart Ltd* [2001] IRLR 591 — Determines that an employer is not permitted to unilaterally reduce other payments to increase the pay of employees in order to comply with NMW.
- *Simap v Conselleria de Sanidad y Consumo de la Generalidad Valenciana* [2000] IRLR 845 — Determined that the time a worker is on call and is required to be present at their workplace should be included in the calculation of that worker's average weekly working time.

Further Information

Publications

- Consultation documents: *A Detailed Guide to the National Minimum Wage*
- PL510 *A Short Guide for Employers and Employees*, Department for Business, Enterprise and Regulatory Reform (BERR)

Organisations

- **Department for Business, Enterprise and Regulatory Reform (BERR)**
  Web: *www.berr.gov.uk*
  The Department for Business, Enterprise and Regulatory Reform brings together functions from the former Department of Trade and Industry (DTI), including responsibilities for productivity, business relations, energy, competition and consumers. It also drives regulatory reform.
- **HM Revenue & Customs**
  Web: *www.hmrc.gov.uk/home.htm*
  HM Revenue & Customs (HMRC) is the department responsible for the business of the former Inland Revenue and HM Customs and Excise. HMRC is responsible for lecting the bulk of tax revenue as well as paying tax credits and child benefit.
- **Low Pay Commission (LPC)**
  The LPC was established as a result of the National Minimum Wage Act 1998 to advise the Government about the National Minimum Wage and assists employees and employers alike with advice.

PAYE and Income Tax

> This topic covers the following:
> - Taxable Income
> - Legal Obligations
> - Record Keeping
> - Operating PAYE
> - Gross Taxable Pay for PAYE purposes
> - Tax Codes for PAYE
> - K Codes
> - PAYE Tax Rates
> - Payment Due to the Collector of Taxes
> - Compulsory Electronic Payments
> - PAYE Year End Returns
> - Penalties and Fines
> - Late Submission
> - Completion Error
> - Compulsory Electronic Filing of Year End Returns

7.493 Pay As You Earn (PAYE) is a method of collecting from employees the income tax due on salaries and wages paid by employers. Employers act as the collecting agent for tax and National Insurance contributions each time an employee is paid.

7.494 At the end of the tax month the employer is required to pay over to the Collector of Taxes the PAYE tax and National Insurance collected from the employees together with the employer's National Insurance contributions.

7.495 Small employers can pay over the PAYE tax and National Insurance contributions every quarter rather than on the monthly basis, where the amount they are due to pay to the Collector each month is less than £1500.

7.496 The Income Tax (Pay As You Earn) Regulations 2003 covering the tax law rewrite became effective on 6 April 2004.

Employers' Duties

7.497 Employers have a duty to:
- operate PAYE properly, making correct deductions for income tax and National Insurance contributions
- keep proper records of pay
- record expenses and benefits paid to all employees
- pay the remittance to the Collector of Taxes either monthly or quarterly
- make complete and correct year end returns for all employees.

Employees' Duties

7.498 Employees have a duty to:
- pay PAYE on their earnings from employment

- notify HM Revenue & Customs of changes to their personal circumstances
- complete self-assessment tax returns where applicable
- supply their new employer with form P45 if they have received one from a previous employer
- complete a form P46 if they do not have a form P45.

In Practice

Taxable Income

7.499 Tax is charged on employment income under the Income Tax (Earnings and Pensions) Act 2003. This includes a contract of service, apprenticeship, holding an office and in the service of the Crown.

7.500 Tax is charged on employee earnings, such as salary, wages, fees, any gratuity or profit or incidental benefit of any kind.

7.501 There is no obligation to deduct tax from payments made to self-employed individuals.

Legal Obligations

7.502 Once an employer starts to pay an employee for doing work they have a legal obligation to set up a PAYE scheme with HM Revenue & Customs (HMRC). Employers have an obligation to:
- operate PAYE properly, making correct deductions for income tax and National Insurance contributions
- keep proper records of pay
- record expenses and benefits paid to employees
- pay the monthly or quarterly remittance to the Collector of Taxes
- make complete and correct year end returns for each employee.

Record Keeping

7.503 Under the PAYE Regulations an employer has a legal obligation to keep a record of the following, each time an employee is paid.
- Remuneration paid including reimbursed expenses and benefits.
- Tax deductions made or tax refunds given to employees.
- Working tax credits paid to employees.
- Student loan deductions collected from employees.
- National Insurance contributions, both the employer's and the employee's.
- Statutory sick pay, statutory maternity pay, statutory adoption pay and statutory paternity pay paid/recovered.
- Gross earnings on which National Insurance contributions are calculated.

7.504 These records must be kept for three years following the end of the tax year to which they relate.

Operating PAYE

7.505 Income tax under PAYE must be deducted from the employment income that an employee receives from holding an office or being in employment. Employment income would include all money changing hands from the employer to the employee. Salaries, wages, bonuses, commission, overtime, fees, statutory sick pay, statutory maternity pay, statutory adoption pay, statutory paternity pay, round sum allowances and cash vouchers are treated as employment income. Where non-cash benefits are provided to employees by the employer, such as a company car available for private use, free fuel for private use and private healthcare, these benefits equate to something that is of direct monetary value or capable of being converted into money by the employee. As such they count as general earnings and are also part of employment income. HM Revenue & Customs collects the tax due on these benefits in kind not directly through the payroll but by adjusting the employee's PAYE tax code.

Gross Taxable Pay for PAYE purposes

7.506 PAYE tax is calculated on the employee's gross pay less certain deductions. These deductions are contributions made, by the employee, into the HMRC approved company pension scheme, additional voluntary contributions into that pension scheme and charitable donations under Give As You Earn. The figure of gross pay less these deductions is known as the "gross taxable pay".

Tax Codes for PAYE

7.507 Each employee is entitled to take part of their gross taxable pay home "tax-free"; this tax-free figure is based on the employee's tax code. An employee's tax code is issued by HMRC and is calculated by reference to the employee's personal circumstances. Each tax year the Chancellor sets the personal allowances in the Budget. For 2007/08 the basic allowance is £5225, this means an employee can earn up to this figure before any tax is due. This allowance would give a tax code of 522L. This code means that an employee earning less than £100 a week and £435 a month will not pay any income tax. Blind people and individuals over 65 and 75 years of age receive additional personal allowances.

7.508 The Pay Adjustment Tables — Table A, issued by HM Revenue & Customs — are a ready reckoner designed so that the individual receives a proportion of their tax code allowance each pay-day throughout the year. The tables are in two parts for weekly and monthly pay periods. If the employee is paid two-weekly or four-weekly, the weekly tables are used at appropriate intervals. For tax code 522L, the tables show that an employee would be entitled to £436.51 take home tax-free each month or £100.74 each week.

7.509 Most tax codes operate on the cumulative basis, which means accumulating the employee's gross taxable pay figures in the tax year to date and then deducting the free pay allowance to date, based on the tax code, to give the taxable pay figure. Sometimes the tax code applicable will be operated on a non-cumulative basis, known as week one/month one. This means that the employee pays tax based only on the earnings for a specific tax week or month. In this case, the earnings in previous weeks and months are ignored when calculating the PAYE tax due for the pay period.

K Codes

7.510 K codes were introduced from 6 April 1993 to simplify the tax affairs of those employees whose personal allowances were exceeded by the taxable value of non-cash benefits, eg company car, fuel, BUPA. Previously in such cases the full amount of tax due on the benefits could not be deducted through the payroll as PAYE only operates on cash sums paid through the payroll. Any additional tax liability had

PAYE and Income Tax

to be collected from the individual after the tax year by HM Revenue & Customs. The purpose of the K code is to collect all the tax due by the employee via the payroll in the tax year.

7.511 The K tax code is calculated by HM Revenue & Customs in the exactly the same way as any other tax code based on the employee's individual circumstances. However this code represents an amount of "additional pay" which is added to the employee's gross taxable pay for the week or month prior to income tax being calculated. The K code is applied in the same way as a standard tax code except that the pay adjustment obtained from Table A is added to gross pay, rather than deducted, to arrive at taxable pay. The remaining steps in the calculation of tax continue as normal, subject to the "Overriding Regulatory Limit" (ORL). The ORL restricts the amount of tax that can be deducted in any one pay period to 50% of actual gross pay after deducting tax-free items. Any tax not recovered in one period will be carried forward to the next period for recovery, unless the code is being operated on a week one/month one basis.

PAYE Tax Rates

7.512 The PAYE income tax is calculated on taxable pay, being gross taxable pay less personal allowances, at the current tax rates for 2007/08. The current tax rates are 10% for the first £2230 of taxable pay, 22% for the next £32,370 (on income from £2231 to £34,600) and any remaining taxable pay over £34,600 is taxed at 40%.

Payment Due to the Collector of Taxes

7.513 Having deducted the PAYE tax and National Insurance from employees, the employer has a responsibility to pay over to the Collector of Taxes the sums collected, known as the remittance. This remittance is due for payment 14 days after the end of the tax month to which it relates, ie by the 19th of the following month. HM Revenue & Customs has the power to charge interest on the tax and National Insurance, not paid to the Collector on time during the tax year and at the tax year end. HM Revenue & Customs' current rate of interest, from 6 September 2004, is 7.5 %. Where payment is made electronically, a later deadline of 22nd of the month applies.

Compulsory Electronic Payments

7.514 From April 2004 large employers have been required to make their monthly remittance payments to the Collector of Taxes electronically. A large employer is one with 250 or more employees. Smaller employers will be required to make their payments electronically at a later date yet to be announced. HM Revenue & Customs will issue "e-payment notices" to employers at the same time as issuing "e-filing notices" from 2004/05. An employer can appeal against an "e-payment notice" if it believes it is not a large employer. Employers can chose between using the BACS (Bankers Automated Credit System) and CHAPS (Clearing House Automated Payments System).

7.515 The payment deadline is 22nd for electronic payments, ie 17 days after the tax month end, and penalties are imposed if the payments are made late. "In year" surcharges apply for late payment and there is also be a default surcharge structure providing for penalties in respect of late payment of PAYE income tax and National Insurance contributions during the tax year. Where an employer is late with a payment this will trigger a default surcharge notice. The surcharge will be based on the total amount of tax due for the tax year and calculated on a set percentage. The surcharge period begins the day after the first late payment and continues until payments have been made on time for a complete tax year.

PAYE and Income Tax

7.516 The rates of surcharge are:

Up to two defaults	0%
3–5 defaults	0.17%
6–8 defaults	0.33%
9–11 defaults	0.58%
12 and subsequent defaults	0.83%

Where defaults have occurred the surcharge notice will be issued to the employer at the end of the tax year and the surcharge is payable within 30 days of issue, subject to any appeal by the employer.

PAYE Year End Returns

7.517 Each employer is responsible for reporting to HMRC at the end of the tax year information on the individuals employed during the tax year. There are three principal returns which must be submitted to HMRC.
1. Form P14/60, Return of Pay, Tax and National Insurance Contributions. This form is prepared for each employee, including leavers, for whom a payroll record, form P11 (Deduction Working Sheet) or computerised equivalent has been maintained. The forms are submitted with the form P35 to HMRC following the end of the tax year to which they relate. The form is a three-part document, the first two pages, the P14, are sent to HMRC, the last page, the P60, should be given to the employee after the end of the tax year. Employees who were in employment at 5 April must receive their P60s by 31 May from their employer.
2. Form P35, Employer's Annual Statement, Declaration and Certificate. This must be filed by 19 May following the end of the tax year, together with the P14. This document lists all the employees for the tax year including leavers and shows the tax, tax credits, student loan deductions, National Insurance contributions, statutory sick pay, statutory maternity pay, statutory adoption pay and statutory paternity pay paid and recovered in respect of those employees. It also records the total remittance paid to the Collector of Taxes during the year.
3. Form P11D or P9D, Return of Expenses and Benefits. This must be filed by the 6 July following the tax year to which the items relate. The form lists all the expenses and benefits provided to an employee during a tax year. The P11D is used for most directors and employees earning at a rate of £8500 per annum or more, including benefits and expenses. The P9D is used for employees earning at a rate of less than £8500 per annum.

Penalties and Fines

7.518 There are penalties for filing the documents late and or completing them incorrectly, whether fraudulently or by mistake.

Late Submission

7.519 For forms P35 and P14/60 there is an automatic penalty of £100 for each group of 50 employees, or part thereof, for each month, or part thereof, that filing is late up to a maximum of 12 months; plus 100% of any PAYE tax and National Insurance contributions outstanding at the tax year end.

7.520 For forms P11D/P9D there is a potential initial fine for late submission of £300 per document plus a further £60 per document per day that failure to file continues. Late filing of form P11D(b) will incur a penalty of £100 per month per 50 employees.

Completion Error

7.521 The fine for a fraudulently or negligently completed form P9/P11D is a maximum £3000 per document. For forms P35 and P14, the maximum penalty is 100% of the tax underpaid.

Compulsory Electronic Filing of Year End Returns

7.522 As part of modernising PAYE procedures employers will be required by law to file their year end returns, forms P14 and P35, electronically in the future. A timetable has been set requiring larger employers to comply at an earlier date than smaller employers. The dates for the change are as follows:
- employers with more than 250 employees — tax year 2004/05
- employers with between 50 and 249 employees — tax year 2005/06
- employers with less than 50 employees — tax year 2009/10.

7.523 Penalties will be imposed where employers that are required to file electronically after having received a notice to do so fail to comply with the notice. The fine is based on the number of employees working for the employer, eg the penalty for non e-filing for an employer with 1000 or more employees will be £3000.

7.524 As an incentive for small employers with less than 50 employees to move to e-filing sooner, HMRC will make a payment to such employers. The incentive payment is £250 for 2004/05 and 2005/06, £150 for 2006/07, £100 for 2007/08 and £75 for 2008/09. If a small employer moved to e-filing for the tax year 2004/05 it would receive the incentive payment each year making a total payment from HMRC of £825.

Training

7.525 It is important that all HR and payroll staff understand the employer's responsibilities under PAYE legislation and regulations. Training should ensure that staff involved with HR and payroll matters:
- understand the regulations and law relating to PAYE deductions
- obtain full information from new employees on forms P45 or P46
- have full knowledge of the meaning of "employment income"
- know the records that an employer must maintain for PAYE purposes
- understand what expenses and benefits have to be reported to HMRC
- know the year end procedure for completion of forms P35 and P14.

List of Relevant Legislation

7.526
- Income Tax (Pay As You Earn) Regulations 2003
- Income Tax (Earnings and Pensions) Act 2003

Further Information

Organisations
- **HM Revenue & Customs**
  Web: *www.hmrc.gov.uk/home.htm*
  HM Revenue & Customs (HMRC) is the department responsible for the business of the former Inland Revenue and HM Customs and Excise. HMRC is responsible for lecting the bulk of tax revenue as well as paying tax credits and child benefit.
- **Department for Work and Pensions (DWP)**
  Web: *www.dwp.gov.uk*
  The DWP is responsible for the Government's welfare reform agenda. Its aim is to promote opportunity and independence for all.

Pensions

This topic covers the following.
- Pension Reform
- Unified Pension Tax Regime from 6 April 2006
- Registered Pension Schemes
- Contracting-Out
- Commercial Pension Schemes
- Pre "A-Day" Schemes
- Tax Relief for Employer Contributions to Registered Pension Schemes
- Investments by Occupational Schemes
- Pension Age
- Age Discrimination
- Administration Issues
- Records
- Registered Pension Scheme Returns
- State Retirement Pension
- Private Pension Provision – No General Duty
- Work-Based Pension Provisions
- Occupational Pension Schemes
- Group Personal Pension Schemes
- Stakeholder Pension Schemes
- Access Requirements
- Relevant Employees
- Exempt Employers
- Deduction from Payroll
- Direct Payment Arrangements
- Payment Record
- Monitoring Payments
- Penalties for Non-Compliance
- Pension Regulation and Protection
- Pensions Advice Tax Exemption
- Pension Inducement Payments
- Settlor of a Trust
- Member-Nominated Trustees
- Implied Duty of Good Faith
- Employment Law Protection for Trustees
- Schedule of Contributions / Payment Schedules
- Contracting Out – Duty to Consult
- Equal Treatment
- Civil Partnerships
- Dispute Resolution
- Pensions Commission

7.527 Work-based private pension provision may take a variety of forms but will generally seek to provide employees with some or all of the following benefits.
- An income stream that will come into payment at some point to the individual member and then continue in payment for the rest of that individual's life, ie the pension.
- A one-off, tax-free lump sum that will be available to the member, usually as a result of the member having chosen in exchange to give up part of the pension rights at the point that the pension is due to come into payment, ie the retirement lump sum.
- A one-off, tax-free, lump sum payable to a third party upon the death of the member before his or her pension has come into payment, ie a death benefit lump sum.

Pensions

- A pension payable to a financial dependant of the member upon the death of the member, whether this is before or after the member's pension has come into payment, ie a dependant's pension.

Employers' Duties

7.528 Employers have a duty to:
- ensure that the pension rules are understood and the necessary processes are in place to accommodate the changes
- check pension scheme rules regularly and make any necessary changes that need to be made in the light of changes to the legislation
- communicate the impact of any legislative changes to employees
- comply with requirements under the simplified pension tax regime applying from 6 April 2006
- pay over Class 1 National Insurance contributions under PAYE so that the employee's right to the basic state pension and state second pension (S2P) is established and maintained
- designate a stakeholder pensions scheme for access by any relevant employees unless the employer is exempted
- comply with the legislative requirements whenever it has entered into a direct payment arrangement
- make payments to a personal pension scheme on behalf of any of its employees where appropriate
- ensure that the promotion of regulated products such as personal pensions and stakeholder pension schemes to employees complies with financial services legislation, although employers who contribute to such schemes can be exempted from the rules governing financial promotions
- comply with their duty as settlor of a trust under the law of trusts whenever establishing an occupational pension scheme
- comply with the employment law principle of the employer's implied duty of good faith when exercising powers under the trust deed and rules of an occupational pension scheme
- comply with the employment law protection measures in relation to trustees
- observe the schedule of contributions or payment schedule relating to employee's occupational pension schemes
- comply with any other requirements of the Pensions Acts 1995 and 2004 or other legislation governing private pension provision
- comply with the age discrimination regulations relating to occupational pension schemes from 1 December 2006
- consider scheme rules in light of the age discrimination regulations and modify scheme rules, if necessary, to include a non-discrimination clause
- unless a specific exemption from the age discrimination regulations exists, ensure that any age discrimination can be objectively justified
- consult with employees when intending to change the nature of the pension provision as required by the Pensions Act 2004.

Employees' Duties

7.529 The main duties of employees are to:
- supply the scheme administrators, often via the employer, with any required information and documentation and to agree to the deduction from their earnings of any required employee contributions
- advise the employer if they wish to contract out of the State Second Pension (S2P).

In Practice

Pension Reform

7.530 It has long been recognised that an ageing population creates a number of challenges, not least in providing security in retirement. In December 2002, the Government set up an independent pensions commission to review the longer-term challenges faced by the pension system and to make recommendations for reform.

7.531 The commission published its findings in November 2004 and set out proposals for meeting the challenge of providing a fair and adequate retirement income for all. This was followed by the National Pensions Debate, in which the views of the public were sought, culminating in National Pensions Day on 18 March 2006.

7.532 In May 2006, the Government published a White Paper, "Security in retirement: towards a new pension system", on which views were sought. The consultation period ran until September 2006.

7.533 The Pensions Bill was published in November 2006, legislates for long-term pension reforms and includes the following measures.
- Restoring the link between the basic state pension and earnings.
- Reducing the number of years it takes to build a basic state pension to 30 years for everyone who reaches pension age from 6 April 2010. It currently takes 44 years for a man and 39 years for a woman to build a basic state pension.
- Making it easier for parents and carers to build a basic state pension.
- Simplifying and improving access to the second state pension.
- Increasing the state pension age over time from 2024 to reflect increasing longevity and to support extending working lives.
- Establishing a delivery authority to start the process for personal accounts.
- Streamlining the regulation of private pensions to make it easier for people to plan and save for retirement.

7.534 The Bill received Royal Assent on 27 July 2007. The measures outlined above will now be introduced under the Pensions Act 2007. For further information, see *www.dwp.gov.uk/pensionsreform*.

Unified Pension Tax Regime from 6 April 2006

7.535 A unified pension tax regime applies from 6 April 2006 ("A-Day"). The unified regime replaced the eight tax regimes that existed prior to that date. Under the unified regime there is a single set of rules that apply to tax-privileged pension savings.

7.536 Employers must ensure that they both understand and comply with the rules.

7.537 For the purposes of the regime, a pension scheme is defined as a scheme or other arrangement that provides benefits to or in respect of a person: on retirement; death; having reached a particular age; on serious ill-health or incapacity; or in similar circumstances. A registered pension scheme is one that is registered with HM Revenue & Customs (HMRC). The tax advantages are only available to registered pension schemes.

7.538 An occupational pension scheme is a specific category of registered pension scheme. Broadly, an occupational pension scheme is one that is established by an employer or employers and which provides benefits for the employees of the employer or employers concerned. More restrictions and conditions apply to occupational pension schemes than to other types of registered pension scheme because of the close relationship between the employer and the employees.

7.539 An employer who establishes or participates in an occupational pension scheme is known as the sponsoring employer. There may be more than one sponsoring employer in relation to an occupational pension scheme. An occupational scheme is subject to special administration requirements.

7.540 Employers can set up their own scheme to provide pension benefits or can join with other employers to set up a pension scheme. If the scheme meets certain conditions it can be registered with HMRC and benefit from the tax advantages available to registered schemes.

7.541 Alternatively, employers can provide pension benefits by means of a scheme established by a financial institution, such as an insurance organisation or bank, rather than setting up their own scheme.

7.542 There is no specific method for setting up a pension scheme. However, the scheme will need a set of rules that cover:
- the types of benefits that are to be provided through the scheme
- how these are to be funded
- when they may be paid
- to whom they may be paid; and
- how the funds may be invested.

Registered Pension Schemes

7.543 To be registered with HMRC as a registered pension scheme, the scheme administrator must provide a declaration that the scheme rules do not offer any person a benefit that is not authorised by HMRC.

7.544 To become a registered pension scheme, certain conditions must be met. In addition:
- the documentation must provide for the appointment of a scheme administrator (there can be more than one scheme administrator); and
- the scheme administrator must be resident in the UK, EU or in an EEA country that is not a member of the EU.

7.545 There are no restrictions on where the scheme may be established.

7.546 The scheme administrator must make the application for registration of the scheme. However, once the scheme has been registered, the scheme administrator can appoint an agent or practitioner to act on behalf of the scheme.

7.547 Registration of the scheme should be done online through the Pension Scheme Service on the HMRC website.

7.548 At the time of registration the administrator can also register to claim tax relief through the relief at source procedure and can apply to contract out.

7.549 The scheme administrator is responsible for fulfilling certain functions and duties in relation to the scheme, including:
- registering the pension scheme with HMRC
- operating tax relief at source on contributions to the pension scheme by claiming tax relief back from HMRC
- completing documents, delivering a pension scheme return and providing accounts, statements and other documents in connection with the return if required by HMRC
- completing certain reports and providing certain information to HMRC as specified in the Register Pension Scheme (Provision of Information) Regulations 2004
- providing information to other people, ie insurers, personal representatives, etc
- accounting for and making quarterly returns of tax under the Finance Act 2004, Part 4
- appealing, if necessary, against decisions of HMRC under the Finance Act 2004, Part 4.

7.550 The scheme administrator is the person liable to certain tax charges under the Finance Act 2004, Part 4. Charges may arise, for example, where there is an unauthorised payment from the scheme to either the sponsoring employer or a member. Where there is more than one scheme administrator, the scheme administrators are jointly and severally liable for any charges and penalties.

7.551 A scheme does not have to be registered with HMRC. However, registration offers tax advantages. However, the tax reliefs are only available up to certain limits.

7.552 There are two controls on the amount of tax relieved savings that an individual can contribute to a registered pension regime. The allowances are as follows:

Annual allowance

Tax year	Annual Allowance
2007/08	£225,000
2008/09	£235,000
2009/10	£245,000
2010/11	£255,000

Lifetime allowance

Tax year	Lifetime Allowance
2007/08	£1,600,000
2008/09	£1,650,000
2009/10	£1,750,000
2010/11	£1,800,000

7.553 If total contributions each year exceed the annual allowance, the excess is taxed at 40%. Similarly, a tax charge arises if pension savings exceed the lifetime allowance. This charge is set at 25% if the additional savings are taken as a pension and at 55% if they are taken as a lump sum.

Pensions

7.554 Individuals are entitled to tax relief on contributions to a maximum of 100% of UK taxable earnings. Employers are entitled to tax relief for contributions they make to a registered pension scheme.

7.555 Individuals can simultaneously be a member of more than one pension scheme. This means that, for example, they may be able to participate in both an occupational scheme and a personal pension scheme.

7.556 An occupational scheme that is not registered is treated as an employer-funded retirement benefit scheme and treated for tax purposes accordingly.

Contracting-Out

7.557 The state pension comprises two elements: a basic state pension and an additional state pension (known as the state second pension (S2P)). A private pension scheme can take responsibility from the state for the provision of the state second pension for some or all of the members. Employees can choose to "contract-out" of the state second pension.

7.558 Contracted-out workers pay National Insurance contributions at a lower rate and receive only the basic state pension. The employer also pays reduced rate contributions. If the scheme is a money purchase scheme, the employer also pays a monthly amount, known as a "minimum payment" to the scheme trustee in respect of each contracted-out employee by the 19th of each month. HMRC also pays a rebate to the scheme in respect of each employee, based on his or her age.

7.559 The contracting out process can be effected online using HMRC's Pension Scheme Service.

Commercial Pension Schemes

7.560 An employer does not have to provide an occupational pension scheme. Alternatively, the employer may choose to offer employees the option to join a commercial scheme. If this option is chosen, the employer needs to decide whether to offer membership of an appropriate personal pension scheme or a scheme that is not contracted-out and to select a scheme accordingly.

7.561 All stakeholder pension plans and many personal pension plans are contracted out appropriate personal pension schemes (APP). Where the APP route is chosen, it is up to each individual member to decide whether to contract out of the state second pension. As the employer is not running the scheme, no further involvement in the contacting out process is required. The employer continues to pay National Insurance contributions at the usual rate to HMRC and HMRC pays a rebate, known as a minimum contribution, to the scheme.

Pre "A-Day" Schemes

7.562 A scheme that had tax approval prior to "A-Day" (6 April 2006) is automatically treated as a registered pension scheme on 6 April 2006. The same is true of former approved superannuation funds.

7.563 In the event that it is preferred that a pre "A-Day" tax-approved scheme is not a registered pension scheme, HMRC must be notified accordingly. If the opt-out notification was not received by HMRC by 6 April 2006, the scheme is automatically treated as a registered scheme from that date. Where a scheme opts out of registration, a 40% tax charge applies on the value of scheme funds.

7.564 After 6 April 2006 an ongoing scheme can only become unregistered if HMRC withdraws registration. This will trigger a 40% tax charge.

7.565 Unapproved schemes in existence before A-Day, such as funded unapproved retirement benefit schemes (FURBS) or unfunded unapproved retirement benefit schemes (UURBS), do not automatically become registered on A-Day. However, such schemes can apply for registration if the registration conditions are met.

Tax Relief for Employer Contributions to Registered Pension Schemes

7.566 There is no limit on the amount that an employer may contribute to a registered pension scheme. There is no set limit on the amount of tax relief that an employer may receive for contributions to a registered pension scheme. However, the relief is not automatic. Relief for pension contributions follows the normal rules for business expenditure.

7.567 Special rules apply when a large one-off contribution is made. Under these rules the tax relief may be spread over several years, rather than given in full in the year in which the contribution was made.

Investments by Occupational Schemes

7.568 Special tax rules apply to investments made by occupational pension schemes that involve certain transactions with the sponsoring employer. There are few restrictions on the types of investments that an occupational pension scheme can make, provided that they are made for commercial reasons. The scheme administrator is responsible for investment decisions.

7.569 Rules are in place to govern the making of loans to the sponsoring employer, pension scheme borrowings and the holdings of shares.

7.570 Where an unauthorised payment is made, a tax charge of 40% of the unauthorised payment is levied. For example, loans made to the employer that do not meet the five tests laid down in the regulations constitute an unauthorised payment and the employer would suffer a 40% tax charge.

7.571 If the unauthorised payment exceeds 25% of the fund value, a surcharge of 15% of the unauthorised payment is also due.

7.572 Tax charges will arise in the following circumstances:
- when the percentage limits for share investments are exceeded
- when a loan to the employer fails to meet the five tests set out in the legislation
- when there is a transaction with the employer that is not at arm's length
- when the borrowing limits are exceeded; and
- where value is shifted out of the pension scheme.

7.573 All unauthorised payments must be notified to HMRC by the scheme administrator by means of an event report. The employer is obliged to report details on any unauthorised payment.

7.574 Where the scheme administrator advises the employer that an authorised payment has been made from the scheme to the employer, the employer must notify HMRC no later than 31 January after the end of the tax year in which the payment was made, of the:
- scheme that made the payment
- nature of the payment
- amount of the payment
- date on which the payment was made.

7.575 The notification should be made to the tax office that deals with the organisation's corporation tax affairs.

7.576 Interest is payable on any tax paid late. Penalties may also be charged if a return is fraudulently or negligently incorrect.

Pension Age

7.577 A scheme must not allow members of a registered pension scheme to take any benefits before they reach the normal pension age. This is age 50 prior to 6 April 2010 and 55 after 5 April 2010. A member does not need to retire to take benefits provided that the normal pension age has been reached. Separate rules apply to pensions paid on grounds of ill health or retirements due to ill health.

7.578 There is no maximum age by which a pension must be taken but stricter rules apply to how benefits can be taken after the age of 75. Where the scheme allows for a tax-free pension commencement lump sum, this must be taken before the member's 75th birthday. If taken after this date, the tax charge on unauthorised payments applies.

7.579 Under the age discrimination regulations — the Employment Equality (Age) Regulations 2006 — an employee has the right to request to continue to work beyond retirement age. The employer has a duty to consider that request.

Age Discrimination

7.580 The Employment Equality (Age) Regulations 2006 prohibit age discrimination in employment and vocational training. The regulations provide compliance with an EU Directive requiring EU countries to outlaw age discrimination by 2 December 2006.

7.581 The regulations apply for pension scheme purposes from 1 December 2006.

7.582 As a result of the regulations, since 1 December 2006, it is unlawful — in relation to pensions — for pension schemes, trustees and employers to discriminate against or harass members or potential members on the basis of age.

7.583 Unless a specific exemption applies, age discrimination in pension schemes is only now lawful if such discrimination can be objectively justified.

7.584 From 1 December 2006, every occupational pension scheme is to be treated as including a non-discrimination rule and managers and trustees are given the power to alter schemes to comply with this rule.

7.585 The regulations introduce a default retirement age of 65. This makes compulsory retirement before the age of 65 unlawful, unless a lower compulsory retirement age can be objectively justified. However, employees have a right to request to continue to work beyond the age of 65 and where such a request is made, employers have a duty to consider that request.

7.586 The Government recognises that pension schemes necessarily have age-related limits and include a number of exemptions to ensure that pension arrangements are disturbed as little as possible, while simultaneously guarding against unjustified age discrimination. The exemptions applying to pension schemes are contained in schedule 2 of the regulations.

7.587 The following age-related rules or practices in occupational pension schemes are effectively exempted from the age discrimination legislation.

- Age-related contributions to defined benefit schemes where contributions increase with age to reflect the increasing cost of benefits in respect of members as they get older.
- Age-related contributions to occupational and personal pension schemes, aimed at producing equal or near equal outcome in pension benefits.
- Flat-rate employer contributions to occupational pension schemes.
- The use of age criteria in actuarial calculations.
- Different amounts of pensions for workers with different lengths of service, provided that for each year of service rights to benefits accrue on the same fraction of pensionable pay.
- A lower age limit below which a scheme member cannot receive an enhanced pension in the event of early retirement — but for existing employees only.
- Different rates of employer contributions to occupational and personal pension schemes for different workers, which are attributable to differences in the remuneration payable to these workers.

7.588 The age discrimination regulations do not affect the state pension, National Insurance rebates, pension sharing on divorce or annuities purchased from insurance companies.

Administration Issues

7.589 Where an authorised payment is made to an employer, the employer must provide details to HMRC by 31 January following the end of the tax year in which the payment was made.

7.590 HMRC can also issue a notice requiring that the sponsoring employer produce or make available certain documents for the period specified in the notice (the Finance Act 2004, s. 252(1) and associated regulations). Documents can be requested in relation to any matter relating to:

- a registered pension scheme
- a pension scheme that has ceased to be a registered pension scheme
- a pension scheme in relation to which an application for registration has been made; or
- an annuity purchased with sums or assets held for the purposes of a registered pension scheme.

7.591 The information must be requested within the period ending six years from the end of the tax year in which the event occurred. The sponsoring employer is given 30 days to produce the information. Such a notice may be given electronically if the employer has consented to electronic communication.

7.592 Where the sponsoring employer is issued with such a notice, the scheme administrator will be informed.

7.593 An employer other than the sponsoring employer can be issued with a notice to produce documents within their possession relating to any matter relating to:

- a registered pension scheme
- a pension scheme that has ceased to be a registered pension scheme
- a pension scheme in relation to which an application for registration has been made; or
- an annuity purchased with sums or assets held for the purposes of a registered pension scheme.

7.594 The request will not relate to documents issued more than six years before the date of the notice. As with notices issued to the sponsoring employer, the non-sponsoring employer is given 30 days to comply. Again, the notice may be issued electronically if the non-sponsoring employer has consented to electronic communication.

7.595 A right of appeals exists against requests to produce documents. An appeal must be lodged within 30 days of the notice. The right of appeal is normal to the general commissions. Where an appeal is lodged, the employer does not need to provide particulars while the appeal is pending.

Records

7.596 The sponsoring employer or the director of an employer's organisation is required to keep certain records in relation to a registered occupational pension scheme.

7.597 Records and documents that relate to:
- any monies received by or owing to the scheme
- any investments or assets held by the scheme
- any payments made by the scheme
- any contracts to purchase a lifetime annuity in respect of a member of the scheme; or
- the administration of the scheme

must be kept for the tax year to which they relate and the following six tax years.

Registered Pension Scheme Returns

7.598 A return must be submitted each year to HMRC in respect of a registered pension scheme. The return is due by 31 January after the end of the tax year to which the return relates, or, if later, three months from the date of the notice requiring that the return be made.

7.599 The responsibility for making the return rests with the scheme administrator.

State Retirement Pension

7.600 Employers are under a duty to:
- pay Class 1 secondary National Insurance contributions
- collect Class 1 primary National Insurance contributions from employees

and pass these on to HMRC.

Payment of Class 1 National Insurance contributions each year will go towards establishing employees' entitlement to be paid state retirement pension on reaching state pension age (currently age 60 for women and age 65 for men). Full pension age equality for men and women at 65 will have arrived by 2020. Women born before 6 April 1950 retain 60 as their pension age, while women born between then and 5 March 1955 have been notified of a pension age between 60 and 65.

The state retirement pension comprises two elements, the:
- basic state pension
- additional pension, now provided by the State Second Pension (S2P).

7.601 Entitlement to the basic state pension is based on the payment of National Insurance contributions for a minimum number of qualifying years. Those who have had caring responsibilities need fewer qualifying years. Contributions can be topped up by the payment of voluntary (Class 3) contributions.

7.602 Entitlement to the additional pension depends on the level of the employee's earnings. However, the current system is designed so that employees on lower earnings receive a larger additional pension as a proportion of earnings than those on higher earnings.

7.603 An employee's additional pension entitlement will be reduced if his or her employment is contracted out of the S2P through the employee's membership of a contracted-out occupational pension scheme. It will also be reduced if, alternatively, an employee chooses individually to contract out through membership of a special kind of personal pension known as an Appropriate Personal Pension.

7.604 Employees can at any time obtain a forecast of their state pension entitlement by completing Form BR19, available from local Department for Work and Pensions offices.

7.605 The state pension is to be reformed (see Pension Reform). The link with earnings is to be restored and the number of years to build a basic state pension is to be reduced to 30 years for people reaching retirement age from 2010. Access to the second state pension is to be improved and the second state pension is to be simplified. However, the state pension age is to be increased over time from 2024 to reflect increased longevity.

Private Pension Provision — No General Duty

7.606 Currently, there is no duty on employers to contribute to the provision of any private pension scheme on behalf of their employees. An exception relates to employees protected by the Transfer of Undertakings (Protection of Employees) Regulations 2005 (TUPE). If they were, or could have become, members of their previous employer's work-based scheme they must be offered pension accrual rights by their new employer which can derive from either a:

- final salary occupational scheme at least capable of meeting the requirements for contracting-out of the S2P, or
- money purchase scheme in which the new employer matches the employee's contributions up to 6% of earnings.

Work-Based Pension Provisions

7.607 The main forms of work-based pension provision are as follows.
- The employer agrees to make a direct contribution into the personal pension or into the stakeholder pension scheme individually chosen by an employee.
- The employer designates a stakeholder pension scheme for the use of some or all of its employees.
- The employer establishes a group personal pension arrangement for the use of some or all of its employees.
- The employer establishes an occupational pension scheme for the use of some or all of its employees.

Occupational Pension Schemes

7.608 Occupational schemes can be set up as:
- a *final salary scheme* where the eventual pension payable will be related to the member's length of pensionable service and to his or her final pensionable earnings shortly before the pension is to come into payment

- an *average salary scheme* where the eventual pension payable will be related to the member's pensionable earnings in each year of membership but with each year's earnings being revalued against some suitable index to protect to some extent their real value
- a *cash balance scheme* where each year a cash balance equal to a defined percentage of the employee's pensionable earnings is allocated to the member's account, and with this amount being revalued against some suitable index to protect to some extent its real value and where the cumulative cash balance is eventually used to secure a pension (eg by buying an annuity from an insurance company)
- a *defined contribution occupational pension scheme* where cash contributions are allocated to each member's accounts and are invested in a fund and if the eventual capital sum invested, less any investment or management charges, is used to secure a pension (eg by buying an annuity from an insurance company). These schemes are often referred to as "money purchase schemes".

7.609 Although no longer required to do so by statute, occupational schemes conventionally offer an Additional Voluntary Contribution (AVC) facility whereby employees can boost their pension rights by paying additional voluntary contributions, sometimes with a direct or indirect employer's subsidy. However, the introduction of stakeholder pensions and the ability to have more than one type of tax-relieved pension plan provided that overall limits are not exceeded has reduced the popularity of additional voluntary contributions.

7.610 An occupational scheme that has tax approval prior to 6 April 2006 automatically becomes a registered pension scheme under the new regime applying from that date and benefits from the associated tax advantages.

Group Personal Pension Schemes

7.611 A Group Personal Pension (GPP) arrangement describes the situation where a particular personal pension scheme which is the product of a particular provider, usually an insurance company, is promoted to the employees of a particular employer or of a particular group of employers.

7.612 A GPP arrangement does not have any legal identity itself. The basis of any GPP arrangement is still a contract between the personal pension provider and each individual member.

7.613 The employer and the employee may also have entered into a contractual relationship (as part of the contract of employment) for the employer to make a contribution to the employee's personal pension.

Stakeholder Pension Schemes

7.614 An employer which is not an exempt employer is under a duty to designate a stakeholder pension scheme for use by any of its employees who do not have access to an occupational pension scheme. The duty is imposed by the Welfare Reform and Pensions Act 1999.

7.615 A stakeholder pension is a type of flexible, low-charge and penalty-free personal pension that can be bought from a commercial financial services company.

Access Requirements

7.616 The access requirements of a stakeholder pension scheme are to:
- designate a stakeholder pension scheme after consultation with the employees concerned or their representatives

- inform those employees which stakeholder pension scheme has been designated
- allow representatives from the stakeholder pension scheme reasonable access to the employees to promote the scheme
- operate a payroll service so that employees, if they wish, can make their own contributions directly to the stakeholder pension via a deduction from their earnings.

Relevant Employees

7.617 A relevant employee is any employee who is not in membership of an occupational pension scheme but who earns at least at the rate of the lower earnings limit (LEL).

7.618 If the employer has no relevant employees, it does not have to designate a stakeholder pension scheme.

7.619 The Stakeholder Pension Scheme Regulations 2001 set out a list of employees who are *not* to be regarded as relevant employees. The access requirement does not apply in their case. Employees who are *not* relevant employees are those:
- who will qualify to join an occupational pension scheme after a waiting period of no more than 12 months
- who will qualify to join an occupational pension scheme when they reach age 18
- who will not now qualify to join an occupational pension scheme because they are less than five years away from the scheme's normal pension age
- who could have joined the occupational pension scheme in the past but declined to do so and are now excluded from membership as a result or who had been a member of the occupational pension scheme but opted out of membership and now as a result are excluded from the scheme
- who have been continuously employed for less than three months
- whose earnings have fallen below the LEL for one or more weeks within the last three months
- who would be ineligible to contribute to a stakeholder pension scheme because they are not at present resident in the UK.

Exempt Employers

7.620 Two classes of employers are exempt from the access requirements of a stakeholder pension scheme.

7.621 The first class of exempt employers comprises any employer with fewer than five employees. An employer with fewer than five employees does not have to offer those employees access to the stakeholder pension. If that employer takes on extra employees to take its total number of employees to five or more, it will then have three months in which to comply with the access requirements.

7.622 The second class of exempt employers are those where there is a term in the contract of employment of every relevant employee over age 18 that specifies that the employer will contribute to a personal pension scheme in respect of that employee of an amount not less than 3% of that employee's gross basic pay, ie the employee's pay excluding bonuses, commission, overtime and similar payments.

7.623 The contract of employment may make this employer contribution conditional on the employee also making a minimum contribution. If this conditional arrangement was already in place on 8 October 2001, the employer's contribution must be equal to, or more than, the employee's contribution. If the condition came into effect on or after 8 October 2001, it must not stipulate that the employee has to pay more than 3% of gross basic pay into his or her personal pension.

7.624 This arrangement will only exempt the employer from the access requirements if the personal pension also does not impose any form of exit charge or penalty on employees who cease to contribute to the scheme or who transfer any funds out of the scheme.

Deduction from Payroll

7.625 An employee who wishes to contribute to the designated stakeholder pension scheme via the employer's payroll must be offered this service.

7.626 Employees have a right to have their contributions cease and the employer must comply by the end of the pay period following the one in which any request to stop paying contributions was made.

7.627 The employer could then impose a six-month period before being obliged to deduct further contributions from an employee's pay. In general, employers can limit any variation in the amount to be deducted in the case of any one employee to one change every six months. These conditions must be given in writing by the employer to the employee when the employee first asks to have contributions deducted.

7.628 Any contributions deducted from an employee's pay must be passed to the stakeholder pension scheme by the 19th day of the calendar month following the month in which they were deducted.

7.629 For new and expanding businesses who may need to offer their employees access to a pension scheme, the Pensions Regulator has produced an information pack: *Pensions Choice in the Workplace*. This pack contains step-by-step guides to setting up a stakeholder pension scheme and paying contributions, and also includes sample letters and a poster that employers can adapt when consulting and informing their staff about stakeholder provision.

Direct Payment Arrangements

7.630 An employer who enters into a direct payment arrangement has a duty to comply with the requirements of the Welfare Reform and Pensions Act 1999 and the Personal Pension Schemes (Payments by Employers) Regulations 2000. A direct payment arrangement is any arrangement where contributions fall to be paid by or on behalf of the employer to a personal pension scheme on:
- the employer's own account but in respect of the employee, and/or
- behalf of the employee out of deductions from the employee's earnings.

Payment Record

7.631 Where there is a direct payment arrangement, the employer must ensure that there is a record of the direct payment arrangement which shows the rates and due dates of contributions to be paid. The record must be maintained and revised when appropriate. The record must include separate entries for the rates of contributions payable on the employer's own account and those deducted from employees' earnings. The contributions may be shown as either a percentage of salary or as a fixed monetary amount. The employer's contribution is paid gross while contributions deducted from the employee's earnings will be net of tax.

7.632 The due date in respect of any contributions payable on the employer's own account is the latest date listed in the direct payment arrangement for paying them.

Pensions

In the case of contributions deducted from employees' earnings, the due date is the 19th day of the calendar month following the end of the month in which the deduction was made.

7.633 Having drawn up the record of payments due, the employer must then send a copy of that record to the personal or stakeholder pension provider before the first contribution payable is due for payment.

Monitoring Payments

7.634 The personal pension provider must monitor the payments made under each record.

7.635 The provider must notify the employee or employees concerned if the payment has still not been made within 60 days from the day following that due date. In cases of such a default, the employees must be informed within 90 days from the day following the due date, even if the payment has subsequently been made.

7.636 If the contributions remain outstanding, and the provider is concerned that the failure is likely to be of material significance to the Pensions Regulator, it should report the failure to the Pensions Regulator and a report should generally be made if the contributions become more than 90 days overdue.

7.637 The personal pension provider must also send each personal pension scheme member a regular payment statement setting out the actual amounts and dates of the payments made under the direct payment arrangement. These payment statements will generally cover a 12-month period and be sent out annually.

Penalties for Non-Compliance

7.638 The Pensions Regulator has power to levy fines on the employer and the personal pension provider for failing to take all reasonable steps to comply with the new requirements. The maximum fine for a single case of non-compliance is £50,000 in the case of a corporate body and £5000 in the case of an individual.

7.639 Employers may incur a fine if they fail to:
- prepare a record of payments due
- keep the record of payments due up to date
- send the record of payments due to the personal pension provider so that it is received by the first due date on the record
- make correct payments so that the personal pension provider receives them by the due date.

Pension Regulation and Protection

7.640 The Pensions Regulator replaced the Occupational Pensions Regulatory Authority (Opra) from 6 April 2005. The Pensions Regulator employs more proactive methods for protecting the pension rights of scheme members and relies on codes of practice rather than on minutely detailed regulations. The Regulator inherited the various sanctions given to its predecessor to deploy against non-compliant scheme trustees, managers and sponsoring employers, including:
- trustee prohibition and suspension orders
- new trustee appointment powers
- improvement orders
- fines
- enforced winding-up orders

Pensions

- post-misappropriation of funds restitution orders.

7.641 The Regulator also has the power of protecting the Pensions Protection Fund (PPF).

7.642 The PPF is designed to go towards making good the losses often experienced in the past when an insolvent employer leaves behind a final salary scheme which, ostensibly well funded, is in practice unable to meet its benefit obligations in full. The PPF's protection is not complete since, while members already receiving their pensions appear well provided for, not yet retired members are in line for only 90% of their accrued rights.

7.643 The PPF is funded by levies on employers sponsoring final salary schemes. A levy based on a straight headcount of members and pensioners added to in 2006 by a levy which asks relatively little from employers whose schemes are well funded and whose own trading futures are judged sound. Relatively much larger levies called on from employers with poorly funded schemes and poor commercial prospects — those, in short, whose schemes are apt to become claimants on the PPF.

7.644 If such differential levies are a useful safeguard for the PPF, they might not still protect it against claims from schemes left short of sufficient assets after some kind of corporate reconstruction. Therefore, the Pensions Regulator is armed with powers to issue contribution notices and financial support directions on employers involved with the reconstruction, which are designed effectively to put an underfunded final salary scheme on a sound financial footing before it can start to be wound up.

7.645 The Pensions Regulator has set out in a "notifiable events" code of practice what is expected by way of notification to the Regulator from trustees and managers of final salary schemes (along with their sponsoring employers) when aware of events which may have an adverse effect on a scheme's funding arrangements.

7.646 The PPF does more than supply the needed cash in post-insolvency situations. It can take over the scheme's assets and liabilities to date and itself be responsible for accrued benefit payments in the future. There have been some examples of where the PPF has negotiated the taking on of part of the equity in the post-reconstruction employer's equity.

7.647 Another part of the PPF's function is to operate the levy-based compensation scheme, set up in 1997 but rarely used, for restoring losses suffered by members whose funds have been misappropriated by fraud or dishonesty.

7.648 From 2005, trustees of all kinds of occupational schemes, in addition to their scheme responsibility and in line with their trust deeds and rules, must be able to display "TKU" (trustees' knowledge and understanding) of their own scheme and the wider UK pensions environment, with particular reference to investment issues. They are not expected to pretend they are investment managers, but are expected to achieve the level of familiarity with the subject which will enable them to challenge the investment advice they are given.

7.649 Members of insolvent employers' schemes left with pensions losses before the PPF was installed may be helped by the taxpayer-funded Financial Assistance Scheme to the extent of £20 million a year for 20 years. So far, only retired members are being assisted.

Pensions Advice Tax Exemption

7.650 Employers can give their employees access to pensions advice via an authorised financial advisor without incurring a tax charge.

7.651 The Income Tax (Exemption of Minor Benefits) (Amendment) Regulations

2004 exempt the benefit of pensions advice and information to encourage employers to boost pensions awareness and take up among their workforce. This exemption will apply only if the benefit is generally available to all employees and up to a limit of £150 for each employee per year. If the cost to the employer is higher than £150 the whole amount will be subject to tax. Other advice on investment and tax or on leisure and legal matters is not covered by this exemption.

Pension Inducement Payments

7.652 Defined benefit scheme can be very costly to the employer. To minimise the overall costs, employers may offer inducement payments to encourage members of a defined benefit occupational pension scheme to agree to a reduction in their benefits or to switch from a defined benefit scheme to a defined contribution scheme. HM Revenue & Customs have confirmed that inducement payment of this nature are taxable and liable to Class 1 National Insurance contributions. Prior to this announcement of 21 January 2007, it was understood that such inducement payments could be made tax-free in certain circumstances.

7.653 Where inducement payments of this nature were paid prior to 21 January 2007, HMRC will not seek to tax or apply National Insurance contributions to the payment. Likewise, tax and National Insurance will not be sought where the offer was made to members prior to 21 January 2007 and reliance was placed on HMRC's former interpretation of the law.

7.654 The revised treatment does not apply to payments that enhance the transfer value of the pension fund and which are included in the funds transferred between schemes. Such inducement payments are treated for tax and National Insurance purposes in the same way as any employer contribution to a registered pension scheme.

Settlor of a Trust

7.655 An employer in the private sector who wishes to provide employees with access to an occupational pension scheme must ensure that the occupational pension scheme is established under trust so that the pension fund is entirely separated from the resources of the sponsoring organisation.

7.656 The employer will therefore be the settlor of a trust and, with the advice of specialist solicitors, will execute a trust deed and rules and appoint the trustees.

7.657 The trust deed and rules will specify the duties, powers and discretionary powers of the employer and of the trustees.

7.658 The trustees must always:
- act in accordance with the trust deed and rules to the extent that its provisions are not overridden by UK statutory law
- act prudently, conscientiously and with the utmost good faith
- act in the best interests of the beneficiaries and seek a fair balance between the interests of different classes of beneficiary, as well as consider the interests of the employer
- take advice on technical matters and any other matters which they do not understand
- invest the pension fund.

7.659 Any power or discretionary power given to the trustees or to the employer must be exercised in good faith and for the limited purpose specified in the trust deed.

7.660 Once executed, the trust deed and rules can be amended but any amendment must be made within the scope specified by the power of amendment clause in the trust deed itself as well as the statutory restrictions on reducing already accrued pension rights set out in s.67 of the Pensions Act 1995 and in future from s.263 of the Pensions Act 2004.

Member-Nominated Trustees

7.661 The Pensions Act 1995 made provision for there to be member-nominated trustees, although there are exemptions for certain kinds of schemes, and the employer can initiate a statutory consultation procedure with the membership to obtain approval for an alternative arrangement. This has led in many instances to the *status quo* being preserved, with trustees being predominantly, or solely, employer's nominees.

7.662 The Pensions Act 2004 replaces the existing provisions and will generally require the trustees of an occupational pension scheme to make arrangements for at least one third of the total number of trustees to be member-nominated trustees in accordance with a Code of Practice to be issued by the Pensions Regulator. The Secretary of State is also given power to raise the minimum threshold for member-nominated trustees from one third to one half.

7.663 "Member-nominated trustees" are trustees who are nominated by a process that, under the Pensions Act 2004, will involve at least all the active members and all the pensioner members of the scheme or organisations which adequately represent the active members and the pensioner members respectively, and who are selected by some or all of the members. There are certain statutory safeguards, eg vacancies must not remain unfilled for an unreasonable length of time and a member-nominated trustee cannot be removed without the agreement of all the other trustees. As before, certain kinds of scheme will be exempt from the requirement to have member-nominated trustees.

Implied Duty of Good Faith

7.664 In exercising any of its powers or discretionary powers granted by the trust deed and rules, the employer may, in many instances, be permitted to look to its own interests while in other cases the employer must exercise the power in question purely on a fiduciary basis under trust law.

7.665 In all circumstances, however, under employment law the employer must always act subject to the "implied duty of good faith". This is to say, as was held in the case of *Imperial Group Pensions Trust Ltd v Imperial Tobacco Ltd*, the employer must not, without reasonable and proper cause, conduct itself in a manner calculated or likely to destroy or seriously damage the relationship of confidence and trust between employer and employee.

Employment Law Protection for Trustees

7.666 The employer is under a specific duty not to discriminate against an employee as a result of decisions that he or she has taken acting in the capacity of a trustee of an occupational pension scheme sponsored by the employer.

7.667 Section 46 of the Employment Rights Act 1996 specifies that an employee must not be "subjected to any detriment" by the employer on the ground that the employee, acting in the capacity of being a trustee of an occupational pension scheme sponsored by the employer, made any particular decision.

7.668 Similarly, s.102 of the 1996 Act has the effect of rendering unfair the dismissal of a trustee of an occupational pension scheme on the ground of performing, or proposing to perform, any functions as a trustee.

Schedule of Contributions/Payment Schedules

7.669 When an employer sponsors an occupational pension scheme, the employer must pay any contributions over to the trustees of the scheme by the due date set in accordance with the scheme's current:

- schedule of contributions in the case of a final salary scheme whose trustees have determined its statutory funding objective on their actuary's advice
- payment schedule in the case of a money purchase occupational pension scheme.

7.670 Also, in any case where the employer deducts employees' contributions from their earnings and passes them over to the trustees, the employer must pay those contributions over by the 19th day of the calendar month following the month in which they were deducted. Further, in line with regulatory guidance, the scheme actuary (in the case of final salary schemes) and the scheme auditor (for all occupational pension schemes) must report to the Pensions Regulator any material failure by the employer to pay the contributions over by the due date. These whistleblowing duties have been extended by the Pensions Act 2004 to other parties.

7.671 Similarly, the trustees must also report material failure to pay contributions by the due date to the Pensions Regulator and also directly to the members affected.

7.672 The meaning of "material failure" has been discussed in regulatory guidance in relation to the actuaries/auditors on the one hand and the trustees on the other. The Pensions Regulator generally will expect trustees to report when contributions remain outstanding 90 days or more after their due date but it also expects trustees to comply with their existing statutory requirement to notify scheme members when contributions are paid 60 or more days late. Trustees must do this within 90 days of the due date. In due course the new Pensions Regulator will issue a Code of Practice on when failure notices need to be issued.

Contracting Out — Duty to Consult

7.673 If an occupational pension scheme is to be issued by HM Revenue & Customs with a contracting-out certificate — so that employees who are members of the scheme are contracted out of the State Second Pension (S2P) — then the employer must comply with the statutory consultation procedure set out by the Occupational Pension Schemes (Contracting-out) Regulations 1996. This consultation procedure also applies to major variations in the contracting-out certificate.

7.674 Those who must be consulted include all employees, both those who are to be contracted out and those who are not to be contracted out, as well as all recognised independent trade unions representing any of the employees concerned.

7.675 It is possible that the contracting-out issue will become controversial when, during the early part of 2006, the Government publishes its intentions over the size of contracting-out National Insurance contribution (NIC) rebates, currently thought to be inadequate to justify contracting-out decisions.

Equal Treatment

7.676 After several years of relying on European Court of Justice decisions over sex discrimination, equal treatment is now codified in UK domestic legislation in the Pensions Act 1995 and the Occupational Pension Schemes (Equal Treatment) Regulations 1995.

7.677 It should be noted that in relation to the following pieces of UK anti-discrimination legislation, measures specifically relating to pensions have been brought into force.

- Employment Equality (Age) Regulations 2006, which came into force in relation to pension schemes from 1 December 2006 (see Age Discrimination).
- Disability Discrimination Act 1995 (Pensions) Regulations 2003.
- Regulation 9A of, and Schedule 1A to, the Employment Equality (Religion or Belief) Regulations 2003.
- Regulation 9A of, and Schedule 1A to, the Employment Equality (Sexual Orientation) Regulations 2003.

7.678 Note that the following anti-discrimination regulations will apply in the context of pensions as with other employee benefits.

- Employment Equality (Age) Regulations 2006 (but note exemptions in schedule 2 applying to pension schemes).
- Fixed-term Employees (Prevention of Less Favourable Treatment) Regulations 2002.
- Part-time Workers (Prevention of Less Favourable Treatment) Regulations 2000.

Civil Partnerships

7.679 From 5 December 2005, civil partnership legislation (the Civil Partnership Act 2004) provides that a same-sex couple officially registering their relationship will acquire many of the same rights (particularly after one of them dies) and responsibilities of married couples. Same-sex couples have had no difficulty in arranging survivor pension treatment from a money purchase scheme or a personal or stakeholder pension. Now, the legislation requires final salary schemes to extend married couple's survivor pension treatment to same-sex couples, at least in relation to pension accruing after they have registered their relationship or, in the case of a contracted-out scheme, the contracted-out element of the pension accruing after April 1988.

Dispute Resolution

7.680 In the context of occupational pension schemes, internal dispute resolution (IDR) procedures are now governed by the requirements of the Pensions Act 2004.

7.681 Pension IDR procedures are the responsibility of the trustees of the occupational pension scheme, not of the sponsoring employer. Pension disputes are also distinct due to existence of the informal dispute resolution service offered free of charge by the Office of the Pensions Advisory Service (OPAS) and of the Pensions Ombudsman, a statutory tribunal which acts to determine pension disputes.

7.682 Pension disputes involving equal treatment or discrimination are, however, normally dealt with by an employment tribunal.

Pensions Commission

7.683 The Government-appointed Commission published what it called "A New Pension Settlement for the 21st Century" in November 2005. If implemented in full it would substantially improve the financial position of lower-paid people retiring after 2020 by:

- gradually raising the state pension age from 65 to (possibly) 68 by 2050 in line with increases in life expectancy
- converting the second state pensions from an earnings-related to a flat-rate addition to the basic state pension, which would be indexed to average earnings
- dropping the NI contributions test for the basic pension if favour of a residency qualification
- phasing out much of the means-tested supplements available for the poorest pensioners today
- improving the position for women with career breaks and for carers.

7.684 The Commission's other key recommendation is the introduction of a National Pensions Savings Scheme (NPSS) under which:
- unless future employees sign up to a work-based scheme just as good, they would automatically be enrolled in the NPSS into which they would pay 4% of relevant earnings, with the Treasury adding another 1% and their employer another 3%
- employees would have the right to opt out if they wish
- the contributions would be subject to low annual management charges and be passed, probably through the PAYE system, to NPSS-appointed fund managers.

7.685 The Government has undertaken to bring its own reform proposals forward in spring 2006. It would be surprising if they did not lean heavily on the Commission's report but Treasury questions about its recommendations' affordability have dominated political and business discussion before as well as after they were officially published. The Commission predicts, for example, that today's gross domestic product percentage spent on pensioners (6.2%) might rise by 2050 to 8% or 7.5% depending on whether by then the state pension age had risen to 67 or 69. And employers' organisations appear deeply divided about the "soft compulsion" implicit in the NPSS' auto-enrolment, with the Engineering Employers Federation finding it acceptable and the CBI and British Chambers of Commerce disagreeing.

Training

7.686 Employers, trustees and scheme administers should ensure that they are familiar with the rules and regulations governing pensions and that they keep abreast of changes. The impact of the changes should be communicated to members.

7.687 It is important that all the trustees of an occupational pension scheme are familiar with the issues with which they are concerned. Under measures contained in the Pensions Act 2004 this will be a legislative requirement.

7.688 Employers, pension scheme managers and trustees should familiarise themselves with the requirements of the age discrimination regulations — the Employment Equality (Age) Regulations 2006, which came into force on 1 October 2006 (but apply to occupational pension schemes from 1 December 2006), and also their requirements under the regulations. They should also ensure that they are aware of any specific exemptions.

7.689 Training should also be given to ensure that the tax implications of the scheme are understood and that the tax obligations are met. Training should ensure that those responsible for tax issues keep abreast of any changes in pension tax law.

7.690 The complexity of administering an occupational pension scheme in-house in practice demands the recruitment of suitably qualified and/or experienced staff.

7.691 The Pensions Management Institute awards a number of qualifications for those working in the field of pensions.
- Diploma in Pension Calculations (DPC).

Pensions

- Qualification in Pensions Administration (QPA).
- Diploma in International Employee Benefits.
- Retirement Provision Certificate (RPC).
- Retirement Provision Diploma (RPD).
- Associateship examinations (APMI).

7.692 The institute does not itself provide training courses commercially but provides lists of training courses which are available.

List of Relevant Legislation

7.693
- Employment Equality (Age) Regulations 2006
- Income Tax (Exemption of Minor Benefits) (Amendment) Regulations 2004
- Disability Discrimination Act 1995 (Pensions) Regulations 2003
- Personal Pension Schemes (Payments by Employers) Regulations 2000
- Stakeholder Pension Schemes Regulations 2000
- Occupational Pension Schemes (Contracting-out) Regulations 1996
- Occupational Pension Schemes (Deficiency on Winding Up etc) Regulations 1996
- Occupational Pension Schemes (Disclosure of Information) Regulations 1996
- Occupational Pension Schemes (Internal Dispute Resolution Procedures) Regulations 1996
- Occupational Pension Schemes (Member-nominated Trustees and Directors) Regulations 1996
- Occupational Pension Schemes (Minimum Funding Requirement and Actuarial Valuations) Regulations 1996
- Occupational Pension Schemes (Modification of Schemes) Regulations 1996
- Occupational Pension Schemes (Payments to Employers) Regulations 1996
- Occupational Pension Schemes (Scheme Administration) Regulations 1996
- Occupational Pension Schemes (Winding Up) Regulations 1996
- Personal and Occupational Pensions Schemes (Pensions Ombudsman) Regulations 1996
- Pensions Act 2007
- Finance Act 2005, Pt. 5
- Finance Act 2004, Pt. 4 and associated regulations
- Pensions Act 2004
- Income Tax (Earnings and Pensions Act) 2003
- Child Support, Pensions and Social Security Act 2000
- Finance Act 2000
- Financial Services and Markets Act 2000
- Welfare Reform and Pensions Act 1999
- Employment Rights Act 1996
- Pensions Act 1995
- Pension Schemes Act 1993
- Finance Act 1989
- Social Security Act 1989 Schedule 5
- Income and Corporation Taxes Act 1988

- Registered Pension Schemes (Standard Lifetime and Annual Allowances) Order 2007
- Financial Services and Markets Act 2000 (Regulated Activities) Order 2001
- Financial Services and Markets Act 2000 (Exemption) Order 2001
- Financial Services and Markets Act 2000 (Financial Promotion) Order 2001

List of Relevant Cases

7.694
- *Preston v Wolverhampton Healthcare NHS Trust (No. 2)* [2001] IRLR 237, HL
- *Unifi v Union Bank of Nigeria plc* [2001] IRLR 712, CAC
- *Barclays Bank plc v Holmes* [2000] PLR 339
- *Outram v Academy Plastics* [2000] IRLR 499, CA
- *University of Nottingham v (1) Eyett and (2) The Pensions Ombudsman* [1999] IRLR 87, HC
- *South West Trains v Wightman* [1998] PLR 113
- *Coloroll Pension Trustees v Russell* [1994] PLR 211
- *Imperial Group Pension Trust Ltd v Imperial Tobacco Ltd* [1991] IRLR 66, HC
- *Scally v Southern Health and Social Services Board* [1991] IRLR 522, HL
- *Barber v Guardian Royal Exchange Assurance Group Ltd* [1990] IRLR 240, ECJ
- *Re Courage Group's Pension Schemes* [1987] 1 AER 528
- *Bilka-Kaufhaus GmbH v Weber von Hartz* [1986] IRLR 317, ECJ

Further Information

Publications
- *Equal Pay, Fair Pay, Equal Opportunities Commission*
- FSA's *Financial Promotion Guidance Instrument 2002* (published May 2002, in force from 1 June 2002)
- FSA's *Guide to the Risks of Occupational Pension Transfers*
- FSA's *The FSA's Regulatory Approach to Financial Promotions*, (April 2002)

Organisations
- **HM Revenue & Customs**
  Web: *www.hmrc.gov.uk/home.htm*
  HM Revenue & Customs (HMRC) is the department responsible for the business of the former Inland Revenue and HM Customs and Excise. HMRC is responsible for lecting the bulk of tax revenue as well as paying tax credits and child benefit.
- **Institute for Payroll and Pensions Management**
  Web: *www.ippm.org.uk*
  The Institute for Payroll and
  Pensions Management aims to promote excellence in the Payroll and Pensions professions.
- **National Association of Pension Funds**
  Web: *www.napf.co.uk*

The NAPF's priority is to ensure aregulatory and fiscal environment that encourages the provision and take up of employer-sponsored pensions, as well as sound stewardship of pension fund assets.

- **Pensions Advisory Service (OPAS)**
  Web: *www.opas.org.uk*
  OPAS is an independent non-profit organisation that provides information and guidance on the whole spectrum of pensions covering state, company, personal and stakeholder schemes.

- **Pensions Management Institute**
  Web: *www.pensions-pmi.org.uk*
  The Pensions Management Institute (PMI) is the Institute for pensions professionals. If you are working in pensions or a related area, such as human resources or payroll, you are a trustee of a pension scheme or you have an interest in pensions, this website will be relevant.

- **Pensions Ombudsman**
  Web: *www.pensions-ombudsman.org.uk*
  The Pensions Ombudsman investigates and decides complaints and disputes about the way that pension schemes are run.

- **Pensions Regulator**
  Web: *www.thepensionsregulator.gov.uk*
  The Pensions Regulator is the regulator of work-based pension schemes in the UK and was created under the Pensions Act 2004.

- **Stakeholder Pension Schemes**
  Web: *www.stakeholderpensions.gov.uk*
  A useful website that includes information on organisations that play important roles linked to stakeholder pensions. They are either Government departments or independent non-profit making bodies.

Statutory Sick Pay

The topic covers the following.
- Qualifying for Statutory Sick Pay
- Period that SSP Applies
- Workers not Covered by SSP
- Period of Incapacity for Work
- Period of Entitlement
- Qualifying Days
- Linked Periods
- Waiting Days
- Notification of Absence
- Evidence of Incapacity for Work
- Records for Statutory Sick Pay Purposes
- Length of Service and SSP
- Payment of Statutory Sick Pay
- Rates of Statutory Sick Pay
- Maximum Liability
- Withholding Statutory Sick Pay
- When to Stop Paying Statutory Sick Pay
- Recovery of Statutory Sick Pay
- Payroll Treatment of Statutory Sick Pay
- Forms for Statutory Sick Pay
- Age Discrimination Legislation
- All employees have a statutory right to receive a minimum payment during a period of sickness, provided they meet the criteria set out in the regulations. This payment is known as statutory sick pay.
- Employers may choose to pay occupational sick pay in preference to statutory sick pay, provided the amount paid is at least equal to the statutory rate. The rate of statutory sick pay is set at the beginning of each tax year and, for 2007/08, is £72.55.
- The HM Revenue & Customs National Insurance Contributions Office has responsibility for administering statutory sick pay. The Department for Work and Pensions (DWP) is responsible for policy and HM Revenue & Customs (HMRC) deals with appeals regarding an employee's entitlement to receive statutory sick pay.
- Self-employed individuals have no right to statutory sick pay while absent from work due to sickness.

Employers' Duties

7.695 Employers must ensure that employees:
- know the requirements for periods of absence
- know the reporting requirements for absence
- are paid the correct amounts for either statutory sick pay or occupational sick pay
- are paid at least the minimum payment for periods of incapacity until exhausted.

Statutory Sick Pay

Employees' Duties

7.696 Employees have a duty to:
- report any absence from work due to sickness within the time specified by the employer or within seven calendar days of the first incapacity
- provide evidence of sickness in the form of a medical certificate or self-certification form, if requested.

In Practice

Qualifying for Statutory Sick Pay

7.697 Since 1 October 2006, Statutory Sick Pay (SSP) has been payable to an employee, regardless of age, whose average weekly earnings equal or exceed the lower earnings limit (LEL) for National Insurance purposes and who satisfy the qualify conditions for SSP. For 2007/08, the LEL is £87 per week.

7.698 To qualify for SSP, the employee must satisfy the following conditions:
- the sickness absence must have formed a period of incapacity for work (see Period of Incapacity for Work)
- the period of sickness must also have formed a period of entitlement (see Period of Entitlement)
- the sick day must be a qualifying day (see Qualifying Days)
- the employee must have provided notification of the absence within the rules (see Notification of Absence).

Freedom from Operating the SSP Scheme

7.699 If an employer pays contractual remuneration, such as wages or occupational sick pay, to an employee at a level that is above the SSP rate for each day of incapacity, the employer can choose whether or not to operate the SSP scheme.

7.700 If the employer chooses not to operate the SSP scheme, the employee's right to entitlement of SSP is unaffected. The employer remains liable to pay SSP for any period of incapacity for work for any day for which contractual remuneration is not paid or is paid at a rate that is less than the SSP rate for that day.

7.701 The employer still needs to record absences from work due to sickness and salary payments made during absences. But the employer can decide whether to take advantage of occupational sick pay and whether to apply it to all employees.

7.702 If an employee's entitlement to occupational sick pay ceases when he or she is still sick, SSP rules will continue to apply where the employer has been unable to apply the easement.

Period that SSP Applies

7.703 Statutory sick pay is payable for periods of "incapacity for work", ie periods

Statutory Sick Pay

lasting four or more consecutive calendar days, which are determined by reference to "qualifying days", ie days which the employee is contracted to work.

7.704 Statutory sick pay is payable from the fourth working day of a period of incapacity for work, after excluding the "waiting days", ie the first three qualifying days of a period of incapacity for work. There is no payment due for periods of sickness lasting three or fewer days, and these need not be recorded for SSP purposes.

7.705 All SSP payments are subject to tax and National Insurance as part of gross salary.

Workers not Covered by SSP

7.706 Some workers are not covered by the SSP rules and these are:
- self-employed individuals
- members of the Armed Forces
- outward-bound international mariners.

Losing Eligibility for SSP

7.707 Eligible employees lose their entitlement to statutory sick pay if on the first day of the period of incapacity for work:
- their average weekly earnings are below the National Insurance lower earnings threshold
- they are sick during the 39-week maternity pay period
- they have already received 28 weeks' SSP from their former employer in a linked period
- they have had a recent claim to certain Social Security benefits, eg Incapacity Benefit, Maternity Allowance, Severe Disability Allowance and Invalidity Benefit, that prevents them receiving Statutory Sick Pay
- they are involved in a trade dispute at their place of employment
- they are in legal custody, under arrest or in prison
- they have done no work under their contract of employment
- they are outside the UK and there is no liability to pay Class 1 National Insurance contributions.

Period of Incapacity for Work

7.708 An employee's absence from work for four or more consecutive days constitutes a period of incapacity for work. This period of incapacity makes an employee eligible for SSP.

7.709 The four-day period includes all days of sickness, including weekends. So if an employee is absent from work on Monday and Tuesday, the employer needs to know whether they were sick at the weekend.

7.710 Any self-certification should therefore ask for both the starting date of the sickness and the first day of absence from work. Where there are less than four days in the period of sickness there is no period of incapacity for work.

7.711 When an employee is sent home from work due to sickness part way through a day or shift, the period of incapacity starts from the next day of sickness, not the working day or shift on which the sickness began.

Example of Period of Incapacity for Work

7.712   The following examples illustrate the period of incapacity for work.

7.713   Jane is off work Thursday and Friday and returns to work on Monday. She was not sick over the weekend. There is therefore no period of incapacity for SSP purposes.

7.714   Sue was off work from Thursday and returns to work on Tuesday, having been sick over the weekend. There were five days of sickness, so there was a period of incapacity for work and this should be recorded for SSP purposes.

Period of Entitlement

7.715   Statutory sick pay is only payable if the day of absence falls within a period of entitlement.

7.716   An employer is only required to pay SSP in any one period of incapacity to work (linked or unlinked) to 28 times the appropriate weekly rate.

Qualifying Days

7.717   Statutory sick pay is only payable for qualifying days. The qualifying days are those days the employee is contracted to work.

7.718   The employer can choose and agree the qualifying days with the employee, providing there is at least one qualifying day in every week. The week always begins on Sunday.

7.719   If an employee does not have to work in a particular week, then the SSP regulations state that the Wednesday of that week is the qualifying day. If the contract is not clear, then all days of the week count as qualifying, except any days agreed as rest days.

Example of Qualifying Days

7.720   The following examples illustrate qualifying days.

7.721   Roger works Monday to Friday under his contract of employment. These days are the qualifying days.

7.722   Jane works on a roster of four out of seven days. She and her employer can agree that all seven days of the week are qualifying days, or they can agree that the days she works within the roster are the qualifying days.

7.723   Charles works from Wednesday through to Friday every other week. The qualifying days in a three-week period would therefore be Wednesday Thursday and Friday in week one, Wednesday in week two, then Wednesday, Thursday and Friday in week three.

Linked Periods

7.724   Where there is more than one period of incapacity for work and the second period starts within 56 days of the end of the first period, the two periods are called "linked" – and count as one period.

Example of Linked Periods

7.725   The following example illustrates linking periods of incapacity for work.

7.726 Ann is sick from 21 August to 27 August inclusive, and then again from 21 September to 12 October inclusive. These two periods of incapacity for work are linked and therefore count as one period.

Waiting Days

7.727 Statutory sick pay is payable for qualifying days only, excluding the first three qualifying days of any period of incapacity for work. These are known as "waiting days".

7.728 If two periods of incapacity for work are linked, only outstanding waiting days, ie up to the maximum of three, have to be served in the second period.

Example of Waiting Days

7.729 The following example illustrates waiting days.

7.730 Arthur works Monday to Friday each week. He is sick one Friday, returning to work the following Tuesday. Friday and Monday are waiting days. Five weeks later, Arthur is sick again from Monday for a complete week. Monday counts as the third waiting day and SSP is payable from Tuesday to Friday.

Notification of Absence

7.731 Before statutory sick pay can be paid the employee must notify the employer that he or she is sick. Most organisations have their own rules on notification of illness, eg a telephone call to say they are sick. For SSP purposes an employer cannot insist that the employee tells them by a specific time on the first qualifying day or more frequently than once a week.

Evidence of Incapacity for Work

7.732 Statutory sick pay is payable to an employee when he or she has met the notification criteria. The employer is entitled to ask for medical evidence but can only withhold SSP:
- for late notification
- where there is reason to believe that the employee is not ill and the employer is waiting for medical evidence to prove otherwise.

7.733 An employee should know what evidence the organisation requires — it is usually a self-certificate for the first seven days and a medical certificate from the eighth day onwards.

7.734 If the employee has two jobs with different employers it is possible to be incapacitated for one and not for the other, depending on the kind of work involved.

Example of When an Employee has Two Jobs

7.735 A supermarket cashier has a broken wrist and cannot work a cash register. However, in the evenings he or she teaches Italian and can continue to do so. In such a case, the supermarket would be due to pay SSP.

Records for Statutory Sick Pay Purposes

7.736 The law requires employers to keep records, for at least three years following the end of the tax year to which they relate. These records are of:
- sickness periods lasting at least four consecutive days for each employee

Statutory Sick Pay

- all SSP payments made during a period of incapacity for work.

7.737 It is useful for employers to keep each employee's medical certificates and self-certificates in case there is a dispute over the payment of SSP. Employers should also keep a copy of the organisation's rules on notification of sickness and information on qualifying days.

7.738 During the course of an audit visit by HMRC these records should be available and accessible.

7.739 The maximum fine for failing to keep these records for three years after the end of the tax year to which they relate is £1000 for any one offence. For continued failure to provide such information after conviction, a further fine of up to £40 a day can be charged.

Length of Service and SSP

7.740 There is no length of service required for an employee to be eligible for SSP. The only requirement is that the contract of employment has started and work has been carried out by the employee, even if only for five minutes.

7.741 Where the employee becomes sick part way through a day, their sickness period runs from the next completed day of sickness.

7.742 Special rules apply to agency workers and to casual workers. Broadly, if a worker is treated as an employee for National Insurance purposes, that worker will also be an employee for SSP purposes.

Defining Incapacity

7.743 There has to be some incapacity for work before SSP can be paid. This means that the employee must be incapable of doing the work he or she is contracted to do, because of some disease or disablement. An employee is also incapable for work if he or she is an infectious disease carrier or convalescent.

Payment of Statutory Sick Pay

7.744 From 6 April 2007, statutory sick pay is payable at a weekly rate of £72.55, provided that the qualifying conditions are met.

Example of Payment of Statutory Sick Pay

7.745 Anne's qualifying days are Monday to Friday and she is off work from Friday to Monday and returns to work on Tuesday. The period of incapacity for work is four days, the qualifying days are Friday and Monday, and the waiting days are Friday and Monday. Statutory sick pay would not be payable.

7.746 If she was off work from Friday through to Thursday, returning to work on Friday, the period of incapacity for work is seven days, the qualifying days are Friday, Monday to Thursday, and the waiting days are Friday, Monday and Tuesday. Statutory sick pay is payable for Wednesday and Thursday only.

7.747 If she was off work for all the days in the above examples and there were six weeks between the two sickness periods, then the periods of incapacity for work can be linked. There are seven qualifying days, the waiting days are the Friday and Monday of the first period of incapacity for work, and the Friday of the second period of incapacity for work. Statutory sick pay is payable for four days, being the last Monday to Thursday.

Rates of Statutory Sick Pay

7.748 The weekly rate for SSP for 2007/08 is £72.55 if the employee's average weekly earnings are equal to or exceed £87 per week (the lower earnings limit for National Insurance purposes for 2007/08). Where the employee's average weekly earnings are below the lower earnings limit, SSP will not be payable, but Incapacity Benefit may be claimed instead. In such a case, the employer must issue a "changeover" form (SSP1).

7.749 Statutory sick pay is paid at a daily rate for the employee's qualifying days only, excluding the waiting days. The daily rate is the weekly rate divided by the number of qualifying days in the week.

Example of Rates for SSP

7.750 In 2007/08, Bill has four qualifying days each week, so his daily rate of SSP is the weekly rate of £72.55 divided by four, which is £18.14. If he had seven qualifying days each week, the daily rate would be £72.55 divided by seven, which is £10.37.

7.751 Helpbook E12 (available from HMRC) contains a daily rate table.

7.752 This rate will eventually be multiplied by the actual qualifying days that an employee is sick. So, if Bill is sick for a working week, whether it be of four or seven qualifying days, he gets the same amount of SSP.

Maximum Liability

7.753 The employer pays SSP for a maximum of 28 weeks in any period — linked or otherwise — of sickness. Once a linked period is broken, the employer's full 28 weeks' liability resumes.

Leaver's Statements

7.754 If a new employee has a period of incapacity within eight weeks of starting, the employer should ask if they have a Leaver's Statement from their previous employment. If the current period of incapacity started within 56 days of the end of a previous period, in the previous job, then the sick pay paid by the previous employer reduces the new employer's liability.

7.755 For example, if the previous employer has paid 18 weeks' SSP in a linked period of incapacity, the new employer will have a maximum liability of only 10 weeks.

7.756 Employers should note that in cases like this the employee still has to serve three waiting days with the new employer before the qualifying period begins.

Withholding Statutory Sick Pay

7.757 Statutory sick pay can be withheld if there is an unreasonable delay in the employee's notification of absence. The rules that enable employers to withhold sick pay for this reason state that the employer must:
- ensure that employees know in advance how to notify their employer
- accept notification at any time on the first day of sickness
- accept notification from someone else on the employee's behalf
- treat notification in writing as made on the day it is posted
- require notification only once a week

- realize that employers cannot require notification before the first qualifying day of sickness
- realize that employers cannot require notification to be in the form of medical evidence.

7.758 The "fall-back" rule states that a written notification of sickness must be accepted up to seven days after the first qualifying day.

When to Stop Paying Statutory Sick Pay

7.759 An employer's liability to pay SSP ends when the employee:
- is no longer sick
- starts her maternity pay period
- is taken into legal custody, arrested or imprisoned
- dies
- has their contract of employment end
- has received 28 weeks' SSP
- has a three-year-long period of incapacity in his or her current employment.

Recovery of Statutory Sick Pay

7.760 Employers may be eligible to recover the SSP they have paid out. To do this, an employer must calculate:
- the gross National Insurance (both the employees' and employer's contributions) for the tax month that the SSP is paid
- 13% of this gross amount.

7.761 If the SSP paid in a tax month exceeds the 13% sum, the employer may recover the excess amount. The excess amount can be deducted from the National Insurance, tax and student loan deduction elements of the monthly remittance paid to the Collector of Taxes.

7.762 The amount of SSP recovered is entered on the tax year-end's P35 Employer's Annual Statement. The amounts of SSP recovered must be disclosed on the employee's P14/P60 — the certificate of earnings and deductions for the tax year.

Payroll Treatment of Statutory Sick Pay

7.763 The payment of SSP is subject to tax and National Insurance deduction just like salary and wages. The amount paid may be recorded separately on the payroll records, although this is not a requirement.

7.764 Where SSP has been paid and recovered, employers must give details on the year-end P14 form — and on the year-end P35 form.

Forms for Statutory Sick Pay

7.765 There are three forms, available from HMRC, addressing different aspects of Statutory Sick Pay:
- Changeover Form
- Leaver's Statement Form
- Record Sheet.

Changeover Form (SSP1)

7.766 This form must be filled in if:
- an employee is not entitled to SSP on the first day of their period of incapacity
- the entitlement to SSP stops but the employee is still sick.

7.767 The form must be filled in by the employer and given to the employee within seven days of the employer being notified that the sickness would last for at least four days. The second section of the form explains how and where to claim Incapacity Benefit.

7.768 SSP1 details why SSP is not being paid. For long-term illness, employers must issue the form at the beginning of the 23rd week of SSP or two weeks before their liability to pay sick pay ends — whichever is the earlier date. Failure to supply an employee with an SSP1 can result in a fine of £1000.

7.769 The information on the form states:
- the last day for which SSP will be payable
- why SSP is no longer payable
- the date the sickness started in the period of incapacity.

Leaver's Statement Form (SSP1 [L])

7.770 New employers must accept a completed Leaver's Statement form if it is handed in before the seventh day after the first qualifying day in a period of incapacity.

7.771 Employers must issue this form to leavers if:
- requested by the employee
- sick pay was payable for a week or more within eight weeks of the leaving date.

7.772 The form must be issued:
- by the seventh day after the employee requested it, or
- on the first pay day in the tax month following the one in which the request was made where it is impractical to issue within seven days.

7.773 Failure to issue the form in the prescribed time can lead to fines.

Record Sheet (SSP2)

7.774 This is an optional form and can be obtained from the DWP for recording SSP information. An employer's own computer-generated records sheet containing the relevant data is acceptable, provided it gives all the required information.

Age Discrimination Legislation

7.775 Prior to 1 October 2006, employees had to be aged 16 and over and under 65 in order to be eligible for statutory sick pay (SSP). These age limits were removed by the age discrimination regulations — the Employment Equality (Age) Regulations 2006 — effective since 1 October 2006.

Training

7.776 It is important that all managers are familiar with the organisation's policy on sickness absence and understand the responsibilities of employers and employees. Training should ensure that managers:
- understand the regulations relating to statutory sick pay

Statutory Sick Pay

- keep abreast of any changes in the law and the practical implications of those changes
- understand the meaning of "sickness" for statutory sick pay purposes
- understand the criteria for an employee to receive statutory sick pay
- obtain adequate proof of absence and sickness from the employee.

List of Relevant Legislation

7.777

- Employment Equality (Age) Regulations 2006
- Social Security (Contributions) Regulations 2001
- Statutory Sick Pay (General) Regulations 1982
- Social Security Contributions and Benefits Act 1992
- Social Security Administration Act 1992

Further Information

Publications

- E14 *What to Do if Your Employee is Sick*, available from HM Revenue & Customs.
- *BERR Redundancy Forms*, Department for Business, Enterprise and Regulatory Reform (BERR).

Organisations

- **Department for Work and Pensions (DWP)**
  Web: *www.dwp.gov.uk*
  The DWP is responsible for the Government's welfare reform agenda. Its aim is to promote opportunity and independence for all.
- **HM Revenue & Customs**
  Web: *www.hmrc.gov.uk/home.htm*
  HM Revenue & Customs (HMRC) is the department responsible for the business of the former Inland Revenue and HM Customs and Excise. HMRC is responsible for lecting the bulk of tax revenue as well as paying tax credits and child benefit.

# Chapter 8
Recruitment and Selection

Advertising and Sourcing Applicants

> This topic covers the following.
> - Recruiting Internally or Externally
> - Advertising
> - Press Advertising
> - Discrimination
> - Writing Good Copy
> - Alternative Sources of External Applicants
> - Being an Employer of Choice

8.1 In each recruitment exercise employers must balance the desire to find the best candidates against the cost of recruiting and the time spent recruiting. To avoid the administrative costs involved in screening a large volume of applications, it is best to try and attract fewer — but higher quality — candidates.

8.2 The first question employers must ask themselves is whether to source applicants internally, externally, or both. If vacancies are filled internally, it is important that they are publicised to all staff and that the process is transparent.

8.3 Some of the ways that employers can attract external applicants include the following:
- press advertising
- the Internet
- recruitment agencies and consultancies
- employee referrals
- networking
- open evenings, milk rounds and recruitment fairs

Whether sourcing applicants internally or externally, it is essential that employers ensure that the recruitment process is free from discriminatory practices.

Employers' Duties

8.4 Employers have a duty to ensure the following.
- Their advertising and recruitment policies and procedures are free from discrimination.
- Any practices which could potentially be indirectly discriminatory are dealt with appropriately.
- Data relating to recruitment and selection are processed in accordance with data protection legislation.

Employees' Duties

8.5 Employees have a duty to:
- be honest in the information they disclose in the recruitment and selection process.

In Practice

Recruiting Internally or Externally

8.6 There is a strong case for giving internal applicants the opportunity to apply for vacancies. Apart from the obvious benefit to the employer, not opening up a vacancy internally can result in loss of morale where employees are looking for progression within an organisation.

The Benefits of Internal Recruitment

8.7 The internal filling of vacancies has benefits both in cost and time savings for the employer.

8.8 Costs savings occur through:
- a shorter induction period — while internal recruits will still need to be inducted into the job, no organisational induction will be required
- no expenditure on advertising or a recruitment consultant's fees.

8.9 Time is saved in the following ways:
- the new recruit will be able to start his or her new job soon after being selected, whereas an external recruit may have to work a lengthy notice period
- internal applicants will generally be available for interview at relatively short notice.

The Disadvantages of Internal Recruitment

8.10 Recruiting internally also has its disadvantages.
- The field of candidates is limited — there may be better candidates available externally.
- Promoting an internal employee who is best at a given job does not necessarily mean that they will be good in another role.
- Organisations sometimes need new employees with fresh ideas and views to avoid complacency.
- Employers may need to recruit to fill a vacancy that has been covered by an internal promotion.

8.11 Whether an employer chooses to source applicants internally or externally, it must make sure that it does not discriminate at any stage of the selection process.

Advertising

8.12 Advertising is one of the most open and transparent means of sourcing external applicants. When considering which method of advertising to choose, employers should consider matters such as the cost, the speed and how best to attract quality candidates rather than simply trying to generate a large quantity of responses.

The Internet

8.13 There are three ways of sourcing applicants via the Internet:
- third party recruitment websites
- trade press and newspaper Internet-only advertising

- organisations' own corporate websites.

Recruitment Websites

8.14 Third party websites can be faster than press advertising as the job is posted virtually instantaneously. However, the advertisement may only reach a small audience unless the employer posts the vacancy on several sites.

Corporate Websites

8.15 The use of corporate websites is particularly appropriate to larger organisations, eg employers recruiting a number of graduates each year often only accept online applications.

8.16 In order to recruit effectively, corporate websites must:
- be easy to navigate
- create an attractive impression of an organisation
- be up-to-date.

Quality v Quantity

8.17 The greatest disadvantage of the Internet is that, as it can be so readily accessed, employers often receive a large number of applications, many from unsuitable candidates. Screening and replying to these can be a major and potentially costly task.

Press Advertising

8.18 Press advertising can be divided into three separate categories:
- local press
- national and regional press
- the trade press.

Local Press

8.19 Local press advertising can be highly effective for general and junior vacancies as it targets a given geographical area. Compared with national newspapers, advertising in the local press is relatively inexpensive, although it may be necessary to place insertions in papers serving surrounding commutable areas as well as the employer's own area.

National and Regional Press

8.20 National newspapers have the widest circulations of any press media — and correspondingly high costs. Different papers specialise in different sectors or disciplines, eg the *Guardian* for both public sector and media vacancies, *The Times* for legal appointments and the *Financial Times* for finance executives.

8.21 Like the Internet, the national press involves some wastage in terms of the percentage of the readership neither living within commutable distance nor willing to relocate. Bearing in mind that applicants for senior posts who are unwilling to relocate are nevertheless usually willing to commute greater distances, it may therefore be worthwhile to advertise for them in regional papers such as the *Yorkshire Post*. Such publications are less expensive than national newspapers and can produce a more targeted response.

Trade Press

8.22 The trade press is the most highly targeted of all media. It may well be the most cost-effective option for many specialist disciplines as well as for certain sector-specific recruitment campaigns. Like the Internet and national press, it has both the advantage and disadvantage of being circulated to people who do not live within commuting distance of the advertiser.

Discrimination

8.23 Advertisements that are discriminatory are now rare. Even if ignorance or carelessness on the part of employers results in the submission of text that could be discriminatory, publishers will normally spot the error and refuse to insert the advertisement until it has been corrected.

8.24 Employers should, however, still take care to ensure that their advertisements are not directly or indirectly discriminatory. Discrimination occurs when a requirement excludes or discourages certain groups from applying. Protected groups include men, women, married individuals, pregnant women, and people undergoing gender reassignment (under the sex discrimination legislation). Race discrimination protects people from discrimination on grounds of race, colour, ethnic origin and nationality. There is protection from discrimination on the grounds of or related to disability. More recent protection is in place from discrimination on the grounds of age, sexual orientation and religion and belief.

Wording for Adverts

8.25 Specifying that a woman is required for a position (eg advertising for a waitress) would result in sex discrimination. Requiring a candidate to be "energetic" could, potentially, discriminate against disabled applicants, or on the grounds of age; and a condition that people should "fit in" could discriminate in a variety of ways, including on the grounds of race, sex, sexual orientation or disability.

8.26 It is also useful to emphasise, usually at the bottom of the advertisement, that the organisation is an equal opportunities employer. There are various forms of words that can be used.

8.27 Some employers state that the position is open to all candidates regardless of gender, ethnicity, disability, etc. Others simply say that they welcome applications from all sections of the community.

8.28 This has the advantages not only of making sure that no category of applicant is omitted but also of taking an inclusive approach rather than tacitly emphasising differences by listing out separate groups.

8.29 If, however, an equal opportunities statement is used, employers must ensure that they do have an equal opportunities procedure in place and that it is followed throughout the recruitment process. Simply paying lip service to equality of opportunity is not enough and will not fend off discrimination claims.

8.30 Wording which was previously acceptable will be open to challenge if it suggests an employer will discount applications on the grounds of age. Seemingly neutral phrases such as "recent college graduate" may imply a certain age range (the vast majority of recent graduates will be under 25). Requiring a certain number of years' experience must be justified and carefully considered — eg what is the difference between five and six years' experience in practice?

Genuine Occupational Requirements

8.31 There may be occasions when it is necessary to advertise for a person of a specific gender when recruiting, based on the fact that a job can only be effectively carried out by a man or a woman. It may also be necessary to advertise for a person of a particular race, eg where the job holder is required to provide welfare services to a particular racial group.

8.32 In such circumstances it is lawful for employers to apply a genuine occupational qualification when recruiting, but it should be borne in mind that this may have to be justified at a later date.

Age Discrimination

8.33 Legislation on age discrimination came into effect on 1 October 2006 and publishers will no longer accept advertisements specifying a lower or upper age limit. Employers should use language and an approach that will appeal to wide age groups. In particular, any advert should avoid discriminatory phrases such as "applicants should be at least 25 years of age" or "would suit young graduates" or "mature drivers required". It would also be good practice to remove the date of birth question from application forms and put it on a separate monitoring form that interviewers do not see.

Writing Good Copy

8.34 In order to attract suitable applicants in a highly competitive market, advertisements need to work. This does not necessarily mean getting as many responses as possible. A well-written recruitment advertisement will actually help those readers who do not fit the bill to realise this as well as encourage those who do match the specification to apply.

8.35 All too often, recruitment advertisements use the same tired old clichés rather than taking the trouble to identify precisely those qualities that are actually required. One of the advantages of using competency frameworks when preparing person specifications is that they provide the kind of detailed and specific information which will help candidates to decide whether or not they should apply for a given post. A good advertisement will concentrate on the most important competencies, not only saying what they are but also explaining why they are essential to the job in question.

8.36 It is important to consider what motivates different types of candidate and what is likely to make them respond to an advertisement. As well as salary and job title, factors such as opportunities for career and personal development, flexible working practices and other benefits need to be brought out in the body of the text if the reader is to be persuaded to apply.

8.37 The language used must be appropriate for the target audience. Skilled copywriters often write advertisements as if they were talking to the person they would like to recruit for the position. Carefully thought-out wording will have a far greater effect on the quality of response than factors such as the size of the advertisement or its position on the page of the publication in which it appears. Remember the age discrimination rules. Making an advertisement look like a flyer for an all-night party is certainly going to discriminate against older readers and is almost certain to fall foul of the regulations.

Alternative Sources of External Applicants

Recruitment Intermediaries

8.38 Recruitment intermediaries account for a significant percentage of the number of permanent job vacancies filled, and for an even larger percentage of temporary vacancies. In the permanent jobs sector, there are three different types of intermediaries.

Agencies

8.39 Recruitment agencies attempt to match job seekers on their registers with vacancies notified by employers. Employers often place vacancies with more than one agency. Agencies operate by:
- being paid only when the person they place starts work with the client
- agency staff being paid a commission.

Executive Selection Consultants

8.40 Selection consultants are effectively just an outsourcing of direct advertising by an employer. They:
- advertise appointments
- sift applications
- interview and test suitable candidates
- present a shortlist of between three and five candidates for a single vacancy to the client, who makes the final selection.

Executive Search Consultants (Headhunters)

8.41 The use of executive search can be an effective if costly way of hiring senior executives. Unlike advertising, executive search targets all potential applicants, including those who are not actively looking for another job. It is sometimes used not only at senior levels but also for identifying and attracting people at lower levels whose talents are in very short supply.

8.42 Search consultants normally operate by:
- agreeing a recruitment brief with a client
- identifying target companies in which suitable candidates for the position in question are likely to be found
- having discussed this list with their client, identifying target individuals within those companies
- making direct approaches to them, with a view to seducing them away from their existing employer to the client organisation.

Volume Recruitment Techniques

8.43 Where the number of vacancies justifies it, employers may use techniques such as:
- university milk rounds
- recruitment fairs
- open evenings.

8.44 Such techniques can be very effective, but involve a significant investment.

JobCentres

8.45 JobCentres are run by the Employment Service. The services of a JobCentre are generally free. JobCentres will advertise either locally or nationally and carry out the initial screening of applicants.

8.46 JobCentres are most appropriate for the advertising of manual or semi-skilled posts.

Recommendations by Existing Staff

8.47 The obvious advantage of applicants recommended by existing employees is that they come free, whereas advertisements and agency fees are expensive.

8.48 Such candidates may well also be more suitable than the average "cold" applicant because existing staff:

- know the culture of the organisation and what a given job entails and should be able to judge whether the person they are recommending will be a good fit
- will be wary of jeopardising their own standing in the organisation by recommending anyone they are unsure of.

8.49 There is, on the other hand, the risk of employees trying to get jobs for their friends, who may not always be of the highest quality. Employers may well find more suitable people by casting their net more widely through an advertising campaign. There are also risks that you may limit the diversity of applications especially if at present the workforce is not diverse and does not reflect the diversity of the surrounding geographical area.

8.50 Where good quality staff are hard to find, some employers positively encourage recommendations from existing staff by offering cash incentives as a reward for introductions. One leading management consultancy practice offered a bounty of 8% of a new recruit's salary, half to be paid on joining and the other half to be paid when the individual had been with the firm for six months. Given that salaries for new recruits ranged from £30,000 to £100,000, this was quite an incentive — but still worked out much cheaper than the 25% of salary charged by agencies or the average cost of an advertising campaign.

8.51 Capital Consulting recently estimated that a company hiring 250 people per year would save £80,000 if only 10% of these came through referrals and a £250 reward was paid for each. The same study found that only 18% of employees work in organisations which encourage them to recommend friends or acquaintances, despite one in every four (24%) knowing someone they could refer immediately.

Networking and Poaching

8.52 The use of personal networks by HR professionals, line managers or the owners or directors of businesses to identify staff is not uncommon, particularly for key positions or for scarce talent. This approach has the same advantages and potential pitfalls as recommendations from existing employees.

8.53 Be aware when recruiting an external candidate that you check that they are not restricted under their existing contract from working for you. This is especially important if they have previously worked for a competitor.

Direct Applications

8.54 Unsolicited applications depend on job seekers being motivated to make direct approaches to a potential employer. Their behaviour is influenced by the image which an organisation projects.

8.55 Some organisations take positive steps to project an image that will assist them in attracting direct approaches from all sections of the community. A large organisation which was opening a new store in an area with a high ethnic minority population might:
- contact community leaders and organisations
- visit youth clubs and religious groups
- generate publicity in the local newspaper and on local radio.

8.56 The time and money which it invested could result in:
- high calibre ethnic minority applicants
- possible savings in recruitment costs
- the stimulation of additional sales revenue as a result of showing an interest in the groups in question.

8.57 Although direct applications are unsolicited, it is nevertheless courteous to reply to them all, even if no suitable vacancy is currently available. If they are retained to be matched with future vacancies, it is vital to:
- have an efficient system for storage and retrieval
- observe the requirements of the Data Protection Act (DPA).

Former Employees

8.58 Employers can keep in touch with high-quality former staff. The cost is minimal but the requirements of the DPA must be observed.

Recent Recruitment Campaigns

8.59 Employers can use applications from previous advertisements within the last few months as a source of recruits. Applicants who were not quite right for the position in question might be ideal for the new vacancy.

8.60 The advantages are:
- low costs
- saved time.

8.61 Once again, the requirements of the DPA must be observed.

8.62 Where agencies are used, it is also possible to go back to candidates who were interviewed but not hired, thus saving time. Although a further fee will have to be paid, it may be possible to negotiate a discount.

Being an Employer of Choice

8.63 Whichever methods of attracting applicants are used, their effectiveness will depend at least to some extent on potential applicants' perceptions of the desirability of working for the organisation. This is a matter of:
- the employer's own image
- the sector in which the organisation operates, which it can do little about.

8.64 Some organisations spend enormous amounts of money on developing and communicating their "employer brand". However, publicity spend is less important than matters such as:
- a genuine commitment to best practice in all aspects of the treatment of existing employees
- the organisation's standards in respect of its products or services
- a commitment to Corporate Social Responsibility (CSR).

8.65 CSR embraces every aspect of the ethical behaviour of employer organisations, ie its behaviour towards:
- the community
- the environment
- customers
- suppliers
- employees, including equal opportunities and diversity, health and safety, the work-life balance.

8.66 The advantage of CSR, as a May 2007 survey conducted by Sirota Survey Intelligence showed, is that employees who are satisfied with their company's commitment to social responsibility have positive views about their employer in several other key areas. The company surveyed 1.6 million people from more than 70 organisations and found that employees who have a favourable view of an organisation's CSR commitment in such areas as environmental awareness were also found to be positive about several factors important to its success, including senior management's integrity and their inspirational sense of direction.

8.67 Additionally, it is vital to pay great attention to the impression conveyed by the actual recruitment process. This is not just a matter of the quality of an advertisement or monitoring the way the employer's chosen recruitment consultants deal with potential employees. It is also a matter of how efficiently the rest of the recruitment process is handled.

Training

8.68 Training in the use of the various methods of sourcing applicants should be a key part of any recruitment and selection course. Although the content of such a course should always provide comprehensive coverage of the discrimination risks involved, these could also be included in courses on diversity and equal opportunities.

List of Relevant Legislation

8.69
- Employment Equality (Age) Regulations 2006
- Employment Equality (Religion and Belief) Regulations 2003
- Employment Equality (Sexual Orientation) Regulations 2003
- Sex Discrimination (Gender Reassignment) Regulations 1999
- Data Protection Act 1998
- Disability Discrimination Act 1995
- Race Relations Act 1976
- Sex Discrimination Act 1975

Further Information

Publications

- *Race Relations Code of Practice for the Elimination of Racial Discrimination and the Promotion of Equality of Opportunity in Employment ("Employment Code of Practice") (1984)*, Commission for Racial Equality
- *Code of Practice on Racial Equality in Employment (Draft Revised Code, 2004)*, Commission for Racial Equality
- *Acas: Age and the Workplace — Putting the Employment Equality (Age) Regulations 2006 into Practice (2006)*
- *The Duty to Promote Race Equality — Code of Practice and Guidance (for Public Authorities)*, Commission for Racial Equality
- *The Race Relations Act 1976 (Amendment) Regulations 2003* — briefing by the Commission for Racial Equality (June 2003)
- *Code of Practice: Sex Discrimination*, Equal Opportunities Commission (EOC)
- *Equal Pay, Fair Pay*

Organisations

- **Commission for Racial Equality**
  Web: *www.cre.gov.uk*
  The Commission for Racial Equality is a publicly funded, non-governmental body set up under the Race Relations Act 1976 to tackle racial discrimination and promote racial equality. From October 2007 this organisation will be replaced by the Commission for Equality and Human Rights.

- **Disability Rights Commission**
  Web: *www.drc-gb.org*
  An independent body established by Act of Parliament to eliminate discrimination against disabled people and promote equality of opportunity. It provides information and advice to disabled people and employers about their rights and duties. From October 2007 this organisation will be replaced by the Commission for Equality and Human Rights (**Web:** *www.cehr.org.uk*).

- **Equal Opportunities Commission**
  Web: *www.eoc.org.uk*
  An agency working to eliminate sex discrimination and put equality into practice in the workplace. From October 2007 this organisation will be replaced by the Commission for Equality and Human Rights (**Web:** *www.cehr.org.uk*).

- **Job Centre Plus**
  Web: *www.jobcentreplus.gov.uk*
  Part of the Department of Work and Pensions, the Job Centre Plus offers help and advice on job hunting and information for organisations.

Induction

> This topic covers the following.
> - Why Induction is Important
> - Who Should be Involved
> - Selling the Idea
> - Corporate v Local
> - Planning and Preparation
> - What Should be Included
> - Providing Handouts
> - Frequency of Induction Events
> - Part-time Employees
> - Inclusion in Business Plans
> - Providing Continued Support
> - Induction for Job Changes
> - Evaluation
> - Record Keeping and Documentation

8.70 Induction is a planned process designed to introduce new members of staff to an organisation as quickly as possible. The induction process should allow new staff to learn about the structure, culture and rules of the organisation. It should help them to settle in and find their way around.

8.71 A number of people in the organisation should be involved in the provision of induction. Line managers or supervisors will be responsible for ensuring staff have access to an induction programme. The training function in larger organisations will probably be responsible for designing the overall programme in conjunction with line managers. Induction needs to be planned carefully so that it lays the foundations for a beneficial working relationship that can be built on in future months and years.

Employers' Duties

8.72 All new staff should be given training in health and safety issues under the Health and Safety at Work, etc Act 1974. There is no legal requirement to provide any other form of induction to new employees. However, induction is an opportunity to introduce employees to the organisation's:
- health and safety policies and practices
- other policies and procedures
- rules
- terms and conditions of employment
- pay and reward
- discipline and grievance
- other informal practices.

Employees' Duties

8.73 Employees have a duty to:

- report any health and safety hazards
- use the telephone, email and Internet in accordance with the organisation's policies
- adhere to any general rules of behaviour
- inform a designated manager if they are unable to attend work due to illness.

In Practice

Why Induction is Important

8.74 It is recognised that induction both helps new recruits to settle into the organisation and contributes towards staff retention. Staff who have been inducted into the organisation effectively have been proven to stay longer, and are also more likely to rate their employer as a "good employer".

8.75 Induction does not sit alone, but instead forms part of an organisation's overall development plan. Induction needs to be part of the philosophy of the organisation and become embedded in its culture. It can help the organisation in the following ways.

- Induction is an excellent time to promote an organisation's image. Notes/packs can be colour coded and can incorporate logos to create a definitive design image.
- Induction gives the organisation an opportunity to present its aims and objectives. For example, if the organisation has strong links with environmental protection issues, the induction process can be used to reinforce that image further. It also allows the organisation to put across important issues such as charitable projects, Investors in People, or its stance regarding corporate social responsibility (CSR).
- Induction will usually be the first interface between new employees and the organisation's training expertise. New recruits in management positions will be watching the way that induction is handled as an indication of the quality of training the organisation offers. Induction also gives the organisation an opportunity to demonstrate the range of training it can provide.
- All employees have a psychological contract with their employer. This contract is not written down; it is an unspoken agreement that the employee will work hard, attend regularly, be loyal and work towards the organisation's aims and targets. This psychological contract can be enhanced if an employee's entry into the organisation is a positive experience.
- Staff perform better when they know what they are working towards both within their team and in relation to the wider goals of the organisation. If the employer is part of a larger conglomerate, it also helps staff to learn a little about the other businesses within the group. When staff understand the big picture, they are more likely to understand how their role fits in.
- Providing new staff with support and information about the organisation, its policies and practices in the first few weeks or months of their employment will make them feel more secure and comfortable.
- New managers are often expected to find their feet immediately in an organisation. They will need to know specifically how the business operates and where they can find the guidelines to help them manage staff effectively. Induction is an opportunity to explain certain processes while issuing relevant procedures or policy documents.
- Induction is an ideal opportunity to find out what staff thought of the recruitment and selection process, and also of the integration of staff into the organisation during the induction period. This feedback can be used to enhance processes and practices for the future.

Induction

- Induction is an ideal process to welcome staff into a business following an organisational merger, takeover, or division. It can also be used effectively for employees joining new teams or moving jobs internally. In fact, the induction process can be used in any situation where staff need to enter a new working environment or relationship.

Who Should be Involved

8.76 A number of different people in the organisation should be involved in the provision of induction. Line managers or supervisors will be responsible for ensuring staff have access to an induction programme. The training function in larger organisations will probably be responsible for designing the overall programme in conjunction with line managers. New employees' work colleagues will also play a major part.

Selling the Idea

8.77 Induction requires resourcing and a business case may have to be presented to management in order to justify the expense. Any cost incurred by this initial investment will be recovered through saving staff time in the early stages of their job, and staff staying longer with the organisation. However, the idea may still need to be sold to the chief executive and to the managers who will need to implement it.

8.78 Whether induction is being introduced or revamped, managers should be involved as early as possible in the design, and their feedback requested and taken on board. Line managers may need training in induction procedures.

8.79 Where a formal proposal is presented to a board, the positive points need to be sold and all costings justified. It should be emphasised that induction needs to be seen as a cultural norm rather than a new initiative, and that it can contribute to strengthening the organisation's image.

Corporate v Local

8.80 Induction can take place anywhere. In some organisations it will take place in the manager's office, while in others it is held in a hotel conference suite. Some organisations will use a split-procedure whereby the corporate induction will take place centrally to ensure that all new staff will hear the same corporate message, while separate local inductions, based around local policy and procedures, are arranged.

8.81 Some organisations ask work colleagues to attend induction presentations so that they can meet new staff members on an informal basis before they move into the working environment.

Planning and Preparation (Local Induction)

8.82 Induction needs to be planned carefully so that it lays the foundations for a beneficial working relationship that can be built on in future months and years. From the moment of recruitment, new staff begin to speculate how life will be in their new jobs. Induction is often the first experience they have of being part of their new organisation. Careful preparation is required to ensure that this experience is a good one and comes across as co-ordinated and helpful. Points for action include the following.

- Involve the new employee's colleagues in the induction process as much as possible. It may be possible to implement a buddy system or simply ask one team member to accompany new staff to lunch on their first day, so that they know where to go.
- Arrange for new employees' desks/working areas to be as tidy and pleasant as possible and, if they are to use computers, ensure that passwords and user names are ready for their first day.
- Arrange for managers to meet new staff at reception on their first day and escort them to their working area. It will give the new employees a good feeling about the organisation.
- Anticipate some of the new employee's early needs, such as where to get lunch or a drink, where they can smoke outside the building, the location of the toilets, how to use the telephone, whether private calls are allowed, and whether personal mobile phones are allowed to be kept on.

What Should be Included (Organisational Induction)

8.83 Corporate or organisational inductions provide more scope for imparting knowledge than local inductions, but the presentations will have to be more general as the information given will be the same for everyone. Some areas to consider covering in an organisational induction are listed below.

- Many organisations are proud of their history and how they were originally founded. Indeed this might even explain why certain structures exist or why decisions are made in a certain way. An organisation's roots will also explain its culture.
- If the organisation works on several different sites, then maps of how to travel from site to site (and within each site) will be invaluable. They will also give new staff a feel for the extent of the organisation. Similarly, internal plans of organisation buildings will help everyone to find their way around, locate toilets, fire exits, snack machines, photocopiers and drinking facilities.
- Most employees need to use the telephone for business and therefore a list of handy numbers will be useful. Also notes on how to use the telephone system – how to dial an outside line, hold a call, transfer, pick up another line, deal with a call waiting, set up voicemail and so forth – will help new employees to be more effective from day one.
- Depending on the size of the induction intake (and the size of the organisation), a split-system could be designed whereby all new staff attend a presentation covering corporate identity, and are then divided into groups for a departmental overview. This would allow new staff to appreciate their role both as part of the bigger picture and in a more local setting. If the intake is insufficient to support this approach a general overview could be supplied by a senior or line manager
- The HR department often has a significant input into induction. It can inform new staff about the terms and conditions of their employment, how various systems (such as sickness absence policies, pension schemes and benefits packages) work, and the paperwork requirements linked with these. HR may also require photographs to be taken for security card passes.
- Health and safety personnel will also play a major role in induction. HR and health and safety will not necessarily need to make a formal presentation. Often a friendly face handing out some leaflets containing useful information and contact details will be sufficient.
- Induction is a good opportunity to present new staff with an overview of the training opportunities within the organisation. New staff will be weighing up the quality of the organisation's training. Where the new staff are managers, the quality of the induction presentation may influence their future choices as regards the training needs of themselves and their staff.

- Consideration should be given to what refreshments are to be offered to delegates and, for a full-day event, whether lunch will be included.
- One way of introducing key staff to new employees is to invite them to a buffet lunch and allow them to mingle. This has the advantage of being informal, while also allowing a lot of people to meet and spend some time with each other, all within a limited amount of time such as one or two hours.
- Key policies and procedures need to be included in any induction event, large or small.
- Any key practices, such as a requirement to use swipe cards to enter buildings or "dress down Fridays", need to be explained during induction.
- If the organisation has a trade union presence it is likely that the union will want to be involved in any induction.
- For a "presentation style" induction event, other guests may be invited, from the chief executive or directors through department heads, to the person who manages the crèche facilities or organises catering. The list could be endless and therefore some people can be invited to put forward leaflets or documentation rather than to give a presentation.

8.84 Remember that staff can get "induction-overload" and feel swamped by too much information. The process should therefore be organised so that information is provided to new employees in separate small chunks over a period of time.

Providing Handouts

8.85 If induction forms part of a strategy for staff development, folders and/or full workbooks may be designed that integrate into the wider system. These folders can then become staff development folders or a place to store certificates and training notes.

8.86 If the induction is a smaller affair, handouts may be more appropriate. However, if handouts are provided, employees should be offered a folder as a place to keep all their induction information for future reference.

Frequency of Induction Events

8.87 The overall design and duration of an induction programme will depend largely on the number of staff being recruited, and how often events can realistically be held. For example, if the organisation has only one intake of graduates each year, then one large-scale event is sufficient. (Note, however, that under the Employment Equality (Age) Regulations 2006, the organisation should not solely be recruiting graduates, as this could discriminate against older people who may be less likely to have attended university.) If, on the other hand, new staff are joining every week but in very small numbers, there might be two or three large scale corporate induction events at different times throughout the year, with individual induction handled through line managers. If there are only a very few staff recruited each year, then a local approach may be more appropriate as a full event would not be justifiable.

8.88 The induction programme, as a whole, needs to be planned carefully so that it starts in some form from day one. From the moment a new member of staff joins an organisation, there should be someone responsible for ensuring that person's learning starts immediately and continues through the next weeks and months. Inductions should not be seen as something that takes place only when there is a sufficient number of new staff.

8.89 The induction programme should be flexible as it will have to meet the needs of a changing workforce and organisation. What might be appropriate in terms of structure, format, content and duration one year may not be suitable the following year. The programme should therefore be revised at least every two years, or following any negative feedback.

Part-time Employees

8.90 The Part-time Workers (Prevention of Less Favourable Treatment) Regulations 2000 entitles part-time employees not to be treated less favourably than comparable full-time staff on account of their part-time status. This general right applies in respect of both contractual and non-contractual terms.

8.91 With regard to training, the regulations specifically provide that part-timers must not be excluded from training just because they are part-time. Employers are therefore under a duty to make sure that new part-time employees are afforded the benefit of any induction programme run by the organisation in full.

8.92 It is recommended also that training should be structured wherever possible so that it takes place at the most convenient times for the majority of staff, including part-time workers.

Inclusion in Business Plans

8.93 Management should make sure that induction is included in the organisational business and/or development plans. This demonstrates commitment to the well-being of staff and a professional approach to integrating new staff into the organisation.

8.94 A robust induction process also supports Investors in People and other quality initiatives.

Providing Continued Support

8.95 Induction does not end once staff have attended their induction briefing. New staff need ongoing support and a point of reference for asking questions, raising concerns and continuing to learn. One option is to pair each new staff member up with a "buddy" — a work colleague who can help with ongoing questions. Another option is to assign each new member of staff a mentor or coach to help support him or her through the first year.

Induction for Job Changes

8.96 Although induction is often interpreted as a programme of education and integration for new employees, it should take place even when employees change jobs within the organisation. Joining a new team can mean working in a completely different way, with new people, new demands and a new business focus. Managers should induct new staff into their team even if they are not new to the organisation.

8.97 Similarly, if an organisation merges with another organisation, an induction programme should be devised for all the new staff in order to provide information about the organisation, reaffirm the organisation's culture and set new standards for the future.

Evaluation

8.98 All induction programmes require evaluation to ensure they are effective in providing the right information to support new employees. The recruitment process may be included as part of this evaluation as recruitment is sometimes difficult to evaluate as a process on its own. Return on investment (ROI) can be demonstrated through measuring the speed at which new employees feel comfortable about their new role within the organisation, how they rate the content of induction as to how helpful it was and how quickly they become effective and efficient in their roles.

Record Keeping and Documentation

8.99 A record of induction training should be kept for each staff member. This could be in the form of a checklist that shows staff have been informed about all relevant policies and practices.

Training

8.100 All new staff should go through the induction training process. Existing staff who are involved in the provision of induction programmes may require training themselves in how to deliver the programme.

8.101 The induction programme should start as soon as the new employee begins work with the organisation. It may include a general induction event at which a group of new employees are presented with information on relevant topics. The frequency of such events will depend on the number of new recruits the organisation takes each year.

8.102 Induction training is most likely to be delivered face-to-face, for instance through talks and exercises. Some aspects of the training could, however, be delivered using distance learning and e-learning, while other topics can be dealt with by the provision of handouts.

8.103 Induction can help an organisation to demonstrate its approach to lifelong learning, training and personal development. For some organisations, induction is the procedure that leads directly into target setting, creating development plans and appraisal.

8.104 Employees may be given personal development folders at induction, within which they can store all their personal data throughout their employment.

List of Relevant Legislation

8.105
- Health and Safety at Work, etc Act 1974

Further Information

Publications
- *Acas Induction Training*
- *B05 Acas Recruitment and Induction*
- *Training Support Directory*, Business Link

Interviewing

> This topic covers the following.
> - Why Does Selection Interviewing Matter?
> - The Purpose of a Selection Interview
> - Selection Interviewing
> - Stage 1 — Preparation
> - Stage 2 — Opening the Interview
> - Stage 3 — Questioning Techniques
> - Stage 4 — After the Interview

Employers' Duties

8.106 Employers have a duty to ensure that:
- no candidate is treated less favourably in the recruitment and selection process on the grounds of age, sex, race, disability, sexual orientation, gender reassignment, religion or belief, or trade union membership or non-membership
- all stages of the recruitment, selection, training and talent management process are monitored to ensure that there is no discriminatory treatment
- consideration is given to any provision, criterion or practice in the person specification or terms of a job which might be indirectly discriminatory
- interview criteria (stated or implied) and interview questions must not discriminate, either directly or indirectly
- interview facilities and arrangements must take account of the needs of disabled workers
- all interviewers are appropriately trained in relation to current legislation and the organisation's policies regarding diversity
- all selection methods are regularly reviewed to ensure effectiveness, reliability, and compliance with current legislation.

Employees' Duties

8.107 Employees have a duty to:
- be honest in the personal information disclosed in the recruitment and selection process
- be honest in any information disclosed at interview
- provide accurate information about past work experience, training courses and qualifications.

In Practice

8.108 While there are many tools available for selecting staff, the interview remains the most popular and the most cost effective. The danger is that most

Interviewing

managers believe that they can interview. An unstructured interview conducted by an untrained practitioner is often highly subjective and a poor indicator of workplace performance. A structured interview which refers to specific and well researched job benchmarks and focuses on a candidate's competencies will be a highly effective tool.

Why does Selection Interviewing Matter?

8.109 Interviewing offers an employer a chance to assess candidates face to face and to explore fully what they have to offer. Conducted well, it becomes a key stage in an integrated policy of recruitment, retention and talent management. It has practical implications for the following key stages:
- predicting workplace performance
- selecting talent
- gaining an awareness of the talent pool
- positively contributing to employer branding.

The Purpose of a Selection Interview

8.110 Selection interviews are used in order to:
- gain information about candidates
- assess candidates' skills, knowledge, motivation and experience
- convey important information about the role and organisation
- assess candidates' commitment to accept a job offer
- establish rapport between the interviewer and candidate
- explore all areas of job criteria with candidates.

Selection Interviewing

8.111 To enable the interviewer to make an effective, fair and legal selection decision, selection interviewing has a number of stages.
- Reference to defined competencies and other job-related documents including job descriptions and person specifications.
- Preparing questions in relation to defined competencies.
- Carefully studying all materials submitted by candidates in documents of application.
- Preparing and, where necessary, adapting competency-based questions.
- Where necessary, forming an interview panel and agreeing an interview structure.
- Providing candidates with useful job-related documents before the interview.
- Providing candidates with clear details about where and when the interview will take place.
- Providing a professional, private, tidy, comfortable, well-lit interview room with appropriate seating.
- Putting a candidate at ease and building rapport during the interview.
- Using appropriate techniques to obtain and confirm information from candidates.
- Using appropriate probing and checking techniques.
- Providing information relating to the job and the organisation.
- Summarising and closing.
- Answering candidate questions.
- Applying selection criteria in a fair, open and effective manner.

- Where appropriate, giving feedback on the interview to candidates or to others outside the interview process.

Stage 1 — Preparation

Having a Clear Picture of the Job

8.112   Begin by reviewing all documents available which:
- define the job — eg the job description
- record the information seen by candidates (eg the job advertisement).

8.113   Next, review any short-listing process which has already taken place — what selection criteria have already been applied? What evidence do you already have about candidates?

Review Candidate Documents

8.114   Your organisation may have a policy restricting the kinds of candidate documents that will be considered (eg your organisation may have a policy of explicitly ignoring CVs or even letters of application). If this is not the case, review in detail all documents submitted by candidates, including any letter of application. Examine points of matching and points of difference. Prepare appropriate interview questions.

Interview Preparation Checklist

Documentation

8.115   Before interviewing, go thoroughly over:
- job description and person specification
- competency framework
- job advertisement
- documents received from candidates
- interview plan/structure
- list of prepared or set questions
- notes of any previous interviews with the same candidate.

Administration

8.116   In order to facilitate the interview process, you should:
- send candidates clear directions and joining instructions
- brief reception on list of candidates and timings
- read all documents as set out above
- prepare any tests and/or equipment to be used
- have relevant documents to hand during the interview, along with paper and pen for notes
- provide refreshments if appropriate
- provide a claim form for travel expenses, if appropriate.

Environment

8.117   Select and prepare an appropriate interview room, ideally one which is:
- well lit, clean, comfortable and at the right temperature
- free of interruptions and background noise
- free of clutter and intrusive equipment such as large computer monitors

- equipped with appropriate seating.

Using Benchmarked Competencies

8.118 Competency statements or frameworks are a highly useful tool in selection, because they begin with the needs of the organisation and help to provide objective, measurable selection criteria.

8.119 There are many ways of defining competencies and the term is often mixed up with skills. A competency is about underpinning knowledge, skills which are used by effective performers, how those skills are used and to what level. Competencies also provide information about the attitude and motivation of successful staff and define their observable behaviours. One way that organisations define competencies is by analysing contributions made by the top 10–20% of staff already in the organisation.

Defining Competencies

8.120 A competency statement will often provide the following key information.
- Knowledge — there are strong correlations between practitioner knowledge and performance in the role. Knowledge assessments need to cater for current and known, or planned assignments.
- Skills — should be defined in terms of content, measurable level and outcomes. Begin by working out which skills are required for success in the role and to what level. Distinguish between low order skills (eg filing) and high order skills (eg delegating). Distinguish between skills which can be acquired quickly through training (eg using a computer application), those which require longer-term acquisition (eg communication skills) and those which are innate (eg a gift for numeracy).
- Attitude and motivation — define the attitudes to work displayed by your top performers, eg staff who are reliable, flexible, prepared to go the extra mile, etc. Also, interview top performing staff about what motivates them to complete the relevant tasks.
- Observable behaviours — list the behaviours which you see in top performers (eg answering correspondence the same day, leaving a tidy desk, etc).

Stage 2 — Opening the Interview

Establishing Rapport

8.121 Most candidates are nervous during a job interview. You're asking them to disclose information about their lives and capabilities, so this is perfectly normal. Thank the candidate for attending. Opening with an ice-breaker statement or question helps — get the candidate to feel relaxed. You may choose to use a low order question here.

8.122 In order to build and increase rapport during an interview, an interviewer ought to:
- provide clear, helpful directions to the interview site
- fully brief reception about candidates arriving for interview
- meet the interview schedule
- remind the candidate of the format and timing of the interview
- begin with low order questions
- demonstrate active listening, eg by positive body language and by summarising

- be prepared to deal with, and able to answer, candidate questions.

Setting the Ground Rules

8.123 You will build up on a good opening relationship by explaining the purpose, timing and format of the interview. Inviting the candidate to ask questions but to keep them until the end of the interview helps keep the discussion on track.

Low Order Questions

8.124 A candidate will generally be nervous at the beginning of an interview. A competent interviewer will recognise this and, in order to help build rapport and settle the candidate, will start with low order questions. The following low order questions are straightforward, easy to answer and therefore require a lower order of processing in the brain.
- "How did you find the journey?"
- "Isn't this weather dreadful?"

Stage 3 — Questioning Techniques

Moving to High Order Questions

8.125 The questions then become progressively more high order, ie require more thinking.
- "Talk me through a typical day at work."
- "What do you find most challenging about your job?"

8.126 As you probe you will gradually ask questions which are higher order.
- "Tell me about a time when you failed to meet a target."
- "Tell me about a time when you had to deal with a team member who was under-performing."

8.127 Ultimately you may ask very high order questions.
- "What do you feel you could contribute to a prospective employer?"
- "How would you describe your weaknesses?"
- "Where would you like to be in five years' time?"

Closed Questions

8.128 Closed questions are rarely useful if they just elicit a yes/no answer, eg "Did you enjoy your last job?" They tend to close a candidate down, limiting response. The following examples, however, can help establish useful facts.
- "When did you pass your driving test?"
- "What class was your degree? Did you complete it?"
- "How many new customers did you win last week?"

8.129 Sometimes closed questions allow candidates to dodge probing questions, eg "Would you describe yourself as computer literate?"

Open Questions

8.130 Open questions are designed to open the candidate up and open up areas of information. The following are a few good examples.
- "Give me an example of a time when you led a team."
- "Tell me about a time when you had to deal with a demanding customer."

Interviewing

- "Why did you leave your last job?"

8.131 The interview should start with open questions to encourage the candidate to talk. Listen carefully to the candidate's responses and probe as necessary, moving gradually towards open high order questions that require a lot of mental capacity and will draw out a candidate's relevant experience, strengths and weaknesses.

Probing Questions

8.132 It is rare that a candidate will give you all the required information from your first question. Probing is the key to a successful selection interview. The questions should be short, simple and in past tense. Following are a few good examples.
- What exactly did you do?
- What feedback did you receive?
- Can you give me an example?
- What was going through your mind?
- What was the outcome?
- How would you do it differently if you did it again?

8.133 Be aware of some appropriate areas for probing questions.
- Past and present ambitions and aspirations.
- Tasks and challenges in present and recent jobs.
- Reasons for previous career decisions.
- Skills obtained and to what level.
- Past challenges and difficulties.
- Reasons for applying for the present position.
- Factors the candidate sees as a strong match for the job.
- Aspects of the job which the candidate might find difficult.

Assessing Competencies

8.134 Competencies are most commonly measured using competence-based questions, either in an application form or in a structured interview.
- Skills — may be assessed by appropriate skills tests, by in-tray exercises and through detailed questioning at interview. Use probing questions to establish the skill ("What exactly did you do?") and the skill level ("What was difficult about this?").
- Attitude and motivation — plan interview questions carefully to draw out actual experiences of attitudes (eg to supervision, deadlines, customers) and motivation (reasons for past job changes or requests for promotion and training).
- Observable behaviours — seek concrete evidence from the candidate of how they dealt with relevant problems in the workplace (eg dealing with a difficult customer). You might also explore typical scenarios ("How would you respond to....").

Competency-based Questions

8.135 These questions should be planned carefully, drawing on the competency framework or statement already produced. They focus on key areas of information.
- What was the nature of the work the candidate has performed? What were the key result areas in their job?
- What specific tasks did the candidate perform?
- What competencies has the candidate needed to carry out previous roles?
- What problems did he or she face?

- What is his/her attitude towards past successes and difficulties?
- Under what sort of conditions and culture did the candidate work?
- How was performance measured and how far were performance criteria met?
- What tangible evidence of success is there to back-up the candidate's claims?
- How did this individual's performance match up with the rest of the team?
- How flexible would this candidate be in transferring these skills to another type of work?

Other Tools in the Interviewer's Kitbag

8.136 To ensure an effective interview, an interviewer should:
- summarise various parts of what a candidate has said to encourage a good relationship and check facts
- probe using the candidate's own words, eg "Tell me a little more about what you mean by 'management responsibility' "
- use active listening to show that you are paying attention
- ensure that body language conveys interest and attentiveness
- make sure that the candidate does most of the talking
- allow pauses for the candidate to think if you are seeking complex information
- not interrupt more than is necessary
- take notes, particularly of positive points, but not lose all eye contact in the process
- encourage the candidate to ask relevant questions.

Stage 4 — After the Interview

Objective Selection

8.137 The following factors assist objective selection of the right candidate.
- The interviewer is conversant with job-related information and criteria.
- The interviewer is conversant with job-related criteria.
- Interview questions and areas of probing are planned in advance
- Candidate responses and experiences are probed.
- All key criteria or competencies are covered by the interview.
- The interview avoids classic objectivity errors.

Interview Evidence

8.138 Utilise interview evidence to arrive at a selection decision.
- Record evidence during and after an interview.
- Ensure that you have covered all the selection criteria.
- Measure candidates against the job, not against each other.
- Use a scoring or matrix system if desired to help score candidates against your wish list.
- Recall evidence about all candidates, not just the most recent or the ones who made the biggest impact.
- Document the reasons for selection.
- Proceed to a written job offer, or seek further candidates for interview.
- If all candidates are unsuitable, review (a) your job criteria and (b) your short-listing method.

Employer Branding and Selection Interviews

8.139 Employer branding is built through impressions and experiences, including the following which relate to the interview process.

- The quality of the documentation and planning which are offered before an interview.
- The speed of response in the recruitment process.
- How candidates are received when they arrive for interview.
- The professionalism of interview arrangements.
- How far recruiters are knowledgeable about the job and the organisation.
- Questions, statements, comments and feedback given during the interview.
- Feedback given at various stages in the process, especially after interviewing and testing.
- How successful and unsuccessful candidates are handled.

List of Relevant Legislation

8.140
- Employment Equality (Age) Regulations 2006
- Employment Equality (Religion or Belief) Regulations 2003
- Employment Equality (Sexual Orientation) Regulations 2003
- Sex Discrimination (Gender Reassignment) Regulations 1999
- Disability Discrimination Act 1995
- Sex Discrimination Act 1975
- Race Relations Act 1976

Further Information

Publications
- Dale, Margaret, *A Manager's Guide to Recruitment and Selection*, Kogan Page, 2003.
- Dale, Margaret and Peel, Malcolm, *Readymade Interview Questions*, Kogan Page, 2001.
- Grout, Jeff and Perrin, Sarah, *Recruiting Excellence: An Insider's Guide to Sourcing Top Talent*, McGraw-Hill Education, 2005.
- Hindle, Tim, *Essential Managers: Interviewing Skills*, Dorling Kindersley, 1998.
- Hackett, Penny *The Selection Interview*, Chartered Institute of Personnel and Development, 1998.

Job Descriptions and Person Specifications

> This topic covers the following.
> - Review the Situation
> - Job Descriptions
> - Job Analysis
> - Review the Existing Job Description
> - Format and Content of Job Descriptions
> - The Person Specification
> - Common Errors
> - Structured Approaches
> - Competency Frameworks
> - Mandatory and Preferred Requirements
> - Direct and Indirect Discrimination

8.141 No recruitment exercise should be allowed to proceed without an up-to-date job description and an objective person specification. In some cases it may be necessary to conduct a job analysis prior to producing the job description. Furthermore, consideration should always be given to whether there actually is a need to recruit at all and, if so, whether or not the job necessarily requires a full-time, workplace-based employee.

8.142 In preparing the person specification, care must be taken to concentrate on factors that are objective and strictly relevant to the job.

Employers' Duties

8.143 Employers have a duty to ensure that:
- no applicant is treated less favourably in the recruitment and selection process on the designated legal grounds
- the provisions on genuine occupational requirements are complied with where appropriate
- consideration is given to any provision, criterion or practice in the person specification or terms of a job which might be indirectly discriminatory
- reasonable adjustments are made for applicants who are disabled
- they do not put pressure to discriminate on any staff involved in recruitment and selection
- they are aware of an employer's potential liability for acts of discrimination in the course of employment even where these are committed by managers and other members of staff
- the terms of an offer of employment are carefully considered to ensure that contractual obligations are fully understood by both parties
- the terms and conditions of employment are consistent with statutory requirements and minimum standards
- checks on health and requests for references are made as appropriate
- checks on the right of the individual to work within the UK are made and copies of the documents retained

- data relating to recruitment and selection is processed in accordance with data protection legislation and guidance from the Information Commissioner.

Employees' Duties

8.144 Employees have a duty to:
- be genuine and honest in providing personal information disclosed in the recruitment and selection process
- facilitate appropriate checks to be made about health and criminal records and any other appropriate checks
- provide, as required, the names of referees
- ensure that they have the right to work in the UK and be able to provide the appropriate documents to the employer when required to do so (normally a passport will be requested)
- abide by an agreement they reach on accepting employment.

In Practice

Review the Situation

8.145 When an employee leaves, HR managers should consider whether there is any need for a replacement. Three simple questions initiate this review process — the same questions can be used to examine requests for additional staff.
- What are the outputs of the job?
- Are these outputs really required?
- Are there alternative ways of achieving these outputs, eg by computerisation or mechanisation, restructuring the department or reviewing systems and procedures.

8.146 Even where a recruitment exercise is necessary, hiring a permanent, full-time, office-based employee may not be the best solution. Outsourcing, home-working, part-time working, job sharing, fixed-term contracts and temporary or contract staff may all be valid alternatives, especially where flexibility is desirable.

Job Descriptions

8.147 It is essential to have an accurate and up-to-date job description. Consider the job's purpose and outputs, its key result areas, tasks and duties. One should not even consider the kind of person who will be required or the way duties will be carried out and results achieved, otherwise assumptions may insinuate their way into the process. Different people may approach a job in different ways and one of the great values of diversity is that a new job holder may find a better way of doing things.

Job Analysis

8.148 Where the job description is out of date, or where the job is a new one, a job analysis should be conducted, involving:
- the person to whom the job holder reports
- the incumbent of the position if appropriate.

8.149 The job analysis should cover:
- the overall purpose of the job
- its reporting relationships
- the extent of the job holder's authority
- the detailed duties
- how performance is to be measured
- any special factors.

Gathering Information

8.150 This information is best gathered by interview and questionnaire. A questionnaire obtains factual information effectively, while the interview can be used to discuss:
- problems encountered in the job
- changes anticipated in the near future, eg in systems or technology.

8.151 In the case of new jobs, it is useful to question other staff who will work closely with the holder of the new job.

8.152 In some cases, eg repetitive manual tasks, job analysis can be conducted by a skilled observer.

Review the Existing Job Description

8.153 Employers should ensure that all job descriptions are reviewed regularly, eg on an annual basis. Reviews could easily be made a part of the appraisal process. A properly conducted appraisal should include a discussion of any changes in the content of a job or the skills needed to perform it. Subjects covered in a review should include:
- whether the purpose of the job has altered
- changes in the organisational structure of the work unit
- alterations in reporting lines or in the number of staff managed
- changes in key result areas
- increases or decreases in the level of budget controlled
- tasks that might have been added to the job
- whether the job holder no longer has any of the duties in the existing job description
- whether the job holder believes any of the current duties are no longer necessary
- anything else that may be relevant to the job description and to the recruitment of a successor.

Format and Content of Job Descriptions

8.154 The format of the job description may vary depending on the nature and level of the post but needs to include seven basic elements:
- job title
- reporting lines
- main purpose of the job
- key result areas
- detailed duties
- working relationships
- special factors.

Job Title

8.155 Make the job title as clear and self-explanatory as possible. It should ideally indicate both the function and the level of the job, eg Marketing Manager, Production Control Clerk, PA to the HR Manager.

8.156 Do not use gender specific terms such as "salesman" or "girl friday". The term "manager" is generally perceived as gender neutral.

Reporting Lines

8.157 State the title rather than the name of the person to whom the job holder reports. This keeps the job description up-to-date even if the line manager moves on.

8.158 State the number of subordinates reporting to the job holder, together with their job titles.

Main Purpose of the Job

8.159 Give a brief description of the reasons why the job exists, identifying the outputs that are expected to accrue from it.

Key Result Areas

8.160 Specify measurable standards by which performance will be judged. It should be possible to apply the procedure to posts at any level.

Detailed Duties

8.161 Classify the detailed duties under appropriate headings in order to give some idea of which tasks are most important and of the percentage of the job holder's time that each of them will take up.

8.162 Duties will normally need to be described in more detail for jobs of a junior nature than for positions higher up the organisation, where job holders are expected to exercise greater discretion and where the achievement of broader objectives is paramount.

Working Relationships

8.163 List the titles of the people with whom the job holder will have to liaise in order to carry out the job.

Special Factors

8.164 Any unusual features of the job should be highlighted, eg:
- the need to travel extensively
- shift working
- the requirement to wear a uniform or protective clothing
- physical factors, such as the need to lift heavy objects.

Format of the Job Description

8.165 Preparation of job descriptions will in practice probably be a joint effort, with:
- HR providing the structure, asking questions and challenging replies
- line managers supplying the detailed information.

8.166 The job description should be in a suitable format to be distributed to applicants so that they can decide, before proceeding with their application, whether they are both interested in and suitable for the position in question. It is therefore important to use clear language.

8.167 Verbs should be used wherever possible to describe the actions that should be performed. Vague statements and terms should be avoided.

8.168 Words such as plans, prepares, produces, implements, processes, provides, schedules, completes, dispatches, maintains, liaises with and collaborates with are useful to put tasks into context.

The Person Specification

8.169 A person specification details the knowledge, skills and experience that a post holder will need to have, and to what level they will need to have them, in order to fulfil the key duties and responsibilities outlined in the job description.

8.170 The person specification must be based on the objective requirements of the job description, not on subjective factors that are frequently irrelevant and may well be considered discriminatory.

Common Errors

8.171 Managers make three common errors when compiling person specifications.
- Specifying requirements out of habit.
- Specifying an ideal candidate.
- Specifying a requirement to "fit in" which may be viewed as discriminatory if the business is not diverse and could therefore perpetuate the lack of diversity.

Habitual Requirements

8.172 Instead of carefully assessing what is actually required for each job, managers sometimes specify requirements out of habit or as a result of preconceived notions. A specification for agility or energy could be seen as discriminating against disabled applicants if these qualities cannot be proven to be necessary for the post.

Ideal Candidates

8.173 Line managers also have a tendency to specify an unrealistically ideal candidate. To avoid this, it helps to separate out mandatory and preferred requirements. This will avoid ruling out candidates who, though not a perfect match, are fully capable of doing the job. Should there be an excess of adequate candidates, it will also provide objective criteria for selecting the candidate who best fits the specification.

Fitting In

8.174 Managers often require employees to fit in with:
- the culture of the organisation
- the team within which the new job holder will have to work
- the person to whom the job reports.

Examples of Fitting In

8.175 In the case of specifying the need to fit in with the corporate culture, there may be some justification, eg an up-market service business may feel that its clients would take offence if it employed people who lacked the expected accent or social graces. But extreme care should be taken as such requirements may very possibly be considered discriminatory.

8.176 Specifying the need to fit into a department or small team can also be discriminatory. Examples include line managers being wary of introducing a man into a team of women (or vice versa) or specifying another young person to fit in with a team whose members are all in their 20s. The assumption here is that an older person, or a person of a different gender, would not fit in the working environment. Not only is this discriminatory, it also underestimates the power of diversity to introduce new challenges and values into the workplace.

8.177 Specifying the need for a job holder to "fit in" with his or her immediate line manager is the most sensitive of these examples. Although managers are not going to hire people they do not feel they can get on with, rejection on these grounds may be very difficult to justify and could lead to claims for discrimination which would be very difficult to defend.

Structured Approaches

8.178 Some employers use a formal approach to counteract the tendency of line managers to allow subjective values to influence person specifications. The two most widely used systems are Alec Rodger's Seven-Point Plan and John Munro Fraser's Five-Fold Grading System. These give certain headings under which the attributes of candidates can be classified.

Rodger's Seven-Point Plan

8.179 The Seven-Point Plan classifies the following attributes.
- Physical make-up, ie appearance, health, bearing and speech.
- Attainments, ie education and experience.
- Intelligence, ie intellectual capacity.
- Special aptitudes, ie mechanical and manual dexterity.
- Interests, ie social, intellectual and physical activity.
- Disposition, ie influence over others, dependability, acceptability and self-reliance.
- Circumstances, ie special demands of the job such as travel abroad.

Fraser's Five-Fold Grading System

8.180 The Five-Fold Grading System classifies the following attributes.
- Impact on others, ie physical make-up, appearance, speech and manner.
- Acquired knowledge or qualifications ie education, work experience and vocational training.
- Innate abilities, ie speed of comprehension and aptitude for learning.
- Motivation, ie individual goals, success rate, consistency and determination in following them.
- Adjustment, ie ability to stand up to stress, ability to get on with people and emotional stability.

Competency Frameworks

8.181 The competency framework is a more flexible, comprehensive and precise technique which assesses the competencies relevant for a particular job and also the degree to which they are required. A typical set of competencies might include:
- communication skills

- decision making
- organising
- leadership
- relationships with other people.

8.182 Once the required competencies have been identified, they can be used as a basis for the person specification, the advertisement, the selection and design of the most appropriate assessment techniques – even the questions that will be asked at interview.

8.183 Building competency frameworks calls for HR staff with the necessary expertise. To keep the framework practical, it is essential to have only six or eight critical competencies.

Mandatory and Preferred Requirements

8.184 It is common practice to divide the criteria listed in the person specification into those that are essential and those that are desirable but not mandatory.

8.185 If requirements are categorised as essential when in fact they are merely desirable, a candidate might claim that he or she has been discriminated against. On the other hand, if essential criteria are omitted from the specification, but are subsequently used to reject certain candidates, then those candidates may justifiably claim that they have been discriminated against.

8.186 It is also important to note that discrimination can occur even if a requirement is classified as "desirable" rather than essential (see *Falkirk Council v Whyte* [1997] IRLR 560).

Direct and Indirect Discrimination

8.187 It is vital when preparing a person specification to avoid both direct and indirect discrimination. Direct discrimination is now rare, apart from those exceptional cases where genuine occupational requirements apply. One area that employers should specifically consider is age discrimination. Legal protection has been in place since 1 October 2006 and employers should have examined any requirements as to age limits within their organisation.

Indirect Discrimination Against Particular Groups

8.188 Indirect discrimination arises when an unjustifiable condition or requirement is imposed, which has an adverse and disproportionate effect on members of one group in relation to another.

8.189 For example, physical requirements relating to the height of candidates would certainly discriminate against women, who are, on average, less tall than men. Such requirements might also discriminate against members of certain racial groups.

8.190 It is therefore vital to ensure that all criteria included in a person specification can be justified as being genuinely necessary for the job. If criteria could potentially discriminate against disabled people, it is important that altering the requirements to accommodate disabled candidates is considered.

8.191 With the new protection against age discrimination having come into force on 1 October 2006, one area of concern is the need to justify any requirement for a set number of years' experience. This could be problematic as the employer must give thought to what skills are increased by experience and there may be difficulties in explaining why, for example, someone with five years' experience is less skilled than someone with six years' experience.

Training

8.192 Training in the preparation of job descriptions and person specifications should be a key part of any recruitment and selection course. Although the content of such a course should always provide comprehensive coverage of the discrimination risks involved, these could also be included in any courses specifically on diversity and equal opportunities.

List of Relevant Legislation

8.193
- Employment Equality (Age) Regulations 2006
- Employment Equality (Sexual Orientation) Regulations 2003
- Employment Equality (Religion or Belief) Regulations 2003
- Sex Discrimination (Gender Reassignment) Regulations 1999
- Disability Discrimination Act 1995
- Race Relations Act 1976
- Sex Discrimination Act 1975

Further Information

Publications
- *Code of Practice: Sex Discrimination*, Equal Opportunities Commission (EOC)
- *Acas: Age and the Workplace — Putting the Employment Equality (Age) Regulations 2006 into Practice (2006)*

Organisations
- **Commission for Racial Equality**
  Web: *www.cre.gov.uk*
  The Commission for Racial Equality is a publicly funded, non-governmental body set up under the Race Relations Act 1976 to tackle racial discrimination and promote racial equality. From October 2007 this organisation will be replaced by the Commission for Equality and Human Rights.
- **Disability Alliance**
  Web: *www.disabilityalliance.org*
  An advice line for disabled people and their advisors.
- **Employers' Forum on Disability**
  Web: *www.employers-forum.co.uk*
  he Employers' Forum on Disability works closely with Government and other stakeholders, sharing best practice to make it easier to employ disabled people and serve disabled customers. It is the employers' organisation focused on the issue of disability in the workplace. It is funded and managed by employers and represents organisations who employ over 20 per cent of the UK workforce.

- **Equal Opportunities Commission**
  Web: *www.eoc.org.uk*
  An agency working to eliminate sex discrimination and put equality into practice in the workplace. From October 2007 this organisation will be replaced by the Commission for Equality and Human Rights (**Web:** *www.cehr.org.uk*).

Job Evaluation

> This topic covers the following.
> - Job Evaluation Defined
> - Purposes of Job Evaluation
> - Benefits of Job Evaluation
> - Assessment of Job Size
> - Who in the Organisation is Affected by Job Evaluation
> - Implementation of a Job Evaluation Scheme
> - Barriers to the Success of Job Evaluation Schemes
> - Analytical Job Evaluation Schemes: The Points-factor Rating System
> - Non-analytical Job Evaluation Schemes
> - The Typical Steps in a Job Evaluation Scheme

8.194 Job evaluation is the process of assessing the relative significance or importance of jobs within an organisation.

Employers' Duties

8.195 Employers should ensure the following.
- Employers need a clear and complete understanding of the various jobs within his or her organisation.
- Ensure that an employer makes any decisions taken by his or her organisation on a rational and defensible basis.
- Assess the success of any evaluation carried out in an organisation.
- Decide whether an evaluation scheme should take in the whole organisation and whether it should differentiate between different sectors of an organisation.
- Determine whether to use an external consultant or ask the HR department to conduct a job evaluation scheme.
- Employers should ensure that job evaluation does not fall into any of the common mistakes and pitfalls of such schemes.
- Ensure that, if a points-factor rating system is used, the factors are not weighted in a discriminatory way.
- Generally, an employer will need to choose a steering committee and a job evaluation panel.
- Confirm that all relevant staff are properly trained to carry out any job evaluation.

Employees' Duties

8.196 Employees should ensure that they:
- fill out any opinion survey by an employer into the pros and cons of a job evaluation scheme
- try to understand the purpose of the scheme and how the employer is aiming to benefit the organisation through the scheme
- complete any questionnaire sent out as part of a job evaluation scheme
- participate fully in any necessary training.

In Practice

Job Evaluation Defined

8.197 Job evaluation is the process of assessing the relative "size" of jobs within an organisation.

8.198 "Size" in this context means significance or importance. It is not an absolute term and can only be measured by comparing the incidence of various factors in a job, such as:
- knowledge and skills required
- level of responsibility
- level of decision-making
- the impact on end results.

Purposes of Job Evaluation

8.199 The key purpose of job evaluation is to provide a rational basis for the management and apportionment of responsibilities and rewards within an organisation.

8.200 However, the external employment market and the acquisition of skills needed to perform roles are equally important factors influencing, in particular, reward structures.

Further Uses of Information Collated During Job Evaluation

8.201 Since the relevant facts about a particular job are analysed in job evaluation, the information collected can be equally useful to organisations for the evaluation of:
- organisation design
- human resource planning
- training and continuous development.

8.202 By emphasising output factors, job evaluation can support change programmes within organisations designed to develop a high performance culture.

8.203 Since job evaluation involves the identification of skills and knowledge, the information gathered can also be used as a basis for encouraging training.

Benefits of Job Evaluation

8.204 The expected benefits of job evaluation are as follows.
- A rational basis is required for making defensible decisions on job grades and rates of pay — such decisions are more likely to be accepted if the logic upon which they are based is clear.
- A consistent approach is required to the management of distinctions between jobs.
- An equitable pay structure is unlikely to be achieved unless a logical method of measuring relative job size exists.
- A formal and analytical method of job evaluation can help to resolve issues over equal pay for work of equal value.

- A reasonably formal approach to job evaluation provides a strategic framework within which rational decisions can be made in response to changing organisation structures and roles, and to market pressures.
- The values of the relevant organisation can be assessed logically and consistently in the context of every role.

Assessing the Benefits of Job Evaluation

8.205 The benefits of job evaluation can be established by the incidence of anomalies in job responsibilities and rewards, and the degree to which the scheme prevents jobs from being overpaid or undervalued.

8.206 The benefits for individual employees can be established through employee opinion surveys.

Assessment of Job Size

8.207 The size of a job can be evaluated in two ways.
- Non-analytical methods — consider the relative size of "whole jobs" on the basis of what are believed to be the key criteria of the job in question.
- Analytical methods — compare jobs by reference to one or more criteria and assessing the degree to which those criteria are present in different jobs.

8.208 In both instances there are two bases upon which comparisons are made.
- One job is compared directly with another.
- All jobs are measured against a set, theoretical scale.

Who in the Organisation is Affected by Job Evaluation?

8.209 Job evaluation can be used for all members of an organisation, though it will not generally be used in the cases of the chief executive and members of the board.

8.210 Typically, there is one evaluation scheme for manual workers and another for managerial, technical and office staff. There are sometimes different schemes for managers and office workers, and professional or scientific staff may also be dealt with separately.

8.211 It is usual to have only one evaluation scheme in an organisation with an integrated pay structure.

Implementation of a Job Evaluation Scheme

8.212 Job evaluation schemes are often introduced to organisations by external consultants, with the help of the organisation's human resources department. The HR department would then normally run the scheme. It is important that the HR department should take ultimate responsibility for the process, and that the process must not only be fair but be seen to be fair.

8.213 Schemes can be developed in-house and tailored to the requirements of the particular organisation. This requires a fair degree of expertise and time.

Proprietary Brands

8.214 There are a number of tried and tested job evaluation schemes offered by external consultants. The organisations offering such "proprietary brands" include Hay, PwC, PA Consulting, P-E International.

Barriers to the Success of Job Evaluation Schemes

8.215 The main problems with job evaluation schemes are that they:
- can never be completely objective — personal views and subjective opinions are always likely to creep in
- involve a considerable amount of preparation and administrative work to introduce and maintain.

Common Mistakes and Pitfalls

8.216 The following are the most common mistakes and pitfalls.
- Introducing a scheme that does not fit the culture of the organisation.
- Taking a scheme "from off the shelf" and not ensuring that the factors used are relevant to the organisation.
- Developing too elaborate a scheme that is unwieldy and difficult to administer and maintain.
- Not involving managers and staff representatives in the design and administration of the scheme.
- Failing to communicate to staff the purpose of the scheme and how they will be affected. It is particularly important to emphasise that the scheme is evaluating jobs, not people. In other words individual abilities and performance levels do not enter into the calculations. It is also vital not only to brief people in advance but also to take great care in informing them about the results of the job evaluation exercise.
- Not appreciating that job evaluation can be an expensive business. Apart from the costs of developing the scheme, which can be considerable, its introduction always increases payroll costs by three per cent or more. This is because if the scheme results in the re-grading of any posts — which is fairly likely — the job holders whose posts have been upgraded will get a pay increase. However, it is unusual to reduce the pay of those whose jobs have been downgraded.
- Applying the scheme too rigidly. In today's more fluid organisations where job responsibilities can change rapidly, an over-bureaucratic approach to job evaluation can inhibit change and development.
- Failing to manage the scheme. Job evaluation schemes tend to erode over time. However hard the HR department tries to control the scheme, managers and staff learn how to manipulate it. The result is "grade drift" (ie jobs being upgraded without good reason).
- Trying to do job evaluation on the cheap, eg by scrimping on the job analysis. This is the foundation of effective job evaluation and, if neglected, can seriously damage the usefulness, fairness and credibility of the scheme.
- Failing to train job analysts and evaluators properly.

Analytical Job Evaluation Schemes: The Points-Factor Rating System

8.217 The most commonly used method of job evaluation is the points-factor rating system. This system breaks jobs down into key factors. A factor is a characteristic within a particular job that can be used as a basis for assessing the job's relative value. "Responsibility", however loosely defined, could be a factor.

8.218 It is assumed that each of the factors will contribute to job size. Points are allocated to the different factors of a job depending on the degree to which each factor is present in a job. The separate factor scores are then added together to give a total score which represents job size.

8.219 Points-factor schemes tend to use between 3 and 12 factors. The factors can broadly be grouped under the following three headings.
- Inputs: these may include technical or professional knowledge, manual and mental skills, interpersonal and team-leading skills, and the education and qualifications required for any of these abilities.
- Process: this is the word used to describe the demands of the job made on the jobholder. Process can include elements such as problem-solving, mental effort, complexity, originality, creativity, judgment, initiative and team working. It can also include physical factors such as stress, physical effort, working conditions and hazards relating to the job.
- Outputs: these are the contributions the jobholder makes to end results. Outputs concern issues such as service delivery, responsibility for resources, decision-making authority and the effect of errors.

Factor Levels and Rating Scales

8.220 When defining factor levels, the aim is to produce a graduated series of definitions that will produce clear guidance on how the factor should be scored. These scores are then set against a rating scale that has been devised to balance out the importance of the various factors. Scoring factors and setting rating scales will to some extent be subjective, but the aim is to provide an objective basis against which all jobs within an organisation can be judged.

Factor Weighting

8.221 Factors could all be weighted equally, but the vast majority of points-factor schemes weight their factors according to each factor's relative importance. Correct weighting is of critical importance, since over-weighting of any one factor could skew the overall evaluation. Care should be taken to ensure that weighting is not discriminatory, eg physical demand should not be over-weighted.

Advantages of Points-Factor Schemes

8.222 The advantages of points-factor schemes are that:
- evaluators are forced to consider a range of factors which will help to avoid the oversimplified judgments made when using non-analytical schemes
- points-factor schemes provide evaluators with defined yardsticks that should help them to achieve some degree of objectivity and consistency in making their judgments
- they at least appear to be objective and this quality makes people feel that they are fair
- they provide a rationale that helps in the design of graded pay structures.

Non-Analytical Job Evaluation Schemes

8.223 The main types of non-analytical (whole-job comparison) job evaluation schemes are job ranking, paired comparison and job classification, as described below.

Job Ranking

8.224 Job ranking is a non-analytical approach that compares whole jobs and does not attempt to assess separately different aspects of different jobs. Following the assessment of all jobs within an organisation, the jobs are then ranked in a hierarchy of job size. Jobs can be ranked within particular categories (eg managers).

Job Evaluation

8.225 Ranking is the simplest and quickest form of job evaluation. For this reason, job ranking is sometimes used to check on the results obtained by using more sophisticated analytical methods of job evaluation.

8.226 The disadvantages of job ranking are as follows.
- There is no rationale to defend the rank order (ie no defined standards for judging relative size). It is simply a matter of opinion, although it can be argued that analytical methods do no more than channel opinions into specified areas.
- The lack of a rationale makes it difficult to defend evaluations.
- Inconsistencies arise because different evaluators give more weight to some aspects of a job than others.
- It is difficult to rank dissimilar jobs.
- It does not provide for any quantification of the differences between jobs, which makes grading an arbitrary process.
- While it will be easy to establish the extremes in a rank order, it may be difficult to discriminate between the middling jobs. Consensus on the current rank order may therefore be hard to obtain.

8.227 These problems can be ameliorated by thorough job analysis, the careful training of evaluators to ensure that they do consider all aspects of the job and by initially ranking a number of key or benchmark jobs whose relative position is easily recognised. This benchmark ranking can then be used as a framework for ranking other jobs.

8.228 Job ranking tends only to be used as the main method in relatively small and simple organisations.

Paired Comparisons

8.229 The paired comparison method is a refinement of job ranking. It is non-analytical and compares whole jobs with one another. A direct comparison between two jobs is likely to be more incisive and revealing than trying to compare a number of different jobs.

8.230 Paired comparisons are made as follows.
1. Evaluators refer to job analyses, usually for a sample of benchmark jobs. It is difficult to carry out paired comparisons for more than about 20 items even with the aid of computers to process the data.
2. Each job is compared in turn with all the other jobs.
3. If it is considered that the size or importance of the job for which comparisons are being made is greater than that of the other job in the pair, it scores two points.
4. If the size is thought to be the same, the job scores one point.
5. If the size is considered to be less, it scores nothing.
6. The total score is added for each job and a rank order is produced, as illustrated in the table below.

Job	A	B	C	D	E	Total score	Rank order
A	—	0	2	0	2	4	2
B	2	—	2	2	2	8	1
C	0	0	—	2	0	2	5
D	2	0	0	—	1	3	3
E	0	0	2	1	—	3	3

8.231 This method is likely to produce more accurate job evaluations than job ranking, but suffers from the same basic disadvantage as job ranking in that paired comparisons lack a rationale for justifying rank orders and do not measure the differences between jobs.

Job Classification

8.232 Job classification compares whole jobs against categorised grade definitions. An initial decision has to be made on the number and characteristics of grades into which the jobs will be classified.

8.233 The grade definitions should take into account discernible differences in skill, competence or responsibility. Jobs are allotted to grades by comparing the whole job description with the grade definition.

8.234 The job classification system is a simple, quick and easily implemented method of slotting jobs into an established structure. Its lack of complexity means that it is suitable for large organisations and decentralised operations.

8.235 However, job classification cannot cope with jobs that do not fit neatly into any particular grade. There is also a danger of the classifications becoming so generalised that they provide little help in evaluating borderline cases.

The Typical Steps in a Job Evaluation Scheme

8.236 The typical steps taken in a job evaluation exercise are as follows.
1. Decide on the objectives and approach to be adopted in the light of an analysis of the requirements of the organisation, its circumstances and culture. At this stage a preliminary view should be taken on the procedure to be followed.
2. Normally, the organisation being evaluated chooses a steering committee and job evaluation panel. The steering committee is often made up of members of the management team. It oversees the project and makes final decisions on the application of the job evaluation results. The job evaluation panel implements the job evaluation process itself: the panel would not normally get involved in grading or pay decisions.
3. Select the job evaluation scheme and train the job evaluation panel in how to carry out the evaluation steps.
4. Choose benchmark jobs. Benchmark jobs are key jobs that represent the various roles and duties within the organisation. The initial analysis and evaluation of these jobs provides reference points with which to evaluate other jobs within the organisation. Benchmark jobs can also be used for external comparison purposes.
5. Analyse benchmark jobs. This involves gathering, analysing and presenting the relevant facts about each job. This process can be very time consuming and it is often desirable to give those being evaluated a standard questionnaire.
6. Evaluate benchmark jobs. This initial evaluation enables the job evaluation panel to make any adjustments necessary before the bulk of the organisation is evaluated.
7. Analyse and evaluate remaining jobs.
8. Review all evaluations and examine any that seem to be inappropriate.
9. Re-evaluate as necessary
10. Present the results of the evaluation to the steering committee.

Training

8.237 Designated human resources staff should be trained to deal with job evaluation within their organisation, and to co-operate with any external consultant brought in to perform a job evaluation scheme.

8.238 Any organisation personnel taking part in either a steering committee or a job evaluation panel will need to be taught the basic processes that are necessary to complete the job evaluation process.

Further Information

Publications
- *B01 Acas Job Evaluation: An Introduction*

Probationary Periods

This topic covers the following.
- Why Use Probationary Periods?
- A Two-Way Process
- Probationary Periods and Salary Increases
- The Legal Situation
- Contracts of Employment
- Duration and Extension of Probationary Periods
- Extending Probationary Periods
- Managing Probationary Periods
- Explaining What is Expected of Employees
- Effective Review Meetings
- Tackling Problems
- Successful Completion of Probationary Periods

8.239 Probationary periods are widely used by employers and included in contracts of employment. This tendency is often seen as empowering employers to get rid of new employees who are failing in their roles. In fact, probationary periods impose obligations on the employer to set clear standards of behaviour, define new employees' roles fully and provide recent recruits with feedback and support. The rules governing probationary periods mean that the benefit to the employer is much less immediate than is commonly supposed.

8.240 Wise employers think carefully about what they want probationary periods to achieve. Probationary periods should be used as part of the wider process of recruiting, motivating and retaining high-quality staff. They are best seen as the first stage in the process of performance management.

Employers' Duties

8.241 Employers have a duty to:
- recognise that placing new employees on probation does not confer a different legal status on them
- recognise that probationary employees are protected in respect of dismissals relating to breaches of contract, equal opportunities legislation and certain statutory rights
- set out the terms of the probationary period in the employee's contract of employment
- state any difference in the amount of notice due during the probationary period
- set out the terms of any extension to the probationary period in writing.

Employees' Duties

8.242 Employees have a duty to:
- comply with reasonable probationary period terms agreed to in their contract of employment.

In Practice

Why Use Probationary Periods?

8.243 Bringing a new member of staff into an organisation is a very expensive business. The costs include:
- the outlay on advertising or agency or recruitment consultancy fees
- providing an induction programme
- the effects on output of the time it takes before a new recruit gets up to speed
- the time of HR staff and line managers at all stages in the process. This cost is significant if priced only on the basis of salaries, but much greater if priced at the opportunity cost, ie the value of what such staff could be doing with their time if it were not being taken up in this way.

8.244 Selection and induction exercises are expensive, even when they are successful. A rough estimate is equivalent to around one year's pay.

8.245 Recruiting a new employee is a high-risk investment. It is very difficult to predict how well a new employee will actually perform in a job, particularly one recruited externally. Interviews are notoriously unreliable and the use of psychometric tests and other extended selection techniques cannot guarantee success.

8.246 It makes sense for employers to use probationary periods to increase the probability of success. Properly managed probationary periods should:
- ensure that the performance of new staff is monitored on a regular basis
- identify problems at the earliest possible stage
- result in such problems being tackled as quickly and effectively as possible
- ensure that new recruits who are not meeting the requirements of the job are dealt with promptly.

8.247 Probationary periods should be constantly managed. Only reviewing them towards the end of the period can result in an:
- employee drifting into permanent employment by default
- acrimonious termination of employment, potentially resulting in a tribunal claim.

A Two-Way Process

8.248 If probationary periods are to be effective, they need the active and positive involvement of the employer, especially the new recruit's line manager or supervisor. This involvement is not just about identifying shortcomings in the new employee's performance. The line manager is also responsible for presenting the employee with opportunities to discuss his or her work concerns — and for dealing with these concerns so as to avoid the employee leaving at or before the end of the probationary period.

Early-Leaver Syndrome

8.249 "Early-leaver syndrome" is a major problem, but one that is often avoidable. Nearly a quarter of new recruits leave within six months; two thirds of this number do not even last a month. Relatively few of these costly departures are due to the employer terminating the contract during the probationary period. Most new joiners leave due to factors such as:

- managers failing to take an interest in them and making them feel unwanted
- the recruit not fitting in with new colleagues or with the organisation's culture
- the job having been oversold at interview
- a lack of proper induction or training.

8.250 As well as picking up on performance shortfalls, probationary period monitoring should identify such problems and prompt corrective action.

Probationary Periods and Salary Increases

8.251 Probationary periods can be used to phase in pay increases. It may be useful when negotiating a remuneration package with an external recruit to agree both an initial salary and an increment, effective at the end of the probationary period and subject to satisfactory performance.

The Legal Situation

8.252 It is essential to recognise that placing new employees on probation does not change their legal status. They have all the legal rights of employees throughout the probationary period.

8.253 Regardless of whether probationary periods are used, it remains easier to dismiss employees with under one year's service, as they acquire additional protection thereafter. Despite this, employees are protected from day one of their employment from dismissal on several grounds, including breaches of:

- contract, relating to the failure to follow correct procedures
- equal opportunities legislation
- statutory rights, covering maternity, health and safety, trade union duties and "whistle blowing".

8.254 With regard to breach of contract, some employers exclude probationers from the application of normal contractual disciplinary procedures. The Government had proposed that the standard dismissal and disciplinary procedure and the modified dismissal and disciplinary procedure would be applied into all employees' contracts of employment, including probationers' contracts. However, following consultation, this proposal is on hold for the time being.

Contracts of Employment

8.255 The terms of the probationary period should be clearly set out in each employee's contract of employment. An example of the basic wording follows: "This appointment is subject to a probationary period of six months, during which time you are expected to prove your suitability for this post. Your performance will be reviewed at regular intervals during this period and again at the end of the six months. We reserve the right to extend the probationary period for whatever reason we see fit. If your performance has not met the required standards either during or by the end of the original probationary period, or by any extension thereof, a decision may be made to dismiss you."

8.256 If applicable, the contract should state whether there will be a difference in the amount of notice the employer will be required to give during the probationary period, compared with the amount that will apply thereafter. The statutory minimum (after one month's service) during the first year of service is one week, whereas many employers' contracts give one month or more.

Duration and Extension of Probationary Periods

8.257 The probationary period must be long enough for employees both to settle into the new organisation and role and to demonstrate whether they are meeting the requirements of the job. These may include:
- the quantity and quality of their work
- their attendance record and timekeeping
- their attitude, especially in customer-contact jobs.

8.258 A six-month period is commonly used, although three months may be considered sufficient.

Extending Probationary Periods

8.259 The main reasons for considering an extension to the period of probation are as follows.
- The employee has been on sickness absence and the amount of time actually worked is consequently not sufficient to make judgments on the probation criteria.
- The employee is failing to meet one or more of the criteria but shows signs of being able to improve. The employer consequently gives him or her more time to reach the required standards. (NB This may well be in both parties' interests. The alternative from the employer's viewpoint will be to incur the time and cost involved in another recruitment exercise — with no guarantee that it will result in the selection of anyone better.)

8.260 An extension would not normally be for more than an additional three months, as the end of the 12-month period (after which it becomes more difficult to dismiss an employee) may become a relevant factor.

8.261 Where the period is extended, it is important to set out the terms of the extension in writing, making clear:
- in what ways the employee's performance has fallen short of the requirements
- the length of the extension
- the performance standards that must be met within such a period.

Managing Probationary Periods

8.262 The most common problem with probationary periods arises when they are not managed at all. Reasons for this include supervisors and line managers:
- taking the view that they can just get rid of employees at the end of the probationary period if they need to
- being too busy or avoiding holding regular review meetings with probationers and not providing them with the help they need to overcome problems.

8.263 Failure to manage probationary periods properly can result in staff whose performance is barely adequate drifting into permanent-employee status. It is essential that supervisors and managers participate fully in the process.

8.264 Active steps should be taken to convince managers of the benefits of managing the probationary period process. Three key benefits are the:
- effect on their department's performance
- time they will save by getting new staff up to speed as quickly as possible
- time and money they will save by avoiding the need for further recruitment if a probationer is dismissed.

8.265 Even if managers are persuaded of the benefits in theory, conflicting demands on their time may prevent them from properly managing probationers. It is, therefore, advisable to insist on some form of reporting to ensure that regular review meetings are taking place between line managers and their probationary employees.

8.266 The HR function should operate a follow-up system to ensure that meetings are taking place. Such a system could send automatic reminders to managers shortly before review meetings become due.

Explaining What is Expected of Employees

8.267 Some employees and managers see the probationary period as a punitive rule. It is essential that managers change perceptions by explaining to recruits the two-way nature of the probationary process. As well as detailing what is expected of them and the key criteria by which their progress will be monitored — performance, attendance and attitude — a good manager will emphasise that probation is a communication process that gives an employee the opportunity to clarify his or her role.

Effective Review Meetings

8.268 Probation review meetings should not be confined to the line manager telling the employee about their shortcomings. Instead the participants should:
- provide positive feedback on achievements
- recognise the areas in which an employee is meeting required criteria
- discuss areas where standards are not being met
- give employees the opportunity to raise concerns about any aspect of the job
- identify any potential grievances, especially with regard to bullying, harassment, and discrimination.

Tackling Problems

8.269 It is vital for both manager and employee to take prompt action against problems identified in the meeting and their causes. Managers should consider what help they can provide the employee. In the case of problems relating to performance, appropriate action might include:
- coaching, either by the manager or by an experienced colleague
- relevant additional training
- a review of the performance criteria, eg where a change in circumstances outside the employee's control has rendered them impossible to achieve.

Successful Completion of Probationary Periods

8.270 No good manager will allow employees to assume that they are performing adequately just because they have got to the end of their probation without any negative feedback. A complacent attitude can be highly de-motivating, giving the impression that the organisation does not care about either its employees or their performance.

8.271 At the successful end of their probationary period, employees should be given a final review at which they are praised for their performance and have their employment status confirmed. This is also a good time to:
- check how they feel about their job and the organisation
- explain how their performance will be managed in the future, eg the appraisal system.

8.272 Continuing to manage performance is absolutely vital, not least because an employee who has successfully completed his or her probationary period may then become complacent. Managers may also fail to provide the ongoing monitoring and support that is required.

Training

8.273 In view of the way probationary periods are frequently mismanaged, there is, in theory, a strong argument for specific training. In practice, it is probably more realistic to include such training in a course covering performance management in general which may well form part of a wider management development programme.

8.274 Managers should also be trained in handling grievance and disciplinary matters, and in the skills required to conduct effective probationary period review meetings. These skills include:
- providing constructive feedback
- understanding different types of questions and when to use them
- active listening
- coaching
- counselling.

8.275 Since they apply to so many aspects of management, training in these skills may also be part of a general management development programme.

List of Relevant Legislation

8.276
- Employment Rights Act 1996

Recruitment — Legal Issues

This topic covers the following.
- Discrimination
- Planning the Recruitment Exercise
- Job Description and Person Specification
- Restrictions on the Employment of Children and Young Persons
- Making an Offer
- National Minimum Wage
- Making Checks
- Data Protection Legislation
- The Employment Practices Data Protection Code
- The Right of Access to Records

8.277 The laws governing discrimination play an important role at every stage of the recruitment and selection process. Rejecting a candidate will generally be unlawful if the underlying reason is the candidate's sex, race, religion, sexual orientation, age or disability. It follows that decisions made during the recruitment and selection process must be non-discriminatory. The various stages of recruitment and selection are legally complex: employers need to handle the process carefully. Employers should judge job applicants against a range of objective criteria, eg skills, knowledge and experience and not on personal factors. Care should be taken not to make assumptions about candidates' suitability, nor to allow personal feelings or preferences to determine the selection decision.

8.278 Employers need also to be aware of other legal requirements, such as legislation on criminal records, and case law on references for those selected for appointment. In addition, data protection legislation applies to the gathering, retention and disclosure of information obtained during the recruitment process.

Employers' Duties

8.279 Employers should make sure that:
- no applicant is treated less favourably on the grounds of age, sex, race, disability, sexual orientation, gender reassignment, religion/belief, or trade union membership or non-membership
- provisions on genuine occupational requirements are complied with where a person specification indicates that someone of a particular sex, race, religion/belief, sexual orientation or age group is required for a specific post
- consideration is given to any provision, criterion or practice (in the person specification) which, although apparently neutral in effect, might, under law, be indirectly discriminatory against particular groups of applicants
- reasonable adjustments are made for applicants who are disabled
- no pressure to discriminate is placed on any staff involved in recruitment and selection
- they are aware of the liability of employers for acts of discrimination by employees acting in the course of employment, including where these are committed by managers and other members of staff
- they are aware that an employer's defence to a claim of discrimination is to show that it took all reasonably practicable steps to prevent the act of discrimination

- the terms of an offer of employment are carefully scrutinised to ensure that contractual obligations are fully understood by both parties
- the terms and conditions of employment are consistent with statutory requirements and minimum standards
- the laws relating to children and young people are complied with
- checks on health, qualifications and/or criminal records, and requests for references are made appropriately
- data relating to recruitment and selection is processed in accordance with data protection legislation and guidance from the Information Commissioner
- the recruitment and selection process is monitored to ensure that there is no discriminatory treatment (this is a duty for public authorities under race and disability legislation).

Employees' Duties

8.280 Employees should make sure that:
- they are honest in the personal information they provide in the recruitment and selection process
- they facilitate appropriate checks that the employer seeks to make about their health, qualifications and criminal record
- they provide, as required, the names of suitable referees
- they abide by any agreement they reach on accepting employment.

In Practice

Discrimination

8.281 Employers have a duty to ensure that job applicants are not subject to discrimination on the grounds of sex, marital status, civil partnership status, trans-gender status, pregnancy, sexual orientation, race, religion or belief, disability, age and, in Northern Ireland, political opinion.

8.282 It is also unlawful to refuse to employ someone on the grounds that he or she is, or has been, a trade union member.

Planning the Recruitment Exercise

8.283 Recruitment, like any other business activity, needs to be carefully thought out and properly planned, if it is to be successful.

Job Description and Person Specification

8.284 There are several ways in which unlawful discrimination might arise in respect of the job description and the person specification.

Job Title

8.285 A job title should be gender neutral so as not to convey that the post is for men or women only, unless a genuine occupational requirement or genuine occupational qualification is applicable.

Job Description

8.286 Any existing job description should be carefully analysed and reviewed, or if no job description exists, one should be prepared for the purpose of recruitment.

Job Duties

8.287 The duties of the job should be listed objectively and should be appropriate to the position advertised. They should not be constructed on the assumption that a person of a particular sex, ethnic group or age will undertake them. The level of the job and the degree of authority it involves should also be objectively stated.

Genuine Occupational Requirement (GOR) and Genuine Occupational Qualification (GOQ)

8.288 Under the various anti-discrimination laws, it may be possible for an employer to assert that it is a genuine occupational requirement of the job that it must be done by someone who:
- belongs to a particular racial group
- holds to a specified religion or belief
- is of a specified sexual orientation (eg gay)
- possesses a characteristic related to age.

8.289 To be a genuine requirement of a job, the individual's race, religion or belief, sexual orientation or age must be necessary for effective performance of the job, and not just preferable.

8.290 In addition, both the Sex Discrimination Act 1975 and the Race Relations Act 1976 contain a limited number of specified genuine occupational qualifications.

8.291 Under sex discrimination law, it is permissible to seek to recruit a man or a woman on the grounds of physiology, authenticity (eg in dramatic performances), decency or privacy, the need to provide special care to residents in a single-sex establishment, the need to provide personal services promoting the welfare or education of men or women, or where workers must live in the employer's accommodation and there is no separate provision for men and women.

8.292 Under race discrimination law, it may be permissible to seek to recruit someone of a specified racial or ethnic group for reasons of authenticity in entertainment, modelling or in an ethnic restaurant, or where the job involves the provision of personal services and those services can be provided most effectively by people of the particular racial group (eg in social work, where knowledge of the culture of a particular ethnic group would be essential in the job).

8.293 A genuine occupational qualification will not, however, generally apply if:
- the employer already has enough men or women, or people from the specified racial group (as the case may be) who can carry out the duties in question, and
- it is reasonable to allocate those duties to these other staff without undue inconvenience.

Person Specification

8.294 The person specification should be drawn up objectively, taking care to ensure that all the criteria included are appropriate and relevant to the performance of the job in question, and not based on the personal opinions of a particular manager.

8.295 Criteria used in recruitment may sometimes amount to indirect discrimination against people in certain groups, eg women, overseas nationals or people in a particular age group. Indirect discrimination occurs where a requirement applied to all job applicants has a disproportionate adverse effect on members of one group compared with another. Unless the criterion in question can be shown to be appropriate and necessary for the effective performance of the job, it will be unlawful.

Age

8.296 Since the implementation of the Employment Equality (Age) Regulations 2006 on 1 October 2006, any criterion for a minimum or maximum number of years of experience in a person specification will be indirectly discriminatory on the grounds of age against younger or older candidates respectively. Employers should therefore take care not to over-estimate how much experience is necessary for the particular job, but should instead focus on the type and breadth of experience that is required, when the job is viewed objectively.

Flexibility

8.297 A range of possible flexibilities may be specified as conditions of employment provided they are relevant and necessary for the job in question. Usually, these will cover work location and working time. It is possible for an employer to specify mobility as a condition of employment, and also flexible working hours, eg shift working and other unsocial hours. It has been established by the courts, however, that such requirements for flexibility can constitute indirect sex discrimination against women with children (see, for example, *Meade-Hill v British Council*, and *London Underground Ltd v Edwards*). Such requirements may, however, be specified if the employer can show that they are justified by the nature of the work as a genuine business need and are not, for example, an excuse to prevent the recruitment of women.

Full-Time Working

8.298 Although full-time working may be specified, a refusal to consider employing a female job applicant who has children on a part-time or job-share basis may amount to indirect sex discrimination against her if she is otherwise the most suitable candidate for the job and the refusal cannot be justified on objective job-based grounds. Therefore, the issue for an employer is whether or not they have a genuine business need for the job in question to be performed full-time by only one person. There is no statutory requirement for employers to provide part-time work or job sharing arrangements. It is, nevertheless, good employment practice, particularly in the context of promoting work-life balance, for serious consideration to be given to these alternative forms of working.

Skills and Experience

8.299 The skills, aptitudes, knowledge, experience, and competence required for the job should be clearly and objectively defined. Employers should avoid unnecessary or excessive requirements, some of which could be unlawful if they are such that people from a particular group are less likely than others to possess them. For example:

- a requirement for a university degree plus a minimum of ten years' experience would discriminate against candidates under age 32 or so
- a requirement to have a UK academic qualification would discriminate indirectly against people who were not educated in the UK, leading to indirect race discrimination.

Attracting Suitable Candidates

8.300 Employers may elect to use a range of methods to attract suitable candidates to apply for the vacant job(s), including media advertising, on-line advertising, employment agencies, head-hunters, job centres and careers fairs. Word-of-mouth recruitment, although not unlawful, is discouraged particularly when an organisation has a predominantly male or predominantly female workforce, as the predominance of one sex is likely to be perpetuated if only this method of recruitment is deployed.

Advertising

8.301 It is important that job adverts promote the organisation as an equal opportunities employer and that they do not contain words or images that express an intention to discriminate or suggest a preference for people from a particular group.

8.302 They should not be written in a way that stereotypes or encourages people to believe that the post is only suitable for certain groups of people. For example, terms such as "dynamic" or "energetic" could discourage applicants with disabilities from applying, or could be interpreted as implying that the employer is seeking to attract only younger applicants.

8.303 Employers should consider carefully which media to use for their advertising in order to ensure that they do not exclude or limit applications from some sections of the community.

Positive Action

8.304 Under discrimination law, it is permissible to take certain forms of positive action to encourage certain groups of people to apply for work.

8.305 This is permitted in circumstances where women (or men) or people from a minority racial group have been under-represented in the workplace in the previous 12 months, or where people from a particular religion, sexual orientation or age group have, in the past, been disadvantaged in employment. An example of positive action could be to place a job advertisement in a particular publication that is read predominantly by women or by people from a particular ethnic group.

8.306 Positive discrimination is not, however, permitted under UK employment law, ie it is only positive action, in other words, encouragement to apply, that is permitted.

8.307 Applicants of all groups should be judged equally and consistently against the pre-determined selection criteria. This means that when the employer is shortlisting, or selecting the successful applicant, the principles of equality must be applied and gender, race, etc must play no part in the decision-making process.

Application Forms

8.308 The law affects application forms in several ways, as follows.
- The information contained in application forms should be treated as confidential.

- Alternative formats should be made available when required, so as to facilitate applications from disabled applicants, eg audio-tape or Braille for people with visual impairments.
- Personal information should be asked for on a separate tear-off portion of the application form, eg gender, marital status, ethnic origin and age, and this should be used only for monitoring purposes and not as part of the selection process.
- Certain personal details should not be asked for, eg the applicant's number of children, unless (exceptionally) the employer can show a genuine need for that information.
- Forms should contain a data protection statement and a requirement for the applicant to sign his/her agreement to the processing of data for recruitment and monitoring purposes.

Shortlisting

8.309 When shortlisting takes place, it should be undertaken consistently and against the objective criteria set out in the job description and person specification.

8.310 An employer's decision not to shortlist an applicant can be challenged under discrimination law at an employment tribunal. If there are clear, non-discriminatory reasons for the non-selection, then the employer should be able to defend the case successfully.

8.311 It is recommended that a record is kept of the criteria under which job applicants are shortlisted.

Interviews

8.312 When questions are asked at interview they should relate to the requirements of the job and be presented objectively. For example, interviewers should:
- take care not to discuss issues such as unsocial hours or mobility in different ways between men and women based on the assumption that women have child-care responsibilities
- avoid questions about child-care arrangements, in particular when interviewing female candidates, as they may be interpreted as direct sex discrimination
- avoid asking questions that would require the applicant to disclose his or her age, eg a question about the date he or she left school
- be aware of the risk of subjective biases and stereotyping affecting the interviewer's judgments.

8.313 Records should be kept of interviews, along with the interviewers' scoring/assessment of each applicant against the pre-determined criteria.

Adjustments for Candidates with Disabilities

8.314 Employers should be aware of the duty to make reasonable adjustments for any candidate with a disability. Examples of reasonable adjustments could include:
- changing the interview location for an applicant who uses a wheelchair
- ensuring there is no background noise for a candidate with a hearing impairment
- allowing an applicant with a learning disability to be accompanied by a helper at the interview
- providing large-print handouts for a candidate with a visual impairment.

Selection Tests

8.315 Selection tests, if used, should be reviewed periodically to ensure their validity and their lack of inherent bias, as it is possible that they may be biased and so discriminatory on the grounds of sex, race or age.

Selection

8.316 Selection should be carried out on the basis of the candidates' relevant skills, experience, knowledge, qualifications and competencies, as measured against the criteria defined in the person specification, and not on the basis on the interviewer's personal preferences. Using more than one interviewer can help to cut down on the potential for bias.

8.317 Provided the criteria for the job have been clearly and objectively defined at the outset of the recruitment exercise, and provided they have been applied objectively to all the candidates, the selection process should be straightforward. It will be a question of selecting the candidate whose background most closely matches the defined criteria, ideally measured by using a points system.

Monitoring

8.318 It is advisable to carry out checks on the recruitment process, ie monitor the numbers of people from both genders, different racial groups, people in different age groups and people with disabilities who apply for employment, who are interviewed, and who are successful in their applications. Any disproportionate outcomes should be investigated thoroughly and appropriate measures adopted to avoid discrimination in the future.

Restrictions on the Employment of Children and Young Persons

8.319 Employers must ensure that the laws relating to children and young people are complied with when recruiting children and young persons. In law, a "child" is a person who is not over compulsory school age; which in most cases means a child under age 16. Young persons are those who are over the minimum school leaving age but have not yet reached the age of 18.

Restrictions on the Employment of Children

Prohibited Occupations

8.320 No school age child may be employed in any "industrial undertaking", that is to say, in any mine or quarry, or in construction or demolition work, or in any premises, such as a factory or workshop, in which articles are manufactured, altered, cleaned, repaired, ornamented, finished, adapted for sale, broken up or demolished, or in which materials are transformed.

8.321 These prohibitions are to be found in the Employment of Women, Young Persons & Children Act 1920. Employers who are uncertain of the extent of these prohibitions should contact their local authority education department for advice.

8.322 Most local authority bylaws prohibit the employment of school age children in hotel kitchens, cook shops, fish and chip shops, restaurants, snack bars and cafeterias, and in any premises in connection with the sale of alcohol, except where alcohol is sold exclusively in sealed containers.

8.323 Furthermore school age children may not be employed in, or in connection with, the sale of paraffin, turpentine, white spirit, methylated spirit or petroleum spirit;

or as window cleaners. A copy of these bylaws is available on request from local authority education departments and will usually be supplied at the same time as a requested application form for an Employment Certificate.

Restrictions on Working Hours and Periods of Employment for Children

8.324 The employment of school age children in offices, shops, hotels, restaurants, tea rooms, etc, or in light agricultural work (eg, at weekends and during the school holidays), is regulated by the Children & Young Persons Acts 1933 & 1963 or the Children & Young Persons (Scotland) Act 1937 (as amended by the Children (Protection at Work) Regulations 1998 and the Children (Protection at Work) (No. 2) Regulations 2000). For Northern Ireland employers, provisions are to be found in the Children & Young Persons (Northern Ireland) Act 1968.

8.325 Under that legislation, often reinforced by local authority bylaws, no child may be employed:

- if under the age of 14
- before the close of school hours on any school day
- before 7.00 am or after 7.00 pm on any day
- for more than two hours on any school day
- for more than two hours on a Sunday
- for more than eight hours (or, if under 15, for more than five hours) on any day (other than a Sunday) which is not a school day
- for more than 12 hours in any week in which he or she is required to attend school
- for more than 35 hours (or, if under 15, for more than 25 hours) in any week in which the child *is not* required to attend school; or
- for more than four consecutive hours on any day without a rest break lasting at least one hour
- at any time in a year unless, at that time, he or she has had (or could still have) during school holidays, at least two consecutive weeks without employment
- to do any work other than light work.

8.326 "Light work" means work of a kind that is unlikely to be harmful to the safety, health or development of children; or to be harmful to their attendance at school or to their participation in work experience, or their capacity to benefit from the instruction received or, as the case may be, the experience gained.

8.327 Under the Education Act 1996, the restrictions on working hours and periods of employment listed above do not apply to schoolchildren engaged in local authority-approved work experience programmes during their last compulsory academic year at school (the GCSE year), always provided that the work in question is not otherwise prohibited by statute or local authority bylaws.

8.328 (The final year of compulsory education runs from the beginning of the summer term prior to the final GCSE year.)

8.329 School age children are not covered by the Working Time Regulations 1998 and are therefore not entitled to the four weeks' paid annual leave prescribed by the regulations. Workers over compulsory school age are, however, covered (*Addison and another t/a Brayton News-v-Ashby EAT* [2003] IRLR 211).

Employing a Schoolchild — Procedure

8.330 Before employing a schoolchild (or within seven days of having done so), an employer must apply to the relevant local education authority for an Employment Certificate. The authority will forward an application form and a copy of its bylaws on the employment of children. The application form will seek a brief explanation of the type of employment in question and will ask for information about daily working hours, intervals for meals and rest, and so on. The local authority may decide to prohibit or restrict the employment of a particular child if it feels that the employment, although not unlawful, may be to the child's detriment.

8.331 A copy of the Employment Certificate (once issued) will be sent, as a matter of routine, to the child's Head Teacher. The local authority will also seek the consent of the child's parents or guardians. Having obtained that consent, it devolves on the employer to inform the parents or guardians of any health and safety risks associated with the type of work in which the child is (or is to be) employed and the steps taken to minimise or eliminate those risks.

Restrictions on the Employment of Young Persons

8.332 Young workers are those who are over the minimum school leaving age but have not yet reached the age of 18. In general, young workers have the same employment rights as adult workers, eg the right not to suffer unlawful discrimination in recruitment.

8.333 The Working Time Regulations 1998 place restrictions on the hours that young people may work and make special provision for compulsory rest days and rest periods and restrictions on night working.

8.334 Employers may in general not require young people to work more than eight hours a day, or more than 40 hours in any one week.

8.335 Young workers are also entitled to more generous rest periods and rest breaks than adult workers as follows.

- *Daily rest* — at least 12 hours' consecutive rest must be given in each 24 hour period. The rest period may be interrupted, however, where the work is either split up over the day or is of short duration.
- *Weekly rest* — a minimum of 48 hours each week must be ensured. This may be reduced to 36 hours where justified by technical or work organisation reasons,
- *Rest breaks* — there must be a minimum 30-minute rest break during the course of any shift lasting (or expected to last) for more than four and a half hours. This entitlement cannot be varied other than for temporary work which has to be done in unforeseen and exceptional circumstances. Compensatory rest must be given within three weeks.
- *Night work* — young people are allowed to work at night only in certain industry sectors, subject to restrictions and provided they are supervised by an adult worker if this is necessary for their protection. They may not, in general work between midnight and 4.00 am.
- A more rigorous health assessment is required for young people, including a consideration of whether the young worker has the physical and psychological ability to do the work.

8.336 The Management of Health and Safety at Work Regulations 1999 require employers to protect the health and safety of young people who work for them.

8.337 Before recruiting young people, employers must assess the risks to their health and safety and decide whether they should be prohibited from doing certain types of work. In making the assessment, employers must take account of young workers' lack of experience, lack of awareness of risk and lack of maturity.

8.338 The provisions in force to protect the health and safety of young workers are not affected by the Employment Equality (Age) Regulations 2006 which expressly allow employers to discriminate on grounds of age if the measures taken are in order to comply with a requirement of another statutory provision.

8.339 For Northern Ireland employers, cognate provisions are to be found in the

Children & Young Persons Act (Northern Ireland) 1968, the Health and Safety (Young Persons) Regulations (Northern Ireland) 1997 (SR 1997/387) and the Working Time Regulations (Northern Ireland) 1998 (SR 1998/386).

Making an Offer

8.340 When an employer proposes to make an offer of employment to an applicant, several factors need to be considered.

- The employer needs to determine carefully the terms of the offer and take account of any promises made at the earlier stages of the recruitment process.
- The offer of employment should clearly indicate a start date and terms that are consistent with legislation on pay, working time, annual leave, etc. If a term is considered discriminatory, it may be void.
- The offer should set out any special conditions relating to the prospective employee, eg a probationary period.
- The offer should state whether it is conditional or dependent on further information being provided, eg a satisfactory medical or criminal records check.
- The offer needs to make clear which terms are contractual and so it is good practice for the full offer to be clearly set out in detail in writing.
- The offer should indicate when there will be an agreement between the applicant and the prospective employer. This is likely to be when the applicant signs a document to state that he or she accepts the employment on the terms offered.

National Minimum Wage

8.341 Employers who pay rates of pay based on the national minimum wage may pay lower rates to workers aged 21 and under. The National Minimum Wage Act 1998 contains three age bands, each with a different minimum rate. The age bands are:
- 16–17 inclusive
- 18–21 inclusive
- 22 and over.

Making Checks

8.342 There are various checks that an employer may want or need to make, depending on the circumstances of the employment. These include:
- a check on the individual's right to work in the UK (see the Recruitment and Migrant Workers topic)
- a medical check
- verification that the employee has the required qualifications
- a request for references
- a check on whether the individual has a criminal record.

8.343 Offers of employment should normally be made conditional on the completion of all these checks to the employer's satisfaction.

Medical Checks

8.344 It is permissible for employers to seek to establish that the person they intend to appoint is medically fit to perform the work. For most jobs, it will be sufficient to ask the prospective employee to complete a general health questionnaire. However, if the requirements of the job are such that more detailed information about an employee's physical and/or mental health are needed, it may be advisable for the employer to require the successful applicant, as a condition of employment, to undergo a pre-employment medical examination with an occupational doctor so that a report can be provided to the employer establishing whether the applicant meets the requisite standard of fitness for the job.

8.345 An alternative to this would be for the employer to seek access to the medical records of the prospective employee through his or her general practitioner. In this case, the prospective employee's written permission must be obtained for a request to be made to his or her general practitioner for a medical report (Access to Medical Reports Act 1988).

8.346 If the employer believes that it is necessary to seek a medical report on the prospective employee, it should be made clear in the recruitment literature why this is the case.

Qualifications

8.347 Employers should always verify that the applicant they wish to appoint has the qualifications that he or she claims to have, provided these are relevant and necessary for performance of the job in question.

8.348 The applicant should be asked to produce documentary evidence of this, eg the original of a degree certificate.

References

8.349 There is no general duty on employers to provide references for existing or past employees. Some employers, however, for example in the finance sector, are required by their regulatory bodies to obtain and provide references for employees.

8.350 Case law has determined that an employer who chooses to provide a reference is under a duty of care to provide a reference that is true, accurate and not misleading (see *Bartholomew v London Borough of Hackney*). A referee also owes a duty of care to the new employer and can be liable for damages if they do not tell the truth (see *Cox v Sun Alliance Life Ltd*).

8.351 Although there is no legal duty to provide a reference, employers should not refuse a request for a reference if the reason for the refusal is that the ex-employee, whilst employed, brought a claim for discrimination against the employer. In these circumstances, the refusal to provide a reference, or the provision of an adverse reference would constitute an act of victimisation and would be unlawful (see *Coote v Granada Hospitality Ltd*).

Criminal Record Checks

8.352 Having a criminal record does not automatically prevent individuals from working for an employer. The nature of the offence, the circumstances, the type of position being offered and the length of time since the offence took place should all be considered. Employment should, in general, not be refused on account of an offence that is irrelevant to the type of work applied for.

8.353 For many types of posts it may be enough to request details from the prospective employee of any unspent convictions.

8.354 It is unlawful for an employer to treat ex-offenders less favourably than other candidates on the grounds that they have a spent conviction although there are many jobs and professions exempted from this provision in which case it is lawful to reject a candidate on grounds of a spent conviction.

8.355 Employers who require more detailed checks have access to prospective

Recruitment — Legal Issues

employees' criminal records through the Criminal Records Bureau (CRB). In Scotland, access is available through the Scottish Criminal Record Office (SCRO).

Rehabilitation of Offenders Act 1974

8.356 Under the Rehabilitation of Offenders Act 1974, a conviction becomes "spent" after a defined length of time has elapsed. The length of time which has to elapse depends on the rehabilitation period and therefore on the type of conviction.

Rehabilitation Periods

Sentence	Rehabilitation Period
Imprisonment, corrective training or sentence of detention in a young offenders' institution for more than six months but not more than 30 months	10 years*
Imprisonment or sentence of detention in a young offenders' institution for a term not exceeding six months	Seven years*
A fine or other sentence not expressly covered by the Act	Five years*
Order for detention in detention centre	Three years
Absolute discharge	Six months
Conditional discharge	One year
Probation	Five years*

The rehabilitation periods given above indicated * may be reduced by half for a person under 18 at the time the sentence was passed. (In the case of a probation order the period is two and a half years from the date of conviction or a period beginning with the date and ending when the order ends, whichever is longer.)

Where a conviction is spent under the Act, the job applicant is entitled to decline to disclose it to a prospective employer (even if asked) and the right not to be penalised for not disclosing it. Unless the job is one on the list of excluded job categories under the Act, the employer must, in effect, treat the job applicant for all purposes as if his or her conviction never happened. It is unlawful for an employer to refuse to appoint a job applicant on account of a spent conviction where the job is not one contained in the list of job categories exempted from the Act.

Exclusions

8.357 Some offences can never become spent. These include a sentence of life imprisonment or any sentence that exceeds 30 months.

8.358 There are also many jobs that are exempt from the Rehabilitation of Offenders Act. For jobs listed in the Rehabilitation of Offenders Act 1974 (Exceptions) Order 1975, it is lawful for an employer to request information on spent convictions as well as unspent convictions and to turn down a candidate for a role on the grounds that he or she has a spent conviction.

8.359 Some of the main excluded job categories are:
- medical practitioners
- nurses/midwives
- dentists, dental hygienists, dental auxiliaries
- solicitors
- barristers

- pharmaceutical chemists
- social services personnel
- chiropractors
- psychologists
- teachers and other posts that involve dealing with children and young people.

8.360 A full list of the excluded categories can be found in the Act. Where the employer is recruiting into one of the exempted jobs, they should explain this fact to job applicants and inform them that they are required to disclose both spent and unspent convictions.

Disclosures

8.361 Where it is appropriate to do so, an employer may seek access to a prospective employee's criminal record through the Criminal Records Bureau (CRB) or (in Scotland) through the Scottish Criminal Record Office (SCRO).

8.362 Three types of certificate are available.
- Criminal Conviction Certificate (or basic disclosure).
- Criminal Record Certificate (or standard disclosure).
- Enhanced Criminal Record Certificate (or enhanced disclosure).

8.363 Only an individual, and not an employer, may apply for a basic disclosure.

8.364 In order to obtain a standard disclosure or an enhanced disclosure, employers must register with the CRB/SCRO.

Basic Disclosure

8.365 A basic disclosure shows details only of unspent convictions under the Rehabilitation of Offenders Act 1974. A basic disclosure is issued to the job applicant only and he or she may use the certificate for any purpose. At present, basic disclosures are only available in Scotland, where they cost £20.00.

Standard Disclosure

8.366 A standard disclosure is issued jointly to the individual and the registered employer and provides information on spent and unspent convictions, warnings, reprimands and cautions.

8.367 Standard disclosures are only available for positions which are exempt from the Rehabilitation of Offenders Act 1974.

8.368 The cost of a standard disclosure is currently (for 2007/08) £31.00 (£20.00 in Scotland).

Enhanced Disclosures

8.369 Enhanced disclosures are also issued jointly to both the individual and the registered employer and include a check of local police records as well as those checks carried out in a standard disclosure. The cost of an enhanced disclosure is currently £36.00 (£20.00 in Scotland).

8.370 An enhanced disclosure would be appropriate for roles that involve caring, training, supervising or being in sole charge of children or vulnerable adults, eg teachers, doctors, social workers, scout/guide leaders, etc.

8.371 People working with children also have to be checked against the lists held by the Department of Health and the Department for Children, Schools and Families of people deemed unsuitable to work in schools or with children.

Protection of Vulnerable Adults Scheme

8.372 The Protection of Vulnerable Adults Scheme (POVA) requires care providers to check the POVA list to ensure that a potential employee has not harmed vulnerable adults in his or her care. This check must be carried out before a care worker is allowed to start work. The current cost is £6.

8.373 Further details on the POVA list and who may access it are available from the Department of Health.

Data Protection Legislation

8.374 Provisions in the Data Protection Act 1998 class certain types of personal information as "sensitive data" including:
- racial or ethnic origins (although it is permissible to gather this information for monitoring purposes)
- religious beliefs
- political opinions
- trade union membership
- physical or mental health
- sexual life
- the commission or alleged commission of a criminal offence.

8.375 Restrictions are imposed on employers in relation to the collection and use of sensitive data. Specifically, the Act states that sensitive data about an individual may not be collected or used unless either the individual has freely consented, or one of a limited list of conditions (which are defined in the Act) is fulfilled, eg if the information is necessary in order to comply with a legal obligation such as the need to carry out a criminal record check in relation to a post involving work with children.

8.376 If employers believe that it is necessary to gather any information about job applicants that constitutes sensitive data, they should ensure that job applicants:
- are told why the information is being gathered
- are told how the organisation intends to use the data
- are assured of the confidentiality of the data and that it will be kept securely
- freely give their written consent to the data being collected and used.

The Employment Practices Data Protection Code

8.377 Employers should seek also to comply with the Employment Practices Data Protection Code, Part 1 Recruitment and Selection, available at: www.ico.gov.uk/Home/what_we_cover/data_protection.aspx.

8.378 Among other things, the Code recommends that employers should:
- collect only information about job applicants that is relevant to the job in question
- not collect information about job applicants' personal lives unless this is necessary in respect of the decision as to whom to appoint
- ask for sensitive data to be disclosed only where the job applicant's explicit consent has been obtained or in circumstances where the collection of such data is in order to fulfil a legal obligation
- inform job applicants as to how the information held about them is to be used
- ensure any tests used as part of the recruitment process are carried out by properly trained and qualified personnel
- retain recruitment records only for as long as they are necessary, based on business needs

- notify any applicant whose details the employer wishes to retain on file after the conclusion of the recruitment exercise, giving him or her the option to ask the employer not to retain it
- ensure the security of all job applications, including those submitted online.

The Right of Access to Records

8.379 Job applicants about whom information is held on a file by a prospective employer have the right to request access to any information held about them, subject to the request being in writing and to the payment of a fee of up to £10.00 (if required by the employer).

8.380 In the event of a valid subject access request, the employer must comply by providing the job applicant with a copy of the information in permanent and intelligible form within 40 calendar days.

Training

8.381 All managers and HR practitioners involved in recruitment and selection should be given awareness training in discrimination law and other legislation that impacts on the recruitment process.

8.382 General and line managers will need a general knowledge of the essential framework of discrimination law. HR practitioners will need more depth of knowledge on the law and on supplementary sources of advice. The training should, ideally, involve both management groups. It should be participative and involve problem-solving scenarios and discussions.

8.383 The following elements would contribute to workshop sessions.
- Discussion, where appropriate, about any new legislative provisions and case law.
- Discussion focused around the organisation's existing documentation to review whether or not it is compliant with the law.
- Use of scenarios — ideally related to the organisation's policy and practice — to discuss problem-solving and the application of the organisation's policy.

List of Relevant Legislation

8.384
- Employment Equality (Age) Regulations 2006
- Employment Equality (Religion or Belief) Regulations 2003
- Employment Equality (Sexual Orientation) Regulations 2003
- Working Time Regulations 1998
- Working Time Regulations (Northern Ireland) 1998
- Health and Safety (Young Persons) Regulations (Northern Ireland) 1997
- Employment Equality Act 1998
- Disability Discrimination Act 1995
- Race Relations Act 1976
- Sex Discrimination Act 1975
- Rehabilitation of Offenders Act 1974
- Children & Young Persons (Northern Ireland) Act 1968
- Children & Young Persons (Scotland) Act 1937 (as amended)

- Children & Young Persons Act 1933 & 1963
- Employment of Women, Young Persons & Children Act 1920
- Rehabilitation of Offenders Act 1974 (Exclusions and Exceptions) (Scotland) Order 2003
- Rehabilitation of Offenders Act 1974 (Exceptions) Order 1975

List of Relevant Cases

8.385
- *Paul v National Probation Service* [2004] IRLR 190, EAT
- *Addison and another t/a Brayton News-v-Ashby* [2003] IRLR 211, EAT
- *Anya v University of Oxford* [2001] IRLR 377, CA
- *Cox v Sun Alliance Life Ltd* [2001] IRLR 448, CA
- *Nagarajan v London Regional Transport* [1999] IRLR 572, HL
- *Coote v Granada Hospitality Ltd* [1999] ICR 100, ECJ Case C-185/97)
- *Bartholomew v London Borough of Hackney* [1999] IRLR 246, CA
- *London Underground Ltd v Edwards (No. 2)* [1998] IRLR 364, CA
- *Jones v Tower Boot Company Ltd* [1997] IRLR 168, CA
- *Meade-Hill v British Council* [1995] IRLR 478, CA
- *Spring v Guardian Assurance plc & ors* [1994] IRLR 460, HL
- *Dekker v Stichting Vormingscentrum voor Jonge Volwassen* [1991] IRLR 27 ECJ
- *Horsey v Dyfed County Council* [1982] IRLR 395, EAT

Further Information

Organisations
- **Advisory Conciliation and Arbitration Service (Acas)**
  Web: *www.acas.org.uk*
  Acas aims to improve organisations and working life through better employment relations. It provides up-to-date information, advice, high-quality training, and works with employers and employees to solve problems and improve performance.
- **Commission for Racial Equality**
  Web: *www.cre.gov.uk*
  The Commission for Racial Equality is a publicly funded, non-governmental body set up under the Race Relations Act 1976 to tackle racial discrimination and promote racial equality. From October 2007 this organisation will be replaced by the Commission for Equality and Human Rights.
- **Criminal Records Bureau (CRB)**
  Web: *www.crb.gov.uk*
  The CRB — an executive agency of the Home Office — is set up to help organisations make safer recruitment decisions.
- **Department of Health**
  Web: *www.dh.gov.uk*
  The Department of Health provides health and social care policy, guidance and publications.

- **Department for Business, Enterprise and Regulatory Reform (BERR)**
  Web: *www.berr.gov.uk*
  The Department for Business, Enterprise and Regulatory Reform brings together functions from the former Department of Trade and Industry (DTI), including responsibilities for productivity, business relations, energy, competition and consumers. It also drives regulatory reform.
- **Disability Rights Commission**
  Web: *www.drc-gb.org*
  An independent body established by Act of Parliament to eliminate discrimination against disabled people and promote quality of opportunity. It provides information and advice to disabled people and employers about their rights and duties. From October 2007 this organisation will be replaced by the Commission for Equality and Human Rights (**Web:** *www.cehr.org.uk*).
- **Equal Opportunities Commission**
  Web: *www.eoc.org.uk*
  An agency working to eliminate sex discrimination and put equality into practice in the workplace. From October 2007 this organisation will be replaced by the Commission for Equality and Human Rights (**Web:** *www.cehr.org.uk*).
- **Home Office**
  Web: *www.homeoffice.gov.uk*
  The Home Office is the Government department responsible for internal affairs in England and Wales.
- **Information Commissioner's Office**
  Web: *www.ico.gov.uk*
  The Information Commissioner enforces and oversees the Data Protection Act 1998 and the Freedom of Information Act 2000. It is an independent UK supervisory authority, reporting directly to the UK Parliament. It has an international role as well as a national one.
- **Low Pay Commission (LPC)**
  Web: *www.lowpay.gov.uk*
  The LPC was established as a result of the National Minimum Wage Act 1998 to advise the Government about the National Minimum Wage and assists employees and employers alike with advice.

Recruitment and Migrant Workers

> This topic covers the following.
> - Asylum and Immigration Act 1996
> - Discrimination
> - Work Permits
> - European Economic Area (EEA)
> - Accession State Registration Scheme
> - Workers from Romania and Bulgaria
> - Applying for a Work Permit
> - Training and Work Experience Scheme (TWES)
> - Employment of Students
> - Working Holidaymakers
> - Highly Skilled Migrant Programme (HSMP)
> - Sectors Based Scheme

8.386 The rules on migration to Britain and on work permits are complex, and there are various different "schemes" under which a UK employer may recruit an overseas national who would not otherwise have the right to work in the UK.

8.387 It is a criminal offence to employ people who do not have the right to work in the UK. Employers must therefore make appropriate checks as part of the recruitment process to ensure that the person they wish to appoint has leave to enter and work in the UK, or alternatively that the person is a British citizen, a citizen of an EEA country, Switzerland or a Commonwealth country. The European Economic Area (EEA) countries are the 27 EU Member States plus Iceland, Liechtenstein and Norway.

8.388 It is important that employers make the same check of every job applicant at the same stage of the recruitment process in order to avoid allegations of race discrimination.

Employers' Duties

8.389 Employers should ensure that:
- checks on each individual's right to work in the UK are routinely made
- they see the original of any document produced by a job applicant as evidence of his or her right to work in the UK
- copies of all documentation relevant to the individual's right to work in the UK are retained on file
- they treat all job applicants in exactly the same way at every stage of the recruitment process, irrespective of nationality.
- work permits are applied for and obtained in advance of the individual starting work
- they carry out a full and thorough search of the resident labour market before applying for a work permit for an overseas national.

Employees' Duties

8.390 Employees should ensure that:
- they facilitate appropriate checks being made about their right to work in the UK
- they provide, when asked, the prospective employer with the appropriate documentation relevant to their right to work in the UK
- they produce, on arrival in the UK, a valid national passport and visa for entry
- if they are from one of eight specified EU countries, they register with the Home Office within one month of commencing employment in the UK.

In Practice

Asylum and Immigration Act 1996

8.391 Any UK employer who employs a foreign national aged 16 or over, who is either an illegal immigrant or does not have the legal right to take up employment while in the UK, is liable to prosecution under the Asylum and Immigration Act 1996.

8.392 The penalty on summary conviction is a fine of up to £5000 for each and every illegal worker hired.

8.393 To avoid prosecution under the Act, employers should devise and implement standard procedures for carrying out pre-employment checks. Under the Act, employers are required to:
- review appropriate documentation appertaining to the job applicant, which may be one document from List 1, or two documents from List 2 (see below)
- verify that the document(s) produced appears to relate to the applicant
- keep a copy of the relevant document(s) on file throughout the person's employment and for six months after he or she leaves.

8.394 As it is unlawful under the Race Relations Act 1976 to refuse employment to a job applicant on the grounds of nationality, it is important that employers ask every prospective employee to produce the relevant documentation at a pre-determined stage of the recruitment process, in order to avoid allegations of racial discrimination.

8.395 The types of documents which employers are required to check are contained in two lists. Employers must check either one document from List 1 or two documents from List 2. The employer must sight the original of the documents, check the details contained in them, eg expiry date, either make a photocopy or scan the documents and retain the copies on file.

List 1
- A passport showing that the holder is a British citizen, or has a right of abode in the UK.
- A document showing that the holder is a national of a European Economic Area (EEA) country or Switzerland.
- A residence permit issued by the UK to a national from an EEA country or Switzerland.

- A passport or other document issued by the Home Office which has an endorsement stating that the holder has a current right of residence in the UK as the family member of a national from an EEA country or Switzerland.
- A passport or other travel document endorsed to show that the holder can stay indefinitely in the UK, or has no time limit on their stay.
- A passport or other travel document endorsed to show that the holder can stay in the UK; and that this endorsement allows the holder to do the type of work the employer is offering if they do not have a work permit.
- An Application Registration Card issued by the Home Office to an asylum seeker stating that the holder is permitted to take employment.

List 2

First Combination

8.396 A document giving the person's permanent NI number and name, ie P45, P60, NI card, or a letter from a Government agency AND one of the following:
- a full birth certificate issued in the UK which includes the names of the holder's parents or
- a birth certificate issued in the Channel Islands, the Isle of Man or Ireland or
- a certificate of registration or naturalisation stating that the holder is a British citizen or
- a letter issued by the Home Office which indicates that the person named in it can stay indefinitely in the UK, or has no time limit on their stay or
- an Immigration Status Document issued by the Home Office with an endorsement indicating that the person named in it can stay indefinitely in the UK or has no time limit on their stay or
- a letter issued by the Home Office which indicates that the person named in it can stay in the UK and this allows them to do the type of work the employer is offering or
- an Immigration Status Document issued by the Home Office with an endorsement indicating that the person named in it can stay in the UK and this allows them to do the type of work the employer is offering.

Second Combination

8.397 A work permit or other approval to take employment that has been issued by the Border and Immigration Agency (BIA) AND one of the following, a:
- passport or other travel document endorsed to show that the holder is able to stay in the UK and can take the work permit employment in question or
- letter issued by the Home Office confirming that the person named in it is able to stay in the UK and can take the work permit employment in question.

8.398 Just because a person is not able to produce the appropriate listed document(s), it is not safe to assume that he or she is living or working in the UK illegally. They should be referred to the Border and Immigration Agency, via the Immigration and Nationality Enquiry Bureau on 0870 606 7766, or to a Citizens Advice Bureau for advice. It may be possible to keep a job vacancy open while this process goes on but that is a decision for the employer, not a requirement.

Discrimination

8.399 The Code of Practice for all employers on the avoidance of race discrimination in recruitment practice (available from the Home Office) provides useful guidance on how to meet the requirements of the Asylum and Immigration Act 1996 without falling foul of race discrimination legislation.

8.400 The Code provides examples of how to avoid race discrimination in recruitment and selection. Employers should ensure that they do not, eg:
- make assumptions about a job applicant's right to work in the UK based on his or her colour, race, nationality, ethnic origin or national origins
- treat applicants differently because of their race, nationality, national origins, colour or ethnic origin
- treat job applicants inconsistently, eg by asking some, but not all, job applicants for a particular post to produce documentary evidence of their right to work in the UK.

8.401 The overall aim should be to treat all job applicants in exactly the same way at every stage of the recruitment process. In this way, an overseas job applicant cannot succeed in a claim for race discrimination if he or she is rejected for the job.

8.402 It is up to the employer to decide at what stage of the recruitment process they wish to introduce the requirement to produce documentary evidence of the right to work in the UK. For example, applicants could conveniently be asked to bring the appropriate documentation along with them to interview, or alternatively the employer may prefer to check only the selected candidate at the final stage of the process.

Work Permits

8.403 On arrival in the UK, every person must produce a valid national passport or other document satisfactorily establishing his or her identity and nationality.

8.404 A work permit holder will also require a visa, which must be obtained before travelling to the UK.

8.405 A foreign national who is not a British citizen, an EEA or Swiss national, or a Commonwealth citizen with the right of abode will not normally be permitted to take up employment during his or her stay in the UK unless in possession of a valid work permit. Work permits are issued by the Border and Immigration Agency (BIA), a shadow agency of the Home Office.

8.406 People who do not fall within any of the above categories will be given leave to enter the UK for limited periods only. Time limits and any conditions attached to their stay in the UK will be endorsed by the Immigration Officer in their passports or travel documents.

Work Permit Exceptions

8.407 The following people do not need work permits.
- Nationals of the European Economic Area (EEA).
- People born in Gibraltar.
- Citizens of Switzerland.
- Commonwealth citizens who are allowed to enter or remain in the UK on the basis that one or other of their grandparents was born in the UK.
- Husbands, wives and dependant children under 18 of people who hold work permits or who qualify under any of the categories as long as the endorsement in their passports places no restriction on their employment in the UK.
- Those who do not have any conditions attached to their stay in the UK.

8.408 The following do not need work permits if the Home Office agrees that they qualify under one of the following categories and they have obtained, where necessary, prior entry clearance at a British Diplomatic Post abroad.
- Those coming to the UK to set up a new business or to take over or join an existing business as a partner or director, or as a sole trader.
- Ministers of religion, missionaries and members of religious orders.

- Representatives of overseas newspapers, news agencies and broadcasting organisations.
- Private servants in diplomatic households.
- Representatives of overseas firms who are seeking to establish a UK branch or subsidiary.
- Teachers and language assistants under approved exchange schemes.
- Employees of an overseas government coming to the UK to do a job for their government or international organisation of which the UK is a member.
- Seamen under contract to join a ship due to leave British waters on an international voyage.
- Senior operational ground staff of overseas-owned airlines based at international airports.
- Seasonal workers at agricultural camps under approved schemes.
- Doctors and dentists in postgraduate training.
- Entertainers and sports people participating in benefit matches and charity events for which there is no fee, or in international competition.
- Entertainers and sports people attending trials and auditions which do not involve a performance to a fee-paying audience.
- Working holidaymakers undertaking employment incidental to their holiday.

European Economic Area (EEA)

8.409 The EEA is made of up of the following countries.

EEA Countries

Austria	Latvia
Belgium	Liechtenstein
Bulgaria	Lithuania
Cyprus	Luxembourg
Czech Republic	Malta
Denmark	The Netherlands
Estonia	Norway
Finland	Poland
France	Portugal
Germany	Romania
Greece	Slovakia
Hungary	Slovenia
Iceland	Spain
Ireland	Sweden
Italy	UK

EEA citizens do not require a work permit to work in the UK.

Accession State Registration Scheme

8.410 Citizens from the following countries that joined the EU on 1 May 2004 are required to register with the Home Office under the Accession State Registration Scheme if they intend to work in the UK for one month or more.

The Czech Republic	Lithuania
Estonia	Poland
Hungary	Slovakia
Latvia	Slovenia

8.411 Employers who employ workers from any of the above eight countries are required to ensure that the workers register with the Home Office within one month of commencing employment. The workers will be provided with registration certificates, valid for 12 months. A registration certificate costs £70.

8.412 It is unlawful to employ a national of one of the eight countries (unless the person has worked legally in the UK for 12 months or more) if he or she is not registered for the job he or she is doing.

8.413 If a worker is a dual national of the UK or Switzerland or of a Member State of the EEA prior to 1 May 2004, he or she does not have to register under the scheme. However, documentary evidence of the exemption must be provided.

Workers from Romania and Bulgaria

8.414 Romania and Bulgaria joined the EU on 1 January 2007. Nationals from these countries now have the right to travel freely to the UK, but do not have the automatic right to work. There is, however, no restriction on their becoming self-employed.

Applying for a Work Permit

8.415 Employers based in Great Britain and Northern Ireland seeking to employ a foreign national who needs permission to work in the UK must apply for a "business and commercial" work permit from the Border and Immigration Agency (BIA) using form WP1X. The application fee is currently £153.

8.416 Applications for permits to work in the Isle of Man, Jersey and the Channel Islands must be sent to specified agencies in those areas.

8.417 It is important to note that it is the would-be employer who must apply for a work permit, not the foreign national. Furthermore, the permit will only be issued for a named person to fill a specified job vacancy within a named business or organisation and for a specified period. The current maximum permit period is five years, although extensions may be obtained.

8.418 Work permits are not transferable and will not enable the holder to work for any other employer in the UK unless that other employer applies for a work permit on the existing permit holder's behalf. A move to a different job within the same organisation will also require a fresh WP1 application to the BIA. A person who has remained in the UK for four years under a full business and commercial work permit may apply to the Home Office for indefinite leave to remain in the UK.

8.419 Forms WP1 submitted by employers who have not previously applied for a work permit (or have not done so within the previous five years) must be accompanied by a copy of the UK organisation's latest audited accounts or a copy of the latest annual report; or, if neither of those is available, any other documents that clearly show that the organisation is a UK based employer. For professional partnerships, a copy of one of the partner's registration with the appropriate professional body (eg the Law Society or the Royal College of Veterinary Surgeons) will suffice.

Criteria for Work Permit Applications

8.420 Applications for a work permit fall under two categories — Tier 1 Applications and Tier 2 Applications. Most employers will wish to apply for a business and commercial work permit and therefore will need to apply under Tier 2.

8.421 An application for a business and commercial work permit will normally be refused if the employer applying for the permit is unable to satisfy the BIA concerning the non-availability of a suitably qualified "resident worker" (a person who is a UK or an EEA national or who has "settled status" in the UK within the meaning of the Immigration Act 1971).

8.422 Work permit applications are considered against four basic criteria.
- Whether the vacancy for which the permit is required is a genuine vacancy.
- The skills, qualifications and experience needed for the job.
- Whether the person named in the application is suitably qualified or experienced.
- Whether there are suitably qualified or experienced "resident workers" available to fill the vacancy in question.

8.423 Certain skills, qualifications and experience criteria must also be met. The BIA will normally only issue work permits for people who have one of the following qualifications or skills:
- a UK degree level qualification or equivalent
- a Higher National Diploma (HND) level occupational qualification which is relevant to the post on offer
- a general HND level qualification plus one year's work experience doing the type of job for which the permit is sought
- at least three years' high level specialist skills acquired through doing the type of job for which the permit is sought; this type of job should be at NVQ/SVQ level 3 or above.

8.424 The Border and Immigration Agency does not issue work permits for low level or unskilled jobs (eg, manual, clerical, secretarial or similar) or for domestic work, such as nannies or housekeepers.

Tier 1 Applications

8.425 Tier 1 applications are given preferential treatment by the BIA and are quicker and easier to process. Employers making applications under Tier 1 do not have to provide evidence that the job cannot be filled in the EEA, and so do not have to advertise the job. Furthermore, less documentation needs to be provided to the BIA. The main advantage with Tier 1 work permits is that they can be issued for up to five years, which qualifies the overseas national for settlement in the UK. The following fall within the narrow ambit of Tier 1.
- Intra-company transfers.
- Board level and equivalent posts.
- Inward investment posts.
- Short supply occupations.

Intra-company Transfers

8.426 This category allows multinational companies to relocate existing employees to the UK. The transferring employee should have at least six months' experience working for the overseas company. To qualify as an intra-company transferee, the UK company must have a direct link to the overseas company by common ownership.

8.427 Employees who are transferred to the UK because of their experience are usually senior employees of overseas companies with offices in the UK with specialist skills, knowledge or experience needed for the job.

Posts at Board Level or Equivalent

8.428 To qualify under this category, the overseas national must either be on the board of the UK company or have a very senior position within the company. The individual's seniority is measured by the degree of influence that his or her decisions have over the company's activities.

Inward Investment Posts

8.429 Work permits are issued under this category where the employment of an overseas national will result in inward investment of at least £250,000 and the creation of jobs for EEA nationals. The investment must be made by an overseas company and not by the individual. Work permits under this category are usually issued initially for one year with a possible extension of up to three years if WP(UK) is satisfied that the investment has taken place and EEA nationals have been recruited.

Shortage Occupations

8.430 Employers may also submit Tier 1 applications in respect of so-called "shortage occupations" for which the BIA acknowledges that there is a shortage of suitably qualified resident workers within the EEA. A list of occupations that fall under this category is available from the BIA. With effect from 29 May 2007, the following occupations were removed from the National Shortage List:
- Senior Physiotherapists.
- Salaried General Dental Practitioners.
- Salaried Assistant Dentists.
- Salaried Vocational Dental Practitioner.

8.431 At the same time, all posts in Scotland covering compulsory schooling were added to the list.

Tier 2 Applications

8.432 All other applications are considered under Tier 2 which undergo more rigorous checks by the BIA.

8.433 Under Tier 2, the BIA will need to be convinced that the employer is unable to train or transfer an existing employee to do the job, or recruit an EEA national, and will need clear reasons why it is necessary for the employer to employ the overseas national.

8.434 The employer should provide evidence that a full, thorough and realistic search of the resident labour market has been carried out. This is normally done by advertising the position in a relevant publication with European circulation. The advertisement(s) should have been placed within the six-month period prior to the work permit application and one month must have been allowed for replies. The employer will need to provide details of their recruitment methods, including copies of job advertisements, details of the response to the advertisements and the number of candidates interviewed.

8.435 The BIA will need to be satisfied that the prominence given to the job advertisements truly reflected the level and nature of the vacancies in question. The employer will also need to explain its reasons for rejecting applicants from within the EEA who applied for the post, including those who might have been capable of doing the job with a little extra training.

8.436 As an alternative to advertising the position the BIA may accept the employer's use of a headhunter to find suitable candidates where a proper search of the EEA has been carried out to fill the post in question.

8.437 The BIA may agree to waive advertising or headhunting in exceptional circumstances.

Extension Applications

8.438 If the employer needs to employ the overseas national for a longer period than that granted by the original work permit, an extension application should be made using form WP1X four to eight weeks before the individual's leave to remain expires. This is the period stamped in the individual's passport by the immigration officer on entry to the UK.

8.439 If the application is still under consideration when the individual's leave expires it will automatically be extended until such time as a decision is made. This allows the overseas national to continue working while the application is being processed, even if subsequently the leave expires.

8.440 Because the overseas national will be in the UK when the extension application is made, the matter will be referred to the Home Office which makes a final decision.

Appeals

8.441 An appeal against a decision to refuse a work permit application must be made within 28 days of receiving the decision. Appeals must be made on the Work Permit Appeal Application Form (WP Appeal).

Training and Work Experience Scheme (TWES)

8.442 The purpose of the Training and Work Experience Scheme (TWES) is to enable individuals to gain skills and experience through work-based learning, which they intend to use on their return overseas.

8.443 An employer's application for a TWES permit will be admissible if, but only if, the person for whom the permit is sought is additional to the employer's normal staffing requirements. In other words, the person in question must not be filling a vacancy that might otherwise be filled by a "resident worker".

8.444 An individual who holds a TWES permit is not allowed to transfer to work permit employment.

8.445 If the person is to occupy a vacant post within the employing organisation, the employer must apply for a normal "business and commercial" work permit (using Form WP1).

Criteria for Applications

8.446 The BIA will not issue a TWES permit unless satisfied that the intended trainee has an adequate command of the English language (in order to benefit from the training and experience offered) and that he or she intends to return overseas at the end of the period specified in the permit. The training or work experience should be for a minimum of 30 hours a week and the intended training should lead to a recognised professional or specialist qualification at postgraduate level.

8.447 The intended work experience should be at managerial, or at least National/Scottish Vocational Qualification (N/SVQ) level 3 or the equivalent. The person should have previous relevant experience or appropriate academic/vocational qualifications to enable him or her to benefit from a work experience programme at this level. The BIA will not normally approve TWES permit applications for people who have neither relevant experience nor any academic or vocational qualifications.

Length of TWES Permits

8.448 A TWES permit for training leading to a professional or specialist qualification will be issued for the average time expected to complete the training up to a period of five years.

8.449 A "work experience" permit will be issued for up to 12 months initially and, exceptionally, for a further period so that the total for the programme is no more than 24 months. Employers wanting to extend a TWES permit should complete form WP1X and explain why the training or work experience programme should be extended and for what period. The BIA will not normally approve requests for extensions unless satisfied that the person in question can successfully complete the training or work experience programme and the extension period is justified.

Employment of Students

8.450 Overseas students studying at UK institutions will normally have in their passports a stamp stating that they cannot work "without the consent of the Secretary of State".

8.451 However, students studying at UK institutions, who are not nationals of an EEA member state, are permitted to take spare time or vacation work or to do sandwich courses or internship placements in the UK without permission, so long as they do not (and are not required to) work more than 20 hours a week during term time (unless the placement with an employer is a necessary part of their education and is endorsed by the college, university or other institution at which they are pursuing their studies).

8.452 Students, however, must not engage in business, self-employment or the provision of a service as a professional sportsperson or entertainer, during their stay in the UK and must not pursue their careers by filling permanent, full-time vacancies.

8.453 Overseas students studying at institutions outside the UK still need permits to undertake work experience in the UK.

Working Holidaymakers

8.454 Young Commonwealth citizens, aged 17–30 inclusive, seeking leave to enter the UK as working holidaymakers, will be permitted to take up employment for no more than 12 months during their extended holidays if they hold a valid visa for entry to the UK in that capacity and if they :

- are unmarried (or married to persons in the same age bracket as themselves and are able and are intending to take a working holiday together)
- have the means to pay for their return or onward journeys; and are able and intend to maintain and accommodate themselves without recourse to public funds
- intend to take employment incidental to a holiday but not to engage in business, be a professional sportsperson or entertainer or pursue careers in the UK
- do not have dependent children aged five years or over (or who will reach that age before they complete their working holidays) and do not have commitments that would require them to earn a regular income

- have not spent time in the UK on a previous working holidaymaker visa
- plan to leave the UK at the end of their holiday.

8.455 Working holidaymakers may take up work in the field in which they intend to pursue a permanent career, so long as this is incidental to their holiday. The 12 months employment may be continuous or may consist of separate shorter periods.

8.456 **Note:** People issued with a working holidaymaker visa before 8 February 2005 do not have any restrictions upon the amount or type of work that they may do.

8.457 Working holidaymakers may be eligible to switch into work permit employment after 12 months in the UK if their occupation is on the list of designated shortage occupations. They may also switch into the Highly Skilled Migrant Programme (HSMP).

Highly Skilled Migrant Programme (HSMP)

8.458 The Highly Skilled Migrant Programme (HSMP) allows highly skilled individuals from overseas to migrate to the UK to either seek employed work or work on a self-employed basis. It differs from the Work Permit scheme in that individuals do not have to have been offered a job in the UK in order to apply. The HSMP fee is currently £400. A full list of fees, effective from 2 April 2007, is available from the Home Office.

8.459 The HSMP is based on a points scheme, where points are scored in the following four areas:
- age (if under 32)
- UK work experience
- educational qualifications
- past earnings.

8.460 Applicants are also required to provide evidence that they meet a mandatory English language requirement.

8.461 In order to qualify as a skilled migrant, the individual must score at least 75 points. Self-employed GPs qualified to practice in the UK may also apply under the programme.

8.462 Permission to stay in the UK is granted initially for up to two years. The individual may, however, apply to stay for a further three-year period provided that he or she is economically active.

8.463 Some categories of workers are unlikely to succeed under the scheme, such as IT specialists, as the Government has deemed that there are enough IT specialists currently working in the UK. An employer taking on an individual under the scheme should ensure that it obtains all the relevant documentation from the individual in question.

Sectors Based Scheme

8.464 Places on the two low-skilled migration schemes for non-EU workers (the Seasonal Agricultural Workers scheme and the Sectors Based Scheme (SBS)), which between them currently have 19,750 places, are now restricted to nationals from Romania and Bulgaria, with numbers maintained at that present level. Initially, food processing and agriculture are the only sectors open to less-skilled nationals from the two latest EU Member States. Industry representatives can however make a case where it is felt similar schemes are needed in other sectors.

8.465 SBS permits are issued for a maximum period of 12 months. It has previously been a requirement that such permit holders had to leave the UK at the end of this period for a minimum period of two months before any further SBS permit would be granted. This requirement has been removed for SBS permit holders from Bulgaria and Romania. Employers may apply for Extension or Change of Employment applications for Bulgarian or Romanian nationals beyond a cumulative 12 months approval period without the SBS permit holder leaving the UK or completing a two month gap between periods of SBS employment. Once Bulgarian and Romanian nationals have been legally employed in the UK on a continuous basis for 12 months, they are automatically exempt from work authorisation requirements and may obtain a registration certificate confirming their unrestricted right to access the UK labour market. This 12-month period commences on the first day of lawful employment in the UK.

Training

8.466 All managers and HR practitioners involved in recruitment and selection should be given awareness training in employing foreign nationals, the duty to make checks under the Asylum and Immigration Act 1996 and the rules and processes on work permits.

List of Relevant Legislation

8.467
- Accession (Immigration and Worker Authorisation) Regulations 2006
- Accession (Immigration and Worker Registration) (Amendment) Regulations 2005
- Immigration (Restrictions on Employment) Order 2004
- Employment Equality Act 1998

Further Information

Organisations
- **Advisory Conciliation and Arbitration Service (Acas)**
  Web: *www.acas.org.uk*
  Acas aims to improve organisations and working life through better employment relations. It provides up-to-date information, advice, high-quality training, and works with employers and employees to solve problems and improve performance.
- **Border and Immigration Agency**
  Web: *www.workingintheuk.gov.uk*
  Formed in 2007 as a Shadow Agency of the Home Office, the BIA has replaced the Immigration and Nationality Directorate. It administers the work permit arrangements on behalf of the UK Government.
- **Commission for Racial Equality**
  Web: *www.cre.gov.uk*
  The Commission for Racial Equality is a publicly funded, non-governmental body set up under the Race Relations Act 1976 to tackle racial discrimination and promote racial equality. From October 2007 this organisation will be replaced by the Commission for Equality and Human Rights.

- **Department for Business, Enterprise and Regulatory Reform (BERR)**
  Web: *www.berr.gov.uk*
  The Department for Business, Enterprise and Regulatory Reform brings together functions from the former Department of Trade and Industry (DTI), including responsibilities for productivity, business relations, energy, competition and consumers. It also drives regulatory reform.
- **Home Office**
  Web: *www.homeoffice.gov.uk*
  The Home Office is the Government department responsible for internal affairs in England and Wales.
- **Information Commissioner's Office**
  Web: *www.ico.gov.uk*
  The Information Commissioner enforces and oversees the Data Protection Act 1998 and the Freedom of Information Act 2000. It is an independent UK supervisory authority, reporting directly to the UK Parliament. It has an international role as well as a national one.

References and Medical Checks

> This topic covers the following.
> - Obligation to Provide a Reference
> - Duty of Care
> - Reasonable Care
> - Implied Term of Trust and Confidence
> - Unlawful Discrimination
> - Victimisation
> - Data Protection Act 1998
> - Guidance on the Use of Data in Recruitment and Selection
> - Data Protection Guidance as to Employment Records
> - Guidance on the Use of Medical Information
> - Disability Discrimination Act 1995
> - Access to Medical Reports Act 1988

8.468 The impact of a reference can have significant financial consequences and references have become an increased source of litigation. The Data Protection Act 1998 (DPA) is now a significant governing factor when dealing with references.

8.469 Medical information sought and obtained for recruitment purposes is also affected by the provisions of the DPA and will need to be treated in appropriate confidence. Recruitment decisions made using information about the medical condition of applicants will also be covered by the Disability Discrimination Act 1995 (DDA).

Employers' Duties

8.470 Employers should be aware of the following.
- There is generally no obligation to provide a reference to a former employee. In certain circumstances the contract of employment can include an obligation to provide a reference.
- A duty of care is owed to the recipient of the reference, so the reference must be true, accurate and fair. The employer's duty will also extend to the employee who is the subject of the reference.
- A failure by an employer to exercise reasonable care could give rise to a potential claim based on negligence or on the implied term contained in all contracts of employment requiring the exercise of due care and skill in the preparation of a reference.
- The implied term of trust and confidence in a contract of employment can also be undermined where a reference is unfair and/or misleading.
- Employers may be legally liable if a reference includes unlawful discrimination.
- Liability may also arise if a reference is found to include unlawful victimisation.
- References and their contents should be treated as data and processed in accordance with the principles of the DPA.
- References should be treated in accordance with the Information Commissioner's guidance as to the use of data in recruitment and selection, and data protection guidance as to employment records.

References and Medical Checks

- Medical information concerning applicants should be treated as sensitive personal data and processed in accordance with the Information Commissioner's Guidance as to the use of medical information.
- Information on sickness absences should comply with the DDA.
- An employer may be justified in not employing a job applicant, or in terminating the employment of an employee, where the individual refuses to consent to medical checks.

Employees' Duties

- A job applicant must give full and frank disclosure, as false statements and/or any material non-disclosure may give the employer grounds for terminating any subsequent contract of employment. Any dishonesty may lead to criminal law consequences.
- An employee or job applicant cannot be compelled to undergo a medical check or answer a medical questionnaire (although an employee may be bound by a contractual clause, which specifically allows for medical checks).
- An employee may be required, in some circumstances, to consent to medical checks. Refusal to consent may allow the employer to refuse employment or to terminate existing employment.

In Practice

Obligation to Provide a Reference

8.471 An employer does not generally have to provide a reference for a present or former employee who is seeking employment elsewhere.

8.472 However, the contract of employment can imply that the employer will provide the employee with a reference. This is likely to be the case if the work is of a kind where it is normal practice to require a reference from a previous employer before employment is offered.

8.473 The employer should also be aware of the fact that refusal to provide a reference is taken by many employers to indicate a problem with the member of staff about whom the reference is requested.

8.474 In such circumstances the employee cannot be expected to enter into the type of employment involved, unless the employer responds to reasonable requests from other prospective employers by providing a full and frank reference.

Duty of Care

8.475 Where the employer provides a reference, there should be a duty of care to the new employer. The House of Lords has confirmed that the duty of care also extends to the subject of a reference.

Reasonable Care

8.476 A reference can be considered unfair if it contains matters of which the employee was unaware (see *TSB Bank plc v Harris* [2000] IRLR 157 EAT) and may give rise to a successful claim of constructive dismissal based upon a breach of the implied term of trust and confidence.

8.477 A reference must be true, accurate and fair, compiled with reasonable care and must not give a misleading impression. However, subject to this, there is no requirement for a reference to be full and comprehensive.

Implied Term of Trust and Confidence

8.478 An employer is potentially liable for damages for negligence where:
- responsible for any negligent mis-statement, or
- liable for any breach of an implied term in the contract of employment requiring the exercise of due care and skill in preparation of references.

8.479 If such a breach is very serious, a current employee may be able to resign and claim constructive dismissal.

Unlawful Discrimination

8.480 A former employee can now bring a claim alleging unlawful discrimination arising out of the provision of a reference. Employment tribunals have jurisdiction to consider a complaint of discrimination that relates only to acts which are alleged to have taken place after the complainant's employment has finished.

8.481 It is important to be consistent in giving references to former employees, otherwise one employee may contend less favourable treatment than another former employee.

8.482 References are often required to deal with sickness absences. If they resulted from a medical condition that amounts to a disability for the purposes of the Disability Discrimination Act 1995, additional care will be needed. Adverse comment arising out of such absences may well be considered discriminatory unless it can be justified.

8.483 As far as the prospective employer is concerned, recruitment decisions that consider sickness records in previous employment can result in unlawful discrimination. Also, there is a duty to make adjustments where any features of the workplace put a disabled person at a substantial disadvantage in comparison with the non-disabled.

Victimisation

8.484 Under EU law, it is illegal for the employer to victimise an ex-employee by withholding references because the ex-employee has asserted his or her rights to equality. The employer is in such circumstances not allowed to use the ex-employee's action as a pretext for withholding the reference.

8.485 Consequently, employers must be aware of the risks involved in giving an unfavourable reference (or refusing a reference), where a current or former employee had made a complaint of discrimination. Under the legislation, such a complaint is treated as a protected act and treating an individual differently because the individual has done a protected act can amount to victimisation.

Data Protection Act 1998

8.486 The disclosure, use and retention of information regarding current and former employees, as well as job applicants, must comply with the provisions of the

Data Protection Act 1998. The Information Commissioner has published an *Employment Practices Data Protection Code* with guidance on the applicability of the Data Protection Act 1998 within the workplace. This Code of Practice has been published in four separate parts:
- Part 1: Recruitment and Selection
- Part 2: Employment Records
- Part 3: Monitoring at Work
- Part 4: Information about Workers' Health.

8.487 The Code, together with supplementary guidance, is available from the Information Commissioner.

Guidance on the Use of Data in Recruitment and Selection

8.488 Key guidance in Part 1 of the *Employment Practices Data Protection Code* dealing with Recruitment and Selection includes the following.
- Where it is necessary to request information about a job applicant from a third party (such as a former or present employer), a signed consent form should be obtained from the applicant, unless consent has been indicated in some other way.
- Where the information from a third party differs from that provided by the applicant, the latter should have the opportunity to indicate any discrepancies.
- Information about job applicants should be deleted where there is no longer any risk of any claim arising and where it is irrelevant to ongoing employment.

8.489 There is a special exemption from the right of access under the Data Protection Act 1998 that applies to a confidential reference when in the hands of the employer who gave it.

Data Protection Guidance as to Employment Records

8.490 Guidance under Part 2 of the Information Commissioner's Code of Practice dealing with employment records includes the key recommendations as follows.
- When giving references, it is recommended that the employer:
  – should have a clear policy
  – be satisfied that the individual is content for a reference to be provided
  – should establish, at the end of employment, whether or not the employee wishes references to be provided to future employers or to others.
- Although an employer does not have to grant access to a reference that it has provided, good practice must be to be as open as possible with employees, who should be able to challenge anything inaccurate or misleading.
- Disclosure of a reference received by an employer to an employee may include information identifying another person, eg the author of the reference. Responding fully to a request for access may lead to the violation of third party rights under the Data Protection Act 1998.

8.491 According to the guidance of the Information Commissioner, where the information from a third party comprises an employment reference received by the employer, it should normally be released to the employee, unless the referee indicates otherwise. However, if this involves the breach of a duty of confidentiality, the information should only be released if it has had or is likely to have a significant adverse impact upon the employee.

Guidance on the Use of Medical Information

8.492 Part 4 of the Information Commissioner's *Employment Practices Data Protection Code* deals with "Information about Workers' Health". Such information will come within the definition of "sensitive personal data" within the Data Protection Act 1998, for which additional safeguards and restrictions are applicable. One of the sensitive data conditions in the Data Protection Act 1998 will need to be satisfied if details about employees' health are processed. The conditions include the following.

- Is the processing necessary to enable the employer to meet its legal obligations, eg to ensure health and safety at work, or to comply with the requirement not to discriminate against workers on the grounds of disability?
- Is the processing for medical purposes and undertaken by a health professional with a duty of confidentiality, such as an occupational health doctor?
- Is the processing in connection with legal proceedings?
- Has the employee given consent explicitly to the processing of his or her medical information?

8.493 For validity, an employee's consent must be informed consent, ie there must be full awareness and any consent must be freely given.

8.494 Where medical checks are being carried out for recruitment and selection purposes, the employer will usually be able to proceed once the job applicant has consented to the medical checks. If the job offer is conditional on the receipt of satisfactory medical checks, this should be made clear in the offer letter.

Disability Discrimination Act 1995

8.495 In seeking medical information about job applicants, an employer will need to be aware that it may relate to disability covered by the Disability Discrimination Act 1995. The Disability Rights Commission has issued a *Code of Practice for the Elimination of Discrimination in the Field of Employment against Disabled Persons or Persons who have had a Disability*. Paragraphs 5.1 to 5.29 deal specifically with recruitment.

Access to Medical Reports Act 1988

8.496 If an employer wishes to obtain a medical report, the individual job applicant or employee has rights under the Access to Medical Reports Act 1988. Before approaching a medical practitioner, the individual's consent must be received and he or she must be informed of his or her rights, including the right to see the report prior to the employer.

Training

8.497 It is important that all managers likely to have to provide a reference are made aware of the legal duty to provide an accurate and fair reference, and the possible legal consequences arising out of breach of this duty.

8.498 Recruitment managers need to receive training to promote good practice and, in particular, awareness of the need to use information provided within any selection and recruitment exercise in a way which is consistent with:

- equal opportunities legislation and guidance
- data protection legislation and guidance
- rights of confidentiality and privacy in respect of medical information.

List of Relevant Legislation

8.499
- Data Protection Act 1998
- Disability Discrimination Act 1995
- Access to Medical Records Act 1988
- Race Relations Act 1976
- Sex Discrimination Act 1975
- Equal Treatment Directive 76/207

List of Relevant Cases

8.500
- *Relaxion Group plc v Rhys-Harper; D'Souza v London Borough of Lambeth; Jones v 3M Healthcare Ltd* [2003] IRLR 484, HL
- *Chief Constable of West Yorkshire Police v Khan* [2001] IRLR 830, HL
- *Kidd v AXA Equity Law Life Assurance Society plc* [2000] IRLR 301, HC
- *TSB Bank plc v Harris* [2000] IRLR 157, EAT
- *Bartholomew v London Borough of Hackney* [1999] IRLR 246, CA
- *Coote v Granada Hospitality Ltd (No. 2)* [1999] IRLR 452, EAT
- *Spring v Guardian Assurance plc* [1994] IRLR 460, HL
- *Lawton v BOC Transhield* [1987] IRLR 404, HC

Further Information

Publications
- *Employment Practices Data Protection Code — Part 1: Recruitment and Selection*, from the Information Commissioner's Office
  Code of Practice and Explanatory Guide for Registered Persons and Other Recipients of Disclosure Information Criminal Records Bureau.

Organisations
- **Data Protection Registrar**
  Web: *www.dca.gov.uk*
  The Data Protection Registrar is responsible in Government for upholding justice, rights and democracy.
- **Information Commissioner's Office**
  Web: *www.ico.gov.uk*
  The Information Commissioner enforces and oversees the Data Protection Act 1998 and the Freedom of Information Act 2000. It is an independent UK supervisory authority, reporting directly to the UK Parliament. It has an international role as well as a national one.

Selection Process

This topic covers the following.
- Screening Applications
- Timing
- Application Forms and CVs
- The Data Protection Act
- Screening Forms
- Formalised Approaches to Screening
- Interviewing
- Panel Interviews
- One-to-one Interviews
- Briefing Candidates
- Conducting the Interview
- Disabled Interviewees
- Extended Selection Techniques
- Appointment Processes — Making the Offer

8.501 Selection is a two-way process. In addition to choosing the best person for the job, it is important to do everything possible to make sure that the chosen individual will accept the offer of employment. This is done by presenting a comprehensive and balanced view of the job and the organisation, and by being courteous, considerate and professional at every stage in the selection process.

8.502 Throughout the process it is also vital to guard against any breaches of discrimination legislation.

Employers' Duties

8.503 Employers have a duty to ensure that:
- no applicant is discriminated against in the recruitment and selection process on any of the designated grounds
- the provisions on genuine occupational requirements are complied with where appropriate
- consideration is given to any provision, criterion or practice in the person specification or terms of a job which might be indirectly discriminatory
- reasonable adjustments are made for disabled applicants
- they do not put pressure to discriminate on any staff involved in recruitment and selection
- contractual obligations in the terms of an offer of employment are fully understood by both parties
- the terms and conditions of employment are consistent with statutory requirements and minimum standards
- checks on health, for work permits, for criminal records and requests for references are made as appropriate
- data relating to recruitment and selection is processed in accordance with data protection legislation and guidance
- the recruitment and selection process is monitored to ensure that there is no discriminatory treatment.

Selection Process

Employees' Duties

8.504 Employees have a duty to:
- be honest about the personal information disclosed in the recruitment and selection process
- facilitate appropriate checks made about health and criminal records
- provide, as required, the names of referees
- abide by any agreement made on accepting employment.

In Practice

Screening Applications

8.505 It is rare for more than 12 candidates to be interviewed for a single vacancy. Therefore if more than 100 people apply for a particular job, less than 10% of applicants will be selected for interview. Inefficient screening is likely to result in better candidates being rejected, leading to:
- a poor return on investment in the selection process
- the risk of illegal discrimination claims.

8.506 Screening must be conducted professionally. Screening criteria must be strictly relevant to the job, based on an objective person specification.

8.507 The amount of work involved in screening can be reduced by encouraging applicants to self-select by such means as:
- advertisements that provide relevant and honest information
- well-designed application packs
- online questionnaires.

Timing

8.508 Where a closing date is set, the process of screening applicants will usually take place as soon as possible after this date.

8.509 If the need to fill the vacancy is particularly urgent, or if it exists in an area of acute skills shortage, the employer may need to call suitable candidates in for interview as soon as they apply or are put forward by agencies.

8.510 Where candidates are known to be scarce, it may be advisable to ask applicants to apply by email or telephone rather than in writing. This allows them to be called straight in for interview. Care must be taken to ensure that an appropriate member of staff is available to take telephone applications at all times — including lunch breaks and evenings — since candidates may not be able to call from their workplace.

8.511 Where there is a large response, it is best to wait until most of the replies have been received before starting to screen applications.

Application Forms and CVs

8.512 Many organisations insist on applications being made on a standard form whilst others accept CVs or alternative forms of application. The sources of candidates and the types of job may be the determining factors here.

8.513 Recruitment agencies usually send out candidates' details in CV format and it would be impractical to get them to fill in forms until they are called in for interview.

8.514 CVs are also the accepted means of application in the private sector at senior and professional levels where response could be damaged by an insistence on completing forms.

8.515 The CV provides an initial indication of an applicant's ability to structure and present information in a clear and succinct manner, which is an important element of many jobs.

8.516 Application forms have distinct advantages over CVs in that they:
- make it easier to compare one applicant with another
- concentrate the attention of screeners on objective factors rather than on presentation
- ensure that all of the information required is actually obtained, whereas CVs tend to be selective
- establish before interview key points such as the compliance by applicants with a vital precondition of employment.

8.517 It is better to have different application forms for different types of candidate, eg manual, clerical, managerial and professional roles.

Personal Information and Equal Opportunities

8.518 Equal opportunities and all personal information should be provided on separate tear-off forms. When application forms are received back from candidates, administrators should remove all personal information before forwarding application forms to the selection panel.

Disabled Applicants

8.519 An employer needs to ensure that the methods of selection do not place a job applicant with a particular disability at a disadvantage compared to other applicants.

8.520 Application forms should include an appropriately worded question to determine whether a candidate is disabled. The employer can then make necessary adjustments for interviewing as well as considering different working arrangements.

8.521 Possible reasonable adjustments include rearranging the venue or the time for the interview or allowing the interviewee to be accompanied by an interpreter or lip reader. The interview may take more time than usual, so allowance needs to be made for this.

8.522 Employers should make it clear that they can provide information to job applicants in formats such as audio tape, large print, Braille or email, and that they are happy to receive applications in such formats.

Equal Opportunities Statements

8.523 It is very useful to add an equal opportunities statement to the application form, eg a simple statement that the employer is an equal opportunities employer and welcomes applications from all sections of the community.

Data Protection Clause

8.524 It is important that a data protection clause is added to the application form so that the applicant gives his or her consent to the processing of personal data.

The Data Protection Act

8.525 Legislation requires selection process records to be handled in a way which respects eight data protection principles. Personal data must be:
- processed fairly and lawfully
- processed for limited purposes
- adequate, relevant and not excessive
- accurate
- not kept for longer than is necessary
- processed in line with the data subjects' rights

8.526 Failure to comply with the Act can bring heavy sanctions including criminal prosecution and an award of damages in the courts.

8.527 In terms of interviews, the legislation imposes upon employers the need to ensure that personal data which are recorded and retained following interview can be justified as relevant to the recruitment process — or for defending the process against challenge.

8.528 The legislation is concerned with data collected at interview and its recording, storage and use as these will constitute processing under the Act. Applicants will normally be entitled to have access to all interview notes about them which are retained as a record of the interview.

Screening Forms

8.529 It is helpful to compile a screening form and attach it to each application form. The screening form lists the key job requirements as defined by the person specification and can be used to rate each candidate against these criteria:
- on a "marks out of five" basis for items such as relevant experience, or
- on a "yes/no" basis for possession of a mandatory professional qualification.

8.530 The use of a screening form ensures that there is an objective record showing why a particular applicant was either selected for interview or rejected. Since the Data Protection Act may allow applicants access to manual as well as to computerised records, it is important to be able to produce such evidence if an applicant challenges a decision.

8.531 There may be some categories of job where neither the application form nor the CV is the best method of application, eg applicants for posts involving a high percentage of telephone or face-to-face communication may best be screened by telephone. In these instances, a screening form should still be used to provide objective ratings.

Formalised Approaches to Screening

8.532 There are three formalised approaches to screening. These ensure that subjective factors are ruled out of the selection process.

Biodata

8.533 The biodata or "biographical data" questionnaire asks applicants to answer

Selection Process

a series of questions designed to predict future performance. The questionnaire may be either a separate document or built into the application form itself. Although apparently scientific, this approach does not automatically satisfy the key requirement of relevance to the vacancy in question. Furthermore, some biodata questionnaires ask about family background and other matters that are both irrelevant and potentially discriminatory.

Competence-Based Screening

8.534 Competence-based screening also uses questionnaires. The technique should be effective provided that the competences used have been carefully selected on the basis of genuine relevance to the job in question. The establishment of a comprehensive competency framework system is a major undertaking. It tends to be adopted only by large organisations that conduct the volume of recruitment to justify the investment.

Psychometric Tests

8.535 Psychometric testing can be either online or offline. Offline testing can be either written or done on a PC. Online testing is a quick and inexpensive method of reducing large volumes of initial applications. Offline testing can realistically be used only when candidates are on the employer's premises. It tends to be used at the interview stage. Ideally, tests should be given before any interview so that the results can be discussed at the interview.

8.536 A candidate can be sent for tests with an occupational psychologist after the employer's own interviews but before making an offer.

8.537 There is controversy over whether job applicants should be ruled out solely on the basis of online tests. There are also special requirements under the Data Protection Act if any screening is only computer-based.

Interviewing

8.538 Well-prepared, structured interviews are essential if organisations want to select and employ the best possible applicants.

The Importance of Preparation

8.539 Studies have repeatedly shown that interviews are an extremely poor predictor of future performance — only slightly more successful than pure chance. One major reason is a lack of preparation on the part of managers and HR professionals. When they hold an interview without planning a poor and costly recruitment decision is likely to result.

Structured Interviews

8.540 Following a pre-determined structure has several advantages. Interviewers can:
- progress smoothly from one subject to another
- ensure that nothing is missed
- avoid embarrassing silences
- be in command and appear professional.

8.541 The structure that is most appropriate depends on the circumstances of individual interviews. When interviewing young candidates with little work experience, it is perfectly reasonable to start with their education and follow through chronologically, ending with their current situation and future plans. If senior candidates with many years' experience are being interviewed, it is far more sensible to home in on the last five years of their career.

Structured Questions

8.542 Structured questioning techniques take the job description, use it to identify key elements of the job, and then design questions that assess how candidates are likely to perform in the work situation. The same questions are put to each candidate and the answers rated or scored by interviewers according to a set system. Structured questions may be either hypothetical or behavioural.

Hypothetical Questions

8.543 Hypothetical questions take the form "What would you do if . . ?". They can be put to all candidates regardless of whether or not they have been in the given situation. The response is likely to be a problematic mix of what the applicant would like to do and what he or she thinks the interviewer wants to hear.

Behavioural Questions

8.544 Behavioural questions elicit from candidates examples of relevant behaviour in past work situations. The candidates' responses are likely to be more realistic than with hypothetical questions. Behavioural questions are based on the principle that analysing what people have done in the past is a good way of predicting what they will do in the future.

8.545 Replies to hypothetical questions can be compared with model answers but this is not so easy with questions based on past performance since each candidate will probably describe a different situation.

Clarification and Honesty

8.546 It is important to study the career details submitted by each applicant selected for interview in order to identify further questions to ask him or her. There may be points requiring clarification or expansion — or even a need to check the honesty of a candidate.

8.547 The areas in which honesty is most likely to be an issue are:
- current remuneration
- qualifications
- gaps between jobs
- short periods of employment
- being unemployed
- health
- criminal records.

8.548 The omission of information can be minimised by making it clear in advertisements and application packs what information is required.

8.549 Deception and lies can be discouraged by:
- including on application forms a warning that false statements may lead to an offer being withdrawn or a contract of employment terminated
- asking applicants to sign the form to show acceptance of this condition.

Panel Interviews

8.550 An organisation's use of a single interviewer — or of a series of single interviewers — greatly increases the risk of personal prejudices influencing any hiring decision.

8.551 Panel interviews have the following advantages over one-to-one interviews:
- they tend to be better predictors of behaviour and performance, provided they are conducted efficiently
- specialists on the panel can concentrate on their own area of expertise
- where a questioner misjudges or misinterprets a reply, another panel member can ask for clarification
- relevant matters are less likely to be omitted
- they reduce the possibility of individual bias — as each interviewer is monitored by the others.

8.552 Panel interviews have the following disadvantages compared with one-to-one interviews:
- the candidate is outnumbered and likely to be defensive
- it is difficult to achieve rapport with the candidate
- being less relaxed, candidates are unlikely to reveal much about themselves
- it is more difficult for an interviewer to follow a line of questioning due to interruptions from other panel members
- they can become a "free for all", limiting the information obtained and creating a bad impression of the employer
- the person who gets the job may be the one who is best at making presentations to groups — a skill which may not be vital for the job
- the time taken to convene a panel of busy managers may result in the loss of potential recruits.

Discrimination

8.553 In order to minimise the risk of discrimination, it is vital that the composition of the interview panel is balanced. Every effort should be made to make the panel as representative of the candidate pool as possible.

Solutions

8.554 There are a number of practices that can maximise the advantages of panel interviews and minimise their disadvantages.
- Ideally restrict the number of people on a panel to three or four at most.
- Ensure that panel members are clear about the person specification and the selection criteria, and that they all understand both the interview structure and the part they are to play.
- Allow time between each interview for panel members to discuss candidates, make notes and prepare for the incoming interviewee.
- Ensure that the panel is efficiently chaired.

8.555 In order to make the candidates feel at ease, consider the following.
- "Soften" the interview environment with potted plants or other human touches.
- Sit everyone around a coffee table rather than a formal table that creates a physical and psychological barrier.
- Arrange seating so that the candidate can readily see, and be seen by, all members of the panel.

One-to-one Interviews

8.556 The physical factors described in Panel Interviews are equally relevant when conducting one-to-one interviews. When individual managers interview in their own offices, they often make the mistake of:

- conducting the interview across the physical and psychological barrier of a desk rather than, say, sitting around a coffee table
- giving a poor impression by littering their desk with papers and files
- failing to prevent disturbances to the interview, eg by not diverting their telephone.

8.557 It is also important, whichever kind of interview is being used, to consider the following.

- Make any necessary adaptations for disabled candidates, eg if interviewing a wheelchair user, using a ground floor meeting room if access to other floors is restricted.
- When making appointments for interviews, bear in mind that some candidates may not be able to attend at particular times of day. This may be because of childcare responsibilities, travel problems or existing work commitments.
- If arranging a series of consecutive interviews, allow for overrunning of the scheduled timings.

Briefing Candidates

8.558 Candidates selected for interview should be sent confirmation in writing. This should cover the:

- date, time and place of the interview — including a map, details of public transport and parking facilities
- policy on reimbursement of travel expenses
- format of the interview, eg panel or one-to-one, and whether any tests, case studies or presentations will be involved
- preparation required, eg for a presentation
- things that candidates should bring with them, eg work samples, proof of qualifications
- estimated duration of the interview
- names of the interviewers and their positions in the organisation
- background information on the organisation.

Conducting the Interview

8.559 The following points are best practice.

- Ensure that candidates are expected and welcomed both at the reception desk and when brought through for interview.
- Try to run to time so that candidates are not kept waiting — during any unavoidable waiting time give them things to do, eg a tour of the premises.
- Begin the interview with appropriate "ice-breakers", eg a question about their journey, but avoid personal matters which could easily be seen as being discriminatory.
- Make the first question an easy, open one that will get the candidate talking and relaxing — you can even invite candidates to ask a question, thus giving them the feeling that they have a share in controlling the session.

Interview Questions

8.560 Throughout the interview, take care to frame questions in the most appropriate way.
- Broach each new topic with an open question, eg "Why did you ...?", "What do you think about ...?".
- Follow up with probing and reflective questions, eg "Can you give me some examples?", "What were the consequences?".
- Use summarising questions to check your understanding of what the candidate has said, eg "So, are you saying ...?".
- Use closed questions, such as "So, you have worked in management before?" sparingly, ie when a "yes" or "no" answer is required to draw a line under a particular topic and move on to something else.

8.561 It is also important to avoid:
- leading questions, eg "Wouldn't you agree that . . .?"
- loaded questions, eg "What do you think of this stupid legislation?"
- multiple questions, eg "When do you see this happening? How do you see this happening?"
- multiple choice questions, eg "If this happened, would you do a..., b..., c..., or d...?".

8.562 It is absolutely vital to "listen actively" to the replies, avoiding:
- being preoccupied with the next question you are going to ask
- filtering what the candidate says through your own assumptions
- being distracted, eg by other members of the interview panel.

Ending the Interview

8.563 At the end of the interview:
- give candidates the opportunity to ask any questions they have
- explain what will happen next, including the timing of the decision or next stage
- thank candidates for attending — remember that last impressions are as important as first impressions.

Disabled Interviewees

8.564 It is unlawful for an employer to refuse to interview or shortlist a disabled job applicant because of the applicant's disability.

8.565 It is permissible to ask about a person's disability at an interview if it is relevant to his or her ability to do the job. If it is relevant it is permissible to ask an applicant to indicate any relevant effects of his or her disability — and to involve him or her in suggesting adjustments that could be made should he or she be employed. Any questions the answers to which might be used to discriminate against a disabled person are unlawful.

Extended Selection Techniques

8.566 Structured interviews conducted by trained interviewers are far more reliable than unstructured ones conducted by untrained interviewers. Consideration should nevertheless be given to the use of additional selection tools.

Psychometric Instruments

8.567 The main types of psychometric instrument are as follows.

- Aptitude tests — which assess an individual's potential for a certain kind of job. These tend to be used at junior levels.
- Ability tests — which assess an individual's current level of ability. The output from such tests can be compared with the requirements of the job. Any shortfall between required and current levels of ability means that further training is required.
- Personality inventories, profiles or questionnaires, the results of which can be compared with the personal qualities required for a job in order to assess suitability and training needs.

8.568 However, it is important to ensure that instruments:
- assess factors that are relevant to the vacancy in question
- are not potentially discriminatory
- are administered by properly trained personnel.

Assessment Centres

8.569 Assessment centres are places in which assessors observe applicants while the applicants complete tests such as in-tray exercises, presentations, group exercises, interviews, ability tests and personality questionnaires. The assessors evaluate the candidates' performance against various criteria. Assessment centres use exercises that simulate the work environment and the testing tends to be thorough: consequently, the results of such testing normally accurately reflect an applicant's future performance.

8.570 However assessment centres are expensive and time consuming. Their use is normally restricted to selection for senior level positions and for graduate intake into management training programmes.

Assessment Centre Techniques

8.571 Where the use of a full assessment centre is not deemed appropriate, individual assessment centre techniques may be added to an interview.

Appointment Processes — Making the Offer

8.572 It is important to minimise the risks of the offer being turned down. Factors to consider include:
- the remuneration package
- timing — candidates should not be kept waiting for the results of the selection process any longer than necessary
- who should make the offer — the HR department, line manager or recruitment agency
- how to make the offer.

8.573 Making an initial offer by telephone has advantages because it:
- is more personal
- provides an opportunity to discuss problems and doubts
- allows the employer to go back to second choice candidates if the offer is rejected by the first choice candidate.

8.574 Offers should be made subject to:
- checking qualifications
- satisfactory references
- a medical examination or questionnaire.

Selection Process

8.575 In the case of particularly important or sensitive appointments, employers may wish to use a security vetting firm.

Handling Rejections

8.576 It is important to advise applicants who have been unsuccessful as promptly and courteously as possible. Particular care should be taken with internal applicants.

Keeping Records

8.577 The Data Protection Act does not specify retention periods for recruitment records, but states that they should not be kept for longer than is necessary. Best practice includes:

- destroying information obtained by a vetting exercise within six months
- considering carefully what information from the application form is to be transferred to the worker's employment record
- deleting information irrelevant to ongoing employment
- once verified, deleting information collected during the recruitment process about criminal convictions (unless relevant to ongoing employment)
- advising unsuccessful applicants if it is intended to keep their names on file for future vacancies
- giving unsuccessful applicants the opportunity to have their details deleted.

8.578 Employers should keep in mind the necessity to retain all records from a recruitment process that might be relevant to defending a claim from an unsuccessful applicant for unlawful discrimination. Although such a claim should be brought within three months, tribunals have discretion to extend this time limit.

Training

8.579 All members of staff who will be involved in the selection process should first be trained in screening and interviewing techniques. Any such course should deal with discrimination issues, although most organisations will also have separate courses that deal specifically with diversity and equal opportunities. Selection training should also cover the best ways to ask questions and active listening skills.

List of Relevant Legislation

8.580

- Employment Equality (Religion or Belief) Regulations 2003
- Employment Equality (Sexual Orientation) Regulations 2003
- Sex Discrimination (Gender Reassignment) Regulations 1999
- Data Protection Act 1998
- Disability Discrimination Act 1995
- Race Relations Act 1976
- Sex Discrimination Act 1975

Succession Planning

> This topic covers the following.
> - The Micro Level: Succession Planning for Key Individuals
> - The Macro Level: Human Resource Planning
> - Identifying Development Potential

8.581 Succession planning may be used in respect of particular positions (eg identifying and grooming a successor to a chief executive) or on an organisation-wide basis. The latter is commonly referred to as Human Resource Planning (HRP).

8.582 In order to be effective, succession planning should be linked to corporate planning, risk management and employee development. Care must be taken to avoid breaches discriminating at all stages of the succession planning process.

Employers' Duties

8.583 Employers have a duty to ensure that:
- no applicant is treated less favourably in the recruitment and selection process on the grounds of sex, race, disability, age, sexual orientation, gender reassignment, religion or belief, or trade union membership or non-membership
- consideration is given to any provision, criterion or practice in the person specification or terms of a job which might be indirectly discriminatory
- all vacancies are communicated in an effective way to all potential applicants
- they are aware of the liability of employers for acts of discrimination even where these are committed by other members of staff
- staff are aware that an employer's defence is to show that where discrimination occurred it took all such steps as were reasonably practicable to prevent the discrimination
- the terms and conditions of employment are consistent with statutory requirements and minimum standards
- data relating to recruitment and selection is processed in accordance with data protection legislation
- they monitor the recruitment and selection process to ensure that there is no discriminatory treatment.

Employees' Duties

8.584 Employees have a duty to:
- be honest in the personal information disclosed in the recruitment and selection process
- facilitate appropriate checks on health and criminal records
- provide the names of referees
- abide by any agreement they reach on accepting employment.

In Practice

The Micro Level: Succession Planning for Key Individuals

Risk Assessment

8.585 Some organisations are heavily dependent on a few key individuals. It makes sense to identify such key individuals and to take steps to minimise the risk posed by their loss. Where this loss can be predicted, for instance if the individual is due to retire or is earmarked for promotion, it will make sense to identify and groom a successor.

8.586 Some losses cannot be predicted. Succession planning should, consequently, be considered as part of broader contingency planning. This may involve everything from providing emergency cover to formal knowledge-management systems and the inclusion of restrictive covenants in contracts of employment.

The Scope of Succession Planning

8.587 Succession planning need not be confined to key appointments. It could be applied to:
- all managerial positions
- all situations where a need for succession can be predicted.

8.588 The major consideration in succession planning is whether to have an overlap period, ie to have the replacement on board by the time the incumbent leaves, or cover the gap while a successor is recruited.

The Question of Timing

8.589 In deciding when to initiate the process of selection planning, the lead time can be calculated by adding together:
- the time needed to identify a successor and for him or her to be released from his or her existing job
- the time it is likely to take for the successor to learn to do the job.

8.590 Employers will generally wish to keep this latter period to the minimum in view of:
- the duplication of costs
- the necessity of keeping the successor motivated.

Internal or External Recruitment?

8.591 The question of timing is easier to handle when an existing employee is chosen to succeed to a specified role, eg when a member of a department takes over from the manager.

8.592 Internal promotions are also more likely when the post becoming vacant requires knowledge of, and experience in, the organisation. Opportunities for internal progression are an important element in an organisation's ability to retain staff. Many employees see a lack of opportunities for career development as a reason for leaving.

Succession Planning

8.593 There are good reasons for external recruitment. It extends the "talent pool" – bringing new blood into an organisation – and can also provide a more diverse workforce.

Equal Opportunities

8.594 Two key questions affecting succession planning are:
- whether considering only internal candidates will mean a less diverse workforce
- whether all internal candidates are given a fair chance.

8.595 In those cases where it can be clearly demonstrated that the post calls for considerable knowledge of or experience in the organisation there should not be a problem.

8.596 In other cases, the question of equal opportunities hinges on the composition of the existing workforce. If the workforce is genuinely diverse and reflects the composition of the community within the employer's catchment area, then internal recruitment need not mean a less diverse workforce. It is helpful to look at that section of the workforce relevant to the job in question, rather than just its overall composition: women, ethnic minorities and disabled employees are often under-represented at senior levels even when they are adequately represented at junior ones.

8.597 It is vital that vacancies are communicated in an effective way to all potential applicants, eg employers should ensure that all staff have access to e-mail if that is the way jobs are publicised. Employers often miss out on candidates and leave employees disgruntled at the lack of opportunities because they fail to publicise vacancies throughout the organisation.

8.598 Unlike external advertising, publicising jobs internally costs very little and need not delay the selection process.

The Macro Level: Human Resource Planning

8.599 There is a strong argument for looking at succession planning on an organisation-wide basis. This is called Human Resource Planning.

8.600 There is no real alternative to HRP. Either HR managers attempt to predict and control the future or they risk falling behind competitors in the supply of human resources. A human resources plan uses the organisation's overall corporate plan to predict its future human resources needs over a period of years. These predictions will normally be broken down over operating locations, levels of staff, types of skills required, etc.

8.601 Once the organisation's requirements have been defined, they can be compared with:
- the resources that are actually available
- resources forecasted on a year-by-year basis, given losses through staff leaving or retiring.

8.602 The plan pinpoints those periods when the workforce will lack adequate personnel. The employer can then set about managing these periods by:
- external recruitment
- the use of training and other forms of development to increase the skill sets of existing members of staff
- encouraging existing members of staff to work beyond normal retirement age
- improvements in operating methods, equipment and systems
- outsourcing.

8.603 Where HRP shows a surplus rather than a shortage of resources it may be possible to re-deploy staff. Planning ahead should enable compulsory job losses to be minimised, eg by natural wastage.

Implementing HRP

8.604 The first step in any HRP exercise is to review corporate objectives. Most organisations have a corporate plan expressed in purely financial terms, with little or no attention to the human resources implications.

8.605 The first step in any workforce planning exercise is to review corporate objectives.

8.606 The extent of the plan's detail depends on the size and sophistication of the organisation. A simple plan may state the number of staff required for each location, level and type of work. A more detailed analysis might define the qualifications, skills and experience required for each role. The involvement of managers and different departments and units in the plan is more important than the details and all plans should take into consideration workforce and service modernisation. The plan needs to be seen as a relevant assessment of future staffing needs, not as an abstract exercise conducted by the HR department.

Reviewing Corporate Objectives

8.607 Organisations need to obtain feedback from the people who are in direct contact with customers in order to formulate a corporate plan that works. An HRP approach recognises the importance of seeking the input of front-line staff in the plan's definition – as well as the importance of communicating the plan to line managers.

8.608 The extent of the plan's detail depends on the size and sophistication of the organisation. A simple plan may state the number of staff required for each location, level and type of work. A more detailed analysis might define the qualifications, skills and experience required for each role. The involvement of managers in the plan is more important than the details. The plan needs to be seen as a relevant assessment of future staffing needs, not as an abstract exercise conducted by the HR department.

Analysing the Current Situation

8.609 The next stage of the exercise is the analysis of the current situation. This includes a detailed breakdown of existing human resources and an analysis of future trends. For example:
- a high proportion of older employees alerts an employer to the danger of losing a significant number of staff through retirement
- a glut of younger people alerts an employer to potential problems of retention where there are not enough opportunities for promotion.

8.610 Staff turnover trends and absence statistics should be studied, as these often function as barometers of motivation.

8.611 External factors should also be considered, including:
- the supply-and-demand situation in the labour market
- how the economy is expected to behave in the near future
- the impact of any anticipated expansion or contraction by other employers in the same sector or geographical area
- the anticipated effect of UK government or EU policies, eg on flexible working, changes in the education system, the availability of skilled staff from overseas

- growing trends in job sharing, part-time working, home working, the use of freelance workers, outsourcing, staff mobility and changes to the work-life balance.

8.612 The organisation also needs to look at:
- the extent to which it may be able to use technology to take over tasks performed by employees
- other ways in which it can alter working methods to achieve greater productivity.

8.613 When the need for the development of existing staff has been identified, supervisors and line managers need to:
- identify the development potential of each member of staff
- select the most appropriate means of achieving development.

8.614 Managers may prefer to adopt a broader, simpler approach by:
- defining the broad categories of staff likely to be required in the future
- comparing them with what is currently available.

8.615 Within an individual department, shorter-term analyses of head-count and skills requirements can also be carried out.

Identifying Development Potential

8.616 There is a close link between succession planning and employee development. Employee potential for further development can be identified in several ways.

Appraisals

8.617 In appraisals managers should discuss career-development aspirations with members of staff. Appraisals are not the best way to do this because:
- they usually only take place once a year
- they can be badly conducted
- managers may not be aware of the range of opportunities available
- managers may value holding on to their staff above encouraging employee promotion
- they tend to be subjective in their assessments.

Psychometric Instruments

8.618 Psychometric instruments provide a more objective approach.
- Aptitude tests assess an individual's potential for a certain kind of job. They tend to be used at more junior levels, eg tests of manual dexterity.
- Ability tests assess an individual's current level of ability. Test results are compared with the requirements of a given job. Any shortfall between required and current levels of ability defines the further training or development that is required.
- Personality inventories, profiles or questionnaires assess an individual's suitability and/or training and development needs. After completion they are compared with the personal qualities required by a given job.

Development Centres

8.619 The use of development centres is usually confined to managers and professional staff, plus graduates with management potential. Development centres:
- use a variety of techniques such as in-tray exercises, presentations, group exercises, interviews, ability tests and personality questionnaires

- are environments in which several candidates or participants are observed by a team of assessors who evaluate performance against various criteria or competences
- use the perceptions of participants, peer and self-assessment to provide in-depth feedback.

8.620 In development centres, there should be a co-operative and collaborative relationship both between the participants themselves and between participants and assessors. There will also be much feedback, since the aim is to help participants to develop the skills they need to progress within the organisation.

8.621 In practice, development centres tend to identify high-fliers rather than the development potential of all participants.

Training

8.622 Managers and other employees who are grooming their successors may need to be trained in coaching and delegation.

8.623 The needs of their understudies will vary greatly. A training needs analysis should be conducted to identify:
- the experience, knowledge and skills required to perform the job in question
- the understudy's current level of such experience, knowledge and skills
- the gaps that exist between the two
- the best ways of filling these gaps.

8.624 The training needs analysis will suggest ways forward, usually a combination of:
- coaching
- formal training
- work experience, eg progressive assignment of projects and delegation of responsibilities by the incumbent.

8.625 Where organisation-wide HRP and employee development are being practised, training and development needs will be identified by techniques such as appraisals, psychometric instruments, development centres and training needs analyses.

8.626 All those involved in the selection process will need to be trained in all aspects of this, including equal opportunities issues.

8.627 All those involved in identifying development potential will need training in their specific field, eg:
- appraisals
- the administration of psychometric instruments
- designing development centres
- acting as assessors at development centres.

List of Relevant Legislation

8.628
- Employment Equality (Religion or Belief) Regulations 2003
- Employment Equality (Sexual Orientation) Regulations 2003

- Sex Discrimination (Gender Reassignment) Regulations 1999
- Disability Discrimination Act 1995
- Sex Discrimination Act 1975
- Race Relations Act 1976

Chapter 9
Termination of Employment

Employment Tribunal Proceedings and Remedies

> This topic covers the following.
> - Statutory Employment Rights
> - Time Limits on Bringing Cases to Employment Tribunals
> - Starting Proceedings
> - The Employer's Response if a Claim is Made Against Them
> - Bringing a Counterclaim
> - Failure to File a Response Form
> - Case Management
> - Disclosure of Evidence
> - Conciliation
> - Withdrawal of Proceedings
> - Interlocutory and Final Hearings
> - Procedure at Hearings
> - Standard Order of Procedure
> - Remedies
> - Costs
> - Right of Appeal
> - Protection From Victimisation

9.1 Most employment disputes concerning the legal rights of employees can be dealt with quickly and relatively cheaply through employment tribunal proceedings. Tribunals are less formal than courts. Legal representation is not required, although the legal complexity of most employment matters means that generally someone involved in a tribunal case would have professional legal assistance.

Employers' Duties

9.2 Employers should ensure the following.
- Employers should recognise that, quite apart from contractual rights arising out of the contract of employment and common law rights arising out of the relationship between employer and employee, employment legislation provides employees with a wide range of statutory rights.
- If an employer wishes to contest employment tribunal proceedings, he or she will need to file a response form within the time limit laid down.
- Parties to tribunal proceedings are under a duty to assist the tribunal in achieving a resolution of the dispute. This means disclosing all relevant evidence and helping with management of the case.
- Employers will be bound by any remedies ordered by an employment tribunal, eg compensation, subject to any right of appeal.
- The right of appeal is limited to questions of law.

Employees' Duties

9.3 Employees should be aware of the following.

- Any individual bringing a case to an employment tribunal should ensure that it is brought within the time limits.
- From 1 October 2005 the claimant must bring their claim on a prescribed claim form, known as an ET1.
- Employment tribunals have a limited power to consider applications for an extension of time for complaints.
- An employee taking a case to an employment tribunal should ensure that the case is ready for presentation at any time.
- In certain cases a party may have costs awarded against him or her.

In Practice

Statutory Employment Rights

9.4 The main statutes providing for complaints to be made to the employment tribunal are as follows.
- Employment Equality (Age) Regulations 2006.
- Transfer of Undertakings (Protection of Employment) Regulations 2006 (TUPE) — this covers complaints about the failure of an employer to inform or consult with employees when a business changes ownership.
- Employment Equality (Religion or Belief) Regulations 2003.
- Employment Equality (Sexual Orientation) Regulations 2003.
- Fixed-term Employees (Prevention of Less Favourable Treatment) Regulations 2002.
- Flexible Working (Procedural Requirements) Regulations 2002.
- Part-time Workers (Prevention of Less Favourable Treatment) Regulations 2000.
- Working Time Regulations 1998 — eg complaints relating to paid annual leave.
- Employment Relations Act 1999 — this deals with the right to be accompanied at a disciplinary or grievance hearing.
- National Minimum Wage Act 1998.
- Employment Rights Act 1996 — this covers complaints as to statements of terms of employment, itemised pay statements, unauthorised deductions from wages, time off work, maternity, adoption paternity and parental leave rights, dismissals, redundancy payments, rights on the insolvency of an employer and victimisation on various grounds.
- Disability Discrimination Act 1995.
- Trade Union and Labour Relations (Consolidation) Act 1992 — this deals with complaints regarding trade union matters in employment (ie the right to time off for trade union duties, victimisation on grounds of trade union membership) and also claims for protective awards arising out of an employer's failure to consult about redundancies.
- Race Relations Act 1976.
- Sex Discrimination Act 1975.
- Equal Pay Act 1970.

Breach of Contract Claims

9.5 As a result of the Employment Tribunals Extension of the Jurisdiction

(England & Wales) Order 1994, tribunals have the jurisdiction to deal with some breach of contract claims, including claims for wrongful dismissal.

Using EC Law in the Tribunals

9.6 Employment tribunals do have a duty to apply European Community law. However, claims relating to EC law must be brought under the relevant provision of UK domestic legislation: claims relying directly on EC legislation cannot be brought.

Time Limits on Bringing Cases to Employment Tribunals

9.7 There are time limits within which complaints must be brought to the employment tribunal. The most common time limit is three months.

9.8 The relevant statutory provision under which a complaint is brought will specify the time limit and the date from which the time limit is to be calculated. The actual date of the act about which a complaint is being made will not be included in the calculation.

9.9 In *Virdi v Commissioner of Police of the Metropolis* [2007] IRLR 24 (a claim for race discrimination), the EAT concluded that, where a claim concerns an alleged discriminatory decision made by the employer, the time limit in respect of bringing the claim runs from the date the decision was made, and not from the date on which the decision was communicated to the employee.

9.10 The three-month time limit is, however, automatically extended to six months in certain circumstances. The circumstances are where the employee has raised a grievance under the statutory grievance procedure specified in the Employment Act 2002, or where the employee has been dismissed and has reasonable grounds to believe that, at the expiry of the usual three-month time limit, the employer was still following through an internal appeal procedure.

9.11 Longer time limits include a six-month limit within which claims concerning redundancy payments and equal pay must be made. Shorter time limits mostly relate to claims for interim relief or to appeals against enforcement and/or non-discrimination notices.

Continuing Acts

9.12 If the act about which a complaint is made to a tribunal took/takes place over an extended period of time (eg a series of instances of harassment), the employee may regard the series of acts as a single course of conduct and can bring a complaint to tribunal within three or six months of the latest in the series of acts.

9.13 However, this provision should not be relied on to delay bringing complaints about earlier acts by the same employer, even if there is a potential connection between the various acts.

Deliberate Omissions

9.14 In discrimination cases, a deliberate omission by an employer will count as an "act".

Notices of Dismissal

9.15 A complaint of unfair dismissal can be made before the contract of employment is actually terminated if notice of dismissal (or resignation) has been given.

Employment Tribunal Proceedings and Remedies

If the Time Limit Expires on a Non-Working Day

9.16 If the last day for a complaint to be received by the employment tribunal is a non-working day and the tribunal concerned has no external letter box, then the time limit will be treated as expiring on the working day immediately before that day. This was the decision of the EAT in *Coldridge v HM Prison Service* EAT (2005) (0728-9/04) in which the principle was upheld that a claimant may reasonably expect a first class letter to arrive two days after the date of posting (excluding Sundays and public holidays). Furthermore, in *Initial Electronic Security Systems Ltd v Avdic* EAT (2005) (0281/05), where a claim is presented electronically the claimant may reasonably expect it to arrive within 30–60 minutes of its transmission.

Clearly the safest course, however, for any claimant would be to make sure that his or her claim is presented well before the last working day.

Limited Extension to Time Limits

9.17 Tribunals have only limited power to admit complaints presented outside the prescribed time limits, and that power is only what is laid down in the relevant statute.

9.18 The two limited possibilities normally open to claimants are as follows.
- It was not "reasonably practicable" for the complaint to be brought within the time limit. This can be used in unfair dismissal cases, but in practice it is very hard to persuade a tribunal to extend the time limit on this basis.
- It is "just and equitable" for the tribunal to extend the time limit. This is the test used in cases of discrimination. This allows the tribunal to take account of the length of the delay, the reason for it, the steps the claimant has taken since the complaint arose and the effect the delay will have on the proceedings. A claimant must have acted with appropriate promptness and diligence.

Starting Proceedings

9.19 From 1 October 2005 a claimant must commence employment tribunal proceedings using a prescribed form (ET1). The ET1 is available from the claimant's local employment tribunal. Alternatively, a claim can be made online using the Employment Tribunals website.

The Employer's Response if a Claim is Made Against Them

9.20 The employer against whom the complaint is made — the respondent — who is subject to a claim should reply within 28 days of the date from which he or she was sent the claim. This is the date when the claim form is stamped by the tribunal.

9.21 The reply is called a Response Form (ET3) and can be provided by the tribunal. The ET3 can be filed online.

9.22 The ET3 should be in writing and should:
- confirm the name and address of the respondent
- state whether or not the claim is contested and, if contesting, on what grounds.

9.23 The respondent can apply within the 28-day period for an extension of time. The tribunal will only grant an extension where it is "just and equitable" to do so.

Bringing a Counterclaim

9.24 The respondent may also wish to make a claim against the claimant. This is

known as a "counterclaim". A counterclaim can only be made in the employment tribunal where the claimant has made a breach of contract claim within three months of termination of employment. Such a counterclaim must be presented to the tribunal in writing and contain:
- the respondent's name and address
- the claimant's name and address
- details of the counterclaim.

Failure to File a Response Form

9.25 If a respondent does not file a Response Form (ET3), he or she can play no part in the subsequent proceedings. The tribunal also has the power to enter a default judgment where no response has been lodged or accepted within the time limit. The respondent may make an application for review within 14 days of the default judgment being sent out by the tribunal. This time limit may be extended by the tribunal if it is considered just and equitable to do so.

Case Management

9.26 Tribunals have a broad range of powers to manage their own cases. Once in receipt of the claim and the response, the tribunal will normally respond with directions given in writing to the parties.

9.27 If either party does not comply with a direction given by the tribunal they may be subject to a costs order. The tribunal may even strike out the whole or part of the claim or prevent the respondent from responding to the claim altogether, depending on which party did not comply with the direction.

Disclosure of Evidence

9.28 The most important directions that a tribunal will normally make to the parties will concern the disclosure of evidence.

9.29 The tribunal has the power to make requirements relating to the:
- production of documents
- provision and exchange of witness statements
- provision of further particulars
- provision of written answers to questions.

9.30 A party to proceedings should aim to ensure that the following four steps are taken, either by agreement with the other parties or through application to the tribunal.
- Where necessary, further particulars should be sought to clarify the other party's case so that it is possible to prepare for any subsequent hearing.
- All documents to be used in the hearing should be exchanged in advance, preferably tidily presented in a bundle with a clear and properly referenced contents list.
- Any witnesses to be used in the case should be identified and witness statements exchanged with the other party. It should be made certain that the witnesses will be available on the day that the hearing is listed to take place.
- Written witness statements should be presented prior to the hearing if so requested by the tribunal. Even if the tribunal makes no such requirement, written statements can bolster a case because they are clearer and easier to present coherently than oral statements.

9.31 The four steps to follow in the disclosure of evidence do not apply to proceedings which include a claim made for discrimination, equal pay or under the Public Interest Disclosure Act (PIDA) provisions in the Employment Rights Act 1996.

Conciliation

9.32 There is in some cases a fixed conciliation period to allow time for the parties to reach an Acas conciliated settlement. Hearings may not be held during the period except for case management discussions and pre-hearing reviews. Straightforward claims, such as unauthorised deduction from wages, have a conciliation period of seven weeks. Other claims, such as unfair dismissal, have a period of 13 weeks. For claims of discrimination, there is no limit to the conciliation period.

Withdrawal of Proceedings

9.33 A claimant can withdraw all or part of their claim either orally at a hearing or in writing beforehand. To do so they must notify the tribunal. Withdrawal does not affect proceedings as to costs, preparation time or wasted costs.

9.34 Where the claim has been withdrawn the respondent should apply to have the claim dismissed. The respondent must do so within 28 days of the notice of the withdrawal being sent to them (or apply for an extension of time which will be granted if it is just and equitable). If the respondent does not apply to have the claim dismissed, it would be possible for the claimant to change his or her mind and make a fresh claim to the tribunal on the same subject matter (provided the time limit for bringing the claim had not expired).

Interlocutory and Final Hearings

Case Management Discussion

9.35 A case management discussion deals with the procedure and management of the case. This is held in private and conducted by the chairperson. It can also be conducted by electronic communication, most commonly a conference telephone call.

Pre-Hearing Review

9.36 A party can request, or the tribunal can order, a pre-hearing review. This will generally be a public hearing. The hearing is designed to hear any interim or preliminary matters relating to proceedings, any case management decisions and oral and written evidence.

9.37 Common examples of issues that might be dealt with at a pre-hearing review include whether or not:
- an extension of a time limit should be granted where the employee's complaint was logged late
- the claimant was an employee, eg in cases of unfair dismissal where employee status is a necessary prerequisite in order for the claim to be brought
- an employee has the necessary length and continuity of service to be entitled to bring a complaint.

9.38 Another purpose of a pre-hearing review is to consider an application for a deposit by either party. This is a procedure for weeding out hopeless cases, and is intended to save time and expense in such circumstances. If the tribunal decides that a case has no reasonable prospect of success, it can order the party concerned to pay a deposit of up to £500 to continue with the proceedings.

Hearings

9.39 Unless the tribunal has indicated otherwise, a case will normally be listed on the basis that all of the issues raised in the claim form will be dealt with at that single hearing. Simple cases will usually be listed for a full hearing without any earlier hearing taking place.

9.40 Where a complaint is upheld, the parties will need to be in a position to settle the matter by agreeing a remedy. However, in the vast majority of cases the tribunal will decide the issue of liability at a full hearing and then, where necessary, list a separate remedy hearing.

9.41 Once the parties know the tribunal's decision on liability, it is often the case that terms of settlement can be easily agreed, so that the subsequent remedy hearing becomes unnecessary.

Procedure at Hearings

9.42 An employment tribunal has wide discretion to conduct hearings in a way that it considers most appropriate to clarify the issues and deal justly with the case.

9.43 Generally the tribunal will sit as a panel of three members, including a chair governing the proceedings.

9.44 A party will usually be entitled to:
- give evidence
- call witnesses
- question any witnesses called by the other side
- address the tribunal.

9.45 A party should always be prepared to present his or her case at the outset of a hearing.

9.46 Normally the claimant will present first, followed by the respondent. However in unfair dismissal cases, the tribunal will generally first hear from the individual responsible for the decision to dismiss.

Standard Order of Procedure

9.47 Subject to the above qualification regarding the flexibility of tribunal hearings, the usual procedure will be as follows.
- Opening discussion.
- Evidence.
- Cross examination of witnesses.
- Re-examination of witnesses.
- Questions by members of the tribunal.
- Submissions.
- Judgment.

Opening Discussion

9.48 The tribunal chair will normally lead a general discussion of the issues involved. Both parties may be expected to outline their cases and explain the practicalities of any evidence they intend to call. Prior key documents provided to the tribunal should prevent any necessity for long, formal opening speeches.

Employment Tribunal Proceedings and Remedies

Evidence

9.49 Traditionally, calling evidence involves putting questions to witnesses and then asking the witness concerned to refer the tribunal to the relevant documents.

9.50 Where written witness statements are being used, it is common for tribunals to expect the history of the case to be fully described in the witness statement. The description should normally be in chronological order as far as is possible, with references to the appropriate page numbers in the document bundle.

9.51 Supplemental questions should then be kept to a minimum, and are often actively discouraged by the tribunal.

9.52 In Scotland, it is not usual for witness statements to be used and instead witnesses are asked questions by their representative in order to draw out the relevant evidence.

Cross-examination of Witnesses

9.53 After each witness has given his or her primary evidence, the other party has the opportunity to ask questions in cross-examination. This is when witnesses who have presented conflicting versions of events can be tackled.

Re-examination of Witnesses

9.54 A witness who has been cross-examined by the other side can then be asked further questions by his or her own side. Technically these questions should relate only to issues arising out of the cross-examination.

Questions by Members of the Tribunal

9.55 The tribunal itself may ask a witness questions after he or she has given evidence, or before re-examination takes place. It is, however, fairly common for the chair of a tribunal to interrupt witness examination with questions of his or her own.

Submissions

9.56 This is when each party has an opportunity to address the tribunal again on the issues, evidence and law. Usually the party whose witnesses gave evidence first will make submissions last.

Judgment

9.57 If the tribunal is sitting as a panel of three members, they will usually adjourn after all the proceedings are complete to deliberate on their decision. The tribunal may give its decision at the end of the hearing or, if the case is complicated or there is little time left in the day, may reserve the decision. However the tribunal must give either oral or written reasons for any judgment. If a judgment is given verbally at the tribunal, written reasons will not be produced unless requested.

Remedies

9.58 The relevant statute under which a case is brought will normally provide for possible remedies. The tribunal can only order remedies that are designated by the relevant statute.

Compensation

9.59 This is the most common remedy provided to someone whose statutory employment rights have been infringed. If the individual who has won the case sustained a loss as a result of the infringement of his or her rights, the tribunal will simply calculate the loss attributable to the relevant infringement.

9.60 The Act under which the case is brought will often specify a formula to be used in calculating an award.

Reinstatement and Re-engagement

9.61 In unfair dismissal cases, the employment tribunal has power under the Employment Rights Act 1996 to order that the employer reinstate the claimant in his or her former job, or re-engage the claimant in comparable or other suitable employment. The tribunal will consider whether it is practicable and just to make such an order.

9.62 In such cases, the tribunal is also likely to specify the terms on which re-engagement should take place, and to order compensation for the period between dismissal and re-engagement. If the employer does not comply with the order, the tribunal will make an additional award of compensation.

Declaration

9.63 A tribunal will often decide on factors that will affect the future relationship between the claimant and respondent. For example, the contract terms between an employee and employer may be clarified by a case. A declaration could have significant impact on the future action of the parties concerned.

Recommendation

9.64 In discrimination cases, tribunals have the power to make a recommendation that the employer should take action to remove a source of discrimination. If the employer fails to comply with a recommendation, further orders for compensation can be made.

Costs

9.65 In most tribunal cases, it is normal for both parties to pay their own costs. Although costs will often be incurred for legal advice or representation, no fee is charged for making a claim to an employment tribunal or for the hearing itself.

9.66 The tribunal does, however, have the power to make a standard costs order against either party for any costs incurred by the other party in certain defined circumstances. The tribunal also has the power to order a party to make payment to the Secretary of State for any witness, expert, assessor expenses or fees paid out in association with the proceedings.

9.67 A costs order may be made where:
- there is an unreasonable postponement or adjournment of the hearing or pre-hearing review
- the party has, in bringing or conducting the proceedings, acted vexatiously, abusively, disruptively or otherwise unreasonably
- the bringing or conducting of the proceedings by a party has been misconceived
- the party has not complied with an order or practice direction.

9.68 Where a party continues with a case after being ordered to pay a deposit at a pre-hearing review and subsequently loses the case, there may similarly be strong grounds for making an order for costs.

9.69 If any of the above circumstances apply, the tribunal may:
- order the offending party to pay the costs of the other party, where the latter has had legal representation, or
- make a "wasted costs award" directly against the representative, or
- where a party has been unrepresented, make a "preparation time order" in respect of the time the party spent preparing for the hearing.

9.70 A tribunal may make a wasted costs award directly against a paid representative to cover the whole or part of the wasted costs of either party in circumstances where:
- there has been an improper, unreasonable or negligent act or omission on the part of the representative, or
- in the light of such an act or omission, the tribunal considers it unreasonable for a party to have to pay the costs in question.

9.71 A "wasted costs award" is, however, only permissible where the representative in question is one who has been paid for his or her services.

9.72 A preparation time order may be made in favour of a party who has not been legally represented at a hearing. "Preparation time" is defined as time spent by the party or his or her employees carrying out preparatory work that is directly relating to the proceedings and/or time spent by the party's advisers relating to the conduct of the proceedings. It does not, however, include the time spent at the hearing itself. An hourly rate of £25 per hour is applied.

9.73 A tribunal may not make both a preparation time order and a costs order in favour of the same party in the same proceedings.

9.74 The tribunal may take into consideration a party's ability to pay when considering whether it should make a costs order and how much it should be for.

9.75 In all cases, the maximum amount of costs that can be awarded by a tribunal is £10,000.

Right of Appeal

9.76 An appeal against the decision of an employment tribunal can only be taken to the employment appeal tribunal on a point of law. An appellant must show that the tribunal made an error of law, such that:
- the tribunal misdirected itself in law, or misunderstood or misapplied the law
- there was no evidence to support a particular conclusion or finding of facts
- the tribunal's decision was perverse in the sense of being one that no reasonable tribunal, directing itself properly on the law, could have reached, or was obviously wrong.

9.77 The time limit for appealing is 42 days from the date that extended reasons were sent to the parties. Although the employment appeal tribunal has the power to extend the time for appealing, the time limit is very strictly applied and rarely extended.

Protection from Victimisation

9.78 An employee who takes a case to an employment tribunal is in some cases, eg claims for discrimination, protected by statute from victimisation that results from bringing the case. This protection does not, however, extend to ex-employees following a complaint of unfair dismissal.

Training

9.79 Managers should be made aware of the procedure used by tribunals in hearing complaints, employees' rights, and the remedies available to employees who win a case at the tribunal.

9.80 Hearings at employment tribunals are public hearings that can be attended by members of the public without any prior arrangement. Simply providing for managers to sit at the back of a tribunal hearing and observe first hand the way in which contested tribunal proceedings are dealt with would amount to a worthwhile training exercise.

List of Relevant Legislation

9.81
- Employment Equality (Age) Regulations 2006
- Employment Tribunals (Constitution and Rules of Procedure) (Amendment) Regulations 2005
- Employment Tribunals (Constitution and Rules of Procedure) (Amendment) (No. 2) Regulations 2005
- Employment Act 2002 (Dispute Resolution) Regulations 2004
- Employment Tribunals (Constitution and Rules of Procedure) Regulations 2004
- Employment Equality (Religion or Belief) Regulations 2003
- Employment Equality (Sexual Orientation) Regulations 2003
- Fixed-Term Employees (Prevention of Less Favourable Treatment) Regulations 2002
- Flexible Working (Procedural Requirements) Regulations 2002
- Part-Time Workers (Prevention of Less Favourable Treatment) Regulations 2000
- Working Time Regulations 1998
- Transfer of Undertakings (Protection of Employment) Regulations 1981
- Employment Act 2002
- Employment Relations Act 1999
- National Minimum Wage Act 1998
- Employment Rights Act 1996
- Employment Tribunals Act 1996
- Disability Discrimination Act 1995
- Trade Union & Labour Relations (Consolidation) Act 1992
- Race Relations Act 1976
- Sex Discrimination Act 1975
- Equal Pay Act 1970
- Employment Appeal Tribunal (Amendment) Rules 2005

List of Relevant Cases

9.82
- *Virdi v Commissioner of Police of the Metropolis* [2007] IRLR 24

- *Commotion Ltd v Rutty* (2005) UKEAT/0418/05 — tribunal practice and procedure — statutory grievance procedures; flexible working requests
- *Thorpe and Soleil Investments Ltd v Poat and Lake* (2005) UKEAT/0503/05 — tribunal practice and procedure — statutory grievance procedures
- *Jones v DAS Legal Expenses Insurance Ltd* [2004] IRLR 218, CA
- *Kovacs v Queen Mary and Westfield College* [2002] IRLR 414, CA

Further Information

Publications
- URN 03/595 Employment Tribunals Service booklet *How to Apply to an Employment Tribunal England and Wales*, available from Employment Tribunal offices and from the ETS enquiry line

Organisations
- **Advisory Conciliation and Arbitration Service (Acas)**
  Web: *www.acas.org.uk*
  Acas aims to improve organisations and working life through better employment relations. It provides up-to-date information, advice, high-quality training, and works with employers and employees to solve problems and improve performance.
- **Department for Business, Enterprise and Regulatory Reform (BERR)**
  Web: *www.berr.gov.uk*
  The Department for Business, Enterprise and Regulatory Reform brings together functions from the former Department of Trade and Industry (DTI), including responsibilities for productivity, business relations, energy, competition and consumers. It also drives regulatory reform.
- **Employment Appeal Tribunal (EAT)**
  Web: *www.employmentappeals.gov.uk*
  The EAT was created by the Employment Protection Act 1975. It is a Superior Court of Record dealing with appeals from the decisions of the Employment Tribunals, the Certification Officer and the Central Arbitration Committee.
- **Employment Tribunals**
  Web: *www.employmenttribunals.gov.uk*
  Contains useful information about employment tribunals, which resolve disputes between employers and employees over employment rights.

Insolvency

> This topic covers the following.
> - Bankruptcy
> - Administrative Receivership
> - Administration
> - Liquidation
> - Termination of Employment
> - Preferential Status of Debts Owed to Employees
> - Principle of Equal Distribution
> - Guaranteed Redundancy Payments
> - Guaranteed Payments from the National Insurance Fund
> - Pensions Contributions
> - Other Statutory Payments

9.83 The insolvency of an employer is likely to have significant ramifications for the contractual relationship between an employer and employee. Three main issues arise.
- The insolvency may bring about the termination of the contract of employment through the dismissal of the employee.
- If the employee is dismissed he or she may be able to recover any unpaid sums due under the contract of employment or statutory employment rights.
- Where the contract of employment continues, liabilities arising out of the employment relationship will be affected by any alteration to the legal status and/or identity of the employer.

Employers' Duties

9.84 The employment responsibilities of insolvent employers will depend upon the specific type of formal insolvency regime under which the insolvency of the employer is regulated, ie:
- bankruptcy
- administrative receivership
- administration
- liquidation.

9.85 The liabilities of an insolvent employer in respect of the termination of employment of employees will vary according to the circumstances of the dismissal, ie:
- prior to insolvency of employer
- on insolvency of employer
- after retention in employment following insolvency.

9.86 Before instigating insolvency procedures, employers have a duty to follow statutory consultation requirements with employees.

Employees' Duties

9.87 Any claims by employees or former employees on debts owed by the employer following an insolvency need to be pursued within the relevant insolvency process. These claims are subject to:

- the preferential status of debts owed to employees — certain debts payable by the employer as remuneration rank as "preferential debts"
- guaranteed redundancy payments — payable out of the National Insurance Fund as "employer's payments" (employees need to apply to the Secretary of State for Business, Enterprise and Regulatory Reform)
- guaranteed payments from the National Insurance Fund — payable in respect of certain debts owed by an insolvent employer to an employee whose employment has been terminated (employees need to apply to the Secretary of State for Business, Enterprise and Regulatory Reform)
- unpaid pension contributions due from an insolvent employer to a pension scheme — payable by the National Insurance Fund
- other statutory payments — statutory sick pay, maternity, paternity and adoption pay — payable by HM Revenue and Customs where payment is not made by an insolvent employer.

In Practice

Bankruptcy

Insolvency of an Individual

9.88 Where the employer is an individual and becomes insolvent, the court process by which the insolvency of the employer is regulated is that of bankruptcy.

9.89 Bankruptcy shifts the liability for any business debts from the employer onto an appointed "trustee in bankruptcy" who is appointed by a court.

Claims Against a Bankrupt Employer

9.90 The Insolvency Act 1986 prevents an employee who is a creditor of a bankrupt employer from pursuing any debts owed by the employer. Instead, the employee needs to submit his or her claim to the trustee in bankruptcy ("trustee"). Until a bankruptcy order is discharged, the employee cannot commence any legal action against the bankrupt employer except with the leave of the court.

Bankruptcy — Effect on Contracts of Employment

9.91 The trustee effectively takes over the contract of employment, since the business of the bankrupt employer has been passed onto the trustee. The financial circumstances of the business may have already resulted in the contract of employment being terminated, especially when the non-payment of wages is likely to amount to a repudiation of the employment contract. Where the employer is made bankrupt, the employee will be able to apply to the court for an order discharging his or her obligations under the employment contract.

Bankruptcy — Liability Under Contracts of Employment

9.92 Where the trustee continues the employer's business, the trustee may decide to continue the employment of the employee or re-engage the employee. Normally, bankruptcy expenses will be met out of the insolvent employer's available assets.

9.93 Expenses incurred carrying on the business have priority over the trustee's own fees. Business expenses will include remuneration due to the employee where his or her employment is continued but are unlikely to cover payments due because of the termination of his or her employment.

Administrative Receivership

The Appointment of an Administrative Receiver

9.94 Where the employer is an organisation, a creditor may be able to appoint a "receiver" to take possession of and turn into cash those assets that can be used to pay off creditors' claims. The receiver is known as an "administrative receiver" when he or she takes possession of all of the assets of a business.

9.95 At the end of the period of administrative receivership, the organisation may continue as a going concern, in which case the organisation's directors resume management of it. It is more likely that the organisation will go into liquidation.

Claims Against the Employer in Administrative Receivership

9.96 An employee is unlikely to be able to enforce any claim against an organisation in administrative receivership as assets in the possession of the receiver are used primarily to pay off the "secured creditor" — a creditor with special rights over the assets because he or she has been instrumental in putting the organisation into receivership. Any claim would need to be enforced against the remaining assets of the organisation, or submitted to a subsequent liquidator.

Administrative Receivership — the Effect on Contracts of Employment

9.97 Employees may continue in employment during a period of administrative receivership. Contracts of employment do not automatically terminate on the appointment of an administrative receiver, although the administrative receiver may take steps that have that result, eg the disposal of the business, replacement of the management team, restructuring.

9.98 Any sale would probably be affected by the Transfer of Undertakings Regulations 2006 (TUPE). The administrative receiver may also enter into new contracts of employment with existing employees.

Administrative Receivership — Liability Under Contracts of Employment

9.99 Legally, administrative receivers are personally liable for any new contracts of employment that they make. They will also be personally liable under any contract of employment adopted by them, although they have a right to compensation from the organisation's assets.

9.100 The administrative receiver's liability is restricted to wages, salary and pension contributions, ie there is no liability for payments arising out of the termination of contracts adopted by an administrative receiver.

9.101 The administrative receiver has a 14-day period after his or her appointment during which he or she cannot be seen as having adopted a contract of employment. Where an employee's services are retained after the 14-day period, a contract of employment will almost certainly be implied.

9.102 In practice, an administrative receiver is unlikely to allow any employment to continue beyond the 14-day period unless the business is in a position to continue to pay the wages, salary and pension contributions involved.

Administration

9.103 Under the Insolvency Act 1986, a court can appoint an administrator to run an insolvent business. This shields the organisation from legal action while the administrator devises a rescue plan that can be approved by the organisation's creditors.

Claims Against the Employer Under Administration Orders

9.104 Once a petition for an administration order has been presented to a court, the consent of the court — or of the administrator if the petition has been successful — will be needed for any proceedings against the organisation. This prevents unfair dismissal proceedings being commenced without the administrator's consent.

Administration — Effect on Contracts of Employment

9.105 The administrator is acting as the agent of the organisation, and has the power to manage its affairs so that contracts of employment are unaffected.

Administration — Liability Under Contracts of Employment

9.106 The administrator incurs no personal liability to employees. However, sums payable under new or adopted contracts of employment entered into by the administrator, ie wages, salaries and pension contributions, are payable out of the organisation's assets before the administrator's own fees and expenses.

9.107 This means that the administrator is unlikely to retain employees if doing so would jeopardise the reimbursement of the administrator's own costs from the organisation's assets.

9.108 Termination payments do not have priority over the costs of the administration. They are "unsecured claims" against the organisation which will be treated in the same way as the claims of other creditors once the period of administration has come to an end.

Liquidation

9.109 Liquidation involves the winding-up of an insolvent organisation either on the basis of a compulsory liquidation, ie through a court order, or on the basis of a voluntary liquidation instigated by shareholders and supervised by creditors.

Liquidation — Claims Against the Employer

9.110 During the presentation of a winding-up order, the court may stop proceedings against the organisation. Where a winding-up order is made, proceedings cannot be started against the organisation without the consent of the court. Employers will need to submit any claim to the liquidator. A voluntary liquidation will not result in an automatic halt to any proceedings but the court may impose such a halt.

Liquidation — Effect on Contracts of Employment

9.111 A compulsory winding-up order will usually result in the dismissal of employees. However, the organisation may continue to trade and retain employees through the liquidator. Contracts of employment will be unaffected by a resolution for voluntary winding-up, as long as the business continues to trade.

Liquidation — Liability Under Contracts of Employment

9.112 In the case of a compulsory winding-up, a court can make provision for payment of the expenses incurred in the course of the winding-up, eg the continued costs of employment. The liquidator is entitled to be reimbursed his or her expenses including the payment of retained employees.

9.113 With a voluntary winding-up, employment costs incurred by the liquidator will be payable out of the organisation's assets and take priority over debts incurred before the liquidation began. The wages of employees employed during the liquidation will still be treated as an expense of the liquidation.

Termination of Employment

Dismissal Prior to Insolvency of Employer

9.114 Where an employer is in financial difficulty with creditors, employees will often be dismissed prior to the employer becoming insolvent. These employees may have claims in respect of sums unpaid under the contract of employment or arising out of the termination. The employee's recourse to legal proceedings depends on the legal status of the employer. Where legal proceedings cannot be taken, these employees can seek to recover any sum owed as a creditor by following the procedures for the different types of employer's insolvency: bankruptcy; administrative receivership; administration; or liquidation.

Dismissal on Insolvency of Employer

9.115 Where employees are dismissed because the employer faces insolvency or becomes insolvent, they may have valid claims for unfair dismissal. Where insufficient notice has been given, the employee may also claim for wrongful dismissal in respect of wages due for the notice period to which he or she was entitled. The employer will usually be able to rely upon redundancy as the reason for dismissal but issues of procedural unfairness may arise, eg over the given levels of warning and/or consultation.

9.116 Any redundancy payment — a sum equal to the basic award for unfair dismissal — will normally be recoverable from the National Insurance Fund administered by the Department for Business, Enterprise and Regulatory Reform (BERR). A claim for a compensatory award for losses incurred as a result of dismissal is unlikely to be worthwhile since the employee would have been dismissed anyway — except where there was the possibility of continued employment for a limited period.

Dismissal After Retention in Employment Following Insolvency

9.117 Where an employee is retained after an employer's insolvency, wages due to the employee are likely to have priority, with an administrative receiver acquiring personal liability for such payments. However, where the continuation of employment is short lived, the employee's termination payments will probably only count as an unsecured claim, ie as a claim without priority, against the organisation.

Insolvency

Statutory Consultation and Notice Periods Prior to Dismissal

9.118 Where the financial situation of the employer may lead to the employer becoming insolvent and/or employees being made redundant, an employee has a right to receive adequate warning and consultation about any proposed redundancies. An employer must follow the statutory consultation requirements as far as is reasonably practicable. This involves a consultation period of at least:
- 30 days where an employer is proposing to dismiss as redundant 20 or more employees at one establishment within a period of 90 days or fewer
- 90 days where the number of employees involved is 100 or more.

Preferential Status of Debts Owed to Employees

9.119 The Insolvency Act 1986 states that there are certain preferential debts payable to employees or former employees on the insolvency of the employer. These include the following.
- Contributions to occupational pension schemes and state scheme premiums.
- Unpaid remuneration payable as wages or salary for the whole or any part of the four month period immediately prior to insolvency, up to a maximum of £800 and including:
  - a guarantee payment to an employee without work to do
  - any payment for time off to look for work or arrange training
  - any payment for time off for ante-natal care
  - any payment for time off for trade union duties
  - remuneration on suspension on medical or maternity grounds
  - remuneration under a protective award for lack of consultation.
- Any accrued holiday remuneration due on the termination of employment, ie pay in lieu of holiday, which is not subject to the £800 cap. (Pay for holiday taken and sick leave are deemed remuneration payable as wages or salary.)

Principle of Equal Distribution

9.120 Employees or former employees will be treated as ordinary unsecured creditors in respect of any sums owed by the employer that are not treated as preferential debts. This means that any assets remaining will be equally distributed, with any shortfall being shared *pro rata* between the creditors.

9.121 The same principle of equal distribution applies where there are insufficient assets to satisfy the full claims of all preferential creditors.

Status of Preferential Debts

9.122 Preferential debts also rank ahead of any "floating charge", ie the general securing of the insolvent organisation's assets that usually results in a receiver being appointed. Only a small proportion of the debts owed by the employer to the employee will have preferential status. In particular, sums due to the employee arising out of the termination of employment, including any award for unfair dismissal or damages for wrongful dismissal, do not have preferential status.

Guaranteed Redundancy Payments

9.123 The Employment Rights Act 1996 provides a guarantee to employees in respect of compensation for redundancy. This covers sums within what is defined as the "employer's payment", ie:
- a statutory redundancy payment

Insolvency

- a payment from the employer to the employee as part of an agreement under which the employee refrains from proceedings relating to statutory redundancy payment — the agreement must meet the requirements of any Acas conciliation or formal compromise agreements
- an agreed payment under a collective agreement approved under collective contracting-out provisions.

Criteria for Guaranteed Redundancy Payments

9.124 The employee will need to meet the following requirements — as well as qualifying for a statutory redundancy payment — in order to recover such a sum from the BERR.
- The employee will need to have made a claim for redundancy payment from the employer within a six-month time limit.
- The employee will need to show that he or she has taken all reasonable steps to obtain payment, and that the employer has refused or failed to make payment — or that the employer is insolvent.

9.125 It may be advisable for an employee to start employment tribunal proceedings to prove that he or she has taken reasonable steps to obtain payment — especially where the employer's liability is in doubt. The employee is entitled to interest on any sum that the employment tribunal orders an employer to pay and if the employer fails to make the payment, the interest can also be recovered from the National Insurance Fund.

9.126 In the event of non-payment by the BERR, an employee has a right to bring a complaint to the employment tribunal. There is no time limit for bringing such proceedings.

Guaranteed Payments from the National Insurance Fund

9.127 The Employment Rights Act 1996 allows an employee to recover the following debts owed to him or her by an insolvent employer, from the National Insurance Fund.
- Arrears of pay up to a maximum of eight weeks, ie the actual pay due over those eight weeks, although this is not restricted to the eight weeks immediately preceding insolvency.
- Statutory notice pay or damages for failure to give the required notice (deductions can be made from any amount owed the former employee for alternative earnings, unemployment benefit and income tax).
- Holiday pay for the preceding 12 months, up to a maximum of 6 weeks, for either "in lieu" or "taken" holiday.
- The basic award for unfair dismissal.

9.128 The term "arrears of pay" also covers:
- statutory guarantee payments
- payments for time off work for public duties
- payments for time off work to look for work and make arrangements for training
- payments for time off work for ante-natal care
- payments for time off work for dependants
- payments for time off work for pension scheme trustees
- payments for time off work for employee representatives
- payments for time off for trade union duties
- remuneration following a suspension on medical grounds

- remuneration following a suspension on maternity grounds
- payment under a protective award for failing to consult as to redundancy.

9.129 Legislation limits the amounts payable out of the National Insurance Fund to £310 per week (for 2007/08). Any tax and national insurance deductions from sums for wages and holiday pay are to be made after the statutory cap has been imposed.

Set-off Debts Owed by the Employee

9.130 The liability of the BERR cannot exceed the liability of the employer, so any "set-off debt" can be taken into account in calculating a payment out of the National Insurance Fund. A set-off debt is one where the employer can subtract a debt owed by an employee from any sum owed the employee.

Criteria for Payment out of the National Insurance Fund

9.131 The following criteria need to be satisfied in order for a payment to be made.
- The employer has been made the subject of formal insolvency measures.
- The employment of the employee has been terminated.
- The employee was entitled to be paid the debt in question which was outstanding on the date in question.

Procedure

9.132 The procedure for obtaining a payment from the National Insurance Fund involves the employee submitting a written application to the BERR, which must be satisfied that the relevant criteria are met. The BERR has the power to require information to be provided in order to verify the claim — from the employer as well. Where a payment is made, the Secretary of State is entitled to take action to recover the sum from the employer.

Employment Tribunal Proceedings

9.133 The employee is entitled to make a complaint to the employment tribunal if the Secretary of State fails to make a payment or fails to pay the full amount. The time limit for making such a complaint is three months from the date the decision of the Secretary of State was communicated to the employee. This time limit can only be extended where the tribunal is satisfied that it was not reasonably practicable for the complaint to be presented before the end of the three-month period.

Pensions Contributions

9.134 Certain unpaid contributions due from an insolvent employer to an occupational pension scheme or a personal pension scheme are also eligible to be paid by the Secretary of State out of the National Insurance Fund.

Extent of Liability

9.135 Any application for pensions contributions would normally be made on behalf of the pension scheme by its trustees. This can be made in respect of arrears of employers' contributions, but also in respect of the employee's contributions where these were deducted by the employer but not paid to the scheme.

9.136 The amount payable by the Secretary of State in respect of employee contributions is limited to the amount deducted from the employee's pay in the 12 months prior to insolvency. Payments in respect of the employer's contributions are also subject to a maximum amount which is the figure for arrears accrued within the 12 months prior to insolvency save where a lower maximum figure applies by virtue of the Pension Schemes Act 1993.

Employment Tribunal Proceedings

9.137 An employee can complain to the employment tribunal regarding pensions payments owed to him or her from the National Insurance Fund. There is a three-month time limit running from the date of communication of the Secretary of State's decision on the application.

Other Statutory Payments

9.138 Certain statutory payments are to be paid by HMRC where an employee is unable to obtain payment from an insolvent employer. These include:
- Statutory Maternity, Paternity and Adoption Pay
- Statutory Sick Pay.

List of Relevant Legislation

9.139
- Statutory Paternity Pay and Statutory Adoption Pay (General) Regulations 2002
- Statutory Maternity Pay (General) Regulations 1986
- Statutory Sick Pay (General) Regulations 1982
- Transfer of Undertaking Regulations 1981
- Insolvency Rules 1986
- Employment Rights Act 1996
- Pension Schemes Act 1993
- Trade Union & Labour Relations (Consolidation) Act 1992
- Insolvency Act 1986
- Directive 2002/74/EC of the European Parliament and of the Council
- Council Directive 1980/987/EEC

List of Relevant Cases

9.140
- *Benson v Secretary of State for Trade and Industry* [2003] ICR 1082, EAT
- *Williams v Compair Maxam Ltd* [1982] IRLR 83, ECJ

Further Information

Organisations
- **Department for Business, Enterprise and Regulatory Reform (BERR)**
  Web: *www.berr.gov.uk*

Insolvency

The Department for Business, Enterprise and Regulatory Reform brings together functions from the former Department of Trade and Industry (DTI), including responsibilities for productivity, business relations, energy, competition and consumers. It also drives regulatory reform.

Redundancy

This topic covers the following.
- Definition of Redundancy
- Avoiding Redundancies
- Obligations of an Employer When Contemplating Redundancies
- Collective Redundancy Consultation
- Individual Consultation
- Paid Time Off to Look for New Work or Arrange Training
- Support for Employees Who are Made Redundant
- Unfair Dismissal Claims
- Redundancy Pay
- Lay Offs and Short Time Working

9.141 An employee may be dismissed as redundant when a business closes down, or if the need for employees to carry out work of a particular kind has ceased or diminished or is expected to cease or diminish. When redundancies occur, the employer has a number of statutory duties towards employees, including the duty to consult them and to pay redundancy pay to those who are eligible.

Employers' Duties

9.142 Employers are under a duty to ensure the following.
- Notify the Secretary of State for Business, Enterprise and Regulatory Reform of any proposal to make 20 or more employees redundant.
- Consult collectively if more than 20 jobs are to be made redundant in one establishment, following the specific procedures laid down in law.
- Give employees whose jobs may be made redundant as much warning as possible.
- Consider whether there are alternative solutions to the proposed redundancies, such as alternative employment.
- Act objectively and reasonably in determining which employees are to be included within the pool for redundancy selection.
- Use objective criteria for selection.
- Give redundant employees proper notice under their contracts of employment.
- Try to find suitable alternative employment elsewhere within the organisation for employees whose jobs are to be made redundant.
- Grant reasonable paid time off work to redundant employees to help them seek new work or make arrangements for training.
- Ensure that a fair procedure is implemented in carrying out any dismissal of employees by reason of redundancy, including the application of the three stages of the statutory dismissal and disciplinary procedure (DDP).
- Pay redundancy pay to employees who have two or more years' continuous employment.
- Not to lay employees off without pay or place them on short time working even in circumstances where the amount of available work has diminished, unless employees' contracts contain an express clause authorising the employer to withhold or reduce pay in these circumstances.

- Keep any relevant documentation that explains why redundancies were necessary, in case the decision should need to be justified at a later date.

Employees' Duties

9.143 Employees are under a duty to ensure the following.
- Take an active part in any consultation process set up by an employer.
- If offered, consider the possibility of volunteering for redundancy.
- Consider carefully offers of alternative employment as an unreasonable refusal of suitable alternative employment may disentitle the employee to a statutory redundancy payment.
- Make use of paid time off to look for alternative employment or training while under notice of redundancy.
- Take advantage of any support offered by an employer, eg help offered to find new work.
- Co-operate with the employer in the carrying out of the statutory dismissal and disciplinary procedure (DDP).
- If a redundancy payment is not made, make a claim at an employment tribunal within six months.

In Practice

Definition of Redundancy

9.144 There are two definitions of redundancy for the purposes of UK employment law. One definition establishes entitlement to redundancy payments and the other establishes the right to be collectively consulted.

9.145 Section 139 of the Employment Rights Act 1996 defines redundancy as a dismissal that is wholly or mainly attributable to the fact that the:
- employer — either generally or specifically in the place where the employee is employed — has ceased or intends to cease carrying on the business for the purposes for which the employee was employed
- requirement of the business for employees to carry out work of a particular kind — either generally or specifically in the place where the employee is employed — has ceased or diminished, or is expected to cease or diminish.

9.146 This is the definition that is relevant to employees' entitlement to redundancy pay, and for the purpose of determining whether there is proper and potentially fair reason for dismissal.

9.147 The Trade Union and Labour Relations (Consolidation) Act 1992, s.195, defines redundancy in the case of collective redundancies as "dismissal for a reason not related to the individual concerned or for a number of reasons all of which are not so related". This is the definition that applies for the purposes of the requirement for collective consultation.

Avoiding Redundancies

9.148 Employers should try to avoid redundancies by developing a formal approach to potential staff reduction requirements. Such a policy should also help to ensure that any redundancy process is fair and consistent.

9.149 Alternative ways of dealing with a need to cut back staff numbers could include:
- reducing overtime
- terminating the engagements of any temporary agency staff
- ceasing sub-contract work
- freezing recruitment or secondments
- reducing hours of work (but only with employees' agreement).

9.150 It is advisable for employers to document carefully the reason(s) why redundancies are necessary and to keep records of steps taken to consider alternative solutions. It is important not only to have evidence that alternative solutions were fully considered but also to show that the employer took all reasonable steps to avoid the need for redundancies.

Obligations of an Employer when Contemplating Redundancies — Summary

9.151 An employer has a variety of obligations if it proposes to dismiss employees as redundant. Employers are under a duty to:
- provide formal notification to the Secretary of State for Business, Enterprise and Regulatory Reform where 20 or more employees are to be made redundant
- consult collectively if 20 or more employees are to be made redundant
- consult with individual employees to ensure dismissals are fair
- follow the three stages of the statutory dismissal and disciplinary procedure (DDP) implemented in October 2004 for each affected employee
- use objective criteria for selection and apply the criteria fairly and consistently
- give redundant employees proper notice under their contracts of employment
- try to find suitable alternative employment elsewhere within the organisation for employees whose jobs are to be made redundant
- grant reasonable paid time off work to redundant employees to help them seek new work
- pay redundancy pay to those who qualify for it.

Department for Business, Enterprise and Regulatory Reform Notification

9.152 An employer proposing to dismiss as redundant 100 or more employees at one establishment within a period of 90 days or less must notify the Secretary of State for Business, Enterprise and Regulatory Reform, in writing, of its proposal at least 90 days before giving notice to terminate any of the relevant employees' contracts of employment.

9.153 An employer proposing to dismiss as redundant 20 or more employees at one establishment within a period of 90 days or less must notify the Secretary of State for Business, Enterprise and Regulatory Reform, in writing, of its proposal at least 30 days before giving notice to terminate any of the relevant employees' contracts of employment.

9.154 This notice should be given on Form HR1. A copy of Form HR1 must be given to each employee representative. Failure to comply with the notification requirements is a criminal offence, which can render the employer liable on summary conviction to a fine not exceeding £5000.

Collective Redundancy Consultation

9.155 This topic is dealt with in more detail in Collective Redundancies. The following points summarise an employer's obligations.

Numbers to Trigger the Duty to Consult Collectively

9.156 The duty to conduct collective consultation arises where the employer proposes to dismiss 20 or more employees at one establishment within a 90-day period. In this case, the employer must begin consultation no fewer than 30 days before the first notices of dismissal are issued. Where 100 or more employees are to be made redundant at one establishment, the consultation period must begin at least 90 days before notices of dismissal are issued. These are the same time periods as are applicable to the statutory duty to provide formal notification of proposed redundancies to the Secretary of State.

9.157 If fewer than 20 employees are to be made redundant, the duty to consult collectively is not activated but the duty to consult individuals and carry out the steps of the statutory dismissal and disciplinary procedure will still apply.

Time Limits for Consultation

9.158 Consultation must begin "within good time", and in any event not fewer than 30 days before the first notices of dismissal are issued by the employer.

9.159 An important decision of the European Court of Justice (*Junk v Wolfgang Kuhnel* [2005] C-188/03C, ECJ) has made it clear that notices of dismissal could not lawfully be issued to employees until the collective consultation period had expired. This is because consultation must be conducted "with a view to reaching an agreement" on (among other things) ways of avoiding redundancies or reducing their numbers, and this cannot be achieved where notices of dismissal have already been issued. It was previously thought that notices of dismissal could be issued during, or even at the start of, the consultation period, but this case decision in effect put an end to that authority. Section 193 of the Trade Union and Labour Relations (Consolidation) Act 1992 was subsequently amended (on 1 October 2006) to reflect this decision.

Appropriate Representatives

9.160 "Appropriate representatives" are elected employee representatives or representatives of a recognised trade union.

9.161 An employer who proposes collective redundancies must consult with:
- the trade union, if one is recognised by the employer, or otherwise
- appropriate representatives of any of the employees who either personally face dismissal or are affected by the dismissals.

9.162 If there are no appropriate representatives within the organisation, the employer must enable fair elections to take place.

9.163 Consultation will also need to take place on an individual basis with the employees themselves.

Consultation Process

9.164 Collective consultation must include consultation about the ways of:
- avoiding dismissals
- reducing the numbers of employees to be dismissed
- mitigating the consequences of the dismissals.

9.165 The employer must approach consultation with an open mind and "with a view to reaching agreement". The employer should give reasons if they do not accept a particular proposal made by the representatives.

Disclosure of Information

9.166 The employer must disclose in writing to the appropriate representatives:
- the reasons for the proposals
- the numbers and descriptions of the employees it is proposed to dismiss as redundant
- the total number of employees of each description employed by the employer at the establishment in question
- how it is proposed to select the employees for redundancy
- the proposed method for carrying out the dismissals, including the period over which they are to take effect
- how it is proposed to calculate redundancy payments (other than statutory redundancy pay) for the employees facing dismissal.

Failure to Consult: Protective Awards

9.167 If an employer does not fulfil the statutory consultation obligations, an employment tribunal may penalise the employer by making an award — known as a "protective award" — in favour of the employees. A protective award will usually be a sum equivalent to 90 days pay for each affected employee.

Individual Consultation

9.168 A redundancy dismissal will be unfair if a fair procedure is not implemented in carrying out the dismissal. Indeed, procedure (or lack of it) is often the main cause of a finding of unfair dismissal at an employment tribunal.

9.169 Employees who are to be included in the selection pool should be given as much warning as possible of potential redundancy. This will help to ensure that the redundancy procedure is considered fair.

9.170 One key requirement for fairness is that each employee is consulted individually about the proposal to dismiss him or her. Each employee should be told of the precise reasons why he or she has been provisionally selected for redundancy and given an opportunity to make representations. Any comments the employee makes should be taken into account, both on selection issues and on any suggested alternatives to redundancy, before any final decision is taken. An employee may, for example, have skills of which the employer is unaware that could be deployed elsewhere in the organisation. Alternatively, he or she may be able to identify another employee within the organisation who — due to experience or length of service — could or should be made redundant in his or her place.

9.171 If a scoring system is used to grade employees against set criteria, each employee should be informed how his or her score was arrived at, and allowed to challenge the score. All this should take place before any final decisions are reached as to who is to be selected for redundancy.

Volunteers for Redundancy

9.172 In order to ensure a fair redundancy process and in an effort to reduce the number of compulsory redundancies, employers often ask for volunteers. The logic is that no one should be made compulsorily redundant when someone else is prepared to leave voluntarily.

9.173 Asking for volunteers is good practice, but the employer may legitimately decline to accept a particular volunteer for redundancy, eg if the volunteer is a vital member of staff, or has special skills that the employer does not wish to lose.

9.174 The employer is not obliged to pay an enhanced redundancy payment to a volunteer, but may choose to do so if it wishes. However, as a voluntary redundancy is still regarded in law as a dismissal (rather than a resignation), statutory redundancy pay will be payable in the usual way.

Definition of the Pool for Selection

9.175 If not all employees are being made redundant, the employer will need to identify a "pool for selection". Factors that should be considered when determining which employees should be within the pool for selection include:
- the reason for the redundancies
- the type of work carried out by the employees
- whether people are interchangeable
- whether other groups of employees are doing similar work.

9.176 It is difficult for an employer's selection to be challenged so long as the employer acts logically and reasonably in identifying the pool for selection.

Determination of Selection Criteria

9.177 If redundancy dismissals are to be fair, the employer will have to act fairly and reasonably when determining and applying criteria for selection to the employees in the selection pool.

9.178 The most common approach to selection for redundancy is the "score sheet" or skills matrix method. This involves:
- marking each employee in the selection pool against agreed selection criteria, weighting the criteria if appropriate
- adding up the resulting scores
- provisionally selecting for dismissal those whose total score is lowest.

9.179 The following factors should be considered when determining selection criteria.
- The criteria should be discussed and agreed with employee representatives where collective consultation takes place, as well as with the individuals concerned.
- The criteria should be factors that can be measured objectively and are not solely subjective opinions. Judgments that could potentially be seen as subjective can be given a greater degree of objectivity if two or more people are involved in the application of the criteria. This approach will also reduce the likelihood of an appeal on the grounds of bias.
- Employers should be wary of taking into account factors that appear to allow excessive scope for an employer's personal prejudice, eg the "attitude" of a particular employee.
- Last in, First Out (LIFO) as a criterion for selection would, in general, discriminate indirectly against younger staff because they are likely to have shorter service than older employees.
- It is important to vet the selection criteria to ensure that they are not directly or indirectly discriminatory, eg on grounds of sex, race, disability, religion, sexual orientation or age. For example, giving preference to full-time employees could indirectly discriminate against women and would also be unlawful under the Part-Time Workers (Prevention of Less Favourable Treatment) Regulations 2000.

Application of the Selection Criteria

9.180 Managers responsible for implementing the selection criteria should be:
- in a position to objectively assess each individual employee in the pool
- given training and guidance on how to apply the selection criteria.

9.181 The manager(s) should jointly consider and mark each individual against the selection criteria. Marking should be done objectively. Personal likes or dislikes and purely subjective opinions that cannot be backed up by facts must play no part in the selection process.

9.182 Each employee should subsequently be informed of his or her score, and allowed to make representations. However, there is no obligation to let employees see the scores of other employees.

Giving Notice

Statutory Notice Periods

9.183 There are minimum statutory notice periods that must be given to employees who are being dismissed by reason of redundancy. The main points are as follows.
- An employee who has been continuously employed for more than one month but less than two years is entitled to receive one week's notice from his or her employer.
- Thereafter the employer must give one week's additional notice for every further completed year of employment, up to a maximum of 12 weeks' notice for 12 years' service.

9.184 If an employee is dismissed without notice or with inadequate notice, the minimum statutory notice period due to him or her will be added to his or her period of continuous service for statutory purposes.

Contractual Notice Periods

9.185 Most contracts of employment are for an indefinite period and will contain an express term specifying minimum notice periods required by both the employee and employer prior to termination of employment. If no notice is specified in the employee's contract, the employer must give either the statutory minimum period of notice due to the employee, or else "reasonable notice" (which may be longer than statutory notice, depending on the circumstances of the employee's employment).

9.186 If an employee's contract of employment provides for less notice than the statutory minimum period to which the employee is entitled, the statutory minimum notice period will prevail. If the contract provides for longer notice, the contractual notice period will prevail.

Payment in Lieu of Notice

9.187 An employee who is to be dismissed as redundant may, at the employer's discretion, be dealt with in one of three ways.
- The employee may be asked to work the notice period, in which case all normal terms and conditions of the contract will continue until employment ends.
- If there is a relevant contractual provision, the employee may be placed on garden leave. This means that the employee continues to be employed during the notice period and is paid normally, but is required not to attend work.

- The employee's contract may be terminated with immediate effect, in which case the employer will make a payment in lieu of notice. For this to be lawful, a term entitling the employer to dismiss with pay in lieu of notice should be included in the employee's contract.

Suitable Alternative Employment

9.188 The employer should always consider whether there are alternative solutions to the termination of employees' employment. In particular, an employer should review the possibility of alternative employment within:
- the organisation
- any associated companies, even if these are outside the UK.

9.189 "Suitable" employment in this context is work which the employee could reasonably be expected to do (in light of his or her qualifications, skills and experience) and on terms and conditions not substantially less favourable.

9.190 An employer should not discount any possibility on the assumption that an employee will not be interested, eg if the job is of a lower status. If in doubt, the best approach is always to discuss all possibilities with the employee.

9.191 In *Fisher v Hoopoe Finance Ltd* EAT 0043/05, the EAT held that, where there are a number of alternative positions that could be offered to a redundant employee, he or she should be notified of the financial prospects of each of these positions in order to enable him or her to make an informed decision

Trial Period in the New Job

9.192 Where an offer of alternative employment has been made which involves a different type of work or different terms of employment, the employee is entitled to a four-week trial period in the new job commencing from the start of the new contract.

9.193 Where the new contract necessitates retraining, this period can be extended by written agreement between the parties. The agreement must specify the date on which the trial period is to end and the terms and conditions that will apply thereafter.

9.194 If during or at the end of the trial period, either the employee or the employer gives notice to terminate the contract, the employee will be treated as having been dismissed by reason of redundancy on the date the original contract came to an end.

Continuity of Service

9.195 Where an employee accepts an offer of new employment as an alternative to redundancy dismissal, continuity of service will be maintained provided that:
- the offer of the new job is made before the old job ends, and
- the new job starts immediately after the old job ends, or no later than four weeks afterwards.

9.196 In these circumstances there is no right for the employee to be paid a statutory redundancy payment because there will have been no dismissal.

The Effect of Refusing an Offer of Suitable Alternative Employment

9.197 An employee loses his or her entitlement to a statutory redundancy payment if he or she unreasonably refuses an offer of suitable alternative employment. In practice, however, this outcome is rare.

Offering an Alternative Job at a Different Location

9.198 If alternative work is potentially available for a redundant employee at a different location, the employer should discuss with the employee whether he or she might be interested in moving to that location, rather than making assumptions about whether the employee would wish to move.

9.199 Even if the job in the new location is in effect the same work as the employee's old job, this does not automatically mean that it will be "suitable" in the context of redundancy (unless there is an agreed mobility clause in the employee's contract). This is because what is suitable will depend not only on the type of work that is available but also on the circumstances of the individual employee.

9.200 Even though the work may be suitable, significant extra travelling time and/or cost, or evidence that the move would cause personal difficulties in relation to family responsibilities would in most cases render an employee's refusal to move to a new location reasonable. Where an employee reasonably refused an offer of alternative employment for a reason of this type, the employer would retain the duty to pay statutory redundancy pay.

Paid Time Off to Look for New Work or Arrange Training

9.201 Employees who are under notice of redundancy and have been continuously employed for at least two years qualify for a statutory entitlement to a reasonable amount of paid time off work to look for another job or to arrange training.

Support for Employees who are made Redundant

9.202 Employers should try to assist employees who are to be made redundant, eg by:
- providing facilities on site for employees to look for new jobs
- inviting employment agencies to talk to employees on site
- contacting other employers about vacancies
- arranging outplacement services, either by way of an on-site clinic or individually (there is a tax concession for such arrangements).

Unfair Dismissal Claims

9.203 An employee who has been dismissed by reason of redundancy may be able to present a complaint of unfair dismissal to an employment tribunal. In order to be eligible to do so, the employee must have been continuously employed by the employer for a minimum of one year as at the date of his or her dismissal.

9.204 A dismissed employee will succeed in his or her complaint of unfair dismissal unless the employer can show that:
- redundancy was the real reason for the dismissal
- the employer acted reasonably.

9.205 Dismissal for redundancy may be unfair where:
- redundancy is not the real reason for dismissal
- the employer handled the dismissal unreasonably, eg by failing to give the employee adequate warning of redundancy, failing to consult the employee or failing to apply objective selection criteria
- the employer failed to follow the three mandatory steps of the statutory dismissal and disciplinary procedure (DDP) prior to dismissing the employee by reason of redundancy
- an employee was unfairly selected for redundancy, eg where objective criteria were not used or where the criteria were applied unfairly to the employee

- the employer failed to consider whether alternative employment was available within the organisation and/or to offer an available alternative job to the employee.

Requirement to Follow the Statutory Dismissal and Disciplinary Procedure (DDP)

9.206 Since 1 October 2004, there is a statutory duty to carry out the statutory dismissal and disciplinary procedure (DDP) in a wide range of circumstances leading to dismissal. The DDP is applicable to redundancy dismissals where fewer than 20 employees are affected (and collective consultation thus not required).

9.207 The three stages of the DDP are to:
- advise the employee in writing that circumstances have arisen under which his or her job may have to be made redundant, inviting the employee to a meeting
- hold a meeting to discuss the matter and allow the employee to make representations and review any alternatives to redundancy; the employee must be allowed to bring a fellow worker or trade union official of his or her choice to this meeting if he or she wishes
- allow a right of appeal if the employee is subsequently dismissed.

9.208 A failure on the employer's part to follow the statutory DDP will render an employee's dismissal automatically unfair, and will also entitle the employee to an uplift on his or her compensatory award.

9.209 In *Alexander v Bridgen Enterprises Ltd* [2006] IRLR 422, the EAT ruled that when an employer is proposing to dismiss an employee by reason of redundancy, the statutory DDP requires the employer to inform the employee at step 2 of the DDP (ie at the meeting) what the basis is for proposing to select him or her for redundancy, providing sufficient detail of the circumstances so as to allow him or her to make representations. This would include telling the employee not only the selection criteria that are being applied, but also the scores that he or she has achieved (where a points system has been used). It would not, however, include a duty to tell the employee of the threshold score that must be achieved to remain in employment, or the scores of other employees in the selection pool.

Remedies for Unfair Dismissal

9.210 An employment tribunal has power to grant the following remedies to an employee if it finds he or she has been unfairly dismissed.
- Reinstatement — this is an order that the employer must re-employ the employee in his or her old job and treat him or her in all respects as if the dismissal had not occurred. Arrears of wages for the period since dismissal through to the date of reinstatement must be paid.
- Re-engagement — in this case, an employee must be re-employed in a job comparable to the one from which he or she was dismissed. Again, arrears of wages must be paid.
- Compensation.

9.211 Before making an order for reinstatement or re-engagement, an employment tribunal must consider whether it is:
- fair and practicable for the employer to re-employ the individual
- "just and equitable in the circumstances" to make such an order.

9.212 If an employer fails to comply with a reinstatement or re-engagement order, the tribunal will make an award of compensation and — unless the employer satisfies

Redundancy

the tribunal that it was not practicable to comply with the order — also make an additional award of compensation. The additional award will be between 26 and 52 weeks' pay.

9.213 Reinstatement and re-engagement are rarely awarded in practice because few dismissed employees request it and/or it is often impracticable for the employer to take the employee back.

Redundancy Pay

Statutory Redundancy Pay

9.214 An employee who is dismissed by reason of redundancy is entitled to a statutory redundancy payment providing he or she has been continuously employed for a minimum of two years at the date of his or her dismissal.

9.215 The statutory redundancy payment is calculated according to a formula involving the:
- number of years' continuous employment
- age of the employee
- amount of the employee's pay per week.

9.216 Broadly speaking, the payment is calculated as follows.
- Calculate the number of complete years of continuous employment (up to a maximum of 20).
- Calculate the employee's gross pay per week, up to a current maximum (for 2007/08) of £310 per week.
- Work backwards from the date of termination and allow one and a half week's pay for each completed year of service while the employee was aged 41 or above; one week's pay for each completed year of service while the employee was between the ages of 22 and 40 inclusive; and half a week's pay for each completed year of service while the employee was under age 21.

9.217 The maximum number of weeks can be read from the redundancy pay table below.

9.218 The maximum statutory redundancy payment entitlement per individual is currently £9300.

Length of Service

9.219 Some absences — such as sickness, injury or temporary shortage of work — can count towards an employee's period of continuous employment, even if the employee's contract of employment was suspended at the time. Absences on maternity leave, adoption leave, paternity leave and parental leave must be counted towards an employee's length of service for the purposes of redundancy pay.

9.220 Working days lost through industrial disputes will not count towards the employee's period of continuous service. Any days that an employee was on strike will therefore be subtracted from his or her total length of continuous employment.

Dismissals Connected to the Transfer of an Undertaking

9.221 Following the implementation of the Transfer of Undertakings (Protection of Employment) Regulations 2006 (TUPE), an employee who is dismissed by reason of an "economical, technical or organisational reason entailing changes in the workforce" (known as an ETO reason) is deemed to have been dismissed by reason of redundancy. Where the redundancy dismissal takes place some time after the employee has transferred to the new employer, his or her length of service for the purposes of calculating statutory redundancy pay will include the total period of continuous service with the previous employer.

Enhanced Redundancy Payments

9.222 Employers may, at their discretion, pay redundant employees a sum of money in excess of the amount due as statutory redundancy pay.

9.223 Where an employer wishes to operate a contractual redundancy pay scheme that enhances the payments made to redundant employees, the scheme must, by and large, mirror the statutory redundancy pay scheme. This means that the scheme must use the same age bands as those used in the statutory scheme, calculate the amounts due to employees in different age groups in the same proportions as are applied in the statutory scheme and not exclude any employee from benefit on the grounds of age. The reason for this requirement is to avoid acting in breach of the Employment Equality (Age) Regulations 2006.

9.224 Specifically, it is permitted for an employer to offer enhanced redundancy payments by doing any or all of the following.
- Increasing or disapplying the limit on a "week's pay" (currently £310).
- Enhancing the multipliers used in the statutory scheme (½ week's pay, 1 week's pay and 1½ week's pay), eg by multiplying them by a figure such as two or three.
- Multiplying the statutory payments due to each employee by a defined number (so long as the same number is used for all employees irrespective of age).

9.225 A contractual redundancy pay scheme that bases redundancy pay on employees' length of service alone (ie one that does not use the age bands and multipliers applied in the statutory scheme) would be indirectly discriminatory against younger staff (who on the whole would tend to have shorter service). Such a scheme would, if implemented, have to be objectively justified.

9.226 Since there is no statutory (and normally no contractual) obligation to provide any payment in excess of statutory redundancy pay, it is open to the employer to attach conditions to such payments. Redundancy payments are tax free up to £30,000.

Employees not Entitled to Redundancy Pay

9.227 There are various categories of employees who have no statutory entitlement to redundancy payment. The categories are listed fully in the Employment Rights Act 1996. They include members of the Armed Forces, Crown servants or employees in a public office and apprentices whose service ends at the end of their apprenticeship contract.

9.228 Employees engaged on fixed-term contracts who have gained two or more years' continuous service and whose contracts expire without renewal are entitled to statutory redundancy pay in the same way as those engaged on permanent employment contracts.

If the Employee or Employer Dies

9.229 If an employer dies and the business stops trading, the personal representatives of the employer will be responsible for any redundancy payments. If an employee dies before receiving a redundancy payment, the payment must be made to his or her personal representative.

Where a Due Redundancy Payment is not Made

9.230 If an employer does not make a redundancy payment where one is due, the employee should take the matter to an employment tribunal within six months. Even if the employee does not make the claim within six months, a tribunal may still order that the payment should be made if the employee takes action within a further six months.

When an Employer Cannot Pay

9.231 If an employer is insolvent and therefore cannot make a redundancy payment, the employee can claim the payment from the Redundancy Payments Office and the office will claim the payment back from the assets of the business.

9.232 To qualify for such a payment, an employee must have applied in writing to the employer for a redundancy payment within six months of the date of employment ending, or have applied successfully to an employment tribunal within six months of that date.

Lay Offs and Short Time Working

9.233 Provisions contained in the Employment Rights Act 1996 prevent employers from suspending employees' contracts of employment without pay rather than declaring redundancies when the amount of available work has diminished. The provisions also provide a method by which an employee in such circumstances can assert his or her right to a redundancy payment.

9.234 A lay off occurs where an employee is not provided with any work by the employer in any given week with the result that the employee is not paid at all for that week.

9.235 Short time working occurs where there is a reduction in the amount of work available for the employee and as a result he or she is paid for less than half a week's pay.

9.236 A week for these purposes means the seven days from a Sunday to a Saturday.

9.237 An employer will only be entitled to lay an employee off or place him or her on short time working if the employee's contract contains a clause authorising the employer to withhold or reduce pay in these circumstances. If the employer has no such right under the contract, but nevertheless reduces or stops an employee's pay, the employee would be able to make a claim for unlawful deduction from wages, resign and claim constructive dismissal and possibly claim a redundancy payment.

9.238 If, however, the weeks of lay off or short time working are wholly or mainly due to a strike or lock out, the employee will not be able to complain to an employment tribunal in respect of any proportionate reduction of pay for those weeks.

Eligibility for a Redundancy Payment when an Employee is Laid Off or Placed on Short Time Working

9.239 An employee will be eligible for a redundancy payment if he or she is laid off or kept on short time working if the employee:
- has been laid off or kept on short time working for four or more consecutive weeks, or for a series of six or more weeks (of which not more than three were consecutive) within any 13 week period
- gives the employer proper notice to terminate his or her contract of employment as per the terms of the contract

- gives written notice to the employer indicating his or her intention to claim a redundancy payment in respect of lay off or short time working. Such notice must be served within four weeks of the end of either the last of four consecutive weeks of lay off or short time working, or the last of six non-consecutive weeks of lay off or short time working.

9.240 The employer may, in defined circumstances resist a claim for redundancy pay by serving a written counter-notice on the employee within seven days of receipt of the employee's notice of his or her intention to claim a redundancy payment. The circumstances in which the employer may do this are where the employer reasonably expects to be able (within four weeks of the employee's notice) to provide the employee with full time working, ie with no further lay offs or short time working, for a period of at least 13 weeks.

Training

9.241 Appropriate training should be provided within an organisation for all managers who are likely to be involved in the redundancy process. They should have a good understanding of an employer's obligations regarding:
- consultation
- the application of selection criteria, in particular an awareness that age must not be used directly or indirectly as a criterion for selection
- suitable alternative employment
- employees' rights to time off during their notice periods
- the duty to follow the statutory dismissal and disciplinary procedure prior to dismissal.

List of Relevant Legislation

9.242
- Employment Equality (Age) Regulations 2006
- Employment Act 2002 (Dispute Resolution) Regulations 2004
- Fixed-Term Employees (Prevention of Less Favourable Treatment) Regulations 2002
- Part-Time Workers (Prevention of Less Favourable Treatment) Regulations 2000
- Employment Act 2002
- Employment Rights Act 1996 (in particular, section 139)
- Trade Union and Labour Relations (Consolidation) Act 1992

List of Relevant Cases

9.243
- *Junk v Kühnel* [2005] IRLR 310, ECJ
- *Kaur v MG Rover Group Ltd* [2005] IRLR 40, CA
- *Lionel Leventhal Ltd v North* [2005] IDS Brief 778, EAT
- *Hardy v Tourism South East* [2004] UKEAT/0631/04

Further Information

Organisations

- **Advisory Conciliation and Arbitration Service (Acas)**
  Web: *www.acas.org.uk*
  Acas aims to improve organisations and working life through better employment relations. It provides up-to-date information, advice, high-quality training, and works with employers and employees to solve problems and improve performance.
- **Department for Business, Enterprise and Regulatory Reform (BERR)**
  Web: *www.berr.gov.uk*
  The Department for Business, Enterprise and Regulatory Reform brings together functions from the former Department of Trade and Industry (DTI), including responsibilities for productivity, business relations, energy, competition and consumers. It also drives regulatory reform.

Resignation and Constructive Dismissal

This topic covers the following.
- Unilateral Termination
- Notice
- Withdrawing Notice of Resignation
- Working During Notice Period
- Heat of the Moment Resignations
- Warning of Dismissal
- Constructive Dismissal
- Exit Interviews

9.244 An employment contract can be brought to an end by an employee offering his or her resignation. Termination by resignation will be lawful, provided that it is done in accordance with the contract. This usually means that the notice required under the contract is provided.

9.245 There are circumstances, however, where resignation is not so straightforward. Examples include an employee:
- resigning in the heat of the moment
- resigning under the threat or possibility of dismissal
- resigning without giving the required notice under the contract.

9.246 An employee may also resign claiming that there was a fundamental breach of contract on the part of the employer, and that this breach caused him or her to resign. This kind of resignation is, in fact, a form of dismissal, commonly known as "constructive dismissal".

Employers' Duties

9.247 Employers should:
- be clear that the resignation is genuine and has not been given in the heat of the moment
- ensure that they do not breach and have not already breached the contract of employment — an act which could lead to claims for unfair constructive dismissal
- make sure that the employee has given the required amount of notice under the contract of employment
- write to the employee stating his or her last working day and effective date of termination
- ensure that the employee is paid all outstanding monies, including accrued holiday pay
- be aware that the employee continues to be entitled to all benefits under the contract of employment during the notice period.

Employees' Duties

9.248 Employees have a duty to:
- make sure that the required amount of notice under the contract of employment has been given.

In Practice

Unilateral Termination

9.249 Where an employee decides to end his or her employment with an employer, he or she resigns. Reasons for resignation vary, but common reasons include the employee:
- being offered a new job
- breaking off from his or her existing career
- not wishing to return to work after a period of maternity leave.

Notice

Notice Period

9.250 An employee should always give the notice required under either statute or the contract of employment, whichever is the longer period.

9.251 The Employment Rights Act 1996 provides that an employee who has been continuously employed for a month or more is obliged to give a minimum of one week's notice. Under the contract of employment, however, the employee may be bound to give more notice and in these circumstances it is this notice period that prevails.

9.252 Where an employee does not give proper notice, in circumstances where the notice is not in response to a repudiatory breach on the part of the employer, he or she is in breach of the contract. In theory, an employer can sue to recover damages for the breach by the employee not giving notice, but in practice this rarely occurs.

Written Notice

9.253 There is no legal requirement for an employee to give written notice of his or her resignation but it is recommended that employers ask employees to confirm a verbal resignation in writing. This can help avoid any doubt as to the fact that the employee has resigned and confirms the date of the resignation. In turn, the employer should write to the employee accepting the resignation and stating:
- when the employee's last working day will be
- the effective date of termination
- payment details, including any holiday pay the employee has accrued but not yet taken.

9.254 The employer could also use the confirmation of resignation letter to invite an employee to attend an exit interview.

Date of Termination

9.255 The effective date of termination is important as, if the employee intends to bring a claim for unfair or constructive dismissal at tribunal after his or her employment has ended he or she will have three months in which to bring a claim from this date. This three-month time limit is, however, automatically extended to six months in circumstances where the employee has raised an internal grievance under the statutory grievance procedure specified in the Employment Act 2002, or in circumstances where, at the expiry of the three-month time limit, the employee reasonably believed that an internal appeal process was still underway.

9.256 Even if an employee resigns on what appears to be good terms, employers should bear in mind that the employee may still apply to a tribunal after the employment relationship has ended.

Withdrawing Notice of Resignation

9.257 A resignation, once given by an employee, cannot be withdrawn unless the employer agrees. The exception, however, is where a resignation is given in the heat of the moment and is then withdrawn quickly.

Working During Notice Period

9.258 An employer may require an employee to work during his or her notice period. In many cases, this is essential as there will be work to be completed and a replacement to be found. If the employee is leaving, however, to join a competitor, it is common to place the employee on garden leave, ie paid leave or absence during the notice period.

Heat of the Moment Resignations

9.259 There have been numerous dismissal cases where resignations given in the heat of the moment have been accepted by the employer, when, in fact, the employer should have given the employee time to cool off.

9.260 In the case of *Langlands and McAinsh Ltd v Shearer*, for example, the Employment Appeal Tribunal held that words spoken in the heat of the moment should not be taken as a serious intention to resign.

9.261 Where an employee resigns in the heat of the moment, a prudent employer should consider whether the employee really intended to resign. Employers should not immediately conclude that words spoken in anger amount to a resignation without first seeking further clarification of the employee's intentions. It is also wise to take into account the employee's length of service and previous good record and perhaps invite the employee to consider the matter and withdraw his or her resignation (See *G Gale Ltd v Gilbert*).

Warning of Dismissal

9.262 It is not unheard of for employees who are being performance managed or undergoing disciplinary proceedings to resign rather than see the proceedings through to the end.

9.263 In these circumstances the employment will terminate due to the employee resigning, rather than due to dismissal, even if, had the disciplinary procedures continued, the end result would have been a dismissal. The only exception would be where the disciplinary procedure had been carried out unfairly, which might provide

Resignation and Constructive Dismissal

grounds for a claim of constructive dismissal. If the employee is working his or her notice, it is open to an employer to continue with the disciplinary procedure during this time.

9.264 The outcome would be different if the employee was pressured into resigning or threatened with dismissal if he or she did not resign. In this case an employment tribunal would be likely to treat the resignation as a dismissal.

9.265 Similarly, if an employee is "invited" to resign on favourable terms set against a background of disciplinary action and a warning that further acts of misconduct or unsatisfactory performance are likely to lead to dismissal, this may constitute a breach of the implied term of trust and confidence and give the employee grounds to claim constructive dismissal (see *Billington v Michael Hunter and Sons Ltd* (2003) EAT (0578/03).

9.266 Where an employee hears that his or her employment is to be terminated in the future — eg due to a potential redundancy situation — and resigns, again the employment will terminate because of the employee's resignation and a dismissal does not occur, even if a dismissal would have occurred at a later date, had the employment continued.

Constructive Dismissal

9.267 Constructive dismissal occurs when an employee resigns claiming that there was a fundamental breach of contract on the part of the employer, and that this breach caused him or her to resign.

9.268 Examples of the kind of behaviour on the part of the employer that could lead to claims of constructive dismissal include:

- harassment of an employee
- unilateral variation of an employee's terms and conditions of employment, eg a change in working hours.

9.269 In order to bring a claim for unfair constructive dismissal, an employee must have at least one year's service and be able to show that the reason for his or her leaving is due to the repudiatory breach of the contract by the employer (See *Western Excavating (ECC) Ltd v Sharp* [1978] IRLR 27).

9.270 The breach of contract must have already occurred (an actual breach) or be anticipated (an anticipatory breach). If the breach is an anticipatory breach, the employer must have clearly indicated that it intends to breach the contract. An employer simply proposing changes in contractual terms would not be enough for an employee to bring a claim for constructive dismissal. Another important condition, therefore, is that employees must not act too hastily. On the other hand, if they intend to bring a claim they should also not delay too long before resigning, as even a short delay may signify acceptance of the breach. In *Kerry Foods Ltd v Lynch* [2005] IRLR 680 EAT, an employee who resigned following his employer's proposal to dismiss him and offer re-engagement on revised terms (including a longer working week and reduced holiday entitlement) failed in his claim for constructive dismissal. The EAT held that there had been no dismissal because the employer had not gone ahead and unilaterally varied the contract, but instead had proposed to give lawful notice in accordance with the terms of the contract. A proposal to give lawful notice under the contract cannot amount to a breach of contract.

9.271 Where a repudiatory breach of contract has occurred, the employee must show that he or she accepts the repudiation and resign. It is not possible for an employee to bring a claim for unfair constructive dismissal without resigning first.

9.272 Since the implementation in October 2004 of the Employment Act 2002

(Dispute Resolution) Regulations 2004, employees are required to implement step one of a statutory grievance procedure in order to be entitled to lodge certain claims with the employment tribunal, including constructive dismissal claims. This involves the employee writing to the employer outlining his or her grievance and then waiting 28 days before lodging the claim.

9.273 Tribunals however, are tending to take a lenient approach to what constitutes a grievance letter. Some general principles upheld by the EAT are that:

- the employee is not required to state his or her intention to raise a "grievance" or even mention the word "grievance" when he or she writes to the employer about a complaint
- the employee's letter need not comply with the employer's contractual grievance procedure in order to constitute a grievance under the statutory grievance procedure
- a grievance can be contained in a letter of resignation
- the employee need not raise the grievance in such a way as to allow the employer to deal with it
- a letter written by an employee's representative or agent (eg a solicitor) can constitute a grievance for the purpose of the statutory grievance procedure
- the employee need not provide every detail of his or her complaint in writing; it will be sufficient that the general nature of the complaint is made clear.

9.274 In essence, all the employee has to do to fulfil step one of the statutory grievance procedure is to set out his or her complaint in writing and give the employer a copy of it. An email, or a series of emails, will suffice for this purpose.

Exit Interviews

9.275 It is rare for employees to be recruited without first having an interview. Yet many employees leave their company without undergoing an exit or termination interview of any kind. Such an interview can provide a source of very useful information and can be used by employers to serve a variety of purposes, eg to:

- establish the root causes of resignations, especially useful if turnover is high
- remedy high turnover
- monitor the effectiveness of recruitment
- identify problems with supervisors, work or morale
- update the job description
- limit the possibility of potential constructive dismissal claims.

9.276 Employees who are about to leave a company usually feel free to comment on such aspects as their place of work, the people they work with, the job they do, etc. The exit interview represents an ideal opportunity for employers to gather feedback on their company and should therefore not be missed.

9.277 The employee's immediate supervisor is usually not the best person to conduct the interview, even though he or she will usually know most about the individual concerned. If the supervisor is the employee's reason for leaving, the truth is not likely to emerge in an exit interview conducted by him or her. It is therefore usually preferable for the employee to be interviewed by a more senior manager or someone from the HR department.

9.278 An exit interview should be carried out as soon as possible after it is known that the employee is leaving. Any attempts to persuade the employee not to leave, if appropriate, are more likely to succeed this way. It is also much better for morale if members of the workforce feel their employer is concerned enough about resignations to ask about one at the earliest opportunity.

Training

9.279 It is important that managers:
- are aware of when a resignation is genuine
- handle resignations appropriately
- are clear of the employee's rights and obligations.

9.280 In addition, training on conducting exit interviews can ensure that the exit interview does not become a mere paper exercise, but instead a useful fact-finding tool.

List of Relevant Legislation

9.281
- Employment Act 2002 (Dispute Resolution) Regulations 2004
- Employment Act 2002
- Employment Rights Act 1996

List of Relevant Cases

9.282
- *Galaxy Showers Ltd v Wilson* [2006] IRLR 83, EAT
- *Mark Warner Ltd v Aspland* [2006] IRLR 87, EAT
- *Shergold v Fieldway Medical Centre* (2005) EAT 0487/05
- *Thorpe and anor v Poat and anor* (2005) EAT 0503/05
- *Billington v Michael Hunter and Sons Ltd* [2003] EAT (0578/03)
- *Western Excavating (ECC) Ltd v Sharp* [1978] IRLR 27, CA
- *Gale BG Ltd v Gilbert* [1978] IRLR 453
- *Langlands and McAinsh Ltd v Shearer*

Retirement

This topic covers the following.
- Contractual Retirement Age
- Discriminatory Retirement Ages
- Exclusion from the Right to Claim Unfair Dismissal and Statutory Redundancy Pay
- Normal Retirement Age
- Flexible Retirement Ages
- Changing Employees' Contractual Retirement Age
- Leading up to Retirement
- Early Retirement
- The Distinction between Voluntary Early Retirement and Voluntary Redundancy
- Age Discrimination Legislation and its Impact on Retirement
- Mutual Consent to Retirement
- The Right to Request to Continue Working beyond Retirement
- Notification of Retirement
- Automatically Unfair Dismissals
- Good Practice
- Pensions

Employers' Duties

9.283 Employers are under a duty to:
- operate any contractual retirement ages so that they are the same for men and women
- ensure that any contractual retirement age applied is defined as an age in years
- make sure that any retirement age to be applied to a group of employees has been clearly specified and communicated, and agreed as part of employees' contracts
- refrain from attempting to raise or lower the age at which existing employees are required to retire without first consulting employees or their representatives to seek agreement to the particular change
- refrain from exerting pressure on employees to leave prior to age 65 (or their contractual retirement age if that is higher or lower than 65)
- review retirement schemes to ensure compliance with the age discrimination regulations.

9.284 Since the implementation of the Employment Equality (Age) Regulations 2006 on 1 October 2006, the following further duties oblige employers to:
- refrain from requiring employees to retire before age 65, unless a younger retirement age can be justified
- take seriously any request from an employee to work on beyond age 65 and follow through a "duty-to-consider procedure"
- give employees approaching retirement age a minimum of six months' (but not more than 12 months') notice of their retirement date and at the same time inform them of their right to request to continue working longer
- hold a meeting with the employee to discuss the request to continue working and, if necessary, hold an appeal meeting.

Employees' Duties

9.285 Since the Employment Equality (Age) Regulations 2006 came into force on 1 October 2006, employees have a duty to:
- not discriminate against any of their colleagues on the grounds of age
- submit any request to continue working beyond age 65 no later than three months before their operative retirement date.

In Practice

Introduction

9.286 The Employment Equality (Age) Regulations 2006 introduced a default retirement age of 65. This is not a mandatory retirement age, but rather the age at or above which employers may (if they wish) require employees to retire without having to provide justification. The Employment Rights Act 1996 was also amended to the effect that the termination of an employee's employment on grounds of retirement is now a potentially fair reason for dismissal.

9.287 This means that employers are entitled, if they wish, to:
- operate a compulsory contractual retirement age of 65
- impose retirement at a defined age above 65
- permit employees to continue working as long as they like, ie have no specified retirement age
- adopt a policy of flexible retirement under which employees may choose to retire at any time within a specified age bracket (so long as the lower age limit is not below age 65).

9.288 Employers are no longer able to require employees under age 65 to retire, unless they can objectively justify such a policy as being a proportionate means of achieving a legitimate aim.

9.289 Voluntary retirement schemes are not affected by the age discrimination regulations so long as any retirement under such a scheme is genuinely voluntary.

9.290 The age discrimination regulations allow employees to request to continue working beyond any retirement date notified by their employer.

Contractual Retirement Age

9.291 Many employers choose to specify a retirement age for their employees by making it a term of their contract that their employment will terminate when they attain a defined age. Any retirement age that is specified must be the same for men as for women. It is, however, permissible for an employer to apply differing retirement ages to different groups of employees (eg the retirement age for professional staff might be set at 68 and for manual staff at age 65). Such differentiations will be lawful provided that the different treatment is not based on or in any way connected with gender, and provided none of the contractual retirement ages is below 65 (unless the employer can show that operating a compulsory retirement age of below age 65 is appropriate and necessary with a view to achieving a legitimate business aim).

Discriminatory Retirement Ages

9.292 It is unlawful under the Sex Discrimination Act 1975 (as amended) to operate different retirement ages for men and women. This change to the law followed the ECJ's ruling in *Marshall v Southampton and South-West Hampshire Area Health Authority (Teaching)* [1986] IRLR 140, ECJ. If an employer does operate discriminatory retirement ages, they will not be enforceable.

Exclusion from the Right to Claim Unfair Dismissal and Statutory Redundancy Pay

9.293 Prior to the implementation of the Employment Equality (Age) Regulations 2006 (on 1 October 2006), employees aged 65 or over were generally precluded from bringing claims of unfair dismissal to tribunal. Similarly, employees who had reached their employer's normal retirement age, or age 65, were not entitled to make a claim for a statutory redundancy payment. These provisions have now been abolished and employees are eligible to claim unfair dismissal and/or statutory redundancy pay irrespective of their age at the time of their dismissals. The one key exception to this is where an employee aged 65 or above is dismissed by reason of retirement.

9.294 In addition, if an employee aged 65 or over is discriminated against on grounds of gender, race, disability, religion, sexual orientation or age, whether during employment or on dismissal, he or she will be able to bring a claim for the discrimination suffered irrespective of his or her age at the time (with the exception of employees who are retired at or above age 65 who are prevented from claiming that their retirement is age discriminatory).

Normal Retirement Age

9.295 An employer's contractual retirement age (if one exists) will usually be their employees' "normal retirement age" provided the contractual retirement age is:
- defined as an age in years
- at or above age 65
- applied consistently to all employees within the group to which it applies
- the same for men and women.

9.296 Prior to the implementation of the Employment Equality (Age) Regulations 2006, complications could arise if an employer regularly disregarded or made exceptions to the implementation of a specific contractual retirement age, and thus regularly permitted employees to work on beyond that age. This could create expectations for other employees that they too would be permitted to work on beyond retirement age if they wished to do so.

9.297 In such circumstances, the employer could no longer rely on the contractual age as a valid reason to terminate employees' employment. Instead employees could reasonably expect to be retired at a different (higher) age or an age of their own choosing. The result could be that an employee required to retire at the contractual retirement age could succeed in a claim for unfair dismissal. Such a claim would be founded on the assertion that retirement was not the real reason for termination and/or that the employee's normal retirement age was some higher age.

9.298 Since the introduction of the retirement provisions contained in the Employment Equality (Age) Regulations 2006, it is not clear whether the difficulties described above are likely to remain. Further new measures in the Employment Rights Act 1996 provide that where an employee's dismissal at or above age 65 is genuinely by reason of retirement and where mandatory pre-retirement procedures (see below) have been fully followed, the dismissed employee cannot challenge his or her dismissal as unfair.

9.299 Employers should nevertheless be aware that regularly departing from the contractual retirement age for some employees can create a precedent for others and ultimately have the effect that employees may develop an expectation that they will be permitted to continue working beyond the stated retirement age, even where the retirement age is clearly stipulated in employees' contracts of employment.

9.300 In *Waite v Government Communications Headquarters* [1983] IRLR 341, the House of Lords confirmed that an employer's contractual retirement age will not always be the normal retirement age for employees. The House of Lords defined the criteria that will be relevant in determining an employer's normal retirement age as follows.

- Where an employer has specified a contractual retirement age, this age will be presumed to be the normal retirement age. However, this presumption may be rebutted if there is evidence that employees regularly retire at a different age or at no specified age.
- If there is evidence that the employer's contractual retirement age has in practice been replaced by another precise higher age, then that higher age will usually be the normal retirement age.
- If the evidence demonstrates that the employer's contractual retirement age is not being adhered to, and employees are in practice permitted to retire whenever they choose, there will be no normal retirement age.
- The overall test will be the reasonable expectation of employees within the specific part of the organisation at the relevant time.

Flexible Retirement Ages

9.301 Many employers nowadays are abolishing compulsory retirement ages and instead introducing a more flexible approach to retirement. Giving employees the choice to work for as long as they are able to is regarded as best practice. In the future, this may become a necessity due to changing demographics in Britain. A report from the Office for National Statistics, *The labour market participation of older people — An investigation into the labour market participation of older people and an examination of the characteristics of older workers*, indicates that by 2024, people over the age of 50 will constitute 40% of the total population. Equally, the number of people under the age of 50 will have dropped, meaning that fewer younger people will be available to replace those who retire.

9.302 Alternatively, a scheme that permits employees to retire at any time between a lower and an upper age (eg between ages 60 and 70) could be introduced. Any such flexible retirement schemes should be agreed with employees or their representatives through a process of consultation.

Changing Employees' Contractual Retirement Age

9.303 An employer may not elect to change the age at which existing employees are required to retire without first obtaining employees' agreement to such a change. This is because any variation to employees' contractual terms and conditions requires agreement from both parties. This should be sought through a process of consultation with the employees or their representatives. Often the best approach is to seek to introduce a bracket between which employees may choose their retirement age. The employer may also wish to consider abolishing compulsory retirement ages altogether.

9.304 In *Bratko v Beloit Walmsley Ltd* [1995] IRLR 629, the EAT ruled that it was not permissible for an employer to introduce a new lower retirement age of 64 for a group of employees whose contractual retirement age had previously been 65 without taking the necessary steps to reach agreement to the change.

9.305 As a result of the implementation of the Employment Equality (Age) Regulations 2006, employers are not now permitted to operate a compulsory retirement age below age 65, unless the policy of applying a lower retirement age can be shown to be appropriate and necessary with a view to the achievement of a legitimate business aim. Where the employer in the past operated a contractual retirement age below age 65, that would have to be changed from 1 October 2006. One effective way of dealing with this requirement is to:

- give all existing employees (who were previously subject to a contractual retirement age below 65) the right to choose to retire at their original contractual retirement age or continue in employment up to a new retirement age of 65 or over; and
- for all new employees, stipulate a contractual retirement age of 65 or above; or
- abolish compulsory retirement ages altogether and permit employees to make their own decisions about when to stop work.

Leading up to Retirement

9.306 It is considered good practice to implement a scheme under which employees are encouraged to reduce their working hours gradually in the period running up to their retirement. This could involve employees working progressively fewer hours or days per week over a period of, for example, one or two years prior to their retirement date, depending of course on the needs of the business.

Early Retirement

9.307 Early retirement is retirement prior to the employee's normal retirement age. Compulsory early retirement is likely to give rise to claims for unfair dismissal and age discrimination. Voluntary early retirement, however, will not constitute a dismissal in law, unless the employer has exerted pressure on the employee to leave prior to his or her normal retirement age. Usually, early retirement will constitute termination by mutual agreement on the basis that it represents an agreement between the parties to bring forward the previously agreed end of the employee's contract of employment. Alternatively, early retirement may sometimes be regarded as a resignation.

9.308 Voluntary retirement schemes are not affected by the introduction of the Employment Equality (Age) Regulations 2006 so long as any retirement under such a scheme is genuinely voluntary.

The Distinction between Voluntary Early Retirement and Voluntary Redundancy

9.309 The position of an employee taking voluntary early retirement contrasts with that of employees volunteering for redundancy. Voluntary redundancy is viewed in law as a dismissal (usually a fair dismissal). It follows that volunteers for redundancy are entitled to statutory redundancy pay in the same way as those selected for redundancy compulsorily by the employer, provided only that a genuine redundancy situation exists in the first place.

9.310 In contrast, employees who retire early are not entitled to a statutory redundancy payment, even in circumstances in which the employer would otherwise have had to make redundancies, eg to cut costs. The same principle applies to those who retire at their employer's contractual retirement age, ie there will be no entitlement to any statutory redundancy payment.

9.311 Whether the termination of an employee's employment constitutes a genuine early retirement or a redundancy dismissal is not always clear. In *Birch and Humber v University of Liverpool* [1985] IRLR 165, CA, the employees who had applied for and been granted early retirement under an existing scheme that made it clear that it was not a redundancy scheme were not entitled to redundancy pay as their termination was by mutual agreement and was therefore not a redundancy dismissal. This was against a background where the employer needed to make substantial cuts to its staff numbers and had invited employees to apply for early retirement. The Court of Appeal nevertheless acknowledged that early retirement can sometimes amount to a dismissal rather than termination by mutual agreement.

Age Discrimination Legislation and its Impact on Retirement

9.312 On 1 October 2006, important new age discrimination legislation was implemented by means of the Employment Equality (Age) Regulations 2006. These regulations, among other things, introduced a statutory default retirement age of 65 for all employers (except the armed forces). This is not a mandatory retirement age, but is simply a means of permitting employers to set retirement ages at or above age 65, but not below this age unless the employer can show that the specified earlier retirement age is appropriate and necessary in order to achieve a legitimate aim.

9.313 Under the regulations, the upper age limits on bringing claims for unfair dismissal and statutory redundancy pay to tribunal were abolished. Correspondingly, retirement has become a potentially fair reason for dismissal. Thus an employee who is genuinely retired at age 65, at a specified higher retirement age or at a lower age that the employer can objectively justify will normally have no grounds on which to succeed in a claim for unfair dismissal (or age discrimination).

9.314 A retirement will constitute a fair dismissal provided all of the following conditions are met:
- retirement is the true reason for the termination of the individual's employment
- it takes effect at the default retirement age of 65, or
- it takes effect at a higher retirement age specified by the employer, or
- it takes effect at a lower age which is the employer's normal retirement age and which is objectively justified
- the employer has provided the employee with written notification of his or her retirement date between six and 12 months in advance
- the employer has properly notified the employee of his or her right to request to stay on
- the employer has complied with the "duty to consider procedure" (see below) in respect of any such request.

9.315 If a retirement does not take place at or after age 65 (or at the employer's own lower retirement age if this is objectively justified), or if proper pre-retirement procedures have not been carried out (see below), then the employee will be able to challenge his or her dismissal. The burden of proof in these circumstances is on the employer to convince the tribunal that the reason for the employee's dismissal was in fact retirement and not a pretext for some other reason, eg redundancy or declining job performance. If the employer is unable to substantiate retirement as the reason for dismissal in these circumstances, the employee will succeed in his or her claim.

9.316 Unless a retirement age below age 65 can be objectively justified in the particular case, an employer that wishes to terminate an employee's employment before he or she reaches age 65 must ensure that it has another fair reason for dismissing the employee and that they follow the statutory dismissal and disciplinary procedure (DDP).

9.317 There is, however, no duty on employers to follow the DDP where the reason for dismissal is retirement, as new pre-retirement procedures apply instead (see below).

Mutual Consent to Retirement

9.318 If an employee volunteers to retire at the employer's normal retirement age, then this will constitute a retirement by mutual consent and will not be a dismissal. In theory therefore, the prescribed retirement procedures (see below) would not have to be followed. Employers would be advised, in these circumstances, to make sure that the employee had genuinely volunteered to leave and that the mutual consent to retirement was clearly recorded in writing and signed by both parties.

The Right to Request to Continue Working beyond Retirement

9.319 Under the age discrimination regulations, employees have the right to request to continue working beyond the age of 65, or beyond their employer's normal retirement age if this is other than age 65. Employers, correspondingly, are subject to a "duty to consider procedure" in respect of any compulsory retirement. The "duty to consider" procedure applies each time an employer wishes to retire an employee (unless the retirement is as a result of a mutual agreement – see above).

9.320 An employee making such a request is under a duty to submit the request in writing no later than three months before the operative date of retirement. The employee also has to specify exactly what he or she wants, ie whether the request is to continue working indefinitely or for a defined limited period. The employee is not obliged, however, to provide any reason for his or her request.

9.321 The duty-to-consider procedure obliges the employer, when a valid request to continue working is received, to hold a meeting with the employee "within a reasonable period" to discuss the possibility of continued working, provide a decision as soon as is reasonably practicable after the meeting and allow a right of appeal against any refusal.

9.322 There is no need for an employer to justify a refusal to permit an employee to work on beyond retirement age, or even to give the employee a reason for refusing his or her request. The duty on employers is only that they must follow through the statutory procedure if a valid request is made. A failure to follow the procedure will, however, render the employee's retirement an automatically unfair dismissal.

Notification of Retirement

9.323 Employers are obliged under the new age discrimination regulations to give employees approaching retirement age between six and 12 months' written notice of their impending retirement date and at the same time notify them of their right to make a request to continue working longer (see above).

9.324 The age discrimination regulations state that employers cannot rely on the terms of an employee's contract or notification of retirement age contained in an organisation's retirement policy or handbook for this purpose.

9.325 Where the employer fails to provide this notice by the date that falls six months before the employee's operative retirement date, the duty to do so continues up until two weeks before the retirement date.

9.326 Where an employer fails to provide written notification to the employee of his or her retirement date, by two weeks before that date, or fails completely to do so, retirement on that date will constitute an automatically unfair dismissal.

9.327 These rules do not restrict employees from electing to take early retirement, if this is an option available to them under their contract of employment or their employer's pension scheme.

Automatically Unfair Dismissals

9.328 In line with the provisions outlined above, termination of employment by reason of retirement will constitute an automatically unfair dismissal if, prior to the retirement date, the employer has:
- failed altogether to notify the employee of his or her proposed retirement date
- informed the employee of the proposed retirement date less than two weeks before that date
- failed to inform the employee that he or she has a right to request to continue working
- failed to comply fully with the "duty-to-consider procedure".

9.329 An employee who has not been properly notified of his or her operative retirement date, or whose employer has not complied with the duty to consider procedure, may bring a freestanding claim to an employment tribunal on either or both of these grounds and may be awarded compensation of up to eight weeks' pay.

Good Practice

9.330 The following good practice is recommended.
- Base retirement policy on business needs while also giving individuals as much choice as possible.
- Ensure that the loss to the organisation of skills and abilities is fully evaluated when operating early-retirement schemes.
- Do not see age as the sole criterion when operating an early retirement scheme (subject to pension rules).
- Avoid making stereotypical assumptions about the capabilities of older employees.
- Use flexible retirement schemes where possible.
- Use phased retirement where possible to allow employees to alter the balance of their working and personal lives gradually and prepare for full-time retirement.
- Offer employees pre-retirement training to help them adjust to and plan for their retirement.

Pensions

9.331 The implementation of a default retirement age of 65 does not impact on the age at which an individual becomes entitled to a state or occupational pension.

9.332 From 1 December 2006, it is unlawful for occupational pension schemes to discriminate against members or prospective members on the basis of age and trustees of such schemes are obliged to disapply or change any age discriminatory rules. There are, however, exemptions applicable to most age-related criteria within occupational pension schemes.

Training

9.333 Employers should make sure that all their line managers are familiar with the organisation's policies and rules on retirement and of the possible implications of deviating from these rules.

9.334 More importantly, training should be given to managers on the implications of the age discrimination legislation — the Employment Equality (Age) Regulations 2006 — to ensure that all managers are familiar with the concept of age discrimination and the practical effect it has on employees' rights in respect of retirement. The training should include the requirement to provide between six and 12 months' notice of retirement and how to fulfil the "duty to consider procedure" when a request to continue working beyond the employee's operative retirement is received.

List of Relevant Legislation

9.335
- Employment Equality (Age) Regulations 2006
- Information and Consultation of Employees Regulations 2004
- Employment Equality (Religion or Belief) Regulations 2003
- Employment Equality (Sexual Orientation) Regulations 2003
- Fixed-Term Employees (Prevention of Less Favourable Treatment) Regulations 2002
- Part-Time Workers (Prevention of Less Favourable Treatment) Regulations 2000
- Transitional Information and Consultation of Employees Regulations 1999
- Employment Rights Act 1996
- Disability Discrimination Act 1995
- Trade Union and Labour Relations (Consolidation) Act 1992
- Race Relations Act 1976
- Sex Discrimination Act 1975

List of Relevant Cases

9.336
- *Bratko v Beloit Walmsley Ltd* [1995] IRLR 629
- *Marshall v Southampton and South-West Hampshire Area Health Authority (Teaching)* [1986] IRLR 140, ECJ
- *Birch and Humber v University of Liverpool* [1985] IRLR 165, CA
- *Waite v Government Communications Headquarters* [1983] IRLR 341, HL

Further Information

Organisations
- **Advisory Conciliation and Arbitration Service (Acas)**
  Web: *www.acas.org.uk*

Acas aims to improve organisations and working life through better employment relations. It provides up-to-date information, advice, high-quality training, and works with employers and employees to solve problems and improve performance.

- **Department for Business, Enterprise and Regulatory Reform (BERR)**
  Web: *www.berr.gov.uk*
  The Department for Business, Enterprise and Regulatory Reform brings together functions from the former Department of Trade and Industry (DTI), including responsibilities for productivity, business relations, energy, competition and consumers. It also drives regulatory reform.

Settlements and Compromise Agreements

This topic covers the following.
- Prohibition on Contracting Out of Statutory Employment Rights
- Settlement of Common Law Rights
- Conciliation Agreements
- Intervention of Acas Conciliation Officer
- Binding Effect of Agreement through Acas
- Effect of Communication of Settlement to Acas
- Drafting of Terms of Settlement Agreed Through Acas
- Agreement to Submit Dispute to Arbitration
- Compromise Agreements
- Requirements for a Valid Compromise Agreement
- Binding Effect of Valid Compromise Agreement
- Enforcement of Compromise Agreement
- Consent Orders

9.337 Employment legislation prevents employers from seeking to contract out of, or waive, statutory employment rights, duties and responsibilities. This is because employers and employees are usually in unequal bargaining positions. It follows that legislation designed to give employees rights would be ineffective if employers could persuade or pressurise employees to agree that such provisions should not apply.

9.338 However, where an employment dispute arises between an employer and an employee, it will often be in the interests of both parties for such a dispute to be resolved by agreement, given the uncertainties of legal proceedings, as they can be protracted and expensive. It is also important that the parties can rely upon any such agreement having binding effect.

9.339 There are a number of ways in which individual employment disputes can be settled by means of a legally binding agreement.

Employers' Duties

9.340 The following duties apply to employers.
- Employers must not impose contractual restrictions on employees' statutory employment rights, and any such restrictions will be deemed to be void.
- If the employer wishes to settle or resolve a claim by the employee in respect of his or her statutory employment rights, they will need to ensure the agreement reached is:
  - a conciliation agreement arrived at through the involvement of Acas; or
  - a compromise agreement which satisfies the requirements for such an agreement, including the requirement that the employee has received independent advice; or
  - a consent order made by the employment tribunal or which forms the basis upon which the tribunal dismisses the proceedings by consent.
- If seeking to use a compromise agreement to settle a dispute with an employee, the employer should ensure all the requirements for a compromise agreement to be valid are met.

Employees' Duties

- The employee should understand that if they enter into any of the following types of agreement, the agreement can be enforced by the employer through the courts.
  - Conciliation agreement arrived at through Acas.
  - Valid compromise agreement.
  - Consent order made by the employment tribunal.

In Practice

Prohibition on Contracting Out of Statutory Employment Rights

9.341 The laws that create statutory employment rights, such as the right not to be unfairly dismissed, also make provision for employees and other workers to complain to an employment tribunal about the infringement of such rights. At the same time, the law prevents employers from seeking to contract out of, or waive, the employment right in question (eg see the Employment Rights Act 1996 s.203).

Settlement of Common Law Rights

9.342 The relationship between employer and employee may give rise to legal disputes that do not involve the employee's statutory employment rights. Personal injury claims arising out of the duty of care owed by an employer to an employee, and breach of contract claims based upon the employee's contractual rights, are very common. These are common law causes of action, capable of being pursued through the ordinary courts.

9.343 At common law, as a matter of general principle, parties to any dispute are capable of coming to an agreement out of court whereby they agree to compromise their dispute, ie settle their claim. The agreement to compromise, once reached, operates as a bar to the further pursuit of the dispute in courts or tribunals, except to the extent of the right to bring an action to enforce the agreement itself.

Conciliation Agreements

9.344 Despite the general restriction on contracting out of employment rights, employers and employees may agree to settle their dispute through the intervention of a conciliation officer from the Advisory, Conciliation and Arbitration Service (Acas).

9.345 The main statutory employment rights that can be the subject of an agreement to refrain from instituting or continuing proceedings, where the agreement is through Acas, are those arising under the Employment Tribunals Act 1996 s.18(1).

9.346 The main employment issues in which Acas conciliates are as follows.
- Unfair dismissal.
- Redundancy pay.
- Failure to provide written reasons for dismissal.
- Failure to provide itemised pay statement.
- Unlawful deductions from wages.

Settlements and Compromise Agreements

- Entitlement to guarantee pay.
- Right to remuneration while suspended on medical grounds.
- Right to equal access to and treatment under occupational pension scheme.
- Time off:
  - for employee representatives for the purposes of consultation on redundancy/business transfers
  - to look for work/training when made redundant
  - for pension fund trustees
  - for public duties
  - for trade union duties/activities.
- Maternity:
  - time off for ante-natal care
  - return to work after maternity leave
  - offer of alternative work before suspension for health and safety reasons
  - remuneration when suspended for health and safety reasons.
- Adoption
- return to work after adoption leave.
- Equal pay.
- Discrimination because of:
  - sex
  - race
  - disability
  - sexual orientation
  - religion or belief
  - age
  - status as part-time or fixed-term worker or employee.
- Detriment (action short of dismissal) on grounds of:
  - trade union reasons
  - employee representatives elected for consultation/business transfers
  - health and safety reasons
  - pension fund trustees
  - whistleblowing
  - assertion of employment rights, such as in respect of working time, Sunday working, etc.
- Refusal of employment or the services of an employment agency because of membership or non-membership of a trade union.
- Consultation through employee representatives about redundancy/business transfers.
- Entitlement to protective award in respect of non-consultation over redundancy/business transfers.
- Trade union regulation:
  - deduction of unauthorised or excessive trade unions subscriptions
  - exclusion/expulsion from trade union other than for a permitted reason
  - political fund contributions
  - unjustifiable trade union disciplinary action.
- Working time.
- Minimum wage.

9.347 Since 1 October 2004, the dispute resolution regulations limit Acas's duty to conciliate to a fixed period for each case.

Intervention of Acas Conciliation Officer

9.348 Under the Employment Tribunals Act 1996 s.18, it is the duty of the conciliation officer to endeavour to promote a settlement of a claim lodged with the employment tribunal, whenever requested to do so by the parties, or on his or her own initiative, if the conciliation officer considers that there are some prospects of a settlement. Provision is also made for the intervention of a conciliation officer in respect of potential claims before tribunal proceedings are commenced, where a request is made by one of the potential parties.

9.349 In unfair dismissal cases, the conciliation officer is required to seek to promote a settlement through the reinstatement or re-engagement of the complainant, save where the complainant does not wish to be reinstated or re-engaged, or it is not practicable.

9.350 The conciliation officer will not give advice as to the merits or demerits of the case, nor recommend what form a settlement should take, but will be able to act as an impartial intermediary to facilitate communication between the parties. In *Clarke and ors v Redcar and Cleveland Borough Council and Wilson and ors v Stockton-on-Tees Borough Council* [2006] IRLR 324, the EAT emphasised also that Acas conciliation officers have no responsibility to ensure that the terms of a settlement are fair to the claimant.

The Employment Tribunals (Constitution and Rules of Procedure) Regulations 2004

9.351 It should be noted that under the Employment Tribunals (Constitution and Rules of Procedure) Regulations 2004 (which came into force on 1 October 2004) amendments were made to the duties of Acas conciliation officers to conciliate in a tribunal claim. In cases which do not involve a claim of unlawful discrimination or protected disclosure there is a fixed period of conciliation. A short conciliation period of seven weeks applies to straightforward claims such as those for breach of contract or unlawful deductions from pay.

9.352 For most other claims there is a standard conciliation period of 13 weeks which can be extended by two weeks only if Acas notifies the secretary in writing that:
- all parties agree to the extension
- a proposal for settlement is under consideration
- all parties probably will settle within the extended period.

9.353 For claims of unlawful discrimination and those involving a protected disclosure, there is no limit to the length of the conciliation period.

9.354 Within the fixed conciliation period, which runs from the date the employee's application to the tribunal is sent to the employer, Acas has a duty to act to conciliate cases but, outside of the fixed time period, they have no such duty although they may, at their discretion, continue to provide conciliation services to the parties in dispute.

Binding Effect of Agreement through Acas

9.355 The effect of an agreement arrived at through the intervention of a conciliation officer is that the employee will be barred from pursuing his or her claim through the employment tribunal. Where a settlement is reached before or without any involvement from Acas, it will not usually be possible to get Acas to confirm and validate such an agreement. In such situations, any such agreement would need to be drawn up as a compromise agreement in order to be valid and binding.

Effect of Communication of Settlement to Acas

9.356 Where the settlement is arrived at through Acas, the wording of the terms of any agreement will be incorporated by Acas into a document referred to as a COT 3 agreement. However, it is well established that an oral agreement arrived at through Acas does not need to have been recorded in writing on a COT 3 form in order to be binding. (See *Gilbert v Kembridge Fibres Ltd* [1984] IRLR 52, EAT.)

Drafting of Terms of Settlement Agreed Through Acas

9.357 While it is permissible to state in an agreement that the agreement is in full and final settlement of all claims arising out of a complainant's employment, or out of its termination, this is likely to be interpreted as only covering claims which were already known about at the time (*Livingstone v Hepworth Refractories plc* [1992] IRLR 63, EAT and *BCCI SA v Ali* [2001] IRLR 292, HL).

9.358 It is normally in the interest of the employer for the wording used in the COT3 form to be as wide as possible in its scope, ie covering all claims arising out of employment. However, in circumstances where the employer knows the specific claims likely to be made by an employee, ie where employment tribunal proceedings have already been issued, it would normally be advisable to include these complaints specifically, together with a term also including all other claims arising out of employment or out of termination of the employment.

Agreement to Submit Dispute to Arbitration

9.359 Another possible route to resolve a dispute is for the employer and employee to agree to arbitration under the Acas arbitration scheme pursuant to the Trade Union and Law Reform (Consolidation) Act 1992 s.212A. The Acas arbitration scheme is intended to provide a voluntary alternative to employment tribunals for the resolution of unfair dismissal disputes and disputes following a request for flexible working. This results in a binding decision on the matter by an arbitrator appointed by Acas.

Compromise Agreements

9.360 The other way for employers to settle an employment law dispute with an employee is through a compromise agreement.

9.361 Compromise agreements represent the other main exception to the prohibition against contracting out of the statutory provisions protecting employment rights.

9.362 The most significant statutory employment rights, in respect of which compromise agreements can be used, are those which arise under the following.
- Employment Equality (Age) Regulations 2006.
- Employment Equality (Religion or Belief) Regulations 2003.
- Employment Equality (Sexual Orientation) Regulations 2003.
- Fixed Term Employees (Prevention of Less Favourable Treatment) Regulations 2002.
- Part-time Workers (Prevention of Less Favourable Treatment) Regulations 2000.
- Working Time Regulations 1998.
- National Minimum Wage Act 1998.
- Employment Rights Act 1996.
- Disability Discrimination Act 1995.
- Trade Union and Labour Relations (Consolidation) Act 1992.
- Race Relations Act 1976.
- Sex Discrimination Act 1975.

- Equal Pay Act 1970.

Requirements for a Valid Compromise Agreement

9.363 The main requirements for a valid compromise agreement are as follows.
- The agreement must be in writing.
- The agreement must relate to the particular complaint or proceedings concerned. In practice, this requirement can be construed as meaning that the only claims that can be settled by way of a compromise agreement are claims that have already been raised by the employee. If a matter that forms the basis of a potential claim has not previously been raised by the employee, then it is doubtful whether a compromise agreement which purports to settle such a claim will be valid. In *Hinton v University of East London* [2005] EWCA Civ 532, the Court of Appeal upheld a tribunal's decision that a compromise agreement must specify the particular statutory claim to be compromised and that a general "catch-all" provision was insufficient. The compromise agreement in this case was drafted to state that all outstanding claims that the employee had were to be compromised and then went on to cite a list of 11 specific causes of action. The list did not, however, include a claim for detriment for making a protected disclosure under s.47B of the Employment Rights Act 1996. The court ruled that the claimant's s.47B claim had not been compromised as it was not itemised in the agreement. Compromise agreements are frequently used for confirming agreement as to severance terms on the basis that the employee agrees not to bring tribunal proceedings after the termination of his or her employment. Before concluding such a compromise agreement, an employer would be well advised to get the employee to confirm in writing all the specific employment complaints he or she has against the employer.
- The employee or worker must have received advice from a relevant independent advisor as to the terms and effect of the proposed agreement and, in particular, its effect on his or her ability to pursue any employment rights before an employment tribunal. This means that advice must have been received from one of the following:
  – a barrister
  – a solicitor
  – a legal executive meeting, with a fellow of the Institute of Legal Executives, provided that the legal executive is properly supervised by a solicitor holding a Practising Certificate issued by the Law Society
  – officers, officials, employees or members of an independent trade union certified by the union as competent to give advice and authorised to do so on its behalf (provided the union is not the employer in question)
  – advisors working at an advice centre who are certified as competent to give advice and authorised to do so (provided the centre is not the employer, and the complainant has not paid for the advice).
- There must be in force, when the advisor gives the advice, a contract of insurance, or an indemnity provided for members of a profession or professional body, covering the risk of a claim by the employee or worker in respect of loss arising in consequence of the advice.
- The agreement must identify the advisor.
- The agreement must state that the conditions regulating compromise agreements are satisfied. In this respect, it is to be noted that the agreement must make reference to the statutory provisions governing compromise agreements in respect of each complaint that is covered by the compromise agreement (see *Lunt v Merseyside TEC Ltd* [1999] IRLR 458, EAT). For example, if the compromise agreement involves a settlement of complaints of unfair dismissal and sex discrimination, the agreement must specifically refer to the conditions regulating compromise agreements in the Employment Rights Act 1996 and the Sex Discrimination Act 1975 being satisfied.

Binding Effect of Valid Compromise Agreement

9.364 A valid compromise agreement will have the effect that the employment tribunal will not be permitted to hear any of the complaints referred to in the compromise agreement.

9.365 A compromise agreement can also validly deal with potential claims in respect of non-statutory employment rights, such as those arising as a result of breach of contract. It is sufficient for the agreement simply to confirm that any claims arising as a result of breach of contract are covered by the compromise agreement, since there are no specific requirements to be satisfied other than common law principles applicable to the validity of agreements.

Enforcement of Compromise Agreement

9.366 In addition to preventing the instigation or continuation of employment tribunal proceedings in respect of the claim concerned, a valid compromise agreement can be enforced through civil proceedings. Thus, if payment of a sum agreed under a compromise agreement was not forthcoming, a civil claim could be brought for the sum due under the agreement.

9.367 Such a claim could also be brought to an employment tribunal, provided that the claim arises or is outstanding on the termination of the employee's employment. The power of the employment tribunal to deal with such a complaint would be subject to the £25,000 limit on its contractual jurisdiction.

Consent Orders

9.368 Employers and employees who have reached a private agreement to settle a dispute may ask the employment tribunal (at the hearing) to validate their agreement.

9.369 The tribunal can make an order in the terms agreed between the parties or, more usually, will simply make an order dismissing the proceedings, by consent, on the basis that the complainant is withdrawing the proceedings, with terms of settlement having been agreed. Once the proceedings have been dismissed in this way, the complainant will no longer be able to bring, continue or reinstitute proceedings in respect of the original complaint. The complainant would, however, be able to take proceedings to enforce the agreement (in the unlikely event that it should be necessary).

9.370 Where an employee voluntarily withdraws his or her tribunal claim, it is advisable for the employer to apply to the tribunal to have the claim dismissed, as described above. If the employer does not do so, it would be theoretically possible for the complainant to change his or her mind and make a fresh claim to the tribunal on the same subject matter (provided the time limit for bringing the particular claim had not expired).

Training

9.371 Managers or human resources professionals directly involved in negotiating and agreeing settlements with employees will need to be trained in the main principles relevant to conciliated and compromise agreements. That said, effective negotiation on behalf of an employer, for the purpose of seeking an acceptable resolution to an employment dispute, also necessitates an understanding of the:
- legal issues involved in respect of the employment right being pursued by the employee

- basis upon which any potential financial liability on the part of the employer would be calculated in the event of a claim succeeding at tribunal
- procedures used for resolving disputes, whether through tribunal proceedings or court proceedings.

List of Relevant Legislation

9.372
- Employment Equality (Age) Regulations 2006
- Employment Equality (Sex Discrimination) Regulations 2005
- Employment Tribunals (Constitution and Rules of Procedure) (Amendment) Regulations 2005
- Employment Tribunals (Constitution and Rules of Procedure) (Amendment) (No. 2) Regulations 2005
- Employment Tribunals (Constitution and Rules of Procedure) Regulations 2004
- Employment Act 2002 (Dispute Resolution) Regulations 2004
- Employment Equality (Religion or Belief) Regulations 2003
- Employment Equality (Sexual Orientation) Regulations 2003
- Fixed-term Employees (Prevention of Less Favourable Treatment) Regulations 2002
- Part-time Workers (Prevention of Less Favourable Treatment) Regulations 2000
- Working Time Regulations 1998
- Employment Act 2002
- National Minimum Wage Age 1998
- Employment Rights Act 1996
- Employment Tribunals Act 1996
- Disability Discrimination Act 1995
- Trade Union and Labour Relations (Consolidation) Act 1992
- Race Relations Act 1976
- Sex Discrimination Act 1975
- Equal Pay Act 1970
- Compromise Agreements (Description of Person) Order 2005
- Compromise Agreements (Description of Person) Order 2004

List of Relevant Cases

9.373
- *Hinton v University of East London* [2005] IRLR 552, CA
- *BCCI SA v Ali* [2001] IRLR 292, HL
- *Lunt v Merseyside TEC Ltd* [1999] IRLR 458, EAT
- *Livingstone v Hepworth Refractories plc* [1992] IRLR 63, EAT
- *Gilbert v Kembridge Fibres Ltd* [1984] IRLR 52, EAT

Further Information

Organisations
- **Advisory Conciliation and Arbitration Service (Acas)**
  Web: *www.acas.org.uk*
  Acas aims to improve organisations and working life through better employment relations. It provides up-to-date information, advice, high-quality training, and works with employers and employees to solve problems and improve performance.

Summary Dismissal

> This topic covers the following.
> - Summary Dismissal
> - Summary Dismissal and Wrongful Dismissal
> - Disciplinary Procedures
> - Appropriate Employer Procedures
> - Before Dismissing an Employee Summarily
> - Mitigation after Summary Dismissal
> - Employer's Options for Employee Dismissal
> - Examples of Gross Misconduct
> - Proof of Conduct to Defend a Claim for Wrongful Dismissal
> - Payment in Lieu of Notice

9.374 Employees guilty of gross misconduct, amounting to a serious breach of their contract of employment, are liable to be summarily dismissed, without benefit of the notice to which they are otherwise entitled to terminate that contract of employment.

9.375 The word "summary" is not synonymous with "instant". Allegations of gross misconduct should be investigated thoroughly before a decision is taken to dismiss the employee in question. If those investigations are likely to take a little time, the employee should be suspended from work on full pay.

Employers' Duties

9.376 Employers must ensure that:
- employees are aware of the organisation's disciplinary procedure, disciplinary rules and the consequences of non-compliance with the rules
- employees are clearly informed of the types of conduct that will be regarded by the employer as gross misconduct leading to summary dismissal
- they follow their disciplinary procedure before summarily dismissing an employee
- their disciplinary procedure incorporates the three mandatory stages of the statutory dismissal and disciplinary procedure (DDP).

Employees' Duties

9.377 Employees must ensure that:
- they do not act in contravention of the employer's disciplinary rules or procedures
- they co-operate with the employer in the application of the disciplinary procedure
- following summary dismissal, they attempt to obtain alternative employment as soon as possible.

In Practice

Summary Dismissal

9.378 Summary dismissal means the termination of an employee's employment without notice or pay in lieu of notice, on the basis of the employee's gross misconduct.

9.379 For summary dismissal to be justified, the actions of the employee must be seen as fundamentally undermining the duty of trust and confidence between employee and employer, to the extent that the employer is no longer required to retain the employee in his employment or be bound by any of the terms of the contract, eg the requirement to give notice.

9.380 Care should be exercised as a summary dismissal can become an unfair dismissal if the correct procedures are not followed.

Summary Dismissal and Wrongful Dismissal

9.381 A dismissal without giving the employee adequate notice or payment in lieu of notice constitutes a breach by the employer of the contract of employment. This allows the employee to claim wrongful dismissal. A wrongfully dismissed employee is entitled to damages equal to the pay and benefits he or she would have received had he or she worked the notice period or been paid in lieu.

9.382 The only justification available to an employer for not giving notice or pay in lieu of notice is that the employee's conduct was so serious that it constituted gross misconduct, ie entitling the employer to dismiss the employee without notice.

Disciplinary Procedures

9.383 Changes to the law implemented on 1 October 2004 mean that it is a statutory requirement for the employer to have a written disciplinary procedure and to include details of the procedure within each employee's written statement of particulars of employment. Alternatively, the written statement can refer the employee to another accessible document which sets out the procedure, eg a staff handbook.

9.384 The employer's disciplinary procedures should provide a list of examples of behaviour which would be construed as gross misconduct and justify a summary dismissal.

9.385 The Acas guidelines on producing disciplinary and grievance procedures show employers how to establish and operate a disciplinary procedure.

Appropriate Employer Procedures

9.386 Although the employer can dismiss the employee without notice following an incident of gross misconduct, the employer should investigate the circumstances thoroughly and carry through a disciplinary procedure before it reaches any conclusion that the employee is guilty of gross misconduct.

9.387 Once the employer is aware or suspects that the employee may have committed an act of gross misconduct, they should meet with the employee and inform him or her of the allegations. This is called an investigation meeting.

9.388 The employer may then choose to suspend the employee, pending the outcome of a full investigation. The employee should remain on full pay for the duration of this suspension.

9.389 As part of the investigation, the employee should be given the opportunity to answer the allegations against him or her, including any evidence provided by witnesses.

9.390 Following the investigation, if there is evidence that the employee may be guilty of gross misconduct, the employer can proceed to a disciplinary hearing. The employer must, at this stage, write to the employee setting out the case against him or her and inviting him or her to attend the hearing. The employee will be entitled to be accompanied at the hearing by a fellow worker or trade union official of his or her choice, if he or she wishes. At the hearing itself, the employee must be given a full opportunity to state his or her case and present any mitigating factors.

9.391 After the disciplinary hearing, if the employer has reasonable grounds to form a genuine belief that the employee did commit an act of gross misconduct, they may proceed to dismissal. The employee should be informed of this outcome in writing and at the same time told that he or she has the right to appeal against the decision to dismiss, and how any such appeal should be lodged.

9.392 The disciplinary hearing should be conducted by an individual within the employer's organisation who was not involved in the initial investigation.

Before Dismissing an Employee Summarily

9.393 Before taking action for gross misconduct, employers should:
- establish a written disciplinary procedure
- provide a copy to all employees
- provide managers with training on this procedure.

Mitigation after Summary Dismissal

9.394 An employee who is summarily, wrongfully or unfairly dismissed is obliged to attempt to obtain alternative employment as soon as possible. The effect of not doing so is likely to be a reduction in any award of compensation in the event of a successful claim at an employment tribunal.

Employer's Options for Employee Dismissal

9.395 If the employer has grounds to dismiss the employee, the options are to:
- ignore the employee's conduct
- discipline the employee
- dismiss the employee with or without notice
- not dismiss the employee but sue him or her for damages — this applies in the event that the employer has suffered financial loss as a result of the employee's actions or omissions.

Ignore the Misconduct

9.396 By ignoring an act of gross misconduct, the employer is accepting the employee's breach of contract. The longer the employer leaves before dismissing the employee, the more likely it is that the employer will be seen by a tribunal as having

Summary Dismissal

accepted the breach. This means that any subsequent decision to dismiss the employee — or any other employee in the event of similar misconduct — summarily is likely to be unfair.

Discipline the Employee

9.397 The employer must follow correct procedures when disciplining an employee. The employer should establish its own procedures or show that a fair process of investigation and discipline, eg the processes outlined in the *Acas Code of Practice on Disciplinary and Grievance Procedures*, is followed at all times.

Dismiss the Employee with Notice

9.398 Dismissing the employee with notice implies that the employee has not committed an act of gross misconduct. A dismissal on notice will also count against any subsequent decision that similar misconduct committed by another employee constituted gross misconduct and justified summary dismissal.

Statutory Minimum Notice Periods

9.399 The statutory minimum notice for employees is outlined in the Employment Rights Act 1996. The relevant notice periods are set out in the table below.

Period of continuous service	Minimum notice to employee
Less than one month	None
One month	One week
Two years	Two weeks
Three years	Three weeks
etc	etc

9.400 The employee has an extra week's entitlement for every extra year of continuous service, up to a maximum entitlement of 12 weeks' notice after 12 years' service.

9.401 The contract of employment can enhance the minimum statutory entitlement but cannot reduce it.

Statutory Dismissal and Disciplinary Procedure (DDP)

9.402 If the employee is dismissed, the disciplinary procedure used must incorporate the three mandatory stages of the statutory dismissal and disciplinary procedure (DDP). These oblige the employer to:

- inform the employee in writing of the details of the case against him or her and invite him or her to attend a meeting
- hold a meeting at which both the employer and the employee have a full opportunity to state their cases
- allow a right of appeal against the subsequent decision to dismiss the employee.

9.403 A failure to follow any one of the above steps will mean that the employee's dismissal will be ruled automatically unfair by an employment tribunal, irrespective of the seriousness of the employee's misconduct.

9.404 For example, in *Masterfoods v Wilson* (2006) EAT 0202/06, a dismissed employee, who was denied an appeal hearing in respect of his dismissal because he had failed to set out the grounds for his appeal in writing within five days as required by his employer's contractual disciplinary procedure, succeeded in his claim for unfair dismissal. The fact that he had not been granted an appeal meant that the dismissal was automatically unfair and the requirements of the employer's own in-house procedure were irrelevant to that fact.

Dismiss the Employee Without Notice

9.405 In cases of gross misconduct, dismissing an employee without notice is often the best option. The conduct must, however, be serious enough to counter claims of wrongful or unfair dismissal, and the employer must act reasonably in all the circumstances. If the employee is summarily dismissed, the disciplinary procedure used must incorporate the three mandatory stages of the statutory dismissal and disciplinary procedure (DDP).

Consistency

9.406 It is important for employers to act consistently in their treatment of employees, eg if one employee is dismissed for a particular offence, then the subsequent commission of the same offence by a different employee should, normally, also lead to the penalty of dismissal. It may be, however, that there are material differences between the circumstances of two incidents in which case there may be justification for differences in treatment. For example, in *Enterprise Liverpool plc v Bauress and Ealey* EAT (2006) (0645/05) two joiners, both recently out of their apprenticeships, had used their employer's van and materials to perform work elsewhere (for profit) during working hours. Both were summarily dismissed. They subsequently argued before an employment tribunal that their dismissals were unfair because another employee who had previously committed the same offence had not been dismissed but given a final written warning instead.

9.407 The EAT held that it was within the band of reasonable responses for the employer to take into account the length of service (30 years) and good disciplinary record of the employee in the earlier case and his admission of guilt at the time. The two joiners on the other hand had short service (about three years) and had lied about their actions.

Do Not Dismiss the Employee, but Sue the Employee for Damages

9.408 Not dismissing the employee and suing him or her for damages instead is worth considering in the event of a breach of specific clauses of the employment contract — and where the employer has suffered financial loss as a result of the employee's actions. Such breaches might relate to restraint of trade or confidentiality or when the employee has taken up employment with a competitor. Alternatively the employer could dismiss without notice and sue for damages.

Examples of Gross Misconduct

9.409 The following is a non-exhaustive list of examples of behaviour that are likely to justify an employer dismissing the employee without notice, providing a fair procedure is followed:
- gross insubordination
- gross neglect of duty
- dishonesty
- theft
- being under the influence of alcohol and/or non-medication drugs at work
- physical violence
- serious bullying or harassment
- fraud or falsification of records

- serious misuse of the employer's computer system
- serious infringement of health and safety rules
- wilful damage to company property.

Proof of Conduct to Defend a Claim for Wrongful Dismissal

9.410 In order to defeat a claim for wrongful dismissal (ie dismissal that is in breach of the employee's contract usually because proper notice has not been given under the contract), the employer will have to justify a dismissal without notice. The key factor to consider is whether there has been a breach of contract by the employee and whether the breach is fundamental in nature. The employer can rely upon factors that come to light after the dismissal. This means that even if the employer had no reason to dismiss the employee when it did, if the employer has since discovered a reason, dismissal may not be wrongful, although it still may be unfair.

Burden of Proof

9.411 In dealing with a misconduct dismissal the employer should refer to the principles established in the case of *British Home Stores v Burchell* [1980] ICR 303. The employer should be satisfied that he or she can demonstrate:

- an honest belief that the employee was guilty of the offence
- reasonable grounds in support of that belief
- that these reasonable grounds resulted from a reasonable investigation of the incidents.

9.412 In assessing whether the employer has met these principles, the tribunal will examine the basis for the employer's belief and then go on to determine whether a reasonable employer would have proceeded to dismiss the employee in such circumstances.

9.413 The employer should also be aware that even where he or she is able to show that a dismissal was made for a fair reason, he or she must also demonstrate that the procedure adopted in carrying out the dismissal was also fair and reasonable.

Payment in Lieu of Notice

9.414 A contract of employment clause may permit the employer to make a payment to the employee in lieu of notice, in the event of dismissal.

9.415 If the contract does not provide for such a payment, it will technically be a breach of contract for the employer to dismiss the employee instantly but pay him or her in lieu of notice. The employee could in theory claim wrongful dismissal although the level of damages would be nil if pay in lieu of notice had been given.

9.416 The employer should be aware of the fact that even a technical breach of the contract of employment is likely to prevent the employer from relying on other clauses within the contract, eg relating to restraint of trade or confidentiality after the employee's contract has ended.

Training

9.417 It is important that all managers are fully aware of the statutory requirements regarding the application of disciplinary procedures, the employer's disciplinary rules and procedures and the kind of behaviour that is likely to constitute gross misconduct. They should also receive full training on their use and application.

Summary Dismissal

List of Relevant Legislation

9.418
- Employment Act 2002 (Dispute Resolution) Regulations 2004
- Employment Act 2002
- Employment Rights Act 1996

List of Relevant Cases

9.419
- *Dubai Aluminium Co Ltd v Salaam* [2003] IRLR 608, HL — in justifying summary dismissal the employer must show that an action was done in bad faith.
- *Rex Stewart Jeffries Parker Ginsberg Ltd v Parker and Another* [1988] IRLR 483, CA — if a contract provides for payment in lieu of notice or the parties agree that the employee shall accept payment in lieu of notice such a payment can properly terminate the contract of employment.
- *Wilson v M Racher* [1974] IRLR 114, CA — the use of obscene language by a normally efficient employee on a solitary occasion, when severely provoked by his employer, would not justify dismissal.
- *Pepper v Webb* [1969] 1WRL 514 — a number of incidents aggregated together can justify the employer acting to summarily dismiss.
- *Sinclair v Neighbour* [1967] 2QB 279 — an employer may summarily dismiss an employee whose conduct, even if not dishonest, has been inconsistent with his duty to his employer and the confidential relationship between them.
- *Laws v London Chronicle (Indicator Newspapers) Ltd* [1959] 1WLR 698 — there is no fixed rule defining the degree of misconduct which will justify summary dismissal.
- *Cluston & Co Ltd v Corry* [1906] AC122 — it is for the court or tribunal concerned, whether the degree of misconduct was inconsistent with the fulfilment of the expressed or implied conditions of service, so as to justify dismissal.

Further Information

Publications
- PL714 *Dismissal — Fair and Unfair*, Department for Business, Enterprise and Regulatory Reform (BERR)
- Acas/CP01 Code of Practice on Disciplinary and Grievance Procedures (2004)

Organisations
- **Advisory Conciliation and Arbitration Service (Acas)**
  Web: *www.acas.org.uk*
  Acas aims to improve organisations and working life through better employment

relations. It provides up-to-date information, advice, high-quality training, and works with employers and employees to solve problems and improve performance.

Transfer of Undertakings

> This topic covers the following.
> - TUPE Defined: A Relevant Transfer
> - When TUPE Applies
> - When TUPE Does Not Apply
> - TUPE and the Contracting Out of Services
> - Who Transfers and When
> - Employees to Whom TUPE Applies
> - When Employees' Transfer Occurs
> - Employees Who Choose Not to Transfer
> - Liabilities and Rights that Transfer to the New Employer
> - Liabilities That Do Not Transfer to the New Employer
> - Contract Terms and Conditions
> - Continuity of Service
> - Non-contractual Benefits
> - Changes to Existing Contracts
> - Collective Agreements
> - Occupational Pension Schemes
> - Insolvency
> - Appropriate Representatives
> - Employee Representative Elections
> - Information and Consultation
> - Dismissals
> - ETO Reasons
> - Avoiding TUPE

9.420 A transfer of undertakings occurs where a business or a discrete part of a business is transferred from one employer to another.

9.421 The rights of employees whose employer changes as a result of the transfer of the business in which they work are to a large degree protected by legislation.

9.422 The original Transfer of Undertakings (Protection of Employment) Regulations (TUPE) 1981 were significantly amended over the years and have now been replaced by the Transfer of Undertakings (Protection of Employment) Regulations 2006. TUPE 2006 applies whenever there is a sale or purchase of a business (other than a share sale), a merger between two or more organisations or where a service contract passes from one contractor to another. It can also apply where part of a business is outsourced, or where a lease or franchise is transferred. In these circumstances, the employees of the business transfer from the original employer to the new employer and their contracts of employment are protected.

Employers' Duties

9.423 The old employer or transferor (ie the employer who disposes of the business concerned) has a duty to:
- adhere to the provisions of TUPE
- be clear about when and which employees are to transfer to the new employer
- provide "employee liability information" to the new employer (ie information about the transferring employees, their terms of employment and any disputes arising in the previous two years)

- if necessary, hold elections to elect appropriate representatives
- provide information in advance about the transfer to employee representatives
- consult the appropriate representatives when required
- ensure that any dismissal implemented for reasons connected with the transfer is for an economic, technical or organisational reason entailing changes in the workforce.

9.424 The new employer or transferee (ie the employer who takes over the business concerned) has a duty to:
- adhere to the provisions of TUPE
- understand the rights of new employees and recognise that all the rights, duties and liabilities of the old employer in connection with the employees' contracts will transfer to the new employer
- be aware that employees will transfer to the new employer on their existing contractual terms and conditions of employment
- comply with the regulations on employees' rights with respect to occupational pension scheme benefits
- recognise employees' continuity of service with the former employer
- ensure that any changes to the contracts of new employees are lawful and not made because of the transfer
- take over any existing collective agreements with recognised trade unions, except to the extent that they relate to occupational pension benefits
- ensure that the appropriate employee representatives are in place, informed and consulted
- ensure that any dismissal of an employee that is made in connection with a transfer of an undertaking is for an "economic, technical or organisational reason entailing changes in the workforce"
- if appropriate, comply with the special provisions when acquiring an insolvent organisation.

Employees' Duties

9.425 Employees should ensure the following.
- If there is any doubt, ie because only part of the business is transferred or employment status is unclear, clarify whether the transfer will affect them or not.
- Tell the old employer before the transfer takes place if they do not want to transfer.
- Be aware of the arrangements for occupational pension scheme benefits in a transfer situation.
- Elect employee representatives for consultation purposes if invited to do so by the employer and ensure that there is proper information disclosure and consultation.
- Raise any individual grievances with the old employer or, if appropriate, the new employer in accordance with the statutory grievance procedure.
- Be aware of the remedies that are available against employers for non-compliance with the TUPE Regulations.

Transfer of Undertakings

In Practice

TUPE Defined: A Relevant Transfer

9.426 There are, broadly speaking, two types of "relevant transfers" under the Transfer of Undertakings (Protection of Employment) Regulations 2006 (TUPE) as follows.
- When a business or undertaking (or part of one) is transferred to a new employer (the transferee). An example of this would be where one business is bought over or merged with another.
- When a "service provision change" takes place. This can arise, for example, if refuse collectors employed by a local authority are outsourced to a private waste management organisation, if a security organisation is awarded a security contract to provide a service for (a bank) in circumstances where the contract was previously held by another contractor, or if a contractor's contract ends and the service is taken "in house" by a local authority.

9.427 The TUPE Regulations 2006 apply to the private, public and voluntary sectors, irrespective of the size of the undertaking. An undertaking may be one person (see *Schmidt* case).

9.428 The effects of TUPE are to:
- transfer automatically employees who work in the undertaking to a new employer
- transfer employees on the same terms and conditions of employment (except any rights to occupational pension benefits)
- ensure that employees are treated as if they had always been employed by the new employer
- guarantee continuity of service for all transferred employees
- make any changes to the terms of employees' contracts of employment unlawful unless they are for an economic, technical or organisational reason entailing changes in the workforce
- transfer completely any outstanding claims against the old employer to the new employer
- make it unlawful for either employer to dismiss employees for a transfer-related reason unless that reason is an economic, technical or organisational reason entailing changes in the workforce.

When TUPE Applies

9.429 TUPE applies to any transfer provided that the business or provision of services is situated in the UK immediately before the transfer. This is the case even if the business is being sold overseas or the employees in the business actually work overseas.

9.430 TUPE only applies if "an economic entity retains its identity" (ie if the business or services transferred retain their identity after the transfer). This means essentially that the business entity post-transfer is for all intents and purposes the same business entity in its operation, etc, as the pre-transfer business entity. However, this usually depends on a factual assessment taking into account all of the relevant circumstances. (See *Spijkers v Gebroeders Benedik Abbatoir CV*.)

9.431 TUPE applies to:

- most business sales
- service provision changes:
  - initial "outsourcing" of services
  - the change in suppliers of services (re-tendering)
  - "insourcing" (when an employer ceases to use a contractor and brings the service "in-house")
- management buy-outs
- transfers of leases
- transfers of part of a business
- intra-group transfers.

When TUPE Does Not Apply

9.432   TUPE does not apply to:
- the sale of shares in an organisation
- the sale of a business if it will be changed significantly by the new owner (ie the economic entity does not retain its identity)
- the transfer of assets alone (without a business)
- transfers of administrative functions between public administrations
- the "one off" (rather than continuing) buying-in of services from a contractor
- the transfer of a contract to purchase goods, rather than services.

TUPE and the Contracting Out of Services

9.433   TUPE applies to all service provision changes, including contracting-out exercises (outsourcing), changes of service provider (eg following a re-tendering exercise) and contracting-in exercises (in-sourcing). All of the employees employed in the business, or relevant part of the business, will therefore automatically transfer to the new employer.

Who Transfers and When

9.434   TUPE applies to employees only — whether full time, part time or engaged on a fixed-term contract.

9.435   TUPE does **not** apply to:
- the self-employed
- casual workers, or
- temporary staff employed through a recruitment agency.

9.436   There can, however, be difficulties in determining the employment status of some workers. For example, agency workers who have worked through an agency for the same employer for over a year could have employment rights against that employer through implication. The Court of Appeal has ruled that an "implied" contract of employment might exist with the client organisation in these circumstances.

Employees to Whom TUPE Applies

9.437   TUPE only applies to employees who are wholly or mainly employed in the part of the business which is to be transferred. If employees are split between different parts of the business then the employer must consider whether they are "assigned" to the part of the business which is to be transferred.

9.438 The employer should consider the following factors in assessing whether employees are properly assigned to the business or part of the business being transferred.
- The amount of time spent on differing parts of the business.
- The amount of value given to the time spent in each part of the business.
- The terms of the employment contract.
- How the cost of the employee's service has been allocated in the organisation's accounting system.

9.439 The employees who will transfer under TUPE must be employed immediately before the transfer. However, if they are dismissed in connection with the transfer prior to it taking place, they are likely to be deemed to be employed at the time of the transfer.

9.440 In *G4S Justice Services (UK) Ltd v Anstey and others* EAT/0698/05, however, the EAT ruled that employees who were dismissed for misconduct before a transfer, but who were reinstated following an internal appeal, were employed immediately before the transfer, even though the original employer's decision to reinstate them was made after the date of the transfer. The EAT held that the reinstatement meant that the dismissals had in effect vanished. The new employer was therefore obliged to employ the individuals following their reinstatement.

When Employees' Transfer Occurs

9.441 Employees automatically become employed by the new employer when the transfer occurs. The transfer itself will not constitute a termination of their employment.

9.442 The transfer will normally occur on the:
- completion of a business sale
- date services commence under an outsourcing arrangement
- date the supplier changes.

Employees Who Choose Not to Transfer

9.443 Employees can choose not to transfer to the new employer. Normally, if they do opt out of the transfer they will be treated as having resigned before the transfer. They will therefore not be entitled to claim a redundancy payment, nor to notice or payment in lieu of notice.

9.444 Where a relevant transfer involves or would involve a substantial change in working conditions to the material detriment of an employee affected by a TUPE transfer, that employee may treat his or her contract of employment as having been terminated by the employer. This right exists independently of the common law right to claim constructive dismissal on account of a breach of contract on the part of the employer.

9.445 The employee could also claim wrongful dismissal, for which no period of qualifying service is required.

9.446 The old employer may wish to retain a particular employee rather than "lose" him or her to the new employer. Since all employees assigned to the part of the business that will transfer automatically become employed by the new employer by operation of law on the date of the transfer, the old employer would have to have re-assigned the employee to another part of the business before the date of the transfer. The employee's consent would be required for such a move.

Liabilities and Rights That Transfer to the New Employer

9.447 TUPE provides that the new employer takes on all the rights, duties and liabilities connected with the relevant employees' contracts of employment, with the exception of some benefits under occupational pension schemes and any criminal liabilities. The relevant employees' rights under their contracts of employment will therefore transfer to the new employer. Any outstanding employment disputes against the old employer (whether as a result of internal grievance or disciplinary procedures, or a claim taken to an employment tribunal or an ordinary court) will also transfer to the new employer.

9.448 Rights and liabilities that transfer to the new employer include:
- all contractual rights under the employment contract — including outstanding holiday pay, non-payment of wages, etc
- any dismissals which the old employer makes that are connected to the proposed transfer and that are not for a permitted reason
- outstanding personal injury liabilities
- liabilities relating to early retirement benefits
- outstanding liabilities under discrimination law or other employment law — although protection against liability transferring to the new employer can be arranged through an indemnity scheme.

9.449 The TUPE Regulations 2006 place a duty on the old employer to provide "employee liability information" in writing to the new employer, normally, at least two weeks before the completion of the transfer. This information includes:
- the identity of the transferring employees
- the ages of the employees
- information relating to any collective agreements which apply to the employees
- instances of any disciplinary action within the preceding two years taken by the old employer where the statutory dispute resolution procedures applied
- instances of any grievances raised by any of the transferring employees within the past two years where the statutory dispute resolution procedures applied
- instances of actual and potential legal action brought by any of the employees.

9.450 A transferee may complain to an employment tribunal if the employee liability information is not provided by the transferor or is defective. Compensation may be awarded of no less than £500 for each employee for whom the information was not provided.

Liabilities That Do Not Transfer to the New Employer

9.451 Liabilities that do not transfer to the new employer include:
- criminal liabilities
- liabilities relating to old-age benefits provided under occupational pension schemes
- liability for pre-transfer dismissals that were either unconnected with the transfer or made in connection with the transfer for an economic, technical or organisational reason entailing changes in the workforce.

9.452 The Court of Appeal has held (in *Cross v British Airways* [2006] EWCA Civ 549) that an employee's normal retirement age will not transfer under TUPE. The court stated that "normal retirement age" is not synonymous with contractual retirement age and is therefore not one of the "rights, powers, duties and liabilities" which automatically transfer under TUPE.

Contract Terms and Conditions

9.453 TUPE provides that the employees transfer to the new employer on their existing contractual terms and conditions of employment, except for:
- the name of their employer — which will be changed to that of the new employer
- rights to receive benefits under the terms of the original employer's occupational pension scheme. If, however, the employee belonged, or was entitled to belong, to an occupational scheme then the transferee must offer a prescribed level of pension provision after the transfer.

Continuity of Service

9.454 TUPE acts to preserve employees' continuity of service that has accrued with the old employer. Furthermore, a person who has worked as an employee for a succession of contractors may, depending on the facts and circumstances, be able to aggregate service with a number of previous employers. Length of service is important in respect of certain contractual rights (eg service-related paid annual leave) and access to certain statutory rights (eg unfair dismissal and redundancy pay).

Non-contractual Benefits

9.455 Non-contractual benefits such as discretionary bonus schemes or discretionary redundancy schemes will not transfer. The transferring employees cannot claim these discretionary benefits against the new employer.

Changes to Existing Contracts

9.456 If the new employer wishes to make changes to existing contracts or offer new contracts of employment to the transferring employees after the transfer, these new terms or new contracts will not be valid if they are made because of the transfer or a reason connected with the transfer which is not "an economic, technical or organisational reason entailing changes in the workforce". Any such contract variation will be void.

9.457 The same prohibition applies to the old employer who is considering changes to terms and conditions of those employees who will be transferred prior to the transfer occurring.

9.458 The TUPE Regulations permit some variations of contracts of employment to be agreed between the employee and either the old or new employer. The reason for the change to the contract must be "an economic, technical or organisational reason entailing changes in the workforce" (or ETO reason). ETO is not further defined in the TUPE Regulations. However, the Department for Business, Enterprise and Regulatory Reform suggests the following as likely definitions.
- Economic — concerning the profitability or market performance of the transferee's business.
- Technical — relating to equipment and production processes.
- Organisational — relating to the structure of the employer's operations.

9.459 More than one of these reasons can occur in any set of business circumstances.

9.460 In *Berriman v Delabole Slate Ltd* [1985] IRLR 305, the Court of Appeal ruled in the context of judging the ETO defence that "entailing changes in the workforce" means changes to the numbers and functions of employees comprising the workforce, and not just changes to the identities of the individuals who make up the workforce. It follows that for a change to employees' contractual terms to be legally enforceable, the change must not only be for an economic, technical or organisational reason, but must also result in changes to the numbers of people employed or changes to the jobs in which people are employed.

9.461 This reasoning was followed in the case of *London Metropolitan University v Sackur* EAT (0286/06). In this case the university sought, following a merger two years earlier, to vary employees' terms and conditions in order to ensure employees were all engaged on a single contract. The employer proceeded to terminate the relevant employees' contracts and offer them new contracts on different terms. On appeal from the tribunal, the EAT held that the dismissals, which were by reason of the transfer (despite the passage of two years since the merger), were automatically unfair. There was no ETO reason underpinning the changes to the employees' contracts as there had been no changes to the number of employees or their job functions.

9.462 In *Power v Regent Security Services Ltd* EAT (0499/06), the EAT decided that, where an employee's contractual retirement age had been increased (from 60 to 65) following a transfer, the employer was not entitled subsequently to compel the employee to retire at age 60. Even though the contractual variation from age 60 to 65 was void, the employee (but not the employer) should be allowed to enforce it if he or she considered it to be to his or her benefit.

9.463 Any changes to the terms of employees' contracts made for an ETO reason must, in compliance with general contract law, also be agreed with the employee(s) concerned.

9.464 As can be seen from the *Sackur* case above, the new rules on permitted variations do not allow for harmonisation of terms and conditions of the new employees with existing employees after the transfer. If the new employer wishes to harmonise, it is recommended that it:

- waits for as long as possible after the transfer to minimise the risk that the changes will be found to be connected with the transfer (note that, in law, there is no stated period of time post-transfer after which changes to employees' terms of employment will be permitted)
- establishes an economic, technical or organisational reason entailing changes in the workforce which is independent of the transfer
- applies the changes to all employees, not just those who transferred.

9.465 In insolvency situations, there is greater scope for contract variation by the new employer. The conditions are as follows.

- The "permitted variation" should be agreed by employee representatives and either the old employer, the new employer or the insolvency practitioner. Such variations must not breach other statutory entitlements (eg under the National Minimum Wage Act 1998 or the Working Time Regulations 1998).
- The reason for the "permitted variation" must be to aim at safeguarding employment opportunities by ensuring the survival of the undertaking.
- The representatives must be union representatives (where a trade union is recognised) or, otherwise, non-union representatives.
- Where non-union representatives are involved then the following must apply.
  - All employees affected by the variation must have a copy of the proposed agreement and some accompanying guidance.
  - The variation agreement must be in writing and signed by each employee representative.

Collective Agreements

9.466 The new employer is required to take over any existing collective agreements with recognised trade unions, except to the extent that they relate to occupational pension benefits.

9.467 In these circumstances therefore, the collective agreement itself will have effect as if it had been made with the new employer. This does not stop the employer from terminating or varying a voluntary collective agreement at a later date, however, as voluntary collective agreements are not normally legally enforceable between the parties.

9.468 Over and above these provisions, any terms that were incorporated from a collective agreement into the contracts of the transferring employees will transfer to the new employer provided the terms were in force immediately before the transfer.

Occupational Pension Schemes

9.469 Employees who transfer under TUPE are covered by special rules with regard to pension schemes. Some of these terms may be contractual.

9.470 Early retirement benefits — which are not occupational pension benefits — will, however, transfer to the new employer.

9.471 From April 2005, under the Pensions Act 2004, new provisions regarding the transfer of pension benefits are in force. If the old employer provided a pension scheme, then the new employer has to provide some form of pension scheme for employees who were members of or eligible to be members of the old employer's scheme. The new pension arrangement will have to comply with defined minimum standards. The new provision can be:
- contributions to a final salary scheme at an equivalent rate and not less than six per cent of the employee's pensionable pay
- benefits under a money purchase scheme subject to a requirement to match the employee's contributions up to a limit of six per cent of the employee's basic pay, or
- a stakeholder arrangement in which the employer matches the employee's contributions up to a limit of six per cent of basic pay.

9.472 After the employee has transferred, he or she and the new employer can agree whatever pension terms they choose. This can include an agreement not to have a pension.

Insolvency

9.473 The TUPE Regulations 2006 introduce new rules affecting the transfer of insolvent businesses as follows.
- Some of the transferor's pre-existing debts to its employees will not pass to the transferee (eg wages, holiday pay, redundancy pay). These will be met from the National Insurance Fund.
- There are greater opportunities for the transferee to vary contracts of employment in insolvency situations.

Appropriate Representatives

9.474 Both the original employer and the new employer involved in a TUPE transfer are obliged to provide information to and to consult with any of their employees who may be affected in any way by the transfer of the business.

9.475 Existing trade union representatives or staff council representatives can be nominated for TUPE information and consultation requirements provided that all of the affected employees are represented.

9.476 If there are already recognised trade union representatives, then the employer must inform and consult them in preference to non-union staff council representatives.

9.477 Appropriate representatives have special rights not to be treated less favourably because they are employee representatives. They also have the right to take paid time off so that they are able to perform their duties.

9.478 Both the old and new employers must arrange for their own affected employees to be represented.

Employee Representative Elections

9.479 If there are no existing appropriate representatives, new representatives must be elected for all the employees who are likely to be "affected" by the transfer.

9.480 There is no minimum number of representatives who must be elected. The employer can decide on a reasonable number and then hold elections to appoint this number of representatives.

9.481 All affected employees employed on the date of the election are entitled to vote. If possible, the vote should be in secret. If the employees fail to appoint representatives, the employer is required to provide information to and consult with the employees directly.

Information and Consultation

9.482 The old and new employers are required in advance to inform and, in some instances, consult their own appropriate representatives about the transfer.

Information

9.483 Both the old and new employer must inform their appropriate representatives in good time before the transfer of the following matters:
- that a TUPE transfer will be taking place
- the date on which the transfer is going to take place
- the reasons for the transfer
- the legal, economic and social implications of the transfer for employees affected by it
- any action envisaged by the new employer (eg reorganisation) that will affect employees. The old employer must tell appropriate representatives about the new employer's proposals regarding any redundancies, changes to terms and conditions of employment or working conditions after the transfer — or that there are no changes planned.

9.484 This information is in addition to the employee liability information that has to be given by the old employer to the new employer.

Consultation

9.485 An employer is only required to consult appropriate representatives of its workforce if there are proposals to make changes to organisational structures, operations, contractual terms or working conditions as a result of the transfer.

9.486 In practice, the new employer and the old employer will often engage in joint consultation with appropriate representatives of the old employer's employees to ensure that the process as a whole runs smoothly.

9.487 The new employer will be required to consult its own employees' representatives if it proposes to make redundancies after the transfer. The consultation process must be meaningful and conducted by the employer with a view to seeking the agreement of the representatives.

Breach of the Information and Consultation Requirements

9.488 If the employer breaches its obligations to inform and consult appropriate representatives, the representatives can bring claims in an employment tribunal. The claims will be for a "protective award" of compensation because of the breach.

9.489 A tribunal can award a just and equitable amount of compensation, up to a maximum of 13 weeks' actual pay per affected employee. In practice, the amount of the award is likely to depend on the extent of the employer's failure to comply with the requirements.

9.490 Where it is the old employer who fails to comply with the information and consultation requirements, both the old employer and the new employer will be jointly liable for the breach and for payment of any protective awards.

9.491 Claims for protective awards must be brought within three months of the transfer.

Employer's Defence to a Claim of Breach

9.492 The employer does have a defence to any claim for breach of the information and consultation requirements. The employer can seek to show that there were special circumstances which meant that it was reasonable for it not to comply with the requirements.

9.493 However, the employer must show that it took all reasonable steps to comply with the requirements given the special circumstances. "Special circumstances" will include an event that was beyond the employer's control.

Dismissals

9.494 If an old employer or new employer dismisses any employees in connection with a transfer, these dismissals will be automatically unfair unless the dismissal was for an economic, technical or organisational reason entailing changes in the workforce.

9.495 However, the employee must have at least one year's service to bring a claim of automatic unfair dismissal in these circumstances. An employee who is unfairly dismissed in connection with a transfer could also bring claims for:

- a statutory redundancy payment (provided the employee has at least two years' service)
- wrongful dismissal (if the employer does not give notice or fails to pay in lieu of notice).

ETO Reasons

9.496 Old and new employers can fairly dismiss employees in connection with a TUPE transfer if they do so for certain reasons necessitating changes in the workforce. These are known as ETO reasons, or "economic, technical or organisational reasons entailing changes in the workforce".

9.497 The reason must also be one that involves changes in the numbers and functions of the people that make up the workforce, thus for example a dismissal for economic reasons alone will not suffice. Dismissals by reason of redundancy are likely to be for ETO reasons.

9.498 In the case of *Hynd v Armstrong and ors* [2007] CSIH 16, the Court of Session ruled that where the original employer — prior to a transfer of an undertaking — dismisses an employee for reasons associated with the post-transfer conduct of the new employer's business, that cannot constitute an ETO reason for dismissal. The ETO defence would be arguable, the Court of Session held, only if the reason for dismissal related to the conduct of the employer's own future business (and not that of the new employer). The new employer had decided that the individual would not be required in their business for economic and organisational reasons, and so they would in all likelihood have been able to use the ETO defence had they dismissed the individual after the transfer, but the dismissal in this case was effected prior to the transfer by the old employer and so the ETO defence was not applicable.

9.499 Although dismissals for ETO reasons will not be automatically unfair, they may still be unfair under the normal principles of unfair dismissal law if the employer does not follow a fair process or act reasonably. The employer will still need to satisfy the normal criteria applicable to dismissals (ie comply with the statutory dismissal and disciplinary procedure and act reasonably towards the employee in a general sense).

Avoiding TUPE

9.500 The following points need to be considered when dealing with TUPE.

- Employers and employees cannot agree to exclude the effect of TUPE.
- Employees cannot waive their entitlements to a protective award for breach of the information and consultation requirements under TUPE.
- A claim for breach of the information and consultation requirements cannot be compromised in agreements with the employer (old or new).
- Employees cannot agree to changes made to their contractual terms and conditions, for a reason connected with the transfer (unless it is an ETO reason), even if the changes are more favourable.
- In practice, employees are unlikely to challenge the validity of improved contract terms at or after the transfer, they are only likely to challenge the validity of new or revised contract terms if the employer attempts to impose new terms that are disadvantageous to them.
- Parties to a transfer will often negotiate indemnities to negate the effect of the transfer of liabilities.

Training

9.501 It is important that line managers are aware of the procedures for appointing representatives and informing and consulting appropriate representatives when a transfer is being negotiated.

9.502 Managers should receive training about their obligations at the start of transfer negotiations.

9.503 Awareness training about the key provisions of TUPE 2006 would also be advantageous to managers so as to make them aware of the extent of employees' rights in a TUPE transfer.

List of Relevant Legislation

9.504

- Transfer of Undertakings (Protection of Employment) Regulations 2006
- Transfer of Employment (Pension Protection) Regulations 2005
- Employment Act 2002 (Dispute Resolution) Regulations 2004
- Pensions Act 2004
- Employment Rights Act 1996
- Transfer of Undertakings Directive 2001/23/EC (Acquired Rights)

List of Relevant Cases

9.505

- *Astle and Others v Cheshire County Council* [2005] IRLR 12, EAT — the EAT held that where an employer's reason for not taking on staff was to avoid TUPE, it would only be one factor, to consider when looking at whether there has been a transfer for the purposes of TUPE. If it is not the principal motive of the transferee to avoid TUPE, then the fact that employees are not taken on is not relevant and does not arise.
- *Celtec Ltd v Astley* C-478/03 [2005] IRLR 647, ECJ — the date of the transfer of an undertaking was the date, at a particular point in time, and not spread over a longer period, when responsibility as employer for carrying on the business of the undertaking moved from the transferor to the transferee.
- *Howard v Millrise Ltd* [2005] IRLR 84, EAT — where there are no recognised trade union representatives or other elected or appointed employee representatives in place, TUPE regulation 10 requires the employer to invite affected employees to elect representatives and, if they fail to do so within a reasonable time, to give each individual affected employee the information required.
- *Fairhurst Ward Abbotts Ltd v Botes Building Ltd* [2004] EWCA, Civ 83 — the transfer of part of a business can be a TUPE transfer.
- *Alamo Group (Europe) Ltd v Tucker* [2003] IRLR 266 — the old employer's liability for failure to comply with the information and consultation obligations transfers to the new employer.
- *Franks v Reuters Ltd* [2003] IRLR 423, CA — determination of employment status of an agency worker who worked over a long period of time for the client organisation. The need to consider the possibility of an implied contract of employment with the client.
- *Beckmann v Dynamco Whicheloe Macfarlane Ltd* [2002] IRLR 578 — early retirement benefits are not excluded from transferring under TUPE.
- *Mitie Managed Services Ltd v French* [2002] IRLR 512 — if the new employer is unable to replicate the old employer's contractual benefit (eg a profit-sharing scheme) the new employer is obliged to provide a benefit of substantial equivalence.
- *Rossiter v Pendragon plc* [2001] IRLR 256 — the new employer must commit a substantial breach of contract for the employee to bring a claim of constructive unfair dismissal.

- *Allen v Amalgamated Construction Co Ltd* [2000] ICR 436 — intra-group reorganisations can be subject to TUPE.
- *University of Oxford v Humphreys* [2000] ICR 405 — the new employer's indication that it would breach the employee's contract was sufficient to allow the employee to resign and claim constructive unfair dismissal against the new employer.
- *Whitehouse v Chas A Blatchford & Sons Ltd* [1999] IRLR 492 — the employee's dismissal for redundancy by the new employer was fair as a permitted reason applied.
- *Wilson v St Helens Borough Council* [1999] 2 AC 52 — changes to contractual terms and conditions connected with the transfer are ineffective unless for a permitted reason.
- *Süzen v Zehnacker Gebäudereingung GmbH Krankenhavsservice* [1997] IRLR 255 — the transfer of a labour-intensive business such as cleaning can be a TUPE transfer even if no assets are transferred.
- *Henke v Gemeinde Schierke* [1996] IRLR 701 — the transfer of a non-economic administrative function was not a relevant transfer.
- *Tuck v BSG Property Services Ltd* [1996] IRLR 134 — the old employer was unable to rely on the new employer's permitted reason when making dismissals before the transfer.
- *Schmidt v Spar-und Leihkasse der fruheren Amter Bordesholm, Keil und Cronshagen C-392/92* [1994] IRLR 302, ECJ — the European Court of Justice ruled that a cleaning service by one person was a relevant transfer. The total absence of transferred assets was not a crucial issue. The decisive criterion was the preservation of identity.
- *Spijkers v Gebroeders Benedik Abbatoir CV* [1986] 2 CMLR 486 — the European Court of Justice said that courts must look at all of the facts in considering whether a business has transferred under TUPE.
- *Berriman v Delabole Slate Ltd* [1985] IRLR 305 — the Court of Appeal ruled that "entailing changes in the workforce" means changes to the numbers and functions of employees comprising the workforce, and not just changes in the individuals who make up the workforce.

Further Information

Organisations

- **Advisory Conciliation and Arbitration Service (Acas)**
  Web: *www.acas.org.uk*
  Acas aims to improve organisations and working life through better employment relations. It provides up-to-date information, advice, high-quality training, and works with employers and employees to solve problems and improve performance.
- **Commission for Racial Equality**
  The Commission for Racial Equality is a publicly funded, non-governmental body set up under the Race Relations Act 1976 to tackle racial discrimination and promote racial equality. From October 2007 this organisation will be replaced by the Commission for Equality and Human Rights.
- **Department for Business, Enterprise and Regulatory Reform (BERR)**
  Web: *www.berr.gov.uk*
  The Department for Business, Enterprise and Regulatory Reform brings together functions from the former Department of Trade and Industry (DTI), including responsibilities for productivity, business relations, energy, competition and consumers. It also drives regulatory reform.

- **Disability Rights Commission**
  Web: *www.drc-gb.org*
  An independent body established by Act of Parliament to eliminate discrimination against disabled people and promote quality of opportunity. It provides information and advice to disabled people and employers about their rights and duties. From October 2007 this organisation will be replaced by the Commission for Equality and Human Rights (**Web:** *www.cehr.org.uk*).

- **Equal Opportunities Commission**
  Web: *www.eoc.org.uk*
  An agency working to eliminate sex discrimination and put equality into practice in the workplace. From October 2007 this organisation will be replaced by the Commission for Equality and Human Rights (**Web:** *www.cehr.org.uk*).

Unfair Dismissal

> This topic covers the following.
> - Termination of Employment
> - Statement of Reasons for Dismissal
> - Potentially Fair Reasons for Dismissal
> - Reasonableness
> - Procedural Fairness
> - Substantive Fairness
> - Automatically Unfair Reasons for Dismissal
> - Right Not to be Unfairly Dismissed
> - Remedies for Unfair Dismissal
> - Contributory Fault
> - Duty to Mitigate

9.506 The Employment Rights Act 1996 enshrines the statutory right of employees:
- not to be unfairly dismissed
- to complain to an employment tribunal against infringements of that right.

9.507 Since 1 October 2004, the Employment Act 2002 requires employers to follow a statutory dismissal and disciplinary procedure (DDP) before dismissing an employee. Failure to adhere to the mandatory steps contained in the DDP will mean the employee's dismissal will be automatically unfair and the employer will be liable to pay an enhanced compensatory award to the employee. The Government has proposed an Employment Simplification Bill of repeal which will include the statutory dispute resolution procedures and is expected to publish details in November 2007.

Employers' Duties

9.508 Employers have a duty to ensure that:
- an employee's termination of employment by way of dismissal is in accordance with the employee's contract of employment
- an employee's dismissal does not involve an infringement of the employee's right not to be unfairly dismissed
- the employee's right to be provided with a written statement of reasons for dismissal is recognised
- the reason for dismissal is one of the six potentially fair reasons for dismissal
- a dismissal decision is reasonable, ie the employer acted reasonably in relying on its reason for dismissal
- they apply the mandatory steps contained in the statutory dismissal and disciplinary procedure (DDP) when dismissing an employee
- they do not dismiss an employee for a reason which is deemed to be one of the automatically unfair reasons for dismissal
- they comply with any remedies for unfair dismissal imposed by an employment tribunal.

Employees' Duties

9.509 Employees have a duty to:
- abide by the contract of employment and the duties placed on employees — breaches may cause the employer to lawfully terminate employment
- co-operate with the employer in the application of the statutory dismissal and disciplinary procedure
- mitigate their loss if unfairly dismissed — compensation for unfair dismissal can be reduced where an employee has failed to take reasonable steps to secure alternative employment.

In Practice

Termination of Employment

9.510 A dismissal is where the contract of employment is terminated in the following circumstances.
- A contract of employment is terminated by the employer, with or without notice.
- A fixed or limited term contract of employment comes to an end without being renewed.
- The employee terminates his or her contract of employment with or without notice as a direct result of an employer's fundamental breach of contract — this is usually referred to as constructive dismissal.

9.511 A dismissal is also likely to be ruled to have occurred:
- where an employer refuses to allow an employee to return to work after a period of maternity or adoption leave, when she or he has a legal right to do so
- in a "forced resignation", ie where an employee is put in a "resign or be dismissed" situation.

Statement of Reasons for Dismissal

9.512 Under the Employment Rights Act 1996, an employee with a minimum of one year's continuous service, who is under notice or who has been dismissed, has a right, on request, to be provided by the employer with a written statement of reasons for the dismissal. This has to be provided within 14 days of the request being made.

9.513 Where a female employee is dismissed while pregnant or on maternity leave, the employer must always provide written reasons for the dismissal, regardless of the employee's length of service, and regardless of whether or not she requests such reasons.

9.514 A failure to provide an employee with a written statement of reasons for dismissal amounts to separate grounds for complaint to an employment tribunal. An employee would also be able to complain on the grounds that the reasons given for dismissal were inadequate or untrue. Where it found such a complaint to be well-founded, the employment tribunal would make a declaration as to what it finds to be the real reasons for the dismissal and the employee would be entitled to an award of two weeks' pay.

Potentially Fair Reasons for Dismissal

9.515 In order to be a fair dismissal, two conditions need to be met. The first is that the main reason for the dismissal must be one of the potentially fair reasons listed in Employment Rights Act 1996.

- Capability — where the employee's inability to do the job is demonstrated by unsatisfactory performance and affected by lack of skill or competence and/or ill health.
- Conduct — where there is misconduct.
- Redundancy — where the need for employees to perform work of a particular kind has ceased or diminished.
- Legal restriction — where it would be illegal to continue to employ the employee.
- Some other substantial reason.
- Retirement.

9.516 On 1 October 2006, when age discrimination legislation — the Employment Equality (Age) Regulations 2006 — was implemented, retirement was added to the list of potentially fair reasons for dismissal. An employee who is genuinely retired at age 65, at a specified higher retirement age or at a lower age that the employer can objectively justify will have no grounds on which to succeed in a claim for unfair dismissal, provided also that the employer complies with certain new pre-retirement procedures.

Reasonableness

9.517 For a dismissal to be fair, a second condition needs to be met: the employer must act reasonably in deciding to dismiss the employee. In practical terms, this involves issues of:
- procedural fairness
- substantive fairness.

The Statutory Dismissal and Disciplinary Procedure (DDP)

9.518 The Employment Act 2002 (Dispute Resolution) Regulations 2004, which were implemented on 1 October 2004, require all employers to operate a dismissal and disciplinary procedure (DDP) when contemplating dismissing an employee on grounds of:
- conduct
- capability
- redundancy, where fewer than 20 employees are affected
- the expiry of a fixed-term contract without renewal
- "some other substantial reason".

9.519 The DDP does not have to be applied in the case of dismissals on the grounds of:
- redundancy, where 20 or more employees are affected (although individual consultation will still, in practice, be necessary in these circumstances in order for the treatment of the employees to be regarded as "reasonable")
- legal restriction
- retirement at or above the employer's contractual retirement age (or if there is no contractual retirement age, at or above age 65)
- the employer's decision to terminate employees' current contracts and at the same time offer new contracts on different terms
- the employees going on strike or taking other industrial action.

Unfair Dismissal

9.520 All employers are obliged under the DDP to do the following.
- Set out the employee's alleged "conduct or characteristics, or other circumstances" in writing and give or send a copy to the employee, inviting the employee to attend a meeting. The written notice must give adequate information to the employee without giving the appearance that the employer has already made up their mind what the outcome will be.
- Hold a meeting to discuss the matter and enable both parties to explain their cases prior to a decision being taken about whether to dismiss the employee or take relevant disciplinary action. After the meeting, the outcome should be communicated to the employee in writing. The employee is obliged to take all reasonable steps to attend the meeting.
- Allow a right of appeal against any decision to dismiss the employee, and if the employee does appeal, hear the appeal and communicate the final decision in writing.

9.521 A failure to follow any one of the above steps will mean that the employee's dismissal will be ruled automatically unfair by an employment tribunal, irrespective of the seriousness of the employee's misconduct.

9.522 For example, in *Masterfoods v Wilson* (2006) EAT 0202/06, a dismissed employee who was denied an appeal hearing in respect of his dismissal because he had failed to set out the grounds for his appeal in writing within five days as required by his employer's contractual disciplinary procedure, succeeded in persuading the tribunal that his dismissal was automatically unfair. In cases where an employee appeals against his/her dismissal, the DDP requires the employer to hear the appeal; the DDP does not prescribe any particular form of appeal nor timescale that the employee must adhere to. The fact that the employee had not complied with his employer's contractual disciplinary procedure did not release the employer from the statutory requirements of the DDP.

9.523 It is also important to note that the DDP represents a minimum level of fairness. There is still a duty to treat employees reasonably in an overall sense, otherwise a dismissal may be unfair even if the DDP has been followed.

Procedural Fairness

9.524 Procedural fairness concerns the steps taken by the employer in arriving at the decision to dismiss. Where employees are dismissed for incompetence or poor performance, the key elements of a fair procedure are:
- appraisal of employee's performance
- informing the employee in writing of the aspects of performance that are unsatisfactory
- discussion of all the performance problems and their causes with the employee
- communication of desired employee performance improvements
- warning of consequences of failure to improve
- providing any necessary support to the employee, eg training
- allowing a reasonable period of time for improvements before considering dismissal
- allowing the right of appeal against any decision to dismiss.

9.525 When considering dismissing for misconduct (which falls short of gross misconduct), the employer should apply a procedure that involves a series of warnings. With dismissals in such circumstances, the key elements of procedural fairness are as follows.
- Except for gross misconduct, no employee should be dismissed for a first breach of discipline.

- Where disciplinary warnings are imposed, the level of the warning, ie from informal verbal warning to final written warning, should be made plain to the employee, should be commensurate with the seriousness of the misconduct, and should take account of whether any previous disciplinary warnings issued remain valid.
- The decision making process leading to a disciplinary warning should be based upon a proper investigation of the misconduct concerned, and should allow the employee to know the details of the disciplinary allegation, and the chance to answer any such disciplinary case.
- In giving an employee a disciplinary warning, the employee should be informed as to the conduct which has resulted in the warning, the consequences of any repetition and the period of time for which the warning will be treated as a "live" warning.
- In dealing with misconduct, it is unlikely to be fair to take account of a previous warning given for misconduct of a completely different kind, unless the earlier warning was in respect of the employee's conduct in general.
- Warnings which have expired should not normally be taken into account in deciding upon an appropriate disciplinary penalty, save that the fact there is a previous record may limit the mitigation available to the employee. In *Diosynth Ltd v Thomson* [2006] CSIH 5, the Court of Session in Scotland ruled that an employee's dismissal was unfair because the employer had taken into account a written warning that had expired a few months earlier. This was despite the fact that the employee's conduct had involved a major breach of safety procedures. The court stated that an employee was entitled to have a reasonable expectation that the employer meant what it said when it stated that the warning would be disregarded after a specified period of time.
- An employee who is at risk of dismissal following non-compliance with an earlier warning should be given a proper opportunity to make representations on the basis that dismissal is one of the options being considered.
- The employee must be granted the right of appeal against any decision to dismiss.

9.526 In capability cases where the issue is one of ill health, the key elements of procedural fairness are:

- obtaining an up-to-date medical report or medical advice
- informing the employee in writing that their ill health absence may lead to the termination of their employment
- consulting and discussing the situation fully with the employee
- considering the likelihood of an improvement in the employee's health
- investigating and discussing the available options, eg alternative employment, adjustments to the job or workplace — bearing in mind the duty of employers towards disabled employees
- allowing the right of appeal against any decision to dismiss.

9.527 In redundancy cases, the guidelines on procedural requirements are as follows.

- The employer should give the employee as much warning as possible of any impending redundancy.
- Consultations should take place on the best way to achieve the desired management results fairly and with minimal hardship to employees.
- The employer should seek to agree with employees or their representatives the objective criteria to be applied in selecting employees for redundancy.
- Each affected employee should be informed in writing that their job may be made redundant and invited to attend a meeting to discuss the circumstances and make representations (before any final selection decisions are made).

- Any selection should be made fairly in accordance with the criteria and take into account representations made on behalf of the employees involved.
- The employer should seek to offer a redundant employee suitable alternative employment within the organisation or any associated organisation.
- The employer must grant the employee the right of appeal against a decision to dismiss.

Substantive Fairness

9.528 Substantive fairness relates to the validity of the reason for dismissing the employee and whether the reason is sufficient to justify the penalty of dismissal. The employer needs to act on the basis of a genuine belief in the circumstances informing the reason for dismissal. Where this validity is subsequently challenged, an employment tribunal will examine whether the employer acted reasonably in arriving at such a belief.

9.529 Before arriving at the decision to dismiss, the employer needs to give consideration to alternatives and to representations made by or on behalf of the employee. Representations include explanations for misconduct or poor performance and mitigating factors, eg length of service and previous employment record.

Automatically Unfair Reasons for Dismissal

9.530 Dismissal will automatically be held to be unfair where the principal reason for it was:
- parental leave
- adoption leave
- paternity leave
- time taken off to care for dependants
- the employee submitting a request for flexible working
- seeking to be accompanied at a disciplinary or grievance hearing
- a spent conviction
- the transfer of an undertaking or a reason connected with it, unless for an economic, technical or organisational reason entailing changes in the workforce
- the employee's trade union membership or non-membership or union activities – except industrial action
- the employee's performance of duties as an occupational pension scheme trustee
- the employee taking action on health and safety grounds
- the employee asserting a statutory employment right
- the employee refusing to do shop or betting work on a Sunday (applicable to retail and betting shop workers only)
- the employee being pregnant, having given birth to a child or taken maternity leave
- the employee whistleblowing.

9.531 An automatically unfair dismissal will also arise where an employee is selected for redundancy on any of the above grounds.

9.532 A dismissal will also be automatically unfair if it is carried out without the full application of the statutory dismissal and disciplinary procedure (DDP).

9.533 Employment tribunals have no jurisdiction to decide whether an employee was fairly or unfairly dismissed where industrial action entitles the employer to terminate the contracts of all those taking part.

Right Not to be Unfairly Dismissed

9.534 Employees have a statutory right not to be unfairly dismissed, as provided for by the Employment Rights Act 1996.

Definitions Regarding the Right

9.535 Employees are defined as individuals who have entered into and work or have worked under a contract of employment.

9.536 A contract of employment means a contract of service or apprenticeship. Its terms may be expressed in writing or orally, or may be implied. Identifying a contract of employment generally involves identifying two key factors:
- mutuality of obligation, ie whether there is an obligation on one party to provide work and an obligation on the other party to do the work
- one party must be subject to the control of the other party.

Exclusions to the Right

9.537 Employees are excluded from the right not to be unfairly dismissed if they have less than one year's continuous service with the employer at the date of their dismissal.

9.538 The qualifying period exclusion does not apply where the complaint is based on dismissal for an automatically unfair reason (except where the reason for dismissal is connected with the transfer of an undertaking or on the grounds of a spent conviction where the one-year qualifying period applies).

Remedies for Unfair Dismissal

9.539 Any person complaining of unfair dismissal can present a complaint to an employment tribunal. There is a time limit for bringing proceedings — normally three months from the effective date of termination of employment. The three-month time period is, however, extended to six months in circumstances where the employee has reasonable grounds to believe that, at the expiry of the three-month time limit, the employer was still following through an internal appeal procedure. The tribunal can, at its discretion, extend the applicable time limit but will only do so if the dismissed employee can show that it was not reasonably practicable for him or her to bring the case within the relevant three or six-month limit.

9.540 Detailed guidance on disciplinary and grievance procedures is provided by the Acas *Code of Practice on Disciplinary and Grievance Procedures*. Non-compliance with this Code of Practice does not automatically cause a dismissal to be unfair, but it is a factor which employment tribunals are entitled to take into account and which will act to the detriment of the employer.

Orders and Remuneration

9.541 The employment tribunal can:
- order the reinstatement of an employee to his or her previous position
- order the re-engagement of an employee, ie order that he or she be placed in employment comparable to that from which he or she was dismissed
- order the employer to pay compensation to the dismissed employee.

9.542 In the event of an order for reinstatement or re-engagement, the tribunal will also order the employer to compensate the employee for loss of wages and benefits from the date of dismissal through to the date of re-employment.

Unfair Dismissal

9.543 Amounts paid to the complainant by his or her employer on termination, eg any ex-gratia payment, will be offset against the sum of compensation awarded.

9.544 Employment tribunals will not make reinstatement or re-engagement orders where it is not practicable for the employer to comply, nor where the dismissed employee does not wish to return to work for the employer.

9.545 Where an employer fails to comply with an order for reinstatement or re-engagement, an additional award of compensation can be made.

Compensation and Awards

9.546 In most cases, the remedy ordered by the tribunal will be an award of compensation. There are two types of award.
- Basic award.
- Compensatory award.

9.547 The basic award is calculated in a similar way to statutory redundancy payments.

9.548 The compensatory award is the amount judged equitable by the tribunal after consideration of the loss sustained by the complainant as a result of the dismissal. There is a statutory cap to the compensatory award payable for unfair dismissal, which is £60,600 (since 1 February 2007).

9.549 Following the case of *Dunnachie v Kingston upon Hull City Council* [2004] IRLR 727, HL, it is clear that compensation for injury to feelings on account of the dismissal, or the manner of the dismissal, is not recoverable as part of the compensatory award for unfair dismissal.

9.550 The Court of Appeal has confirmed (in *Burlo v Langley and Carter* [2006] EWCA Civ 1778) that an employee who was absent from work due to sickness when (unfairly) dismissed was not entitled to compensation equivalent to full pay in respect of the notice period where the contract of employment allowed for only statutory sick pay to be paid during periods of sickness absence.

Uplift/Reduction on the Award of Compensation

9.551 An enhanced award of compensation will be awarded to an employee where the employer has failed to apply the statutory dismissal and disciplinary procedure (DDP).

9.552 The reverse also applies, ie an employee's compensation will be reduced where the employee has failed to co-operate with the employer in the application of the procedure, or failed without good reason to exercise their right of appeal. The uplift/reduction in compensation is a minimum of 10% and, at the tribunal's discretion, up to 50%. The statutory cap of £60,600 still applies, however, irrespective of any uplift in the employee's compensation.

Contributory Fault

9.553 The tribunal is required to reduce the compensatory award if it finds that the dismissal was caused or contributed to by the employee's actions, eg misconduct.

Duty to Mitigate

9.554 The tribunal is also required to take account of any failure by the employee to mitigate his or her loss. The employee has a duty to seek alternative employment to make good any loss caused by the dismissal. Where the employer satisfies the

Unfair Dismissal

tribunal that the employee could have obtained another job after dismissal but did not do so, the compensatory award can be reduced by the amount which would have been earned through such employment.

Training

9.555 Individuals involved in making any decision as to the possible dismissal of an employee, including the hearing of any appeal, will need appropriate training.

9.556 Training should be based on the Acas *Code of Practice on Disciplinary and Grievance Procedures*.

List of Relevant Legislation

9.557
- Employment Act 2002 (Dispute Resolution) Regulations 2004
- Employment Act 2002
- Public Interest Disclosure Act 1998
- Employment Rights Act 1996
- Disability Discrimination Act 1995
- Trade Union and Labour Relations (Consolidation) Act 1992

List of Relevant Cases

9.558
- *Sahatciu v DPP Restaurants Ltd* (2007) EAT 0177/06
- *Masterfoods v Wilson* (2006) EAT 0202/06
- *Copsey v WWB Devon Clays Ltd* [2005] IRLR 811, CA
- *Cross v British Airways plc* [2005] IRLR 423, EAT
- *HM Prison Service v Beart (No. 2)* [2005] IRLR 171, EAT
- *Lionel Leventhal Ltd v North* [2005] IDS Brief 778, EAT
- *Marks & Spencer plc v Williams-Ryan* [2005] IRLR 562, CA
- *Omilaju v Waltham Forest London Borough Council* [2005] ICR 481, CA
- *Street v Derbyshire Unemployed Workers' Centre* [2005] ICR 97, CA
- *Asda Stores Ltd v Thompson (No. 2)* [2004] IRLR 598, EAT
- *Ramsay v Walkers Snack Foods Ltd* [2004] IRLR 754, EAT
- *Dunnachie v Kingston upon Hull City Council* [2004] IRLR 727, HL
- *McGowan v Scottish Water* [2004] IDS Brief 771, EAT
- *X v Y* [2004] IRLR 625, CA
- *Iceland Frozen Foods v Jones* [1982] IRLR 439, EAT
- *Williams v Compair Maxam Ltd* [1982] IRLR 83, EAT
- *Weddell and Co Ltd v Tepper* [1980] IRLR 96, CA
- *British Home Stores Ltd v Burchell* [1978] IRLR 379, EAT — in misconduct cases, the employer must have carried out as much investigation into the matter as was reasonable in all the circumstances of the case by the point in time at which any conclusion of misconduct was reached.

Further Information

Publications
- PL714 *Dismissal — Fair and Unfair*, Department for Business, Enterprise and Regulatory Reform (BERR)
- *Acas/CP01 Code of Practice on Disciplinary and Grievance Procedures (2004)*

Organisations
- **Department for Business, Enterprise and Regulatory Reform (BERR)**
  Web: *www.berr.gov.uk*
  The Department for Business, Enterprise and Regulatory Reform brings together functions from the former Department of Trade and Industry (DTI), including responsibilities for productivity, business relations, energy, competition and consumers. It also drives regulatory reform.
- **Advisory Conciliation and Arbitration Service (Acas)**
  Web: *www.acas.org.uk*
  Acas aims to improve organisations and working life through better employment relations. It provides up-to-date information, advice, high-quality training, and works with employers and employees to solve problems and improve performance.

Wrongful Dismissal

> This topic covers the following.
> - Termination of Employment
> - Entitlement to Notice
> - Payment in Lieu of Notice
> - Resignation by the Employee
> - Lawful Dismissal without Notice
> - Summary Dismissal
> - Defence to a Wrongful Dismissal Claim
> - Damages for Wrongful Dismissal
> - Deductions from Damages for Wrongful Dismissal
> - Restraining a Wrongful Dismissal
> - Jurisdiction of Employment Tribunals

9.559 Employees will mostly seek to challenge a dismissal by bringing a complaint of unfair dismissal. This is provided for under the Employment Rights Act 1996 and results in proceedings in the employment tribunal. The main issue becomes the dismissal's fairness (as defined by the statute).

9.560 However, a dismissal can also lead to legal proceedings for wrongful dismissal. This is essentially a common law claim. The normal forum for common law claims is the County Court (or the High Court in high-value cases) or, in Scotland, the Sheriff Court. The main issue would be whether or not the dismissal was in breach of contract, in the sense of being in breach of the contractual rights of the employee.

9.561 Most contracts of employment make provision as to the means by which the contract can lawfully be terminated by the employer (and also by the employee), ie what notice is required to terminate the employment relationship. Usually this involves a stipulation as to the amount (in time) of notice required. It follows that the most common form of wrongful dismissal claim involves the employee claiming that he or she has not been given the required amount of notice.

9.562 The amount at stake would normally be the amount of remuneration, plus a sum equivalent to the value of other contractual benefits, to which the employee would have been entitled during the notice period. The jurisdiction of the employment tribunal extends to allow such claims, up to £25,000 in value, to be brought as proceedings in the employment tribunal.

9.563 Since 1 October 2004, the Employment Act 2002 requires employers to follow a statutory dismissal and disciplinary procedure (DDP) before dismissing an employee. Failure to adhere to the mandatory steps contained in the DDP will mean the employee's dismissal will be automatically unfair and the employer will be liable to pay an enhanced compensatory award to the employee. The Government has proposed an Employment Simplification Bill of repeal which will include the statutory dispute resolution procedures. Details are expected in November 2007.

Employers' Duties

- The termination of a contract of employment should be in accordance with any stipulations in the contract providing for the termination of employment.

- In particular, in terminating a contract of employment, an employer will need to comply with the employee's entitlement to notice by giving the employee such period of notice as provided for under the contract.
- The need to give notice may not arise where the contract entitles the employer to terminate the employment by means of a payment in lieu of notice.
- A lawful dismissal without notice may arise where the contract of employment is terminated by operation of law, such as in an insolvency case or where it is brought to an end as a result of an external event amounting to frustration.
- An employer will need to be able to justify a summary dismissal on the basis of action by the employee, such as gross misconduct, that amounts to a repudiation of the contract of employment.
- The employer must conduct appropriate investigations and carry out a proper disciplinary procedure before deciding to dismiss an employee summarily.
- The employer's defence to a wrongful dismissal claim will involve seeking to show that conduct by the employee gave the employer the legal right to terminate the contract summarily.
- The employer should avoid taking any steps which amount to a repudiation of the contract of employment, since in such circumstances resignation by the employee may give rise to a claim for wrongful dismissal and/or constructive unfair dismissal.

Employees' Duties

- Employees will need to conduct themselves in a way which is in accordance with and consistent with the provisions and purpose of the contract of employment, since to do otherwise may amount to gross misconduct and/or action repudiating the contract, thereby justifying a summary dismissal.
- A contract of employment will normally stipulate the period of notice.
- The unlawful termination of a contract of employment will entitle the employee to seek damages for wrongful dismissal .
- Deductions from damages for wrongful dismissal will include deductions to take account of the effect of taxation and any receipt of state benefits, but deductions may also be made where the employee fails to fulfil the duty to mitigate the loss.
- In very limited circumstances an employee may be able to take enforcement proceedings restraining a wrongful dismissal.
- Employees' claims for wrongful dismissal, up to £25,000 in value, are within the jurisdiction of employment tribunals.

In Practice

Termination of Employment

9.564 Wrongful dismissal occurs where an employer terminates a contract of employment in a way which is in breach of contract, and therefore unlawful. A contract of employment will usually contain provisions allowing for the lawful termination of the contract, such as:
- upon expiry of a fixed term
- upon completion of the purpose of the contract
- by giving notice.

9.565 A termination of the contact of employment which is otherwise than in accordance with such provisions will involve a breach of contract and will potentially amount to a wrongful dismissal. The employees will be able to seek a remedy in an ordinary court of law for the infringement of their common law rights. Such claims, up to £25,000 in value, can also be heard in employment tribunals (but there is no ceiling for claims brought to the ordinary courts).

Entitlement to Notice

Contractual Notice

9.566 Contractual notice is normally the period of notice required in order to terminate a contract of employment. It may be stipulated by the contract of employment itself, and the parties to the contract will be bound by such a provision. Employers are required by statute to provide employees with a "written statement of particulars of employment" which has to include "the length of notice" which the employees are obliged to give and entitled to receive to terminate their contract of employment.

Statutory Notice

9.567 In the event that a contract of employment is silent as to the length of any notice period, the employer and employee have statutory rights to minimum periods of notice.

9.568 Employees who have been employed continuously for one month or more are entitled to a minimum of one week's notice. If the period of continuous employment is two years or more, employees are entitled to not less than one week's notice for each completed year of service (up to a maximum of 12 weeks' notice).

9.569 These statutory requirements will be treated as having been incorporated into individual contacts of employment. Breach of such requirements would therefore entitle the employee to proceed by way of a claim for damages for breach of contract.

Reasonable Notice

9.570 Where the contract of employment is silent as to the required notice period, the employee may be able to assert a common law right to reasonable notice, the length of which will depend upon the circumstances, such as the type of employment involved.

9.571 An employee who has been employed for less than one month, so as not to have a right to the minimum statutory notice, may nevertheless be able to claim entitlement to reasonable notice. In some circumstances, a court or tribunal might find that reasonable notice necessitated a period in excess of the minimum statutory period of notice.

Payment in Lieu of Notice

9.572 Where a contract of employment specifically provides for the contract to be terminated either by the giving of notice of a certain period, or by a payment of salary for that period in lieu of notice, no breach of contract or wrongful dismissal will be involved if the contract is terminated with pay in lieu. This is because any termination by way of payment in lieu of notice will be in accordance with the contractual provisions for termination.

9.573 By contrast, in a case where the employer gives the employee wages in lieu of notice, which the employee accepts, without the employer having any contractual right to terminate the contract in this way, the dismissal will amount to a summary and wrongful dismissal. This will be the case even if the wages paid in lieu of notice represent the measure of damages to which the employee would ordinarily be entitled in respect of such wrongful dismissal. This has two important consequences from the employer's perspective:

- it is hardly worth the employee making a claim once the payment has been made since he or she would not stand to gain financially
- the breach of contract has the effect of rendering any post-termination clauses in the contract unenforceable.

Resignation by the Employee

9.574 An employee will be entitled to terminate the contract summarily if the employer is in breach of a significant term or behaves in a way which amounts to a repudiation of the contract. In this case, the employer would be liable for damages for wrongful dismissal. The employee may also be able to bring a claim for constructive (unfair) dismissal if he or she has had a minimum of one year's continuous service.

Lawful Dismissal Without Notice

9.575 There are circumstances where a dismissal without notice will not amount to a wrongful dismissal.

9.576 Where the contract of employment is terminated by operation of law, such as in an insolvency case, this will not be treated as a dismissal giving rise to remedies for wrongful dismissal.

9.577 A contract of employment may also come to an end as a result of "frustration of contract". Frustration of a contract occurs when an external event affecting the contract takes place that:

- was not reasonably foreseeable at the time the contract was made
- renders further performance of the contract totally impossible or something radically different from what the parties bargained for.

9.578 The courts will treat such a contract as discharged by operation of law. Typical instances of frustration might be a change in the law that makes the contract illegal or the death of one of the parties.

9.579 If frustration is deemed to have occurred, dismissals will not give rise to remedies for wrongful dismissal.

Summary Dismissal

9.580 The most common situation giving rise to a claim of wrongful dismissal is where there is a summary dismissal of an employee. A summary dismissal is a dismissal without notice or pay in lieu of notice. However, a summary dismissal will not amount to a wrongful dismissal where it can be justified. This is because the law recognises the right of either party to a contract of employment to treat the contract as terminable without notice by reason of conduct of the other party which is in fundamental breach of the contract.

Disciplinary Procedures

9.581 Although gross misconduct on the part of the employee may justify the employer in carrying out a summary dismissal, this does not mean a dismissal without going through the normal procedures prior to taking the decision to dismiss. Even though a summary dismissal will involve a situation in which disciplinary warnings are not appropriate, the employer will still need to carry out a proper investigation, conduct an interview with the employee and consider all the circumstances before deciding to dismiss.

9.582 The Employment Act 2002 (Dispute Resolution) Regulations 2004, which were implemented on 1 October 2004, require all employers to apply a dismissal and disciplinary procedure (DDP) when contemplating dismissing an employee and any dismissal implemented without the full and correct application of the DDP will be automatically unfair.

9.583 The Advisory, Conciliation and Arbitration Service (Acas) *Code of Practice on Disciplinary and Grievance Procedures* points out that "'summary' is not synonymous with 'instant' and incidents of gross misconduct will usually still need to be investigated as part of a formal procedure."

Fundamental Breach

9.584 Summary dismissal is justified where the conduct of the employee amounts to a repudiation of the contract by the employee. Clearly not every breach of the contract by an employee will have this effect. A repudiatory breach of contract is sometimes described in terms of a significant or fundamental breach which goes to the root of the contract. Thus, it could be said to involve the employee acting in a way which is in conflict with, and is inconsistent with, the contract itself.

9.585 Thus, a single act of gross misconduct can be said to amount to a repudiation of the contract, whereas an instance of less serious misconduct is unlikely to do so, save in the case of repeated misconduct where the misconduct continues after appropriate disciplinary warnings.

Defence to a Wrongful Dismissal Claim

9.586 Where the contract of employment is terminated summarily, ie without notice, the employee has the right of common law to bring proceedings for breach of contract.

9.587 Where the employer's summary termination of the contract was in response to an action on the part of the employee, the employer's defence will be to seek to show that the employee's conduct amounted to a fundamental breach of a key term of the contract or a repudiation of the contract which entitled the employer to terminate the contract summarily.

9.588 In addition to gross misconduct, disobedience to lawful orders and negligence may also justify summary dismissal.

9.589 Contracts of employment frequently list, by way of example, the types of conduct which will be treated as gross misconduct. However, it is not so much the label or description of the conduct which matters, as the seriousness of the conduct. Clearly the seriousness of the employee's act will depend upon the circumstances, including the type of employment.

Damages for Wrongful Dismissal

9.590 Damages for wrongful dismissal will normally be limited to the losses sustained by the employee in the period until the date when the employer could lawfully have terminated the contract. Thus, damages will normally be limited to the employee's earnings during the notice period. However, employers may be able to claim unfair dismissal in addition to wrongful dismissal, although there can be no double recovery of losses.

Fixed-Term Contracts

9.591 If a fixed-term contract of employment (with no provision for notice during the currency of the contract) is terminated early in circumstances other than gross misconduct, the employee will be able to claim as damages any earnings which would have been received during the remainder of the fixed term. Any such claim would be limited to the amount to which the employee would have been entitled if the employer had fulfilled its legal obligations.

9.592 Recent cases show that an employee may be able to claim non-contractual payments such as discretionary bonuses following a wrongful dismissal. In *Horkulak v Cantor Fitzgerald International* [2004] IRLR 942, CA the Court of Appeal held that, even though the claimant's contract stated that the employer "may pay" an annual discretionary bonus, the fact that the discretionary bonus clause existed as part of the contract created a right for the employee to be paid something. The bonus clause stood "to be read as a contractual benefit to the employee, as opposed to being a mere declaration of the employer's right to pay a bonus if he wishes".

9.593 Other cases demonstrate that an employer is not entitled to refuse to make such payments if this would involve acting irrationally or in bad faith and/or in breach of the implied term of trust and confidence. (See *Clark v Nomura International plc* [2000] IRLR 767, HC and *Clark v BET* [1997] IRLR 348).

Injury to Feelings

9.594 It is well established that a wrongfully dismissed employee cannot claim damages by way of compensation for the manner of dismissal or injury to reputation or for injury to feelings (see *Addis v Gramophone Company Ltd* [1909] AC 488, HL).

Damages for Reputation

9.595 Stigma damages, ie damages for loss of or damage to reputation and future employment prospects (eg as where caused by an employer conducting a dishonest or corrupt business, see *Malik v BCCI* [1997] ICR 606, HL) cannot be claimed in an ordinary wrongful dismissal case, but may be claimed in other breach of contract cases (eg where a breach of the implied term of trust and confidence has occurred during employment rather than on termination.

Damages for Deprivation of Financial Benefits

9.596 Damages for deprivation of financial benefits and rights may be recoverable in an action for wrongful dismissal. This arises in cases where the wrongful dismissal of an employee without notice deprives the employee of the opportunity to become eligible and qualify through service for particular rights, such as redundancy rights or rights under permanent health insurance (PHI) schemes. In PHI cases, courts are likely to rule that the termination of an employee's contract on the grounds of long term sickness absence is unlawful if the effect would be to deprive the employee of benefits under a PHI scheme provided as part of the employment package.

9.597 The Court of Appeal has held, however (in *Harper v Virgin Net Ltd* [2004] TLR 174), that a employee dismissed shortly before attaining the necessary one year's service to qualify for the right to claim unfair dismissal cannot recover damages for the loss of the right to claim unfair dismissal on account of being dismissed without the full period of notice due under the contract.

Deductions from Damages for Wrongful Dismissal

Mitigation

9.598 In wrongful dismissal cases employees will be under a duty to take reasonable steps to mitigate their loss, ie find another job to replace the lost source of earnings. What is reasonable will depend upon the circumstances of the case.

9.599 It may be reasonable for employees initially to seek employment which equates to their former position, but after a while it may become reasonable to expect them to take a lesser paid job. Compensation for loss of earnings can be reduced where employees have failed to take reasonable steps to mitigate their loss.

Effect of Pay in Lieu of Notice Clause

9.600 No duty to mitigate will arise where the contract gives the employee a contractual right to payment of a sum in lieu of notice. However, where the contract gives the employer discretion to terminate the contract by way of a payment in lieu of notice, rather than allowing the employee to work out his or her notice, there will still be a duty to mitigate. (See *Cerberus Software Ltd v Rowley* [2001] ICR 376, CA).

9.601 Earnings from new employment will normally be taken into account and offset against any award of damages to the employee in respect of loss of earnings.

Taxation

9.602 As a general rule damages are not taxable in the hands of the claimant. So that the employee is not placed in a better position than he or she otherwise would have been in, *British Transport Commission v Gourley* [1956] AC 185, HL establishes that damages for loss of earnings should be calculated and awarded net of tax. However, the Income Tax (Earnings and Pensions) Act 2003 provides for post-cessation receipts from employment to be taxed to the extent that they exceed £30,000. Thus, any damages for wrongful dismissal which exceed £30,000 will be calculated and awarded gross.

State Benefits

9.603 Where a wrongful dismissal claimant seeks damages for loss of earnings it is possible that the claimant will have been receiving state benefits for part or all of the period of the claim. There is no automatic provision for the recoupment of such benefits from any damages for wrongful dismissal (unlike the position with damages for personal injury). In wrongful dismissal cases, courts will calculate the loss suffered by the claimant so any amount calculated as loss of earnings is likely to be reduced by the figure for any state benefits already received.

Private Insurance and Pension Benefits

9.604 Private insurance and pension benefits are unlikely to be deducted from any award for damages for loss of earnings on the basis that such benefits are received as a right and as a result of the foresight of the claimant in taking out any such policy and paying the necessary contributions over a period of time.

Redundancy Payments

9.605 Redundancy payments will normally be deducted from awards of damages for wrongful dismissal, except possibly where the employee would have been made redundant anyway.

Wrongful Dismissal

Reduction for Accelerated Receipt

9.606 Where damages for wrongful dismissal represent loss of earnings over a significant period of time, the amount awarded will usually be reduced to take account of the fact that the payment of damages will provide the claimant with the full sum immediately (with the possibility of increasing it by investment), but also to take account of the uncertainties of life, such as the possibility of the employment being terminated for other reasons before the end of the period concerned.

Compensation for Unfair Dismissal

9.607 The rule against double recovery will prevent the same losses for the same period being awarded twice over as compensation for wrongful dismissal and compensation for unfair dismissal.

Restraining a Wrongful Dismissal

9.608 There is a general rule against enforcing a contract of employment, even for the notice period. However, it is not a fixed rule of law, as established in *Hill v C A Parsons & Co Ltd* [1972] Ch 305, CA, and there are limited circumstances in which enforcement action may be considered, including restraining unlawful disciplinary action (see *Peace v City of Edinburgh City Council* [1999] IRLR 417, OH), and restraining a dismissal in breach of procedure (see *Irani v Southampton & SW Hampshire* HA [1985] ICR 590, HC).

9.609 The factors taken into account by courts in enforcement proceedings in deciding whether or not to restrain breaches of a contract of employment can be summarised as shown below:
- whether there is continuing mutual trust between the parties
- the stage at which intervention is being sought, in that the courts will be more likely to restrain a breach of contract which may lead to dismissal, rather than the purported dismissal itself
- whether damages will be an adequate remedy
- whether any order made by the court will be likely to be effective.

Jurisdiction of Employment Tribunals

9.610 As a result of the Employment Tribunals Extension of the Jurisdiction (England & Wales) Order 1994, employment tribunals have the jurisdiction to deal with breach of contract claims including claims for wrongful dismissal.

9.611 The key points are as follows.
- The main requirement for an employment tribunal to have jurisdiction is that the claim must arise or be outstanding on the termination of the employee's employment.
- The restricted jurisdiction in breach of contract claims also means that the employment tribunal does not have the power to award more than £25,000 in respect of breach of contract.
- Tribunals have no jurisdiction to deal with proceedings relating to the breach of a restrictive covenant.
- If breach of contract proceedings are to be brought in the employment tribunals it is important to remember the three-month time limit which is normally applicable.
- Employers may bring a counter-claim for breach of contract against the employee. A counter-claim must be brought within six weeks of receipt of the employee's claim.

- It will often be worthwhile for employees to bring a wrongful dismissal claim at the same time as an unfair dismissal claim. Different principles are involved, so there is a possibility of one claim succeeding where the other does not.
- A practical consideration is that where a summary dismissal for gross misconduct is found to be unfair, there will often be a reduction of the award for unfair dismissal to take account of contributory fault, while such a deduction would not be made in a claim for wrongful dismissal.

Training

9.612 Wrongful dismissal claims usually arise out of summary dismissals. It is therefore important that those employees responsible for deciding whether or not to implement a summary dismissal have appropriate training for handling disciplinary matters, which might appropriately be based upon the Acas *Code of Practice on Disciplinary and Grievance Procedures*, as well as focusing upon the legal and contractual issues involved in the termination of employment.

List of Relevant Legislation

9.613
- Employment Act (2002) (Dispute Resolution) Regulations 2004
- Income Tax (Earnings and Pensions) Act 2003
- Employment Act 2002
- Employment Rights Act 1996
- Employment Tribunals Extension of Jurisdiction (England and Wales) Order 1994

List of Relevant Cases

9.614
- *Dunnachie v Kingston upon Hull City Council* [2004] IRLR 727, HL — When assessing compensatory award on unfair dismissal, the loss suffered by an employee for which compensation can be awarded by an employment tribunal is financial loss only. There is no power in unfair dismissal cases for a tribunal to award compensation for non-economic "loss" such as injury to feelings, just as there is no power for a tribunal to award aggravated or exemplary compensation by way of penalisation of the conduct of the employer.
- *Harper v Virgin Net Ltd* [2004] TLR 174, CA — Dismissal of employees before they have one year's service.
- *Horkulak v Cantor Fitzgerald International* [2004] IRLR 942, CA.
- *Johnson v Unisys Ltd* [2001] IRLR 279, HL — Dismissal without going through a disciplinary procedure.
- *Cerberus Software Ltd v Rowley* [2001] IRLR 160, CA — Pay in lieu and duty to mitigate.
- *Clark v Nomura International plc* [2000] IRLR 767, HC.
- *Neary v Dean of Westminster* [1999] IRLR 288 — Gross misconduct undermining trust and confidence.
- *Peace v City of Edinburgh City Council* [1999] IRLR 417, CS — Restraining unlawful disciplinary action.

- *Clark v BET plc* [1997] IRLR 348, HC — Claiming of bonuses and implied trust and confidence.
- *Malik v BCCI SA (in compulsory liquidation)* [1997] IRLR 462, HL — Employer conducting a dishonest business.
- *Aspden v Webbs Poultry & Meat Group (Holdings) Ltd* [1996] IRLR 521, HC — Dismissal provisions cannot be used to disentitle an employee from benefits under a permanent health insurance (PHI) scheme.
- *Irani v Southampton and South-West Hampshire Health Authority* [1985] IRLR 203, HC — Restraining a dismissal in breach of procedure.
- *Hill v CA Parsons and Co Ltd* [1972] Ch 305, CA — Restraining a wrongful dismissal.
- *British Transport Commission v Gourley* [1956] AC 185, HL — Damages awarded net of tax.
- *Addis v Gramophone Co Ltd* [1909] AC 488, HL — Damages for injury to feelings.

Further Information

Publications
- PL714 *Dismissal — Fair and Unfair*, Department for Business, Enterprise and Regulatory Reform (BERR)
- Acas/CP01 *Code of Practice on Disciplinary and Grievance Procedures (2004)*
- Inland Revenue Guidance on Payments in Lieu of Notice (PILONs) in *Tax Bulletin*, Number 63 (February 2003).

Organisations
- **Department for Business, Enterprise and Regulatory Reform (BERR)**
  Web: *www.berr.gov.uk*
  The Department for Business, Enterprise and Regulatory Reform brings together functions from the former Department of Trade and Industry (DTI), including responsibilities for productivity, business relations, energy, competition and consumers. It also drives regulatory reform.

Appendix
Key Rates and Data

Statutory Sick Pay

Weekly Rates of SSP

Tax year	Lower Earnings Limit	SSP
2006/07	£84.00	£70.05
2007/08	£87.00	£72.55

SMP, SPP and SAP

Statutory Maternity Pay

Tax year	Set rate
Before 1 April 2007	£108.85
From 1 April 2007	£112.75

Statutory Paternity Pay

Tax year	Set rate
Before 1 April 2007	£108.85
From 1 April 2007	£112.75

Statutory Adoption Pay

Tax year	Set rate
Before 1 April 2007	£108.85
From 1 April 2007	£112.75

Redundancy Pay

Portion of a Week's Wages

Age	Portion of week's wages
under 21	half
22 to 40	one
41 and over	one and a half

Maximum Week's Pay

Period	Maximum week's pay
From 1 February 2006 until 31 January 2007	£290
From 1 February 2007 until 31 January 2008	£310

Statutory Redundancy Pay — Ready Reckoner

To calculate the number of weeks' pay due, read off the employee's age and number of complete years' service.

Age in years	_	_	_	_	_	_	complete years' service												
	2	3	4	5	6	7	8	9	10	11	12	13	14	15	16	17	18	19	20
*17	1																		
18	1	1½																	
19	1	1½	2																
20	1	1½	2	2½	—														
21	1	1½	2	2½	3	—													
22	1	1½	2	2½	3	3½	—												
23	1½	2	2½	3	3½	4	4½	—											
24	2	2½	3	3½	4	4½	5	5½	—										
25	2	3	3½	4	4½	5	5½	6	6½	—									
26	2	3	4	4½	5	5½	6	6½	7	7½	—								
27	2	3	4	5	5½	6	6½	7	7½	8	8½	—							
28	2	3	4	5	6	6½	7	7½	8	8½	9	9½	—						
29	2	3	4	5	6	7	7½	8	8½	9	9½	10	10½	—					
30	2	3	4	5	6	7	8	8½	9	9½	10	10½	11	11½	—				
31	2	3	4	5	6	7	8	9	9½	10	10½	11	11½	12	12½	—			
32	2	3	4	5	6	7	8	9	10	10½	11	11½	12	12½	13	13½	—		
33	2	3	4	5	6	7	8	9	10	11	11½	12	12½	13	13½	14	14½	—	
34	2	3	4	5	6	7	8	9	10	11	12	12½	13	13½	14	14½	15	15½	—
35	2	3	4	5	6	7	8	9	10	11	12	13	13½	14	14½	15	15½	16	16½
36	2	3	4	5	6	7	8	9	10	11	12	13	14	14½	15	15½	16	16½	17
37	2	3	4	5	6	7	8	9	10	11	12	13	14	15	15½	16	16½	17	17½
38	2	3	4	5	6	7	8	9	10	11	12	13	14	15	16	16½	17	17½	18
39	2	3	4	5	6	7	8	9	10	11	12	13	14	15	16	17	17½	18	18½
40	2	3	4	5	6	7	8	9	10	11	12	13	14	15	16	17	18	18½	19
41	2	3	4	5	6	7	8	9	10	11	12	13	14	15	16	17	18	19	19½
42	2½	3½	4½	5½	6½	7½	8½	9½	10½	11½	12½	13½	14½	15½	16½	17½	18½	19½	20½
43	3	4	5	6	7	8	9	10	11	12	13	14	15	16	17	18	19	20	21
44	3	4½	5½	6½	7½	8½	9½	10½	11½	12½	13½	14½	15½	16½	17½	18½	19½	20½	21½
45	3	4½	6	7	8	9	10	11	12	13	14	15	16	17	18	19	20	21	22
46	3	4½	6	7½	8½	9½	10½	11½	12½	13½	14½	15½	16½	17½	18½	19½	20½	21½	22½
47	3	4½	6	7½	9	10	11	12	13	14	15	16	17	18	19	20	21	22	23
48	3	4½	6	7½	9	10½	11½	12½	13½	14½	15½	16½	17½	18½	19½	20½	21½	22½	23½
49	3	4½	6	7½	9	10½	12	13	14	15	16	17	18	19	20	21	22	23	24
50	3	4½	6	7½	9	10½	12	13½	14½	15½	16½	17½	18½	19½	20½	21½	22½	23½	24½
51	3	4½	6	7½	9	10½	12	13½	15	16	17	18	19	20	21	22	23	24	25
52	3	4½	6	7½	9	10½	12	13½	15	16½	17½	18½	19½	20½	21½	22½	23½	24½	25½
53	3	4½	6	7½	9	10½	12	13½	15	16½	18	19	20	21	22	23	24	25	26
54	3	4½	6	7½	9	10½	12	13½	15	16½	18	19½	20½	21½	22½	23½	24½	25½	26½
55	3	4½	6	7½	9	10½	12	13½	15	16½	18	19½	21	22	23	24	25	26	27
56	3	4½	6	7½	9	10½	12	13½	15	16½	18	19½	21	22½	23½	24½	25½	26½	27½
57	3	4½	6	7½	9	10½	12	13½	15	16½	18	19½	21	22½	24	25	26	27	28
58	3	4½	6	7½	9	10½	12	13½	15	16½	18	19½	21	22½	24	25½	26½	27½	28½
59	3	4½	6	7½	9	10½	12	13½	15	16½	18	19½	21	22½	24	25½	27	28	29
60	3	4½	6	7½	9	10½	12	13½	15	16½	18	19½	21	22½	24	25½	27	28½	29½
**61	3	4½	6	7½	9	10½	12	13½	15	16½	18	19½	21	22½	24	25½	27	28½	30

*The same figure should be used when calculating the redundancy payment for a person aged 61 and above.

* The table starts at age 17, as it is possible for a 17-year-old to have 2 years' service. Compulsory school leaving age can be 15¾ or 15⅘ where a child is 16 before 1 September. Particular care should be taken when calculating an individual's redundancy pay when they joined as an employee below the age of 16.

** The table stops at age 61 because, for employees age 61 and over, the payment remains the same as for age 61.

(Source: Department for Business, Enterprise and Regulatory Reform)

Guarantee Pay

Period	Daily Rate
From 1 February 2007 until 31 January 2008	£19.60

National Minimum Wage

Category	1 October 2006	From 1 October 2007
Main rate (22 years old plus)	£5.35	£5.52
Development rate (18–21 years only)	£4.45	£4.60
Youth rate (16–17)	£3.30	£3.40

Income Tax

Personal Allowances

Tax year	Personal Allowance	Married Couple's Allowance
2005/06	£4895	£2280*
2006/07	£5035	£2350*
2007/08	£5225	£2440

*Notional

Annual Rates of Income Tax

Tax year	Taxable Income	Rate	Cumulative Tax
2005/06	£1 – £2090	10%	£209.00
	£2091 – £32,400	22%	£6877.20
	Over £32,400	40%	—
2006/07	£1 – £2150	10%	£215.00
	£2151 – £33,300	22%	£7068.00
	Over £33,300	40%	—
2007/08	£1 – £2230	10%	£230.00
	£2231 – £34,600	22%	£7344.40
	Over £34,600	40%	—

Age Allowances

Tax year	Single 65–74	Single 75+	Married 65–74	Married 75+	Income limit
2005/06	£7090	£7220	£5905	£5975	£19,500
2006/07	£7280	£7420	£6065	£6135	£20,100
2007/08	£7550	£7690	£6285	£6365	£20,900

Blind Person's Allowance

Tax years	Allowance
2005/06	£1610
2006/07	£1660
2007/08	£1730

Calendars

Bank and Public Holidays

Bank and Public Holidays in England and Wales: 2007–2009

Dates with asterisks are bank holidays which have been introduced since the 1971 Banking and Financial Dealings Act, and are routinely proclaimed each year by the Queen. All other dates have been designated bank holidays under the Banking and Financial Dealings Act 1971.

Holidays	2007	2008	2009
New Year's Day	1 January*	1 January*	1 January*
Good Friday	6 April	21 March	10 April
Easter Monday	9 April	24 March	13 April
Early May Bank Holiday	7 May*	5 May*	4 May*
Spring Bank Holiday	28 May	26 May	25 May
Summer Bank Holiday	27 August	25 August	31 August
Christmas Day (or in lieu of 25 December)	25 December	25 December	25 December
Boxing Day (or in lieu of 26 December)	26 December	26 December	28 December

Bank and Public Holidays in Scotland: 2007–2010

Holidays	2007	2008	2009
New Year's Day	1 January	1 January	1 January
2 January (or day in lieu of 2 January)	2 January	2 January	2 January
Good Friday	6 April	21 March	10 April
Early May Bank Holiday	7 May	5 May	4 May
Spring Bank Holiday	28 May*	26 May*	25 May*
Summer Bank Holiday	6 August	4 August	3 August

Holidays	2007	2008	2009
St Andrew's Day	30 November†	1 December†	30 November†
Christmas Day (or in lieu of 25 December)	25 December	25 December	25 December
Boxing Day (or in lieu of 26 December)	26 December*	26 December*	28 December*

*Subject to Royal Proclamation.
†Subject to confirmation by the Scottish Parliament.

Bank and Public Holidays in Northern Ireland: 2007–2009

Dates with asterisks are bank holidays which have been introduced since the 1971 Banking and Financial Dealings Act, and are routinely proclaimed each year by the Queen; dates in italics are subject to Proclamation by the Secretary of State for Northern Ireland and are not included in the Royal Proclamation. All other dates have been designated bank holidays under the Banking and Financial Dealings Act 1971.

Holidays	2007	2008	2009
New Year's Day	1 January*	1 January*	1 January*
St Patrick's Day	17 March	17 March	17 March
Good Friday	6 April	21 March	10 April
Easter Monday	9 April	24 March	13 April
Early May Bank Holiday	7 May*	5 May*	4 May*
Spring Bank Holiday	28 May	26 May	25 May
Battle of the Boyne (Orangemen's Day)	*12 July*	*14 July*	*13 July*
Summer Bank Holiday	27 August	25 August	31 August
Christmas Day (or in lieu of 25 December)	25 December	25 December	25 December
Boxing Day (or in lieu of 26 December)	26 December	26 December	28 December

Bank and Public Holidays in the Republic of Ireland: 2007–2008

Holidays	2007	2008
New Year's Day	1 January	1 January
St Patrick's Day	17 March	17 March
Good Friday	6 April	21 March
Easter Monday	9 April	24 March
Public Holiday	7 May	5 May
Public Holiday	4 June	2 June

Holidays	2007	2008
Public Holiday	6 August	4 August
Public Holiday	29 October	27 October
Christmas Day	25 December	25 December
St Stephen's Day	26 December	26 December

Islamic Religious Holidays and Festivals: 2007 – 2008

Holidays	2007	2008
Al-Hijra (Islamic New Year)	20 January	10 January
Ashura	29 January	19 January
Prophet Muhammad's Birthday	31 March	20 March
Lailat-Ul-Isra' Wal Mi'raj	11 August	31 July
Start of Ramadam	13 September	2 September
Eid Ul-Fitr (End of Ramadam)	13 October	2 October
Al-Hijra (Islamic New Year)	20 December	8 December

Some dates are approximate and may vary by a day either side of the one stated. In most cases they are subject to the visibility of the new moon at Mecca and the traditions of the local community.

Hindu Religious Holidays and Festivals: 2007 – 2008

Holidays	2007	2008
Holi (Spring festival)	3 March	21 March
Navratri (1st day)	12 October	30 September
Diwali	9 November	28 October

These are the main dates in the Hindu calendar.

Sikh Religious Holidays and Festivals: 2007 – 2008

Holidays	2007	2008
Birthday of Guru Gobind Singh Ji	5 January	5 January
Vaisakhi	14 April	14 April
Martyrdom of Guru Arjan Dev Ji	16 June	16 June
Birthday of Guru Nanak Dev Ji	24 November	13 November
Martyrdom of Guru Tegh Bahadur Ji	24 November	24 November

The dates for Sikh festivals are taken from the Nanakshahi calendar.

Jewish Religious Holidays and Festivals: 2007 – 2008

Holidays	2007	2008
Purim	4 March	21 March
Pesach (Passover) (1st day)	3 April	20 April
Shavuot (Pentecost)	23 May	9 June
Tisha B'Av	24 July	10 August
Rosh Hashana (Jewish New Year)	13 September	30 September
Yom Kippur (Day of Atonement)	22 September	9 October
Succot (Tabernacles) (1st day)	27 September	14 October
Chanukah (1st day)	5 December	22 December

All Jewish holidays begin at sundown the day before shown.

Chinese Religious Holidays and Festivals: 2007 –2008

Holidays	2007	2008
Lunar New Year	18 February	7 February

Because the start of the Chinese New Year is based on lunar cycles, it can occur anywhere between late January and the middle of February.

Index

A

Acas arbitration scheme 3.304–3.305
  agreement to submit to 9.359
  appeals 3.309
  Arbitration Agreement 3.306
  hearing 3.307
  industrial disputes 5.63–5.68, 5.234
  procedure 3.306
  remedies 3.308
Acas conciliation 3.286–3.288, 5.232, 9.344–9.350
  binding effect of agreement 9.355
  conciliation period 9.32, 9.351–9.354
  COT3 agreement 3.286, 9.356, 9.358
  drafting terms of settlement 9.357–9.358
  effect of communication of settlement 9.356
  industrial disputes 5.63–5.68, 5.232
  unfair dismissal 9.32, 9.349
accident records
  data protection 2.295
  retention 2.310
accredited training
  abolition 7.454
administration 9.103
  claims against employer 9.104
  contracts of employment
    effect on 9.105
    liability under 9.106–9.108
  see also insolvency
administrative receivership
  appointment of administrative receiver 9.94–9.95
  claims against employer 9.96
  contracts of employment
    effect on 9.97–9.98
    liability under 9.99–9.102
  see also insolvency
adoption leave 6.2, 6.302–6.303
  annual leave entitlement and 1.10
  complaints 6.31
  disrupted placement 6.26
  early return 6.25
  general qualifying conditions 6.5–6.8
    adoption from overseas 6.10
    adoption within UK 6.9
  keeping in touch days 6.27–6.30, 6.323–6.326
  notification
    adoption from overseas 6.14–6.17
    adoption within UK 6.11–6.13
    employer's response 6.18–6.19
  paternity leave and 6.303
  reasonable contact 6.27–6.30
  remedies 6.31
  statutory rights during and after 6.20–6.24
adoption rights 6.1–6.2
  parental leave 6.143
  statutory paternity leave after adoption 6.186–6.188
  see also adoption leave; statutory adoption pay
advertising *see* recruitment advertising
age discrimination 4.1–4.3
  accredited training, abolition 7.454
  application of regulations 4.13–4.15
  bullying 3.28
  burden of proof 4.87
  claims 4.82, 4.207
    burden of proof 4.87
    questionnaire procedure 4.84–4.86
    time limits 4.209–4.215
    unfair dismissal rights 4.83, 9.293–9.294
    vicarious liability 4.88–4.89
    see also discrimination claims
  defining 4.6–4.8
  direct 4.20, 4.22
  during employment 4.39–4.60
  employee share and share option schemes 7.385–7.390
  exceptions 4.18–4.20
  harassment 4.26–4.28, 4.324
  indirect 4.20, 4.23–4.24
  Irish case law 4.90
  justification 4.20
  monitoring 4.91
  notification of retirement 4.73–4.78
  pensions 4.79–4.81, 7.676–7.678, 9.331–9.332
    pension age 7.580–7.588
  person specification 4.305–4.306
  promotion 4.51–4.52
  qualifying conditions 4.16–4.17
  questionnaire procedure 4.84–4.86
  recruitment 4.10, 4.29–4.34, 8.296
    advertisements 4.31, 8.33
    best practice checklist 4.38
    person specification 4.305–4.306
    positive action 4.35–4.37
    skills and experience 8.299
    see also discrimination in recruitment
  redundancy pay 4.54, 9.293–9.294, 9.313
    contractual redundancy pay schemes 4.55–4.60
  redundancy selection 4.53

request to continue working beyond
   retirement   4.66–4.72, 9.319–9.322
retirement age   4.61–4.65, 9.290,
    9.312–9.317
sabbaticals   1.176
scope of law   4.9–4.12
service-related benefits and
    4.43–4.45, 7.89–7.93
sickness and health schemes
    4.46–4.50
statutory sick pay and   7.775
terms and conditions of employment
    4.40–4.42
training opportunities   4.51
transfers   4.51
unfair dismissal   4.83, 9.293–9.294,
    9.313
vicarious liability   4.88–4.89
victimisation   4.25
agency workers
  annual leave entitlement   1.9
  Draft Directive on   2.557–2.558
  employment status   2.391–2.392,
    2.497, 2.545–2.556
  working time   1.364
  see also employment agencies and
    employment businesses
alternative dispute resolution (ADR)
    5.231
  see also Acas arbitration; Acas
    conciliation; conciliation; mediation
annual hours' contracts   7.474–7.476
annual leave
  entitlement
    agency staff   1.9
    definition of a "leave year"   1.23
    definition of a "week's leave"   1.22,
    1.435
    long-term sick leave and   1.11–1.14
    minimum entitlement   1.15–1.21
    part-time workers 1.17, 1.122–1.124
    periods of absence   1.10–1.14
  payment during   1.36–1.38
  Working Time Regulations
    1.434–1.436
  see also holidays
annualised hours contracts
    2.532–2.536
ante-natal care
  time off work   1.246, 1.255–1.258
appearance and dress codes 2.1–2.2
  gender reassignment   2.33–2.34
  human rights   2.28–2.32
  long hair   2.14–2.16
  race discrimination   2.2, 2.20–2.23,
    4.470–4.474
    justification   2.24–2.27

religion or belief discrimination   2.2,
    2.20–2.23, 4.566–4.569
  justification   2.24–2.27
  long hair   2.16
sex discrimination   2.2, 2.7–2.8,
    4.661–4.663
  men with long hair   2.14–2.16
  proving   2.9–2.10
  shirts and ties   2.17–2.18
  skirt wearing   2.11–2.13
staff handbooks   2.17
application forms 8.308, 8.512–8.517
  data protection clause   8.308, 8.524
  disabled applicants   8.520, 8.522
  discrimination   8.308
  equal opportunities information   8.518
  equal opportunities statement   8.523
  personal information   8.308, 8.518
  screening   8.529–8.531
appraisals   8.617
apprenticeships
  apprenticeship agreements
    2.559–2.570
  apprenticeship plan   2.567
  breach of contract   2.396, 2.569
  employment status   2.571–2.572
  fixed-term contracts   2.570
  government-sponsored
    Apprenticeships   2.395–2.397,
    2.566–2.570
  national minimum wage and   2.573
  no obligation to provide work   2.397
  redundancy pay   2.569
  time off for training   2.568
  traditional apprenticeships
    2.560–2.565
arbitration see Acas arbitration
  scheme
Asylum and Immigration Act checks
    2.173, 4.498–4.500, 8.391–8.398
  List 1 documentation   8.395
  List 2 documentation   8.396–8.398
attachment of earnings   7.4–7.5
  against whom orders cannot be made
    7.9–7.10
  assessment of attachable earnings
    7.15–7.19
  attachable earnings less than
    protected earnings   7.28–7.29
  Attachment of Earnings Act 1971 7.5,
    7.6–7.36
  Child Support Act, orders under
    7.55–7.57
  consolidated order   7.14
  contents of order   7.21
  Council Tax Attachment Orders
    7.51–7.54

deduction-making procedure 7.24–7.27
employer's procedure on receipt of order 7.22–7.23
income support deduction notices 7.58
meaning 7.1
new employee with existing order, notification 7.33
non-priority orders 7.13
Northern Ireland orders 7.49–7.50
notification of earnings 7.32
priority orders 7.12
priority of orders 7.59
protected earnings 7.20
sanctions for non-compliance 7.60–7.61
Schedule 5 attachment of earnings orders 7.36
Scotland
  conjoined arrestment order 7.43–7.45
  current maintenance arrestment 7.42
  Debtors (Scotland) Act 1987 7.5, 7.37–7.48
  earnings arrestment 7.38–7.41
  failure to comply with order 7.46–7.48
types of order 7.11–7.13
variation of order 7.30–7.31
weekly payment of monthly wage 7.34–7.35
when orders can be made 7.7–7.8
atypical workers see casual workers; fixed term employees; home workers; part-time workers; temporary workers

B

bank holidays 1.24–1.30, 1.360
  part-time workers 1.125
bankruptcy
  claims against bankrupt employer 9.90
  contracts of employment
    effects on 9.91
    liability under 9.92–9.93
  insolvency of individual 9.88–9.89
  trustee in bankruptcy 9.89
  see also insolvency
benefits 7.64–7.66
  age discrimination and service-related benefits 4.43–4.45, 7.89–7.93
  categories 7.79–7.81
  communication programme 7.84
  company cars see company cars
  company vans see company vans
  compliance obligations 7.145–7.148
  cost base 7.76–7.77
  dispensations 7.135–7.138
  employee attitudes 7.78
  employee car ownership schemes 7.238–7.239
  flexible benefits package 7.70–7.75
  lateral view 7.82–7.83
  manual workers' allowance and benefits 7.98–7.100
  maternity leave and 7.94
    additional maternity leave 7.97
    ordinary maternity leave 7.95–7.96
  National Insurance and 7.122–7.123
    Class 1A contributions 7.124–7.131
    Class 1B contributions 7.132–7.134
  non-cash benefits 7.85–7.88
  salary sacrifice arrangements 7.101–7.105
  taxation
    dispensations 7.135–7.138
    P11D employees and directors 7.117–7.118
    PAYE settlement agreements (PSAs) 7.139–7.144
    salary sacrifice arrangements 7.105
    tax exempt benefits 7.119–7.121
    tax rules 7.106–7.111
    valuing benefits for tax purposes 7.114–7.116
    [009c]8500 threshold 7.112–7.113
  see also employee share and share option schemes
bereavement leave 1.268, 1.269, 1.277–1.283
  religion or belief discrimination 1.284–1.285
blind persons
  disability discrimination 4.121
breach of contract 2.40–2.41, 2.222–2.224
  anticipatory 9.270
  apprenticeships 2.396, 2.569
  breach of trust and confidence 2.74, 8.478–8.479
  bullying 3.26
  claims prior to employment 2.72–2.73
  constructive dismissal 9.267–9.274
  contractual terms 2.44–2.48
  damages
    employees 2.70, 2.74, 2.75
    employers 2.41, 2.51–2.52
  deductions from wages 2.41, 2.54–2.55
  employees' remedies 2.56–2.59
  employer discretions 2.65
  employer's rights 2.49–2.53

employment tribunal claims 2.40,
  2.57–2.59, 2.78–2.82, 9.5
fundamental breach 2.53, 2.60,
  9.548–9.545
injunctions
  employees 2.77
  employers 2.41, 2.50
injury to feelings 2.75–2.76
repudiatory 9.269–9.271
summary dismissal 2.66–2.71, 9.396,
  9.584–9.585
variation of contract
  imposed variation 2.589, 2.596,
    2.603–2.604
  unilateral variation 2.61–2.62
  variation clauses 2.63–2.64
  withholding wages 2.41, 2.54–2.55
Bulgarian workers 1.70, 1.71, 8.414,
  8.464–8.465
bullying 4.323–4.330
  breach of contract claims 3.26
  counselling 3.41–3.42
  disciplinary rules and procedures 3.43
  discrimination claims 3.28
  effects 3.15–3.19
  examples 3.8–3.14
  grievance procedure 3.243
  harassment 3.11, 3.13
  health and safety at work claims
    3.23–3.25
  investigating 3.38–3.40
  personal injury
    claims 3.14, 3.20–3.22
  policy development 3.36–3.37
  suspension 3.44–3.46
  unfair dismissal claims 3.27
  unfounded allegations 3.47
  vicarious responsibility 3.28
  see also harassment

C

cancer
  disability discrimination 4.120
capability
  dismissal on grounds of 1.218,
    1.219–1.220
career breaks
  advantages to employer 1.157
  disadvantages and dangers
    1.168–1.170
  duration 1.167
  initiating 1.155
  return of employees 1.184–1.187
  see also sabbaticals
cars
  employee car ownership schemes
    7.238–7.239

see also company cars
casual workers 1.113, 2.542–2.544
  employment status 2.389–2.390,
    2.496
  working time 1.364
  see also temporary workers
Central Arbitration Committee (CAC)
    5.314–5.315
  trade union recognition applications
    5.441–5.442
changing facilities
  religious discrimination and 4.570
children
  employment of 2.398–2.402
  prohibited occupations 8.320–8.323
  restrictions 8.320–8.331
  schoolchildren 8.330–8.331
  working hours and periods of
    employment 8.324–8.329
  see also young persons
  see also parental leave
civil partnerships
  discrimination 4.700
  pensions 7.679
classic cars 7.181
  see also company cars
collective agreements 2.381, 5.1–5.2
  incorporated terms 2.190
  scope 5.36–5.46
  transfer of undertakings and
    9.466–9.468
  variation of contract and 2.210
  working time 1.437–1.438
  opt-outs 1.401
  see also collective bargaining
collective bargaining 5.1
  bargaining scope 5.44–5.46
  bargaining unit 5.37–5.39,
    5.443–5.444
  consultation 5.308–5.309
  disclosure of information 5.32–5.33
  effect on individual employment
    contracts 5.34–5.35
  failure of bargaining process
    5.56–5.57
  conciliation, mediation and
    arbitration 5.63–5.68
  imposing a settlement 5.58–5.59
  industrial action 5.60–5.62
  inequality of power 5.9–5.10
  information about proposed
    redundancies 5.262
  Regulations 2004 5.69–5.73
  joint regulation 5.11–5.13
  level of bargaining 5.40–5.43
  meaning 5.5–5.8
  method 5.452–5.454

non-unionised employees 5.51–5.54
parties
  employers 5.23–5.24
  employers' associations 5.25–5.26
  Trade Union Congress (TUC) 5.22
  trade unions 5.19–5.21
process of bargaining 5.55
recognition of unions for bargaining
  5.27–5.30, 5.31
rights 5.398
usefulness of
  pluralist perspective 5.17
  unitarist perspective 5.15–5.16
workforce agreements and 5.49–5.50
Working Time Regulations and
  5.47–5.48
works councils 5.192–5.197
see also employee representatives; trade unions
collective redundancies 5.75–5.76
calculating numbers to be dismissed
  5.84–5.86
consultation 5.263–5.269, 9.155
  appropriate representatives
    9.160–9.163
  disclosure of information 9.166
  employee representatives
    5.163–5.167,
    5.263–5.269, 9.160–9.163
  failure to consult
    consequences of 5.121–5.123
    other rights and claims
      5.133–5.134
    protective awards 5.127–5.131,
      9.167
    "special circumstances" defence
      5.124–5.126
    unfair dismissal 5.132
  individual consultation 9.168–9.171
  meaningful
    consultation 5.101–5.102
  numbers triggering the duty to
    consult 9.156–9.157
  period of 5.81–5.83
  process 9.164–9.165
  subjects for consultation
    5.115–5.120
  time limits 9.158–9.159
  when employer should consult
    5.99–5.100
  who should be consulted
    5.103–5.104
  works councils 5.138
definition 5.79–5.80, 9.147
"dismiss as redundant", definition
  5.90–5.91

employee representatives see employee representatives
employers' obligations when contemplating redundancies
  9.151–9.154
European dimension 5.137–5.138
information to representatives/
  employees 5.112–5.114
notification to BERR
  5.95–5.98, 9.151, 9.152–9.154
"one establishment", definition
  5.92–5.94
selection for redundancy see redundancy
works councils 5.138
Commission for Equality and Human Rights (CEHR) 4.348
common law rights
settlement of 9.342–9.343
company cars 7.151–7.152, 7.157–7.158
accessories 7.178
allocation policy 7.159–7.167
appropriate percentage 7.183–7.191
calculation of taxable benefit
  7.195–7.198
capital contributions 7.179
cars with no carbon dioxide emissions
  figure 7.192
cash alternatives 7.236–7.237
classic cars 7.181
fuel benefit 7.201–7.203
  advisory fuel rates 7.208–7.211
  example 7.204–7.207
  mileage allowance payments
    7.212–7.217
list price 7.174–7.177
NI contributions
  approved mileage allowance
    payments and 7.244–7.246
  Class 1A contributions 7.240–7.243
  compliance 7.247–7.251
passenger payments 7.218–7.220
periods of unavailability charge
  7.193–7.194
pooled cars 7.199–7.200
price cap 7.180
price of car 7.173–7.177
taxation 7.168–7.172
see also company vans
company share option plans (CSOPs) 7.292, 7.321–7.322
compliance 7.334
conditions relating to shares 7.323
exercise of options 7.328–7.329
grant of options 7.327
option price 7.324–7.326

performance targets 7.330
tax liability 7.331–7.333
see also employee share and share option schemes
company vans 7.153, 7.221–7.228
  allocation policy 7.164–7.166
  pooled vans 7.234–7.235
  van fuel benefit 7.229–7.233
  see also company cars
compassionate leave 1.277–1.283
compromise agreements 3.296, 9.360–9.362
  binding effect 9.364–9.365
  confidentiality 3.303
  enforcement 9.366–9.367
  exempt claims 3.297
  qualifying conditions 3.298–3.300
  requirements for valid agreement 9.363
  risk of constructive dismissal claims 3.301–3.302
conciliation 5.232
  Acas see Acas conciliation
conciliation agreements 9.344–9.347
confidential information
  protection 2.131–2.134
  restrictive covenants 2.124
confidentiality
  clauses 5.493
  compromise agreements 3.303
  whistleblowing and 5.493
consent orders 9.368–9.370
constructive dismissal 9.246, 9.267–9.274
  breach of contract 9.267–9.274
  bullying 3.27
  claims arising out of disciplinary procedures 3.198–3.199
  compromise agreements 3.301–3.302
  length of service 9.269
  repudiatory breach of contract 9.269–9.271
  statutory grievance procedure and 9.272–9.274
  variation of contract 2.589
  see also resignation
consultation see information and consultation
contract formation see formation of contract
contract terms 2.228–2.231
  breach see breach of contract
  custom and practice 2.194–2.195
  disciplinary rules and procedures 2.266–2.267
  discretionary terms 2.48, 2.228, 2.257
  dismissal procedures 2.266–2.267
  dispute resolution procedures 2.266–2.267
  employee's duties
    duty to be loyal 2.255
    duty to obey employer's orders 2.253
    duty to work with reasonable care and skill 2.254
    mutual duties 2.256
  employer's common law duties 2.377–2.379
    duty of care 2.250
    duty to pay costs and expenses 2.251
    duty to pay wages 2.248
    duty to provide a reasonable period of notice 2.252
    duty to provide work 2.249
    mutual duties 2.256
  express terms 2.45, 2.182–2.184, 2.228, 2.235–2.242, 2.373, 2.577
    incorporated terms 2.240–2.242
    oral terms 2.238
  implied terms 2.45–2.47, 2.185–2.186, 2.228, 2.243–2.247, 2.373, 2.578–2.579
    incorporated terms 2.187–2.190, 2.240–2.242
  mutual duties 2.256
  statutory terms 2.191–2.192, 2.380
  variation see variation of contract
  void terms and illegality 2.193
  Written particulars of terms of employment, complaint to tribunal 2.230–2.231, 2.263–2.265
contracts of employment
  annualised hours contracts 2.532–2.536
  breach see breach of contract
  collective bargaining and 5.34–5.35
  confidential information 2.131–2.134
  contracts of service and contracts for service 2.500–2.503
  deductions from pay, provision for 7.266
  employer discretions 2.65
  fidelity clause 2.101–2.103
  fixed-term see fixed-term employees
  flexibility agreements 2.135–2.138
  flexibility clauses 2.63, 2.125
  formation see formation of contract
  garden leave 2.93–2.96
  implied terms 2.45–2.47, 2.586
    trust and confidence 2.46, 2.141, 8.478–8.479

insolvency of employer
  administration   9.105–9.108
  administrative receivership
                            9.97–9.102
  bankruptcy   9.91–9.93
  liquidation   9.111–9.112
intellectual property rights
                            2.128–2.130
job-share   2.386, 2.528–2.529
medical examinations   2.139–2.141
mobility clause   2.125–2.127
nil hours contracts   2.540–2.541
non-dealing clause   2.116
non-solicitation clause   2.116
permanent full-time contracts   2.382
permanent part-time contracts   2.383
probationary periods   8.239,
                            8.255–8.256
reimbursement of training costs
  clause   2.142–2.143
restrictive covenants *see* restrictive
  covenants
search, right to   2.97–2.100
secondments   1.179
temporary contracts   2.387–2.388,
                          2.530–2.531
transfer of undertakings and
                          9.456–9.465
see also contract terms; employment
  status; formation of contract;
  job-share contracts; variation of
  contract
copyright
  email and Internet   2.337
COT3 agreement   3.286, 9.356, 9.358
Council Tax Attachment Orders
                              7.51–7.54
counselling   3.41–3.42
criminal offences outside
  employment   3.66–3.67, 3.190–3.194
Criminal Records Bureau checks
                    2.172, 8.352–8.355

D

data protection   2.271–2.274
  access to records   2.300–2.303,
                            8.379–8.380
  data controller   2.281–2.282
  discipline, grievance and dismissal
                                  2.308
  disclosure requests   2.306
  email   2.333–2.334
  employee monitoring   2.311–2.314
  employment records   8.490–8.491
  equal opportunities monitoring   2.297
  fraud detection   2.298–2.299

insurance schemes   2.296
Internet   2.333–2.334
medical records   2.315–2.316,
                         8.469, 8.492–8.494
  access   8.496
mergers and acquisitions   2.307
outsourcing data processing   2.309
pension schemes   2.296
personal data
  conditions for processing
                      2.277–2.278, 8.525
  meaning   2.277
  penalties   2.283–2.285, 8.526
  sensitive personal data   2.279–2.280
records
  collecting and storing   2.294
  recruitment records   2.292–2.294
  retention   2.292–2.293, 2.310
  sickness
    and accident records   2.295
  recruitment and selection process
                            8.374–8.376
  applications   2.286–2.287
  data protection clause in application
    form   8.308, 8.524
  Employment Practices Data
    Protection Code   8.377–8.378
  pre-employment checks   2.291
  retention of recruitment records
                            2.292–2.294
  right of access to records
                 2.300–2.303, 8.379–8.380
  shortlisting   2.289–2.290
  verifying applicants' claims   2.288
references   2.304–2.305,
                        8.468, 8.486–8.487
  guidance   8.488–8.494
  medical information   8.492–8.494
sensitive personal data
  meaning   2.279
  processing   2.280
workers' access to own information
                            2.300–2.303
deductions from pay   7.256
  breach of contract   2.54–2.55
  categories   7.269–7.280
  contract of employment provision
                                  7.266
  contractual deductions   7.272
  correction of wages paid in error
                           7.278–7.280
  enforcement   7.281–7.283
  one-off authorisation by worker
                           7.267–7.268
  overpayments   7.278–7.280
  retail trade   7.273–7.275
  SMP   6.228

stakeholder pension schemes 7.625–7.629
underpayment of wages 7.276–7.277
voluntary deduction 7.270–7.271
when pay can be deducted 7.261–7.265
whose pay can be deducted 7.259–7.260
see also attachment of earnings

dental appointments
time off work 1.272–1.273, 1.289–1.291

development centres 8.619–8.621
disability discrimination 4.97–4.100, 4.331–4.333
application forms 8.520, 8.522
blind persons 4.121
bullying 3.28
cancer 4.120
claims 4.172
burden of proof 4.182
compensation 4.186–4.187
employer's defence 4.177
public sector disability duty 4.173–4.176
questionnaire procedure 4.178–4.181
time limits 4.209–4.215
vicarious liability 4.183–4.185
see also discrimination claims
compensation 4.186–4.187
conditions not to be treated as impairments 4.122–4.123
in the course of employment 4.164–4.171
definition of disability 4.107–4.111
blind and partial sight 4.121
cancer, HIV and multiple sclerosis 4.120
long-term effects 4.116–4.117
mental impairment 4.113–4.114
physical impairment 4.112
progressive conditions 4.118–4.119
"substantial" 4.115
direct 4.125
disability-related discrimination 4.126
employer's defence 4.177
harassment 4.26–4.28, 4.130–4.135, 4.324
HIV 4.120
job specifications 4.148–4.150
long-term sickness absence 1.215–1.217
medical examinations 2.168, 4.161–4.163
medical information 8.469, 8.495
mental impairment 4.113–4.114

mobility clauses 2.127
monitoring 4.188–4.190
multiple sclerosis 4.120
partial sight 4.121
person specifications 4.148–4.150
physical impairment 4.112
post-employment discrimination 4.171
pre-employment health checks 4.161–4.163, 8.495
progressive conditions 4.118–4.119
promotion 4.169
public sector disability duty 4.173–4.176
qualifying conditions 4.105–4.106
questionnaire procedure 4.178–4.181
rates of pay 4.168
reasonable adjustments,
duty to make 4.136–4.146, 4.279, 4.332–4.333, 8.314
recruitment 4.147–4.163
advertisements 4.151–4.155, 8.302
applicant information 4.156
application forms 8.520, 8.522
interviews 4.157–4.159, 8.564–8.565
job specifications 4.148–4.150
person specifications 4.148–4.150
pre-employment health checks 4.161–4.163, 8.495
testing of applicants 4.160
redundancy selection 4.170
scope of law 4.101–4.104
selection process
application forms 8.520, 8.522
interviews 4.157–4.159, 8.521, 8.564–8.565
terms and conditions of employment 4.166–4.168
training opportunities 4.169
transfers 4.169
vicarious liability 4.183–4.185
victimisation 4.127–4.129
disability harassment 4.130–4.135
disabled children
parental leave 6.142
disciplinary rules and procedures 3.100–3.101, 9.397
Acas Code of Practice 3.110–3.111
appeal right 3.83, 3.152–3.158
breach of contract claims 2.68
bullying 3.43
constructive dismissal claims 3.198–3.199
criminal offences outside employment 3.66–3.67, 3.190–3.194
demotion or downgrading 3.81
drawing up 3.56–3.58, 3.106–3.108

email and Internet misuse	2.342	bullying	3.28
examples	3.59	civil partnership discrimination	4.700
grievance arising out of	3.195–3.197, 3.212	claims *see* discrimination claims	
		complaints procedure	4.291–4.295
gross misconduct	3.62, 9.384	disability *see* disability discrimination	
hearing		employment status and	2.419–2.420
arranging	3.119–3.120	gender reassignment discrimination	
conducting	3.122		2.34, 4.701–4.704
deciding the outcome	3.124–3.125	interviews 4.312–4.313, 8.312–8.313	
mitigating factors	3.123	disability discrimination	
purpose	3.121		4.157–4.159, 8.564–8.565
right to be accompanied		job descriptions	4.301–4.302
	3.159–3.162, 5.149–5.155, 5.373–5.374	disability discrimination	4.148–4.150
		marital status discrimination	4.699
inter-relationship with statutory		overseas workers	1.88–1.93
disciplinary rules and procedure		pensions	7.676–7.678
	3.188–3.189	age discrimination	4.79–4.81,
investigating a disciplinary offence			7.676–7.678, 9.331–9.332
	3.112–3.115	disputes	7.682
key features	3.109	pregnancy	
misconduct	3.60–3.61	discrimination	4.697–4.698, 6.129
proof of	3.151	race *see* race discrimination	
need for	3.54–3.55, 3.104	recruitment *see* discrimination in	
poor performance	3.63–3.65	recruitment	
record keeping	3.200–3.201	religion or belief *see* religion or belief	
remedies for inappropriate		discrimination	
disciplinary action	3.90–3.95	retirement age	
sanctions	3.68	age discrimination	
demotion or downgrading	3.81		4.61–4.65, 9.290, 9.312–9.317
dismissal with notice	3.84–3.86, 3.139–3.141	sex discrimination	4.705, 9.292
		sex *see* sex discrimination	
summary dismissal	3.87–3.89, 3.142–3.146, 9.397, 9.402–9.404	sexual orientation *see* sexual	
		orientation discrimination	
suspension	3.44–3.46, 3.82, 3.116–3.118, 3.149	**discrimination claims**	4.198–4.200
		age discrimination	4.82, 4.207
transfers	3.81	burden of proof	4.87
sanctions short of dismissal		questionnaire procedure	4.84–4.86
	3.147–3.150	unfair dismissal rights	4.83
statement of reasons for decisions		vicarious liability	4.88–4.89
	3.127	appeals	4.248–4.251
dismissal	3.126	bullying	3.28
statutory procedure *see* statutory		burden of proof	4.200, 4.236–4.238
dismissal and disciplinary procedure		age discrimination	4.87
summary dismissal and 9.383–9.385,		disability discrimination	4.182
9.397, 9.402–9.404, 9.581–9.583		race discrimination	4.516–4.517
suspension from work	3.82, 3.116–3.118	religion or	
		belief discrimination	4.622
bullying and	3.44–3.46	sex discrimination	4.715
without pay	3.149	sexual orientation discrimination	
transfers	3.81		4.790
warnings *see* warnings		tribunal proceedings	4.236–4.238
written statement of particulars of		compensation	4.252–4.260
employment	3.54–3.55, 3.105	disability discrimination	4.172
discretionary schemes *see* company		burden of proof	4.182
share option plans		compensation	4.186–4.187
discrimination		employer's defence	4.177
age *see* age discrimination			

public sector disability duty
    4.173–4.176
questionnaire procedure
    4.178–4.181
  time limits   4.209–4.215
  vicarious liability   4.183–4.185
employment tribunal proceedings
    4.227
  appeals   4.248–4.251
  beginning proceedings 4.228–4.230
  burden of proof   4.236–4.238
  case management   4.231–4.232
  costs   4.261–4.271
  decision   4.245–4.247
  hearing   4.239–4.244
  questionnaires   3.278–3.279
  remedies   4.252–4.260
  striking out claims   4.233–4.235
grounds   4.203–4.208
part-time workers   1.127–1.129
persons bringing   4.204–4.208
questionnaire procedure 3.278–3.279
  age discrimination   4.84–4.86
  disability discrimination 4.178–4.181
  Northern Ireland   4.435
  race discrimination   4.512–4.515
  religion or belief discrimination
    4.618–4.621
questions procedure   4.218–4.221
  time limit for response   4.226
  use in tribunals   4.222–4.225
race discrimination   4.511
  burden of proof   4.516–4.517
  compensation   4.525–4.526
  harassment by customers, suppliers
    and other third parties 4.521–4.524
  questionnaire procedure
    4.512–4.515
  time limits   4.209–4.215
  vicarious liability   4.518–4.520
religion or belief discrimination   4.617
  burden of proof   4.622
  compensation   4.630–4.631
  harassment by customers, suppliers
    and other third parties 4.626–4.629
  questionnaire procedure
    4.618–4.621
  time limits   4.209–4.215
  vicarious liability   4.623–4.625
sex discrimination   4.710
  burden of proof   4.715
  compensation   4.723–4.724
  harassment by customers, suppliers
    and other third parties 4.719–4.722
  questionnaire procedure
    4.711–4.714
  time limits   4.209–4.215

  vicarious liability   4.716–4.718
sexual orientation discrimination 4.785
  burden of proof   4.790
  compensation   4.799–4.801
  harassment by customers, suppliers
    and other third parties 4.795–4.798
  questionnaire procedure
    4.786–4.789
  time limits   4.209–4.215
  vicarious liability   4.791–4.794
time limits   4.209–4.215
  extension   4.216–4.217
who can bring   4.204–4.208
discrimination in recruitment 4.300,
    8.277, 8.281–8.282
advertising *see* recruitment advertising
age discrimination   4.10, 4.29–4.37,
    8.296
  advertisements   4.31, 8.33
  best practice checklist   4.38
  person specification   4.305–4.306
  positive action   4.35–4.37
  skills and experience   8.299
application forms   8.308
  application forms   8.520, 8.522
application process   4.307
disability discrimination   4.147
  advertisements   4.151–4.155, 8.302
  applicant information   4.156
  application forms   8.520, 8.522
  interviews 4.157–4.159, 8.564–8.565
  job specifications   4.148–4.150
  medical examinations   4.161–4.163
  pre-employment health checks
    4.161–4.163
  testing of applicants   4.160
flexibility requirements   8.297
full-time working requirement 8.298
genuine occupational qualifications
  and requirements
  advertising   8.31–8.32
  race discrimination   4.487–4.490,
    8.288–8.293
  religion or belief discrimination
    4.598–4.607
  sex discrimination   4.681–4.683
  sexual orientation discrimination
    4.767–4.774
interviews 4.312–4.313, 8.312–8.313
  disability discrimination 4.157–4.159
job descriptions   4.301–4.302, 8.286
job titles   8.285
migrant workers   8.388, 8.394,
    8.399–8.402
panel interviews   8.553
person specifications   4.303–4.306,
    8.294–8.295

age discrimination 4.305–4.306
direct discrimination 8.187
disability discrimination 4.148–4.150
indirect discrimination 8.187, 8.188–8.191
  mandatory and preferred
    requirements 8.185–8.186
positive action 4.318–4.320, 8.304–8.307
  age discrimination 4.35–4.37
  race discrimination 4.491–4.493
  religion or belief discrimination 4.608–4.609
  sex discrimination 4.684–4.685
  sexual orientation discrimination 4.775–4.776
race discrimination 4.451, 4.486
  advertisements 4.494–4.497
  Asylum and Immigration Act checks 4.498–4.500
  best practice checklist 4.501
  genuine occupational qualifications and requirements 4.487–4.490, 8.290, 8.292, 8.293
  positive action 4.491–4.493
  skills and experience 8.299
  references 4.317, 8.480–8.483
religion or belief discrimination 4.547, 4.597
  best practice checklist 4.610
  genuine occupational requirements (GORs) 4.598–4.607
  positive action 4.608–4.609
selection 4.314–4.316, 8.316–8.317
selection process 8.502
selection tests 4.160, 8.315
sex discrimination 4.647, 4.679–4.680
  advertisements 4.686–4.689
  best practice checklist 4.690
  genuine occupational qualifications (GOQs) 4.681–4.683, 8.290, 8.291
  job titles 8.285
  positive action 4.684–4.685
sexual orientation discrimination 4.740, 4.766
  best practice checklist 4.777
  genuine occupational requirements (GORs) 4.767–4.774
  positive action 4.775–4.776
shortlisting 8.309–8.311
skills and experience 8.299
testing of applicants 4.160, 8.315
trade union membership 8.282
dismissal
capability grounds 1.218, 1.219–1.220, 9.515, 9.526
consistency 9.406–9.407
constructive *see* constructive dismissal
disciplinary sanction
  dismissal with notice 3.84–3.86, 3.139–3.141
  summary dismissal 3.87–3.89, 3.142–3.146
economic, technical or organisational (ETO) reasons 9.221, 9.458, 9.496–9.499
employee representatives 5.187
fair dismissal
  potential reasons 9.515–9.516
  reasonableness 9.517–9.529
flexible working applications and 6.60
industrial action and 5.210–5.211
maternity and 6.130
misconduct 9.515, 9.525
notice
  contractual notice 9.185–9.186, 9.566
  payment in lieu 9.187, 9.414–9.416, 9.572–9.573, 9.600–9.601
  reasonable notice 9.570–9.571
  statutory minimum 2.409
  statutory notice 9.183–9.184, 9.567–9.569
parental leave and 6.170
procedural fairness 9.524–9.527
reservists called out for whole-time service 1.322
retirement 9.516
sanction short of 3.147–3.150
statement of reasons for 9.512–9.514
substantive fairness 9.528–9.529
suing employee as alternative to dismissal 9.408
summary *see* summary dismissal
termination of employment, meaning 9.510–9.511
trade union membership and 5.380–5.383
safety complaints and representation 5.384–5.385
transfer of undertakings 9.494–9.495
  economic, technical or organisational (ETO) reasons 9.221, 9.458, 9.496–9.499
  redundancy pay 9.221
under a year's service 3.187
unfair *see* unfair dismissal
with notice 3.84–3.86, 3.139–3.141, 9.398
  statutory minimum notice period 9.399–9.401
without notice *see* summary dismissal
written statement of reasons 3.126

wrongful *see* wrongful dismissal
see also statutory dismissal and disciplinary procedure
dispute resolution 2.266–2.267, 3.260
  Central Arbitration Committee (CAC) 5.314–5.315
  pensions 7.680–7.682
  Regulations 2004 5.159–5.161
  see also Acas arbitration scheme; Acas conciliation; alternative dispute resolution; compromise agreements; conciliation; employment tribunals; mediation
dress codes *see* appearance and dress codes
drivers' hours and records 1.439–1.440
  breaks from driving 1.440
  daily rest period 1.440
  domestic hours laws 1.440
  driving time 1.440
  total daily driving 1.440
  total driving time in a fortnight 1.440
  weekly driving 1.440
  weekly rest period 1.440
  work records 1.440
  see also working time

E

early-leaver syndrome 8.249–8.250
email 2.321–2.322
  contract law 2.336
  criminal and other offences 2.338–2.341
  data protection 2.333–2.334
  human rights 2.335
  monitoring communications 2.326–2.329
    legislation 2.327, 2.329, 2.330–2.332
  policy on use 2.343–2.346
employee *see* employment status
employee benefits *see* benefits
employee car ownership schemes 7.238–7.239
employee handbooks *see* staff handbooks
employee representatives 5.142–5.144
  benefits of employee representation 5.198
  collective redundancies 5.163–5.167, 5.263–5.269, 9.160–9.163
  election process 5.106–5.110, 5.184
  employers' duties on election of representatives 5.105
  failure to elect representatives 5.111
  right to consultation 5.163–5.167, 9.160–9.163
  elections 5.179–5.181, 9.479–9.481
    election process 5.106–5.110, 5.184
    employers' duties 5.105
    failure to elect representatives 5.111
    post-election 5.185
    preparation for election process 5.182
    prior to election 5.183
  health and safety representation 5.171
  paid time off to perform duties 1.246
  right to be accompanied 5.149–5.155, 5.159–5.162
    extra rights to accompaniment 5.158
    person requesting flexible working 5.157
    time off to accompany 1.251, 5.156
    trade union officials 5.373–5.374
  right to consultation 5.162
  collective
    redundancies 5.163–5.167, 5.263–5.269, 9.160–9.163
  consultation mechanism 5.188–5.191
  European companies 5.176–5.178
  health and safety representation 5.171
  Information and Consultation of Employees Regulations 2004 5.172–5.175
  transfer of undertakings 5.168–5.170, 5.270–5.274, 9.474–9.492
  rights 5.186
    not to be dismissed or victimised 5.187
  time off work 1.252, 5.285
  right to be accompanied and 1.251, 5.156
  transfer of undertakings and 5.270–5.274, 9.474–9.492
    consultation 5.168–5.170
  works councils 5.192–5.197
  see also collective bargaining
employee share and share option schemes 7.286–7.289
  age discrimination 7.385–7.390
  HM Revenue & Customs
    tax rates approval 7.296–7.297
    unapproved schemes 7.294

see also company share option plans; enterprise management incentive schemes; savings-related share option schemes; share incentive plans; unapproved share option schemes
employer/employee relationship see employment status
employment agencies and employment businesses 2.426–2.427, 2.429–2.432, 8.39
  distinction between 2.430–2.431
  implied contracts of employment 2.457
  industrial disputes 2.433
  information to be provided
    by hirer 2.447–2.448
    to hirer 2.449–2.456
  payment of workers 2.434–2.436
  prohibition orders 2.458
  restrictions on fees charged
    to employers 2.439–2.443
    to work-seekers 2.437–2.438
  terms and conditions between employment business or agency and hirer 2.444–2.446
  see also agency workers
Employment Appeal Tribunal (EAT) 3.284–3.285
  discrimination claims 4.248–4.251
employment references see references
employment relations skills 5.240
employment status
  agency workers 2.391–2.392, 2.497, 2.545–2.556
  apprentices 2.571–2.572
  casual workers 2.389–2.390, 2.496
  contracts of service and contracts for service 2.500–2.503
  discrimination and 2.419–2.420
  employee
    meaning 2.360–2.362
    office holder distinguished 2.367
    worker distinguished 1.114, 2.363–2.365, 2.368–2.370, 2.504–2.509
  fixed-term contracts 2.384–2.385, 2.517
  home workers 2.496, 2.537–2.539
  job-share 2.386, 2.528–2.529
  nil hours contracts 2.540–2.541
  office holders 2.367
  self-employment 1.6, 2.351, 2.366, 2.500–2.503
  worker see worker
  see also contracts of employment

employment tribunals 3.263, 9.1
  appeals 3.284–3.285, 4.248–4.251, 9.76–9.77
  breach of contract claims 2.40, 2.57–2.59, 2.78–2.82, 9.5
  case management 9.26–9.27
  discussion 9.35
  claim form (ET1) 3.266, 3.270, 4.228, 9.19
  compensation 9.59–9.60
  costs 3.289–3.295, 9.65–9.75
    ability to pay 3.292, 9.74
    discrimination claims 4.261–4.271
    maximum amount 3.292, 9.75
    preparation time orders 3.293–3.294, 9.72–9.73
    wasted costs awards 3.295, 9.69–9.71
  counterclaim 9.24
  declarations 4.252, 4.253, 9.63
  default judgment, application to review 3.272
  deposits 3.276
  disclosure of documents 3.274
  disclosure of evidence 9.28–9.31
  discrimination claims 4.227
    appeals 4.248–4.251
    beginning proceedings 4.228–4.230
    burden of proof 4.236–4.238
    case management 4.231–4.232
    costs 4.261–4.271
    decision 4.245–4.247
    hearing 4.239–4.244
    part-time workers 1.127–1.129
    questionnaires 3.278–3.279
    remedies 4.252–4.260
    striking out claims 4.233–4.235
  EC law 9.6
  employer's response 9.20–9.23
    failure to file 9.25
    response form (ET3) 3.270–3.271, 4.229, 9.21–9.22
  equal pay cases, questionnaires 3.278–3.279
  further particulars 3.273
  hearings 3.275, 9.39–9.41
    cross-examination of witnesses 9.53
    discrimination claims 4.239–4.244
    evidence 9.49–9.52
    hearing panel 3.281
    judgment 9.57
    open discussion 9.48
    procedure 9.42–9.57
    procedure at 3.282–3.283
    questions by tribunal members 9.55
    re-examination of witnesses 9.54

standard order of procedure
    9.47–9.57
  submissions   9.56
mediation   3.310
National Insurance Fund payment,
  failure to make   9.133, 9.137
notification to employer   3.270
overriding objective   3.264–3.265
pre-hearing review   9.36–9.38
preparation time
  orders   3.293–3.294, 9.72–9.73
prohibition orders   2.458
recommendations   4.252, 4.260, 9.64
reinstatement and
  re-engagement   4.252, 9.61–9.62, 9.210–9.213, 9.541–9.545
remedies   9.58
  compensation   4.252, 4.253–4.260, 9.59–9.60
  declaration   4.252, 4.253, 9.63
  recommendation   4.252, 4.260, 9.64
  reinstatement and
    re-engagement   4.252, 9.61–9.62, 9.210–9.213, 9.541–9.545
settlements   3.286
starting proceedings   9.19
statutory employment rights   9.4–9.6
striking out claims   3.277, 4.233–4.235
time limits   3.267–3.269, 9.7–9.11
  continuing acts   9.12–9.13
  deliberate omissions   9.14
  expiration on non-working day   9.16
  limited extension   9.17–9.18
  notices of dismissal   9.15
victimisation, protection from   9.78
wasted costs
  awards   3.295, 9.69–9.71
withdrawal of proceedings   9.33–9.34
witness orders   3.280
written statement of particulars of employment, complaints as to   2.230–2.231, 2.263–2.265, 3.55
wrongful dismissal
  claims   9.5, 9.610–9.611
enterprise management incentive (EMI) schemes   7.292, 7.335–7.337
  annual return   7.358
  basic criteria   7.338
  conditions relating to shares   7.347
  disqualification of options   7.351
  eligible employees   7.341–7.343
  exercise period   7.349–7.350
  HM Revenue & Customs notifications   7.357
  maximum
    value of option   7.345–7.346
  option granted "by reason of employment"   7.344
  option price   7.348
  performance targets   7.352
  qualifying company   7.339–7.340
  tax liability   7.353–7.356
  see also employee share and share option schemes
equal opportunities
  monitoring   4.334–4.335
    data protection   2.297
    Northern Ireland   4.336–4.338, 4.392
  policy   4.283–4.290
  sabbaticals and   1.176
  statement in staff handbook   2.487
  succession planning   8.594–8.598
equal pay   4.346–4.348
  audits   4.373–4.379
  comparators   4.357–4.359
  indirect discrimination in pay arrangements   4.387
  job evaluation   4.380–4.382
  job-sharers   4.383
  "like work"   4.360
  material differences other than sex   4.365–4.367
  part-time workers   4.383
  pay disparity   4.349–4.354
  pensions   4.384–4.386
  policy   4.355
  questionnaire procedure   3.278–3.279, 4.368–4.372
  remedies   4.254–4.255
  right to   4.356–4.364
  work of "equal value"   4.362
  work rated as "equivalent"   4.361
European companies
  consultation for   5.176–5.178
European Works Councils *see* works councils
exit interviews   9.275–9.278

F

fertility treatment
  time off work   1.271, 1.286–1.288
fidelity clause   2.101–2.103
fixed-term employees   1.130–1.133, 2.515–2.517
  comparable permanent employee   1.137–1.138
  continuous service   2.385, 2.516, 2.524, 2.525–2.527
  damages for wrongful dismissal   9.591–9.593
  definition   1.134–1.136
  employment status   2.384–2.385, 2.517

government-sponsored
  Apprenticeships   2.570
  less favourable
    treatment   2.520–2.521
  notice   2.518–2.519
  Regulations 2002   2.408
  right not to be treated
    less favourably   1.139–1.143
  temporary cessation
    of work   2.525–2.527
  termination   1.144, 2.522–2.524
  waiver clauses   1.145–1.146
flexibility agreements   2.135–2.138
flexible working   1.223, 6.35–6.37
  appeals   6.51, 6.52–6.53
  application for   6.44–6.45
    employer's response   6.46–6.51
    unresolved applications   6.56–6.59
  carers of adults   6.36
  case studies   6.64–6.79
  detriment or dismissal   6.60
  qualifying conditions   6.37
  right to request   6.35–6.37, 6.41–6.43
  sex discrimination   6.61–6.62
  time limits   6.54–6.55
formation of contract   2.150–2.151
  acceptance
    conditional   2.163–2.164
    means of acceptance   2.161
    oral   2.161
    reasonable period   2.161
    unconditional   2.162
  conditional offers   2.165–2.174, 8.340
    Asylum and Immigration Act
      checks   2.173
    Criminal Records Bureau
      checks   2.172
    medical or health check 2.168–2.170
    qualifications   2.167
    references   2.166
    rehabilitation of offenders   2.171
  custom and practice   2.194–2.195
  by email   2.336
  employee handbooks *see* staff
    handbooks
  express terms   2.182–2.184
  implied terms   2.185–2.186
  incorporated terms   2.187–2.190
  misrepresentation   2.175–2.176
  mutual obligations   2.196–2.198
  offers   2.155, 8.340
    conditional *see* conditional offers
      above
    oral offers   2.156–2.158
    written offers   2.159–2.160
  reference documents   2.201–2.202
  staff handbooks *see* staff handbooks

statutory terms   2.191–2.192
transfer of undertakings   2.216–2.221
variation *see* variation of contract
void terms and illegality   2.193
written statement of particulars
                                2.177–2.178
  excluded employees   2.179
freelance workers
  working time   1.364

G

garden leave   2.93–2.96
gender reassignment
  appearance and dress codes
                                  2.33–2.34
  discrimination   2.34, 4.701–4.704
government-sponsored
Apprenticeships *see* apprenticeships
grievance procedure *see* statutory
  grievance procedure
gross misconduct
  disciplinary rules and procedures
                                3.62, 9.384
  examples   9.409
  summary
    dismissal   2.183, 3.142–3.146,
                    9.374–9.375, 9.384, 9.409
  see also misconduct
group personal pension schemes
                                7.611–7.613

H

harassment   3.13, 4.323–4.330
  age harassment   4.26–4.28, 4.234
  complaints procedure   4.291–4.295
  by customers, suppliers and other
    third parties
    racial harassment   4.521–4.524
    religious harassment   4.626–4.629
    sexual harassment   4.719–4.722
    sexual orientation harassment
                              4.795–4.798
  disability harassment   4.130–4.135,
                                      4.324
  grievance procedure   3.243
  intentional harassment claims   3.29
    protection from claims   3.30–3.35
  meaning   3.11
  racial harassment   4.324,
                4.478–4.485, 4.521–4.524
  religious harassment   4.324,
                4.590–4.596, 4.626–4.629
  sectarian harassment   4.410–4.412
  sexual orientation
    harassment   4.324, 4.760–4.765

by customers, suppliers and other
    third parties 4.795–4.798
sexual and sex-based harassment
    4.324, 4.668–4.678
see also bullying
health checks *see* medical checks
health and safety
    bullying and 3.23–3.25
    information
        and consultation 5.257–5.261
    overseas workers 1.97–1.99
    record retention 2.310
    statutory grievance procedure 3.245
health and safety representation
    5.171
see also safety representatives
health schemes *see* sickness and
    health schemes
**Highly Skilled Migrant Programme
    (HSMP)** 8.458–8.463
HIV
    disability discrimination 4.120
holidaymakers
    working 8.454–8.457
holidays
    accrual of holiday in first year of
        employment 1.39–1.41
    agency staff 1.9
    annual leave *see* annual leave
    bank holidays 1.24–1.30
    carrying over holiday entitlements
        1.47–1.48
    deductions for holiday taken in excess
        1.53
    employees' notice of intention to take
        holiday 1.42
    employer's right
        of counter-notice 1.43–1.46
    extended leave 1.54
    payment during annual leave
        1.36–1.38
    payment in lieu of holiday 1.49–1.52
    policy and procedure 1.7
    public holidays 1.18, 1.24–1.25
    religious holidays and festivals
        1.31–1.33, 4.577–4.579
    specifying particulars of holidays
        1.34–1.35
    timing of holidays 1.42–1.46
    worker, definition 1.4–1.6
    see also long-service leave;
        sabbaticals
home workers 1.113, 2.403
    employment
        status 2.496, 2.537–2.539

human rights
    appearance and dress codes
        2.28–2.32
    email privacy 2.335

I

income support deduction notices
    7.58
income tax 2.404
induction 8.70–8.71, 8.244, 8.249
    business plans 8.93–8.94
    continued support 8.95
    corporate or organisational induction
        8.80–8.81, 8.83–8.84
    documentation 8.99
    evaluation 8.98
    frequency of events 8.87–8.89
    handouts 8.85–8.86
    importance 8.74–8.75
    job changes 8.96–8.97
    local induction 8.80–8.81
        planning and preparation 8.82
    part-time employees 8.90–8.92
    record keeping 8.99
industrial action 5.203
    alternative dispute resolution 5.231
    Acas arbitration scheme 5.63–5.68,
        5.234
    Acas conciliation 5.63–5.68, 5.232
    mediation 5.63–5.68, 5.233
    ballot requirements 5.412
    categories of dispute 5.206
    debrief 5.242
    employees' protection
        from dismissal 5.210–5.211
    employer's response 5.213–5.215
    employment businesses and 2.433
    failure of collective
        bargaining process 5.60–5.62
    forms of action 5.207
    legal action 5.220
    legality 5.208–5.209
    management skills 5.229
    obligation to resolve 5.221–5.223
    payment of wages 5.224–5.227
    resolution of disputes 5.216–5.220
    role of HR practitioners 5.235
    seriousness of disputes 5.212
    subjects for dispute 5.204–5.205
    trade unions
        ballot requirements 5.412
        employees' protection from union
            5.238
        illegal union action 5.228
        immunity from legal proceedings
            5.236–5.237

right to be balloted 5.411
workplace dispute procedures 5.230
information and consultation
  5.245–5.250
achieving effective consultation
  5.310–5.312
benefits 5.255
case studies 5.324–5.360
collective bargaining *see* collective bargaining
collective redundancies *see* collective redundancies
disclosure of information 5.316–5.319
  exceptions 5.320
  types of information 5.321
disputes 5.314–5.315
European Works Councils
  5.281–5.285, 5.530–5.532
existing arrangements 5.305
failure to consult 5.313
health and safety 5.257–5.261
Information and Consultation Agreement (ICA)
  negotiations 5.298–5.299
  proposing 5.294–5.297
  provisions of negotiated ICA
  5.300–5.301
occupational and personal pensions
  5.275–5.280
Regulations 2004 5.69–5.73,
  5.246–5.247, 5.286–5.307
rights to 5.256
staff handbook and 2.471–2.473
strategic thinking 5.303–5.304
trade unions 5.306–5.307
  consultation rights 5.393–5.397
  information rights 5.390–5.392
transfer of undertakings 5.168–5.170, 5.270–5.274
transnational organisations
  5.281–5.285
variation of contract 2.592–2.594
works
  councils 5.501–5.502, 5.520–5.524
  European Works Councils
  5.281–5.285, 5.530–5.532
insolvency 9.83
guaranteed payments from National Insurance Fund 9.127–9.129
  criteria for payment 9.131
  employment tribunal proceedings
  9.133
  procedure 9.132
  set-off debts owed by the employee
  9.130

guaranteed redundancy payments
  9.123–9.126
individual *see* bankruptcy
pension contributions 9.134
  employment tribunal proceedings
  9.137
  extent of liability 9.135–9.136
preferential status of debts owed to employees 9.119
  principle of equal distribution
  9.120–9.121
  status of preferential debts 9.122
statutory payments 9.138
termination of employment
  dismissal after retention in employment following insolvency
  9.117
  dismissal on insolvency of employer
  9.115–9.116
  dismissal prior to insolvency of employer 9.114
  statutory consultation and notice periods prior to dismissal 9.118
  transfer of undertakings and 9.473
see also administration; administrative receivership; liquidation
institutional racism 4.510
insurance schemes
  data protection 2.296
Internet 2.321–2.322
copyright 2.337
criminal and other offences
  2.338–2.341
data protection 2.333–2.334
policy on use 2.343–2.346
recruitment and 8.13–8.17
  corporate websites 8.15–8.16
  recruitment websites 8.14
interviews 8.106, 8.538
briefing candidates 8.558
candidate documents 8.114
clarification and honesty 8.546–8.549
competencies
  assessing 8.134
  benchmarked competencies
  8.118–8.119
  competency statements 8.118, 8.120
  competency-based questions 8.135
  defining 8.119, 8.120
conducting the interview 8.559–8.563
disabled interviewees 4.157–4.159, 8.557, 8.564–8.565
discrimination 4.312–4.313, 8.312–8.313
  disability discrimination 4.157–4.159, 8.521, 8.564–8.565
employer branding and 8.139

877

ending the interview	8.563
importance	8.109
interview evidence	8.138
objective selection	8.137
one-to-one interviews	8.556–8.557
opening	8.121–8.124
panel interviews	8.550–8.555
discrimination	8.553
preparation	8.112–8.117, 8.539
purpose	8.110
questioning techniques	8.560–8.562
behavioural questions	8.544–8.545
closed questions	8.128–8.129
competency-based questions	8.135
high order questions	8.125–8.127
hypothetical questions	8.543, 8.545
low order questions	8.124
open questions	8.130–8.131
probing questions	8.132
structured questions	8.542
rapport	8.121–8.122, 8.552
stages	8.111–8.139
structured interviews	8.540–8.541

J

job descriptions	8.141, 8.147
content	8.154–8.164
discrimination	4.301–4.302
disability discrimination	4.148–4.150
format	8.165–8.168
job analysis	8.148–8.152
review	8.153
job evaluation	
benefits	8.204–8.206
definition	8.194, 8.197–8.198
equal pay	4.380–4.382
job size assessment	8.207–8.208
purposes	8.199–8.200
schemes	
barriers to success	8.215–8.216
implementation	8.212–8.213
job classification	8.232–8.235
job ranking	8.224–8.228
paired comparisons	8.229–8.231
point-factor rating system	8.217–8.222
proprietary brands	8.214
typical steps	8.236
job references *see* references	
job specifications *see* job descriptions; person specifications	
job-share	
employment status	2.386, 2.528–2.529
equal pay	4.383
indirect sex discrimination and	4.696, 8.298

JobCentres	8.45–8.46
jury service	
loss of earnings allowances	1.242
subsistence allowances	1.243
time off work	1.240–1.245
travel allowances	1.244
unfair dismissal and	1.245

L

lay offs	9.233–9.238
liquidation	9.109
claims against employer	9.110
contracts of employment	
effect on	9.111
liability under	9.112
see also insolvency	
long-service leave	
policy and procedure	1.8
see also holidays	
long-term sickness absence	1.205
disability discrimination	1.215–1.217
holiday entitlement and	1.11–1.14
management	2.11–2.18

M

manual workers' allowance and benefits	7.98–7.100
marital status discrimination	4.699
maternity allowance	6.216
maternity leave	
additional leave	6.84–6.85
duration	6.92
EWC before 1 April 2007	6.85, 6.90–6.91
returning from	6.117–6.119
rights during	6.108–6.109
additional maternity leave, benefits during	7.97
annual leave entitlement and	1.10
benefits during	7.94–7.97
compulsory	6.115
contact during	6.120–6.124
detrimental treatment	6.129
dismissal and	6.130
employee notification	6.93
change of start date	6.94–6.95
response	6.96
going on leave	6.97–6.98
keeping in touch days	6.120–6.124
miscarriage	6.126–6.127
ordinary leave	6.83, 6.89
duration	6.89
pay rises awarded during	6.105–6.107
returning from	6.116
rights during	6.104–6.107

ordinary maternity leave, benefits
  during   7.95–7.96
pay rises awarded during 6.105–6.107
qualifying conditions   6.89–6.92
redundancy and   6.128
returning to work notification
  EWC on or after 1 April 2007
                              6.111–6.114
  EWC before 1 April 2007   6.110
small employer exemption   6.125
stillbirth   6.126–6.127
maternity rights   6.82–6.86
ante-natal care,
  time off for   1.246, 1.255–1.258
discrimination   4.697–4.698
dismissal   6.130
pregnancy-related
  absences   6.99–6.102
mediation   3.310–3.313
industrial disputes   5.63–5.68, 5.233
procedure   3.311–3.312
medical appointments
time off
  work   1.272–1.273, 1.289–1.291
medical examinations
contracts of employment 2.139–2.141
disability discrimination   2.168,
          4.161–4.163, 8.495
pre-employment   2.168–2.170,
   4.161–4.163, 8.344–8.346, 8.469
medical records
access   2.141, 8.496
data protection   2.315–2.316, 8.469,
                          8.492–8.494
mental impairment
disability discrimination   4.113–4.114
mergers and acquisitions
data protection   2.307
migrant workers   8.386–8.388
Accession State Registration
  Scheme   8.410–8.413
Asylum and Immigration Act checks
    2.173, 4.498–4.500, 8.391–8.398
  List 1 documentation   8.395
  List 2 documentation   8.396–8.398
  Bulgarian workers   1.70, 1.71, 8.414,
                          8.464–8.465
European Economic Area (EEA) 8.409
Highly Skilled Migrant Programme
  (HSMP)   8.458–8.463
holidaymakers   8.454–8.457
low-skilled workers   1.71
overseas students   8.450–8.453
race discrimination   8.388, 8.394,
                          8.399–8.402
Romanian workers   1.70, 1.71, 8.414,
                          8.464–8.465

Sector-Based Scheme (SBS)
                            8.464–8.465
Training and Work Experience
  Scheme (TWES)   8.442–8.445
  criteria for applications 8.446–8.447
  length of permits   8.448–8.449
work permits see work permits
see also overseas workers
misconduct
examples   3.60–3.61
proof of   3.151
see also gross misconduct
mobile workers
working time see working time
mobility clause   2.125–2.127
discrimination   2.127
variation of contract   2.597–2.598
multiple sclerosis
disability discrimination   4.120

N

National Insurance
benefits and   7.122–7.123
  Class 1A contributions 7.124–7.131
  Class 1B contributions 7.132–7.134
Class 1 contributions
  calculation   7.415–7.425
  definition of earnings   7.405
  earnings, meaning   7.411
  earnings period   7.401–7.402,
                          7.412–7.414
  exact percentage
    calculation method   7.424–7.425
  liability   7.395
  non-cumulative calculation   7.401
  payment   7.397
  tables calculation method
                          7.415–7.423
Class 1A contributions
  benefits   7.124–7.131
  calculation of payment 7.128–7.130,
                          7.426–7.427
  company cars   7.240–7.243
  employer-only   7.406
  exceptions from charge   7.127
  liability arising   7.125
  liability to pay   7.126
  when payable   7.131
Class 1B contributions   7.132–7.134,
                                  7.428
company cars
  approved mileage allowance
    payments and   7.244–7.246
  Class 1A contributions 7.240–7.243
  compliance   7.247–7.251
contributions   2.405

disclosure rules 7.440–7.443
fund *see* National Insurance Fund
interest 7.437–7.438
lower earnings limit 7.398
number 7.396
payment to HM Revenue & Customs
 7.434–7.436
penalties 7.439
primary contributions 7.399, 7.404
rates and limits 2007/08 7.408
record keeping 7.429–7.431
returns 7.432–7.433
secondary contributions 7.400
share incentive plans (SIPs) and
 7.378–7.381
unapproved share option schemes
 and 7.367–7.369
National Insurance Fund
 guaranteed payments 9.127–9.129
  criteria for payment 9.131
  employment tribunal proceedings
   9.133
  procedure 9.132
  set-off debts owed by the employee
   9.130
 pension contributions 9.134
  employment tribunal proceedings
   9.137
 extent of liability 9.135–9.136
national minimum wage (NMW)
 7.447–7.454
 accredited training, abolition 7.454
 age bands 8.341
 apprentices 2.573
 deductions 7.485–7.486
 determining 7.460
 enforcement 7.449, 7.489
 hourly rate of pay 7.487–7.488
 hours counted as
  having been worked 7.465–7.468
 meaning of "worker" 7.461–7.464
 output work 7.471–7.473
 pay for the work 7.479–7.482
 rates 7.450–7.453, 7.457–7.459
 reductions 7.484
 reference period 7.478
 salaried work and annual hours'
  contracts 7.474–7.476
 time work 7.470
 unmeasured work time 7.477
night work 1.359, 1.422–1.428
 calculating average hours
  1.429–1.433
 derogations 1.369
 health assessments 1.426
 meaning of "night-time" 1.485
 mobile workers 1.428, 1.483–1.485

young persons 1.427, 8.335
nil hours contracts 2.540–2.541
non-dealing clause 2.116
 see also restrictive covenants
non-solicitation clause 2.116
 see also restrictive covenants
Northern Ireland
 affirmative action 4.423–4.425
  recruiting from unemployed workers
   4.428
  redundancy selection 4.426
  targeted encouragement 4.427
 attachment of earnings orders
  7.49–7.50
 Equality Commission 4.438
 fair employment monitoring
  4.336–4.338
  monitoring returns 4.418–4.419
  registration 4.415–4.417
  reviews 4.420–4.422
 harassment 4.410–4.412
 redundancy selection 4.426
 religious or political discrimination
  4.393–4.395
  burden of proof 4.433–4.434
  complaints 4.429–4.435
  direct 4.400–4.402
  indirect 4.403–4.406
  justification 4.407–4.408
  liability 4.413–4.414
  protected workers 4.396–4.398
  questionnaire procedure 4.435
  remedies 4.436–4.437
  sectarian harassment 4.410–4.412
  victimisation 4.409
 sectarian harassment 4.410–4.412
notice
 dismissal
  contractual notice 9.185–9.186,
   9.566
  reasonable notice 9.570–9.571
  statutory minimum 2.409
  statutory notice 9.183–9.184,
   9.567–9.569
  payment in lieu 9.187, 9.414–9.416,
   9.572–9.573
   contractual right to 9.414,
    9.600–9.601
 resignation
  notice period 9.250–9.252
  withdrawing 9.257
  working during notice period 9.258
  written notice 9.253–9.254

O

occupational pension schemes
 7.608–7.610

additional voluntary contributions
   (AVCs) 7.609
automatic registration 7.610
average salary scheme 7.608
cash balance scheme 7.608
defined contribution scheme 7.608
final salary scheme 7.608
information and consultation
   5.275–5.280
internal dispute resolution (IDR)
   7.680–7.681
investments by 7.568–7.576
transfer of undertakings and
   9.469–9.472
see also pensions
office holders 2.367
overseas
  workers 1.58–1.62, 2.393–2.394
  discrimination claims 1.88–1.93
  health and safety 1.97–1.99
  policy and procedure 1.100
  Posted Workers Directive 1.70–1.76
    enforcement 1.77
  redundancy 1.95
  risk assessment 1.97
  statutory employment rights 1.94–1.96
  unfair dismissal 1.81–1.87
  war zones 1.98
  working outside Europe 1.78–1.80
  written statement of particulars of
    employment 1.65–1.69, 2.393
  see also migrant workers; work
    permits

P

parental leave 6.134–6.136
  a week's leave
    fixed working hours 6.145
    varied working hours 6.146
  adopted children 6.143
  annual leave entitlement and 1.10
  caring for a child 6.147–6.148
  change of employer 6.144
  contractual entitlement 6.162
  detriment 6.170
  disabled children 6.142
  dismissal 6.170
  entitlement 6.141–6.144
  failure to return to work 6.165–6.166
  postponement 6.156–6.159
  qualifying conditions 6.139–6.140
  record keeping 6.160–6.161
  redundancy selection 6.171–6.172
  refusing leave 6.168–6.169
  returning to work 6.163–6.164
  rights and obligations during 6.167
  schemes 6.149–6.151
    enhanced 6.136
    statutory fall-back scheme 6.152
      documentary evidence 6.153
      how leave may be taken 6.155
      notice of intention to take parental
        leave 6.154
      postponement of parental leave
        6.156–6.159
  victimisation 6.170
part-time workers 1.104–1.106,
    2.510–2.514
  annual holiday
    entitlement 1.122–1.124
  annual leave
    entitlement 1.17, 1.122–1.124
  bank holidays 1.125
  comparable full-time worker
    1.111–1.112, 2.512
  contractual benefits 2.407
  definition 1.109–1.110
  equal pay 4.383
  indirect sex discrimination and 4.696,
    8.298
  induction 8.90–8.92
  permanent contracts 2.383
  public holidays 1.125–1.126
  redundancy selection 2.514
  Regulations
    2000 1.113–1.121, 2.406–2.407
  remedies for less favourable
    treatment 1.127–1.129
  written statement of reasons for
    unfavourable treatment 1.128, 2.513
paternity leave 6.178–6.179
  adoption leave and 6.303
  annual leave entitlement and 1.10
  notification requirements
    adoption 6.192–6.194
    birth 6.191
  declaration of right to take statutory
    paternity leave 6.195–6.196
  period of leave 6.189
  qualifying conditions 6.182–6.184
  statutory paternity leave
    after adoption 6.186–6.188
    after birth 6.185
    commencement 6.198–6.202
    declaration of right to take
      6.195–6.196
    further notice 6.202
    right to return 6.205–6.207
    terms and conditions during
      6.203–6.204
    unfair dismissal rights 6.208–6.210
    variation of start date 6.201
PAYE 7.493–7.496

compulsory electronic filing of year
   end returns   7.522–7.524
compulsory electronic payments
   7.514–7.516
gross taxable pay   7.506
K codes   7.510–7.511
legal obligations   7.502
operation   7.505
Pay Adjustment Tables   7.508
payment due to collector of taxes
   7.513
penalties and fines
   completion error   7.521
   late submission   7.519–7.520
record keeping   7.503–7.504
tax codes   7.507–7.509
tax rates   7.512
taxable income   7.499–7.501
year end returns   7.517
payment in lieu of holiday   1.49–1.52
payment in lieu of notice   9.187, 9.414–9.416, 9.572–9.573
   contractual right to   9.414, 9.600–9.601
pension fund trustees
   employment law protection
   7.666–7.668
   member-nominated   7.661–7.663
   time off work   1.254
pensions   7.527
   administration issues   7.589–7.595
   advice   7.650–7.651
   age discrimination   4.79–4.81, 7.676–7.678, 9.331–9.332
      pension age   7.580–7.588
   civil partnerships   7.679
   commercial pension schemes
   7.560–7.561
   contracting-out   7.403, 7.557–7.559
   duty to consult   7.673–7.675
   data protection   2.296
   direct payment arrangements   7.630
   discrimination   7.676–7.678
      age discrimination   4.79–4.81, 7.676–7.678, 9.331–9.332
      disputes   7.682
      pension age   7.580–7.588
      sex discrimination   7.676
   dispute resolution   7.680–7.682
   employment law protection for
      trustees   7.666–7.668
   equal pay   4.384–4.386
   equal treatment   7.676–7.678, 7.682
   funded unapproved retirement benefit
      schemes (FURBS)   7.565
   group personal pension schemes
   7.611–7.613

implied duty of good faith   7.664–7.665
inducement payments   7.652–7.654
information and consultation
   5.275–5.280
insolvency of employer   9.134
   employment tribunal proceedings
   9.137
   extent of liability   9.135–9.136
internal dispute resolution (IDR)
   7.680–7.681
member-nominated trustees
   7.661–7.663
monitoring payments   7.634–7.637
occupational schemes *see*
   occupational pension schemes
payment record   7.631–7.633
payment schedules   7.669–7.672
penalties for non-compliance
   7.638–7.639
pension age   7.577–7.579
   age discrimination   7.580–7.588
pension reform   7.530–7.534
pensions advice tax exemption
   7.650–7.651
Pensions Commission   7.683–7.685
pre-"A-Day" (6 April 2006) schemes
   7.562–7.565
private pensions   7.527
   no duty to contribute   7.606
records   7.596–7.597
registered pension schemes
   7.543–7.556
   returns   7.598–7.599
   tax relief for employer contributions
   7.566–7.567
regulation and protection   7.640–7.649
schedule of contributions   7.669–7.672
settlor of a trust   7.655–7.660
sex discrimination   7.676
stakeholder pension schemes *see*
   stakeholder pension schemes
State Retirement Pension
   7.600–7.605
unapproved retirement benefit
   schemes (UURBS)   7.565
unified tax regime from 6 April 2006
   ("A-Day")   7.535–7.542
work-based pension provisions   7.607
permanent full-time contracts   2.382
permanent part-time contracts   2.383
person specifications   8.141–8.142, 8.169–8.170
   age discrimination   4.305–4.306
   common errors   8.171–8.177
   competency frameworks   8.181–8.183
   discrimination   4.303–4.306, 8.294–8.295

direct 8.187
disability discrimination 4.148–4.150
  indirect 8.187, 8.188–8.191
  mandatory and preferred
    requirements 8.185–8.186
Fraser's Five-Fold Grading System
      8.180
  mandatory requirements 8.184–8.186
  preferred requirements 8.184–8.186
  Rodger's Seven-Point Plan 8.179
  structures approaches 8.178–8.180
personal injury claims
  bullying 3.14, 3.20–3.22
personal pensions
  information and consultation
      5.275–5.280
poaching of customers
  restrictive covenants 2.114–2.116
poaching staff 8.52–8.53
  restrictive covenants and 2.108, 2.120–2.121
poor performance
  dealing with 3.63–3.65
prayer facilities
  provision of 4.571–4.576
pre-employment checks 8.342–8.343
  Asylum and Immigration Act checks
    2.173, 4.498–4.500, 8.391–8.398
  Criminal Records Bureau checks
    2.172, 8.352–8.355
  data protection 2.291
  disability discrimination 4.161–4.163, 8.495
  medical checks 4.161–4.163, 8.344–8.346, 8.495
  migrant workers 8.387–8.388
  protection of vulnerable adults (POVA)
    scheme 8.372–8.373
  qualifications 2.167, 8.347–8.348
  references *see* references
  rehabilitation of offenders 2.171, 8.356–8.373
  verifying applicants' claims 2.288
pregnancy discrimination
    4.697–4.698, 6.129
press advertising *see* recruitment advertising
probationary periods 8.239–8.240
  contracts of
    employment and 8.239, 8.255–8.256
  duration 8.257–8.258
  early-leaver syndrome and
      8.249–8.250
  extension 8.259–8.261
  legal situation 8.252–8.254
  management 8.262–8.266
  reasons for using 8.243–8.247

review meetings 8.268
salary increases and 8.251
successful completion 8.270–8.272
prohibition orders
  employment agencies and businesses
      2.458
**protection of vulnerable adults
(POVA) scheme** 8.372–8.373
psychometric instruments
    8.567–8.568, 8.618
public duties
  unpaid time off 1.233–1.235
public holidays 1.18, 1.24–1.25
  part-time workers 1.125–1.126
public interest disclosure *see* whistleblowing

Q

qualifications
  pre-employment
    checks 2.167, 8.347–8.348
questionnaire procedure 3.278–3.279
  age discrimination 4.84–4.86
  disability discrimination 4.178–4.181
  equal pay 3.278–3.279, 4.368–4.372
  race discrimination 4.512–4.515
  religion or belief discrimination
      4.618–4.621
    Northern Ireland 4.435
  sex discrimination 4.711–4.714
  sexual orientation discrimination
      4.786–4.789

R

race discrimination 4.443–4.445
  appearance and dress codes 2.2, 2.20–2.23, 4.470–4.474
    justification 2.24–2.27
  bullying 3.28
  burden of proof 4.516–4.517
  claims 4.511
    burden of proof 4.516–4.517
    compensation 4.525–4.526
    harassment by customers, suppliers
      and other third parties 4.521–4.524
    questionnaire procedure
      4.512–4.515
    time limits 4.209–4.215
    vicarious liability 4.518–4.520
    see also discrimination claims
  comparable person 4.456–4.457
  compensation 4.525–4.526
  direct 4.459–4.460
  grievance procedure 4.455
  harassment 4.26–4.28, 4.324, 4.478–4.485

by customers, suppliers and other
  third parties 4.521–4.524
indirect 4.461–4.464
dress
  codes 2.20–2.23, 4.470–4.474
identifying a "legitimate aim" 4.468
provision, criterion or practice 4.465
"put at a disadvantage" 4.466–4.467
test of proportionality 4.469
institutional racism 4.510
migrant
  workers 8.388, 8.394, 8.399–8.402
monitoring 4.527–4.530
post-employment discrimination 4.506
promotion 4.504
qualifying conditions 4.454–4.455
questionnaire procedure 4.512–4.515
race equality schemes for public
  bodies 4.507–4.509
recruitment 4.451, 4.486
  advertisements 4.494–4.497
  Asylum and Immigration Act checks
    4.498–4.500
  best practice checklist 4.501
  genuine occupational qualifications
    and requirements 4.487–4.490,
    8.290, 8.292, 8.293
  positive action 4.491–4.493
  skills and experience 8.299
  see also discrimination in
    recruitment
redundancy selection 4.505
scope of law 4.446–4.452
terms and conditions of employment
  4.503
training opportunities 4.504
transfers 4.504
vicarious liability 4.518–4.520
victimisation 4.475–4.477
**race equality schemes for public
bodies** 4.507–4.509
racial harassment 4.478–4.485
customers, suppliers and other third
  parties 4.521–4.524
recruitment 8.1–8.3
advertising see recruitment advertising
agencies 8.39
application forms see application
  forms
being an employer of choice
  8.63–8.67
children see children
data protection 8.374–8.376
  applications 2.286–2.287
  data protection clause in application
    form 8.308, 8.524

Employment Practices Data
  Protection Code 8.377–8.378
pre-employment checks 2.291
retention of recruitment records
  2.292–2.294
right of access to records
  2.300–2.303, 8.379–8.380
shortlisting 2.289–2.290
verifying applicants' claims 2.288
direct applications 8.54–8.57
discrimination see discrimination in
  recruitment
executive search consultants
  8.41–8.42
executive selection consultants 8.40
former employees 8.58
headhunters 8.41–8.42
intermediaries 8.38
internal recruitment 8.2
  benefits 8.7–8.9
  disadvantages 8.10–8.11
Internet 8.13–8.17
  corporate websites 8.15–8.16
  recruitment websites 8.14
interviews see interviews
job descriptions see job descriptions
job evaluation see job evaluation
JobCentres 8.45–8.46
medical reports, access 8.496
migrant workers 8.386–8.388
migrant workers see migrant workers
monitoring 8.318
networking 8.52–8.53
offers of employment 8.340
person specifications see person
  specifications
poaching 8.52–8.53
pre-employment checks see
  pre-employment checks
recent recruitment campaigns
  8.59–8.62
recommendations by existing staff
  8.47–8.51
record keeping 8.577–8.578
recruitment intermediaries 8.38
retention of recruitment records
  2.292–2.294
selection see selection process
shortlisting 2.289–2.290,
  8.309–8.311
trade union membership and
  5.376–5.378
verifying applicants' claims 2.288
volume recruitment techniques
  8.43–8.44
young persons see young persons
recruitment advertising 8.12

discrimination 4.308–4.311, 8.23–8.24, 8.301–8.303
  age discrimination 4.31, 8.33
  disability discrimination 4.151–4.155, 8.302
  genuine occupational requirements 8.31–8.32
  race discrimination 4.494–4.497
  sex discrimination 4.686–4.689
  wording for adverts 8.25–8.30
press advertising
  local press 8.19
  national press 8.20–8.21
  regional press 8.21
  trade press 8.22
  writing good copy 8.34–8.37
redundancy 9.141
  avoiding redundancies 9.148–9.150
  collective redundancies *see* collective redundancies
  definition 9.144–9.147
  employers' obligations when contemplating redundancies 9.151
  lay offs 9.233–9.240
  maternity leave and 6.128
  notice
    contractual notice period 9.185–9.186
    payment in lieu 9.187, 9.414–9.416
    statutory notice periods 9.183–9.184
  overseas workers 1.95
  parental leave and 6.171–6.172
  pay *see* redundancy pay
  procedural fairness 9.527
  selection 5.87–5.89
    age discrimination 4.53
    application of selection criteria 9.180–9.182
    assistance for selected employees 5.135–5.136
    definition of pool for selection 9.175–9.176
    determination of selection criteria 9.177–9.179
    disability discrimination 4.170
    Northern Ireland 4.426
    parental leave and 6.171–6.172
    part-time workers 2.514
    procedural fairness 9.527
    race discrimination 4.505
    religious discrimination 4.614
    sex discrimination 4.706–4.708
    sexual orientation discrimination 4.782
    trade union membership grounds 5.379
    unfair 9.205, 9.531
  volunteers 9.172–9.174
  short time working 9.233–9.240
  statutory dismissal and disciplinary procedure, requirement to follow 9.206–9.209
  suitable alternative employment 9.188–9.191
    alternative job at different location 9.198–9.200
    continuity of service 9.195–9.196
    refusal, effect of 9.197
    trial period in new job 9.192–9.194
  support for employees made redundant 5.135–5.136, 9.202
  time off to look for new work or arrange training 1.246, 1.261–1.264, 9.201
  unfair dismissal claims 9.203–9.205
  voluntary redundancy 9.172–9.174
  voluntary early retirement distinguished 9.309–9.311
redundancy pay
  age discrimination 4.54, 9.293–9.294, 9.313
  contractual redundancy pay schemes 4.55–4.60
  apprentices 2.569
  death of employee or employer 9.229
  deductions from damages for wrongful dismissal 9.605
  dismissals connected to transfer of undertaking 9.221
  due payment not made 9.230
  employer unable to pay 9.231–9.232
  enhanced payments 9.222–9.226
  guaranteed 9.123–9.126
  ineligible employees 9.227–9.228
  insolvency of employer 9.116
    guaranteed payments 9.123–9.126
  lay offs 9.239–9.240
  length of service 9.219–9.220
  Redundancy Payments Office, claiming from 9.31–9.32
  short time working 9.239–9.240
  statutory redundancy pay 9.214–9.218
    waiver clause 1.146
  transfer of undertakings 9.221
references 8.349–8.351, 8.468
  data protection 2.304–2.305, 8.468, 8.486–8.487
  guidance 8.488–8.494
    medical information 8.492–8.494
  discrimination 4.317, 8.480–8.483
  duty of care 8.350, 8.475
  implied term of trust and confidence 8.478–8.479

obligation to provide 8.349–8.351, 8.471–8.474
offers conditional on reasonable care 2.166
    8.476–8.477
sickness absences 8.482–8.483
victimisation 8.351, 8.484–8.485
see also pre-employment checks
rehabilitation of offenders
declaration of unspent convictions
    2.171
disclosures 8.361–8.371
protection of vulnerable adults (POVA)
  scheme 8.372–8.373
rehabilitation periods 8.356
spent convictions 8.356
  exclusions 8.357–8.360
reimbursement of training costs
  clause 2.142–2.143
reinstatement and re-engagement
    4.252, 9.61–9.62, 9.210–9.213, 9.541–9.545
reserve forces see reserve forces
religion or belief discrimination
    4.537–4.540
appearance and dress codes 2.1, 2.20–2.23, 4.566–4.569
  justification 2.24–2.27
  long hair 2.16
bereavement leave 1.284–1.285
bullying 3.28
burden of proof 4.622
changing facilities 4.570
claims 4.617
  burden of proof 4.622
  compensation 4.630–4.631
  harassment by customer, suppliers and other third parties 4.626–4.629
  questionnaire procedure
    4.618–4.621
  time limits 4.209–4.215
  vicarious liability 4.623–4.625
  see also discrimination claims
comparable person 4.552–4.554
compensation 4.630–4.631
dietary issues 4.580–4.582
direct 4.559
during employment 4.611–4.614
harassment 4.26–4.28, 4.324, 4.590–4.596
  by customer, suppliers and other third parties 4.626–4.629
indirect 4.560
  appearance and dress codes 2.16, 2.20–2.23, 4.566–4.569
  dietary issues 4.580–4.582
  identifying a legitimate aim 4.563
  prayer facilities 4.571–4.576

provision, criterion or practice 4.561
"put at a disadvantage" 4.562
showering and changing facilities
    4.570
Sunday working 4.583–4.586
test of proportionality 4.564–4.565
time off for religious festivals etc.
    4.577–4.579
monitoring 4.632–4.634
Northern Ireland see Northern Ireland
outside the employment field
    4.555–4.557
post-employment discrimination
    4.615–4.616
prayer facilities 4.571–4.576
promotion 4.613
qualifying conditions 4.550–4.551
questionnaire procedure 4.618–4.621
recruitment 4.547, 4.597
  best practice checklist 4.610
  genuine occupational requirements (GORs) 4.598–4.607
  positive action 4.608–4.609
  see also discrimination in recruitment
redundancy selection 4.614
scope of Regulations 4.541–4.549
showering facilities 4.570
Sunday working 4.583–4.586
terms and conditions of employment
    4.612
training opportunities 4.613
transfers 4.613
vicarious liability 4.623–4.625
victimisation 4.587–4.589
religious holidays and festivals
time off work 1.31–1.33, 4.577–4.579
religious or political discrimination
see Northern Ireland
relocation 2.125–2.127
see also mobility clause
reserve forces
reinstatement in civil employment
    1.320–1.321
  application for reinstatement 1.323
  continuous employment 1.332–1.333
  dismissal of employees called out for whole-time service 1.322
  notification of availability for work
    1.324
  obligation of employers to reinstate employees 1.327–1.329
  reasonable and practicable reinstatement 1.330–1.331
  reinstatement committees
    1.334–1.336
  renewal of application 1.326

settlement of disputes 1.334–1.336
whole-time service 1.325
time off work 1.296
  call-out 1.300–1.303
  exemption or deferral 1.304–1.308
  financial assistance 1.309–1.314
  time limits 1.315–1.316
  Reserve Forces Appeal Tribunals
    1.317–1.319
training and duties 1.297–1.299
resignation 9.244–9.246
date of termination 9.255–9.256
exit interviews 9.275–9.278
heat of the moment resignations
  9.259–9.261
notice
  notice period 9.250–9.252
  withdrawing 9.257
  working during notice period 9.258
  written notice 9.253–9.254
unilateral termination 9.249
warning of dismissal 9.262–9.266
wrongful dismissal and 9.574
see also constructive dismissal
restrictive covenants 2.104–2.110, 2.174
confidential information 2.124
duration 2.119
non-dealing clause 2.116
non-solicitation clause 2.116
poaching of customers 2.114–2.116
poaching of staff 2.108, 2.120–2.121
removal of invalid sub-clauses
  2.111–2.113
scope 2.117–2.119
stability of workforce and 2.108, 2.120–2.121
trade secrets 2.124
transfer of undertakings 2.122–2.123
retirement
age see retirement age
automatically unfair dismissals
  9.328–9.329
early retirement 9.307–9.308
  voluntary early retirement and
    voluntary redundancy distinguished
    9.309–9.311
good practice 9.330
leading up to 9.306
mutual consent 9.318
notification 4.73–4.78, 9.323–9.327
request to continue working beyond
  retirement 4.66–4.72, 9.319–9.322
time off for retiring
  employees 1.274, 1.292–1.294
retirement age 9.286–9.290

age discrimination 4.61–4.65, 9.290, 9.312–9.317
contractual retirement age 9.291
  changing 9.303–9.305
default retirement age 9.286
discriminatory retirement ages 9.292
flexible retirement age 9.301–9.302
normal retirement age 9.295–9.300
sex discrimination 4.705, 9.292
statutory redundancy pay and
  9.293–9.294
unfair dismissal claims and
  9.293–9.294
Romanian workers 1.70, 1.71, 8.414, 8.464–8.465

S

sabbaticals 1.149–1.151
advantages to employer 1.156
age discrimination 1.176
contact during 1.180
continuity of employment 1.177
definition 1.149
disadvantages and dangers
  1.168–1.170
duration 1.167
equal opportunities and 1.176
initiating 1.154
pay and benefits 1.177
policy on 1.8, 1.175–1.177
purpose 1.177
qualifying service 1.177
return of employees 1.177, 1.184–1.187
timing 1.177
see also career breaks
safety committee 3.245, 5.258, 5.260
safety representatives 3.245, 5.171, 5.258–5.259
time off 1.249
salary sacrifice arrangements
  7.101–7.105
savings-related share option schemes 7.292, 7.299–7.301
annual return form 7.320
compliance 7.320
conditions 7.302
exercise of options 7.313–7.315
grant of options 7.306–7.312
option price 7.303–7.304
save-as-you-earn contract agreement
  7.305
tax liability 7.316–7.319
see also employee share and share
  option schemes

887

Scotland
attachment of earnings
conjoined arrestment order
  7.43–7.45
current maintenance arrestment 7.42
Debtors (Scotland) Act
 1987 7.5, 7.37–7.48
earnings arrestment 7.38–7.41
failure to comply with order
  7.46–7.48
search, right to 2.97–2.100
secondments 1.149–1.150
 benefits 1.163–1.166
 contract 1.179
 definition 1.149
 disadvantages and dangers
  1.171–1.174
 duration 1.167
 initiating 1.158
 management 1.181–1.183
 return of employees 1.184–1.187
 scope 1.159–1.162
 setting up 1.178–1.179
selection interviews see interviews
selection process 4.314–4.316,
  8.316–8.317, 8.501
 application forms see application
  forms
 appointment processes 8.572–8.575
 assessment centres 8.569–8.571
 CVs 8.512–8.517
 disability discrimination
  application forms 8.520, 8.522
  interviews 4.157–4.159, 8.521,
   8.564–8.565
  discrimination 8.502
 extended selection techniques
  8.566–8.571
 interviews see interviews
 making the offer 8.572–8.578
 psychometric instruments
  8.567–8.568, 8.618
 record keeping 8.577–8.578
 rejections 8.576
 screening applications 8.505–8.507
  application forms 8.529–8.531
  biodata 8.533
  competence-based 8.534
  formalised approaches 8.532–8.537
  psychometric tests 8.535–8.537
  timing 8.508–8.511
 selection tests 8.315
 shortlisting 2.289–2.290
self-employment 1.6, 2.351, 2.366,
  2.500–2.503
 maternity allowance 6.216

workers from Romania and Bulgaria
  8.414
working time 1.364
 drivers 1.386–1.388, 1.461–1.464
see also employment status
settlement of common law rights
  9.342–9.343
sex discrimination 4.642–4.643
appearance and dress codes 2.2,
  2.7–2.8, 4.661–4.663
 men with long hair 2.14–2.16
 proving discrimination 2.9–2.10
 shirts and ties 2.17–2.18
 skirt wearing 2.11–2.13
bullying 3.28
burden of proof 4.715
civil partnership status 4.700
claims 4.710
 burden of proof 4.715
 compensation 4.723–4.724
 harassment by customers, suppliers
  and other third parties 4.719–4.722
 questionnaire procedure
  4.711–4.714
 time limits 4.209–4.215
 vicarious liability 4.716–4.718
 see also discrimination claims
comparable person 4.651–4.654
compensation 4.723–4.724
direct 4.656–4.657
during employment 4.691–4.698
flexible working 6.61–6.62
gender reassignment discrimination
  4.701–4.704
harassment 4.26–4.28, 4.324,
  4.668–4.678
 by customers, suppliers and other
  third parties 4.719–4.722
indirect 4.658
 job-sharing 4.696, 8.298
 justification 4.660
 part-time work 4.696, 8.298
 provision, criterion or practice 4.659
justification 4.660
marital status discrimination 4.699
mobility clauses 2.127
monitoring 4.725–4.726
pensions 7.676
post-employment discrimination 4.709
pregnancy discrimination 4.697–4.698,
  6.129
promotion 4.694–4.695
qualifying conditions 4.649–4.650
questionnaire procedure 4.711–4.714
recruitment 4.647, 4.679–4.680
 advertisements 4.686–4.689
 best practice checklist 4.690

genuine occupational qualifications
  (GOQs) 4.681–4.683, 8.290, 8.291
  job titles 8.285
  positive action 4.684–4.685
  see also discrimination in
    recruitment
  redundancy selection 4.706–4.708
  retirement ages 4.705, 9.292
  scope of law 4.642, 4.645–4.654
  terms and conditions of employment
    4.692–4.693
  training opportunities 4.694–4.695
  transfers 4.694–4.695
  vicarious liability 4.716–4.718
  victimisation 4.664–4.667
sexual harassment 4.668–4.678
  by customers, suppliers and other
    third parties 4.719–4.722
sexual orientation discrimination
  4.735–4.738
  bullying 3.28
  burden of proof 4.790
  claims 4.785
    burden of proof 4.790
    compensation 4.799–4.801
    harassment by customers, suppliers
      and other third parties 4.795–4.798
    questionnaire procedure
      4.786–4.789
    time limits 4.209–4.215
    vicarious liability 4.791–4.794
    see also discrimination claims
  comparable person 4.745–4.746
  compensation 4.799–4.801
  direct 4.751
  during employment 4.778–4.782
  harassment 4.26–4.28, 4.324,
    4.760–4.765
    by customers, suppliers and other
      third parties 4.795–4.798
  indirect 4.752
    identifying a legitimate aim 4.755
    provision, criterion or practice 4.753
    "put at a disadvantage" 4.754
    test of proportionality 4.756
  monitoring 4.802–4.804
  outside of employment field
    4.747–4.749
  post-employment discrimination
    4.783–4.784
  promotion 4.781
  qualifying conditions 4.743–4.744
  questionnaire procedure 4.786–4.789
  recruitment 4.740, 4.766
    best practice checklist 4.777
    genuine occupational requirements
      (GORs) 4.767–4.774

    positive action 4.775–4.776
    see also discrimination in
      recruitment
  redundancy selection 4.782
  scope of Regulations 4.739–4.742
  terms and conditions of employment
    4.780
  training opportunities 4.781
  transfers 4.781
  vicarious liability 4.791–4.794
  victimisation 4.757–4.759
share incentive plans (SIPs) 7.293,
  7.371–7.373
  annual return 7.383–7.384
  approval conditions 7.382
  features 7.374–7.377
  free shares 7.374
  matching shares 7.374
  optional features 7.377
  partnership shares 7.374
  tax and NIC advantages 7.378–7.381
  see also employee share and share
    option schemes
shift workers
  working time 1.441–1.445
short time working 9.233–9.238
showering facilities
  religious discrimination and 4.570
sickness absence 1.193–1.195
  dismissal on capability grounds 1.218,
    1.219–1.220
  identifying reasons for absence
    1.199–1.203
  improving levels of absence 1.223
  keeping in touch with absent
    employees 1.221–1.222
  long-term absence 1.205
    holiday entitlement and 1.11–1.14
    management 2.11–2.18
  management commitment 1.206
  policy and procedure 1.204–1.205
  pregnancy-related 6.99–6.102
  references and 8.482–8.483
  self-certification 1.200
  short-term absence 1.207–1.210
  persistent 1.205, 1.208–1.210
sickness and health schemes
  age discrimination 4.46–4.50
sickness records
  data protection 2.295
staff handbooks 2.44, 2.199–2.200,
  2.240, 2.241, 2.376, 2.462–2.465
  access to 2.262
  appearance and dress codes 2.17
  consultation during development
    2.481
  content 2.484–2.485

889

possible topics 2.486–2.491
disciplinary rules and procedures
 2.260
format 2.477–2.478
Information and Consultation of
 Employees Regulations 2004
 2.471–2.473
key terms of employment 2.474
purpose 2.468–2.470
structure 2.475–2.476
style 2.479–2.480
updating 2.482–2.483
variation of contract and 2.204
stakeholder pension schemes
 7.614–7.615
access requirements 7.616
deduction from payroll 7.625–7.629
exempt employers 7.620–7.624
relevant employees 7.617–7.619
see also pensions
statutory adoption pay (SAP) 6.2,
 6.214–6.220, 6.297–6.304
average weekly earnings calculation
 6.311
continuous employment 6.308–6.310
dismissal of employees with under a
 year's service 3.187
entitlement 6.305–6.306
insolvency of employer and 9.138
keeping in touch days 6.323–6.326
legislative changes 6.219–6.220,
 6.343–6.346
matching week 6.307
notification and evidence 6.312–6.315
overseas workers 1.96
payment 6.319–6.322
period of payment 6.225
rates 6.225
relationship with SSP 6.329
returning to work 6.330
SAP1 (Change Over Form) 6.331
start date 6.316–6.318
stopping payment 6.327–6.328
**statutory dismissal and disciplinary
 procedure** 2.266–2.267, 3.163–3.164
appeals 3.83
exemptions 3.168
financial sanctions for failure to
 comply 3.182–3.186
general requirements 3.179–3.181
inter-relationship with employer's own
 procedure 3.188–3.189
modified two-step procedure
 3.174–3.178
requirement to follow 9.206–9.209
scope 3.165–3.167

standard three-step procedure
 3.169–3.173
unfair dismissal and 9.402–9.404,
 9.507, 9.518–9.523, 9.532
wrongful dismissal and 9.563
see also disciplinary rules and
 procedures
statutory employment rights 9.4
during time off for dependants 1.354
overseas workers 1.94–1.96
prohibition on contracting out 9.337,
 9.341
statutory grievance procedure 2.595,
 3.207–3.208, 3.218–3.221
appropriate management skills 3.246
bullying 3.243
constructive dismissal and
 9.272–9.274
grievances 3.207
 definition 3.219
disciplinary procedures
 giving rise to 3.195–3.197, 3.212
 failure to deal effectively with 3.247
 gravity of issue 3.213–3.215
 issues giving rise to 3.211–3.212
 minor issues 3.214
 serious issues 3.215
harassment 3.243
health, safety and welfare 3.245
issues giving rise to grievances,
 disciplinary rules and procedures
 3.195–3.197
modified two-step
 procedure 3.220, 3.226–3.231
 general requirements 3.232
public interest disclosure 3.244
records 3.248–3.250
requirements 3.217
role of HR practitioners 3.216
sanctions for failure to comply
 3.233–3.238
 exceptions 3.239
 financial sanctions 3.240–3.241
standard three-step procedure 3.220,
 3.222–3.225
 general requirements 3.232
variation of contract 2.595
whistleblowing 3.244
statutory maternity pay (SMP)
 6.214–6.220, 6.227–6.232
average weekly earnings calculation
 6.275
change of circumstances 6.276
continuous employment rule
 6.239–6.240
deductions 6.228
entitlement 6.233–6.238

890

evidence and notification 6.246–6.248
expected week of childbirth 6.232
ineligibility 6.241–6.245
insolvency of employer and 9.138
keeping in touch days 6.266–6.271
legislative changes 6.219,
 6.336–6.342
MAT B1 form 6.232
maternity pay period 6.232
overseas workers 1.96
payment 6.249–6.265
qualifying week 6.232
rates 6.223, 6.274
records 2.310, 6.281–6.282
recovery 6.229–6.231
relationship with SSP 6.272–6.273
returning to work 6.277
small employers 6.229–6.231
SMP1 (Change Over Form) 6.278
SMP2 (Record Sheet) 6.279
SMP3 (Checklist) 6.280
statutory paternity pay (SPP)
 6.214–6.220, 6.283
 average weekly
  earnings calculation 6.288
 continuous employment 6.286–6.287
 entitlement 6.284–6.285
 evidence 6.289
 insolvency of employer and 9.138
 not payable when 6.295–6.296
 overseas workers 1.96
 payment 6.290–6.292
 rates 6.224
 relationship with SSP 6.293
 SPP1 (Change Over Form) 6.294
statutory redundancy pay
 9.214–9.218
 waiver clause 1.146
 see also redundancy pay
statutory sick pay (SSP)
 age discrimination 7.775
 freedom from operating
  SSP scheme 7.699–7.702
 incapacity for work
  defining 7.743
  evidence 7.732–7.735
 ineligible workers 7.706
  losing eligibility 7.707
 insolvency of employer and 9.138
 leaver's statements 7.754–7.756
 length of service and 7.740–7.742
 linked periods 7.724–7.726
 losing eligibility 7.707
 maximum liability 7.753
 notification of absence 7.731
 payment 7.744–7.747
 payroll treatment 7.763–7.764

period of application 7.703–7.705
period of entitlement 7.715–7.716
period of incapacity for work
 7.708–7.714
qualifying conditions 7.697–7.698
qualifying days 7.703, 7.717–7.723
rates 7.748–7.752
records 2.310, 7.736–7.739
recovery 7.760–7.762
SAP and 6.329
SMP and 6.272–6.273
SPP and 6.293
SSP1 (Changeover Form)
 7.766–7.769
SSP1 [L] (Leaver's Statement Form)
 7.770–7.773
SSP2 (Record Sheet) 7.774
stopping payment 7.759
waiting days 7.727–7.730
withholding 7.757–7.758
statutory time off see time off
students
 employment of overseas students
  8.450–8.453
succession planning 8.581–8.582
 appraisals 8.617
 development centres 8.619–8.621
 equal opportunities 8.594–8.598
 external recruitment 8.593
 human resource planning (HRP)
  8.581, 8.599–8.603
 analysis of current situation
  8.609–8.615
 implementation 8.604–8.606
 reviewing corporate objectives
  8.607–8.608
 internal recruitment 8.591–8.592
 psychometric instruments 8.618
 risk assessment 8.585–8.586
 scope 8.587–8.588
 timing 8.589–8.590
summary
 dismissal 3.87–3.89, 9.378–9.380,
  9.405, 9.575–9.579, 9.580
 appropriate employer procedures
  9.386–9.392
 breach of contract 2.66–2.71, 9.396,
  9.584–9.585
 consistency 9.406–9.407
 contract terms 2.183
 disciplinary rules and procedures and
  9.383–9.385, 9.397, 9.581–9.583
  statutory procedure 9.402–9.404
 gross misconduct 2.183, 3.142–3.146,
  9.374–9.375, 9.384, 9.409
  ignoring 9.396
  justification 9.379

meaning 9.378
mitigation after 9.394
wrongful dismissal and 9.381–9.382
see also dismissal
Sunday working
  religion or belief discrimination
    4.583–4.586
suspension 3.82, 3.116–3.118
  bullying and 3.44–3.46
  without pay 3.149

T

temporary workers 1.113,
    2.387–2.388, 2.530–2.531
  see also casual workers
termination of employment
  deductions for holiday taken in excess
    1.53
  fixed-term employees 1.144
  see also dismissal; redundancy;
    retirement; summary dismissal;
    unfair dismissal; wrongful dismissal
time off 1.229
  accompaniment to hearings, right of
    1.251, 5.156
  adoption leave *see* adoption leave
  ante-natal care 1.246, 1.255–1.258
  bereavement leave 1.268, 1.269,
    1.277–1.283
    religion or belief discrimination
      1.284–1.285
  compassionate leave 1.277–1.283
  dental appointments 1.272–1.273,
    1.289–1.291
  for dependants 1.223, 1.268,
    1.340–1.341
    excluded employees 1.344
    general qualifying conditions 1.344
    meaning of "dependant" 1.345–1.348
    notification requirements
      1.350–1.351
    reasonable time off 1.352–1.353
    reasons for time off 1.349
    statutory rights during 1.354
  employee representatives 1.246,
    1.252, 5.285
  employer's discretion 1.268–1.274
    bereavement leave 1.268, 1.269,
      1.277–1.283
    religion and belief 1.284–1.285
    compassionate leave 1.277–1.283
    dental appointments 1.272–1.273,
      1.289–1.291
    fertility treatment 1.271, 1.286–1.288
    medical appointments 1.272–1.273,
      1.289–1.291

reserve force *see* reserve forces
retiring employees 1.274,
    1.292–1.294
  territorial duties 1.295
European Works Council
  Representatives 1.246, 1.253
fertility treatment 1.271, 1.286–1.288
jury service 1.240–1.245
medical appointments 1.272–1.273,
    1.289–1.291
paid time off to perform duties
    1.246–1.264
pension fund trustees 1.254
reasonable time off 1.236–1.239
redundancy and , time off to look for
  new work or arrange training 1.246,
    1.261–1.264, 9.201
refusal to allow 1.229
religious festivals etc. 4.577–4.579
reserve force *see* reserve forces
retiring employees 1.274, 1.292–1.294
safety representatives 1.249
territorial duties 1.295
trade union activities 1.235,
    1.247–1.250, 5.365, 5.386–5.389
unpaid time off to perform public
  duties 1.233–1.235
young employees 1.259–1.260
trade secrets
  restrictive covenants and 2.124
Trade Union Congress (TUC) 5.22
trade unions
  collective bargaining *see* collective
    bargaining
  de-recognition 5.456–5.457
  discrimination on grounds of
    membership 8.282
  dismissal
    on membership grounds
      5.380–5.383
    safety complaints and representation
      5.384–5.385
  employers and 5.416
  expelling members 5.399–5.403
  grievance procedures 3.256–3.257
  independent trade unions 5.423
  industrial action
    ballot requirements 5.412
    employees' protection from union
      5.238
    illegal union action 5.228
    immunity from legal proceedings
      5.236–5.237
    right to be balloted 5.411
  information and consultation
    5.306–5.307
    consultation rights 5.393–5.397

financial information	5.410	**training costs**	
information rights	5.390–5.392, 5.410	reimbursement	2.142–2.143
membership	5.363–5.412	**Training and Work Experience Scheme (TWES)**	8.442–8.445
recruitment and	5.376–5.378	criteria for applications	8.446–8.447
rights of employees	5.372	length of permits	8.448–8.449
rights of members	5.375	*see also* migrant workers	
political activity and funds	5.408–5.409	**transfer of undertakings**	2.216–2.221, 9.420–9.422
purpose	5.422	collective agreements and	9.466–9.468
recognition	5.424–5.428		
application to CAC	5.441–5.442	continuity of service	9.454
approaching the employer	5.437	contract terms and conditions	9.453
bargaining unit	5.443–5.444	contracts of employment,	
benefits	5.434	changes to	9.456–9.465
business transfers and	5.458	dismissals	9.494–9.495
for collective bargaining	5.27–5.30, 5.31	economic, technical or organisational (ETO) reasons	9.221, 9.458, 9.496–9.499
costs	5.433		
de-recognition	5.456–5.457	redundancy pay	9.221
determination as to award	5.445–5.446	employee representatives and	5.270–5.274, 9.474–9.492
gaining	5.435–5.454	consultation	5.168–5.170
holding a ballot	5.447–5.451	employees choosing not to transfer	9.443–9.446
making award of recognition	5.448		
recognised trade unions	5.429–5.432	information and consultation	
		requirements	5.270–5.274
voluntary agreement	5.438–5.440	breach	9.488–9.491
recruitment and	5.376–5.378	compromise agreements and	3.297
redundancy selection	5.379	consultation	5.168–5.170, 9.485–9.487
representatives	5.368–5.371		
recognition and rights	5.455	employee representatives	5.168–5.170
rights	5.420–5.421	employer's defence to claim of	
collective bargaining	5.398	breach	9.492–9.493
consultation	5.393–5.397	information	9.483–9.484
financial information	5.410	insolvency	9.473
information	5.390–5.392	liabilities	
of members	5.375	not transferring to new employer	9.451–9.452
not to be unjustifiably disciplined	5.404–5.407	transferring to new employer	9.447–9.450
time off for duties and activities	1.235, 1.247–1.250, 5.365, 5.386–5.389	non-contractual benefits	9.455
safety committee	5.258, 5.260	occupational pension schemes and	9.469–9.472
safety representatives	1.249, 3.249, 5.171, 5.258–5.259	redundancy pay	9.221
		restrictive covenants and	2.122–2.123
statutory right to be accompanied and	5.373–5.374	rights transferring to new employer	9.447–9.450
time off for duties and activities	1.247–1.250, 5.365, 5.386–5.389	time of transfer	9.441–9.442
		trade union recognition and	5.458
unfair dismissal		TUPE	9.422
membership of union	5.380–5.383	application	9.429–9.431
safety complaints and representation	5.384–5.385	avoiding	9.500
		continuity of service	9.454
unjustifiable disciplinary action	5.404–5.407	contract terms and conditions	9.453
		contracting out of services and	9.433

contracts of employment, changes to 9.456–9.465
dismissal for economic, technical or organisational (ETO) reasons 9.496–9.499
effects 9.428
employees affected by 9.434–9.440
inapplicable transfers 9.432
information and consultation 9.474–9.478
insolvency 9.473
occupational pension schemes and 9.469–9.472
relevant transfer 9.426–9.428
time of transfer 9.441–9.442
trustee in bankruptcy 9.89

U

unapproved share option schemes 7.294, 7.359–7.362
compliance obligations 7.370
National Insurance liability 7.367–7.369
performance targets 7.363
tax liability 7.364–7.366
see also employee share and share option schemes
unfair dismissal 9.506
Acas conciliation 9.32, 9.349
age discrimination 4.83, 9.293–9.294, 9.313
automatically unfair 9.328–9.329, 9.530–9.533
bullying 3.27
collective redundancies, failure to consult 5.132
compensation and awards 2.416–2.418, 9.546–9.550
contributory fault 9.553
duty to mitigate and reduction of award 9.554 9.552
rule against double recovery 9.607
uplift of award 9.551
duty to mitigate 9.554
flexible working applications and 6.60
jury service and 1.245
overseas workers 1.81–1.87
parental leave and 6.170
pregnancy or childbirth, related to 6.130
redundancy dismissal 9.203–9.205
reinstatement and re-engagement 4.252, 9.61–9.62, 9.210–9.213, 9.541–9.545
remedies 9.539–9.552
right not to be unfairly dismissed 9.534–9.536

exclusions 9.537–9.538
statutory dismissal and disciplinary procedure and 9.402–9.404, 9.507, 9.518–9.523, 9.532
statutory paternity leave and 6.208–6.210
termination of existing contract 2.588
territorial jurisdiction 1.81–1.87
trade union grounds
membership of union 5.380–5.383
safety complaints and representation 5.384–5.385
variation of contract 2.588, 2.589, 2.605–2.606
waiver clauses 1.145–1.146

V

variation of contract 2.203
by agreement 2.204–2.207
breach of contract
imposed variation 2.589, 2.596, 2.603–2.604
unilateral variation 2.61–2.62
variation clauses 2.63–2.64
collective agreement 2.210
consensual variation 2.584
constructive dismissal 2.589
consultation 2.592–2.594
employee's response to imposed changes 2.601–2.605
employer cannot impose changes 2.596–2.600
express acceptance 2.602
express provision within contract for flexibility 2.582, 2.585
grievance procedure 2.595
implied acceptance 2.602
implied terms as to 2.586
imposed 2.589
incorporating right to vary within contract 2.208–2.209
information and training 2.600
justification 2.591
lawful and reasonable instructions 2.599
mobility clause 2.597–2.598
principal reasons for variation 2.582
resignation of employee 2.605–2.606
staff handbook and 2.204
statutory restrictions 2.590
suing the employer 2.603–2.604
termination of existing contract 2.587–2.588
unfair dismissal
claims 2.588, 2.589, 2.605–2.606
unilateral variation 2.61–2.62, 2.211–2.215

variation clauses 2.63–2.64
vicarious liability
  age discrimination 4.88–4.89
  disability discrimination 4.183–4.185
  race discrimination 4.518–4.520
  religion or belief discrimination
    4.623–4.625
  sex discrimination 4.716–4.718
  sexual orientation discrimination
    4.791–4.794
victimisation 4.296–4.299
  age discrimination 4.25
  disability discrimination 4.127–4.129
  employee representatives 5.187
  employment tribunal claims and 9.78
  examples 4.298
  Northern Ireland 4.409
  parental leave and 6.170
  race discrimination 4.475–4.477
  references 8.351, 8.484–8.485
  religion or belief discrimination
    4.587–4.589
    Northern Ireland 4.409
  sex discrimination 4.664–4.667
  sexual orientation discrimination
    4.757–4.759

W

waiver clauses
  fixed-term employees 1.145–1.146
warnings 3.69–3.72
  content 3.75
  formal 3.132–3.133
  informal 3.128–3.131
  levels 3.73–3.74
  lifespan 3.134–3.138
    extending 3.78–3.79
    indefinite 3.138
  previous warnings 3.76–3.77
  verbal 3.72
whistleblowing 5.461–5.464
  cases 5.490–5.491
  confidentiality clauses 5.493
  enforcement 5.492
  exceptionally serious cases
    5.488–5.489
  good faith 5.476–5.477
  grievance procedure 3.244
  internal disclosure 5.474–5.475
  internal policy 5.478–5.482
  prescribed regulators 5.483–5.484
  protected disclosures 5.473
  qualifying disclosures 5.470–5.472
  "reasonable in all the circumstances"
    5.487
  scope of legislation 5.467–5.469

  wider disclosure 5.485–5.486
work permits 8.386, 8.403–8.406
  appeal against refusal 8.441
  applications 8.415–8.419
    criteria 8.420–8.424
    extension applications 8.438–8.440
    intra-company transfers 8.426–8.427
    Tier 1 applications 8.425–8.431
    Tier 2 applications 8.432–8.437
  exceptions 8.407–8.408
  inward investment posts 8.429
  posts at board level or equivalent
    8.428
  shortage occupations 8.430–8.431
  see also migrant workers
worker
  definition 1.4–1.6, 2.363–2.365
  national minimum wage and
    7.461–7.464
  employee
    distinguished 1.114, 2.363–2.365,
      2.368–2.370, 2.504–2.509
  see also employment status
workforce agreements
  collective bargaining and 5.49–5.50
  working time 1.437–1.438
  see also collective agreements
working time 1.357–1.360
  48-hour weekly maximum 1.357,
    1.378–1.381
  annual leave 1.360, 1.434–1.436
  application of regulations 1.363–1.365
  calculating the weekly average
    1.390–1.395
  children 8.324–8.329
  collective agreements 1.437–1.438
    opt-outs 1.401
  collective bargaining and 5.47–5.48
  domestic workers 1.374
  drivers' hours and records
    1.439–1.440
  exemptions 1.369–1.374
    compensatory rest 1.371–1.372
    excluded sectors 1.366–1.368
  mobile workers 1.380
    calculating average weekly working
      time 1.481–1.482
  daily rest breaks 1.409
  daily rest periods 1.414
  drivers' hours and records
    1.439–1.440
  night work 1.428, 1.483–1.484
    meaning of "night-time" 1.485
  occasional mobile workers
    1.465–1.466
  on-call time 1.384

periods of availability 1.383, 1.470–1.473
record keeping 1.489–1.493
reference period 1.476–1.480
rest breaks 1.383, 1.486–1.488
Road Transport (Working Time) Regulations 2005 1.382–1.389, 1.450–1.451
  application 1.458–1.460
  enforcement 1.494
  self-employed drivers 1.386–1.388, 1.461–1.464
  weekly rest periods 1.420
  working time 1.467–1.469
  working week 1.474–1.475
night work 1.359, 1.422–1.428
  calculating average hours 1.429–1.433
  derogations 1.369
  health assessments 1.426
  mobile workers 1.428, 1.483–1.485
on-call time 1.384, 1.415
opt-out agreements 1.378, 1.396–1.399
  collective agreements 1.401
  restrictions 1.400–1.402
record keeping 1.403–1.404
rest
  breaks 1.360, 1.383, 1.486–1.488
  daily 1.405–1.409
  derogations 1.369, 1.371
  monotonous work and 1.410–1.411
rest periods 1.360
  daily 1.412–1.417, 1.440
  weekly 1.418–1.421, 1.440
shift workers 1.441–1.445
unmeasured working time 1.375–1.376
workers employed outside GB 1.377
workforce agreements 1.437–1.438
young persons 1.358, 1.365, 1.379, 1.399
  daily rest breaks 1.408
  daily rest periods 1.413
  night work 1.427
  weekly rest periods 1.419
works councils 5.501–5.502
collective bargaining 5.192–5.197
collective redundancies and 5.138
European Works Councils 5.197
  Agreement 5.518–5.519
  consultation 5.176–5.177
  enforcement of rules 5.536–5.541
  information and consultation 5.281–5.285, 5.530–5.532
  members' protection 5.533–5.535
  statutory 5.525–5.529

time off for representatives 1.246, 1.253
information and consultation 5.501–5.502, 5.520–5.524
European Works Councils 5.281–5.285, 5.530–5.532
organisations covered by rules 5.505–5.509
special negotiating body 5.513–5.517
valid requests 5.510–5.512
written statement of particulars of employment 2.177–2.178, 2.229, 2.352, 2.374–2.376
complaint to employment tribunal 2.230–2.231, 2.263–2.265
disciplinary rules and procedures 3.54–3.55, 3.105
employment tribunal claims 2.230–2.231, 2.263–2.265, 3.55
excluded employees 2.179
general obligations 2.258–2.262
overseas workers 1.65–1.69, 2.393
wrongful dismissal 2.412–2.414, 9.559–9.563
burden of proof 9.411–9.413
damages 9.590
  deprivation of financial benefits 9.596
  fixed-term contracts 9.591–9.593
  injury to feelings 9.594
  reputation 9.595
deductions from damages
  compensation for unfair dismissal 9.607
  mitigation 9.598–9.599
  pay in lieu of notice clause and 9.600–9.601
  private insurance and pension benefits 9.604
  reduction for accelerated receipt 9.606
  redundancy payments 9.605
  rule against double recovery 9.607
  state benefits 9.603
  taxation 9.602
defence to claim 9.586–9.589
employment tribunal jurisdiction 9.5, 9.610–9.611
proof of conduct as defence to claim 9.410–9.413
resignation and 9.574
restraining 9.608–9.609
statutory dismissal and disciplinary procedure and 9.563
summary dismissal and 9.381–9.382
termination of employment 9.564–9.565

Y

young persons
- employment of 2.398–2.402
- restrictions 8.332–8.339
- time off work 1.259–1.260
- working time 1.358, 1.365, 1.379, 1.399, 8.335
- daily rest breaks 1.408
- daily rest periods 1.413
- night work 1.427, 8.335
- weekly rest periods 1.419

see also apprenticeships; children